Christian Home Educators'

CURRICULUM MANUAL:

ELEMENTARY GRADES

by Cathy Duffy

GROVE
Publishing

Disclaimer:

We do our best to ensure that the information presented in this book is accurate and up to date. However, we cannot make any guarantees since we depend upon so many other people to provide us with information. Also, reviews are necessarily based upon opinions. We cannot guarantee that any particular product will perform as described in every situation.

Grove Publishing
16172 Huxley Circle
Westminster, CA 92683
www.grovepublishing.com
714.841.1220

Acknowledgments

This book has gone through major changes with each new edition. Many people have helped with various editions over the years, and I'm grateful for their assistance. Valerie Thorpe has always been heavily involved in the process, contributing some of the material on teaching art and physical education plus assisting with reviews and editing.

You can identify reviews written by someone other than myself since at the end they say [V.Thorpe], [Maureen Wittmann] or the name of another reviewer. If another person has worked on a review with me, both their name and my initials appear at the end of the review.

I'm always absorbing input from homeschoolers who actually use the resources, distributors who sell them, and publishers who produce them. Consequently, many reviews reflect assistance from unnamed others. I greatly appreciate such assistance because it broadens my perspective about what works in different situations.

As most of you are aware, the publishing business has become computer-dependent. This has, in turn, made me dependent upon others who know more about computers than I do—primarily two of my sons. My eldest son Chris does all the graphics and design work and also fixes some of my hardware and software problems. My second son, Josh, is the network, hardware, and emergency fix-it expert. Without their help, I'd be lost!

My husband, Mike, deserves special thanks for his patience and forbearance each time we get ready to publish new editions. As we rush to meet deadlines, everything else—meals, laundry, housecleaning—has to wait. He always pitches in so that the really important things still get done.

Most of all, I give thanks to our Heavenly Father who makes all things possible, and through whose grace we accomplish anything worthwhile.

- Cathy Duffy

Table of Contents

Introduction and How to Use This Book

Attempting to write a curriculum manual that will be helpful to the majority of home schoolers is quite an undertaking when you consider the diversity among our families—even among the children within each family. With this intimidating task at hand, I set out to make recommendations that are concrete enough to be of use to those who have no idea where to turn for curriculum materials. At the same time, I want those recommendations to also be helpful to those who are re-evaluating what they have used and are interested in knowing what else is available.

It is impossible to be completely objective concerning curriculum. I have tried to accommodate various educational viewpoints in materials and methods, and I have chosen to include materials that suit a broad range of learners and situations. Many materials are included even though I have some reservations about them. I've used a code system at the end of reviews: **(S)** means this is not a Christian product, but I haven't identified objectionable content; **(SE)** means it's not Christian and it likely has some content that you might want to skip over, but it's still worth the bother. I have omitted materials that fall too short in educational quality. After all, if you can't say at least one nice thing about a product, better to not say anything at all.

If you find that I have omitted something which you feel should be included, please write and tell me about it. A lot of my research originates from recommendations from individuals. If you disagree with my comments, please write and share your viewpoint. Ultimately, much of this is based on opinion, and opinion is subject to change.

It would be impossible for me to do in-depth reviews of every item mentioned in this book. You can generally identify products I have spent more time reviewing by the length of the reviews. Shorter reviews often reflect less familiarity with the resource Occasionally, it just means I was unimpressed. Please compare my reviews with those in other sources so that you have broader counsel upon which to base your decisions.

As you read through the book, you will find that most resource titles are followed by a publisher's name in parentheses. Look up these items under the publisher's name in the Appendix for ordering information. (Some publishing companies have names that sound like a person's first and last name. Consider these to be company names and look under the first name, alphabetically. For example, Diana Waring-History Alive shows up alphabetically under "d".) In a few instances, the name of the item and the "publisher" are identical, so no publisher's name appears. Look for these items under the given title. Following the publisher's names are prices. I include prices so that you can decide whether a product is appropriate for your budget before you waste time getting more information. Prices change frequently, so check with the publisher or distributor before ordering. You will also need to ascertain shipping, handling, and tax costs to determine your actual cost. In cases where no price appears, it might be for a number of reasons such as the publisher did not supply it, the price is set by various distributors with large variations from one to another, or the item is out-of-print or too new for a price to have been set. In these situations, contact a publisher or distributor for more information.

Inevitably, some publishers go out of business and some items go out of print. I appreciate it when potential customers tell me this has happened (or suspect it has happened), because I sometimes do not discover such problems until months later.

One other stylistic choice deserves mention. I have chosen to use the generic "he" in most cases to refer to either girls or boys. I do not intend to be sexist, but constant references to he/she or alternation of the two terms is unwieldy and awkward.

Now I know you are anxious to skip to the reviews, but if you have been diligent enough to read through this introduction, persevere just a little longer to read the first few chapters before finding out what I have to say about *The Phonics Game* or *Saxon Math*. You can save yourself much grief if you tackle curriculum selection in an orderly manner. And please stay tuned in to the Holy Spirit for His guidance as you try to sort things out.

- Cathy Duffy

Chapter 1

How to Choose Curriculum

Making the decision to home educate our children was hard enough. Now we have to figure out how to actually do it!

Planning a program for home education can easily seem an overwhelming proposition. When our family began home schooling in the early 1980's, there was little information available to us. We had no idea there were numerous choices and decisions to make. Our biggest concern was often finding educational publishers who would sell anything at all to us. Many of them feared some awful consequences if teachers manuals or answer keys got into the hands of unsupervised home educators.

We now have the opposite situation (most of the time) where publishers are more than willing to supply curriculum. The concern facing home schoolers today is how to choose from among the thousands of options. On top of that, the number of different approaches to teaching from which we are able to choose can make us feel that we need a degree in curriculum and methodology before we even begin.

I hope to simplify your decision making by helping you set concrete goals and learn how to choose methods and materials that are right for you.

Goal Setting

Where are you going? Are you like Alice in Wonderland, asking the Cheshire Cat which fork in the road to take? The Cat asked her where it was she wanted to go. Alice replied that she did not actually know where she wanted to go. The Cheshire Cat then replied that it did not really matter which road she took, since both would take her somewhere!

Are you just going "somewhere"? If so, then perhaps it does not matter what curriculum you choose. They all lead somewhere. However, if you have somewhere specific to go you had better choose the curriculum and methods that are going to take you in that direction.

Perhaps you thought that teaching your children would be simpler than this. After all, the schools seem to have it down to a pat formula. If you would like to raise a child that is a duplicate of the typical public-school product, then perhaps home education is not for you. If you desire something different, then read on.

Perhaps you have not thought about your goals. If so, you are certainly not alone. Few of us have been faced with the need to clearly state our goals in life, much less come up with specific goals for educating our children. So where do we begin?

Why

Before setting educational goals, we must set forth clearly our basic philosophy, that is, our beliefs about life and its purpose, about man's relationship to God, and about parental rights and responsibilities. There's not enough space here to deal with these very basic questions. You need to do it on your own. I encourage you to write out a simple statement of your basic philosophical beliefs before you begin. Ask yourself questions such as:

"For what am I preparing my children?" (e.g., To make lots of money, or to serve God in whatever capacity God has planned for them?)

"Who owns our children?" (The State, parents, or God?)

"What is man's nature?" (Is there a sin nature that must be overcome, or is man basically good unless corrupted by society?).

The answers you give to such questions have a direct bearing on your choices of materials and methods. Those answers provide the WHY of home schooling. They need to be the motivational force behind your efforts.

How

The next area to consider is still philosophical, but it is the HOW part of our philosophy. It is, specifically, our philosophy of education. Here there is much room for debate. Christians differ on the proper approach to educating children. We need to understand that there is no exclusively right way to teach our children. We will probably agree with one philosophy of education more than others for a number of reasons. Some of those reasons will have to do with the education we received. Some will reflect what we see in our own children—their special needs and gifts. Some of those reasons may be the result of the influence of people whose opinions we respect. Arriving at our own philosophy of education will take some time (possibly years) and experience. Do not expect to begin with a clear and unchangeable philosophy.

We will encounter advocates of early learning, delayed learning, and everything in between. There are advocates of traditional approaches that depend on memorization and drill and advocates of discovery/experiential learning. There are those who believe that children will do best if left to their own devices and those who believe that children need guidance and direction at all times.

We must look past labels to understand the true philosophy behind any educational approach. Some people use the same terms to describe very different things. An excellent example is the term "child-centered learning." To some people child-centered learning means the child is the best judge of what he or she needs to know. They believe the child should have primary control over his schooling, choosing what, when, and how to learn. To others, child-centered learning means an individualized approach that takes into account the unique gifts of each child and the fact that God has a different plan for each. In this view, the parent directs what is taking place. The parent chooses methods and materials that work best with each child and which will help develop the special talents that God has given to each.

Another example would be "individualized program." One publisher uses the word "individualized" to mean that you choose the rate at which each student progresses through his workbooks. Individualized to someone else means the child chooses his own subject matter as in the first definition of child-centered learning above. Individualized to still another person means something more similar to the second definition of child-centered learning. This can be very confusing!

Books to Read

To form our own philosophy, the best thing to do is read. We should begin with the Bible, because whatever ideas about education we choose to follow must be in agreement with God's Word. Then, we need to read books and magazines presenting different viewpoints so we can compare and judge for ourselves the validity of each. We also should talk with other parents, weighing opinions and experiences according to their sources and circumstances. Keep in mind that what works for the family with ten children that lives self-sufficiently on their own farm out in the country is likely to be different from what works for the family with two children who live in an apartment in a heavily-populated community.

There are many books on the philosophy of education and more each year that focus on home education. Following are some of the worthwhile books you should consider reading. I have listed them in alphabetical order rather than preferential order. The issues that concern each of us vary, so the books that will best address our concerns will be different for each of us.

Better Late Than Early
$9 or
School Can Wait
$10
by Dr. Raymond and Dorothy Moore
(The Moore Foundation)

Both these books present Dr. and Mrs. Moore's ideas on the integrated maturity level and delaying formal academics. While both books cover the same topics, *School Can Wait* offers more scholarly documentation, while *Better Late Than Early* was written for the average reader. Dr. and Mrs. Moore have written several other books related to home education such as *Home Grown Kids* [$9], which tells about successful home school families, and *The Successful Homeschool Family Handbook* [$11] which warns about pitfalls to avoid and suggests positive alternatives. Dr. Moore describes these alternatives as low-stress, low-cost, high-achievement learning methods. Their newest book, *Minding Your Own Business* [$10], deals with home management, home industries, money management, and altruistic service.

The Big Books of Home Learning
by Mary Pride
(Alpha Omega)
$25 each

The *Big Books* are now available in their fourth editions. Presented in three volumes, the first two are of interest at this level: *Getting Started* and *Preschool/Elementary*. (If you prefer a "computer" version, all three volumes will be combined on a single CD-ROM with a price of about $50.) With delightful and witty commentary, Mary presents her philosophy of education and hundreds of product and program reviews. Mary and I differ in our opinions on many products, so it should be very helpful to compare our comments before making up your own mind.

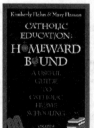

Catholic Education: Homeward Bound
by Kimberly Hahn and Mary Hasson
(Ignatius Press)
$14.95

This book reflects the growing popularity of home education among Catholic families. Hahn and Hasson present the rationale for home education but spend most of their time on what to do and how to do it. As you might expect, they strongly stress spiritual purpose and focus throughout our educational endeavors. The book deals with teaching all ages.

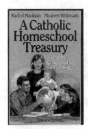

A Catholic Homeschool Treasury: Nurturing Children's Love for Learning
compiled and edited by Rachel Mackson and Maureen Wittmann
(Ignatius Press)
$14.95

A Catholic Homeschool Treasury is a great introduction to home education for Catholic families as well as an encouragement and help to those who aren't Catholic. It features a number of articles on getting started, philosophy of education, resources, enrichment, support, and "how we do it" stories from different educational philosophy viewpoints. Stories are real rather than idealistic, which makes it very practical. Many of the articles offer specific suggestions of resources and methods to use, creating an overall balance in the book between philosophical and practical help. This *Treasury* contains articles by the two editors plus numerous other homeschooling moms and dads. Appendices include addresses, phone numbers, and some web sites for Catholic groups, vendors, and products.

Catholic Home Schooling: A Handbook for Parents
by Mary Kay Clark
(Tan Books)
$18

Catholic Home Schooling was primarily written by Mary Kay Clark, director of Seton School, but it also includes a few chapters by others. This is a comprehensive handbook (452 pages) covering the philosophical and theological bases for home schooling as well as the mechanics. Mary Kay's extensive experience in home educating her own sons and assisting thousands of families is evident in her very practical suggestions for planning, scheduling, and teaching. I found her suggestions for homeschooling large families some of the most realistic and helpful I've read. (The first edition of this book was published in 1993. The review is of the updated, 1998 edition.)

Charlotte Mason Companion
(Charlotte Mason Research and Supply Co.)
$18.99

Karen Andreola's *Charlotte Mason Companion* is a compelling, in-depth journey through Charlotte Mason's philosophy of education— "the gentle art of learning"—that many will find to be a much more practical source than the original volumes by Mason. Andreola emphasizes how a loving home environment provides an atmosphere for establishing good habits and motivation for children to learn by means of their own curiosity. The reading of real, living books and retaining knowledge

through narration (oral retelling) develops students who ultimately are able to educate themselves. From the novice to the well-seasoned home educator, this guide offers a Godly design of purpose, inspiration and encouragement.[Debbie McCullough]

The Charlotte Mason Research and Supply Co. also carries other resources supportive of Charlotte Mason's methodology as well as back issues of the *The Parents' Review: A Quarterly Magazine for Home Training and Culture*. For those who wish to follow Mason's directives, this company is an indispensable resource.

A Charlotte Mason Education
$8.95
More Charlotte Mason Education
$13.95
by Catherine Levison
(Charlotte Mason Communiqué-tions)

Both these books also do an excellent job of conveying Charlotte Mason's ideas in a user-friendly format. You might want to read the second book before the first since it offers more broad advice about scheduling, selecting materials, teaching methods, and philosophy of education. It also includes using the methodology with high schoolers, creating a "century book," and lengthy, recommended-book lists. Quoting frequently from Mason's work, Levison explains and clarifies Mason's ideas while also adding her own ideas resulting from her years of experience teaching this way in a home school setting. The first book focuses on methodology by subject areas such as literature, spelling, science, and art appreciation, while it also includes chapters on narration, handicrafts, citizenship and morals, and the formation of habit. I found these books extremely practical and thoughtful.

The Christian Home School
by Gregg Harris
(Noble Books)
$12.95

In *The Christian Home School*, Gregg Harris shares some philosophy of education and child-training as he discusses basic decisions in beginning home education. He is sure to convince fence-sitters that home education is the only way to go. (This is a good book for "reluctant" fathers.)

Countdown to Consistency: A Workbook for Home Educators
by Mary Hood, Ph.D.
(Ambleside Educational Press)
$8.95

Countdown to Consistency, is subtitled "Understanding and Clarifying Your Educational Philosophy." Hood proposes four philosophical categories of home educators, of course allowing for much overlap. She does a superb job of describing philosophies so that novices can understand basic differences. She then ties in related areas—assumptions about life and learning; educational goals; teacher/student roles and relationships; curriculum design; methods of planning, instructing, and evaluating; and selection of materials. She includes worksheets to help us think through different areas and record our conclusions. At only forty-five pages, with much blank space for our own notes, this book offers a quick jump-start for developing a philosophy of education.

Creating the Balance [video]
(KONOS Character Curriculum)
$150

KONOS Character Curriculum has created a seven-hour video in which *KONOS* author Jessica Hulcy demonstrates how to organize school, home, and family while planning and using *KONOS*. Settings include the single family and a small co-op group. Jessica has such great ideas and covers so much territory, that even those using other curricula will learn much from this video. This series is a good investment for a support group.

Dads: The Men in the Gap [video]
(Konos Character Curriculum)
$35

Wade Hulcy hosts a group of veteran homeschooling dads in this 1 1/2 hour video. Group discussion is interspersed with photos and illustrations to keep it interesting. Key themes grow out of the discussion as the fathers address the very real challenges they face. This is a tremendously encouraging video as well as one that upholds a high standard of involvement and responsibility. It comes with a study guide that helps focus fathers on the key ideas, giving them practical activities to evaluate their effectiveness as "provider, priest, protector, principal, and partner."

Designing Your Own Classical Curriculum: A Guide to Catholic Home Education, revised third edition
by Laura M. Berquist
(Ignatius Press)
$14.95

This specialized resource should have particular appeal for Catholics and those pursuing a classical form of education. It reviews the foundations of a classical education, although not as thoroughly as does Wilson in *Recovering the Lost Tools of Learning*. However, Laura Berquist devotes much more attention to outlining a recommended course of study for grades K-12. She divides studies according to her "translation" of the Trivium, then shares specific recommendations for each grade level. Drawing on her experience in actually constructing and

teaching this curriculum, she adds personal comments explaining her preferences and how they might work for other families. She recommends a broad mixture of resources from Catholic publishers and distributors, Seton's correspondence program, BJUP, Saxon math, *Learning Language Arts through Literature*, and other highly- regarded resources as well as "real" books. She includes recommended reading lists for each level, and she uses a helpful key to show us where we might obtain almost all of the resources. Even those who are not particularly enthusiastic about the classical approach but who prefer a truly Catholic education will find this book an invaluable source for locating resources. Laura Berquist's new book, *The Harp and Laurel Wreath* (Ignatius Press) [$19.95] helps parents implement the classical approach with poetry and dictation for all age levels. See the review under "Literature for a Classical Curriculum" in Chapter Nine. Laura has also written complete Syllabi for grades K-4, 7, and 8 for implementing classical education as recommended in her book. (Grades 5 and 6 are in production.) See the review under "All-in-One Studies" in Chapter Five.

Dr. Beechick's Homeschool Answer Book
by Dr. Ruth Beechick
(Mott Media)
$12

Drawn from the questions homeschooling parents have asked Dr. Beechick over the years, *Dr. Beechick's Homeschool Answer Book* gives common sense advice in a question-and-answer format. Among the topics included are educational philosophy, choosing curriculum, reading, writing, math, Bible, preschoolers, high school, and testing. Dr. Beechick's answers are always supportive and encouraging. (Dr. Beechick's answers were selected and edited by Debbie Strayer.)[V.Thorpe]

Educating the Whole Hearted Child
by Clay and Sally Clarkson
(Whole Heart Ministries)
$20.95

Educating the Whole Hearted Child is much more than a book about the philosophy of education. The preface to the books says, "...this book provides a model for home education that will help you sort out the books and materials that weary your body (and your child) from the ones that will enrich you and your child. The Home Centered Learning model in this book shows you how to turn your home into a heart-filling, rich and lively learning environment using a whole book, literature-based approach to home education." *Educating the Whole Hearted Child* accomplishes this and much more. It is directed to parents of children approximately ages 4 - 14 and covers such topics as discipleship, home organization, methodology, resource selection, learning styles, lifestyle, creativity, and support groups. It includes a recommended reading list, resource addresses, and reproducible planning forms. This book is loaded with information and inspiration and will be helpful to all homeschoolers no matter their choice of curriculum.

For the Children's Sake
by Susan Schaeffer Macaulay
(Crossway)
$12.99

For the Children's Sake is based upon the work of Charlotte Mason, an educator who lived at the turn of the century. Both Mason and Macaulay beautifully present a philosophy of education for young children that identifies the home as the ideal setting for a real-life education using "real" books, nature, and everyday activities as tools for learning. I recommend this book to almost all parents starting to home school children in the elementary grades.

Freedom Challenge: African American Homeschoolers
edited by Grace Llewellyn
(Lowry House)
$16.95

African American homeschoolers encounter all of the same problems other families have, plus others unique to their situations. However, this book is not really about the "black experience" so much as it is about homeschooling when you're not part of the mainstream group. This collection of stories and interviews by and with parents and children will stretch your thinking about not just the nuts and bolts of home education, but the homeschooling groups you join and how you interact with other families. These families represent a broad social and religious spectrum. Also, some are world travelers. The diversity of ideas and experiences they present is bound to expand your thinking about home schooling.(S)

Gifted Children at Home: A Practical Guide for Homeschooling Families
by Janice Baker, Kathleen Julicher, Maggie Hogan
(Castle Heights Press, Inc.)
$24.95

Written by homeschooling moms who've "been there," this book addresses concerns about homeschooling gifted children ranging from "How do I know if they're gifted?' to "How do I deal with the college admission process?" These moms have also worked with hundreds of other parents, so they draw from a wide range of experience when they address issues such as teaching methods, curriculum choices, discipline, and dealing with special problems created by these children's extraordinary needs. The book is very practical with "what to do" lists, resource recommendations, and contacts. Much of this book would also be helpful for any homeschooling parent wonder-

ing how to provide both challenging and appropriate learning opportunities for their children.

Home Educating with Confidence
by Rick and Marilyn Boyer
(Holly Hall)
$9.99

In *Home Educating with Confidence*, the Boyers share from their sixteen years of experience with their thirteen children. Using anecdotes and a "friend-to-friend" style, they encourage us to examine Scripture and design home school programs that reflect God's priorities. They help us get away from the "school-at-home" approach all the way through high school into college and career preparation.

The Home School Manual 🖥
by Ted Wade
(Gazelle Publications)
$30

Now in its seventh edition, *The Home School Manual* is one of the most comprehensive books available. Ted covers all the basics of home schooling and offers a very balanced presentation of the pros and cons of home schooling. Special sections by guest authors add extra depth. There is much help here for both beginning and veteran home schoolers.

Since the book is well over 500 pages, Ted provides six "guided tour" options, which list pertinent chapters to read depending upon your situation--investigating home education, teaching young or preschool children, just beginning to teach elementary grades, continuing elementary grades (veterans), high school at home, and teaching children with physical and/or educational challenges or disabilities. Chapters reviewing resources, although not nearly as extensive as those in the *Curriculum Manuals*, should be helpful to compare with those in this book. Addresses are listed for home schooling organizations and government education offices for all states, for Canadian provinces, and for 18 overseas countries. Ted also enlisted the skills of organizing expert, Marilyn Rockett, to create a number of reproducible charts and forms that appear at the back of the book. If you have children preschool age up through early elementary years and 500+ pages are too overwhelming, Mr. Wade has distilled from *The Home School Manual* the absolutely most important information about working with young children. He has published these excerpts in a 64-page book titled *Early Years at Home, When Life Patterns Are Set* (Gazelle Publications) [$4]. It addresses crucial topics regarding teaching preschoolers, the timing and how-to's for introducing academics, and teaching values. Current lists of suppliers and magazines are included.

Ted Wade's *The Home School Manual* (Gazelle

Publications) is now also available on CD-ROM [$34] for machines running Windows 95 or higher. (Note: the brochure says that the program is "mostly accessible with the Mac as well.") Since the print edition is a huge book, this is a space saver as well as a convenience in many other ways. The interactive index and table of contents as well as word search capability within chapters allow you to quickly locate information. Footnotes are accessible in sidebars with the click of a button. Related information also pops up automatically in the sidebars. The "tours" from the original book are even more usable on the disks. Links to web sites and e-mail addresses are included.

Homeschooling Almanac 2000-2001
by Mary and Michael Leppert
(Prima Publishing)
$24.95

Homeschooling Almanac offers getting started help for homeschoolers of diverse religious or non-religious persuasions. It covers the basic questions for making the decision as to whether or not to homeschool. Then it helps parents figure out where they fit in relation to three basic "philosophies" of education: the parental approach, unschooling, and the eclectic approach, although it does describe various other specialized approaches (e.g., Charlotte Mason). Interviews with experienced home educators (parents and children) add "real life" pictures of what homeschooling is really like for different people. The book is fairly balanced as it presents different options, but the Lepperts clearly favor experiential, enjoyable homeschooling that responds to the needs and interests of both parents and children. Helpful, but limited, contact lists for resources and organizations are at the end of the book along with some valuable coupons for free or discounted magazines that might even offset the cost of this book.(S)

How to Get Your Child off the Refrigerator and on to Learning
by Carol Barnier
(YWAM Publishing)
$8.99

The subtitle of this book, "Homeschooling ADHD, Distractible or just Plain Fidgety Kids," might make you think this is only for parents with learning disabled kids. But while it has some brilliantly-practical ideas and insights for such situations, I think just about all parents would love the help Carol offers for those days when the kids just can't stop fidgeting. The bulk of the book is creative games and teaching ideas that work with the Wiggly Willy child. (See the section on learning styles a few pages further on in this chapter.) Most of Carol's ideas are low-cost, minimal work, and they address most subject areas—even ways to plan field trips for optimal success. I've come to many of the same conclusions as has Carol, and I've tried some of the methods she has with great success. So,

as long as you have children who are not always placid and compliant, you'll find this book useful. Carol's humorous approach and encouragement might actually get you to laugh at your child's next "creative incident" rather than loose your cool.

How to Homeschool the Primary Years [video tape series]
(Dave Exley)
$99

Ever been to a homeschool convention and wished you could have attended only the best parts of the best sessions? This six tape set of videos makes it happen. Presentations by some great presenters have been edited to varying degrees to create these videos that cover the most important topics for those teaching children through the primary grades. Even better, specially taped interviews with some presenters along with commentaries by Dr. Ruth Beechick expand upon or focus in on crucial areas. The result is a "best of the best" collection of presentations that you can watch any time you want to. Featured speakers in addition to Dr. Ruth Beechick are Cynthia Tobias, Debbie Strayer, Vicky Goodchild, Elizabeth and Dan Hamilton, Dr. Dale Simpson, Jane Hoffman, Monty and Karey Swan, Jackie Winner, Dr. Walter Drew, Pat Wesolowski, Barry Stebbing, Chris Osborne, Dr. Jeff Bradstreet, and Steve Shapiro. The Preview tape is a 13-minute overview of all presentations. Volume 1 addresses social and family issues in addition to some of the bigger questions folks have when they are deciding whether or not to home educate. Volume 2 treats very practical issues regarding learning such as learning style, scheduling, and teaching reading. Volume 3 focuses on teaching math and science, and it also includes a wonderful segment with the Swans on "Teaching to the Heart of Your Child." Volume 4 stretches beyond the 3 R's with presentations on creative play as a primary learning tool; how to help your children become lifelong, independent learners; why and how to teach art; and software and computers for grades K-3. Volume 5 deals with two challenging issues: teaching children who have learning difficulties, and teaching with toddlers present.

Let Us Highly Resolve
by David and Shirley Quine
(Cornerstone Curriculum Project)
$10

David Quine has developed an entire line of math, science, art, and music curriculum all based upon a biblical Christian world view and reflecting the ideas of Francis Schaeffer. In *Let Us Highly Resolve*, a book David coauthors with his wife Shirley, the Quines give us a "handbook" for raising our children according to that world view. From building upon the biblical foundation and teaching our children absolutes and proper reasoning, we can build our families up in faith, truth, and knowledge, equipping them to carry the message of the gospel to the world. The Quines show us how we can raise our children to "challenge our culture with the truth of Christianity." You might consider this a foundational book on the philosophy of raising families and of education. Some of the ideas are very profound and challenging, but the Quines translate those ideas into real life with many stories from their own lives and experiences. If you are interested in doing more than just "getting through school" with your children, this is a must read.

No Place Like Home...School
by J. Richard Fugate
(Foundation for Biblical Research)
$6.95

No Place Like Home...School packs a lot of basic information for new home educators into only 136 pages. This book is actually a compilation of the "best of" two earlier books by Fugate—*Successful Home Schooling* and *Will Early Education Ruin Your Child?*—and some of his most popular presentations that he gives at home schooling conventions. He deals with the major questions we face making the decision to begin. He addresses the practical questions such as how mom and dad divide up home schooling responsibilities, choosing how to set up your school, should we use Christian curriculum, and whether or not to use standardized testing. Four chapters deal with the question of when to begin teaching, with Fugate advocating early education if a child is mature enough to learn. He does not try to address specific curriculum choices or programs, but he includes a recommended reading list and a list of key addresses. While all prospective and new home educators should read this book, I suspect its conciseness and straightforwardness will be especially appealing to dads looking for encouragement, conviction, and practical advice.

The Relaxed Home School
$10.95
The Joyful Home Schooler
$12.95
by Mary Hood Ph.D.
(Ambleside Educational Press)
Relaxed Record Keeping
by Mary Hood, Ph.D.

(Elijah Company)
$5

In *The Relaxed Home School*, Mary Hood (who is also the author of *Countdown to Consistency*) describes her own philosophy of education. She covers some of the background territory such as I do in the first few sections of my book. Then she goes on to "demonstrate" her philosophy in action in her own family by telling us how they tackle each subject. Mary's

approach is, as the title indicates, relaxed. She is a Christian home educator but does not rely on a Christian-textbook approach to learning. She stresses the need for goals, coupled with an openness to many ways of attaining them. Her children have significant input into goal and strategy decisions, reflecting their own personal goals, talents, and interests. I highly recommend Mary's book for great advice on how to actually apply your own as well as your children's creative ideas to learning.

Mary Hood has also authored *Relaxed Record Keeping* which tells us how to keep records via journaling and creating portfolios. She shows how to put together reports to turn in to authorities describing educational progress of our children, while still maintaining a "relaxed" homeschool atmosphere. With plenty of examples, she makes it look easy to do.

Mary's latest book, *The Joyful Home Schooler*, has over 200 pages of encouragement and wisdom from one who has " been there." Included are chapters on trusting God, discovering your real role, educating children at all age levels, and overcoming adversity and spiritual attacks.[V. Thorpe]

The Right Choice: The Incredible Failure of Public Education and the Rising Hope of Home Schooling
by Christopher Klicka
(Noble Books)
$14.95

The Right Choice presents the case for the success of home education. If you are hoping to be talked out of home educating your children, avoid this book like the plague. I don't see how anyone can read it and still defend placing their child in a public school. Author Christopher Klicka accurately, but mercilessly, nails public school failures in the areas of academics, morality, and philosophy. He then contrasts the home school's advantages in all of these areas. Assuming we have been convinced to begin home schooling, the next section includes a few chapters contributed by Gregg Harris on starting your own home school. Klicka takes over again on the legal front, describing anti-home education tactics of social workers, school officials, and teachers' unions. Lest we be intimidated by bureaucratic attacks, Klicka delineates parental rights under the Constitution and demonstrates courtroom strategies used to protect those rights. Since homeschooling continues to come under attack, even in states with the best laws, the next section deals with ongoing legislative awareness and involvement as well as defensive actions such as obtaining positive media coverage for home education. Since Klicka is a lawyer with the Home School Legal Defense Association, he appropriately adds an encouragement to join HSLDA.

While there are numerous books that cover many of the topics addressed here, Klicka has done us a favor by pulling it all together into one book. His documentation is thorough with plenty of statistics and studies. (This is an essential resource for anyone doing a presentation or paper on home education.) The inclusion of real-life examples and stories keep us from zoning out from data overload. If you are easily overwhelmed, you can skip around in the book rather than reading straight through its 462 pages. This is another of those basic "must-have" books for home educators. New home schoolers need it just to know what this is all about, and veterans will appreciate having so much useful information at their fingertips.

The Simplicity of Homeschooling
by Jack and Vicky Goodchild
(HIS Publishing Company)
$20

The Simplicity of Homeschooling is a book and audio tape set by homeschooling pioneers that reflects the conclusions that many pioneer families have come to share about what home schooling and the home school lifestyle ought to be. The book, by Vicky, is for both beginners and veterans. It addresses some of the beginner's questions with encouragement and reassurance. Vicky then describes seven primary homeschool methods, mentioning resources for more information and/or curriculum for each. Obviously, she prefers unit study approaches the most, but, like many experienced home educators, she also believes that the best home schooling pulls in elements of a number of different approaches to tailor what we do to fit our own families. Vicky also covers the question of what to do with preschoolers, homeschooling high schoolers (with lots of specific helps), curriculum suggestions, goals, scheduling, support organizations, and resource and curriculum suppliers (selective lists). A theme throughout the book is the importance of developing a "learning lifestyle," of creating a home where education is encouraged and enjoyed rather enforced. The audio tape by Jack Goodchild is directed to dads who might be more likely to listen than to read the book. It summarizes the importance and value of home schooling with some practical suggestions for dads, then ends with a beautiful song by Monte and Karey Swan.

The Three R's and You Can Teach Your Child Successfully
by Dr. Ruth Beechick
(Mott Media)
Three R's set - $12; You Can Teach... - $14

The Three R's are discussed under math, reading, and language since this is a set of three separate booklets on each of those topics. These are for parents teaching children in grades K-3. You Can Teach Your Child Successfully is a 388 page book for parents of children in grades 4-8. Dr. Beechick has a remarkable talent for demystifying the educational process. She explains what we need to accomplish, then presents easy and practical ways to meet our goals. She stresses the impor-

tance of parent-child interaction, real-life experience, and the value of reading "real" books. Anyone teaching young children absolutely must read the Three R's! They are tremendous confidence builders. You Can Teach... is loaded with practical teaching/learning strategies that help parents as their children move on to more challenging learning experiences. Dr. Beechick's explanation of the "narration" method of learning is especially helpful. Both these resources belong in your home-school basics library.

Timeless Teaching Tips
by Joyce Herzog
(Simplified Learning Products)
$14.95

Described as "A collection of wisdom from more than 30 years experience working with children," this is a super-practical, encouraging book for homeschooling parents. It deals with "how to home school" questions as well as basic parenting. Joyce does a masterful job of balancing parental control and authority with recognition of the needs and individuality of each child. Ideally, parents should read this book before they even have children so that they can learn how to fulfill God's calling upon them to be their children's teachers even if they choose not to homeschool. As an added bonus, Joyce uses personal stories to help illustrate her points which makes the book easy to read, understand and remember.

The Ultimate Guide To Homeschooling
by Debra Bell
(Thomas Nelson, Inc./Tommy Nelson)
$19.99

One of the most current and thorough guides to home-schooling, The Ultimate Guide To Homeschooling is great for those investigating homeschooling as well as veterans. Author Debra Bell begins by answering "Why would we want to do this?", carefully balancing the pros and cons. She includes a "Family Worksheet" with questions to help you decide if homeschooling is for your family. Once past the foundational questions, she covers topics such as choosing curriculum, using the library, organization, preventing burnout, raising responsible kids, what to teach (plus when and how to do it), homeschooling teenagers, computers, creative solutions to challenging problems, and evaluation methods.

She adds a resource guide with lists of organizations, publications, and suppliers. She includes some non-sectarian contacts (e.g., Growing Without Schooling), although she primarily lists those of interest to Christian home educators. Part of the strength of this book lies in Debra's inclusion of real-life examples of what she has done in her own family and what she has observed in hundreds of others. The book is exceptionally detailed with strategies, checklists, and suggestions. I would quibble over some of Debra's recommendations (e.g., Hakim's

History of Us series) and I would take issue with her praise for state-sanctioned diplomas for homeschoolers and her encouragement to homeschoolers to work toward access to public school sports programs (both of which I consider very dangerous). However, anyone who writes a book as detailed as this is bound to step on toes here and there. Overall, this is one of the most useful and readable books on homeschooling.

The Well-Trained Mind: A Guide to Classical Education at Home

by Jessie Wise and Susan Wise Bauer
(W.W. Norton & Co.)
$35

A mother and daughter team has written the most thorough guide to classical education. Jessie educated her daughter Susan, and Susan educates her own children using the ideas they present in this book.

While they have tried to maintain religious neutrality to be helpful to non-Christians, they still stress the importance of worldview and religious training periodically throughout the book. However, they don't suggest specific resources for such purposes.

They present classical education as the correct way to educate rather than as just another option you might select. They seem to have spent a good deal of time researching curriculum choices and making excellent choices. While they do sound fairly dogmatic about many of those choices, they let us know why they selected each and why they think it better than others.

The Well-Trained Mind lays out comprehensive, detailed programs for all grade levels with a strong college-prep emphasis. It tells what subjects to cover, which resources to use, how much time to spend, what methods to use, and sources for resources. Sections at the back deal with basic homeschooling questions for newcomers plus college preparation questions. This is a treasure trove for anyone who wants to do classical education.

Workshop-in-a-Box: Beginning Homeschooling 📼

by Trudy Abel
(H.O.M.E. Inc.)
complete kit with video - $239.98; complete kit with audio tape - $199.98; video and packet - $149.98; cassette and packet - $119.98. Mention *Christian Home Educators' Curriculum Manual* and get a 50% discount on any of these packages

The heart of *Workshop-in-a-Box: Beginning Homeschooling* is a 57-minute video introduction to home education. This presentation is also offered on audio tape rather than video. It covers the basic points in a very condensed but efficient fashion. Experienced home educator and consultant, Trudy Abel, discusses the basic concerns parents

have about homeschooling, what the research says, how to succeed, learning styles and personalities, how to choose curriculum, and an overview of the primary homeschool approaches. The video also includes a "pitch" from HSLDA. Trudy simplifies the options to help parents get started with confidence. The video comes with a packet that includes a tool for determining learning styles, a booklet summarizing homeschool research facts, an annotated bibliography, and an HSLDA application with information. You can also choose to purchase the complete "kit" which includes Trudy's recommended set of basic books: *The New Dare to Discipline, The Way They Learn, Home Schooling: Answers to Questions Parents Most Often Ask,* and *A Survivor's Guide to Homeschooling.*

Your Child Wonderfully Made

by Larry Burkett and Rick Osborne
(Moody Press)
$18.99

Sometimes the responsibility for guiding our children seems overwhelming. How do we help them realize and develop their abilities? How do we help prepare them for life as adults? *Your Child Wonderfully Made* is a relatively small, easily understood book that gives sensible advice and help in this area. The authors begin with the idea that each child is unique and has been specially made with his particular strengths and abilities by God to fulfill His purposes. They continue by supplying advice in personality testing (tests included in the back of the book), character training, motivations in career choices, and how to discern and do God's will. Each chapter is brimming with encouragement and practical suggestions. At the end of each chapter are questions that help us apply insights from the chapter to each child and explain to our children how to know and do God's will. One of the last chapters deals with setting goals and includes inventory forms that will help older children realize and set goals. This book will help you celebrate your child's uniqueness and give you practical steps in helping him plan his future.[B. Parker]

Cassettes

There is a wealth of knowledge and experience available to us on audio tapes from home school workshops and seminars. Cassette tapes are probably available from home schooling events in every state. Many of these deal with philosophy of education. While you could contact every state to find out what's available, an easier solution is to contact O.T. Studios (address listed in appendix), a company that has recorded presentations at many such conferences and seminars. Request their free catalog.

Inge Cannon audio tapes
(Education PLUS+)

Recordings of Inge Cannon's presentations are available on audio tape. Send for the Education PLUS+ brochure so that you can choose from among their constantly expanding list of titles. I would like to recommend to you two particular tapes [$6 each]: *Identifying Dangerous "High Places" in Education* and *Schooling or Educating: Which are you doing?* The *High Places* tape helps us avoid false dependence on test scores, improper use of curriculum, and other traps that sidetrack us from our important goals. *Schooling or Educating* helps us sort out our philosophy of education on the practical level. Inge has also put together a syllabus that you will want to purchase along with the tapes; in *How to Pattern Learning Upon Scripture* [$16], Inge includes outlines, diagrams, charts, resource lists, and other "handout" type material to accompany most of her tapes. You purchase the book as a companion to the above-mentioned tapes as well as 13 other tapes you can buy from Education Plus+.

Magazines

Home education magazines will expose you to a broader range of educational philosophies than you will usually find in any one book or tape, and they will keep you up to date on events, resources, and teaching ideas. There are a number of Christian and non-sectarian home education magazines.

The Teaching Home
bimonthly, $15/year

The Teaching Home magazine includes news, some of which is provided by HSLDA. Articles, including a topical section in each issue, letters from home schoolers, columns, teaching tips, and advertisements round out the content. Each issue also includes a brief presentation of the gospel. Topical sections are extensive treatments of important issues such as learning disabilities and teaching subject areas, each addressed by a range of contributing authors. Advertisements are carefully screened for product content that will not conflict with Christian values. *The Teaching Home's* web site includes their "Question and Answer Brochure" in both English and Spanish, a calendar of events, and a list of state organizations and home school suppliers with links to their sites.

Home School Digest
(Wisdom's Gate)

quarterly , $18/year—special offer to readers of *Christian Home Educators' Curriculum Manual*: purchase a full-year subscription,and you can include a one year subscription for a friend for free

Home School Digest offers a wide variety of topics in every issue, with the emphasis on information rather than news.

They generally carry lengthier articles than do the other magazines. They describe their content: "...practical tips, simple suggestions, and bold biblical challenges that make up an open forum for wrestling through the complex issues that affect all homeschooling families." *Home School Digest* has compiled two volumes of perennially-relevant articles from earlier issues in *The Best of the Home School Digest*, Volumes 1 and 2 [$19.95 for one volume, $35 for both (postage paid)].

Homeschooling Today ®
bi-monthly,$19.99/year

Homeschooling Today strives for practicality with features such as pull-out lessons we can put to immediate use, how-to articles, literature reviews, and more. Their "Understanding the Arts" pull-out center section offers a serious art study, complete with color illustrations, in each issue This magazine has always been especially helpful for families with younger children, but over the last few years it has developed a stronger emphasis on history, culture, and Christian world view ideas. Among the excellent writers contributing to this magazine are Shari Henry, Jeff Myers, and Cafi Cohen.

Practical Homeschooling
(Home Life)
bi-monthly, $19.95/year

Practical Homeschooling is Mary Pride's entry in the magazine arena. PHS tackles challenging and "leading edge" topics, addressing hot issues as well as some of the deeper questions about why we do what we do as Christian home schoolers. Also, it wouldn't be a "Mary Pride" magazine without lots of product reviews. None of the other magazines can compare with the in-depth special reviews of *PHS*.

Growing Without Schooling
(Holt Associates)
bi-monthly, $26/year

The *Growing Without Schooling* magazine/newsletter, published by Holt Associates, Inc., presents the "unschooling" philosophy, primarily through letters with a this-is-what-we-did flavor. This is a non-sectarian publication that has been existence longer than any of the others. The very first twelve issues of *GWS*, originally published 1977-79, are now available in a single bound book. This is fascinating reading for both veterans and novices that shows what it was like for the "real pioneers."[$29.95] (S)

Home Education Magazine
bi-monthly, $24/year

Home Education Magazine covers a wide range of home schooling options, including articles from many philosophical perspectives. However, they have taken a strong stand against some Christian home schooling organizations. A free sample issue is available upon request.(S)

The Link
free publication

The Link is a non-sectarian newspaper that is sent free to subscribers. It features a broad range of articles, some about topics of special interest to Christians, plus news, reviews, and advertisements. They sometimes run lengthier articles than you typically find in the magazines. Examples of some of their contributors are John Taylor Gatto, Lori Harris, Cafi Cohen, Catherine Levison, Andrew Pudewa, and Jacki Orsi, This is a top quality production you shouldn't miss, especially since the price is right.(S)

El Hogar Educador
free to Spanish-speaking families

El Hogar Educador, is a home-school magazine for Spanish-speaking families. This international publication features both original and translated articles from periodicals such as *The Teaching Home*.

El Hogar Educador also produces 36 audio cassette tapes in Spanish at very reasonable prices ($2-3 per tape). These tapes are high quality translations of presentations of speakers such as Gregg Harris, Mike Farris, and Chris Klicka. Contact them for titles and prices.

Publishers' Philosophies

As we examine offerings from various publishers, we often overlook crucial information. Publishers have particular philosophies of education underlying their materials. Some are quite obvious, and some are not. Many publishers offer pamphlets or flyers explaining their philosophy of education. If not, ask them about it. (Read Chapter Four "Major Publishers" for information on some publishers you might be considering.) The philosophy of the publisher dictates the methods presented in their material, just as it should be in our homes that our philosophy of education dictates our methods of teaching.

The point is, if we have a certain philosophical approach to education, we should try to be fairly consistent in choosing our materials so that our learning tools are not doing battle with our educational philosophy. Sometimes we are not aware of philosophical conflict, but we know that whatever we are using is not working for us.

An example of this type of conflict would be a situation where the family is working with a traditional curriculum that is heavy on written work and memorization while mom and dad's educational philosophy leans toward experiential, activity-oriented learning. The curriculum is at odds with the parents' philosophy of education. Too often, such conflicts produce frustrated moms and tearful children.

We can adapt materials to match our educational philosophy by changing methods of presentation and other ways we use the materials; however, this requires both an awareness of the conflict and extra work.

Curriculum Choices

When we combine the WHY and the HOW, we can determine the WHAT—that is, what methods and materials are appropriate choices for us. There will most likely be a tremendous number of choices at this point since we now have many excellent materials from which to choose. The most important thing to remember, especially if we are just starting, is there is no perfect curriculum! We can actually use any curriculum there is and adapt it to suit our needs. It boils down to the question, "How much adapting do we want to do?" In this manual I hope to give you information that will help you choose materials that will require the least adaptation.

Before we delve into specific curriculum choices, we must first stop to examine some important factors such as the ages of our children, our experience and confidence, our level of support, and our knowledge of God's Word. These play important roles in our choices.

Dealing With Reality

Logistics

How many children are we teaching? What is their age span? How much time do we have to devote daily to teaching? How much responsibility can Dad assume?

These are crucial questions. If we have three or more children including a toddler or baby, if we have to work part time, or if we have a handicapped child or disabled dependent relative living with us, our time is more limited than if we are teaching one or two children with few outside demands on our time. Time restrictions, whatever their source, may force us to use a program that requires less advance preparation and less personal supervision. Remember though, that effective teaching for either beginning learners or older children who learn poorly on their own requires much one-on-one work. We cannot expect younger children, or even some children up to the ages of twelve or thirteen, to work primarily on their own. They rarely learn well in this manner.

Teaching Background or Experience

Next, we consider the teacher. How much experience do we have teaching our children or other children? We may think we have none, but remember the questions our children have asked that we struggled to answer on their level? Questions like, "Where is heaven?", "Why is the sky blue?", or "How does a cow make milk?" Answering those questions provided us with teaching experience!

Have we taught Sunday School or Vacation Bible School, provided day care or informal teaching in our home, or helped our children with homework? Do not discount this valuable experience. If we realize that we have some experience, we will feel a little more confident in approaching home education. Our experience, however limited, might have alerted us to our own teaching style, and we might already have some ideas of what approaches we would like to try.

If you are truly a novice to education, then it might be wise to choose a more structured program in the beginning to give you a sense of security.

Teacher's manuals will be of great value if they offer background information on teaching techniques that apply to the home situation, suggestions for follow-through on the lesson (practical application), and problems to watch for and methods of dealing with them. All teacher's manuals do not include such information. They vary greatly in content even within one publisher's materials. Some manuals offer little more than an answer key (which might be all we need in some situations). Others sometimes deal so extensively with classroom situations, that they are of little practical use for the home school. Since teacher's manuals are not necessary for all subjects, always check to see if they will be useful to you!

If we have some experience, we will probably be able to work with less-structured (informal) approaches, especially in areas other than math and language. Since math and language rely so much on building concept upon concept, we must know more about what we are teaching and how to present it in an orderly way. Most curricula for math and language provide us with this information both in the actual presentation of the material in the student texts and in the teacher's manuals. Some of the less-academically-structured math and phonics programs still provide us with basic teaching information.

Confidence-Support

How confident are we? Do we feel we lack creative ideas? Do we feel more comfortable with someone looking over our shoulder? Are we afraid of teaching the wrong thing?

If we lack confidence, as do many new home schoolers, we must remember that God is the primary source of wisdom, and He has promised to give wisdom to those who ask (James 1:5). If God has led us to home educate our children, He will see us through. As Christians, we should be relying on God before relying on man to meet these needs.

That does not mean we should not get extra help. Sometimes it is wise to sign up under an Independent Study Program, Correspondence School, or School Service for support (See "Sources for Materials").

These organizations provide varying degrees of service, but usually they will give us suggestions, help us over problem areas, give us encouragement, and hold us accountable for educational progress.

Be certain if you sign up with a program or school that it will provide the amount of support you need. The best way to know if they will be as available as they say (often a weak point of these programs) is to talk to home schoolers who have previously signed up with them.

Often local support groups offer that same kind of encouragement and assistance without requiring that we sign up with a formal organization. However, we must not take other people for granted. We should ask them if they are willing AND have the time to give us advice and assistance. Some of the more experienced home schoolers are so deluged with people needing advice and assistance that it interferes with their own families' needs.

If you choose to sign up under any program or school, find out what curricular materials (if any), testing, and paperwork will be required. (Paperwork might vary from brief quarterly reports to daily lesson plans.) Some programs will limit your choices of materials, and you must decide before enrollment if those materials will be appropriate for your child. If you object to testing young children, be sure that this will not be a requirement.

Independent Study Programs vary greatly as far as curriculum requirements. Some will accept an informal academic approach (although they rarely have time to help you plan this type of program). Others will require that you choose from standard school materials.

Correspondence courses are usually quite rigid in requiring that you use the material they send, responding with finished lessons by certain dates.

School services and independent study programs both are usually more flexible than correspondence courses in allowing you to make your own curriculum choices.

In Chapter 22, I discuss many of the options available across the country. Check with your local support group for options available in your state or community.

Christian or Secular Books?

We can create lessons from events and objects around us if we understand that God is the author of all truth and the creator of all things, including opportunities for education. While events and objects are fairly neutral teaching materials, books are not. Every book reflects a point of view—some innocuous, some not. Choosing secular books as supplements and choosing them as basic textbooks are two different matters. With supplemental books, it is easier to choose which parts of the books to use. When considering secular textbooks, it is wise to read the entire text to discern the underlying philosophy which can be easily overlooked upon superficial examination. The subtlety of false philosophic attitudes can influence a textbook tremendously without providing obvious specific examples which are objectionable (although there are certainly enough secular textbooks with obviously objectionable content). New

Christians and those lacking familiarity with the Bible might find it very difficult to identify problems on their own.

Those of us who are weak in our knowledge of philosophy and the conflict of Biblical and humanistic ideas might want some help in understanding and teaching how God's truth integrates with all subject areas. Ruth Haycock wrote a book to do just that. *The Encyclopedia of Bible Truths for School Subjects* (Association of Christian School International) [$49.95] is a large, hardbound volume organized by subject areas. For each area, it explains the subject's relationship to Biblical concepts and provides the appropriate Scripture references. Parents should use this as a reference tool.

Those who feel confident in their ability to spot erroneous ideas, can use a wider variety of books, even those containing evolution and other unbiblical concepts. By using such books as tools to point out that not everything written in books is true and that there is often accurate information mixed with false or misleading information, we are providing our children with tools for discernment they will need later. Non-Christian books, used with discernment, also help us to stretch our understanding of what and why other people believe. Both we and our children need to know how other people think and reason if we ever hope to communicate about philosophical issues. If we know only the Christian viewpoint and never consider the framework of other belief systems, we will have a difficult time communicating because we cannot address the issues which are important to adherents of other beliefs. For instance, if we understand the doctrine of reincarnation, we can discuss with Hindus the purpose of life and the Bible's teaching about eternal life in contrast to their beliefs.

All of this relates to a topic, popularly called "world views." World views are the philosophical/religious frameworks through which we view and interpret all of life. Our personal beliefs about all areas of life should not contradict each other, but rather should make a coherent, consistent whole or world view. An increasing number of resources can be found that deal with world views.

A simple summary of world views is available in *Comparing World Views* (Family Protection Ministries)[$5 postpaid]. This booklet summarizes the Christian world view and compares it with secular humanistic and cosmic humanistic (New Age fits in here) world views in chart form. The implications of how our world views shape our lives are also shown.

Summit Ministries has earned praise for their life-changing, two-week summer world view courses for teens. Dr. David Noebel, director of Summit, has compiled background course content into a hefty book on world views entitled *Understanding the Times* (available from Summit Ministries). In the book, world views are broken down into four basic categories: Biblical Christian, Marxist Communist, Secular Humanist, and New Age (addressed in a separate chapter).

Within each category Dr. Noebel addresses ten significant areas of life, demonstrating how beliefs result in actions.

We lay a foundation for studying world views by first teaching our children about God and His revealed truth. They have to know truth before they can identify "untruth." From that foundation there are many ways to proceed.

History and literature are both great vehicles for studying about worldviews. One great way to begin is with reading biographies with your children, identifying the beliefs of the hero or heroine, then examining how those beliefs were reflected in their lives. By continually raising questions about what people (historical figures, literary characters, and real-life people) believe about God and how they live their lives, children begin to understand that what you believe makes a difference in the way you live your life. Gradually, they learn to develop their own discernment and awareness of the importance of beliefs, including their own.

Because of limited space here, I recommend to you Diana Waring's *What in the World's Going on Here?* tape set as a great starting place to explore and apply worldview ideas with your children. Also, the *Junior/Senior High* volume of *Christian Home Educators' Curriculum Manual* has an entire chapter devoted to the topic.

Methodology

Almost everyone discovers that what works this year with this child might not work two years down the road. Children change as they mature, and their learning needs reflect these changes. Sometimes we have no idea what is normal for children at different ages. Our eldest children are often the "guinea pigs" as we figure all of this out! Inge Cannon helps us look ahead to what we should expect with a basic course in child development on audio tape titled *Growing in Wisdom and Stature: How to Make the Most of Each Stage in a Child's Development*. She teaches about ages and stages in sets of audio cassette tapes. Volume 1 [$13] covers Toddlers and Preschoolers. Volume 2 [$13] covers Primary Years and Intermediate Years. Volume 3 [$17] covers Adolescents, Teenagers, and Young Adults. Tapes come in albums and are ordered through Education PLUS+. An understanding of child development will help us sort out some of the curriculum and methodology choices for different age children.

One of the major issues in education is choosing between formal and informal learning approaches. Traditional schooling represents a formal academic approach to learning, one based primarily on workbooks, writing, and rote drill. Informal learning means learning which takes place outside a standard textbook or workbook, or which uses methods that emphasize creative, investigative approaches to learning. Informal learning may be done with library books, hands-on materials, games, or practical application of skills or concepts.

The decision doesn't have to be exclusively for one or the other approach—informal or formal. You might find a mixture best for your children. For example, you might use a formal style curriculum (a curriculum with teacher's manual and textbooks) as a guideline, teaching the material in an informal manner. To do this, the teacher studies the next concept to be learned as presented in the text, then presents it in a less formal manner. Using a formal curriculum as a guideline often gives us more confidence as we are just beginning home education because a sequence has already been laid out to follow. Techniques like this can be used at all age levels.

I, personally, prefer more informal methods for young children because they fit more easily into everyday life and inspire in children an enthusiasm for learning. There are certainly some young children who will thrive on the formal academic approach, but I think they are a smaller percentage. When I talk about informal teaching for young children, I mean such methods as teaching beginning numbers and letters by pointing out those within the child's experience. We can use shop signs, food packages, addresses, phone numbers. We can talk about numbers and letters, including sounds of the letters, as we drive, walk, and do dishes. Game playing is a great learning tool. Yet another benefit of informal methods for busy moms is that when we tune in to this type of teaching, we discover how easily children can learn without much pre-planning on our part.

Other activities I would recommend for the young child rather than formal academics are cutting, drawing, and pasting for small muscle development; helping with laundry and dishes to learn sorting, classification, and other skills; cooking to begin to learn about measurement and following directions; and gardening for science and an appreciation of God's creation and provision. These types of activities will also give our child a sense of purposefulness in his contribution to the family.

Shifting from Informal to Formal

For five-year-olds, using plastic alphabet letters to make words is very appropriate, but if a ten-year-old still needs plastic letters, there is a serious problem. As our children mature, they very naturally shift to more abstract ways of learning, using books, paper, and pen rather than concrete objects and experiences. By fifth or sixth grade (if not before) they should certainly be able to handle formal academics. They need to develop good study habits (if they have not already)—learn how to study, learn the self-discipline needed to study independently, and begin to learn how to pace themselves appropriately. As our children become more independent, textbooks become a more practical learning tool.

At the same time, we should continue to include informal or less-structured learning situations occasionally as our children grow older. Unfortunately, when we turn toward textbooks we often have a tendency to turn totally away from informal,

hands-on, experiential learning. Yet, some children still have a strong need for hands-on learning (especially with math and science) at older levels. Others need more times of unstructured learning to explore their own ideas, developing creativity and skills. By expecting them to work totally out of texts or workbooks, we sometimes make learning more difficult or unpleasant than it need be, or we sometimes limit their opportunities to develop interests and abilities which God has given them.

Informal learning for older children can include such things as applying math skills to life situations, researching subjects of interest, and planning for events such as birthday parties and campouts.

For example, if our son is interested in building things with his hands, we have him use math to plan exactly what he will need, figure the cost, do the measuring, and so on. He can also research the background of whatever he has chosen to build (e.g., the history of soap box racing when he builds a soap box racer or a study of birds when he builds a birdhouse).

Developing Self-Government

One of our most important goals should be that our child becomes self-governed (under God's direction). This means he will be able to choose wisely what he will do when and how he will use his time and resources. Young children are rarely self-governed, and it is not easy for them to become so. Most children are not self-motivated and need a lot of encouragement and supervision to follow through on lessons. Some children tend to be lazy; some have a short attention span. Other children have such easygoing temperaments that nothing much matters to them, and some are easily discouraged. We will need to spend a great deal of time training our children to follow through with assignments and to persevere when things are not easy. This requires diligent supervision and follow-through on our part. As our children develop good work habits and self-motivation, our task becomes easier.

We next need to focus in on each child we will be teaching. We want each child to be challenged by what he is learning, yet we do not want the level of difficulty to be so challenging that it produces frustration. We want to use methods which appeal to our child, yet we do not want to fall into the trap of catering to his whims and moods. Many home educators shift back and forth between the desire to provide learning situations that are enjoyable for their children and expectations that they be doing something that resembles "real school."

This is probably the most challenging part of home education. The balance is difficult to achieve and almost impossible to maintain for any length of time without adjustments. If we have formulated our own philosophy of education, it will help us keep on track while performing this balancing act. For example, if we believe that some drill and memorization is essential, we incorporate that goal while considering a variety of methods or resources that provide practice in drill and memorization.

Most children are quite flexible and will go along with whatever we choose. However, if our child has been in school and under excessive pressure to perform academically, we might need to begin with a very cautious approach. Such a child might need some unstructured time to undo some of the harm done by inappropriate schooling. Using a rigidly structured program can do more harm than good. It will be necessary to be extra careful in selecting learning materials and methods.

Individualizing - Matching the Curriculum to the Child

We may have opinions about how education should take place. Structure, organization, and schedules will be important to some of us, while exploration, creativity, and flexibility will better describe another person's view of home school. Whatever our opinions, we need to be aware that each child learns differently and our preferences might not meet their needs. We can improve the learning environment in our home school by tailoring each child's curriculum to his learning style so far as this is practical.

As I discuss learning styles here, you must keep in mind that this is a very subjective topic. Even the experts cannot agree on one method of defining and applying learning styles because there are so many variables involved. In spite of the lack of unanimity among scholars, I have found that by identifying learning styles according to any of the systems people have come up with, we can better decide which methods and materials will work most effectively with our children. Rather than present all the research, I will concentrate on one view of learning styles which I have found effective and easy to use.

Learning Styles

By identifying learning styles, we are able to choose teaching methods and materials that are more likely to be successful for each child and adapt what we are doing to teach them more effectively. Dr. Keith Golay, in his book *Learning Patterns and Temperament Styles* (Manas Systems), discusses four basic learning styles or temperaments that help us discover strengths and weaknesses in the ways each of our children learn. The following information is adapted from Dr. Golay's book.

However, there are a number of learning style and personal-

Chart 1	ADULT LEARNING STYLES

Wiggly Willy
- Has trouble organizing and following through
- Would rather play and have fun than work
- Tends to do things impulsively
- Probably did poorly in school (often due to lack of interest or boredom)
- Looks for creative and efficient solutions to tasks
- Dislikes paperwork and record keeping
- Prefers activity over reading books
- Prefers to teach the fine arts, physical education, and activity-oriented classes

Perfect Paula
- Likes everything neatly planned ahead of time
- Likes to follow a schedule
- Is not very good at coming up with creative ideas
- Is comfortable with memorization and drill
- Gets upset easily when children don't cooperate
- Worries about meeting requirements
- Often prefers to work under an umbrella program for home educators
- Prefers to teach with pre-planned curricula
- Is more comfortable with "cut and dry" subjects than those which require exploration with no clear answers

Competent Carl
- Likes to be in control
- Thinks and acts logically
- Likes to understand reasoning and logic behind ideas
- Is selectively organized
- Likes to work alone and be independent
- Is impatient with those who are slow to grasp concepts and those who are disorganized
- Is often uncomfortable in social situations and has trouble understanding others' feelings and emotions
- Tends to avoid difficult social situations
- Likes to make long-term plans
- Prefers to teach math, science, and other logic-related subjects rather than language arts and social studies

Sociable Sue
- Enjoys social interaction
- Likes to belong to groups, especially for activities
- Worries about what other people think
- Tends to be insecure about how well he/she is doing with home education
- Is idealistic about expectations and goals
- May or may not be organized, depending upon accountability
- Is more interested in general concepts than details
- Prefers to teach subjects related to language arts, social studies, and, possibly, the fine arts

ity "systems," none of which is exclusively better than all others. I chose this particular system to work with because Dr. Golay had already begun studying its application with children in education. Before I go on, I want to mention some other learning style and temperament books you might want to investigate.

Discovering Your Child's Learning Style by Mariaemma Willis and Victoria Kindle Hodson (Prima Books) is reviewed elsewhere in this chapter. *People Types and Tiger Stripes: A Practical Guide To Learning Styles* by Gordon D. Lawrence (Center for Applications of Psychological Type) is another basic introduction. These two books, along with Golay's book, are based upon the work of Isabel Briggs Myer. For a different approach, read *In Their Own Way* by Thomas Armstrong (Penguin Putnam Inc.) [$11.95]. All these are non-Christian in philosophy.

For a comprehensive yet easy-to-read examination of five different learning style models from a Christian perspective, read Cynthia Tobias' *The Way They Learn* [$15] (Tyndale House). Cynthia also has a newer book, *Every Child Can Succeed* (Tyndale House) [$16.99]. It briefly reviews the various ways of identifying learning style and personality, then spends more time on practical issues of discipline and motivation. Although written with traditional schooling in mind,

much of this is very helpful to homeschooling parents.

Your Child Wonderfully Made by Larry Burkett and Rick Osborne (Moody Press), which is reviewed in Chapter One, also deals with learning styles from a Christian perspective.

The starting place when addressing learning styles is with ourselves. Before trying to determine each child's learning style, we should try to identify our own, since learning style conflicts arise from the contrasts between our own learning/teaching style and those of our children. Refer to Chart 1 for descriptions of adult learning styles. Try to disregard the names at this point. It is easy to deny our actual personality traits, particularly those that are less admirable or less desirable in our eyes, and the names themselves might influence our objectivity.

Do not expect to find any one style that fits perfectly to the exclusion of traits shown in the other styles. Look for the type that has the most characteristics that describe you, then note which of the other learning styles describe you to a lesser extent. If you find very little or none of your character traits in a learning style, take note of that also.

Keep in mind that any attempt to categorize people of any age is bound to fall short because each person is unique. Categories are seldom as clear cut as they are made to sound. Usually, people fall into untidy places between categories or

Chart 2	CHILDREN'S LEARNING STYLES
(The names assigned to the four learning styles do not reflect an exclusivity of each learning style to either irs or boys.)	

Wiggly Willy

Wiggly Willys are those children who learn best by doing—the hands-on learners. These children are usually not interested in deep thinking or analysis. They like to be free to act spontaneously, without restraint, and they dislike planning and organizing. However, they often do very well with hands-on projects. These are carefree children who live for the moment. They have short attention spans (unless doing a task of their choosing), are difficult to motivate, and can be disruptive in groups. Sometimes these children are labeled as having attention deficit disorder, although the real problem is that, because of their age and temperament, they really need to be moving around more than is allowed in a typical classroom.

Perfect Paula

I call our second type of learner Perfect Paula. This is the responsible child who likes to see that everything is done correctly. She likes things to be clearly structured, planned, and organized. Perfect Paulas seldom act spontaneously and are uncomfortable with creative activities that lack specific guidelines. They follow rules and respect authority. They like to follow a typical school curriculum and feel that they are accomplishing the same things as other children their age. They prefer to be part of groups, and they need approval and affirmation to let them know that they are doing what is proper.

Competent Carl

Competent Carl likes to be in control of himself and his surroundings. He tends to be analytical, constantly trying to understand, explain, and predict. Problem solving is something he enjoys. Competent Carls are self-motivated and enjoy long-term, independent projects. They value wisdom and intelligence. Subject areas that tend to be strong are math and science. On the other hand, social skills tend to be a weak area. Often they have difficulty understanding and relating to their peers. Because of this, and sometimes simply by choice, they enjoy solitary activity.

Sociable Sue

Sociable Sues are, of course, sociable. They often have warm, responsive personalities. They are interested in people, ideas, principles, and values. Because of this they tend to look for meaning and significance in things. Concepts are more interesting to them than details and technicalities. They can be very excited about a new project or assignment, but easily lose "steam" once the novelty has worn off. They like to be known, recognized, and acknowledged, and because of this they will often be over-achievers, putting out extraordinary effort to impress people. They are vulnerable to conflict and criticism. They dislike competition, preferring cooperation so that others' feelings are not hurt.

offer interesting combinations of more than one learning style. You will no doubt find this to be true with these categories we are discussing.

We tend to be most comfortable with teaching methods that suit our own learning styles, yet those methods might be very unsuitable for our children. We must guard against making choices that suit our style but not our child's.

Look next at the Children's Learning Styles (Chart 2). As you read through the chart, remember that people change and grow. Some learning style characteristics, especially for Wiggly Willys, reflect immaturity as much as anything else. Children will often change greatly in their learning style as they mature. We must allow our children room to grow and change and not use these categories as limitations.

It is possible that with these limited descriptions, you might find it difficult to identify your child's learning style. Most of the learning style/personality books I've mentioned include tools which can be used for you and your children to identify learning styles.

I find that both tests and categories have limited application for younger children (eight years or younger) because personality is still in such a formative stage. Most younger children learn best through activity-based approaches—learning that involves both large and small muscle movement—rather than simply listening, seeing, speaking, and writing. A high percentage of young children will appear to be Wiggly Willys just because short attention span, constant activity, and other characteristics of that learning style are developmentally normal for all young children and should be expected. On the other hand, some young children are more passive in their outlook, waiting for information to be "fed" to them. Such children might be content to have you read or teach them without any pizzazz. While they might not appear to be Wiggly Willys, it might be difficult to clearly see them within any of the other three categories at this stage of development.

The simplest way of ensuring that we are effectively teaching young children is to teach through all the senses--sight, sound, and feel—multi-sensory learning.

It is important for many children that the "doing" activities involve both large and small muscles—the whole body rather than just the hands. Even with this simplified approach, we might notice strengths and weaknesses.

Sight, sound, and feel describe learning modalities, an aspect of learning styles with which many people are already familiar. Some children will learn better by hearing, some by seeing visual aids, some by experiencing hands-on activity. The simplest differentiation is between children who learn best by hearing (auditory learners) and those who learn best by seeing and doing (visual-spatial learners).

A simple test for identifying learning modality strengths and weaknesses is to use a list of numbers. (Begin with five numbers, increasing to about eight or nine numbers.) First say them

Reflective Educational Perspectives

Reflective Educational Perspectives offers another learning style approach in a format that is easy for homeschoolers to use. They use a system of five learning styles, four of which correspond to those used in this book (Wiggly Willy = Performer, Perfect Paula = Producer, Competent Carl = Inventor, Sociable Sue = Relator). It further breaks each style down by disposition, preferred modality, best study environment, interests, and talents. Their book, *Discover Your Child's Learning Style,* [$16.95] (Prima Publishing)(S) includes Learning Style Profiles that can be used with the whole family for a fairly detailed analysis.

A primary theme of the book is that we should work with learning styles to encourage eagerness for learning in each child while helping him accomplish learning goals. The book is for all parents, no matter their educational choice.

The Homeschooling Manual and Curriculum Guide (Reflective Educational Perspectives) [$25] is a companion to the book and was specifically developed for homeschoolers. It contains practical information, including tips for setting up a school day, programs, and curriculum that work best with different styles.

The whole system (book and manual) walks us through the process of using the profiles, then applying what we discover in areas of curriculum and methodology, environment, motivation, time, and areas for growth for all family members. It suggests ways to overcome learning style conflicts in situations where there are significant differences between parent(s) and child(ren). Lists of resources for various modalities and styles take the recommendations to the practical level. (Note: Many of the recommended items are reviewed in the *Christian Home Educators' Curriculum Manuals,* and you should read my complete descriptions of as many of these products as possible before making choices.)

Reflective Educational Perspectives offers other related materials. *A Self-Portrait Interactive Styles for Parents and Teachers* includes 2 Interactive Styles profiles and a follow-up booklet for $12.50. In addition they have materials on relationships, teachers in the classroom, and on the workplace.

to your child, in order, and ask your child to repeat as many back to you in order as he can. Then write a list of numbers, show it to your child, and ask him to again repeat them out loud back to you. You might notice a significant difference in how many numbers your child is able to recall in each situation. A child who recalls more of the spoken numbers is stronger auditorially (hearing), while a child who recalls more written numbers is a stronger visual-spatial learner.

Whatever your observations about learning modalities, you will see that they sometimes fit within the learning styles approach I use throughout this book. The kinesthetic modality is the obvious fit with Wiggly Willy learners. Visual and auditory strengths cross the learning style boundaries much more frequently, and should be taken into account no matter which type learner our child seems to be. Learning styles includes awareness of children's preferred learning modalities, but it goes further to look at other personality traits such as desire to work with other people or independently, an orientation toward either the big picture or the details, and preferences for a more or less structured environment.

Teaching Methods to Suit Each Child

Studying characteristics of different personalities and learning styles will show us that teaching methods which are appropriate for one type of learner might be ineffective for another type. This does not mean that we teach each type of learner only with methods that suit his personality and temperament. For some children, it would be all fun and games, and they would learn no self-discipline. The proper approach is to use methods which work best for each child when introducing new or difficult subject matter. Once they have grasped a concept, we can use other, more-challenging methods when they are less likely to be stressful or produce failure. We can help to strengthen students' weak areas, such as short attention span or lack of creativity, by working on these problem areas within subjects that are especially interesting to our child or subjects in which they excel. For example, most Wiggly Willys do not like writing assignments, but reading an exciting historical adventure or biography aloud (which they will likely enjoy) and asking them to draw a picture about the story and write a few descriptive sentences will develop writing skills in a more enjoyable way than workbook activity. After initial instruction, we review and reinforce learning through methods that will help each child stretch himself and strengthen his weak areas. For example, a very active Wiggly Willy can learn math by using objects, without paper and pencil. Once he has mastered a concept, he can do review and practice in a workbook.

To sum it up, with both younger and older children we should teach new concepts through a child's strongest sense (learning mode) or learning style and then review and practice through the other senses (modes) or learning styles.

It helps if we recognize those subjects that are easier and those that are more difficult for each child. While there are some typically strong subjects within each learning style, there are many, many exceptions. Wiggly Willys usually prefer physically-active subjects such as music, the arts, and athletics. Perfect Paulas like more structured "book and paper" subjects like math, spelling, history, and geography. Competent Carls often excel in math and science, exhibiting less interest in the humanities. Sociable Sues will often prefer whatever subjects are presented with the most enthusiasm and interaction, but their strong areas tend to be writing and literature, languages, social studies, and performing arts. These are very general observations that may or may not apply to your child.

Chart 3	PREFERRED AND DISLIKED LEARNING SITUATIONS		
WIGGLY WILLY **Prefers:** • variety in methods • audio-visual aids • short, dynamic presentations • construction activity • hands-on activity • freedom to act • physical involvement • full control of his own project (with supervision) **Does Not Like:** • long range goal setting • complicated projects • planning • paper and pencil tasks • workbooks **Needs Help Developing:** • study habits • self-discipline to persevere	**PERFECT PAULA** **Prefers:** • workbooks • consistent structure • routine • lecture following an outline • repetition and memorization • drill and review • time to prepare for any discussion **Does Not Like:** • creative activities such as role playing, dramatization, imaginative writing • changes in a planned schedule • constant changes in the curriculum **Needs Help Developing:** • creativity • thinking skills that stretch • beyond the obvious	**COMPETENT CARL** **Prefers:** • talking rather than listening • logically organized lessons • clear sense of purpose for lessons • long-term projects • independent work • problem solving • debate • brainstorming **Does Not Like:** • listening to peer group discussion • wasting time on excessive written work or previously mastered material • repetition **Needs Help Developing:** • social skills • non-technical creativity	**SOCIABLE SUE** **Prefers:** • small group discussion • social interaction • enthusiastic presentation • creative writing • role playing • situations where she is personally recognized and valued • (needs but does not necessarily enjoy) repetition for detail **Does Not Like:** • (boring) drill • competition • being ignored **Needs Help Developing:** • attention to detail • perseverance and follow-through

You must observe which subjects consistently are handled with ease and which cause frustration. Then, for the frustrating subjects, consider using other teaching methods which better fit your child's learning style.

Chart 3 identifies learning situations that each learner often prefers followed by learning situations each type typically does not like. When a child struggles with a subject, consult the chart for another method which might make it easier for him to learn.

Avoid using a child's "weak" methods until he understands the basic concept and has reached a review or application stage. I have also pointed out areas of character training, self-discipline, or challenge typical for each type. These problems are basic to development of both Godly character and successful life skills and must be addressed.

Motivation

As you might guess, each type of learner responds to different types of motivation. Wiggly Willy responds to prizes, special trips, play time, or food. Perfect Paula can be motivated simply with happy faces, stickers, stars, and grades. Competent Carl, who enjoys being independent, can be motivated by self-designed contracts, or rewards of free time or money. Sociable Sue, more interested in people and relationships, can be motivated by personal affirmation (praise) and recognition.

Motivating our children is one of the biggest challenges we face in home education. If we can make learning more enjoyable for children (not that it always will be!), we solve part of the motivation problem. By using creative approaches and relating learning to the interests of our children, we make learning more of a partnership than a struggle.

Teaching Specific Subjects

I have talked in generalities about teaching methods, but I will delve further into learning styles for specific subjects in future chapters. When I address learning styles in each subject area, I will point out particular weaknesses to look for with different types of learners that will need special attention. You might find such extremes in your children that you cannot begin to tackle these "Needs help to" areas right now. Don't let this discourage you. These are presented as suggestions to help improve weaknesses, but you may be content to have them at least learning, even though only through their areas of strength.

This process of selecting methods and materials may seem overwhelming to those new to home education. It certainly can be! We have all wasted money at one time or another on materials that did not work well in our situations, so you will be in good company if you make mistakes in your curriculum choices. But I do believe that by knowing your children and their learning styles better, your choices will become more and more accurate and your schooling more successful.

Disguised Learning Disabilities

A word of caution is needed here. Sometimes we can mistake the characteristics or evidence of a learning disability for a learning style. If a child is still unable to do paper and pencil work after he should be developmentally able, and for subjects he has already learned through other methods, he might be hindered by a learning disability that needs to be dealt with. Sometimes a child will appear to be a Wiggly Willy because a learning disability interferes with reading, writing, or thinking processes.

If you suspect that your child has a learning disability, or if your child has other learning problems, you should first read one or more of the books I suggest in Chapter 21. Then, you might want to seek help from a developmental specialist in your area or contact one of the people or services which are described in that same chapter.

Realistic Strategies

We can see how complicated choosing curriculum materials can be. If you feel overwhelmed, a helpful strategy is to talk with other home schoolers who have children of ages similar to your children to find out what they use and how they like it. The purpose is not to discover which curriculum gets the most votes but rather to gather information about materials in actual use. The questions to ask are, "What do you use?" AND "What do you like or dislike about it?" You will soon find out which materials appeal to you and which to avoid, especially as you identify moms with children similar to yours.

Learning styles is an important factor in choosing resources, but it's not the only factor.

We usually end up compromising in one way or another. For example, we might like to use a discovery/experience approach to learning, but we have five children of widely varied ages and a limited budget. Therefore, we might choose workbooks for math and language (and maybe other subjects) on each age level and use *KONOS* (See "Unit Studies") for occasional group activities. Or because of a lack of confidence, we might choose to use the Calvert correspondence course for the first year to give us confidence and direction even though we would prefer something less structured.

These choices are not bad! Many times our home schooling choices will be less than our ideal because of circumstances. It is important to remember that selection of a particular curriculum or the amount of money spent on learning materials will rarely be the determining factor in the success of our home education. Materials are only tools to achieve our goals. Use whatever resources you have, trying to adapt to learning styles when necessary and feasible.

Do-It-Yourself

I can't conclude this chapter without saying that purchasing textbooks or other educationally-designed material is not always necessary to teach our children properly. Yes, you can actually do school without school books!

A few talented home educators have done an excellent job by finding and making all of their own resources.

Borg Hendrickson has made it practical for even those of us who feel less talented to create our own curriculum. In her book, *How to Write a Low Cost/No Cost Curriculum for Your Home-School Child* (Mountain Meadow Press) [$14.95], she says, "If you elect to use...a commercial curriculum, or the scope and sequence of a textbook series, a private school curriculum, or your state's public school curriculum, you will be giving over the educational philosophies, lifelong learning aims, lesson objectives, and perhaps modes of teaching and selection of materials to the educators who wrote those curriculums. While you may obtain soundly written curriculums, perhaps useful as references, they will not be your own. They cannot truly, fully reflect your educational intentions nor your child's educational needs or desires" (p.2).

The alternative is to determine your own educational phi-losophy, lifelong learning aims, lesson objectives, along with the methods and materials to accomplish them. Borg Hendrickson helps us to do just that, all while keeping in mind state-mandated requirements. She shows us how to create our own curriculum from the ground up for any grade level and also how to incorporate purchased materials to use as tools to help us accomplish our goals. Hendrickson does an excellent job of breaking the do-it- yourself process down into bite-size chunks, while helping us maintain a clear focus on what we are trying to accomplish. Even those who are purchasing curriculum will find help here for choosing which parts of that curriculum to use to work toward their own goals.

Controlling Your Curriculum

Most of us begin homeschooling with little (if any) understanding of what it will really be like. The "security blankets" many brand new home schoolers opt for are a complete grade level package from one publisher or enrollment in a correspondence course that makes all the decisions for us. I am increasingly reluctant to recommend either of those options to new homeschoolers, no matter how desperate they are. Too many will burn themselves out in that first year, trying to com-

---

CO-OPING

The Complete Guide to Successful Co-oping for Homeschooling Families
by Linda Koeser and Lori Marse
(Successful Co-oping)
$14.95

Personally, I think co-oping is one of the best strategies for home schooling. Of course, it will not work for everyone, but if it does, it can be the highlight of your homeschooling. Some of you are probably asking yourselves, "What's co-oping?" As with most home school strategies, there are probably a number of ways you might define co-oping, but essentially it means home schooling families joining together (from as few as two or three families to as many as you can handle) to plan joint learning activities where parents somehow divide up teaching tasks. Co-ops have been organized in a number of ways. For example, parents take turns once a week planning an entire days activities for all the children around a theme, parents take turns teaching various classes on the same day, parents hire a teacher or teachers to teach classes, or parents split up older and younger children into two or three groups and do special activities with each. There is no single correct way to do this. Co-ops might be formal arrangements with membership or tuition fees, but some of the most successful have been less formal situations where like-minded parents simply work together.

This brief description of co-oping still leaves dozens of unanswered questions. Linda Koeser and Lori Marse, successful co-oping moms, have pooled their experience and advice in a book, *The Complete Guide to Successful Co-oping for Homeschooling Families*. They describe their various co-oping experiences in detail, warning of potential pitfalls, suggesting ideas and resources, and, most of all, encouraging us with the benefits and blessings we can derive from successful co-oping. They talk about schedules, family philosophies of education and discipline, sharing costs, working with various age spans, record keeping, resources and relationships. Lots of photos throughout the book help us "see" what co-oping looks like. Three "lesson plans" for co-op days, complete with resource lists, are included as examples. Linda and Lori emphasize the blessings of lifelong relationships and the sense of extended family that develop within small co-ops. Having participated in a great deal of co-oping through our homeschooling years, I can heartily endorse what they say.

Another aspect of co-oping is that it can be especially helpful for new homeschoolers. This is a way to work closely with more-experienced moms and better understand the possibilities inherent in home education. Veterans can also gain a renewed enthusiasm for homeschooling that comes from working with and encouraging one another, and, sometimes, by enjoying a day off now and then.

plete all the pages of all the texts on an approved schedule. In the process, all they experience is the pain of schooling at home and none of the joy of real home education. It is not surprising that many don't make it past year one when they select such options. So, I am more and more convinced that even new homeschoolers are better off with some sort of "pick-and-choose" solution than restrictive packages. Fortunately, we now have "pick-and-choose" packages, preplanned unit studies, counselors, and flexible school services that can show where and how to start if we don't have the confidence to pull it together on our own. Programs like Sonlight Curriculum; a number of the all-in-one unit studies reviewed in Chapter Five; school services like Hewitt Research Foundation, Sycamore Tree Center for Home Education, and the Moore Foundation; and Curriculum Cottage's Custom Homeschool Packets are just some examples of what I would consider better choices to help you get started.

Barbara Edtl Shelton has also written a book, ***The Homeschool Jumpstart Navigator for Younger Children*** (Homeschool Seminars and Publications) [$8] that will help you through the beginning stages of home education and putting together your own curriculum. She combines the philosophical (why-to) and practical (how-to) for the novice who wants someone to hold her hand and show her step-by-step what to do.

I do not mean to say that complete packages and correspondence courses are anathema. There are certainly situations where they are useful and appropriate. The most important factor here is that parents must exert some control over the goals and implementation of curriculum; they must be able to adapt whatever they do to family situations and each child's needs.

Granted, most of us will still choose published curriculum and learning materials rather than doing without or creating them from scratch. Still, we cannot let them rule our home school! We should not be afraid to change materials if what we are using is not successful.

We should try to pick-and-choose materials from different publishers, to assemble the best resources we can for each subject each year. We should not be afraid to modify a specific resource, omitting some chapters and/or adding extra material of our choosing. As we do this, we must constantly evaluate and re-evaluate what we are doing in light of our goals. It is easy to get so caught up in "just getting through the books" that we lose sight of our original goals. This is what controlling the curriculum is all about.

Summary

We often face the dilemma in our home schools of balancing freedom and creativity with structure and legal pressures. We are faced with schools, relatives, and others looking over our shoulders, judging us and comparing us with "regular schools."

We face the danger of legal problems if we try to push our freedom too far. Legally, it is easier to defend our methods of home education if we are doing what most everybody else is, that is, following an acceptable, standard curriculum. (This does not mean that using other teaching methods is not defensible!) For most of us, it is easier to follow a prepared curriculum since it saves us time in preparation and gives us a certain amount of confidence and security.

On the other hand, the best learning usually takes place in those situations where the material learned is real, vital, and useful to the learner. This happens most often when we are not using the standard curriculum but are using more creative approaches.

There is a difficult balance to achieve between these contrasting pressures, but we should, ideally, be able to mix both standard curriculum and creative learning in a way that suits our needs. No single approach will be suitable for everyone. We are all so different—that is one of the primary reasons that many of us home school! Choose what works best for you, your children, and your family.

Whatever you do, keep good records—both a teacher's plan book and a journal for comments if you can. (See Chapter Two.) This is not only for legal requirements, but to be able to see what you have accomplished and to evaluate progress and make appropriate adjustments.

Seek God's direction for yourself and each of your children. And I pray that God will richly bless your efforts.

Chapter 2

Planning, Organizing, and Scheduling

You've probably heard the saying, "Those who fail to plan, plan to fail." Unless we intend to be home school "casualties," we had best do some preliminary research and planning.

Making an Individual Plan:
Goal Setting

How do we know what to teach? Assuming you have thought about your own philosophy of education, you should have some ideas about what is most important. These ideas should produce goals. For example, if you decide that education is about spiritual development as much or more than anything else, then developing Christian character will probably

appear high on your list of goals for your children. But since we do not operate in a self-contained universe, we have to consider more than just our own goals. We determine which subjects we plan to teach by combining our goals with the legal requirements for our state. Most states require that home educated students be taught a program equivalent to that taught in public schools. The wording of laws varies greatly as does the strictness of such requirements. Check for legal requirements in your state by getting in touch with your local home schooling organization. If they can't answer your question, they will steer you to someone who can. You might also need to know about peculiar circumstances in your county or local school district. If you have trouble contacting a support group, people at *The Teaching Home* and *Growing Without Schooling* (mag-

CULTURAL LITERACY AND YOUR COURSE OF STUDY

Dr. E. D. Hirsch roused public interest in the typical course of study followed by schools in his provocative book, *Cultural Literacy*. He expressed concern for the lack of historical and literary study, much of which would be considered part of a classical education. He went on to list specific topics he considered necessary for a good education.

Many people agreed with his assessment, but they asked, "How and when do we teach these topics?" Hirsch and his associates answered by compiling *The Core Knowledge Sequence* (The Core Knowledge Foundation) [$22.50], a scope and sequence organized by grade levels K-8 and subject areas within those levels. Subject areas addressed are language arts, American civilization, world civilization, geography, fine arts, visual arts and architecture, mathematics, life and physical sciences. This scope and sequence is not intended to be comprehensive. For instance, spelling and handwriting skills are not included in language arts. They expect that the *Core Knowledge Sequence* should be used as the foundation for about 50% of the curriculum. The remainder should then be determined by the school. The authors have tried to maintain unity whenever possible between subjects for each grade level, so topics will often lend themselves to unit study. Christians will find some areas lacking as well as some heavily weighted toward a secular humanist world view. In spite of this, most home schoolers will find it useful.

To help implement this scope and sequence, Hirsch has written a series of books, one for each grade level. They are entitled *What Your Kindergartner Needs to Know, What Your First Grader Needs to Know, What Your Second Grader Needs to Know,* etc. (through "*Sixth Grader*"). The books, published by Doubleday, are available from either The Core Knowledge Foundation or bookstores.

The books are designed to be used as supplements to a child s education in school. It is recommended that parents spend fifteen minutes a day following the guidelines and using the written material in the book. All subject areas are covered. Hirsch s goal is to provide a thorough backup which will fill any gaps and probably extend learning beyond school instruction. Because of criticisms that *Cultural Literacy* emphasized western civilization to the detriment of other cultures, we find more multi-cultural emphasis in the grade-level books than in *Cultural Literacy*.

Home educators might consider using either *The Core Knowledge Sequence* or a grade level book as the foundation for their own scope and sequence, although they will need to use something more to put together a complete curriculum.

Books to Build On: A Grade-by-Grade Resource Guide for Parents and Teachers (The Core Knowledge Foundation) [$12.95] provides even more assistance. This book is a descriptive bibliography by grade level and topic of recommended books to use for teaching. It should be especially useful for those of us who wish to construct our own curriculum using real books, but who appreciate some help in organizing and finding resources.

azines), as well as the folks at the National Center for Home Education, can provide help in locating home school organizations. Also, the Home School Legal Defense Association (HSLDA) is probably the most up-to-the-minute source for legal information about home education in all states. HSLDA will provide you with a free one-page summary of the current law for your state.

I also encourage you to consider joining HSLDA. Membership provides legal representation if you should be contacted by government/school officials regarding your right to home educate. This is an investment in peace of mind as well as for the protection of home schoolers as a whole. You can often receive a discount on your membership fee by joining through your local support group or independent study program.

Course of Study

Most states require that private schools keep certain records. One of the most common requirements is a course of study for each grade level that outlines the total program for each child. The course of study lists which subjects (and what specific area[s] of each subject) will be covered, usually accompanied by a list of materials or texts that will be used.

The state will usually require that your course of study be similar to that of the public schools, requiring that you teach the same basic subjects. This still leaves plenty of leeway in determining which details of each subject you wish to cover, and texts and methods are generally left up to you. Again, check with your local home schooling organization for your state's requirements.

Some of us have no idea what is taught in the public schools, so we have no idea which subjects we should be covering. Some public schools will provide us with their course of study, but this information is easily available from a number of sources. One of the most popular is World Books' *Typical Course of Study*, a very inexpensive (sometimes free from your encyclopedia salesperson) booklet showing lists of topics covered under various subject headings at each grade level.

Actually, there is great variation in courses of study when we look at the particulars. Compare what is covered in Bob Jones University Press, A Beka, and Rod and Staff with free scope and sequence information available from each publisher to see the variations even among Christian publishers.

In the spring preceding each school year, you should begin planning which subjects you will cover, making a general outline of goals in a notebook. There are too many variables to start filling in charts until a little bit later; nevertheless, this remains your "behind the scenes guide." From this outline, you proceed to plan the details of your courses. Often you will plan the details and select curriculum simultaneously, even though ideally you should know what you want to teach, then select

the materials that teach it. What happens with most of us is that we stumble across, hear about, read about, or otherwise discover some wonderful-sounding curriculum we want to use. The curriculum is so appealing that we compromise or ignore any sequential plan we might have had.

Despite my recommendation about a course of study, in actuality, it makes little difference what order you cover topics in most subjects, with math being the most important exception, followed by a few exceptions in the language arts areas. So if something inspires or enthuses you, it might be the best choice for that fact alone. However, it is important that you do have an overview of what subjects you are teaching so that you don't become lopsided with language arts and history while ignoring math and science.

Let's assume you are going about this in an orderly fashion rather than on impulse. First, you select primary texts or resources that will serve as the foundational structure for your program. These are the texts or materials that will keep you on target, giving you an orderly approach for teaching particular subjects.

Keep in mind that all subjects do not carry equal weight or importance. If you are teaching a child in kindergarten through third grades, your emphasis will probably be on basic arithmetic and reading skills. At older levels, your emphasis will more likely be on writing skills, math, science, and history.

When you decide which subjects will be your primary objectives you do not dismiss the other subjects. Instead, you will allot them less time or maybe even postpone teaching them until they can be given proper attention. It can be more effective to cover a subject such as science, art, music, or foreign language in depth during one year rather than giving it minimal attention over three years. Another option might be to rotate less important subjects, focusing on each for a month at a time.

Most of us are so accustomed to the idea that we have to cover every subject every day, that it is often difficult to conceive of doing things differently. Yet, there is no reason not to be creative with your scheduling (aside from possible legal restrictions) if it works for you.

Next, you plan your schedule and select textbooks in light of your priorities. You should choose materials for the most important subjects first and determine as best you can how much time will be required to use them. Secondly, keeping in mind the time available, you choose books and materials for the subjects of lower priority.

Finally, you choose supplementary books and resources you would like to use. Included here are math materials such as *Math-It, GeoSafari,* games; language materials such as *Grammar Songs* (Audio Memory), special science classes, foreign language, music, and art. (See recommendations under each subject heading and also "Creative Teaching Ideas.")

Recording Your Course of Study

Copy Chart A, Course of Study, which you will find at the end of this chapter, to use in planning your course of study. (Make a copy for each child.) As you read through specific curriculum recommendations and make choices, fill in that information on the chart. Then refer to the Appendix for information on where to best obtain the material, and record that information under "Source."

If you choose to use a unit study approach, you should still use this chart, showing which subject areas are covered within the unit study.

Keep the Course of Study on file with your important school records.

Placement

We should not arbitrarily place our children in third grade material because they are eight years old or in fifth grade material because they are ten. Instead, we should determine what level our child has achieved in the learning sequence for different subjects or what knowledge or skills he has already mastered. This is most important for math and language arts at all levels, and less so for other subjects until upper elementary level. Math and language arts should be learned in a sequential manner. For example, children learn the values of numbers before they learn to add numbers. They learn sounds of letters before they write words. They learn words before they write sentences. Language arts includes so many areas—grammar, composition, spelling, handwriting, etc.—that we have increasingly broad options about what to teach once we move beyond phonics and beginning writing.

Sometimes we already have an accurate knowledge of our child's educational level, but often we use tests to help us. Standardized tests such as the *Iowa* or *SAT 9* tests are often of minimal help when it comes to placement in subjects. If our third-grader scores at fifth grade level on such a test, it does not mean we should place him in fifth grade curriculum. The grade level result of the test reflects the level at which our child becomes frustrated. He or she should be working one or two levels below the frustration level. (See the chapter on testing for more information about using test results.) To be of real value, a standardized test should provide us with detailed breakdowns of performance within subject areas. What we really need to know is information such as whether or not a child knows how to multiply fractions.

Diagnostic tests are often more helpful than standardized tests. The booklet versions of diagnostic tests available from Alpha Omega and School of Tomorrow for math and language will help us pinpoint areas of competence and areas of weakness. These tests were written for those particular curricula and have some questions that your child might be unable to answer because he learned a concept by a different method. Be aware of such idiosyncrasies and, if you can identify them before testing, have your child skip them. Generally, you will start your child in these diagnostic tests a few levels below where you think he should be, then have him work through as far as he can until he is continually missing questions.

We are _not_ looking for a grade level placement as we examine results of these diagnostic tests but are looking at particular concepts within subject areas to determine what are the next topics to be learned. It is usually best to start into new material with some review level concepts as students familiarize themselves with new texts or materials.

Science and history topics vary greatly from publisher to publisher, so there is no specific body of knowledge that must be mastered before going on to something else. Although states are developing standards to try set a predetermined sequence of study for both subject areas, these are likely to have minimal impact on most homeschoolers for a number of years. Because of this, I don't include scope and sequences for these subject areas. See my comments about selecting topics for these subject areas in the science and history chapters.

Using a Scope and Sequence

Textbook publishers and other educational organizations print scope and sequences showing which details of a subject are covered at each grade level within their curriculum. We need to work with a scope and sequence like this to identify the details of a subject to be studied and the order in which we intend to cover them. We might borrow a publishers scope and sequence, either using it as a guideline or adopting it as our own. On the other hand, we might choose to write our own.

It is useful to compare at least two different scope and sequence lists to see how they differ from one another. You can get them in various forms from such sources as textbook publishers—Bob Jones University Press, Rod and Staff, Alpha Omega, and School of Tomorrow all offer scope and sequence information; local school districts; Hewitt Homeschooling Resources; Heart of Wisdom Publishing; Simplified Learning Products; The Weaver; and at the website www.Home2school.com.

Using a scope and sequence can be a little tricky, since they vary from state-to-state and publisher-to-publisher. Even so, up until recently, there has been a great deal of similarity in all the different lists. However, the national standards movement has caused significant shifts in the content and methodology being adopted by schools across the country. Many of these changes reflect philosophies of education and worldview with which we might disagree—evolution, whole language, and deconstruction ("constructing your own truth") being some major examples.

Consider the math standards as an example. Mathematics specialists, working in many groups across the country, have each written up lists of math standards, almost all reflecting the goals and standards created by the National Council of Teachers of Mathematics (NCTM). The math standards movement promotes more mathematical reasoning and analysis in the early years than was previously taught. Young students are introduced to estimation, probability, and statistics far earlier than before. They are supposed to learn how to read and create many types of graphs and charts during the elementary years, and calculators are to be used in the primary grades. To spend time on these concepts means that time is usually taken away from traditional math skills.

As you might have guessed, many people, myself among them, disagree with the direction the standards movement has driven math instruction, yet most math programs are written to reflect those standards since they are used to create questions for standardized tests. This presents a dilemma to home educators: teach to the new standards so that your children understand material presented on standardized tests, or teach in a more traditional fashion that stresses mastery of computation skills. Certainly there's middle ground between the extremes, but you need to make a conscious choice. If your children have to pass a high-stakes standardized test every year or so—score above a certain percentile or put your children back in school consequences, you will more likely be concerned about covering concepts in line with the new standards (hopefully, in addition to a solid foundation in basic skills). If you are not under significant "test pressure," you should choose to do what you believe is best for your children, whether or not it aligns with the standards.

Personally, I think calculators should wait till junior high or high school so that children develop excellent computation skills. I would save probability and statistics till at least fifth or sixth grade, and I would also introduce chart and graph interpretation much more slowly.

Language arts standards are less controversial. If you provide your children with a solid skills foundation, they will easily surpass the standards. They won't be hindered if they don't learn "guessing" strategies instead of phonics or if you fail to encourage them to use "temporary" or "invented" spelling. If you examine your "state standards" you might also notice the inclusion of non academic goals such as developing conflict resolution skills. This sort of social engineering seems to be popping up in standards across the country. Again, this shouldn't pose a problem on standardized tests.

I include scope and sequence lists for math and language arts in this chapter. I originally planned to include both my own scope and sequence lists (which I developed based on more traditional scope and sequences and courses of study) and another list from state standards. However, because of space limitations and the "mushiness" of so many of the state standards, I decided to include only a representative sample of goals from the California standards for comparison.

The simplest way to use these lists is to read through the goals, considering what your child already knows, identifying at what grade level he or she seems to be working. Watch for topics that might have been missed at earlier levels.

We must also watch for readiness before pushing ahead. Just because our child has mastered addition, we cannot assume he is ready to move on to subtraction. When in doubt, the best thing to do is progress by small steps and watch how they handle things. For children who struggle with new concepts, we introduce them in a different fashion, and if they still do not understand what is happening or get very frustrated, we should save it for later—they are not mature enough.

Whatever scope and sequence you refer to (those from publishers, that in this book, or another you might have), be aware that it is only a guideline which can be changed as you wish.

At the end of this chapter, the Curriculum Worksheet, Chart B, is a form you may copy and use for creating a personalized scope and sequence for each subject. You do this by listing the detailed goals (scope and sequence) of each subject you will teach this year. With subjects where you will be following a textbook closely, it is likely that you can list your goals by copying the table of contents. For subjects where you will be pulling together a variety of materials and activities, this form will help you see clearly what you will be accomplishing.

Let me add a caution here. You need to guard against a mechanical approach to schooling where you feel bound to stick closely to a scope and sequence. You should instead seek God for what is appropriate for your child to learn at this time. Perhaps reading will wait a year or two, even if all the other children his age are learning to read. Or maybe your child is ready to learn to write the alphabet at age three. And, what character traits need development at this stage? Perhaps your child needs to work on large and small muscle development and coordination. As you progress, you need to pray for God's guidance as to whether or not you need to make any changes. Even with all the guidelines, none of us can know as well as God the particular needs of each child.

Assuming you've got personalized lists of goals written down, next you determine which materials (textbooks, hands-on materials, etc.) to use that are appropriate for that level. Remember, materials from different publishers vary in what is covered at different grade levels. Although the order for presentation of new concepts is very similar, some publishers push more concepts in earlier grades than others.

For example, if you identify that your child knows basic addition and subtraction and is ready to begin multiplication, you see on the scope and sequence that multiplication is usually introduced in second grade and seriously dealt with in third grade. But when you look at multiplication in publishers' scope and sequences you find that A Beka gets heavily into multiplication in second grade and Modern Curriculum Press does not really do much with multiplication until the middle of third grade. You would then choose whichever material you prefer but at the appropriate grade level, either second or third grade, depending upon the publisher you choose.

To make sure your curriculum lines up with your goals, once you have chosen to use a particular publisher's material, you should ask for their scope and sequence and identify the level in their curriculum where your child should begin. A little review is good, but too much is boring and, possibly, counterproductive. Make sure that you are not requiring your child to do excessive review. Also, watch that you are not skipping important concepts to push children ahead into the "proper" grade level.

Following is my own scope and sequence covering math, language arts, and reading plus excerpts from California's standards for comparison. I've included progress boxes with my list in case you wish to use these with your children. Reviews of more extensive, book-format scope and sequences (which I mentioned earlier) follow these.

Traditional Scope and Sequence

Mathematics

Concepts are listed in an approximate sequence which builds skill upon skill. Use the boxes to the right of each goal to track your child's progress. Grade levels are also approximations. Programs that are advanced will cover skills at a faster rate than shown here.

Kindergarten level

	Introduced	Practicing	Mastered
• Comparison: same/different; larger/smaller; shorter/taller; long, longer, longest	☐	☐	☐
• Classification: by color, shape, size, common characteristic	☐	☐	☐
• Correspondence: matching items one for one, recognizing like amounts	☐	☐	☐
• Duplicate or extend given pattern by color or shape	☐	☐	☐
• Identify four basic shapes—circle, square, rectangle, triangle	☐	☐	☐
• Recognize numbers 0 - 10	☐	☐	☐
• Order objects and numbers 0 - 10	☐	☐	☐
• Count and print numbers 0 - 10	☐	☐	☐
• Identify more/less-larger/smaller of numbers 0 -10	☐	☐	☐
• Compare numbers of objects	☐	☐	☐
• Perform pictorial addition 0 - 10	☐	☐	☐
• Name coins: penny, nickel, dime	☐	☐	☐
• Name the days of the week	☐	☐	☐

Approximately 1st grade level

	Introduced	Practicing	Mastered
• Count backwards from 10 to 0	☐	☐	☐
• Add numbers 0 - 10	☐	☐	☐
• Match set with numbers 0 - 20	☐	☐	☐
• Add numbers 0 - 20	☐	☐	☐
• Subtract numbers 0 - 10	☐	☐	☐
• Subtract numbers 0 - 20	☐	☐	☐
• Count, read, and write numbers to 100	☐	☐	☐
• Recognize smaller/larger numbers to 100	☐	☐	☐
• Count backwards from 20 to 0	☐	☐	☐
• Recall addition facts to 10	☐	☐	☐
• Recognize that 2 + 4 is the same as 4 + 2 (commutative property)	☐	☐	☐
• Recognize addition and subtraction in various formats— horizontal and vertical	☐	☐	☐
• Recall subtraction facts for numbers 10 or less	☐	☐	☐
• Recognize quarters (money)	☐	☐	☐
• Count coins to $.25	☐	☐	☐
• Recognize time to the hour and half hour	☐	☐	☐
• Recognize fraction shapes 1/2 and 1/4	☐	☐	☐
• Count by 10's to 100	☐	☐	☐
• Represent two digit numbers in place value form as tens and ones	☐	☐	☐
• Read, write, and use expanded notation (e.g., 60 + 9 for 69)	☐	☐	☐
• Perform two digit addition and subtraction without carrying	☐	☐	☐

	Introduced	Practicing	Mastered
• Read calendar, know days of week/months	☐	☐	☐
• Select correct operation for problem solving (addition/subtraction)	☐	☐	☐
• Think about practical application of arithmetic	☐	☐	☐
• Identify and continue simple patterns	☐	☐	☐
• Select, collect, record or organize data using tallies, charts, graphs, tables	☐	☐	☐

Approximately 2nd grade level

	Introduced	Practicing	Mastered
• Use symbols for "greater than" and "less than"	☐	☐	☐
• Count by 2's and 5's to 100	☐	☐	☐
• Represent three digit numbers in place value form as hundreds, tens, and ones	☐	☐	☐
• Read and write 3 digit numbers	☐	☐	☐
• Select largest or smallest of numbers to 999	☐	☐	☐
• Recall addition and subtraction facts to 9 + 9 (some children will need additional time before mastering subtraction)	☐		
• Perform two digit addition with carrying (regrouping)	☐	☐	☐
• Perform two digit subtraction with borrowing (regrouping)	☐	☐	☐
• Introduce multiplication concept	☐	☐	☐
• Represent simple multiplication concepts with numbers	☐	☐	☐
• Identify halves, thirds, fourths	☐	☐	☐
• Know value of penny, nickel, dime, quarter, half dollar	☐	☐	☐
• Count coins to $1.00	☐	☐	☐
• Recognize time to quarter hour	☐	☐	☐
• Work with simple measurement: linear, liquid, weight	☐	☐	☐
• Interpret bar graph	☐	☐	☐
• Solve one-step word problem with addition or subtraction	☐	☐	☐

Approximately 3rd grade level

	Introduced	Practicing	Mastered
• Do multiplication to 9 x 9 = 81 (Note: Mastery of times tables might not occur this year.)	☐	☐	☐
• Introduce division concept pictorially or with hands-on materials	☐	☐	☐
• Identify place value in 4 and 5 digit numbers	☐	☐	☐
• Read and write up to 5 digit numbers	☐	☐	☐
• Recognize odd and even numbers	☐	☐	☐
• Do three digit sums and differences with regrouping (carrying/borrowing)	☐	☐	☐
• Do division with 1 digit divisors	☐	☐	☐
• Recall multiplication and division facts to 9 x 9 = 81	☐	☐	☐
• Do 1 digit times 2 digit multiplication with regrouping (carrying)	☐	☐	☐
• Identify missing function (+,-,x,÷)	☐	☐	☐
• Identify and complete more difficult patterns/sequences	☐	☐	☐
• Recognize 1/2, 1/3, and 1/4 of different objects	☐	☐	☐
• Read and write time to nearest 5 minutes	☐	☐	☐
• Understand a.m. and p.m.	☐	☐	☐
• Count, add, subtract money using $ and decimal point	☐	☐	☐
• Measure length, capacity (liquid measure), and mass (weight) using both English and metric measurements	☐	☐	☐
• Interpret simple line and bar graphs	☐	☐	☐
• Identify patterns and relationships from organized data; draw conclusions	☐	☐	☐
• Solve one-step word problems using addition, subtraction, multiplication, division	☐	☐	☐
• Perform mental computation	☐	☐	☐
• Recognize reasonable and unreasonable estimates in simple problem solving	☐	☐	☐
• Make up word problems from given data	☐	☐	☐

	Introduced	Practicing	Mastered
• Interpret and make up codes	☐	☐	☐

Approximately 4th grade level

	Introduced	Practicing	Mastered
• Identify place value in digits up to 7 numbers	☐	☐	☐
• Read and write numbers with 7 digits	☐	☐	☐
• Do any addition and subtraction with whole numbers	☐	☐	☐
• Do 2 digit times 3 digit multiplication	☐	☐	☐
• Round off numbers and estimate multiplication and division answers	☐	☐	☐
• Do division with 2 digit divisors	☐	☐	☐
• Show remainders in division as whole numbers and as fractions	☐	☐	☐
• Introduce addition of fractions with like denominators	☐	☐	☐
• Understand fractions as ratios	☐	☐	☐
• Perform addition and subtraction of fractions with like denominators	☐	☐	☐
• Recognize and create equivalent fractions	☐	☐	☐
• Define, identify and use factors, multiples, greatest common factors, least common multiples	☐	☐	☐
• Simplify fractions (reducing to lowest terms)	☐	☐	☐
• Identify fractions on number line	☐	☐	☐
• Read and write time to nearest minute	☐	☐	☐
• Do all operations with money; make change	☐	☐	☐
• Work with more difficult levels of measurement: length, capacity, mass	☐	☐	☐
• Determine perimeter of any polygon	☐	☐	☐
• Be familiar with lines, segments, cubes, pyramids	☐	☐	☐
• Construct bar graph	☐	☐	☐
• Add/subtract mixed numbers	☐	☐	☐
• Multiply and divide fractions	☐	☐	☐
• Identify and complete more complicated patterns	☐	☐	☐
• Solve more complicated (two-step) word problems	☐	☐	☐
• Use data to construct word problems	☐	☐	☐
• Determine missing data for problem solution	☐	☐	☐
• Analyze problems	☐	☐	☐
• Define and find averages	☐	☐	☐
• Identify values of Roman numerals	☐	☐	☐

Approximately 5th grade level

	Introduced	Practicing	Mastered
• Determine prime factors	☐	☐	☐
• Read and write up to 9 digit numbers	☐	☐	☐
• Introduce decimals other than in money	☐	☐	☐
• Read and write decimals to thousandths	☐	☐	☐
• Do any addition, subtraction, multiplication, division problems with whole numbers	☐	☐	☐
• Add, subtract, and multiply any decimals	☐	☐	☐
• Divide whole numbers by decimals	☐	☐	☐
• Express division remainders as decimals	☐	☐	☐
• Use ratio	☐	☐	☐
• Work with more difficult measurements	☐	☐	☐
• Determine area of rectangles and squares	☐	☐	☐
• Introduce concept of volume with cubes	☐	☐	☐
• Round whole numbers or decimals	☐	☐	☐
• Accurately estimate answers	☐	☐	☐
• Recognize congruence and symmetry	☐	☐	☐

	Introduced	Practicing	Mastered
Define and draw diameter and radius of circle, angles, parallel lines, perpendicular lines, and intersecting lines	☐	☐	☐
Construct and interpret line graphs	☐	☐	☐
Compute area of triangle	☐	☐	☐
Apply math skills to life situations	☐	☐	☐
Perform mental computation	☐	☐	☐
Apply logical thinking to problems and life situations	☐	☐	☐
Work with Roman Numerals	☐	☐	☐

Approximately 6th grade level

	Introduced	Practicing	Mastered
Read and write numbers up to 12 digits	☐	☐	☐
Read and write all decimals	☐	☐	☐
Understand and use terminating and repeating decimals	☐	☐	☐
Do any computation with fractions and decimals	☐	☐	☐
Convert fractions to decimals and decimals to fractions	☐	☐	☐
Determine circumference and area of circles	☐	☐	☐
Use protractor to measure and draw angles	☐	☐	☐
Measure and make triangles (include some that are not equilateral)	☐	☐	☐
Interpret circle graphs	☐	☐	☐
Convert measures from one type of unit to another within the same system	☐	☐	☐
Formulate and apply problem solving strategy (application of logic)	☐	☐	☐
Change percents to decimals	☐	☐	☐
Understand and apply percentage	☐	☐	☐
Introduce integers	☐	☐	☐
Introduce exponential notation	☐	☐	☐
Define, explain, and use simple probability	☐	☐	☐
Analyze and evaluate simple statistics	☐	☐	☐

Reading

Note: Goals for reading and the rest of language arts are separated in my lists, but combined in the California Standards list.

The following are some of the initial steps to reading that follow a general progression. There are much more detailed lists that break goals down by particular phonograms and other phonic elements.

	Introduced	Practicing	Mastered
Name letters of the alphabet (Some authorities think the names of the letters are confusing and irrelevant for beginning readers, and they prefer to introduce names at a later time.)	☐	☐	☐
Learn sounds of the letters (short vowels before long)	☐	☐	☐
Recognize upper and lower case letters	☐	☐	☐
Recognize that sounds make up words	☐	☐	☐
Learn the left to right sequence used in reading	☐	☐	☐
Learn how to blend sounds of letters together	☐	☐	☐
Make simple words from a movable alphabet	☐	☐	☐
Read aloud simple words	☐	☐	☐
Learn and recognize patterns	☐	☐	☐
Recognize blends, digraphs and diphthongs (but not these terms that identify them!)	☐	☐	☐

Note: If your child is progressing well, you might not have to be concerned with each detailed area, but if he is having difficulty, breaking reading skills down into steps might help overcome problems.

	Introduced	Practicing	Mastered
• Recognize some basic sight words	☐	☐	☐
• Recognize root words	☐	☐	☐
• Recognize some suffixes	☐	☐	☐
• Read aloud	☐	☐	☐
• Read aloud including "oral punctuation" (e.g., stopping at ends of sentences and raising the voice for sentences that ask questions.)	☐	☐	☐
• Use context to help understand the meaning of unfamiliar words	☐	☐	☐

Reading comprehension becomes important once children have mastered phonics and have actually begun to read. Until they are reading about 100 words per minute, their comprehension level is likely to be very low because they are expending most of their concentration in decoding words. Comprehension activities for beginning readers should include ordering events of a story, retelling, and answering questions about what has been read. These can and should be done orally most of the time rather than with workbook pages.

Improving reading skills:

At the next level, which is about second or third grade reading level in most programs, children are improving skills, solidifying phonics knowledge, increasing vocabulary, and gaining comprehension skills.

Children should:

	Introduced	Practicing	Mastered
• Recognize and form compound words	☐	☐	☐
• Recognize the number of syllables in 2 syllable words	☐	☐	☐
• Understand and apply phonics skills consistently	☐	☐	☐
• Read basic sight vocabulary	☐	☐	☐
• Recognize contractions	☐	☐	☐
• Read and recognize common prefixes and suffixes	☐	☐	☐
• Recognize homonyms, synonyms, and antonyms	☐	☐	☐
• Identify two or more syllables in words	☐	☐	☐
• Relate a story they have read	☐	☐	☐
• Follow written directions	☐	☐	☐
• Read for pleasure	☐	☐	☐
• Continually develop new vocabulary	☐	☐	☐

By approximately fourth grade reading level, children should have mastered phonics skills and be able to read just about anything. However, they are still limited by vocabulary and their lack of knowledge and maturity. Individual students' reading skills vary greatly in upper elementary levels, and some might still need remedial work. If so, *Sound Track to Reading* (Professor Phonics), *Winning* (International Learning Systems of North America, Inc.), one of the basic phonics programs, or a phonics workbook might be of use. If a child reads too slowly to comprehend well, this is the time to work on improving reading speed.

The emphasis shifts now to reading for information, wisdom, and pleasure. Various comprehension skills such as discerning the main idea, making inferences (understanding that which is implied by the written words but not directly expressed), perceiving cause and effect, drawing conclusions, and retaining information become more important.

Advanced reading skills:

	Introduced	Practicing	Mastered
• Understand prefixes and suffixes on a more difficult level (include study of Greek and Latin influences)	☐	☐	☐
• Read aloud with increasing skill and expression	☐	☐	☐
• Use reading skills to locate information	☐	☐	☐
• Follow more difficult written directions	☐	☐	☐
• Listen to adult reading (good listening skills will improve reading skills)	☐	☐	☐
• Use alphabetical and guide word skills to discover meaning and pronunciation of words from dictionary	☐	☐	☐
• Develop practical reading skills: newspaper, advertisements, schedules, etc.	☐	☐	☐
• Identify author's point of view	☐	☐	☐
• Read materials for literary value	☐	☐	☐

	Introduced	Practicing	Mastered
• Read and study a variety of forms of prose and poetry	☐	☐	☐
• Analyze reading materials for theme, technique, personal appeal, effectiveness	☐	☐	☐
• Become familiar with some renowned authors and their works	☐	☐	☐
• Compare authors and their works	☐	☐	☐

Learning Goals for Composition and Grammar

These goals are listed in sequential order to give you an idea of the sequence followed by most schools and publishers. This is not a comprehensive listing but will give you an idea of the types of skills typical for different levels. Remember that grade level is not necessarily determined by age but rather by each child's readiness and needs.

Approximately 1st grade level

	Introduced	Practicing	Mastered
• Speak in complete sentences	☐	☐	☐
• Follow oral directions	☐	☐	☐
• Tell short stories	☐	☐	☐
• Say name, address, and phone number	☐	☐	☐
• Recognize rhymes	☐	☐	☐
• Listen to others reading	☐	☐	☐
• Relate simple stories, verses, or rhymes orally	☐	☐	☐
• Write simple sentences ending with periods	☐	☐	☐
• Capitalize first letters of sentences, proper names, and the pronoun "I"	☐	☐	☐

Approximately 2nd grade level

	Introduced	Practicing	Mastered
• Follow oral instructions	☐	☐	☐
• Add suffixes *s, ed,* and *ing*	☐	☐	☐
• Recognize some uses of apostrophes	☐	☐	☐
• Alphabetize by first letter	☐	☐	☐
• Follow a series of instructions	☐	☐	☐
• Introduce syllables	☐	☐	☐
• Use simple dictionary	☐	☐	☐
• Write original *short* stories, notes, reports	☐	☐	☐
• Capitalize days, months, cities, streets, states, references to God and the Bible	☐	☐	☐

Approximately 3rd grade level

	Introduced	Practicing	Mastered
• Follow oral directions	☐	☐	☐
• Write and relate short original stories, reports, etc.	☐	☐	☐
• Use simple punctuation	☐	☐	☐
• Recognize and use complete sentences	☐	☐	☐
• Use some prefixes and suffixes	☐	☐	☐
• Follow logical sequence in telling or writing stories, reports, etc.	☐	☐	☐
• Use dictionary	☐	☐	☐
• Alphabetize	☐	☐	☐
• Recognize number of syllables in words	☐	☐	☐
• Identify nouns, verbs, pronouns, adjectives	☐	☐	☐
• Identify subjects and predicates	☐	☐	☐

Approximately 4th grade level

(Note: Grammar becomes a more important aspect of language arts as children learn proper word usage to improve their writing skills.)

	Introduced	Practicing	Mastered
• participate in discussion	☐	☐	☐
• Write simple stories, poems, letters, reports, etc.	☐	☐	☐
• Simple punctuation used correctly: period, comma, exclamation point, and question mark	☐	☐	☐

	Introduced	Practicing	Mastered

- Use periods after abbreviations and initials ☐ ☐ ☐
- Commas used in word series, dates, greetings and closings of letters ☐ ☐ ☐
- Use apostrophes in some contractions and in possessive words ☐ ☐ ☐
- Use adjectives and adverbs in writing ☐ ☐ ☐
- Group related sentences to form paragraph ☐ ☐ ☐
- Write simple letter and address envelope ☐ ☐ ☐
- Capitalize initials ☐ ☐ ☐
- Identify nouns, verbs, pronouns, adjectives, articles, and adverbs ☐ ☐ ☐
- Dictionary skills ☐ ☐ ☐
- Use correct verb forms-singular/plurals, present, past, future ☐ ☐ ☐

Approximately 5th grade level

(Note: In most programs, grammar and other concepts are repeated at increasing levels of difficulty each year. The emphasis shifts to writing and vocabulary skills since phonics and foundational language skills should have been mastered by this level.)

- Interpret oral information, judge content and presentation ☐ ☐ ☐
- Participate in discussions ☐ ☐ ☐
- Give oral reports ☐ ☐ ☐
- Use punctuation correctly, including quotation marks around titles and direct quotations ☐ ☐ ☐
- Underline titles ☐ ☐ ☐
- Write notes, invitations, book reports, original prose and poetry ☐ ☐ ☐
- Proofread and edit their own written work ☐ ☐ ☐
- Identify nouns, verbs, adjectives, adverbs, pronouns ☐ ☐ ☐
- Identify subjects, predicates, direct objects ☐ ☐ ☐
- Recognize subject-predicate agreement ☐ ☐ ☐
- Use verbs correctly ☐ ☐ ☐
- Identify prepositions, conjunctions, interjections ☐ ☐ ☐
- Recognize agreement between pronouns and antecedents ☐ ☐ ☐
- Recognize irregular plurals ☐ ☐ ☐
- Diagram subjects and predicates* ☐ ☐ ☐
- Diagram direct objects* ☐ ☐ ☐
- Diagram adjectives and adverbs* ☐ ☐ ☐
- Diagram prepositions and conjunctions* ☐ ☐ ☐
- Recognize indirect objects ☐ ☐ ☐
- Diagram indirect objects* ☐ ☐ ☐

Approximately 6th - 8th grade levels

Note: Goals will vary greatly according to each student's progress. I include goals through eighth grade so you can better plan a long-range schedule of when to accomplish which goals.

- Give oral reports ☐ ☐ ☐
- Participate in discussions ☐ ☐ ☐
- Use plural possessives and contractions ☐ ☐ ☐
- Recognize and write compound sentences ☐ ☐ ☐
- Identify and write topic sentences ☐ ☐ ☐
- Write outlines ☐ ☐ ☐
- Write using correct punctuation, including quotation marks, indentation, colon, and semicolons ☐ ☐ ☐
- Write compositions, dialogue, simple poetry, short research paper, book reports ☐ ☐ ☐
- Write business and friendly letters ☐ ☐ ☐

	Introduced	Practicing	Mastered
• Write with unity and coherence	☐	☐	☐
• Proofread and edit their own work	☐	☐	☐
• Use dictionary to locate word origins, dictionary spellings (pronunciations), usages	☐	☐	☐
• Recognize appositives and direct address	☐	☐	☐
• Recognize helping and linking verbs	☐	☐	☐
• Identify predicate adjective and predicate nominative (noun)	☐	☐	☐
• Recognize and diagram basic parts of speech: subject, verb, adjectives, adverbs, prepositions, conjunctions*	☐	☐	☐
• Diagram more complicated sentences*	☐	☐	☐
• Recognize prepositional phrases	☐	☐	☐
• Diagram predicate nominative and predicate adjective*	☐	☐	☐
• Do dramatic oral presentation	☐	☐	☐
• Understand use of italics	☐	☐	☐
• Recognize and use simple similes and metaphors	☐	☐	☐
• Use thesaurus	☐	☐	☐
• Take notes from printed and oral material	☐	☐	☐
• Know how to use card catalog or library cataloging system and other reference materials	☐	☐	☐
• Organize information from reference materials for reports	☐	☐	☐
• Write research paper including brief bibliography (7th-8th grade)	☐	☐	☐
• Apply proper word usage in writing and speech	☐	☐	☐

   * or use *Winston Grammar* (Precious Memories Educational Resources) or Montessori methods for identifying parts of speech

California Standards

Excerpts from California Standards. You can view the complete standards on the web at www.csun.edu/~hcbio027/k12standards/.

(Note: I've rewritten some of these for brevity and/or clarity.)

Math Standards

Grade One
Standard 1. Number and Operations
Students demonstrate their knowledge of basic skills, conceptual understanding, and problem solving in number and operations.

For example, students in grade one who meet the standard will:

Compare two groups of objects (up to 20 objects in each group) and identify which group has more or less in it and count how many more are in one group.

Combine groups of objects up to a total of 20 objects and write the correct addition equation.

Count orally by ones and tens to 100 and by twos and fives to 50 and write numerals to 50.

Separate up to 20 objects into two groups and write the correct subtraction equation.

Figure out all addition facts (sums to ten) and related subtraction facts, with and without the use of concrete objects, orally and in writing.

Identify halves and wholes by using concrete objects in simple situations.

Identify and give the value of common coins.

Standard 2. Geometry and Measurement
Students demonstrate their knowledge of basic skills, conceptual understanding, and problem solving in geometry and measurement.

For example, students in grade one who meet the standard will:

Sort and classify two- and three-dimensional shapes.

Use words, such as "in front of" and "behind," "right" and "left," and "above" and "below," to represent the position and direction of objects.

Use nonstandard units to measure length by using a number of the units end to end.

Order three objects by length.

Standard 3. Function and Algebra
Students demonstrate their knowledge of basic skills, conceptual understanding, and problem solving in function and algebra.

For example, students in grade one who meet the standard will:

Identify, extend, and build patterns.

Translate patterns from one material or symbol to another.

Standard 4. Statistics and Probability

Students demonstrate their knowledge of basic skills, conceptual understanding, and problem solving in statistics and probability.

For example, students in grade one who meet the standard will:

Use concrete materials to organize small amounts of data.

Fill in a symbolic graph based on a concrete or pictorial graph.

Read simple bar graphs for information.

Standard 5. Problem Solving and Mathematical Reasoning

Students solve problems that make significant demands in one or more of these aspects of the solution process: problem formulation, problem implementation, and problem conclusion.

Problem Formulation (Students participate in the formulation of problems when given the basic statement of a problem situation.)

For example, students in grade one who meet the standard will:

Use concepts and skills acquired through previous activities.

Explain what materials to use, when possible.

Problem Implementation (Students make the basic choices involved in planning and carrying out a solution.)

For example, students in grade one who meet the standard will:

Find a solution that is correct and makes sense.

Tell what their solution is and how they know it works.

Problem Conclusion (Students provide closure to the solution process through summary statements and general conclusions and make connections to, extensions to, and/or generalizations about related problem situations.)

For example, students in grade one who meet the standard will:

Show the solution with another material or in another way when directed to do so.

Standard 6. Mathematical Communication

Students communicate their knowledge of basic skills, conceptual understanding, and problem solving and demonstrate their understanding of mathematical communications of others.

For example, students in grade one who meet the standard will:

Use appropriate mathematical vocabulary; for example, words for simple shapes, attributes, and numbers.

Show ideas by drawing; by using words and numbers; by building with a variety of concrete materials, such as connecting cubes, pattern blocks, buttons, beads, and color tiles; and by pasting paper representations of materials.

Explain strategies used in solving problems.

Share ideas responding orally, when probed by the teacher, and in writing and drawing (even though responses may lack some coherence or organization).

Understand oral directions for appropriate mathematical activities.

Language Arts

Grade One

Standard 1. Reading/Literature

Listen to and experience texts representative of a wide range of self-selected and teacher-selected materials, including traditional and contemporary literature from a variety of cultures (e.g., picture books, nursery rhymes, poems, legends).

Listen to and experience texts representative of books, newspapers, magazines, and visual media across the curriculum.

Standard 2. Reading/Comprehension

Read, comprehend, interpret, and begin to evaluate materials appropriate to the grade level.

Select favorite books and stories.

Identify setting and characters.

Retell stories and events, using a beginning, a middle, and an end.

Recognize the topic or main idea.

Relate previous experiences to what they read.

Make predictions about content.

Distinguish between fantasy and realistic narrative.

Standard 3. Reading/Skills and Strategies

Demonstrate increasing proficiency in basic reading skills.

Begin to develop reading vocabulary and fluency in grade-level-appropriate text.

Demonstrate knowledge of how print is organized and read.

Read from left to right and top to bottom.

Match spoken words with print.

Identify letters, words, and sentences.

Identify all letter names and shapes.

Identify some (more than 40) high-frequency words.

Use conventions of written language, such as periods and question marks, when reading aloud.

Demonstrate phonemic awareness.

Identify beginning, middle, and ending sounds of words.

Change beginning, middle, and ending sounds of words to make new words.

Accurately clap syllables in words and sentences.

Apply knowledge of letter-sound correspondences (phonics) when reading.

Use beginning and ending consonants in decoding single-syllable words.

Use vowel sounds in decoding single-syllable words.

Blend beginning, middle, and ending sounds to recognize and read words.

Recognize most word families and patterns.

○○○○○○○

Grade Five
Standard 1. Reading/Literature

Read fiction extensively, including self-selected and teacher-selected traditional and contemporary literature from a variety of cultures.

Read nonfiction extensively, including books, newspapers, magazines, textbooks, and visual media across the curriculum.

Read several books in depth (or book equivalents, such as essays, stories, groups of poems, articles, or magazines) about one issue or subject, or several books by a single writer.

Standard 2. Reading/Comprehension

Respond to fiction, including poetry and drama, using critical, interpretive, and evaluative processes.

Demonstrate a thorough understanding of the text.

Relate what they have read to prior knowledge and experience.

Identify recurring themes across works in print and media.

Make inferences and draw conclusions about contexts, events, characters, and settings.

Explain the differences among genres.

Discuss the impact of authors' word choice and content.

Read nonfiction text and informational materials to develop understanding and expertise.

Relate new information to prior knowledge and experience.

Make connections to related topics and information.

Define and sequence information needed to carry out a procedure.

State the main idea in material read or heard and the significant details in his/her own words.

Distinguish between significant and minor details.

Standard 3. Reading/Skills and Strategies

Read aloud accurately familiar materials of the quality and complexity illustrated in the district's adopted reading list.

Self-correct when subsequent reading indicates an earlier miscue.

Use a range of cueing systems, e.g., letter-sound correspondences (phonics), meaning, grammar, and overall context to determine pronunciation and meanings.

Use a rhythm, pace, and intonation that sounds like natural speech.

Determine the meaning of unknown words using context, glossaries, and dictionaries.

Standard 4. Writing/Process

Generate and organize ideas for writing.

Include appropriate facts and details.

Revise work by combining sentences, adding details to support the content, and adding or changing work to make the meaning clear to the reader.

Proofread their own writing or the writing of others, using dictionaries and other resources.

Standard 5. Writing/Communication

Write to inform the reader.

Provide appropriate facts and details from more than one source to develop the subject.

Organize the writing in such a way that a reader can easily follow what is said.

Write to tell a story (fictional or autobiographical).

Provide an engaging beginning that establishes the situation, moves through a sequence of events, and concludes in a logical way.

Use literary elements, such as creating a situation, plot, point of view, setting, conflict, and characters, with increasing facility and detail.

Use dialogue with increasing skill.

Use a variety of literary techniques, such as suspense, dialogue, episodes, and flashbacks.

Write to describe and express ideas.

Explore ideas and/or observations.

Maintain a consistent focus.

Orient the reader and use relevant and well-chosen detail to elaborate on ideas.

Exhibit clear thinking.

Analyze ideas by looking at them from more than one angle and/or moving through successively deeper layers of meaning.

Write to persuade the reader, e.g., creating point-of-view pieces or responses to literary works.

Clearly state the writer's judgment and/or point of view.

Provide supporting evidence through a variety of strategies, such as references to a text or personal knowledge.

Anticipate the reader's concern or counterarguments.

Standard 6. Writing/Conventions

Use appropriate conventions of written language, which include grammar, spelling, punctuation, language usage, capitalization, and sentence structure.

Use a variety of sentence structures with appropriate capitalization and punctuation.

Use paragraphs to organize information and ideas.

Use conventional spelling by referring to resources when needed.

Use appropriate and varied word choice.

Standard 7. Speaking and Listening

Ask appropriate questions and respond to the questions of others.

Use appropriate grammar, word choice, and pacing during formal oral presentations.

Paraphrase and summarize to increase understanding.

Listen responsively and respectfully to others' points of view.

Use clear and specific language to communicate ideas to the intended audience.

Use language and gestures expressively.

Participate in role-playing activities that extend a story ending or elaborate on a historical event.

Other Scope and Sequences

Evaluating for Excellence by Teresa Moon (Beautiful Feet Books) [$17.95] covers scope and sequence and placement along with much more extensive treatment of diagnosing children's learning needs and evaluating progress. See the review under "Accurate Evaluation" later in this chapter.

Learning Objectives for Grades One Through Eight, an eighty-page book from Hewitt Homeschooling Resources [$10.95], does an excellent job of breaking subject area goals down into skill areas (e.g., Language objectives are broken down under the skill headings of Listening, Speaking, Handwriting, Capitalization, Punctuation, Grammar/Usage, Composition and Writing, Literature, Reading, and Spelling).

What Your Child Needs To Know When by Robin Scarlata Sampson (Heart of Wisdom) [$24.95] is significantly expanded in the 1996 edition. The first half of the book discusses the history, purpose, and goals of education, followed by a presentation of Robin's "Heart of Wisdom" approach to learning—a Bible-centered unit study type approach that stresses development of language arts skills, particularly writing. Some traditional texts might be used to complete some subject areas, but she emphasizes the value of using real books and hands-on activities. The second half of the book consists of skills evaluation check lists for math, science, language arts, and social studies reflecting a scope and sequence in line with most of the standardized tests. Robin cautions us about the limitations of standardized tests and recommends the benefits of using a check-off chart for evaluation rather than a test. She also includes character trait charts, Bible reading schedules (for covering the entire Bible every year), and reproducible forms for evaluating spiritual fruits, work and study habits, attitude, responsibility, and character traits for each of our children. You can view dozens of excerpts at http://homeschoolfaq.com

Luke's School List by Joyce Herzog (Simplified Learning Products) [$39.95] offers extensive checklists for kindergarten through eighth grade, even including detailed objectives for history, science, and cultural knowledge. Organized by topics rather than grade levels, *Luke's School List* does indicate typical grade levels for many skills and concepts. It also provides

three columns so that you can indicate progress toward mastery or record progress of more than one child in a single book. This book is so detailed that you could actually create your own curriculum from it. Also, forms are included for creating Individualized Education Programs (IEPs) for your children.

Creative Home Teaching sells Susan Fernald's *The Basic Skills Book: What Your Child Should Learn in Grades 1-8* [$14]. Susan's approach reflects an understanding that home educators rarely stay strictly on grade level. She divides skills under three levels (grades 1-3, 4-6, and 7-8). I also like the way Susan uses three columns for recording introduction of a concept, progress in learning it, and mastery. History and science goals are little more than topic headings in contrast to the detailed skill breakdowns provided for math and language arts. An extra section allows us to record progress on character development. Dolch sight word lists and spelling rules are helpful extras at the back of the book. At 54 pages, this is a happy medium between the super-detailed approach of the other "scope and sequences" reviewed here and the condensed versions we get from publishers.

Skills Evaluation for the Home School from The Weaver [$20], is a very detailed scope and sequence with check-off boxes for planning and recording as students progress. The goals listed are similar to those of a typical school. If you wish to make sure you are doing everything the schools do, you might want to use this.

Home2School.com (www.Home2School.com) offers free access to grade-level scope and sequence lists for each state for math and language arts on-line. By entering a child's grade level after registering at this website (no charge for this!), you get charts with check off boxes that provide detailed objectives such as what level of difficulty in working with commas a student should be achieving at seventh grade level. On-line you can find detailed teaching information regarding each objective—definitions, ways to teach, and examples. A separate section at this same site offers two-minute parent tutorials on most (if not all) topics covered in the objectives. Print out lists for your own record keeping and use the on-line information whenever you need clarification or assistance. Recommended reading lists are also available through this site, but they include adult books written at younger grade levels and need much screening to be useful. It's surprising to find such extremely helpful information available at no charge!

Using Our Goals to Keep on Target

At this point, we should be aware of what our child already has learned, know what is typically taught next, and have made some decisions according to the criteria already covered as to how we wish to proceed and what we wish to cover this year. We now have our goals!

We must keep these goals at hand as we choose materials which will help us achieve them. We will probably find nothing that perfectly meets all our criteria, but we should choose that which comes closest. If the material we purchase covers things that we prefer to cover next year, we have the prerogative to save those sections for next year, or even skip them. We should feel free to substitute supplemental materials to enrich our program. However, in most cases, we should not try to use supplements and complete the entire textbook besides. We must use materials to meet our educational goals, not because we have invested money in them or because someone else thinks that we should use them.

We need to refer frequently to our original goals to see if we are still on target. It is easy to wander. Sometimes the wanderings are very helpful, but sometimes they are unproductive and prevent us from meeting our objectives.

Often we feel that we are doing an inadequate job. The way to determine the truth is to refer to our goals and ask ourselves if we are heading in the right direction. We might be moving more slowly than we should. We must then determine if our original expectations were realistic or not and adjust if necessary.

If we are totally missing a goal, we should question ourselves first as to the validity of the goal. Home educators who feel the most inadequate are often those who are overwhelming both themselves and their children with unrealistic expectations, usually with too many subject areas at a time, and not enough time allowed to cover all of the work. This "overwhelming" often occurs because we have a totally unfounded belief that classroom teachers actually cover everything in every textbook and thoroughly teach every subject. Or sometimes we feel overwhelmed when we compare ourselves with other home schoolers who are doing more than we in a particular subject, who are comparing themselves with others, etc., etc., creating a vicious cycle of impossible expectations.

Make sure that the goals you set were realistic and appropriate for your children, then make any adjustments or changes you need to get back on track.

Changing Programs

What material has your child used in the past?

If your child is used to working with a particular curriculum already and you are satisfied that it is appropriate for your child, then it might be wise to continue with that material simply because it is familiar. We should not change curriculum just on the chance that we might find something better, unless we are dissatisfied with it. (On the other hand, some children thrive on variety and get bored with the same approach year after year. This might be reason enough to change.) There is no perfect curriculum, and we can waste much time and money trying everything available.

Often parents have had their children in an academic Christian day school program for kindergarten before deciding to home school them for first grade. Some children do fine in these kindergarten programs, yet they have been pushed fur-

ther than necessary. We can continue to work with them in workbooks or a structured curriculum, but it is wise to put less emphasis on the formal academic activities and instead broaden their education with more oral reading together, hands-on activities, and discovery learning.

If a child already has negative school experience to overcome, give him a year of "refreshment." Do only informal academics with lots of fun, experiential learning.

Read to him, take field trips, share your learning discoveries with him. The object is to refresh his attitude toward learning. If we continue to work with formal academics with a burned-out child, his entire schooling experience is likely to be totally frustrating, if not a failure.

Scheduling

Many home educators make excellent learning material choices but never reap the advantage of their investments because of poor planning. They never find time to use half of what they buy because the pressure of uncompleted textbook exercises consumes all their time. Whether or not we have already chosen learning materials, we must realize that the choices are only half the battle. Planning how we will use the materials is crucial to our success. There are many ways to tackle the challenge, but some techniques will be useful in any situation.

Master Schedule

The Master Schedule will help us put our Course of Study into a practical format so that we can make the best use of our time, energy, and materials. Make a photocopy of Chart C (at the end of this chapter) for your own use and a copy for each child old enough to benefit from it. Fill in your tentative time schedule for subjects to cover each day with each child. You will do this just once a year unless you make major changes. This will help you get a clear view of how you will accomplish your goals in the time available. Keep in mind household chores and demands when making your schedule. Plan time for the entire family to learn together when you know the time can be uninterrupted, whether it be early morning or in the evening with Dad. Then stagger subjects you know will need one-on-one work so you are available when each child needs you.

A program for a younger child may be quite informal, in which case a master schedule might not be useful. We must plan to set aside a block of time to devote to learning activities such as reading to our child or cooking together, even if it is not scheduled under subject headings. Otherwise we tend to get too busy and end up neglecting these activities.

I realize that in most families we don't have buzzers sounding time for one period to end and another to begin. A schedule seems kind of silly to some of us once we actually start homeschooling. Sometimes children will work on their assignments in whatever order they choose, at whatever speed they are capable of working. If this happens, you can simply assist each child when needed, asking the one waiting to go on to another subject until you are available to help him.

The Master Schedule is still valuable for two reasons. It helps us to realistically allot time before we begin. Many home educators have a list of twenty subjects they want their children to study. When they look at it in terms of fitting it into a schedule, they can see how unrealistic their expectations are and make the necessary adjustments. Probably the most valuable use of the schedule is that we have a chart which shows our child what is expected for each day. This forestalls some of the "Aren't we finished yet?" and "You didn't tell me I needed to do that!" comments. Children can easily refer to the Master Schedule (or to an assignment list) to find out what needs to be done.

If you need additional help establishing and maintaining a schedule, you might want to invest in Steven and Teri Maxwell's *Managers of Their Homes* (Managers of Their Homes) [$25] . This 174- page book offers the most detailed, comprehensive approach to scheduling I have encountered. It covers both the rationale and very detailed how-to's. It also features pages and pages of sample schedules for families, parents, and children, most of which were submitted by families who have used this "program." Some families will find tremendous security as they incorporate such schedules into their family life. The book comes with a complete scheduling kit with charts, forms, and instructions to get you going.

Assignments

Different systems of scheduling assignments work for different families. After experimenting, we found that a system using assignment books for each child worked best for us. Each child's assignments for each subject were written on the assignment sheet. (See Chart D at the end of this chapter for an assignment sheet form that can be photocopied and put into a notebook.) Younger children were given one day's assignments at a time to avoid intimidating them, while older children were given assignments for a few days to a week ahead so they can make more choices about how to budget their time. Preparing any of these charts a week in advance might save lost school time and problems arising from lack of preparedness.

As assignments are completed, the child puts a check mark next to the assignment. Assignment books are handed in with the work (when applicable) to be checked off or recorded by mom in her plan book.

If you use my assignment form, record creative alternatives at the bottom of the chart, identifying the subject assignments they can replace. You might offer math games as an alternative to workbooks. You might offer creative writing (e.g., applying challenging language skills such as the use of dialogue) as an alternative to a language workbook. Parental approval should be required for alternate choices or this can get out of hand.

Other possibilities for assignment sheets are the reproducible forms in Noble Book's *Home School Organizer* or *Assignment Sheets For Home And School* (Sycamore Tree Center for Home Education) [$4.95], which has twelve different forms. A plain, spiral notebook will suffice for assignments if you do not have easy access to reasonable photocopy services, but there are complete sets of preprinted assignment forms available. Common Sense Press offers a packet of preprinted *Record Keeping Sheets*, three-fourths of which are color coded (for three children) assignment pages. Castle Heights Press publishes *The Homework Assignment Book* [$7.95], specifically dated for each school year. It allows for an extended school year, with dates beginning with August and ending with June. Subject areas listed are Bible, English, Foreign Language, History, Math, Science, and Other. Because of the subject headings, and also since writing space is limited, this book will work better with older students than with younger.

Christian Liberty Press offers the *Class Lesson Planner* [$7.95], which at first looks like other lesson plan notebooks. However, it has us enter lessons as "daily assignments" with a space for noting "main concepts to cover" for each subject each day. Each assignment also has boxes for grades and completion date. A section at the end of each week's assignments, for recording items sent in to CLASS, reveals that the book was designed for those using that program, but that in no way limits its use to those in CLASS. Other reproducible forms for field trips, academic planning, report cards, health records, etc., are included at the back.

Planning and Record Keeping

If you choose to work informally, you'll find that subject areas often overlap. "Hmm? Was that biography we just read for history or literature?" This can be difficult to break down into subject headings to fill in a teacher's plan book. In this case, a journal of some kind, such as a spiral notebook, works well for writing down everything our child does. It is increasingly easy to find plan books at teacher supply stores that feature two-page spreads with large sections rather than small boxes. Although these are usually designed for thematic studies and/or whole language, they work well for unit studies or other less structured learning.

Most of us will find that a typical teacher's plan book, divided into six or seven subject columns, will work well for our record keeping. We can use one or two of the columns for the notes on informal learning activities and list textbooks or more subject-specific work under each appropriate subject heading. Teacher's plan books are very inexpensive and available at any teacher's supply store or from Bob Jones University Press [$7] or Rod and Staff [$3.95].

We need to record attendance (in some states), what is done each day (for our own benefit, if not for the State's), and grades (only if we wish to or if it is required). Some teacher's plan books have recording pages for attendance and grades. We might need to keep these records separately if they need to be used for specific purposes (e.g., to turn in to authorities or independent study programs).

A basic teacher's plan book will suffice for most people, and the planning pages then become our records which saves the effort of duplicate recording. However, more extensive organizers are available that help with organizing both home and school. Although organizers are not essential, many home educators have found them very helpful for getting started with record keeping and then also for keeping track of family and school activities that are strongly interrelated.

Noble Books publishes the *Home School Organizer* [$34.95] which includes most planning and record keeping pages we might need for our home school. The pages most families use are preprinted, and there are reproducible master pages for more specialized forms. This is a fairly complex but comprehensive system for organizing and record keeping. *The Noble Planner* (also from Noble Books) is a newer product, more similar to a *Day Runner* than a teacher's planning book. It deals with time management, family hospitality, and household organization in an 8 1/2" by 5 1/2" format.

Cherry Patterson's personal organizer called the *Personal Touch Planner* (Personal Touch Planners) is also more like a *Day Runner* than a typical teacher's planning book. It is specially designed to meet the organizational needs of Christian mothers at home. (Others certainly can use it by selecting the forms that meet their needs.) It covers just about every area of life most moms encounter. We find here the "standard" forms for weekly, monthly, and yearly planning; weekly lesson plan forms; "to-do" sheets; address lists; library loans; and goal planning. But it includes much more with forms for family information; medical permission; health records; checklists for picnics, camping, or travel; correspondence records; gift ideas; comparison shopping; menu planning; grocery lists; family spiritual growth; prayer requests and more. The complete binder includes either single or multiple copies of all forms, a movable plastic marker to easily locate "today," and a plastic zip pouch with a few note and recipe cards, Post-Its, and hole reinforcers. The lightweight binder itself is padded, washable vinyl, but washable cloth covers are available at extra cost. Packets of complete binder refills or masters for all forms are sold separately, although we may reproduce all forms for our own use. We can even purchase individual form masters if we wish. Customization can occur on several levels: we can purchase the complete binder, selecting only those forms we intend to use. We can purchase specialized forms (standard 8 1/2" x 5 1/2" three-hole punch) to use with other planners (e.g.,

Franklin Quest). We can select a cloth cover for a different look. Its compact-size makes this planner small and light enough to carry everywhere, while still functioning as far more than an ordinary calendar. This is a very efficient way to carry information for the mom-on-the go. Personal Touch Planners also offers a *Kid's Planner* designed by Cherry Patterson's daughter Cami [$17.50]. [Prices: Deluxe package (binder, dividers, pages, masters, plastic accessories/cards) - $58; filler package with multiple copies of forms - $20; masters - $20; cloth covers - $20] [Diane Eastman/C.D.]

Cary Gibson (Gibson's Curriculum and Counseling Services) publishes the *Complete Homeschool Planner* as a Master Pack of forms (one of each) for us to copy as needed. While it is particularly suitable for home educators in California, those in other states will probably find it equally useful. Forms included are Purpose of Homeschooling, School Year Calendar (year-at-a-glance without dates), Monthly Calendar, Weekly Lessons, Monthly Progress, Goals, Attendance, Faculty Qualifications (CA requirement), Course of Study, Quarterly Progress Report, Grades, Field Trip Record, Lending/Borrowing Record, Reading Book List, Student Assignments, Student Weekly Record, Repeating Schedule, Scripture Memory Record, and High School Planning Record. We can purchase these forms either as the Master Pack only or as a complete set with a binder, tabs, and a copy of the World Book *Typical Course of Study*. This is an excellent assortment of forms that will suit most families. [Master Pack - $15; complete with binder - $25]

School Forms for Home and Classroom (Sycamore Tree Center for Home Education) [$4.95 per set] has fewer forms than *The Home Educator's Lesson Plan Notebook*, but they are more specialized and might be a useful supplement. They include reproducible forms for school entry medical examination, curriculum listing, weekly lesson plans, weekly schedule, attendance chart, grade sheet, report cards, work contracts, and achievement and completion certificates. Their separate *Assignment Sheets For Home And School* has twelve different monthly, weekly, and daily assignment forms including charts for chores, extracurricular activities, and practical arts.

The Home Education CopyBook and Planning Guide by Kathy von Duyke (Tim and Kathy von Duyke) [$25] is unlike any of the other resources described here. It grew out of the Von Duyke's unit study approach to education and their own personal philosophy of family life and education. While there are forms of all sorts (lesson plan, journals, objectives, unit study plans, cumulative records, resource lists, high school logs, and much more), Kathy also shares practical strategies of family and time management from her own experience with 10+ children. With plenty of examples, she shares specifics of how she has set goals, selected and used materials, and kept records. She includes practical issues like dealing with toddlers, illness, and household chores as essential aspects of home education. The *CopyBook* is probably most useful for the eclectic, creative home schooler who needs to put some structure into the process, but others should also find constructive ideas and useful forms for their situations.

Some families want something compact, but ready-to-use. *The Home Schooler's Journal* (FERG N US Services) [$7.95] is one of the least expensive options. While it looks more like the inexpensive teacher planning books found in teacher supply stores because of its size, wire binding (so that it opens flat), and the fact that no photocopying is required, it expands beyond the typical plan book. Included are field trip logs, check-off list for yearly requirements, a 2-year calendar, a linear calendar, objective/resource pages, a test score keeper, a borrowing/lending page, resource cost page, and individual pages for library lists. A wide NOTE column allows recording of unusual activities. An unusual feature for families who don't always follow the typical school week is the list of initials for Sunday through Saturday along the left-hand margin for each day so that we can customize our school week. We simply fill in the circle of the appropriate day's initial. This *Journal* also allows for multiple students and grade levels. Another plus is the "Jelly Proof" cover.

The Home School Lesson Planner (Soteria) [$24.98] has taken yet another approach with a very different looking lesson planner. Instead of a variety of forms, it consists primarily of large (13" x 10") printed envelopes. There are 36 of these envelopes, comb-bound between laminated covers. On the front of each envelope is a lesson planning chart for one week. On the reverse are a cumulative attendance record, a grading record, and a sizable space for comments. The envelopes are then used for keeping sample pages, legal documents, field trip records, book reports, or any other records pertinent to that week. Aside from a two-page "year-at-a-glance" chart and instructions that include sample lesson plans, that's it. Moms who want special forms for field trips, book reports, and hospitality need to look elsewhere, but moms who want to do the least possible amount of work to keep records should find this fits the bill.

Homeschooled student, Sarah Crain, worked with her mother to devise *The Homeschool Planbook* (The Homeschool Planbook) in various editions to meet specialized needs. Every edition has enough pages to keep records for seven days a week, twelve months a year. Each planner also includes pages for goals, subject overviews, state requirements, curriculum planning, test scores, tally sheets for hours, calendars, field trips, projects, reading lists, Scripture memory, other memory work, report cards, and weekly planning. Key differences between editions lie in the number of students that can be recorded in a single book and weekly planning pages. The Anniversary Edition [$9.50] is for one student, while the Family [$15] and Unit Studies [$15] editions can be used for up to four children. The Family Edition has room for individ-

ualized plans for each student in each subject, while the Unit Studies Edition has individual spaces for language arts and math, but combined space for other subject areas. These two are punched for a three-ring binder (not included), but the Anniversary Edition is spiral bound.

Those whose schooling activities don't fit well under subject headings might prefer to use *My Special School Journal* (Bookworm Books of TN) [$8.95]. These perfect-bound journals come in your choice of six colors, and a separate one is required for each child. At the beginning are a few "memory pages" for personal thoughts and memories, family tree, and health history. Then we find pages for recording field trips, books read, and curriculum resources and goals. The bulk of the book consists of identical pages for daily records. Half of each page is lined for recording subject matter accomplishments, while the rest of the page is set aside for recording things like "Something I Learned Today," "Something Funny Today," "A Prayer Request," and "A Goal for Tomorrow." This format leaves minimal room for recording academic detail, which might be just fine for some families.

A compromise approach for lesson planning/record keeping is available from Hewitt Homeschooling Resources. Hewitt's *Blueprints Organizer* [$9.95] is primarily designed for the elementary grades. The *Blueprints Organizer* stresses goal setting, including worksheets to help us work from general to specific goals. Suggestions and instructions are included. Master copies of various forms are included for us to copy as needed. Monthly calendar pages plus weekly lesson plan/recording pages will be the bulk of the organizer, while monthly and yearly progress report forms can be used to summarize progress. Photocopy permission for the family is granted.

Home School Helper (K.T. Productions) [$25] is yet another binder-organizer. This one has forms for attendance, weekly planning, quarterly test grades, yearly overview, yearly curriculum, report cards, field trips, weekly jobs, rotating menus, books read, books/videos lent, and health records, plus dividers, a section for us to insert support group calendar and mailing list, and large envelopes labeled for awards/certificates, art work, and unit study projects (possibly pictures of projects rather than projects themselves). There are six of each form, so the weekly planner is likely to be the only one we will need to copy for a long time. *Home School Helper* lacks the professional typography and graphics of some of the others, but it does have a unique combination of forms. The publisher also offers separate packets containing one of each form if we choose to photocopy our own [$11.85], or individual forms [$1 each] if we prefer to purchase extras.

Those with computers might prefer one of the resources that allow us to customize forms and print them out ourselves as needed. Ted Wade's computerized *Home School Manual*, reviewed in Chapter One, includes both school and home organization forms by organizing expert, Marilyn Rockett.

It does not matter what particular method we choose for organization and record keeping as long as we have some sort of system. Experiment until you find what works best for your family.

Report Cards

After recording what happens educationally day-to-day, you usually need to keep briefer summaries of academic history. One form is the report card—something with which most of us are already familiar. Although I hesitate to recommend grading and report cards for the elementary grades, in some cases it will be necessary or desirable.

Report cards are available from Bob Jones University Press [$3.50 each], Educational Support Foundation (customized in sets of 10 plus a master to make more of your own) [$14], and Sycamore Tree Center for Home Education [$.75 each]. A special kindergarten report card/anecdotal record called *My Growth in Kindergarten* is available from Sycamore Tree Center for Home Education for $2.95. (Report card forms also appear in a number of the organizers/planners.) Sycamore Tree also sells sets of reproducible forms packaged as *School Forms for Home and Classroom* [$4.95]. Within this set are three different report cards for kindergarten, grades 1-8, and grades 9-12. In addition there are forms for lesson plans, medical records, work contracts, completion certificates, curriculum planning, and scheduling.

Accurate Evaluation

While report cards have long been the standard form for summarizing educational progress, portfolios are becoming increasingly popular. Teresa Moon's book, *Evaluating for Excellence* (Beautiful Feet Books) [$17.95], describes many different ways of evaluating and recording student progress, including creating a portfolio. At the beginning of this book, Teresa Moon tells us, "If... we will first diagnose where our students are and project goals based on their needs and guide them with a course of study that addresses their needs, we can usually evaluate whether or not we are making progress on our own." In this statement she sums up the heart of home education as I see it: developing our own program for each child and then using tools that measure whether or not we have met our own goals rather than those set by some standardized testing company.

Moon divides the book into four sections, reflecting the four steps in this process that work in a cyclical manner. We start by diagnosing where our child is in a particular area. Next we project where each child should be at the end of the school year—goal setting. Once we have goals, we can guide our children by deciding specifically how we will reach each goal. Then we evaluate what has been done to determine if we have been successful. These four steps—diagnose, project, guide, and evaluate—then repeat as your evaluation leads you to diagnose what needs to be learned next. Each section is introduced with a few pages of explanation, followed by sample forms already completed as examples of how we might accomplish each step. An appendix then includes reproducible master forms for all four steps. This is a super tool for reclaiming control of our curriculum. If we control the evaluation process ourselves, as this book teaches us to do, we have a much better handle on where we actually stand in our home education endeavors.

Cumulative Records

A useful form for long range record keeping is the cumulative record, the form most schools use for maintaining long-term records on each student. Usually printed on heavy card stock, the cumulative record is used for recording yearly grades, attendance totals, standardized test scores, and other such information that might be passed on if a student enters another school. Bob Jones University Press sells such a form, called *Academic Record*, either individually [$3.50 each] or in packages of 25. Shekinah Curriculum Cellar lists a cumulative file with medical form, sold individually, and Sycamore Tree Center for Home Education sells single copies of the *Christian Cumulative Record* (same as that used by Christian schools) [$1.95 each].

Help!

If all of the steps of the planning stage as I have described them here seem frightening and overwhelming, and there are no "How to Home School" seminars in the near future in your area, there is somewhere to turn for more help. Gayle Graham has put her introductory seminar into a manual entitled *How to Home School, A Practical Approach* (Common Sense Press) [$20]. The manual covers just about any area you might need: philosophy, organization, record keeping, planning assignments, unit study planning, goals, evaluation, working with your large family, and more. Her suggestions for language arts, math, and unit studies are solid and practical. The manual also includes informational pages, sample charts, and blank charts—all very nicely put together. There is an optional packet of pre-printed Record Keeping Sheets (weekly unit study planning sheets and student assignment sheets color coded for 3 children). This is a terrific resource for those who need a bit more help.

Special Memories

On the personal side, many of us like to keep our own records just to look back on and remember the highlights. *My Homeschool Year* is a "yearbook" from Sycamore Tree [$8.95] with places for anecdotes, family news, subjects taken, friends, pets, field trips, unusual learning experiences, church activities, and photos. Many of these would not be items you would share with authorities, but they reflect the heart and soul of schooling at home.

Course of Study

Student _____ School Year _____

Subject	Texts or Materials	Source
Bible/Religion		
Math		
Language: Composition/Grammar		
Reading/Literature		
Supplementary Reading Materials		
Spelling		
Handwriting		
Science		
History/Social Studies		
Fine Arts		
Physical Education		

Curriculum Worksheet

Student_____ Subject_____

_____

School Year _____ Approximate Grade Level _____

_____

Subject Focus _____

Goals:

1._____

2._____

3._____

4._____

5._____

6._____

7._____

8._____

9._____

10. _____

Materials to be Used:

_____

_____

_____

_____

Methods to be Used:

_____

_____

_____

Chart C

53

Master Schedule

Name _____ School _____ Year _____

Time	Monday	Tuesday	Wednesday	Thursday	Friday

Alternate Choices:

_____

_____

_____

_____

Chart D

Assignments

Name _____ Week of _____

Time	Monday	Tuesday	Wednesday	Thursday	Friday

Alternate Choices: _____

_____

Chapter 3

Curriculum Recommendations

DO NOT SKIP THIS CHAPTER

Information in this chapter will help you understand how to use the entire book.

Tips to Remember:

In choosing textbooks and materials, there are some important points to remember:

Textbooks are only tools

Textbooks and other learning materials are only useful if they help us accomplish our goals. Before choosing resources, carefully examine your goals. (Consult the scope and sequence lists in this book or others if you need help setting educational goals.) First, try to think of the easiest way to accomplish each goal— textbooks being only one of the available choices. For instance, we can teach a child to count by 5's by adding nickels rather than by filling out a workbook page. If it is evident that particular resources will be useful in helping meet your goals, then you should purchase them. If you can do as good or better a job without that resource, then why waste your money? As you read through recommendations for various subjects, pay close attention to alternatives and extras listed under each. Often, the "supplemental" choices will serve as primary curricula. Also, since many of these supplemental materials were designed for one-on-one or small group use, they actually work more effectively than classroom-designed textbooks.

Publishers follow different scope and sequences

Materials from different publishers vary quite a bit in the order and rate in which they present concepts. Choosing between two sixth grade math texts can be like comparing apples and oranges. One sixth grade text might cover what we list as goals for fifth grade level, while another is much more advanced, covering many of our seventh grade level goals. To avoid problems, you must know where your child is in each subject—through personal knowledge of your child, by comparison against a scope and sequence or curriculum outline, or by testing. Next, look at the scope and sequence or curriculum outline from the publisher of the material you wish to use.

Choose the text that covers topics your child needs to learn next regardless of the grade level stated for the text. Since grade levels are only approximations of what the "average" child might be ready to learn at a certain point you cannot rely on age/grade level labels to identify the appropriate text for your child.

Set priorities

You can easily get overwhelmed if you try to cover every subject in depth. You must establish priorities. Concentrate on the most important subjects, then add other subjects as you are able to handle them. If you never seem to get to music or art, try alternating your emphasis on the lower priority subjects—spending more time on music one year, switching to art the next year, or perhaps studying each subject for only one semester of the school year. Keep in mind that some subjects need daily attention while once or twice a week is sufficient for others.

Use teacher's manuals only if they're useful

Teacher's manuals or guides and teacher's editions might or might not be necessary. If they provide information that will help you do a better job, and if you have time to use that information, you should purchase them. If you know a subject fairly well and have good ideas for presenting it, you might not need teacher's manuals. On the other hand, some serve as answer keys, and the time they save you might justify their cost.

Continually re-evaluate

Re-evaluating texts and materials periodically, sometimes switching or supplementing with other materials is essential. Check your child's progress against your goals periodically. Ask yourself, "Are the materials I'm using helping us to reach those goals?"

Look before your buy

Whenever possible, examine texts before buying! When publishers or distributors allow returns, the cost of postage to receive and, possibly, return resources is money well spent.

Get the big picture first

Be sure to read the section "Major Publishers" for an

overview of the strengths and weaknesses of the major publishers before reading subject area recommendations. This will help you decide if any of the major publishers is likely to have resources that suit your needs. It will also help you understand some of the major differences among even Christian publishers.

Evaluating Content

IMPORTANT! READ THIS TO UNDERSTAND MY CONTENT CODING SYSTEM!

I began researching materials by first reviewing those from Christian publishers, then seeking out secular materials secondarily. Sometimes Christian texts fall short in quality. Often secular books or materials offer a more effective learning strategy or more interesting presentations. I use the following code to help you differentiate between Christian and secular materials. While some secular books do contain material objectionable to Christians, many are worth using while applying our own "editing" process. Those that are likely to need some "editing" are indicated. I cannot read every page of every book mentioned, so it is possible that you will still discover material that needs editing in books that don't have the "SE" code.

(S) = Secular publisher. I am not aware of objectionable material in these, but I offer no guarantees.
(SE) = Secular publisher. These will require some editing.

Identifying Sources

Almost all books or resources reviewed show the name of the publisher or source in parentheses after the title. Look up the publisher's or source's name in the appendix. Publishers with names that include what sounds like a person's name are listed alphabetically under the first name (e.g., Gibbs Smith, Publisher is listed under "G"). Publishers with names that start with initials are included alphabetically rather than at the beginning of each section; e.g., AIMS Education Foundation will come after Advanced Training Institute and before Alpha Omega. A few items show no publisher or source in parentheses. These are listed under the title itself. The appendix will also help you locate sources for purchasing each of the products.

Ready, Set, Go

It would be difficult to write a book such as this without my own personal philosophy showing through from time to time, and I suspect you will have a good idea of my philosophy by the time you have finished reading. Since I do not believe there is only one way to educate every child, I have tried to present a balance of materials representing a range of viewpoints. Each child and each situation is unique, and God has graciously pro-

vided us with a multitude of suitable materials to please most everyone.

Consider my opinion along with those of other homeschoolers and reviewers, pray, experiment with different materials, and choose what is best for you.

Chapter 4

Major Publishers

I provide information on the major Christian publishers here since there are general characteristics of each publisher's curriculum that are easier to deal with here than within each individual review. Each publisher has a distinctive philosophy of education. You will usually be more successful with resources that reflect your own philosophy of education.

A Beka Book

A Beka Book offers materials for pre-kindergarten through twelfth grade including supplementary materials. A Beka also offers enrollment in their own A Beka Correspondence School or video courses.

A Beka's philosophy is conservative, Christian (Protestant), and patriotic. Their approach to education is traditional with an emphasis on drill, repetition, and memorization. Children are expected to memorize information first, then develop conceptual understanding later. Learning takes place through direct instruction, workbook activities, drills, and oral responses. Hands-on activities are limited to some science experiments, construction of social studies reports, and arts and crafts.

All material is written from a Christian perspective. Although this is very evident in the science and history books, it is much less obviously so in most of the math and language arts books. Conservatism and patriotism are most evident in reading/literature and history.

A Beka books are colorful and appealing to children except for the amount of work involved. Many are paperback, making them both less expensive and less durable than hardbound books. Worktexts, used in many subjects, are definitely not reusable.

A Beka sells teacher curriculum guides, teacher's editions (sometimes equivalent to answer keys), and texts at retail prices to individuals. Subject area curriculum guides/lesson plans lay out lesson plans and offer teaching suggestions. A Beka is unusual in that they sometimes separate answer keys (teacher's editions) from teaching information (teacher curriculum guides), although this is not true of most of the newer editions. In new editions of some of their books, A Beka is creating teacher editions with instructional information in the first half of the book and student pages in the last half. Sometimes answers to questions are overprinted on the student pages. The organization of teacher material is not the same for all courses, which creates some confusion. In some instances, you will want both teacher's edition and teacher curriculum guide. But, with only a few exceptions, curriculum guides are not very useful to home educators.

The math and language worktexts include instruction on new concepts, but you will sometimes need teacher's editions for additional instruction and for answer keys, especially when the material gets too difficult to correct without them.

The arithmetic program for the early years requires the curriculum guides. The colorful, revised arithmetic programs for grades 1-3 include demonstrations with manipulatives and application (word) problems, but they also require some one-on-one teaching. Arithmetic texts for the elementary grades constantly review concepts already learned. The scope and sequence is more advanced than some other programs, so be cautious about expecting all children to work at the listed grade level.

Language arts programs review much of the same material year after year. Students are able to work independently through much of the material in the Language worktexts.

The reading program is based upon phonics, although the complete age-graded reading program for each grade level is cumbersome for home educators. A Beka does push reading at a very early age, so you will have to judge which level is appropriate for each child. A Beka uses a number of readers at each level rather than a single series.

History books for first and second grades are not very "meaty" but are good as starting points to do further research and kindle an interest.

Science books continually reinforce Biblical truths and an understanding of God as Creator. However, like most science texts for the early grades, the first and second grade books lack substance. Revised science books for grades 4-6 separate health topics into separate health science texts.

One frequent complaint about A Beka materials is that there are too many quizzes, drills, and tests, and they tend to focus on detailed, rote learning rather than concepts. A Beka does include quite a bit of busy work in their material. Watch carefully and do not require your child to complete everything in each lesson unless the practice is necessary.

A Beka materials can be ordered directly from A Beka by writing for a catalog and order form.

A Beka also offers courses on video cassette. See the

description of A Beka's Video Home School under "Sources, Correspondence Courses."

Alpha Omega

Alpha Omega LifePac materials are unlike typical school textbooks in a number of ways. Children are placed at the appropriate starting point in each subject area in the program, and they work sequentially through a number of workbooks, called LifePacs, as they master the material in each one. These small workbooks contain instruction, information, questions (with blanks), and tests. Although Alpha Omega LifePacs are similar in format to School of Tomorrow PACEs, Alpha Omega includes a variety of questions to encourage deeper thinking rather than simple recall of factual information.

Children take tests as they complete each section of a workbook before proceeding to the next. Tests check on student mastery of current subject matter and also review previously mastered material. A second test is included within each LifePac to be used as needed.

Alpha Omega offers full curriculum for grades 1-12, including Bible. The newest editions, called LifePac Gold, are printed in full color. LifePacs consist of ten booklets for each subject each year. These are now available in complete sets for each subject for each grade level. Each boxed set includes 10 LifePacs and a complete teacher's guide which includes all answer keys, tests, and teacher helps for the subject for that year in a spiral-bound volume. (Grade 1 teachers' guides are in two volumes because of their size.) Subject areas are Bible, Math, Language Arts (English), Science, and History and Geography (the latter two subject areas combine within one LifePac strand) for the elementary grades. Only five of the LifePacs require the use of a supplementary book to complete the course. Non-denominational Christianity is integrated throughout the material. Students can work at their proper levels in all subjects rather than being regimented into a single grade level for all subjects.

Unlike School of Tomorrow, Alpha Omega emphasizes their material should not be used by a child working totally independently but that parents need to be involved, supplementing with activities and other interaction from the teachers' manuals to ensure an effective program. Even though the LifePacs enable children to work independently, parental involvement is essential for providing the complete learning experience intended by the publisher. Unfortunately, there is a tendency among home educators to ignore the teacher's manuals and allow children to use the material completely on their own. Because this happens so frequently, I recommend that LifePacs be used with learners who are independent, self-motivated, and who do not need much hands-on experience to learn well. However, if parents plan to use the material as designed by the publisher, then it can work with learners who need more parental interaction.

The LifePac approach can be a real boon to parents with many children (especially when there are large gaps between oldest and youngest) or to parents who feel inadequate to help their children in particular subjects.

Materials are available through correspondence courses, through home school suppliers, or by direct order from the publisher.

Alpha Omega offers a *Parent Starter Kit* [$19.95] which includes some basics for beginning homeschoolers, a scope and sequence for the curriculum, the book *The How and Why of Home Schooling*, plus step-by-step instructions on how to use the LifePacs which covers organization, administration, and record keeping.

Diagnostic tests are available for Bible, Language Arts, History and Geography, Math, and Science. These are $5 each or $19.95 for the set. Tests are not timed and they are parent-administered. Step-by-step instructions show us how to administer the tests, grade them, analyze the results, and determine which Alpha Omega LifePacs to order. The diagnostic tests might be useful as a general testing tool for others as explained in Chapter 21.

Alpha Omega also publishes the *Horizons* program: *Mathematics* for K-6 and a new *Language/Phonics* program, due out April 2000. See the complete reviews of these products in their respective chapters. [Note: *Horizons* courses are quite different from the LifePacs and they follow a more advanced scope and sequence. The *Horizons Math* program is generally a more challenging and more effective math program than the LifePac Math courses. Math LifePacs are being revised to bring them closer to the advanced pace of *Horizons*, beginning with Math LifePacs for grades 4-6. For example, students moving from *Horizons Mathematics 3* into the revised LifePac Gold for grade 4 should have no problem. However, students moving from the as yet unrevised LifePac Gold 3 into LifePac Gold 4 will find introductory lessons reviewing content covered in *Horizons Mathematics 3*, but not previously covered in LifePac Gold 3. The LifePac Gold 4 then picks up the pace quickly and moves at a faster pace than the old editions of the math LifePacs. (The LifePacs for levels 4-6 are fairly similar to Saxon's *Math 54, 65*, and *76* in their scope and sequence.) This minor problem will be remedied as new LifePacs for K-3 math, become available.

Switched On Schoolhouse is a computerized version of the LifePac curriculum available for grades 3-12. See the complete review in Chapter Five.

Bob Jones University Press (BJUP)

BJUP's philosophy is conservative and Christian (Protestant). Educationally, they seem to have balanced their curriculum with teaching methods that suit most learning styles, although much of the necessary information to properly teach to all the learning styles is contained in the teacher's editions rather than in student books.

BJUP offers a mixture of softbound and hardbound student texts with separate teacher's editions. Most classroom teacher's editions are in a revised format—spiral binding with a hardback cover. The pages will not rip out of these as they might from binders, and the hardback cover lends rigidity for easier handling. Reproduced student pages within many teacher's editions are printed in black and white, although student books themselves are printed in color. (New teacher's editions will have color reproductions of student pages.) Teacher's editions seem expensive, and home educators sometimes try to work without them. However, they often contain material essential to proper use of the texts. Sometimes teacher's editions contain the student text without answers so a separate student text might be unnecessary. (Check with the publisher about each teacher's edition.) Recognizing that the cost of teacher's editions has sometimes deterred homeschoolers from purchasing these volumes, even when they are essential, BJUP now offers less expensive home teacher's guides (along with support materials) for most of their courses for the elementary grades.

Throughout BJUP's curriculum, student material is colorful and well presented. It also has strong Biblical teaching incorporated in a very effective manner. BJUP also has less busy work than A Beka.

The cost might be higher than other publishers since many texts are hard cover and you will often need the teacher's editions. However, quality and durability are good, and many of the books can be resold after use.

BJUP begins reading instruction in kindergarten. The phonics program is contained within *Beginnings K/5* and *Phonics and Reading 1*. *Beginnings K/5* provides all we need for kindergarten aside from math curriculum and Bible instruction. The goal of the K/5 program is exposure to beginning concepts without pressure. *Phonics and Reading 1* continues with phonics and correlates that instruction with other language arts areas. While there are a variety of informal activities in the K-1 programs, they lean toward more formal learning than some find necessary in the home school. You might use other methods for early elementary levels (particularly kindergarten), switching to BJUP when you feel it is appropriate.

The math program does not stress advanced computation skills as does A Beka's. BJUP math strives to develop understanding of math with manipulatives and thought-provoking word problems. This approach requires more one-on-one presentation than do some other math programs.

BJUP uses a slant printing/handwriting system very similar to ScottForesman's *D'Nealian* that is very popular with some home schoolers and teachers.

Science books for first through fifth grades are more activity-oriented than traditional science texts. This makes them more useful for children with different learning styles. BJUP has done a good job melding high quality content with activities.

Families with only one or two grade levels to teach generally find they can make use of BJUP texts and teacher's editions more easily than families with more grade levels to teach. The problem of getting through the large amount of material in the teacher's editions (even in home school teacher editions) sometimes causes families to use only the texts or workbooks, thereby eliminating essential parts of many courses. Check under individual course reviews whether the teacher's edition is essential or not, then determine if you have time to utilize the material properly.

Christian Liberty Press

Christian Liberty Academy was one of the pioneers in home education. They have offered educational assistance through their home education program at extremely low cost because they view their role as one of ministry. They promote solid, Bible-based (Protestant) education and a very conservative (limited government) political philosophy.

We can enroll in their correspondence course or purchase materials separately. In their efforts to keep the cost of home education as affordable as possible, they have begun publishing many of their own books under the Christian Liberty Press imprint. Many of these books in the past were reprints from the last century, but these have largely been replaced with newly-written books. The quality improves with each new edition. All CLP books are very inexpensive.

An assortment of readers is available for all levels. Since they differ significantly from one another, check the reviews for each level. The *Nature Reader* series (for grades 1-5) are reprints, many of which have been reformatted from the original to make both print and pictures larger. However, they are not substitutes for basal readers but are useful as supplemental reading material.

CLP has put together inexpensive reading kits for both beginning and remedial instruction that incorporate their books along with others. CLP's set of beginning phonetic readers are an excellent tool that might be used along with other phonics programs. Also, check out *Noah Webster's Reading Handbook*, a self-contained, uncluttered approach for teaching phonics.

The *Handwriting* series for grades K-4 features the traditional ball and stick/Palmer method. While they are not visually exciting and colorful, they do the job of teaching handwriting. The *Building Spelling Skills* series (for grades 1-8) takes a very rule-oriented approach to teaching spelling, building first upon phonetic skills.

The history books are an eclectic assortment of reprints and new books that can be used at various levels from first through eighth or ninth grade. Some of the readers are also quite useful for history coverage. See the reading and history sections of this book for details.

The new science books seem to be a real contrast to the general Christian Liberty approach, because they are very experiment-oriented with plenty of thought-provoking questions. (Only science books for grades K through 3 are available at present.)

Bible books are available for grades K-8. Younger levels are useful, and the higher levels of the *Studying God's Word* series (books E-H) are excellent.

All history/civics textbooks, *Building Spelling Skills* (except Book 1), and the *Studying God's Word* series have teacher's manuals written by CLP staff, sometimes at no extra cost. The manuals are very brief, containing answer keys and teaching suggestions. Even briefer teacher's notes come with the handwriting books.

Among supplementary CLP books are biographies of Saint Patrick, Robert E. Lee, George McClellan, Stonewall Jackson, Charles Spurgeon, David Livingstone, and George Washington; two good books on the Pilgrims; and an interesting little book entitled *Training Children in Godliness*.

If you are not satisfied with CLP books, they may be returned within thirty days of shipment; however, you will be charged a ten percent restocking charge.

Christian Light Education

Christian Light publishes a curriculum, much of which is similar in concept to Alpha Omega's LifePac curriculum. Originally an adaptation of that curriculum, Christian Light has gone on to create much of their own original material. Christian Light's Mennonite beliefs (Anabaptist doctrine) are reflected throughout much of their curriculum.

First graders begin with ten "Learning to Read" Lightunits. After completing these, they are ready to move into five basic strands of Lightunits: Bible, language arts, math, science, and social studies.

In addition, Christian Light publishes some textbooks designed primarily to meet the needs of Mennonite students but of interest to many other home schoolers: *God's Marvelous Gifts* (fifth grade science), *Living Together on God's Earth*, *Into All the World*, *North America is the Lord's*, and *God's World - His Story* (social studies texts for grades 3-6). An elementary-level Canadian social study unit is available, and Canadian studies are also covered in a set of four special Lightunits used typically at seventh grade level.

Christian Light also carries a broad line of supplementary books and resources. Christian Light curriculum is available by grade level, subject, or individual unit. They also offer school services through Homeschool Plus. See the description under "Independent Study Programs, Correspondence Schools, and School Services" in Chapter 22.

Landmark's Freedom Baptist Curriculum

Landmark offers a complete curriculum for grades K-12. Students can enroll in the complete program or purchase individual courses. See details under "Independent Study Programs, Correspondence Schools, and School Services" in Chapter 22.

LFBC believes that it is parents' responsibility to pass on knowledge, wisdom, and values to their children, so the curriculum is strongly oriented toward inculcating a Judeo-Christian value system. Most people would describe the philosophy as very conservative. History shuns modern social studies, choosing to concentrate on history and geography.

English takes a back-to-basics approach with phonics, reading (using *McGuffey Readers*), parts of speech, diagramming, and plenty of writing. Science is Bible based, teaching the creation science viewpoint. Bible courses use the KJV. The courses are uneven in quality, both graphically and in content, but they are gradually being revised and improved. The curriculum is very academic through the elementary grades. See reviews of the kindergarten program in Chapter Five and reviews of specific subject courses in some of the other chapters.

Customized samples (samples from two subject sets of the customers choice and a Scope and Sequence) are available for $5.

LFBC allows parents to purchase materials to use as they wish, but they encourage home schooling families to work under the auspices of some oversight organization for accountability.

Rod and Staff

Rod and Staff is a Mennonite publishing company that is very supportive of home schooling.

The curriculum relies heavily upon Biblical material in all subject areas. Among the distinctives of the Mennonite philosophy are nonresistance and separation, including the belief that the church should not involve itself in government, and this is reflected in their texts. Mennonite philosophy also emphasizes hard work and diligence, and this is very evident throughout the material. Learning occurs via reading, lectures, and memorization rather than through experimentation and discovery.

There is much busywork and extra material in Rod and Staff's textbooks since they were designed for classroom use. So you should not try to use everything in every book. If you know your goals and use curriculum as a tool, you can use Rod and Staff effectively by choosing how much of the material to have your child do.

Their readers are appealing to those who desire strong Biblical content since they feature retold Bible stories and character-building stories based on Biblical principles, rejecting the fantasy, science fiction, and fables found in most other readers.

The *Building Christian English* texts are solid, traditional courses for second through eighth grades, that follow an accelerated scope and sequence.

Science books have excellent content, but they present science experiments to illustrate what has been taught rather than as a means of discovery learning.

Rod and Staff offers Reading for 1-8; English for 2-8; Math for 1-8; Spelling for 2-7; Penmanship for 1-4; Social Studies for 2-6; History for 7; Health for 2 and 4; Music for 1-7; and Science for 2-4 and 7-9. They also offer Spanish readers for 1-3 and Math (in Spanish) for 1-3.

School of Tomorrow

School of Tomorrow materials are designed for children to work independently. No lesson preparation or presentation by the parent is necessary. Children work through individual worktexts, called PACEs (12 per course, per year, although the rate can be varied to suit each child).

School of Tomorrow diagnostic tests are important for determining placement of our child in the material. They will identify learning gaps, performance levels, and levels of mastery. The tests are also useful to those who are not using their material. (See Diagnostic Tests" under " Testing in Chapter 21.) These tests are shorter than the CAT, Iowa, or SAT 9 tests and are not timed. Diagnostic testing is now also available on CD-ROM.

Once children have been placed at the proper performance level in each subject area, they work sequentially through the PACES as they master the material in each one. This methodology is called "Mastery Learning." Students might be working at different levels in different subjects according to their individual abilities and needs.

These small workbooks contain instruction, information, questions (with blanks), and tests. Children take quizzes as they complete each section of a worktext before proceeding to the next. Especially at younger grade levels, tests generally cover only what has recently been studied, relying largely on short-term memory.

School of Tomorrow has materials for grades K-12, most of it printed in full color. Subjects are covered under general headings of Bible, Math, Language Arts (English), Word Building (spelling and vocabulary) for grades 1-9 only, Science, and Social Studies. Because School of Tomorrow views acquiring Biblical wisdom as a major educational goal, they have added "wisdom lessons", Scripture memory, and Biblical values throughout the curriculum.

Bible Reading curriculum is available for three levels (approximately grades 2-4). The Bible Reading courses have children read Scripture, then fill in blanks with one-word answers taken verbatim from the text.

Word Building reinforces phonics, then works on vocabulary and etymology at upper levels. *Word Building* tests with digitized speech are now available on CD-ROM, which makes it much easier for students to complete the *Word Building* PACEs independently.

School of Tomorrow social studies is big on the "social" end (e.g., the first half of the seventh grade level is entirely devoted to careers) along with church and Bible history, but lacking in comprehensive coverage of world and United States history and geography until high school level.

Supplemental books are required or recommended with a number of courses, more so at the upper levels than in the early elementary grades, but these are increasingly being eliminated as PACEs are rewritten to stand alone, with the exception of their new *Literature and Creative Writing* course which includes a number of readers essential to the course.

School of Tomorrow designed the material to move slowly at the primary levels with much attention given to drill. For instance, there is no multiplication until fourth grade. The difficulty curve rises quickly at upper elementary levels.

School of Tomorrow's biggest weakness is that the material relies heavily upon simple recall rather than deeper thinking. Students can scan for the correct answer without having to really think about the material. There is little to encourage deeper thinking. From about fifth grade and up, more thinking and application skills are required, but the curriculum never operates at the same thinking-skill levels as curriculum from other major Christian publishers.

While no lesson preparation is required with School of Tomorrow PACEs, parents should use preparation time to develop activities that correlate with lessons to enhance the child's learning experience. Parents should also discuss PACE material with students to ensure that they are understanding rather than simply going through the motions of completing their worktexts.

School of Tomorrow also has preschool material (*Preschool with Ace and Christi*) which covers readiness topics. A separate course for beginning reading is entitled *A B C's with Ace and Christi*. It is presented in a more traditional format, requiring teacher presentation of lessons.

Some School of Tomorrow materials are also available in Spanish. School of Tomorrow sells a *Home Educator's Resource Kit* for $39.95. This includes a video for parents, a home school manual, scope and sequence book, and an Activity Pac. They also offer a *Quick Start Kit* [$49.95] which includes a Diagnostic Test Kit, Record Keeping Kit plus the all items in the *Home Educator's Resource Kit*. Either of these kits will help you figure out how to get started in the curriculum much more easily than if you try to do it on your own.

Chapter 5

Unit Study, All-In-One Studies, and Computer-based Curriculum

Unit Studies

Before delving into the confusion of textbook choices, you need to be aware of an alternate approach that is popular with many home educators.

Unit study appears under many different names and guises but can be recognized by the presence of a unifying theme. Unit study is not a new or radical idea, yet it is usually a departure from the structured, traditional-curriculum approach which is most familiar to us. Rather than approaching each subject and topic as an isolated thing to be learned, information is presented in context as part of a whole. By integrating information, children learn with more understanding, resulting in better retention of subject matter. (At least that's the theory.)

Unit study approaches often (but not always) use hands-on experiences or activities for more effective learning. The value of such experiences and activities is based upon the belief that children retain much more of what they learn by doing than they retain from only hearing and/or seeing. The discovery approach is also frequently used, wherein the child learns a truth by actually experiencing or discovering a truth through experimentation, observation, and study. To guard against faulty conclusions, it is necessary that parents act as guides in the discovery learning process.

We can pursue unit studies either with purchased materials that have planned the foundations of the study for us, such as *KONOS, The Weaver*, and *Alta Vista*, or with materials that we collect and plan ourselves. A unit study can also be presented by simply choosing sections of textbooks that all relate to a theme and teaching them together. For instance, if we are studying about the California Gold Rush, we could study those sections in a California history textbook and sections about mining and minerals from a science textbook. We might also integrate a language arts activity by assigning a creative writing task related to the Gold Rush.

Unit study might encompass many subject areas or may be limited to one subject area. The major published unit studies generally encompass everything except math and language arts. On the other hand, *Developing Godly Character in Children* is a unit study approach that covers only the Bible/religion subject area.

Unit studies typically outline a series of topics under each theme as the foundation on which to build other studies. Topics and themes vary tremendously among published unit studies and are unlimited for those we might choose ourselves.

An example of a typical unit study comes from the first chapter in *KONOS Volume 1* on the character trait, attentiveness. We choose an aspect of attentiveness we wish to study first, such as listening and sound. We study related Scriptures, then study about the human ear (science), listen to music (music), make musical instruments (crafts), study about musical composers (music history), practice listening games (character development), study about and apply the speeds of sound and light to thunder and lightning (math and science), and write a headache commercial describing irritating noises (language). These ideas are only a fraction of what is offered within a typical unit study!

Unit study programs presently available usually try to cover most subject areas other than math and language. We are expected to supplement with math and language programs (including phonics/reading) of our choosing since both subjects need to be presented in a more sequential manner than other subjects.

A unit study approach can be used to simultaneously teach children of different ages, assigning more in-depth follow-up work for the older student. It is not necessary for the parent/teacher to have thorough knowledge of a subject beforehand because the parent is also involved in the learning process along with the child.

Research is essential. Most unit studies require that we rely on outside sources such as library books for full information on specific topics. (Publishers could not possibly fit all information on all subjects covered in one large book.) Unit studies encourage children to think beyond the confines of textbook material. Learning is enhanced as we deal with questions and situations that arise out of unit studies.

One drawback is that unit studies sometimes require more preparation and presentation time from the teacher than typical textbook studies. (Sometimes when we get into a unit study, we discover interesting sidetracks to explore which may take more time than was planned.) One possible solution is to use unit study as a supplement rather than the main part of our program. This gives us the freedom to devote more or less time to it as we are able.

While unit methods vary in topics, they also vary in the amount of preparation work which has already been done for us, the resources we will have to search out, the amount of step-by-step guidance provided, and the cost.

Tapes and workshops on implementing unit study methods are available from KONOS. Their tapes (both audio and video) are loaded with practical information and examples based on the experiences of the authors themselves and others who have used *KONOS*.

I recommend the book *KONOS Compass: An Orientation to Using KONOS* [$25] to anyone using *KONOS*. It gives an overview of all three volumes along with a comparison to typical state requirements so that we can see we are covering the necessary material. *KONOS Compass* also provides teaching information and sample lesson plans. Another alternative is *How to Use KONOS Curriculum*, a set of six, hour-long audio cassettes [$25].

The Weaver publishes a book, *Teaching Tips and Techniques* [$30], that applies to both general teaching methods and unit study. This book is loaded with specific ideas, concentrating most heavily on language arts, the area lacking in most published unit studies. The combination of one of the *Weaver* volumes, *Wisdom Words, Teaching Tips and Techniques,* and a math text makes a complete program for students in middle elementary grades who have already mastered phonics.

Published Unit Studies

There are presently a number of choices for published unit study material. Most of those listed here offer activities across many subject areas.

The ABC's of Christian Culture
by Julia M. Fogassy
(Our Father's House)
Level A - $93; Level B - $69.95

Julia Fogassy has created a comprehensive unit study for Catholic families that focuses on world views. Students ages 10 and up can cover most of their subject studies within the curriculum with the exceptions of math, foreign language, high school science, and some religion courses. History, geography and language arts are the primary subject areas.

History is the organizing theme, with the presentation arranged around 10 historical periods, some of which overlap each other. The ten periods reveal the religious worldview orientation: Egypt, Greece, Rome, Israel, Early Church, Patristic Church, Growth of Church, High Middle Ages, Divided Christendom, and Modern Times.

The program is designed such that we cover each of the ten periods every year, albeit with varying amounts of time and attention given to each from year to year. I was a bit concerned about this arrangement until I reviewed Level B and saw how the selected focus changed in addressing each period. For example, Egyptian history is covered in broader scope in Level A, then with a narrow focus on a single dynasty in Level B. Nevertheless, it would not be difficult to divide the material up differently, focusing on fewer selected periods each year. Programs are labeled, Levels A, B, etc. Levels A and B are available thus far, with C and D nearing completion.

Two primary goals of the program are that children remember what they learn and that they understand the context for that knowledge. Consequently, Fogassy incorporates multi-sensory learning activities for more effective learning as well as the use of timelines to help children place people and events in proper historical context.

Level A is the starting point for all families. Two audio cassette tapes explain to both parent and student how to use the program. A three-ring binder provides additional explanation for the teacher, map masters printed on heavy card stock, "write ideas," tests for both time periods and map studies, record keeping instructions and forms, and student notebook dividers. Along with the binder we receive a wall chart and a set of cards, all of which are laminated for durability. The wall chart features a miniature timeline showing the ten time periods, their overlaps, and the color coding used throughout the program. Sixty color-coded "people and monument" cards can be used for teaching and inclusion on each child's timeline.

While children can share the set of cards, they will each need a set of notebook dividers to create their own notebooks [$15]. The notebook dividers are heavily-laminated pages that precede each of the 10 time periods in binders children will each create. Binders become the repository for map work and written assignments. Children will continue to add to these binders as they work through future levels of the program.

I mentioned the map masters and "write ideas" in the teacher's manual, but these deserve special attention as the "meat of the program." The map masters come with questions that help students learn geography as well as some history. Children trace and label maps, perhaps two or three times each. Map tests verify mastery of the information. The "write ideas" section in Level A offers 41 writing assignments that incorporate a wide range of language arts skills. "Some assignments, such as writing a biographical sketch, are straightforward and require only basic research and writing skills, while other assignments are very complex and require in-depth research, comparison and analysis of data and solid documentation of evidence." Select activities that are appropriate for the skill level of each student.

Numerous outside resources will be required, so Fogassy includes recommendations for each of the ten time periods, although you might use others not on her lists. Locating these resources and making appropriate assignments for each child will be very time consuming compared to traditional textbooks. Parents will probably want to read many of the selections aloud as a family, discuss assigned readings, and present many of the multi-sensory activities Fogassy suggests for each period (e.g., "Make plaster map of the course of the Nile. Include the delta and all the water falls.") Although "write idea" assignments are fairly detailed (including assignments of tracing and labeling map masters whenever appropriate), other activity ideas are sketchily presented. That means that parents looking for a detailed "road map" through the curriculum might quickly get lost. This program will work best for those who like to use real books and tailor activities to suit their children's needs and who also have the time and energy to do so.

This program also requires serious research, reading, and writing from students. No direct language arts instruction is provided for these assignments. You will probably need to use other resources for these areas, but, at a minimum, I suggest purchase of a handbook such as Writers Inc to be used for reference and review.

The ABC's of Christian Culture will work especially well in a group class where students help to motivate one another, although it will work for individual students. Obviously, a good deal of each student's work must be done independently, which will require a certain level of maturity and self-direction.

Level B, as I have found with most such programs, provides even more assistance than the first level. It features 80 "write idea" projects in contrast to the 41 assignments in Level A. It also has 63 more history cards, 21 map masters with questions, and directions and masters for making 13 medieval flags. Students must complete Level A before beginning Level B. I expect to see expansion and development of ideas to make this program easier to use over the next few years. Nevertheless, the present editions offer an excellent outline and tools based on a solid philosophy of education. Students who work through these lessons are bound to develop writing and thinking skills as well as a knowledge base well beyond that typical of traditional programs.

Across America

(Hewitt Homeschooling Resources) $129.95 for complete package; supplemental manuals for either first grade or combined third/fourth grades

Hewitt offers other complete grade level packages, but this second grade package differs from the others because it integrates all of the subject areas around studies of the states. Math and language arts (including reading) are covered, unlike most other unit studies. Social studies, science, art, Bible/character, music, health, and studying and thinking skills comprise the rest of the content coverage. The complete package includes a three-ring binder Teacher's Manual that explains the program, describes the scope and sequence for each subject,

then provides detailed daily lesson plans. A student binder contains worksheets primarily for math and language arts. In addition to the two binders the package comes with the *Across America Reader*, the game *Rummy Roots*, *States and Capitals Songs* (map and cassette tape), and state map stickers.

Themes for the units are drawn from the study of each state as well as from character traits, although they are not as thoroughly developed as we find in *KONOS* or the *Weaver*.

The program incorporates multi-sensory learning through songs, games, crafts, hands-on learning of concepts, oral work, and listening along with more traditional worksheet activities. Generally some extra items are required for each unit, but a list at the beginning of each helps us plan ahead. Items required are generally easily accessible, e.g., paper sacks, tracing paper, crayons, books, pictures, ingredients for recipes, burlap, and magnets.

Parent involvement is essential throughout the program, because there is a great deal of discussion and interaction. Parents who like a structured program that lets them know what to do each day, yet who want to provide the variety and fun of unit study for their children should find this a good compromise solution. Since it was written for home educators, the activities are practical in the home setting. We can purchase extra student binders for additional students in our family.

Hewitt has published supplements for either first graders or third and fourth graders that come in three-ring binders. These supplements allow us to teach the same topics to children at all these grade levels while still targeting necessary skills at each level.

The *Grade-1 Supplement* includes a reading program and instructions for teaching arithmetic by using Addison Wesley's *Mathematics 1* and *Unifix Cubes*. Appropriate activities for younger students are frequently described for the other subject areas also. This Supplement includes *My Book of States,* which serves as a beginning reader, and state flag stickers. You may also purchase a package that includes the above plus the math text and *Unifix Cubes* for $69.95.

The *Grades 3 & 4 Supplement* expands lessons on Bible/character, social studies, reading, and science/health to offer age-appropriate challenges. Time line charts printed on heavy card stock and a U.S. map with transparency overlays are tucked in the pockets of the binder. This supplement also includes the *American Tales Reader*, a collection of biographical tales about famous people, each followed by comprehension/discussion questions. Both supplements must be used along with *Across America*; they do not stand on their own.

Alta Vista Curriculum

$95 per unit; Instructor's Handbook - $35; $35 for materials for each extra student

Alta Vista Curriculum differs from other published unit studies. The novice unit study teacher who needs a lot of ideas and direction will find security with the detailed, step-by-step approach of this material. *Alta Vista* stresses that teachers will not need to spend much time in advance preparation with these units but rather will learn along with her children. Units are packaged in three-ring binders with removable student pages contained within the binder. A separate *Instructor's Handbook* provides detailed "how to," "why to," and learning styles information, as well as scope and sequence charts, evaluation and portfolio guidelines, lists of recommended children's literature, and activity instructions (e.g., how to make collages and salt dough). *The Instructor's Handbook* is required for first-time purchasers because it is vital for understanding the program. The regular price is $45, but only $35 when purchased with your first unit.

Learning Styles and Tools (Alta Vista) [$15.95] excerpts, adapts, and expands information from the *Instructor's Handbook* on learning styles, child development, and assessment and evaluation. See the description of this book under the discussion of learning styles. Parents who do not use the curriculum can have access to this information to aid in all teaching situations. The information on child/student development helps us know what to expect with the average child at different stages. Assessment information includes explanations of portfolios, evaluation by observation, and other non-traditional methods of evaluation. Forms for evaluation make it a little easier for us to note attainment of some objectives. However, a few of the forms are strictly for classroom situations.

The *Alta Vista Curriculum* is fairly easy to deal with. Students need to do some research outside the curriculum, but the student text (with accompanying worksheets) is the primary learning tool.

The layout of the curriculum is quite unusual. It is divided into four levels: A (K-1), B (2-4), C (5-7), and D (8-10), although units are not complete at all levels, and only one is available for level D at this time. Within each level are five units: Plants, Animals, Earth and Space, People in Groups, and People as Individuals. The People in Groups unit is slated for division into two separate units in the future: People in Political Groups and People in Ethnic Groups. When this happens, there will be six units for each level. These unit themes are repeated at each level, but the content within each theme at each level is different, so we are addressing different subject matter if we are teaching out of two or more levels. (If our children are three or four years apart, we might be able to stretch one unit a year or two either way rather than buying two different levels.) When using two different levels, there will be a few points where joint field trips or activities will work but do not count on much overlap. Each unit has fifteen lessons, emphasizing different subject areas, generally presented in the same order within each unit. Since each lesson should take about one week to complete, each unit should require about one semester to complete (although we can easily take longer

if we choose). The schedule should work out such that we complete two units per year—six over a three-year period. We should purchase only one unit at a time, according to our child(ren)'s interest, since there is no particular order to be followed in the use of units. While most units are now available for levels A and B, there are four for level C.

We find very creative ideas throughout the curriculum. There is a definite sense of a concept-upon-concept building process taking place—something that is missing in most unit study approach lessons. Large amounts of material (factual knowledge) are not covered as you would find in A Beka or Bob Jones, but topics are covered in great depth. Emphasis is on learning how to observe, think, analyze, synthesize, and evaluate—all steps to higher levels of thinking. Lessons are constructed with four parts to each: introducing, presenting, practicing, and responding. The introduction is designed to interest children in the topic with a personal experience. Presenting means conveying the knowledge content, which often includes projects. Practicing offers opportunities for children to assimilate knowledge, and responding activities have children apply the knowledge. Activities are designed to address all learning style needs at one point or another.

Alta Vista makes no attempt to cover math and language skills in a thorough fashion, so we must supplement with other programs. However, they now sell a separate language arts curriculum for K-3 that easily correlates with the A and B units. The curriculum, by Marlene and Robert McCracken is literature-based and organized by units such as "Animals," "Myself," and "The Sea and Other Waters." *Alta Vista* also will provide customers with recommendations for math and other language arts programs which they feel coordinate well with their material.

For detailed information on the philosophy behind the program and costs, request their free brochure. Samples of *Earth and Space*, Lesson 1, from Levels A, B, and C are available for $5 ($8 overseas). With the sample lessons you receive a coupon for $5 credit on your first purchase.

Beyond Five in a Row, volumes 1-3
by Becky Jane Lambert
(Five in a Row Publishing)
$24.95 each

Some of you might be familiar with the original *Five in a Row* literature-based unit studies for younger children. These were authored by Jane Lambert. Becky Jane Lambert, her daughter, has developed a series of studies for older students. These excellent, one-semester courses are suggested for ages 8-12, but might easily stretch to include junior high students. Four books for each volume are the foundation for each unit study. For example, Volume 1 includes *The Boxcar Children, Thomas A. Edison - Young Inventor, Homer Price,* and *Betsy Ross - Designer of Our Flag.* Subject areas covered include literature, some language arts, history, composition, science, and fine arts.

A *Christian Bible Supplement* [$9.95 each], also by Becky Jane Lambert, stretches to include Bible-based character study that might comprise your Bible course. We need to supplement for math, grammar, spelling, and penmanship but history, science, Bible (using the *Supplement*), fine arts, and a significant part of language arts will be covered for children in grade 3-6.

Lessons are set up so that we read a chapter from the book, then work through our choice of the suggested activities which vary greatly from day to day. Quite a bit of historical and scientific information is included within the book, but we need to use outside resources for additional research. Many such resources are suggested in the lessons. Lessons often include "Internet Connection" activities for students to do research at a particular site or sites on a topic related to the study. About half of the lessons include an essay question; you will need to tailor requirements on these to suit the age of each student. Occasional "Career Paths" sections help students consider career possibilities and offer suggestions for further research and/or experience in the field. Timelines are recommended as a means of helping students understand chronological relationships between people and events. Numerous hands-on activities are included: art projects, cooking, science experiments, learning sign language, etc. A list of all topics covered (a form of scope and sequence) is located at the back of each book; this will help you for both planning and tracking your accomplishments.

Christian Cottage Unit Studies (four volumes)

(Fountain of Truth Publishing Division)
Volume I - $75; Volumes II and III - $59.95 each; Volume IV - $75

Students from primary grades through high school can participate in this unit study curriculum. Each of the four volumes is a one-year program designed especially for home educators. However,the publisher suggests that families cycle through the four volumes twice, covering a total of eight years.

Volumes follow each other chronologically: Volume I, *In The Beginning, God!: From Creation to the Middle Ages*, Third Edition. Volume II, *For God So Loved the World*, studies various regions of the Eastern Hemisphere with special emphasis on Asia, Africa, and the Orient. (Note: Volume II is being updated and expanded. The new edition should be available July 2000 for $75.)Volume III, *God Bless America*, studies the Western Hemisphere plus American history from exploration through the revolution. Volume IV, *Blessed to Be a Blessing*, continues American history from 1800 up through the present day.

The curriculum was developed through actual use by home schoolers in Christian Cottage Schools. Units were "initially taught to groups of 10-12 children ranging in level from kindergarten to eighth grade." To make it easier to teach various age levels, resources and activities are suggested for primary, elementary, intermediate, and advanced levels. Younger students do more hands-on activities and less book work, while older students do more book and written work and fewer hands-on activities. Overall, hands-on, experiential learning plays an important role in this curriculum as it does in many other unit studies.

Instructions and expanded information for most subjects was limited in the first volume, but that shortcoming has been corrected in the most current edition of Volume I as well as in the following three volumes—making them similar to the *Weaver*, *KONOS*, or other more extensive unit studies.

Christian Cottage Unit Studies feature activities and studies designed around the theme of each lesson, buttressed by the use of texts and other resource materials. Three days a week are identified as "book days." On book days, students work primarily through workbooks, texts, and other learning materials, with unit study activity taking a 30 to 90 minute slot. One day is set aside for intensive unit study activity such as a project, art, field trip, or event. The fifth day is "writing day" for discussing, creating, and rewriting.

The publisher recommends that we purchase one history text and one science text for the year for the oldest student. Supplemental textbooks are optional for elementary students. These are used as resource books from which we make assignments, read aloud, and draw information as needed. (Note: Textbooks seem to be more and more optional as we move to newer editions.) Lists of annotated recommendations at the beginning of each volume help us identify which textbooks will be most useful.

Each unit within a volume also includes annotated lists of historic fiction and classics, videos, and other resources. Each unit's activities are broken down into the four levels—primary, elementary, intermediate, and advanced—so that we can identify main points of study, vocabulary words, and daily activities appropriate for different learners. (The main points of study also serve as an aid for test preparation.) Typically, for the three "book days," there is one activity provided, with instructions added for the various levels when necessary. The activity for the fourth day of each week does not seem any more comprehensive than do the first three days' activities, which leaves us to determine what else we might do as a field trip, event, project, etc. for the rest of the day. (Perhaps this is a day to spend more time on math, language arts skills, foreign language, etc.) The fifth day's "writing assignment" is often extensive. For example, on the tenth day of the "Roots and Relations" unit, students make stone soup, write up family recipes, and make a padded, fabric cover for a previously begun project, a Family Heritage Book.

Subjects covered in all volumes are Bible, astronomy, life science, physical science, geography, government, history, creative writing, literature, home economics, music, and art. History coverage in Vol. I is selective, which is fine for elementary grades but inadequate for junior and senior high students. (The publisher expects that *In the Beginning, God!* will be serving as a supplement to most junior and senior high studies rather than as the main course, so it is not intended to be comprehensive for the upper grades in all subjects.) The units are arranged to cover "history and the story of creation simultaneously," so emphasis shifts back and forth between the two subjects in alternate units. The publisher suggests two additional options for arranging the units, depending upon your purpose; one option arranges units in a chronological approach and the other arranges them according to the seasons.

Because history coverage is selective rather than comprehensive, supplementing with a text for continuous, thorough coverage for older students makes sense. However, you should not require students to read an entire textbook and also complete all of the unit study activities. Use texts as a resource to fill the historical gaps or flesh out a topic. This is especially important for older students.

Volume II, *For God So Loved the World*, is especially strong in geography, government, and cultural studies. It is arranged by Eastern Hemisphere geographical units: Mediterranean Region, Western Europe, Eastern Europe, African Safari, Southwest Asia, Central Asia, The Orient, and Oceania. It also covers wildlife, technology, weather, and other topics. Information on countries is up-to-date, more current than in most textbooks.

Volume III, *God Bless America*, studies North America, Central America, South America, explorers, missionaries to the New World, early settlers, and the establishment of the United States of America. For science it covers anatomy, wildlife, geology and weather. Even more polished than Volume II, it offers quite a bit of background information and teacher helps to make it easier to prepare lessons.

Volume IV, *Blessed To Be A Blessing*, continues American history and technology from 1800 up through the present day, focusing also on government and the Constitution. Science topics featured are horticulture, veterinary science, physics, electricity, disease prevention, and the senses. The last unit in this volume, "Christianity 2000," is a study of "end times." This volume retains the strong emphasis on activities and hands-on learning characteristic of the entire curriculum.

An encyclopedia such as *World Book* would be extremely useful. The recommended topical books and literature can be found at the library, although some families will find it easier to invest in books of their own.

The overall approach of the Christian Cottage Unit Studies is user-friendly. The authors have provided great activities balanced with textbooks and other easy-to-use resources so that the work involved is manageable. Suggestions for scheduling and some basic teaching tips are especially helpful to those who worry about how much is enough of each subject. I consider this an excellent way for families to try unit studies with fewer choices and less work than is required by programs such as *KONOS* and *Weaver*.

The Classics

(The Helping Hand)
Combo Set - $199, individual units - $75

The Classics is a unit study approach based primarily on literature that relates to American history. There are ten units (volumes) from which to choose. The scope and sequence shows American history coverage beginning with exploration and colonization of North America in the first unit, up through World War I and the Great Depression in the tenth unit.

Each unit consists of a Teacher's Edition and a Student Activity Book with reproducible pages. These are packaged together within a single binder that has divider tabs. Extra Student Activity Pages (specific for either grades 3-4 or grades 5-6) are available if we choose to purchase them rather than reproduce pages.

Lessons are geared for students in grades 3-6, although they might be stretched without much difficulty for younger and older students. Activities within the lesson plans are given approximate grade level designations so we can easily spot those likely to be appropriate for each child. Each unit should take 12 to 15 weeks to complete, although most families are taking longer. There are a number of lesson plan options presented so each family can work out a schedule that suits them.

Each unit revolves around a single novel, with all subject areas except math taught in reference to the novel. Subject areas are divided into language arts, history and geography, science and health, and moral and ethical values. (Moral and ethical teaching is tied to the Bible and Christian principles, although there is no sectarian doctrine involved.) Language arts is further divided into creative writing, vocabulary, English, reading, critical thinking, and spelling. Daily lesson plans are provided for language arts, then we choose from the other subject areas according to the level of each child. (We should not attempt to do everything in the book.) While the Student Activity Book is rather bulky, the variety of activities included prevents comparison with typical workbook activity. In fact, some of the student pages are activity descriptions rather than work sheets. We can reproduce student activity pages if we wish for our own children, but some parents will find it more practical to purchase packets of student activity pages.

Teacher's Editions include unit evaluation pages which are designed both for testing itself and to provide students with practice filling in little circles as they do on standardized tests. Answer keys are included along with a bibliography of fiction, non-fiction, and biographies for supplemental reading.

The language arts instruction seems to be a very strong area. The feedback I receive from users of *The Classics* praises the writing instruction and daily writing activities, typically a weak point in most other curricula for these grade levels.

The titles of available units are *The Witch of Blackbird Pond, Johnny Tremain, The Best Christmas Pageant Ever, Ben and Me, Little House on the Prairie, The Adventures of Tom Sawyer, Across Five Aprils, Old Yeller, Mama's Bank Account,* and *Charlotte's Web.*

A variety of learning methods has been included to help meet children's learning styles. Parents who need structure while their children need variety and hands-on activity will find this a comfortable option that provides the security they need. It differs from *KONOS* and *The Weaver* in its use of work pages, inclusion of complete language arts instruction, a more-structured approach, and indirect, sporadic Bible-related teaching. (Most of us will want to provide Bible instruction in greater depth than is provided here.) Activities generally require inexpensive materials that are usually found around the home. Most of the lesson preparation work has been done for us.

We do need a copy of the novel that accompanies each unit, as well as a math program, and an encyclopedia. (They recommend and sell *World Book*.) They also recommend the handwriting program *A Reason for Writing*.

The Helping Hand catalog shows sample pages and describes the curriculum in detail. To begin, I recommend that you commit to this approach for one year, and purchase the Combo Set which includes three different units of your choice. I am impressed with the wealth of material included in *The Classics*, the thoroughness of topic coverage, and the ease of use.

Education PLUS: Patterning Learning Upon Scripture, Genesis 1-11, Parts I and II and Genesis 12-50, Parts I and II
by Inge and Ronald Jay Cannon
(Education PLUS+)
Part I of each study - 99 each; Part II of each study - $79 each

This is actually an interdisciplinary study rather than a unit study. The Cannons describe it: "It is true that interdisciplinary study is built from units. Interdisciplinary study, however, enables the 'whole' to be greater than the sum of its parts." In contrast to unit study where activities and learning often relates to the same topic, but rarely to each other, interdisciplinary study includes discussion of the interrelationships between subject areas and activities. There is an underlying theme to the curriculum; volume 1 (presented in two parts) centers around and is titled *Genesis 1-11*. The second volume

is *Genesis 12-50* (also presented in two parts). Proceeding in Scriptural order, each chapter has a title/theme with key concepts for each lesson that serve as foundations for other studies. For example, in volume one, chapter 1's topic is "The Beginning." The key concept for lesson 1 is "Genesis is foundational—to the rest of Scripture and to the development of faith." The parent/teacher prepares and presents lessons using a variety of resources. There is time when the entire family, all age levels, works together, then time when various ages separate to work at their appropriate grade levels. Chapters are outlined for four lessons each. Families may choose to spend whatever time they wish on each chapter, using the curriculum for a full year or even two.

Volumes of *The Preacher's Outline and Sermon Bible (POSB)* are used throughout all of the studies and the required volume that coordinates with *Genesis 1-11* comes with the purchase of Part I of that volume. In lesson 1 we begin with Scripture reading and singing the featured hymn. We continue with readings from *POSB* and other sources as well as discussions about the book of Genesis itself, the author of Genesis, and "prehistoric man." Next, we perform research on "how sociologists believe written communication began," get into Scripture study using a Concordance and other tools—a great deal of information is provided within the curriculum, but you will need to build an extensive library as you use *Education PLUS.*

Following these foundational lessons are subject area assignments divided into four levels: up through age 7, ages 8-12, ages 13-18, and ages 16 and up. Subject areas covered are language arts/literature, history, sciences, business/economics, government/law, mathematics, and fine arts. All subjects are not covered every day. Subject area assignments are a variety of textbook readings, reading from other resources, discussions, research, and hands-on activities, most related to the general theme of the lesson or chapter. For example, science studies related to "The Beginning" for ages 8-12 include researching, "What does it mean to *evolve*? How do the words *evolution* and *evolve* relate?" (See *Life Science*, BJUP, pp. 81-87.) For ages 13-18, one assignment is, "Natural revelation involves those things that we can observe and therefore know. Work through Chapter 1, 'Science and the Bible' (*Basic Science*, BJUP, pp. 1-19) to understand the limitations of science." Many assignments from level to level address closely related or identical topics, but at more challenging levels, so your children might be studying the same ideas, simplifying the teacher's task. Textbook assignments do not necessarily follow the textbook's order of presentation, but are selected as they address specific topics. *Genesis 1-11* includes orientation information for parents plus supplements for teaching literature and keeping records.

Math and language arts need separate, sequential coverage, although language arts does receive a good deal of attention in this program. While there are some hands-on activities, especially at the lowest level, this is primarily book-based study. We can find some resources at the library, but it will be necessary to purchase quite a few. Among those required for all volumes of *Education PLUS* are the complete sets of BJUP history, science and literature textbooks for high school level; the above mentioned *Preacher's Outline and Sermon Bible* (additional volumes come with each volume of *Education PLUS*); *Strong's Concordance; Major Bible Themes* by Lewis Sperry Chafer; *Encyclopedia of Bible Truths for School Subjects; Etiquette PLUS: Polishing Life's Useful Skills; God, Man, and Law: The Biblical Principles* by Herbert W. Titus; *The Timetables of History*; a hymnbook; a dictionary; a thesaurus; a grammar handbook; and *Best Books for Kindergarten through High School*. Another list of 22 books, mostly creation-science oriented titles, is required for teaching *Volume 1, Genesis 1-11*. Still more books are listed as optional for the complete series and for the *Genesis 1-11* volume. Although this requires a large financial investment, having a library at your fingertips makes teaching much easier.

Education PLUS combines the benefits of unit study with the convenience of textbooks in an unusual fashion. I expect that the inexperienced home educator might find this a little overwhelming since you still have to make a number of decisions about what to do with each child. But experienced home educators seeking a Biblically-based, unified program should check this out. An *Orientation Kit* [$6] includes orientation pages and the first 37 lesson pages of *Genesis 1-11* plus a 60-minute audio cassette with answers to frequently asked questions. I highly recommend that you review the *Orientation Kit* first to check out the program before purchasing. Additional volumes are planned: *Exodus, the Life of Christ, Acts, Revelation and Prophecy, Old Testament History,* and others.

Five in a Row

by Jane Claire Lambert
(Five in a Row Publishing)
Vol. 1 - $19.95; Vol. 2 - $24.95; Vol. 3 - $19.95

Five in a Row is a less intense approach to unit study than *KONOS, Weaver, The Classics*, etc., primarily so because it is geared for ages 4 through 8. All three volumes available in the series follow the same format, but with differing numbers of unit studies per volume. For each volume, author Jane Claire Lambert has selected a number of outstanding books for children, then built unit studies around each one. Volume 1 has 19 units, Volume 2 has 21 units, and Volume 3 has 15.

Each study should take one week, with more or less time spent each day depending upon which lesson elements we choose to use. While there are no Biblical references in the primary volumes, *Five in a Row* repeatedly teaches positive character qualities that tie easily to Scripture (e.g., forgiveness, compassion, honesty). Likewise, the selected stories are not overtly Christian, but reflect godly principles. For those who want more explicit Christian "connections, a separate *Five in a Row Bible Supplement* [$17.95] contains more than 200 Bible lessons relating to the 55 studies in volumes 1 through 3.

Examples of selected books are *The Story About Ping, Who Owns the Sun?, Mike Mulligan and His Steam Shovel, Clown of God, Katy and the Big Snow, Wee Gillis, Make Way for Ducklings, All Those Secrets of the World, Harold and the Purple Crayon,* and *Gramma's Walk*. Each story is to be read aloud every day for one week (five days). Then we select activities for social studies (the term loosely used to cover character qualities, and relationships in addition to geography, history, and cultures), language arts, math, science, and art. There are numerous hands-on activities and projects, although much of the detailed lessons is presented as "talk about this" type activities. An example of the activities are "story disks" in each volume, one per unit. These are to be cut out and laminated (by mom) then used by students to locate where stories take place on a world map. (These disks are also available as a ready-to-use set, printed in color and laminated for $15 for the set of 55.)

We can select only one subject area per day or combine a variety of activities from among the subject areas. Activities range from those appropriate for non-writers and non-readers to those for children who have mastered these skills. Thus, we can use the lessons to meet the academic needs of older learners. This is not intended to be a complete curriculum for math and language arts. It does not teach phonics, writing, or math in any sequential progression. In fact, we are encouraged to use stories in whatever order we please. (A calendar linking stories to calendar events suggests a possible progression we might follow.) For younger children, the material might be more than adequate to meet their learning needs. For six- and seven-year-olds, the social studies, science, and art will be much better than what they might get from textbooks, so we might want only to add basic phonics and math, and possibly other language skill development for the oldest children. An index lists what is covered under each subject area, sometimes broken down further under subheadings. This helps us if we have specific goals of our own. A reproducible planning sheet helps us with weekly lesson plans. Instructions for activities are quite detailed. Lambert includes valuable tips on questions to ask our children to guide discussions. *Five in a Row* seems to be extremely user-friendly, especially for the inexperienced homeschooler. *Before Five in a Row* [$24.95] is a product developed for children ages 2-4. Plenty of activities center around 23 books written for young children. Check this one out if you have preschoolers.

History Links
by Jennifer Alles and Barbara Little
(Wooly Lamb Publishing)
units - $15 each

In the past, I (Maureen Wittmann) have used Greenleaf Press' Study Packages for teaching ancient history. I like their approach, and their program fit well into my homeschool. However, since we are a Catholic family, I knew that once we reached the Reformation era, we would want to use a different program since Greenleaf presents their material from a Protestant viewpoint.

Enter *History Links*. I had the privilege to field test History Link's *Ancient Greece* unit. Like Greenleaf, *History Links* moves through history chronologically thus giving our children the foundation that they need to truly understand history as well as current events. In addition, *History Links* provides a Catholic perspective, demonstrating both God's involvement and the beauty of His Church throughout our history lessons.

History Links can be used with any grade level and is designed so that it may be used over and again, making it affordable and economical for growing families. The authors have provided a coding system that allows you to simply skim the columns to find activities appropriate for each child's age. They even provide activities for preschoolers, a blessing for those of us with toddlers underfoot. While your teen is searching through encyclicals, your grade schooler could be studying Greek roots and prefixes, all while your toddler is kept busy with a game of dress up.

The *General Studies* unit is the foundation of the other units and must be used first. It was recently revised and now does a much better job of handling the Church's guidance on interpreting Sacred Scripture. It incorporates some "writing helps" from Andrew Pudewa's *Teaching Writing: Structure and Style* seminar, which is reviewed elsewhere in this manual. Pudewa granted the authors of *History Links* permission to use some of his material here. [Note: Pudewa's methodology works particularly well with *History Links*.] It also lays the foundation for study of other subject areas, somewhat similar to the Principle Approach in concept. For example, in the section on archaeology, students first research, discuss, and define what archaeology is; the activities you select will depend upon each child's level. Then, in keeping with *History Links'* desire to incorporate hands-on activities, you create an artificial "dig" using one of a number of creative suggestions supplied (these sound like great fun!). Students read and research through other resources on the topic, taking notes, then giving an oral or written report.

History Links is very much a "worldview" program in that topics are continually linked back to theology and the world of ideas. For example, one activity in the Ancient Greece study says, "We see images of the Greeks' religious beliefs in their art work, in their poetry, in their literature, in their recreation, etc. How is religion reflected in the activities of our culture? If our culture were unearthed in 2000 years, what would the archaeologists think we valued highly?" Throughout the units, students (especially at older levels) are encouraged to read from the Great Books and classical works as well as the Bible, the *Catholic Catechism,* encyclicals and other resources that help them think through the important life questions.

As the title of this unit study series suggests, *History Links* is strongest in history/social studies providing complete coverage for that subject area. In addition, it provides partial coverage for language arts, religion, science, math, physical education, and arts and crafts depending upon the unit studied and the activities selected. For example, studying their *Creation* unit can provide adequate science coverage equivalent to a full year's course. Math activities will always be supplemental to sequential studies. Language arts coverage might depend upon whether or not a student is ready to focus heavily upon composition skills primarily based upon assignments from a unit. Students who need more grammar instruction might be using a text on the side, or students might be working through Pudewa's seminar.

Other units currently available include *Creation, Mesopotamia, Ancient Egypt, Ancient Israel,* and *Ancient Greece,* with *Ancient Rome* due soon. The *General Studies* unit should take about 2 months to complete, while the other units should take from 2 to 4 months each according to the authors. However, I can easily envision a family spending longer than 4 months on some of these!

Each of the succeeding units follows the same arrangement. At the beginning are brief notes pertinent to the particular unit; prayers and hymns; a library resource list, including video titles, and internet addresses; a vocabulary word list; timeline entries; and subject symbol codes. These pages are followed by the bulk of the unit study which is similar in arrangement to many others with activities to select under each topic heading. An appendix in each volume contains maps, readings, and other helps pertinent to the unit. Guides are each 70 to 80 pages in length. Additional resources will be essential. A few, such as the *Catechism*, you will need to purchase, but others you might be able to find at the library.

Lessons require planning and preparation time, although how much time will depend upon the mix of hands-on and book-based activities selected. You will need to work with younger students throughout most of the studies, while older students will most likely be doing more independent reading, research, and writing. Units are designed such that older students might easily help instruct younger students since they will be studying the same topics. *History Links* lends itself particularly well to use with a group of three or four families who share the preparation and presentation activities. [Maureen Wittman, partially reprinted from a review printed in *TORCH,*

June, 1998)/C.D.]

Waring's Study Guides for *What in the World's Going on Here?*
(Diana Waring-History Alive!)
Vol. 1 - $19.95; Vols. 2 and 3 - $22.95 each

This three-volume series of study guides build upon some of the ideas presented in Diana Waring's two-volume audio tape series, *What in the World's Going on Here?*. (See the review of the tapes in Chapter Fifteen.) The tapes are only one element of a fairly comprehensive unit study approach Diana presents in each book. The first two tapes of Volume 1 of *What in the World...* correspond with the first Study Guide book: *Ancient Civilizations and the Bible*. The second two tapes of Volume 1 correspond with the Study Guide *Romans, Reformers, and Revolutionaries*. The third book corresponds to Volume 2 of *What in the World...* and is titled *World Empires, World Missions, World Wars*.

These Study Guides can be used with children about fourth grade and up, and many of the books and activities lend themselves to participation by the entire family. In *Ancient Civilizations,* study is broken down into twelve units, arranged chronologically as on the tapes. The other two volumes are presented in nine units each.

For each unit, there is a list of recommended reading with age designations. Most books are available through libraries, although there is a good mix of secular and Christian resources. Combined with the audio tapes and discussion questions provided in the book, the books from this list form the core of your study.

You can choose which topics to emphasize, which activities to do, and which resources to use. Timeline, research, and reporting activities, followed by a vocabulary list, shift students into more academic work. However, Diana includes lots of projects and activities relating to geography, art, music, and cooking. The final section for each unit features suggestions for creative writing, drama, and art. It should take a full school year to complete the studies in each book.

These unit studies will be comprehensive for history/social studies and, possibly, English for some students, but coverage of other subjects will require additional resources. Math is not covered at all. English coverage will depend upon how much reading (lots of real books recommended for each unit), grammar, and composition parents integrate into the unit study. Research and reporting activities can easily stretch to challenge older learners in many subject areas. Basic instruction (e.g., grammar) needs to be presented when necessary for each student. Although some science is included, older students, especially, will need additional study. The arts are amply covered with numerous arts and crafts, music, and drama activities. Recipes reflective of different cultures, feasts, or holidays round out each unit.

Keep in mind that the entire series will take about three years to complete. The last Study Guide ventures into U.S. History, so you will be able to satisfy World History and at least part of U.S. History requirements. Individual Study Guides will stand on their own if you don't have time to complete them all.

Diana's background in and enthusiasm for Protestant missionary efforts is evident throughout the Study Guides, and most strongly in the third volume. However, especially in *Romans, Reformers, and Revolutionaries,* she takes a fairly evenhanded approach that should work well for Catholics, Orthodox, and others as long as they add a few resource books (e.g., on church history) reflecting other viewpoints. Diana addresses early church history, the Church Fathers, Councils, and early missionary efforts. She devotes attention to Eastern Orthodoxy, a subject breezed over in most history texts. She raises key questions in regard to church history that are likely to instigate some thought-provoking research and reporting.

Diana is also creating a series of *Activity Books* [$11.95 each] that will be extremely useful to those with children in grades K-6. The first volume which correlates with volume 1 *(Ancient Civilizations)* is available thus far. Parents with children fourth grade and up should be using the primary study guide with the *Activity Book* as a supplement. Those with younger children can use only the *Activity Book* since it includes discussion questions and activities sufficient for grades K-3. Games, crafts, puzzles, skits, and recipes are only some of the ideas you will find here. Of course, whichever books you use, all are dependent upon the tape series *What in the World's Going On Here?*

You might also want to supplement with the *Maps and Timeline Pack* for each level [$19.95 each] and the *True Tales from the Times of...* [$8.95 each] audio tapes Ω. The *True Tales* tapes feature Diana telling intriguing stories about people and events from each time period. Learn more about Attila the Hun, Heinrich Schliemann who discovered the ancient city of Troy, the great Byzantine emperor Justinian, and many other fascinating characters. These are great both for the historical content and for entertainment, and there's a tape to go along with each volume of the unit study guides.

KONOS Character Curriculum, Volumes 1, 2, and 3
Curriculum - $95 per volume; time lines - $59.95 per volume; curriculum/timeline combo - $144.95; Index - $20; KONOS In-A-Box - $175; KONOS In-A-Box manual - $60

KONOS features character traits as unit topics for children in grades K through 8, with a recently published high school level volume. Subjects included in the

KONOS program are history (primarily American history), Bible, social studies, science, art, music, some language, and some math. The authors suggest we use other math and language programs when our children are ready. Because the authors believe children learn best by "doing," this program is strong on activity—an ideal program for Wiggly Willys.

While Volume 1 should probably be the first volume used with children in grades K-3, any volume, including the third, could be used at any level with good results. Activities are not broken down by specific grade levels as in *The Weaver*, but it is not very difficult to pull out those that seem appropriate or interesting for our children. Lesson plans in each volume will assist you in choosing activities if you wish to use them.

The strength of *KONOS* is in the number of activities to choose from. There are many, many more ideas than we could possibly use. Some people are overwhelmed at the choices, but so many alternatives allow us to choose how much time we spend, the amount of hands-on activity, field trips, books, etc. that fit our situation. The percentage of listed hands-on activities is probably greater in *KONOS* than in any other unit study, so there are plenty of ideas for very active learners.

Each volume of *KONOS* can be used for two years. *KONOS* provides detailed background information on some activities but not all. Library books and other sources will be needed to round out the lessons. Detailed lists of resources and activities are under each heading. It is necessary to plan ahead to get books and other resources that will be needed. For those who have difficulty getting books at the library, *KONOS* has arranged with Lifetime Books (see "Sources") to carry a line of books specifically correlated to *KONOS* units. With many, many titles to choose from, we can be guaranteed the availability of appropriate resources.

KONOS was originally designed without specific lesson plans so parents would feel free to choose the ideas that best suit the needs of their children. However, many parents found it difficult to sort through so many good choices and figure out what would be appropriate for different aged children, so *KONOS* has incorporated lesson plans into each volume, listing materials and preparation, then recommending specific activities for younger, middle, and older aged children. The lesson plans are a tremendous help to those who are overwhelmed when there are too many choices and also to those who want just a little help in quickly sorting through all the ideas.

For those who have some experience with home education, this program will still give some structure, yet leave much room for individualizing. (Moms who prefer a set structure and routine might have trouble using *KONOS*, while those who prefer variety will likely enjoy it. Those who are unsure might want to view the *Creating the Balance* video described below before deciding whether or not KONOS is for them.)

Because history is covered in a non-sequential fashion, we should use time lines to tie historical events together coherently. We can make or purchase time lines. *KONOS* sells beautifully laminated *Time Lines* that coordinate with each volume of the curriculum, plus a *Bible Timeline* and an *Artist and Composers Timeline*. The five different *KONOS Timelines* can also be used with other curricula.

The *KONOS Index* shows which topics are covered where in each volume of *KONOS*. This is most valuable to those who have accumulated two or more *KONOS* volumes. If they want to locate information on a particular topic the *Index* will help them find it.

If we use all three volumes of *KONOS*, we will cover material typically covered in history and science programs in school with the exception of world history which *KONOS* reserves for higher levels. Those with older students who would like to continue this style of teaching through high school should be aware of the newest addition to *KONOS, History of the World*, written for high school students.

Those who like the methodology of *KONOS* for their children, but who feel overwhelmed with what it requires from the parent/teacher will love *KONOS In-A-Box*. These are 9 to 12 week unit studies derived from the original *KONOS* volumes. However, they are laid out with detailed, daily lesson plans, and they come with just about everything you need. No more frantic trips to the library and the craft supply store. The *Obedience* unit we received for review contained the teacher's manual/curriculum (which is also offered separately), craft materials (e.g., copper foil, wire, brads, whistle, tapestry set, fake jewels), eight resource books, and timeline characters, all packaged in a sturdy cardboard case with carrying handle.

Within the *Obedience* study there are three divisions: the first week is a study about authority and light; the next four weeks focus on kings and queens; and the last four weeks are about horses. It will take four such nine-week unit studies to comprise a full school year. Another *KONOS In-A-Box* unit, *Orderliness,* is available, with other units on *Attentiveness* and *Trust* on the drawing board to complete the one-year program.

KONOS In-A-Box is more comprehensive than the original *KONOS*, particularly in the area of language arts. The new studies cover science, history, social studies, art, music, literature, reading (not including phonics), language arts, health, critical thinking skills, practical living, drama, character training, and Bible. Math and phonics are not covered. Of course, there are still some choices to be made. The studies can stretch to meet the needs of students in grades K-8, but you must choose which activities to require of older and younger students. For example, when it says, "Write five simple sentences on index cards about what you learned yesterday about light," you might ask your third grader to write only three sentences, and spend time with your kindergartner on basic reading skills while older students write their sentences.

While some preparation time will still be necessary, it will be a fraction of that required for the original *KONOS*. If you've always wanted to try unit studies, but felt that it might be too overwhelming, this is a terrific way to try it out. Many families are finding that after using *KONOS In-A-Box*, they can easily handle the regular *KONOS* volumes.

Watch for *KONOS In-A-Bag*, a brand new, easy-to-use option for studying countries, continents, cultures, and character traits.

Lessons from History - four volumes
by Gail Schultz
(Hillside Academy)
$19.95 each

Lessons from history are essentially unit study outlines that the author recommends for grades K-9. My judgment is that they best suit students up through eighth grade. Four volumes cover four different eras: Creation to 100 B.C., 1400's to 1700's, 1800's, and 1900's. (A fifth volume is in the works.) At the front of each volume is a scope and sequence chart for covering history, social studies and science, geography, Bible, and the arts. Key people, events, or movements anchor each week's study. For example, the 1800's volume's beginning lessons are on the American revolution, the Louisiana Purchase, the Lewis and Clark Expedition, and Robert Fulton. Lesson outlines for the week provide background information (e.g., a biographical overview), suggested books to read, related areas of study, projects, and discussion questions. Obviously, we need to adapt any of these to suit the ages of our learners. Recommended books vary in difficulty, although most seem to be children's titles.

Since each week's lesson outline is only a few pages long, this is clearly not a comprehensive, self-contained curriculum. It serves as a framework and outline for us to create our own lessons. Suggestions at the front of the book tell us how to put together weekly lessons, including language arts and field trips. At the end of each book are pictures that can be used to create a time line (instructions provided also).

There is a distinctive Christian flavor throughout the books, although it is not always obviously stated. For example, the lesson on cowboys raises questions about character, responsibility, and family. However, sometimes it is obvious, such as in the questions about Louis Braille that require students to refer to Scripture verses. The books are well-organized and presented as well as nicely illustrated with appropriate clip art. Those who like unit studies but also like to have a great deal of control over the form it takes will find these

books to be excellent resources.

Life in America series
by Ellen Gardner
(Life in America)
$54.95 per volume

Seven books are projected for this unit study series, with the first three volumes available thus far. Following a chronological progression through U.S. History up through WWII, students cover history, science, and geography comprehensively, with plenty of additional work in Bible, language arts, and arts and crafts. Designed for students in grades K through 8, the studies are ideal for the middle of that spectrum and will stretch up through high school or down to lower levels. You should be able to complete approximately two volumes per year. Lessons are arranged into six units with six lessons within each unit. The number of days required for each of these lessons will vary, but following the suggested schedule in each book should work out to a semester per volume.

Titles in the series are *Life in a New World (1000-1763)*, *Life in the Colonies (1764-1789)*, *Life Establishing a Nation (1790-1849)*, *Life in a Nation Divided (1850-1866)*, *Life on the Frontier (1867-1898)*, *Life in a Victorian Age (1899-1931)*, and *Life in a World at War (1932-1945)*.

As with many unit studies, we choose from activities suggested for each lesson. However, lessons are designed to follow the 4MAT process under the headings interest, inform, integrate, and innovate. Consequently, we should select at least one activity under each of these four steps (headings) in each lesson. Activities are designed to suit all types of learners by using combinations of reading, writing, research, construction, drama, and art.

Some reference material is provided for us within each volume, which saves some time digging for information. However, we still will need additional resources. The most vital seem to be *The American History Explorer CD* (Parsons Technology), *Considering God's Creation, A History of US* series (Oxford), and *The Write Source* handbooks (Great Source). (The Life in America Company carries these resources plus age-appropriate literature.) Each volume also lists optional resources. In some lessons, extra resources will be essential, especially for older students who will need a great deal more content than is included within each volume. For example, when students study the respiratory system, less than two pages of information is included. For most students, you will want to use one or more of the six optional resources. You might also wish to utilize each lesson's key words for library or Internet research. The recommended Zane CD-ROM software might also be a desirable option for many families.

Preparation time will depend greatly upon which activities and resources you choose. Obviously, making a model Indian village will take much longer and require more preparation than reading a chapter in the *History of US*.

The text of the lessons is written at about sixth grade level. However, writing assignments are connected to *Write Source* handbooks so each student receives instruction at his or her level in grammar and composition skills.

Many make-a-list and draw-a-picture type activities allow younger students to participate along with older siblings.

Note that the *A History of US* series is often referred to as a reading option. This series has some serious content problems. Gardner mentions a few problems, but you will have to be on watch for others: e.g., depicting Abraham's sojourns as the wanderings of a restless man rather than those of a man directed by God, or misrepresentation of relations between the Spaniards and the Moors during the Moorish occupation of Spain. (These two problems crop up on only the first few pages of the second volume in the *History of US* series and reflect widespread inaccuracies throughout the series.) Some *Life in America* users choose other resources to try to avoid such problems.

Overall, *Life in America* should be fairly easy to use for parents who do not mind making choices and pulling together or purchasing the necessary resources. Lessons are well organized with objectives and progression easy to identify. The program's strategy of breaking lessons down into chunks that take from 2 to 5 days to complete also makes it less overwhelming than some other unit studies that work in larger time span segments. Since this is a new curriculum, you might find an occasional problem. For example, more explanation at the beginning would help with activities like creating a time line. (Students are told to create a symbol for their time line, but instructions on making a time line do not appear until volume 2.)

Thoroughly Christian in perspective, the series frequently refers to the Bible and pays extensive attention to religious events and influences throughout history from a Protestant perspective.

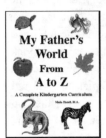

My Father's World From A to Z: A Complete Kindergarten Curriculum
by Marie Hazell
(My Father's World)
$95

This is a unit study approach to beginning reading, math, and science, appropriate for children who are just ready to begin learning letters and sounds. The other activities, which form the bulk of the book, might also include younger or older children. Although *My Father's World* was written for either home schools or regular day schools, it has elements of classroom organization and scheduling. However, the overall flavor reflects Susan Schaeffer Macaulay and Charlotte Mason's philosophies of education as presented in Macaulay's book, *For the Children's*

Sake. (That book is referred to a number of times in *My Father's World*.)

Lessons should take 60 to 90 minutes per day, and there are sufficient lessons here for a full school year. Lessons are presented in two parts—reading lesson and science lesson—although lessons are structured differently for the first ten days. Those first ten days follow integrated lesson plans wherein the Biblical creation story is taught along with letters and their names. From day eleven on, we integrate lessons for teaching sounds and beginning blending (short-vowel words only) with science lessons. All learning is multi-sensory, combining worksheets, oral work, listening, movable alphabet, flashcards, and hands-on activities.

For example, Lesson 11 teaches about insects, emphasizing the Biblical concept of diligence. Ants, bees, and ladybugs are used as examples. Children are advised to look at the "Ant" article in *World Book Encyclopedia*, and make observations from the illustrations. The book *Ant Cities* by Arthur Dorros is recommended along with creation and maintenance of an ant farm.

Simple science experiments, craft projects, and literature are built into the lessons. Reading lessons present a new letter every six days (which coordinates with the six days for presenting each science lesson), then use a wide variety of activities to teach the sound, letter formation (handwriting), recognition of sounds in spoken words and pictures, and, when ready, blending. Directions for a few of the reading activities are sometimes presented in two different ways, for either classroom or homeschool. A variety of worksheets are provided, including some cut-and-paste. Many learning activities use textured letters (you will need to obtain a set), tactile activities (e.g., finger jello cut into letter shapes, pancakes formed as letters), and verbal responses.

Day six in each lesson is "Book Day" for reading a "real" book and engaging in related activities. Math is often integrated in lessons; for example, sorting leaves by color and size or cutting an apple in half. When math skills do not integrate easily into the topic, they are presented as supplemental lessons. Skills covered include shapes, comparing and sequencing, measuring, calendar, money, time, counting, and writing numbers.

The program includes a lovely, full-color set of *A to Z Alphabet Flashcards*. These 5" x 8" flashcards feature illustrations from nature and a typestyle that looks like manuscript printing. These flashcards are also sold separately for $7.95, and they might be used with other reading courses.

My Father's World is clearly structured with easy-to-understand instructions. Lesson preparation time will be required primarily for gathering necessary materials; planning ahead is essential. In addition to the textured letter set mentioned above, you will need a Bible and access to either a set of appropriate encyclopedias such as World Book or children's non-fiction library books. My Father's World sells a set of textured letters [$7.95] and some of the recommended books through their web site. Some inexpensive art supplies such as clay, watercolor paints, and paintbrushes will be required; a few more such as tempera paints and colored pencils will be optional. You will also need an extra set of Student Worksheets for each additional student [$24.95].

A Sample Pack is available for $4.

My Father's World First Grade: Reading and Language Arts, Social Studies, Art, and Bible
by Marie Hazell
(My Father's World)
$120

This first grade program very quickly reviews letters and sounds, then begins with short-vowel words, presenting words by word families. All basic phonic concepts are presented this year. Spelling and writing both receive much more emphasis this year. Unlike the kindergarten program, the first grade program does not include science. Instead, the authors recommend a Charlotte Mason approach using real books and activities. A list of first grade math goals and ideas for informal math activities are included. If you prefer more structure and/or lesson plans, you will need a separate resource for math.

The first grade program includes the teacher's manual, student workbook, student worksheets, timeline and figures, *Bible Reader, Alphabet Flashcards,* and *Bible Notebook*. The *Bible Notebook* is a "blank" book with lines and spaces for children to create their own notebook from the lessons they study. The *Bible Reader* features simple retellings of Bible stories. (The *Bible Reader* is also available separately for $15 or for $25 with more than 30 cardstock timeline figures.) Weekly memory verses from Proverbs reinforce key lesson ideas and are used for developing handwriting skills as well.

This program builds a very strong familiarity with the Old Testament since it uses lengthy readings in many lessons as well as the *Bible Reader*. Children also learn the names of the books of the Bible this year. Minimal lesson preparation is required. Daily lesson plans provide detailed instruction and are easy to follow. Some cut-and-paste activities are used from time to time, and there are a few projects you might use if you so choose (e.g., celebration of Purim).

Children are asked to draw in many of the lessons, and the author suggests using the book *Drawing with Children* for developing drawing skills. The book *Celebrate the Feasts of the Old Testament in Your Own Home or Church* is also a recommended extra.

The Prairie Primer
by Margie Gray
(Cadron Creek Christian Curriculum)
$45

Primer might be slightly misleading in the title, since this volume is more similar to a *KONOS* or *Weaver* volume than any primer I have seen. It differs in that it is more of a do-it-yourself approach than the aforementioned programs. (It reminds me somewhat of the original *KONOS* volume that was a fraction as big as the present volume.) *The Prairie Primer* is one large, plastic-spiral-bound volume that accompanies the nine books in the *Little House* series. Each *Little House* book has one unit in the Primer, and it should take from one to two months to complete each. The learning level encompasses grades three through six, covering "...U.S. History in the 1800's, U.S. geography, science, language, practical living, health and safety, nutrition, music, and art. With the exception of a grammar, spelling and math program, the *Primer* is a well-rounded scholastic program" (quote from the Introduction). Specific topics covered within the curriculum are listed under subject area headings for all but writing and grammar, for which scope and sequence suggestions are broken down by grade levels.

The Primer and the Bible are the primary resources, but we also need reference resources (encyclopedia and library access). Daily lesson plans provide comprehension questions related to reading from the *Little House* book. Activity suggestions follow next to subject area headings. In most cases the activity is outlined in general rather than in detail. For example, study bears and their hibernation patterns, habitats, and food; write a report on what you have learned. Since a number of the activities listed for any single day might be as involved as this example, we must pick a reasonable number of activities to accomplish rather than attempting to do them all. A planning guide at the beginning of each week's lessons lists topics for which we will need information, suggested reference resources for some of them, items needed, and field trip ideas. Space for our own planning notes is allowed. Although lesson plans are listed for each day, it might be more realistic to take two days for each so that you can fully develop some of the suggestions. Scripture readings and principles are strongly integrated throughout the curriculum. At the end of the book are an appendix on motivational gifts and a list of resource sources.

The Prairie Primer could be overwhelming for the new home educator, but veterans who already know how they like to present lessons should appreciate the wealth of ideas assembled in this volume. (The publisher tells me they have gotten positive feedback from first-time homeschoolers using *The Prairie Primer*, as well as comments from veterans who found it less overwhelming than other unit studies.) The fact that the cost is significantly less than the other major unit studies is likely to give it extra appeal.

Rebirth and Reformation

by Vivian Doublestein
(The Master's Press)
$40; art activities kit - $20

Vivian Doublestein offers classes through the Master's Academy of Fine Arts where students meet one day per week. Since everyone cannot participate in the classes, she decided to put together a unit study curriculum to reflect her teaching methodology and her interest in the fine arts. The first volume, packaged in a three-ring binder, focuses primarily on the Medieval/Renaissance period although it begins with the fall of Rome and ends with the Renaissance without really getting into the Reformation. The study is not age-graded, and it is open-ended enough to work with all ages. You might spend up to two years to complete the study, depending upon which activities you choose to use. Study is divided into four main sections: The Church; Medieval Life; Barbarians, Explorers and Merchants; and The Renaissance. Each section has a number of subsections. For example "The Church" includes sections such as "Art and Architecture of the Roman Catholic Church," "Monasticism," "Education," and "The Crusades." Each of these subsections begins with a historical overview, followed by a list of activities for Bible, reading, writing, science, geography, math, arts, and field trips. We need to consult other sources for information in most cases. For example, reading suggestions might be biographies or a finding information on a particular topic. A musical tape with appropriate selections is included. An appendix has a bibliography plus instructions for a medieval feast complete with "Mummer's Play."

A Christian worldview is evident throughout the study (including a reference to Francis Schaeffer's *How Should We Then Live?*). The study seems to take a non-judgmental position on Catholic theology, pointing out the meaning of the liturgy and the support and encouragement of music and the arts that occurred within the Catholic church.

You will be surprised at the physical appearance of this resource; even though it is only $40, it is printed with many full-page illustrations on high quality paper. Considering that it also includes a CD, the price is unbelievable.

History By the Book!: Historically Based Arts Activities is an optional, companion art kit for the Medieval/Renaissance period. It includes complete supplies for six projects; all you'll need to find at home are glue, tape, scissors, pencil, and containers for water and paint as you work. The six projects are a Byzantine cross, a triptych, a tile mosaic, stained glass simulation with tissue paper, tapestry (created on burlap with yarn), and a plaster frescoe. Complete instructions are included. These activities are especially appropriate for children in the elementary grades, but you will need a separate kit for each child.

The Weaver Curriculum
The Interlock
$110; Interlock Sample - $4

The Interlock program, designed for preschool and kindergarten, studies Genesis 1-10. The program includes manipulatives, visual aids, a music tape, math, and a writing program. This is a low-key approach, covering social studies, science, language arts, arithmetic, observation projects, art, physical education, health, memory work, music, and penmanship. It is designed to meet the developmental needs of the young child, so lessons are provided for only three days per week.

Volumes One - Five
$145 each; Volume I 10-Day Sample - $5

Each volume of *The Weaver Curriculum* comes in a large three-ring binder. Any of the five volumes can be used for any number of students in first through sixth grades, and each volume should take about one year to complete. (*The Weaver* can be expanded to cover grades 7-12 with *Supplement* volumes.) Each chapter is divided into subject areas, and each subject area is divided into grade levels. This makes it easy to organize our own lesson plans according to the learning level of each child. Bible, health and safety, and art are offered as group lessons rather than on individual grade levels. Many language arts activities are included. *Wisdom Words* (another resource from The Weaver, described under Language Arts) provides a foundation for a complete language program when used in conjunction with *The Weaver*. We must still supplement with basic math and phonics instruction, except at kindergarten level.

Each volume of *The Weaver* gives recommendations for specific books that can be found at the library to be used as supplements. They also offer supplemental resource books that we can purchase. These resource books are from the Usborne line, and also include titles from Milliken Publishing Company that are easier to use as teaching tools. The Milliken books also contain higher-grade-level material that makes them usable with other *Weaver* volumes and for older children.

The Weaver provides much information within the program itself for parents to present to the child orally. It uses less hands-on, activity-based learning than *KONOS*, although there should be plenty of hands-on ideas for most families. *The Weaver* should appeal most to Sociable Sues and others who like creative approaches to learning but who do not need as much activity as Wiggly Willys.

The Weaver offers a sample and video for $7. I recommend that you view the video and study the *Volume One 10-Day Sample* before leaping into the program.

Volume One uses Genesis 1:11-50, following the Scriptural chronology, as the underlying organizational theme with topics including cities, archaeology, and transportation for unit organization. The Scriptural emphasis is stronger than in *KONOS*. Daily lesson plan guides for all five Weaver volumes ,called *Day by Day* [$50 each], help make using *The Weaver* very easy. Each volume lists the needed materials and sequence for the objectives for each level, harmonizes the objectives with the Bible lessons, lists pages of the Resource Section that go with the lessons, and lists selections from *Wisdom Words* to be used for language arts. This should cut preparation time to a minimum.

Volume One and Wisdom Words come with a cassette tape to walk us through the program as we begin.

Volume Two is based upon Exodus and the Books of the Law. Although it is recommended as a sequel to Volume One, it can be our starting point. Examples of topics are royalty and respect, families and responsibility, and deserts and humility.

Volume Three covers Joshua, Judges, Ruth, and I Samuel through verse 10. Topics covered are exploration and navigation, espionage and communication, recording of history, fortifications, music, thinking skills, United States history from 1789-1860, time, social structures and the family, and service.

Volume Four covers the period of the Kings and Prophets. Topics are spiritual giants; civil war; the wisdom of Solomon (includes an introduction to biology); the temple; ancient civilizations of Assyria, Babylon, Persia and Greece; and introduction to the Roman Empire.

Volume Five studies the Life of Christ through the gospels and in relation to the Old Testament. Topics covered are World and American History from 1865 to the present, the concept of covenant, government, ancient Rome, families, reproduction, the solar system, stars, the human body, miracles, biographies of men and women of faith, agriculture and stewardship, geology, map making, the temple.

The Weaver also sells math materials and a complete phonics program, *1-2-3 Read!*, to help complete your curriculum.

Zephyr Unit Studies

(Zephyr)

$18 each

Zephyr publishes 24 topical unit study guides for the elementary grades. Among these are titles such as *The Americas, Ancient Egypt, Ancient Greece and Rome, Astronomy, Ecology, Marine Biology, Paleontology, The Renaissance, Science Fiction, U.S. Constitution,* and *U.S. Immigration.* These guides briefly introduce the topic, then lay out a framework for investigations to learn more about the topic. A bibliographical list of filmstrips, books, and games is included at the back of each book. These books do a good job of posing questions that will guide the investigations. They are designed for gifted students who will do much of their research independently. They are not Christian in outlook, but the activities are so open-ended that they can be guided in whatever direction we choose. We might wish to look for resources in addition to those listed since the recommended resources most likely will reflect a secular

humanistic viewpoint. These unit studies do not incorporate other subject areas as extensively as the major programs such as *Weaver* and *KONOS* but instead emphasize the use and development of study, research, and thinking skills.(SE)

Limited Unit Studies

The following unit study materials are narrower in scope than those already listed.

My First Reports

(Hewitt Homeschooling Resources)

$5.95 each; set of 14 - $49.95

Don't settle for spoon feeding information to your children. Help them ask questions and develop research skills with these great little packets. Currently 21 packets are available, among which are *Birds, Marine Life, Music, Pets and Farm animals, Weather, Solar System, Transportation, Sports,* and *Outdoor Activities.* Each packet contains 12 sub-topic pages, and each page contains six to eight questions which students will have to research in order to make their report. Reproducible, lined sheets in three different sizes are included for the actual report writing. If you use one sub-topic per week, one packet will last an entire quarter. There are also unit study ideas for those of you who want to enlarge upon the chosen subject, with suggested activities relating to Bible, language arts, math, science, history, music and art. Field trip ideas and a list of books about each topic are included. With so many interesting ideas, these low-priced packets offer a good way to try out a unit study approach without a big investment. These are designed for grades 3-4, but can also be used with younger students with more help from a parent.[V.T.]

Night Owl Creations unit studies

(Night Owl Creations, Inc.)

curriculum prices range from $11.95-$14.95; packages range from $20-$53

Night Owl produces a number of *Delightful Treasures* topical unit studies that can be used for grades K-8, but which are keyed to course objectives for grade levels K-2, 3-5, and 6-8. Thus far in the *Delightful Treasures* series are the titles *Weather, Inventions, Thanksgiving and Christmas, The Arts, A Tour of Europe, Ancient Greece, Ancient Rome, Explorers, Wilderness Survival, Energy, First Aid and Safety, Australia, Colonial America, Beautiful and Historical Florida,* and *Marine Life.* Unlike any of the others, each of these studies also has a companion *KT Folder. KT Folders* are preprinted pages to be cut, pasted, folded and otherwise "beautified" by each child to create a report/presentation booklet. You will need to supply scissors, glue, markers, string, paint, and other craft supplies. The studies include activities addressing science, history, geography, Bible, music, arts and crafts, creative writing, and composition, although all subjects do not receive equal coverage in every study. Biblical applications are the only consistent items that appear in every lesson. These will supplement most subject areas, while providing complete coverage for some sections of your curriculum such as your study of Ancient Greece and Rome. Most of the studies require one or two resource books. For example, the *Wilderness* study uses *The Boy Scout Handbook*, the *Wilderness Survival Badge* book, and *Survival Cards*; *Weather* requires the book *Weather and Climate*. These additional resources can be purchased as part of a complete package for each study that includes the basic curriculum, a *KT Folder*, and the resources. Everything can also be purchased separately. Other books are referenced throughout the various studies, but you can choose to use them or not. Most of these can be found at your local library. Instruction or information for each of the three learning levels is included wherever appropriate.

All studies are designed to be easy for teachers. Complete lesson plans direct you through each step. Materials required are listed, and directions are provided when necessary. Much background information is provided within the curricula so we need not search out information before we can begin. We will need to reproduce some of the pages in the main curricula, and we need to purchase a *KT Folder* for each student creating a folder. Watch for new titles from Night Owl Creations, Inc.

Pioneer Boys
by Pat Hirst and Camilla Pait
(Hirst/Pait)
$19.95

Before you skip over this one since it is only for boys, you must know that it includes a *Resource Guide for Girls* also so that you can focus some of your reading selections on topics of likely interest to girls. This is a unit study on pioneer life intended to be used with groups of children in grades K-6. You could spend an entire year on this study, using it as the primary resource from which you will construct all social studies. You could use it as a once a week (or more frequent) supplement or alternative to other history studies, or you could condense the study to complete it in a few months, selecting fewer activities to do and books to read. The study is organized into ten sections: heritage, pioneer homes, everyday life, school days, diet, money, medicine, symbols of America, music, and "what we have learned." Each section includes a narrative of background information, discussion questions, creative writing topics, and activities and crafts. Brief biographies that might be used throughout the study are at the front of the book. Additional biographies on women are in the *Resource Guide for Girls*. Book lists are included, and it is intended that we acquire some of these books from the library or elsewhere to flesh out the information provided. (Library call numbers are included to

save time.) Books are not cross-referenced to each section, so it will be up to us to determine which to read when. Instructions for activities and games are quite detailed, saving us time where it probably matters the most. This is not full-blown unit study like *KONOS* or *Weaver*. While we get some coverage of language arts and a little science, this is primarily social studies we are covering. There are about 70 pages total in the book and *Resource Guide* combined, so you can see that this is not as extensive as some other resources. However, this is much more extensive than Amanda Bennett's *Unit Study Adventures,* which are more like outlines with much less specific information than we find here. I suspect that this will appeal to parents who like the idea of unit study but are not prepared to jump into a total unit study approach like *KONOS*. Printed in black-and-white and bound with a plastic comb, this is not a fancy production, but it should serve well as the foundation for a pioneer unit study for the entire family. Occasional references alert us to the fact that the authors are Christian, but Christian content is limited to occasional references and some of the recommended books. [Valerie Thorpe/C.D.]

Developing Godly Character in Children
by Beverly Caruso, Ken Marks, and Debbie Peterson
(Hands to Help Publishing)

This is a unit study type curriculum in a single volume that aims to help our children develop Christ-like character. See the full review under Bible materials.

For Instruction in Righteousness: A Topical Reference Guide for Biblical Child-Training
by Pam Forster
(Doorposts)
$25 spiralbound; $27 looseleaf binder

Like *Developing Godly Character in Children*, this unit study focuses on character qualities from a Biblical perspective. See the full review under Bible materials.

God's World News for Kids
single-copy price for 26-issue subscription (through the school year): $17.95 for children 3rd grade and under; $19.95 for children grades 4-9; three or more subscriptions sent to the same address - $6.95 -$7.50 per child.

God's World News for Kids is a weekly, current events newspaper offered on four different grade levels (preK-1, 2-3, 4-6, and 7-9)—the only current events papers written from a Christian perspective. Subject areas covered are social studies/history, language, art, science, and math. The two older-level editions use a different format, which, although not categorized into subject areas, includes material that can be shaped into unit studies or research projects. The Teacher's Helper highlights key topics and suggests methods of integrating the papers into our curriculum. The Teacher's Helper for the two youngest levels is loaded with unit study ideas centered around a topic covered in that issue.

God's World News subscriptions now also include two bonus issues and eight supplements with posters, maps, and other extras.

Huge discounts apply when three or more copies of the same edition are sent to a single address. This is a tremendous resource for a bargain price.

Interdisciplinary Units
(Teacher Created Materials)
$14.95 each

All of Teacher Created Materials' *Interdisciplinary Units* are on the "Challenging" level, appropriate for 5th through 8th grade. These units take one topic, such as heroes, and build an in-depth study of the topic, using activities from several subject areas. The biggest emphasis is on literature and reading, but social studies, math, science, and the creative arts are also represented. Each section suggests more books for deeper study, research topics, and a bibliography of books and videos. Some of the activities are more oriented to the traditional classroom, such as bulletin board suggestions for the teacher. But why not use that to your advantage, and have the students in a family come up with a "bulletin board" on the topic?

The *Interdisciplinary Unit Heroes* which I reviewed is divided into ten sections ranging from Super heroes to Sports Heroes to Medical Heroes. These units include both imaginary or legendary heroes and real-life heroes. Each section gives short biographies (included in the book) of four figures with suggestions for activities throughout the curriculum that are related to those people or characters. Medieval Heroes includes King Arthur, Robin Hood, Joan of Arc, and Vassilissa (a Russian princess). A variety of Americans are included without regard as to their race or gender. Only the section on Heroes of Social Causes seems to be weighted toward the multicultural end of the spectrum, with Mother Teresa, Cesar Chavez, Martin Luther King, Jr., and Corazon Aquino. Abraham Lincoln is suggested as recommended reading. I appreciated the fact that Wartime Heroes was one of the sections.

Individual books and videos recommended need to be screened on an individual basis. I question the inclusion of some such as *Henry V* for children of that age because of the film's violence. Other books included on the lists such as Pyle's *King Arthur* and the D'Aulaires' *Book of Greek Myths* are excellent. Some parents might object to the inclusion of super heroes or mythological heroes. However, I can see them as a great starting point for a child who is already interested in a super hero, as a way to bring the child to the study of real heroes.

Interdisciplinary Thematic Units in addition to *Heroes* are *Ancient Egypt, Ancient Greece, Ancient Rome, Courage, Early Humans, Energy, Freedom, Native Americans, Shakespeare, Survival,* and *World Religions.* You will need to vet most of these titles for political correctness and other such problems, but most should be useful resources for home schoolers.(SE)[Kath Courtney]

Teaching With God's Heart for the World
by Ann Dunagan
(Family Mission/Vision Enterprises)
two volumes - $49.95 each or $89.95 for the set

Missions, evangelism, intercessory prayer, and God's heart for the lost are foundational themes in this one-year unit study. There are two metal-comb bound volumes of more than 250 pages each, which should take about one semester each to complete. They are not as comprehensive as *KONOS, Weaver,* or *Alta Vista* in coverage. While Bible, history, geography, reading, language arts, foreign language, math, science, music, and art all receive attention from time to time, this program will need additional supplementing in all areas other than music and art. This is especially true for students beyond about third grade level. The curriculum is geared for a wide span of ages, although much of it seems appropriate for middle through upper elementary grades. Many of the foundational activities can be used with the entire family.

Beyond the foundational Bible- and mission-oriented lessons (called "Family Devotions" in daily lessons), history, geography, and language arts receive significant attention. Supplemented with some of the suggested resources (historical novels, biographies), lessons for history and geography should be adequately covered for primary grade students. Language arts/reading areas will need additional work depending upon the needs of each student. Beginning readers will need separate instruction, while students who can read will need occasional grammar instruction. There are plenty of writing assignments, even for older students. A reproducible form can be used to create individualized spelling lists for each student. Additional teaching tips, alternate assignments, and creative ideas are provided.

The suggested schedule shows history, geography, and science each being taught one day per week. Foreign language study is scheduled for four days a week, reading/writing/language arts and math are scheduled everyday. Arts and crafts, music, a family field trip, and an international meal for dinner are each scheduled one day per week. Even though math and foreign language are shown in the schedule we need to select our own curriculum. However, a weekly math lesson deals with some type of practical math application.

At the beginning of the book are sections explaining the philosophy of the curriculum, its Biblical basis, and a brief summary of the history of world missions. A reproducible report card form reflecting this curriculum is included, as well as descriptions of international holidays, timeline tips, history and geography research forms, and maps.

Aside from the curriculum itself, we also need two additional books: *Operation World* and *From Jerusalem to Irian Jaya*. (These are books I recommend to everyone!)

Other books are highly recommended for high school and adult students but are not essential: *World Mission in a Three Part Manual* (William Carey Library), *Unveiled at Last* (YWAM Publishing), and either *The History of the World in Christian Perspective* (A Beka) or *Streams of Civilization* (Christian Liberty Press). Lengthy descriptions of these and other resources are included at the end of Volume 1 along with ordering information. (Many of these resources can also be ordered through Family Mission/Vision Enterprises through their separate catalog.)

Instructions for "Family Devotions" are fairly detailed, while those for other areas are generally briefer. Sometimes, the amount of work suggested for a day sounds impossible to cover, so it is obvious that we must choose between the various options. Some of this is intended for high school students and adults so you must not try to do everything with the entire family. For example, the first week of the curriculum outlines serious Bible study lessons (really designed for teens and adults) that might take far more time and attention that either parents or children have for any one day. Day 4 covers the arrangement and message of the Bible, proof that it is divinely inspired and reliable, and all of the basic Bible doctrines. However, this is unusual in comparison to the rest of the curriculum. You might want to use some of these ideas with the entire family, but don't try to do it all. Feel free to stretch units out, taking the time you need to teach it properly without overloading your children. Overall, the curriculum is very practical for home educators. Some preparation time is required to gather books and resources, but it provides adequate guidance for the foundational lessons, even for new home schoolers.

The curriculum was written and produced by families who have spent years in the mission field themselves, and it reflects their deep desire to stimulate others to participate in efforts to take the Gospel into all the world. This curriculum admirably meets that goal with interesting and stimulating lessons that build from a strong foundation of Bible knowledge, prayer, and Christianity put into action.

This curriculum should also be an excellent option for Sunday Schools or afterschool programs that would focus on only the foundational parts of the lessons.

Unit Study Adventures Guides series
by Amanda Bennett
(Holly Hall)
$13.99 each

Amanda Bennett has written a series of *Unit Study Adventures Guides* for grades K-8.

These are not comprehensive unit studies such as *KONOS* or *Weaver* but guides that present outlines and activity ideas so that we can thoroughly develop our own topical unit studies. Titles in the series are *Baseball, Christmas, Electricity, Gardens, Home, Computers, Elections, Oceans, Pioneers, Thanksgiving, Dogs*, and *Olympics*.

These guides feature detailed outlines, both a condensed one in the front of the book and an expanded "working outline" with space to fill in our own details regarding resources and teaching plans. Each guide shares the same organizational structure which includes lists of recommended resources for both reference and reading; spelling/vocabulary lists and a few assignments (at two levels); writing assignments; subject word list; activities; writing ideas; recommendations for games, videos, and software; "room decoration" ideas and resources (with addresses); internet resource addresses; field trips; "trivia" questions and answers; and reproducible timelines and worksheets. Guides seem to range from about 110 to 140 pages, and some of them include Christian content (e.g., the *Oceans* outline begins with "History of the oceans in the Bible", and *Christmas* and Thanksgiving are thoroughly Christian).

The guides can be used throughout the elementary grades, although younger children should not be expected to cover all of the material that older students do. Recommended books are available at the library and through home school distributors. [No prices are listed by some of the resources, so it is difficult to determine which will be affordable. Price information would be especially useful on the government agency publications whose prices can range from free to outrageous.] There is plenty of material in each guide to keep you busy for many months, so you might get through no more than two of these a year. Parents will probably also want to invest in the *Unit Study Adventures Journal* [$7.99], a book of reproducible forms to be used along with any of the volumes in the series. These forms are essentially organizing and recording tools for parents to use for planning a study, recording details about resources to use, making schedules and assignments, planning field trips, and making reading lists. A few completed samples are included.

****

With so many alternatives available, it is good to experiment with different types of unit studies, perhaps trying the Weaver's sample or ideas from *God's World* to get started without a large investment. The major unit study methods mentioned here—*Alta Vista Curriculum, KONOS, The Classics*, and *Weaver*—are all distinctly different from each other, but all will provide an exciting alternative to traditional methods of schooling. Once you get the idea of how unit studies might be done, you will find the topics are limitless. With a little experience, you will probably be creating your own unit studies.

Creating Your Own Unit Studies

To "do-it-yourself" requires a bit of preplanning and work, but you can tailor your studies to suit your children more exactly. I will share two examples from unit studies we created on our own.

We studied many of the body systems, system by system. Following is a summary of our study of the nervous system.

1.) Read from William Coleman's *More about My Magnificent Machine* a selection on the brain from a Godly perspective.

2.) Look at poster illustrating the brain and nervous system.

3.) Read about the brain and nervous system in *Blood and Guts* (Brown Paper School Books) by Linda Allison, and in *Junior Body Machine* by Dr. Christian Barnard. Both books, but especially *Blood and Guts*, have evolutionary doctrine included. Select only the parts that are true and appropriate.

4.) Sit in a circle and hold hands. Pass "squeezes" from hand to hand to illustrate how neurons pass messages in the nervous system.

5.) Look at a slide of a neuron.

6.) Dissect a cow's brain.

7.) Test reflexes in our bodies (described in *Blood and Guts*).

8.) Discuss and test for brain hemisphere dominance in individuals (described in *Blood and Guts*).

9.) Participate in outdoor activities demonstrating dominance (described in *Blood and Guts*).

10.) Write report on brain studies to accompany photographs taken of unit study activities.

Although we did not include all subject areas in this particular study, you could add mathematical exercises on such things as computing the speed of reflex reactions and the percentage of body weight for the brain. It is not necessary that your study be as complex as ours.

Another example comes from our study of Ancient Rome. I found numerous library books on life in ancient Rome to help my children understand the people and the culture. Then we studied Roman soldiers and their armor and compared it to Ephesians 6:14 on the armor of God. My children made their own armor or costumes, wrote about living in Roman times, learned Roman numerals and did some math with them. A biography of Julius Caesar, read aloud, provided material for discussion of ethics, power, social pressures, and much more. Excerpts from Shakespeare's play *Julius Caesar* added a literary aspect to the study. Books for this study are easily available from the library.

Do-It-Yourself Helps for Unit Study

Guides to History Plus
by Kathryn Stout
(Design-A-Study)
$14

Those who want to center unit studies around historical time periods or cultures will appreciate the help that is available through *Guides to History Plus*. This book can be used as a teacher resource guide for teaching grades 1-8 or it can be used as an independent study guide by high school students for developing their own history unit studies. The same basic approach is used for studying any time period. Study is divided under the headings: customs, religion, government, achievements, changes, geography, and climate zones. Under each heading are a list of questions. For instance, under government, students must answer such questions as, "How was it governed?", "How were leaders chosen?", and "What were some of the basic laws? (Compare them to the Ten Commandments.)" The geography section includes some key terms and a few blackline masters.

The rest of the book supplies helpful ideas and guidelines from which we can select those that are useful to flesh out the course. The first of these supplementary sections has recommended activities for composition, vocabulary/spelling, music, art, science, health/nutrition, math, and geography so that the study can tie together across the curriculum. Next is a general outline of objectives for history coverage, with more detail for high school courses and little more than topics for lower grades. A helpful section of key concepts for history, geography, government, and economics will be especially helpful for older students. Another section, "Practicing Making Connections," suggests composition or discussion questions/topics arranged by topic.

The final section is quite lengthy. It features annotated lists of books, games and videos by topic.

This is not a lesson-by-lesson study guide, but one from which we tailor our own questions and activities on each topic to be studied. Teachers and students must search out the reference sources for answers to questions posed in each section. Because of the work involved this is not a method for those who are short on time or energy. However, those who want to develop their own history-based unit studies will find it a valuable tool.

The Maya is a sample of how the *Guides to History Plus* is applied to that topic [available for $5]. It follows the outline from *Guides to History Plus*. The questions have been answered and answers presented as a report. Activities are suggested that apply specifically to the Mayan study, but following the *Guides* subject headings. *The Maya* can be used as a basis for our own study of that culture or as a sample to better understand how to use *Guides to History Plus*.

Author Kathryn Stout also has an audio tape, *A Chronological Unit Approach to History* [$4.50], that should help us do a better job of helping our children develop a historical overview. ☊

How to Create Your Own Unit Study
by Valerie Bendt
(Common Sense Press)
$16

If you have been avoiding unit studies because the work involved in planning all the activities sounds overwhelming, this book is for you. Valerie has developed unit studies that are primarily based on the use of books rather than a tremendous amount of activities. This is a do-it-yourself guide for putting together your own unit studies based upon your families' goals and interests.

In the beginning of the book, Valerie presents a philosophy of education drawn from Charlotte Mason, Susan Schaeffer Macaulay, and Dr. Ruth Beechick.

The language arts receive complete treatment within unit study related activities. Everything is not rigidly tied to the current topic, yet the topic provides a central theme and direction for study.

World geography is the unit study topic Valerie uses most frequently to illustrate her ideas throughout the book. Expanding to other topics will be a small challenge for those who lack creativity, but most of us will find it easy to transfer the ideas to whatever topic we prefer.

Throughout the book, Valerie passes on great teaching hints that she has discovered. I particularly appreciated her explanation of how to teach a full language arts course with dictation and copying as primary activities. She has done the best job I know of in translating theory into a practical sounding strategy.

Descriptions of resource books and methods for a number of different unit studies are included, but even more valuable is the last one-third of the book, "A General Guide to the Reference Section of the Children's Department of the Public Library." Here we find the reference tools that will save us enormous amounts of time in our search for materials for our own unit study topics. Many, many such reference books are listed and described. One example: "*World History in Juvenile Books*: JR028.52. By Metzner. Books are categorized by country. Each division includes biographies, fiction, and non-fiction. The title, author, number of pages, and grade level are given, but descriptions are not included" (p. 82). So, if we are studying about Egypt we can easily locate biographies of key characters, historical fiction, and factual information resources. This "Guide" portion of the book alone will prove extremely useful to those of us who are unfamiliar with the wealth of resources available at the library. The entire book

will help those who want to design their own curriculum.

Valerie followed up by writing *The Unit Study Idea Book* [$14] (also published by Common Sense Press). Here Valerie shares information about the books and methods they have used for studying many topics such as Sign Language, Ants, Birds, Electricity, Aviation, as well as literature-based units for books such as *Heidi* and *Swiss Family Robinson*.

⚬⚬⚬⚬⚬⚬⚬⚬

I would encourage you to try the do-it-yourself approach to some extent if at all possible. It enables us to tailor our studies to best suit our children and our situation. No matter whether we choose pre-published or do-it-yourself unit studies, we should soon find that our children begin to see the interrelationships of subject matter very clearly, and learning should become much more enjoyable for both us and our children.

If all this seems a bit overwhelming, remember that we make our plans, counting on God to direct our path (Proverbs 16:9) as He so faithfully does. Proverbs 16:3 also reassures us that if we commit our work to the Lord, it will succeed. In my experience, God's direction is much more evident when we design our own unit studies than when we use formal curriculum. As we choose topics and activities we are more open to God's leading than when we work with curriculum that has already been designed by someone else.

All-in-One Studies

There are a number of programs that look like unit studies, yet lack a unifying theme. Instead, projects, assignments, readings, etc., for each study area are outlined according to a schedule. The benefit of this approach is in the time it saves us in creating lesson plans—it is all done for us. We only need gather the books and materials needed for each lesson.

A Bee Sees
(Hewitt Homeschooling Resources)
complete program - $109.95; teacher's manual and readers - $74.95

A Bee Sees, is an alternative first grade unit study program from Hewitt that might be used after their *Training Wheels* curriculum or any other kindergarten curriculum that has taught the names and sounds of the letters, counting up to 20, how to write their own name, and other beginning skills. In *A Bee Sees*, children briefly review letters and sounds and almost immediately begin reading short-vowel words. The language and reading move at a slightly slower pace than they do in Hewitt's other first grade study. Hewitt *Early Readers* and the companion *A Bee Sees Reader* are used with the lessons presented from the 500+ page teacher's manual. The complete program also includes Addison-Wesley *Mathematics* 1 and *Unifix Cubes*. Animals, birds, insects, and other creatures are the themes for each unit. Daily lesson plans cover Bible/character education, math, reading, social studies, language arts, physical education, science/health, and art, although all subjects are not studied each day. Key concepts, objectives, and materials needed are listed at the beginning of each unit. Lessons should take about 2 to 2 1/2 hours per day. Multi-sensory learning via flash cards, games, art and craft projects, puppets, read aloud, discussion, and math manipulatives make this a more informal approach than programs such as A Beka's, Christian Liberty's, or Bob Jones's. There are some reproducible activity and game pages at the back of the teacher's manual. Lessons will require some preparation time, and a few additional resources such as recordings of particular types of music, pictures (e.g., a diagram of the ear or a picture of a trumpet), bean bags, kite, hymnal, and potato. Most of these are easily found around the house, but some might take a little more effort to secure. This curriculum is great for the parent who wants daily lesson plans already provided but who does not want to use too much in the way of formal academics.

Beginnings K/5
(Bob Jones University Press)
K/5 kit - $169

BJUP has put together a foundational kindergarten program that covers phonics, language arts (handwriting, comprehension, composition), science, social studies, music, motor development, and art. All we need to add for a complete program are Bible and math. Lessons are correlated and follow unit-study themes as do *KONOS, Weaver*, and other thematic studies. Home-School Teacher's Manuals make the program much more practical for homeschoolers than did the previous classroom-designed manuals, although the program is still a formal academic approach to education. Teacher's Manuals come in three volumes. Other components are three student worktexts, 13 slim readers, phonics response cards, songs cassette, phonics charts, teaching visuals, and flip charts. Components can be purchased separately, but the kit price is less than the cost of individual components. The Teacher's Manuals are the heart of the program, and it is most practical to use the entire program as laid out within those volumes.

See the review of *Beginnings* under "Phonics Programs" for more information about teaching methodology.

Champion Baptist Kindergarten Program
(Landmark's Freedom Baptist Curriculum)
teacher's kit - $125; student kit - $75

Phonics/reading, writing, math, and Bible are foundational subjects in this "almost complete" kindergarten program. Brief suggestions and activities are given for science, history, health and safety, and fine arts. You might want to supplement these areas with other resources and activities.

Reading begins with letter and sound recognition. Phonics

is taught with consonant-vowel combinations first (ba, be, bi, bo, bu), then word families. 8 1/2" by 11" cards for key words/letters, numbers, some phonogram blends, and alphabetical Scripture verses come packaged with the program.

Phonics covers both long and short vowel words as well as sight words that enable students to read beginning *McGuffey's Eclectic Primer* and the *Beginner's Champion Phonics Reader* that accompany the program. Math introduces numbers and continues up through addition up to sums of 10; counting by 2's, 5's, and 10's; telling time; and money recognition. Handwriting and spelling skills are also stressed. This program is more academic than many, and about equivalent to A Beka's kindergarten program. There are a few hands-on activities such as working with flash cards and counting pennies.

Daily lesson plans, presented in one volume, give us step-by-step instructions, including what to say. Although written for the classroom, the curriculum can easily be adapted for home schools. The kindergarten program is packaged into two kits: one for teacher or parent and the other for the student. The first package includes teacher manual with lesson plans, the two readers, flashcards mentioned above, and a 1 to 100 Numbers Chart. The student kit includes copies of the two readers, Letters and Numbers Pads (3 separate pads that total 389 pages), a Letters Writing Tablet, Numbers Writing Tablet (these last two are each about 1 inch thick), a K5 report card, a K5 diploma, chart for Bible memory verse records, and small numbers flash cards. We need a separate student kit for each student, but only one teacher's kit.

Common Sense Learning for Kindergarten Skills
(Common Sense Press)
$60

Common Sense Learning for Kindergarten Skills is a combination of five resources which comprise a complete kindergarten program. Those resources are *Early Education at Home, A Study in Wisdom, Language and Thinking* (by Beechick and Nelson), *Common Sense Math*, and *First Learning Activity Books* (actually four separate Usborne activity books).

Phonics, language arts, and math instruction all utilize hands-on and activity methods more than workbooks as primary learning tools. Phonics is essentially learning letters and sounds; see the review of *Early Education at Home* for details. (Some children might be ready to move beyond this level, and Common Sense Press' *Common Sense Reading Program* is designed to follow this level.) *A Study in Wisdom* is a six-week study of Proverbs. *Language and Thinking* is reviewed elsewhere. It covers broader language arts skills than phonics. *Common Sense Math* teaches kindergarten math skills using blocks, games, discs, and other hands-on approaches, with instructions given in the Teacher's Manual. (Manipulatives are included.) The Usborne *First Learning Workbooks* used are

Starting to Add, Ready for Writing, Ready for Reading, and *Opposites.* Children will enjoy these twenty-four-page books because of their colorful, heavily-illustrated format.

A weekly lesson guide is included so we know how to coordinate the different components of this program. Because all the resources were not originally written to be used together they will not fit as smoothly together as do components of some other kindergarten programs. However, parents who wish to implement Ruth Beechick's philosophy will find that this program lines up with her recommendations for less workbooks and more real learning; lots of discussion; and plenty of age-appropriate activity.

Early Education at Home: A Curriculum Guide for Parents of Preschoolers and Kindergartners
by M. Jean Soyke
(Elijah Company)
$19.95

I am reluctant to recommend most curricula that I see for preschool and kindergarten because generally the programs are too academic for home school use, especially for preschoolers. They usually spend a great deal of time creating artificial situations to teach children skills that can easily be learned by simply participating in household activities with the family. However, I know many parents are uncomfortable trusting household activities and unstructured learning (such as reading to a child) to meet the developmental and learning needs of their children. Searching for a happy medium which provides some structure yet is not heavy with time-wasters can be frustrating.

Early Education at Home is one of the few resources that achieves that balance, fits the home school situation, and appropriately addresses the learning needs of young children. This preschool-kindergarten curriculum is contained within a single spiral-bound book. It includes general teaching information, skills checklists, descriptions of activities and materials to help children develop those skills, suggested schedules, weekly lesson outlines, ideas for learning centers, tangram patterns, recommendations of computer software, reproducible planning sheets, and an alphabetical index to topics (e.g., airplanes, animals, ants, etc.). The weekly planning sheets detail math, language arts, science, and social studies activities for the week. They also tell us which of the letters, numbers, colors, or shapes are to be learned each week, with parents then choosing appropriate activities from those suggested. Subjects are staggered so every subject is not scheduled every week, with the exceptions of letters and numbers. Specific Bible stories, real books, and field trips are suggested as well as snack ideas that tie in with the week's topics. Snack ideas often involve following recipes provided in the book to make goodies such as homemade pretzels, fruit leather, granola, "igloos," and kabobs—wonderful learning activities in themselves.

There is a strong emphasis on constructive play and craft activities such as playing grocery store and making placemats for the family. Plans for 36 weeks—about one school year—are included.

Early Education at Home allows us flexibility in choosing activities to meet learning style and developmental needs, yet provides us with structure and ideas so less planning time is required than if we do it on our own. Because the book is written to be used with both preschool and kindergarten children, it is less academically structured than others written only for kindergarten.

Early Learner's Packet for Preschool - Kindergarten and First Grade
(Bealls' Learning Games)
$35

This is an all-in-one approach, but it does not claim to be comprehensive. There is plenty here for a casual approach to preschool and kindergarten, but it does not provide the thorough coverage of some of the other programs. It is strictly a supplement at first grade level. This is not a curriculum but a collection of games and activities for learning such basics as letters, shapes, colors, counting, printing numbers and letters, and time telling. It comes in a three-ring binder with a number of laminated game/activity boards, reproducible pages, and instructions. Included are three colorful card decks, a wipe-off felt marker, storage pockets, and the reversible gameboard: "Teddy Bear on a Picnic" on one side and "Tubin' Down the River" on the other. Children will love the super-bright colors and cute illustrations.

Here I Grow!
(Hewitt Homeschooling Resources)
$59.95

Here I Grow! is a first grade continuation of *Training Wheels.* The topics covered are the same as in *Training Wheels* so that we can teach much of the material to children at both levels simultaneously; however, *Here I Grow!* takes a more in-depth approach. Both volumes can also be used independently of one another.

Here I Grow! comes as a package which includes the three-ring binder teaching manual, a single reader that covers two reading levels, and a *Link 'N Learn Suitcase Set* and *Activity Book.* The package comprises a complete curriculum. It presupposes that a child has already learned to read, incorporating reading practice in the first lesson. (Some children will need more work on blending and word reading before beginning the readers, and some might need more math preparation. Appropriate resources are offered by Hewitt.) The entire program should take two to two and a half hours per day, and it allows flexibility regarding which subjects are covered each day. Subject areas covered are the same as in *Training Wheels*.

Parents who need structure will find security here. Daily plans are provided, although parents are encouraged to adapt the schedule to suit their family. Science and social studies topics are often presented as outlines for discussion, research, or activities rather than textbook-style lessons. The introduction urges parents to allow children to make their own selections of reading material, music, art, and P.E. activities one day a week so that children learn how and are encouraged to pursue areas of personal interest. The program also takes into account children's preferred learning modalities, offering teaching tips for best meeting the needs of auditory, visual, or kinesthetic learners. Because of this, games, songs, art activities, visual teaching aids, etc. are built into the program. The variety of learning activities should be appropriate for most learners although those who have Wiggly Willy learners will need to make good use of the more active ideas to keep their children's attention. The inclusion of the *Math Links* (colored plastic links) and an overall hands-on approach to math lessons ensures that the needs of active learners are addressed in math. There are reproducible worksheets included at the back of the binder, but only one per unit (or week).

Having two linked programs such as these for kindergarten and first grade levels offers an added benefit of the flexibility of having a child work at a higher level in one subject and a lower level in another.

I Love To Read! I Love To Write!, Levels K-II
by Denise Griney
(S & D Publications)
complete sets: Kindergarten - $125; Level I - $220; Level II - $250; Level III - $310; Level IV- $310
extra sets of Student Papers: K-$60; I - $75; II - $90; III - $90; IV - $200
literature study guides - $7.50 each; books - $6 each; vocabulary books - $15 each

This is a complete Christian language arts curriculum for approximately grades K-6, suitable for either home schools or traditional classrooms. Level numbers in this program do not translate directly to grade levels. Kindergarten level goes beyond language arts to provide a complete curriculum. The first four levels (K-II) focus most heavily on building a solid phonics/reading foundation for the primary grades, while Level IV provides a means of completing the elementary grades' language arts skills within the same methodological structure. Each level comes as a set with one or two Teacher's Manuals in three-ring binders and a set of Daily Student Creative Activity Papers. All levels beyond kindergarten also include reading books, and Levels II-IV include study guides for literature. The first thing I noted when reviewing this program is how massive it looks. Teacher's Manual binders for K-III are from 3 to 4 inches thick each, with two such binders for

kindergarten. Student pages are up to double the amount of teacher pages. However, these are not all lesson plan and worksheet pages. Many are instructions for teaching, reference charts or lists, game ideas, evaluation pages, and other components, while much of the bulk consists of heavy, colored paper with flash cards and manipulatives students will use. Students are provided with preprinted worksheets for most activities, although by fourth grade level they will be writing many compositions on other paper. Student Papers are consumable, so an additional set must be purchased for each child.

While this program is expensive, it offers lots of time and frustration-saving help and does an excellent job of "instructing the instructor" and providing easy-to-follow lesson plans. The lesson plans in some levels even include occasional "reminders" that teachers might pass on to students to make learning easier. Pre-tests and periodic evaluations help the teacher identify student strengths and weaknesses. Detailed lesson plans save on preparation time and instill confidence, telling you everything you need to know as well as how to present it. Lessons DO need to be taught. This is not self-instructional material until Level IV.

Denise Griney has included activities for multi-sensory learning to meet the needs of almost all types of learners. While you are free to use everything provided, you will probably find that when working with one child, you will be able to skip some of the activities when you see that your child has already mastered a concept. In fact, Griney encourages parents to use their own discretion in selecting activities.

I Love To Read! I Love To Write! seems to have combined the "best of two worlds": the content and rules-oriented coverage of programs like A Beka *Language* with the creativity, applications, and incorporation of literature found in programs like *Learning Language Arts Through Literature*. It also provides continual reminders about the importance of individualizing lessons in terms of student progress, activity choices, and amount of work.

Kindergarten level is a comprehensive kindergarten curriculum covering math, Bible, and readiness skills as well as language arts. It includes a manuscript printing program, letter flashcards, and an interactive Bible study. It teaches letters and sounds of the 26 letters and introduces blending at the end of the year. This is not complete phonics coverage. Numbers through 100 are introduced along with the concepts of value and sequencing. Children also learn introductory addition and subtraction as well as beginning time telling and coin identification. Bible instruction and memory verses are integrated throughout the lessons. Daily lessons follow a consistent format: teaching the letter and number of the week with a variety of multi-sensory activities. The teacher can select from game ideas in an appendix to add variety or alternate learning methods. Children learn manuscript printing with practice sheets showing letter and number formation provided. (Because letter and number models are hand drawn, they exhibit an inconsistency in shape that might be improved upon.) Flashcards and worksheets are ready to use (cutting sometimes required). Periodic evaluations are built into the program so that we can easily assess student progress. The teacher might need to secure supplemental materials or read-aloud books, but preparation time required will be minimal. As with just about every kindergarten program, this one does require teacher presentation and interaction. While I, personally, don't find it necessary to do this much work with kindergartners, this level (or some other form of teaching that covers similar concepts) is necessary before tackling Level I.

Level I reviews the basics and moves on into blends, digraphs, and other phonic concepts. Overall, language arts coverage is similar to most first grade level programs. Level I comes with 12 short-vowel and 9 long-vowel readers (illustrated with black-and-white line drawings). It moves students quickly into easy readers while also teaching beginning grammar, spelling, and composition skills. One thing would make it just a little easier to use the first two levels: page numbers on student pages directing us to some of the extra sections (at least at the beginning as we familiarize ourselves with the program). Level II - IV do have page numbers on student pages.

Level II covers typical second grade material and then some. It might be used by older students who lack a solid language arts foundation. Before beginning this level, students should be able to read simple chapter books; identify nouns, verbs, pronouns, and adjectives; write a short paragraph; spell simple words using phonetic principles; be able to alphabetize; and have some beginning grammar concepts.

Level II includes study guides and books for *Frog and Toad Treasury, The Bears of Hemlock Mountain, The Courage of Sarah Noble,* and *Helen Keller.* Extra student activity pages, a bag of unusual buttons, and a packet of sunflower seeds are packaged for use with the *Frog and Toad Treasury.* Level II starts with a review of blends and digraphs, then continues through presentation of advanced reading skills, spelling, grammar, composition, use of reference tools, and some Greek and Latin roots, prefixes, and suffixes. A cursive writing chart is included with Level II, but you will need another resource if you need assistance with direct instruction. Non-denominational Bible study suggestions are offered at the beginning of each section. Since these are not integrated into daily lessons, you will have to make an extra effort to use them. Some students will need longer than one year to complete Level II.

Level III, a two-year program, builds upon Level II. The teacher is referred back to Level II for assistance and review periodically if students need more foundational work. Level III will serve as a third-fourth grade program in most cases, but Griney stresses the importance of moving more slowly or more quickly with children in accordance with their abilities. Children beginning Level III are expected to have learned topics covered in Level II, including knowledge of some Greek and Latin roots, prefixes and suffixes; familiarity with the writing process; knowledge of parts of speech up through interjections and conjunctions; and some other topics which might not have been covered in other second-grade language arts programs.

The Level III set includes the teacher's manual (almost 600 pages), teacher's Appendix binder, student papers (about 1,000 pages), study guides and books for *The Cabin Faced West; True Animal Stories; A Lion to Guard Us; Sarah, Plain and Tall; The Wright Brothers; The wind in the Willows;* and *Squanto.*

One of the goals of this level is to help children become more independent learners, however, it still requires a good deal of direct instruction and interaction between teacher and student. Mastery of phonics is another goal, so phonics review is coupled with plenty of reading, spelling, and writing to reinforce and develop basic skills.

The program provides thorough coverage in reading, grammar, spelling, writing, and research skills. Literature studies incorporate literary elements, analysis, and Biblical applications. Handwriting models for cursive are provided, but handwriting is not covered extensively. You might choose to supplement with another program, although it is not essential. Two other features of this program—oral reports and self-editing—enhance development of language arts skills. In addition, instructions for Bible "journaling" are included.

Level III is divided into four "phases" which are simply divisions of the lessons. Each phase is divided into introduction lessons, then review and evaluation. However, even in the introduction lessons, students are continually reviewing and applying previously-learned material.

The appendix binder includes program objectives, charts of phonics families, a glossary, rules and guidelines (e.g., comma rules), reproducible forms, game ideas, answer key to puzzles, vocabulary and literature activities, and additional evaluations. The program was originally written as a one-year program, but their was too much content to cover in a year. Griney includes instructions for using it as a two-year program, but it takes a little bit of adjustment (e.g., cutting lessons in half) on our part. This should not be very difficult to do.

Level IV should be used with students in grades 4 through 7 but is probably best for most students in grades 5 and 6. Developed from the beginning as a two-year program, it comes in two sections. Its format is quite different from earlier levels with a major shift toward student independence. The teacher's manual at this level is very small, while the daily lesson plans are, for the most part, found in the student's notebook.

In Level IV students complete extensive book studies of *Skylark, Mr. Popper's Penguins, Samuel Morris,* and *Little Pilgrim's Progress.* These studies use a "whole language" approach, incorporating all the language art skills within each study to varying degrees. Between time devoted to book studies, students complete daily lessons from their notebook which are partially teacher-directed. Students write numerous compositions, including poetry, and create their own dictionaries, all which are kept in tabbed-sections in their own binders. The methodology is quite similar to that of Level III with the primary difference being students reading and following instructions on their own.

Learning at Home: Preschool and Kindergarten
(Noble Books)
$49.95
Learning at Home: First Grade and Learning at Home: Second Grade
(Small Ventures)
$49.95 each

While this is not a unit study approach with learning integrated around a central theme, it covers all the necessary subjects in one volume at each of three levels. Since it covers many subjects, it is similar in many ways to the published unit study materials. Because it covers each subject in the daily schedules, it cannot be listed under individual subject areas without much repetition, so I include it here.

Learning at Home meets the needs of many home educators who are interested in presenting academics but are easily overwhelmed with the process. Instead of a half dozen texts and teacher's editions from which you compile lessons, you can have one basic manual with detailed daily lesson plans that does it all for you. This book, along with a few basic resources, provides everything you need.

Learning at Home: Preschool and Kindergarten is the first volume. It is designed to be used over two years. This low-key program for preschool covers readiness activities along with Bible, history, science, art, music, and physical education. Lesson plans are laid out for each day with instructions for each subject area, including pages to be read from specific books. Recommended books are to be borrowed from the library. Many suggested titles are listed, but others on the same topic can be substituted. Ideas listed in *Learning at Home* can easily be used with preschool and kindergarten children together. At the end of the book a more formal, second-year program outlines phonics and math, but leaves us on our own for other subjects. The formal phonics and arithmetic can either be substituted in the daily lesson plans or used during a second year. The scope and sequence of the math and phonics is more advanced here than it is in most other programs, and this outline could easily be used at first grade level rather than kindergarten. The book, *The Writing Road to Reading*, can be purchased to use for the formal reading program following the lesson plans within *Learning at Home*. However, author Ann Ward now suggests using *Phonics for Reading and Spelling* instead. While the second half of *Learning at Home* might

seem too formal for some, the book is well worth its cost even if you were to use only the first part of it.

Learning at Home: First Grade follows the first volume with the same format of daily lesson plans covering reading (including spelling), writing, English, music, arithmetic, health, manners, responsibility, Bible, art, character building, physical education, history, geography, and science. Children learn about God within every subject area. Language arts/reading instruction is from The Writing Road to Reading. The scope and sequence for the math has slowed down from the first volume, bringing it closer in line with most others. However, English instruction goes beyond typical first grade level, including identification of nouns, pronouns, verbs, adjectives, and adverbs. There are a number of paper and pencil tasks so it is important to make sure that children are capable of doing these tasks without frustration. If they are not, either substitute other activities or omit the tasks. The academic approach is balanced with purposeful art activities, stories and activities relating to the Pilgrims, puppet shows, and an emphasis on service to others. Author Ann Ward has even written many learning songs (sung to familiar traditional tunes such as "Yankee Doodle") to be used as learning aids for geography, health, and manners. While the general approach here is quite academic, it is still less formal than typical school curriculum because of the emphasis on parent-child interaction and inclusion of many activities for multi-sensory learning. A lengthy, annotated bibliography is included at the end of the book, listing more than 340 books with information on print size, number of words, and reading level.

Learning at Home: Second Grade carries on where *First Grade* leaves off. Reference is made to the Ayer's Spelling Lists and phonograms, both included in *The Writing Road to Reading*. Language arts covers slightly more skills than in most traditional programs, with written work done in a three-ring binder and on practical-application forms (such as letter and journal writing). The arithmetic scope and sequence is now equivalent to most other programs. American history and world geography are studied through supplementary books as directed by daily lesson-plan outlines. Science topics are geology, botany, meteorology, astronomy, human anatomy, and zoology, again studied with supplementary books. Bible study and memorization, character building, physical education, art, and health, manners, and responsibility continue as in earlier levels. Many new songs have been added to help students learn and remember information. This volume does not include a bibliography such as that found in the *First Grade* volume. While *Second Grade* has been written as a follow-up for the *First Grade* volume, it can be used as your starting point if your child has learned concepts that have been taught in earlier volumes.

Overall, the *Learning at Home* series moves fairly rapidly into formal academics, although without textbooks. Some activities and multi-sensory learning help to balance the program. However, the first and second grade program will not work as well for very active learners—most Wiggly Willys, those with short attention spans, and those who need to delay reading and writing activities until they are more mature—as it will for mature learners who are ready for formal academic work that includes much reading and writing.

Mother of Divine Grace School Syllabi for grades K-8
by Laura Berquist
(Mother of Divine Grace School)
K-2 - $20; 3-8- $25

Many parents who read Laura Berquist's book, *Designing Your Own Classical Curriculum,* feel they need additional help to implement the ideas. Laura has provided that help with *Syllabi* for each grade level K-8 and selected high school subjects. Each *Syllabus* provides day-by-day lesson plans for all subjects for a full school year. Subject areas covered are religion (Catholic), math, phonics, language arts, poetry, science, history, geography, foreign language (Latin and Greek), art, and music. Younger students will need more one-on-one interaction than will older students. You might combine subject areas like history, science, music, and art with children close in grade level, drawing from only one *Syllabus* for your lesson plans in those areas. I particularly appreciate the detailed planning for the arts since this is an area frequently given short shrift in both planning and actual learning.

Recommended resources are primarily those described in *Designing Your Own Classical Curriculum* such as TAN history books, *Wordly Wise, English from the Roots Up, Our Roman Roots,* A Beka *Arithmetic,* and *Saxon Math.* Many supplementary "real" books are also suggested.

The format of each *Syllabus* is somewhat similar to that of Sonlight Curriculum's grade level teacher manuals with specific instructions for what to do each day in each subject area. A major difference between the two would be the classical approach's emphasis on memorization in the early grades and the inclusion of Catholic religious instruction rather than Protestant. Another difference is that composition skills are developed through regular oral and written composition activities rather than skill instruction through most levels, although skill instruction does occur at some grade levels. Most composition activity occurs within history and religion assignments.

To maintain consistent worldview instruction, Protestants can substitute other resources for Religion, and they might also wish to substitute for some of the selected history books. In doing so, parents will have to create their own lesson plans for those resources, but they can follow the patterns for use of the other resources.

The Noah Plan™: A Complete Educational Program in The Principle Approach ◖
(Foundation for American Christian Education)
$60 per level; subject guides - $25 each

The Noah Plan is presented in two volumes—one for K-8 and one for high school. Each program notebook is a large, three-ring binder with audio cassette tapes. Each presents a complete curriculum using the Principle Approach. The first part of this review pertains only to the K-8 volume.

Based upon years of application in both traditional Christian school and home school settings, this curriculum is the most complete resource for those wanting to use the Principle Approach. It includes a self-directed "seminar" for teachers at the beginning of the binder; in the past, it has been necessary for those interested in this methodology to attend seminars to learn how to teach this way. This seminar teaches the foundational principles and how they are translated into the "Notebook Approach" that includes the four steps: research, reason, relate, and record. Divided into nine lessons, the seminar requires teachers to do additional reading, reflection, and writing as they learn. The two audio cassettes are used with this part of *The Noah Plan.*

The seminar is followed by curriculum "Guidelines." The Guidelines introduce the actual curriculum with an overview of subjects to be studied and reproducible forms to be used. Next are guidelines for each grade, including a suggested schedule (geared toward traditional classrooms), a classroom constitution (agreement between student and teacher about attitude, getting work done, etc.), student supply list, a sample weekly goal sheet, and subject overviews. The subject overviews are the most helpful part for homeschoolers; they lay out the purpose and goals, principles to be taught, key definition, quarter-by-quarter topics to be covered, grading standards, notebook standards, texts, and recommended resources.

The Guidelines should be used in conjunction with the subject Curriculum Guides also published by F.A.C.E. for art, literature, English grammar and composition, history and geography, and reading. Guides for math and science, classical and modern languages, and Bible are in production. These guides get even more specific about what and how to teach for grades K-12. They include a teaching plan, model lesson plans, teaching methods, sample student notebooks or records (as for art), and lists of required resources.

I was able to review the *Reading Curriculum Guide* by Martha Barnes Shirley, *The Literature Curriculum Guide* by Rosalie June Slater, *English Language Curriculum Guide* by Carole Goodman Adams, *The History and Geography Curriculum Guide* by Elizabeth L. Youmans, the *StoneBridge Art Guide* by Wendy Giancoli and Elizabeth Youmans.

The *Reading Curriculum Guide* is quite extensive in scope. It outlines a reading curriculum that recommends the *Writing Road to Reading* program and also uses the Bible for reading material. (Children's versions of the Bible are used for the early grades.) It includes explanation of the rationale and organization of the curriculum; charts for each grade level showing purpose, objectives, scope and sequence, definitions, suggested teacher and student resources, and specific skills to be developed within sub-areas of reading (through eighth grade level, with a "Reading with Reason" enrichment course provided for high school); "Foundations for Teaching Reading"—teaching principles; extensive how-to-teach information; and an appendix of recommended resources, reading lists for children, and reproducible forms.

The English Language Curriculum Guide outlines a complete language arts program aside from the reading instruction already covered in the *Reading Curriculum Guide*. Maintaining consistent methodology, language instruction also utilizes the *Writing Road to Reading* methodology for handwriting and spelling. More extensive than most language programs, this Guide explains how to teach the foundations of English language, orthography (spelling/phonics, elocution, penmanship), syntax (sentence structure/grammar), composition (including various forms of public speaking), and prosody (understanding the forms of and writing poetry and prose). One-page charts outline what is to be covered within each area for each grade level K-12. The *Guide* offers a mix of background for teacher training and specific helps. I particularly like the presentation on diagraming and sentence patterns—one of the clearest I have seen.

The History and Geography Curriculum Guide by Elizabeth L. Youmans focuses heavily on the basic philosophy behind the Principle Approach. History has always been its strongest focal point within subject areas since the "Red Books" that first presented the ideas dealt primarily with history. Curriculum charts for each grade level (K-12) for history are two pages each with a great deal of detail. Most teaching information is background for the teacher with strategies for using timelines, biographies, source documents, and activities. Developing a Biblical Christian worldview is a dominant theme throughout the curricula.

About half the book explains how to teach geography with curriculum charts for grades K-8. A great deal of factual information and map masters are included. Detailed instructions show how to teach students to create accurate maps. Among the suggested texts and resources for this Guide are Genevieve Foster's *George Washington's World* and Christian Liberty Press's *Streams of Civilization*.

The *Literature Curriculum Guide* is similar to the *Reading Curriculum Guide* in format, but it is much larger (368 pages). It charts purpose, objectives, etc., although it focuses on content more than skills as is appropriate for the study of literature. It supplies some content coverage within the *Guide*. The *Guide* is very helpful, but it is uneven in the amount of information given from topic to topic. For example, extensive

guidelines help us to teach Shakespeare, while we are referred to other syllabi for teaching the classics.

The *StoneBridge Art Guide* differs some from the *Reading Curriculum Guide* since it was developed for a once-a-week art class at StoneBridge School. Time limitations and the nature of art study demand a slightly different application of the 4R methodology (less notebook work being the most obvious). Homeschooling parents might choose to expand the lessons given more time. The *Guide* presents the rationale for an art curriculum built upon biblical principles of art. It then translates the ideas into application through scope and sequence for grades K-8, sample lesson plans, background information for teaching, suggested projects, and timeline and illustrations showing how artists fit the model of Christianity's westward movement. Articles at the end of the book provide additional background for the teacher on art plus the basics of the Principle Approach.

The Noah Plan follows a challenging scope and sequence incorporating foreign language instruction throughout all grade levels in French, Latin, and Greek; research papers in the elementary grades; and other high-level, challenging, academic goals.

In all subjects, students create their own notebooks as they "four R" each subject. In addition to the subject Curriculum Guides, you will need to get a number of other resources such as the *American Dictionary of the English Language,* the "red books" by Verna Hall and Rosalie Slater, and subject textbooks (but not for all subjects). Many of the books you acquire in the process of teaching this program will be the foundation of an excellent library.

The Noah Plan needs to be taught by the teacher, as is true with any Principle Approach program. The teacher must first master the material, which means quite a bit of work for parents.

Remembering God's Awesome Acts

by Susan Mortimer
(Susan Mortimer)
teacher's manual and one student notebook - $35; additional student notebooks - $20 each

More limited in scope than most resources reviewed in this section, this unit study focuses primarily upon Bible and history while also providing some coverage in art, writing, speech, drama, geography, social studies, linguistics, anthropology, and archaeology. The eight units in the study deal with creation, man, the fall, the flood, the dispersion, God's chosen people, Egypt, and the Exodus. Each unit integrates Bible study with historical/cultural studies as the foundation. History and social studies cover historical data about the Sumerians, Babylonians, and Egyptians in a somewhat random fashion, but religious beliefs are highlighted and often examined in great depth. Lessons at the beginning of the book coupled with these on non-Christian belief systems and mythology provide a strong introduction to world views upon which we can continue to build through the high school years.

From history and Bible-based lessons, the course branches out to activities in the other subject areas, all still related to the primary theme of each unit. Brief instructions for each lesson are given in the teacher's manual, but most of each lesson is derived from and requires the student notebook. The pages in the student notebook serve as sources of information and activity pages/worksheets that become a "permanent" notebook when the course is complete. These heavily-illustrated pages offer a great deal of variety and visual interest. Each student will need his or her own notebook.

The course is suggested for grades 5 and up. While some of the content is introductory level, much of it is challenging enough for junior high and, possibly, even the beginning of high school. However, even when the content is challenging, many of the activities seem a little young for junior high students. There is good bit of cut-and-paste, coloring, puzzles, filling in the blanks with words from a word bank, and other such activities more typical of the elementary grades.

Three subject areas deserve special mention. Drawing exercises interspersed throughout the book teach basic shapes, shading, drawing from life, drawing faces, and perspective, although instruction on each of these skills is very limited. Linguistics receive a great deal of attention in the unit on the dispersion from Babel. Students are exposed to a number of different languages and dialects (e.g., Turkish, Waroni [Ecuador], Vietnamese). Languages are approached in the context of country studies drawing on the book *Operation World.* (See review in Chapter Fifteen.) You might expand this section beyond those countries for which studies are provided, following the models used for those lessons. Speech and drama activities require students to present orally before groups. To make this easier for them to do, scripts for Bible stories/teachings that use "object lessons" are provided within the teacher's manual. You, the parent/teacher, first presents each lesson to your student(s), then they are to familiarize themselves with the script and props and present the lesson to a Sunday School class, a backyard Bible study, or other appropriate audience. This is a wonderful way for our children to learn the value and basic skills of public speaking.

While this study includes sufficient Bible study, you will probably want to use it in conjunction with a text or other resources for more thorough history coverage. For other subject areas it is supplemental. Lesson preparation is fairly minimal, but you must look over lessons ahead of time in case you need to gather any books or materials. Lesson presentation time will vary from day to day; you can often expand or contract lessons as you choose. Students will complete parts of most lessons on their own. The NIV Bible is used; using other versions will require minor adaptation on some activity pages.

Training Wheels: A Kindergarten Curriculum for Home Schoolers
(Hewitt Homeschooling Resources)
$79.95 for complete program

This complete kindergarten program is primarily contained in the *Training Wheels* book (one-inch thick, spiral bound, and handsomely printed). Along with the book come the *Human Body, Food Pyramid,* and letter felt sets.

The program is set up with daily lesson plans, giving specific instructions for each subject area for each day. Yet, the learning activities use primarily informal, activity-based methods. Some lesson preparation is necessary, such as locating magazines with pictures of areas suffering from famine or making up a tray of assorted shapes, colors, and substances for children to separate and classify. Subjects covered are Bible, social studies, math, language, reading, science, health, physical education, music, and art. Reading instruction includes learning letters and sounds along with simple blends and some sight words. Math skills take children through the typical topics including counting up to 100. Children are instructed in proper techniques for writing numbers and letters.

This curriculum is slightly more structured and academic in approach than the *Common Sense Kindergarten* program, yet is definitely more informal (less workbook and textbook oriented) than Bob Jones, A Beka, and other traditional curriculum publishers. Although the book is set up like some unit studies, the subject areas are not developed around themes. Nevertheless, some subjects flow naturally into one another because the topics are purposely related to each other. Often the topical relationships grow out of each unit's Bible lesson. This seems even more true of *Here I Grow!* (first grade) than *Training Wheels.*

Some subjects are alternated in the schedule. Bible lessons and physical education are included every day, while social studies, language, and music are scheduled for Monday-Wednesday-Friday, and math, science, health, and art are done on Tuesday and Thursday. Teaching each day should take about one and a half to two hours.

A cassette tape and songbook of the Bible songs used in *Training Wheels* and *Here I Grow!* is available for $5.95. Children can sing along with other children on side one of the tape, or they can sing along to the musical accompaniment on side two.

Computer-based Curriculum

Only programs that are advertised as being core curriculum—offering complete coverage for a subject at the specified grade level—are reviewed here. Supplemental computer programs are included under the relevant chapters.

A+ LS Home ™

(American Education Corporation)
$69.95 per title

A+LS Home is a series of CD-ROM computer programs for Windows or Macintosh systems. The home version will be the choice for most home educating families. The same basic format is used throughout the series. Each program features separate lessons covering a number of topics within the designated subject area, with the total amount of content equivalent to a textbook. However, some of these programs will serve as stand-alone courses, while others should be used as supplements. Courses available that are targeted toward the elementary grades include *Reading I-II, Vocabulary I-VI, Grammar and Usage I-IV, Language Skills I-VII, Writing I-IV, Mathematics I-VI, The Sciences I-VI, U.S. Geography, U.S. History I-II, World Geography,* and *World History I-II.*

Lessons offer four basic options: study (instruction), practice, test, and essay. The study portion consists of explanation of the topic or rule with examples. It would be nice if the information could be presented in a more interesting manner, but instead we get a dry presentation of factual information. Computer illustrations are used whenever it is appropriate, and often students are directed to identify features on the illustrations as they read through the instructional information. In practice sessions the child attempts to answer questions, and he is given immediate feedback with access to hints and instructional information. The test section presents a series of questions which are scored at the end. The student can go back and change answers until he actually tells the program that he is done. When a student logs on to the program he types his name, and his test results are recorded. The student can also review his test to see which errors he made. After completing a test, if he earns enough "bonus points," the student can play the *Letter Lightning* game. *Letter Lightning* is a hangman type game using phrases and a slot machine to offer letter options.

There are editing options for the administrator to add, delete, or revise study material and questions. The administrator may add or edit users, access reports, and get printouts of tests, answer keys, and study material. Administrators can also access reports on individual student performance. The program does a thorough job in terms of management and reporting. If we prefer to have "paper" evidence of student progress, we can print out tests and have students complete them the old-fashioned way.

Screen presentation is colorful and includes pictures. Programs allow children to move at their own speed. There are no time limits. The subject matter is drawn from typical topics taught at the various grade levels. Because of the structure of

the program, the emphasis is on memorization of facts. All of the *A+LS Home* programs for various subjects follow this same format.

Language Usage I-III develop and strengthen basic grammar and word use skills typically taught in grades 1-3. These titles also assists in mastery of subjects and predicates, nouns and pronouns, adjectives, subject-verb agreement, capitalization and punctuation, plurals, contractions, and more. We could begin to use the appropriate lessons for instructing a first grader, adding additional lessons when appropriate. Aside from actual writing experience, grammar instruction within this program should be sufficient for the early grades.

Language Usage IV-VII work on basic grammar and word use skills typically taught in grades 4-7. They cover sentence structure, subjects and predicates, nouns, and pronouns, verbs, adjectives and adverbs, prepositions, conjunctions, contractions, abbreviations, and more.

Grammar and Writing I and *II* are both for grade levels 1-3, and *Grammar and Writing III* and *IV* are for grade levels 4-6. The emphasis in these programs is on correct usage. There is some grammar review, but most attention is given to topics such as subject/verb agreement, noun/pronoun agreement, verb tenses, and use of singulars and plurals. Little actual writing is involved. For the most part, students move words to create and correct sentences, select the correct word choice, and in other ways correct or change what appears on the computer screen. There is a little overlap with content in the *Language Usage* programs.

Writing I and *II* are both for grades 1-3 and *Writing III* and *IV* are for grades 4-6. Examples of topics covered: types of sentences, capitalization, punctuation, subject/verb agreement, identifying overused words, writing descriptions, sentence combining, organizing ideas for writing, and writing letters. As with Grammar and Writing programs, much of this is accomplished by moving and selecting words on the computer screen, although students also do some writing. There is some overlap with topics in *Language Usage* and *Grammar and Writing*.

Reading I and *II* are for grades 1-3 and 4-6 respectively. These programs help develop reading comprehension skills such as identifying the main idea, drawing conclusions, identifying cause and effect, alphabetizing, understanding analogies, using context clues, differentiating between fact and opinion, and identifying plot elements.

Building Vocabulary I-VI are targeted at grades 1-6. These programs are more general language arts tools than vocabulary-specific ones. They cover topics such as phonetic sounds, sight words, prefixes and suffixes, alphabetical order, abbreviations, compound words, homophones, homonyms, synonyms, homographs, antonyms, similes, metaphors, and "tricky words."

The Sciences I-VI are suggested for grades 1 through 6.

These programs cover topics similar to those found in typical science textbooks: For example, the third grade level covers matter, energy, the human body, ecology, plants, animals, the earth, weather, and space. Since emphasis is on factual information, it is vital that we supplement such a resource with hands-on science activities and/or discussion to develop fuller understanding.

I could not find any references to evolution in the obvious places; the entire presentation seems to have been designed to be non-controversial. We find some overlap in content from program to program, as is also true of textbooks, although material is written differently for the various levels.

World History I covers up through the Middle Ages, while *World History II* begins with the Renaissance and Reformation and continues up through modern times. Information is geared for students in grades 6 through 9. The emphasis is on factual information because of the nature of the programs so these are not substitutes for good history texts or a "real book" approach. They might work very well alongside real books because they can provide continuity and coverage of detail that might otherwise be missed. Not having seen the actual programs, I cannot vouch for the philosophical viewpoints expressed. Even though they concentrate on factual data, there is still room for interpretation via choices of which data is used and how it is presented. One section likely to present problems is the "prehistory" coverage of early man. If there are no content problems otherwise, they should be useful supplements to help children absorb factual information in a more interesting format than most texts.

U.S. History I and *II* divide our country's history in two parts: the first part covers exploration and colonization up to the Civil War, and the second part begins with the Civil War and continues up to modern times. Topics seem to be fairly well-balanced in comparison to some of the newer textbooks, but I have not reviewed these programs, so I cannot vouch for the content. Emphasis is on factual information because of the nature of the programs, so you will want to read and discuss U.S. History in other formats for deeper understanding as I've also recommended for World History I and II. These programs are recommended for grades 4 through 8.

U.S. Geography makes geography much more palatable than do most textbooks. This program covers geography basics such as latitude and longitude, the tools of geography, landforms, bodies of water, etc., but spends most of the time on features of the U.S. Some history is intermixed, e.g., information about the original explorers and settlers of Arizona, New Mexico, Oklahoma, and Texas. The emphasis is on factual data, so use this as an adjunct to your U.S. History studies to make it more interesting. The content should be equivalent to a textbook-based geography course. Recommended for grades 4-8.

World Geography is designed for grades 6-9, so wait until the upper elementary grades before tackling it. The program reviews the basics, so it might be used on its own. It then intermixes some historical information with geography lessons about continents, countries, and, occasionally, specific, localized geographical features. I was impressed that lessons seem to draw out major characteristics and important features or locations for identification rather than descending into nitpicking detail.

Mathematics I-VI are for grades 1 through 6. These programs strongly reflect the new math standards with inclusion of concepts such as graphs, estimation, and symmetry included in the first grade program. On-screen graphics help children to visualize concepts, many of which are taught with visual manipulatives. Children learn to use an on-screen calculator beginning in second grade. These are intended to be comprehensive programs. However, the only review seems to be in tests at the end of each program, except in fifth and sixth grade where there are more frequent review tests. I expect that most parents will need to use a supplemental workbook or other tools to provide more practice and review of previously learned concepts.

The Learning Odyssey: ChildU 💻
(The Learning Odyssey)

The Learning Odyssey is comprehensive on-line curriculum to which you subscribe. Prices: 1 student - $69/month or $699/year; 2 students - $99/month or $999/year; 3 students - $129/month or $1299/year. Course work is offered in language arts, math, science, social studies, art, music, technology, and life skills, but we do not subscribe per class, but to the service. Curriculum is non-sectarian and is tied to national and state standards, so you can expect that there are likely to be occasional "content conflicts" over topics like evolution. A placement test helps students begin at the right place in each subject, not necessarily at the same grade level in all subjects. There are over six hundred learning activities for each grade level. Testing is included, and a certified teacher monitors student progress through the course work.

The heart of lesson presentation is printed text on the screen. But text is supplemented by illustrations, animations, and occasional interactive activities. Questions in a variety of formats are integrated into lessons. If a student demonstrates a poor grasp of a topic on tests, he is given a different type lesson presentation and additional questions. Students can move from page to page as quickly as they are able; there's little time wasted on graphic downloads. Students can review prior topics or look up information on specific topics whenever necessary.

"Guide Tips" can be accessed on just about every page. These offer extended activities and hot links or other web sites to investigate, but they are directed toward parents. If children work through these lessons independently, as I suspect will happen almost all the time, I don't see how parents will be accessing these tips without going through lessons themselves.

Parents can view a summary of concepts students will be covering each day, which might alert them to lessons to which they might wish to pay particular attention.

Yellow boxes on some lesson screens direct students to write in their notebooks, do an activity or experiment, take a quiz, etc. The idea is to have the students working off the computer some of the time. Green boxes suggest activities, many of which are accessed via links to other sites. Blue boxes list other recommended resources on the topic. There are also highlighted words that serve as internal links to flashcards, animations, graphic images, video clips, etc. Occasionally, a free response box asks students to write on a topic and submit this to the TLO teacher who will respond with comments within 24 hours. Students can contact TLO teachers for help when needed, and parents can get progress reports on students through the site.

Students can complete coursework on whatever schedule they (or their parents) choose, beginning any time of the year. TLO can be accessed from any computer with an internet connection, so it will work even for travelers.

This is planned to be a complete curriculum for grades K-12, but only grades 3-6 are on-line thus far, with grades 1-8 slated to be ready by September 2000.(SE)

Robinson Self-Teaching Home School Curriculum, version 2.0 [computer program for IBM or Macintosh computers] 🖥

(Oregon Institute of Science and Medicine and Althouse Press)
$195

When Laurelee Robinson, home schooling mother of six, died suddenly, her husband, Dr. Arthur Robinson, determined to continue home schooling. The children, ages 17 months through 12 years at that time, worked with their father to devise a plan whereby they could home educate themselves. Dr. Robinson reports that during the past seven years he has spent less than 15 minutes a day teaching his children. What the Robinsons developed out of necessity, presents an option for many families who lack the time or expertise to provide more traditional learning opportunities. The program is fairly simple. The children learn to read using a phonetic method. Once children are able to read, they are introduced to a vast array of good books to read for history, science, and literature. Many of these books are classics, some are college level texts, some are non-fiction books, and some are old encyclopedias. The Saxon math series from level 5/4 up through Calculus covers mathematics instruction. The children each write an essay per day. The children essentially teach themselves, achieving high levels of academic competence with very minimal parental input and supervision.

The Robinsons spend five hours per day, six days per week, twelve months per year with occasional days off for special

activities. As you might expect from such a schedule, the older Robinson children are tackling college curriculum ahead of schedule and taking advanced placement exams to secure college credit for those courses.

The *Robinson Self-Teaching Curriculum* is not comprehensive in itself, although Dr. Robinson includes suggestions for rounding out your program to create a comprehensive program. What we get are 22 CD-ROMs that contain facsimile copies of more than 230 books, the 30,000-page 1911 *Encyclopedia Britannica*, the 400,000-word 1913 *Webster's Dictionary* (these last two resources include special on-screen reading software), 6000-word vocabulary flashcard system, 2000 historic illustrations, progress exams for some of the books, and vocabulary/comprehension quizzes for some of the literature. We can print out copies of these books as needed, and, since they are facsimile images, they look just like the original. (The drawback here is that we can't search for words, select paragraphs, or otherwise play with the text in facsimile copies.)

Dr. Robinson also includes articles about teaching the various subject areas, creating a study environment, and other helpful insights. This has been expanded to serve as a more thorough course of study based upon feedback Dr. Robinson has received from many families who used the first version.

The books themselves form the core of a valuable library and are worth the cost of the program if for no other reason than to have access to such books. Some of the titles in the curriculum are the *McGuffey Reader* series, Josephine Pollard's *George Washington* and *Life of Christopher Columbus, Just So Stories,* the *Five Little Peppers* series, *Tom Sawyer, The Swiss Family Robinson, The Hound of the Baskervilles, Do and Dare* by Horatio Alger, *Two Years Before the Mast, Little Women, Little Men, Don Quixote, Diaries of George Washington, The Spy, Circulation of the Blood* by William Harvey, *Faraday's Lectures, The Prince* by Machiavelli, *Julius Caesar* by Shakespeare, *The Autobiography of Theodore Roosevelt, The Federalist Papers, Institutes of the Christian Religion* by Calvin, and *Paradise Lost.* Version 2.0 also features complete science texts for high school, including advanced texts for students who need to work at more challenging levels. Dr. Robinson recommends the Saxon math series and offers discounts on these if you wish to purchase them through Oregon Institute of Science and Medicine.

We install the foundational programs on our hard drive, then access the various disks as needed. The program is easy to install and operate.

The curriculum requires parents to determine which books to offer their children at which time. It also leaves us to determine for ourselves how and if to supply specific instruction in areas such as beginning mathematics, writing, spelling, grammar, and science. So, while Dr. Robinson offers suggestions for many of these areas, we cannot rely on the CD-ROM disks to be a comprehensive curriculum by themselves. The Robinsons plan to add to the curriculum as they are able, so we should think of this as a curriculum in process.

I am thoroughly convinced of the value of reading worthwhile books as a major component of our home schooling, and this is a very affordable way to obtain more than 120,000 pages to build a library. Dr. Robinson's approach to homeschooling offers a model that most of us can glean from even if we do not follow it exactly. It also suggests a much broader realm of possibilities for many families who are reluctant to home school or who consider it beyond their capabilities. While such an independent, reading-based approach to education might present problems for auditory (hearing) and kinesthetic (hands-on) learners, the Robinsons have proven it successful with their own children. The Robinsons welcome comments and recommendations.

Check for special upgrade prices if you already own version 1.0.

SkillWorks [computer curriculum] 🖥

(Milliken Publishing)
packages: K - $159; 1st grade - $169; 2nd grade - $189; 3rd grade - $199; combined K-3 - $399

Designed to run on either Windows or Macintosh systems, SkillWorks is advertised as "core curriculum educational software" for grades K-3. In reviewing SkillWorks, I found that these CD-ROM programs do not come close to offering complete coverage in any of the three subject areas mentioned. Packages actually include only math and phonics in the K-2nd grades, and only math and reading in the 3rd grade. There appears to be significant repetition of material from level to level. The scope and sequence is unusual; essential phonic skills are spread out too much, with critical elements such as soft "c" not taught until second grade. Because of this, it seems the only sensible choice is to purchase the combined K-3 program so that you can use lessons at the proper time for each student.

Lessons are high-quality multimedia presentations; you must have a sound card in your computer. The program is fairly intuitive; children can figure out what to do with most lessons easily. One thing seems to be missing: on screen help if a student can't figure out how the lesson works. However, there is help for the academic concept if needed.

Reading is phonics-based. It will help with the alphabet, sounds, blending, and other skills, but do not expect your child to rely on this program for all of his reading instruction. Reading comprehension lessons in the 3rd grade level work on identifying cause and effect, main ideas and details, sequence, and inferences. Math lessons begin with number readiness activities, then continue through addition, subtraction, multiplication, and division. Other concepts covered are "laws of arithmetic," number theory, time, money, fractions, word problems, and estimation. A few simple games are built into the program for a bit of fun.

Pre- and post-tests help assess children's skill levels. Management tools allow up to three teachers and five students to use the program. (It might be possible for families to share a single program.) Teachers can individualize assignments, selecting order of lessons as well as the sequence of activities within a lesson. You can turn visual and auditory "rewards" on or off, set the percentage of right answers needed for mastery, and choose whether or not to allow students to proceed if they haven't yet mastered a particular lesson. Detailed tracking information on student progress can be accessed by the teacher.

My biggest complaint is the price. The K-3 combined program is a useful educational supplement, but you could buy quite a few stand-alone programs for the same money that could do the job as well. A free demo is available at their website.

System requirements are: Windows '95 or '98, 16 MB RAM, 250 MB disk space, SVGA or better; Macintosh 7.5 or above, 16 MB RAM, and 500 MB disk space.(S)

Switched On Schoolhouse [computer curriculum] 🖥

(Alpha Omega)
$61.95 per subject or $259.95 for complete 5 subject set

Alpha Omega's LifePac curriculum is also available for grades 3-12 in a completely computerized form that includes full-color graphics, videos and slides, sound, and internet excursions. Students can work independently. Parents need to set up the initial program, customize lesson plans if necessary, check student progress which can be viewed in "teacher mode" on the computer, and review writing assignments. Of course, parents are always free to add additional assignments on their own.

Computer equipment should be fairly current for smooth viewing of video clips and use of sound. Listed requirements are a Pentium 133 or better multimedia PC with CD-ROM player, sound card, and Windows 95/98. Web excursions are not essential to the curriculum, so an internet connection is not absolutely necessary. However, the web links should add extra interest and additional learning opportunities.

Bible, Math, Language Arts, Science, and History/Geography courses can be purchased individually or as a complete grade level set. The programs follow the general format of the LifePacs, although they are not identical. Students begin with vocabulary in each lesson. If there are more than two vocabulary words, the program offers students the option of playing "Vocabulocity," multiple choice drill in a game-quality graphic environment. As far as I can tell, the exact same graphics are used for Vocabulocity in every subject which makes it unappealing after a certain amount of use. Whether or not students play the vocabulary game, they need to have an understanding of the vocabulary words and definitions before proceeding. Then they read through a section of the material on the screen, hit "next" and answer the questions. Questions are presented in crossword puzzles, fill-in-the-blanks, multiple choice, sorting, and matching. Incorrect answers are immediately identified, although students are not allowed to correct them until later on. In subject areas other than math, students can scan the "text" material to figure out what the correct answer should be much of the time, but sometimes they must make inferences, read maps, or interpret data to arrive at correct answers. Math programs require students to solve problems. If students miss questions, those that were answered incorrectly are presented again. Sometimes hints are given such as pointing out that the error was in the spelling or indicating a map to which a student might refer to find the answer. However, such hints seemed few and far between. Once students have answered all questions correctly for a set number of lessons, they take a quiz. Some written responses are required in the exercises and quizzes, and parents/teachers must score these themselves. The program alerts parents/teachers to exercises that need grading while the program is in "teacher mode." Exercises and quizzes are scored by the computer, although parent/teacher override is permitted.

The program is very professional (much improved from the first edition of *Switched On Schoolhouse*). It allows parents control over which lessons are to be assigned in which order, how lenient or tough to be with spelling of answers, grade format, and access to the internet. It truly allows students to work independently—a tremendous help for parents with little time to oversee schoolwork. Parents also set up a school calendar which allows the computer to schedule each student's rate of progress. The computer then alerts students if they get behind schedule.

Extra graphic boxes that expand to add additional information are generally very helpful. The programs move at a fairly good pace for the most part so there's not a lot of wasted time as in software of the "edutainment" sort. While answers are each followed by a verbal affirmation (it would be nice to be able to turn these off and just have something like a green light/red light signal), there are no "cute" graphics wasting time between answers and subsequent questions.

Like the LifePacs, content is non-denominationally Christian throughout all subjects. Biblical concepts appear throughout all subjects, although less so in math than others.

The Bible program offers solid content, including some Scripture memorization. Map identification is added to the typical questions and answers.

The Language program covers reading skills, grammar, composition, spelling, and vocabulary. Periodic writing projects stretch skills beyond the short answers they write within the lessons themselves.

History and geography are combined, with geography and map work intermixed throughout lessons. Essays, reports, and special projects expand learning beyond the computer.

Science programs also include a few experiments, essays, observations, and other non-computer activities.

There are some flaws in the program, some of them inherent to the computer format. Installing new subjects was not difficult, but the instructions in the manual were not quite as complete as they should be. Sometimes I had to guess where to go to accomplish a task. Occasionally, it was not clear what to do next and no help was available at that point in the program. Again, I could eventually figure it out without too much trouble.

As I have encountered in many other computerized programs, requested answers seemed highly debatable. Teacher overrides are helpful in dealing with such situations, but that requires more immediate oversight. I am continually surprised at questions curriculum authors write that have little value or might even be deemed incorrect by some children. For example, the science curriculum in one lesson focuses at least two questions on defining geraniums as plants that often grow in window boxes. Here in Southern California, geraniums are a common ground cover or bush and only rarely appear in window boxes since they grow too fast for such containers.

Vocabulocity is appealing at first, but once you have done it a few times, watching the same dramatic graphics before you can answer the next question begins to feel like a time waster. Students can simply skip the game playing if they wish. It would have been nice to have a few different game options for vocabulary drill.

A problem cropped up in the math program immediately with the presentation of addition and subtraction problems with regrouping. Given 3-digit numbers, students will generally work from right to left to solve each problem, yet the cursor begins on the left, and it is a bother to get it to enter numbers in the logical order.

In the language program, students are frequently working from reading selections, answering questions regarding content. Unfortunately, some of the questions are too nit-picky. For example, one question asked students how many trees were in the backyard (13) in a story about family members being friendly to birds and animals. The number of trees was irrelevant.

In summary, I expect that many parents will find *Switched On Schoolhouse* the tool that makes homeschooling possible for them. I still suspect that, like the LifePacs, many students will ultimately find this frustrating and boring. Even though I have concerns over the narrowness of learning in this format as compared to reading a book and discussing it together, *Switched On Schoolhouse* does offer a self-contained learning system.

The 2000-2001 release of Switched On Schoolhouse addresses some of my concerns and includes some enhancements. Web links, which are troublesome to set up in the present programs, will not need this extra step. Video teacher tips, called "tiny-tutors," will be added to each lesson. A "Spelling Bee" will be added to work with each vocabulary list. Vocabulary lists will print out, with or without definitions, to be used for both vocabulary and spelling study. Science CD's will contain printable lists of all experiments and supplies needed. Science for grades 4-9 will have video-supported experiments.

Tomorrow's Promise 💻
(Compass**Learning**)
$159.95 per subject per grade level except for spelling programs which are $99 each (monthly rental plan also available)

Tomorrows Promise offers core programs in reading, math, and language arts instruction with history and social studies integrated within those subject areas. Spelling is offered for only grades 1 and 2. How comprehensive coverage of the various subjects is difficult to determine. They tell us, "Compass**Learning** offers 100% objective coverage in most grades and subjects to the Jostens Learning Comprehensive Assessment Test (JCAT). JCAT is based on the core objectives of the Comprehensive Test of Basic Skills (CTBS); California Achievement Test (CAT); Iowa Test of Basic Skills (ITBS); Metropolitan Achievement Test (MAT-7); and the Stanford Achievement Test (SAT)." A Compass**Learning** representative told me that they viewed the programs as supplemental—not a complete curriculum. However, the reading program is clearly intended to be comprehensive in terms of skills taught, while language arts and math might be. History and science are integrated without serious intent to provide complete coverage. However, for K-2 these areas receive what many will consider adequate coverage within the reading program. Units at each level are divided under the headings Science, Health and Safety, Home and Neighborhood, and (except for kindergarten) Nation and the World. Once past second grade, social studies and science topics are scattered with very selective coverage of topics such as whales, dinosaurs, "The Real Yankee Doodle," and Sequoyah. Keep in mind that any curriculum presented on the computer, no matter how comprehensive it might seem, should be supplemented with "off the computer" activities and interaction.

All lessons present instruction, practice, and testing, with introductory/exploratory lessons and initial diagnosis sometimes included. Lessons vary in form of presentation, but typically, students read through instructional material, practice answering questions then take a test on that material, with tests closely resembling the practice material and format. A sound card is required since parts of the programs are presented auditorially. *Tomorrows Promise* features outstanding graphics throughout all of the programs. Animation, full-color, and variety make these programs very appealing for children. Even

if the material sometimes lacks excitement (as will happen from time to time in any course), the program design helps keep children engaged.

Tomorrows Promise goes beyond simple recall answers into challenging application and analysis questions. Additionally, the language arts program walks students through actual writing assignments, although screen boxes sometimes impose limits on sentence or paragraph length that seem unrealistic. *Tomorrows Promise* software has been created for greater learning efficiency than many other programs I have seen. Most move slowly between questions or get bogged down while cute little animated characters provide unnecessary diversion. While this sometimes happens in *Tomorrow's Promise*, especially in spelling and in younger level programs, the programs proceed at a decent pace at upper levels.

Tomorrows Promise suffers from the same limitations as do many workbooks. Some skills are taught as isolated bits of information, and it is expected that somehow they will come together into a coherent whole. While such exercises can be useful, they cannot adequately serve as a complete curriculum on their own. Recognizing such limitations, *Tomorrows Promise* solves part of the problem by building into the program integrated activities that require students to research a topic on the internet, then use that information in activities that stretch across other subject areas.

While *Tomorrows Promise* lessons appear to be comprehensive, parents must understand that children cannot learn only through these programs. For example, children must read aloud to someone as they develop their reading skills. Also, children require interaction to discuss course content, ask questions, explore topics not covered in the curriculum, and cover other aspects of learning that cannot be handled by the computer (or only by workbooks for that matter). Teacher's guides include additional activity suggestions to help meet such needs.

Tomorrow's Promise makes planning, grading, and record keeping easy by including a built-in Personal Compass. Student work is tracked with scores recorded on the appropriate lessons. Parents can quickly access student records to view their progress. Teachers Guides for each subject area and each level offer general suggestions for some activities that might be used to accomplish these goals.

Since modules can be purchased individually by subject and grade level, I will now focus on individual subject area programs.

Reading is offered for K-8. The methodology is explained in their teaching guides: "Compass**Learning** Reading 2 employs the whole language approach to reading, coordinated with skill instruction in phonics, vocabulary, and comprehension. Students are exposed to a variety of narrative and expository texts from original stories. Themes are incorporated from many areas, including anatomy, machines, geography, careers, and voting." Phonics is spread out very gradually through the program; for example, "ck" and the rules concerning the sounds of "c" and "g" are taught in second grade. The broad range of reading skills, such as main idea, cause and effect, and identifying the author's purpose, is covered fairly thoroughly. Those who want an intensive phonics foundation might use another phonics course for initial instruction, switching to *Tomorrow's Promise* once children have mastered the basics and are reading fairly well. Reading material includes selections from biographies, fantasy, humor, mysteries, poetry, history, and science, all typical of the type of material encountered in secular texts. Other, reading-related skills covered are using reference materials, graphs, and study skills.

Language Arts, offered for grades 3-8, covers mechanics and usage of language plus a few writing activities. Some thematic sections cross into social studies and science topics, but not in-depth as we find in the reading programs. As with most language arts curriculum, there is a great deal of repetition and reinforcement of the same material from level to level, with gradually increasing difficulty. Grades 7 and 8 include significantly more practice and challenge in writing assignments with modules focused on general writing skills as well as essay writing. It is possible for a student to work through a writing activity, filling in nonsense on the screen, so this area will require more oversight than do the others. The writing activities can be printed out for individual evaluation by the parent/teacher. The activities within the program do require the student to perform self-evaluation as they look for various required elements (e.g., use of particular voice, use of adverbs, introductory topic sentence), so the diligent student will have some assistance as he or she works through each lesson.

Math, offered for K-8, meets the objectives of standardized tests and is aligned with the NCTM recommendations. Because of this, math instruction, beginning in the early grades, includes a number of strands. For example, kindergarten level includes number readiness, whole number concepts, geometry, addition and subtraction of whole numbers, measurement, and statistics and probability. Fractions and money are added in first grade. A calculator tutorial first appears in third grade, although an on-screen calculator is available in earlier levels. Coverage of topics increases in level of difficulty from level to level. For example, geometry in kindergarten is merely recognition of plane figures. However, the scope and sequence is different from that encountered in traditional mathematics approaches, and parents need to check that activities are appropriate for each child. For example, in the second grade program, children encounter basic addition and subtraction facts, but then stretch to division with remainders (although this level of difficulty seems to be a solitary exception). Parents should watch for any skill instruction that seems inappropriate and have children skip those lessons. Word problems and practical applications are integrated

throughout lessons, increasingly so through the progressive levels. The seventh grade program features a large, separate section of problem solving/puzzle type activities that work particularly well to provide practice and application. While topic coverage is comprehensive, there is not enough practice on most concepts within the programs for mastery. Consequently, you should use other resources for additional practice.

Spelling differs significantly from the other *Tomorrow's Promise* programs. Available for only grades 1 and 2 at this time, the programs are more game-like than the others. Children may choose from an array of activities to learn spelling skills. Many of these are simple recognition activities rather than true spelling exercises. The words studied are drawn from the Dolch list and other most-frequently-encountered words. Grade 1 begins with short-vowel, three-letter words, progressing to more-complex words. Common word elements are emphasized in each lesson's group of 10 words, although all phonetic elements in each of those words have not been taught. For example "br" words include "brown," "brick," and "broom" although not direct instruction has been given on the "ow", "ck", and "oo" elements. Teachers can customize and/or assign word lists to students. Companion workbooks for each level provide actual writing practice, although they, too, rely more on recognition skills than actual spelling mastery. Workbook pages are grouped to correlate with word list groups in the program, but it is up to the parent to determine which pages to use.

Animals living at Farnsworth Farm provide entertainment, instruction, and feedback throughout the program, and this is a very entertaining program that children will love. Activities are divided into three areas: the farm itself with 14 different readiness, practice, and extension activities; the West Field with games; and the East Field with assessment. Students must earn at least 25 ears of corn in the farm activities before they will be allowed to play games in the West Field. Assessment activities (spelling bee, pretests, and posttests) can be accessed at any time. While the spelling programs are extremely well done, I wish there were less recognition and more true spelling activity.

System requirements are fairly demanding for these programs. They will run on either Windows 3.11 (or higher) or Macintosh platforms. Macintosh computers must be 68040/40 or higher and system 7.1 or later. PC systems must be 486 DX or higher. While a 2x CD drive will work, a faster drive will be much better. You will also need 8MB of available RAM and 5MB disk space (10 MB for spelling programs). These are very complex programs and speed will be an important issue if you desire education efficiency. Consequently, I recommend using these on systems that exceed the minimum requirements if at all possible.(SE)

Chapter 6

Bible

In the subject area called "Bible" many of us are concerned about finding the most effective way of teaching the material. We often forget that we already have the best textbook available, the Bible, and try to improve on it unnecessarily. This is not a criticism of Bible curriculum materials. These can be valuable assets for exploring and applying what has already been learned. But we often would do better to use the Bible, in an appropriate version for whatever age level we are dealing with, as our primary textbook for learning about God and things of God. As in other areas of our lives, we often reject the simple and obvious methods and go after the complicated and less effective.

[Note: While some families will choose to use Bible versions written especially for children or in easier language, choosing to use the KJV or another adult version provides a consistency for Bible memory as well as fodder for vocabulary lessons.]

I strongly recommend reading through the entire Bible, front to back, possibly skipping a few sections here and there. This gives children the big picture of God's relationship with man. They learn to know God through his love, mercy, and justice. It's hard to get this sort of foundational understanding by reading only snatches of stories from Genesis, Esther, Kings, Samuel, and the Gospels. Reading of isolated stories and passages is certainly worthwhile, but it's sort of like watching only selected scenes from a movie—you might learn an object lesson here and there, but you miss the plot.

The key ideas conveyed within Scripture really do evolve in a logical story line for the most part.

1.) Who God is: Reading through the Old Testament you learn God's character, His love, mercy, patience, judgment, direction, and so on. (Genesis, Exodus, Deuteronomy, Joshua, although not to the exclusion of other books of the Bible)

2.) Who we are in relation to God: His unconditional love, His sacrifice for us, redemption, our sinfulness, our need for salvation and an ongoing relationship. (Judges, Samuel, Kings, Chronicles, Job, Prophets, Gospels)

3.) Our relationship to God: How we relate to God through prayer, worship, thanksgiving, songs, intercession, as friends, and as children, always seeking His direction. (Numbers, Deuteronomy, Psalms, Gospels, and Epistles)

4.) How God works in our lives: Fitting us for His service; molding us as the potter molds the clay. (Gospels and Epistles, also going back to the Old Testament to see how God fitted His servants for service)

5.) How we relate to the world and those around us: The Church, believers and non-believers, relationships, marriage, and family. (Gospels, Acts, Epistles and Proverbs)

6.) Future things: prophecy of things to come and our eternity with God and the family of believers. (Revelation, Daniel, Ezekiel)

I believe that familiarity with the Bible is essential as a foundation upon which we can build other knowledge. As we view things around us in light of God's plan and perspective, we see how it all fits together—we make sense of the world. We should spend much time discussing and tieing other subject areas into what we have learned from the Bible. Remember that "Bible" should not be an isolated subject but an integral part of our daily lives (Deuteronomy 6:6,7).

Now, on to more mundane, practical issues like which version of the Bible to use. Most of us are aware that translations vary in their accuracy. Yet, some of the "looser" translations are much more understandable, especially for the Old Testament. The *Living Bible* and *The Child's Story Bible* by Catherine Vos (William B. Eerdmans Publishing Co.) are two such translations I recommend for use with young children. *The Child's Story Bible* omits much of the detailed information, such as in Numbers, and sexual references that would be beyond a young child. It still remains quite true to the original, adding occasional background information for clarity.

Regarding Scripture memorization, memorize from the version you prefer, but if you use King James, make sure children understand what they are memorizing. (Explain to them the meaning of "thee," "thou," "ye," etc.) The *Living Bible* and other story Bibles are not generally appropriate for memorization because the wording is so different.

If you have "antsy" children who find Bible reading boring, try to add some multi-sensory activities. Try using the Family Worship Set Bible felt figures (by Betty Lukens or Little Folk Visuals) for children to arrange as you read a story from the Bible, or have your children draw a picture illustrating Scripture that is being read. The beauty of using the felt figures is that all ages can be involved together, and the excellent visual aids bring the stories to life. Drawing their own pictures encourages children to think about the Scripture and translate it into something concrete. The *Family Worship Set* comes in an economy set with all of the felt figures for $16.95 or a deluxe version that includes a board and filing system for $35.95. Since there are many figures in the set, I highly recommend the deluxe system so your figures will be easy to find and use. Maps, charts, timelines, coloring books, audio tapes, and other resources can also help stimulate and maintain interest.

It is important that our Bible study be part of our family life. There are numerous resources available to help us go further in depth with our study, many of which can easily be used by a father with little or no preparation time. Leading family Bible study is the ideal place for fathers to be involved with teaching their children.

Following are reviews for many resources that might be used for family time and/or as part of our educational program.

Family Time and Supplemental Resources

Adam and His Kin
by Ruth Beechick
(Mott Media) $9

Dr. Beechick has extended her imagination beyond the boundaries of Scripture to flesh out the Old Testament Bible stories in Genesis 1-11. She tries to stick carefully to the implications of Scripture, but adds color and interest to help us imagine the thoughts, feelings, and struggles of our Biblical ancestors. Dr. Beechick's research in astronomy, archaeology, and other scientific areas adds to the book's credibility. This is a good choice for a read-together book for those with children from about ages four through ten.

Adventure Bible Handbook
(Zondervan House)
$16.99

Every child needs to know about the Bible. Teaching the Bible to a seven-year-old is a complicated task. It might become confusing for some children. The *Adventure Bible Handbook* does an excellent job of explaining many parts of the Bible. Funny cartoon characters journey through the Bible with you to help you understand it. This book covers topics such as the Israelites in the Wilderness, Joseph in Slavery, the Tower of Babel, John the Baptist, Saul's Conversion, the Last Supper, and numerous others. Besides all of this, it explains other important things about the Bible. It addresses questions such as what the Bible is, where it came from, what it means to believe in God, why Jesus had to die on the cross, and more to help your child understand his Christian faith. [Matt Duffy]

The Amazing Book [video cassette tape] 📼
(Bridgestone Multimedia)
$9.95

The creators of *The Music Machine* and *Bullfrogs and Butterflies* have applied their talents to instruction about the Bible with great success. Cute cartoon characters, Doc Dickory and Dewey Decimole, help energetic young Revver to learn about the most amazing book ever written. Catchy songs serve up the information in such an entertaining way that your children will be singing the names of the books of the Bible after seeing and listening to this tape only once or twice. *The Amazing Book* is recommended for ages two through ten, but home schooled children do not seem to outgrow childhood as quickly as others. At ages twelve and fourteen, our boys still enjoyed Mary Poppins and thought The Amazing Book was okay, so I would guess that other older home educated children might not mind watching it along with their younger brothers and sisters.

Bible Builder [computer game for IBM compatibles]
(Bridgestone Multimedia Group)
$12.95

Everbright Software produces a Bible study game called *Bible Builder*, which is distributed by Bridgestone Multimedia Group. This game mixes the fun of a regular video game and Bible knowledge. Younger players should be able to read and have some knowledge of the Bible, although it is recommended for ages 7 to adult. As you play this game you learn about verses from the Bible, when different Biblical events took place in history, the Ten Commandments, locations of Biblical cities, and different hymns which you might sing in church. There are several types of questions you might get to answer. In some you have to tell what happened in a particular part of the Bible using multiple choice answers, while in others you identify verses.

As you play this game you are assisted by the angel Michael. He helps you understand the Bible. Also, to help you understand it better, there are animated scenes and extra notes that add interesting facts to your game. You can play this game at several levels of knowledge. Some of the questions repeat frequently throughout the game but I consider this helpful. Answering the same questions a few times will help increase retention of information. This game comes with a NIV Bible to assist you when you play.

The program comes on a CD, and a sound card is recommended to enjoy the digitized sound effects. [Matt Duffy]

Bible Maps & Charts

(Beacon Hill Press)

$14.99

This set of 8 maps and 10 charts makes great visual aids for Bible study. It's especially useful for larger families when you need map illustrations larger than those in the back of your Bible. Full-color charts and maps are printed on both sides of sturdy, heavy-duty poster paper. All but one are approximately 22" x 17". The *Old Testament Time Line/Life of Christ Time Line* is almost twice as long. Maps are similar to those you find in the back of many Bibles. Among the charts are *Old Testament* and *New Testament Book Groupings, The Kingdom Period,* and *Exile and Return.* These and other charts primarily show relationships between events and chronologies. The set includes a booklet with reproductions of the charts and an index to people and places on the charts.

Big Book of Books and Activities, Religious Supplements: Old Testament and New Testament

by Dinah Zike

(Dinah-Might Activities)

$12.95 each

Dinah Zike has created two craft books, one for the Old Testament and one for the New Testament. We photocopy the pages in this book, then cut and paste them to make dioramas, mobiles, unique picture books, and other unusual teaching aids. We can do these ourselves and use them to illustrate Bible stories, or children can make them. I would guess that children should be about age seven or eight for these projects because of small, accurate cutting required on many projects. Activities are similar to those found in some Sunday school curricula, although they range from quick and simple to time consuming and involved. If you are teaching straight from the Bible or using a book-only curricula, these make good supplements for adding an arts-and-crafts dimension.

Butler's Lives of the Saints [CD-ROM]

(Harmony Media, Inc.)

$29.95

This CD-ROM runs on either Windows or Macintosh systems. It includes the entire four-volume *Butler's Lives of the Saints* plus *A History of Christianity* by Paul Johnson, *Saints and Heroes Speak* by Fr. Robert J. Fox, meditations/devotionals, and cross references through a calendar, lists of patron saints, popular saints, historical figures, an historical timeline, and numerous indexes. The *Butler's Lives* volumes feature brief, easy-to-read biographical sketches. Unlike Butler's volumes, *Saints and Heroes Speak* is not organized according to the calendar, but, instead features lengthier biog-

raphies on fewer, selected saints. Told in first person style, each is followed by discussion questions and an activity suggestion. Background music and occasional illustrations add multi-sensory appeal.

Captain Bible in Dome of Darkness

([computer game for IBM compatibles] (Bridgestone Multimedia Group)

$12.95

When parents mention memorizing Bible verses to their kids, a common attitude is, "But Mom, they're so boring." If you have not yet found a way to make learning Bible verses interesting, here it is: *Captain Bible in Dome of Darkness.* It takes the fun of a computer game, then combines it with Bible verses and a way to understand and apply them in a game which can be played by anyone.

The story is that the enemy has taken over part of the city called the Dome of Darkness. This tower is deceiving people into believing God doesn't love them and that He is not real. You, with your Bible, will have to travel through levels, find these people, and set them straight with the Word of God, teaching and converting them. (Great practice for witnessing!) The people are then used to help you run a large robot which will destroy the Dome of Darkness, set the people onto the right path following God, and help you win the game.

Throughout your journey robots will try to convince you the Bible is wrong. You must use the Bible to prove they are lying by picking verses which contradict what they say. Then you fight the robots. The combat option may be turned off if parents choose. (The combat makes it more like a regular video game, but this is not a major element.) Full color, animated graphics and sound make this game entertaining.

We can choose from King James, New International, Revised Standard, and Living Bible translations for the verses, all within the single program. This game uses complete rather than abbreviated verses. There are three levels of difficulty, but the difficulty is in the game rather than the Bible verses. I would recommend using this game for ages 7 and up.

The program comes on a CD and a sound card is recommended to enjoy the digitized sound effects.[Matt Duffy]

Celebrate the Feasts of the Old Testament in Your Own Home or Church

by Martha Zimmerman

(Bethany House)

$8.99

This is a great resource for Christians who wish to celebrate the Old Testament feasts. Chapters on the Sabbath, Passover, Festival of the First Fruits, Rosh Hashanah, Yom Kippur, and Sukkoth provide Scriptural and cultural background and practical guidelines for celebrating the feasts in our homes. The feasts are for the entire family, so all ages can get involved in activities, crafts, and food preparation as well as the ceremonies. Zimmerman even provides scripts for us to follow and recipes for the foods to prepare. This is a beautiful way to teach our children the symbolism and fulfillment of the Old Testament feasts.

Character Building For Families, Volumes 1 and 2

by Lee Ann Rubsam
(Full Gospel Family Publications)
$13 each or $25 for both purchased together

Volume 1 of *Character Building for Families* is a terrific Bible Study and character training program for the whole family. It might be used for "school" or for family devotion time with little ones as young as three or four years old up through ages eleven or twelve. (Teens should have already studied and learned most of this.) It features detailed, daily lessons for one school year in the character traits of obedience, orderliness, diligence, loyalty, deference, cheerfulness, gentleness, contentment, gratitude, truthfulness, service, and hospitality. The number of lessons devoted to each trait varies. Some lessons might be completed in as little as ten minutes, but most should take about twenty minutes or a little longer. Each lesson should ideally be done by the entire family together, although Mom might lead it if Dad is unavailable. Each lesson directs us in Scripture reading, discussion, and prayer. Typical is an obedience lesson that begins with memorization of Philippians 4:13 and Luke 22: 42b. Next, we read John 8: 28, 29. This is followed by questions: "Who was directing Jesus' life and actions?" and "What did Jesus say about His obedience to His Father?" These questions are followed by statements we can read or restate: "We should make it our goal to let our lives be guided by the Holy Spirit, as Jesus did. We should want to always please the Father, too." After this, we read Mark 14:36 and "review what is happening in this verse." The lesson continues in this vein through one more Scripture passage and some discussion, ending with prayer. Answers to questions are shown in parentheses when appropriate. Lessons often deal with practical application such as a lesson that stresses practicing kindness with our tongues to other family members. I appreciate the occasional reminders to review a basic concept and reinforce memory verses and principles. An unusual feature of this program is the inclusion of Mom and Dad in the study. For example, parents' responsibility before God is mentioned frequently, and suggested prayers are often for the entire family to grow in Godly character rather than just children. I like the "real family" feel of this program. Too often in other programs, scripted questions sound phony and cannot be used without rephrasing them, but in this case the questions sound natural and can be used as is. The mix of Bible reading, memorization, discussion, and prayer is just right to keep the atten-

tion of wiggly young ones and impatient older ones. Well, we might lose the preschoolers after five minutes, but this is one of the most practical and worthwhile no-frills programs for Bible study or family devotions I have seen.

Volume 2 is similar in format to Volume 1. It is divided into five units: stewardship, teachableness, mercy, patience, and desire for Jesus. Volume 1 should be completed before moving on to Volume 2.

Character Sketches [Three volumes]

(Advanced Training Institute International)
$39 per volume; three volume set - $105

Scriptural character traits are exhibited either positively or negatively in nature stories. Sometimes a dramatic animal story presents a moral lesson, a la Aesop's fables. A Bible story relating to the same character trait is introduced with a question that helps tune children in to the story. Detailed background information with illustrations on both the animal and the Bible story are included, but can be used as much as is appropriate for the age levels of our children. Because of the wealth of science-related information, I have also listed these books as science resources. They are a good investment for your family library.

Child's Story Bible

by Catherine Vos (Wm. B. Eerdmans Publishing Co.) $25

This is one of the few Bible story books directed to children that is true to the Bible in format and content. It retells the Bible in language children understand but edits parts that are beyond the range of a child's experience. Children can understand the "big picture" of God's plan by hearing almost all of His Word in context rather than in the isolated Bible stories that are usually offered to children. You might want to also use felt figures to make the stories come alive as you read.

Everyday Life in Bible Times

by Arthur W. Klinck and Erich H. Kiehl
(Concordia Publishing House)
$9.99

The whole family will enjoy this book on life in Bible times. The authors examine occupations, agriculture, vineyards and orchards, food and drink, homes and their furnishings, trades carried on in both homes and shops, arts and sciences, travel, trade, commerce, social customs, and family life. Instead of brief dictionary-style entries, each topic is allotted enough space to include details that will hold the interest of both children and adults. It is interesting enough to read straight through, or you can use it as a reference book. If you read it straight through, you can use the discussion questions as the end of each chapter. Either way, you might want to try some of the research and hands-on activities also found at the ends of chapters.

Facts in Acts
(Creative Teaching Associates)
$8.95

These four-sided "dominoes" work just like the other great *Match Wits* games from CTA. *Facts in Acts* uses people and places from the book of Acts to create information match-up challenges. For example, on one of the four sides of one domino it might say, "A centurion who lived in Caesarea," and it needs to be connected with another domino with the name "Cornelius." There are four possibilities on each domino, and part of the challenge is to connect more than one of the facts when you place your domino. Point values are shown on each domino. And they are totaled according to the number of connected facts. There are two sets of 30 dominoes each. One deals with people and the other with places. This is a great way to reinforce Bible knowledge. (A "Reference Sheet" is included if we need help verifying answers. Suggested for ages 10 and up.

A Family Guide to the Biblical Holidays
by Robin Scarlata Sampson
(Heart of Wisdom)
$39.95

This 600+ page volume is an activity-based approach to learning about Biblical holidays that is designed for the entire family. It can be used as a home school curriculum for an entire year or only for certain seasons (instructions for these options are included). It also includes instructions for use in Bible study groups, church groups, Sunday or Sabbath schools, and co-op groups. There is a special home school section at the back of the book that outlines nine thematic unit studies incorporating activities for literature, writing, history, geography, art, science, and the use of library resources.

The first section of the book is overview, background, and historical study of the Hebrew roots of the feasts. This section also includes crafts and activities that might be used for any one or more of the feasts. Next, are sections on each of the feasts: Passover, Unleavened Bread, First Fruits, Weeks, Trumpets, the Day of Atonement, Tabernacles, Hanukkah, and Purim. Sabbath celebration is then presented as a weekly feast.

Each of the Biblical feasts from the Old Testament is examined for historical and spiritual significance. Original Jewish customs are described. Charts are used for such things as comparing aspects of each feast's observance in one column with the Messianic significance in a second column. Next, are extensive suggestions and instructions for conducting your own celebration of the feast, including recipes. Reproducible

activity pages are appropriate for elementary grade children. As part of your curriculum, this will primarily be a Bible curriculum, serving supplementally for all other subject areas. This is wonderful for whole family participation or even combining with other families to share the celebrations.

Dozens of excerpts can be viewed at http://biblicalholidays.com.

For Instruction in Righteousness: A Topical Reference Guide for Biblical Child-Training
by Pam Forster
(Doorposts)
$25 spiralbound; $27 looseleaf binder

This 300+ page book can be used in a number of ways. It can be the foundation for unit studies on character traits. We might incorporate it into other unit studies, especially those dealing with character traits such as *KONOS* or *Developing Godly Character in Children*. It might serve as a reference when we deal with character issues in our children.

The book is organized into eight main sections dealing with character defects or sins: Sins of a Proud Heart, Sins of Discontent, Sins of Unbelief, Sins of an Undisciplined Life, Sins of the Tongue, Sins of an Unloving Heart, Sins in Relationships, and Comparisons of the Obedient and the Disobedient. Under each section we find such topics as pride, hypocrisy, defiance, vanity, covetousness, fear, laziness, haste, gluttony, immodesty, gossip, flattery, poor manners, and bad friendships. Under each topic we find Bible references with summarized descriptions. The next section suggests what happens or what should happen to persons committing the sin, usually followed by a suggestion for an object lesson. For example, according to Titus 3:9 we should avoid the contentious person, so the suggested object lesson is to isolate the arguing child or to disallow friendships with contentious children. These object lessons help us apply Biblical discipline related directly to Scripture. The next section tells us to what each sin is likened [e.g., envy and jealousy are cruel as the grave (Song of Solomon 8:6)]. Following this is a list of Bible stories illustrating the consequences of the sin with the references and a brief summary. Finally, there is a list of Bible stories illustrating the opposite character trait plus verses to memorize (either KJV or NKJV). At the beginning of the book is a great section on Biblical teaching techniques which discusses object lessons, parables, proverbs, stories, songs, history, memorials and celebrations, and covenants. The entire approach is solidly Biblical with a very literal perspective for the most part. We might easily overwhelm both our children and ourselves if we try to tackle too much of this too quickly. It is a terrific resource for instituting Godly rather than arbitrary discipline, but use it with prayer and selectivity. It's available in either spiralbound or looseleaf binder format. [Valerie Thorpe/C.D.]

The Game of Pilgrim's Progress

(Cactus Game Design)
$24.99

The Game of Pilgrim's Progress, a high-quality board game based on Bunyan's spiritual classic, was created to provide entertainment that encourages Christian families to spend time and grow spiritually together. Players move their pieces (tiny pilgrims with detachable burdens) around a large, complex path. Two different dice control the moves, and at various points the player can obtain cards such as "The Armor of God" and "Forgiveness" to help him through the obstacles of the game. Each player must land on one of several "cross" squares to be released from his burden and eventually be able to enter the Celestial City.

The game is competitive, rather than cooperative, unless players choose to allow the option of sharing their Prayer, God's Guidance, and Encouragement cards. There are enough pitfalls and complications that a player might surge ahead in the beginning but become bogged down enough that another can win. The game follows the narrative of the book very closely, but the element of luck that the developers have introduced assures that the game is not merely a reiteration of the book. It would be fun to play the game while reading the book as a family.

The entire game "package" is very professionally presented, and the instructions are well-written and printed in booklet form. This is a high-quality game that many ages can enjoy playing together (not much reading is required), in addition to being one that will help children learn spiritual truths. [Kath Courtney]

GENESIS, Finding Our Roots

by Dr. Ruth Beechick
(Mott Media)
$17.50

This unusual book defies classification. It is primarily a unit-study-style theological study, but it also covers a good deal of science, history, geography, literature, art, and linguistics. It consists of six units, all based on the book of Genesis, plus appendices. The six units are entitled, "God's Book of Creation," "Book of Adam," "Book of Noah," "Book of the Sons of Noah," "Book of Shem," and "Book of Terah." Each unit begins with Scripture and Scripture study. Following next are a series of topical studies. For example, in the first unit on creation some of the topics addressed are dragons, "day," the origin of the week, and creation myths for comparisons. Short readings from other sources are often included, such as selections from two unbiblical "creation" myths. A final section offers suggestions for further study: correlated readings that fit

in directly with the study (primarily from *Adam and His Kin* by Ruth Beechick and *The Genesis Record* by Henry Morris), science text topics to look for to expand knowledge, other topical areas for further reading, and writing assignments. Questions and activities are interspersed throughout each unit; they vary in difficulty from simple to challenging so we can select those that are appropriate for each of our children. Some will require outside reading and research and will clearly be best suited for older students. The KJV is used throughout, although we can substitute another version if we prefer. The perspective is that of a literal interpretation of the Bible, supporting a young earth. There might be areas where you might hold a different viewpoint. Some might be major (e.g., the age of the earth and length of each of the days of creation) and some might be less crucial (e.g., in talking about the writing of Chapter 1 of the book of Genesis, she states that God either wrote the words Himself or told Adam the words to write). Throughout the study, Dr. Beechick brings out the importance of developing a Biblical Christian worldview.

This is a hardcover book, only about 112 pages in length, so it should take less than a semester to complete. It should work best for family Bible study time, perhaps led by Dad, with Mom then incorporating much of the extended topical studies into school time. The book is heavily illustrated and nicely formatted.

How the Bible Came to Us

by Meryl Doney
(Lion Publishing)
$13.95

This book traces the history of the "Book That Changed the World" in a colorful format with lots of pictures and graphics. The book was written for elementary levels, but all ages would find it interesting.

Leading Little Ones to God

by Marion Schoolland (Wm. B. Eerdmans Publishing Co.)
$18

This is a classic Protestant book for teaching children about God. Written in a devotional format, it talks about who God is, what He does, sin, Christ's work, the Holy Spirit, the Christian life, prayer, and the church. It is written in a conversational style to children and has full-color illustrations.

Learning for Life Series Family Activity Books

by Rick Osborne and others
(Moody Press)
$9.99 each

This series is based on the idea that teaching children about God and the Bible does not happen only during scheduled lessons but should be a part of our activities all day long. In order to prepare parents to do this, these 110-page large format paperbacks give background information, Bible verses, trivia questions, and ideas for working mini-lessons into everyday life. Scripture is taken from the New International Readers' Version, but you could easily substitute another translation if you prefer. Cheerful, multi-cultural drawings by Ken Save add interest and humor.

Your Child and The Bible gives an overview of the Bible: the way it is put together, the types of literature represented, and the history of its development into the form we know today. Also given are two summaries of the entire Bible story; one, a short version for younger children and the other a little longer. If you feel a little shaky in your knowledge of the Bible or have trouble simplifying your knowledge enough to teach children, this book should help give you the confidence you need. It also presents factors to consider when choosing a Bible for your child and three age-appropriate reading plans to guide your children through the most significant and interesting parts of the Bible story (and keep them from getting bogged down and discouraged halfway through Leviticus.)

Your Child and the Christian Life covers a variety of basic subjects such as salvation, prayer, obedience, stewardship (including budget ideas), relationships, and witnessing. Since a big part of teaching is living and modeling the Christian life, be prepared for a commitment rather than a lesson plan. [V. Thorpe]

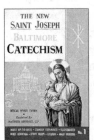

The New Saint Joseph Baltimore Catechism No. 1, No. 2, and First Communion Catechism
by Father Lovasik
(Catholic Book Publishing Co.)
No. 1 - $2.75; No. 2 - $3.25; First Communion - $2.25

Don't let the inexpensive price on these books fool you. These catechisms are worth their weight in gold. Based on the Baltimore Catechism which was first approved by the Archbishop of Baltimore, James Cardinal Gibbons, in 1885, these books are inviting with their illustrations and easy-to-use format. The New Saint Joseph version goes beyond the simple question-and-answer format of the original catechism. It incorporates Holy Scripture with each lesson and includes discussion questions, a fill-in-the-blank section, and suggested Bible readings at the end of each lesson. The pictures themselves are great teaching tools as they illustrate spiritual truths.

Memorizing the questions and answers of the catechism provides the opportunity to build a religious foundation. This basic Catholic doctrinal foundation gives children the tools necessary to defend their faith when they are old enough to apply reason and logic (much like memorizing the alphabet before learning to read and analyze literature).

In addition to memorization of the question and answers, I copy the accompanying Scripture on 3" x 5" cards. The children and I memorize the Scripture verses, then discuss how it applies to the week's lesson. I am careful to emphasize the Scripture as a part of a whole picture rather than putting too much weight on individual verses. We review the Q&A and Scripture each day for a week, before moving on to the next lesson.

First Communion Catechism (65 pages) - This is a simple book to be used in the child's First Communion year (usually 2nd grade). It emphasizes Jesus in the Eucharist and the sacrament of Reconciliation. There are discussion questions at the end of each of the 11 lessons, but the fill-in-the-blank and Scripture references are not included in this book as they are in books No. 1 and No. 2. The book begins with prayers for everyday and ends with an explanation of the Holy Mass.

No. 1 - The Baltimore questions and answers are divided into three parts: The Creed, The Commandments, and The Sacraments and Prayer. Usually used in grades 3 to 5. 192 pages.

No. 2 - Has the same division and order as book No. 1, but the lessons are more in-depth for the older student. Usually used in grades 6 to 8. 264 pages. [Maureen Wittmann]

Pearables
(Pearables)
$15 per volume

The *Pearables* are character-building stories told in parables. Most of them follow a "king and kingdom" format, beginning with introductions such as, "There was once a mighty King who ruled over all the land as far as the eye could see." Each story goes on to address an important teaching about faith and character. Examples of titles: "The Viewing Box" (about entertainment and television), "The Governor's Plot" (about homeschooling), "The Beauty" (about inner and outer beauty), and the self explanatory titles "Faith," "Patience," and "Brotherly Kindness." Biblical applications and verses are at the end of each story. Delightful black-and-white illustrations create storybook appeal. Each story is about 20 pages in length, so we can read through a story in a single sitting or spread it out into two or three sessions for younger children. Stories are presented in three volumes, with 8 stories per volume.

Proverbs for Parenting: A Topical Guide for Child Raising from the Book of Proverbs
(Lynn's Bookshelf)
$15.95; coloring books individually - $2.50 for 1, $1.75 each for 2 or more; book plus coloring book set - $16.95

Proverbs, in KJV and NIV, are arranged topically under Reverence for God, Obedience, Self-Control, Work, etc. When your child needs help in a certain area, turn to this book for help in finding applicable Proverbs. With this book as a tool, you can explain to your child how God wants him to act and why. The book is beautifully bound in hardcover. *A Coloring Book of Bible Proverbs* and *A Coloring Book of Bible Verses from the Epistles* (in both KJV and NIV) are also available from the same source.

Science and the Bible; 30 Scientific Demonstrations Illustrating Scriptural Truths, volumes 1 and 2

by Donald B. DeYoung
(Baker Book House)
$8.99 each

Any of 30 short and simple science demonstrations from each of these books can be used as "hooks" to lead into Bible lessons for a group (family, Sunday school class, etc.). Emphasis is primarily upon Bible truths rather than scientific knowledge, although scientific explanations are given. These books can be used with various age groups since object lessons such as these interest just about everyone. Information for the actual Bible truth presentation is offered, but it will be up to the presenter/teacher to determine the best way to do that. This is a great tool for dads to use for family devotion time. [Valerie Thorpe/C.D.]

Searching for Treasure: A Guide to Wisdom and Character Development

by Marty Elwell
(Noble Books)
$19.95

Scripture is the most powerful character changing "resource" available to us, and this guide offers a simple, effective arrangement of Scriptural studies on character traits.

Study is divided into seven major themes (understanding wisdom, developing right relationships, controlling yourself, controlling what you say, avoiding the way of the wicked, and following the way of the righteous), with each theme then divided into three or four, week-long units (for a total of 20 lessons). Daily lessons are fairly brief—the introductory lesson for each week will probably take more time than each daily lesson. The introduction opens with discussion questions leading up to the Scripture reading, then follows up with more discussion questions, prayer suggestions and the key verse for the week. Delightful line-drawing illustrations of the Scripture reading can be reproduced for coloring. The next four days, we delve into specific aspects of wisdom relating to the week's topic with Scripture reading and discussion questions. For example, the first week's lesson asks questions such as, "How would you define wisdom?" On the second day, we read Proverbs 1:1-9, then answer from Scripture four questions: "How does wisdom help us?", "What is called the beginning of wisdom?", "What is it that fools despise?", and "What persons should you listen to?" An additional, optional memory

verse is given for each day. A sixth day can be used to do the summary for the week-long lesson, or it can be squeezed into the weekday studies. Lessons can be used on different levels depending upon the ages of children. Younger children can color pictures, listen to the Scripture readings, and learn simplified versions of the memory verse(s). Older children can participate at whatever level beyond that which is appropriate for them. At the end of each week's lesson are "Questions for parents" that help us reflect on our example and child training methods as well as upon our children's spiritual growth. The appendices are essential to the program since they contain both a craft and a game activity to accompany each week's lesson, suggestions for organizing a family night where you might use the activity ideas, memory verse cards printed on card stock, and a fold-out board game designed to reinforce both memory verses and Scriptural principles. The whole idea of this book is simple, but effective and fun.

Teaching Bible History to Children (of All Ages) series

by Kathryn L. Merrill and Kristy L. Christian
(Infinite Discovery Inc.)

In Jesus' Time (published by Rainbow Books, Inc. but can be ordered from Infinite Discovery) [$16.95], *Moses and the Law, Paul and Early Christianity Volume I*, and *Paul and Early Christianity Volume II* [the last three - $19.95 each] are the first four titles in a projected series of ten books. Other titles to be published are *How the Bible Began, The Patriarchs, David: From Shepherd Boy to King, Women in the Bible, Prophets and Prophecy, Healings in the Bible*, and *Letters to the Seven Churches in Asia*. The books are non-denominational Bible history study tools that can be used over a wide age span. Children (beginning at about fourth/fifth grade level) can participate in reading, listening, and discussing Scripture and historical events. Many activities involve interpretation and analysis appropriate for students junior high and high school level, so we must choose how far to take each lesson with each child. One book is needed for any size family or group. Instruction is presented by the parent/teacher, with students using Bibles, a concordance, and activity pages (reproduced from the book) to work on lessons. Older children can do most of their study independently. Some supplementary books are recommended, but a Bible and concordance are the mainstays. Many activities involve the use of charts (from the book) which are filled in as children learn about various topics. This method makes the book particularly age-adaptable since younger children might fill in a word or two while an older child might write more detailed information. Detailed maps are included for study and activities along with flash cards, memory verses, crossword puzzles, and other learning tools. Even with the inclusion of these "extras," this is not typical busy-work Bible curriculum but in-depth study of both Bible history and Bible content. The authors do a fairly good job of keeping the study non-denominational, yet occasional glimpses of theological interpretations peek through from time to time. Because the books are strongly research-based, extensive bibliographies appear at the back. Helpful glossaries are also found there. *In Jesus' Time* has 20 lessons while *Moses and the Law* has 16. The authors suggest that each lesson take about one hour; however, it appears to me that some of these lessons could easily take more than twice the suggested time. If using the books for daily lessons, I would plan to spend about two months per book rather than one. The print and paper quality of the books is excellent, a helpful factor since all work pages and maps have to be reproduced. This resource helps us study Bible history beyond what we find in most curriculum written for students below high school level.

Treasury of Bible Subjects

(Rod and Staff)
$8.05

This *Treasury* presents Scriptural references, arranged topically, to fit in with typical school topics. It serves as a resource to help us connect learning in other subject areas with God's Word. Included are suggestions for the teacher on presentation methods.

Vision Book series

(Ignatius Press)
$9.95 each; any 3 for $25: 6 for $45; all 16 for $119

This is a wonderful series for Catholic children about saints and spiritual heroes. Among the seventeen titles in the series are *The Curé of Ars, St. Dominic and the Rosary, Edmund Campion, Francis and Clare: Saints of Assisi*, and *St. Pius X*. They span a broad historical and geographical range. Each story is an "expanded" biography, based upon historical fact. They should be especially good for family read aloud with children in the elementary grades. Books such as these provide marvelous examples of "living Christianity" to inspire our children.

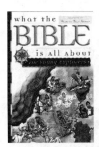

What the Bible is All About for Young Explorers

(Regal Books)
$10.99 pb; $15.99 hc

This overview of the Bible is geared for upper elementary and junior high but is still interesting for adults. Maps, charts, plenty of illustrations, background information, chapter summaries, and archaeological information provide either an excellent introduction or a foundation for in-depth study of the Bible. *How the Bible Came to Us* would be better for younger children, this book for older children.

Wise Words: Family Stories that Bring the Proverbs to Life

by Peter Leithart
(Great Christian Books/Full Quart Press)
$9.99

At first glance, this appears to be a collection of 18 fairy tales. But closer inspection reveals fairy tales unlike those of the "Grimm" tradition because they draw upon Biblical stories and proverbs for themes, plots, characters, and principles. However, none of the stories seem to be clear allegories for any single Bible story, but rather a mixture of many. For example, in the story "Ivy and the Prince," Ivy is first lured into forbidden territory (parallels with Eve) by a rabbit which is transformed into a dragon as soon as both step past the dividing thicket. Ivy is rescued by a handsome young prince who kills the dragon. The prince leaves her with a token but returns to his golden castle in the clouds. No one knows when he will return. The story proceeds through mixed metaphors about the prince knocking at the door, having oil in their lamps, and the prince's eventual, abrupt arrival and rescue of Ivy. The publisher suggests the book for children ages five to twelve, but I have reservations about the ability of children to sort out the metaphors without becoming thoroughly confused about the original Bible stories and their meanings. On the other hand, these stories are thoroughly enjoyable and offer wonderful opportunities for unraveling Biblical analogies for those willing to take the time. I would recommend reading and discussing them with older children, perhaps up through the teen years.

Your Story Hour [audio cassettes] ⌒

12-tape albums - $43.50; Great New Stories - $21.50 each; Acts of the Apostles - $28.50; Bible series - $210

Your Story Hour features dramatized Bible and character-building stories, as well as biographies of famous Godly people, on audio cassettes. Christian values are presented through all of these stories, and children will listen to these tapes over and over again. (All of these tapes are from the popular series of radio programs which has been on the air since 1949.) The above stories are offered in albums of twelve tapes each. There are eleven such albums to choose from. *Great New Stories*, Volumes 1, 2 and 3, are six-tape albums of new stories. *Acts of the Apostles* is an eight-tape set about the lives of the apostles. *The Bible* series is a five-album dramatized retelling of the Bible.

Bible Memory

Bible Memory "Review" Cards

(Bealls' Learning Games)
$5.95

These index cards are great for helping children review

Bible verses. They have a picture of a Bible with a blank banner on one side and an open Bible with lines for writing verses on the reverse. Children can color these with crayons or felt pens and write the "address" for the verse on the banner. Store the cards in a file box and keep them handy. There are 50 cards in the pack, tips on how to use them, and a card listing Old and New Testament books.

Bible Memory by Memlok

(Bible Memory by Memlok)
traditional card set - $49.95; PC Memlok - $59.95

Memlok was one of the first Bible memory programs to use rebus-type visual cues as an aid to Scripture memorization. Visual clues on memory verse cards illustrate beginning or key words of verses to act as memory cues. Some of the clues are silly, some stretch for the connection, some are great; but the overall idea is that by establishing a visual connection for each verse, the verses (with references) are recalled much more easily. Verses are arranged under 48 topics, with over 700 verses on 550 cards (the size of a business card) included. We learn the verses under whichever topic we choose. The verses are stored in the clear, plastic cardholders for review. The visual clues are all incorporated onto one summary card, providing another memory device to recall related verses.

Memlok should work for all ages, although older family members will have to help non-readers with beginning memorization until the clues are easily recalled. The entire family can share one *Memlok* book (an 8 1/2" X 11" spiral notebook) by having each member choose a different topic to work on or by keeping memory verse cards in a central location in the home. There's enough memory work here to last a family for twelve years. The program should take only five to ten minutes a day, and long term retention of verses should be greater than with other programs because of the review system. Accountability is stressed. There is a Completion Record sheet to be initialed by whoever hears us recite the verses, but we must make our own arrangements for that person to check on our progress. Memlok comes in NIV, KJV, NKJ, and NAS versions of the Bible.

PC Memlok is a computerized version of the traditional card set with enhancements. The program runs on Windows 3.1 and higher systems. It prints "business" cards in color for all 700 verses. It also prints out 8.5" x 11" pages that can be colored. One Bible translation of your choice is included. Automatic review ensures that review takes place. A number of users can be working on the same verses at the same time, with progress of each tracked by the computer. We can print out pages as needed. One program feature allows us to attach personal notes; another provides a practice pad for self-testing; and yet another lets the user erase portions of verses to learn a phrase at a time. If you have a suitable computer, this version makes the most sense for families. This is probably why *PC Memlok*

has become even more popular than the traditional card set.

SanctiFinder®

(Providence Project)
$5

Using the same idea as in other Providence Project products such as *CalcuLadder, SanctiFinder®* focuses on memorizing the names and order of the books of the Bible. This is a 48-page book with eight different timed drills. There are six copies of each drill since a student practices the same drill up to six times, both to memorize and develop speed. Suggested time goals for two different levels of learners are noted at the bottom of each page. The drills are mazes, fill-in-the-blanks, circling, and writing names of books of the Bible that come before and after each listed book name. The book is not reproducible, so you need separate books for each family member.

Scripture Memory Fellowship International

This organization, with many, many years of experience, offers Scripture memory programs for preschoolers through adults, along with awards to be earned as memory students progress. They provide each "student" with a memory book which the memorizer selects according to grade level or previous experience in memorizing God's Word. For the most part, verses are in King James Version and are all arranged topically. You are enrolled as a family, one person, a church class, or a neighborhood group. You also select your supervisor who encourages you and helps keep track of progress. You may either purchase the memory books outright or enroll with rewards which you select from their list contained in the *Scripture Memorizer*. These incentives (rewards) are primarily Christian books—selections for all ages and a variety of interests. There are memory books for memorizers at all levels, including easier adult programs for those new to Scripture memorization. They suggest that fall is the best time to enroll but enrollments are welcomed at any time of the year. Each September a new list of rewards is available. The enrollment fee is kept to a minimum and represents about one-third of their actual cost; the remainder is subsidized by supporters of the ministry. No one is turned away.

N. A. Woychuk, the developer of the memory books, has also written a 161-page paperback titled *You Need to Memorize Scripture* that presents encouraging testimonials and offers some memorizing tips that others have found helpful.

Word Maps-Memory Aid Posters

(Hear An'Tell Adventures)
$15 for book and tape set

This is a book of illustrated Scripture posters for your children to color. The illustrations explain the meaning of Scripture so a child can understand it. Scripture is also set to lively music on the accompanying audio cassette. Photocopying posters is allowed for family use. Verses are in

KJV.

Church History/Missions

Kids for the World: A Guidebook to Children's Mission Resources

(U.S. Center for World Mission)

$10.25

Anyone searching for methods and materials for teaching about missions should have Gerry Dueck's resource book, *Kids for the World: A Guidebook to Children's Mission Resources* (second edition published in 1996). This is a comprehensive compilation of information about resources rather than a "read-through" book. The first section lists and briefly describes resources of all types—curricula, books, stories, activities, visual aids, audio-visuals, songs and music. The second section describes 52 simple lesson plans, expanded lesson plans on "hidden peoples," stories to be used with some of the lessons, and directions for a number of activities. Next is a list of contacts—writers, resource people, and speakers we can contact for more information or help. Four supplementary readings about missions are included, along with indices for People Groups and countries and a list of sources with their addresses. All of this is offered to help get us started rather than to serve as complete missions curricula. Resources are keyed, showing for which age group (preschool through adult) they are appropriate. A free 1999 Supplement is included when you order the book. (You might also want to check their web site for a comprehensive listing of resources.)

Sketches from Church History: An Illustrated Account of 20 Centuries of Christ's Power

(Banner of Truth)

$19.99

I suspect the format of this book is the biggest factor that accounts for its popularity among home schoolers. The text is broken up into manageable chunks rather than overwhelming chapters. Frequent illustrations add visual variety. Topically, it sticks with the Protestant side of Christianity aside from a brief look at Islam (beginnings of the religion and the Crusades). Also, you can read a section from the middle of the book which pertains to other topics in which you are interested without having to read the entire book. Because it focuses on the Protestant Church, early church history is not adequately covered and an anti-Catholic bias is evident.

It is written at adult level, so it will not serve as a student book. It might be read aloud with fifth or sixth graders, but I suspect that most of them will be overwhelmed if it is not pre-read and summarized by parents. I recommend this book for the benefit of parents at this stage more than for the children. When your children reach junior high and high school levels, they can read it themselves.

Bible/Religion Curriculum

Bible curriculum sometimes turns vital topics into just another school subject, trivializing truths with word searches and crossword puzzles without challenging children's hearts and minds. However, there are times when Bible curricula or religion courses can be useful tools. When looking for a curriculum, remember that children's spiritual growth is even more unpredictable than that in academic areas. We must take into account the needs of each child and which Scriptural principles or topics will best help them grow in Godliness at this time in their lives.

Alone With God Bible Studies

by Karen Mohs

(Greek 'n' Stuff)

13-week studies - $6.95 each; Acts study - $20.95

This series of Bible study guides can be used by the entire family or independently by students who can read on their own. Each study covers a book (or part of a book) of the Bible, proceeding verse by verse. Daily lessons for Monday through Saturday are set out, with a single memory verse provided for each week. Each lesson begins with prayer and reading or recitation of the memory verse. Check-off boxes are provided so that these crucial steps are not omitted. Next, students read through the Scripture verses covered that day, then answer questions in the workbook regarding those verses. Questions are recall, factual questions rather than interpretive or application. At the end of the week, a "Think and Pray About It" section raises some of the deeper issues. Many, but not all, daily lessons add an extra comment or explanation relating to the verses. The actual lessons (after prayer and memory work) should take less than 10 minutes a day, unless you choose to expand discussion yourself. Non-reading, younger children (ages 4-6) can participate in such studies, since they need only listen carefully to answer questions. No teacher preparation time is needed. These studies should suit those looking for Bible curriculum that provides continuity without a lot of work. Titles in this series all read *I Can Study* [insert "Esther" or another book of the Bible here] *Alone With God*. Books of the Bible for which there are 13-week studies include Jonah and Ruth (in a single book), Esther, and 1 Samuel (Part One now available with two more parts due). Acts is a 52-week study.

Bible Study Guide for All Ages

by Mary Baker

$29.95 per unit; wall maps/time-line - $19.95; pictures and names label packets - $9.95 for first set, $5.595 for up to 7 more sets; song tape - $12.95

Four separate units covering the Bible are the essential part of the non-denominational program. Other options are Children's Songs tape and Wall Maps/Time-Line. This is the most comprehensive program I have seen at such a low price. The entire Bible is studied over the four years or less you spend going through all four units. Buy the first unit to begin. It is recommended that you use them in order because of the chronological nature of the study and because of the built-in review. Although study begins with Joseph, Daniel, and Jesus, there is a foundation laid that helps students understand the rest of the Bible. All units are designed to review old information, then go on to teach something new. Each one-page lesson includes drills on basic Bible knowledge, a learning activity (see descriptions farther on), reading of the Biblical text and related Scriptures, definitions or explanations of terms encountered in the reading, questions (coded for review use in future lessons) that emphasize recall of factual information from the reading, map work (map outlines are provided in the back of the book), singing a children's song (on the extra song tape) and a hymn, memory work and discussion, prayer time, and drawing of a story page from the lesson. Lessons are neatly arranged on a single page, although you do refer to other sections of the book for drill, activity instructions, and visual aids.

Visual aids are casually drawn with stick figures. Although these are not examples of good art, they demonstrate that everyone can quickly sketch the basic story without regard to artistic skill. When children create their story pages at the conclusion of the lesson, they need not worry about artistic ability, and when parents illustrate lessons, they too can concentrate on the story rather than the art.

The *Wall Maps and Time Line* add more visual impact to lessons. It includes three large, colored maps and a timeline which is more than six feet long. Both are printed in color. Movable Bible character pictures and name labels, which can be attached and removed with tacky tape, can be placed on the wall maps and timeline as studied.

There are many different types of activities incorporated into the lessons. Some examples are familiar activities such as making murals, role playing, puzzle pictures, and finger plays, while others are creative twists on familiar games such as "Knock, Knock" and "Twenty Questions." (There are at least forty game ideas from which to choose.) Some of these activities work as visual aids in telling the Bible stories, while others are used for review and reinforcement of lessons.

Although lessons are not taught in chronological order all of the time, there is a chronological sense to the layout of lessons. Children learn the background of the Old Testament and how the New Testament is the fulfillment of the Old. Especially helpful is the teaching of prophetic books simultaneously with the historical books to which they correlate. The time line is a big help here.

Thorough knowledge of the Bible is the goal throughout the curriculum. Personal application of Biblical lessons is also stressed and impetus for application occurs at the end of each lesson.

The lessons are designed for teacher presentation rather than independent study. The inclusion of activities helps the active learner, although there is much classroom-like instruction. (In fact, this material makes excellent Sunday school curriculum.) All ages can work through the material together, although it will be important to choose activities (as permitted) according to the ages in your family. You do not need to purchase anything except one single binder for one unit to use the program (although the song cassette will be helpful to some). Some families might choose to take longer with each lesson so they have time to do everything while others might adapt lessons to save time by skipping some parts.

Bible Truths for Christian Schools

(Bob Jones University Press) student books grades 1-4 - $9 each, grades 5-6 - $10 each; teacher editions - $37 each; student materials packets for grades 2-4 - $6.50 each

Newly revised third editions of Bible Truths 2, 3, and 4 are available. Second editions for K5, 1, 5, and 6 are scheduled for updates over the next few years.

Key components are the spiral-bound (for grades 1-4) or three-ring-binder (for grades 5 and 6) teacher edition plus the student worktext. The *Bible 1* text features an insert of memory verses and color paste-ups. There is an optional music cassette to provide accompaniment for songs and hymns in the curriculum. The second grade book, titled *A Servant's Heart,* has an optional Student Materials Packet (memory verse bookmarks and timeline) and two supplementary novels: *Pelts and Promises* and *A Question of Yams* [$6.49 each]. The second grade student book has catechism questions and answers at the back. The third grade book, titled *Following Christ,* has supplementary books: *Escape* and *Peanut Butter Friends.* The fourth grade book, *God and His People,* has two supplementary books: *Captive Treasure* and *With Daring Faith.* Both third and fourth grades have optional Student Materials Packets and an optional CD/cassette. For grades 5 and 6, there is a separate *Elementary Bible Truths Handbook* [$5.50] with catechism, a glossary, and "Bible Action Truths."

These courses encourage student involvement and application of concepts presented through a variety of activities such as songs, stories, and crafts. Students study catechism questions and learn traditional hymns and memory verses. The Scripture perspective is strongly conservative and fundamentalist. *Bible 1* is fairly chronological, focusing primarily on the Old Testament, but also teaching about the Life of Christ.

Levels two through four are fairly chronological and are structured around application themes. Bible study skills are included in the revised books. *Bible Truths* for grades five and six are surveys of the New and Old Testaments, respectively. They stress application of Biblical principles to everyday living.

Developing Godly Character in Children, A Handbook and Resource Guide for Parents and Teachers

by Beverly Caruso, Ken Marks, and Debbie Peterson
(Hands to Help Publishing)
$20 from Hands to Help (or $23.95 retail)

This is quite different from standard Bible curriculum. Unlike *KONOS* character curriculum, *Developing Godly Character in Children* concentrates primarily on the Bible. Concepts are based upon the authors' backgrounds in Youth With A Mission and Christian day and home schools. They are also influenced by the teachings of Bill Gothard.

Nine main character qualities are used as the foundation for nine units of study, with 95 related sub-qualities included under the various units. Most home educators will only be able to cover about three of the nine units in a year, making this is a three-year curriculum. Each main and sub- character quality is introduced and defined in children's terms; Scripture memory verses are also given for each sub-quality. A catechism approach is then used to teach some key concepts. A traditional hymn relating to the quality is learned, and a list of simple, commonly-known choruses is provided. In addition, we are given a list of projects/activities that help teach the character qualities in each unit, along with lists of useful resources (books and both audio and video cassettes). A reproducible lesson plan form can be used to organize the activities you choose.

Many ideas presented in this curriculum are so broad they can easily be used with all ages. The more narrowly focused ideas will suit selected age groups. The result is a curriculum that can easily be used to include the entire family.

This also makes an excellent Sunday school or children's church curriculum for creative teachers.

Discover 4 Yourself Bible Studies for Kids

by Kay Arthur
(Harvest House)
$8.99 each

Kay Arthur, who popularized inductive Bible study methodology, has worked with various co-authors (including Cyndy Shearer of Greenleaf Press) to create a series of Bible study books for children about fourth grade and up. Using a movie-making analogy, children learn to identify key elements of each chapter of a book, drawing a short storyboard for illustration. Identification and marking of key words, a critical component of the adult methodology is also incorporated. Fill-in-the-blank questions, charts, questions requiring full-sentence answers, and word puzzles are used as learning tools. Children work from reprinted text of the New American Standard Bible. Thus far there are two books in this series: *Jesus in the Spotlight, John 1-10*, and *Wrong Way Jonah, Jonah*.

Faith and Life series

(Ignatius Press)
texts: grades 1 and 2 - $6.50 each; grades 3 and 4 - $6.95 each; grades 5 and 6 - $7.95 each; grades 7 and 8 - $8.95 each; activity books - $3.95 each; teacher's manuals - $10.95 each

This a very popular religion series among Catholic homeschoolers. The content is solid and does not water down instruction as many other modern religious texts do. The series incorporates the questions and answers of the Baltimore catechism for memorization work.

The teacher's manuals for each grade level are very helpful and necessary to complete each course. Especially helpful is the suggested background reading for teachers. Lesson plans are supplied for both one-day and five-day presentations. The one-day presentations are designed for CCD (PSR) classes, while the five-day presentations are designed for daily use in the Catholic classroom or homeschool. Some homeschoolers use the one-day presentation as the backbone of their religious studies and supplement with Bible study, Saint stories, liturgical celebrations, daily Mass, and so on. There are approximately 30 lessons per grade level. The activity books reinforce the lessons learned in the textbooks. They are helpful, but not absolutely necessary.

With the exception of the second grade book, the texts are filled with beautiful works of religious art that lift one's heart up to the Lord. (Art credits are listed in the back of the books so that the parent/teacher might easily incorporate the religious studies with art appreciation.) Each text ends with prayers to memorize and vocabulary words with complete definitions.

Our Heavenly Father (Grade One) provides basic instruction in prayer, the Trinity, the life of Jesus, and salvation. Growing in love and trust in God is accentuated.

Our Life (Grade Two) prepares the student for Reconciliation and First Holy Communion. Children are taught God's law (which we obey through love), that forgiveness is found through Jesus' sacrifice, and the true presence of Jesus in the Eucharist. The order of the Mass is emphasized and the praying of the rosary is taught.

Our Life with Jesus (Grade Three) continues the lessons taught in the second grade book on Confession, Communion, and the Mass. God's plan for our salvation is stressed through lessons on the Old Testament covenant, the Incarnation, and Pentecost.

Jesus Our Guide (Grade Four) seeks to aid students in understanding their purpose and goals in their lives with Jesus showing the way. Grace received in the sacraments is shown to give strength in doing God's work. The text ends with Advent/Christmas and Lent/Easter supplements.

Credo: I Believe (Grade Five) is a complete and thorough study of the Apostle's Creed, line by line. It guides students to understand the truths which we profess in the Creed.

Following Christ (Grade Six) focuses on God's Law and how it brings order to our lives and, in turn, true happiness. Deeper explanation of the Holy Mass is taught. Also covered are death, judgement, and the end of the world. An appendix provides explanations of sacred vessels and vestments. [Maureen Wittmann]

Image of God Series
(Ignatius Press)
text/activity books: grades 1, 2 - $8.95 each, grades 3-5 - $10.95 each, grade 6 - $12.95; teacher's manuals: $16.95 each; Mass text/activity book - $4.95; Confirmation text/activity book - $7.50; Confirmation teacher's manual - $7.50

This Catholic religion series combines text and activities in a single student book for each level. Early grades use crossword puzzles, coloring activities, plays, and more to enhance the lessons. Later grades include more thoughtful activities and questions to challenge the older student. Lessons are filled with Scripture, lives of the saints, contemporary stories, and solid church doctrine to help train the young mind.

The detailed teacher's manuals offer activities, vocabulary words, and practical ideas. Although the teacher's manual is not absolutely necessary, it does complete the program and add considerably to the study.

Ignatius Press also publishes the *Faith and Life* series. *Image of God* is clearly designed for daily lessons while *Faith and Life* offers scheduling options so that lessons might be taught daily or once a week.

Notes on each level text follow.

Who Has God's Life (grade one) student book - 66 pp., teacher's - 166 pp.: Simple activities and colorful drawings to teach the little ones about Jesus and His Church. Introduces the very basics of God's love, grace, and the sacraments.

Who Loves Me Always (grade two) student book - 172 pp., teacher's - 276 pp.: Prepares children for the sacraments of Reconciliation and Holy Communion. Teaches children how they can participate more fully in the Sacrifice of the Mass.

Who Is Our Example (grade three) student book - 269 pp., teacher's - 217 pp.: Highlights the mystery of God and the Trinity. Forming a moral conscience and recognizing how God wishes for us to act are emphasized.

We Celebrate the Sacrifice of Love: The Mass (supplement to 1st through 3rd grade courses): Children are introduced to the Holy Sacrifice of the Mass through photographs and the actual text of the Mass.

We Follow Jesus (grade four) student book - 199 pp., teacher's - 224 pp.: Children learn how God created everything from the angels to the universe to people, all out of love. Students are taught that through the grace of Jesus, we sinners can be redeemed.

Our Mission of Love (grade five) student book - 228 pp., teacher's - 208 pp.: Our creation in the image of God is accentuated. The birth, function, and mission of the Church are introduced. A deeper learning of the sacraments, grace, and prayer is emphasized.

God's Merciful Love: The Old Testament (grade six) student book - 372 pp., teacher's - 241 pp.: Centers on an extensive study of the Old Testament, with a special emphasis on the book of Genesis.

Confirmation (supplement) student book - 73 pp., teacher's - 31 pp.: Using Scripture, Vatican II documents, and the lives of the saints and popes, Confirmation candidates are prepared to spread and defend the faith. Emphasis is placed on serving the community, fruits of the Holy Spirit, apologetics, and more. This can be used whatever year students make their confirmation. [Maureen Wittmann]

Know & Grow Bible study series
by Janice Southerland
(Children's Inductive Bible Study)
$15 each; Teaching Guides - $5 each

This is a series of inductive Bible studies for children based on the approach used in the well-known *Precept Upon Precept* studies. Children learn how to dig into Scripture as they work through the lessons. Thus far in the series are *Know & Grow in 2 Timothy, Know & Grow in Understanding God,* and *Know & Grow in Sermon on the Mount, Parts I* and *II.* Large-print copies of 2 Timothy and a section of Ephesians (New American Standard version) are at the back of the book for students to work with. They identify key words by marking them with special symbols. They explore the who, what, where, when, and why for selected people and events. They make topical lists of facts. Periodic review reinforces the learning. Lessons are completed with an action—something to put the learning into practice. The author sums it up well: "The student will glean basic facts from the text of Scripture (knowledge), learn how these truths fit together in context with the whole counsel of God's Word (understanding), and begin to see how the reality of these truths can make a difference in their lives now (wisdom)." The beauty of this type of study is that it teaches children how to search out the Scriptures for themselves. The fifteen lessons in this book can be completed as a family study or used for independent study. However, each student should have his or her own book since there is a great deal of written activity plus Scripture worksheets students use frequently. (Books are not reproducible.) Children who are not yet writing can do much of the work orally.

Teaching Guides come in two formats: individual or group. The Teaching Guides outline the lessons, provide additional Scripture references, teaching tips, and answers (when appropriate).The individual Guides include more information about the tools being taught, more cross-references, and suggested music to help "anchor the truth to their hearts through a melody." Group Guides add group discussion ideas with more cross references and applications.

This is not an activity-oriented study; the only activity I spotted was making a "salvation bracelet or necklace" to be used as both a personal reminder and a witnessing tool. The *Know & Grow* approach should work well in home schools, day schools, or Sunday schools.

Landmark's Freedom Baptist Curriculum: Bible
(Landmark's Freedom Baptist Curriculum)
$35 per course

Bible curriculum for grades 1 through 12 is theologically Baptist and uses the KJV Bible. The format is somewhat similar throughout the series. Lessons are designed to take one week each, with six parts to each lesson. One of those parts is Scripture memory which will be worked on throughout the week. The other five parts can be spread over five days or combined. Typically, the opening lesson is vocabulary, with following lessons varying from level to level. Older levels require students to read significant portions from Scripture, then accompany that reading with some commentary. Younger levels retell the Biblical stories or concepts of each lesson, selecting appropriate memory verses that represent a primary lesson concept. Activities for younger levels include fill-in-the-blanks, multiple choice questions, short essay questions, and matching, while upper levels require both brief answers and lengthy compositions. There are no Sunday school type puzzles and games, just straightforward Bible teaching with an emphasis on both comprehension and understanding. Each lesson has a space for a selected person to sign off when the student demonstrates mastery of their memory verse or verses. Answer keys and quizzes are included in each course. Topics for each level from first through sixth grades are Old Testament Characters, Stories of Israel, New Testament Characters, Miracles of Christ, The Book of Acts, and Bible Survey (of the complete Bible). These are easy to use and require no significant teacher preparation.

My First Communion Catechism
(The Neumann Press)
$6

This little book was originally published in 1942 and is based on the *Baltimore Catechism*. The small size and lovely illustrations naturally draw children into the book. It begins with Catholic prayers and follows with 25 lessons written to prepare second graders for their First Holy Communion. *My First Communion Catechism* could be used as the sole text for second grade or along with another religion text. [M. Wittmann]

Plants Grown Up: Projects for Sons on the Road to Manhood
by Pam Forster
(Doorposts)
$40

Parents interested in training sons rather than just raising them should appreciate this book full of ideas for projects to build Godly character in their sons. The title is drawn from Psalm 144:12 which says, "That our sons may be as plants grown up in their youth...." Some of the topics covered are leadership, Bible study, self-control, courage, perseverance, relationships, serving cheerfully, obedience, contentment, communication, teaching skills, and finances. These are arranged under seven headings drawn from II Peter 1:5-7—virtue, knowledge, temperance, patience, Godliness, brotherly kindness, and charity.

Each chapter features ideas appropriate for both younger and older sons, arranged in a helpful, approximately chronological order so that we choose from the first ideas for young boys and from the latter ideas for older boys. However, many of the ideas are easily adaptable for a wide range of ages. For example, one activity is to "Read through *How the Bible Came To Us* by Meryle Doney. Write a summary of the book's content. Do some of the activities suggested in the book." We might have a young child simply narrate back to us some of the key ideas in the book, while we would require a written assignment from an older child.

A variety of planning, organizing, and worksheets are included for those who wish to use them. There are character evaluation questions at the end of each chapter that ensure practical application of each lesson. A lengthy section of reproducible memory verse pages (KJV) with check-off boxes is at the end of the book. *Plants Grown Up* is easy-to-use and extremely flexible, allowing us to choose which ideas to use for our family. Activities vary to suit different learning styles, so there is something to appeal to everyone. While the "lessons" will touch on other subject areas, you should probably consider this the Bible study part of your curriculum. *Polished Cornerstones*, follows the same format for girls. See the review below. [Valerie Thorpe/C.D.]

Polished Cornerstones
by Pam Forster
(Doorposts)
$40

See the review of *Plants Grown Up* above. This volume follows the same format, this time focusing on raising girls to meet the standards of the Proverbs 31 woman. It tackles subjects like money management, housekeeping, organization, meal planning, church activities, and teaching. It recommends resources such as *Beautiful Girlhood, Christian Character* (by Gary Maldaner), *The Excellent Wife* (by Martha Peace), *Hidden Art of Homemaking* (by Edith Schaeffer), *Homework Manual for Biblical Living* (2 volumes), *Nave's Topical Bible, Shorter Catechism for Study Classes* (2 volumes), *Strong's Exhaustive Concordance*, and the *Westminster Standards*. Many other resources are recommended, but those listed are the most essential.

A number of activities and recommended resources duplicate those found in *Plants Grown Up* since the goal in spiritual development is the same. This makes it easy to teach both sons and daughters using both volumes. You can use the similar lessons from one or the other volume for all your children (watching for age propriety), then pursue the other activities more appropriate for girls or boys.

An optional comb-bound book, *Polished Cornerstones Memory Verses* [$5], contains the suggested memory verses for this volume. This makes personal study and memorization much more convenient.

As with *Plants Grown Up*, this volume will easily provide adequate Bible study, but coverage of other subjects will depend upon activities you select. It will not be comprehensive for any of your basic academic subjects for older students, although you might find it sufficient for the early elementary grades for social studies.

Pro Series Bible Curriculum
(Positive Action for Christ)
K5 - grade 6 student workbooks - $9.30 each; all teacher's editions - $30.75 each; cassette tapes - $7.95 each

Although this curriculum is written for the classroom, almost everything is easily adaptable for the home school. This is a "meaty," non-denominational Bible-based curriculum with a strong emphasis on character development. In grades K5-6, Bible reading, illustrative stories, hymns and choruses, Scripture memory, and seat work make up each lesson. Because of preferences for different versions of the Bible, the curriculum (both student and teacher books) is available in either KJV or NIV versions. The bulk of each lesson is contained in a three-ring binder teacher's manual, while a student workbook has activity pages (dot-to-dots, puzzles, fill-in-the-

blanks) that reinforce lessons. Since the teaching comes primarily from the teacher's manual, this is not an independent study curriculum, but one that requires teacher/parent involvement. However, a minimal amount of lesson preparation is required because the teacher's manuals are well-designed.

Each year of curriculum contains thirty-five lessons (about one per week) developed around a unifying theme. (Different lesson plan options are suggested in the beginning of each volume.)

Kindergartners are introduced to "the basics": God's character, Bible doctrines, and Scriptural principles. First graders learn about God's gifts, including the gift of salvation. God's promises are the topics for second grade. Christian growth is studied through the lives of Joseph and Daniel in third grade. Fourth grade is a survey of the New Testament, focusing on the life of Christ, the work of the Holy Spirit, and the apostle Paul. A survey of the Old Testament is presented in fifth grade. An athletic theme challenges sixth graders to put their Christian faith into action while focusing on a deeper study of God's word and foundational doctrines. Because children (and adults) often need repetition before truly learning something, both character traits and Scripture verses are reviewed every few years in greater depth. Their detailed scope and sequence booklet shows developmental activities, "target truths," God's promises, and character traits covered in each lesson so we can easily choose the level that meets the needs of our child/children.

An important feature of the curriculum is that it recognizes various levels of thinking skills and goes beyond simple recall of facts to develop understanding and application of knowledge.

Both traditional hymns and choruses are incorporated into the curriculum. Cassette tapes of hymns and choruses are available for those of us who are not familiar with those that are used. The publisher also sells Dr. Al Smith's *Treasury Of Hymn Histories* [$25], which briefly tells the story of each of the selected hymns and provides the sheet music. This adds an extra dimension of understanding as children learn the hymns. *Sing and Be Happy* [$15.95] is the music book for the choruses used in grades K-6. Words for all hymns and choruses are found in both teacher and student books, but you will need the two above-mentioned resources for the music. A single cassette tape for each grade also has all of the hymns and choruses.

By including character traits, thinking skills, and deeper music study, this curriculum attempts to be more comprehensive than most others.

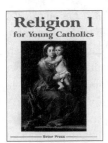

Seton Home Study School Religion Courses/Religion for Young Catholics

(Seton Home Study and Seton Press)

Seton offers Catholic religion textbooks as well as religion correspondence courses based on the *Baltimore Catechism*. In the correspondence courses, all levels except kindergarten study the *Catechism*, guided by a textbook. Texts are provided for church history, and miscellaneous smaller books on a variety of topics are also included. Courses are available for kindergarten and above.

Seton publishes its own textbooks for grades K-3 [$10-12 each], which can be purchased independent of the correspondence courses. For kindergarten, Seton offers *Kindergarten Catechism* [$10], an introductory course which uses about 50 key catechism questions as springboards for expanded explanations. Levels 1-3, called *Religion for Young Catholics,* are serious courses covering the Ten Commandments, the sacraments, creation and the fall, the life of Jesus, and basic doctrine every year. The first two levels also include prayers. (The content has been approved by the Archdiocese of Arlington.) The above topics are covered in varying depth at the different levels with continual repetition and review of key concepts. Lessons are designed to focus on a group of catechism questions each week which must be memorized then reviewed throughout the year. Levels 2 and 3 incorporate some questions within the daily lessons, and answer keys are provided with the texts. Black-and-white illustrations add visual interest. Minimal direction is provided for parents within the texts, but it seems evident that lesson content should be discussed to ensure that children understand what is being taught. Of course, interaction is also required for catechism work.

Star Light/Star Ways Bible Curriculum

(Praise Hymn)
teacher manual and student book sets for grades 1 to 3 - $19 each; for grades 4 to 6 - $20 each; extra student books - $4.98 each; Songs cassette - $4.98

Although written for Christian day schools, this curriculum can be adapted easily for home school. Lessons are presented from the teacher's manual and students complete activities in student workbooks. Teacher's manuals are clearly laid out with daily lesson plans which require some advance preparation. Some object lessons and activities are suggested for which we will need to gather materials, but we can choose which of these to use. Study at each level is a survey course of the Bible in chronological sequence. This means we repeat or review some of the same material from year to year. However, the authors have wisely selected different sections of the Bible to focus upon each time around. For example, in first grade students study a great deal about Moses and the entry into Canaan while in second grade the focus shifts to Joshua and the conquests. By the end of the series, students will have studied every major Old Testament story and all books in the New Testament.

The *Star Light* series covers grades 1 through 3, while *Star Ways* covers grades 4 through 6. KJV, NKJV, NAS, or NIV Bible will all work with the *Star Light* series, but it is easier to work through *Star Ways* using either KJV or NIV.

Student books are printed in black-and-white, but they are still very appealing. Excellent, sometimes humorous, illustrations coupled with fun (and for the most part worthwhile) workbook activities offer more variety than we find in most Bible curricula.

Teaching centers around Bible story-telling, some Scripture reading, and practical applications, all of which should take about 15 to 20 minutes per day. This is not as challenging as some studies, but it might be an especially good choice for those with children who need a "lighter touch."

As with any Bible curriculum, we need to adapt lessons that present doctrinal positions or interpretation with which we might disagree (e.g., earth was created in an "old" state.) Quite a bit of personal interpretation and application is included in the teacher's manuals, so feel free to substitute your own thoughts and interpretations.

It is not necessary to stick with the right grade level book for each student, although they are designed to reflect grade level abilities. Each level might stretch for children a year or so older and younger, but not much more than that. So if you have more than one child to teach you might have trouble using this if they are very far apart. Otherwise, select one level and adapt lessons as much as possible to suit all of your children. Purchase additional student workbooks for each child who needs one.

You will probably want to also purchase the *Star Light Songs Cassette* if you are using any of levels 1 through 3.

Studying God's Word, Books A-H [for grades K-7]

by Darrel A. Trulson
(Christian Liberty Press)
Books A-H - $7 each; teacher's manuals - $1.95 each

Books A and B introduce this nondenominational Bible study series. Book A features faithful retellings of some of the most important Bible stories from both Old and New Testaments using language suitable for young children. Comprehension questions are included after most of the stories. Book B focuses on Bible doctrine at a level appropriate for young learners. Each week's lesson is introduced in catechism format with one or more doctrinal questions and answers. Throughout the week parents read related Scriptures with their children, help them complete fill-in-the-blank exercises, and direct the weekly activity (craft, game, coloring, crossword, or object lesson). Book B seems to take a more serious, purposeful approach than does Book C. Book C uses stories from the Old Testament to illustrate basic truths. The text of each lesson may be read by or to the child. The lesson text is followed by a page or pages that require filling in blanks, coloring, cut-and-paste work, mazes, matching, and other traditional workbook activity. Print is appropriately large for young eyes. An inexpensive teacher's manual/answer key is also available.

Book D is subtitled, "Exploring the Truths of the Life of Christ for the Young Reader." Like Book C, instead of following a chronological presentation, it is foundational in coverage. It uses stories from the life of Christ to illustrate basic truths and doctrine. Readings are all from the gospels. There are some cut-and-paste activities, but more written work—filling in the blanks, crosswords, word searches, matching exercises—than in Book C. Because of the interests and attention spans of young learners, books A-D do not follow the comprehensive chronological approach we find in books E-H, but instead offer Bible study via different approaches in each book.

The remaining books use a chronological approach. Book E covers from Genesis to Ruth, Book F covers First Samuel to Malachi, Book G covers the message and ministry of Jesus Christ, and Book H studies the Book of Acts. CLP plans to continue the series through the New Testament. Books of the Bible are taught chronologically rather than in the order they appear in the Bible. For instance, when studying through the books of Kings, lessons from other Biblical books that correlate are inserted in their proper places. I almost hate to list this series under "curriculum" because the emphasis is on the Bible more than in typical curricula. Lessons reinforce Bible knowledge rather than developing slightly connected topics as do many so-called Bible curriculum lessons. The historical books are given more attention because the goal is to get the overview of God's plan as I have recommended in the introduction to this section. The Scripture passage(s), lesson goal, and a memory verse are listed at the beginning of each lesson along with a small timeline to help us place events in context. This is followed by background and explanatory information, then questions that require both recall and thinking. Thought questions prompt students to apply Scripture to their lives. Supplemental exercise (crosswords, word searches, mazes, etc.) are included after many of the lessons. Constant references to a time line help students to keep the "big picture" in sight. Unit tests are also in the student book.

CLP sells very inexpensive and very brief Teacher's Manuals for all levels. The few pages of introduction are essential reading. The remainder is your answer key. Although each book is recommended for a grade level, they need not be limited to those levels. Books C and D are the most limited because of the younger style activities, but the other books can be used across much wider age spans. If just beginning the series with students past third grade, you will probably want to begin with Book E. Books E through H can be used interchangeably for students in grades 4 through 8. These upper level books offer interestingly-written, good, solid Bible study—one of the most effective, yet relatively inexpensive options you'll find.

Train Up a Child...in Sound Bible Doctrine
by Lori Verstegen
(Berean Bible Ministries)
$17.50

This is a self-contained, creative Bible curriculum, originally written for home Bible clubs, but easily adaptable for home school, Sunday school, or other settings. There are no extra student books or answer keys to purchase.

Lessons center around basic, non-denominational Bible doctrine—God, the Bible, creation, the fall, sin, redemption, salvation, our position in Christ, and the fruit of the Spirit.

Lessons are laid out very clearly. The objective is stated, followed by a list of materials needed (photocopies of cut-out pages from the book, craft materials, etc., but nothing very expensive or hard to find). The lesson is presented from the book, using visual aids in the book or a flannel board. (Patterns for flannel board items are in the book.) Every lesson includes both a craft and an activity, and these more closely reinforce the lesson objectives than do most crafts and activities in other Bible curricula I have reviewed. Memory verses and songs are also incorporated into each lesson. There are a total of fifteen lessons, so the book will take about four months to complete. Lessons should take about an hour and a half in a larger group—less time with one or two children. For practical purposes, home schoolers should do parts of each lesson each day (following the author's suggestions for how to do so) rather than an entire lesson in one day. The author suggests using the curriculum with children ages 5-11, but it seems to be most appropriate for the early elementary grades—children up to about ages 8 or 9. Consider having an older child prepare and present the crafts and activities for younger siblings.

Train Up a Child is also a good introduction to the idea of conflicting world views. A number of lessons use pictures of sheep (to be cut out as cards) with doctrinal statements that sound correct. While some of the statements are true, some of them are what the world would have us believe instead of the truth, so, if you flip the card over, there is a picture of a wolf on the reverse. Children use the cards as a game activity to see if they can separate truth from falsehood.

Chapter 7

Thinking and Reference Skills

Thinking

It is far too easy to jump into familiar subject areas and overlook a very important area of curriculum that does not appear on the list of "required subjects"—thinking skills. Even the government schools have discovered you can stuff a child full of facts and not produce an educated person. If the student has not acquired the ability to think, he is effectually uneducated.

Thinking skills are being stressed more in recently published materials, particularly those from secular publishers, but you cannot rely on curriculum material for this. It requires interaction between teacher and student in a way that provokes thoughtful analysis of what has been learned, application of that learning by combining and drawing from accumulated knowledge, and evaluation of the thinking process itself.

In some families this process happens without any conscious planning. Ideas are discussed and weighed. Newspapers provide fuel for discussion. Parents and children welcome the interplay of differing perspectives on an issue. (Mind, we are not talking about whether Johnny is supposed to obey his parents or not, but about discussions of issues such as our city's authority to forbid the use of Safe and Sane fireworks.)

Some families shun such discussions either because they are not interested or because the intense feelings and emotional turmoil resulting from them is too uncomfortable. These families especially need to look at some of the thinking skills materials, either as motivational tools or as a means for developing thinking skills while keeping discussions under control. Discussion-prone families may not need the stimulation of these materials to stretch their thinking, but they might enjoy using them for the fun of it.

Educators have chosen their guru in the field of thinking skills—someone who put everything into nice neat little categories that make good topics for workbook chapters. Benjamin Bloom's work on thinking skills is summed up in his book, *Taxonomy of Educational Objectives*: *Cognitive Domain* (Longmans, Green, and Co., 1956.) [Note: While I recognize the value of acknowledging different levels of thinking, there is much in Bloom's book that conflicts with our purposes and goals. This reference to his work is not intended to be an endorsement of all of his writings.] Bloom's theory is the most popular tool for teaching thinking skills. Without agreeing with his philosophy or other ideas, we can better understand thinking skills by looking at the way he has arranged them. He organized thinking skills into a hierarchy of:

- Knowledge
- Comprehension
- Application
- Analysis
- Synthesis
- Evaluation

Bloom explains that we begin at lower levels and progress to higher levels. This hierarchy has been incorporated into a number of learning materials, sometimes subtly, sometimes obviously. Any resource that talks about "higher order thinking skills" is at least indirectly referring to Bloom's Taxonomy.

The following materials provide a springboard into the application of thinking skills throughout the curriculum if you pay attention to the types of questions and thought processes involved. These are not your typical textbooks. Use materials from any of them whenever appropriate. They will serve as supplements to whatever else you are doing.

Resources

Analogy Adventure
(Learning Works)
$6.95

Suggested for grades 4-8, this reproducible 48-page book teaches students how to solve and how to construct analogies. Most lessons present analogies to solve with multiple choice answers. There are a few pages to use as forms for student-created analogies, plus some pages of lists (e.g., synonyms and antonyms) that might serve as sources for these analogies. Instructions for a create-it-yourself analogy game plus an answer key complete the book.(S)

Brain Teasers

(Teacher Created Materials)

$19.95 each

This is a series of six reproducible books for grades 1-6. Each features a variety of thinking skill activities appropriate for that grade level. The first grade book has dot-to-dots, word searches, mazes, codes, scrambled letters, identification, matching, simple logic, visual puzzles, antonyms, and more. More-challenging activities are added at each level such as completing cliches, "making a list of things with holes," analogies, logic grid puzzles, research trivia, and acrostics. By sixth grade, students are challenged to name the individuals who originated famous quotations, connect inventors with their inventions and geographic sites with their countries, create rhymes, solve riddles, and brainstorm word lists. Students will need to go look up some information for some of these, especially at the higher levels. Answer keys are included within each book.(S)

Brain Teasers [computer program]

(Teacher Created Materials)

$9.95

This CD-ROM program will run on either Windows or Macintosh systems. It is a tool for teachers rather than a student program. It has 250 *Brain Teaser* worksheets, similar to those in the printed books from TCM, which can be printed out for student use. Worksheets represent most subject areas—math, language arts, thinking skills, social studies, geography, and science at intermediate grade levels (approximately grades 4-6). These worksheets are strictly supplemental—not primary curriculum. You can bring up thumbnail pictures of all pages from each category, but you'll need to bring up the full page view to be able to figure out what each one is actually covering. Answer keys can be read on screen or printed out. The great thing about this program is that for a lower cost, you have access to far more worksheets than if you purchased Brain Teaser books.(S)

Critical Conditioning

by Kathryn Stout

(Design-A-Study)

$12

When parents choose to use good literature rather than a textbook-based reading series as the foundation of their reading program, they sometimes neglect some of the reading comprehension skills. This guide covers all the comprehension skills that are usually taught from kindergarten through eighth grade. A key goal throughout the guide is to develop an active rather than passive approach to reading. Children are taught thinking skills and are encouraged to apply them in reading and research activities. Explanations are given for the purposes of various activities, then parents are given questions to ask

and ideas to use with their children. Vocabulary development, study skills, note taking, and some writing activities are included. Skill lists and a checklist at the back of the book are handy tools to help us plan and evaluate progress in these areas. While it is primarily written for grades 1-8, it is also useful for those teaching high schoolers.

Critical Thinking: Reading, Thinking, and Reasoning Skills

(Steck-Vaughn)

$10.54 each; teacher's edition - $8.95 each

Each book in this series for grades 1-6 is quite comprehensive. Exercises develop skills in classification, identifying facts or opinions, outlining and summarizing, comparing and contrasting, identifying main ideas and relationships, drawing inferences, evaluating, logic, and more—a good variety of exercises to work on both thinking and reading skills. These books could be used as replacements for reading workbooks, particularly at upper levels. Teacher's editions are essential. They include reduced student pages and answers plus lesson plans. Lessons all follow a five-step lesson plan: define the skill, identify the steps, demonstrate the skill, practice the skill, and provide feedback.(S)

Critical Thinking Books & Software

Critical Thinking Books & Software specializes in the area of thinking skills with many outstanding books and computer programs from which to choose.

Books such as *Building Thinking Skills* and *Mind Benders* are available from teacher supply stores and home school distributors. CTBS also publishes books that help develop thinking skills within various subject areas (e.g., math, language arts, science, U.S. history). See reviews of *Developing Critical Thinking through Science, Mathematical Reasoning through Verbal Analysis*, and *Cranium Crackers*. Send for their catalog to determine which resources best suit your needs.

The *Building Thinking Skills* series is probably the most basic, comprehensive resource for thinking skills at all levels. Each reproducible student book is accompanied by a teacher's manual that offers a combination of lesson plans and teaching information. Lessons use student worksheets, hands-on materials (only with the *Primary* book), and interaction between teacher and student(s). Each lesson should take about ten to twenty minutes to do and requires just a few minutes of teacher preparation.

The first three books in the series are written for the levels addressed in this manual. The first book, *Primary Building Thinking Skills*, is suggested for grades K-2. The required hands-on materials are attribute blocks, pattern blocks, and interlocking cubes. Manipulative activities are performed with these materials before students complete the worksheet. In the 246-page *Primary* book, children deal with similarities and differences, sequences, classifications, and analogies. Visual-figural skills get a workout in these lessons, too. Examples of two activities: 1.) "Use PATTERN BLOCKS to make figures that look like the pictures below." [Four different, complex arrangements of pattern blocks are illustrated]; 2.) "Use INTERLOCKING CUBES of any color to construct and cover each figure in the top box. [7 figures are pictured.] Move all 1-cube figures into the first small box and all 2-cube figures into the second. Trace the figures and color the pictures to match the cubes." Children who are already reading fairly well should probably move into the next level, *Book 1*.

Book 1 (271 pages), suggested for grades 2-4, uses interlocking cubes for some lessons and broadens activities beyond the primarily visual-figural approach of the *Primary* book. Children work on the same skills as in the *Primary* book but add discussion of five types of analogies, following directions, antonyms and synonyms, "deductive reasoning, parts of a whole, map skills and directionality, logical connectives, spelling and vocabulary building, Venn diagrams, pattern folding, rotation, tracking, mental manipulation of two-dimensional objects," and more.

Book 2 (296 pages), suggested for grades 4-7, does all of the above, expands to seven different types of analogies, and adds branching diagrams, overlapping classes, and more. The idea of "implications" is also introduced. Activities vary in difficulty, so select those that seem most appropriate for each child.

Building Thinking Skills student books are $23.95-$25.95 each, while teacher's manuals range in price from $14.95 to $18.95.

The *Mind Benders* series consists of sets of smaller (28-30 page) books. Each book is self-contained with brief teaching information and an answer key in the front or back of the book. Children organize clues (some direct and some indirect) in grids (except in introductory lessons in lowest levels) to derive logical conclusions. For example, in a very introductory lesson, students are told, "Edmund, Ida, Joanne, and Tony are two sets of twins. Tony is a month younger than Edmund. Joanne is a month older than Ida." Students must then answer two questions, "Which pair is the younger set of twins?" and "Which pair is the older set of twins?" The Warm-Up book is for grades K-2. For grades 2-6, there is a series of books, *A-1, A-2, A-3,* and *A-4*. Some older students will be ready to move up to the second series, *B-1* through *B-4*, suggested for grades 6-10. These activities appeal to children, because they are like "detective work" as students try to match clues with identities. *Mind Benders* are $8.95 each. The *Instructions/Solutions* book covering all of them is $10.95.

Organizing Thinking: Graphic Organizers, Books I and II [$34.95 each] offer a totally different format for developing thinking skills. Both books cover the basic subject areas of math, writing, science, language arts, and social studies, as well as enrichment topics and problem solving. They use graphic organizers such as Venn diagrams, flow charts, and time lines that provide visual organization structures for information. Each organizer is presented as a blank "chart" and also as a particular lesson, accompanied by a lesson plan and background information. We can try the sample lessons to become familiar with the use of each organizer, then branch out on our own. Organizers are reproducible, and when there are predictable answers for sample lessons, they are entered in non-reproducible blue ink to serve as an answer key. The organizers are also available on computer disks for the Macintosh, so that either we or our students can adapt or write information on the original forms. *Book I* is suggested for grades 2-4 and *Book II* for grades 4-8, however, both books might be used over even wider age spans. Since the lessons themselves address specific topics such as comparing and contrasting Abraham Lincoln and Frederick Douglass, we must choose lessons that relate to subject areas appropriate for our children. (Some topics are more general and thus easier to use with more students.) The books themselves are hefty (342 pages in *Book II*) with so many sample lessons to choose from that we can get a lot of mileage out of a book without getting beyond the sample lessons.(SE)

Dandy Lion Publications

Dandy Lion has a whole section of books on logic and thinking skills in their catalog that I like. Books are reproducible and answer keys are in the back. All but *Lollipop Logic* and the *Logic Safari* series are illustrated by Dean Crawford. His drawings have a "silly" touch to them that most children will enjoy.

Lollipop Logic [$9.95] was written to introduce pre-readers to logic activities such as sequencing, relationships, analogies, deductive reasoning, patterns, making inferences, and analysis. Since it is suggested for grades K-2, some children will be able to read and do these activities on their own, but most will need parents to read and explain the directions.

Primarily Logic [$9.95], written for grades 2-4, has a great mix of activities including topics such as analogies, relationships, deductive reasoning, problem solving, and organizing information. Cute illustrations, lots of variety, and engaging activities introduce students to some pretty sophisticated logic in a way they will enjoy.

"Blast Off with Logic" is a series of three books [$9.95 each] which build upon one another at increasing levels of difficulty.

Logic Countdown, written for grades 3-4, introduces relationships, analogies, sequencing, "all" and "no" statements, syllogisms, if-then statements, deduction, and inferencing. *Logic Liftoff* for grades 4-6 reviews and expands all of these topics, continues into deeper logical reasoning, and introduces logical notation. *Orbiting with Logic* for grades 5-7 builds on the previous two books, expands logical notation, and adds logic diagrams and logical fallacies. While it is possible to use any one of the books alone, they really work best as a sort of continuous course. Grade designations are not hard and fast. If an older child hasn't gone through the first two books, use some of the lessons from those to begin with. Most of us parents will find many of the lessons new and challenging, so we should tackle them right along with our children to improve our own thinking skills.

Another series focuses on analogies, those problems that read like, "maple is to elm as rose is to _____." *Analogies for Beginners*, suggested for grades 1-3, includes pictorial analogies as well as word analogies. Answers in this and the other two books are all multiple choice. *Thinking Through Analogies* for grades 3-6 [$7.95] has some illustrations on the pages, but the analogies at this level are all words and no pictures. *Advancing through Analogies* for grades 5-8. This one even throws in a few math analogies. Books are $6.95 each.

Logic Safari [$6.95 each] is yet another series of three books for three levels. These books feature grid matrix logic puzzles at increasing levels of difficulty. These are the puzzles that pose problems like, "There are four children, Joe, Bob, Sue, and Ann. They each have a different pet—a cat, a dog, a bird, and a hamster." Then through a series of statements and working with the grid, children deduce which child owns which pet. Book 1 is for grades 2-3. Book 2 is for grades 3-4. Book 3 is for grades 5-6.(S)

Primary Analogies

(Educators Publishing Service)
Book 1 or 2 - $4.65 each; book 3 - $5.50; teacher's guides - $4.50 each

Help your child develop flexible thinking skills by studying analogies with this series of workbooks for the primary grades. These books are useful also in preparing children to do well on standardized tests. Book 1, for grades K-1, and Book 2 for second grade present problems with pictures and/or words to match up. The child should already have some reading skills to be successful. Book 3 for third grade uses only words and symbols. You will need the teacher's guide and answer key for each book which will give you ideas for teaching your child how to approach analogy problems and will also save you from needless frustration trying to figure out the occasional, ambiguous (or in one case, erroneous) drawing. At the end of each book, the child is invited to make up his own analogies from words in a word bank.(S)

Ridgewood Analogies

(Educators Publishing Service)
$5.85 each; teacher's guide - $2.30 each

Teach your child how to solve five kinds of analogy problems with these workbooks. Each kind of analogy is studied at four skill levels, from finding an analogy that corresponds to a given analogy, to creating two analogies that correspond to one another in a given relationship. Book 1 is for fourth grade, Book 2 for fifth grade, and Book 3 for sixth grade.

Reference Skills

A truly educated person knows how to teach himself. He knows how to search out information from many different sources. The person who relies only on pre-digested textbook information, learns from only one narrow viewpoint on each topic. We need to equip our children with the skills to search out information through various reference materials such as encyclopedias, thesauruses, special reference works such as *The Reader's Guide to Periodical Literature*, atlases, "real" books, videos, and the internet. We want them to be able to teach themselves well, searching out the best sources of information on each topic rather than the most convenient.

Instruction on the use of reference tools is usually covered at some point in most language programs, but it should be an ongoing practice, incorporated into daily school work. We can accomplish this by encouraging our children to look up more colorful words for their writing from a thesaurus, locate on a map the cities where stories they are reading take place, read the books or the encyclopedia to discover more about new topics, etc. Of course, they should also be using dictionaries, indexes, glossaries, and tables of contents every day.

I must add a word about encyclopedias at this point. First of all, an encyclopedia is not absolutely essential. If you have easy access to a library, it is actually better for children to learn to go directly to sources on particular topics than read encyclopedia articles. However, many of us do not have easy library access, in which case an encyclopedia is a great investment. Also, our children sometimes have questions to which they want immediate answers; a trip to the library next week will miss the teachable moment when they are really interested in the answer. An encyclopedia can supply that quick answer. Another reason you might need an encyclopedia is if you use a unit study program that relies heavily upon the World Book Encyclopedia, as do a few of those I review in this book.

While the cost of encyclopedias made them an impractical investment for many families in the past, computer CD-ROM versions and on-line encyclopedias have changed the situation dramatically in a short time. While many of us will still prefer actual books, I suspect that these will largely be replaced with electronic versions in the next few years.

World Book seems to be the clear frontrunner for homeschoolers because of the high quality of articles, the reading level, colorful illustrations, and breadth of topics. Articles are accessible for mid-elementary grade students, yet there is enough detail to maintain the interest of even an adult audience. *World Book* is available in both print and CD-ROM formats as well as by subscription on-line at www.worldbookonline.com.

Another useful CD-ROM encyclopedia that is sometimes recommended by unit study programs is Microsoft's *Encarta*. Encarta is a wonderful starting place with lots of colorful illustrations and short, easy-to-read text. You can easily purchase a copy at a very reasonable price at software outlets, and you might even get it bundled with pre-installed software on your computer.

Encyclopedia Britannica upset the encyclopedia world with their announcement that they were making their entire encyclopedia available on-line for *free* at www.britannica.com. In many ways, this on-line version is even better than a print encyclopedia. When you search for a topic, the web site brings up encyclopedia articles plus magazine article synopses and an annotated web site list. This is useful even when the *Encyclopedia Britannica* doesn't have an article on a topic. For example, I searched for "creation science," a topic for which the *Encyclopedia* lacks any articles, but the other books, magazine articles, and websites that came up might be even better sources. *Encyclopedia* articles you pull up include highlighted topics you can click on to move to other articles. All articles include lists of additional topics (and, sometimes, books) in which you might be interested. This is an adult level encyclopedia, but it should be an excellent tool for older students and parents. There are some advertisements on the site pages, but they are not very obtrusive. Surprisingly, you don't have to sign up for anything or provide personal information to access the *Encyclopedia*.

There are other free, on-line encyclopedias or research URLs, although most are not as extensive as *Encyclopedia Britannica*. Other on-line reference resources sometimes have the added benefit of hot links to other web sites with related information. I particularly like the **Kids' Almanac** site at http://kids.infoplease.com/. It includes the *Columbia Encyclopedia, Information Please Almanac*, a dictionary and other sources. When you enter a topic, it brings up a list of the resources where it is mentioned, including the dictionary definition.

Certainly, there are numerous other encyclopedias to choose from. You might find that you want to own both print and CD-ROM versions of encyclopedias so that your child who loves to curl up in the beanbag chair with books as well as the computer lover both have opportunity to explore these resources.

Reference Skill Resources

Facts Plus
(Instructional Resources Company)
Almanac, $15.95; Activity Book $19.95

Two separate books can be purchased as a set or individually. The first book is *Facts Plus: An Almanac of Essential Information*. One might describe it as a 250-page mini-encyclopedia. It is divided into ten sections: time and space, science and health, the Earth and its people, the United States, maps, libraries and books, the English language, writing/music/art, math and numbers, and handbook. Each of those sections is further divided under subtopics. Information is geared for grades 4-6 but will be useful for older and, possibly, younger students. An extremely comprehensive index makes it easy to locate appropriate information. This book can be used on its own as a reference tool.

The second book is *Facts Plus: Activity Book*. The *Activity Book* helps students learn how to locate and use information. It can be used with other resource books, including encyclopedias, but it is keyed (with page numbers) to the *Almanac*. Too often, without aids such as the *Activity Book*, students do not get enough experience actually using whatever reference books we have, so I recommend it also. Games, worksheets, charts, time lines, map outlines, a make-it-yourself passport, and other pages are used with the lesson instructions for a wide variety of learning activities involving research. (The geological periods and events activities reflect evolutionary assumptions, so adapt as needed.) The books were originally written for the classroom, so there are a few suggestions that are impractical in a small setting (e.g., having a rubber stamp custom-made to use on the passports). However, most activities will work well with a single child, small group, or a child interacting with an adult.(SE)

Information, Please!
(D.P. & K. Productions)
$16 per volume except for Getting Started - $20

Designed particularly for home educating families, the *Information, Please!* books are the perfect tool for helping our children become proficient information seekers. There are four books: *Getting Started, Beginning, Intermediate,* and *Advanced*. Reading skills are prerequisite, but most third graders should be able to answer most of the questions from the *Getting Started* level. *Getting Started* is an introduction to the use of reference materials, appropriate for almost any student who is just beginning to work with such tools. It also has 12 practice pages similar to the content of each of the other three books (four pages per book). These will give you a better idea of how the books work and also help you pinpoint the appropriate level for students. *Beginning* is best for grades 1-5. *Intermediate* should be appropriate for grades 6-8. *Advanced* should be best for grades 9 and up.

Each book has forty pages with ten questions per page. Many children might need some assistance initially as they learn where to look for answers, but soon they will be able to identify the correct sources and find it for themselves. The research, especially once we are past the *Beginning* level, goes beyond the standard dictionary/thesaurus/encyclopedia/globe approach found in most other classroom designed materials. Some of the information can be found at home, but you will probably want to plan a weekly trip to the library to "do research." A child can work alone or with a parent's assistance. We can photocopy these pages for children in our family so they can compete to see who can find all the answers first. We might give different sheets to different students if we prefer to avoid competition. Questions are extremely eclectic. A few examples from *Beginning* level: "How much postage is required to mail a postcard?", "How many degrees are in a circle?", and "What are the duties of a public relations specialist?" Examples from the *Intermediate* level: "What causes the blackness under an injured fingernail?", "Which two countries had the highest casualties during WWII?", and "What does 'P.S.' stand for at the end of a letter?"

Even better, the author is a Christian home schooling parent, so we also encounter Scripture-related questions. Answers will vary from single word to lengthier explanations, and answer keys are included. *Information, Please!* seems more like a game than a part of the curriculum, yet it accomplishes a major educational goal in equipping our children to do their own research.

Library Skills for Christian Students
(Peggy Pickering)
$25; teacher manual - $10

Familiarize your children with the library by working through this course. The student book is approximately 220 pages with information and mostly fill-in-the-blank type activities. Students learn about everything from basic "how to find it" skills, card catalog (physical catalog or computerized catalog), and Dewey Decimal System through use of specialized reference works. This is intended to be a three year course for grades 4-6. (Pickering also offers *Library Skills Introduction* for younger students which I have not reviewed.) Most activities do not require actual trips to the library, maybe an advantage for many families, but a deficiency in my opinion. I would love to see more of these activities adapted so that students need to actually search through the library to apply what they are learning. Still, the information in this course is far more comprehensive than students will find in any language arts course, most of which cover library skills in a cursory fashion. The teacher manual offers additional information and serves as

an answer key.

Study Skills [Introductory and Intermediate Levels]
(Essential Learning Products)
$2.95 each

These two, half-size workbooks are geared toward fourth through sixth grades. They are both subtitled "Using Books and Libraries." Topical areas are the same in both books—dictionary skills, parts of a book, kinds of books (e.g., thesaurus, atlas, almanac), and library skills—with lessons more difficult in the intermediate level book.

Essential Learning Products has four other *Study Skills* books, A-D, which emphasize study skills such as goal setting, organization, test taking, paying attention, and remembering. They should fit grades 1-4, using them in alphabetical order. Answer keys are at the back of each book.(S)

Teaching Children to Use the Library
by Mary Hood, Ph.D.
(Elijah Company)
$5

Parents learn how to teach their children to use the library with this "5-step program for parents" by home education consultant Mary Hood. This 20-page book is for parents of children of all ages. It starts at the beginning, describing the parts of a book and the difference between non-fiction and fiction. Next, we learn how to locate materials in general using the Dewey Decimal system and the less common Library of Congress system. Detailed information about the "shelving" of fiction and non-fiction books, such as special coding, helps simplify our book or topic searches. The last step is learning to use library resources to do research. This section will help us teach our children how to make use of the adult reference section rather than relying on children's resources. Two appendices, "Using the Library to Develop a Curriculum for Teaching Your Children at Home" and "Recommended Children's Books and Resources for Parents" will help us take full advantage of the wealth of material available at our library.

Chapter 8

Introduction to Language and Reading

Language arts has to do with all areas of communication. To keep from overlooking important skills, I have divided language arts into individual areas. Reading is the key area and the first to be addressed.

In developing reading skills, we concentrate on phonics at beginning levels, shifting the emphasis to reading comprehension and other reading skills, then literature at older levels. Some children will work on phonics longer than others. Some will need to reinforce phonics principles with exercises in supplemental phonics workbooks and/or phonetic spelling programs. Some will need to work on reading comprehension skills much more than others.

We need to gradually develop other language skills as children are ready. Writing (both handwriting and composition) skills will be dependent upon the development of small motor coordination. My personal opinion is that spelling should not come into the picture until children can read and understand the words they spell, and they are also able to write comfortably enough to think about spelling as they write. Grammar study can begin once children are able to compose sentences but should keep pace with a child's ability to apply what he learns in his writing.

Goals and Motivation

One of the primary goals of education for us as Christians should be learning how to communicate the message of salvation to others. The communication tools we need are reading, so we can first obtain knowledge for ourselves, then writing and speaking, so we can pass our message on to others.

We should also have secondary goals having to do with communication for survival in this world. Reading for information, forming and maintaining relationships, employment, filling out forms, and making purchases all have to do with effective communication. The list of goals could be endless.

We generally set goals for our children's education that reflect our own education. For instance, because most schools teach cursive in second or third grade, we expect that everyone must learn cursive at that point, or because we learned the eight parts of speech in fourth grade, so should our children.

We need to recognize that both goals and methods are often debatable. For example, some folks have decided to skip manuscript (printing) and begin with cursive instruction. Others have reacted to their children's resistance to learning cursive by teaching them to print efficiently and use the computer.

We need to carefully set and examine our goals, questioning whether each one is valid or simply based on "tradition." We need to believe strongly in the goals we set. Then a large part of our job is to help our children recognize and appropriate these goals for themselves, although don't expect this to happen before upper elementary grade levels. This will happen most easily when children are allowed to experience real-life need for each skill, whether it be reading, writing, speaking, spelling properly, and so on. When our children feel a need to communicate, they will be more motivated to learn the required skills. Just as children most often become interested in learning to read when they have been introduced to the wonders hidden in printed words by being read to, they also become interested in writing when they see something worthwhile happening with their written communication. Telling a seven-year-old boy that practicing his printing will enable him to get a better job when he is an adult, provides little motivation, but finding a pen pal who wants to exchange letters may give him just the needed impetus.

If our children grasp the purposes for developing their communication skills, both teaching and learning will be much easier.

Chapter 9

Reading

Educational Goals

Thousands of books and programs have been written about the mechanics of reading instruction, so there's no reason for me to repeat the wealth of information available elsewhere. Instead, I lay out some basic guidelines of what is typically covered at younger and older levels. However, keep in mind that children are ready for reading instruction at different ages, and each child will progress at his own rate. Do not choose a level based solely upon your child's age. Also, the sequence for learning to read can vary with the individual, so be sensitive to your child's abilities and needs.

Learning to Read - Readiness

Readiness activities such as matching and classifying are supposed to help lay a framework for actual reading skills. Such activities as matching identical shapes help children to recognize and remember letters. Discrimination skills that will help children differentiate between *b*'s and *d*'s are developed by having children identify subtle differences between objects.

Readiness activities are offered in abundance in kindergarten programs but are often repetitive of everyday activities that happen incidentally in the home. For example, matching practice and discrimination take place as your child helps you sort socks into pairs. Do not waste time having your children fill in workbook pages to learn skills they acquire more naturally by helping around the house.

Examples of readiness skills about which you should be concerned:

- auditory discrimination (understanding what people are saying, distinguishing between different sounds)
- listening skill (staying tuned in to what someone is saying)
- visual discrimination (identifying visual similarities and differences)
- directionality (up, down, above, below, right, left)
- lengthening attention span, fine motor skills (ability to hold and write with a pencil or crayon with relative ease)
- identifying attributes (e.g., an object is large, the color red, has stripes, etc.)

Reading Materials and Methods

Readiness

There is some controversy over the time to begin reading instruction with children. Research (see Dr. Raymond Moore's *School Can Wait* and *Better Late Than Early*) indicates that children who are pushed to read before they have reached a certain maturity level often have difficulty that hinders their reading for the rest of their lives. On the other hand, young children often show an interest in reading and express a desire to learn. Whether they are actually ready to begin reading will have to be determined on an individual basis, but you can begin readiness activities with any young child. If they are not ready to proceed beyond readiness activities, it will be apparent in their short memory of the names of the letters and/or in their confusion of sounds. A young child might be ready and <u>can</u> be taught to read, but it might require much repetition, and this approach might be detrimental in the long run if it is forced.

Read Aloud

Reading aloud to children is one of the most important factors in developing children who read well. As they hear well-written, imaginative language, their vocabulary grows along with their appreciation for and interest in the written word.

I cannot over stress the importance of reading aloud to our children. We are giving our children the message that we value books, and that reading is something that we choose for enjoyment and for other purposes. On the other hand, if we have few books around the house and seldom pick one up other than when forced to, we are effectually telling our children that books have little value in life. Most children desire to be like their parents, and they most likely will adopt our attitudes toward reading.

It is generally best to choose books above the child's reading level for reading aloud to them. Their comprehension vocabulary is usually higher than we give them credit for. Introducing them to the beautiful sounds of language in the hands of a skillful writer opens a new dimension in their lives.

Many parents have trouble figuring out what types of books our children should or should not read. I have been told by many home educators that they allow their children to read only books that are true. But they overlook an important aspect of literature when they do this. When an author writes a biography about a person who lived a century or more in the past, there is often little first hand information about him or her (such as diaries, eye-witness reports, letters to friends, etc.). They must ask how much of that biography will be true and how much is manufactured to fill in the blanks of the author's knowledge. Do such biographies constitute truth any more than do stories that are written about fictional characters but based upon real-life events?

The only written work that is wholly true is the Bible. Everything else has the possibility of containing untruth. If we do not want to restrict our children's reading to only the Bible, we must wrestle with the issue of what is acceptable. Books such as *Reading Between the Lines* and *A Landscape with Dragons* will help you think through these issues and learn how to make your own decisions.

Rather than give a comprehensive list of specific authors and books for you to read with your children in this publication, I would advise that you purchase and refer often to one or more of the following books.

Books Children Love

by Elizabeth Wilson
(Crossway)
$14.99

This is an excellent source for recommended books which have been selected by a Christian author. She has grouped recommendations (with descriptions of each) by areas of interest and designated appropriate ages. She has been very selective in choosing only books most Christians would find acceptable.

Best Books for Kindergarten through High School

(Bob Jones University Press)
$9.95

This is a compilation of annotated listings of recommended fiction arranged by levels. Books have been chosen for literary merit and propriety for Christian children. For junior and senior high levels, there are additional listings of worthwhile literature that requires some discussion because of questionable elements. (Those elements are described for us.) Another section lists biographies and autobiographies. At the end are excellent guidelines for choosing books.

A Family Program for Reading Aloud

by Rosalie Slater
(Foundation for American Christian Education)
$16

This is more than just a list of recommendations. It outlines the Principle Approach as applied to literature and a study of American history. It features great recommendations for those who want to read for more than just enjoyment.

For the Love of Reading

by Valerie Bendt
(Common Sense Press)
$15

Author, Valerie Bendt, is an experienced home school mom who wants to encourage us to inculcate a love for books in our children. In her book, Valerie uses anecdotes from her own family to show how listening to stories can lead to story telling and then to reading. She gives suggestions about how to foster a love for reading and how to extend learning by writing and game playing. Although this is not a step-by-step instruction book, it is inspirational.

Hand that Rocks the Cradle

by Nathaniel Bluedorn
(Trivium Pursuit)
$5

Hand that Rocks the Cradle is a booklet listing recommended fiction, presented in both alphabetical order by author and by subject area. Some titles are described with time settings, publication date and story summaries. It includes some modern fiction but mostly "classic" titles from authors such as Marguerite De Angeli, Daniel Defoe, Frank Gilbreth, Marguerite Henry, C.S. Lewis, E.B. White, Mark Twain, and Jack London.

Honey for a Child's Heart

by Gladys Hunt
(Zondervan Publishing House)
$10.99

This long-time favorite encourages Christian parents to read to their children and gives specific recommendations.

How to Grow a Young Reader

by Kathryn Linskoog and Ranelda Mack Hunsicker
(Harold Shaw Publishers)
$14.99

While most people will purchase this book primarily for the reading recommendations, Linskoog and Hunsicker also use the first four chapters to accomplish broader goals. They first make a case for modern children's literature to be read in addition to "classic" literature. They discuss "enemies" of reading—things like television and video games that have negative influences on the brain and thinking skills as well as on a child's motivation to read. The third chapter presents some strategies to get the family "into books." The fourth chapter is a condensed history of children's literature which might have appeal for some readers. From there we move on to the annotated recommendations of more than 1,800 books for children of all ages. They are presented in categories such as classics, fantasy, realistic fiction and biography, picture books, and books that provide "Christian nurture and values." General age levels are suggested. The viewpoint is definitely Christian, although there are certainly some recommendations that Christians will quibble over. The annotations/descriptions are lengthier and more helpful than in many other such books, making this a helpful tool for parents in guiding children's selection of reading material.

How to Raise a Reader
by Elaine K. McEwan
(Baker Books)
$9.99

Originally published in 1987, this book is now available in a new, updated edition. It begins by making a case for the importance of reading, both for the child and for the impact reading together has upon relationships. McEwan points out the failure of many schools to provide this necessary foundation and encourages parents to assume this task. She tells us, "You don't need to be remarkably learned about education and psychology. You need only a remarkable respect for the mind of a child, a willingness to be consistent, lots of patience, and hundreds of good books." A good part of the book consists of book recommendations, arranged by topics and levels. She begins with books for children up to about three years old, followed by those for ages 4 to 7, and ending with recommendations for ages 8 to 12. Most parents will appreciate that her selections for the last group lean toward "classic" titles rather than modern, high-interest books. Bible story books, Bibles, and Christian literature are included. Resources lists help parents find phonics programs, help for children with reading problems, and information about other reading-related issues.

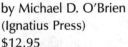

A Landscape with Dragons
by Michael D. O'Brien
(Ignatius Press)
$12.95

Do you avoid tales of monsters, dragons, and evil beings when it comes to children's literature? Michael O'Brien suggests that there is tremendous value in mythology and other forms of fiction when symbols are properly used, reflecting spiritual realities. Just as Scripture uses images of the dragon and the serpent to represent Satan, some classic tales incorporate similar images to create battles between good and evil. Good literature becomes a morality tale.

In contrast, some modern children literature (as well as movies) have corrupted such symbolism. Dragons are now heroes, and serpents have been unreasonably maligned. Such literature can undermine spiritual truth by creating fictional falsehoods.

Other spiritually positive and destructive elements appear throughout children's literature. O'Brien presents a four-tiered method of categorizing literature in relation to spiritual truth and danger. Using examples, he shows how he determines the categories for various books. As O'Brien explains, categories are sometimes ambiguous, but it does present a framework for helping us make judgments.

This book is particularly helpful in alerting us to the subtle spiritual dangers we often miss. For example, he tells us, "A powerful falsehood is implanted in the young boy by heroes who are given knowledge of good and evil, given power over good and evil, who play with evil but are never corrupted by it."

The last third of the book features more than one thousand recommended books arranged in categories of increasing level of difficulty.

Let the Authors Speak: A Guide to Worthy Books Based on Historical Setting
by Carolyn Hatcher
(Old Pinnacle Publishing)
$18.95

Those who prefer a more classical approach to literature should check out *Let the Authors Speak*. Hatcher uses the first half of the book to explain the rationale for using real books for learning and for literature, basing her ideas upon those of Charlotte Mason, Susan Schaeffer Macaulay, Marva Collins, and others. The second half lists books, first by historical setting (time period, location), then by author. A supplemental section lists myths/legends, fantasy, folk tales, fables, and allegories by time period. Few recommendations of drama and poetry are listed, and few 20th century titles appear since most have not yet had time to establish themselves as classics. Brief comments accompany each entry. Hatcher works from a Judeo-Christian world view and leans toward a western-civilization background, which is reflected in the lists. However, all books listed are not necessarily Christian.

Reading Between the Lines: A Christian Guide to Literature
by Gene Edward Veith, Jr.
(Crossway Books)
$14.99

Reading Between the Lines helps us sort through the different factors relating to our Christian faith, literary value, and enjoyment when choosing reading material. Veith, a university instructor, loves literature, and because of this he promotes guidelines some of us might feel are too liberal. However, as you read this book, you will probably do some rethinking about your view of literature. Even with the area of fantasy, which seems to be one of the biggest problem areas, Veith does an excellent job of explaining how to differentiate between that which is worthwhile and that which is not.

For those of us with a poor literary background, this book

provides an excellent mini-course in literature. Veith piques our interest by quoting from various authors and whetting our appetites for "the whole story." You are likely to find yourself making a list of books you need to read. Some of us might feel overwhelmed if we try to read this entire book straight through. I recommend taking a leisurely approach, reading those sections that are most pertinent to your concerns first and others as you find the time or need.

They're Never Too Young for Books: A Guide to Children's Books for Ages 1 to 8
by Edyth McGovern and Helen Muller
(Prometheus Books)
$16.95

I realize that some readers of my book are looking for a broader selection of recommended books for children than those in the other resources such as *Honey for A Child's Heart*. *They're Never Too Young for Books* reflects popular psychological views about child training, views with which many of my readers might disagree. However, this resource is still useful for Christian homeschoolers since it lists a huge number of books according to categories we do not find in the others. A sampling of these categories: tall tales, security and safety, family life (adoption, new baby, siblings, etc.), competence and self-esteem, behavior and misbehavior, friendship, sexual identity, moving, divorce, illness, death, peace-related, monsters, animals, seasons, ethnic groups, poetry, bilingual books, songs with music, informational books, and books that emphasize skills. Each book is described with a sentence or two. While this resource recommends a huge number of books, it does so on "literary merit" only. Recommendations do not take into consideration objections Christian parents might have to the treatment of some topics. Thus, we are not forewarned, but must preview questionable books on our own.(S)

Sources for Quality Literature

A number of Christian suppliers offer quality reading material we can trust. BJUP publishes "real" books for reading in addition to their textbook line. Check the "Sources" section for other suppliers who carry reading books for children. While many suppliers sell literature along with other books

Scholastic has a catalog that is exclusively dedicated to supplementary reading books. Books for kindergarten through twelfth grade are sold as grade level collections or individually at very reasonable prices. While they carry classics, they also carry a wide range of modern literature from which you will need to make careful choices.(SE)

Finding Classic Literature

Many of us turn to books that are considered classics, since the content is generally much better than that found in most modern literature. However, while abridged versions of classics make difficult books accessible to a wider audience, some abridged versions mutilate the original story in content and/or style.

Troll Books sells a series of abridged classics (twenty-nine titles available) that have exceptionally beautiful illustrations [$3.95 each]. You will need to check the content yourself on these. Troll also lists more than one hundred titles in their Watermill Classics line at very low prices. These are unabridged versions of such favorites as *Black Arrow, Gulliver's Travels, Heidi, Red Badge of Courage,* and *Wind in the Willows* [$2.95 to $3.95 each].(SE)

Another source for classics is **Scholastic, Inc**. Send for their catalog for complete listings of available titles.

Audio Classics

Those seeking unabridged audiobooks need to check out the extensive catalogs of **Blackstone Audiobooks** or **Books on Tape, Inc.** Both sell and rent unabridged books, while Blackstone also offers selected plays, speeches, and special programs.

The Blackstone catalog is so large that tapes are categorized under headings like "Literature of the 20th Century," "Literature" (i.e., classics), "Children's," "Non-fiction," "Politics," and "Religion." Among books for children are such titles as *The Five Little Peppers and How They Grew, The Railway Children, Anne of Green Gables, The Princess and the Goblin,* and *The Secret Garden*. Prices depend upon the length of each work. For example, *Robinson Crusoe* is produced on eight 1 1/2-hour cassettes, sells for $56.95, and rents for 30 days at $12.95. *The Wind in the Willows* fills five 1 1/2-hour cassettes, sells for $39.95, and rents for 30 days at $10.95.

Books on Tape also has a huge 500+ page catalog with books categorized under eleven categories including "Books for Young Readers" and "Classics." They carry an excellent collection of truly classic literature such as books by James Fenimore Cooper, Alexandre Dumas, Nathaniel Hawthorne, and Charles Dickens as well as works such as Machiavelli's *The Prince* and Plato's *Apology of Socrates/Crito/The Republic*. An example of pricing: Charles Dickens' *Great Expectations*—twelve 1 1/2-hour cassettes—rents for $14.95 and sells for $96.

Greathall Productions offers audio cassettes of literary classics [$9.95 each] that can be used with children who are pre-readers or reluctant readers, or with children whose best learning modality is auditory. Greathall's brochure indicates a non-judgmental, "new-age" philosophy, so select tapes with that in mind. In spite of that caveat, the tapes, performed with dramatic flair by storyteller Jim Weiss, are very well done. Weiss seems to have an unlimited repertoire of voices, and combined with sound effects, the result is far more entertaining than most storytelling. Some possibilities I might suggest are *The Jungle Book, Greek Myths, The Three Musketeers/Robin Hood, Arabian Nights, King Arthur and His Knights,* and *Sherlock Holmes for Children.* Most titles can also be purchased in CD format [$14.95 each]. These are all one-hour-long, mostly-abridged versions, recommended for ages 5-12, but older children will also enjoy some of these. Don't expect the flowery language of Howard Pyle's version of *Robin Hood* or of the unabridged *Arabian Nights* (although *Arabian Nights* comes closer to the original than does *Robin Hood*). The vocabulary straddles the fine line of being understandable to children without talking down to them or alienating adult listeners.(SE)

The **Children's Classics Library** and **Family Classics Library** audio tapes (Newport Publishers) [$49.95 each set] are a mixture of abridged and unabridged versions of classics. There are forty audio cassette tapes in each of these sets. The *Children's Classics* set is only slightly younger in content than the *Family Classics.* All tapes are recorded with sound effects and a variety of voices. Some of these are full-length, unabridged presentations, some are "mildly" abridged, and some are extremely short presentations—little more than plot summaries.

Examples of titles in the *Children's Classics Library* are *The Adventures of Huckleberry Finn* - 6, *Gulliver's Travels* - 4, *The Legend of Sleepy Hollow* - 2, *The Wind in the Willows* - 6, *Pinocchio* - 5, *Peter Pan* - 1, *Fiction and Fantasy* - 1, *Sleeping Beauty* - 1. (Numbers following titles indicate the number of tapes for each presentation.)

Examples of titles in the *Family Classics Library* are *The Pickwick Papers* - 1, *Les Miserables* - 6, *The Call of the Wild* -1, *The Count of Monte Cristo* - 1, *A Tale of Two Cities* - 9, *A Christmas Carol* - 3, *Great Expectations* - 5, and *The Scarlet Letter* - 4.

Quality varies from presentation to presentation. For example, *Gulliver's Travels* was hard to understand and the use of speeded-up and slowed-down voices for tiny people and giants did not work well. The retelling of *Little Red Riding Hood* on the *Fiction and Fantasy Tape* featured a distressing combination of professional and amateur reading voices. On the other hand, *A Tale of Two Cities* and *The Count of Monte Cristo* are both quite good. Most of the tapes, with the exception of a few single tapes (e.g., Fairy Tales, *Aesop's Fables,* Nursery Rhymes), are for an audience at least in their teens rather than for younger children, partly because of the vocabulary level and partly because of length and children's attention span. The value of these tapes for homeschoolers is exposure to stories that might not be read in their original versions. (I'm not recommending such substitutions as a major part of a literature program, but only as a supplement to expand familiarity and possibly stimulate interest in the original version.) Although the quality and age appropriateness vary greatly from tape to

tape, if we consider either set as an investment for the entire family they are a bargain.(S)

Reading Readiness Activities

Preparing your child to read requires activities besides reading aloud. As mentioned previously, numerous books and programs on the subject are available, so we will not attempt to outline a readiness program. However, one important idea is sometimes ignored by reading programs and should be briefly mentioned here. You should try to introduce the sounds of letters with a movable alphabet—plastic, wooden, posterboard, magnetic, sandpaper, felt, etc. It is very helpful to have vowels in a different color than consonants to demonstrate the special role vowels play. The *Magnetic AlphaBoard* (Educational Insights) [$19.95] features 36 each of capital and lower case letters (besides numbers and math symbols). Although they are not color-coded, they are very practical. We can use the letters on the portable board or stick them on the refrigerator where they are handy for spur of the moment use. After introducing letters, point out letters in the environment for children to practice letter recognition and identification of sounds. Another source for magnetic letters is **Peter Parker's Magnetic Learning Systems.** They sell 42-letter *Magnetic Alphabet* sets of either upper or lower case letters [$8.95 each set]. Vowels are red, and consonants are blue. Peter Parker's also sells sets of *Phonics Magnets* which have vowel blends, silent "e" endings, consonant blends, and digraphs [$8.95]. Magnetic boards, pages, binders, and mats are also available starting at $3.99 each.

Do we need a program?

We can teach our children to read without a reading program. Some children might even teach themselves if we're not careful! If they are brought up to love books, they might just decide to go ahead without us. Many children zoom ahead on their reading after a little instruction on beginning phonics.

Reading can and should be fun. If we are working too hard and having no fun, perhaps we are going about it the wrong way. By just working with letters around us—on signs, cereal boxes, in our child's name, or with silly games we create—we can introduce sounds of letters in a more effective way than through a program. For reading material we are neither required to use nor limited to the use of readers.

We can instead use the library or other sources for "real" books, children's magazines, and Bible stories to serve as reading material. We can choose simple books to begin with such as P.D. Eastman's *Go, Dog, Go!* or Dr. Seuss' *Green Eggs and Ham.* Since these materials are not strictly vocabulary controlled, we have children read words they know while we read the unknowns. Gradually we expand their vocabulary using phonetic guidelines such as those in *Professor Phonics* or *Noah Webster's Reading Handbook* to know which words to introduce next. It is not necessary to limit a child to learning only words that fit in a proper phonetic order, but working systematically will help us know what to expect and when to urge them to attempt different words.

Reading favorite books over and over and over again, then having our child begin to read familiar words is a good beginning. Children can begin by reading only one or two words whenever they occur in a story. As they learn new sounds and words (that we may have taken from a phonics manual and taught our child informally), they gradually try to read more words. This approach is more of a game than a lesson, but it works. When children are familiar with the text already, they do a bit of sight reading, but at the same time they begin to apply phonics concepts as we teach them. The success they experience with a familiar book is a strong impetus to further progress.

Some books that work well with this approach:
- *Green Eggs and Ham; The Cat in the Hat; Oh Say Can You Say?; Hop on Pop; Fox in Socks;* and *One Fish, Two Fish, Red Fish, Blue Fish* by Dr. Seuss (Random House)
- *Frog and Toad, Frog and Toad are Friends,* and *Frog and Toad Together* by Arnold Lobel (Harper and Row)
- *Katy and the Big Snow* by Virginia Lee Burton
- *Are You My Mother?* and *Go, Dog, Go!* by P.D. Eastman (Random House)
- *Best Word Book Ever* by Richard Scarry (Western)
- *Little Bear* by Elsa H. Minarik (Harper and Row)
- "Beginner Books" from Random House by Theo LeSieg (aka Dr. Seuss) and Robert Lopshire such as Lopshire's *Put Me in the Zoo.*

On a more challenging level:
- *Frog and Toad All Year* by Arnold Lobel (Harper and Row)
- *The Bear Scouts* by Stan and Jan Berenstain (Random House) (Note: Berenstain Bear books make dad look foolish.)
- *Make Way for Ducklings* by Robert McCloskey (Viking)
- *Curious George* by H.A. Rey (Houghton Mifflin)

Children are so different in what strikes their fancy. If they have a favorite book or type of books, choose that in preference to any on a recommended list as long as it meets with your approval.

It is often easier to supplement with some beginning phonetic readers such as those from the *Bob Books* series or Modern Curriculum Press phonetic readers or with lists of words such as those found in the *Victory Drill Book.*

It is necessary to make sure children do have a knowledge of phonics for future "decoding" efforts and spelling. But acquiring that knowledge can be surprisingly easy.

Teaching a child to read does not need to be an overwhelming task, although some methods make it seem like it. A little, twenty-eight page booklet, *A Home Start in Reading* (Mott Media) by Dr. Ruth Beechick, outlines a simple phonics pro-gram along with hints on teaching spelling. Even if you choose to use another program, this little book is a gold mine of hints and helps for teaching reading. (When purchased as *The Three R's* set [$12] with Beechick's other two books on math and language, we get a two-sided phonics/math chart that provides a simple summary of phonics.) With so many good choices, the thing to do is to choose the method that provides us with the amount of guidance we desire and with which both we and our child are comfortable.

Consider Your Child's Learning Style

New beginning reading programs are popping up constantly. Most of us are convinced phonics is the way to go, but you will probably find that Wiggly Willys have a bit more difficulty learning phonics rules than other children, usually because they would rather be moving than sitting still. For Wiggly Willys we might choose a program that teaches phonics through games, actions, and songs such as *Sing, Spell, Read, and Write; Listen and Learn with Phonics;* or *Play 'N Talk.* However, make sure they get enough actual reading practice and do not become dependent on recalling jingles before they can decode words. Perfect Paulas and Competent Carls who do not have learning disabilities should do well with just about any phonics program. Programs such as Romalda Spalding's *Writing Road to Reading*, which might not work as well with Wiggly Willys and Sociable Sues because of their dislike of detail, should work better for Perfect Paulas and Competent Carls. "Willy" and "Sue" might feel overwhelmed with the multitude of rules that would appeal to"Paula" or "Carl." Problems that crop up with such programs can be overcome by paying close attention to a child's responses and varying teaching methods, such as using more oral work rather than written work, to best suit each child.

Our learning style (as the teacher) is also likely to have some influence over what material we choose. We need to be cautious that we are meeting our child's needs as well as choosing a program with which we can work.

Whether or not we choose to work with a reading program, it is vital that we also have our child read real books as soon as possible. For reading material, choose types of literature that appeal to each type of learner to stimulate reading interest, and then challenge them to try other types of literature to help them grow. If we want to find literature on a particular theme, the library usually has such lists available. Some home education distributors list books thematically (especially historical novels and biographies), and the *The Unit Study Idea Book* (Common Sense Press) has recommendations under a limited number of themes.

LEARNING STYLES
Wiggly Willy Prefers:
- an activity-oriented approach to learning phonics and reading

- reading from context
- exciting or humorous stories
- mysteries and adventure stories

Wiggly Willy needs help and encouragement to concentrate on phonetic rules, analyze stories, and read for information

Perfect Paula Prefers:

- phonics
- word lists
- work sheets rather than oral work
- oral reading if she is prepared

Perfect Paula needs help and encouragement to read from context and to read beyond literal meaning

Competent Carl Prefers:

- reading in subject area of personal interest
- efficient phonics programs without too many extras
- mystery stories
- technical reading

Competent Carl needs help and encouragement to read outside his narrow areas of interest

Sociable Sue Prefers:

- phonics that is not overly detailed in presentation
- stories about people or moral values
- fables and parables

Sociable Sue needs help and encouragement to read more technical textbooks

Readiness Programs

(Note: Some readiness programs include basic subject areas in addition to phonics.)

ABC-123
(A Beka Book)
$10.25; lesson plans - $59.95

This book falls into the readiness category if you consider knowing letters and sounds plus numbers and counting up to 20 as pre-kindergarten skills. A Beka uses this book as part of their K-4 or early kindergarten program. However, some might use it earlier or later, depending upon the child. You should be using A Beka's *Phonics/Reading/Writing Curriculum/Lesson Plans* to understand their method of presenting phonics (consonant-vowel pairs on ladders); *ABC-123* is not designed to be used alone. Children learn to write letters and numbers, but they do not write whole words in this book. Most exercises require circling correct answers and connecting lines between items.

Common Sense Learning for Kindergarten Skills
(Common Sense Press)

This program serves as a readiness program. See the complete review under "All-in-One Studies."

Hearts and Hands
by Darrel A. Trulson
(Christian Liberty Press)
$6

Subtitled "Beginning Drill in Letters, Phonics and Numbers," this worktext is similar in concept to those from A Beka (especially *ABC-123*). Number and letter recognition and writing are taught along with letter sounds. Teaching instructions are in the introduction and on each page as needed. No teacher's manual is needed. The lack of a teacher's manual and CLP's already low prices make this an inexpensive choice. The 150-page book is printed in two colors (black and red), with large type and clear, line-drawn illustrations. Children will be able to do many activities without parental help but will require assistance on some. This is a practical resource for use before a phonics program that assumes children already recognize letters and individual sounds.

A Home Start in Reading
by Dr. Ruth Beechick
(Mott Media)
sold as part of the Three R's set for $12

With some pre-existing confidence in our ability to teach reading, we can actually teach our child how to read with only this book! This 28-page book has five sections covering the five essential stages of reading: prereading, beginning, blending, decoding, and fluency. Dr. Beechick includes charts of phonetic sounds (including combinations of letters) and lists of basic sight words. She also describes simple yet effective reading readiness activities that all children should experience.

Sing, Spell, Read, and Write Pre-Kindergarten ⌒
(International Learning Systems of North America, Inc.)
$69.95

Sing, Spell, Read, and Write, *Kindergarten* and *Level 1* programs contain some readiness activity, but the *Pre-Kindergarten* kit focuses much more on age-appropriate readiness activities for young children. The *Pre- Kindergarten* kit includes a teacher's manual, 5 cassette tapes and one CD (use one or the other), alphabet/key word cards, a package of worksheets, an alphabet placemat (with a chart for marking progress on reverse), alphabet puzzle cards, laminated clock and picture of shoes for learning time telling and shoe tieing, popsicle sticks, stickers, and a small alphabet/number strip. Cassettes and the CD feature children's songs relating to the various concepts being learned: the alphabet, shapes, numbers, etc. (Words and some of the music are printed in the teacher's manual.)

This kit works on basic readiness activities: letter/sound recognition, counting from 1 to 10, colors, shapes, classifying skills, sequencing skills, direction concepts, attributes of objects, and seasons.

The teacher's manual provides daily lesson plan suggestions, suggestions for related children's literature to read, and a number of hands-on activities from which to choose. Some activities depend upon a classroom setting, but most are easily adaptable for home schoolers. The program requires one-on-one presentation. Worksheet activities (used as worksheets to be done at home with parents for traditional classroom groups) involve coloring, drawing, cutting, and pasting.

This kit is appropriate for children about age 4 (even though it is not necessary to use a program at this age). It is not necessary for all students to use the *Pre-Kindergarten* kit before beginning either of the more advanced kits.(S)

Other books

Many inexpensive readiness books are available at teacher supply stores, markets, and department stores. *Golden Step Ahead* books are an example of this type of book.

Teaching Phonics

You might choose to work with any one of the excellent phonics programs available. These programs are similar in content but vary greatly in presentation. Some programs offer leeway for a less formal presentation while others are more rigid and detailed. Some teach combinations of vowels and consonants as nonsense syllables while others combine letters only in words.

I have reviewed programs here that are easily accessible, appropriate for the home school, and that approach reading instruction from a variety of educational philosophies. There is certainly something for everyone amidst all the choices.

Placement

Sometimes, especially when children have already attended school, we are uncertain as to where they should be begin. Some might already have grasped short-vowel words, but not long-vowel words. Some might have learned the basics, but need to work with simple vocabulary. The easiest way to determine placement in a phonics program is to have a child attempt to read from the program's reading material. We can easily identify where their skills are lacking. However, many of us need to place our children BEFORE we purchase a program. If we can borrow vocabulary controlled readers or reading lists from someone else, we can use them to get an approximate idea of what a child does and does not know.

For those who find this approach impractical, two reading placement tools are easily available to home educators. The first is the *Swift Placement Screen for Reading: A Quick Assessment of Reading Level* (Swift Learning Resources) [$7.95]. It includes ten reading level lists with 30 words per list for preprimer level up through level eight. A "window" page is used so children read only 11 words at a time.

A more complex tool is *The Blumenfeld Oral Reading Assessment Test* (Paradigm Company) [$19.95]. It tests decoding skills plus broader literacy from beginning through adult levels. There are 380 words arranged in numbered columns (indicating increasing difficulty). Two versions of the test are provided so we can retest if necessary. Five "Marking Copies" for each version are included for scoring of five to ten different students. (More Marking Copies can be purchased from the publisher.) Detailed explanatory information is included along with an audio cassette tape of pronunciations of all words used in the tests.

Both of these tools will be more valuable with older students than with those at beginning levels, since there is a minimal number of very simple words in either instrument. Blumenfeld's assessment separates short-vowel words, putting them first, followed by long-vowel words. Swift's mixes all types of words, drawing from those most frequently used rather than following a short to long vowel progression. You might choose your assessment tool based upon whatever reading methodology your child has been exposed to. If a child is coming out of a school which has used either whole language or a whole language/phonics combination, he might do better with the *Swift Placement Screen*. A child who has been introduced to intensive phonics might do better with Blumenfeld's.

Phonics Programs

(arranged in alphabetical order)

The A B C's with Ace and Christi
(School of Tomorrow)
$145.60

School of Tomorrow publishes a good, phonics-based course for beginning reading. The teacher's manual is the heart of this course which relies on teacher presentation. The course also includes a student workbook, flash cards, phonics tapes, and other extras.

Action Reading Fundamentals
by George O. Cureton, developed and taught by Jeanie Eller
(Action Reading, Inc.)
$139

Six audio cassette tapes and a workbook are the heart of this complete phonics reading program. Jeanie Eller teaches the concepts as well as instructing students when to use the accompanying workbooks or the flashcards and games that come with the workbook. There is no teacher manual—not even a note to teachers! This is a very easy program to use! Parents/teachers follow along with students to offer reinforcement and assistance. Parents need to listen as children read aloud, and they need to oversee workbook activity and play the games with their children. On each cassette, Eller indicates to children when to stop the tape either to do an activity or at the end of the lesson. Instruction is straightforward rather than cute or gimmicky, and Eller teaches with enthusiasm.

One minor caution: Listening to one tape, I was bothered by her reference to money as being "my favorite thing," an attitude I do not want to foster. I did not listen all of the way through every tape, but found no other objections to what I did hear.

Eller teaches letters by their sounds rather than their names to prevent confusion. She teaches a slant print (or precursive) style of writing in the workbook, although models of typeset, cursive, and ball-and-stick letters are provided. Reading practice material as well as comprehension and writing exercises are found in the workbook. Large print and appropriate amounts of written work make workbooks suitable for most young learners.

The program comes with a 45-minute video aimed at both parents and children, which explains the origins of our language and offers suggestions to enhance the program.

Parents who like to have someone else do the teaching will love this program. Action Reading offers an unusual 100% satisfaction guarantee without a time limit.

An Acorn in My Hand
by Ethel Bouldin
(Thoburn Press)
$11.95

An experienced teacher, Ethel Bouldin, shares a large dose of her refreshingly practical philosophy of education along with a basic outline for teaching reading, writing, and spelling for kindergarten and first grade. She summarizes the rules and gives us an outline of simple steps to follow for successful teaching. We make our own phonogram cards, and we use the information and word lists in the book to produce our own "reading program."

Words are introduced by "families," that is, those with similar sounds such as bad, bed, and bid. Children are instructed to write letters and words as they learn them, and spelling lessons are then also incorporated into reading and writing. Suffixes and syllabication rules are taught at the end.

This is one of the most inexpensive, bare-bones approaches for teaching, yet it can be just as effective as more costly programs. You might want to use simple readers for extra practice.

Alpha Omega Language Arts 1
(Alpha Omega)
complete boxed set - $85.95

Alpha Omega's Language Arts (new LifePac Gold edition) combines reading, spelling, penmanship, composition, grammar, speech, and literature. At this level, the emphasis is primarily upon reading skills, although the other areas of language arts are included. This level begins with single-syllable, short-vowel words, assuming that children already know their letters and sounds. Unlike LifePacs for older levels, this course

must be taught by the teacher. Instructions are included in two hefty teacher manuals. While there are a few reproducible worksheets in those manuals, students also complete ten LifePacs. (Student LifePacs are printed in full color.) Beginning readers are inserted into the middle of five of the LifePacs so that students get plenty of reading practice. This course does a decent job of combining language arts skills in one place which is particularly helpful for parents uncertain how to cover other skills when they purchase a phonics-only program. Christian content appears throughout the course.

Alpha-Phonics
by Sam Blumenfeld
(The Tutoring Company)
$35

Alpha-Phonics, Sam Blumenfeld's classic course in phonics is again available as a separate book. (For a few years it has only been available as part of the complete *Blumenfeld's Alpha-Phonics* kit, but those kits have gone out of production.)

Alpha-Phonics provides comprehensive phonics instruction in a simple, straightforward manner. Rules are presented along with lists of words and syllables, and, eventually, sentences. A parent works through lessons with his or her child, working from the book. You can add extra activities, practice readers, or games if you wish. Print is very large, suitable for young readers.

The methodology is solid phonics. Blending is taught via the vowel-consonant method, with initial consonants added next: e.g., "am" taught first, followed by "Sam" and "ham." Words are taught in families (e.g., an, ban, can, Dan, fan, Jan). However, many nonsense syllables are included in the early stages to help students develop phonetic fluency. Some of the practice lists of such syllables get quite silly as students read through syllables and words like: "gab, gac, gack, gad, gaf, gag, gal, gam, gan, gap, gas, gat, gav, gax, and gaz." Students practice with quite a few such lists, but they also move quickly into reading actual sentences.

This program does not use pictures for key words as do many other programs. The intent is that students concentrate on the letters themselves so that they immediately recognize the sounds associated with a letter rather than taking an extra mental step to recall a key word associated with a picture.

Alpha-Phonics teaches 44 different sounds for the letters of the alphabet. It teaches basic phonic rules, but not so many rules as we find in other programs like *Writing Road to Reading* and Saxon's *Phonics.*

Also see the review of *PhonicsTutor,* a CD-ROM version of *Alpha-Phonics.* Of additional interest might be Sam Blumenfeld's *How to Tutor* [$24.95, from Elijah Company] which includes a section that is, in fact, a phonics manual covering essentially the same material that is in Alpha-Phonics. However, the print is much smaller, making *How to Tutor* impractical to use directly with young children.(S)

Alphabet Island Phonics

(Eagle's Wings Educational Materials)
A.I. Phonics Level I - $69.95; A.I. Phonics II - $84.95; A.I. Phonics Complete (both I and II) -$119.95

Alphabet Island is more similar to *Sing, Spell, Read, and Write* than anything else, but it really is unique. The *Alphabet Island* program introduces letters and their sounds by creating characterizations through stories, poems, and songs telling about *Alphabet Island* (a fictional place) and the letters who live there. The character pictures and characterizations are a little complicated but very interesting. However, the characterizations might be overly distracting for children with reading difficulties. Some children might not need or enjoy the detail, in which case it can be omitted after the initial introduction of the letter. The phonics presentation is excellent; rules are clear and understandable, without being excessive.

The complete kindergarten program includes three parts: *Getting to Know Alphabet Island* covering phonetic sounds, alphabet sequence, and letter formation; *Learning to Read in Alphabet Island* introducing reading and spelling of short vowel words; and *Kinder-Math* covering basic kindergarten level arithmetic concepts and then some. (See review of *Kinder-Math* under "Arithmetic.") By combining phonics and arithmetic the publisher has made this a comprehensive program for the academic basics. *Kinder-Math* is included free with the purchase of *A.I. Phonics Complete*, but it may also be purchased separately.

The advanced first grade to third grade program, *Alphabet Island Phonics II*, includes *Phonics Fun in Alphabet Island* and *Spelling in Alphabet Island*. (Choose materials for all other subjects from other publishers.) It quickly reviews the material contained in the kindergarten level. Older students just beginning phonics can probably start with this advanced level. It then moves on to long vowels and all the other phonetic concepts.

While the components are separately titled *Phonics* and *Spelling*, both subject areas are covered in both books, although the emphasis shifts. There is excellent instruction and application practice with both phonics and spelling rules.

Songs and stories are included on cassette. Workbooks and teacher's manuals are included for each component along with alphabet cards, game boards and cards, and flashcards. The *Alphabet Flashcards* for *Alphabet Island Phonics* are laminated and printed in full color. All subjects are taught largely from the teacher's manuals, and workbooks are for reinforcement. The workbooks are a big improvement over those in *Sing, Spell, Read, and Write.*

The entire program is unusually sensitive to developmental needs of children since it has larger print, more large-muscle activity, and entertaining presentation. It does require one-on-one presentation and a large initial time commitment in preparing materials and becoming familiar with the program.

(See also the review of *Eagle's Wings Comprehensive Handbook of Phonics.*)

At Last! A Reading Method for Every Child

by Mary Pecci
(Pecci Educational Publishing)
$29.95

If you really want to understand how to teach reading, you might find everything you need in this one book: how to teach reading, how to cure reading failure, how to compare and evaluate methods, how to test reading ability in 15 minutes, how to prepare seatwork, and more.

If a particular reading program or method you have tried didn't seem to "fit" your child, Mary's book will provide the reason/s why as well as the understanding of what will work. She simplifies the process into fewer steps than most phonics programs. With this method, children are able to use other beginning reading material besides just phonics readers.

For example, Mary shows you how to integrate intensive phonics into a developmental, sight, basal reading series. In this way, you get the best of both worlds: (1) "natural" English sentences to read right from the beginning, which provide motivating stories and a meaningful context that helps students decode words; (2) intensive phonics skills which lead to independent reading. Mary points to years of success using this method. <u>Every</u> word is decoded phonetically.

This approach "deals the blow to the dragon of reading failure"—sight words—and overcomes what she calls the "phonics bottleneck." If your present phonics method is confusing your child, Mary shows you how to succeed with phonics the easy way.

Mary also provides "seatwork" that is actually fun for kids. Her *Super Seatwork* books have large, simple activities and exercises, including some cut-and-paste, some writing, and some drawing. The variety and simplicity are much more appealing to kids than the typical phonics workbooks. Titles include: *Color Words, Content Areas, Letter Recognition, Linguistic Exercises, Number Words, Phonic Grab Bag* [$12.95 each], and *Word Skills* [$18.95]. *Letter Recognition* includes alphabet cards and strips, Bingo, follow-the-dots, letter-match games, puzzles, and more. *Linguistic Exercises* includes short vowel families, long vowel families, sight families, and 40 phonic review sheets. *Phonic Grab Bag* covers all basic phonic skills: consonants, blends, digraphs, long and short vowels, phonograms, and more. *Word Skills* covers skills related to reading such as contractions, possessives, prefixes and suffixes, alphabetizing, and dictionary skills. All *Super Seatwork* books are reproducible in 8 1/2" by 11" format.

Mary Pecci maintains a message board to answer any questions you might have at www.OnlineReadingTeacher.com.

[Patty Alberg/C.D.]

Beginnings K5 and Phonics and Reading 1

(Bob Jones University Press)

K5 kit - $169; Phonics and Reading 1 - approx. $149

BJUP incorporates phonics into their foundational kindergarten program. This program introduces all 44 sounds and practices them in phonograms, with children learning to read simple primer material. BJUP's method has children work with vowel-consonant patterns, then adds beginning consonants, although this method is more evident at the first grade level. Handwriting and other appropriate language arts skills are incorporated into *Beginnings*.

Phonics and Reading 1 is the continuation of *Beginnings K5*, reviewing all of the skills taught in *Beginnings K5* at a faster pace. It correlates language arts instruction in phonics, vocabulary, handwriting, grammar, and reading. (See *Phonics and Reading 1* below.)

Beginning Reading at Home

by Elizabeth Peterson

(Individualized Education Systems)

$35.00

This program beautifully suits the young learner ages 3 to 6, with simple, age-appropriate introduction to letters and sounds, accompanied by development of basic reading skills. A simple readiness test is included which helps you figure out when your child is ready to begin. The format is unusual—ten sets of 8 1/2" by 5" cards, tied together as books. Each book includes blue letter/picture cards for introducing letters and their sounds (plus some blends and sight words); green cards with raised-surface, lower-case letters so that children can feel the shapes; orange cards with one-syllable words for children to learn to blend sounds together, then practice reading; and yellow cards that can be separated from each book to make nine simple storybooks which are illustrated with cute line drawings. The separate sets allow children to learn a few letters and sounds, put those letters together into words, and then read a simple story with those words. Short vowels and consonants are taught first in the first six kits. "Ch," "sh," "wh," "ck," and "th" are taught in kits seven and eight. Long vowels are in kit nine. Kit ten teaches some sight words, opposites, and a few phonetic "fun words." The card format is great for young children, because they can handle the cards themselves and the large letters will not cause eyestrain. A Parent's Guidebook gives simple instructions and suggestions for games. *Beginning Reading* is a low-stress phonics program that does a good job building a foundation. It does not cover all of the phonograms ("ou," "igh," etc.), and it introduces only one-syllable words, but it will be easy enough to continue on from here with or without a program.(S)

Bring Phonics to Life

(Learning Wrap-Ups)

$19.95

An 85-page activity book is used in conjunction with two audio cassette tapes to introduce children to the 40 basic sounds of our alphabet. The tapes use stories and music along with "letter characters" such as Agnes the Alligator, Cry-Baby Cecil, and Fergie the PHantom F to teach the concepts. This "dramatized" presentation is a particularly appealing method for reluctant learners because it seems more like story-time than school. The activity book has reproducible coloring pictures, teaching notes on presenting the various phonograms and how they function in words, and activity suggestions for each sound. (There are a few errors in the teacher notes, so have another reference source handy if you are not familiar with the phonograms.) Although it is not a complete reading program it is a good introduction for younger children.(S)

Christ Centered Phonics

(Christ Centered Publications)

Teacher Basic Program - $179.95; Student Program A - $39.95; B - $63.95; C - $46.95

Christ Centered Phonics does an excellent job of incorporating Scriptural principles, Bible stories, and Christian character development into their program. This program encourages brief academic periods for three-year-olds, with gradually longer teaching periods for four-year-olds and up. The sequential format with lots of repetition makes this possible. This is a very detailed, structured program with accompanying teacher's guides that are necessary to the program. Word-for-word lessons make it easy for the inexperienced teacher to present lessons.

There are three levels within the phonics program: A, B, and C. Four *Phonics Lessons* books (which use various visual aids) introduce the 118 cards in the *Phonics Flashcards* set plus spelling rules, beginning grammar, vocabulary development, dictionary skills, and writing exercises. Beginners use only one or two of the lesson books; older students go through the full series. The A, B, and C level *Phonics Workbooks* reinforce the lessons. Each level is geared to the capabilities of a particular age group. The *Phonics Cassette* offers practice on the letter sounds contained in the *Phonics Flashcards* set. Phonics materials are useful through second grade.

Blend and *Word Drill Charts* plus three small readers (used with Levels A and B) and *Noah's Vowel Song* and *Vowel Lane Houses* (used with Level A) are also available. There are additional phonics materials, some of which are included in the *Teacher Basic Program*.

The *Christ Centered Teacher's Manual for Early Childhood* provides the background philosophy for the program, teaching and child training helps, coordination for the complete early childhood program, and help for detecting learning disabilities.

Although the phonics program can be used without this book, it will help us to truly understand how to best use the material in a meaningful context.

All program components are available individually, but the most practical way to buy is to get the package deals. The foundation is the *Teacher Basic Program* which includes the *Teacher's Manual*; Doreen Claggett's book *Never Too Early*, which fully explains the philosophy; the *Phonics Cassette*; flashcards; lesson books; numerous supplemental items; plus the basics for *Christ Centered Math*. We then choose the appropriate level or levels according to the needs of our child; Student Programs A, B, and C provide the remaining components for phonics and math. Level A is for four-year-olds or five-year-olds who need a slower pace. Most five-year-olds should begin with Level B, skipping Level A. Any older child who is just beginning formal reading instruction should also begin here. Level C follows Level B. The *Teacher Basic Program* is a one-time purchase covering all levels. See the review of *Christ Centered Math* for information about that part of the program.

Codebusters

by Betty J. Ward, M.A.
(Codebusters)
$9.95; album set of workbook and tapes - $29.95

Betty Ward developed this reading program based upon her thirty-year career as a teacher and reading specialist. This is an inexpensive phonics program that can be taught from a single book. The task is easier if you purchase the complete set which includes the book plus four audio tapes, packaged in a sturdy album. Using the book alone requires careful attention to the written directions in the footnotes on each page. However, instructions on the tapes are easier to follow and actually do the teaching for us. Betty tells the students when to complete each page, how to sound out letters, etc. Even though lessons are presented on the audio tapes, it is vital that parents work with children on both oral and written work. Letter sounds and rules are taught through ten verses sung to the tune of the *ABC Song*. The organization is unusual: the fifteen most common consonants are taught first, in alphabetical order, followed by the five short vowel sounds. Students learn to write each letter, listen to its sound in the key word, then compare and write it under picture words having the same sound as the key word. Spelling is introduced and all sounds are reviewed as they recycle through these first twenty pages, completing the spelling of each picture word. Although these are three-letter words containing only the sounds that have been presented, adult guidance is essential.

The next section presents the remaining consonants, "k, q, v, w, y, and z" and adds consonant blends in four-letter words. Phonics learning progresses to long vowels, modified vowel sounds, digraphs, and diphthongs in the second half of the

workbook. In the middle of this, students are introduced to verb endings ("s, ing, ed") and irregular verbs (e.g., see, saw, go, goes, going, went)—an unusual strategy. Students are working with three and four letter words very early in the program, but it will be vital for parents to ensure that each child is ready before tackling these lessons. This program combines reading, writing, and spelling as does *The Writing Road to Reading*. However, it teaches each skill in a far less comprehensive manner. (Remember that *Writing Road to Reading* is intended to be a comprehensive language arts program covering up through about third grade level.) This might be sufficient for some students, but most will need more work, especially with spelling unless parents spend intensive time working through spelling exercises and additional activities suggested by *Codebusters*. For example, some students will need assistance to spell words in the dictation exercises because they might have had insufficient experience with words to be able to identify proper spellings. (The author repeatedly tells us to "help" or "guide" students.)

Each lesson includes instructions, generally at the bottom of each page, with the remainder of the page serving as a student worksheet. A variety of activities are described within the instructions for each lessons (e.g., cut and paste pictures of words starting with a certain letter, copy words to the student "dictionary" in the back of the book, alphabetize picture words), and we can choose those that are appropriate for each child. Students are encouraged to begin reading books with simple words after they have completed the first twenty pages in the book. Overall, the book is comprehensive in teaching phonics basics, but the suggested activities and reading practice will be essential to provide sufficient coverage. The course is helpful as a beginning handwriting and spelling tool for kindergarten and first grade levels. You will probably want to use other programs for handwriting and spelling as your children move beyond those levels. The graphics and tape quality are less polished than programs such as *Sing, Spell, Read, and Write*, but the cost of *Codebusters* is only a fraction of the cost of the others. Spanish tapes are also available for those learning English as a second language.

Color Phonics [CD-ROM computer program] 🖥

(Alpha Omega)
$39.95

Color Phonics, a product distributed by Alpha Omega, can be used as your basic phonics program, but I think it will work better as a supplement. It uses a color-coding system to identify sounds, coupled with slanted letters for alternate sounds and thin letters for silent letters. A set of coordinated colored pencils comes with *Color Phonics* for students to mark up other books they might be using with the *Color Phonics* coding. Five CDs are each used in succession. No installation is required. Up to fifty students can be tracked on each CD. The program scores and records their progress.

Consonants are taught before vowels, and words are taught in sound families (e.g., all vowel combinations that make the "long a" sound) rather than similar spelling families. Children practice with both letter and sound recognition on every one of the CDs, although they can skip this if they wish. While this practice is essential at first, it shouldn't be after students have completed the first few CDs. A "reference" section on each program offers instruction on each concept. The largest part of each program uses brief instruction followed by recognition activities. The first two CDs work on consonants, vowels, combinations, and blends within single words. The others continue with more challenging phonograms, but shift into actual story-like reading material where students practice word recognition. As students correctly identify words, the picture accompanying each story bit-by-bit changes from distorted to clear.

The "teacher center" on each CD allows the parent/teacher to select phonetic concepts to be learned, and it provides student progress/mastery information. Students can work with or without time limits, and settings for this are found in the teacher center. 80% correct is the default requirement for students to proceed, but teachers can change this if they wish. Apparently, teachers cannot short cut students through the lessons themselves. For example, students must complete all preliminary practice before getting to actual reading material on the third CD.

Sound is used throughout the program, and all sounds are carefully enunciated. Illustrations of the throat with descriptions of how sounds "feel" help students learn proper pronunciation as well as how to differentiate between sounds. The printed Teacher Handbook that comes with *Color Phonics* summarizes this information concisely.

The Teacher Handbook outlines the content of the CDs and lists the sounds/words taught in each section. The entire text of each of the reading selections are also printed here.

My primary criticism of *Color Phonics* is the same leveled at most educational software. It takes far longer to get through the material because of the time spent watching cute characters fly, jump, drive, etc across the screen; listening to affirming feedback; and waiting for the CD to find and present the next piece of information (which becomes less of a problem the faster your CD-ROM player). I found myself calculating that a child could probably complete an entire workbook page in the time it took for two questions to be answered in the program.

The program rates high for graphic and auditory quality; it really is very well put together. For reluctant learners, the visual appeal might well be worth the time it takes to use the program. However, I can't help but think that most children will soon reach the same point of frustration I did, feeling like "Why can't they just skip the guys buzzing across the screen each time and get on with it?" Ultimately, it's up to parents to decide what works best with their own children.

Teaching tips, extra activity ideas, suggestions for teaching ESL and remedial students, developmental information, and vocabulary lists are all found in the Teacher Handbook. Christian content seems to be isolated to two of the reading sections.

The Blue Book Common Sense Reading Program
(Common Sense Press)
$95

The *Learning Language Arts Through Literature* series begins with this complete beginning phonics and language arts program, a successful blending of integrated language with phonics instruction. Based on Ruth Beechick's ideas about teaching young children, this program integrates instruction for phonics, reading, spelling, handwriting, grammar and higher order thinking skills. It teaches with a great deal of hands-on activity and incorporates real books along with the program's readers.

The program comes in a boxed set including *The Blue Book* teacher manual, *The Blue Book Student Activity Book,* three sets of beginning readers, and a materials packet. *Student Activity Books* may be purchased separately for additional students [$25].

The teacher manual outlines daily lesson plans. Some preparation time is required. You will need to collect materials like glue, crayons, markers, popsicle sticks, and old catalogs or magazines. You will, occasionally, need books from the library, for which you will need to plan ahead.

Many types of activities are built into the lessons so that students learn through all of their senses. This approach is especially good for Wiggly Willys. Students work with color-coded letters, phonograms, and words as well as with specially-designed letter dice. Right after students learn the first few letters and sounds, they are introduced to the first readers to experience the fun of actually reading. Along with instruction, parents/teachers read stories to the student from storybooks pulled from the student activity book and from popular children's books that can be easily found at the library. Many of the included stories are fanciful, including some *Aesop's Fables* and other tales. The content is wholesome, but not overtly Christian.

Spelling and grammar instruction is truly integrated within the lessons, rather than being treated as two more isolated subjects as we find in most programs. Handwriting receives more isolated attention as students receive instruction in letter formation and practice. The style of handwriting is unusual: it is a straight up and down manuscript style, but it has an unusual "calligraphy/slant print" look because most horizontal lines and curves are drawn on a slant. This style is used throughout the handwriting lessons, but not on the movable-letter cards or in the readers. This is neither good nor bad, just different. You can select another handwriting style to teach, but you will need to reconstruct the handwriting worksheets to do so.

The phonics coverage begins with letters and sounds and continues through long- and short-vowels, and consonant blends. However, you will need to continue with *The Red Book* for the next level to complete coverage of all phonograms.

The program impresses me as being one of the most interesting from a child's point of view, but it is likely to require more preparation and presentation time by the parent/teacher than many other programs.

Eagle's Wings Comprehensive Handbook of Phonics and Spelling

(Eagle's Wings Educational Materials)
$19.95

This basic book for instruction in phonics and/or spelling can be used for kindergarten and up, either alone or with another program that is weak in the phonics presentation. (It is included with the *Alphabet Island Phonics 2* program.) The *Handbook* contains thorough explanation of the phonics rules and how to present them along with complete word lists. The "heart" of *Alphabet Island's* teaching methodology is here but with less of the activity work. However, it does include phonetic rules in poetic form (as in *Alphabet Island*) plus many game and activity ideas. Lesson plans are included to keep us from getting overwhelmed by the amount of material offered in this book.

First Reader System

by Phyllis Schlafly
(First Reader System, Inc.)
$79.95

Early in our home schooling days, I was at a conference where I heard Phyllis Schlafly describe how she taught her children to read at home, then sent them to school after she made certain they had that vital foundation. She taught them phonics without any of the fancy games, songs, and other extra enhancements. Thousands of other parents have probably heard her story, and she has frequently been asked to recommend other phonics program that will help parents do what she did. She felt that there was nothing on the market that fit the bill exactly, so she put together her own reading course.

First Reader comes in a sturdy, vinyl case. In it are the *First Reader* book, a workbook, two audio cassettes, and two "fat" pencils. On the cassettes Mrs. Schlafly introduces the program, then gives parents lesson-by-lesson instructions. The instructions are also printed in the back of the book, so it is not necessary to listen to the cassettes for daily lessons. In fact, once we are past the first ten lessons, each day's instructions are generally only a few sentences to a paragraph long, so you probably won't want to bother getting the tape player out for it.

The book uses a simple picture-code system for identifying words that are sounded out, sight words, words that follow unusual rules, words with silent letters, silent-e words, and phonograms that have more than one sound. Letter sounds (lower and upper case together) are taught and immediately practiced within short words. Vowels are combined with consonants following "ma, mi, me, mu, mo" patterns, although children practice reading words rather than the nonsense syllables.

As soon as children learn the short vowel sounds and the letter "m," they are taught the sight words "the" and "a," then given simple sentences to read such as "Mick met Meg on the mat." Obviously, children have not yet learned the other consonants and they will not be reading this all on their own (although I don't see that explained in the program). Schlafly explains that we are to spend as much time as necessary on each page, so some might spend a long time on the first lessons with words as they learn to blend sounds together. This might be the weak point of the program.

Some children (and parents) might need more help with the blending stage than is provided. All of the phonograms are taught, and reading practice material is built into the book. Some of the word lists remind me of those in the *Victory Drill Book*, although they are not as extensive. As with most reading programs, some children might need extra reading practice at different stages, but it is easy to supplement with any of the many choices mentioned elsewhere in this manual.

The *First Reader* book deserves commendation for its appearance. This is a lovely hardbound book, printed on high-quality paper with beautiful, water-color illustrations. The illustrations themselves are cute and warmly appealing. The entire book looks and feels more special than regular school books, sending children the message that phonics is special.

The *First Reader Workbook* is printed in black and white, although it has a full-color cover. Using the ball-and-stick method, it teaches children proper letter formation and reinforces phonics concepts with simple written exercises. Lines are properly spaced for young learners. About half of the letter-writing exercises provide dotted-line patterns for children, so that they are working more on letter formation than spelling knowledge at this point. One criticism of this workbook that holds true for some others: there are a few pages with assorted pictures where instructions say to draw lines from the picture to the letter whose sound is heard in the word for each picture. Sometimes it is difficult to know what word is meant by the picture without instructions or a key. This workbook compounds the problem by asking children to identify the sound in the middle of the word when there might be more than one choice. For example a picture of pancakes (which might also be called hotcakes) is used as an example with a line to the letter "c." How do we know that "n" is not the letter desired? There are only three of these "middle of the word sound" pages so this is not a major problem. Workbook pages are keyed to the text at the bottom of the each workbook page, so it is easy to know when to use each one. Some children might need more workbook/writing activity than is provided here, especially as they get toward the end of the book. We can easily supplement with something like the Modern Curriculum Press *Phonics* or *Explode the Code* (Educators Publishing Service) workbooks.

Overall, *First Reader* is a very practical option for parents who want a no-nonsense phonics program, but who also want a well-organized program that tells them how to present the lessons. Think of it as a "full-service" version of *Professor Phonics*.

The Gift of Reading
by Trudy H. Palmer
(The Gift of Reading/Homeschool Instructional Services)
book - $15.95; kit - $59; flash cards - $18.95; phonics tape - $8.95

Trudy draws on her wealth of experience teaching and tutoring to put together an intensive phonics reading program. *The Gift of Reading* book is the main ingredient. Trudy has information in here that anyone teaching a child (or person of any age for that matter) to read can draw on to better understand the process. The first section describes the stages of reading. The second chapter teaches us about the phonemes or sounds of English, including explanations and illustrations of mouth/tongue movement for the different groups of sounds. (This is also very useful for speech therapy.) The next few sections cover language development and pre- and early-reading skills. All of the foregoing is foundational knowledge which will help us do a better job of teaching reading no matter what program we use. Next are instructions for actually teaching phonics. Trudy draws on many of the ideas from *The Writing Road to Reading*. However, the *Gift of Reading* differs in a number of ways with an important difference being the approach to spelling. Trudy stresses pre-reading and blending activities throughout the teaching of the phonograms, so that reading usually takes place before spelling. Then she includes her own spelling list, concentrating on more in-depth work with closed-syllable words (single-vowel syllables which end with a consonant) before moving on. Two chapters cover topics neglected in most other programs: one is on oral reading, silent reading, and the evaluation of reading, and the other is on correcting reading difficulties using oral reading as a diagnostic tool. As in *The Writing Road to Reading*, children learn and practice by recording their lessons and exercises in a composition book (available through The Gift of Reading). Because of the incorporation of writing, there is an appendix explaining proper position for writing.

The Gift of Reading Phonogram Flash Cards are also extremely useful. These large cards provide the child's flash card on one side and teacher's information on the other that includes example words, instructions for forming the letter(s), and hints for properly teaching the phonogram. Exceptions are

also noted on these cards. These cards are so good they are almost a program by themselves.

The Gift of Reading Audio Tape teaches the 73 phonograms directly to students, which is a big help for parents who feel uncertain of their own ability to properly present the sounds.

While all of these can be purchased separately, I recommend that you purchase one of the kits. The Classic Kit [$59.95] includes all of the above plus *My Spelling Notebook*. The Beginner Kit [$59.95] includes the book, cards, tape, and Trudy's book, *In One Ear and (Hopefully Not) Out the Other!*. The Deluxe Kit [$79.95] includes book, cards, tape and both books.

In summary, this is a multi-sensory approach to reading, writing, and spelling, which provides much detail and explanation to help us teach these subjects. Because of common roots, I must compare it to Bonnie Dettmer's *Phonics for Reading and Spelling*. Trudy provides more technical background on the reading process, and because she has worked so much with learning disability problems, she has more information for those situations. In contrast, Bonnie provides more detail for actual lesson presentation which makes her program a little easier to teach from.

The Great Saltmine and Hifwip [also known as Vertical Phonics
(Teach America to Read and Spell)
$38.50

Frank Rogers liked the way Romalda Spalding's method in *The Writing Road to Reading* taught all of the phonogram sounds at one time, but he thought those methods needed to be presented in an easier and more effective manner. After performing a computer analysis, he came up with a program that fit the bill, *The Great Saltmine and Hifwip*, also known as *Vertical Phonics*.

Children should learn the names of the letters before beginning this program. Students then learn the phonograms (letter/sound associations of phonics) as in *Writing Road to Reading*, but children start decoding words after learning just four phonograms. Children drill on the phonograms, using timed practice to improve their speed of recognition. Rogers also felt that reading should precede writing and spelling, so he does not have children learn to write and spell until later, unlike Spalding who teaches reading, writing, and spelling simultaneously. (I understand that in her seminars Spalding says writing and spelling do not have to be taught simultaneously.) Students who use this program <u>do</u> learn to spell the 500 most often occurring words that make up sixty percent of common written vocabulary, so spelling is not ignored. The basic reading package includes the manual (which is the basic book used by both teacher and student), three-ring binder, flash cards, and two dictation exercise books.

You can begin with the *Penny Primer Starter Set* which

includes the *Penny Primer*, a sample lesson, a sixty-minute audio cassette that explains the program, and some general background information on teaching phonics. The *Starter Set* is included in the *Great Saltmine and Hifwip* package, but it may be purchased by itself for $15.

This program is very effective with remedial students. No readers come with the program, but A Beka's *Reading for Fun Enrichment Library* is recommended. Parents with poor reading skills will find this program easy to use as well as an aid for improving their own reading skills.

For those curious about the name: *Saltmine* represents the first eight letters taught in the program and *Hifwip* is the acronym for High Frequency Words In Print.

A Handbook for Reading phonics textbook
(A Beka Book)
student book - $8.20; teacher edition - $17.70

This is A Beka's basic phonics program that starts with letters and sounds and continues through almost all of the phonograms. The *Phonics/Reading/Spelling Curriculum/Lesson Plans* covers much of the same teaching instructions provided in the Teacher Edition of this book, so you won't need both. A Beka uses the "consonant-vowel" approach for teaching blending (ba, be, bi, bo, bu). Some reading specialists criticize this use of nonsense syllables to teach blending. Their reasoning is that since vowel sounds are determined by what follows rather than what precedes, children have to relearn to a certain extent when they actually form complete words. While reading specialists quibble about this, most children do not have trouble with this method and some actually seem to learn better using "consonant first" blending. Whatever the critics say, this method is used successfully by many major publishers.

You will probably want to get A Beka's alphabet flashcards, phonics flashcards, and phonics charts to use along with this book. The Teacher Edition has only slightly reduced, full-color pictures of pages from the student book, so it might be possible to work from only the Teacher Edition.

However, most young children like to have their own book in hand as they learn to read, so I recommend getting a copy for each child. Even though instruction in the Teacher Edition is geared for classrooms, it is easy to use at home. *A Handbook for Reading* correlates with A Beka's *Letters and Sounds* books 1 and 2 and some of their readers. *Writing with Phonics* books 1 and 2 might also be used along with it.

Happy Phonics
by Diane Hopkins
(Family Resources, Inc.)
$19.95; ready made flashcards - $3.95

I repeatedly say that you don't have to buy an expensive program to teach reading. But most parents want more direction and more activity than they get with a minimalist approach like *Professor Phonics* or *Noah Webster's Reading Handbook*. Diane Hopkins has solved the problem by creating *Happy Phonics*. A 22-page, stapled teacher's guide directs you through a step-by-step process from learning letters and sounds into reading real books. The rest of *Happy Phonics* is heavy-duty, brightly colored paper stock printed with an alphabet desk strip, flash cards, words, letters, game pieces, and stories. These are cut apart and used for their various duties as explained in the instructions. The games are more manipulative learning materials than competitive devices, but young children love the matching, flipping cards, and moving things around. They contain some of the same elements you find in reading workbooks or texts, but the format is more appealing, and the games are definitely more fun. Yes, it does take some time to put this together, but it's not overwhelming. A simple chart in the instructions shows which parts of *Happy Phonics* are used at which stages of learning. Diane does recommend using *Explode the Code* workbooks as part of your reading program and mentions other reading tools such as the *Bob Books* that you might wish to use. She also encourages you to make your own beginning readers. A few suggestions for writing and spelling are included, but coverage of those topics is minimal. Diane suggests making your own alphabet cards with lower case letters on one side and capitals on the other. Family Resources sells a very inexpensive alphabet set in case you would rather not do it yourself. If you dislike cutting things out and organizing, this program might not work for you, but if you are looking for a low cost, fun phonics program with games, this is it.

Hooked on Phonics Learn to Read 🎧
(Gateway Learning Corporation)
$249.95

Forget everything you've ever heard before about *Hooked on Phonics*. This is an entirely redesigned program. The only features left from the original are the name, the same toll-free phone number, and high quality presentation.

While the original *Hooked on Phonics* had some significant shortcomings, this new version is outstanding. It offers a solid base of phonics, and it also incorporates phonetic readers so that children can quickly experience the joy of reading.

The program starts with alphabet and letter/sound recognition. (If children already know the alphabet and letter sounds, they can begin with the second "kit.") *Hooked on Phonics* teaches children how to blend sounds to make words using the "word family" approach: e.g., cat, mat, bat, rat. It spends a significant amount of time on short vowels and short-vowel words to form a solid foundation. Then it moves on to long vowels and more complex phonograms. Children learn sight words so they are able to read the stories, although some of these "sight words" are really phonetic but contain phonograms children have not yet learned.

The program contains six colorful boxes or kits. The first is your "starter kit" with instructions, and lessons for learning the alphabet and letter sounds. Children who already know these can begin with the next kit. Each kit contains one or two audio cassette tapes, heavy-duty flashcards (a set for the phonograms and a set for sight words to be learned at each level), a student "workbook," and full-color readers.

Audio tapes provide direct instruction to children, including drill exercises where children follow along through the flashcards or workbook. The workbook provides reading practice material but no written exercises as you would expect. This program does not teach or require any writing, so you will need to supplement with other resources if you wish your child to learn to write simultaneously.

One of the most appealing features of this redesigned program is the readers. Written especially for *Hooked on Phonics,* these storybooks compare well to children's storybooks on the library shelves with their beautiful illustrations and entertaining story lines. However, the stories are written for a non-sectarian audience and use talking animals and fantasy which some parents might not appreciate.

Although children can listen to the tapes on their own, parents should listen along, especially to their child's responses to the tapes. Parents will also need to spend time as their children practice reading aloud. *Hooked on Phonics* makes teaching reading an easy, enjoyable task, even for the parent with no phonics background.

Horizons American Language Series Beginning Reading and Language

(Alpha Omega)

$249.95 complete language arts program. All components are available individually.

This beginning language arts program is based on the *Little Patriots* material (originally published by Mile-Hi), but those who have seen *Little Patriots* will hardly recognize the similarities at first glance since this is a first class, colorful, inviting-looking program. They have tried to accommodate the variety of learning styles better than in *Little Patriots* by adding cassette tapes with songs (no rock beat, rap, or other objectionable musical styles here). There are actually only six phonics songs, although it looks like more because they are on three separate tapes. This does not compare with the amount of auditory presentation in programs like *Play 'N Talk* or *Sing, Spell, Read, and Write* but it does assist auditory learners.

A section of the teacher's manual has games, songs, and poems that are to be used at the teacher's discretion. It might be easy to skip them since they are not built into the lessons, but they will help reach more active learners or those whose interest is piqued by songs or poems. I have started with the "learning style extras" so that you understand this is not just a repackaged *Little Patriots* program. However, the Horizon American Language series retains the emphasis on developing mental discipline and a sound knowledge foundation. They also lean toward "early is better than later," teaching reading, writing, and spelling skills in this beginning program. If used for kindergarten, Horizon American Language's scope and sequence puts their kindergartners at the level of some other first grade programs. If you like the program but want to wait until your child is six or seven, there is no grade level indication on the program and it will work fine.

Let's look at the whole package. A very large, very heavy box contains your complete language arts program—reading, writing, and spelling. It consists of two teacher's binders—one will be your primary volume with lesson plans you will use everyday. The other is a phonics/spelling manual. It is a 500-page reference book that describes the philosophy and methodology of the program, along with detailed explanations of phonetic rules and visual aids. You should read through the various sections as they relate to the primary teacher's manual.

There are four audio-cassettes: the three song tapes mentioned earlier plus a lengthy introduction tape by the program author. (Listen to this tape before you begin the program!) There is a beautiful set of animal alphabet flash cards—great wall decor. There are two *Phonics & Reading* workbooks and two *Spelling, Writing, & Vocabulary* workbooks. Yes, this is "a lot of workbook" for kindergartners, but Alpha Omega's philosophy includes introduction of concepts, followed by recurring opportunities to practice and develop skill with each one. This takes more time and work than a program that teaches each concept one time. The workbooks are not quite as overwhelming as they appear at first. The *Phonics & Reading* workbooks require very little actual writing—drawing lines, circling items, etc., are typical activities. The *Spelling, Writing, & Vocabulary* workbooks do require writing, but the amount per page is reasonable <u>if</u> a child is ready to begin writing. All workbooks are heavily illustrated in full-color, but pages are not too crowded. Finally, there are six vocabulary-controlled readers. Reading material is wholesome with Bible stories included, beginning with the third book. Godly character, obedience, and practical life experiences are common themes.

All of these components are carefully cross-referenced in the teacher's manual. The program begins with the introduction of letters, sounds, and their formation. It moves quickly into blending with children reading short words in the earliest lessons. It follows the consonant-vowel approach in teaching blending—"la, lo, le, li, lu." The beginning program limits itself to single-syllable words, but it does a thorough job introducing all the basic phonetic rules that might be applied to such words.

This is a rule-oriented program. Words are taught in terms of rules, then reviewed with reminders about which rules they represent. It somewhat resembles *The Writing Road to Reading* in the rule orientation and the combined teaching of reading, writing, and spelling.

One of the pluses for this program is that it has been very carefully designed for the inexperienced teacher. Everything is explained; nothing is assumed. However, you must read through all of the material to catch the details. Some teacher preparation time is required, and the program must be taught. It is not designed for independent learning.

Since *Horizons Mathematics K* is intended to be used with the beginning level of *Horizon American Language* you should also read that review.

Christian Light first grade language arts program

(Christian Light Publications, Inc.)
Learning to Read - $56.70; I Wonder - $19.85; Language Arts 100 - $28.85; Reading 200 - $50.70

Christian Light's first grade program for language arts actually consists of three separate courses. Children begin with *Learning to Read*, which consists of 90 lessons, taking a little over half the school year. The *Language Arts 100* course is brought in beginning the second month and continues through the end of the school year. *I Wonder* slightly overlaps *Learning to Read*, then continues through the end of the year. Clear instructions and charts are provided to show the coordination of resources, so it's not as complicated as it sounds.

These courses are part of Christian Light's new *Sunrise* curriculum. All *Sunrise* courses have accompanying, inexpensive Teacher's Guidebooks [$5.95 each] which contain answer key inserts, so it is not necessary to purchase separate answer keys.

Learning to Read consists of ten LightUnits, a Teacher's Guidebook, Word Flash Cards, Phrase Flash Cards, and a primer. This course focuses on phonics, while also providing other introductory language arts instruction. Although it begins with letters and sounds, it moves very quickly into challenging concepts that would be overwhelming for most kindergartners, so be cautious about beginning it with younger students. The course recommends teaching sounds of the letters rather than letter names, but it provides presentation for teaching both simultaneously. Lessons are scripted for teacher presentation which is a tremendous help to the inexperienced mom who lacks confidence. However, the language is likely to seem a little stilted if you try to follow the script exactly. The course does not presume that students have had prior phonics instruction. It introduces blending with consonant-vowel combinations (e.g., da, di, du....). Sight words are presented from the very beginning, so some words that are actually phonetic are taught early in the program as sight words (e.g., "ring," "is," "brown"). The program's stress on learning sounds carries throughout the course as students learn dictionary spellings and letter/sound representations such as the schwa and "ö". (The pronunciation symbols might differ from those

in your dictionary!) This approach is meant to standardize all similar spellings representing a single sound representation, but it is an unusual way to do it. In the process children learn to use correct terminology such as "macron" and "breve."

This course as well as the other two language courses stresses practice and repetition for mastery. The two sets of flash cards serve the same purpose. However, to save money, you can make up your own from lists provided in the Teacher Handbook, although it will take a great deal of time and energy. Supplemental ideas for activities to appeal to different types of learners are included.

I Wonder is actually a continuation of *Learning to Read*, consisting of a hardcover reader, Teacher's Guidebook, and four Learning Sheet booklets (which look just like LightUnits). It continues with phonics instruction, but it increasingly focuses on reading comprehension.

Language Arts 100 correlates with the other two courses,  reinforcing phonics instruction and teaching penmanship, spelling, and introductory grammar (e.g., capitalization, punctuation). These latter two courses are not scripted like *Learning to Read*, but they do provide detailed lesson plans.

Reading, handwriting, spelling, and beginning grammar are integrated throughout the components of all three first grade language courses, rather than any one component focusing exclusively on one skill area. You really need to use all three together.

Christian Light's *Reading 200* course continues reading instruction for second grade. It can be used on its own or alongside CLP's *Language Arts 200*. It consists of ten LightUnits, two Teacher's Guidebooks, and two hardcover readers. The methodology is the same as for the first grade program, and it might be difficult to switch from another method of teaching phonics to this for second grade level. This course continues to review and reinforce phonics, but it expands lessons to teach children to read for meaning and understanding. Students will be able to do much of the work on their own, but they should be required to do daily oral reading to ensure decoding skills as well as to develop reading fluency. The two readers are titled *Helping Hands* and *Happy Hearts*.

All these courses were designed for classroom presentation, but they require minimal effort to adapt for individual students. As with other Christian Light courses, things of God receive a great deal of attention. The warm and gentle stories and poems in the readers often start with a Scripture verse and teach lessons about thankfulness, honesty, unselfishness, and other godly attitudes and character traits. A few stories that take place in other lands and cultures are included. There are no fairy tales, but imagination is not excluded; in one delightful story a boy comes to his own house pretending to be a helpful stranger. Illustrations reflect Mennonite culture and values with modestly clothed figures, women and girls always in dresses, and rural subject matter. Simple one- or two-color illustrations enhance the text, making these readers a good choice for those who find full-color pictures in a reader too distracting. Readers are very low cost for such high-quality books.

Learning Wrap-Ups

$7.95

See the full description of how Wrap-Ups are used in the math chapter. For phonics there is one set of ten phonics Wrap-Ups. This set can be used to supplement phonics instruction as children match illustrations of words with beginning sounds and rhyming endings. Some of the illustrations are a little difficult to identify, so help your children with picture identification if needed.

Lickety Split®, The Reading Board Game

(Mary Sturgeon Educational Games)
$54.95 US

Lickety Split® is a different approach to teaching phonics. This circus-theme board game, developed by a reading specialist, gives beginning readers practice reading letter sounds, blends, and whole words while simultaneously helping them memorize phonics rules.

A parent or other "reader" is needed to play the game. Some phonics instruction and practice should precede the game; however, a separate phonics program is not necessary since the rules to be learned are contained in the *Ringmaster's Magic Tricks* booklet, and the word cards from the game can be used for practice.

The game can easily be modified to fit each child; if he finds a certain phonics rule especially confusing, you can remove that card for awhile. (You might also wish to remove the reference to the circus fortune teller.) The basics are here, but I couldn't find any discussion of "ough" as in "rough," and treatment of suffixes and prefixes is very superficial. Since phonics programs vary in coverage, these might not be major issues to many parents, but some might still prefer the security of a more comprehensive phonics program that is laid out in lessons, using *Lickety Split* for reinforcement and practice rather than as the primary teaching tool. Parents with a good knowledge of phonics might do very well using the game, adding comments or extra help as needed.

Special features of this game include separate cards for three levels of readers and the inclusion of computer vocabulary words. The board and cards are bright and colorful with appealing art work. While *Lickety Split* is definitely a teaching tool, it has enough game features to make it seem more fun than most programs. It is recommended for children ages 6-10, but it is probably best for ages 6-8. Younger siblings can play

along by using only the letter cards. A free colorful brochure with sample cards is available.(SE) [Valerie Thorpe]

Listen and Learn with Phonics ⌒

(Career Publishing, Inc.)
$89.95

The basic set includes three cassette tapes with instruction in phonics for children to listen to while looking at the five beginning word books which are correlated to the tapes. The set also comes with a parent's guide, a game envelope containing six games, two beginning readers (*I Can Read My Name* and *Let's Read*), four additional follow-up readers, a separate phonics game, and a 24-page phonogram dictionary.

Children can work fairly independently, and instructions are simple and clear. While this is not as comprehensive as *Sing, Spell, Read, and Write* or *Play 'N Talk*, it is a good, orderly phonics program that does a lot of the work for us. If we have a *Wiggly Willy* learner we might also want to use *Shortcuts to Reading* with *Listen and Learn*. Many students of all learning styles might need more extensive practice than is provided here. (See "Readers" for extra reading material or consider supplementing with an inexpensive phonics book or supplement.)(S)

The Literacy Primer Packet

(Literacy Press)
$41.25 for all components

The Literacy Primer Packet is similar to but more detailed than *Professor Phonics*. The basic set consists of *The Literacy Primer* (the basic text containing phonics rules, lessons laid out in a very workable format, and reading material), a *Spelling Board Kit* (a movable alphabet with pocket chart for formation of words without writing), a teacher's supplement, and a packet of practice words for word games. Also available are three phonetic readers to be used at the completion of the primer.

This program effectively covers the different methods of learning by incorporating seeing, hearing, feeling, and saying in all presentations but without the games and songs/poems found in the most expensive programs. It quickly gets the child into real reading. The *Spelling Board Kit* is also sold separately for $3.50. If you are teaching more than one child, you might want to have a kit for each.

Little Angel Readers

by Linda Bromeier, M.Ed., B.S.
(Stone Tablet Press)
Readers A-C - $10 each; Reader D - $12; workbooks A-D - $7 each; teacher's manual - $26; complete set - $90

Stone Tablet Press has developed a complete phonics program which not only reflects Catholic thought and traditional values, but delivers solid instruction for kindergarten through second grade. *Little Angel Readers* include four readers and corresponding workbooks which can be purchased separately or as a set with a teacher's manual. The manual rounds out the program with daily lesson plans, multi-sensory activities, and spelling and handwriting instruction.

If you are content with your current phonics program, the readers and workbooks may be used for enrichment. The workbooks reinforce lessons. The readers are phonics-based and use a word family approach (e.g., "man," "ran," "van" taught together). Sight words are kept to a minimum and appear in boldface when they first appear. Rebus pictures are sometimes used in place of sight words. The illustrations employed throughout the books are inviting to young children; I especially like the depictions of guardian angels looking out for the little ones in the stories.

If you are using this as a complete program, the teacher's manual provides approximately fifty 45-minute lessons for each of the four readers. Lessons include drill and review, art projects and fun activities, plus spelling and writing practice. Workbooks are similar in concept to the Modern Curriculum Press *Plaid Phonics* series with a variety of activities and large print. Spelling lessons are closely tied to the phonics lessons. Reading readiness and reading disabilities are addressed in the manual as well.

The readers and workbooks are recommended as follows: Level A - advanced kindergarten or 1st grade, B - 1st grade, C - 1st or 2nd grade, and D - 2nd grade. The author has included recommended readers at the end of the teacher's manual for continuing lessons past the second grade. [Maureen Wittmann]

Little Stories for Little Folks: Catholic Phonics Readers

by Nancy Nicholson
(Catholic Heritage Curricula)
$18.95

Little Stories for Little Folks is an uncomplicated phonics program, affordably priced for the typical one-income home-schooling family. It can be used as a complete phonics program or as enrichment to other programs. A 6-page parent's guide, Catholic flashcards, and 45 readers are included. The readers are printed on 8 1/2 x 11 sheets of paper and made to be folded into four pages to form small booklets. The booklets are color coded to distinguish reading levels for pre-K through first grade levels. The stories are brief and plainly illustrated, much like the popular *Bob Books*. What separates these two products is the way that Little Stories weaves the beauty of the Catholic faith into each tale.

Little Stories uses word families to teach phonics, and it quickly allows children to read whole words in sentences. This is not an intensive phonics program, so if you feel you need more direction and assistance, you might want to use a more comprehensive program and use these readers as supplements.

The 45 readers are reproducible for all the children in your family, which makes the ultimate cost even lower. (I recommend keeping the original and making photocopies for each child as they begin their journey into the world of reading.) Children can have the added treat of coloring each booklet as it is mastered. [M. Wittmann]

McOmber Reading Program

(Swift Learning Resources)
72 Storybooks with flash cards, Teacher Guide, and word stand - $139.95; a more complete set includes the foregoing plus Writing Activity Books for $199.95; CD-ROM version - $59.95

The *McOmber Reading Program* uses a "word family" approach to phonics (e.g., "hat," "rat," and "sat" taught together). This is a complete program that begins with the alphabet. 72 small storybooks provide children with plenty of reading practice as they learn new skills. Readers are illustrated and are more interestingly written than many other vocabulary-controlled readers.

The teacher guide outlines how to teach the program. *The Writing Activity Books* are two binders containing 70, 14-page, reproducible workbooks (over 900 lessons) that are correlated to the storybooks. Reading comprehension, spelling, and writing are all included.

In the complete program, *McOmber* uses a straightforward approach to teaching reading, writing, and spelling. Children are introduced to the new letters/sounds they will encounter in the next storybook. They practice taking dictation. Then students make words to form word families and write them on their worksheets. Once children are familiar with new words, they read the story. Next, we might use worksheet pages for drawing a picture and writing a "story" if appropriate. On the following four worksheets, children practice matching sentences to pictures (comprehension), filling in missing letters, circling the correct words to identify pictures, and writing complete words. Answer keys are included within each section.

The storybooks themselves offer an interesting mix of silliness and character building lessons. I read about a dozen of the 72 in the complete set and encountered no content problems (as long as talking animals and silliness doesn't bother you). The illustrations are prominent in the storybooks, which makes them more appealing to children, but also provides sight-reading hints. However, once students are beyond the easiest levels, the text is too complex for sight reading.

The storybooks can also be used alone to teach phonics (using information on the inside cover of each book) or in conjunction with other phonetic programs.

I received last minute notice that Swift also has a CD-ROM version of this program. Contact them for details.

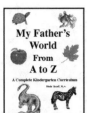

My Father's World From A to Z: A Complete Kindergarten Curriculum

by Marie Hazell
(My Father's World)
$95

See the review in Chapter Five. A major part of this program is reading instruction. *My Father's World First Grade* continues phonics instruction.

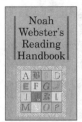

Noah Webster's Reading Handbook

(Christian Liberty Press)
$7

This has got to be just about the cheapest resource for teaching phonics/beginning reading! It does a very adequate job, which should not be surprising since it's an updated version of Webster's original *Blue-Backed Speller* which was used to teach thousands (at least) of children.

It follows a fairly standard progression, introducing short vowels first, then using consonant-vowel practice to help beginning readers learn to blend. (This is the same method used by A Beka and *Sing, Spell, Read, and Write.*) Practice words and sentences are included on each page as soon as is appropriate. Lengthier reading selections (Bible-based) are at the back of the book. Rules are presented in boxes at the bottom of pages. A few pages of technical information are at the back of the book for parents who want to better understand the functions of the alphabet and sounds.

No frills, no confusion, straight-to-the-point phonics, and there seems to be little missing other than more work on sight words and complete treatment of the "ough" sounds. Add this to your list of possibilities if you're looking for a simple, uncluttered approach. This book also suits remedial learners of all ages. If using it with beginning readers, consider using CLP's *Adventures in Phonics* workbooks Levels A and B (and other levels as they become available) for written practice and reinforcement.

Pathway Publishers Reading Program

Written for Amish children in Amish schools, Pathway's program is a traditional approach to teaching phonics which uses workbooks and readers. Content is God-honoring and wholesome, and it also reflects the agrarian environment in which many Amish live.

Phonics instruction is presented by the teacher with reinforcement provided by workbook activities.

Instruction begins with three workbooks and a preprimer. The three workbooks are *Before We Read, Learning through Sounds Book 1*, and *Learning through Sounds Book 2*. The preprimer is titled *First Steps.* A single teacher's manual covers the preprimer and *Before We Read* workbook, while another teacher's manual covers the two *Learning through Sounds* workbooks. Flashcards are also available.

Following the preprimer, students move on to other hard-bound readers and workbooks which are available through the eighth grade level.

The method is similar to *Professor Phonics, Sing, Spell, Read, and Write,* and others in that it teaches blending with an initial consonant followed by a vowel, later adding an ending consonant.

Books are printed in black-and-white with simple illustrations, yet there is quite a bit of variety in types of exercises within the workbooks. Print is appropriately large to prevent unnecessary eyestrain.

Phonics and Advanced Phonics 2 [audio cassette/workbook] 🎧

(Twin Sisters Production)
$9.98 each

These are two separate audio cassette tapes, each with a companion activity book. On the first tape, *Phonics,* children reinforce sound/letter identification by listening and singing along to the rap-style music. The second tape, *Advanced Phonics 2,* moves on to more complex phonograms plus rhyming words, compound words, synonyms, and antonyms. These tapes do not comprise a complete phonics program. Teach the sounds first, providing explanations from a complete phonics program, then offer your child this tape for independent listening. The 24-page activity book in each set features puzzles, cut-and-paste pages, and other activities plus lyrics to all of the songs.(S)

Phonics for Reading and Spelling

by Bonnie L. Dettmer
(Small Ventures)
$69.95

Bonnie Dettmer has gathered the key elements from the *The Writing Road to Reading* type of methodology and presents them along with her own teaching ideas in a comprehensive, well-organized program. As in *The Writing Road to Reading,* phonics, reading, writing, and spelling are all taught together to provide multi-sensory reinforcement for learning. Children first learn basic phonograms and how to write them. Then they begin spelling and reading. Once children have begun to actually read, they will need outside reading material such as beginning readers or easy-to-read literature. (In Bonnie's program, children begin actually reading much sooner than in *WRTR.*) There are no separate workbooks or student books. Rather than writing in workbooks, children create their own notebooks of all that they learn. See the review of *The Writing Road to Reading* for more about the methodology. This program can be used with all ages. *Phonics for Reading and Spelling* comes in a large, seven-ring binder. Included are the

Basic Phonogram Tape, a set of *Basic Phonogram Cards,* and the *Spelling Scale for Home Educators.* There is nothing consumable, so a one-time investment can be used to teach many students.

Many extra features add to the value of *Phonics for Reading and Spelling.* Bonnie has included teaching tips that go beyond the basic topics of instruction, plus language history, spelling word lists (with words marked according to the unique methodology of the program), reference charts, help for selecting reading material and working on comprehension skills, flowcharts to help us teach students beginning at different skill levels, spelling rules, and several appendices (lists of specialized words, "Latin and Greek Roots," and "Spelling Word List Index").

Prior to teaching, parents will need to spend time familiarizing themselves with the methodology, but after that, minimal preparation time is needed. Lessons must be presented to students and require verbal interaction as well as the student's work in his or her notebook. The program is well-organized, so even novice teachers should have no problem teaching from it. Those who would like more training or preparation for teaching the program should check out Bonnie's *Phonics Seminar Tapes* [$29.95]. This is an actual workshop presented on four audio tapes with a booklet containing pictures of the overheads so that the listener can "see" what is being discussed.

Bonnie makes this intensive phonics method of reading instruction usable by parents without the need for hours of training.

The Phonics Game

(Games 2 Learn)
$199.95

The Phonics Game reviews the sounds of the letters, so you can start at this level with six- or seven-year-olds without first using *The Phonics Game Junior* or another program, although children should have done some prior work with letter recognition. (*The Phonics Game Junior* from the same company provides introductory lessons, or you can cover them using another resource or by using ideas such as Ruth Beechick presents in her small book *A Home Start in Reading.*) *The Phonics Game* then introduces six different games designed to teach phonics and reading. Older children (and even adults) can breeze through the introduction and review of letters, while younger children will need to take more time.

A thing to be aware of if students using this program have already received beginning phonics instruction in any program other than *The Phonics Game Junior* is that this program teaches that both "y" and "w" are sometimes vowels, something I don't recall encountering anywhere else. (In case you are wondering how "w" can be a vowel, they tell us that "w"

acts like a second vowel to make the first vowel long in words such as "low" in the same way that "y" does in words such as "day.")

The Phonics Game includes three video tapes, eight audio cassette tapes, six 2-part card decks, *American Heritage Children's Dictionary* (a "free gift included with the game, but not an essential component), phonics charts, and an excellent instruction book, all packaged in a sturdy case. *The Fun Zone* CD-ROM and a set of ten phonetic readers are optional.

We begin the program with either the first video or the first audio tape. The first video introduces the program and provides an overview. The second video and the first audio tape both cover basic letters and sounds as well as instructions for the first game. If students are just beginning in phonics, the video will be most helpful since children can see how the hostess moves her mouth for pronunciation. Otherwise, either the video or the audio tape provides essentially the same information and instruction, although the presentation is quite different on the two formats. This is true with the rest of the video and audio tapes, although, obviously, they do not correspond exactly to each other. The videos are hosted by Barbara and Ellen, assisted by children and adults of all ages. The audio tapes are hosted by Jonelle and Mike. Self-esteem talk (e.g., responding to the invisible child supposedly listening to the tape with comments like "That was perfect!") is a minor annoyance that we can ignore. Lessons are presented in conjunction with each card game. The concepts are taught on tape directly to the student. Parents need to listen in so that they can play the games with their children. The hostess provides most of the instruction, and she does an excellent job of teaching proper enunciation of the sounds, describing the way the tongue, mouth, and lips move for each sound.

The first game moves immediately into blending sounds together for three- and four-letter, short-vowel words. The second game teaches long vowels. It includes some consonant blending for words such as "globe" and "plane," although I could not find any specific instruction to students on such blends. Still, the progression is sensible and should not pose a problem for most children. If your child struggles with blending, take the time for additional instruction and practice on your own at this point. The third game teaches secondary sounds for some of the letters. The optional phonetic readers [$34.95] provide reading practice as children progress through each of the games. Sight words are introduced in the program, but often they are introduced briefly at the bottom of the reading selections. Again, practice in extra reading material will be helpful for developing proficiency with sight words.

The fourth game covers some of the more challenging phonograms such as "au," "aw," "ou," and "ow." The fifth game, called "Oddballs," deals with some sight words, unusual phonograms such as "ough," "psy," and "gh." The sixth game teaches rules of syllabication. Each of these six games features a two-part card deck, with the second half generally more challenging than the first. Scattered through each deck are rule cards that reinforce instruction on the tapes. Jokers, "Give," and "Take" cards add game-playing elements to make learning more fun.

An adult or older child will need to assist a younger child with reading instructions from the manual. Most of the instruction is already on the tapes, so you should not need to read the entire manual, but it saves time if you've already gone through the tapes and want to verify the rules for the games or some other detail.

One of the few oddities in *The Phonics Game* is the instruction for beginning readers to read and explain these rules which are written at a reading level that they have supposedly not yet attained. A note in the instruction book suggests that someone else might need to help them, but reading the rules is actually part of the games themselves. An additional tape, "Sounds and Spelling," works on spelling skills.

The components of *The Phonics Game* all work together; instruction is contained on the tapes, in the instruction book, and in the card games themselves. If you use all of the components as instructed and supplement with more reading practice, coverage is quite thorough.

Games 2 Learn also sells *The Fun Zone* CD-ROM (runs on either Windows or Macintosh systems) [$49.95]. This is an excellent program with six games corresponding to each of the card decks. Heavily animated with great sound, the CD-ROM provides a welcome change of format for more practice. The only problem I encountered was with one game, "Double Trouble," where the player has to hear the sound then identify words with that sound. There's no way to repeat the sound, and sometimes sounds were hard to decipher with my computer speakers of average quality. When players make an error, the game presents the phonics rule in question.

The time needed to work through all of the levels of the *Phonics Game* will vary greatly depending upon the student. You must spend as much time as each child needs at each stage until he or she masters the concepts. The game format makes it much easier to spend that time since children are likely to enjoy playing the games over and over. *The Phonics Game* should also work very well with older children with a poor or nonexistent phonics background since it does not have the feel of a program designed particularly for young children and also because they can move through the various games quite quickly to fill gaps in their knowledge.

Phonics rules are taught so thoroughly and in-depth that *The Phonics Game* provides a great foundation for spelling skills. However, since the primary goal is to teach the student how to read, there is no instruction on handwriting or composition.

Even though some of the instruction is presented auditorially, this program should work well for kinesthetic and visual learners because of the instruction about how it actually feels

to make the letters. The video presentation might be more helpful than the audio tapes for children who need the visual input. Also, the program suggests that students use a mirror to watch their mouths as they form letters. This attention to detail helps prevent potential problems that arise from sloppy enunciation.(S)

The Phonics Game Junior
(Games 2 Learn)
$159.95

The Phonics Game Junior is a precursor to the more well known *Phonics Game*. It comes in an impressive package that includes three short videos, a game board, bingo-type games, card games, one beginning reader, two large wall charts, and an instruction book. Everything is high quality from the full-color printing through the video production. Each video introduces each of the three levels in *The Phonics Game Junior*.

Video #1 teaches the alphabet using one of the wall charts, the alphabet song, the bingo type game, and other learning activities. The videos are professionally presented almost like a prime time children's television show, complete with a muppet-like character named Ed. Children and parents should watch the video together the first time, then children will probably want to watch again on their own. Parents must read the *Junior Phonics Play Book*, an instruction manual that expands upon the instruction given on the video with further detail plus suggestions for other learning activities. Video #2 teaches the sounds of the letters, stressing proper pronunciation. Primary sounds of the consonants and short vowel sounds are taught. Children also begin blending letters to read short vowel words. Video #3 advances blending skills and teaches children to recognize common vowel sounds within words. The various bingo, card, and board games all reinforce letter, sound, and reading skills. Children should play the appropriate games until they have mastered each level. No written work is required, although you might choose to do letter formation activities with your child. Children should be able to read books with only short vowel words once they have complete *The Phonics Game Junior*. At that point, you can move on to *The Phonics Game*. It is possible to skip *The Phonics Game Junior* and begin with *The Phonics Game* as long as you spend plenty of time introducing letters and sounds before tackling the first card game in *The Phonics Game*.

Phonics Intervention: An Incremental Development
(Saxon Publishers)
teacher manual - $100; "classroom materials" - $66.67; student book - $20

Lorna Simmons, author of Saxon's *Phonics* program for the

early grades, has created this remedial phonics program for students grade 4 through adult. It follows a very systematic, incremental approach to teach reading, spelling, and vocabulary. It teaches students "coding"—marking letters and groups of letters with both common and specialized marks (e.g., macrons for long vowels) to show their sounds within words. The program is designed to be taught from the extensive teacher's manual. Lessons are scripted and include detailed instructions and tools for using all components of the program. Student workbooks are essential, but they are not self-contained and do not provide instruction. The Classroom Materials component of this course includes an audio cassette for pronunication, a set of classroom master forms (for assessment and record keeping), plus six sets of laminated cards: letter cards (letters and letter clusters), picture cards (key words), spelling cards (teach regular patterns), sight word cards, and affix cards (prefixes and suffixes). This is an excellent program, but it's not for the fainthearted. It will require a good deal of presentation and interaction. But, if you have an older child who is not yet reading, this might be the best investment of your time.(S)

Phonics Made Plain: Wall Chart and Flashcards

by Michael S. Brunner

(Mott Media)

$19.99

This is a surprisingly simple method for teaching phonics based on phonograms (similar to Spalding's *Writing Road to Reading*). The large chart clearly identifies the basic phonograms (sounds made by letters or groups of letters) while also listing prominent exceptions. Flashcards have the phonogram on one side and sample words, cross references to the wall chart, and extra teaching hints on the reverse. One card contains basic reading instruction information. Children can use any beginning readers with these cards. The teacher is instructed to refer to that reader for new phonograms children will encounter and use those phonogram cards for instruction. Even inexperienced parents should find this program fairly easy to use. There is no extra fluff, and you choose your own reading material.

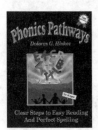

Phonics Pathways

by Dolores G. Hiskes

(Dorbooks)

$32.95

One large, 256-page book contains a complete phonics program for beginning or remedial readers. Sounds of the letters are taught, beginning with short vowels. As each consonant is taught, it is immediately used to begin making blends with the short vowels. (Beginning blends are arranged "consonant-vowel", i.e., ba, bi, bo...) Multi-sensory learning methods (hearing, saying, tracing, writing) are used with each letter. Upper and lower case letters are shown from the beginning, although children work primarily with lower case letters. (We might need to take some extra time to work specifically on recognition and writing of upper case letters, although this could be done late in the program.) Because of the quick movement into blending practice, children are reading three-letter words very soon. Each new concept taught is followed by words, phrases, or sentences for practice, so no extra reading material is necessary. Reading practice is designed to improve tracking skills from left to right, which is especially important for preventing dyslexic problems. Some of the phrases and sentences are purposely nonsensical or humorous to keep it entertaining. The "Dewey the Bookworm" character and proverbs are also used throughout the book for the same reason. The program covers all phonetic sounds, diacritical markings, suffixes and prefixes, plurals and possessives, contractions, and compound words. Teaching instruction is on each page. It is brief enough that no significant preparation time is needed. Complete spelling rule charts and two pages of "Vision and Motor Coordination Training Exercises" are found at the back of the book. Try some of these exercises if you have a child who seems to have minor learning disabilities. *Phonics Pathways* is very reasonably priced for such a comprehensive program.

Three beginning phonics activity books, *The Dorbooks*, are also available for those who would like extra practice in sounding and blending [$9.95]. These shorter reading workbooks are primarily for younger students (preschool through third grade). Each book increases in both size and difficulty, working up through three-letter, short-vowel words. The unusual art work helps to interest the slow or struggling learner, and the author continually reminds us to be patient and go as slowly as we need to with each child. While the *Dorbooks* are worthwhile, *Phonics Pathways* can be used without them.

Other supplementary books, card games, board games, and readers are available, providing extra practice in sounding and blending. Of particular interest might be the *Pyramid* book [$17.95]. It uses a gradually widening pyramid to help students "strengthen eye tracking, develop blending skills, increase eye span, and teach syllabication." This might work well alongside other programs that use the same introductory approach (e.g., *Sing, Spell, Read, and Write*) to help students struggling with tracking and blending. One problem in this program that is most obvious in *Pyramid* is that when students begin with consonant-vowel combinations, then add following letters, they cannot at first determine the proper vowel sound. That sound is determined by what comes next. When children start reading long vowel words, they need to be taught to scan ahead for signals such as silent "e" that determine the vowel sound. (This problem is most apparent on page 50, but I suspect that most children will automatically scan ahead by this stage to figure it out for themselves and it will not be a major issue. The author tells me that diacritical markings will be added to the next edition in places where this might cause any confusion.) The other supplements should also work well with most other phonics programs. Contact the publisher for more information.(S)

PhonicsTutor [computer CD-ROM] 🖥

(4:20 Communications)

$99.95; teacher's manual - $49.95; school version (program and teacher's manual) - $139.90; reader - $29.95; workbook - $29.95

PhonicsTutor for Macintosh or Windows 95 (or higher) computers includes a CD-ROM disk and a small instruction manual, not to be confused with the Teacher's Manual. However, the "school version" includes the Teacher's Manual.

This program is based on the book, *Alpha-Phonics*, by Sam Blumenfeld. The CD-ROM disk features all 128 lessons from the book, but lessons are presented with sound and allow student interaction, all of which lets a student work independently most of the time. Parents will need to set up the program (a little trickier process than you might expect from such a program), then help children get started. Once children understand lesson progression and the functions of the arrows and question mark on the screen, they can work alone. Parents must read through the small manual that comes with the program to understand its capabilities and options as well as to pick up supplemental teaching ideas. Each lesson is presented in eight modes: "Presentation," "Investigation," "PhonicsConst," "WordReading," "WordSounding," "SayIt," "WordSpelling," and "SentenceSpell." "Presentation" introduces the new phonograms, words, or sentences for the lesson with sound. Sound is incorporated through all lessons. "Investigation" familiarizes the student with simple identification exercises. "PhonicsConst" instructs students to type in the spoken phonogram. Correct letter responses appear on the screen, but incorrect responses do not. Prompts (audible, context-sensitive help) are available by hitting the question mark on the screen. "WordReading" requires students to identify the spoken word from among a number of words on the screen. If a student identifies an incorrect word, the correct word is highlighted.

Homonyms pose potential problems in some lessons, but generally one phonogram is taught at a time which limits confusion. For example, "igh" is taught with words like right, sigh, and fight. When students are asked to spell "right," they might wonder if the desired word is "write" if they are not paying attention to the phonogram currently being covered. Generally, this should pose no problem. However, some lessons substitute "WordSounding" mode for "WordReading" specifically to work on homonym identification. "SayIt" requires the student to read aloud the word on the screen, then compare their pronunciation/identification to the computer's. "WordSpelling" mode asks students to spell each word in the lesson. "SentenceSpell," which occurs once students are past beginning lessons, pronounces complete sentences which students must write with correct capitalization and punctuation. Instruction in basic capitalization and punctuation is included within the program.

Students are identified and tracked within the program, and their lessons automatically begin at the place where they left off last time. Parents/teachers really should work with students, assisting them with instruction whenever they need it rather than leaving it to the program's timing. Such assistance might also be necessary if a student struggles with a particular phonogram or concept. The Teacher's Manual comes in handy in such cases. The parent can read and see screen shots of exactly what's being presented in the program, then focus on problem areas. Charts of spelling rules are included in the Teacher's Manual.

Parents should also be encouraging their children to apply their developing reading skills whenever possible. A new 200-page Student Reader will provide reading practice that extends beyond that provided with *PhonicsTutor.*

A new Student Workbook will provide writing activities correlated to the program lessons plus questions for stories from the Student Reader. Parts of speech and beginning composition skills will also be covered.

The CD-ROM adds two lessons not found in the *Alpha-Phonics* book: one introduces letters and sounds, and the other teaches "an extended Orton Gillingham phonogram list." The latter is especially useful for a number of reasons. It puts the key phonogram rules in one location. It can be used before the rest of the program, concurrently, or however you wish.

There is a minor problem you might encounter—it is sometimes difficult to correctly identify the spoken phonogram. Some are difficult to differentiate, especially if you have poor speakers for your computer or you can't achieve a loud enough volume. If a child already has weak auditory discrimination, this can be particularly frustrating.

While the price seems a little high, this is a fairly sophisticated program that offers comprehensive, straight-forward, efficient, phonics instruction. It's not "edutainment" but solid instruction.

Students who need lots of reinforcement and practice can get it from the program even when mom is not available. Students who quickly grasp a lesson can skip ahead to the next lesson. The multi-sensory combination of seeing, hearing, speaking, and writing also enhances the program's suitability for different types of learners while developing all these skill areas. You can preview this program by checking out the free demo at their web site.

Note: equipment requirements for Macintosh are 4 MB RAM, and system software 6.0.6 or 7; equipment requirements for IBM compatibles are Windows 95 or NT 4.0, 8 MB RAM, 4MB free space, SVGA, and a Win 95 sound device.

Although the program described above stands on its own, 4:20 Communications is also producing two new books that are great enhancements to the program—*PhonicsTutor Student Reader* and *PhonicsTutor Student Workbook*. Each book should be about 200 pages in length. The *Reader* is far more than the typical reader. It extends lessons from the program, provides additional practice in both reading and writing. It features word lists (words with common elements) similar to those in *Victory Drill Book*, phrases, sentences, and stories to read. As students progress, the "stories" actually get quite entertaining. The *Reader* also includes some grammar and usage instruction (e.g., punctuation, comparative adjectives, verb tenses) plus other language arts skills such as reading dictionary entries. The workbook provides opportunity for students to test and apply their knowledge. You shouldn't need any other language arts course if you use all these components for the early grades.

Play 'N Talk 🎧

cassettes version - $250; CDs version - $350; computer version - $395; Basic Course - $119; diskettes - $45

Play 'N Talk is based upon a phonics program developed and used by the Isabelle Buckley Schools. It was published in 1961 and has been successfully used by many thousands of children ever since. *Play 'N Talk* requires practically no preparation by the parent. All the teaching is done by the speaker on cassettes or CD's. Clear pronunciation is modeled and emphasized. Calm music provides an introduction and closure for each lesson. Rules and instruction are often in poetic form. Children can listen to the recordings on their own for basic instruction, although parents should listen also. Parents need to verify that children have learned and are properly applying material taught in the lessons, and they should be prepared to play the games and use other *Play 'N Talk* components with their children.

The entire program becomes a computer-based multi-media course with the addition of four diskettes to the complete course. (The diskettes come with the computer version of the course or you can purchase the diskettes for $45 if you already own the complete course with CD's.) Diskettes run on either IBM compatible or Macintosh computers and are used in conjunction with the CD's. Diskettes include al the visual material from the textbooks, notes on how to use the program, and "management" programming to direct component usage. Textbook pages appear on the computer screen just as in the books. All the other components of the complete set come with the computer version.

If we are purchasing *Play 'N Talk* to use without the computer, we can choose either the cassette or CD option. The cassette option includes 14 instructional tapes and two informa-

tional tapes, while the CD version includes seven compact disks. (I recommend CD's since they are so much easier to search to find the correct lesson.) Both versions include 13 books (4 of which are student texts); large alphabet cards (like those mounted above the chalkboards in classrooms); a large Manuscript Alphabet Chart showing how to form letters; Phonics Wall Chart; *Slide 'N Sound* word construction set (includes 43 laminated plastic strips with a card that works like a slide ruler for combining letters and phonograms into words); *Riddles 'N Rhyme* phonics reinforcement game; *Spell Lingo* (24 diagnostic bingo games for practice in recognition and differentiation); *Ring 'N Key* typing program (for reinforcement of spelling and reading plus instruction in keyboard skills); *Flash Card Pattern Book;* a three-hour teacher training video cassette tape; and an *Instructor's Manual*.

The cassettes and compact disks are color-coded to the text books and some of the related items to make it easy to identify what goes with what. No workbooks are used in the program although children who are able can practice with writing activities as directed in the program.

Play 'N Talk allows for developmental variables so that the different aspects of the program (reading, spelling, writing, typing) can be paced to the child. Teaching methods include hearing, seeing, saying, and doing, with extra activity suggestions that can be used according to the needs of each student. Though not designed for children with learning disabilities, *Play 'N Talk* has been used with great success for dyslexic children and also for remedial work. Children work with syllable families (at, am, ab, etc.) rather than letter combinations (ba, be, bi, bo, bu, etc.), practicing both decoding and encoding. The syllabic encoding work helps students develop spelling skills. Reading practice takes place within the student books, *Slide 'N Sound, Spell Lingo, Ring 'N Key*, and other activities, but extra reading practice is recommended. Rules are narrated in rhyme without music. Children need to practice working with concepts to move beyond dependence upon the rhyme. This is accomplished with the various *Play 'N Talk* components and with the addition of supplemental readers.

The *Instructor's Manual* gives detailed step-by-step instruction and correlation of all *Play 'N Talk* components. The video tape provides additional information about phonics instruction plus ideas for setting up a tutorial program for helping people other than family members learn to read. *Play 'N Talk* has built in spelling instruction. The structure of learning teaches children to spell while they learn to read. It eliminates the need for a separate program.

This is really a comprehensive phonics program. Also, it does provide much more than most phonics programs. It begins with introduction of the letters, something often assumed to be already mastered at the beginning of other programs. It covers all phonetic concepts so that children completing the program can read (decode, not necessarily understand) any reading material. Materials are durable and non-consumable, so this one-time investment may be used for many children. This is a good example of "you get what you pay for." While the investment cost is significant, *Play 'N Talk* provides much more than most other programs. *Play 'N Talk* is probably the easiest-to-use, most complete program available. The only thing you might possibly add would be more practice readers. There are no consumables in *Play 'N Talk,* so everything can be used over and over again with a number of children.

If the price for the complete program is prohibitive right now, you can, instead, start with the new *Basic Course* for $119. This includes 6 audio cassettes (or 4 CD's) plus the companion books covering the first two "series" out of the four series in the complete program (essentially covering both short and long vowel single-syllable words up to six letters in length). The *Basic Course* also includes a 36-page *Instructor's Manual*, flashcards, Manuscript Alphabet Chart, Giant Phonics Wall Chart, Resource Manual, and Reading Test with key. When your child completes the *Basic Course*, you can purchase the *Advanced Course* which includes the complete *Instructor's Manual*, the remaining CD's or cassette tapes, *Ring 'N Key* keyboarding kit, and the *Flash Card Pattern Book*. A *Reinforcement Game Package* [$100] includes optional items which are included in the complete *Play 'N Talk* set: *Spell Lingo, Riddles 'N Rhyme, Slide 'N Sound*, and the 3-hour teacher training video.

To preview the program, write or call to request the *Resource Manual* and *Literacy First Aid Kit* which includes a 90-minute cassette with information about the program, phonics test with key, sample lessons, and samples of other program components. The 88-page *Resource Manual* describes the program in detail, offers many testimonials, and compares it with other major phonics programs.

Play 'N Talk provides the *Resource Manuals* and *Literacy First Aid Kits* at no cost. (Support groups can request multiple copies.) Indicate the age level of your children, so they can send the appropriate information.

Professor Phonics Gives Sound Advice

by Monica Foltzer, M.Ed.
(Professor Phonics-Educare)
$15; teacher manual - $7; alphabet cards - $8; spelling word list - $3; Sound Track to Reading (text and instructor's manual) - $15; Sound Track student book only - $12; training tape - $40; 4-part primary set - $33

This is an simple approach for teaching beginning phonics and reading. Start with the alphabet cards, introducing letters for identification and sounds. Then use the student's manual

containing all phonics rules and some reading material. These two items plus a very simple teacher's manual is included along with a spelling word list in the *Four Part Primary Set*. Since the included reading material is minimal, you might wish to purchase a set of phonetic readers to use with this program. Both *Merrill Linguistic Readers* (SRA)(S) and *Phonics Practice Readers* (Modern Curriculum Press)(S) are recommended by the author for this purpose. The *Victory Drill Book* is another good supplement. *Sound Track to Reading* (combined student text and instructors' manual) is for advanced students or remedial work with older students. All components are also sold separately. *Professor Phonics* is a solid phonics course without any fluff. It does the job at a lower cost than many other programs. An optional, two and one-half hour video tape, *Professor Phonics Training Tape*, shows how to teach phonics using these five components.

Recipe for Reading

(Educators Publishing Service)
manual - $17.50

Here is a simple presentation in a single book, similar to *Professor Phonics*. It offers a clearer outline for the teaching of each letter than does *Professor Phonics*.

A valuable extra is an appendix in the back that shows a choice of readers from numerous publishers that would be appropriate at each stage of phonics instruction. The list includes a number of options from their own publisher, Educators Publishing Service, and also the *Merrill Linguistic Readers* (SRA).

Recipe will probably progress too slowly for the bright child but will work well for average to slow learners. The instructions for teacher presentation are excellent for parents lacking confidence.(S)

Ringbound Reading™

(Ringbound Enterprises)
$67.95

Convenience is the distinguishing feature of this phonics program. A 28-page manual, 382, 3" x 9" flashcards, and three large metal rings comprise this unique system. We teach from the flashcards, moving them from storage rings to the "active learning" ring. Some cards have single letters. Some have phonograms such at "kn." Some have long vowel words with silent "e" at the end which can be folded under to demonstrate the difference the silent e makes. Some have pictures for key words or matching games which can be colored with the crayons that come with the program. Cards are divided into three main "decks." The Core deck and the Supplemental deck cards are transferred to the ring that has the smaller Alphabet deck. This becomes the active learning ring. We continually review previous concepts by going through the active cards. Flashcards are color-coded. There are some matching and identification games included. For some of these, we cut one or more cards into squares which are then stored in a 3" x 9" plastic pouch that also goes on a ring. Extra games and activities using the cards are suggested at the end of the manual. Spelling is to be incorporated as students complete each "color" section of cards. Spelling can be oral or written; general instructions about spelling are included in the manual. This program teaches fewer "rules" than programs like *Writing Road to Reading,* so when there are only a few words that follow a particular pattern, they are treated as sight words.

You need to pay careful attention to instructions for letter pronunciation; the manual tells us to "say, 'B, buh, ball,' being careful to isolate the beginning sound of the word 'ball.'" Inclusion of "uh" after a consonant sound can be confusing, but the intent here is to get the teacher to focus on the /b/ sound rather than /bu/.

The manual directs us to our own choice of beginning readers for more practice once children have mastered enough concepts. A list of suggested readers is included.

Cards are nicely done, but they are hand-lettered and the drawings are sketches, which make them look less professional than they might. A big advantage to the system is portability. You can carry these in the car or to the doctor's office without losing anything. The variety of learning methods utilized also appeals to many different learners. Moving the cards around is probably more appealing to Wiggly Willys than more traditional methods. If you choose to have a child color in pictures, but want to use the program with another child, you can purchase additional sets of the "picture" cards for only $16.50.

Saxon Phonics K
(Saxon Publishers, Inc.)
homestudy kit - $110

Saxon Phonics applies the same incremental, spiralling principals that are used in their math program. New content is taught in small increments, then continually applied and reviewed to achieve mastery and retention.

The methodology is somewhat similar to *Writing Road to Reading's* in that it is rule oriented: many, detailed rules are taught throughout the program. (Both programs are based on Orton Gillingham methodology.) Also, both programs use their own coding systems to mark all word elements according to the rules, although Saxon's is a little closer in appearance to standard dictionary markings than *WRTR's.* Both programs teach phonics, spelling, and handwriting simultaneously. However, *Saxon Phonics* does allow for more leeway in offering children oral or hands-on options if they are not yet able to do the writing. Such options, along with the inclusion of letter

tiles and a number of games make the Saxon program very suitable for hands-on learners.

Saxon Phonics K focuses on phonemic awareness—recognizing letter and sound correspondence. However, the program is far more extensive than simply introducing letters and sounds. In addition to the basics, children also learn digraphs and combinations (e.g., ch, ck, ar, er), a portion of the coding system used throughout the program, one spelling rule, and simple syllabication.

Even while students are learning phonograms, they are also learning to blend the sounds into words, applying the necessary phonics rules. Some words will probably be learned even before children master blending as they learn to identify words that contain specific sounds (e.g. identifying the word "cat" because it contains the /a/ sound). After lesson 25, they should have learned skills to read words like "log", "hog", and "hot".

The Homestudy Kit consists of 500+ page teacher's manual, two student workbooks, a colorful alphabet strip, three sets of "Kid Cards" for games, letter cards, key word cards, spelling cards, letter tiles, 15 self-constructed readers, reading word list booklet, rule book, audio pronunciation tape, and introductory video. (The same video and audio tape come with each of the three levels of *Saxon Phonics.*) All of the components work together to provide multi-sensory learning experiences. In my judgment, it might not be necessary to use all of them with children who learn quickly and easily. Workbooks are set up for students to complete one page a day for four days of the week with a parent's help. A weekly oral assessment is to be completed on the fifth day; forms for each are found in the workbooks.

The alphabet strip features block manuscript on one side and D'Nealian (slanted) letters on the other. We can choose whichever style we prefer to teach our child. Since worksheets are all printed in Time Roman typestyle (so that students learn to recognize letters found in books), students do not use letters on workbook pages as models for their own handwriting, but, instead, use the alphabet strip. In their daily lessons, children practice spelling sounds as well as forming the letters to write the sounds. (I found little direct instruction as to how to present the penmanship within the program.)

Although "spelling tests" are given, they involve a child recognizing individual sounds of letters rather than being able to spell entire words from memory.

Kid Cards and the other card decks are used to work on skills such as lower/upper case letter recognition, letter/sound identification, rhyming, spelling, and blending. The card decks are all on perforated sheets to be separated and formed into the different decks.

The program needs to be taught. The teacher's manual lists all items needed for each lesson. Then each lesson is laid out in step-by-step detail, telling the teacher/parent what to do and what to say. The audio pronunciation tape will help parents who are unfamiliar with phonetic sounds themselves. The basic lesson should take about 30 minutes to complete, with games, reading and other activities taking additional time. Of course, the time can be split up if a student's attention span requires it.

This program is extremely thorough and well-thought out in its presentation of phonics. On the other hand, it requires a great deal of time and effort from both parent and child compared to some of the other kindergarten level programs. Because it was originally constructed for classrooms, it is designed as a three year-program. It allows for the likelihood that many children will not complete the entire kindergarten program because of time constraints, and it also recognizes the fact that some children will encounter the first grade program without first having gone through level K. Consequently, there is more here than we should feel obligated to accomplish. The first grade program will again cover the basics, although at a much quicker pace. Those parents who have already been introducing their young children to letters and sounds might find that it works to skip the Level K and begin with *Saxon Phonics 1*.

Scaredy Cat Reading System

by Joyce Herzog
(Simplified Learning Products)
Level 1 - $39.95; Level 2 - $34.95; Level 3 - $54.95; Level 4 - $54.95

This phonics-based reading and spelling program was written by a teacher with much experience teaching children with learning disabilities. She has designed a user-friendly method that appeals to both child and parent. Recognizing problems some children have with letter/sound identification, she has created "stories" to help children learn and remember. These stories originate from a comic which accompanies the program, "The Story of LetterMaster Who Gave the Vowels Their Jobs." Within the story is the rationale used in the system to teach letters and sounds; the behavior of the letters creates the inconsistencies of English letter/sound correspondence. (The comic is the introduction and will probably only be needed at the beginning of the program.)

There are four spiral-bound books, each with instructions, games, puzzles, and accompanying audio tapes. All students need not use all levels of *Scaredy Cat*. (Write for their free brochure, which will help you determine which levels you need.) The *PreReading Kit* (Level 1) covers the alphabet, beginning sounds, and an introduction to the vowels via songs on cassette tape, a script for the songs, sound pictures, games, and puzzles.

The *Beginner's Book* (Level 2) moves through three-letter Consonant-Vowel-Consonant (CVC) words (lessons on tape). Students who have had previous reading instruction but have progressed poorly can begin with the third or fourth step. *Advanced Beginner's Book* (Level 3) reviews CVC and continues through second-grade reading and spelling concepts (again with lessons on tape). *Rules and Fun* (Level 4), in fifteen rules, covers all phonics concepts from the CVC pattern through prefixes, suffixes, and foreign words and sounds, with a song for each rule on tape. Students with learning disabilities might need to use both levels 3 and 4, while the average student can probably jump straight to level 4.

Variety is the hallmark of *Scaredy Cat*. Herzog has included games, lots of reading material (some illustrated), and many activity suggestions. The wealth of ideas reflects her years of practical experience and also makes it easier for us to adapt the program to suit the needs of different learners. We can do more auditory (listening to the tapes), visual (working with written materials in the book), or kinesthetic (hands-on) activities depending upon the need. The materials are non-consumable and can be used to teach more than one child at a time.

The presentation of phonetic rules is a little unusual. The primary emphasis at first is on vowels since they present the most difficulties. The first rule about vowels has a number of exceptions that are covered in more depth elsewhere in the program. The book makes us conscious of the exceptions so we can acknowledge them if our child spots them.

Christian supplements are available: *Graded Bible Quotes* for reading practice after Rule One, and *Character Building Songs* which take us from the (not always exemplary) behavior of the letters to Biblical concepts.

While rule-oriented phonics programs appeal to some teachers and learners, many others will prefer *Scaredy Cat's* simplified approach which teaches only fifteen rules. Simplification of the reading process is one reason why this program is ideal for those with learning difficulties. Additionally, the use of the comic reduces the intimidation factor. The program does require lesson preparation and some one-on-one instruction, but many of the games and activities can be done by children independently.

Shortcuts to Reading

(Career Publishing, Inc.)
$7.95

This inexpensive, oversized book with simple, cartoon-style illustrations can be used to teach basic phonetic sounds. The format is very appealing to children, inviting the active participation that so many learners require. The instruction is orderly yet not as comprehensive as a complete program. A minimal amount of practice and application is included. Use Modern Curriculum Press' *Plaid Phonics A*, Modern Curriculum Press' *Phonics Practice Readers* or other materials to build a complete program. It also works well with older learners who need remedial help.(S)

Sing, Spell, Read, and Write, Kindergarten, Level 1, *and* Level 2 🎧

(International Learning Systems)
Level 1 - $175; combo kit - $235

This multisensory, phonics-based language arts program, appropriate for children ages 5 through 8, is especially good for active learners such as Wiggly Willys. It covers phonics, reading, comprehension, spelling grammar, manuscript handwriting, and composition. The Level 1 set includes 17 full-color, phonetic, storybook readers; 6 cassette tapes with simple, catchy songs introducing sounds; a CD presentation of the songs (use either the tapes or the CD); 5 phonics games; a cardboard treasure chest with prizes; a phonics placemat; raceway chart and raceway car for tracking progress; teacher's manual; two consumable student workbooks; an assessment book; and a teacher training video. It is packaged in a sturdy box. The back cover of the *Raceway* student book is a wipe off writing "slate" as is the back of the placemat; a wipe-off marker and eraser for theses are included. The revised second edition is more polished, more colorful, and features modest changes to improve a few weak spots that were in the first edition.

Sing, Spell, Read, and Write, along with many other reading programs, uses the "consonant-vowel" approach (ba, be, bi, bo, bu) to teach reading. (See comments regarding this in the review of A Beka's *A Handbook for Reading phonics textbook*.)

Sing, Spell, Read, and Write is a <u>fun</u> program, fairly easy to use, that has had mostly positive success for those using it. Instruction is provided by the parent with assistance from the cassettes and the detailed Instructor's Manual. Lesson plans coordinate program elements plus lessons in grammar, reading, comprehension, and writing that are presented from the Manual. The program is truly multi-sensory as it incorporates all learning modalities.

The first workbook, *Off We Go*, provides readiness activities plus an introduction to letters, their sounds, and their formation. The second, the *Raceway Book*, is far more intensive, beginning with blends and continuing through all phonics instruction, while also working on manuscript handwriting, comprehension, and some grammar and spelling. There are 36 "steps" in the program, and progress is tracked on the Raceway Chart as children master each step.

The songs are pleasant, child-oriented tunes that children will sing along to. The games, raceway chart, and prizes add extra fun and incentive to both levels of the program. *The Assessment Book* (a new addition to this second edition) offers assessment pages to be used after each reader to check on word recognition and comprehension. It also has three achievement tests to be used at different points in the program.

The inclusion of phonetic readers saves us the trouble of looking elsewhere for practice material. There are more than 1000 pages in these readers. The last few readers in the set are often unnecessary, because by this point many children have mastered phonics well enough to read many real books. Still, the last few books cover the "oddities" of the English language such as "ph" making the sound /f/, and these do need to be covered at some time.

Some parents have found that the Level 1 kit moved too quickly for their kindergartners or that the workbook lines were too small or required too much writing. So, International Learning Systems has created a Kindergarten level presentation that covers the first 15 of the program's 36 steps in a slower fashion with a separate set of workbooks and six more readers. The two workbooks, *All Aboard* and *On Track*, spend more time on readiness activities and have larger print, more white space, and move at a slower pace than the presentation in Level 1. If you use the Kindergarten materials, you can probably skip a good part of the lessons covering these same steps in the Level 1 program. The Kindergarten books only cover a portion of what is in Level 1, so you will still need both programs if you start with the Kindergarten materials. These are sold as the Combo Kit. You cannot purchase the Kindergarten materials by themselves; they are designed to be used with the tapes and other components from the Level 1 kit. Some parents who used the earlier edition of *Sing, Spell, Read, and Write* felt that their children needed more reading practice at the "short-vowel" stage. Using the Kindergarten program provides that needed expansion for many children. (Reading readiness activities for preschool level children are in a separate *Pre-kindergarten Kit*. The *Pre-kindergarten Kit* teaches colors, shapes, categorizing, sequencing, audio discrimination, and sound and letter recognition.)

Level 2 is presented as a complete language arts program for second grade. It includes phonics review and also covers grammar, handwriting, composition, vocabulary, spelling, proofreading, and reference skills. A Phase I set is available at this time, but the full set should be available for Fall 2000. The complete set comes with two, very colorful workbooks, answer keys, teacher manual, 17 charts, 5 games, 6 audio cassettes or one CD with phonics songs, 1 cassette or CD with songs of the states/geography/parts of speech, a dry erase marker, and eraser.

The approach is fairly traditional, although multi-sensory activities are built into lessons as described in the teacher's manual. Much of this is classroom oriented and will not be useful for homeschoolers. If you use the workbooks alone, as I suspect many will be tempted to do, children will be missing crucial parts of the program—interaction with charts, songs, games, and other class activities.

Workbook activity consists of filling in blanks, matching columns, circling, underlining, writing spelling words, unscrambling words, completing crosswords and word search puzzles, occasional writing sentences, and practicing manuscript printing (book I) or cursive (book II).The back cover of each book is a "wipe-off slate." The one on the back of book I has blank lines, but the back of book II has cursive models for practice.

Workbooks are titled *Grand Tour I* and *II*. The Grand Tour theme is also reflected in the readers which feature stories about the states.

Level 3 works on grammar and spelling. See the review of Level 3 in Chapter Ten.

Sue Dickson, author of *Sing, Spell, Read, and Write*, has also written *Winning* [$175], an older level reading program, designed for those fourth grade and up who are working at remedial levels. *Winning* is packaged for special appeal to older students and adults. The kit includes a Sony Stereo Cassette Walkman, 6 song cassettes, a VHS instructional video, a backpack, two card games, four student books and four instruction manuals. The methodology is very similar to that of *Sing, Spell, Read, and Write*, using songs, games, and books. Songs feature blues, rap, country, and swing arrangements to appeal to older learners. Reading material progresses from appealing comic-book format to something more akin to newspapers and magazines. 70 special learn-to-read stories and comprehension tests are included. *Winning* is great for teaching reading to an older student who needs to learn phonics and spelling from the ground up.

Teach Your Child to Read in 100 Easy Lessons
by Siegfried Engelmann, Phyllis Haddox, and Elaine Bruner
(Simon and Schuster)
$20

This reading program is based on the Distar method, a phonetic system developed from a great deal of research. This volume has adapted the method for use in the home with young children who have not yet had any reading instruction. Because it uses an unusual orthography (formation of letters to represent the various sounds) it would probably be confusing to use with a child who has already begun reading instruction in another method. Distar uses forty-four different letter formations to create a regular alphabet to simplify the decoding process for beginning readers. This eliminates problems such as the different sounds of the letter "t" when used alone or in conjunction with the letter "h" (e.g., "t" as in tan and than). Some letters, such as "long e" simply appear with the macron (long mark line) over the letter. Others join two letters such as the "th" to illustrate that sound. Miniature letters indicate those that are silent. The system presented here does not attempt to provide a regular symbol for every possible sound. The authors feel that it is important for students to recognize that irregularities will appear in words such as "to." They include a few such words in the text, then expect that those remaining can be dealt with after the transition has been made to the use of the

normal alphabet. (The transition begins in lesson seventy-five.)

Each lesson is very carefully scripted (telling the teacher what to say at each step) and controlled to prevent any confusion. (Author's note: While confusion might be a problem in a large group of children, I think it is quite easy to identify and deal with any confusion when dealing with only one child. Because of this, I am not convinced that sticking to the script is as crucial as the authors suggest. However, parents who lack confidence will likely the script very helpful.) Everything necessary for instruction is contained in this single volume, including words, sentences, and stories for reading practice. Because the program is written for instructing young children, the words introduced at the end of the program are on a level young children will understand. A few pages at the end of the book provide suggestions for covering additional phonetic sounds along with suggested books for reading. You are likely to find that your child will not need any other program to learn how to decode the remaining sounds, but can easily learn them as you read real books with them. If you feel you would like to check your child's accomplishments against a complete phonics program, you might review *Professor Phonics* or *Noah Webster's Reading Handbook* to pick up missing concepts.

I have hesitated to recommend this book because of the "distorted" alphabet. I have not seen the need for introducing all of the supplementary letter symbols and have viewed it as an unnecessary complication. However, the reports I get back from those using the program are almost uniformly positive. The general opinion is that the book is much easier to use than many other reading programs, practice stories are entertaining, and the transition to the regular alphabet seems to be a fairly simple process. ISBN #0671631985.(S)

Victory Drill Book
$14.95; teacher's guide - $17.95; worksheets - $22.95; cassette tape - $6.95; Pre-Drill Book - $8.75

You can purchase either the *Victory Drill Book* alone or the book along with other program components, depending upon your need. The entire program can be used to teach phonics, yet the *Victory Drill Book* itself can be used along with any other phonics program for practice and developing reading fluency. The book consists mostly of lists of words arranged according to phonetic relationships. Sentences for practice reading are interspersed. At the end of the book is a summary of thirteen key phonetic rules, eleven spelling rules, a list of nine phonetic vocabulary words we should know (like diphthong, syllable, etc.), and ten rules for syllabication. Children are to be timed as they practice reading through the lists, improving their speed as words become more familiar. Many children are able to decode yet never become good readers because they are just too slow. They have difficulty making the change from decoding each word to actually reading by sight recognition as fluent readers do. The *Victory Drill Book* will help many children overcome such problems. Since some older students who are struggling with reading also have trouble tracking across a line on a page, it might be helpful to place a sheet of paper under a line, then have students read words across the page instead of down the columns.

The book has brief instructions in the front and can be used alone. Other components turn this into a complete phonics program as well as a spelling program. The *Victory Pre-Drill Book* (to be used prior to the *Victory Drill Book*) introduces letter, sounds, and blends in a consumable workbook. It progresses through short vowels and consonants only. The *Teacher's Guide for Victory Drill Book Reading Program*, a necessary tool for those wishing to use *Victory Drill* as a complete phonics program, contains more detailed teaching instruction, ideas for games, reproducible worksheets on phonics and spelling rules, and spelling charts. A cassette tape will help with pronunciation. Teachers with poor phonetic training will find the cassette useful. The *Victory Drill Book Worksheets* provide paper and pencil practice to accompany each page in the *Victory Drill Book*. The worksheets are reproducible, and an answer key is provided. The overall approach is one of formal academics. A few children (especially those who learn to read rapidly) will balk at reading word lists rather than sentences or stories and will resist this type of drill. Although your child might be one of those few, most children will find this type of drill helpful for developing phonics proficiency.

Aside from its usefulness as a phonics program, *Victory Drill Book* might also serve as a spelling program for those who like to teach spelling with words grouped according to common rules.

The Writing Road to Reading

by Romalda Spalding
(Spalding Education Foundation)
$17

This thorough, intensive phonics program consists of a single manual (book) instructing the teacher how to present phonics, writing, and spelling in great detail as a unified, multisensory language arts program. If we use *The Writing Road to Reading*, it contains everything we need to teach those subjects through approximately third grade level, covering all phonics and spelling rules. The heart of the program is the learning of phonograms which the children practice saying, reading, and writing in their notebooks. Some parents feel overwhelmed by the amount of work required to both figure out and present *The Writing Road to Reading*, but for those who have persevered, the results have been excellent. (Most parents need to attend workshops or else use one of the other programs that more clearly explain the methodology.) This program should appeal more to Perfect Paula and Competent Carl learners *and* teachers who do not mind detail as much as other learners. Some

learning disabled children who need much repetition and very complete, specific instruction have also benefitted very much from this method. To teach this program, the teacher needs *The Writing Road to Reading* book and phonogram cards (which can be purchased or made); the child needs pencil and paper (or notebook). Supplementary materials such as the phonogram cards are available from the Spalding Education Foundation, Back Home Industries, Parents as Teachers, The Riggs Institute, and others.

Training courses are offered, and I strongly recommend them to those considering this method. Organizations offering training courses include the Spalding Education Foundation, The Riggs Institute, and Back Home Industries.

If training courses are not practical for you, consider using one of the books that will make using the basic book much easier. *Learning at Home: Preschool and Kindergarten* has detailed lessons plans for presenting the course. *Handbook for The Writing Road to Reading* (Small Ventures) is a 32-page booklet which helps you to organize Spalding's book into a more easily usable form. *Teaching Reading at Home & School* by Wanda Sanseri (Back Home Industries) is a lengthier book that also provides such help in the form of step-by-step instruction. Small Ventures' *Phonics for Reading and Spelling* actually replaces *The Writing Road to Reading*, but utilizes a very similar method. (See reviews below.)

Writing Road to Reading Related Resources

Basic Spelling and Usage Dictionary

(Riggs Institute)
$26.50

Useful for anyone teaching the *WRTR* method for kindergarten through second grade levels, this dictionary has 4,832 words marked with the unique Spalding markings plus 1200 illustrations.

Grammar Works

See the review under "Ungraded Curriculum for all Levels" in Chapter Ten. This resource was originally designed for use alongside any *WRTR* program.

Handbook for The Writing Road to Reading

(Small Ventures)
$4.95

Bonnie Dettmer has, like Wanda Sanseri, developed tools to make using *The Writing Road to Reading* easier to use. In her small booklet, she offers suggested lesson outlines for beginning readers at kindergarten or first grade level; for older beginners who have had no previous phonics teaching; for second graders who have had previous teaching in phonics and/or spelling, but with another method; for third graders with previous training under other methods; for fourth and higher grades new to this system; and for second and following years with students who have used *The Writing Road to Reading* from the beginning. Bonnie suggests only a few minor changes in using the basic book, but simplifies things by telling us "when to do what."

Her handbook makes the entire process much easier than if we were to try to work with *The Writing Road to Reading* on our own. Small Ventures also carries the special composition books and paper recommended for the program.

My Spelling Notebook
by Trudy Palmer
(The Gift of Reading/Homeschool Instructional Services)
$21.95

This book summarizes spelling rules based on the approach used in *The Writing Road to Reading*. Even more specific, it reflects Trudy Palmer's adaptations of that methodology as she presents it in *The Gift of Reading*. (*The Gift of Reading Kit* includes *My Spelling Notebook* .) Rules are broken down into detailed components so we have the following sections: marking for spelling words, consonant sounds and rules, vowel sounds and rules, suffixes, stresses, and syllabication. Some student recording pages are included so children can write words which reflect the particular rules as they encounter them. (There are pages for only some of the rules.) This book is not laid out with step-by-step lessons, but rather serves as a resource for parents who want to familiarize themselves with the rules so that they can better instruct their children. (A suggested schedule appears in *The Gift of Reading*.) To make the book easy to use, Trudy includes three levels of *Spelling Lists*. *Levels 1* (K-2), *2* (grades 2-3), and *3* (grades 3-4) present lists of words arranged by spelling "generalizations" or rules. Syllabication rules receive more attention here than in any other spelling programs I recall. While it can be used apart from *The Writing Road to Reading* or *The Gift of Reading, My Spelling Notebook* will be easier to use if they match up with a phonics program using similar methodology.

Phonics for Reading and Spelling
by Bonnie L. Dettmer
(Small Ventures)

See the complete review under the general reviews of all phonics programs.

Phonics Fun
(Small Ventures)
$15.95

Phonograms are an essential part of *Phonics for Reading and Spelling, The Writing Road to Reading*, and numerous other phonics programs, although the specific phonograms taught vary from program to program. Children should have no problem figuring out the phonogram cards no matter which phonics program they have used. This set of 144 cards includes two groups of 72 phonograms—one pink and one blue—plus instructions for four games. Three of the games are take-offs on old standards: Concentration, Old Maid, and Fish. The fourth game is played by forming words from the cards. Phonogram cards can be very helpful in everyday phonics work for creating words. *Phonics Fun* helps "lighten up" intensive phonics instruction, and it might also be used as a game approach for remedial phonics instruction. These cards are laminated for durability, and it should be easy to wipe off peanut butter and jelly fingerprints with no trace.

Phonics Treasure Chest
(Phonics Treasure Chest) $19.95

This set of eight games (plus variations) was designed to accompany Trudy Palmer's *Gift of Reading* program. However, it will work with other phonics programs, particularly those using phonograms similar to those of *The Writing Road to Reading*. Rules for five card games are like those for Concentration, Go Fish, and other fairly simple card games. Two double-sided game boards and a set of Bingo-style cards are used for more phonogram recognition games. Boards are printed with black ink on brightly colored paper and then laminated for durability. Cards are printed on bright-colored heavy card stock. Since this type reading methodology tends to be rather intensive and work-oriented, these games make a great balance, particularly for learners who like fun and games.

Phonogram Activity Sheets
(Small Ventures)
$19.95

This set of reproducible activity sheets helps reinforce phonogram knowledge through cut, color, and paste type activities.

Phonogram Fun Packet
(Bealls' Learning Games)
$22.95; $18.95 supplement

Although designed to reinforce phonograms and spelling rules as taught in *The Writing Road to Reading*, this set of games can actually be used along with many other phonics programs. While there are instructions and materials for ten games in the set, variations enlarge the actual number. A full-color, double-sided, lightweight game board is the most appealing part of the set with its cute art work. Bingo type cards, phonogram and spelling rule card decks, a spelling rule/phonogram master list, assorted playing pieces, and instructions complete the set. Many games can be played by players of differing skill levels. For example, both game boards are follow-the-path style games. One player can advance by properly identifying phonograms while another player properly completes spelling rule statements. The Bingo type game is called Go the Row, and there are eight cards for three different levels. The remaining games are played with the card decks. For older students, you can order the Supplement which includes all the above components except the game board.

Beall's Learning Games used to produce *Math, States and Capitals, Early Learning*, and *Geography* packets, which were designed to be used along with the basic game board, but these have been discontinued. However, by spring 2000, they should have masters for some of the components of these other packets so you can produce your own. Card decks are available for phonograms, spelling rules, addition, subtraction, multiplication, division, preschool kindergarten deck (including colors, shapes, number patterns, numbers, letters, time), states and capitals, and geography [$3 to $5 each]. Contact them for details.

Primary Learning Log for Language Arts
by Wanda Sanseri
(Back Home Industries)
$4.50

Instead of just a totally blank notebook for the student to build as a spelling text, Wanda has now designed a 36-leaf student book. The spelling pages have two columns for ten spelling words in each column. At the bottom of the page students are to rewrite neatly and correctly their best original sentence for that lesson. Spelling concepts are formatted directly in the back of the *Learning Log*. Students add example words.

The Riggs Institute

The Riggs Institute offers *America's Spelling and Reading with Riggs* [$43.50] by Myrna McCulloch, a "274-page Teacher's Edition with student teacher dialogue and full scope and sequence, [which] includes grammar and vocabulary development ideas." This is a thorough explanation of teaching techniques that instructs us as to when, why, and how to present lessons. Every aspect of teaching the *WRTR* is covered. The purpose of the Riggs Institute's materials is to enhance the *WRTR*, make it easier to use, and "extend the method to cover instruction in grammar, syntax and vocabulary development." The original *WRTR* is an essential part of the Riggs program.

Local "mentor" instructors offer training seminars at various locations across the country. A 360-hour correspondence course using the Riggs materials is offered for credit through Southern Arkansas University. This is a comprehensive college course, offered for either undergraduate or graduate credit, which incorporates actual teaching time as part of the course. The audio tapes and books used in the course are also available directly from the Riggs Institute for those who prefer to learn independently. The 3-hour taped *Self or Home Study Course* [$17.50] is extremely detailed and easy to understand.

Even though there are only three hours of video to watch, the course should take about one year to complete. *The Daily Lesson Plans* [$14.95] features both daily and weekly lesson plans and helps us through the first six months of teaching the program.

The Riggs Institute also publishes other items essential for the program: *70 "Orton" Phonogram Cards* [$20] (each card has a "script" for what the teacher says as she teaches sounds and letter formation), *"Orton" Phonograms with Spelling Rules for Teachers and Students* (cassette tape) [$6.50], and composition notebooks [$2], along with the optional book, *A Basic Spelling and Usage Dictionary* (reviewed elsewhere in this section). Some home educators might also want to get the article "Phonetics, Spelling, Whole Language: How We Put Them Together for the Best of Both Worlds" [$2]. Contact the Riggs Institute for a detailed brochure.

The Riggs Institute also publishes the four-page "A Mini Phonetic Spelling Kit," which very concisely summarizes the phonograms, spelling rules, and letter formation information. Send a SASE (self-addressed, stamped envelope) for a free copy.

Spelling Scale for Home Educators
(Small Ventures)
$1.50

The Writing Road to Reading recommends the *Morrison-McCall Spelling Scale* as a tool for evaluating spelling skills. *The Scale* is out of print, so Bonnie Dettmer of Small Ventures has composed a similar scale including instructions for use. Although designed to correlate with *The Writing Road to Reading*, others might wish to use it as an evaluation tool. It is not intended to be a spelling list/instruction tool. *The Scale* is designed to test students at all grade levels through the first year of college.

Teaching Reading at Home & School
by Wanda Sanseri
(Back Home Industries)
Core Kit - $69; TRHS book alone - $19.95

Wanda Sanseri has written a teacher's manual for teaching the first four years of language arts-phonics, penmanship, spelling, reading, composition, logic, and introductory grammar. Her book can be used as a supplement to *Writing Road to Reading*, but now can be used instead with her newest book, *The Wise Guide for Spelling*. Other helps including the *70 Basic Phonogram Cards, Phonogram Cassette Tape*, student spelling notebooks, *TRHS Charts, The Alpha List, The New England Primer*, and a *Teaching Reading at Home* video are also available from Back Home Industries. *TRHS, The Wise Guide*, the *Phonogram Cards* and cassette tape are sold at a lower price than what we pay when purchasing individual items. Wanda and ten other teachers she has trained and endorsed offer seminars for interested groups across the country and in Canada.

I have received many positive reports from those who have attended Wanda's seminars and used her materials. They tell me that Wanda gives them practical instruction that really works for homeschoolers while clearly explaining the basics so they have confidence in their knowledge and ability to teach their children.

The Wise Guide for Spelling

by Wanda Sanseri
(Back Home Industries)
$35.00

The Wise Guide covers 2000 basic words (plus hundreds of derivatives) to teach the foundational principles of English spelling. This culmination of ten years of work replaces the spelling list in *Writing Road to Reading* as a required resource with *Teaching Reading at Home & School*.

The word list draws from some of the best of leaders in the field including Ables, Ayres, Bishop, Fry, Hanna, Irish, Orton, Spalding, and Webster.

Lesson plans are provided for each set of twenty words. Recommended preliminary activities are suggested including warm-up drills and motivational comments for introducing the lesson. Sentences are provided to illustrate each word. Selections come from literature, quotes of famous people, or instructive comments. Each word is divided into syllables and highlighted to amplify spelling rules. Information to explain the spelling is provided.

Creative ways to reinforce spelling words are suggested. Rather than uninspiring activities like copying a word five times, students actively use spelling words in a creative variety of ways. The teacher is given simple instructions and the student works from the words dictated for him to write into his spelling notebook. No worksheets are needed. Enrichment activities involve a wide variety of topics: literature, grammar, antonyms, synonyms, derivatives, etymology, contractions, compound words, alphabetizing, keyboard instruction, punctuation, alliteration, homonyms, analogies, words of comparison, oxymorons, figures of speech, verb conjugation, poetry, plurals, subject and verb agreement, Greek and Latin roots, possession, and appositives. Assignments utilize art, pantomime, refrigerator magnetics, deaf signing, and games. Numerous approaches are used to improve composition including: creative writing, letter writing, diary work, vivid word selections, descriptive writing, feature writing, and dictation.

Supplemental Materials

Beginning Readers

The Alphabet Series
(Educators Publishing Service)
$56.25

This set of 21 short vowel readers correlates with *Recipe for Reading* from the same publisher. I found a couple of the stories objectionable, but these could easily be omitted. These work well with *Recipe for Reading* and will also serve as reading material for most phonics programs.(SE)

Basic Phonics Readers
(A Beka Book)
$11.40 for all 12; teacher edition - $14.20

These are 12 small, colorful readers, divided into three sets of four books each. The sets progress in difficulty, reflected in the set titles: "I Learn to Read," "I Do Read," and "I Can Read Well." They begin with short-vowel words, shift into long vowels by the fourth book, and continue up through words like "south," "ground," and "bright." You can purchase the individual books or you might purchase the teacher edition which includes all of the readers in one comb-bound book.

Bob Books First, Bob Books Fun, Bob Books Kids, Bob Books Pals, and Bob Books Wow
(Scholastic, Inc.)
$16.95 per set

These five sets of beginning readers are phonetically organized with controlled vocabulary, yet the stories are more interesting than many other such readers. The first set of 12 little books, *Bob Books First* (#914544), concentrates on short-vowel words. The second set of 12 slightly longer books, *Bob Books Fun* (#912198), continues with short vowel, consistent words, adding double consonants, blends, endings, some sight words and longer stories. The last three sets continue to add more complex phonics. The books get longer, so there are fewer per set. *Bob Books Kids* (#914546), has 10 books with eight stories and two activity books. They continue work on short vowels words. *Bob Books Pals* and *Bob Books Wow!* each have four books of 16 pages each and four books of 24 pages each. *Pals* adds new blends, more sight words, and longer compound words. *Wow!* introduces long vowel words.

Illustrations are simple black-and-white line drawings that children can imitate and color, and both the stories and drawings have an appealing child-like character. Teaching instructions are short and simple. These readers will work with any orderly phonics program.

Catholic National Readers

(Neumann Press)

[Note: This same series is also reprinted by Our Lady of Victory/Lepanto Press]

Speller/Word Book - $16; Primer/Book One - $15; Book Two - $17; Book Three - $19; Book Four - $20; Book Five - $22; Book Six - $25; Complete Set - $125

Published in the 1890's the *Catholic National Readers* are suggested for grades K-8. The entire set, consisting of a speller and six readers (including the primer), are often referred to as the "Catholic McGuffeys." The books may also be purchased individually. They do not correspond to grade levels, and Book Six may easily be used past the eighth grade. The books increase in size from the 128-page primer to the 480-page Book Six. The phonics-based primer uses diacritical marks and includes handwriting (script) lessons. Later readers include vocabulary and language lessons with most stories. They are filled with great literature and sound Catholic sentiment. The later books presume some understanding of Greek and Roman classics.

Kolbe Academy publishes question and answer guides to supplement the *Catholic National Readers*, which are available for sale to the general public. See the appendix to contact Kolbe Academy for more information. [M. Wittmann]

Hewitt Early Readers, Sets I and II

(Hewitt Homeschooling Resources)

$7.95 per set

There are five books in each of these two sets of beginning readers. Each twelve-page reader is illustrated with whimsical, black-and-white line drawings. The readers are phonetic in that they use a controlled vocabulary and include a chart at the beginning of each book showing which phonograms and which sight words students will encounter. However, even the first reader mixes short- and long-vowel words, making even Set I most useful after students have been introduced to most of the phonograms. Vocabulary difficulty increases only slightly in Set II, but there are more words per page. Books feature animal or insect themes (e.g., bats, worms, foxes, turtles), but the injection of humor into the illustrations makes them unreliable for scientific content (e.g., a turtle with his shell drawn to look like an actual house). I would not use these readers for drill of basic phonograms, but I would use them for supplementary reading material once the phonograms have been learned.

It is Fun to Read, Pals and Pets, A Time at Home, and It is a Joy to Learn [set of four readers]

(Christian Liberty Press)

$11 per set of four

These four reading books can be used along with any phonetic program for practice with short- and long-vowel words. The first two readers concentrate on short-vowel words beginning with sentences containing three-letter words, while the last two continue through long vowels and the remaining phonograms. In the new second editions of these readers, full-color illustrations accompany the text which is now in an improved, easy-to-read typestyle. The content is Christian with references to Jesus and God, along with character building themes. This is one of the least expensive sets of phonetic readers available, although there is not a lot of practice for each level. These work well in combination with CLP's *Noah Webster's Reading Handbook* and *Adventures in Phonics* Level A.

Little Companion Readers

(Paradigm)

$19.95

These readers were designed specifically to accompany *Alpha-Phonics*, but they will work with other phonics programs that introduce short vowels first. There are 10 illustrated readers, all concentrating on short-vowel words.

Phonics Practice Readers

(Modern Curriculum Press)

$19.50 per set

MCP offers three different series (*A, B,* and *C*) of these readers to choose from for variety's sake. We need not purchase them all. Within each series are four sets: short vowels, long vowels, blends, and digraphs. Each set consists of ten eight-page books. We might need only short and long vowels before children are ready for many beginning reading books. These are inexpensive and colorfully illustrated.(S)

Phonics Round-Up

(Creative Teaching Associates)

$14.95 each

Your child can practice phonics skills while playing a game. Spin the spinner and then match the sound to the colorful pictures on the game board. A block of four markers wins. The game called *Consonant Blends* has a large spinner color-coded to 5 different game boards so the game could be used with a group as well as individually. Other titles in the series are *Vowels, Beginning Consonants, Digraphs/Diphthongs, and Silent & Ending Consonants/Bossy"R"*. Recommended for grades K-3.

Reading for Fun Enrichment Library

(A Beka Book)

$33.95

Fifty-five small readers come in a boxed set. While they do not follow as strict a phonetic progression as the Merrill or MCP readers, they do begin with short vowels and gradually increase the phonetic complexity. (For most children, you will still need additional practice with short vowel words beyond these readers.) While there are a few Bible stories and some character-building stories, most are about children, fairy tales, nature, and other common subjects. Books are illustrated in full color. The price is very reasonable for so much good quality reading material.

Short and Long Vowel Readers

(Thoburn Press)

$14.95/set

These are actually two separate sets of readers from the Fairfax Christian Curriculum Series—*Short Vowel Reading Series* and *Long Vowel Reading Series*—with ten, 16-page books in each series. Each book actually has a story with a message about Christian living. (Scriptural references are provided at the end.) Stories are illustrated with black-and-white line drawings done in a child-like style. Type is large and easy-to-read, and the stories are quite entertaining for beginning readers. These books can be used with any orderly phonics program. These sets are among the least expensive beginning readers available.

Phonics Workbooks

Note: Workbooks are included in many of the phonics programs reviewed above.

Adventures in Phonics, Levels A and B

(Christian Liberty Press)

student workbook - $8 each; teacher manual - $7 each

Adventures in Phonics teaches phonics in a traditional manner. It is similar in concept to the Modern Curriculum Press *Plaid Phonics* series, but it is a little more challenging. In Level A, basic phonics is covered along with some suffixes and the articles "a" and "an." Letters and sounds are taught along with practice in letter formation. Little attention is given to teaching how to blend the sounds together for words. Instead, children practice writing and saying simple words. Parents might need to work with children a little more at the blending stage if they don't pick it up quickly.

Vowel sounds are taught in families (e.g., all the ways of making the long "o" sound). Almost all phonograms are taught in Level A, and by the end children should be able to read simple sentences. Level B reviews previously taught information, then continues with more challenging phonics, syllabication, the use of apostrophes, synonyms, antonyms, and homonyms.

The student workbook and teacher's manual are both essential for whichever level you are using. The workbook is dependent upon the teacher's manual for lesson presentation, and the teacher's manual includes a set of phonics flashcards and charts.

Workbook pages are mostly typical fill-in-the-blank or circle-the-correct-answer exercises. The teacher's manual has brief, easy-to-follow lesson plans, and it also shows how to use the workbook pages and flash cards. *Adventures in Phonics* is best used as an adjunct to a basic handbook such as *Noah Webster's Reading Handbook* (also from CLP). Using the *Handbook* with both levels of workbooks provides a solid grounding in phonics and reading. Add a few practice readers (such as those published by CLP) for a complete program. (CLP offers such a package in their catalog, although it doesn't include Level B.)

Levels C and D, planned for future publication, should provide continuing practice and reinforcement for older students.

Explode the Code

(Educators Publishing Service)

$6.20 each; teacher's key for Books 1-5 and 1 1/2-4 1/2 -$1.90; teacher's key for Books 6-8 - $1.90

There are fourteen separate workbooks available in this series, although we might not want to use them all. The books review phonetic concepts individually rather than attempting to review concepts over and over at increasing levels of difficulty as we find in Modern Curriculum Press' *Plaid Phonics* series. They also feature large print and less of it per page than MCP, making them a good choice for children who can do only limited amounts of writing or have trouble focusing. Books 1-8 are the most important. Content of each is as follows: Book 1—short vowels; Book 2—initial and final consonant blends; Book 3—open syllables, silent e rule, digraphs, and simple diphthongs; Book 4—syllable division rules; Book 5—word families, three-letter blends, qu, -ey, and the three sounds of -ed; Book 6—more difficult diphthongs and r-controlled vowels; Book 7—soft c and g, silent letters, sounds of ear, ei, eigh, and the digraph ph; Book 8—suffixes and irregular endings. Books 1 1/2, 2 1/2, 3 1/2, 4 1/2, 5 1/2, and 6 1/2 offer more practice on topics covered within books 1, 2, 3, and 4 respectively. Post-tests are included within each book. One Teacher's Key covers Books 1 through 5 and 1 1/2 through 5 1/2, while another covers Books 6 through 8. Keys include program description, answers, and dictations for the post-tests.(S)

Letters and Sounds K or 1

(A Beka Book)

K - $9.95; grade 1 - $11.55

Use *Letters and Sounds*, either book *K* or *1*, as seatwork after initial presentation of letter and sound recognition. These books should be used along with A Beka's *Phonics and Reading* Kindergarten and Grade 1 Teacher's Guide/Curriculums. These are colorful workbooks that are not overwhelming as long as you are not pushing a child into reading before he or she is ready. The kindergarten book requires a minimal amount of writing—mostly drawing lines between things, circling, and selecting the right answer until the end of the book where they fill in some blanks. However, children are expected to be able to read three-letter, short-vowel words early in the book. *Letters and Sounds 1* repeats much of what is covered in *K*, but moves further, especially with fill-in-the-blank writing activities.

Phonics for Young Catholics K, 4, and 5

(Seton Press)

4 - $15; 5 - $13

Phonics for Young Catholics K and *4* are similar in concept to the *Plaid Phonics* series, although there is more content per page, work is at a higher level than in *Plaid Phonics*, and content is definitely Catholic. The kindergarten program is presented in two volumes. (Volume 1 is completed, but Volume 2 is still in progress.) It begins with readiness activities, then introduces letters and sounds. In *Phonics 4*, some work is very easy for fourth grade level (e.g., matching words with pictures), especially at the beginning, but the level of difficulty increases dramatically as students progress. Exercises review basic phonic rules and require students to analyze word structures. They also cover suffixes, inflections, plurals, possessives, prefixes, roots, synonyms, antonyms, homonyms, and syllabication. The book is a consumable worktext, and it comes with an answer key.

Phonics for Young Catholics 5 is in an older edition which I did not review since I expect it to be revised in keeping with the format of the fourth grade book. Phonics for first grade is in progress.

Plaid Phonics level K, A, or B - 1998 editions

(Modern Curriculum Press)

student editions: K - $8.75, A - C - $9.95 each; teacher's resource guide - $44 each

The MCP *Plaid Phonics* workbooks can be used for phonics instruction or reinforcement, although most homeschoolers use them as workbook supplements to other phonics programs. The 1998 editions are colorfully illustrated and have large print, so they are not intimidating to children. Use these to help build both auditory and visual discrimination of sounds and letter. Level K introduces letters and sounds (short vowels only), working on identification and discrimination of individual letters. Level A reviews, then adds long vowels, blends, digraphs, contractions, and inflectional endings. Level B reviews more rapidly, then adds compound and two-syllable words, *R*-controlled vowels, plurals, suffixes, prefixes, vowel pairs and digraphs, diphthongs, synonyms, antonyms, and homonyms. Some "whole language" activities have been added to the latest editions. For example, children make their own storybooks with pages from the workbook. Other whole language activities (e.g., suggestions for related story books to read aloud) are in the teacher's resource guide. The guide offers these and other lesson-expanding helps as well as lesson presentation instructions and workbook answers. However, answers are fairly obvious, and much of the guide's content is classroom oriented and unlikely to be used by many home educators. On the other hand, the teacher's guide is a must for those who want to use *Plaid Phonics* as a more central part of their phonics instruction.(S)

Phonics Skills Practice Books

(Essential Learning Products Co.)

$3.99 each

These five, 96-page books are especially good for slow learners or those with poor writing skills, although they make a good supplement for those who want a limited amount of writing practice with phonetic concepts. The workbooks are half-size with large print so there is less work per page than in other such books. However, the total number of pages does add up to a substantial amount of practice. Workbooks are titled *Initial Consonants, Medial and Final Consonants, Short and Long Vowels, Vowel Combinations,* and *Blends and Digraphs.*(S)

Intermediate and Advanced Readers and Reading Programs

A Beka Book Readers

(A Beka Book)

In the past, A Beka Book has combined readers from a number of series to create sets of readers for each grade level, but they are gradually replacing many of those with their own new readers and novels. Most of them seem to be collections of stories and poems, old and new. Especially at older levels, we find stories by well-known authors.

In each book, new vocabulary words are highlighted at the beginning of each story. At the end of each story are questions, most of which focus on comprehension but with a few that challenge children to think at deeper levels. All of the books emphasize Godly character development. These books are beautifully printed in full-color throughout with illustrations and lovely borders across the tops of all the pages. Teacher editions of these readers are available, but they are not necessary for the early grades. Readers correlate with the reading program presented in *A Handbook for Reading* at the early grade levels. A Beka recommends up to nine or ten readers per level in grades 1 through 3, but you might not feel that you need all of them.

Three unusual readers deserve mention. *Adventures in Nature, Adventures in Greatness* [$7.70 each], and *Adventures in Other Lands* [$8.20] are speed reading/comprehension texts for approximately fourth through sixth grades. Short, interesting selections are timed with the total number of words shown for determining reading speed. Comprehension questions sometimes follow the story, or they are on quiz pages at the back of the book. Books are meant to be consumable with children writing answers in the book, although answers can be written elsewhere if desired. An answer key is at the back of each book.

Alpha Omega LifePacs

(Alpha Omega)
Language Arts 300, 400, 500, and 600

Alpha Omega incorporates reading into the Language Arts LifePacs. The first number of the course signifies grade level, i.e., 300 = third grade level. You should supplement with more reading material than is included. See description of each *Language Arts* LifePac course under "Composition and Grammar.

Bob Jones University Press Reading Program
Phonics and Reading 1
Home School Kit - $149

Phonics and Reading 1 replaces the rather complicated *First Grade English Skills* program previously offered by BJUP. Listening, comprehension, composition, and handwriting activities work with the theme of the phonics lesson to give a correlated set of lessons. Then in the same teacher manual, the lesson plans for *Reading 1* apply the phonics skill just learned. The two-volume teacher manual includes "how to teach" instructions and reduced pictures of student worktext pages (with answers). The student materials in the kit include two hard cover readers, *Reading 1-1* and *Reading 1-2*, and four worktexts: *Phonics and Vocabulary, Handwriting 1*, and a set of two smaller worktexts to accompany each of the reading texts. Extra teacher materials in this new kit include a home teacher packet, Teaching Visual flip chart, two songs cassettes, and *Write Now! Activity Sheets*. Skills are presented in a traditional developmental sequence, using word families but no nonsense syllables. We can find hands-on and multi-sensory learning ideas in the home teacher manual.

The readers have well-written, interesting stories, so even if

you use other materials than BJUP's for phonics instruction, you might still want to use the BJUP readers [$18.50 each] and companion worktexts [$9] which are also sold individually. However, the lesson plans and answers for these are contained in the *Phonics and Reading 1* two-volume manual.

Reading for Christian Schools 2
set of all components - $95

The second and third grade programs are the first in the series to be published as second editions. For second grade, student materials include two readers and a single worktext. There is also a two-volume Teacher's Edition with reduced, full-color student readers pages. The Teacher's Edition correlates lesson presentation and use of readers and worktext. A free copy of *Reading for Life* video is included in each homeschool kit. A Teacher's Edition of the worktext has answers overprinted on student pages, but instruction for worktext activities is in the primary Teacher's Editions. The program directs a significant amount of phonics review from the Teacher's Editions, while also working on comprehension, oral reading skills, and vocabulary development. Characters with personalities are introduced to help children learn relationships and functions of letters in words (similar in concept to *Alphabet Island*, but not as involved). Reading selections are a broad mix of genres, including some fantasy. Bible truths are incorporated throughout the lessons. The full-color illustrations are visually appealing. Activities for various learning styles are used in lesson presentation by the teacher. Supplementary activities (e.g, games, searching newspapers for examples) are offered, although most will require extra work to collect resources and/or prepare materials. A set of 108 Service Word Cards is used for teaching irregular words. Reading 2 Teaching Visuals Flip Chart helps with lesson presentation. Three supplemental novels can be used for grade 2 enrichment: *The Treasure of Pelican Cove, Carolina's Courage,* and *Pulling Together*. *BookLinks* guides offer lesson plans for study of each of the three books. Sets of each book and its companion *BookLinks* are $12.99 each.

The program is academically sound and thoughtfully put together. However, it does take more preparation and presentation time than do many other phonics programs, and you will have to select from among presentation activities those that are useful with your child.

Reading for Christian Schools 3
$95

The third grade program is similar in format to the second grade. Three supplemental novels can be used for enrichment: *The Case of the Dognapped Cat, Jenny Wren,* and *These are My People. BookLinks* are $12.99 for each set.

Reading for Christian Schools 4
$73 for all essential components

The basic package includes a hard cover student reader, a Teacher's Edition, a worktext, a worktext teacher's edition, and the novel *Medallion*. The reader is good, but this particular worktext is more challenging than those for earlier levels, focusing on higher levels of comprehension. Consequently, more direct teaching and supervision may be necessary when using this worktext than those at lower levels. The novel *Medallion* is studied with teaching information included within the Teacher's Edition. The following Book Links/novels are available for grade 4: *Sheriff at Waterstop, Medallion*, and *Mountain Born*.

Reading for Christian Schools 5
$107.99 for all essential components

This reader has a variety of interesting stories. An accompanying worktext helps students further develop reading skills. The Teacher's Edition includes study information for the novel *Derwood, Incorporated*.

Reading for Christian Schools 6
$73 for all components

Components are the student's hard cover reader, worktext, teacher's edition for the reader, worktext teacher's edition, and the novel, *A Father's Promise*. Study information for the extra book is provided within the teacher's edition.

The Christian Eclectic Readers and Study Guide
by William H. McGuffey; revised and edited by Charles and Betty Burger
(Wm. B. Eerdmans Publishing Co.)
$50

McGuffey's original readers have received yet another rejuvenation. This latest edition is the best yet. The editors have worked form the original readers rather than later editions. Grammar and vocabulary have been updated. Stories have been edited and some omitted to remove grisly or inappropriately disturbing references. However, the general flavor is still that of the early nineteenth century in both style and content. A few other minor changes have been made from the originals. Diacritical markings found in the originals have been omitted. Also, the originals included lists of words, their definitions, and pronunciations, while the new editions ask the reader to define and learn to spell the listed words.

There are four books in the series, and like the originals, these do not correspond to grade levels. Students must have a prior introduction to phonics and beginning reading. The first story in the *First Reader* begins, "Here is John" which is obviously already beyond simple three-letter, short-vowel words. The readers can be used all the way into high school. The *Fourth Reader* especially emphasizes articulation and rhetoric with "rules" presented at the beginning of most lessons to be practiced and applied.

The content of these readers, as with the originals is thoroughly Christian with frequent Biblical references and constant themes of morality and godly character.

One of the most important features of this new series is the inclusion of a study guide by Betty Burger. An experienced home schooling mother, Betty has presented some basic tools for using the readers, then follows with themes and assignments for each of the reading lessons in all four volumes. She reinforces the Biblical teaching throughout the study guide, and, at the upper levels, she incorporates worldview type questions that will challenge students to think through and apply their faith. For example, one lesson for the *Fourth Reader* asks, "Is our God part of His creation or separate from it? Answer in an essay how Christian doctrine differs from pantheism and why that is important."

Children used to fast-moving entertainment might struggle with the prose which seems convoluted compared to modern writing (and especially that aimed at children). I expect some children will be put off by the style while others will find it intriguing and entertaining. Perhaps this is a good tool to "expand children's literary horizons" in small steps rather than with entire works such as *David Copperfield*.

Christian Liberty Press Readers
Meeting New Friends
$6

This 150-page, illustrated reader is for first grade level. Reading is fairly simple, essentially providing practice for phonics application. Phonics charts and vocabulary drill are included.

Beautiful Stories for Children
$7

Children who have mastered phonics fundamentals can stretch their reading skills with this 190-page, illustrated reader. Reading selections were apparently originally written in an earlier era, and they teach godly character through real-life stories and poems about children, families, and nature. (No fables, fairy tales, talking animals, etc. appear in this book.) Vocabulary words and definitions are provided at the beginning of each selection, but they appear because they are part of the selected stories rather than because they are part of a controlled-vocabulary approach to reading. There are no comprehension questions and no teacher's manual.

Lessons From the Farmyard
$3.50

This book reads like Beatrix Potter (*Tales of Peter Rabbit*) with a delightful, moralistic lilt. Most of the book is a series of stories about a rabbit family, featuring two brother-rabbits, Lapino and Trottino. There is some continuity, so these stories should be read in order. At the end is a poem, "Minna's Thanksgiving." The book very definitely purposes to teach positive character traits to children, so there are teaching suggestions for each section to help us reinforce the stories' lessons. It will be a difficult book for most second-graders to read on their own, so use it for shared reading or a read-aloud book.

History Stories for Children
$6

This 250-page reader is listed as being for third grade level, but it can actually be used by children in a much wider age/grade level span (both younger and older). Stories are short and are written in narrative form so they are interesting to children without being overwhelming. Large print makes reading easier for developing eyes. Topics range from Bible history through world and U.S. history, although the majority would fall under U.S. history. Many stories tie in with holidays and anniversaries such as "Saint Valentine," "Easter Lilies," and "Hatchets and Cherries." This is an excellent way to introduce children to heroes, especially since the stories emphasize godly character traits. A "Note to the Teacher" follows most stories with very brief background information and/or teaching suggestions. A separate page of questions comes with the book, but no questions are included in the text.

Stories of The Pilgrims
$6

This updated and revised edition of the original book about the Pilgrims by Margaret B. Pumphrey tells of this brief but important time in America's history in story form. The reading level is appropriate for third or fourth graders, but it makes a good read-aloud book for younger children. Comprehension questions follow most, but not all, chapters. The print is large and dark with a few black-and-white illustrations scattered throughout the book.

Boys and Girls of Colonial Days
$5

This revised and edited edition of an original book by Carolyn Sherwin Bailey is an excellent supplement for children from about third grade up through fifth or sixth grade, even though it is listed in the CLP catalog as a fifth grade reader. It contains twelve stories about children in colonial days. In many of the stories the children meet famous people such as Benjamin Franklin, Samuel Adams, George Washington, and Betsy Ross. The writing style sounds like the original was written in the nineteenth century, yet it is very understandable for children. The book also has numerous black-and-white illustrations; most are of an older-appearing etched style in keeping with the text. This book is printed in large type in a 6" by 9" format, thus eliminating small-print problems for young readers. There are no questions in the book, but a separate page of questions comes with the book along with an answer key.

The Story of Inventions
$8

This 350-page reader about inventions and inventors is recommended for sixth grade. (Cover science and reading at the same time!) Illustrations help children visualize what they are reading, and comprehension questions at the end of each chapter help students retain what they have read.

Landmark's Freedom Baptist Curriculum
Literature 1 (LSGX105)
$35

This first grade level course from Freedom Baptist curriculum uses the *McGuffey First Eclectic Reader* as its main text and provides worksheet activities to round out the reading program. The main emphasis is on phonics exercises to support the *Reader*, although there are also character trait instruction and Scripture verses to memorize or practice writing. Opportunities for art and creativity are included. There are many activities that deal with our American heritage, such as Thanksgiving, the flag, and President Lincoln. The exercise book comes comb-bound so that it will lie flat for young students. Illustrations are in black-and-white but are attractively done. It seems a useful resource for use with the *McGuffey Reader*. Quizzes and answer keys are included. [Kath Courtney]

Literature 2
$35

This literature course includes *McGuffey's Second Eclectic Reader*; the *Art-Literature Reader, Book 2*; student study guide; quizzes; and answer keys in one complete package. Lessons include reading, vocabulary, and comprehension skills as well as a few broader language arts activities such as dictionary skills and sentence writing. The study guide consists of daily lessons that students who are fairly proficient readers can read on their own, completing a variety of exercises such as matching columns, filling in blanks, identifying the number of syllables in words, arranging words in alphabetical order, and answering in complete sentences. Students are directed to read assignments in their readers upon which many of the questions are based. Weekly quizzes and answer keys are included. Parents will need to listen to a child's oral reading to ensure that they are learning proper pronunciation as well as developing the ability to read expressively and with understanding. The content is morally uplifting, occasionally mentions God, and features related Bible verses in "boxes" within lessons.

Literature 3
$35

This literature course includes *McGuffey's Third Eclectic Reader*; the *Art-Literature Reader, Book 3*; student study guide; quizzes; and answer keys in one complete package. This course is very similar to Literature 2, although the readers and questions are at a higher level.

Literature 4
$35

This literature course includes *McGuffey's Fourth Eclectic Reader*, student study guide, quizzes, and answer keys in one complete package. Lessons include reading, vocabulary, and comprehension skills as well as a few broader language arts activities such as book reports, dictionary skills, and sentence writing. The studyguide consists of daily lessons that students can read on their own, completing a variety of exercises such as matching columns, filling in blanks, and answering in complete sentences. Students are directed to read assignments in their reader upon which many of the questions are based and from which vocabulary words are drawn. Weekly quizzes and answer keys are included. Book reports are required every six weeks, and instructions and forms for the book reports are included in the study guide. Parents will need to listen to a child's oral reading to ensure that they are learning proper pronunciation as well as developing the ability to read expressively and with understanding. Parents also need to oversee completion of lessons, signing off when students are ready for their quizzes and approving book report selections. The content is morally uplifting, occasionally mentions God, and requires memorization of some Bible verses.

Literature 5
$35

This course is very similar in format to Literature 4, although it includes *McGuffey's Fifth Eclectic Reader*. Vocabulary development receives the most attention with weekly quizzes focusing exclusively on vocabulary words drawn from current reading lessons. Three book reports are required, two written and one oral. Instructions and forms for the book reports are included in the study guide. Parents need to oversee completion of lessons, signing off when students are ready for their quizzes and approving book report selections.

Literature 6
$35

This course is similar to those for fourth and fifth grades, although it includes *McGuffey's Sixth Eclectic Reader* and adds lessons on essay writing. While vocabulary development receives much attention, weekly quizzes focus on both vocabulary and reading skills. Book reports are required every three weeks, with one-third of these presented orally.

McGuffey Readers, Christian School Edition
(Thoburn Press)
$44.95 per set in paperback; $69.95 in hard cover

Seven readers, available individually or as a set, are unedited facsimiles of an early version of the classic readers, including the original illustrations and typesetting. Both paperback and hard cover editions are available. They are not the originals (which are published by Mott Media) but are slightly different. Like the originals, they begin with a primer and then

cover, essentially, all grade levels but not corresponding by number and grade level. As with the other "McGuffey" readers, each book can be used over two or more grade levels. The First Reader might be best toward the end of first grade through second grade.

Thoburn Press also publishes workbooks to accompany the primer and the first two readers.

> Note: "McGuffey" Readers include many stories that are archaic. Some children find this interesting, others find it boring or hard to relate to. Borrow one before purchasing a series for your child.

Moore-McGuffey Readers
(The Moore Foundation)
$15 each

This reading series covers a wide skill level span so it must be used at a slower pace than other readers. Readers have excellent discussion questions. You will want to use more reading material than what is included here to complete your program. This is an updated version of the *Original McGuffey Readers* which are published by Mott Media.

The first reader is suitable for first and second graders, and for some third graders. The second reader should be appropriate for third and fourth graders, although some third grade level students might not be ready yet for Book 2 because of the level of the comprehension questions. It also increases significantly in difficulty from beginning to end. Most fifth graders will be able to handle Book 3. It should be used for two or more years, being suitable for fifth through seventh or eighth grade levels.

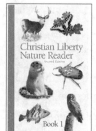

Nature Readers
(Christian Liberty Press)
Book 1
$6

Spiders, insects, birds, and animals are themes for reading selections in this book. Large print with two-color line drawings make the book easy-to-read and appealing. We get excellent reading material and a "science text" in one little book. The "science," rather than being dry, is very entertaining and interesting, and it is likely to encourage children to be more observant of animal life.

Book 2
$3

Crabs and other marine life, bees, wasps, and spiders are the subjects for reading selections in this book. This book is by a different author than Book 1, and this author uses unusual structures for paragraphs and sentences that I suspect might confuse a child who is just learning to begin paragraphs with indentations and include all related sentences. Reading material is worthwhile but not as interesting as Book 1.

Book 3
$3.50

Excellent reading material and a "science text" are in one little book. The "science," rather than being dry, is very entertaining and interesting; it is likely to encourage children to be more observant of animal life.

Book 4
$4

This excellent little book is a good example of the type of real book Charlotte Mason would recommend. It is good for all ages, so please do not limit it to your fourth grader. It is informative, practical, and well-written rather than "textbookish." Topics include, poison ivy, many varieties of birds and insects, toads, bats, beavers, turtles, snakes, and the stars. Questions and both indoor and outdoor activities follow each chapter. Black-and-white illustrations and a glossary are helpful extras.

Book 5
$5

Reading topics are the human body and animals. Questions are included. The reading level is not very difficult, although the content directs it toward older children. This book has been revised with larger print in a 6" by 9" format.

New England Primer of 1777
edited and expanded by Gary and Wanda Sanseri
(Back Home Industries)
$14.95

More than just a beginning reader, the *New England Primer* also includes the Lord's Prayer, the Creed, the Ten Commandments, the Shorter Catechism, and poetry. Practically every page uses or relates to Scripture. This is the *Primer* where we find the well-known pictures and introductions to the sounds of letters that begins, "In Adam's Fall We Sinned All." This nicely bound, hardcover edition has updated print style, syllable divisions, and other minor details to make it easier to use. The Sanseris have added some helpful extras to this edition: a list of the 70 basic phonograms (as used in *The Writing Road to Reading*), 20 basic spelling rules, a list of 99 most-frequently-used words, an extra story section, and a summary of the gospel.

Original McGuffey Readers
(Mott Media)

This series is in the original language, including some archaic expressions, but with very Biblical, character-building content. These are the precursors to the *Moore-McGuffeys* above. The level of difficulty throughout the series is higher than other readers so do not equate readers with grade level numbers.

First Reader
$12.99

The level of difficulty is higher than most first-grade-level readers and might be suitable for late first grade through second grade.

Second Reader
$15.99

The second reader should be started with advanced second graders or average third graders, and it should take about two years to complete.

Third Reader
$16.99

Recommended for average fifth graders, this reader should be used up through about seventh or eighth grade.

Pathway Publishers Reading Program

See the description of the basic phonics instruction above under *Pathway Publishers Reading Program*. The *Pathway* readers can be used after phonics instruction has been presented using any other program. The stories, while not filled with excitement and adventure, are true to life and engaging. Most stories take place in rural/farm settings, although some take place in other countries. Workbooks reinforce phonics knowledge and help develop reading comprehension and thinking skills.

Students start with the preprimer. Following the preprimer, first graders move on to two more readers: *Days Go By* and *More Days Go By*. There is a workbook for each reader. A single teacher's manual covers both readers, and a separate teacher's manual covers both workbooks. Teacher's manuals are highly recommended for proper presentation of lessons.

Second grade readers are *Busy Times, More Busy Times*, and *Climbing Higher*. A workbook accompanies each reader. A single teacher's manual covers the first two readers. Answer keys are in the teacher edition of the workbook. The workbooks are more challenging than some others at this level, working on things such as diacritical markings and rules for suffixes in more depth than usual for second grade.

Third grade readers are *New Friends* and *More New Friends*. Workbooks are available for both readers along with teacher's editions of the workbooks.

The fourth grade reader is *Building Our Lives* and the fifth grade reader is *Living Together*. A workbook and a teacher's edition of the workbook are available for both readers.

The sixth grade reader is *Step by Step*. A workbook and answer key are also available.

Rod and Staff
(Rod and Staff)
Bible Nurture and Reader Series for grades 1-4

Rod and Staff readers use Bible stories for reading material, and many people love these readers for the Godly content and emphasis on Christian character development. Reading workbooks, worksheets, and phonics workbooks are available that correlate with the basic textbooks. Problems with the previous version such as dialect, uneven progression, and inappropriate content have been remedied, although there is still a lot of busy work that should be used only as needed.

First Grade

prices for sets including reader, workbooks, phonics workbook, worksheets, printing practice, and teacher's manual: Unit 1 - $25.50; Units 2 and 3 - $36.95; Units 4 and 5 - $36.80

This revised edition consists of three basic texts covering five units (*Reader for Unit 1, Reader for Units 2 and 3*, and *Reader for Units 4 and 5*).Three teacher's manuals cover all program components. They are designed to provide instruction in reading, phonics, language, spelling, and penmanship. Flash cards and additional readers are available at extra cost.

Second Grade

complete program (readers, workbooks, phonics workbooks, and teacher's manuals) - $78.20

Two readers with five reading workbooks and three phonics workbooks cover reading and phonics. The reading workbooks are closely correlated with the texts, but the phonics workbooks are not as closely associated, allowing more flexibility in their use. Readers and reading workbooks can be used without the phonics workbooks if you are using another method of phonics instruction. Bible stories provide most of the content in the readers. Two teacher's manuals cover both texts and the workbooks.

Third Grade

$52.15 - price includes readers, workbooks, and teacher's manual

This revised edition includes two hardback books with five reading workbooks. Phonics is reviewed, and reading skills are developed. Language is covered in the separate text, *Building Christian English*. A single teacher's manual, covering text and workbooks, contains answers to workbook exercises and pointers for oral reading and lesson discussion.

Fourth Grade

price includes reader, workbooks, and teacher's manual - $28.05

This revised edition includes one hardback student text, three workbooks, and one teacher's manual. Most of the reading selections are Bible stories. Phonics skills are reinforced while oral reading and comprehension skills are developed.

Readers for Grades 5-6

A Time to Plant

pupil text - $12.15; teacher's manual - $8.05

For fifth grade level, one hardcover textbook contains reading selections plus questions and exercises. Reading selections include prose and poetry other than Bible stories. Goals at this level are to develop listening, speaking, vocabulary, compre-

hension, study, and writing skills while encouraging an interest in good literature. The teacher's manual contains answers to exercise questions and some teaching instruction.

A Time to Build

price includes pupil text, teacher's manual, workbook, and teacher's workbook manual - $25.30

This text is similar in format to the fifth grade text, *A Time to Plant*, but it has added emphasis on vocabulary development for sixth graders. A student textbook and teacher's guide are available, as well as a workbook of vocabulary exercises.

Saxon Phonics 1

(Saxon Publishers, Inc.)

homestudy kit - $130

See the complete review of *Saxon Phonics K*. Level 1 reteaches the basic letters and sounds already taught in Level K but at a much quicker pace. It goes on to cover more complex phonograms such as "tch", "dge", and "eigh"; prefixes and suffixes; compound words; and more complex syllabication. Homestudy Kit materials are similar to those in *Phonics K,* with the addition of an irregular spelling booklet and three more sets of "Kids Cards." Students also have 52 self-constructed readers this year. The teacher's manual is almost 800 pages in length, and the heftier student workbooks include two worksheets per lesson. Students complete one of these worksheets with a parent/teacher and the second can be used for independent work, to extend a specific concept, or for extending the lesson for a child who needs additional work. The number of rules taught this year expands along with the various program components in keeping with the expanded concepts to be covered. Weekly spelling tests at this level include sight words for memorization along with the phonetic words using spelling rules taught this year.

Throughout *Phonics 1*, the level of difficulty increases significantly. Lessons should take about 45 minutes per day with games and other activities requiring additional time.

Saxon Phonics 2

(Saxon Publishers, Inc.)

homestudy kit - $125

See the complete review of *Saxon Phonics K*. Level 2 briefly reviews vowels and consonants, then continues reviewing combinations, digraphs, sight words, and rules already taught in *Phonics 1*. If a child (second grade or older) is not solid with all the vowel and consonant sounds, he/she should begin with *Phonics 1*. *Phonics 2* expands into more advanced prefixes and suffixes (e.g., mono, bi, tri, quad); additional final, stable syllables (e.g., sion, tion, tious); and more-challenging elements of phonics, spelling, and syllable division. Much of the program is a reinforcement of concepts already learned, but with the integration of more complex vocabulary—lengthier, and more-complex words. For example, lesson 88 teaches words such as launch, auction, and canine. There are two worksheets to be completed each day. The first requires parent/teacher direction, while the second can be used for independent work or to extend a specific concept. Lesson time should require about 30 minutes per day with additional time required for games and other activities.

The Homestudy Kit is similar to that for *Phonics 1*, but it does not include letter tiles since children should no longer need these.

Reviewing Phonics

By third or fourth grade level, most children should have a good foundation in phonics. If a great deal of foundational work is needed, consider using one of the complete programs recommended for beginners. If just a bit of review work is needed, you might use the *Victory Drill Book*, Modern Curriculum Press' *Plaid Phonics C* or *Phonics Word Study D*, or *Explode the Code* (Educators Publishing Service). You might wish to reinforce phonics concepts by also using Modern Curriculum Press' *Spelling Workout* on the same level as their phonics.

By fifth or sixth grade, students should be reading well without having to look for vocabulary controlled reading materials. Many will still prefer easier books until their vocabulary and speed have increased. If a child still needs work with phonics at this level but does not need an intensive program, you might use *Professor Phonics Sound Track to Reading*, a short manual for remedial phonics or *Noah Webster's Reading Handbook* (Christian Liberty Press).

If review at a more minimal level is needed, you might use Modern Curriculum Press *Word Study D* or *E* (Modern Curriculum Press) [$9.85 each; teacher's guides - $44 each]. These books are the continuation of the *Plaid Phonics* series for the younger grade levels, but they broaden into dictionary skills, critical thinking, listening and speaking, usage, and reading comprehension. It might be helpful to reinforce these with *Spelling Workout* (Modern Curriculum Press) of the same level since the two books correlate with each other.

Reading Comprehension Supplements

Reading comprehension skills are best handled with oral questions to ensure comprehension at early levels. Until a child is reading about 100 words a minute, his comprehension is usually not very good, so do not be overly concerned if a younger child is concentrating on decoding and not doing very well on comprehension.

If you choose not to use a complete reading program (with readers and workbooks), but use either real books or readers without companion workbooks, you might wish to supplement reading with comprehension activities by using one or more of the following books. There are many reading workbooks to choose from, but I have listed the following ones because they are interestingly presented and educationally worthwhile.

Across the Centuries: Teaching Units for Timeless Children's Literature from a Christian Perspective
(LifeWay Christian Resources)
$19.95 each level

These Christian guides for the study of full-length books were designed for the classroom but will work well for homeschoolers. There are six levels that go up through high school level. The first four levels, A-D, are for grades K-6. Suggested grades levels are Level A - Kindergarten, Level B - grades 1-2, Level C - grades 3-4, and Level D - grades 5-6. There are two volumes for each level, although Volume 2 for Level A is not yet complete. Most families will complete one volume per year.

There are from 3 to 7 books covered within each volume—more books at younger levels, decreasing as books become longer for upper levels. For example: Level B, Volume 1 covers the books *Ira Sleeps Over, The Snowy Day, Ox Cart Man, Little House in the Big Woods,* and *The Hundred Penny Box*. The 176-page guide for this volume provides a story summary, author background, numerous discussion and comprehension questions to be used orally, many activity suggestions (e.g., 15 for *Ira Sleeps Over*), comprehension quizzes, and blackline masters. Activities range from word searches and writing assignments, to science and craft projects. The blackline masters make some of these activities particularly quick and easy, but some activities will take much longer and require other materials. Some activities are designed to be "cross-curricular"—focusing on subjects like math or science in relation to the story. .You will need to be especially careful to select activities for first graders for which they have acquired the necessary skills. The teacher guide includes answers (or possible answers in some cases) for all activities.

Discussion questions and some activities reflect a Christian viewpoint. For example, when the question of obedience comes up, children are asked, "What does the Bible say about obeying quickly?" Relevant verses are given in the teacher guide, but you will want to have your Bible handy. There are a number of other novel study guides, but few with the Christian outlook we find here.

Use these book studies as supplements to your other lessons. They focus on reading skills/comprehension but not on phonics. There is quite a bit of writing activity and incidental coverage of other subject areas unless you choose to expand an activity (e.g., studying about different types of bears) for a particular subject.

The format is similar in other levels. Level A is easier, dealing with beginning reading skills. Level C has more written work and more-challenging activities. Level D includes writing, research, discussion, crafts, etc. at levels appropriate for older students.

Critical Thinking: Reading, Thinking, and Reasoning Skills, Books 2-6

(Steck-Vaughn)

I probably would not start using this series before Book 2 for second grade, so that I could focus on basic phonic skills first. This worktext is designed to develop both thinking and reading skills through a variety of challenging activities. See the lengthier description under "Thinking Skills."(S)

Gates-Peardon-LaClair Reading Exercise Books

(Teachers College Press)

$3.95 each; teachers manual - $2.95

There are three strands in this series, each represented by books for two or three different levels. The three strands are *Read and Remember* (basic reading comprehension), *Read Beyond the Lines* (more challenging reading skills), and *Follow Directions* (activities where students follow written directions to draw, create crafts, or fill in the blanks). These exercises are not timed. Exercises in the first two books should take no more than five to ten minutes each to complete. *Follow Directions* exercises often require drawing, cutting, and/or pasting which might take significantly longer.

Level A of each book is suitable for mid-first grade through second grade reading levels. Level B of these books is suggested for third and fourth grade reading level. Only *Read and Remember* and *Read Beyond the Lines* are available for level C, which is suggested for students at fifth and sixth grade reading levels.

Teaching instructions for all three books and answer keys for the first two books are included in a single teachers manual for all levels of all three books. *Follow Directions* does not require an answer key. Scoring charts are in the back of the first two books for students to track their own progress.(S)

McCall-Crabbs Standard Test Lessons in Reading, Books A - F

(Teachers College Press)

$2.95 each; teacher's manual - $1.50

The McCall-Crabbs books offer 60 short reading passages followed by 8 multiple choice questions. Questions are set up like standardized test questions to familiarize children with that format. They focus on both comprehension and inferential skills. These exercises can be used in a number of ways. The optimal use is to allow exactly three minutes for a student to read the passage and complete the questions. Grade equivalents corresponding to each score (number correct) are shown at the bottom of each page. This gives us an immediate, although not always accurate assessment of how they are doing. Tracking these scores through a number of lessons

gives us a much more accurate picture. For some students, the time pressure will be inappropriate, so we can use the lessons untimed, ignoring the grade equivalent scores. In such cases, oral reading of the passages might even be appropriate. There are six books in the series, labeled A-F. These correspond roughly to grade levels 3-8, although children can vary dramatically in reading levels at the same ages. A single teachers manual provides instructions and answer keys for all six books.(S)

Read and Think 4, 5 and 6

(A Beka Book)

$5.65-5.75 each

These books contain timed reading exercises to be used at fourth, fifth, and sixth grade levels. The goal is to improve reading speed and comprehension. Each reading is followed by a comprehension quiz. The emphasis is primarily on simple recall rather than on higher levels of thinking. However, it seems that in the sixth grade book some questions do require students to understand inferences and draw some conclusions.

Reading Comprehension series, Books A-F

(Essential Learning Products)

$3.99 each

There are six, half-size books in this series for grades 1-6. They are printed in two colors with illustrations and fairly large print so that they are less intimidating than full-size workbooks. Each book is divided into four main sections. "Reading for You and Me" helps beginning readers connect with written material and understand the value of both reading and writing. "Reading and Doing" are reading comprehension activities that require students to also read between the lines to make inferences. "Reading the Facts" helps them analyze written material. "Reading Stories and Poems" includes some comprehension work, but it also directs students to "construct their own meaning" by relating their own interpretations, feelings, and ideas. There are a variety of activities even within each of these sections. Answer keys are at the back of each book. At 80 pages each, these books will not take long for most children to complete.(S)

Reading for Comprehension series, Books A-F

(Continental Press)

$5.95 each; teacher's guide - $2.75 each (prices for both series)

Book A is a beginning level reading comprehension book which has very short, interesting stories followed by fairly simple questions. In Book B, students are only required to check or circle answers to comprehension questions. Book C features half-page stories followed by multiple choice questions. Some children will be ready for this level in second grade. Books D-F increase in length and difficulty of reading passages, but all use the multiple-choice question format. While the D-F levels correlate to grades 4-6, many home-schooling students will find the book for the next grade level a better match for their reading skills. Children generally find these fun to read and not overly-challenging. The series is slightly revised for their new *Reading for Comprehension 2000* series.(SE)

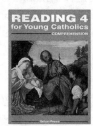

Reading for Young Catholics series 4-8

(Seton Press)

$10 each

Reading comprehension, analysis, and vocabulary are addressed in this series, although vocabulary receives minimal attention in book 4, with gradually increasing emphasis up through book 8. Reading selections are worthwhile writings of particular interest to Catholics: e.g., "What is a novena?" and "Homily of St. Bernard." Question style varies from book to book; the younger levels feature more yes/no and multiple choice questions than older levels, but they also require students to sometimes write complete paragraphs. Older levels require increasingly-individualized answers. Some questions will even be for discussion rather than writing. Each workbook includes a separate answer key, but subjective answers will require personal attention.

Reading Comprehension series, Books 1-4

(Instructional Fair)

$2.95 each

These half-size, inexpensive workbooks from Instructional Fair's Homework Booklet series are printed with large, black-and-white lettering and feature a variety of comprehension activities. An answer key is included in each book. Book numbers correspond to grade levels.(S)

Reading Skills, Books 2-4

(Instructional Fair)

$2.95 each

These half-page size workbooks from Instructional Fair's Homework Booklet series feature large, black-and-white print. They differ from Instructional Fair's Reading Comprehension series with more focus on analysis than recall. There is a good variety of exercises, and an answer key is included in each book.(S)

Reading Strands: Understanding Fiction

(National Writing Institute) $22.95

This ungraded teacher's resource book is useful from the early grades all the way through high school. It begins with a discussion of goals and objectives. We are then referred to the index of objectives in the back of the book from which we will choose appropriate lessons for each child. The primary method the author uses to show us how to teach concepts is dialogue. He first describes the idea we need to get across to our children, then provides a sample dialogue (about a book we have read to our child or our child has read to him or herself) showing how we can help children think beyond the surface of stories. We might need to read the books we will be discussing with our children (particularly if our child has weak comprehension skills) so that we can direct the conversation usefully. The author tries to address the needs of various age groups throughout, although some of the ideas (such as parody, satire, and complicated voice/point of view) will need to be reserved for junior or senior high level. In the back of the book are extensive reading lists which, while they are very useful, also include many books that are popular but unacceptable. However, the lists should be useful in directing us to well-written books at appropriate reading levels.(S)

Reading Strategies for Literature and Reading Strategies for Nonfiction

(Curriculum Associates)

student books - $6.95 each; teacher guides - $3.95 each

Curriculum Associates publishes two series of books for grades 1-8 which help students understand and interpret what they read. Student books feature lessons with either a literature or nonfiction excerpt accompanied by instruction and exercises for developing better reading skills. Students work on basic comprehension, main idea/details, predicting, etc. Visual organizers are frequently used. These are helpful for basic skill development. Lessons should be presented by parents using the appropriate helps from the teacher guides. Answer keys are in the teacher guides. Select the appropriate book by your child's reading level, and choose either or both workbooks for working with literature or nonfiction.(S)

Reading-Thinking Skills, 3rd - 6th Grade Level

(Continental Press)

$6.95 each; teacher's guide - $3.25 each

This series is more challenging than Continental Press' *Reading for Comprehension* series, but it provides excellent coverage of a wide range of reading skills. You might use both Continental Press books since both are fairly small workbooks. *Reading-Thinking Skills* workbook activities will take more time to complete than *Reading for Comprehension*. You might be able to manage the third and fourth grade books without teacher's guides, but you will definitely want them for fifth and sixth grade level books.(SE)

Readmaster [MS DOS computer program] 🖥
(School of Tomorrow)

$280 levels 1-12 kit; $69.95 for kits for fewer grade levels

Readmaster is a computer program for improving reading speed and comprehension skills for students reading at grade levels 1-12. Students read through character-building reading selections, then answer questions on screen. The computer corrects and evaluates student responses, tabulating reading rates and scores on questions answered. The computer tracks and reports on students' scores so busy moms can check on progress when it is convenient rather than on a particular schedule.

Kits are available for groups of grade levels: 1-3, 4-6, 7-9, and 10-12. Each kit consists of a program manual, a diagnostic disk which must be used first to place students at the correct level, the appropriate story disks, and three student disks that will allow a student to access up to 108 stories. Additional student disks are $4.50 each.

If we initially purchase story disks for a limited number of grade levels, we can add others as needed. There are 36 story sessions per grade level, the same number that are allowed by the student disk. Each session should take from five to fifteen minutes to complete. If used once a week, a level should take one school year to complete. I suspect home school students will work through them faster since they do not have to take turns at the computer with a classroom of students. Students must pass each session by answering a sufficient number of questions correctly, or else the computer returns them to the same story for review and retesting.

Some families might be interested in the complete kit which includes all grade levels, one diagnostic disk and two student disks. Components can be purchased individually, but all (diagnostic, student, and story disks) are necessary to operate the program.

Teaching Reading with "Real Books"

You can use "real" books instead of or in addition to readers. This becomes much easier once basic phonics has been mastered and children have the tools to sound out most words. They are then limited more by vocabulary and lack of speed.

Many children prefer reading full-length, real books to reading the short anthologies in readers. Many reluctant readers learn to enjoy reading when allowed to use books of particular interest to them for reading material. All children benefit from the inclusion of at least some full-length books in their reading as well as discussions that arise in relation to their reading. This becomes increasingly important as children move into the upper elementary grade levels.

Recommended reading lists abound. Check the recommended reference books under "Read Aloud" at the beginning of this chapter. Reading lists for different levels can be found in books such as *The New Read Aloud Handbook*(S) and *Honey for a Child's Heart.*

For younger children, it is best to concentrate on literature written from a Christian perspective even though it might not mention God or Christianity. Young children sometimes have difficulty separating fantasy from reality. But, more importantly, they learn basic concepts about good and evil from symbols and imagery in literature that reflect reality. That symbolism and imagery should accurately and consistently reflect a Christian world view so that children form correct concepts about spiritual truths. See the review of the book, *A Landscape with Dragons*, for further explanation.

Literature for a Classical Curriculum

The Harp and Laurel Wreath
by Laura Berquist
(Ignatius Press)
$19.95

Laura Berquist has already written one of the most helpful books on the Classical approach to learning, *Designing Your Own Classical Curriculum* (Ignatius Press). In that book, she recommends the use of poetry and prose for the different stages of learning (grammatical, dialectical, and rhetorical stages). Students use well-written models to memorize, copy, take through dictation, analyze, present orally, and as subjects for compositions. Berquist makes numerous poetry and literature recommendations in *Designing Your Own Classical Curriculum*, but she has done a great service by compiling a superb collection of prose and poetry in a single volume, *The Harp and Laurel Wreath*. The large majority of the book consists of poetry and verse with less space given to speeches, documents, and literary excerpts. In addition to being well-written, selections are often inspiring and character-building. I was very impressed with the selections—the poems really do represent some of the greatest works with which you would like your children to be familiar. Favorite, traditional children's poems and rhymes are also represented. A few titles from the works included are "The Children's Hour," "Psalm 100," "The Charge of the Light Brigade," "O Captain! My Captain!", "scenes from *Hamlet*, and "The Second Inaugural Address of Abraham Lincoln." Among the included authors are Longfellow, Stevenson, Stephen Vincent Benét, Carroll, Millay, Shelley, Shakespeare, Wordsworth, and Yeats. Berquist also explains how to use the readings, dividing them up according to the different stages of learning. Study questions are included after each piece in the "rhetorical" section, with suggested answers provided at the back of the book.

Even if you are not implementing a classical curriculum, this volume is probably the best source for poetry and readings for use in any homeschool.

Study Guides and Other Literature Helps

Many publishers offer study guides to help us make the most of our reading adventures. Some options follow.

Classics at Home
by Ann Ward
(Noble Books)
$19.95

The *Classics at Home* is a study guide for four books of classic children's literature: The Works of Beatrix Potter, Charlotte's Web, Winnie the Pooh, and *The House at Pooh Corner*. The guide can be used with children of widely varying ages. If children are interested in the stories, they will be motivated to learn vocabulary words. Comprehension questions are a combination of recall, interpretation, and application, but nothing much beyond the capabilities of first and second graders. A "Learning More" section transfers story topics into the realms of science, art, social studies, Bible study, and other areas of language arts. Books and stories are broken down into manageable sections so we don't try to cover too much each day.

Classics for Children series
(Calvert School)
each complete course - $125

Thus far there are two courses in the Classics for Children series, one of which is appropriate for children ages 5 to 8 or 9, and the other for ages 8-11. The younger course is *Beatrix Potter: Her Life and Her Little Books*. This course includes a reading guide, a biography of Beatrix Potter written for children with color illustrations and photographs, supplies for all the activities, and ten hardback storybooks. "The supplies include a Beatrix Potter writing set with pencils and a ruler, and other Beatrix Potter items such as a pencil sharpener, an eraser, and stickers. You also receive watercolor paints, paper for painting and tracing, modeling clay, and a Calvert notebook." The reading guide directs reading and activities centering around each of the ten Beatrix Potter storybooks. Parents need to work with their children as they read and discuss the books and work on vocabulary words. As with other Calvert courses, you can take longer than a regular school year to complete the course. Those who already have the storybooks can purchase the course for $65.

The second course is a study of the Laura Ingalls Wilder *Little House* books, which is divided into 2 segments, one for ages 8-10, and the other for ages 9-11. The complete course includes reading guides, *Little House* Books, and *Laura Ingalls Wilder Country*. The reading guides by themselves are only - $70. The reading guides and *Laura Ingalls Wilder Country* can be purchased for $90. More reading courses are being developed.(S)

Favorite Books Activities Kit
(Prentice Hall)
$28.95

The word "Kit" in the title might be a little misleading since this is simply a 324-page book. The word kit is supposed to reflect the completeness of the resource book, which includes quizzes, project ideas, and activity sheets for 48 books appropriate for grades 4-8. Books are divided up into groups of four per month, with attempts to group them seasonally or with a holiday. The four books reflect a range of reading levels, so we could use the easiest books the first year with a fourth grader, then move up to more difficult books in subsequent years. Three different, reproducible comprehension tests are included for each book, although we only use one. Comprehension questions operate at the lower thinking levels, for the most part avoiding analysis or deeper thinking. Reproducible activity work sheets for each book generally works on language arts skills such as grammar and writing, and sometimes on reading skills. Project pages list a number of wide-ranging ideas such as rewriting a scene from the story, making a poster, and making a model of a room. Selected books are popular children's literature, which means you and I might not want our children to read all of these books. Short synopses of the books are provided at the beginning of each section so we can be selective. Answers are in the back of the book, and record keeping charts help us track children's reading and scores on tests, activities, and projects. The value of such a resource is that it saves us having to read all the books our children are reading, yet provides a method of checking up on their comprehension. ISBN #0876283091.(SE)

Inside Stories, Books 1, 2, 3, and 4
(Dandy Lion Publications)
$12.95 each

Each of these books offers in-depth study of ten different novels. Higher level thinking skills are brought into play, but not so obviously as in some other books of this type. Study must be teacher-directed (one-on-one). There are no workbook pages to complete. Books are read and studied in groups of chapters. (I have trouble keeping my children from reading ahead if the book is good, making this approach impractical unless the book is re-read for the study.) Vocabulary and discussion questions accompany each group of chapters. At the end, there are conclusion and summary questions followed by optional activities. Work on characters, themes, motivations, comparison and contrast is included. The activities really stretch students' creativity beyond the bounds of the story. For instance, an activity for *Little House in the Big Woods* has the student research pioneer recipes, choose and prepare one, then give an oral report about pioneer food preparation. Book 1 for grades 3-4 includes such titles as *Little House in the Big Woods; Sarah, Plain and Tall; Charlie and the Chocolate Factory; Charlotte's Web;* and *Soup and Me*. Book 2 for grades 4-5 includes *Caddie Woodlawn; Ben and Me; The Door in the Wall; The Lion, the Witch and the Wardrobe; Island of the Blue Dolphins;* and others. Book 3 for grades 5-6 studies *Sounder, The Cay, The Pushcart War, Rabbit Hill, The Railway Children,* and *Tuck Everlasting* plus others. Book 4 for grades 6-7 includes such books as *Johnny Tremain, Bridge to Terabithia, Sing Down the Moon, The Witch of Blackbird Pond,* and *Wrinkle in Time*. While these are recognized as excellent books from a literary standpoint, we need to discern which of these books are appropriate for Christian children to study.(S)

Literature Units
(Teacher Created Materials)
$7.95 each

Comprehensive literature study "units" (books) are available in reproducible formats. Each unit covers one novel with units available for three levels: primary, intermediate, and challenging. Three titles available for primary level are *Where the Wild Things Are, If You Give a Mouse a Cookie and If You Give a Moose a Muffin,* and *Strega Nona* (an Italian story). Several titles are listed for intermediate level. Among these are *Charlotte's Web, Island of the Blue Dolphins, The Secret Garden, The Sign of the Beaver,* and *Charlie and the Chocolate Factory*. Among titles for the challenging level are *Where the Red Fern Grows, Julie of the Wolves, Old Yeller, Anne of Green Gables, Bridge to Terabithia, The Hobbit,* and *Book of Greek Myths* (by the D'Aulaires).

We might not necessarily feel that these are all books that we want our children to read, so use your own discretion on selecting titles. The novels are broken down into chapter groupings for study. Activities for each grouping range across the curriculum (whole language approach) including writing, vocabulary, geography, art, music, math, science, and social studies.

Quizzes and answer keys are included within each unit. A few of the lesson plans show a multicultural emphasis (Indians, ecology), but some of these activities could easily be skipped. Some activities would work best in a small group, and others are oriented to the traditional classroom; however, at the price of $7.95 for each book, you still get plenty of material, even if you don't cover it all.(SE)[Kath Courtney/C.D.]

Progeny Press Study Guides for Literature
(Progeny Press)
lower elementary level - $9.99 each, upper elementary and middle school levels - $12.99 each

Within the Progeny Press series are a number of study guides geared for the primary grades. They are for the books

The Bears on Hemlock Mountain; Clipper Ship; The Courage of Sarah Noble; The Drinking Gourd; Frog and Toad Together; The Josefina Story Quilt; Keep the Lights Burning, Abbie; The Long Way to a New Land; The Long Way Westward; A New Coat for Anna; Ox-Cart Man; Sam the Minuteman; and *Wagon Wheels*. Another guide, *The Minstrel in the Tower,* straddles primary and middle grade levels.

Study guides geared for the upper elementary grades include the titles *The Best Christmas Pageant Ever; The Bridge; The Cricket in Times Square; Crown and Jewel; The Door in the Wall; The Two Collars; Farmer Boy; Little House in the Big Woods; Sarah, Plain and Tall; Charlotte's Web;* and *In the Year of the Boar and Jackie Robinson*.

Middle school titles stretch sometimes as low as fifth grade and up through eighth grade. Among them are *Number the Stars; Amos Fortune, Free Man; Bridge to Terabithia; The Bronze Bow; Carry On Mr Bowditch; The Hiding Place; The Giver; Island of the Blue Dolphins; The Indian in the Cupboard; Johnny Tremain; The Magician's Nephew; Maniac Magee; The Sign of the Beaver; Roll of Thunder, Hear My Cry; The Secret Garden; Shiloh; Where the Red Fern Grows;* and *The Lion, The Witch and the Wardrobe*.

These study guides, although written by different authors, all come from a Christian perspective. Thus, we find questions that refer to Scripture such as "Read Proverbs 17:17. 'A friend loves at all times, and a brother is born for adversity.' Tall John was Sarah's friend. At the end of Chapter 7, how did he comfort her?" (from *The Courage of Sarah Noble* study guide).

The study guides deal with both literature as art and literature as a reflection or source of ideas, although, at the primary level, children study vocabulary and meaning with little attention to literary constructions or style.

The format varies from one study guide to another but with many common characteristics. A synopsis and some background are first. Ideas for pre-reading (and sometimes mid- and post-reading) activities are next. Then studies are divided up to cover groups of chapters at a time. Each study section has vocabulary activities along with comprehension, analysis, personal application, and thought questions. A variety of vocabulary activities are used within each guide, so the studies maintain a higher level of interest than those which use the same format for every lesson. *The Courage of Sarah Noble* study guide includes some art, craft, game, and cooking suggestions, and I suspect other primary guides will also include such extras.

Students might be able to work through the study guides independently if their reading skills are adequate, although discussion enhances any literature study. Answer keys are found at the back of each book, so each study guide is self-contained aside from the novel itself. All study guides are 8 1/2" by 11", looseleaf, and are reproducible for your family.

Quizzes for 220 Great Children's Books, 1996 revised edition

by Polly Jeanne Wickstrom
(Teacher Ideas Press)
$24.50 pb

Home educated children often read more books than parents can begin to keep track of. If you would like to maintain some sort of academic accountability for your child's reading, this book might be helpful. It has descriptions of each of the 220 books (divided into age group categories for grades 3-8); lists of books by categories such as courage, crime, or death/dying; instructions on how to set up this reading/accountability system (including contracts, points, and record keeping); and a reproducible page of multiple choice and true/false questions for each book. An answer key in the back has the answers to these questions, but it also assigns a point value to each book which is arrived at by category level and the number of pages. Books are those usually easily found at the library and include those by authors such as Judy Blume, Beverly Cleary, Robert Lawson, E. B. White, Lois Lenski, Laura Ingalls Wilder, Betsy Byars, Louisa May Alcott, C.S. Lewis, Scott O'Dell, Charles Dickens, and Elizabeth George Speare. With only multiple choice and true/false questions, you will only be checking on recall of details and basic comprehension rather than more comprehensive reading skills.

Still, this is one way to make sure that your children are actually reading all those books they claim to read.

Responding to Literature: Writing and Thinking Activities, Grades 1-3

(Spring Street Press)
$15.95

58 reproducible worksheets can be used with any books children read to integrate reading, writing, and thinking activities. The key areas addressed are plot, character, and setting, with lesser attention to areas such as vocabulary, poetry, categories, and judgments. A variety of approaches are used to tackle each area so we can select one that best meets each child's learning style needs. For example, to identify and describe the plot, one child might write what happened first, next, and last. Another child will draw pictures that will act as a filmstrip of the story. Still another child might write and illustrate a postcard to a friend concerning the story. Since the book is geared for grades 1-3, there is a range of difficulty evident in the activities. With 13 activities relating to "plot" alone to choose among, there is certain to be something appropriate for almost any child whether we are working on plot, character, or setting. Since the activities can be used along with any books, we are not limited to a prescribed or even recommended reading list. At the end of the book are eight reproducible reading record sheets—some are variations of book report forms and others are designed for recording number of pages read, books read, or student evaluations of books read. Simple instructions and objectives are on the back of each activity page, so very little preparation or presentation time is required. This is an ideal resource for home educators because of the tremendous flexibility.(S)

Responding to Literature: Writing and Thinking Activities, Grades 4-8

(Spring Street Press)
$15.95

Similar to the book of the same title for grades 1-3 (reviewed above), this one has 75 reproducible worksheets that can be used with any books children read to integrate reading, writing, and thinking activities. The key areas addressed at this level are plot, character, setting, and literary forms with subtopics such as mood, theme, historical fiction, biography, autobiography, plays, folk tales, mysteries, poetry, vocabulary, judgments, and analyzing an author's purpose. Learning style activities are similar to those mentioned above, but on a more challenging level reflecting skill abilities of children in grades 4-8. Choose activities that seem appropriate for each child.(S)

Strategies for Reading Nonfiction: Comprehension and Study Activities, Grades 4-8

(Spring Street Press)
$15.95

Note that this resource deals with nonfiction, an area slighted by many other study guides or comprehension workbooks. There are over 40 reproducible activities that can be used with a wide range of non-fiction books, be they textbooks or topical books. Students learn how to read with purpose, identifying what type of information they should be looking for before they begin. They practice taking notes and summarizing what they have read. They think about and analyze information. And, since new words are often crucial to new knowledge, vocabulary activities are included. The activity pages follow various formats, most of them functioning as organization maps to help students. The graphical/visual creativity makes it easier and more appealing to work on these activity pages than doing the same things with blank paper. Simple instructions (and objectives) are on the back of each activity page, and most students will be able to figure out how to use these on their own.(S)

Total Language Plus

(Total Language Plus, Inc.)
$17.95 each; advanced level guides - $18.95 each; set of four guides - $68; teacher's manual - $3.75

Total Language Plus "...covers reading, comprehension, spelling, grammar, vocabulary, writing, listening, and analytical and critical thinking with a Christian perspective." Each volume is a student workbook that accompanies a novel. Students read sections of the novel each week and answer comprehension questions. The week's study also includes vocabulary work consisting of four lessons working with words drawn from the reading. There are also four activities for a list of spelling words from the reading. Grammar worksheet activities include dictation exercises and grammatical work with the dictated material that serves to review rather than teach grammar. Students create their own glossary toward the back of the book by entering definitions and parts of speech labels for their vocabulary words each week. Vocabulary review tests and an answer key are both at the back of the book. At the front of each book are projects, drawing, and writing activities, as well as Enrichment/Writing suggestions and a puzzle. These activities, with the exception of the Enrichment/Writing, are not tied directly to any one chapter so we can use them when, if, and how we wish. Enrichment/Writing suggestions are repeated within pertinent lessons. We can select more activities to turn our study into an in-depth unit study or choose fewer and stick to the basics. The activities are presented as suggestions rather than as fully-developed plans, so they will require independent research and work beyond what is presented here.

The number of lessons in the various volumes of *Total Language Plus* ranges from five to eight, so some books are likely to take longer to study than others. Generally, a volume should take from 9 to 10 weeks to complete. (Plan to complete one per quarter.) If impatient students want to read through the novel quickly rather than spread it out, they can do so covering the comprehension and critical thinking questions as they go and working through the remainder of each week's lessons on a slower schedule. The only supplementary items needed are the novel and the small teacher's manual which serves for all volumes in the series. A "Note to Teachers and Students" in each book explains how to use each study guide.

Total Language Plus's effectiveness in developing broader writing skills is dependent upon your selection of assignments from the Enrichment/Writing as well as upon your work with your children on the writing process within those assignments.

Books have been selected to meet the needs of various age levels and interests. The catalog features very complete descriptions of each study guide as well as a synopsis of each novel. Available titles in the series thus far are *My Side of the Mountain; The Cricket in Times Square; The Light in the Forest; The Lion, the Witch, and the Wardrobe; A Wrinkle in Time; Johnny Tremain; Words by Heart; Julie of the Wolves; The Witch of Blackbird Pond; The High King; The Bronze Bow; Caddie Woodlawn; The Giver; Wheel on the School; The Trumpeter of Krakow; Where the Red Fern Grows; The Call of the Wild; The Hiding Place; The Swiss Family Robinson; Carry on, Mr. Bowditch; The Yearling; Rifles for Watie; Anne*

of Green Gables; The Scarlet Letter; Oliver Twist; The Scarlet Pimpernel; To Kill a Mockingbird; and *Jane Eyre.* The last five titles are advanced high school level. *Total Language Plus* complements a program of grammar and composition instruction, and it also works well as a break from traditional curriculum.

Book Reports

I am reluctant to recommend book reports at all. Teachers use them as a means of checking to see whether or not students have actually read assigned books. We can ask a few questions if that is our goal. Some children might choose not to read when they know a book report awaits the final chapter, or else they develop a habit of never finishing books. If you still wish to require book reports, they should be on only a few of the books children read, not on the majority.

Instead of traditional book reports, consider using one of the other approaches that will encourage children to read beyond the surface. One of my favorite ideas is to have children write book reviews instead of book reports. They can provide a plot summary (without giving away the end of the story) along with their own opinion as to why they might or might not recommend the book to other readers. As an example, *Inside Stories*, described above, helps children to focus on what they are reading and apply some thinking skills.

Book Report Beagle and *Book Report Backpack* (Learning Works) [$6.95 each] offer creative formats for book reports as well as other ideas for multi-sensory activities based on books children read. *Book Report Beagle* is suggested for grades 2-4. It features reproducible forms and instructions that involve writing, drawing, arts and crafts, oral activities, and drama. Actual writing required is fairly minimal in keeping with the suggested age group.

Book Report Backpack jumps up to grades 4-6. In addition to general activities for either fiction or non-fiction books, there are a number of activities targeted at specific kinds of books such as historical fiction, animal stories, sports, and mythology. While activities include arts and crafts, drama, and oral reports, the writing assignments are more numerous and require much lengthier responses than in the younger level book. A Book Report Checklist, a reproducible form for creating your own "book review" card catalog, and a list of additional suggestions on the last page expand the usefulness of this book even more.(S)

Chapter 10
Composition and Grammar

Materials and Methods

Foundations

Learning to read and write are prerequisite to learning other language skills. Once a child has begun to read and form simple words into sentences, we can then begin to work on other language skills. These skills are now divided into five areas: composition (writing), grammar, literature, spelling/vocabulary, handwriting, and speech. We will cover grammar and composition in this section, although there is some overlap into the other areas.

At early elementary levels, we can work on these areas without a text as long as we have a clear idea of what we wish to teach. Beginning concepts can be taught most effectively with an informal approach. Have children begin to work on sentence construction in ways that are meaningful to them such as short letters or thank you notes, stories about events in which they have participated, or even "made-up" stories. But, remember to keep them short! I strongly recommend that you read Dr. Ruth Beechick's, *A Strong Start in Language* (Mott Media) [sold as part of the *Three R's* set for $12] for a good perspective on what is important and what methods work best. If you want specific ideas of language arts activities to use with your kindergartners and first graders, look at both *A Strong Start in Language*, *Language and Thinking for Young Children* (Mott Media), or *Writing Strands, Level 1.*

Some beginning language goals, as listed above, are already covered in beginning reading programs. Check your reading/phonics programs for the extent of coverage before looking for other materials for language.

Writing

Most Christian publishers' traditional language programs are weak in writing skills in comparison with some of the books written particularly to address composition skills at one level or another. While Bob Jones *Language* series is stronger than others, resources such as the *Wordsmith* series (Common sense Press), Marjorie Frank's *Complete Writing Lessons* books, *Writing Step by Step* (Builder Books), and others often do a better job because we can select a resource that targets skill development needs of each child. We can help them with

beginning sentence and paragraph construction with Teacher Created Materials' *How to Write a Sentence* or *How to Write a Paragraph.* Help them learn to structure both basic and complex paragraphs with *Writing Step by Step.* Help them learn the writing process with *Complete Writing Lessons.* Expose them to different forms of writing with *Writing Strands.* Such resources have the added benefit of being more fun than typical textbooks.

Also, if we want children to enjoy writing, they need to feel that what they are doing has some purpose. Simply grading papers, then filing them, can cause children to question the value of their work. Of course, some writing will simply be done for skill improvement, but we can develop more eager writers by providing writing outlets. These can take many forms: letters, articles for newsletters, letters to the editor, stories that are shared, writing incorporated into art projects, etc. Writing may be shared with dad when he gets home from work, with grandma and grandpa when they come to visit, with other home schooling friends, or with pen pals. Wherever and however, sharing is an important encouragement tool. Those who have trouble finding a place to share might check out their local home school newsletter or else consider nationally published newsletters or magazines.

Evaluating Writing

Many parents question their own ability to evaluate their children's writing because they do not feel that they know how to write well themselves. It is very difficult to identify problems if we do not have a good grasp of the mechanics of writing. We can enlist the help of a friend who is more proficient than we are to either work with our child individually or, even better, with a group class.

Group classes are wonderful for motivation and stimulation of ideas. Children in a group class can act as co-editors to help with improving and polishing written pieces and as an audience for sharing and encouraging.

In situations where group classes are not possible and no help seems to be available, we can take advantage of long distance help. **Lightsource Editing Service**, a ministry of the Kustusch family, is a new business that enrolls families for $25 per year, then edits all work for $1 per page editing fee. No grades are issued, but helpful suggestions for improvement are included. I have a feeling that the Kustusch family is likely to be overwhelmed with response since their charges are so reasonable.

Writing Assessment Services, a web-based service operated by Cindy Marsch, M.A., charges $2.50 per 100 words sent by e-mail. This service is best for students fifth grade level and above. Cindy also offers writing tutorials on grammar and usage, essay writing, and other forms of writing.

An even better strategy is for parents to sharpen their own evaluating skills. National Writing Institute's *Evaluating Writing* [$19.95] is designed to do just that. Author Dave Marks shows keen insight into the problems both parents and children face. He describes common writing problems and how to correct them. (Read straight through that section for a valuable mini-writing course.) Next, he presents numerous samples of student writing along with evaluation comments and suggested conversations so we truly understand how to approach the process. Many examples are from *Writing Strands* lessons, so they will be especially useful to those using that series. Examples come from writers at all levels so we get a good idea of what we might expect, although Marks emphasizes the individuality of each child and the impossibility of setting identical goals for all. An appendix suggests "rules" for writing the various drafts of writing assignments and also includes lists of spelling rules and commonly misused words.

Grammar

Learning grammar is not a goal in itself, but grammar is learned as a tool for more effective writing and speech. When we want to help our children write more colorful sentences, we can use the common vocabulary of adjectives and adverbs to describe things more fully. If the antecedent of a pronoun is unclear, we can discuss the functions of nouns and pronouns. Grammar helps us efficiently identify what we are discussing or writing.

Knowledge of grammar carries over to the study of foreign languages. We can identify equivalent functions of words in both English and the language being studied. For instance, if we understand that adjectives describe nouns, then we can discuss agreement of adjective endings with the nouns they describe in languages such as Spanish and Latin.

Grammar is introduced at different levels and by different methods by publishers. It is repeated throughout elementary grades and sometimes in high school. We are free to choose for ourselves the best time and method for introduction of grammar. We are also free to determine how much repetition is needed—probably much less than is found in most programs.

Learning the parts of speech is a major part of grammar. Traditional diagramming is simply one of a variety of methods for learning parts of speech. We can choose traditional diagramming, a non-diagramming method, or a combination for learning parts of speech. However we choose to teach gram-

mar, that method may be included in a total language program or presented by itself. Keep in mind that if we choose a resource that teaches only the parts of speech such as *Winston Grammar* (Precious Memories Educational Resources), we still need to use other methods and materials to cover other elements of grammar such as punctuation and verb usage.

Learning Styles

We should take into consideration our child's learning style when choosing the approach we will take. (See "Individualizing-Matching the Curriculum to the Child" in Chapter One.) For example, Perfect Paulas do well when writing assignments are clear cut and well defined as they are in most typical language textbooks, but they struggle when asked to write creatively. These students should be stretched with "story starters" or books that deal specifically with creative writing. Wiggly Willys and Sociable Sues are likely to respond better to texts that emphasize creative writing rather than grammar but unlikely to do as well in more traditional language arts program such as A Beka's or Rod and Staff's. *Winston Grammar* might be a better approach for teaching grammar to those who find diagramming confusing. Bob Jones University Press includes various teaching methods that are appropriate to more types of learners. Yet, in their language arts program early introduction of parts of speech is not appropriate for all learners. A Beka is likely to appeal more to Perfect Paulas and Competent Carls. The following lists show what approaches might work best with each type of learner.

Wiggly Willy Prefers

☛ language games

☛ application of concepts as they are learned

☛ writing stories and poetry

☛ an active approach to learning grammar

☛ incorporating writing with preferred subjects (e.g., art, P.E., music)

☛ using a computer rather than writing neatly by hand

Wiggly Willy needs help and encouragement to tackle reports and research-related writing and to review what he writes, learning to spot his mistakes.

Perfect Paula Prefers

☛ grammar drill

☛ worksheets or workbook approach

☛ well spelled-out assignments

☛ assigned writing topics with story starters or help getting started

Perfect Paula needs help and encouragement to write creatively.

Competent Carl Prefers

☛ diagramming

☛ to write with a straightforward, factual style rather than descriptive

☛ studying structure of language

- word origins and roots
- vocabulary
- technical writing

Competent Cart needs help to write creatively.

Sociable Sue Prefers

- language games
- poetry
- plays
- writing about ethical questions
- creative writing

Sociable Sue needs help to rewrite and to pay attention to details such as proper grammar.

Other Language Skills

Language skills include both the written and spoken use of words. Some skills are easily overlooked, such as making introductions and speaking before a group. Some language courses incorporate all the different skills, including vocabulary, speech, composition, and study skills, while others concentrate on grammar and usage. Sometimes some of these other skills are included in other texts from the same publisher but might be overlooked once we obtain a language textbook. For instance, A Beka covers grammar well in their language texts, but at older levels we need to also use their *Creative Writing* or another writing supplement. In addition, we should consider using tools such as A Beka's *Oral Language Exercises* [$10.80] for improving speaking skills. We must be certain we are covering all the necessary language skills in one way or another.

> **Resource Recommendations**

Basic Resources for Parents

For parents of children at many levels of writing skills, I recommend the following reference books and resources:

Any Child Can Write

by Harvey S. Wiener, Ph.D.
$13.95
(Oxford University Press)

Mary Pride discovered this book when it was out of print. She was so excited about it that she motivated the author and publisher to come out with this updated, revised edition.

At the beginning of the book, Wiener addresses parents of preschoolers with ideas for stimulating interest and abilities in writing. He seems to share the same viewpoint as Dr. Ruth Beechick in encouraging lots of positive activity without an unhealthy concern for perfection or "correctness" during these early years. Throughout the book he includes pictures of examples of what we can typically expect from different age groups. He includes charts of general writing goals for age

groups but adds a strong caution about the need to be aware of the development of each child as an individual.

Although Wiener originally wrote for parents who wanted to help their children with their schoolwork in the after-school hours, in this revised edition he includes references to the home school situation. He generally expects that students will be doing typical school activities, so he offers suggestions for assisting children with such assignments. However, he adds many creative ideas that can be used apart from any other curriculum. He believes that autobiographical writing—writing that draws upon the writer's personal experience—is best, since the child has a wealth of knowledge about himself and his experiences which he lacks about other topics. Many word games and writing activities are included to build knowledge and positive attitude. Some activities are brief suggestions, while some are fully developed "lessons" with examples.

Many parents will find Wiener's helps for judging "correctness" a valuable aid. Too often we are uncertain about how much correction we should be doing. Charts of guidelines by age group help us determine which aspects of the writing process should concern us, and they also alert us as to what our expectations should be.

Comprehensive as it is, this book is not a complete writing curriculum. However, parents of children of preschool age and beyond will find here a combination of guidance, specific suggestions, and encouragement that cannot be found elsewhere.(S)

Clear and Lively Writing

(published by Walker and Co., but order from Bob Jones University Press)
$16.95

This book emphasizes listening and reading as prerequisites to writing. It covers expressive language—speaking and gesturing, along with problems particular to writing—mechanical problems, disability problems, problems of approach. It has many games and ideas to work on all these areas and to stimulate general creativity. Ideas in this book span the needs of kindergartners through adults.(S)

If You're Trying to Teach Kids How to Write, You've Gotta Have This Book!

by Marjorie Frank
(Incentive Publications)
$16.95

Yes, that is really the title. This is a "teacher's manual" to be used as a resource book, not a student text. It is good for about fourth grade level through high school. Although it is a little confusing at first glance because of the overwhelming graphics, this book contains a gold mine of ideas for helping your children develop a love for writing. It covers the writing process briefly, talks about methods that turn children on to writing, then presents a zillion (almost) ideas to try. The emphasis is on creative writing of all sorts. Once children can write sentences, we can begin using ideas in this book, choosing ideas that are age appropriate. This book is my personal favorite for creative writing. Those who prefer organized lesson plans rather than ideas will appreciate Frank's two books, *Complete Writing Lessons for the Primary Grades* and *Complete Writing Lessons for the Middle Grades*. In these books she turns ideas from *If You're Trying...* into lesson plans with accompanying activity sheets.(SE)

Teaching Your Child to Write
by Cheri Fuller
(Penguin Putnam, Inc.)
$12

Parents of children of all ages will find this a goldmine of guidelines and suggestions for turning children into writers. Fuller sets the stage by telling us how to create a home environment that develops writers through encouragement of reading and "word play." She discusses ages and stages in regard to writing: what should children be able to do at each age level and how do we help them develop the necessary skills. Then she focuses in on vehicles for writing—letter writing, e-mail, family newsletters, book reports, journals, story writing, creating books, family history stories, games with words, and writing poetry. Since Fuller encourages sharing at least some of children's writing productions, she adds a chapter on "Helping Young Writers Break into Print" and addresses of magazines that publish young authors. Parents will also appreciate the guidelines for evaluating children's writing, found at the end of the book along with a concise grammar guide. Fuller uses lots of examples and stories throughout this book, so, while it is informative, practical, and inspiring, it is also enjoyable. Although not targeted only to parents home educating their children, this is an ideal book for us. ISBN # 0425159833.

Trudy Palmer's Writing Workshop
(The Gift of Reading)
$15.95

Trudy Palmer's Writing Workshop includes two audio cassettes and a book from a live presentation. This is a great way to learn Trudy's strategies and ideas for teaching writing to children of all ages. She covers basic sentence and paragraph construction while helping us spur our children toward more colorful and engaging writing. You will want to re-listen to this seminar every so often to renew your enthusiasm and prompt you with different strategies.

Ungraded Complete Programs for all Levels

NOTE: Following this section are two more sections reviewing ungraded resources focused on only grammar and only writing and composition skills. Following those two sections are reviews of programs that are grade-level specific.

Understanding Writing: A Christ-centered, Mastery-oriented English Language and Composition Curriculum for Grades 1-12
by Susan Bradrick
(Bradrick Family Enterprises)
$65

In *Understanding Writing* Susan Bradrick has successfully combined the teaching of language and composition skills in a format that adapts easily to multi-level teaching and is totally Christ-centered in philosophy. This is an approach to writing that places equal emphasis on development of skills and development of godly character. Comprehensive as it is, there are some areas of language arts not included. These are phonics, penmanship, reading, spelling, and literature. Junior high level grammar is taught by combining *Understanding Writing* instruction with the grammar materials recommended in the text. Also, the text teaches students to refer to a dictionary, a thesaurus, and the recommended English handbooks at all levels.

This one-inch-thick book is divided into three parts: "Part I, 'Rethinking Writing' deals with the theory behind an effective approach for studying English composition; Part II, 'Understanding the Basic Elements of Writing,' discusses the elements of content, style, and mechanics essential for effective writing and gives examples of each; Part III, 'Teaching the Basic Elements of Writing,'...provides detailed lessons for teaching your child to master the content, style, and mechanical skills of effective, God-honoring written communication."

Although Part III is divided into twelve levels, they need not necessarily correlate to grade levels. Instead, we should use the Diagnostic Check List in the Appendix to identify which goals have been accomplished within each level, then determine from there a starting point for each child. Children of varying skill levels can easily be instructed at the same time upon a new concept, then work at their ability level in their individual writing time. (The Bradricks have used this method successfully with their nine children.) Each child maintains an "English notebook" (folder or three-ring binder containing drafts of written work rather than copied exercises), and there is no need to purchase student books other than dictionaries or thesauruses.

This is not an independent study curriculum. Lessons are dependent upon teacher presentation at all levels, although students in junior and senior high should be able to do most of their grammar work and some of their writing independently. Lessons are structured in units with daily assignments which include a balance of discussion and writing time that varies according to a child's level. While most lessons require no parent preparation time, the few that do state this clearly at the beginning of the lesson. For example, instruction at the beginning of a second level lesson says, "Read the sections on adjectives and adverbs in your English handbooks."

Children write about personal experiences and observations rather than fiction until the high school level. Suggested topics are included in the Appendix. Because the thrust of this curriculum is mastery of God-honoring communication, most composition assignments are to be written for a specific reader. They are also to be actually delivered (usually in letter form) to that individual so that a habit of skillful, genuine communication is the result of the student's writing study.

A reproducible "Composition Planning and Evaluation Sheet" is used to help students think through their composition before they begin, then provide key areas for parents to address in their evaluations. (These sheets are also available from the publisher in pads of fifty, three-hole-punched sheets.)

With the book, we also receive a special template for making lines on unlined paper so unskilled writers can still use nice stationery without their writing wandering all over the page.

Understanding Writing should be an excellent curriculum for those who like well-structured material with clear goals that retains flexibility enough for multi-level teaching.

Wisdom Words

(The Weaver)

$40

The Weaver has produced one large book in a three-ring binder that covers language (language, composition, and handwriting but <u>not</u> phonics/reading or spelling) for grades K through 6. (Spelling is found in *Success in Spelling*.) This is a teacher's manual with a few reproducible worksheets for specific assignments (not busywork). The introductory section outlines the overall approach, then the "Directives" section is color coded by grade level, listing specific topics to be learned with brief information for each. Activity approaches to learning are incorporated, using cards on heavy paper which are provided with the book. Both oral and written language are emphasized. For composition, reproducible worksheets with instructions are provided that help both parent and child learn skills for constructing paragraphs and longer essays. Writing takes place every day in one form or another. Younger children are encouraged to use drawing and verbal expression until they are developmentally ready for writing. Creative writing ideas are included throughout the book to help students practice concepts that have been taught. Grammar is only introduced at young levels, then concentrated upon in later grades.

Diagramming is included only at sixth grade level as a reinforcement of basic grammar and sentence construction. This book eliminates much of the repetition present in most language textbooks. Creative teaching suggestions for each topic provide activity, practice, and reinforcement. A "Forms" section is reproducible, but the "Manipulatives" printed on heavy paper are not. This program must be taught one-on-one and requires some preparation time. Only one volume is needed for all of our children in the elementary grades.

Ungraded Resources and Supplements for Grammar

Building Sentences with the Humpties

by Ellen Hajek

(Builder Books)

$8.95

This 43-page book is intended to be used as a follow-up to the introductory *Humpties* book, reviewed below. Cartoon characters and illustrations are used to show relationships between words in sentences rather than relying on definitions presented only with words. It covers both simple and compound subjects and predicates plus direct objects. Children learn how to diagram these simple sentences. They also learn basic types of sentences.

Noun and verb "humpties cards," about 1 inch square each, are cut from pages in the center of the book to be used by children as they identify those parts of speech within sentences. In addition to using the "humpties cards" and diagramming, children fill in blanks, underline, draw pictures, solve puzzles, and write complete sentences. Periodic reviews are included. This is a short course, but it does include a range of multi-sensory activities to aid learning. It should be appropriate for children working at about second to fourth grade levels, depending upon their prior grammar instruction. It might also be used with older students who need a gentle introduction to beginning grammar.

Diagramming—the key to understanding grammar

by Ellen Hajek

(Builder Books)

$15.95

Parts of speech are introduced in Chapter One with rules, examples, and exercises. From Chapter Two on, diagramming skills are taught. However, children should have some basic instruction before beginning this course, since it covers the parts of speech in very cursory fashion. For example, instruction about nouns essentially teaches that "a noun is a person, place, or thing." Discussion about the various roles that nouns may play within a sentence is scattered through lessons on subjects, direct objects, indirect objects, and predicate nouns without thorough instruction. The heart of this book (and the reason you should use it) is the diagramming lessons. Simple through complex sentences are taught, including participles, infinitives, and gerunds. Sentences to diagram are widely spaced on pages so that students can work within the book. Answers are at the back. Diagramming lessons are interspersed with brief writing assignments so that students can apply grammatical knowledge to their own sentence construction. As a diagramming tool, this is less complex and has fewer exercises than AMG Publisher's *Learning English with the Bible*, but it does offer more variety in exercises.

Editor in Chief series

(Critical Thinking Books & Software)
Books A1, A2 - $14.95 each; Books B1, B2 - $15.95 each; Books C1, C2 - $16.95 each; bundles: A1, B1, C1 OR A2, B2, C2 - $42.95 each

Children can improve their spelling, punctuation, and grammar skills in context with the brief exercises in *Editor in Chief*. A reading selection is accompanied by a picture and a caption. The problem is to identify errors and make proper corrections. An editing checklist is at the front of each book to alert students to types of errors they should watch for. A substantial "Guide to Grammar, Usage, and Punctuation" is at the back of each book for handy reference. Extensive answer keys identify and explain errors (helpful for us parents who will have trouble finding some of them ourselves). There are 33 lessons per book which works out to about one per school week in a normal school schedule. Books A1 and A2 are recommended for students working at 4th - 6th grade levels. Books B1 and B2 are recommended for those working at 6th - 8th grade levels. Books C1 and C2 are recommended for eighth grade level and above. *Editor in Chief* is also available as computer programs for either Windows or Macintosh systems. A demo is available at Critical Thinking's web site.(S)

F.L.A.G.S.

by Letz Farmer
(Mastery Publications)
$29.95

Children who need hands-on learning and those who enjoy games will appreciate *F.L.A.G.S.* (FUNdamental Language Arts Games Supplement). This is a set of 37 game boards, bound into a book, along with phonics cubes (which we assemble ourselves) and Spelling Squares. They introduce and review language arts concepts from beginning letters through parts of speech (pre-kindergarten through about fourth or fifth grade levels). Games may be played by players of differing skill levels using suggestions in the Parent's Manual. There are over 150 suggested variations, so it is unlikely that you will ever use everything. The games are fairly simple in concept—essentially bingo games and "loop" games. The variations come from the manual's suggestions; e.g., if a bingo game has words such as breathe and cloth, younger students simply identify the word correctly while older students must name the part of speech of each word. The loop games have children move a pawn around the game boards by performing such tasks as reading words, supplying missing letters, making contractions, spelling abbreviations, and identifying parts of speech. Flash cards and spinners (which we cut apart) come with the set.

The 18 Roll-A-Word Cubes are rolled like dice for children to practice constructing their own words. They are particularly useful for children who are at the blending stage of phonics. Spelling Squares are color-coded manipulatives for working with roots, prefixes and suffixes.

Everything is printed with black ink on solid color paper. Laminating or covering with contact paper will increase durability. Use the games for alphabet recognition, color and number words, sight vocabulary, phonics, contractions, abbreviations, prefixes and suffixes, antonyms, synonyms, homonyms, syllabication drill, auditory sequencing, visual sequencing, and parts of speech. Although not intended to be a complete program, *F.L.A.G.S.* is a practical language arts supplement for a wide range of ages.

An important side note: Mrs. Farmer compared lists of the most common words in current primers with those from 1950. Words like "government," "public," and "system" have replaced words like "please," "thank," "funny," and "kind." So she has incorporated many of the "old" words into her games so children practice working with a kinder and friendlier vocabulary.

The Grammar Key

by Robert L. Conklin
(The Grammar Key)
instructor's manual - $19.95; student workbook - $19.95; computer program - $59.95; video - $29.95

The beauty of *The Grammar Key* is simplicity, consistency, and efficiency. Choose the book, video, or computer version—all follow the same presentation and lesson design. Conklin introduces parts of speech along with their sentence functions, using key questions to help with identification. Key questions are repeated and memorized as are lists of helping verbs, linking verbs, determiners, pronouns, etc. Students mark sentences with labels, arrows, circling, and underlining. Although diagramming is presented within the instruction for each topic, students are never required to diagram sentences themselves (a plus or a minus, depending upon how you view diagramming). Lessons build continually so knowledge is integrated rather than taught in isolation. The course begins with noun recognition and continues through verbals (infinitives, participles, and gerunds). A single book is used from the middle elementary grades through high school.

The instructor's manual presents the lessons in such a fashion that students can read it on their own. After the instruction, students shift to the workbook to complete exercises. Periodically they encounter "Writing Practice" assignments which have them identify sentence elements that they have studied thus far within their own short compositions. The exercise answers are found in the instructor's manual. Lessons are not intended to encompass all areas of grammar (e.g., no verb tenses or subject-verb agreement lessons), although, at the end of the instructor's manual there are some helpful mnemonic (memory-assisting) devices for capitalization and commas. This means that you still need to cover some usage and mechanics as well as writing instruction elsewhere. (*The Grammar Key Mechanics* is in the works.) *The Grammar Key* essentials are summarized on a large, folded card which students can use for quick reference as needed. These three components—instructor's manual, student workbook, reference card—can stand alone, although you may substitute computer or video options. (The reference card comes with the instructor's manual, the student workbook, or the computer program.)

The computer program runs on either Macintosh or Windows systems. The program won't dazzle you with speed and sophistication, but it does a straightforward job of presenting both the instructional material (from the instructor's manual) and student exercises. The program requires at least eight hours of work to cover all of the topics, but this should be spread out so that students have time to absorb and apply the information as well as time to complete the other written assignments from the workbook. The computer monitors student progress, with the capability of tracking unlimited students from the same program. The publisher asks only that purchasers buy a program for each computer that will be used. The program does not allow students to progress to the next level until they pass the present level, so students cannot skip ahead even if they have previously mastered topics. Occasionally, the program is hypersensitive to placement of the sentence tags, rejecting appropriate answers if they are not placed just so, but the program signals clearly when all of the correct labels are in place. If the computer seems to be rejecting a tag that the student feels is correct, he should try it twice in case the computer is not registering it. The computer program allows for a more independent-study approach than the books since it monitors and tracks progress, but students should also have the student workbook since it has more practice sentences than the program and includes the writing activities which the program lacks. In fact, students are directed by the computer program to complete corresponding sections in their workbooks.

The eighty-minute video serves as a tutorial although it is not as comprehensive as the instructor's manual. Students who learn better via audio or multi-media presentations might find this option better than the instructor's manual, but I recommend that those purchasing the video also purchase an instructor's manual for complete course information. Whatever the case, students still will need the workbooks to complete their exercises.

The Grammar Key is a practical solution for students either learning or reviewing parts of speech.

Grammar Songs, Learning with Music
(Audio Memory)
$19.95 cassette; $22.95 CD

The basic set includes a cassette with sixteen songs, a student workbook, and teacher's guide that together teach parts of speech, punctuation, capitalization, sentence construction, Greek and Latin prefixes and suffixes, and more. Some student writing activities for reinforcement are in the workbook. The teacher's guide helps us know when to use the tape and workbook and provides a few extra ideas along with an answer key. Some songs are more effective than others, and they range in style from very calm to almost "rock." Listening to these songs is a great introduction to learning the parts of speech. Children find it much easier to identify nouns, verbs, etc. from the definitions and examples in the songs. While the songs are best suited for about third grade level through junior high, many older students and adults will also enjoy them.

Grammar Works
by Jay W. Patterson
(Holly Hall Publications)
$49.99

Grammar for grades K-8 is covered in a single 500+-page book. It is designed to complement the *Writing Road to Reading* and other phonics-based reading programs. *Grammar Works* requires students to create their own grammar notebook just as they do when they learn the phonograms and rules in *WRTR*. *WRTR* methodology is also evident in manuscript handwriting instruction and in the multisensory approach where students see, hear, say, and do each new skill or concept. Repetition for mastery is stressed.

The course is divided into 44 lessons. Within each lesson is material for five levels: LK (kindergarten, L12 (grades 1-2), L34 (grades 3-4), L56 (grades 5-6), and L78 (grades 7-8). The author advises grade level designations be used only as rough guidelines, and that we move students through the various levels as they exhibit mastery. Older students just starting the program must begin at the lowest level and proceed at whatever pace they can up to their appropriate level. Once a student has been through material for a lower level, we repeat the course, using material for the next level, reviewing as necessary. Each student fifth grade or above compiles a notebook that will be used throughout the course for however many years it takes to develop mastery. They write definitions, rules, examples, word lists, conjugations, and other information needed to equip students to write clear, concise sentences. Everything is done to exact specifications to help students learn to pay attention to details. For example, students are instructed to write on specific lines on specific pages in their notebooks. Likewise, word-for-word grammar instruction in each lesson is specific and detailed, covering parts of speech, punctuation, capitalization, sentence patterns, and basic syntax. During analysis, sentences are kept intact and marked with abbreviations and brackets instead of using diagramming. Although the text is not designed to teach a comprehensive approach to composition, some skills such as outlining, letter writing, and book reports are covered. Students are encouraged to practice composition skills such as outlining or writing summaries in other subject areas.

This is not a comprehensive program, nor is it intended to be. Some grammar skills are taught within *WRTR* programs—prefixes, suffixes, syllabication—so they are purposely omitted from *Grammar Works*. However, still other skills typically covered in the elementary grades are also missing—skills such as subject-verb agreement, comparison of adjectives and adverbs, and abbreviations. Because of its design, this course is a perfect adjunct for those using a *WRTR* course. For those using other resources than *WRTR*, the value of this text is in its word-for-word, step-by-step instruction and the sequential, incremental presentation that allow parents to teach grammar precisely and with confidence. Using it for a few years will build a solid foundation in those skills the program covers.

Reading Works and Advanced Grammar Works will supplement and expand this course in the future.(S)

The Great Editing Adventure Series, Volumes 1 and 2

(Common Sense Press)
$15 each; Student Activity Book - $10 each

Escape the drudgery of endless workbook grammar review by switching to *The Great Editing Adventure Series*. If our children have already been studying grammar for a few years, and they have a handle on the basics of punctuation, spelling, and grammar, these books will provide plenty of material to review, reinforce, and stretch their learning. In each book, there are 90 lessons, appropriate for grades 4-8, so each will provide either a year of lessons

occurring every other day or a half-year with daily lessons. The lessons are derived from three complete short stories. For each lesson we write a few sentences from the story (in order) on a chalk or white board. (If you don't have time to get those sentences on the board each day, purchase the *Student Activity Book* which has each day's sentences printed on a page. Underneath them are lines for students to write their corrected versions.) The sentences contain grammatical (usage, parts of speech, capitalization, punctuation, etc.), structural (letter writing and addressing envelopes) and spelling errors that children must spot, vocabulary words with which they need to become familiar, and words for which they must discover synonyms. The authors have covered language arts concepts typical for 4th through 6th grades. (The book functions as review material for grades 7-8.) Everything needed to present each lesson is contained within the teacher book for each volume, although students will need to have a dictionary and thesaurus handy. Answers as well as explanations are provided in the teacher book, so we can actually teach or reteach a concept that poses problems for a student without having to go elsewhere for assistance. The stories themselves are entertaining, as we might guess from some of their titles: "Incredible Kooky Inventions," "The Adventures of a Sheep Named Bill," and "Around the World with the Roaming Detectives." Take a break from grammar texts for awhile and see if this isn't at least as effective and a lot more fun.

The Great Grammarian

(Great Grammarian)
$49.95

This board game has questions, some serious and some zany, that help your children review parts of speech, spelling, punctuation and proper word usage as they move around the board collecting gold stars. It is set up for team play, but it should work just as well if students play as individuals--games will just take longer. Questions range from fairly easy for typical fourth graders to quite challenging for sixth graders. Children should have studied grammar for a number of years before playing this game. Questions on correct spellings, usage, homonyms, etc., also assume at least fourth grade level learning, and sometimes higher. The board is quite large so it easily accommodates a "crowd." (S) [V.T.]

Hands-On English

by Fran Santoro Hamilton
(Portico Books)
$9.95; activity book - $14.95

This 8" x 10 3/4" paperback is a useful grammar reference that covers parts of speech, types of sentences, punctuation, spelling, and proper word usage. It also contains information on word roots, proofreader's marks, footnotes and bibliographies, including how to show e-mail sources. A unique feature of this book, and one that would be especially helpful for visual learners, is the use of small drawings of objects to symbolize the functions of the parts of speech, such as a block for a noun and a spring for an action verb.

The Activity Book to Accompany Hands-On English makes the reference book even more useful. It includes 158 reproducible worksheets and answer key with notes in a looseleaf binder. Students work on parts of speech, usage, sentences, sentence patterns, capitalization, punctuation, and basic spelling rules, with some coverage of reading, writing, vocabulary. Diagramming is included.

These two books together provide a solid, foundational grammar course for students grades 4 through about nine.(S)[V.Thorpe/C.D.]

"How To" Series
(Teacher Created Materials)
$7.95 each

Teacher Created Materials offers a series of books on three levels which includes a number of titles for working on grammar skills. The three levels are grades 1-3, grades 3-6, and grades 6-8. Some titles are repeated at more than one level. *How to Use Parts of Speech* and *How to Punctuate* are available for the lowest and highest levels. *How to Capitalize* is available as a separate book for the first level and is combined for the second level in *How to Capitalize and Punctuate*. The second level also includes *How to Spell Homophones*. These books offer short lessons that can be used for focused instruction, but they do not provide the type of spiral coverage found in complete programs such as A Beka's. You might want to use the gentle introduction of these books for a student in the early grades, moving on to a more comprehensive course the next year.(S)

Humpties: Parts of Speech with "Eggceptional" Personalities
by Ellen Hajek
(Builder Books)
$8.95

If you want to introduce recognition of parts of speech to children in the elementary grades, this is the type of tool that will make the job easier. Nouns, pronouns, verbs, adjectives, adverbs, conjunctions, prepositions, and interjections are taught. Definitions are very simple. Each part of speech is represented by a cartoon figure that should help children recall its definition. For example, the description of nouns begins, "The noun is the father of the Humpty family parts of speech. You can see by his top hat and glasses that the noun has a very important job. He <u>names</u> everything! Anything that you might point to or look at has a name that is a noun." This is followed

by examples. After each part of speech is introduced, you cut out the 1" x 1" pictures of the cartoon figures from the back of the book, then students use them to identify nouns (or whatever parts of speech are being studied) in a short set of sentences. This method allows children to learn parts of speech without the pencil and paper work required by workbook exercises. The presentation is definitely for young children both because of the wording and because lessons are strictly introductory. The author suggests using the book with grade levels 3-5, but I think that most fifth graders will find it too young. It can be used with second graders if you choose to teach parts of speech at that level (something I do not necessarily recommend).

A follow-up book, *Building Sentences with the Humpties*, covers basic sentence structure and introduces diagramming.

Language Arts, Book One
by Alyce-Kay Garrett
(Tools for Godly Living)
$15

Copying and dictation are the core methodology of this one-year program. It can be used with students in mid-elementary grades through junior high, depending upon their background. It is best for grades 4-6. It uses verses from Joshua, Psalms and Proverbs; the Ten Commandments; and the songs "Jesus Loves the Little Children," "Battle Hymn of the Republic," and "The Star Spangled Banner" first for copying then for dictation. Using methodology based upon Ruth Beechick's approach to language arts, these passages are used for grammar and composition assignments for each week. Students study parts of speech, punctuation, alphabetizing, and other grammar skills while they also memorize the selected passages. Weekly composition assignments do not include instructions on how to write, so most children will need additional instruction. The Introductory Note to the book suggests that junior and senior high students might also use this book for independent work, but most older students should already have mastered the grammatical concepts taught in this book. Also, copying/dictation selections are really too short and lack the range of grammatical constructions appropriate for older students. However, many composition assignment topics seem to be designed for older students (e.g., from an assignment dealing with the commandment, "Thou Shalt Not Commit Adultery,"—"What can you do now to practice the skills needed to remain true to your husband or wife someday? What character qualities would it be helpful to work on?"). Focusing clearly on a narrower range of students abilities might have been more helpful.

The real value of this book seems to me that it sets up a process of regular copying and taking dictation. Copying samples the first time eliminates the frustration of guessing which of a few possible constructions an author might have selected. Taking dictation then challenges the student to master punctuation, capitalization, and spelling in both prose and poetry. More books are planned for this series.

Learning English with the Bible series

by Louise M. Ebner

(AMG Publishers)

Two basic texts, subtitled *A Systematic Approach to Bible-Based English Grammar* [$7.99; answer key - $4.99] and *Using Punctuation and Capitalization* [$7.99], focus on grammar basics and can be used whether or not you choose to teach diagramming. Ungraded, they can be used with all ages, although I would suggest ages 8 or 9 and up. A separate answer key is included for the first textbook.

AMG also offers a third book in this series, subtitled *English Grammar Diagrams Based on the book of Joshua* [$6.99]. This was the original book that attracted my attention. It offered the most thorough treatment of diagramming I had ever seen. Assuming a foundational knowledge of parts of speech, it demonstrates simple to extremely complex sentence diagrams using Scripture verses. Students are given sentences to diagram, and "solutions" are shown at the back of the book. It serves as a companion to the other books, but it can also be used to teach diagramming on its own. *A Systematic Approach*, its answer key, and *English Grammar Diagrams* are available as a set for $17.99.

Learning Grammar through Writing

(Educators Publishing Service)

$8.95

This book contains grammar and composition rules with reference numbers. It can be used for third through twelfth grades, although it is not detailed enough for most junior and senior high students. (I recommend it particularly for students in the middle to upper elementary grades.) It covers basics of grammar but skips some of the "fine tuning" details that we find in more extensive grammar handbooks or reference works. The teacher marks student's work with reference numbers for the student to identify his own errors. Basic teaching of rules must be done first. This method encourages children to think about their errors and then determine how best to correct them.(S)

Rules of the Game

(Educators Publishing Service)

$8 each; answer keys - $3.70 each

This is a series of three, softbound workbooks that teach grammar by the inductive method. That means that rather than telling students a "rule" and following it with exercises, students are led to discover a general principle or definition for themselves. In actuality, the amount of discovery is quite minimal, but it still is a more interesting way to introduce

grammar concepts. Once the concept has been presented, students practice with a variety of exercises. Like *Easy Grammar*, this is a more concise means of learning grammar, and it can be used with children of widely varying ages—from about fifth grade through high school. Book 1 covers nouns, pronouns, subjects, verbs, capitalization, punctuation, sentences, contractions, possessives, adjectives, adverbs, prepositions, interjections, conjunctions, compounds, and subject/verb agreement. Book 2 briefly reviews the above, then continues with direct and indirect objects, linking verbs, predicate nouns and adjectives, appositives, objects of prepositions, prepositional phrases, and punctuation. Book 3 works on dependent clauses, complex and compound-complex sentences, and verbals, while also supplying comprehensive application exercises for all previously learned grammatical elements. These inexpensive books are not reproducible so purchase one for each student. Answer keys are available at minimal cost.(S)

Simply Grammar

(Charlotte Mason Research and Supply Co.)

$24.95

Simply Grammar is an ungraded resource book for teaching grammar. It is a modernized version of Charlotte Mason's original book published in 1928. According to Mason's philosophy, grammar is not taught directly until around fourth grade. Thus, this book is written for students in grades 4-8. However, I expect that many third graders will be ready for these lessons. *Simply Grammar* also works especially well for those who have just completed *English for the Thoughtful Child.* It utilizes much more oral work than written, implementing Mason's method of teaching through narration. (Narration means that children describe, explain, summarize, and relate as a primary means of developing language art skills.) *Simply Grammar* features 50 full-page, nineteenth-century illustrations which are used as subjects for learning. For example, one illustration shows a mother, her daughter, and an infant. Students are told, "Deborah is a helper. Look at the picture on page 44 and make six sentences, with the verb in the present tense or time." There are some fill-in-the-blank questions and some requiring brief answers, but these should be done orally or on separate paper, since this book is not intended to be consumable. Some of the language sounds "young" for eighth graders, but the grammar content is sufficient through junior high level. It includes sentences, subjects, predicates, nouns, verbs, adjectives, prepositions, adverbs, pronouns (all the various types), conjunctions, interjections, subject/verb agreement, number, cases, tenses, and moods. Some additional practice exercises and an answer key are at the back of the book. The print is large and uncrowded.

Obviously, there is not as much practice and drill here as in grammar programs that have new books for each year, but remember that those books cover essentially the same material over and over. If you begin in this book in fourth grade, remember that your child need not learn all of the lessons in a single year. In fact, he or she probably needs to wait a few years before tackling questions like, "Give the person, number, and gender of the relative pronoun in given sentences...." (p. 148) If you want more practice or review than is provided here, supplement with *Daily Grams*.

The foregoing description fails to capture the emotional warmth of this book. The delightful pictures, trailing-vine page borders, and the gentle approach give a distinctly different flavor than typical grammar books. The publisher will send sample pages to those who send along two first-class postage stamps with their request.

Winston Grammar

(Precious Memories Educational Resources)
$40; extra Student Packet - $13.50; supplemental workbook and answer key - $17.50

Instead of traditional diagramming, you might prefer to use the *Basic Winston Grammar Kit. Winston Grammar* uses key questions and clues for word identification. Rather than constructing diagrams, students use symbols and arrows to "mark up" sentences, showing parts of speech. In the use of colored cards for different parts of speech, it mimics Montessori methodology. (For comparison, A Beka uses a combination of symbolic marking and diagramming while Rod and Staff uses diagramming.) The *Basic Winston Grammar* set teaches parts of speech, noun functions, prepositional phrases, and modifiers. It includes a teacher manual, student workbook, cards, and tests. Extra *Student Packets* (student workbook and set of cards) can be purchased.

In addition to the above, there is also a *Supplemental Workbook* for extra practice. This workbook corresponds exactly with the original in content and difficulty, offering "more of the same" for those students who need it. It comes with an answer key, but workbooks can be purchased alone for additional students [$11].

Once students have mastered the basic course, they should continue with *Advanced Winston Grammar* [$35], but it should probably wait until students are at least junior high level.

Precious Memories also publishes *Winston Word Works: A Usage Program* [$26.50]. This is a complementary program that focuses on the most common usage errors such as subject-verb agreement, use of personal pronouns, use of who/whom, correct forms of indirect object pronouns, and comparative and superlative forms of adjectives. This course builds upon the basic *Winston Grammar* procedures for identifying sentence elements. It will be most useful after completing both *Basic* and *Advanced* programs.

Ungraded Resources and Supplements for Writing

Complete Writing Lessons for the Primary Grades
by Marjorie Frank
(Incentive Publications)
$12.95

If you like creative writing, this is the book to use for beginning writing! Marjorie Frank combines fantastic creative ideas with instruction in the writing process. Each lesson is laid out step-by-step so that it is ideal for the novice teacher yet helpful for the experienced. Children can begin some of the lessons as soon as they can write, although I think second grade level (when children are able to write and spell a fairly large number of words) is the best time to start. Lessons are appropriate for children through third and fourth grades (and possibly beyond).

Thirty lessons focus on many different aspects of writing, including sentences, paragraphs, questions, poetry, definitions, metaphors, recipes, letters, characterization, riddles, advertisements, conversations, and stories. The writing process is clearly explained at the beginning of the book, then reflected in each lesson outline.

Children generally enjoy the lesson themes which are silly and sometimes nonsensical. Since these books are written for the secular classroom, you might have to do a little adapting to fit the home school situation.

Student activity pages are reproducible, so one book per family is all you will need. This approach requires interaction between student and teacher and is even more effective when more than one student is involved. (SE)

Complete Writing Lessons for the Middle Grades
by Marjorie Frank
(Incentive Publications)
$12.95

Children beginning in fourth or fifth grade up through junior high will enjoy writing lessons that can best be described as "zany." Marjorie Frank, the author, first wrote *If You're Trying to Teach Kids How to Write, You've Gotta Have This Book!*, but found that many teachers wanted more specific lesson plans for applying her ideas. This book presents those lesson plans explaining and developing the writing process while students work on creative writing projects. In fact, this is one of the best books for teaching writing because it effectively teaches skills in an enjoyable way and is easy for teachers to use. Topics covered include paragraphs, questions, explanations, directions, reports, character studies, idioms, suspense, news articles, fables, myths, posters,

Young Writers Institutes

The Young Writers Institute is a terrific opportunity for fledgling writers (grades 3- 12), or even reluctant writers, to attend a one or two day workshop with two outstanding Christian authors learning about "real" writing. Authors participating at present are Sigmund Brouwer, author of The Accidental Detectives, CyberQuest, and other popular novels; Bill Myers, author of McGee and Me, Wally MacDoogle and other titles; Nancy Rue, author of Focus on the Family's Christian Heritage series and Raising the Flag series; plus Robert Elmer, T. Davis Bunn, Angela Elwell Hunt, Stephen Bly, and Rob Randall. The focus is on creative writing, with students separated into two grade levels.

In a morning keynote address, authors introduce themselves and share from their own experience. The keynote address is followed by a book signing time and a lunch break. During the afternoon, students are divided into their grade-level groups and attend topical workshops with one or both of the authors. Parents are welcome at all sessions. There is some down time for students while the other grade-level group is in their workshop with the authors, and parents are required to supervise their children during these periods. Students may register for one or both authors on each day.

YWI works with a local contact person and a regional or state home school group to schedule an event with YWI bearing all of the costs.The YWI has visited over 40 cities thus far. Contact them for information about events in your area or about hosting one yourself. (The YWI is a sister organization of the Home School Resource Center; both organizations were founded and are owned by Debra Bell.)

advertisements, jokes, diaries, and poetry. Some activities are done on reproducible student pages. This approach requires interaction between student and teacher and is even more effective when more than one student is involved.(SE)

Comprehensive Composition

(Design-A-Study)

$14

This is a teacher's resource book for writing instruction for grades 1-12. The author's goal was to provide a vehicle for writing instruction based upon integration of writing assignments with other subjects being studied rather than depending upon textbook composition topics. The author provides thorough instruction in skills with some sample topics to get students started. Students then can apply the skills to other topics being studied.

The writing process is developed throughout the book with general guidelines provided for what should be expected at different levels. Specific guidelines are given for various types of writing (essays, descriptive writing, writing a news story, etc.).

One section of the book deals with elements of style and grammar in sentence construction. Another chapter is a grammar reference source. Although it does not cover the parts of speech, it does cover capitalization and punctuation.

One of the most valuable parts of the book is the final section of sample lessons. In each sample, the assignment topic is given and we are shown how the lesson was presented or how the student worked to develop his composition. Then we read the final (and sometimes intermediate) results.

The book is not intended to be used in strict sequence but in the order best for each learning situation.

This has to be one of the most concise, yet comprehensive books for teaching the writing process available to home educators. Material for early grades is rather limited, but for middle elementary through high school level it should be excellent.

Kathryn Stout has a 60-minute audio tape, How to Teach Composition, that will also help you learn how to teach and evaluate composition skills [$4.50].

Easy Writing

(ISHA Enterprises)

$20.95

From the author of Easy Grammar, Wanda Phillips, comes a new approach to teaching writing. This is not a comprehensive writing program but one that concentrates on sentence structure. Children learn how to write more interesting sentences by using conjunctions, subordinate clauses, participial phrases, and other more complex structures. Each unit within the book is divided into an easier level and a more difficult level. Some children instinctively construct interesting sentences but many do not. This book will help those children (and parents) who have difficulty writing sentences more interesting than, "The boy chased the dog."

EZ Writer

by Gerald R. Wheeler, Ed.D. and Vance Socash

(Wheeler Applied Research)

$39.95

EZ Writer helps students improve their expository writing skills with a systematic approach to sentence and paragraph writing. Training students to automatically write more creative and complex sentences and paragraphs than do most unskilled writers is the basic goal of the program. The system asks students to write numerous five-sentence paragraphs, each containing five different types of specified sentences. I won't reveal the "key" for the five different sentences since that's the heart of this program, but it has much to do with various parts of speech. This is a great tool for helping students see how learning parts of speech can translate into improved writing skills. Instruction begins with a 70-minute video tape covering the basic principles of the program. The video periodically tells the student to stop the tape and do some actual writing. This breaks up the passive time for those who have difficulty just sitting and watching. The video overlaps the first seven pages of the student book. Once finished with the video, students continue on through the book. A brief, 10-page teacher's guide offers parents guidelines for using the course. A tear-off pad of "Scrubbers" is included. Scrubbers are half-page sheets for students to evaluate and improve their own work. It features check off boxes next to 11 key things to recheck to "scrub their writing clean." The program urges students to substitute synonyms for over-worked words, for which they should use a thesaurus. However, the suggestion to use a thesaurus is buried in the teachers' manual, so remember to have one handy to use along with this program. Towards the end of the book we find examples and suggestions for tackling academic reports, both those that can be contained within five sentences and lengthier pieces. A Book 2 from *EZ Writer* plans to continue with techniques for writing persuasive paragraphs, media copy, and dialogue. Appendices assist students with capitalization and punctuation rules, lists of adverbs, prepositions, and pronouns, and a four-step strategy summary. While *EZ Writer* focuses upon only one part of your language arts program, it is an excellent tool for developing and refining writing skills. Students as young as fourth or fifth grades will probably need lots of teacher assistance, but junior and senior high students should be able to go through most of it on their own.(S)

"How To" Series
(Teacher Created Materials)
$7.95 each

Teacher Created Materials offers a series of books on three levels which includes a number of titles for teaching writing skills. The three levels are grades 1-3, grades 3-6, and grades 6-8. Some titles are repeated at more than one level. In such cases, the books follow the same outline, but present the material at a higher level of difficulty.

These books are especially useful for breaking skills down into manageable chunks. Reproducible worksheets combine with discussion and fun activities to teach and reinforce concepts. Some activities are classroom oriented, but most can be used by homeschoolers, sometimes with slight adaptation. Multi-sensory activities help children with different learning styles master skills. One title repeated at all three levels covers a crucial topic: *How to Write a Paragraph. How to Make a Book Report* is also available for all three levels, while *How to Write a Sentence* and *How to Write a Story* are offered for the first two levels. The first level also includes *How to Write a Simple Report* (which is actually quite challenging for even most third graders!). The second level adds *How to Give a Presentation, How to Write a Poem,* and *How to Write a*

Research Report. Book Report titles offer a number of different approaches for relating the contents of a book as well as creative activities that spring from the book's contents (e.g., writing a letter as if you were a character from a book). *How to Write a Story* works on both organization and style while developing basic writing skills. Other books in the "How To" series work on grammar and punctuation skills.(S)

The "How to Write" Book
(Teaching & Learning Company)
$10.95

The publisher suggests using this resource for grades 5-6, but I suggest trying some of the ideas with younger students to develop a proper attitude and approach to writing before they get stuck in a typical workbook approach to writing. Author Ellen Hajek stresses thinking and planning before writing. Within that process, students identify their audience and purpose, crucial steps in good writing. This workbook can be used by students working independently for the most part. Models and simple instructions make the writing process "non-threatening." Children work with an assortment of assignments that range from very short and simple, such as circling topic sentences, through the complex tasks of writing formal reports, poetry, essays, and short stories. Along the way they learn about paragraphs, planning, topic sentences, letter writing, book reports, news reports, outlines, titles, mechanics, style, and proof reading. Many of these topics are dealt with briefly, but taken all together, this is a good resource for developing writing skills. The one criticism I have, and one that most of your children will pick up on immediately, is the amateur art work. The book is self-contained. There are only a few of the exercises that have definite answers, and those answers are provided at the back of the book.

The Institute for Excellence in Writing [video course]
(Institute for Excellence in Writing)
Teaching Writing seminar - $130; Student Writing seminars - $99 each; Student Workshops - $19.95 each

In spite of the development in recent years of excellent resources for teaching writing, many parents hesitate for lack of confidence. Andrew Pudewa presents writing seminars for parents and students that overcome the confidence barrier better than anything else I've yet seen. Since attending Andrew's seminars is not practical for many parents and teachers, he now offers those same seminars in the *Teaching Writing: Structure and Style* video course. The course consists of four video tapes (6 ½ hours of viewing), workbook/syllabus, your choice of a *Student Workshop* video, free toll-free phone consultation, feedback on practicum assignments, and a certificate of completion.

The course teaches both structure and style in such a way that students acquire a repertoire of techniques. Much of this is practical for use with students as young as second and third grade, although some will apply more to upper elementary through high school. Parent/teachers learn how to teach both creative and expository writing. Students continue to develop and apply the techniques through actual writing activities taught throughout the course. Parents may watch the entire course all at once or spread it out over weeks or months. Students might watch with them, but this really is focused on teacher training. [Special note: I.E.W. offers $9 per tape refund for tapes returned within 2 months of purchase. The syllabus does cover the same material in abbreviated form. So if you work through the seminar carefully, then refer to the syllabus as you teach your students, you can save money by taking advantage of this generous offer.]

Pudewa does not try to cover all types of creative and expository writing, but focuses on basic structures and approaches. However, this foundational development should be excellent preparation for students to build upon as they explore other forms of writing.

One of the strategies Pudewa uses is to have students begin by making notes from a model composition. Students come up with key words to convey main ideas. Then they work from their notes to reconstruct the piece, not attempting to copy it, but using their own words, expanding with their own ideas and expressions. This strategy works very well since it provides a secure starting place so students are not worrying excessively about what to say. Instead, they concentrate on structure and style.

The course as presented to students, consists of nine units: Note Making and Outlines, Summarizing from Notes, Summarizing from Narrative Stories, Summarizing References and Library Reports (2 units), Writing from Pictures, Creative Writing, Essay Writing, and Critiques. Once past the first few lessons, we can use the lessons in whatever order seems best for our students. The syllabus includes reproducible models that are an essential part of each lesson.

What I like most about this course is that Pudewa walks us through each strategy in detail. His teaching experience is very evident as he identifies and deals with the problems that tend to crop up for both teacher and student. The lessons move along slowly enough for us to think and work through the process with his "live" audience. This means we are more likely to end up with a really solid grasp of the course content.

As mentioned above, the seminar set includes your choice of a *Student Workshop* video. *Students Workshops* are recordings of hour-long classes conducted with different age groups: elementary (grades 2-4), intermediate (grades 5-7), and high school (grades 8-12). These serve as demonstration classes. You might have students work alongside the "on-tape" class to introduce them to some of the methods of this course.

Even more help is available through *Student Writing Intensive* videos. These are four-tape sets of actual classes, running about 10 hours per set of videos. Three age-designated sets are available: grades 4-5, grades 6-7, and grades 8-10+. Video classes in each set focus on selected lessons from the syllabus. A set of reproducible papers (models, checklists, reference sheets, worksheets) comes with each set of tapes. As with the *Student Workshop* videos, students may work through these along with the "on-tape" classes.

I.E.W. also offers other related resources in their catalog, including a group package for the video seminar that you should investigate if you want to do a group class.

A few homeschoolers were so impressed with I.E.W. that they went out of their way to make sure I reviewed it. My impression is that their enthusiasm was well-founded.(S)

Learn to Write the Novel Way
by Carole Thaxton, M.S.
(Konos Connection)
$39.95; teacher's guide with answer key - $5.95

It's easier for students to learn language skills when they have a purpose for doing so. This course uses writing a novel as the context for applying all writing skills in a dedicated project. This consumable workbook breaks the process into thirteen manageable steps, each with three sections. In the first section of the lesson you work with your child on the new concept being taught. Then a short practice exercise is assigned for the student to complete on his own. Finally, the student is instructed to apply the concept to his own developing novel, which will be kept in a separate notebook. At each step the parent checks the student's work before going on to the next lesson. It might be necessary to devise extra practice lessons from some other source for students who have not mastered a particular lesson. The more time you can devote to "coaching" your child's writing, the more he will benefit from this book.

This program covers grammar and proper word usage and can be counted as a full year of English for grades 5-12. For the younger students, you might wish to continue a separate spelling program. A word processor is necessary.[V. Thorpe]

Newspaper Reporters: An Introduction to Newspaper Writing
(Teacher Created Materials)
$7.95

Students are usually much more interested in purposeful writing than in writing essays about what they did on their summer vacation. Writing articles for their own newspaper is a purposeful writing activity that most children greatly enjoy. This forty-eight-page book provides a framework for teaching about newspapers through activities, then it has children create their own newspaper.

The first section introduces children to the parts of a newspaper through hands-on activities. Reproducible activity pages help them prepare before they start searching through the newspaper looking for articles, stories, and information. A variety of writing assignments are scattered throughout the lessons. The technical aspects of layout, typesetting, and printing are briefly covered with activities included.

Then students begin to work on creating their own newspaper articles. They learn how to write different types of articles and headlines. They work on organization, note taking, and other writing skills. They conduct interviews, do background research, compose advertisements, and prepare puzzles and comic strips.

Children can work through the activities individually, but I suspect it will be most successful when used with two or more children who can share ideas and encourage one another.

Teacher Created Materials also offers "blank" newspapers [$7.95] for children to use as they work. The newspaper forms come fifteen to a package with each paper having four 11" x 17" pages, folded tabloid style. Red and black outlines and some headings are preprinted on the forms. Lined sections are designed for students to fill in their articles. Boxes are set aside for advertisements, pictures, a puzzle, an editorial cartoon, and a comic strip.

I suggest allotting a month or two for each child to work on creating his or her own newspaper, working on all of the different types of writing and creating puzzles, cartoons, and advertisements. The publisher suggests using these materials with children in grades three through six.(SE)

The Poetry Corner
(Good Year)
$12.95

This book offers instruction on all types of poetry along with reproducible activity sheets to encourage students to experiment.(S)

Poetry Parade
(Learning Works)
$6.95

Suggested for grades 4-6, *Poetry Parade* provides lessons on a variety of poetic forms appropriate for these grade levels. The first section focuses on poems that follow patterns (e.g., haikus, quinzaines), followed by rhyming poems. Next are an assortment of assignments that include some arts and crafts activities and lots of creative ideas. Another section includes an optional "poetry contract" with a requirement that students copy five poems that they especially like, a marvelous way for children to develop a "feel" for poetry. Reproducible pages at the end of the book are used by students to create their own "mini-book of poetry" from the various assignments.(S)

Storybook Weaver Deluxe [computer program]
(The Learning Company)
$14.95

Get those reluctant writers motivated with this CD-ROM for either Windows or Macintosh systems. Children assemble a background scene by matching a top with a bottom, and then add drawings or choose from a wide variety of "stamps" of people in various positions, objects, cars, animals etc. These stamps can also be painted on, modified or resized. Then students can make the sleeping boy snore or water drip by choosing from a variety of sound effects that can be applied to the objects. Background music sets the mood. When their picture is complete, they can write about it on the bottom of the same page. (The computer will read back what they type, but the clarity is not as good as that in some other programs.) A spell check and thesaurus help the writing process.

For those who don't know where to start, there are a variety of story starters in English or Spanish to complete. Also, think about letting two or more children try a co-operative story. Fun for grades 1-6.(S)[V. Thorpe]

Teaching English Through Art
by Sharon Jeffus
(Visual Manna)
$17.95

Teaching English Through Art would be a fun supplement to an upper elementary language arts program. The idea is an excellent one: to get away from language arts worksheets which really cannot teach either writing or creativity. Many of the writing assignments are inspired by black-and-white art that is reproduced in the book; one section requires writing different types of paragraphs based on pictures or art work. Suggestions are included to make a writer's portfolio, which is an excellent record keeping technique as well as inspiration for the author. Some of the ideas are of particular interest to Christians. For example, instead of writing just any type of business letter, the author suggests writing a letter of appreciation to a famous person.

As with other books from Visual Manna, the authors need to be more careful in proofreading their text. Some of the directions could use a bit more explanation. One assignment is to write a poem from a picture, using "as many mood capturing words as possible" with no discussion of what these words might be. There are also no guidelines for critiquing the student's writing. Because of these limitations and the fact that the book is not complete in its coverage of topics, I would use it only as a supplement. Despite this caveat, there are enough unusual or inspiring assignments to recommend it. I envision using Teaching English through Art on a Friday as a respite from more traditional work.[Kath Courtney]

Ultimate Writing & Creativity Center

(The Learning Company)

$39.95

This CD-ROM is designed to give children instruction and help with all phases of the writing process. A rather annoying talking pen named Penny is available with simple advice for each step. If children don't know what to write about, they can visit four different "idea lands" where they see a scene, such as the Southwestern Desert, with various plants and animals. Click on one of these and it does something silly and then, usually with poetry or pun, gives an idea for writing that is related to that plant or animal. Or click on "Writing Projects" for report ideas or "Did You Know?" for interesting facts about the desert.

For graphics, students can go to the "Picture Place" and choose a scenic background. Then they click on the stamp tool to view objects they can place on their scene. Each scene shows the stamps that are related to that scene, which is good for those who get overwhelmed with too many choices; the forest background has forest animal stamps and the spooky house has ghosts and witches. For some reason, the space background has a few multi-ethnic super-heroes as well as astronauts and aliens. There are several fairy tale type backgrounds as well as a blank one with stamps of multi-ethnic teen paper dolls and clothing. Children can also use the art tools and draw or paint on the backgrounds or graphics. If they want to make their picture really silly they can apply one of the animated "critters" from the idea lands to their page.

For writing help the student can access a spell check, thesaurus or dictionary; "Writing Tips" has models for idea organizers, types of letters, book reports and poems. When the writing is finished the child can go to the "Presentation Theater" and hear his words read by the computer.

In the school version [$69.95] an accompanying binder contains tutorials and ideas for student activities. The whole program is rather school oriented (you even save your work in a "backpack"), but it can be adapted for home use. Best for grades 2 to 4.(S)[V. Thorpe]

WIN Program

by Dr. Les Simonson and Peter Joel

(Elijah Company)

Book A:Story Writing by Dictation - $5.95, *Book B: Seven Sentence Story* - $5.95, *WIN Program* - $20, Expository Writing Handbook - $5.95; *Essay Handbook* - $10

The *WIN* (Story Writing by Dictation) program does designate approximate grade levels for their materials, but I list it here because it should be seen as a whole rather than as individual resources. *Book A: Story Writing by Dictation* (for grades K-1) and *Book B* (for primary grades) are books of about 30 pages each. The *WIN Program* (for grades 3-7+) is a much larger, comb-bound book. For about sixth grade through

high school level, there are the smaller *Expository Writing Handbook* and the lengthier book, *The Essay Handbook* .

All of the *WIN* books use a "formula" approach to story writing. There are designated lines and/or boxes for conveying specific information. Wordy writers will have to learn to be concise. While the idea of writing to a formula is somewhat constricting, it does teach the importance of organization and planning very well. There are key elements essential to a story, and none will be omitted if students work through these lessons. The presentation of the *WIN* Program makes it very easy for the inexperienced parent to successfully teach her (or his) children to write.

Book A: Story Writing by Dictation introduces young children to story writing through organized formats. Story writing at this level is divided into four basic parts: the setting, the problem, the solution to the problem, and the conclusion. Children select topics guided by their parents, then tell stories following simple guidelines. These are short stories. There are three different dictation forms (or models) in the book. The first two are student-dictated and teacher-written, while the third might be written by the student. The first has small squares for student illustrations and space rather than lines for the story. The second has lines but no picture space. The third has large lines appropriate for beginning writers. Examples are included. We should begin with the first form, then move on to the others as is appropriate. An important part of the *WIN* methodology is planning and discussion before writing, and it is stressed even at the beginning level.

Book B: The Seven Sentence Story is similar in concept to *Story Writing by Dictation* but expands into paragraphing and other details such as indentation of the first word of the paragraph. In *Book B*, we are still working with the four basic elements of a story, this time using lined boxes. It is not necessary to use *Story Writing by Dictation* first. *Book B* will help prepare students for the *WIN Program*, although it is not a prerequisite.

The *WIN Program* will stand alone and makes an excellent introductory writing course. It is suggested for grades 3-7, but older students could also benefit from it. There are no grade level indications, and content is not necessarily "young," so I see no problem with students even up through high school beginning here. It works with the same four basic story elements as *Book B*, this time presented as setting, story problem, action-solution, and conclusion. Instruction covers both mechanics and style, although it is by no means a grammar course. Students work through a number of models/forms, studying examples and gradually building upon basic skills. They continue to work in controlled boxes. Although they are limiting, they teach discipline and organization. In the appendices are additional exercises and helps for lively story starters and dialogue, lists of more colorful synonyms for commonly-used words, an editing chart, reproducible forms, plus guides for capitalization and punctuation. While it might be possible to work through all of this in a year, it will probably take a few years to bring students up to the advanced levels of writing demonstrated here. The WIN Program would be a good resource to use for a group writing class.

The *Expository Writing Handbook*, suggested for grades 6-12, teaches students how to write 500-600 word compositions. It uses a highly structured format, requiring students to first fill in forms with the main topic, sub topics, and supporting details, before fleshing this out into the composition itself. Reproducible forms are included in the book. A completely developed model composition is used as an example for instruction.

The *Essay Handbook* focuses on this particular writing form, which is so essential as students progress into high school and college. As with other *WIN* books, this is a formula approach to essay writing that helps students develop a thorough understanding of the elements of a good essay. The essay-writing process is tackled in four steps: outlining, planning (expanding upon notes), rough draft, and final draft. Reproducible worksheets for each step walk students through with explicit instructions. Samples are provided. The Appendix includes instructions, sample, and forms for writing an eleven-sentence essay—a great way to introduce students to the concepts taught in this book without overwhelming them.

Both *Expository Writing* and *Essay* books emphasize organization, reasoning, and logical presentation rather than style. Check out *Writing with a Point* (Educators Publishing Service) or lessons in the *WIN Program* to work on style. However, the particular value of these books lies in their being user-friendly—they make the writing process simpler for students to understand and easier for teachers to teach.

Wordsmith: A Creative Writing Course for Young People

by Janie B. Cheaney
(Common Sense Press)
$14; teacher's guide - $5

Many students at upper elementary and junior high level have learned the basics in grammar and need some help transferring grammatical knowledge into their writing.

Wordsmith assumes the student knows basic grammar. It moves on from there to work with grammar through written applications. For example, one assignment has them come up with vivid action verbs to replace weak verbs accompanied by adverbs. The goal is to sharpen writing skills by choosing words carefully for the best effect.

After working on grammar, they tackle sentence construction, again with the goal of writing more interesting yet concise sentences. Once grammar and sentence structure are under control, they can apply those skills to composition writing.

Although *Wordsmith* does not teach all the different forms

of writing such as reports, research papers, etc., it covers techniques that can be applied in most any writing situation. Lessons work on skills such as describing people, narrowing the topic, and writing dialogue. At the end, students write their own short story. Helps on proofreading and editing are included.

The student book may be written in or used as a reusable text by doing the brief activities in a notebook. Lesson organization is clear and well-designed. Most students should need a year or more to work through all of the lessons. Some teaching, primarily in the form of discussion and evaluation, is required, although students will do much of the work on their own. The author's humorous touches scattered throughout the book add special appeal.

Parents who lack confidence in their ability to teach students how to write will appreciate the inexpensive teacher's guide. It includes answers, lesson plans, teaching suggestions, and ideas for expanding lessons. Parents with strong writing skills will probably be able to manage without it.

Other books attempt to meet the same goals, but the presentation here is better than anything similar at this level.

Wordsmith Apprentice

by Janie B. Cheaney
(Common Sense Press)
$16

Wordsmith Apprentice is a "prequel" to one of my favorite junior high writing programs, *Wordsmith: A Creative Writing Course for Young People*. Cheaney translates the same enthusiasm, humor, and energy that so impressed me in the older-level course to this course for students ages 9 to 12. Using a newspaper-writing approach, she creates interesting writing activities that develop both grammatical and composition skills. For example, in the first section teaching about sentences, students learn the four types of sentences then write four sentences to describe a news photo, mixing declarative, interrogatory, and exclamatory sentences. Stretching beyond the limitations of the newspaper format, students also write invitations, letters, and thank-you notes. "Comic-strips" introduce each new section. Topics covered are nouns, verbs, sentences, modifiers, prepositions, paragraphs, synopsis writing [often neglected!], dialogue, opinion writing, and more. These are covered within the context of newspaper tasks such as writing classified ads, travel articles, book reviews, articles, headlines, as well as editing. Examples and some forms are included, not to stifle or limit students, but to help stimulate their imaginations and give them organizing tools. Cheaney writes from a Christian perspective, although it comes through subtly; for example, students learn to recognize good synopses by deciding which one of three synopses most accurately conveys the story of David and Goliath, then an assignment follows to write three synopses, one of which is for the story of "The

Good Samaritan."

This study is designed for students in grades 4 through 6, and it can be used by students working independently (with parents reading and responding to exercises and assignments) or by a mixed age and ability group. Students who have already been introduced to grammar basics will find this a great way to apply what they have learned. Those without prior grammar instruction will need supplemental study defining and identifying grammatical concepts. All students will need a thesaurus and they should also have a newspaper to consult for examples. (It need not be current, so you can carefully select and edit a newspaper for objectionable content.)

The Write Book for Christian Families
by Robert Allen
(Bob Jones University Press)
$9.95

The title of this book nicely sums up its purpose: assisting Christian parents teach their children how to serve God through writing. *The Write Book* gives idea after idea of activities to encourage children to put pencil to paper. Robert Allen has not written this book specifically for homeschoolers, and it is not designed as a writing course. But it does provide suggestions on writing for any family.

Chapters, whose titles all continue the pun of write/right (such as "Write Away" and "The Write Gift"), feature a a variety of fun writing activities that vary from brief to lengthy. Some of the shorter, easier ideas include making lists, various word games, gift coupons, and cartooning. The lengthier writing suggestions include newsletters, writing tracts, writing songs, and making a family Bible commentary. Throughout the book, Mr. Allen shares examples from the writing of his own children.

This small paperback book would be especially helpful for parents of younger children who have not done much writing. It is also valuable for families who want to learn how to incorporate writing into family life. The activities in this book can help make writing a fun, daily part of your family life and an opportunity to serve God.[Becky Parker]

The Write Stuff Adventure: Exploring the Art of Writing
by Dean Rea
(Great Expectations Book Co.)
$19.99

Developed through use with different age groups of homeschoolers, this writing program easily adapts to students from about fifth grade through high school. Beginning lessons work on basic concepts. The first few lessons are designed to get kids writing in a non-threatening manner. The first section also draws attention to punctuation, some parts of speech, phrases, clauses, and complete sentences. Very creative writing topics keep these lessons from being mechanical experiences.

Lessons become more challenging, moving on through such activities as interviews, letters to the editor, essay writing, poetry, creating family history "pieces," writing non-fiction articles, writing a family newspaper, and writing feature articles. The last few sections stretch into writing radio scripts, creating editorial cartoons, and working on forms of visual communication—areas not typically covered in writing programs.

Lessons are designed to be presented by the teacher—this is a teacher's manual, rather than a student book. It will work well for a parent working with just one child, but it would be more fun in a group. You will need to be selective about which lessons to use since there is a wide range in level of difficulty. Most lessons can be used with older students, challenging them to perfect skills even with the easiest lessons. However, younger students might need to take more time at various levels as they develop new skills.

I like this program for many of the same reasons I like Cheaney's *Wordsmith*—it combines some practical grammar application within lessons that are creative and encouraging, all the while developing significant writing skills.

Writing Step by Step: Developing Paragraphs by Asking Questions
(Builder Books)
$9.95

This is a teacher's manual with reproducible "maps" to help children (and parents) organize thoughts and put them easily into paragraph form. Models of different strategies are given, showing how to brainstorm, develop ideas, organize, and construct paragraphs.

The methods can be applied to many types of expository writing. The first part of the book is directed to lower grades. The second part of the book, directed toward older students, continues beyond basic paragraph writing to teach them how to develop more difficult compositions including steps in a process, comparison and contrast, problem/cause, and cause/effect. Ideas from both sections can be used according to the needs of each child, regardless of age. *Writing Step by Step* makes it so <u>easy</u> to write paragraphs; it helps many of us overcome this major stumbling block in teaching our children writing skills.

Writing Strands, Levels 1-6
by Dave Marks
(National Writing Institute)
Level 1 - $14.95; Levels 2-4 - $18.95 each; Levels 5-6 - $20.95 each

Writing Strands is a series of books that can be used selectively or sequentially.

Level numbers do not necessarily correspond to grade levels.

Writing Strands 1 is a small book that can be used with children who are at the prewriting stage (preschool through early elementary). It encourages parents to interact with their children through "word" activities. Games, stories, rhymes, and conversations are described which help children to broaden their experience with words before they begin writing. Many of the ideas are fantastical and silly, designed for fun as much as learning.

Writing Strands 2 needs to be presented by the teacher/parent. Students do their actual writing in a separate notebook. They are introduced to a variety of writing skills, among which are the use of adjectives, writing paragraphs, grouping information, story writing, dialogue, writing about personal experiences, and imaginative writing. Some grammar skills are taught within the lessons, but this is not intended to be a comprehensive grammar course. There are fifteen lessons, each of which might take anywhere from a couple of days to a week or more. Author Dave Marks offers suggestions about how much of each lesson might be covered each day, but you will need to make your own plans depending upon the ability and interest of each child. *Writing Strands* does a better job than most curricula do in teaching writing skills in the primary grades because lessons are purposely organized and content is interesting enough to motivate reluctant writers. Free worksheets are available on their web site which can be used with children who need a slower pace and/or more guidance as they work through Level 2.

Writing Strands 3 provides help for parents who lack confidence in their ability to teach their children how to write. The author speaks directly to the students, providing explanations with lengthy examples of concepts being taught. Parents still need to be involved in the lessons with students to varying degrees—more so with younger students, less so with older. Third graders can start at this level, but older students new to *Writing Strands* might also begin with Level 3. The emphasis throughout all levels is on writing itself rather than grammar and mechanics. However, children are instructed at the end of each assignment to look up solutions to grammatical problems in a grammar handbook (*The Write Source* or *Learning Grammar through Writing* can be used for just such a purpose.) Level 3 includes four strands: creative writing, basic writing skills, descriptive writing, and organization. Time schedules are laid out for each writing task, e.g., seven days are planned for learning how to create and resolve conflicts in writing fiction. Instruction and assignments are then given for each day's work, although lessons might take more or less than the allotted time. The tone is friendly and easy to understand—more inviting than most textbooks. The ideas for teaching writing are very creative and unlike those found in most textbooks.

Writing Strands 4 is similar to the third book, advancing slightly in level of difficulty. Level 4 refers back to Level 3, so

you should probably start with that level first.

Writing Strands 5 should follow levels 3 and 4, even if a child is just starting in *Writing Strands*.

In *Writing Strands 6*, lessons are clearly broken down into three writing strands: explanatory, creative, and report, with heavy emphasis on report and research writing.(S)

Writing to God's Glory: A Complete Creative Writing Course from Crayon to Quill
by Jill Bond
(Homeschool Press)
39.99

Jill Bond translates her wealth of experience as a published author into a valuable resource for parents and teachers who want to stimulate and guide their own, sometimes reluctant, budding authors. This 300-page book is divided into two primary sections: a teacher's guide and student pages.

An introductory section of about 50 pages "teaches the teacher" with specific guidelines for teaching this program as well as more-universal writing instruction guidelines under headings such as, "Grading and Other Forms of Torture," "Kevorkian Teaching Techniques" (which tend to kill off budding authors), and "Light, Salt, and Red Marks" (the proper use of encouragement and red pens). As you might guess from these headings, Jill uses a humorous approach throughout the book. Within this initial section, we also find "Action Learning," ten terrific, pre-writing activities that develop skills such as observation, characterization, identifying shades of meaning, and use of the five senses.

The remainder of the teacher's guide and the section containing the student pages are both organized into five divisions: Writing Well (the writing process or mechanics of building a story), Craftsmen Exercises (work with grammar), Outlet Journal (preparing and sending pieces for publication), Ideas (worksheets and a checklist for planning stories), and Favorites (favorite quotes, story ideas, fun words, examples, and more). Writing Well and the Craftsmen Exercises form the bulk of the activities.

Throughout the book, rather than tackle all types of writing, Jill focuses on story writing. However, she observes that the skills for writing an interesting story transfer readily to writing interesting essays and reports. Writing Well lessons alert students to techniques for describing setting, developing characters, outlining plots, identifying conflicts, ensuring that a story has a conclusion, and developing style. It also stresses a "Christian" approach to writing in purpose, content, and presentation.

The Craftsmen Exercises are not a primary teaching tool for grammar, but, through creative exercises, they help students understand how grammar rules apply to their actual writing.

Parents and children can actually learn to write together

through *Writing to God's Glory*. It can be used with children of all ages if we adjust the activities in keeping with the ages and abilities of the writers. (We'll skip some activities with younger children.) We can use most of the activities in whatever order we please, although, if students are tackling a complete story, they should first work through the lessons on character development, plot, etc. in the Writing Well and Ideas sections.

The teacher needs to invest time reading the first section, then looking through lessons to select those most appropriate. Once those steps are accomplished, lesson preparation time is minimal. We need to reproduce the student pages, which students should maintain in a three-ring binder, divided into the five sections reflecting the organization of the book. Lessons are presented by the teacher, then students spend varying amounts of time completing their writing assignments. Some of the activities are very brief, but if students write stories, they will obviously invest much more time.

This is an inspiring, user-friendly approach with tremendous flexibility and Godly purpose.

Writing with Results

by JoAnne Moore
(Books for Results)
$28 U.S.

Writing with Results is a fun writing resource that can be used in grades one through six, and can, in fact, be used over again from year to year, or with several students of different ages. Though clearly written with the traditional classroom in mind, this book is easily adaptable to the home setting. At only $28, it can be a real bargain, especially if you plan to use it with several students.

Perhaps the feature that will be of most interest to home schoolers is the author's distinction between writing that uses the *idyllic* imagination and writing that uses the *moral* imagination. (*Idyllic* is used here to mean stories that are simply escapist, with no clear standard of right and wrong; *moral* encourages the development of a standard of right and wrong.) Mrs. Moore encourages the moral imagination in both reading and writing, and her assignments are geared toward the moral. Many of the writing assignments are inspired by good literature. The author also easily mixes Christian and secular examples of excellent writing.

The first half of the book is devoted to writing stories, with a Three Point Outline for developing plot and a central character. The second half includes a veritable wealth of different writing assignments from newspapers and book reports to poetry and paragraphs. A simple plan for writing research reports covers outlining, note taking, and citing references. One interesting assignment practices proper style for writing letters by having the student pretend that he is a character in a book or story writing to another fictional character. Some of the step-by-step lesson plans are geared toward the traditional classroom, but they could be easily used in the home school. Worksheets to be copied are included where appropriate.

The final section of *Writing with Results* contains a grade-by-grade list of objectives for writing, and a variety of references for the teacher (spelling, punctuation, and grammar). I wouldn't worry about keeping in step with the lists, but instead would let the child's writing skills develop at his own pace. The appendices are mostly for classroom use.[Kath Courtney]

Writing Works

(Pencils Writing Resources)
$8.95

Racking your brain for interesting writing topics?*Writing Works* serves up 300 "story starters" and writing assignments, suitable for just about all ages. Some ideas are silly, some are serious.

Ideas are presented in a 4 1/2" x 6" comb-bound book. Three related ideas per page center around topics like fruit, dogs, teachers, books, self-image, cereal, and animals. The first idea is a "quick thinking activity" that might be completed in 5 to 10 minutes. The second might be considered a journal topic that might take 10 to 15 minutes. The third is a lengthier creative writing assignment that might take 20 to 60 minutes or more. These different activities might easily be assigned to various age groups in home educating families, with briefest assignments given to the youngest students and lengthiest to the oldest. This takes no advance planning to use. Pull it out in the morning, give everyone an assignment, then compare results later in the day.(S)

Resources by Grade Level
1st Grade Level

A text is not necessary and might be more of a handicap than an asset at this level. It is often better to have our children write words and sentences about things that are part of their lives and play games with letters, words, and sentences. Copying is also good for children at this age, although it is important that what they copy be uncrowded and in large print. Some children will have difficulty focusing and finding their place when either copying or writing on their own. If so, let them wait until their eyes, brain, and muscles are mature enough. Use some of the aforementioned basic resources if you need ideas for a non-academic approach.

Alpha Omega Language Arts 1

(Alpha Omega)
$85.95

Alpha Omega's Language Arts combines reading, spelling, penmanship, composition, grammar, speech, and literature although the main emphasis is on reading skills. This is a LifePac-based program. See the complete review under "Phonics Programs."

Language and Thinking for Young Children
(Mott Media)
$7.99

This book is described by the publisher as an oral language manual to be used by parents and teachers of kindergarten and primary children. Dr. Ruth Beechick is one of the authors, so those familiar with any of her other books will understand her emphasis on age-appropriate learning methods. Rather than having children begin writing in workbooks at early ages, the authors suggest ideas that encourage children to explore lan-

Writing Their Own Books

Rather than a text at this level, have your child write "books." At beginning levels, these books can be sentences dictated to the parent to accompany a child's drawings. They can be very short descriptions of photographs from a recent field trip or event. They can be a story written by the child with illustrations drawn by a parent or cut from magazines.

This idea can be used for many years with increasing levels of difficulty. As soon as children are able, they can begin to write their own story text. Keep it short and manageable. Rather than holding children accountable for perfect grammar and spelling, ask that they make sure they check for particular grammatical concepts, such as capitalization and placement of periods, that they have already mastered. The goal is to encourage writing rather than to discourage children over mechanical shortcomings. Also, there is much greater incentive to learn to write correctly when children have a personal goal and something concrete to show and share when they are finished.

Creating "blank books" for our children to write in can be a project in itself, but we have a ready-made option in the *Family Adventure Photo Books* available through Atco School Supply that are perfect for our purposes. These 8 1/2" by 7" blank books are available in different thicknesses. The covers are attractive, very-heavy paper (140-pound index) while pages are smooth, white, low-acid content, heavyweight paper (90-pound index). These sturdy books are put together with plastic comb binding. They even come with an instruction/suggestion sheet. In looking over our collection of photo books, I find that most of ours are in the 10-page range, so you might stock up on quite of few of that size and a couple of larger books. (You can add and remove pages to adjust the sizes of your books.) [prices: 10- sheet books, $1.50 each; 20-sheet books, $2.00 each; 30-sheet books, $250 each]

Children who prefer arts and crafts to writing might also enjoy the approach used in *Making Big Books with Children: Resource Book and Reproducible Patterns* (Evan-Moor) [$11.95]. Twenty full-size patterns and instructions for "shape" books are provided along with story starter suggestions for both picture and word stories. After children create their books, they write in or on them. The patterns for covers come in 2 sizes_11"x17" for big books, or 6" for mini-books. Patterns include bunny, elephant, apple, house, clown, and fifteen more. For each pattern, you get literature recommendations, extension activities such as stick puppets, and a simple story and poem which you can use to make big books for reading instruction. Ideas can easily be adapted for readers or non- readers. This book is geared to children in grades K-2. Volume 2 is similar, as is a third Seasonal volume.

How to Make Books with Children is a series of books that are similar in concept to the *Making Big Books* series, although completed books are generally smaller. (Evan-Moor) [$16.95] There are four books in the series that target grades 1-6: *Literature and Writing Connections, Read a Book-Make a Book, Holidays and Celebrations,* and *Science and Math*. These books include background information on the selected topic, recommended reading list (or a required book in *Literature and Writing Connections* or *Read a Book-Make a Book*), instructions, reproducible patterns, plus writing ideas for a wide span of skill levels. A fifth book, *Beginning Writers* is appropriate for grades K-2. It includes "cloze" forms where students fill in words and complete sentences for some of the activities, making the writing aspects easier. Some of the projects in the books for grades 1 -6 are quite complex, while those in *Beginning Writers* are much simpler. Each volume features different types of books. For example *Read a Book-Make a Book* includes lift-up books, pull-down books, pop- up books, double-hinged books, and other styles while *Holidays and Celebrations* features flap books, pull-through books, shape and flip books. The last book is broadly inclusive in its choice of holidays, so you will probably end of using only a few of the holiday ideas as presented. However, you might be able to adapt the book-making ideas to other holidays or feast days.(SE)

Creating Books with Children (Common Sense Press) [$18] is yet another option, but one written by a home schooling mom for home schooling families. Valerie Bendt, author of *How to Create Your Own Unit Study* and *The Unit Study Idea Book*, expands her creative ideas with this new book. Here she explains in thorough detail how to help our children create their own books from start to finish. She shares examples of book projects completed by children from three-years-old up through high school. The book itself is divided into six parts: pre-writing activities, writing the stories, text layout and editing, illustrating the books, developing the beginning and ending pages and the book jackets, and assembling the books. You can see that a lot of time goes into the artistic end as well as the construction of the book. The amount of time devoted to the actual writing will probably vary according to each child's interest and ability. The first two sections offer lots of help for the writing process. Valerie also recommends *Write Source 2000* for additional help in this area. The combination of examples, detailed instructions, and suggestions for stimulating creativity found in this book are a successful formula for helping children develop both writing and art skills.

guage orally and with activities. Unit topics are Stories, Vocabulary and Thinking Skills, Language Games, Memorizing, Learning About Telephones, Enjoying Poetry, Manners, and Learning on Trips. Ideas also include number and arithmetic activities. Language arts goals I have listed for first grade, with the exception of sentence writing, are covered in this book. This book is especially recommended for parents who choose to delay formal academics with their children or to be used with children who have reading difficulties in the early grades since it avoids typical academic approaches that rely heavily upon reading and writing skills.

Phonics and Reading 1

(Bob Jones University Press)
Home School Kit - approx. $190

See the review under "Bob Jones University Press Reading Program" in Chapter Nine.

Language 1

(A Beka Book)
$11.55

Language 1 is designed to be seatwork exercises for students that correlate with A Beka's phonics and handwriting resources. It is intended to be used with the Curriculum/Lesson Plans for this level, but I think that most parents can use it without them. This full-color worktext integrates grammar, spelling, handwriting, creative writing (minimally), and reading through a variety of exercises. It assumes that children are already able to read at least short vowel words at the beginning of the book, so it will be advanced for some children.

Extra busywork is included since it was written for classroom use, so do not require your child to complete every item on every page. The amount of actual writing done at the beginning of the book is minimal, gradually increasing as children progress. Some people choose A Beka *Language* books for their thorough coverage and repetition which reinforces learning. For others, this is the very thing that cause them to avoid A Beka.

Since A Beka has switched to cursive penmanship from the very beginning of their program, eliminating manuscript (printing), children are shown cursive models alongside standard print in many lessons. However, you can still use this book if your child has learned manuscript rather than cursive. A Teacher's Key is available but unnecessary.

The Shurley Method

(Shurley Instructional Materials)
kits - $70 per level

The Shurley Method is an English language arts program for grades 1 through 7 that covers grammar and composition. It does NOT cover phonics, reading, spelling, or literature. Children memorize jingles to learn some grammar basics. They learn a "question and answer flow" whereby they learn

to attack sentences by asking exact questions to determine subject, verb, direct object, etc. Workbooks carefully present sentences with particular elements, adding questions to the "question and answer flow" as sentences become more complex. The combination of visual, verbal, and written activity helps children with different learning styles. Children become proficient in identifying parts of speech and their syntax, and they also learn proper usage (e.g., verb tenses), capitalization, and punctuation. Once children have mastered enough grammar, they begin writing, constructing sentences according to "formulas"—(e.g., article, adjective, subject noun, verb, adverb). From there they go on to paragraph construction and longer compositions.

This program is highly structured. Lessons are taught with continual teacher-student interaction. Students then complete worksheets or writing assignments from their workbooks. Cassette tapes present jingles and the question and answer flows for different types of sentences. The Resource Booklet explains the methodology and offers useful teaching tips and some creative ideas.

Each grade level kit includes a teacher's manual, student workbook, resource book, and cassette tape. Extra workbooks are available for additional students. Workbooks are NOT reproducible. You can combine students within a grade level of each other since there is quite a bit of repetition from year to year. You can begin to use this program at any level—you need not go back to level 1.

New "Home School" editions are in development at this time. These new editions will have more writing, with writing instruction spread throughout the year rather than saved for the last part of the school year. New books for grades 1 - 4 might be ready for the 2000-2001 school year.(S)

Voyages in English, Book 1

(Our Lady of Victory/Lepanto Press)
$6

This consumable worktext is a reprint of the 1958 edition of the *Voyages in English* series. (See the reviews of the newer, heavily revised editions published by Loyola Press.) These "originals" are distinctively Catholic. Content is less challenging at the lower levels than in the newer editions. Little grammatical vocabulary is used. For example, in presenting plural forms they use the heading, "Words for More than One." If you are concentrating on phonics, beginning reading, and handwriting, this will give you adequate coverage of language arts for first grade. No answer key should be necessary.

Voyages in English, Grade 1, 1995 edition

(Loyola Press)
student edition - $10.25; teacher edition - $26.95

The *Voyages in English* series has been used since the 1940s, primarily in Catholic schools. The series still retains the traditional, solid coverage of grammar and composition for which it was so well known, but it has been updated in many ways. Short literary pieces are used as springboards for grammar and writing instruction in a nod to whole-language methodology. Plenty of writing practice also incorporates group and peer editing activities (which can still be used with a single student). Multicultural influences show up in some literary examples and pictorial illustrations. Although Loyola is a Catholic publishing company, there is little to no evidence of that in this series. In the first grade book, I found only a reference to a church picnic and a picture of a church used for teaching top, middle, and bottom—both totally generic. On the other hand, there are mentions of "magic witch hats" and the inclusion of fables and fantasy. Such references are not as problematic as they are in most secular texts. Throughout the series there is a subtle but pervasive use of positive character building elements through stories and practice sentences that produces a "kind and gentle" flavor.

Voyages in English focuses primarily upon grammar and composition while also including listening, speaking, literature, vocabulary, spelling, study skills, and thinking skills. Literature, vocabulary, and spelling is supplemental rather than comprehensive. The scope and sequence is a little advanced: first grade includes introductory instruction on nouns, verbs, adjectives, and pronouns. The first and second grade level programs are designed to be taught from the teacher edition. Reduced reproductions of student pages are surrounded by instructional information. Many activities are suggested here that do not appear in the student books. The teacher editions include blackline masters for letter writing, book reports, developing writing ideas, letters to parents, and other things, although none of these are indispensable. Student editions are full color, soft cover, consumable books. They include minimal writing and grammar "handbooks" plus cut-and-paste pages at the back of the first grade book. The size of the print and space for writing are appropriately large. Student editions are self-explanatory enough that parents might use these without the teacher edition, foregoing the additional instruction and activities in the teacher edition.

New 1999 editions of student books have minor structural changes, but the teacher's editions are greatly expanded with material for classroom teachers which isn't useful for homeschoolers. The 1995 editions will be less expensive, more practical choices for homeschoolers as long as they are available.

Writing, Books A-F (for approximate grade levels 1-6)

(Essential Learning Products)
$3.99

Book A

Book A assumes students have mastered basic writing skills sufficient for writing short sentences in a personal journal.

Because of this, older students (up to about ages 7 or 8) might find *Book A* to be an appropriate starting point, even though it can be used by younger students. This half-size, 96-page book helps children learn to express themselves in a variety of ways, although there is no instruction on the mechanics (sentence structure, punctuation, capitalization, etc.). It offers guided lessons—some done in this little workbook, while others are completed in a journal, on nice note paper, or in a homemade "book." Children write about themselves and their feelings, but I give the publisher extra points for avoiding the "I am wonderful" syndrome common to most such books. There are a number of imaginative writing exercises about such things as made up creatures, talking animals, jokes, riddles, and things children wonder about. (Skip pages 26-27 about writing a magic spell.) Children write plans, letters, and lists as well as observations about the weather and their surroundings. They also compose a book about themselves (using some of the material they wrote in earlier exercises) and their families. Used as a supplement, this book offers some structure for developing writing lessons for young children, although it cannot stand alone without additional instruction in mechanics. However, some parents might wish to use this as the idea book, supplying "mechanical" instruction on their own as needed. Either way, it is a very inexpensive source for writing ideas.(S)

2nd Grade Level

A text is not necessary at this level. Involving children in worthwhile language activities is better than using a textbook. One of the best activities is to have children write their own books as described above.

If you would like a text:

Daily Guided Teaching and Review for Second and Third Grades

(ISHA Enterprises)
$18.95

This book can be used as the primary teaching tool for these levels, although it can also be used as a supplement. Lessons need to be taught rather than used independently, although by third grade students might be doing a good part of the work on their own. Each daily lesson consists of four to five types of exercises which include capitalization, punctuation, alphabetizing, dictionary work, parts of speech, prefixes/roots/suffixes, synonyms, homonyms, antonyms, rhymes, and sentence combining. Rules or explanations are provided in the lessons for each topic that is likely to be new or in need of review. Answers are provided at the back of the book. The book has 180 lessons divided into parts one and two (90 lessons each). Half of the lessons (part one) can be used every other day at second grade level with the other half reserved for third grade.

Or, the entire book can be used in one year with one lesson per day. All principal parts of speech up through interjections and conjunctions are introduced in part one (a very brief introduction of each of the more difficult parts of speech), so consider this when deciding at what level to use it.

English for Christian Schools 2 [Writing and Grammar]

(Bob Jones University Press)
home school kit - $47; worktext - $11.65; teacher's edition - $39

The student worktext and teacher's edition are both needed for a complete program. Second grade covers nouns, verbs, and adjectives at an introductory level. This early introduction of parts of speech may be premature for some children, and we might wish to skip those lessons. The course includes some composition work and organizes instruction around the theme of a missionary family in Grenada.

English for the Thoughtful Child: A First Course

(Greenleaf Press)
$18.95

Cyndy Shearer's search for language arts materials reflecting Charlotte Mason's ideas led her to a book written in 1903 by Mary Hyde. Cyndy updated and revised the book, making it available to home educators. The book assumes that a child has developed basic writing (or printing) skills and is ready to compose sentences. Instead of endless workbook pages, there is a mixture of oral composition (or narration), memorization, written composition, and language exercises. Interesting old pictures are used as prompts for discussion, narration, and writing. Basic grammar skills necessary for writing—complete sentences, types of sentences, capitalization, and punctuation—are taught. Literary excerpts used throughout the book are from fables, mythology, and poetry. The single volume has teaching instructions in small print and student material is written in very large print. While students could do some of the exercises in the book, we might want to have them work in a separate notebook. (Families can reproduce pages for their children rather than buying separate books for each child.) English for the Thoughtful Child is a low-pressure, yet effective introduction to language arts.

You might also use some of this book with a first grader who is reading well. A good follow-up to this book is *Simply Grammar* by Karen Andreola.

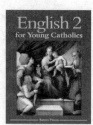

English for Young Catholics 2

(Seton Press)
$13

Using a very traditional approach to teaching English, Seton is developing this thoroughly-Catholic series of worktexts. Books for grades 1-4, 6 and 8 are available thus far. In this second grade book, a variety of exercises are used to teach alphabetizing, types of sentences, nouns, verbs, adverbs, pronouns, and adjectives. Among other skills covered are diagramming (introduced at the end of the book), contractions, letter writing, and story writing. Focus is primarily on grammar rather than composition. I have concerns that some lessons expect students to move too quickly from beginning skills to advanced. For example, students choose among a group of sentences the best one to complete a paragraph, then, in the next lesson, write their own stories. The book has some black-and-white illustrations and some spot color, and it comes with an answer key. A revised edition of this book is due out Summer of 2000.

Grammar, Practice Books A-F

(Essential Learning Products)
$3.99 each

Book A in this series is appropriate for students at about second grade level. It provides practice with nouns, verbs, sentences, capitalization, and punctuation. This half-size workbook is good for those who want to keep grammar instruction to a less intensive level than is found in most other resources. It can also be used as a supplement to another curriculum for children who need more practice. I can foresee it being used along with one of the *Learning Language Arts Through Literature* books, *Wisdom Words*, or *Understanding Writing* for independent student practice, since it provides a small amount of reinforcement for lessons that can be used as needed. Answer keys are in the back of each book. The lengths of the books range from 96 to 112 pages.(S)

Language 2

(A Beka Book)
$11.55

This full-color worktext thoroughly covers advanced second grade level concepts with plenty of reinforcement practice. This is a seatwork book which requires little or no lesson preparation. However, parents will need to work with most second graders to expand upon concepts covered in this seatwork book and instruct them as to how to complete the exercises. The level of work is more difficult than some other second grade programs, and it does require quite a bit of writing. Some parents might choose *Language 1* for a second grader who is not advanced. *Language 2* covers capitalization, end-of-sentence punctuation, complete sentences, suffixes and pre-fixes, compound words, rhyming words, antonyms, synonyms, plurals, possessives, contractions, alphabetizing, and creative writing. The teacher key has answers overprinted on student pages. You should not need the teacher key, but should be able to figure out answers well enough from just the student text.

Extra busywork is included since it was written for class-room use, so do not require your child to complete every item on every page. Some people choose A Beka *Language* books for their thorough coverage and repetition which reinforces learning. For others, this is the very thing that cause them to avoid A Beka. A Teacher's Key is available but unnecessary.

Learning Language Arts Through Literature, The Red Book package
(Common Sense Press)
$85

The 1998 version of this program reflects the same signifi-cant improvements we find in all the latest editions in this series. It is more comprehensive and easier to use than the first edition, although it retains much of the original material and ideas that made the first edition a good product.

The program comes in a boxed set containing the teacher manual, student activity book, and six readers. It is organized into 36 lessons, each of which takes about five days to com-plete, providing a solid year's worth of instruction geared toward second grade level students.

This comprehensive language arts curriculum is based upon Ruth Beechick's ideas about how to best teach young children. It incorporates a great deal of literature throughout the lessons, frequently using literature as the springboard into grammar, writing, spelling, and other language arts learning. The litera-ture serves to motivate greater interest in both the lessons and the books themselves. The student activity books incorporate great variety into learning activities, and this helps stimulate and maintain students' interest. A student book is included in the package, but extras are available for $25 each.

The program was designed for home educators and provides plenty of detailed instruction on lesson presentation. Minimal lesson preparation is required, but lessons do need to be pre-sented by the parent/teacher. While lessons are multi-sensory and interactive, students will occasionally work on assign-ments in the student activity book on their own.

Six illustrated readers come with the program, but you will also need to borrow or purchase eleven additional children's books for a number of lessons.

Phonics is reviewed at this level, but instruction also covers beginning composition skills, handwriting (printing), gram-mar, reading comprehension, spelling, critical thinking, and beginning research and study skills. A skills index at the back of the teacher's book shows which skills are covered in which lessons. If a child has already mastered phonics, you might skip those parts of the lessons and focus on new material instead.

Periodic assessments help parents/teachers determine how well their students are progressing.

The books are written by Christians and reflect Christian attitudes, but religious perspectives are not dealt with in most lessons. A few excerpts from the Bible are used for reading.

Printing instruction is a bit strange. Students are asked to write full sentences from the very first lesson in the book, how-ever, lesson five requires students to trace and print letters and two-letter words. In addition, the style of letter presented for tracing and emulation is more like calligraphy than ball-and-stick or slant-print , but it is presented without explanation. I find this confusing and suggest using another tool for teaching handwriting, either manuscript or cursive.

One other minor complaint: bingo charts and flip books that are to be cut out and put together need to have cutting lines clearly marked as well as some explanation of how flip books are to be put together.

The Red Book provides a great alternative to traditional workbooks and programs that isolate subjects and skills. It should be fairly easy for even beginning homeschoolers to use.

The Shurley Method
(Shurley Instructional Materials)
kits - $65 per level
See review under "1st Grade Level."

Voyages in English, Book 2
(Our Lady of Victory/Lepanto Press)
$8

Book 2 for second grade is similar in format to Book 1. Again, content is less challenging than most other language programs for the early grades, but it should be adequate. No answer key should be necessary.

Voyages in English, Grade 2
(Loyola Press)
student edition - $10.25; teacher edition - $26.95

See the complete review under "1st Grade Level." Second grade level adds adverbs to the parts of speech to be studied, and it continues work on prefixes, suffixes, contractions, sub-ject-verb agreement, and other grammatical concepts. Writing activities include friendly letters, "how-to" paragraphs, and very short reports. The only Catholic reference I found here was the inclusion of abbreviations for Father and Sister as forms of address. While some fantasy appears in the literature, I found nothing objectionable. As with the first grade program, the teacher edition is intended to be the source of instruction, but the student books can be used on their own for less thor-ough and comprehensive coverage.

Composition and Grammar

Writing, Books A-F (for approximate grade levels 1-6)

(Essential Learning Products)

$3.99

Book B

Book B carries on in the same vein as Book A, although the exercises encourage children to use larger writing vocabularies and better-developed ideas. Two significant additions are writing plays—one for sock-puppets and another for people, stuffed animals, dolls, or other types of players. I am skeptical about the ability of most seven-year-olds to stick with this lengthy a project. However, many young children can successfully tackle such a project with lots of help from parents or older siblings, so I suggest using the plays for family projects. Although designated for second grade level, this book might also suit older students. (There are no "spells" or other objectionable content in Book B.)

3rd Grade Level, Complete Programs

(Note: Children's abilities vary dramatically at this stage, and many profit more from actual writing experience as described above under "Writing Their Own Books" than from workbooks.

Building Christian English 3, Beginning Wisely

(Rod and Staff)

student book - $11.40; teacher's manual - $14.25; worksheets - $2.90; tests - $1.90

This hardback text is excellent for those who prefer a formal academic approach, although it is not exciting. Scriptural content as well as frequent references to farm life also serve to differentiate this program's content from most others. Lessons require teacher involvement and allow for some independent work. At this level it introduces nouns, pronouns, verbs, adjectives, and adverbs as well as noun usage as subject or direct object. Diagramming is taught along with each part of speech. (This reflects a scope and sequence advanced beyond others I have reviewed.) Dictionary work, capitalization, punctuation, and oral communication are also taught at this level. It includes extra busywork for classroom purposes, so it is not necessary for children to do all exercises. Both oral and written exercises are included within each lesson. The amount of writing might be too much for some third graders, in which case more exercises can be done orally. Original composition work is included, but there is a very minimal amount in comparison to written exercises. Oral reviews and written quizzes are provided in the teacher's manual; there are also an accompanying set of worksheets and a test booklet. However, the teacher's manual states that the worksheets, oral reviews, and written quizzes are not required for the course. Children do not write in the textbook, so it can be reused. The teacher's manual

includes teaching instructions plus answers to student exercises, but students can complete much of the work independently.

English for Christian Schools 3 (Writing and Grammar)

(Bob Jones University Press)

home school kit - $47; worktext - $11.65; teacher's edition - $39

The student worktext and Teacher's Edition are both needed for a complete program; both are included in the home school kit. This level reviews nouns and verbs and adds study of pronouns, antonyms, synonyms, homonyms, verb usage, and composition skills. Music for some grammar songs is in the teacher's edition. Much of the lesson presentation in the teacher's edition is geared for classroom use, but there are some essential items found there such as the correlation of lessons and exercise pages. There are 135 lessons that would take from 30 to 60 minutes of classroom time but which take much less time in the home setting. A farm theme is woven throughout the lessons, but we can choose how much attention we devote to developing the theme. Students worktexts are consumable while the Teacher's Editions are not.

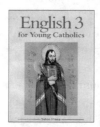

English for Young Catholics 3

(Seton Press)

$13

This is the third grade level book in this Catholic English series. Very traditional in its approach, it is presented in a worktext format. This level presents more instruction on composition than does the second grade book, especially as it works on paragraph development. Using a variety of exercises, it reviews and expands coverage of nouns, verbs, pronouns, adjectives, adverbs, punctuation, capitalization, library/dictionary skills, and sentence diagramming. As in the earlier book, diagramming is presented in lessons at the end of the book. Illustrations are mostly black-and-white, mainly of saints and religious events in keeping with the thoroughly Catholic content of the book. (The content is actually so strong an education in Catholic history and thought that it might seem more important than the English skills being taught!) An answer key comes with the book.

English 3 [E115]

(Landmark's Freedom Baptist Curriculum)

$35

This complete course covers grammar, composition, and spelling skills in a traditional worktext format, somewhat similar to A Beka's, although in a less intensive manner. Included are the student studyguide, quizzes, and answer keys for both. Among topics covered at this level are sentences, capitalization, punctuation, nouns, pronouns, verbs, adjectives, subjects, predicates, contractions, homonyms, dictionary use, and composition of letters and short "essays." Spelling is taught via separate lessons for each week found at the back of the studyguide. Students are held accountable in their compositions for only those skills and spelling words they have already learned. Many of the lessons will take little time to complete, but the occasional lengthier writing assignments and compositions will probably require much more time. Students should be able to complete most of their lessons independently, but at this grade level they will still need some teaching assistance. Also, parents will need to evaluate writing assignments.

Language Arts 300
(Alpha Omega)
$42.95 for complete set

Alpha Omega LifePac curriculum for language arts combines reading, grammar, handwriting, composition, and spelling with strong Scriptural content. Grammar covers nouns through adverbs and adjectives. There is enough handwriting practice, but we need to supplement with more reading material. This is a more formal approach that better suits Perfect Paulas and Competent Carls than Wiggly Willys and Sociable Sues. The complete set includes ten LifePacs and a complete Teacher's Guide.

Language 3
(A Beka Book)
$11.95; teacher edition - $22.80; curriculum - $29.95

This consumable, full-color student worktext includes sentence construction, word usage, composition skills, punctuation, suffixes and prefixes, dictionary skills, contractions, and beginning diagramming. Children learn about nouns, verbs, adjectives, and articles. There are more than enough practice exercises, so students need not do every one. It is possible to work only from the student worktext, but you should probably also purchase the Teacher Edition. The Teacher Edition has student pages overprinted with correct answers, explains how the program is to be used, and provides the first ten daily lesson plans from the *Language Arts 3 Curriculum*. This gives you the opportunity to see how useful the Curriculum might be to you before purchasing it. The *Language Arts 3 Curriculum* includes 172 daily lesson plans, suggestions for oral and written review and practice, ideas for creative writing and journal entries, instructions for book reports, and bulletin board ideas. It was written for classroom teachers, so some of it will not apply to home schools.

A Beka is very comprehensive in grammatical instruction. The 1996 edition of *Language 3* improves composition instruction and practice over earlier editions. Some of that instruction comes from the separate Curriculum book, but the assignments in the student book and blank journal pages at the end of the book (for weekly entries) both demonstrate a greater attention to composition than in the past. A "Handbook of Rules and Definitions" towards the end of the student book is handy for reference.

Learning Language Arts Through Literature, Yellow Book
(The Common Sense Press)
student book - $20; teacher book - $25

The new editions of *Learning Language Arts Through Literature* have been significantly expanded and rewritten to make them more thorough, easier-to-use, and more age-appropriate. Written for third grade level, but adaptable for a little wider age span, the *Yellow Book* should take one school year to complete. A Skills Index at the back of the Teacher Book shows which skills are covered on which pages. The broad range of language arts skills are covered: grammar, composition, cursive handwriting, spelling, listening, oral presentation, dictionary skills, and more, plus critical thinking.

Following recommendations by Dr. Ruth Beechick, models from good literature are used as springboards for developing other skills. Students copy, and sometimes take by dictation, short passages from prose and poetry. Parts of the ensuing lesson refer back to the passage (e.g., identify personal pronouns in the passage). Grammar, spelling, handwriting, and other skills all receive extensive attention.

Four "Literature Link" units interspersed throughout the book offer two options: read the recommended book and work with questions and activities that refer to the book, or read the lengthy alternate passage included within the text and use the appropriate questions. The four recommended books for these units are *The White Stallion, Madeline, Meet George Washington,* and *The Courage of Sarah Noble.*

Extra enrichment activities found in the Student Activity Book (e.g., word puzzles, projects, critical thinking and grammar activities, analogies) can be used for challenge or enrichment. Lessons feature a great deal of variety. Unlike the earlier edition, the new edition Student Activity Book is essential since it contains numerous workbook type assignments, periodic reviews and assessments, and some pages that need to be cut out for some activities. The new edition remedies an earlier-edition weakness by providing more composition and grammar activity. Lesson preparation time is minimal, and answers are in the Teacher Book. While the book is obviously Christian, it is less obvious than in some other books in this series.

Literature and Creative Writing PACE course
(School of Tomorrow)
$51.20

See the review of the fourth grade level course. This second grade level course incorporates one-page stories. The focus is upon developing beginning writing skills, and it also includes handwriting practice and development of reading fluency. This course includes 12 PACEs and 4 keys. Additional grade levels are being developed for this series each year.

Voyages in English, Book 3
(Our Lady of Victory/Lepanto Press)
student text - $10; teacher's manual - $6; exercise book - $9; key to exercises - $2

This is part of the "original" *Voyages in English* series reprinted by Lepanto Press. (Do not confuse these with the new Loyola Press series of the same title.) The preface of one of the books in this series says, "The child growth that is sought in *Voyages in English* is growth toward a Christian adulthood that is truly cultured, that accepts social service as a sacred duty, and that can render social service the better because it has been taught to think clearly and to express itself clearly." These are the sentiments that produced one of the most effective language art series ever used in Catholic schools.

These books are distinctively Catholic. Character building is embedded throughout the books. Content is broader and more challenging than newer books as you move past the early grade levels. A variety of exercises accompany each lesson in the text. Many of these exercises should be done orally, but some must be copied from the book. Optional, Exercise Workbooks are consumable. (Answer keys to Exercise Workbooks are available.) The Exercise Workbooks might be used in place of some of the exercises within the text (especially for students who have much difficulty with writing), or both might be used for students who need a great deal of practice and reinforcement. On the other hand, you might find that text exercises are adequate without additional workbook activities. The second half of each text focuses on grammar, while the first half covers the range of other English activities.

Teacher's manuals include some instructional information, but they serve primarily as answer keys. The Book 3 text for third grade and succeeding levels are all printed as hard cover books, but Exercise Workbooks are consumable.

Voyages in English, Grade 3
(Loyola Press)
student edition - $18.95; teacher edition - $22.95; *Exercises in English* workbook - $7.95; teacher edition for *Exercises* - $8.95

The *Voyages in English* series has been used since the 1940s, primarily in Catholic schools. The series still retains the traditional, solid coverage of grammar and composition for which it was so well known, but it has been updated in many ways. Poems and short literary pieces are used as springboards for grammar and writing instruction in a nod to whole-language methodology. (Some sources for literary excerpts are

Charlotte's Web, Encyclopedia Brown, The Phantom Tollbooth, and *A Wrinkle in Time.*) Composition skills are emphasized with plenty of instruction and numerous writing assignments. Multicultural influences show up in some literary examples and pictorial illustrations. Although Loyola is a Catholic publishing company, there is no evidence of that in the third grade book. Some fables and fantasy are used but in ways that will not be objectionable unless you object to the genres themselves.

Voyages in English focuses primarily upon grammar and composition while also including listening, speaking, literature, vocabulary, study skills, and thinking skills. Literature and vocabulary are supplemental rather than comprehensive. The scope and sequence is a little advanced: students begin sentence diagramming with nouns, verbs, adjectives, adverbs, and pronouns in third grade. Writing activities are more challenging than in most other language programs.

The program for grades 3-8 uses a different format than does the program for the first two grades. Hardcover student textbooks and teacher editions are necessary for the complete program for these levels. The text is divided into two parts: composition and grammar. The teacher is expected to move back and forth between these two sections, incorporating grammar lessons in whatever order she wishes. This might be challenging to some teachers and parents, but, if in doubt about how to do it, try alternating lessons from each section. Lessons are designed to be presented by the teacher rather than for independent work. The teacher edition is essential, since some activities are intended for oral work rather than written, and this is indicated only in the teacher edition. In addition, listening activities require the teacher to read from the teacher edition, then students answer questions which appear in their student text. The teacher edition is an enlarged student text with the extra margin space used for teaching information and answers. Texts are printed in full color with appealing illustrations.

Exercises in English workbooks offer extra work on grammar skills and are supplemental. These are printed in two colors with few illustrations. These are most useful for students who need additional practice or for those who have trouble copying grammar exercises from the *Voyages in English* text. The teacher edition of *Exercises in English* is a reproduction of the student book with answers overprinted. Students can use the *Exercises* book for independent work.

New 1999 editions of student books have minor structural changes, but the teacher's editions are greatly expanded with material for classroom teachers which isn't useful for homeschoolers. The 1995 editions will be less expensive, more practical choices for homeschoolers as long as they are available.

Wisdom Words
(The Weaver)
See description under "Ungraded Resources for All Levels"

earlier in this chapter. This is not a textbook but a manual for the teacher.

Grammar or Composition Extras for 3rd Grade

NOTE: See "Writing Their Own Books" earlier in this chapter.

Daily Grams: Guided Review Aiding Mastery Skills for 3rd and 4th Grades

(ISHA Enterprises)

$18.95

This grammar review book is from the publisher of *Easy Grammar*. One page for each day is used to reinforce grammar skills. Each page has exercises in capitalization, punctuation, general review, and sentence combining. Answers are at the back of the book. Books are progressively more difficult. Students should have already been instructed in basic grammar before beginning Daily Grams, although *Daily Guided Teaching and Review for Second and Third Grades* (ISHA Enterprises) can provide basic instruction if that has not yet been covered.

Daily Writing

(GROW Publications)

$23.95 per level

Daily Writing manuals are available for grades 1 through 6 (grades 7 and 8 due summer, 2000), although I think that you probably won't need this sort of reinforcement until at least third grade. *Daily Writing* activities are intended to be used as supplements, possibly to use at the beginning of language arts "class" time. Rather than a primary teaching tool, they are intended to be used for practice, reinforcement, and application. Activities cover six general areas: writing process, "author's craft," mechanics, parts of speech, grammar and usage, and sentence structure. These are brief activities that should take no more than five to ten minutes a day. In the book, they are arranged three to an 8 1/2" by 11" page. While GROW offers other classroom styled options, you will probably want to purchase the manual with blackline masters. You can reproduce the pages and cut them apart or not as you wish. Teacher's instructions and answers (when appropriate) are on facing pages. There are 144 activities per book, except for Grade 1 which has only 129. Most grammatical activities in *Daily Writing* seem to be at lower levels than our children encounter if they are using A Beka, BJUP, Alpha Omega, or most of the other publishers popular in the home school market. Composition activities in *Daily Writing* are as challenging or more so than in those same programs. You might want to choose a level higher than the grade level of your language arts program as long as you have been developing you child's composition skills.(S)

Easy Grammar Grades 3 and 4

Easy Grammar: Grades 3 and 4

(ISHA Enterprises)

$24.95; workbook - $13.95

This is the first level of the *Easy Grammar* series. Concepts are introduced on a basic level. Using ISHA's highly effective "prepositional" approach (see review of *Easy Grammar Plus*), this text introduces only 28 prepositions. Simple explanations and practice exercises help students grasp the basic parts of speech and their functions within sentences. Unit reviews, unit tests, cumulative reviews, and cumulative tests help students retain previously taught concepts. This level covers most of the same concepts we find in upper levels—even interjections and conjunctions are introduced, but lessons are on a simpler level with less print per page in a larger typeface.

Grammar from the Ground Up

(Grammatica Press)

See the review under fourth grade.

Grammar, Practice Books A-F

(Essential Learning Products)

$3.99 each

Book B is appropriate for third grade level. See the description under second grade. Topics in this book are sentences, verbs, nouns, subjects and predicates, pronouns, capitalization, punctuation, and letter writing.

Practice Exercises in Basic English C

(Continental Press)

$5.95; teacher's guide - $2.75

This inexpensive workbook covers basic skills more briefly than others. Use with a writing supplement from the list below. Short narratives are often used to develop language exercises—a more interesting approach than fill-in-the-blanks grammar. This requires less formal academic work than other choices for this level.(S)

The Shurley Method

(Shurley Instructional Materials)

kits - $65 per level

See review under "1st Grade Level."

Sing, Spell, Read, and Write, Level 3: Grammar Plus Kit

(International Learning Systems of North America, Inc.)

$35.50

The third level of *Sing, Spell, Read, and Write* is called the *Grammar Plus Kit*, accurately reflecting the shift to grammar and spelling that occurs once children have mastered basic reading skills. The kit includes two student workbooks, *Trophy Book I* and *Trophy Book II*; a teacher's manual that is essentially an answer key to the student books; and a cassette tape of two songs. Topics covered in the kit are alphabetizing, sentence structure, types of sentences, capitalization, punctuation, word usage, parts of speech, introductions, writing letters, writing stories, practical reading skills (reading for information), and spelling. Lessons do not flow in a natural progression of development but cover each skill, then move on to the next, with spelling being the exception. I suggest using the lessons in whatever order seems most appropriate for each student; e.g., begin introducing nouns and verbs, then come back to other parts of speech later, or follow punctuation lessons with a story writing activity for application practice. Spelling words are drawn from previous *Sing, Spell, Read, and Write* lessons, the 1000 most frequently spoken English words, and the 100 most difficult-to-spell English words. Words are presented in alphabetical order with "a" words in the first lesson and "z" words in the last. This means there is no graduation in difficulty from the first lesson to the last. Some of the words might be difficult for young learners (e.g., sergeant, particularly, spaghetti) so use the lists and words with this in mind. These words actually serve as a "mastery level" checkup for the first two levels of *Sing, Spell, Read, and Write*. Lessons are, for the most part, self-contained within the workbooks. Instructions are at the top of each page. Spelling lessons need some teacher presentation. The audio cassette features two songs, one on parts of speech and the other on prepositions. These are helpful tools, especially for auditory learners. Consider the grammar lessons as introductions rather than as comprehensive coverage. The writing lessons do instruct students in letter writing, but they do little in the way of teaching composition skills. You might think of these workbooks as a scaled-down version of the traditional grammar workbook approach to language; however, lessons are less overwhelming and are assisted by the audio tape.

Writing, Books A-F (for approximate grade levels 1-6)

(Essential Learning Products)
$3.99
Book C

Book C encourages children to maintain a journal using methods similar to lower level books. It then adds letters-to-the-editor and other letter writing ideas, informational signs, factual writing (describing things, explaining, narrating events, and reasoning), more work on writing poems and stories, writing television commercials, and newspaper writing. As befits the increasing attention span length of eight- and nine-year-olds, these are often multi-part exercises which carry over for a number of lessons. Although designated for third grade level, ideas are useful up through about fifth. (No content problems here.)(S)

Complete Programs

Building Christian English 4, Building with Diligence

(Rod and Staff)
student book - $14.15; teacher's manual - $18.85; worksheets - $2.90; tests -$1.90

This hardback text for fourth grade offers a solid, traditional approach to grammar, writing, listening, and speaking. The grade four text includes all basic parts of speech except interjections, along with diagramming. This is an earlier introduction of those topics than is found in most other curricula. Original composition writing is included, but it teaches within limited patterns reflecting Rod and Staff's educational philosophy. Emphasis is on organization and clear writing rather than upon creativity. Rod and Staff's books are printed in black and white with simple drawings so they are not as visually appealing as many others. Some of the examples and writing assignments reflect Mennonite life so strongly that non-Mennonite children may have trouble relating to them. Lessons are designed to be presented by the teacher from the teacher's manual, although most work in the student text is done independently. There is a great deal of written work within the textbook, so it is unnecessary to purchase the extra worksheets. There is also an accompanying test booklet; answers are found in the teacher edition.

English for Christian Schools 4 [Writing and Grammar]

(Bob Jones University Press)
home school kit - $47; worktext - $11.65; teacher's edition - $39

The student worktext reviews grammar and emphasizes composition skills. The teacher's edition contains some basic instruction and includes extras such as music for grammar songs. The teacher's edition also includes suggested reading and resource materials for expanding the course's theme of "Forest and Forest Products." It introduces the steps for investigating a report topic and gives five alternatives to the traditional book report. Both worktext and teacher's edition are included in the home school kit.

English for Young Catholics 4

(Seton Press)
$13

See the review of the third grade level book in this series. The format is similar, with content more advanced in difficulty.

God's Gift of Language A

(A Beka Book)

$12.40; teacher's edition - $22.80; test book - $4.20; test key - $8.95

All eight parts of speech are taught along with traditional diagramming. Composition skills, word usage, report and letter writing, dictionary and encyclopedia skills are also covered. The student book is in worktext format and can be used without the *Grade 4 Language Arts Curriculum*. The book is 296 pages and provides comprehensive coverage. The teacher's edition serves as an answer key. A test booklet is also available.

Language Arts 400

(Alpha Omega)

$42.95 for complete set

Alpha Omega's LifePac Language Arts curriculum combines reading, grammar, handwriting, composition, and spelling. Most work is done within the LifePacs, but be sure to use the writing assignments found in the Teacher's Guide. You should supplement with additional reading material. The complete set includes ten LifePacs and a Teacher's Guide.

Learning Language Arts Through Literature, Orange Book

(The Common Sense Press)

student activity book - $20; teacher book - $25

The new editions of *Learning Language Arts Through Literature* have been significantly expanded and rewritten to make them more thorough, easier-to-use, and more age-appropriate. The *Orange Book* targets fourth-grade-level skills. A Skills Index at the back of the book shows which skills are covered on which pages. The broad range of language arts skills are covered: grammar, composition, spelling, listening, speech, dictionary skills, etc.

Four books are used as literature sources for lesson material: *The Boxcar Children, Wilbur and Orville Wright, Benjamin Franklin*, and *The Sign of the Beaver*. A Book Study of each is followed by additional lessons that integrate literature, vocabulary, grammar, spelling, and composition skills. Read each book at the beginning or as you progress through the lessons. Periodically, students copy short literary excerpts or write them from dictation, depending on their abilities. Units on research, journal writing, poetry, newspaper writing, and story writing/book making are interspersed between the book studies. There are 32 lessons which might take from one to two weeks each to complete. Extra enrichment activities found in the Student Activity Book (e.g., word puzzles, projects, logic activities, analogies) can be used for challenge or enrichment. Lessons feature a great deal of variety. Unlike the earlier edition, the new edition Student Activity Book is essential since it contains numerous workbook type assignments as well as some cut-and-paste activities. The new edition remedies an earlier-edition weakness by requiring more composition and grammar activity. Lesson preparation time is minimal, and an answer key is in the Teacher Book.

Literature and Creative Writing PACE course

(School of Tomorrow)

$51.20

Twelve PACEs (numbers 1037-1048) present this new fourth-grade level course from School of Tomorrow. Structured similarly to their other courses, it includes six books to enhance the literature component: *Choice Stories for Children, Charlotte's Web, Saved at Sea, Children's Missionary Library, The Red Rag Riddle*, and *The Little Green Frog*. These books coupled with the PACE content produces a thoroughly Christian course that stresses godly character development. Another significant feature is the inclusion of lessons for sequential development of composition skills. Children do some copying, a useful way to build familiarity with sentence structure. They also learn to write sentences with proper capitalization and punctuation, then combine sentences into paragraphs. The number of writing assignments is limited, but the progressive development leads children through such activities as writing a new ending for a story, writing a letter, writing an invitation, and writing a full page "sketch." Spelling, handwriting, and vocabulary might be covered adequately for some students within this course. Others might need more targeted practice in those areas. This course comes with four answer keys. Additional grade levels of *Literature and Creative Writing* are being developed each year.

Voyages in English, Book 4

(Our Lady of Victory/Lepanto Press)

student text - $10; teacher's manual - $7; exercises workbook - $11; key to exercises - $3

See the review of Book 3.

Voyages in English, Grade 4

(Loyola Press)

student edition - $18.95; teacher edition - $22.95; *Exercises in English* workbook - $7.95; teacher edition for *Exercises* - $8.95

See the review under "3rd Grade Level." Fourth grade expands into story writing (plot, characters, etc.), outlines, short reports, more challenging oral presentations, and more challenging grammar concepts.

Wisdom Words

(The Weaver)

See description under "Ungraded Resources for All Levels" earlier in this chapter. This is not a textbook but a manual for the teacher.

Alternatives or Extras, 4th Grade Grammar

Daily Writing
(GROW Publications)
$25 per level
    See the description under "Extras for Third Grade."

Easy Grammar Grades 3 and 4
(ISHA Enterprises)
$24.95; workbook - $13.95
    See the review under "Grammar or Composition Extras for 3rd Grade."

Easy Grammar: Grades 4 and 5
by Wanda Phillips
(ISHA Enterprises)
$24.95; student workbook - $13.95
    This volume includes teacher helps, a thorough presentation that's easy to understand, and cumulative review that helps students retain what they've learned. You can use the primary 520+ page volume to teach any number of children, photocopying student pages for them to use. If you wish, you can purchase student workbooks so that you don't need to copy pages for them. Answers and teaching instructions are in the main book which is essential. It covers all eight parts of speech, punctuation, capitalization, and letter writing. Some advanced concepts within these areas as well as a few other topics are covered in *Easy Grammar Grades 5 and 6* and *Easy Grammar Plus*. This volume begins with prepositions (only 40 at this level as compared to 53 at higher levels) as do the other *Easy Grammar* books. By first learning to recognize prepositions and prepositional phrases, identification of other parts of speech is much simpler. Wanda has included more teaching tips here than in any other of her books. She outlines how we should use this book at the very beginning. She strongly recommends that we teach grammatical concepts in order since the book includes cumulative review of previously covered topics. The exceptions would be punctuation, capitalization, and letter writing which can be taught whenever we choose. In contrast to A Beka's Language series, sentences are fairly short which makes identification exercises easier. Also, there are far fewer exercises per lesson than we find in A Beka. Nevertheless, coverage is more than adequate considering that students will be reviewing and relearning most of this material again in another *Easy Grammar* book or another program. If you want additional practice, consider supplementing with ISHA's *Daily Grams*. Use *Daily Grams Grades 3 and 4* for students with minimal grammar background or *Daily Grams Grades 4 and 5* for those who have already learned the basics. If you are new to *Easy Grammar*, note that instead of dia-gramming, students use underlining, circling, and letter abbreviations to identify sentence components.

Daily Grams: Guided Review Aiding Mastery Skills for 3rd and 4th Grades and Daily Grams: Guided Review Aiding Mastery Skills for 4th and 5th Grades
(ISHA Enterprises)
$18.95 each
    These grammar review books are from the publisher of *Easy Grammar*. One page for each day is used to reinforce grammar skills. Each page has exercises in capitalization, punctuation, general review, and sentence combining. Answers are contained at the back of the book. Books are progressively more difficult. Students should have already been instructed in basic grammar before beginning either of these levels of *Daily Grams*. *Daily Guided Teaching and Review for Second and Third Grades* or another source for grammar basics should have already been completed, and *Easy Grammar: Grades 4 and 5* (ISHA Enterprises) might be used concurrently if not already completed. Consider using *Easy Grammar: Grades 4 and 5* in fourth grade, then concentrating on composition skills in fifth grade while using *Daily Grams for 4th and 5th Grades* for grammar review.

Grammar, Practice Books A-F
(Essential Learning Products)
$3.99 each
    See description under second grade. Book C is appropriate for fourth grade, although other books might also be useful, depending on what your child has already learned. Topics in Book C are sentences, subjects and predicates, nouns, pronouns, verbs, adjectives, adverbs, capitalization, punctuation, and proofreading.(S)

Practice Exercises in Basic English D
(Continental Press)
$5.95; teacher's guide - $2.75
    This inexpensive, small workbook works well with *Winston Grammar* or other resources that concentrate on parts of speech. *Practice Exercises* covers the rest of English grammar. Use other resources for composition work..(S)

The Shurley Method
(Shurley Instructional Materials)
kits - $65 per level
    See review under "1st Grade Level."

Writing
See "Writing Their Own Books" above

Writer's Express Handbook
(Great Source)
$12.50

This handbook follows the same format as *Write Source 2000*, but it is designed for students at fourth and fifth grade levels. See the review of *Write Source* under sixth grade for more information.(S)

Writing, Books A-F (for approximate grade levels 1-6)
(Essential Learning Products)
$3.99
Book D

Journal writing is the introductory lesson, followed by extended activities for developing journaling skills. Letter writing exercises are especially useful because they include prompting questions or topics (although these naturally reflect the interests and activities of non-Christians). An example of one of their useful suggestions when writing to an older person is, "...you might tell about a problem you have and ask for advice." Organizing activities such as writing lists and creating and maintaining a "recommended books" card file are helpful. A lengthy section of exercises on evaluating, then writing television commercials is actually quite useful for developing both writing and thinking skills, but it will present obvious problems for TV-less families. The same problem crops up in the next section where students write a TV show then turn it into a play. The last project is writing a "best seller" story. Excellent step-by-step instructions walk students through development of plot, setting, characters, organization, and book-binding the final product. There are good ideas here to use with students up into the junior high years.(S)

5th Grade Level

Basic Texts

Building Christian English 5, Following the Plan
(Rod and Staff)
student - $14.55; teacher edition - $19.40; worksheets - $2.70; tests - $1.90

This comprehensive text covers the eight basic parts of speech, writing skills, speaking and listening. The *Building Christian English* series covers grammar more quickly and thoroughly than others. Students do written work in a separate notebook of their own, so textbooks are usable with more than one child. Optional workbooks offer supplementary practice. If you are looking for thorough coverage and are selective about the busywork, this is a good choice.

English for Christian Schools 5 [Writing and Grammar]
(Bob Jones University Press)
home school kit - $47; worktext - $11.65; teacher's edition - $39; Listening Skills cassette - $11

This is a worktext with a good balance of grammar and writing skills, although the presentation is unexciting. It includes lessons in paragraph development and writing to persuade, and it presents a series of lessons on writing a piece of fiction. Students also learn "...note taking, outlining, and paragraph development for use in writing a short report at the end of the year." Listening lessons include instruction in note taking and feature an audio tape with three sermons (purchased separately) for children as practice material. The teacher's edition is necessary for a complete program. Both worktext and teacher's edition are included in the home school kit.

God's Gift of Language B
(A Beka Book)
$12.40; teacher's edition - $22.80; test book - $4.20; test key - $8.95

Both writing and grammar skills receive comprehensive coverage in this edition. Writing instruction covers topic sentences, paragraphs, and transitions. Outlining, taking notes, and preparing bibliographies are also taught in the context of report writing. Capitalization, punctuation, and parts of speech are reviewed. The text also introduces complements and teaches diagramming, adding diagramming of prepositional phrases to reviewed concepts. The teacher's edition serves as an answer key. A test booklet is also available.

Language Arts 500
(Alpha Omega)
$42.95 for complete set

Alpha Omega's LifePac curriculum for language arts combines reading, grammar, handwriting, composition, vocabulary, and spelling. There is stronger emphasis on reading skills at this level than earlier. Children can work fairly independently in this program, but be sure to discuss topics with them for better learning. If children are weak in any single area of language arts, supplement with other material. Be sure to use writing assignments from the Teacher's Guide. The complete set includes ten LifePacs and a complete Teacher's Guide.

The Latin Road to English Grammar, Volumes I-III
(Schola Publications)

This program serves as both a Latin and an English grammar course for elementary students. I suggest some introduction of grammar before beginning the course, although it is not absolutely necessary. See the complete review under Latin programs.

Learning Language Arts through Literature, Purple Book
(Common Sense Press)
student book - $20; teacher book - $25

The 1998 edition is geared toward fifth grade level and is very similar in format to the *Orange Book* for fourth grade. See that review under "Basic Textbooks" for 4th grade level. The four books studied this year are *Farmer Boy, Trumpet of the Swan, Meet Addy,* and *Caddie Woodlawn.* Students focus particularly on oral presentations, poetry, tall tales, folk tales, and speech making. As is appropriate for this level, the Student Activity Book requires more writing and little cut-and-paste activities. Like the other new editions in this series, the Student Activity Book is essential. It contains much of the material students will need to work with as well as questions and assignments. Enrichment activities found only in the student book stretch into research, analogies, and logic.

The Shurley Method
(Shurley Instructional Materials)
kits - $65 per level

See review under "1st Grade Level."

Voyages in English, Book 5
(Our Lady of Victory/Lepanto Press)
student text - $12; teacher's manual - $7; exercises workbook - $12; key to exercises - $3

See the review of Book 3. Grammar concepts are more complex, and topics such as articulation, choral speaking, and interpretation of diacritical markings are covered. Illustrations are minimal, so even though some are dated in appearance, it matters very little. Among topics covered in Book 5 are group discussions, "judging talks," parliamentary procedure, choral speaking, paragraph construction, outlines, writing poetry, dictionary use, letter writing, book reports, drama, radio broadcasts, and a wide range of grammatical concepts including parts of speech through prepositions, interjections, and conjunctions. Diagramming instruction begins with this level.

Voyages in English, Grade 5
(Loyola Press)
student edition - $18.95; teacher edition - $22.95; *Exercises in English* workbook - $7.95; teacher edition for *Exercises* - $8.95

See the review under "3rd Grade Level." The fifth grade text instructs students in paragraph, report, story, and letter writing, all at more challenging levels. It continues to cover speaking, listening, library, dictionary, and reference skills. Grammar coverage continues to expand, adding prepositions, conjunctions, and interjections with diagramming.

Alternatives or Extras, 5th Grade: Grammar

(Note: *Winston Grammar, Easy Grammar,* or *Learning English with the Bible* can be used to teach parts of speech. All of them can be used for more than one year. The presentation of *Learning English with the Bible* is on an older level; it must be presented by a parent in a suitable manner or used at an older level.)

Daily Grams: Guided Review Aiding Mastery Skills for 4th and 5th Grades or Daily Grams: Guided Review Aiding Mastery Skills for 5th and 6th Grades
(ISHA)
$18.95 each

These grammar review books from the publisher of *Easy Grammar* become progressively more difficult. One page for each day is used to reinforce grammar skills that have already been learned. Each page has exercises in capitalization, punctuation, general review, and sentence combining. Answers are at the back of the book. Choose the lower level for a student with weak skills and the higher level for a stronger student.

Daily Writing
(GROW Publications)
$25 per level

See the description under "Extras for Third Grade."

Easy Grammar Grades 5 and 6
(ISHA)
$26.95; workbook - $13.95

This book covers essentially the same type of content found in *Easy Grammar Plus*, using the same approach. The difference is that there are more worksheets, unit reviews, cumulative reviews, and tests. It is recommended for grades 5 and 6, but it can be used with younger and older students. As with *Easy Grammar Plus*, extra workbooks with only the student pages are available. See the review of *Easy Grammar Plus*.

Easy Grammar Plus
(ISHA Enterprises)
$28.95; workbook -$13.95

Easy Grammar Plus is one big book covering the basics of grammar, although it is stronger on parts of speech than on usage. This program is unique in presenting prepositions before other parts of speech. By teaching students to identify prepositions and prepositional phrases before other parts of the sentence, it eliminates such problems as confusing the object of a preposition with the subject. Parts of the sentence are designated by underlining, circling, and making notations rather than diagraming. In addition, it covers phrases, clauses, punctuation, capitalization, types of sentences, sentences/fragments/run-ons, and letter writing. Each concept is presented briefly. Examples are given followed by a practice page. Answers are on the opposing page in the book. Separate workbooks are also available, but we are given permission to photocopy work pages for our immediate family.

We find more grammatical detail taught in Rod and Staff and A Beka than we do here, but the essentials for the elementary grades are here. The format is very repetitious and would be enhanced by using it with *Grammar Songs* (below) or another form of learning to add variety. Grammar topics are taught one at a time without significant integration of topics. However, *Easy Grammar Plus* includes reviews, tests, cumulative reviews, and cumulative tests which helps students retain previously taught information.

While this is not a complete language program, it provides an easy alternative for teaching grammar basics. However, *Easy Grammar: Grades 4 and 5* provides a more comprehensive foundation at this level, so I would recommend using it before *Easy Grammar Plus*.

Daily Grams (also from ISHA) provide brief, daily review once the basics have been mastered.(S)

Grammar, Practice Books A-F

(Essential Learning Products)
$3.99 each

See description under second grade. Book D is appropriate for fifth grade level although other levels might also be useful. Topics covered are sentences, nouns, verbs, subjects and predicates, direct objects, pronouns, conjunctions, compound sentences, adjectives, adverbs, prepositions, capitalization, and punctuation.(S)

A Journey through Grammar Land, Parts 1, 2, 3, 4 and 5

(Wordsmiths)
$15 each

Wordsmiths' workbooks are written by a Christian teacher and designed to work in either home school or regular school settings. They are entirely self-contained; answers are included as is appropriate in each case. They can be used as consumable workbooks, or students can write answers in notebooks to preserve the books for other students. The author has designed the *Grammar Land* books to be used for grades 5-7, although any older student lacking a foundation in grammar should probably begin with this series. The books are well designed for independent study. "These books are in allegory format and tell the story of how Tank, a young fellow with grammar and writing problems, travels through *Grammar Land* meeting all sorts of folks and learning about the language in the process." The first half of the book is the story (with illustrations); the second half is the exercises, which are called

scrolls within the story. As students read through the story, they are actually receiving grammatical instruction. Every so often, the character is assigned to work on a particular scroll (exercise) which is a signal to the student to do that exercise. Helpful notes, definitions, and examples are scattered through the exercise section. Examinations are included.

Part 1 covers subjects, predicates, nouns, rules for noun plurals, inflectional and derivational suffixes, pronouns (person, case, gender, and number), antecedents, possessive nouns and pronouns, reflexive and indefinite pronouns, and punctuation. Part 2 reviews and expands upon the previously covered topics with an emphasis on verbs (complete predicates, action verbs, linking verbs, verb tenses, etc.). Part 3 deals with adjectives and adverbs. Part 4 covers prepositions and conjunctions. Part 5 teaches complex sentence and clause structures.

Concepts are reviewed periodically to ensure retention of knowledge. An answer key is at the back of the book along with very brief notes for teachers. Since *Grammar Land* can be used independently by students, no teacher preparation time for the lessons is necessary, but it is helpful if parents take a few minutes to read through page 54 in Part 1 which explains how to use the book. Students should be able to complete one or more books a year, depending upon what type of schedule is established.

The *Grammar Land* books should be useful for a broad range of home schooling situations because they are so user-friendly. However, some students will find the pace too slow because of the interjection of the story.

Practice Exercises in Basic English E

(Continental Press)
$5.95; teacher's guide - $2.75

This small workbook covers basic grammar concepts and works well in combination with *Winston Grammar* or another resource that provides complete instruction on parts of speech. Supplement for writing with one of the recommendations below.(S)

Writing

(Also see "Writing Their Own Books" above.)

Writer's Express Handbook

(Great Source)
$12.50

This handbook follows the same format as *Write Source 2000*, but it is designed for students at fourth and fifth grade levels. See the review of *Write Source* under sixth grade for more information.(S)

Writing, Books A-F (for grade levels 1-6)

(Essential Learning Products)

$3.99

Book E

Students continue developing journal writing skills with added emphasis on developing observation skills. Persuasive letter writing skills are practiced, then students produce a community brochure for which they do interviews and research as well as writing activities. A lengthy story-writing section is somewhat like that in Book D. The final section has students create a chronicle using writing and visual aids which they then present to an audience. The book suggests that this ideally be done as a group or family project. You might want to skip the "Just for Fun!" activity on pages 76-77 which deals with zodiac signs, horoscopes, and character traits. As with the other books, this one should stretch to cover older students also.(SE)

6th Grade Level

Basic Texts

Building Christian English 6, Progressing with Courage

(Rod and Staff)

student - $16.50; teacher edition - $22.95; tests - $1.90; worksheets - $3.05

This text reviews and expands upon previous levels. There is heavy emphasis upon grammar. It might be too detailed for some students, but Rod and Staff covers the grammar well in elementary grades so that students can concentrate on other language skills in high school. Writing, listening, reading, and speaking skills are also taught. The student text is hardback so students do their written work in separate notebooks. Answers are found in the teacher edition.

English for Christian Schools 6 [Writing and Grammar]

(Bob Jones University Press)

home school kit - $47; worktext - $11.65; teacher's edition - $39

The home school kit includes a student worktext and the Teacher's Edition. The Teacher's Edtion contains essential elements of the course, including lessons on writing an adventure story and report writing. There is a good balance of writing and grammar in the complete program.

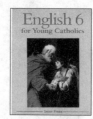

English for Young Catholics 6

(Seton Press)

$15

This is the sixth grade level book in this Catholic English series. The approach is very traditional, and it is presented in a worktext format. A minimal amount of instruction, often appearing in a box at the top of a lesson, is coupled with student exercises to provide plenty of practice with grammar concepts. Topics covered include all eight parts of speech, sentences, phrases, clauses, punctuation, capitalization, and letter writing. Forms of usage of the various parts of speech are covered (e.g., pronouns used as predicate nominatives). Curiously, students at this level are required to write many sentences, but the only longer composition work is a brief lesson on letter writing at the very end. Also, diagramming is not included as it is in the younger level texts in this series. (Seton does include a section on diagramming in their Lesson Plans for students enrolled in their grade 6 correspondence course, but if you use this text apart from the correspondence course, you might also wish to use a supplemental book on diagramming.) While the content is very Catholic, that content doesn't weigh more heavily than English instruction as it seems to in the third grade book. An answer key comes with the book.

God's Gift of Language C

(A Beka Book)

$12.40; teacher's edition - $22.80; test book - $4.20; test key - $8.95

Grammar, composition, and mechanics are given thorough review at this level. If grammar has been studied in a "hit or miss" fashion up to this point, this is a good book for reviewing and making sure that everything has been covered. The writing process is taught with explanations and demonstrations. Material for teaching writing is incorporated into the student text. "The Student Writer's Handbook" is a helpful reference tool at the end of the text. The student book is in worktext format. The teacher's edition serves as the answer key. A test booklet is also available.

Language Arts 600

(Alpha Omega)

$42.95 for complete set

Alpha Omega's LifePac curriculum for language arts combines reading, grammar, handwriting, composition, vocabulary, spelling, and practical application skills. Many supplemental writing assignments are available in the Teacher's Guide. Children can work fairly independently in this program, but be sure to discuss topics with them for better learning. If children are weak in any single area of language arts, supplement with other material. The complete set includes ten LifePacs and a complete Teacher's Guide.

Learning Language Arts through Literature, Tan Book and Green Book

(Common Sense Press)

Tan Book

student book - $20; teacher book - $25

The new edition of the *Tan Book* is much improved over the first edition. It is dramatically different from its predecessor with far more material in a format that is much easier to use. The format follows that used in the lower levels, so that students will sense a continuity in the series that seemed lacking in early editions. That format is described in the review for the *Orange Book* under Basic Textbooks for 4th grade level. The four books studied this year are *Carry On, Mr. Bowditch; The Bronze Bow; Big Red;* and *The Horse and His Boy.* There are special units on research and writing the research essay. Lessons are increasingly challenging as students work through activities for reading, grammar, composition, vocabulary, spelling, library skills, and thinking/logic. Again, the Student Activity Book is essential.

Green Book

student book - $20; teacher book - $25

Some students will be ready to go into the *Green Book*, even though it is designated for grades 7-8. It covers grammar, including diagramming; poetry; book study (Patricia St. John's *Star of Light*); creative writing; topic studies; speech making; and research papers. Supplemental books, *Star of Light* and *Adam and His Kin*, are necessary.

The Shurley Method

(Shurley Instructional Materials)

kits - $65 per level

See review under "1st Grade Level."

Voyages in English, Book 6

(Our Lady of Victory/Lepanto Press)

student text - $12; teacher's manual - $9; exercises workbook - $12; key to exercises - $3

See the reviews of Book 3 and Book 5.

Voyages in English, Grade 6

(Loyola Press)

student edition - $18.95; teacher edition - $22.95; *Exercises in English* workbook - $7.95; teacher edition for *Exercises* - $8.95

See the review under "3rd Grade Level." At sixth grade level, students work on improving writing, speaking, listening, and grammar skills. Among composition activities are various types of paragraphs, note taking, story writing, book reports, creative writing, letter writing, and filling out forms. Grammar reviews previously taught material, then presents more complex concepts, expanding into study of phrases and clauses.

The Write Source

(Great Source)

This is a different approach to language arts The *Write Source* is an entire line of language arts materials designed to produce better writers. A student handbook, *Write Source 2000* [$12.50], serves as the foundation, and it is used for reference and instruction. It includes grammar and usage rules coded by number, guidelines for various forms of writing including research papers, student models of writing, and reference tools. There is also a teacher's guide to the handbook [$15.95]. These are designed to be used for sixth through eighth grades. The handbook can be used alongside any other grammar/composition resources you might use.

In addition, Great Source publishes a classroom-designed language arts program [$125] plus other resources targeted at grades 6, 7, and 8 that correlate with the handbook: *Daily Language Workouts* [$15.95 each], *Skillsbook* [$7.95 each], and *Skillsbook* teacher's edition [$11.95 each]. You might run into content problems, particularly in the examples, since these are written for public school students.(SE)

Alternatives and Extras, 6th Grade: Grammar

Daily Grams: Guided Review Aiding Mastery Skills for 5th and 6th Grades or Daily Grams: Guided Review Aiding Mastery Skills for 6th-adult

(ISHA Enterprises)

$18.95

Daily Grams may be used to reinforce learning from any grammar program. There is one page for each day to reinforce grammar skills. Each page has exercises in capitalization, punctuation, general review, and sentence combining. Answers for *6th to Adult* are contained at the bottom of the page, and answers for *5th and 6th Grades* are at the back of the book. Books are progressively more difficult. Choose the lower level for a student with weak skills and the higher level for a stronger student. (Students should have already been instructed in basic grammar before beginning *Daily Grams*.)

Daily Writing

(GROW Publications)

$25 per level

See the description under "Extras for Third Grade."

Grammar, Practice Books A-F

(Essential Learning Products)

$3.99 each

See description under second grade. Book E is appropriate for sixth grade, although lower levels might also be useful. Topics include all parts of speech, sentences, subjects and predicates, direct and indirect objects, capitalization, punctuation, editing, and writing notes and letters.(S)

A Journey through Grammar Land, Parts 1, 2, 3, 4 and 5
(Wordsmiths)
$15 each

See description under "5th Grade Level."

Practice Exercises in Basic English F
(Continental Press)
$5.95; teacher's guide - $2.75

This small workbook covers the basic concepts and works well in combination with *Winston Grammar* or other resources that concentrate on parts of speech.(S)

Writing

Creative Writing
(A Beka Book)
$7.55

This writing skills workbook is suitable for sixth grade through high school. The emphasis is on creativity rather than technique, and it includes handwriting practice exercises.

Report Writing
(Continental Press)
$6.75

This 64-page book lays out a step-by-step approach to writing a research report that is very easy to follow. This is the best resource I have seen for learning to write research reports at this level. It is suggested for grades 5 and up.(S)

Writing, Books A-F (for approximate grade levels 1-6)
(Essential Learning Products)
$3.99
Book F

Journal writing continues at this level with exercises that help students describe feelings. Similes, metaphors, and personification techniques are introduced. Students also write letters, invitations, thank-you notes, and a series of exercises about an invention they create. "Comparison and contrast" skills are introduced through exercises about each student's community now and fifty years ago. Poetry received brief attention in younger level books, but more types of poetry are introduced here as well as skills for students to write their own. The final section is entitled "A Project of My Own." It provides minimal guidelines under which students work to create a writing project. Guidelines are more vague and open-ended than those for lengthy projects in earlier levels, so I would choose which book to use, keeping in mind how much guidance each student is likely to need. Self-directed students will probably manage at this level, but others might need the guidance provided in younger level books.(S)

Speech and Listening Skills

Speaking and listening are crucial to communication. We actually have more opportunities to develop these skills at home than at school because of the significantly lower student-to-teacher ratio. The following materials should be helpful.

In One Ear and (Hopefully Not) Out the Other!
(The Gift of Reading)
$21.95

This unique book is designed to work on auditory processing and listening skills for all preschool and elementary age students, but especially for those with difficulties in those areas. It is divided into seven different sections: building vocabulary, auditory categorizations, auditory memory, auditory discrimination, auditory association, auditory reception, and syntax/morphology. The exercises/activities can be used to diagnose problems, review and reinforce previously learned language skills, supplement a therapy program, provide daily exercises, enhance children's language skills, and focus on problem areas. There are some reproducible pages in the back, but one book may be used with your entire family.

Oral Language Exercises
(A Beka Book)

See description under fourth grade.

Play by the Rules
(Tin Man Press)
$11.95

Help children in grades 2 to 6 develop listening and direction-following skills with the fun exercises in this book. Most of the activities are done with basic supplies like paper, pencils, rulers, scissors, and crayons. A few of them require elbow macaroni and soda crackers. Introductory exercises are fairly easy, but they progress fairly quickly to complex levels. For example, in one activity students draw 16 numbered circles, then follow directions drawing lines connecting the circles according to specific instructions. Circles and lines that meet specified criteria are then colored according to instructions. Some of these activities produce silly results such as the face drawn with a tracing of a fist as the basic pattern. Do not expect your second and third graders to be able to do all of these. Time required will depend upon the activity and maturity of children.(S)

Chapter 11

Spelling and Vocabulary

We supposedly teach spelling to help our children spell correctly. However, spelling books are not necessarily the way to accomplish that goal. Some children will go through years of spelling books yet still be unable to spell well. Others will learn to apply spelling rules to words they encounter; for them spelling books might be worthwhile.

An understanding of phonics will help a child spell more words correctly, but phonics cannot tell him which of three possible ways to spell a certain sound is correct in a given word. Good readers (word decoders) are not always good spellers, although plenty of reading practice does help many children more easily recognize correct spelling. Good spellers tend to visualize words in their minds. They have a strong sense of what "looks" correct. Some very intelligent people never do become good spellers, even as adults, because they lack the ability to visualize words.

This does not mean we should just forget about teaching spelling. Rather, we need to judge whether the approach we are using is producing results. If not, we need to try a different strategy. In some cases, it might mean providing our child with the tools he needs to overcome what could be a lifelong handicap—tools such as a poor-speller's dictionary which lists common misspellings followed by correct spellings, or a computerized spelling aid.

Personalized Spelling Lessons

One of the most effective methods for teaching spelling is to select words our child commonly uses in both writing and speaking and use those words for a spelling list. Add words that are misspelled in written work, basic sight words from his reading program, and words of special interest to him. I believe it is still a good idea to review spelling rules as needed if we use this method for choosing spelling words.

A resource which has creative activities that can be used along with personalized spelling lists is **Spelling Works** (Learning Works) [$6.95]. This 48-page reproducible workbook is suggested for grades 4-8. Each page describes a different type of activity; some are simple and some are involved so choose those appropriate for each child. Examples of the types of activities include finding antonyms for ten words selected from the spelling list, creating a game of charades with spelling words, identifying words according to placement of accent marks, and writing a phone message to a friend using at least ten of the spelling words. Appealing illustrations make the work pages look like fun.(S)

Game Playing

Games can also help develop spelling skills. However, children with very poor spelling skills are often intimidated by spelling games, especially those which are very competitive. Most such games involve visual skills to organize random letters into words. Because a visual weakness is often the cause of their difficulty, such games pose a problem. They might help a child improve his visualization or they might reinforce his negative feelings about his lack of spelling ability. While most children will not have this problem, be cautious about using spelling games if your child is a very weak speller.

Many of the game and activity ideas in the **Big Little Spelling Book of Fun** (The Helping Hand) are great for children who have visual weaknesses. This is a great place to start looking for fun approaches to try with your children. (See the review elsewhere in this chapter.)

When to Begin Using Spelling Curriculum

My educational philosophy regarding spelling differs from that of many publishers. I do not recommend that a separate spelling curriculum begin before children are able to read. A child's reading vocabulary is generally much greater than his spelling vocabulary. He may be able to recognize or decode a word, but it is much more difficult for him to spell the word on his own before it has been encountered in reading many times. Because of this, be cautious about spelling materials for the early grades. Some reading programs such as *The Writing Road to Reading* incorporate spelling, while others such as A Beka and BJUP correlate their language arts materials so that spelling practice reflects what is being taught in other language arts materials. These programs are careful to see that children first work on reading the words before spelling them. However, some children might need more practice seeing the words before attempting spelling.

Assessment for Placement

If we need to assess our child's spelling ability, Mott Media has reprinted Leonard Ayer's book, *A Measuring Scale for Ability in Spelling* [$8.99], which lists the most commonly used words divided by grade levels. We can use the lists for assessment and then use them for spelling lessons. A similar tool is the *Spelling Scale for Home Educators* (Small Ventures).

The Writing Road to Reading recommends the *Morrison-McCall Spelling Scale* as a tool for evaluating spelling skills. The *Scale* is out of print so Bonnie Dettmer of Small Ventures has composed a similar scale including instructions for use which is called *Spelling Scale for Home Educators*. Although designed to correlate with *The Writing Road to Reading* and *Phonics for Reading and Spelling*, others might wish to use it as an evaluation tool. It is not intended to be a spelling list/instruction tool. *The Scale* is designed to test students at all grade levels through the first year of college.

> *Being able to spell a word on a test does not indicate mastery. Mastery is the consistently correct spelling of a word in written work.*

Spelling Resources

The Alpha List: A Dictionary Focusing on the Logic of English Spelling
by Wanda Sanseri
(Back Home Industries)
$14.95

Whatever spelling method you choose to teach, this book is likely to be a handy accessory. If you are using any of the *Writing Road to Reading*-inspired systems, it will be doubly valuable. *The Alpha List* features alphabetically the 2000 words in the *Wise Guide for Spelling*. Included are the most frequently used and many of the most frequently misspelled words in English. But these are more than simple lists. Words are written in syllables and marked with special spelling highlights. To the right of the words are several columns. The first tells us which chart in Wanda's own program, *Teaching Reading at Home & School*, teaches each word. The second designates which of 29 spelling rules apply to that word. (The list of rules is at the back of the book.) The third adds a helpful comment—maybe a trick to help remember the spelling, related forms of the word to learn, or the root word. The foundational rules are spelled out in *The Alpha List* so we need not use any specific program to benefit from this reference book. Included are the 70 basic phonograms, 29 spelling rules, an

explanation of the spelling highlight system used, rules for syllabication, prefixes and suffixes, rules for doubling consonants and spelling plurals. Words wrongly considered rule breaker words are explained—e.g., why we drop the "e" in tracing but not in traceable. I think the this book will be best for students who have already been introduced to spelling rules but who still make occasional errors in their writing. We can look up the word in this book, mark the error with spelling highlights that apply, and hand our student the book to determine how to correctly spell the word and why.

Beyond Phonics: Word Pattern Stories
by Nancy D. Nelson
(Training for Life Publications)
$29.95; workbook - $12.95

Despite the title, this is not a phonics program, although it certainly reinforces and builds upon phonics. It uses stories, songs, poems, and activities primarily as mnemonic devices to reinforce spelling patterns. According to the author, "This program provides a necessary bridge between beginning reading and higher level spelling, between phonics and the word memorization needed to apply phonics principles with automaticity" (p.2). It should be especially useful for students who lack a strong visual memory which enables them to recognize correctly and incorrectly spelled words. These are the students who often show little progress when using more traditional spelling programs.

This program can be used on its own or in conjunction with other phonics or spelling programs that teach words by grouping them according to common phonograms or sounds. Stories, written to appeal to all ages, are designed to reinforce Christian character and Biblical principles while also incorporating basic, non-denominational doctrine. Lessons are arranged under letter patterns such as "-ff, -zz," "-ci- as sh," or "age." For each lesson, we introduce the words and discuss the spelling pattern or patterns. Next, we read the story; one of the briefer ones reads: "Usually, I work like **crazy**. I'm not **lazy**, but sometimes I like to **laze** around and **gaze** at the stars. My eyes **glaze** over and my mind goes **hazy**. I'm in a **daze**. Within minutes, I am asleep." Discussion of the moral and character lessons should follow the story, but that's optional. The teacher then rereads the story, dictating the bold words for students to write. An optional workbook provides the story in fill-in-the-blank form plus word lists from which students can work. The workbook will save a tremendous amount of time, so I recommend purchasing it.

This system can be used with all ages once they have at least begun to learn phonics. We need to be selective about lessons, choosing those appropriate for various skill levels. We might also adapt lessons with more challenging words, by only having younger students write the simplest words in those stories. While the example above would be suitable for young students, a lesson that includes the words "mother, of, discovered, covetousness, quarrelsome, and confession" would need some adaptation.

Only one textbook is needed for the entire family for all levels. Also each student needs only the one workbook to cover all levels.

Big Little Spelling Book of Fun

(The Helping Hand)
$10.95

Whether you make up your own spelling lists, teach spelling informally, or use a spelling program, you can make it more fun with the ideas in this book. This is not a program or a workbook but a book full of creative ideas from among which you can pick and choose. Some involve activities such as writing, looking words up in the dictionary, and arranging words in alphabetical order, while others suggest super-creative activities like spelling out words with Legos on the large Lego "green-grass" boards, decorating cookies with word parts that students have to assemble to create words, and playing a truth or consequences spelling game. We even find some of the highly recommended, multi-sensory approaches for teaching spelling to hands-on learners like drawing their words in sand or salt, or spelling words rhythmically while jumping rope or jumping on a trampoline.

Building Spelling Skills

(Christian Liberty Press)
Books 1-6 - $8 each; answer keys - $3 each

Book 1

This self-contained student first grade worktext serves as much for phonics reinforcement as it does for spelling. All but the last two lessons are designed around a phonics rule. (The last two work on syllables.) The first five lessons cover the short vowels, working only on words with the designated short vowel sound. Almost all of the phonograms are covered in Book 1. A variety of exercises induce the child to practice writing words over and over. The number of words per lesson seems a little large in comparison to other programs, and the difficulty level also is advanced. Examples of the more difficult words are voyage, poison, grudge, because, awkward, and laundry. Space for children to take their weekly tests is provided at the back of the book. Teaching instructions are at the front. Some content and inserted verses and quotations identify the curriculum as Christian. This is not an exciting program, but it does reinforce phonics more than do most spelling programs at this level. No answer key is available or needed.

Book 2

This book accelerates the emphasis on phonics rules with some intense phonics vocabulary. Weekly word lists are intro-

duced with definitions of the phonetic concept such as consonant digraphs and voiced/voiceless consonants, or rules of syllabication. Some of the lessons deal with root words, prefixes, and suffixes. There are plenty of practice opportunities, but as in Book 1, the word lists are more advanced than in other second grade programs. Examples of the more difficult words: adage, foreign, cyclone, musician, disappear, although, exodus, and accomplish.

Book 3

This book seems to build on Book 2, assuming that much of the phonetic vocabulary is familiar. (The phonics background information does appear at the back of the book for reference.) Like Book 2, it is very rule-oriented, reviewing previously covered phonetic rules, then moving on to still more. The difficulty level still seems advanced with words such as audience, dynamite, and luncheon but not quite as much so as the first two books.

Book 4

This book continues in the same vein but moves on to accents, more complicated prefix and suffix work, contractions, possessives, and calendar and measurement vocabulary/spelling words.

Book 5

Book 5 is subtitled *The World of Words*. The first nine units deal with geography-related words. Remaining units feature individual topics such as birds, sports, anatomy, and economics. Exercises are very eclectic rather than following similar formats throughout. One might have students practice with antonyms or suffixes, while others concentrate on the unit topic with vocabulary and practical usage. One example of the latter type of lesson is one on titles for civil officers. Throughout most of this lesson, students learn job descriptions for mayor, notary, auditor, magistrate, constable, assessor, etc. Book 5 strikes me as one that can be used whenever this type of study seems appropriate for a student rather than at a particular grade level.

Book 6

Book 6 reviews the basic spelling rules students most likely encountered in the early elementary years. This is a good time to review because most students have forgotten there are patterns to help them figure out the spelling of unfamiliar words, even if they use that knowledge without realizing it. Review does not take students back to one-syllable words but introduces challenging words. Suffixes and prefixes (including Latin and Greek prefixes) are also addressed in depth. Spelling rule coverage is not as thorough as that found in *The Writing Road to Reading* or other resources dedicated specifically to spelling rules. However, this book should be very useful for the student who either never learned the rules or does not use them as a tool when needed. Many junior high students would do well to go through these lessons.

Calvert School Interactive Spelling & Vocabulary, 5th and 6th Grades [CD-ROM] 🖥
(Calvert School)
$20 each

Calvert's spelling and vocabulary CD-ROM programs are each intended to provide a full year's practice in both subjects, although spelling instruction is better than vocabulary. Sound and graphics are used to provide a multi-sensory learning experience. The spelling program focuses on words that are most commonly encountered and used by students at each level rather than on words sorted by common phonetic elements. No spelling rules or generalizations are taught. On the other hand, students hear the words used in context, and they are given multiple opportunities in the "spelling lab" to actually spell words correctly rather than just recognize pre-typed words as in some spelling programs. As with every comparable program I've seen, the program itself doesn't register typed in responses as quickly as many students can work. Time is lost while the computer cycles through the program.

Vocabulary lessons are stronger on graphic presentation than educational content. Words are presented with three possible definitions to choose from; that's the entire extent of the daily lesson. Review lessons are more challenging since students must then fill in missing letters of a word used in the context of a sentence. Still, this is minimal help in vocabulary development in comparison to resources like *Wordly Wise*.

The program tracks a number of students, but only in regard to lessons completed, not how well students performed on daily lessons. It is possible for parents to tell how many spelling words are missed in pretests by looking at the study lists the computer compiles for students. Parents and students are also able to add troublesome words of their own to student's study lists.

The program's graphics vary in quality from outstanding to mediocre. The program requires computers running Windows 3.1 or higher with a sound card.(S)

The Child's Spelling System: The Rules
(Educators Publishing Service)
$7.15

This is a thorough presentation of the rules including some ideas for presentation. It is appropriate for middle elementary through junior high.(S)

The Common Sense Spelling Book, Part 1
by T. W. Butcher, revised by Teresa Walker
(Republic Policy Institute Press)
$19.95

Originally published in 1913, this two-volume book has been slightly revised for this new edition. Both volumes are enhanced by the addition of Teresa Walker's lesson plans which come with each volume. Part 1, the first volume, covers grades 1 through 8. (My review of Part 2 appears in the *Christian Home Educators' Curriculum Manual: Junior/Senior High*. Price when both *Parts* are purchased together is $36.90.) Building on a phonetic base, this spelling book incorporates character building poetry in spelling instruction that relies heavily upon learning diacritical markings, syllabication, and spelling rules. The single volume serves as both teacher and student book, although the *Lesson Plans* should be used alongside to understand how to use the material. The poetry can be used for both spelling and memory exercises. Children <u>do</u> need access to a dictionary, since some instructions require them to identify and/or write the words with syllable divisions, placement of accent marks, and diacritical marks. You need to compare the marking system used by your dictionary with that used in this book to ensure uniformity or alert your child to alternative markings. Students should keep a notebook to record spelling and capitalization rules as they study them. [Note: the letter "w" is introduced as sometimes being a vowel. This approach is uncommon, and it is encountered in at least two sections without explanation: sections 60 and 71 (e.g., the "ow" in owl in taught as a diphthong, or two vowels pronounced together). "Ow" is the most common example encountered.] The vocabulary and level of language study is definitely more challenging than that of typical spelling texts. I strongly encourage you to develop vocabulary exercises to help children master the meanings of the words encountered. Some words are archaic, but, even so, most of them will be encountered in literature if not in common usage. Overall, I think this is a valuable tool for teaching spelling if you also want your children to master the use of the dictionary, know how to properly divide words between syllables, and develop a sophisticated vocabulary.

Excellence in Spelling 🎧
(Institute for Excellence in Writing)
$99 per level

This unusual spelling program is targeted for children ages 9 and up. It is offered at three levels of difficulty, with the third level geared for students at least sixth grade, but more likely high school level. An introductory video presentation demonstrates how the program works. It is possible to figure out how to use the program from the eight-page booklet that comes with it, but the video clarifies and demonstrates exactly how it works.

The same set of flashcards is used with all three levels. There are 47 lessons/flashcards in the set.

These half-page size flashcards feature pictures and names of animals on the front which exemplify particular spelling rules or hints for each lesson. On the back is the rule, a jingle, or hint to be learned. There are also three lists of words, arranged by levels A, B, and C. Children only work with those words that are on their level. Every fifth flashcard is used for personal spelling words that are collected from other spelling challenges a child encounters during the week. Parents can introduce each flashcard and work with children, especially introducing each new lesson. Or children can work with the flashcards independently.

Instead of a workbook, children work with words by listening and writing. Five CD's for each level direct the child in independent study through most of each lesson. Rules, jingles, and hints are presented. (This might be a repeat of a parental presentation, but that's not a problem.) Students are encouraged to study the words on the flashcards before beginning to listen to the lesson on the CD. On the CD each of the fifteen words is pronounced and used in a sentence. Children prepare a piece of paper upon which they will write the words as they hear them. After all fifteen words have been presented, children check their own work by listening to correct spelling on the CD. One technique I don't see explained in the directions, but which is demonstrated on the video, is to have children write the correct spellings as they listen to them on the CD in the process of correcting their own papers. I would have a child ONLY write the words from the pronounced spelling (next to each word they wrote on the first time through the lesson that day) and not try to check words at this point. After they have written all of the words, they should compare their original and the correct spelling. A child might not SEE his misspelling until the correctly-spelled word is written next to it. Students repeat each lesson, writing the words each time, continuing until they are able to score 100% two times in a row with the same list. Children should use headphones to help them concentrate on the auditory input and to keep them from being distracted. The CD presentation also frees parents from lesson preparation and presentation while still providing children with the focused input they need.

This program should be especially good for children who are strong auditory learners. The idea is that as children listen to the words being spelled to them, writing as they listen, the sequential order of the letters is reinforced in the brain. The authors do not claim this is the best program for every child, and they offer a money-back guarantee if it does not work for your child.

The independent nature of this program might work very well for some children. (Parents should check from time to time to ensure honesty.) This removes some of the embarrassment children experience in other programs. It also allows children to go through each lesson as many times as they need with no stigma. If they score 100% the first two times, they can complete a lesson in only two days.

The selection of words seems to have been determined by the need to use words as exemplars of rules. Thus these are not the most commonly used words but an eclectic mix. For example, lesson 26 includes the following words for level A: "true, bluebird, avenue, have, value," and "due"; level B includes "groove, eave, mauve, tissue, flue," and "cue"; level C has "continue, queue, subdue, valve, dissolve," and "starve." Canadians will appreciate alternative spellings in parentheses such as "neighbor (neighbour)."

How to Teach Any Child To Spell
by Gayle Graham, M.Ed.
(Common Sense Press)
$8

How to Teach Any Child To Spell and its companion, *Tricks of the Trade: A Student's Individualized Spelling Notebook* [$12], are designed for children who struggle with spelling. Some children work through spelling workbooks and memorize word lists yet still frequently misspell words in their written work. Often, the problem is they can't see that words look "funny," a natural ability for the good speller. Gayle Graham offers a solution by combining Ruth Beechick's suggestion to create individualized spelling lists of words each student misses with focused instruction on the pertinent spelling rules. She stresses the need to keep the rules simple, pointing out that most children struggle with only a few key rules. *How To Teach Any Child To Spell* is a small teacher's manual that outlines the approach, presents the phonics rules for daily structured phonics review, and lists the six key spelling rules. Put Gayle's ideas into practice with *Tricks of the Trade*, purchasing one book for each student with whom you will be working. *Tricks of the Trade* includes "Clue Sheets" showing phonetic sounds and essential rules for spelling. This is followed by the bulk of the book, the child's personal spelling "dictionary." In this dictionary, children write the words they miss under sound or "rule" headings rather than in alphabetical order. They then concentrate on studying only the rules that apply to those words. Gayle outlines four-step, daily spelling lessons that include general phonics review, review of the misspelled words following Gayle's strategy, oral reading incorporating exercises to help the child develop visual perception, and writing time. This system works best for children who have already learned to read and write, but whose spelling skills lag behind. It should even work for teens who might have decided that spelling skills are not in their repertoire, but who really do want to be able to spell words correctly.

The Month by Month Spelling Guide
by Kathy von Duyke
(Tim and Kathy von Duyke)
$10

This *Spelling Guide* features lesson plans for teaching spelling according to the *Writing Road to Reading*. It is simpler to understand than the *WRTR*, and it is also more specific in providing instruction for parents.

My Spelling Notebook

by Trudy Palmer

(The Gift of Reading/Home School Instructional Services)

This teacher's resource book presents spelling rules in detail following the type of methods found in *The Writing Road to Reading*. See the review under "Supplemental Materials to Use with *The Writing Road to Reading*."

Natural Speller

(Design-A-Study)

$22

Everything necessary for spelling instruction for grades 1-8 is included in this 78-page book. Note that *Natural Speller* is not a student text but a parent/teacher resource book. Basic word lists are given for each grade with words containing similar patterns grouped together. Special word lists (e.g., calendar words, contractions, measurements, homophones, Latin roots) are also provided. Kathryn Stout strongly advocates keeping separate those words with similar sounds which are formed by different letter combinations (e.g., though, bow, sole). Lessons can be developed from the word lists or with words of our own choosing. Instructions are provided for teaching spelling and for studying words. Greek and Latin roots and activities included in the *Natural Speller* should be used primarily with students in grades 6 to 8 as an aid to vocabulary development. Spelling rules are provided with charts that include suffixes and prefixes along with phonic and writing rules.

Oh Scrud!

$7.95

Boggle, Scrabble, and other familiar games can be great tools for improving spelling skills. There is a another, newer game I really like because of its flexibility, called *Oh Scrud!* This is a card game in which we race to form words from letters and phonograms. There are negative cards that force us to turn in good cards we have been accumulating. Everyone plays at once, drawing and discarding cards at random which makes it rather exciting (or pressured depending upon your perspective). To enable varying ages to play together, younger children can be allowed to form short words while older players are required to make longer words. However, you might find as I did that the adults might be the ones who need the advantage.

Prescriptive Spelling Program, Books One, Two, or Three

(McGraw Hill)

student editions - $8.91 each; teacher editions - $8.91 each

These books review spelling rules and apply them to spelling lists. They are frequently recommended for students who have had difficulty in spelling. Reading levels of the three

books are grade levels 3.5, 4.5, and 5.5. respectively. (Ordering numbers for the student books are 45065058, 45065059, and 45065060 respectively. Numbers for accompanying teacher editions are 45065069, 45065070, and 45065071.)

This series is especially good for the child fourth grade or above who struggles with spelling problems because he or she never learned spelling rules.

A Reason for Spelling

(Concerned Communications)

$39.98 per level

A Reason for Spelling is designed for those who want lots of activities in their spelling lessons. Each level consists of a Teacher Guidebook and student workbook. Both are hefty books: the three student books I reviewed ranged from 206 to 254 pages and the Teacher Guidebook was 350+ pages. Levels A - F are appropriate for grades 1 - 6. Lessons are very dependent upon the Teacher Guidebook and presentation by a parent/teacher. Lessons begin with a Scripture verse and lengthy "themed story." The stories convey spiritual lessons and might even be considered part of your Bible or religion class. They are well-told but do not seem to have a crucial connection to any other parts of the lesson. (For $29.98, you can purchase a four-audio tape set of the stories for each grade level.) Discussion activities following the story help you evaluate your child's comprehension as well as expand upon the theme. Next, students are given a pre-test on this weeks words, a combination of words with common phonetic elements plus some sight words in the earlier levels, moving toward most-commonly-used words at upper levels. Because of the classroom-driven design of the program, there's no suggestion that you might skip lessons if students already can spell all the words. If you do choose to skip some lessons for this reason, note that some of the themed stories are continued over a number of weeks, and you might need to read stories from skipped lessons to maintain continuity.

The first workbook activity is fitting spelling words into word-shape boxes, then marking common elements as directed. Then chalkboard activity helps students build visual memory. Activities for different learning styles (e.g., shaping your spelling words out of *Play Doh*) are presented. Next are more typical workbook activities such as filling missing letters, putting words in dictionary order, and identifying rhyming words. Naturally, these activities increase in complexity and difficulty for higher grade levels. Dictation exercises require students to write dictated words to fill in blanks within sentences. Proofreading exercises offer students multiple choice options in standardized test format to recognize which word is misspelled. (I suggest skipping such exercises with students who have poor visual memory. They only become more confused when they get reinforcement with incorrect images.) Optional games are probably only marginally useful for single students, but might be useful if you have other students who can join in. Students are also supposed to write weekly journal entries. Post-tests are given at the end of the week. Supplemental activity pages in the Teacher Guidebook can be photocopied for use with advanced students or those who need the extra work.

Student workbooks are very colorful, featuring super cartoon illustrations. While this program is probably great for classrooms, there is more here than most homeschoolers need. You might select the most useful activities, skipping others as long as you have the time to sort through all of your options.

Spelling
(Association of Christian Schools International)

Research is the foundation for the methods used to teach spelling in this series. Three strategies used for spelling instruction reflect that research: sound-letter relationships, visual memory, and meanings. Sound-letter relationships (phonics) are taught first, then work on visual memory helps students to identify which of the various phonetic possibilities is correct. "Meanings" refers to the fact that many words are related (derived from the same base words), and by studying bases, prefixes, and suffixes, we can identify words of related meaning, thus making connections that also help with spelling. While all three strategies are used throughout the program, sound-letter relationships are emphasized in the first two grade levels.

Word lists are purposely not presented as word families but instead are designed to teach most-frequently-used words as well as spelling rules. Room for the addition of what are called "Home Base" words—extra words that are added to the list by the teacher—is allowed within each lesson along with space to practice writing, using those words.

Writing/composition activities are a major part of each spelling lesson at all levels, and a number of these incorporate Bible topics. Teacher's editions are useful for understanding the philosophy behind the program and for understanding such things as the use of the "First Look" test process and "Home Base" words. This "front" information is the same for all levels. Activities, sample sentences, related devotional suggestions, and reduced copies of student pages with answers are also found in the teacher's editions. If sample sentences and an answer key are not important to you, I still suggest purchasing one teacher's edition (even if you are teaching more than one student level) because of the"front" information.

Prices: grades 1-6 student worktexts - $11.25 each; teacher editions - $37 each

Grade One

In the first grade book, there are no spelling lists for the first twelve weeks' worth of lessons. Instead, attention is first devoted to phonetic foundations. This feature makes this one of the better spelling programs for beginners. Children also work on visual memory and writing activities, where they are encouraged to use invented spellings for words they do not know. Large print and colorful format following a circus theme make the book appealing and easy-to-use. Activities stretch beyond spelling to include practice with alphabetizing, synonyms, sentences, punctuation, capitalization, contractions, and other skills.

Grade Two

At second grade level "The Neighborhood" is the theme. Students work on rhyming words, context clues, definitions, antonyms, poetry, creative writing, and letter writing, in addition to skills introduced at first grade level. Word lists appear in both manuscript and typeset formats but not in cursive. Students are encouraged to begin work on a Dialogue Journal (described in teacher's edition).

Grade Three

"Transportation" is the theme for this level, and the emphasis shifts from phonics to visual memory although phonics is not ignored. Word lists appear in manuscript, cursive, and typeset formats. There is more work with words in context, use of the dictionary, and definitions than in earlier levels.

Grade Four

Phonetic principles are reviewed, and visual memory skills are developed. Word lists appear in cursive and typeset formats. New skills are syllabication, accented syllable, the use of the schwa, and higher level thinking skills. This level is different from others, adding suggestions for small group or partner activities (usually not useful for home educators), and strategies for meeting needs of children having different learning styles.

Grade Five

The emphasis changes to word meaning for fifth and sixth grade levels. In addition to spelling word lists, most lessons also include charts of words related to the spelling words. All basic phonics principles and spelling rules are reviewed through the fifth and sixth grade levels. Exceptions are also studied. Skills incorporated include vocabulary development, use of words in context, word origins, prefixes and suffixes, expanding forms of words, parts of speech, proofreading, dictionary work, and research. The fifth grade book uses the theme "The Word Power Team" with characters such as Captain Consonant and Sam Synonym.

Grade Six

The theme for this level is "Sports." Many writing activities involve Bible-related topics or verses.

Spelling and Poetry 1, 2, or 3
(A Beka Book)

Student books for grades 1-3 - $7.20 each; teacher editions - $12.70 each

The grades 1-3 spelling books use a "...straightforward teach/practice/test approach...." rather than the expanded workbook approaches found in *Spelling Workout, Spelling for Christian Schools*, and most others. Lessons are intended to be taught rather than given to students as independent work. However, there are a few seatwork activities with each lesson in student workbooks. Words are arranged phonetically and are coordinated with other A Beka language, reading, and writing lessons at each grade level. Word lists reflect an above average level of difficulty, so you might choose to abandon the coordination with other A Beka materials and choose whichever book seems to be most appropriate for each student's ability. *Spelling and Poetry* books can be used apart from other A Beka materials with no problem. Poems are included at the back of the book for memorization. Some vocabulary work is included beginning with the second book. The teacher editions, available for grades 2 and 3, include reduced copies of student text pages, teaching information, answers, sample sentences for all words, and study helps. There are no teaching instructions in the student books, so unless you already know how to teach spelling, you will probably want to get the teacher editions.

Spelling by Sound and Structure series
(Rod and Staff)
Second Grade
$10 for both pupil and teacher books

This workbook divides each lesson into two parts: Part A works on synonyms, antonyms, definitions, picture clues, context clues, and categories of words; Part B works on phonetic patterns and word structure (syllables, plurals, verb forms, etc.). There are 34 weekly lessons with some of those being review lessons. This is a very formal, academic approach, although the level of difficulty of the spelling words is average. Word lists in all Rod and Staff books reflect both their Christian beliefs and their view of a kinder, gentler society.

Third Grade
$10.15 for both pupil and teacher books

This series has a strong phonetic emphasis. New word lists are presented in both printed and cursive forms. Words are grouped by phonetic or structural similarities so children can learn the pertinent rules. There are 34, two-page lessons with 13 words per lesson except in review lessons. Word lists in all Rod and Staff books reflect both their Christian beliefs and their view of a kinder, gentler society. Each lesson has three parts: A develops familiarity with word meanings, B teaches the phonetic and structural principles, and C works on dictionary skills. Although student workbook pages are fill-in-the-blank approach, the teacher's edition offers a number of activities for oral or expanded written work. Consider adding or substituting some of these when appropriate. Student books are consumable.

Fourth Grade
$14.70 for both pupil and teacher books

This worktext is more detail-oriented than other series at this level. Lessons are divided into four parts: A "...introduces one or two speech sounds and teaches the most common spellings of these sounds....," B helps familiarize children with word meanings, C teaches dictionary skills, and D works on a variety of other skills such as syllabication. Because the amount of material covered increases at this level, the print is smaller and more crowded. Although the student workbook is consumable, some students might find it easier to do their written work in a separate notebook. A spelling word dictionary at the back is handy for reference.

Fifth Grade
$14.80 for both pupil and teacher books

The fifth grade level book in this series is very similar in format to that of the fourth grade book.. Although there is a great deal of detail and drill, the word lists reflect an average level of difficulty.

Sixth Grade
$18.90 for both pupil and teacher books

At sixth grade level, the student text switches from soft cover to hardbound textbook. There are 34 lessons with 20 words per lesson except for review lessons. Spelling, pronunciation, meanings, structural patterns, abbreviations, contractions, syllabication, and other concepts are taught and reviewed. Challenge activities are included for advanced students. A Speller Dictionary at the back is handy for reference. The teacher's edition provides teaching tips and answer keys.

A Spelling Dictionary for Beginning Writers
(Educators Publishing Service)
$4.50

This is a thin book you purchase for each child. It uses large, easy-to-read type with plenty of space between words. It lists most commonly used words to be used as spelling lists as well as special word banks for such things as home, sports, and weather. It also allows space at the back to add each child's own words. Especially handy is the word bank, a mini-thesaurus at the back, which will give children an easy way of finding "more colorful" words to spice up their writing. This ungraded book is good for all elementary students.(S)

Spelling for Christian Schools
(Bob Jones University Press)

BJUP has written special home school teacher's editions for their spelling courses that save us both time and money. All home teacher editions are $20 each; student books - $11 each; home educator's kits - $29 each

First Grade

At this level, spelling reinforces the phonics and spelling patterns taught in *Phonics and Reading 1*. One section, "King's English," ties one word in each weekly list to Scripture. The home teacher edition presents strategies for teaching spelling, including beginning dictionary skills.

Second Grade

This text teaches spelling patterns based upon phonics and common structural generalizations. It also includes an introduction to dictionary skills and composition work.

Third Grade

This worktext teaches generalizations using word families and also includes journal writing and interesting information about the history of words.

Fourth Grade

In this worktext students continue to work on structural analysis while learning more about word histories (interesting!) and dictionary skills. They also learn to spell the names of the books of the Bible.

Fifth Grade

This worktext includes the study of word origins and dictionary use as well as writing experiences. Students continue to study structural patterns within words, particularly looking for relationships between similar words that will help with spelling and meaning. The teacher's edition is recommended primarily for answers but also for the methods for teaching topics such as related word pairs.

Sixth grade

At this level, word origins and their relationship to spelling is emphasized as students continue to study patterns and word relationships. Writing exercises for application are included. The Home Teacher's Edition is useful as an answer key and also for the lists of Greek and Latin prefixes and meanings.

Spelling for Young Catholics series

(Seton Press)

Spelling 1 - $8.50; Spelling 2-8 - $6.50 each

This is a spelling series "in transition." The first grade book is of the new, workbook design, while the rest of the books, as of this review, retain the prior "text" format. The older style presents each week's lesson on a single page, then requires students to practice writing words and sentences in a spiral notebook. A suggested sequence of activities has students look up definitions of words and write them in complete sentences in addition to basic study, writing, and testing activities. Older books are clearly rule-oriented, presenting spelling rules immediately after word lists. Both are followed by a lengthy paragraph on a faith-related topic (e.g., biography of a saint), which includes some words from the lesson. (I actually prefer this older format over the new, although it does require more work by both teacher and student.)

The new edition switches to a workbook format. The first grade book presents ten words per lesson, grouped by common sounds or phonograms. Bonus words are a mixture of sight words and additional words relating to the featured sound/phonogram. Lesson presentation is very brief. Brief workbook exercises for each day (fewer for the first few weeks of school to ease children into the program) may be supplemented with activities from those suggested in the front of the book. Exercises are fairly simple, but they vary to include alphabetizing, identification of vowels and consonants, and proofreading. Content of all books is explicitly Catholic. Watch for revised editions of the rest of the series.

Spelling Plus: 1000 Words Toward Spelling Success

by Susan C. Anthony
(Instructional Resources Co.)
$19.95

One perfect-bound, 168-page reproducible book can serve as your spelling book for kindergarten through sixth grade. The entire program focuses on 1000 most commonly used and misspelled words, teaching 10 in kindergarten and 165 at each of the remaining six grade levels. Children are pretested to determine the appropriate beginning level. Words for each level are broken down into eleven lists. Many of the words are associated by phonetic characteristics, prefixes, etc. Homophones are included in each lesson. Notes to the Teacher provide valuable information pertinent to each list. At the front of the book are background information concerning spelling, teaching tips, and techniques. A unique feature is the use of dictation for review and reinforcement. Each student also personalizes his list by choosing five personal words each week. This is important when you realize that there are only about five words per week provided within the program itself. Extra word lists at the back of the book feature words related to geography, geometry, and math. I recommend that you also purchase the companion volume, *Dictation Resource Book*, and consider the useful, but less crucial *Homophones Resource Book*. The program is quite easy to use, especially with the assistance of the resource books.

The *Dictation Resource Book* ($12.95) consists of short sentences and paragraphs to be dictated to students after each spelling list in *Spelling Plus*. It will save you the time and energy of dreaming them up yourself. The book also features reference tools such as letter formats, extensive capitalization rules, postal abbreviations, common abbreviations, punctuation rules, prefixes and suffixes, charts and definitions of parts of speech, bibliographic form information, lists of Latin and

Greek roots, and a word history dictionary containing all the words used in *Spelling Plus*.

Homophones Resource Book ($15.95) features all homophones already in *Spelling Plus* along with quite a few more. Tips for teaching each pair of homophones are included. The bulk of the book is reproducible activity sheets where students complete sentences by filling in the blanks with correct homophones. Lessons are coordinated with spelling lessons or suggested for particular grade levels, making it easy to determine which ones to use. It would be possible to skip this volume if your child/ren are not having any particular difficulty with homophones.(S)

Spelling Power
by Beverly L. Adams-Gordon
(Castlemoyle Books)
$49.95

Spelling Power can be the only spelling book you use with all of your children through all of their schooling. The basic program is designed for students third grade to adult, but there are also instructions for modifying lessons for children between the ages of five and eight. In order to use this program, the student should be able to write easily and copy words correctly. Children with writing disabilities should get handwriting instruction before beginning this program.

This very comprehensive spelling program uses a base list of about 5,000 frequently used words. (A list of the 12,000 most frequently used and misspelled words is included as a separate section. It codes each word showing when it should be taught, by grade level and in correlation with *Spelling Power*. These words can be used to supplement the basic 5000 already selected.) The 5000 words are broken down into groups with common elements. Diagnostic tests place the students at the proper beginning point in the list. Then each student progresses at his own rate, studying only those words with which he is having trouble. Frequently used words are reviewed periodically to insure retention. A ten-step study process is used for each word to be learned. (This ten-step process should help even poor spellers improve their skills.)

The "Quick Start Introduction" at the beginning of the book walks you through placement and instructions for using the program.

Parental/teacher involvement is essential, although we can note daily activities on the study sheet for older students to do on their own. As children mature and become familiar with the program, they should be able to do much of their work independently.

The interaction required between teacher and child actually makes this program more ideal for home schoolers than for the regular classroom. Reproducible study, test, dictionary and record keeping forms and a whole section of game and activity ideas are included. Castlemoyle Books also offers *Spelling Power Activity Task Cards* (reviewed next) to facilitate our use of games and activities. [V.T./C.D.]

Spelling Power Activity Task Cards
by Beverly Adams-Gordon
(Castlemoyle Books)
$29.95

The author of *Spelling Power* has created a set of 365 color-coded, 4" x 6" *Activity Task Cards* that can be used along with *Spelling Power* or any other phonic-based spelling program. The brightly-colored cards are filed in a sturdy box for easy use. Cards are divided into five categories: drill activities, skill builders, writing prompters, dictionary skills, and homonyms and more. Within each category, cards are further color coded into four categories responding to age/skill level groupings covering all grade levels. Activities designed for auditory, visual, kinesthetic, and tactile learning modalities provide learning opportunities for all children. Examples of a few of the activities are games, dot-to-dots, painting, puzzle making, as well as a variety of writing activities. Most activities can be done by a single student although a few require a partner. The *Activity Task Cards* come with a very helpful Teacher's Manual. The manual tells us how to use the *Activity Task Cards*, offers suggestions for making our own letter tiles, cross references to *Spelling Power* lessons, and includes answers for the appropriate cards. Cards can be used as supplements to lessons or sometimes in place of lessons. If you are using *Spelling Power*, I highly recommend this set as both a time saver and lesson enhancer. For those using other programs, it will help supplement lessons through all grade levels.

Spelling Rule Cards
by Wanda Sanseri
(Back Home Industries)
small - $7.95; large - $12.95

According to Wanda Sanseri, author of *Teaching Reading at Home & School*, the two essential tools for learning the logic of English spelling are the phonogram cards and the spelling rules. These cards provide a visual memory jogger of the rules for easy review and reinforcement. For example, on the front of one card are the letters "XS" covered by the international symbol for no (a circle with a slash through it). The back of the card has the rule being illustrated which is: "X is never followed by S." While based on the 28 rules taught in *Teaching Reading at Home* and *The Writing Road to Reading*, these cards can stand alone as a beneficial aid for anyone teaching spelling. Cards are available in two sizes: small - 4.25" x 5.5" or large - 8.5" x 5.5".

Spelling, Vocabulary, and Poetry

(A Beka Book)

Level 4 - $7.95; teacher edition - $12.95; Levels 5 and 6 - $7.95 each; teacher editions - $12.95 each

Level 4

This spelling program is significantly more difficult than others at this grade level, comparing with those for fifth grade from some publishers. A Beka spelling books use a "...straightforward teach/practice/test approach...." rather than the expanded workbook approaches found in *Spelling Workout, Spelling for Christian Schools,* and most others. Lessons are intended to be taught rather than given to students as independent work, yet there are quite a few workbook activities in student workbooks. Words are arranged phonetically and are coordinated with other A Beka language, reading, and writing lessons for fourth grade level. Word lists reflect an above average level of difficulty, so you might choose to abandon the coordination with other A Beka materials and choose whichever book seems to be most appropriate for each student's ability. *Spelling, Vocabulary, and Poetry* books can be used apart from other A Beka materials with no problem. Poems are included at the back of the book for memorization. The teacher edition includes reduced copies of student text pages, teaching information, answers, sample sentences for all words, and study helps. There are no teaching instructions in the student books, so unless you already know how to teach spelling and don't mind working without an answer key, you will probably want to get the teacher edition. Related optional items: student test booklet, teacher key to the test booklet, *Spelling Challenges,* and *Fourth Grade Poetry Cassette Tape..*

Level 5

Following the same format as Level 4, Level 5 continues to be advanced beyond other publishers' courses. Level 5 focuses on usage, pronunciation, and word analysis skills. Poems are included at the back of the book for memorization.

Level 6

Following the same format, Level 6 focuses on Latin and Greek suffixes, prefixes, and roots, stressing vocabulary, spelling, and word origins. Poems are included at the back of the book for memorization.

A Spelling Workbook for Corrective Drill for Elementary Grades

(Educators Publishing Service)

$11.70

Written for fourth through sixth grade students who have difficulty with spelling, this 120-page workbook takes a multi-sensory approach. Phonetic drills are used with kinesthetic (body movement) reinforcements. Rules are taught and words are grouped by families. Syllabication and pronunciation are also reviewed.(S)

A Spelling Workbook for Early Primary Corrective Work, Books I, IA, and II

(Educators Publishing Service)

Books I and IA - $9.90 each; Book II - $10.50

These three workbooks are recommended for second and third grade students who have reading and spelling difficulties. *Book I* and *Book IA* are identical in content, but *Book I* uses cursive writing rather than manuscript since some dyslexic students are taught cursive from the beginning to prevent reversal problems. *Book II* may be used with either cursive or manuscript writing. Phonetic elements and spelling rule generalizations are used.(S)

Spelling Workout A - F

(Modern Curriculum Press)

$7.55 each; teacher's edition - $7.30 each

The *Spelling Workout* series, books A-F, correlates with MCP *Plaid Phonics* A-C and MCP *Word Study D-F,* although *Spelling Workout* may be used alone. Spelling is taught from a phonics perspective and reinforces phonetic principles. Riddles and activities, plus the use of poetry, limericks, and excerpts from literature make these more interesting than many other spelling workbooks. These spelling workbooks are generally very effective for home educators, although, in my opinion, it is not necessary to use this or any other spelling program with first graders. *Spelling Workout* is fairly efficient, requiring a reasonable amount of time for lesson activity. Teacher's editions are needed only for checking answers at higher levels.(S)

Spellwell series

(Educators Publishing Service)

$5.40 each; keys - $3 each

The *Spellwell* series targets grades 2 through 5 with two worktexts per grade level. Books are designated A and AA for second grade level, B and BB for third grade level, C and CC for fourth, and D and DD for fifth. Teacher keys are single books that each cover the two books for a grade level. This series designs lessons around spelling rules or generalizations. Some of these are "discovered" by students as they look for patterns, while others are specifically identified. One or more "outlaw" words appear in each lesson, and space is provided for you to add your own words to be studied.

Lessons begin with a pretest. Students who get most or all words correct are then given an additional list of more-challenging words to study. A variety of age-appropriate activities help students recognize spelling patterns. Other thinking skills come into play in activities such as identifying rhyming words, words that fit the same categories, and antonyms and synonyms. There are also puzzles, scrambled letters, crosswords, and other more-entertaining activities.(S)

Success in Spelling series

by Rebecca L. Avery

(The Weaver)

Success in Spelling reflects my belief, stated above, that spelling should be taught after children have become fluent readers. Thus, this program recommends Level 1 for students "...in second grade and above, and only when the child is reading fluently." Phonics rules are reviewed, and spelling rules are taught throughout the program. Sight words and most-commonly-used words are also taught but separate from lessons emphasizing rules. Daily lesson plans explain how to introduce the spelling words (including the applicable rule), provide an activity (games, drawing, written work, etc.—something different every lesson), pretest, review, and final test.

Level 1

$8

Level 1 has daily lesson plans for 19 weeks, plus another 17 lists of sight/common words that can be used for weekly lessons. The book itself is the teacher's manual, and there is no student workbook. Instead, we reproduce (only for our family) "Spelling Pretest" pages. These pages are divided into three columns. The spelling words are in the left hand column. Students study the words, then the page is folded so only the center column is visible for the pretest on day 3. Misspelled words are rewritten in the third column. The final test encompasses only the words missed on the pretest. The vocabulary is wider ranging than that found in typical second grade books, including words like smite, whine, clasp, and bane.

Level 2

$10

Some third graders will begin with Level 1, while others will be ready to move on to Level 2. There are 46 lessons beginning with long vowels and working through blends and digraphs. Accented syllables and simple diacritical markings are also taught. The level of difficulty is slightly higher than most spelling programs for third grade level with the exceptions of A Beka's, Rod and Staff's, and Christian Liberty's.

Level 3

$12

Level 3 has 57 lessons which build directly upon lessons taught in earlier levels. It continues with "...digraphs, vowels under the accent, trisyllables, diacritical marking and special spelling rules." Daily lesson plans are sometimes grouped when lesson plans are almost identical; for example, Lessons 1-3 follow the same lesson plans but use a different list of words each week. The word lists are significantly more challenging than other mid-upper elementary programs in terms of both spelling difficulty and vocabulary. Examples of some of the more challenging words: plenitude, rectitude, derogate, immolate, plausible, chancery, and debauch.

Level 4

$14

Level 4 has 66 lessons detailing homophones, accented syllables, special spelling rules and short and long vowel spelling possibilities....Emphasis is placed on diacritical marking and syllabication."

Level 5

$18

Level 5 has 75 lessons with from 3 to 12 words per lesson. There are daily lesson plans (five per week) for each lesson/word list, although most of us will move more rapidly through some of the lists. If we actually spent a full week on each list, it would take 820 days! So adapt the lessons, using suggestions as is appropriate for each student. Level 5 covers homophones, suffix and prefix meanings and spelling rules, exceptions to spelling rules, accented syllables, six- to seven-syllable words, and hard-to-spell words. The word choices grow increasingly unusual. (They began to do so in earlier levels.) Examples of unusual words: flagitious, absolutory, circumjacent, disembarrass, cognoscible, and flageolet. Although I find no directions for vocabulary study, students are required to write the words in sentences in their final tests. Because many words are likely to be unfamiliar, we will probably need to develop some method for vocabulary study on our own. Even though Level 5 is recommended for sixth graders, I suspect that many older students will struggle through some of these lessons.

Super Spelling Book One

by Mary F. Pecci

(Pecci Educational Publishers)

$19.95

Mary Pecci, author of *At Last! A Reading Method for EVERY Child!*, has created a companion spelling program, based on the same simplified phonics principle. "Teach only the reliable facts." Pecci illustrates her approach with a stairstep hierarchy of language skills beginning with listening, then moving up through speaking, reading, and spelling, ending with written language. Thus, she stresses the need for children to learn to read before learning to spell, although she is not demanding total reading mastery before spelling begins. (Spelling begins one month after reading instruction.) A good example of how this works is that rather than having first graders do any creative or independent writing, Pecci has them copy or follow closely along with teacher instructions, receiving step-by-step guidelines as they learn how to produce correct sentences. This approach contrasts with whole language theory that would have children writing anything for the sake of learning to express themselves without regard to conventions.

Another unique feature of this spelling book is a focus on high-frequency words (e.g., dog, the, run, can, big) rather than lists consisting of rhyming words (e.g., cat, sat, hat, rat) or topical words (e.g., colors: red, yellow, blue). This enables children to write intelligible sentences using familiar words.

She uses fewer rules, treating words that don't follow the rules as "study words." Pecci uses her own very simple system of marking digraphs and "study" words. Rather than simply memorizing the spelling of words that don't follow rules, students learn to analyze them in ways that will help them remember their correct spelling.

Daily lessons help students to master weekly spelling lists, beginning with five words each week, but increasing to ten per week by the end of the year. Lessons are directed by the teacher, with daily lesson plans provided in the book. There is no student workbook. Students begin writing isolated words in their daily practice, but increase to complete dictated sentences. Sentences include only words that students have already mastered. Periodic reviews are built into the course.

As they learn to write sentences, students learn the four types of sentences and basic punctuation. Lessons include weekly additional practice activity such as filling in the missing spelling word, unscrambling, and adding punctuation to sentences, beginning after lesson 3.

Little to no lesson preparation time is required, but parents must work with children each day. *Super Spelling* should be good for the child (and, perhaps, the parent) who is easily overwhelmed by numerous rules. While it can be used alongside most other phonics programs, it will work best with those using Pecci's reading program.

Think Speak and Write Better! [computer program] 🖥

(Smartek Software)
Levels A-J - $49.95 each

Think Speak and Write Better! is an efficient and effective vocabulary and spelling program. It comes on a CD-ROM that runs on either Macintosh or IBM compatible computers with a sound card. There are ten different levels, each a separate CD that you purchase. On each level, there are from 9 to 13 groups of 20 words each that are the "core words" studied. One of the advantages of this program is that it teaches via the three learning modalities: seeing, hearing, and doing.

Except in Volume A, words are introduced with closely related synonyms, then used in exercises with four "common misconceptions"—words or meanings which people commonly confuse. The result is about 1400 words with which students become familiar at each level. There are five learning modes for each word group. The first mode is "multiple choice with audio discussions." One word from the word list is highlighted and five options are listed to the right from which to choose the meaning. We hear the word used in a sentence, then select the answer. Once the proper word has been selected, we hear and view the "audio discussion." We can read the screen while listening to an expanded definition, word origin and history,

and usage information. The audio pronunciations are very helpful, although they are not always accurate. (Perhaps this is a problem with computer voices, but it is not nearly as bad as the manufactured computer voices we hear from places such as telephone directory assistance.) The next mode is "flashcards." Here, a phrase or sentence uses the synonym identified with a list word in the multiple choice lesson. We are given a short time to answer mentally, then the list word appears on the flashcard. The next mode is "column matching," then the fourth mode is "sentence completion." To complete sentences, we must fill in the blank with the correctly spelled word from the list. The list is not displayed unless we call it up on the screen. If the spelling is close but not perfect, we get another chance. If it is too far off, the properly-spelled word is displayed to the right on screen. The "laser review" mode is a multiple choice game where we shoot the correct synonym.

The down side to these programs is that words are presented with only one meaning throughout all the different exercises, while, in reality words often have a number of meanings. Additionally, the selected meaning in the program is sometimes not a common usage of the word. I found this to be a significant problem in Volume A, but less so at upper levels.

The program allows tremendous flexibility to enter and leave at any time and to access audio discussions or helps. Sound effects and excellent graphics make it visually and auditorially interesting. The program also tracks and records scores in the appropriate modes. Learners can select whichever modes are most effective for them or use all of them. Words are based on the research of linguist Johnson O'Connor for developing effective vocabulary improvement programs. We find a mix of commonly-used and challenging words from levels A through J. Volume A "contains the most common words and Volume J contains words unknown to 90% of adults." Volume A is titled *Word Adventure*, and has additional graphics to appeal to younger learners. I don't like Volume A as well as the upper levels for reasons mentioned above. However, most students in the elementary grades should begin with Volume A or B; they are unlikely to get beyond the first five or six volumes.(S)

Word Building 🖥

(School of Tomorrow)
Levels 2 and 3: PACEs - $38.40, tests on CD-ROM - $49.95; Levels 4-6: PACEs - $43.20; tests on CD-ROM - $49.95

School of Tomorrow's *Word Building* PACEs for grades 2-8 build vocabulary and teach spelling. Worktext pages are colorful with enough variety to maintain student interest. Spelling rules are taught and practiced. Tests for *Word Building* can now also be done on computer if you have a CD-ROM drive. CD-ROM disks use sound card and speaker to orally drill students. Student responses are monitored and scored by the computer.

This option can save busy moms a great deal of time. The disks will run on IBM compatible computers. A printer is needed to print out test results.

Spelling Alternatives

At higher levels, we might use a book which explains and gives examples of the spelling rules for reference. We make notations on the student's papers for the reference page or number of the spelling rule which applies to the word they have misspelled. The student looks up the rule and determines how he has violated it. This helps students increase their mastery of spelling rules and overcome their own common errors. One book that will work like this is **The Child's Spelling System: The Rules** (Educators Publishing Service). See the review under "Spelling Resources."

Vocabulary Resources

Spelling courses often contain elements of vocabulary lesson development. But, especially at higher grade levels, it helps to focus more purposefully on vocabulary.

English from the Roots Up: Help for Reading, Writing, Spelling and S.A.T. Scores
by Joegil Lundquist
(Literacy Unlimited)
$27.95; flashcards - $17

Children as young as those at second grade level can begin to understand the roots of the English language that are found in the Greek and Latin languages. The goal is similar to that of *Vocabulary from Classical Roots* (from Educators Publishing Service); this book uses more interactive, teacher-directed teaching methods, while *Vocabulary from Classical Roots* is a workbook approach. In this approach, index cards, a file box, and a good dictionary are the primary tools for learning vocabulary. Actual teaching information provided is brief but loaded with activity suggestions. The teacher is on her own to implement the ideas, although pre-printed flash cards are now available which will save a great deal of preparation time (highly recommended). Examples of activity ideas: for the root "graph," a number of related words are presented with accompanying ideas; e.g., "Telegraph - Let someone present a research report on Thomas Edison's early days as a telegrapher. Let someone do a report on Morse code and give a demonstration of it." Or "Lithograph - Discuss the process of lithography and talk about Currier and Ives. Their lithographs are still used every year as Christmas cards. Make potato or linoleum block prints." These activity ideas could be turned into great unit studies. This resource will be especially suited to the creative teacher who prefers general guidelines rather than detailed lesson plans.

Our Roman Roots
by Dr. James R. Leek
(The Leonine Press)
$44.99

Our Roman Roots comes with three components: spiral-bound student worktext, teacher's manual, and audio cassette. Suggested for grades 4 - 8, this course will accomplish some of your English language arts goals in vocabulary, grammar, and composition and it will introduce your children to the study of Latin. Vocabulary is the primary emphasis, building English vocabulary based on study of Latin root words. In the process it also teaches some history, character development, and Catholic traditions. This sounds like an eclectic mix of goals, but it blends together very nicely.

Each lesson begins with a Latin quote for the day and its English translation. Students try to connect words that correspond to one another. Each day a new Latin word is introduced with a list of English derivatives and their definitions. Children create their own notebooks where they copy this information. (They will add to this notebook as they complete other parts of each lesson.) Memorization of oral passages from the cassette are next, followed by grammar and vocabulary exercises. Some written exercises can be completed in the student worktext, while others will need to be entered into the student's notebook. Optional extension activities include such assignments as reading excerpts from classical works and responding with drawing or writing, telling a story related to the day's character lesson, identifying human rights in the Declaration of Independence, and researching examples of freedoms lost during wartime. As you can see, some of these activities are quite challenging, so you will need to use your own judgment about which of these your children will do. Continual review is built into the lessons and periodic quizzes are included. Students will need access to a good English dictionary as well as a Latin dictionary. We can teach lessons almost exclusively from the student text—students will complete much of their work independently. However, the teacher's manual does add a few teaching suggestions as well as serve as your answer key. [Note: While the course can be taught by a parent without prior knowledge of Latin, an important explanation is missing in the first few lessons: in Latin, adjectives change their endings to reflect the case and gender of the noun they modify.]

Rummy Roots Card Game
(Eternal Hearts)
$11.95

Rummy Roots is a card game that offers an alternative to book approaches for studying Greek and Latin roots. It is exceptionally well designed for learning purposes, because it includes instructions for four different games using a card deck of Greek and Latin roots plus English meanings. The first game helps us learn the meanings of the roots with a "Go Fish" type game. (Lists and glossaries for this and other games are included so we need not have a dictionary at hand.) Once we are somewhat familiar with root meanings, we move on to the next game of combining two roots to make an English word. The method of play is different, plus it includes the use of "bonus" and "stump" cards for fun. Players are supposed to say the meanings of their words, but we added that step after we played the game first just figuring out how to combine roots. (Take time to make sure players know the meanings of the roots before moving on to higher levels.) The third game allows players to make words combining up to three roots. Stump cards are now used to challenge players on word definitions. The fourth game adds yet another dimension of difficulty.

Some educational games are so busy teaching that they forget that games are supposed to be fun. *Rummy Roots* avoided that mistake by adding enough game elements, especially once we get past the introductory game.

Rummy Roots teaches "...42 Greek and Latin roots, 193 vocabulary words, and the knowledge to decipher half of over 2000 other words." The publisher says the game is for players ages 8 to adult, but younger players will probably need to play mostly at the first two levels. Do not be in a hurry to push them on to levels where they might become frustrated. This game is best for older students.

More Roots, a second game from Eternal Hearts [$11.95], teaches an additional 42 new Greek and Latin roots using the same methods as *Rummy Roots.*

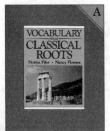

Vocabulary from Classical Roots, Book A

by Norma Fifer and Nancy Flowers
(Educators Publishing Service)
$8 - student book; $6.25 - teacher's guide

This is an excellent approach to vocabulary, especially for bright students who can easily remember root words and recognize them in unfamiliar words. Words with similar roots are grouped thematically for ease of study. A variety of exercises including work with synonyms, antonyms, analogies, and sentence completion help students develop full understanding. Two unusual extras are included: literary, historical and geographic references help develop cultural literacy; suggestions for extended writing activities help students to apply new vocabulary. A Teachers' Guide and Answer Key for Book A contains teaching suggestions, exercise answers, and a helpful glossary.(S)

Wordly Wise, Books One, Two, and Three

(Educators Publishing Service)
student books - $7.10 each; teacher's key - $5.50 each

I highly recommend *Wordly Wise* vocabulary workbooks. Words are studied in a variety of contexts that help students better understand their meanings and usage. The strength of this book as compared to others is in the study of multiple definitions for most words. Children must then truly understand meanings to complete the activities. Crossword puzzles at the end of each unit reinforce learning from earlier lessons. Vocabulary is somewhat advanced, so keep children in lower level books if you want them to study vocabulary they are more likely to encounter and use. You might want to start students in this series about fourth grade. See also the review of the new *Wordly Wise 3000* series.(SE)

Wordly Wise 3000, Books 1, 2, and 3

(Educators Publishing Service)
$7.70 each; keys - $3.00 each

I expect that this new series will eventually replace the original *Wordly Wise* series. It retains many of the elements of the original that made it so outstanding. The series also features some significant changes. Each lesson presents the lesson's words with definitions, while we had to look up definitions in the back of each book in the originals. This is much more convenient. As in the originals, students work through a number of exercises with each week's words to learn not just a single definition, but alternate meanings and usages of other forms of some of the words. They have added a narrative section which incorporates words from the lesson. Students read the narrative, then answer 15 questions in complete sentences. This activity will require more time, but it definitely enhances learning. Vocabulary words are a little more familiar than those in the original books. Words were selected from "current literature, textbooks, and SAT-prep books" to include words children are likely to encounter. While the words might be a bit more familiar, they are not necessarily easier. For example, in lesson 5 from Book 1, suggested for fourth graders, the first six words on the list are "abrupt, achieve, attempt, contempt, entertain," and "glimpse." In the original Wordly Wise, Book 1, lesson 5, some of the words are "assist, avoid, exile, mar, navigate," and "vat."

After every fourth lesson, there is a vocabulary puzzle—an enjoyable feature retained from the original series. The first three books in the series are suggested for grades 4-6. Children with above average vocabularies might tackle a book a year beyond their grade level. Parents will need to watch the content; I'm getting reports that political correctness is a problem in this new series. The reasonably-priced student books are consumable and NOT reproducible. You will also want to purchase answer keys for these books.(SE)

Chapter 12

Handwriting

There is some division of opinion on handwriting methods, which we are especially aware of since our major Christian publishers have chosen different methods. If we use one publisher's materials for some subjects and another publisher's for others, we might run into problems when handwritten material is presented differently in each one. This only occurs in the language arts subject area, and it usually presents no problem at all.

The two primary methods offered are the traditional ball and stick manuscript printing with "Palmer method" cursive, and the alternative, slant print with a simplified cursive form. Italic style offers a third, less widely known option. We actually have yet another choice—whether to skip manuscript printing and begin with cursive instead.

Proponents of slant print believe it is simpler for children to learn a form of printing more similar to cursive, and it is easier to form the slanted letters which have children keep pencil on paper for the entire letter rather than lifting for directional changes as in ball and stick. (This helps to prevent letter reversals.) They also feel that the less ornate cursive is easier to form than the traditional cursive. Adherents of the traditional method believe some children will have greater success with the ball and stick because they have difficulty making directional changes without lifting their pencil. They also point out that the slant is more difficult for some children than the perpendicular stick form. As you can see, there are valid reasons for preferring either method.

Some would say that rather than wasting time on either manuscript or slant print, we should teach cursive from the beginning. This skips the transition step entirely. The only caution against this approach might be small motor development problems. If children have trouble keeping pencil to paper while changing directions, they might find it more frustrating than the ball and stick method or even Italic style.

If we consider our own handwriting, we will probably find that it little resembles the method we were taught in school. We each seem to develop our own personal style as adults, regardless of what we have been taught. So the importance of this issue is debatable. It will ultimately be a choice based on what works best for each child and other factors that influence the overall choice of curriculum materials.

Let's Write and Spell (Educators Publishing Service)

[$9.75] is not for handwriting instruction itself. Perceptual skills are developed through pattern and copying exercises. Perception, discrimination, and hand-eye coordination are stressed. Use this along with any other handwriting program for children who have been introduced to cursive but who are having difficulty.

Writing Skills for the Adolescent by Diana King (Educators Publishing Service) [$10.65] covers cursive handwriting, spelling, grammar and composition instruction methods for dyslexic and dysgraphic students, fourth grade and up. This is the only resource I am aware of that integrates all of these areas for students with learning difficulties. ***Writing Skills, Books 1*** and *2* (Educators Publishing Service) [$7.50 each] "present the material and method discussed in *Writing Skills for the Adolescent* in workbook form." Many home schoolers will prefer to use these two books instead of the original.

Some students might be interested in learning calligraphy. Calligraphy will not replace basic handwriting, but it often improves a child's handwriting as he or she learns to pay attention to details. Parkwest Publications has books for all levels. *Calligraphy for the Beginner* and The Anatomy of Letters look like possible tools for the mature student.

Handwriting Materials

Traditional Method/Ball-and-Stick

The traditional handwriting method most of us learned in school is used by A Beka, School of Tomorrow, Christian Liberty Press, and Alpha Omega, while Bob Jones University Press and Rod and Staff offer the slant print method. Rod and Staff prefaces the learning of slant printing with the traditional ball and stick, resulting in a "two-transition" handwriting curriculum—ball and stick to slant print to cursive. A Beka Book offers the option of either manuscript printing or cursive for kindergarten.

A Beka Book's Handwriting Program

(A Beka Book)

A Beka Book's handwriting program in the early grades combines handwriting with phonics in their

Writing with Phonics texts. If our primary purpose is writing, and phonics needs only a little reinforcement, we might choose these books; but if phonics is the primary goal, look for a better workbook. Either manuscript or cursive is taught even in the *K4* program for young kindergartners [$7.95], although children learn only lower case letters. *K5* [$8.35] also teaches lower case letters, then adds capitals and requires children to write complete sentences. Slant guides that can be place underneath any lined paper a student might use help them develop proper slant from the very beginning. The newest editions of the *K4* and *K5* books are printed in full color. Separate *Writing Tablets* are also available for both *K4* and *K5* [$7.65 and $7.50 respectively]. *K4*, in this case, includes capital letters. You should choose either a *Writing Tablet* or *Writing with Phonics*, but not both. Penmanship lessons continue through *Writing with Phonics* for grades 1 and 2 [$10.55 each] or *Writing Tablets* [$3.95-$5.45]. As they move into second grade, students learn to reduce the size of their writing. The *Cursive Writing Skillbook/Writing with Phonics 3* [$11.55] expands into a variety of writing formats, and includes creative writing, phonics review, and dictionary work.

The Art of Writing for Young Catholics

(Seton Press)

$8 each

The Art of Writing for Young Catholics, books I-V teach traditional manuscript and cursive, making the transition to cursive in book II. The series is suggested for grades 1 through 5, although you need not necessarily use them at those grades. Practice sentences are from Scripture, Church history, and other Catholic writings. The books are uneven in quality. In book II, instruction is hand-printed above and around lines, but that printing is frequently uneven, overwritten, or otherwise below the standard you would expect. Books IV and V, on the other hand, are excellent with in-depth instruction on technique and letter formation. Seton also offers optional handwriting tablets and practice books. A revised edition of book I is due out in Summer of 2000.

Christian Liberty Handwriting

(Christian Liberty Press)

$5.50 each

The *Christian Liberty Handwriting Series* (Christian Liberty Press) consists of five books, two for traditional manuscript and three for cursive, for grades K through 4. The highest level book can be used with students beyond fourth grade who need to improve their cursive. One possible problem to be aware of is that lines in the early books might be too small for young children. In all books, instructions are usually given to write a word that is only shown in typeface, but not in cursive.

It would help if more models of actual handwriting were shown. In the cursive books, some fun activities are included along with exercises that work on other language skills such as alphabetizing and letter writing. Home school personalities from the past are featured in the last three books. *Handwriting Practice Pads* for either the lower or higher level can be purchased for $.95 each.

E-Z AS A-B-C Penmanship course, Books A, B, and C [Fairfax Christian Curriculum Series]

(Thoburn Press)

$5 per book; Teacher's Guide - $9; complete set - $24

The ball-and-stick method is used for kindergarten level or older students who need help with manuscript (printing) in this series of three workbooks. Information in the Teacher's Guide is largely classroom oriented but provides many helpful tips on how to teach printing. A single Teacher's Guide covers all three workbooks. Book A covers individual letters and numbers and some blends. Book B teaches short words and some simple sentences towards the end. Book C has almost entirely Scripture-related content, including a number of simplified Bible verses for writing practice. Large, one-inch lines used throughout are sized right for young children.

Handwriting Practice Books 1-5

(Essential Learning Products)

$4.49 each

These books might be all you need to teach your child both manuscript and cursive writing. Using traditional ball-and-stick, the first two books teach manuscript. The third book teaches cursive, which is practiced in the next two books. Every book covers both upper and lower case letters, beginning with single letters and continuing up through words and sentences. Numbers are also taught in each book. Students copy models for almost every exercise, with just a few exercises such as "write your name and address." Line spacing begins very large and decreases with each book. The books are half-size like other ELP books which makes them less intimidating for those who have difficulty with paper and pencil tasks.

Happy Handwriting

(Mastery Publications)

$12.95

Happy Handwriting comes from Letz Farmer, creator of *F.L.A.G.S.* and *Mastering Mathematics*. This handwriting workbook features the basic ball-and-stick method. Cute illustrations and plenty of space for inexperienced writers to have wiggle room appeal to children. A letter/sound activity accompanies each lesson along with numerous examples of how each letter might appear using various print styles (or sign language!). Identification exercises use Christian content.

Sequencing skills (numerical order and alphabetical), capitalization, numerals, consonants and vowels also receive attention. The workbook is consumable, but we are allowed to photocopy the necessary pages for children in our family.

LFBC Penmanship
(Landmark's Freedom Baptist Curriculum)

Landmark's Freedom Baptist Curriculum's *Penmanship* course [$25] suggests teaching penmanship to students three years in a row, in second through fourth grades. Their course features Palmer method, although it differs from some others in that it stresses ending letters with a tail that reaches up to the mid-line. It seems to me that one of the commonest features of sloppy handwriting is letters that end abruptly, either going straight down to the line or trailing off in a variety of inconsistent styles. Consequently, stressing proper "tails" might well improve the appearance of a child's handwriting. Lessons include instruction and questions regarding penmanship vocabulary. Students trace and copy exercises throughout the text, as well as on weekly quizzes and quarterly tests. Content is clearly Christian and it includes some Bible verses. Print quality in the text is uneven, and the black-and-white style is not as appealing as some of the more-colorful options, but instruction is sound and thorough. Worktext, quizzes, tests, and answer key are included.

Peterson Directed Handwriting

Peterson Directed Handwriting should be very appealing to home educators for two reasons: it is inexpensive and it is thorough. Both teacher and pupil books for each level cost about $5.50 all together. New home school handwriting kits include the teacher and pupil books plus the new self-adhesive Position Guide, and pencils or pen (depending upon the level) [kits: K - $14.95; grades 1, 2, or 3 - $9.95; grade 4 or advanced - $6.95].

The teacher's handbooks offer step-by-step teaching instruction as well as extra strategy helps and explanations about some of the research and theories behind the methodology. It covers types of pencils, how to hold them, desks and sitting positions, tips for teaching left-handed students, and more. This is one of the few handwriting programs where the teacher's manual is a necessity because it contains so much useful information.

The methodology is standard ball-and-stick, based on learning basic movement patterns to reinforce left-to-right tracking. "Printwriting" begins with the traditional one-stroke-at-a-time process. In second grade, slant print is introduced using a "no-lift" rhythm called "threading" in the jargon of motor control specialists. Transition to a traditional cursive takes place in third grade. Form, slant, size, spacing, smoothness, and control are continually emphasized. Songs and rhythms that assist in teaching handwriting skills are available on an optional audio cassette [$5]. Materials are available for kindergarten through eighth grade. A special teacher booklet, *The Left-Handed Writer*, is also available [$2.05]. Peterson also lists in their catalog many other supplemental items such as reproducible lesson-sheets, wall alphabets, pencil grips, as well as special education materials. Of particular interest might be *Shirley's Books* [$6.95 each], a four-book series of vertical manuscript, slant print, and cursive reproducible practice books.(S)

Peterson also sponsors yearly cursive handwriting contests for each of grades three through eight. Information is available on their web site. The web site also offers research information about handwriting.

Primary Fonts [computer programs]
(Teacher Created Materials)
$19.95

Primary Fonts I is a CD-ROM for either Windows or Macintosh systems that allows you to add several useful fonts to your computer. Samples for handwriting can be printed out, as well as dotted line letters for tracing practice. These come in manuscript or cursive, with or without lined backgrounds. (If you use a D'Nealian handwriting program, get *Primary Fonts II*.) Also included are fonts with math symbols and pictures to help you print out your own professional looking math lessons.

ReadyWriter®
(Providence Project)
$17.95

ReadyWriter® is an introductory penmanship program for students ages 4 through 7 which uses the standard ball-and-stick style. It includes motor skills practice with basic strokes which is essential for consistent, legible penmanship. However, the format is much different from any others reviewed here. Pictorial exercises (farm scenes), wherein students complete pictures using what are essentially handwriting strokes, make it more interesting than simply making strokes on blank lines. It is presented in a single book with 12 copies each of 16 different exercises (printed on colored paper), an instructor's guide, and achievement certificates. Purchasers may photocopy workbook pages for use within their own families.

A Reason for Writing program
(Concerned Communications)
student books - $10.98 each; teacher guidebook - $12.98

Concerned Communications offers a handwriting program called *A Reason for Writing*. This curriculum uses the traditional method with Scripture as the writing material. An unusual feature is the set of decorated border sheets in the back of the books for children to write their verse of the week and color the border. These completed pages are attractive enough to hang in prominent places, use as family memory verses, or send to grandparents and relatives. Seven different books are offered with schools in mind. The first book, entitled *God Made My World*, is an introduction to manuscript (printing) for kindergarten level. The next two books, *Words of Promise* (Psalms and Proverbs) and *Words of Jesus* (Gospels), teach manuscript, covering the same skills but with different Scripture selections. *Words of Jesus* also has a section added for transition to cursive writing for schools who begin transition in the second grade. Lines have more space than *Words to Live By*, so children don't become frustrated by lack of space. The fourth book, *Words to Live By* (Epistles), covers the transition from manuscript to cursive for schools who prefer to transition in the third grade. Some children will need to use both the third and fourth levels as they make the adjustment to smaller lines. Some children might need to use both levels to experience adequate practice. And some children will be able to master cursive quickly using only one of the "transition books." The last three books, *Words of Love* (Gospels), *Words of Praise* (Psalms), and *Words of Wisdom* (Proverbs), all cover the same basic skills of cursive. If you do not need to use all of the books, choose according to Scripture content. The Teacher Guidebook, which covers all levels, includes principles of handwriting, teaching tips, vocabulary and skill lists for each student workbook, reproducible master forms for student progress records, plus supplemental exercises, games, and ideas.

Sycamore Tree's Border Pages

(Sycamore Tree)

$7.95 each

Pretty Pages and *Beautiful Border* (Sycamore Tree Center for Home Education) are border pages with lovely line drawings similar in concept to those in *A Reason for Writing*. They are available in two versions, one for manuscript and one for cursive. Each version has one each of 36 different designs.

Slant Print/Simplified Cursive

Handwriting for Christian Schools

(Bob Jones University Press)

Bob Jones University Press' *Handwriting for Christian Schools* program concentrates on handwriting with the emphasis placed on a clear, legible style. Children begin by learning slant print letter formation. Transition to a simplified cursive form takes place in second grade. Workbooks are appealingly illustrated in full color. I particu-

larly like the way they use shaded, slanted gray sections on the lines to help students maintain correct slant in their own printing and cursive in the first two books. Student worktexts are $9.65 each for grades 1-6. The teacher's material for the first grade book is incorporated into the Home Teacher's Manual that also covers phonics and reading. However, you can probably manage without it. There is a separate teacher's edition for second grade [$25] that provides presentation methods as children make the transition from printing to cursive. The student book, alone, does not explain how to make the transition. You should not need teacher's editions for other grade levels. The third grade student book can be used on its own to practice or learn basic cursive forms. It offers students a great deal of practice, including models to copy.

D'Nealian Handwriting

(ScottForesman)

ScottForesman offers their own slant print called *D'Nealian*. This is very similar to BJUP's program. Good, colorful workbooks and optional, supplementary activity books make it appealing to children. Cursive is introduced in second grade. There are Home School Packages for grades K-3 for $34.35 each. However, you should be able to work with only the student workbooks in most cases. The teacher's editions have reproductions of student pages, lesson presentation outlines, and supplemental activity pages. Student workbooks for K-6 are $8.58 each, and regular teacher's editions are $49.35. Order numbers for the 1999 editions follow, showing student workbook number followed by the teacher edition number for the same grade: K -#59213-8/#59219-7, 1 - #59214-6/#59220-0, 2 -#59215-4/#59221-9, 3 -#59216-2/#59291-X, 4 - #59217-0/#59292-8, 5 - #59218-9/#59224-3, 6 -#59225-1/#59227-8.(S)

The Writing Rhino and The Writing Warthog

(Learning Works)

$6.95 each

These two books provide lessons for learning and practicing letter formation. *Rhino* teaches "modern manuscript" or slant print for the early grades while *Warthog* teaches "modern" or simplified cursive. Each page provides a line each for practice on upper and lower case forms for a single letter. There are two such pages per letter. There is no printed instruction but models with arrows show directionality. After working on letter formation, children practice writing a tongue twister sentence which features many uses of the featured letter such as, "Gigi Gerbil gulped as she gazed at the giraffe's long, gooey tongue." Cute drawings illustrate each sentence. At the end of each book is a "reminder" list for students to check height, shape, slant, spacing, resting on base line, and neatness. This encourages them to analyze their handwriting for particular errors. These books are probably most useful for practice after students have already learned to form the letters since all letters are used in the practice sentences from the first lesson onward.

Italic Style

Italic Handwriting series
by Inga Dubay and Barbara Getty
(Portland State University)
individual books - $5.75 each;
starter set of any 3 books plus
instruction manual - $23

Italic style handwriting, typically thought of as our third option, can be taught with this series of inexpensive handwriting worktexts. Italic is similar to slant print in appearance, but letters are formed differently. The method is more like a very basic calligraphy than anything else, although the writing instrument is lifted far less often than in calligraphy. Italic letter forms for printing and cursive are basically identical, with entrance and exit strokes added to the "printed" forms for joining letters in cursive. This makes transition from printing to cursive almost effortless. These books teach students to use a "look, plan, and practice" approach to evaluate and improve their own work, beginning with the first step in Books A-C, then using all three steps in D-G. The books have full-color covers, and the print explaining lessons matches the Italic style. The teacher's manual (one book for student books A-G) [$5.75] contains the scope and sequence for the series; discussion of materials; tips for teaching left- or right-handed writers; and techniques for teaching and evaluating shape, strokes, size, slope, spacing, and speed of writing. It also has black-line masters for various sizes of ruled-line paper, three letter formats, and an envelope. Italic looks impressive without requiring extraordinary effort. Many schools are now using this as their basic handwriting program. This method might also be a good choice for children who have struggled with or have very sloppy handwriting and need a new approach. Introducing italic style to children with handwriting difficulties has proven very successful in some cases. It gives them a fresh start, and the results can look good with little skill. Students need not begin in Book A (kindergarten level) but can start with the book for their grade level.

Blackline masters [$6.75 a set] are available for use with children who need even more practice than that supplied within the workbooks. To make teaching italic style easier, they have produced a video which sells for $29.95. These two teaching aids should make it easier than before to teach italic style printing and writing.

For those who prefer more efficient instruction within a single book rather than child-oriented worktexts, the authors have

written *Write Now* [$12.95]. Although written for adult learners, children from about ages eight or nine should be able to learn from it, although they might need some adult assistance. *Write Now* teaches basic italic handwriting with plenty of examples and practice exercises. Unlike the workbook series described above, it goes beyond simple italic into the use of different types of pens and more complicated calligraphy. Following the instruction is a brief, illustrated history of the alphabet. Lined guide sheets are also included.

Handwriting Without A Text

After the foregoing discussion, I must tell you it is not necessary to use a program or textbook for teaching handwriting. It often works just as well to teach your child how to form letters, then simply allow him to practice as much as he needs. "Letter strips" or charts showing how letters are formed (following whatever method you prefer) are valuable for reference. Inexpensive, erasable mats with letter models as well as letter strips or charts can be found at teacher supply stores and from many of the publishers and distributors listed in this manual.

For "Lefties"

Cursive Writing Skills by Diana Hanbury King (Educators Publishing Service) [$7.15 each] is available in both right- and left-handed editions, so be sure to specify which you are ordering. Each forty-eight page book teaches about posture, grip, paper position, lower and upper case letters, and joins, then provides copy practice. The left-handed student is taught a "backhand" cursive. These books can be used with young students or older students who have not previously been able to master cursive writing. The publisher recommends them for ages seven through adult.(S)

Typing

Children usually love to type on a typewriter or keyboard. This is especially true when they are just learning cursive and are finding it laborious to think about letter formation and connections and neatness. There is a strong temptation to quit fighting the cursive battle around ages nine and ten, and instead let children work on a computer. Don't! Developing familiarity with the keyboard is worthwhile, but do not let a child avoid the self-discipline needed to develop fluency in his cursive writing. It just takes some hard work for a while until it comes more easily. Ten to twenty minutes a day of diligent copying will help children develop the necessary fluency so that they can write and think at the same time. (Children who have impaired motor skills might be the exception, in which case, using a keyboard rather than laboring over cursive might be the best choice.)

Assuming our child is not looking for an easy out from cursive, teaching them keyboard skills is recommended. Although few of us own typewriters (or have them anywhere they might be used even if we do still own one), typing manuals can be useful for learning basic keyboard skills. However, instructions for "carriage returns" and special key functions will need to be covered.

Children will find typing lesson books written especially for them easier to use than those written for adults. One such book

 is *Type It* by Joan Duffy (Educators Publishing Service) [$12.15]. It uses a phonetic approach that will help to reinforce reading and spelling skills.

Many excellent typing programs for computers are available. You can hardly go wrong with any of those you find on the market these days.

School of Tomorrow sells a typing program presented as lessons. *Typemaster* ▄ consists of six diskettes, each containing twelve complete tutorial lessons. Lessons are appropriate for the approximate grade levels 1-6, but students should be able to read before they begin. The six diskettes are divided into two levels, *Typemaster I* and *Typemaster II*, with three diskettes for each. *Typemaster I* teaches key location and typing of single words. Programs are animated and very colorful to appeal to young learners. Older learners perform letter pattern drills, and type sentences and paragraphs. Character values are also taught within lessons. *Typemaster I* and *Typemaster II* each sell for $49.95, making this a significantly more expensive option than more common programs. *Typemaster* requires IBM compatible- computers with VGA graphics adapters and 3.5" floppy drives.

Chapter 13

Mathematics

Many of us learned to hate math in our early school years because it was taught in ways that made it seem pure drudgery. We developed a negative attitude that stuck with us through the multiplication tables and fractions and on into algebra and geometry. We often see our own negative attitude reflected in our children as we try to teach them math. They quickly pick up on our uncertainties and our body language messages that say, "Math is really awful, but we have to get through this."

Math need not be the low point in home education. We can do things differently so that math is far more interesting than it was for us as children. But, on the other hand, math cannot be all fun and games. As soon as math begins to require more thinking, many of us (parents and children alike) decide it is a difficult and boring subject. We need to use more interesting approaches to math to help prevent this negative attitude from taking control. Fortunately, there are lots of interesting programs available to us, some of them written specifically for home educators.

Learning Styles

In choosing the type of material(s) to use, we must remember to consider our child's learning style.

Wiggly Willys will often do poorly with programs that consist only of workbooks or textbooks. Wiggly Willys need lots of manipulative (hands-on) work along with practical application to catch their attention and enable them to understand. Sociable Sue is often bored with problem solving without meaningful application, so she sometimes has trouble with programs lacking that application. Programs such as *Miquon Math, Moving with Math*, and *Making Math Meaningful* are usually more successful with Wiggly Willys and some Sociable Sues. We should use more learning materials and games for a Wiggly Willy than we would with others. Wiggly Willys and Sociable Sues will both like to play math games, but the Willys might intimidate the Sues with their strong competitive spirit. Sociable Sues will usually prefer cooperative rather than competitive games. For both types of learners look for variety in methods for practicing their math facts. Sociable Sues might also enjoy the Biblical symbolism of numbers taught in *Christ Centered Math*.

Perfect Paulas are comfortable with book-based math pro-grams lacking manipulatives if they are not above their grade level, but we must make sure they understand concepts and do not learn solely by rote. Perfect Paula is often more comfortable with workbooks that follow a consistent format day after day than with programs that use different methods and formats for each lesson. Thus, Modern Curriculum Press or Saxon (past third grade) are likely to be better choices for Perfect Paula than *Miquon, Making Math Meaningful*, or other hands-on programs for the early grades.

Competent Carl will probably have little problem with any math program unless it is too repetitious, does not offer him explanations of concepts, or is too easy. We can supplement most math curriculum with "brain teasers" or logic books for extra interest. Bob Jones University Press, Modern Curriculum Press, and Saxon (*Math 54* and above) math programs are all good choices for Competent Carls since they offer challenging thinking and application problems.

If you run into problems with math, refer to the list below and consider trying alternate teaching methods. Try to help your child overcome his learning style weaknesses by giving him easier or review work when using learning methods that are difficult for him.

Wiggly Willy Prefers
- math games
- short, varied tasks
- practical application of concepts
- manipulatives
- incentives

Wiggly Willy needs help to do pencil and paper work, to develop a longer attention span, and to do long word problems.

Perfect Paula Prefers
- workbooks
- consistent format
- drill

Perfect Paula needs help to apply arithmetic to word problems that require imaginative thinking.

Competent Carl Prefers
- math principles and theory
- real-life problems
- math puzzles
- computer

Sociable Sue Prefers
- background of math discoveries
- people in relationship to math
- hands-on math that involves group interaction

Sociable Sue needs help to pay attention to detail

Characteristics of a Good Math Program

Math materials vary greatly in format and content. Look for the following characteristics for a good math program:

1.) A format that constantly reviews and reinforces previous material is better than one that covers single topics then drops them to go on to the next.

2.) Math often requires a visual demonstration or hands-on experience of the concept for understanding, especially with young children. Many children continue to need these types of experiences throughout the primary grades and beyond. Some children <u>need</u> concrete experiences to understand concepts because they cannot yet form the abstract concept in their mind without hands-on experience. Even those children who do not need it will usually benefit from some hands-on work, gaining increased understanding and more enjoyment as they discover concepts for themselves. (A few children, usually Competent Carls will find hands-on learning to be a waste of their time.) Some publishers include ideas for hands-on methods in the teacher's manuals. If not, you will need supplemental materials for this purpose.

3.) Word problems and practical application are vital parts of a good math program to ensure understanding.

4.) Some drill is necessary, but drill can be made more enjoyable and sometimes more effective when done with games or approaches other than workbooks. Some teacher's manuals include fun ideas for drill and interesting drill pages, but you should also look for supplemental materials and ideas.

Mathematics Materials

I recommend the use of informal approaches to teach math at kindergarten level and sometimes beyond. Many of the available programs for kindergarten and first grade rely heavily on workbooks with insufficient hands-on experience for understanding of concepts. While hands-on programs take more time, they actually can be more efficient in teaching concepts in the long run. Many children in the early grades have the ability to grasp concepts presented with manipulatives while the same concepts presented in the traditional paper/pencil mode would be too difficult. You will generally find that with manipulative-based programs you have to do less reteach-

ing and reviewing. Because of this, I have concentrated reviews for the early grades on programs that I consider more developmentally appropriate. However, I have included some others for those who feel that such an approach is best for their children and for those who have a different philosophy of education.

To help you sort out ideas about appropriate math programs, I recommend Dr. Ruth Beechick's little book, *An Easy Start in Arithmetic* (one of three books in *The Three R's* set from Mott Media) [$12] . It will help you understand what is essential in teaching math in the early grades and what is just "school stuff."

As we move up in grade level, we still have some hands-on programs to choose from, but we are increasingly faced with a number of textbook-based options. If you choose to use textbook-based programs, you might want to have some manipulatives (hands-on materials) to use as a supplement. Textbooks basically offer two format choices: books children write in and books that are not written in. A book a child writes in might consist of worksheets which accompany lessons which have been taught by the teacher, or it might be a worktext which contains both the instruction and problems to be solved in one place. Books that are not written in are usually hardback textbooks from which students must copy problems before they can solve them. For many children with poor small-muscle coordination, the extra step of copying problems is an unnecessary obstacle that discourages them. If your child hates to write or has poor small motor coordination, choose a workbook or worktext in which he can write so he is not doing too much written work copying problems. Another alternative is for you to take the time to copy problems out of the book for him.

Other Choices for Readiness Programs

Refer to the "Readiness" section of "Reading Materials and Methods" in Chapter Nine for materials or programs that can be used with preschool and kindergarten aged children if desired. Many of those listed under reading also cover basic number skills. Some of the inexpensive workbooks available in markets and department stores as well as teacher supply stores are appropriate for young learners. They offer just enough without being as overwhelming as programs designed for the classroom.

Ungraded Programs for Preschool through Second Grade

Beginning Math at Home
(Individualized Education Systems)
$13.50

This is a simple introductory math program for ages 3 to 6. It consists of four kits of 4" by 5 1/2" cards (about 90 cards altogether). Kit one covers shapes, tallest and shortest, and longest and shortest. Kit two teaches counting to 10, more than and less than, and time telling to the hour. Kit three covers addition combinations adding up to 10, while kit four teaches subtraction with numbers up through 9. Visual representation (pictures of objects or dots) helps young children understand number concepts. Suggestions are offered for other math activities using objects around the house. I suspect that young children will stay at the kit-one level for some time, since most three-year-olds do not easily grasp "more than" or "less than" concepts taught in kit two. Don't rush children through but wait until they are ready to move on. A simple little teacher guidebook shows parents how to teach using the kits. A one-page game can be used for addition and subtraction practice. A pre- and post-test booklet can be used to verify progress, but be cautious of discouraging young children by asking them to do math problems they have never before seen. "Program" might be a generous description of *Beginning Math*, since it is more of a bare bones approach to basic math skills than a comprehensive program. Still, for parents who want to use a low-key, non-workbook approach, this is a good place to begin.

Math Sense Building Blocks Program

(Common Sense Press)
Math Pack - $38; Math Bag - $26;
Math Sense Manual - $16

Math Sense Building Blocks can be used to supplement another math curriculum that lacks manipulatives (such as A Beka's), or they can be used as the foundation of your own self-designed program for the early grades. The blocks are colored manipulatives that snap together, sort of a combination of *Unifix Cubes*® and *Cuisenaire Rods*®. Each length manipulative is a different color and the "rods" are marked off in units so that students can easily see the numerical differences between them. The heart of the program is the 68-page *Math Sense Manual* which tells us how to use the manipulatives for grades K-6. Rather than a general manual about how to teach with the manipulatives, it presents detailed lessons for presenting various math concepts. Even though activities give specific directions (e.g., "Put a Green 3-Block horizontally next to each Pink 4-Block square."), in most cases, the strategy can then be used over and over again to work with various numbers. The bulk of the book is divided into two sections: one for grades K-3 and the other for grades 4-6. Some of the upper level ideas are also useful beyond sixth grade level. The Appendix includes reproducible pages that are used for some of the lessons.

Since the *Math Sense Manual* is written for use with unique *Math Sense Building Blocks*, you probably want to purchase either the *Math Pack* or *Math Bag*. The *Math Pack* includes the *Manual*, reproducible activity sheets, a 104-piece set of blocks, and color-coded dice, all packed in a back pack. The *Math Bag* is roll bag stuffed with a 104-piece set of blocks and a mini-manual that demonstrates how to teach basic math concepts with the blocks.

The *Math Sense Building Blocks*, although designed differently, are the same size as *Cuisenaire Rods*, so they may also be used with any of the excellent Cuisenaire activity books.

Fun at the Beach

(Little Folk Visuals)
$17.95 - economy; $27.95 - deluxe

In this hands-on math program, felt beach balls, coconuts, seals, buckets, and so on are used for children to experience math concepts. Then they apply what they learn to math problems. A teacher's manual and 182 felt figures come in the economy set, or you can spend more and get the deluxe set which includes a storage box and file sheets to help keep all the pieces organized. You need to supply your own "flannel board" on which to place the pieces. If you need a flannel board, Little Folk Visuals offers one for $12.95. In terms of academic concepts, there is enough here to work through kindergarten, first, and second grades. This approach works well with active learners and also lets you include the preschoolers in math lessons.

Miquon Math

(Key Curriculum Press)
$53.95 for complete Homeschool Set; set of *Cuisenaire*® Rods - $8.95

This inexpensive program, based on the use of *Cuisenaire*® Rods, is advertised for first through third grades. However, because of unique methods of teaching arithmetic concepts, younger children can begin to learn arithmetic through the hands-on activities, and older children can also benefit from *Miquon* used as a supplement. The child uses the *Rods* to discover mathematical concepts. He also does written work as he records his findings, moving towards more written work as he masters concepts. Essential components are *Lab Sheet Annotations* (the teacher's guide), *Notes To Teachers* (a small, inexpensive book), and student workbooks (two for each grade). I also recommend the *First-Grade Diary* which tells how the program actually worked in one classroom situation. This is probably one of the least expensive options in terms of effectiveness and cost for early elementary children who need active learning. We hear many glowing reports of success from those who have used it, although a few parents (typically Perfect Paulas) find it too confusing. You might want to supplement this program with inexpensive workbooks for computation practice.(S)

Kindergarten Level Programs

Christ Centered Math

(Christ Centered Publications)
See prices under the review of *Christ Centered Phonics*; the math manipulative package is $34.50

This program provides a strong Scriptural foundation for arithmetic. *Math Workbook A* covers beginning number concepts and simple addition and subtraction. *Math Workbook B* includes number facts up to 20, place values in the 100s, money, time, and fractions. This is a formal program that teaches concepts in sequence with lots of repetition so it can even be used with three- and four-year-olds, covering material up through what is considered first grade level. It begins with hands-on activity followed by workbook exercises. However, no workbooks are recommended for three-year-olds. At the youngest level the emphasis is not quite so academic but more activity oriented. Colorful *Math Flashcards* are also available that use animal families and character traits adapted from Bill Gothard's *Character Sketches*. The *Math Lesson Guides* are revised editions that combine drill with plenty of hands-on learning using manipulatives.

Program components may be purchased as part of the complete *Christ Centered Curriculum* (see the review of *Christ Centered Phonics*) or individually. A separate set of math manipulatives—snap cubes, place value pocket chart, place value sticks, *Base Ten Blocks*, and a place value mat—is essential to the program, although we can purchase individual items if we already have some of these.

Creative Oral and Written Drill Math Series
[Workbook 1 for preschool and kindergarten]

by Rosemary S. Thoburn
(Thoburn Press)
$18.95; teacher's edition - $14.95

Beginning with number recognition, tracing, and counting, this book might be used with preschoolers but is probably most appropriate for kindergartners. It does an excellent job of teaching counting (up to 120) and beginning addition (up to 9 + 9) with activities and workbook exercises. Even though the hefty, 388-page student book looks fairly complete, essential demonstrations and activities are explained in the Teacher's Manual, so you need to purchase both. Presentation is written for the classroom setting but should adapt easily to the home school. I spotted just a couple of Scripture verses in the student book that would make this "Christian" curriculum, but it is about as minimal as possible. Coverage of shapes and introduction of coins, typical kindergarten goals, are missing, but both concepts are easily covered in other ways. Workbook exercises are quite varied. Used along with lesson activities from the Teacher's Manual, they should provide an appropri-

ate balance of large and small motor activities for most young children. Children who have trouble with the written work can do more activity work and less workbook pages. *Animal Number Families Flash Cards* [$9.95] are also available to use with the program. Thirty large cards, printed in black on white, are used to teach numbers and number families. Animal stories, outlined in accompanying teacher information pages, are used throughout to show number relationships.

Kinder-Math

(Eagle's Wings Educational Materials)
$14.95; *Kinder-Math* is included with the *Alphabet Island Complete Phonics* program at no extra cost

Kinder-Math includes a workbook and teacher's manual, flash cards, simple games, and clock board. (Time telling and addition may be introduced too early for some children.) Large print and interesting presentations through games and activities favorably impress me. Concepts covered: number recognition and formation, simple addition, counting, time telling, "larger than/smaller than," and simple geometry.

Visual aids printed on tag board are included—clock, coins, counting chart, number cards, "domino patterns." Since children are usually fascinated by money, coins are used for many activities. Counting is emphasized. Children learn to add numbers up to ten, but because of their familiarity with other numbers from counting, they also add small numbers to large, e.g., 85 + 2.

Making Math Meaningful, K

(Cornerstone Curriculum Project)
Level K - $30; manipulative packet - $15

See the review under "1st Grade Level." While the program includes a kindergarten level course, you can skip it and begin with first grade. (Kindergarten level covers concepts that can be taught as effectively in informal situations around the home. See Ruth Beechick's An *Easy Start in Arithmetic* for ideas.) Nevertheless, some parents will appreciate the security of having such a program to give their children a good start in math. As is appropriate for young learners, student worksheets are used infrequently at this level, while manipulatives are used frequently.

Math K5 for Christian Schools

(Bob Jones University Press)
home school kit - $44

BJUP's K5 math program comes with a Home School Teacher's Edition which streamlines the program for home use. It is designed to build a foundation for understanding math concepts. The kindergarten theme centers around a farm, featuring Farmer Brown, Mrs. Brown, and their mouse Cheddar.

This program is designed to be taught from the Teacher's Edition, with the student worktext used for practice and reinforcement. Review activities are in the Teacher's Edition. Manipulatives (e.g., *Unifix Cubes* and counters) play an important role in introducing new concepts. The Student Materials Packet provides manipulatives for the student, although the Teacher's Edition offers suggestions for substitutes and make-it-yourself manipulatives. The Home Teacher Packet contains essential teaching aids and worksheets used in the lessons. The Teaching Charts Flip Chart contains teaching charts. In addition to the student worktext, an activity book offers optional enrichment activities. The *Math K5* Home School Kit includes all of the essential components.

Math-U-See

See the review under first grade. Kindergartners can start at either *Introduction* or *Foundations* level, but they must first learn number recognition, counting, and one-to-one correspondence. Then they can move ahead through either level. Be careful to allow them as much time as they need rather than pushing them to do a consistent number of pages per week, especially if you start in *Foundations* level. You might not need the fraction kit yet, so you can wait until later to purchase it.

Horizons Mathematics K
(Alpha Omega)

$60.95 for the kindergarten math set; manipulatives are extra

The *Horizons's Mathematics K* program follows an advanced scope and sequence closer to many publishers' first grade programs. Students are doing addition and subtraction (two digits plus or minus one digit) with no regrouping by the end of the year. However, lessons are taught with visual aids and manipulatives to better help young children grasp concepts. The program consists of the teacher handbook and two student books. Lessons are taught from the teacher handbook with a combination of oral, hands-on, and written activities. Only some of those activities appear in the student books, so the student books do not stand alone. Manipulatives and visual aids are primarily things we find around the home like egg cartons, calendar, index cards, and paper plates. However, you will need to either purchase or create some of them like a flannel board and objects to use on it, an abacus, beads, clock models, and flash cards. The number line and number chart are used extensively throughout the curriculum, but they are provided. Supplementary worksheet masters are in the teacher handbook, and you will need to photocopy these. *Mathematics K* follows a developmental approach wherein concepts are introduced then retaught and practiced at regular intervals. The student books are very attractive and colorful. Although there are many workbook pages for kindergarten, they do not appear

overwhelming. The authors have taken care to balance drill exercises with more oral than written practice at this level. The Teacher Handbook outlines every step of the lesson, listing objectives, materials needed, stories, poems, and games. Some preparation time is needed, and lessons must be taught. However, lessons are purposeful; they don't waste time on peripheral topics as occurs in some other new math programs for younger levels (Saxon being an example of such). This program was designed very much with home educators in mind, so we find few classroom-only type activities that must be adapted or skipped. For home educators who want an academic math program for kindergarten, this is a practical solution. For those uncertain about their child's readiness for this program, there is a Horizons Math readiness test at the back of Alpha Omega's math diagnostic test booklet.

Math-U-See, Introduction level
(Math-U-See)

teacher's manual - $10; student book - $15; extra practice sheets - $15; Introduction video - $15; blocks - $30; skip-counting tape and coloring book - $10

The *Introduction* level covers essential number concepts needed before going on to *Foundations*. It teaches number recognition, writing numbers, place value, counting, simple addition, skip counting, shapes, time, and money (pennies, dollars, and dimes since they correlate to our number system). There are 30 lessons, but children use manipulatives far more than in succeeding levels as well as far more than in most kindergarten math programs. If you choose to use a program for kindergarten, I consider this one more developmentally-appropriate than most.

Moving with Math, Pre-K/Kindergarten or Level A or Grade 1

(Math Teachers Press - MTP)
Pre K/Kindergarten: Teacher Resource Manual and student activity book - $61.90; $110 for complete package
Level A package: Skill Builders, three student workbooks, Math Capsules, Home School Instructions, Using Models: Addition and Subtraction - reproducible version - $67.90 OR non-reproducible - $42.90; manipulatives also sold through MTP
Grade 1 set: student book and teacher manual set - $95.90; complete set - $170

See the complete program descriptions of Level A and Grade 1 under first grade. We can begin with Level A, but there is a preschool-kindergarten program which has more thorough coverage of concepts for younger levels. It is very much a hands-on approach, but it also uses artificial activities to teach concepts that can easily be taught using informal real-life opportunities as described in Ruth Beechick's *An Easy Start in Arithmetic* (Mott Media). If you are working informally with your children to cover beginning math concepts, skip the Pre-K/Kindergarten program and begin with Level A or Grade 1. Many kindergartners will be able to easily work at this level. Like most classroom-oriented resources, much of what is taught children learn on their own in a home where children are involved in daily household activity that teaches them the difference between short and tall, biggest and smallest, and other concepts.

This program offers a compromise between the extremes of a totally manipulative-based approach such as *Math-U-See* and a workbook approach such as A Beka (fourth grade and above). The Pre-K/K level of *Moving with Math* is more structured than the other levels. There is one student workbook, and the lessons are organized to be used in order. (Other levels allow us to diagnose children's needs, then choose appropriate lessons.) The first three chapters are geared for preschool, while the last seven address kindergarten-level concepts, so choose the appropriate beginning point for each child.

The Pre-K/K level is taught from the teacher resource manual. There are three parts within the manual: the teacher guide with daily lessons plans, skill builders reproducible activity sheets, and "math capsules"—reproducible tests, record sheets, and daily review. The 176-page student book is consumable. Some manipulatives are essential to the program—*Unifix Cubes*, a *Unifix Number Stair*, teddy bear counters, pattern blocks, and attribute blocks. Optional manipulatives are *Cuisenaire Rods*, dinosaur counters, farm animal counters, toy vehicle counters, and the *Teddy Bear Balance Scale*. Themes such as teddy bears or trains are used within single lessons or groups of lessons. Related storybooks are suggested in some lessons. Since the program was written for classroom use, there are activities designed for groups. Some of these can be easily adapted for one or two children. As with other hands-on programs at this level, lesson preparation and presentation time are greater than with a totally workbook-based program. The time required is offset by the value of interactive and hands-on learning for young children. The complete package includes the manual, student book, and essential manipulatives.

After Pre-K/K, *Moving With Math* is divided into four levels: A for grades 1-2, B for 3-4, C for 5-6, and D for 7-8. Level A is offered both in its original format (which covers two grade levels) or broken down into two separate packages for Grade 1 and Grade 2. These all differ in format from the Pre-K/K level.(S)

Saxon Math K

(Saxon Publishers)
home study kit - $57.75

The publishers of *Saxon Math* have developed math materials for the early grades that are extremely different from the rest of their program. The K-3 *Saxon Math* programs stand apart from upper level books with totally different formats. The kindergarten program differs still more in that it has no student books as do the grade 1 through 3 programs. Levels K-3 all use manipulatives (bear counters, *MathLink Cubes*, geoboard, tangrams, etc.) and scripted presentations by the parent/teacher. The incremental approach which Saxon uses at upper levels is still very evident in the early levels. Children review previously learned concepts continually, while adding new learning in small segments that build upon each other. Level K consists of teacher-directed instruction and activity, so this is not a program for independent learning. Optional written work comes from reproducible master sheets in the teacher's manual.

The methodology very much reflects the new math standards. Children spend a great deal of time on mathematical thinking and related topics. The program does teach traditional math skills but at a slower pace than programs such as A Beka, Horizons, or Bob Jones. Each day's lesson begins with "The Meeting" where parents direct discussion and activity related to time, temperature, money, counting, patterns, and problem solving. After "The Meeting," a new concept is introduced (usually with manipulatives) and previously taught concepts are reviewed. At kindergarten level, oral counting, acting out addition and subtraction stories, sorting, identifying and counting coins, measuring, and telling time are the types of activities that replace workbooks.

The K-3 programs were originally written for classroom use. In the new home school versions, the teacher's manuals, key components at each level, have been rewritten to eliminate the classroom activities. The home school kit for kindergarten includes the teacher's manual and the Meeting Book. We need to purchase the necessary manipulatives. A *Home Study Manipulative Kit* [$65] designed for the Saxon program is sold through ETA (contact ETA at 620 Lakeview Parkway, Vernon Hills, IL 60061 or 800-445-5985.) The same manipulatives will be used throughout the K-3 programs. While the program does a thorough job of covering a multitude of concepts, the price is likely to discourage many home educators from using it. Also, those who prefer more natural learning are likely to be uncomfortable with all of the artificial classroom-type presentations of knowledge and skills that children acquire quite naturally just being around the home and interacting with their parents.

1st Grade Level

Arithmetic 1
(A Beka Book)
$11.55; teacher curriculum guide -
$39.95; teacher edition - $20.95;
Speed Drills and Tests - $4.60; key to
Speed Drills and Tests - $8.95; flash-
cards, felt objects, manipulatives, and
games are extra.

A Beka's arithmetic program for grades 1-3 has been redesigned. The student workbook is dependent upon instruction
presented by the teacher from the curriculum guide. All of the
topics to be taught in each lesson are outlined in the curriculum guide, but all are not shown in the workbook. The curriculum guide includes numerous classroom-designed review
activities for each lesson, most of which can be used by home
schoolers. For each lesson, one page from the workbook is
intended to be used in class with another used for independent
work. The student Test and Speed Drill Booklet is supposed to
be used in daily lessons. The separate teacher edition has
reduced pictures of student seatwork pages with answers. It
also lists the lesson objectives and a few activities.

First Grade Program Without a Text

At kindergarten and first grade levels, it is not necessary to
use a textbook for math. If we know our goals, we can put
together our own program with learning materials and games.
If you are inexperienced this might sound a bit overwhelming,
so I have included an example here of how to do this.

Following is the list of educational goals for first grade with
suggestions for teaching each concept. There is space to offer
only one suggestion for each goal, but the ideas themselves
should suggest other ideas to you.

- Counts backwards from 10 to 0—Use a number line or
  Wonder Number Game Board or 100's chart (chart num-
  bered 1-10 across, 11-20 second row, etc., to 100).
- Add numbers 0 to 10—Use objects such as beans, blocks,
  LEGOS, etc.
- Matches set with numbers 0 to 20—Write numbers on a
  large number line. Glue beans to popsicle sticks to repre-
  sent each number. Match popsicle sticks to number line.
- Add numbers 0 to 20—Use objects.
- Subtract numbers 0 to 10—Use objects, *Wonder Number
  Game Board*, or a *One Hundred Board.*
- Subtract numbers 0 to 20—Use objects.
- Count, read, write numbers to 100—Count houses on your
  street, leaves on a branch, etc. Use chalkboard for writing.
- Recognize smaller/larger numbers to 100—Play war with
  card deck.
- Count backwards from 20 to 0 using objects.
- Recall addition facts to 10—Make or buy triangle flash
  cards. (*Triangle Flash Cards* have addends of one color in
  the bottom two corners, the sum in a different color in the
  third (top) corner. Cover the number to be answered.)
- Recognize that 2 + 4 is the same as 4 + 2 (commutative
  property)—Do with objects.
- Recognize addition and subtraction in various formats- horizontal and vertical—Show on chalkboard.
- Recall subtraction facts for numbers 10 or less—Use
  Triangle Flash Cards. Covering an addend rather than the
  sum changes the problem from addition to subtraction.

- Recognize quarters (money)—Use real money.
- Count coins to $.25—Use real money.
- Recognize time to the hour and half hour—Use a play
  clock with movable hands that has minute markings. The
  Judy Company makes small (approx. 4") clocks that sell
  for a dollar or two at most teacher supply stores.
- Recognize fraction shapes 1/2 and 1/4—Cut bologna,
  pizza, sandwiches, etc.
- Count by 10s to 100—Use dimes, *Wonder Number Game
  Board* or 100's chart.
- Represent two digit numbers in place value form as tens
  and ones—String beads in groups of tens, keeping some as
  singles. Show how much easier it is to handle one group of
  ten that is strung together than ten single beads. Place
  value is one of the most crucial concepts!
- Read, write, and use expanded notation (60 + 9 for
  69)—Using your beads, show numbers as separate groups
  of tens and ones.
- Perform two digit addition and subtraction without
  carrying—Use the beads.
- Name the days of the week—Read the calendar every day.
- Select correct operation for problem solving (addition/sub-
  traction)—Give oral word problems that apply to real life
  situations. Ask them to explain how they arrive at their
  answer. Discuss the process.
- Find practical applications of arithmetic—Explain how
  math helps you in the grocery store, in making other types
  of purchases, or in building projects.
- Identify and continue simple patterns—Play a "What
  comes next?" game—Give numbers such as 2,4,6,8, and
  ask, "What comes next?"
- Select, collect, record or organize data using tallies, charts,
  graphs, tables—Record weather on chart and tally in chart
  form how many leaves each child collects.

[Ruth Beechick's *An Easy Start in Arithmetic* (Mott Media)
  and *Maximum Math* (Design-A-Study) also explain ways
  to teach concepts without textbooks for the early grades.]

Hands-on Activity

Any formal curriculum at younger levels should be supplemented with lots of hands-on activity and experience.

Following is a list of resources that can serve as part of your math program. Also check the "Helps for Teaching, Drill, Review, and Fun" section for more ideas.
• money—real money or a cash box of play money
• clocks
• abacus
• chalkboard or whiteboard
• dominoes

• *Triominoes* (3-sided dominoes game available at toy and game stores)
• dice
• household items (especially in the kitchen) e.g., beans, measuring cups, ruler
• games that involve counting, number recognition, sequences, simple addition, money, and number relationships (e.g., *Yahtzee*®, numerous games from Creative Teaching Associates, and old favorite board games such as *Monopoly*®).

The new version is an improvement over the old because it uses more visual aids, games, and activities. (I suggest you purchase the curriculum without these aids, then go through it to figure out which of them you need, which you can make or find yourself, and which you need to order.) Another improvement is that they have jazzed up the student workbook with lots of illustrations and color. However, the basic philosophy remains the same, emphasizing rules, memorization of math facts, review, and drill. For the most part, new concepts still depend on verbal explanations rather than demonstrations with manipulatives. (E.g., carrying is taught simply by talking about place value, rather than by demonstrating with objects how groups of 10 must be moved to the next column.)

While the program is intended to be dependent upon the curriculum guide, I suspect some home educators will skip it, figuring they can teach the the objectives listed in the teacher edition on their own. However, every once in a while an activity relies on the teacher reading questions from the curriculum guide, and we won't know what is intended in those instances. Also, the bulk of each lesson is spent on review and drill activities, much of it directed from the curriculum guide. Some home educators will hand their students the workbook and consider that their entire program. While lesson presentations and activities in the curriculum guide are useful, it is possible for students to learn the necessary material from the worktext with some extra assistance from parents on new concepts. There is plenty of work within the student worktext, but it does lack explanations. Those who want to use the curriculum as intended will want both the curriculum guide and teacher edition. A Test and Speed Drill Booklet is available, and instructions as to when to use it are in the curriculum guide.

This curriculum best suits the Perfect Paula and Competent Carl learning styles. It can work with other learners who need more hands-on experiences by supplementing with *Cuisenaire Rods* ® or other manipulatives.

Beginning Arithmetic, 1991 edition (Grade 1)
(Rod and Staff)
teacher's manual - $14.25; 2 pupil workbooks - $6.40

each; speed drills - $1.55; blackline masters -$13.10; flash cards - $16.10

Rod and Staff's arithmetic program reflects their educational philosophy that eschews experiential learning and games, preferring a no nonsense teaching of the facts. Lessons are presented by the teacher, who uses visual aids to teach concepts. A flannel board and flash cards are essential to teach the lessons as presented in the teacher's manual, with other visuals playing minor roles. Rod and Staff sells a set of large flash cards to be used along with the lessons, although we might choose to make these ourselves. (The only difficulty occurs with the number order flash cards. Some flash cards have particular numbers arranged out of order; these are used to help children identify the proper order for numbers.) We are told to create a small set of flash cards for each student for some of the drill practice. You might let a single small set serve for lesson presentation and student practice.

Lessons are divided into class time, seatwork time, and "after class" time. (Remember the program is designed for the classroom.) Most of all three parts of the lesson actually occur during what would be considered math class. The main lesson is presented at class time. Students complete speed drills every other day at the end of class time, then complete the lesson page in their workbooks during seatwork time. They might also complete some of the blackline pages. The "after class" time, which is directed by the teacher, is intended for practice, review, or introduction of a new topic.

The amount of seatwork is similar to that in A Beka or Alpha Omega's *Horizons Math* programs, but there is a larger amount of math fact drill and less variety in methodology than we find in most math programs. Student workbooks are illustrated, but everything is printed in brown ink on white paper. You will almost certainly want the blackline masters since these pages correlate with the lessons.

The teacher's manual lists blacklines for each lesson in descending order of importance, so we need not use them all. Some dot-to-dots and more interesting pages are found in the blackline set. The scope and sequence is slower than some of the other Christian publishers; first grade covers double-digit addition and subtraction but without any carrying or borrowing. Rod and Staff directs the teacher to handle and manipulate objects to demonstrate concepts. At home it should be practical to have children do more of the handling themselves, increasing the hands-on dimension for those learners who need it. The teacher's manual has complete instructions for lesson presentation, patterns, reduced student pages with answers, and explanation of the design of the program.

Developmental Mathematics
(Mathematics Programs Associates, Inc.)

student workbooks for Levels 1 - 16 - $8.50 each; instruction guides for levels 1 - 9 - $3.50 each; solution manuals for levels 10 - 16 - $8.50 each; level set for levels 1 - 9 (student workbook and instruction guide) - $10.50 each, and for levels 10 - 16 (student workbook and solution manual) - $15.00 each; student set of all student workbooks for levels 1 - 16 - $120.00 each; complete set of all student workbooks, instruction guides, and solution manuals for levels 1 - 16 - $200.00 each

This unusual math program has a distinct philosophy of education behind it. The author, Dr. Saad, believes arithmetic is best taught in a sequential order without jumping from topic to topic or including "extraneous topics" such as time-telling, temperature, and measurement. (He believes these should be taught through life experience.) Much time is spent on achieving mastery of concepts. Dr. Saad uses deductive methods through which the child draws upon previously learned knowledge to understand new concepts. While no hands-on materials are used or recommended, pictures are used to introduce new concepts. The material is designed for independent study. The child studies a number of examples at the beginning of each lesson, then completes the exercises, essentially teaching himself. (Young children will need assistance if they are unable to read independently.)

There are sixteen books or levels in the series, and each should be completed at whatever pace is comfortable for each child. The material covers all arithmetic skills from number and object recognition through fractions and decimals, and including ratio, percent, and proportion.

I am impressed with the development of thinking skills in this program. Each concept is presented in many ways, including application/word problems to ensure understanding. According to Dr. Saad, students are ready for pre-algebra after completion of level 16. Since negative numbers and square roots have not been covered, students should move from level 16 into a pre-algebra program such as Saxon's *Algebra 1/2*. In addition, those "extraneous topics" mentioned earlier have not been taught specifically, although money is used extensively in word, picture, and number problems. You can easily obtain supplementary books on these subjects if you need them.

Because of the unique design of *Developmental Mathematics*, it is important to properly place a child. Dr. Saad cautions that we should start a child at as low a level as is necessary to provide a strong foundation without concern for grade level. Level 1 is suitable for kindergartners. Level 2 teaches simple addition, assuming foundational knowledge has been learned. Placement help is provided in the free information packet, Placement Tests (available upon request), and on the internet at www.greatpyramid.com All student workbooks come with a "diagnostic" test to be used *after* completion of that level. Review tests and progress charts are also included within each workbook.

The Instruction Guides for lower levels provide some teaching helps, but primarily serve as answer keys. The Solutions Guides for upper levels are student books with overprinted answers. Lesson preparation time is little to none.(S)

Exploring Mathematics Grade 1
(ScottForesman)

student text - $22.74; teacher's edition - $115.68; manipulatives kit - $195.45

ScottForesman's *Exploring Mathematics* was designed for government schools and correlates with the new math standards. Student books are colorful and appealing to children. Teacher's editions are large, spiral-bound volumes with hard backs and soft front covers. They include reduced pictures of student pages on the appropriate teaching pages. ScottForesman also publishes a kindergarten level program, but I am not recommending it because, like most classroom designed programs, it spends far too much time and costs too much for what it accomplishes. It teaches number recognition, counting, and number writing, while introducing simple addition, subtraction, and other math skills. (Use other resources or make up your own program for kindergarten.) The Grade 1 program reviews numbers and counting briefly, then teaches addition and subtraction facts through 9 + 9 = 18 and it's reverse; introductory geometry and measurement; place value, counting, and number patterns through 99; money; time; and introductory fractions and probability.

In keeping with the new math standards, manipulatives are used throughout the program. A core manipulatives kit for each grade level includes enough manipulatives for a classroom. I suggest that you purchase only what you need (play money—coins only, clock, counting figures like teddy bear counters, and a set of *Unifix Cubes*®) from other sources. Many of these same items are used again for higher grade levels. Manipulatives are used to teach concepts, then students are gradually shifted into paper and pencil work. The amount of manipulative work is similar to that of Saxon's program and a bit less than used in Horizons. However, both Saxon and Horizon have significantly more workbook activity with two workbooks rather than the single volume for ScottForesman.

Topics are presented sequentially with little review. This is not a significant problem at this level, but might be at higher levels.

Exploring Mathematics' scope and sequence moves more slowly than do those of Saxon's books and *Horizon Math* (which might be fine for some learners). It spends more time developing each topic and emphasizing new standards' ideas such as group learning, cross-curriculum connections, and mathematical thinking and application. It also devotes time to bringing topics such as probability, graphing, and calculator use down to the earliest grade levels. If you want to introduce calculators to your first grader, you can purchase a calculator separately. (The TI-108 is the one they are using.)

The program is written to be presented by the teacher with workbooks used as integral parts of most lessons. It is possible to accomplish what you need to for first grade level by using only the student workbook, but you will encounter occasional lessons that depend upon the teacher's edition. Each chapter opens with a story, found in the teacher's edition. While all stories have some math connection, some are included for multi-cultural content or other social goals. Most of them are innocuous talking-animal stories. You will not miss much without them. Cooperative work is stressed throughout the teacher's edition, and even shows up in the student book with workpage instructions that sometimes direct students to "work with a partner." Determine which of these are necessary, then have a sibling be the partner or do so yourself. Although not absolutely essential, I recommend that you purchase the teacher's edition.

Additional program components are available, but not essential. Of most interest should be three extra workbooks, one for practice, one for reteaching, and one for enrichment. You might choose one or more depending upon the needs of your child. Each of these has a separate, inexpensive answer key.(S)

Fun at the Beach
(Little Folk Visuals)

See "Ungraded Programs."

Horizons Mathematics 1
(Alpha Omega)
$70.95 for the first grade math set; manipulatives are extra

Most of you will be surprised when you check out Alpha Omega's new math program, because it is very different from their LifePacs. Although each level does have two student workbooks, the Teacher Handbook is the main part of the program. Totally different from the old Alpha Omega math program, it now uses a variety of manipulatives throughout first through third grades. Manipulatives used are a number line, number chart, play money, place value materials, flannel board and numbers, and flash cards, along with household items such as bags, a calendar, an egg carton, a ruler, and straws. The nec-

essary manipulatives should be available through Alpha Omega's Catalog or other sources. Worksheet pages are generally reinforcement or practice for the lessons, although in *Mathematics 2* and *3* they are more integral to lessons than in *Mathematics 1*. All instruction is provided through one-on-one teacher instruction, demonstrations, and hands-on activity. The program provides regular practice and review to improve understanding and retention. Within each lesson is instruction on a new concept and practice or review of previously learned concepts. Unlike many programs where review is cursory, each lesson includes a number of activities that require inter-action between teacher and student, often with hands-on materials. For example, one lesson includes paper and pencil work with a hundreds chart, regrouping demonstration with place value manipulatives, oral number chart work, time telling practice using small clocks, written place value practice, addition practice, writing the words for large numbers, and word problems.

Alpha Omega explains their scope and sequence and course layout in great detail at the beginning of each Teacher Handbook, making it very easy to see what should happen when. A readiness evaluation is also found there, so we can make sure that each child is ready for this level and also to point out weaknesses. The Teacher Handbook is very well designed with each part of the lesson clearly labeled. Novice home educators, especially, should appreciate the easy-to-follow layout. Activity instructions are numbered and spaced so they are easy to locate and read quickly. The Teacher Handbook also has a wealth of practical, supplemental material not found in many other teaching guides. Within the student workbooks, simple instructions are included with each activity. Students have two separate workbooks (each about one-half inch thick) to cover each level. This is a lot of workbook, but they are appealingly designed with full color, large print, and variety in the layout. Supplemental, reproducible worksheets are included in the back of the Teacher Handbook.

The first grade program begins with concepts such as counting by twos, fives, and tens; cardinal and ordinal numbers; addition facts; and place value. This means that a solid foundation in number recognition and meaning along with other kindergarten concepts is essential before beginning this level. This foundation is laid in *Mathematics K*.

The scope and sequence is advanced throughout this series, becoming more obviously so as we move into *Mathematics 2* and *Mathematics 3*. Choose levels according to appropriate skill levels rather than equating them to grade levels.

Each level is a complete math program that goes beyond most other programs by spending more time on development and practice of concepts and skills. Keep in mind the advanced speed of the program and slow down if necessary, or skip some of the practice work if a student has already thoroughly mastered the concept. The scope and sequence is purposely advanced in keeping with the stiffer standards suggested for public schools across the country.

Alpha Omega's educational philosophy is very evident in this program. They believe repetition and review are essential until a subject has been mastered to the point where it becomes second nature. They view math, in particular, as both a basic functional skill and a communications skill that develops precision in thinking. Within this framework which emphasizes mental discipline, they have done an excellent job of breaking tasks down into manageable increments and also building in learning methods that address the needs of various learning styles.

Making Math Meaningful, Level 1, second edition

(Cornerstone Curriculum Project)
$40; manipulative packet - $15; extra student books - $18.75 each

The beginning levels each consist of a Parent/Teacher Guide and Student Book for presenting and practicing math concepts, and a separate packet of math manipulatives—links, large chips, and *Unifix* cubes. While the program, designed for home educators, also offers a kindergarten course, we can skip it and begin with first grade.

Unique methods of presentation are based on sound research and a biblical Christian worldview. Teachers are given detailed, word-for-word instruction. Lesson plans chart out "What I am to do" and "What I am to say" for each lesson. This means lessons must be presented one-on-one. The Student Book has 160 pages for individual student work, but a significant amount of the work is drawing, recording or representing manipulative activity, and other work that develops conceptual understanding rather than workbook practice on computation skills. *Making Math Meaningful* seems to move more slowly than other math programs at this level because the goal is a very thorough understanding of concepts. However, students are learning algebra by seventh or eighth grade in this program. A few concepts (time and calendar reading) taught in most programs are not covered here, but these are easily taught on their own. Supplement with another resource if children need additional work on computation skills.

Mastering Mathematics

(Mastery Publications)
complete program - $129.95

This complete math program was developed by a Christian school teacher/curriculum developer-turned-home schooling mom. Like *Developmental Mathematics*, it concentrates on one skill at a time. Once that skill is mastered, a child moves on to the next. Number recognition and other such kindergarten skills must be learned before starting the program. The program begins at what would be considered first grade level with beginning addition and continues through about sixth grade level material. However, some topics, such as the use of exponents and variables, do move beyond that level. The program is divided into six student books: *Attacking Addition, Subduing Subtraction, Mastering Multiplication, Defeating Division, Perfecting the Point* (place value, decimals, and percentage), and *Finishing Fractions*. More concepts are taught than are indicated by those titles. Time, money, stewardship/consumerism, measurement, check writing, thermometer reading, graphing, area, perimeter, Roman numerals, and others are covered either at the ends of the various books or through information provided in the teacher's manual. One large teacher's manual covers all six books. The manual is outstanding. There is extensive information on teaching children of varying abilities from "higher functioning Down's Syndrome" children through gifted. Learning style needs are addressed with suggestions for adapting lessons to suit the learner. Extra suggestions are provided for advanced learners. We are strongly urged to adapt the program rather than blindly assign page after page. Using the program in this manner will require some daily lesson preparation and varying amounts of one-on-one teaching. Children with average to above average skills might be able to work independently most of the time.

Manipulatives in the form of card stock "counting strips" and "fraction picture proofs" are used in place of the rods or cubes used with some other programs. Additionally, flash cards and games are included in packets which are part of the teacher's manual. Suggestions for the use of beans, M&M's, and other materials as manipulatives are also provided. Visual representations such as pictures of dominoes help young children transfer from representational to abstract thinking at the beginning of each lesson. Lessons are very clearly laid out with instruction provided on each workpage. Parents need to read through the fairly brief teacher's manual before beginning each of the six books but from then on will usually be able to present each day's lesson by simply following instructions in the child's book and using appropriate flash cards and games.

Large print, ample white space, the lack of distracting pictures, blank pages facing the work sheets, and short assignments give *Mastering Mathematics* probably the least distracting page layout in a complete curriculum for home schoolers. (Some children with learning disabilities <u>need</u> uncluttered pages to maintain concentration on their work.)

Older children needing remedial help or beginning the program after having already learned some arithmetic skills should be given placement tests at the front of the addition, subtraction, multiplication, and division books (depending on how far they have progressed). It is then very easy to use the prescriptive information in the teacher's manual to know where to begin with the various skills.

Memorization of facts and drill for speed is an important part of the program. Additional assistance in drill is available with *Mastering Mathematics IBM Practice Disk* 💻 [$9.95]. This is a very simple, "pop-in-the-disk-and-go" program. It does not have any cartoon figures or mazes but uses a "fill-in-the-grid" format for drilling addition and multiplication. (If children know addition and multiplication well, they almost automatically know their inverses—subtraction and division.) The screen is colorful, and there is great flexibility for choosing which number facts to drill and whether to present them in numerical or random order. Although the program is designed so we can easily identify which level is appropriate according to our child's place in *Mastering Mathematics*, it could be useful for any child learning math facts.

Mastering Mathematics goes beyond facts, drill, and rote learning with many of the suggested activities and games and especially with the very practical word problems. (This is also where the Christian content shows up.)

Each family has permission to copy workbook pages for their own children which keeps the overall cost low. A protective clear sheet is provided for children to write on with a wipe-off marker on pages (such as drills) that we might wish to use over and over. This can also be used for children to work out of the same book without photocopying pages.

Some unusual choices have been made with scope and sequence. Explanation of the rationale for place value has been delayed until *Perfecting the Point*. In earlier lessons, children simply learn the method. Decimals are taught before fractions. Children learn how to work with very large numbers within each concept area (addition, subtraction, etc.) before moving on to the next concept. The author presents some valid reasons for making these choices, and there should be no problems because of them. (The only consideration might be placement of a child when switching to another program in the middle of the sequence.)

We can purchase the entire program, individual programs (e.g., *Attacking Addition* with related teacher's manual), combination programs (e.g., addition and subtraction sold as a unit), or additional workbooks. The computer program is sold separately in all cases. We save the most money when purchasing the complete program.

This looks like a great program for the parent who wants flexibility and creativity yet has little lesson preparation time.

Mastery Publications now has a separate *Skill Inventory* [$10.95] that can be used to assess your child's math skills, both computational and noncomputational, such as time, money, and calendars. These are extensive assessments that can be used for *Mastering Mathematics* as well as for other math programs so that you can select lessons on which to concentrate. You will need both the parent and student manuals. The student pages are reproducible for your immediate family but not for school groups.

Math 1 for Christian Schools

(Bob Jones University Press)
Home School Kit - $44; tests with answer key - $10; activity books - $9 each; activity book answer keys - $4.50 each

BJUP has revised their math program for levels K-6. The Home School Kit for *Math 1* includes a streamlined Home School Teacher's Edition, student text, Student Materials Packet, and Home Teacher Packet. The first grade theme centers around the community and features Digit the Clown and his seal Cecilia. The program is designed to be taught from the Teacher's Edition using the manipulatives and activities. The student worktext is used for practice and reinforcement. Review activities and reduced pictures of the worktext pages with overprinted answers are also found in the Teacher's Edition. The Home Teacher Packet contains essential teaching aids and worksheets used in the lessons. Manipulatives such as *Unifix Cubes* and counters play an important part in introducing new concepts. The Teacher's Edition offers suggestions for substitute and make-it-yourself manipulatives. The Student Materials Packet is used by the student in conjunction with the worktext.

In addition to the student worktext, there are separate student activity books for additional practice which are not included in the Home School Kit. Activity books are written at three levels: remedial, average, and advanced. Choose only one of these according to the skill level of the child. It is not necessary to complete all pages in all of these resources, but they are there for us to use as much as is needed. These activity books, their companion answers keys, and tests for the entire program are optional. While correlating and using all of the program components is more time consuming than for some other programs, this new edition does a good job of meeting learning style needs with a variety of teaching/learning methods.

Mathematics, Level A

(Modern Curriculum Press)
$9; teacher's edition - $20.15

The worktext format includes lots of hands-on work and emphasizes understanding of concepts and thinking skills. The teacher's manual outlines concrete methods of presentation and also gives an error pattern analysis that will help you find out why children make certain errors and then reteach the topic. A weakness is that it deals with only one subject per lesson, reviewing previously learned concepts at infrequent intervals on tests. Supplement with other means of review, or do as one mom suggested—skip occasional problems in each lesson , then come back and use those for review.(S)

Mathematics 100

(Christian Light Publications, Inc.)

LightUnits - $22.90; Teacher Handbook - $5.95; answer keys - $22.90

Christian Light's first grade math program is a solid, traditional course which is inexpensive, yet thorough. It begins with numbers and counting, so it is not necessary for students to have completed a prior math program. It continues through addition and subtraction to 18. It also covers telling time to the half hour, counting to 100, measurement, money (pennies and dimes), geometric shapes, sets, and number order. The Teacher Handbook is a very slim volume which is easy to use. It sometimes includes suggestions for presenting lessons with inexpensive visual aids or hands-on materials. Many activities presume a classroom setting, but group activity is not critical for any of the lessons. I expect that most parents will work directly from the student LightUnits, providing instruction as needed. Lesson preparation time is very minimal. Answer keys are not necessary at this level.

LightUnits are printed with green ink on white paper, and they use numerous line-drawn illustrations. Although the costumes and figures throughout the course reflect Mennonite culture, there is no religious content. While this course lacks some of the extras (e.g., calendar reading, story problems) found in Saxon's first grade program and some others, it does cover the essentials upon which young children need to focus. However, parents with Wiggly Willys will have to be creative to make it into a true hands-on program.

Math-U-See, Foundations level

(Math-U-See)

teacher's manual - $20; student book - $15; extra practice sheets - $15; foundations video - $15; blocks - $30; skip-counting tape and coloring book - $10

Steve Demme, creator of *Math U-See*, combines hands-on methodology with incremental instruction and continual review in this manipulative-based program that is a complete curriculum.

There are four levels—*Introduction, Foundations, Intermediate*, and *Advanced*—that cover approximately K-8, followed by *Basic Algebra/Geometry , Algebra 2* and *Trigonometry. Introduction* is intended for kindergarten with the other three levels taking approximately 2 to 2 ½ years each to complete. For each of the first four levels there are one or two instruction videos (varying in length from one to four hours of content), a teacher's manual, a student workbook, and a book of Extra Practice Sheets. There is also a *Skip Count Tape* with coloring book in either Christian or secular versions. The program also uses plastic blocks, color-coded to correspond to each number. The blocks snap together like *LEGOS* because of their raised surfaces. One set will be used throughout all the levels.

Parents should watch the videos to understand the basic concepts which are the foundation of the program. On the videos, Demme works each level lesson-by-lesson, demonstrating and instructing. After the initial viewing, parents and children can watch and work through lessons together, or parents can review the presentation, then present it to their own children. Demme's style is very engaging. He explains why and what he is doing clearly. He throws in lots of "math tricks," the kind that make you scratch your head and ask why they never taught us that in school. Although concepts are explained briefly in the lessons in the books, the video presentation is critical.

The *Introduction* level covers essential number concepts needed before going on to *Foundations*. It teaches number recognition, writing numbers, place value, counting, simple addition, skip counting, shapes, time, and money (pennies and dimes since they correlate to our number system).

The *Foundation* level book is divided into 36 lessons. The teacher manual has one or more presentation pages (teacher instructions) per lesson, reduced pictures of student pages with answers, tests, word problems, and a few extra drill practice sheets. The student book has four worksheet pages per lesson. There is also a book of Extra Practice Sheets since most students will need more practice than is in the student book. (These sheets are clearly linked to corresponding lessons.) The presentation has the child work with manipulatives. It might take a day or more of presentation and practice before students tackle the problems in each lesson. Once students have grasped a concept, they can practice and do problem pages on their own with occasional assistance. Each lesson should be mastered before going on to the next. Taking a tip from Saxon, Demme has used a spiral design for the problem pages, continually reviewing and practicing previously learned concepts. The teacher's manual includes answer keys, tests, and word problems.

Children learn concepts with the manipulatives. They verbalize what they are doing. They listen to the *Skip-Count Tape* to build a foundation for multiplication and division auditorially. And they do paper and pencil work, some of which drills them on their math facts. This is a true multi-sensory program.

Concepts covered in *Foundations* are place value, counting from 0 to 100, reading and writing numbers to 1000, solving for unknowns, addition facts, regrouping (carrying and borrowing), column addition, subtraction, skip counting facts from the two's through the ten's, multiplication through the 10s, graphing, square units, area of rectangles, perimeter, geometric shapes, thermometer, inequalities, time, money, and ordinal numbers. *Foundations* is approximately equivalent to a grades 1-3 program, although the methods used allow children to learn concepts usually reserved for older grade levels.

The *Skip Count Tape* help students to grasp multiplication/division facts as they count by 2s, 3s, 4s, 5s, and so on with catchy musical rhymes. There are other skip count tapes I like better, although this is the one recommended by Steve Demme. See reviews of others under "Helps for Teaching, Drill, Review, and Fun."

Miquon Math

(Key Curriculum Press)

See "Ungraded Programs for Preschool through Second Grade."

Moving with Math, Level A OR Grade 1

(Math Teachers Press - MTP)

Level A (Skill Builders, three student workbooks, Math Capsules, Home School Instructions, Using Models: Addition and Subtraction) - reproducible version - $67.90 OR non-reproducible version - $42.90; teacher's guides set - $22.85; manipulatives also sold through MTP

Grade 1: $95.90

This program offers a compromise between the extremes of a totally manipulative-based approach or a workbook approach. It also offers two options for first/second grade level in terms of flexibility and individualization. The original *Moving with Math* program, Levels A-D, offer tremendous flexibility for designing the program to fit your child's needs using the diagnostic/prescriptive tools and instructions that come with the program. The alternative Grade 1 and Grade 2 programs that can be used in place of Level A are organized more like other programs and lack this flexibility.

The original program, which I will describe first, is divided into four levels: A for 1-2, B for 3-4, C for 5-6, and D for 7-8. There are three basic components at each level: *Math Capsules, Moving with Math* (student workbooks), and *Skill Builders*. We can purchase packages with reproducible *Skill Builders* and *Math Capsules* or the packages with non-reproducible versions of these two items. Student workbooks are consumable in either case, and separate sets must be purchased for each student. If you are teaching only one or two children, you should probably choose the non-reproducible version. If you will use the program with more than two children, you will save money with the reproducible version.

Much of the instruction comparable to that found in a teacher's manual is in *Skill Builders. Skill Builders* also contains activity pages, some of which are paper-and-pencil activities and others which are for use with manipulatives. This is a substantial part of the program.

Moving with Math workbooks include basic instruction and practice along with instruction for some manipulative activity. There are separate, brief answer keys for each workbook, although these should be unnecessary for levels A and B. Answers are also contained in the optional teacher's guides. It

is not absolutely necessary to use manipulatives with the workbooks, but it is strongly recommended.

Math Capsules contains pre and post tests for the entire level; however, there are also pre and post tests for each chapter or unit in each *Moving with Math* workbook. It contains a detailed key to the objectives, but you can see the objectives by simply reading the table of contents in each book—they read like a scope and sequence list. The part you should be most interested in is "Maintenance tests"—reproducible, short tests to be used for continual review of previous concepts. Every question in each maintenance test is matched to an objective so parents always know what their child does and does not know. Another feature of the Level A *Math Capsules* component is "Oral Drill" exercises to be used along with the "Maintenance tests."

To use the program, you identify which objective you wish to work on, then plan a combination of both the workbook and *Skill Builder* sheets and activities that are most appropriate. This sounds more confusing than it actually is, so the publishers have put together teacher's guides that lay out step-by-step lesson plans keyed to the program components. If you use the teacher's guides, you should still be making the underlying decision of whether or not your child actually needs to do each lesson. MTP recommends that most home schooling parents purchase the teacher's guides to understand how to organize instruction and teach with the manipulatives. I suspect that many home educators will want the guides since they will save much time in lesson planning. MTP also provides to home educators guidelines for breaking down program material into one-year programs and suggestions as to how many days to spend on each objective.

Level A is for grades 1-2, although some kindergarten level material is included. Level A has three workbooks: Parts I (numeration), II (addition and subtraction), and III (fractions, geometry, and measurement). It reviews basic number activities taught in kindergarten, so it is possible to begin arithmetic instruction with Level A. The Level A package integrates one more component that is especially useful to those with no experience teaching with manipulatives—*Using Models to Learn Addition and Subtraction Facts*. Manipulatives needed for Level A include either *Base Ten Blocks* (or *Cuisenaire®ꞏ Rods* with "hundreds squares") and *Unifix* cubes, both available from MTP.

Math Teachers Press has an hour-long video, "Moving with Math: An Overview for Home School," which describes the philosophy and components of the program, the role of manipulatives in bridging the gap from concrete to abstract, and practical suggestions from a home-school parent. It also shows students from various levels working with manipulatives. The video is free with orders over $125 or it can be purchased for $19.95.

The Grade 1 and Grade 2 programs teach the same objectives as Level A, but separate the material into two parts. These versions are enhanced by the integration of children's stories (from the library or bookstore) which are integrated with the math lessons. There is no diagnostic/prescriptive feature in these programs. Student books are combined into a single book for each of Grade 1 and Grade 2. You will need a student book for each student plus the Teachers Resource Manual. The Teachers Resource Manual for each grade includes detailed lesson plans. They are scripted, telling us what to say as we follow each step-by-step lesson plan. Reduced pictures of student pages show correct answers. Within the lesson plans are suggestions for using over 280 children's trade books and extensive activities that help children see math in the real world. Combined with additional art activities, this approach is more appealing to children with literary or artistic "bents."

Also in the Teachers Manual are the reproducible Skill Builders and Math Capsules that come as separate books in Level A. The Grade 1 and 2 versions offer more security for parents who are uncertain about their teaching ability and require less decision making and planning.

Trained educational consultants are available at Math Teachers Press' toll free number to answer questions.(S)

Primary Mathematics 1A and 1B
(Family Things)
1A and 1B sets - $18.50 each; teacher's guides - $15 each

Everyone has heard how well Asian students do in math compared to U.S. students, but few people understand why this is so. You will understand clearly why Asian students excel if you peruse this math program. Apparently, this program is typical of those used in many Asian countries. Also called *Singapore Math* (the name by which this program was referred to me), *Primary Mathematics* is published (in English) by the Curriculum Planning & Development Division of the Ministry of Education in Singapore.

There is a huge difference in the scope and sequence between this and all other programs I have reviewed; *Primary Mathematics* is far more advanced. The program uses a three-step process, taking children from concrete, to pictorial, then abstract approaches to learning.

Each level has two coursebooks (A and B) which are the heart of each lesson. There are two student workbooks for each coursebook up through level 4, then one workbook per coursebook for levels 5 and 6. Teacher Guides—one per coursebook—are available, although they are not very useful at this level. They do have a few answers to workbook exercises, but it is quite easy to figure these out without a key, and the key isn't complete. Many of the concrete activities are presented in the Teacher Guides, but I suspect that most homeschoolers will rely on the pictorial lessons and oral activity for most lesson presentations. I would recommend that you purchase at least

one Teacher Guide so that you understand what they offer.

The program requires one-on-one teaching throughout most lessons for the younger grades. This is always true for activities directed from Teacher Guides (if you choose to use them), and almost always true for coursework lessons. The coursework books present pictorial lessons to introduce new concepts. Parents do these orally with children. Correlated workbook exercises are indicated at the end of each coursebook presentation. Full-color coursebooks are not consumable and are not intended to be written in, although they are inexpensive enough that you might choose to have your children sometimes write in them. Children should be able to work through workbook exercises independently once they can read directions without problems. The 1A Part One workbooks are 80 pages each, while the 1A Part Two workbooks are 88 pages each. These are about 10 by 7 ½ inches, with uncrowded, large black-and-white print, so they are not overwhelming in the amount of written work required of children. There are no answer keys—you won't need them.

The level 1 course begins with an assumption that children already have a basic sense and recognition of numbers. It begins with counting to 10, but by the fourth lesson, students are learning addition. Subtraction is introduced on page 38 of the 88-page 1A coursebook. Single-digit multiplication is taught about half way through 1B, with division introduced immediately after. I suspect that one of the reasons this program works well is that each concept is presented in a number of different ways so that children really do learn to think mathematically.

The methodology reflects many ideas of "new math." It stresses conceptual understanding over math-fact drill at this level. (You might want to provide opportunity for more practice with math facts using other resources, but level 2 does offer much more practice with multiplication facts.) Practical applications are used in lesson presentation and word problems. In addition to the four arithmetic operations, level one teaches ordinal numbers, shapes, measurement, weight, time telling, money, and graphs.

Because the books were originally written for students in Singapore, they use the metric system and bills and coins from Singapore (which are actually similar in denominations to ours for the most part). The few other cultural differences such as names of fruits and people's names are relatively insignificant. Note, also, that some of the spellings and vocabulary are British, e.g., metre instead of meter, colour instead of color, petrol rather than gasoline, and, probably most important, the word brackets instead of parentheses.

Coursebook lessons provide little assistance for the teacher in how to talk about each lesson. I think that parents who have a strong foundation in mathematical thinking and confidence in their teaching ability will be able to use these books without much difficulty, but those who want teaching guidance and those unfamiliar with the concrete and pictorial teaching methods might find it difficult to figure out how to teach the lessons.

Family Things has an 14-day return policy for full refund minus shipping.(S)

Saxon Math 1

(Saxon Publishers)
home study kit - $89.255; extra student workbook set - $33.60

Level 1 is somewhat similar to Cornerstone Curriculum's *Making Math Meaningful* in format with a script for the teacher to follow and use of manipulatives to teach concepts. Unlike *Making Math Meaningful*, this program tries to cover a plethora of math related concepts in keeping with the new math standards accepted and promoted within the government-controlled educational system. That is not to say it is a bad program, but it does spend a lot of time covering topics children pick up quite simply on their own or with minimal amount of instruction. For example, children are taught in math lessons how to identify the weather, morning, afternoon, evening, night, days of the week, seasons, and months.

Each day's lesson begins with "The Meeting"—together time for working on time, temperature, money, counting, patterns, problem solving, and the calendar. "The Lesson" introduces a new concept which will be reviewed and practiced over and over again in future practice sessions. During the lesson children complete one page in their workbook. Later in the day they are to do a second workbook page on their own. Frequent assessments, both written and oral, verify their mastery of the material. This program requires preparation and presentation time. It is not designed for independent student work other than the second worksheet page. Manipulatives are used to teach new concepts, and manipulative activities are vital components of children's learning tasks. We need to purchase the necessary manipulatives since they do not come with the basic kit. A Home Study Manipulative Kit [$65] designed for the Saxon program is sold through ETA (contact ETA at 620 Lakeview Parkway, Vernon Hills, IL 60061 or 800-445-5985.) The same manipulatives are used throughout the K-3 programs.

The program was originally written for classroom use. Saxon has redesigned the teacher's manuals for home schoolers, eliminating or rewriting class-based activities. The teacher's manual is the heart of the program. It provides scripts and detailed instructions for lesson presentation. The home study kit for Level 1 also includes The Meeting Book, two student workbooks (Parts One and Two), and fact cards. The assessment pages are the most obvious holdover from the classroom-formatted program with space for recording progress for 32 students.

The program is expensive, but I think a bigger concern is the time wasted. This program appears to take far more time without accomplishing significantly more of importance than less expensive, less time-consuming alternatives. For example, regrouping for addition is introduced in three lessons in Level 1, but Level 2 does not return to the concept until the middle of the year. This is slower progress on this vital concept than in programs such as A Beka's or Alpha Omega's. I think the clue as to why this is so is in the brochure Saxon sends out titled, "National Standards Correlations." They are correlating their objectives for first grade to standards such as "Believe that mathematics makes sense," "Construct number meanings through real-world experiences and the use of physical materials," "Develop intuitions about the relative effect of operating on numbers," "Reflect on and clarify their thinking about mathematical language and symbols," and "Acquire confidence in using mathematics meaningfully." I am a strong proponent of using manipulatives to understand math concepts and of applying arithmetic in real-life situations, but teaching children to develop intuition and construct meaning is not what I want to teach.

On the plus side, inexperienced home schoolers can follow the script and feel confident they are covering everything that would be covered in a classroom; manipulative-based learning builds a strong conceptual foundation; repeated review ensures that students hang on to what they have learned; and students are drilled on basic math facts with mastery by the end of third grade as the goal. The bottom line is that the program does teach math and does use some good methods to do so, but it might not be the most efficient way to accomplish our goals.(S)

Using Inexpensive Workbooks

Sometimes when we choose to create our own program, we still desire to have a workbook that can be used for those days when mom is otherwise occupied. Rather than buying a text that will seldom be used, purchase one of the inexpensive little workbooks from a teachers' supply store, the market, or toy department of most department stores. *Golden Step Ahead* books, Frank Schaffer books, and many others will do for this purpose.

Other alternatives to workbooks that give children practice in writing math solutions are dot-to-dot style workbooks, where children solve problems, then use answers to connect the dots, making a picture. This method is self-checking and provides a useful incentive for most children. Check your teacher supply store for books such as this.

2nd Grade Level

Arithmetic 2

(A Beka Book)
$11.55; teacher edition - $20.95; teacher guide/curricu-

lum - $39.95; speed drills and tests - $4.60; key to speed drills/tests - $8.95; flashcards, felt objects, manipulatives, and games are extra.

This new arithmetic program follows the same format as *Arithmetic 1*. See the review under first grade. It requires quite a bit of one-on-one presentation and uses manipulative demonstrations for concept understanding. Second grade level covers addition and subtraction with regrouping using four-digit numbers, multiplication and division with multipliers and divisors up through the number 5, and place value to the hundred thousands.

Developmental Mathematics

(Mathematics Programs Associates, Inc.)

See description under "1st Grade Level."

Exploring Mathematics Grade 2

(ScottForesman)

softbound student text - $22.74; teacher's edition - $115.68; manipulatives kit -$265.83

See the review under "1st Grade Level." Grade 2 continues the same format as Grade 1. It covers addition and subtraction up through three digits with regrouping. Multiplication and division are introduced—multiplication shown in numerical sentence form, but division only introduced conceptually. Place value through 999; number patterns; skip counting by 2s, 5s, and 10s; time; measurement; money; fractions (identification of fractional parts such as 3/4); probability; graphing; and geometry (shape identification and perimeter measurement) are taught at this level. The stories at the beginning of each chapter begin to get objectionable. They are primarily dumb, original fairy tales, but one about a tortoise and rabbit race actually teaches dishonesty as a means of problem solving. It is no loss to just skip the stories. You will need to add *Base Ten Blocks®* to your stock of manipulatives for Grade 2. Very brief chapter review tests check progress. A separate test booklet and an answer key are available for about $30, but you probably do not need them at this level. As with Grade 1, topics are taught without continual review. This might not be a problem, but if it becomes one, you might want to purchase one or more of the supplemental workbooks for practice, reteaching, or enrichment. The scope and sequence still lags behind those of Horizons and Saxon but is similar to BJUP on basic arithmetic.(S)

Fun at the Beach

(Little Folk Visuals)

See description under "Ungraded Programs." This program might serve either as foundation or supplement at second grade level. Some children will be ready for more than is covered within *Fun at the Beach*, in which case we should use it to demonstrate new concepts and for review while using some-

thing else for the basic program.

Horizons Mathematics 2

(Alpha Omega)

$70.95 for the second grade math set

See the description under first grade. *Math 2* follows the same format as *Math 1*. The scope and sequence is advanced throughout this series, becoming more obviously so as we move into *Math 2* and *3*. Choose levels according to appropriate skill levels rather than equating them to grade levels.

Math 2 expects that children have learned two-digit addition and subtraction with carrying and borrowing, but it still reteaches the concepts, then moves on to larger numbers. Multiplication facts for 1-10 are taught along with place value, number order, sets, correspondence, cardinal and ordinal numbers, shapes, graphs, fractions (1/2, 1/3, 1/4), measurement, temperature, estimation, ratio, the calendar, time, money, area, perimeter, volume, and decimals (in money).

Each level is a complete math program that goes beyond most other programs by spending more time on development and practice of concepts and skills. Keep in mind the advanced speed of the program (reflecting the higher math standards intended for public education), and slow down if necessary or skip some of the practice work if a student has already mastered a concept thoroughly.

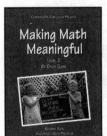

Making Math Meaningful 2, second edition

(Cornerstone Curriculum Project)

$40; manipulative packet - $15; extra student books - $18.75

This program uses unique methods of presentation based upon sound research. Detailed, easily understood instruction is given for the parent/teacher in the Parent/Teacher Guide. The manual directs parents in what to say and do, so the program must be presented one-on-one. Students complete pages in their Student Book in conjunction with lesson presentations. Student Books are insufficient without lesson presentation from the Parent/Teacher Guide. Student books are consumable; extras are available for additional students. This level continues to use the same package of manipulatives that is used with earlier levels for hands-on learning.

Mathematical thinking and understanding of concepts is stressed, so concepts are introduced at a slower pace than in most other programs. However, by the end of the second grade book, children have learned mathematical concepts relating to equations, fractions, algebra, and other topics that often are not taught until much, much later.

The revised version of the second grade program is very well developed. It is very easy to understand, has a well-designed format, and does an excellent job of presenting concepts. With the older version, it was sometimes difficult to switch from another program into *Making Math Meaningful* at this level, but this is no longer a problem. Occasionally there is a small amount of lesson preparation, but for most lessons we can just pick up the manual and teach.

Mastering Mathematics

See description under "1st Grade Level."

Math 2 for Christian Schools
(Bob Jones University Press)
Home School Kit - $44; activity books - $9 each; activity book answer keys - $4.50 each; flip chart - $15; tests with answer key - $10

The second grade level has been revised. See the review for the first grade program which is similar in format. The theme is "Homes Around the World," featuring Matt, the builder, and his companion, Paddy Beaver. The *Math 2* Home School Kit includes the student worktext, Student Materials Packet, Home Teacher's Edition, and Home Teacher Packet. Tests, flip chart, and activity books are optional.

Lessons are taught from the Home Teacher's Edition. The second grade student book is a softbound workbook that will definitely NOT work without the instruction from the Teacher's Edition. There are two pages per daily lesson in the workbook. One is done along with the lesson presentation, and the other is done as seatwork. Work with manipulatives is foundational to the lessons. Quite a few different items are required if you want to follow the Teacher's Edition's lesson presentation; many of these come in the Home Teacher Packet. Still, lesson preparation time is substantial, making this a challenging curriculum to use if you are teaching numerous children at different levels.

Aside from the preparation and presentation requirements, the curriculum does an excellent job in presenting concepts in a variety of ways to reach different learning styles. Since much learning occurs through activity and discussion, workbook learning is a minimal part of each lesson. However, workbooks are colorful and appealingly illustrated.

The scope and sequence is about average (neither advanced nor slow), covering addition and subtraction up through three-digit numbers, and introducing division readiness and multiplication by one-digit multipliers. Review activities are presented in the Teacher's Edition and their new *Math 2 Review Activity Book.* This book includes cumulative, concept, and fact reviews to give students extra practice.

We can supplement with one of the three Math Activity Books for second grade. At each level there is one each for remedial, average, and advanced students. Separate answer keys are needed for these.

Mathematics Level B
(Modern Curriculum Press)
$9; teacher's edition - $20.15

See description of Level A under "1st Grade Level."(S)

NOTE: Horizons, A Beka, and BJUP continually review material covered so that students remember concepts learned in past lessons. Modern Curriculum Press' weakness is the lack of this continual review. A supplement like *ADD-Arithmetic Developed Daily* works well with *MCP Math.*

Math-U-See, Foundations level

See review under "1st Grade Level."

Miquon Math
(Key Curriculum Press)

See description under "Ungraded Programs." If your child is just beginning in this program, whether or not he has used any other math program previously, it would be best to begin in the first books since they introduce the *Rods* and familiarize children with this method of learning. Older children will move very quickly through early lessons, perhaps skipping those that cover concepts already mastered.(S)

Moving with Math Level A OR Grade 2
(Math Teachers Press)
Level A (Skill Builders, three student workbooks, Math Capsules, Home School Instructions, Using Models: Addition and Subtraction) - reproducible version - $67.90 OR non-reproducible version - $42.90; teacher's guides set - $22.85; manipulatives also sold through MTP
Grade 2 package - $95.90; complete package - $170

See comprehensive description under "1st Grade Level."

The Grade 1 and Grade 2 programs teach the same objectives as Level A, but separate the material into two parts. Those just entering the program with a child functioning at second grade level, should begin with the Grade 2 program. The Grade 2 package includes student book, teacher's manual, and essential manipulatives.

Primary Mathematics 2A and 2B
(Family Things)
2A and 2B sets - $18.50 each; teacher's guides - $15 each

See the review of *Primary Mathematics* 1A and 1B. Level 2 covers addition and subtraction with renaming, multiplication and division (focusing on the math facts), measurement, money, introduction of fractions, time telling, graphs, and very introductory geometric shapes and area. The two coursebooks for this level are 104-pages each and the four workbooks are 88 pages each. Teacher's Guides for this level are not very helpful. No answer keys are available.(S)

Saxon Math 2

(Saxon Publishers)

home study kit - $91.75; extra student workbook set - $34

See the review of Level 1 under first grade. Level 2 teaches renaming for subtraction, multiplication by numbers up to 5, and division by the number 2. As with the other levels, it teaches a multitude of math-related concepts including such topics as identifying lines of symmetry and oblique line segments, graphing ordered pairs on a coordinate plane, conducting surveys, and creating and reading Venn diagrams. Aside from, or maybe in spite of all the extras covered, the program does a decent job teaching basic arithmetic. Manipulatives need to be ordered separately as described in the review of Level 1. The same manipulatives are used with all levels.(S)

Working Arithmetic 2, revised edition

(Rod and Staff)

workbooks - $29.10; teacher's manuals - $21; blackline masters - $9.25

Rod and Staff's second grade arithmetic program is packaged differently from most others. Student work is divided into five units, each a tear-out workbook. Then there are two teacher's manuals, the first covering the first two student units and the last covering units 3-5. Teacher's manuals give directions for class-time drills, coordinate blackline sheets with lessons, and have reduced student pages with answers. The blackline pages reinforce lessons taught throughout the program and also introduce multiplication and division which are not taught in the rest of the second grade program. Carrying and borrowing are covered at this level. Continuous review is built in throughout the year with the last ten lessons of the program providing a systematic review of the course. The emphasis leans toward memorization and drill rather than experiential learning.

For Extra Help

Continue to use hands-on materials listed above and add games and resources such as the following (reviews are under "Helps for Teaching, Drill, Review, and Fun)":

ADD-Arithmetic Developed Daily, Grade 1 or Grade 2
Addition Facts or *Subtraction Facts in 5 Minutes a Day*⊳
Addition, Subtraction, and *Multiplication Songs Kits*
Addition Teaching and Learning Made Easy
Arithmetic Practice Books, Addition or *Subtraction*
CalcuLadder®
Coins Make Change Bingo
Creating Line Designs
Designs in Math
Flashcards for Kids (website: www.edu4kids.com/math/)

Focus on Problem Solving B
The Good Steward game
Holey Cards
Key to Measurement series
Learning Wrap-Ups
Little Spender
Math Drillsters
Mathematical Reasoning through Verbal Analysis, Book 1
Mathematicians are People, Too, volumes one and two
Mental Math, Second Grade
Moneywise Kids
Muggins and other games
Multiplication, Addition, Subtraction, Division audio tapes
   and workbooks from Twin Sisters
Musical Math Facts Level 1
One Hundred Sheep, Skip Counting Songs from the Gospels
The Original Skip Count Kid or *The Skip Count Kid's Bible*
   Heroes
The Quarter Mile Math Game
Quick Thinks Math, Book A1
Scratch Your Brain Where It Itches
Triangle Flash Cards
Turbo Math Facts

∽∽∽∽∽∽∽

In addition to the specific recommendations above, there are numerous other possibilities. Look for books of word/thinking problems from teacher supply stores and home school distributors. Don't forget the practical experiences children get if they help in the kitchen. Cooking, reading, and measuring for recipes involves math skill application.

Help for Sloppy Number Crunchers

Many children have more difficulty with the paper and pencil end of arithmetic than they do with the actual problem solving. A major cause of errors is mistakes in number alignment. This can easily be solved by simply turning line paper sideways (columns) or by using graph paper. If children assign one number to a box, any misalignments show up immediately. I recommend using graph paper with squares no smaller than four per inch. Young children might do better with even larger squares. To get something larger, we have to use centimeter graph paper. Masters for centimeter graphs that can be photocopied are available in some math activity books that are used with *Cuisenaire® Rods.*

Working Without a Text

It becomes increasingly difficult to do everything without a text at older levels, although it can be done through second or third grade with little problem. In *An Easy Start in Arithmetic* (Mott Media), Dr. Beechick outlines arithmetic courses without texts for first through third grades, although third grade would probably be easier with a text or program. (*The Three*

R's set [$12] which includes *An Easy Start in Arithmetic* also comes with a two-sided math/phonics chart. The math side shows a "Hundred Chart" and describes both easy and advanced activities to be used with it.)

At older levels, a text can serve as a guideline to help us cover all the concepts for the grade level. We can supplement with manipulatives (objects for learning math concepts), games, and activities. At all levels, try to substitute experience and activity for workbooks whenever possible. Children can experience the usefulness of math through such activities as budgeting and grocery shopping; planning, measuring, and building a project out of wood; or keeping records of their own income and expenditures.

3rd Grade Level

Arithmetic 3
(A Beka Book)
$11.55; teacher curriculum guide - $39.95; teacher key - $20.95; speed drills and tests - $4.60; key to speed drills and tests - $8.95; flashcards, felt objects, manipulatives, and games are extra.

This new arithmetic program follows the same format as *Arithmetic 1*. It also requires quite a bit of one-on-one presentation and uses manipulative demonstrations for concept understanding. See the review of *Arithmetic 1*. *Arithmetic 3* covers multiplication by two-digit multipliers, short division up through divisors of 12, and adding and subtracting fractions and decimals.

Developmental Mathematics
(Mathematics Programs Associates, Inc.)
See description under "1st Grade Level."

Exploring Arithmetic
(Rod and Staff)
pupil textbook - $11.95; teacher's manual - $13.70; speed drills - $4.45; blackline masters - $4.05

The philosophy and methodology for third grade are similar to what I have described for the first and second grade programs—*Beginning Arithmetic* and *Working Arithmetic*. The third grade format changes to a single hardbound student text. There are fewer blackline masters than at previous levels. Students copy problems from their text to solve on paper, but curiously, there are rarely any instructions in their book. Most of the exercises are obvious; the first lesson page is always computation practice. A good part of the second page of each lesson is also obvious, but occasionally students will need an explanation of what is expected. The scope and sequence remains on the slow to average side with multiplication and division facts through the 9s introduced in the last three-

fourths of the course.

Exploring Mathematics Grade 3
(ScottForesman)
softbound student text - $29.43 or hardbound student text - $41.76; teacher's edition - $98.85; manipulatives kit - $234.12

ScottForesman's *Exploring Mathematics* was designed for government schools and correlates with the new math standards. Student books are colorful and appealing to children. For Grade 3, we have a choice between soft or hardbound student books. Teacher's editions are large, spiral-bound volumes with hard backs and soft front covers. They include reduced pictures of student pages on the appropriate teaching pages. Addition and subtraction are reviewed, and multiplication and division with single-digit multipliers and divisors are taught. Fraction and decimal recognition is taught along with place value, time, measurement, money, and geometry (shape identification, perimeter, area, introduction of volume, and congruence). Statistics, probability, and graphing are taught at introductory levels.

In keeping with the new math standards, manipulatives are used throughout the program. A core manipulatives kit for each grade level includes enough manipulatives for a classroom. I suggest that you purchase only what you need (play money—coins and bills, *Base Ten Blocks*, and a plastic template for drawing various geometric shapes, although the last item is optional). Manipulatives are frequently used to teach or illustrate concepts, but students are still required to do quite a bit of paper and pencil work. At this level, practical application, mathematical thinking, and word problems receive a great deal of attention, one of the positive reflections of the new math standards. The math standards also encourage practice with estimation, but this program often has children make guesses out of the blue and label these exercises as estimation. Group learning and multiculturalism also are heavily stressed throughout the program in both teacher's edition and student text. Determine which of the group learning activities are necessary, then have a sibling be the partner or do so yourself. Most of the multicultural connections in the program are quite interesting, but, even so, these might be an unnecessary distraction from the primary task of developing basic math skills. Use them as time allows.

Another helpful "extra" found in the teacher's edition for most lessons is a "problem of the day." Problems of the day are intended to be presented from a separate flip-chart book, but we can present most of them ourselves by simply copying them on to a white board. Answers/solutions are in the teacher's edition. The Problem Solving and Critical Thinking Workbook pages are correlated with lessons within the teachers' edition. These should be helpful for those looking for extra thinking skills work. Answers are shown in the teacher's edition.

Throughout the program, topics are presented sequentially with limited review. For example, while students are studying measurement, they practice addition and subtraction only within the context of measurement. There are additional exercises for review, enrichment, or practice at the end of each chapter from which we can pull some review material, and there are a few pages on remedial topics at the end of the book for students who might need to go back even further. The teacher's edition offers brief "warm-up reviews" in the margins of each lesson, but these usually pertain only to topics taught within that chapter. The lack of regular review on all previously-taught topics might be a problem for some students who need to keep their arithmetic skills sharp with more frequent practice. Supplemental books are available for reteaching, enrichment, or extra practice, but you might do better with supplemental tools that focus primarily on computation skills (e.g., *CalcuLadder, Math-It*, or a computer math drill program.).

Exploring Mathematics' scope and sequence moves more slowly than do those of A Beka and Horizon (which might be fine for some learners), but it is fairly comparable to those of BJUP and Saxon. Saxon's program is most similar since it, too, follows the new math standards. *Exploring Mathematics* for Grade 3 also devotes time to bringing topics such as probability, graphing, and calculator use down to the earliest grade levels. If you want your child to learn how to use a calculator for simple arithmetic at this level, you can purchase a calculator on your own. They have chosen the TI-108 to work with.

Overall, this program is more appealing than some others because of both appearance and the variety of activities and exercises. On the other hand, the lack of continual review starts to become a problem at this level and so it might sometimes require adaptation or supplementation.

The program is written to be presented by the teacher with workbooks used as integral parts of most lessons. It is possible to accomplish what you need by using only the student workbook, but you will encounter occasional lessons that depend upon the teacher's edition. Lessons are clearly presented in the teacher's edition and require minimal preparation time. The teacher's edition also has answers overprinted in red and, sometimes, printed in the margins. Although not absolutely essential, I highly recommend that you purchase the teacher's edition.(S)

Horizons Mathematics 3 (or 2)

(Alpha Omega)
$70.95 for the third grade math set

See the description of *Mathematics 1* under "1st Grade Level." *Mathematics 2* and *Mathematics 3* both follow the same format as *Mathematics 1*. The scope and sequence is advanced throughout this series, and this becomes more obvi-

ous as we move into *Mathematics 2* and *3*. Choose levels according to appropriate skill levels rather than equating them to grade levels.

Mathematics 2 expects that children have learned two-digit addition and subtraction with carrying and borrowing, but it still reteaches the concepts then moves on to larger numbers. Multiplication facts for 1-10 are taught along with place value, number order, sets, correspondence, cardinal and ordinal numbers, shapes, graphs, fractions (1/2, 1/3, 1/4), measurement, temperature, estimation, ratio, the calendar, time, money, area, perimeter, volume, and decimals (in money).

Mathematics 3 covers the same topics as *Mathematics 2* but at more challenging levels; e.g. multiplication covers up through four-digit multipliers, division works up through two-digit divisors with remainders. Algebraic thinking is introduced with equations like $n + 5 = (7 + 2) + 4$.

Each level is a complete math program that goes beyond most other programs by spending more time on development and practice of concepts and skills. Keep in mind the advanced speed of the program (reflecting the higher math standards being implemented in public education). Slow down if necessary or skip some of the practice work if a student has already mastered a concept thoroughly.

Making Math Meaningful 3, second edition

(Cornerstone Curriculum Project)
$40; extra student books - $18.75 each; manipulative kit - $15

See description under "2nd Grade Level." Level 3 consists of a Parent/Teacher Guide and Student Book. You will also need the Manipulative Kit (cubes, links, and counters). Lessons also call for some other household items such as toothpicks and coins. Lessons are scripted for the parent teacher, explaining in detail what to say and do. Students complete workbook pages in conjunction with the lesson presentations. While this program appears to move at a slower pace than others, the emphasis is upon building a strong foundation in mathematical thinking rather than simply learning math facts. Children are actually learning more challenging mathematical concepts even if the computation work does not seem as difficult as in other programs. The result of this approach is likely to be better understanding and retention, which translates into greater success with math at older levels.

Some students might need additional computation practice which can be accomplished with any of a number of supplemental resources. Student books are consumable and may be purchased separately.

Mastering Mathematics

See description under "1st Grade Level."

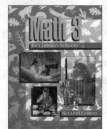

Math 3 for Christian Schools

(Bob Jones University Press)
Home School Kit - $44; activity books -
$9 each; activity book answer keys -
$4.50 each; tests with answer key -
$10

The third grade level has been revised.
See the review for the first grade program
which is similar in format. The *Math 3* Home School Kit
includes the student worktext, Home Teacher's Edition,
Student Materials Packet, and Home Teacher Packet. The
Teaching Charts Flip Chart, activity books, and tests are
optional.

Lessons are taught from the Home Teacher's Edition. The
theme centers around national parks and features the photographer Hal and his squirrel Horatio. The third grade student
book is a softbound workbook that will definitely NOT work
without the instruction from the Teacher's Edition. There are
two pages in the workbook per daily lesson. One is done along
with the lesson presentation, and the other is done as seatwork.
Work with manipulatives is foundational to the lessons. Quite
a few different items are required for lesson presentation, but
many of these are in the Home Teacher Packet. Nevertheless,
lesson preparation time is substantial, making this a challenging course to use if you are teaching numerous children at different levels.

Math 3 covers multiplication by single-digit multipliers and
division with single-digit divisors. Students master their multi-
plication/division facts this year. Unlike many other programs
at this level, *Math 3* does quite a bit of work with fractions and
decimals. Lots of word problems help develop application
skills. Review practice is found in the Teacher's Edition.

We can supplement with one of the three Math Activity
Books for third grade or one of the three available for second
grade depending upon each child's need. At each grade level
there is one activity book each for remedial, average, and
advanced students. Separate answer keys are needed for
these.

Mathematics Level C

(Modern Curriculum Press)
$9.55; teacher's edition - $20.15

See description for Level A above under "1st Grade Level."
Students can work fairly independently through this worktext,
although manipulative ideas and oral math exercises are
included in the Teacher's Edition. Thinking skills and understanding of concepts are both emphasized. This program is for
the average to above average student. Check out the *ADD* program, described under "Helps for Teaching, Drill, Review, and
Fun" for second grade, for review work.(S)

Math-U-See, Intermediate level

(Math-U-See)
teacher's manual - $20; student book - $15; Intermediate
video set - $35; Extra Practice Sheets - $17.50; blocks -
$30; fraction overlays - $30

Read the review under "1st Grade Level" to understand the
layout of the program. The *Intermediate* curriculum reviews
the basic concepts of the *Foundations* level for those just
beginning the program with older children. In addition to the
manipulative blocks used with earlier levels, you will need the
Intermediate videos (2 tapes), teacher's manual, student book,
and *Fraction Overlays*. *Fraction Overlays*—flat, colored plastic sheets in combination with clear grids—are also used with
Advanced and *Basic Algebra and Geometry* levels.

Concepts covered at this level are reading and writing numbers to 1,000,000, expanded notation, multiplication and division with multiple digits, fraction functions, mixed numbers,
converting fractions to decimals and percents, nine-overs
(casting out nines), rounding, averaging, Roman numerals,
estimating, factors, tallying, linear measurement, equations,
and positive and negative numbers. These concepts are similar
but not identical to those covered in typical courses for grades
3-6. Most programs do not introduce positive/negative numbers until later. The conceptual understanding taught thus far
makes it easier for students as they move on into more difficult
concepts. An answer key is included in the teacher manual
along with tests and word problems. A book of *Extra Practice
Sheets* should be helpful for most students.

Miquon Math

(Key Curriculum Press)
$53.95 for complete Homeschool Set; $8.95 for set of
Cuisenaire rods

This inexpensive program based on the use of *Cuisenaire®
Rods* is advertised for first through third grades. However, it
will also help older students understand arithmetic concepts.
The child uses the rods to discover mathematical concepts,
then does written work as he records his findings, moving
towards more written work as he masters concepts. Essential
components are *Lab Sheet Annotations* (the teacher's guide)
and student workbooks (two for each grade level). Also recommended are two inexpensive little books that will give us a
better feel for the program: *Notes to Teachers* and *First-Grade
Diary*. Although the *Diary* refers to first grade, the methods
apply to all levels. *Miquon* users report that children actually
learn concepts beyond third grade level in this program.
Students need to start in the first book of the program, although
they can complete them as quickly as they are able. They cannot start in the middle.(S)

Moving with Math [Level B for 3rd-4th grades]
(Math Teachers Press-MTP)
Combined Home School Set - reproducible version
$67.90 OR non-reproducible version - $42.90; combines
teacher's guides - $25.85; manipulatives sold separately
by MTP

There are three primary components: *Skill Builders B*; three
Moving with Math workbooks—Part I (Numeration, Addition,
and Subtraction), Part II (Multiplication and Division), Part III
(Fractions, Geometry, and Measurement); and *Math Capsules*.

The layout and components for Level B are similar to those
of Level A described under "1st Grade Level" but with the
omission of "Oral Drills." Likewise, there are two options:
either a consumable version or a reproducible version.

Multiplication covers through two-digit multipliers, but
division covers only through single-digit divisors. Considering
that this level is supposed to cover through fourth grade level,
the program's overall rate of progress is slower than that of A
Beka, BJUP, and Modern Curriculum Press. Part of the reason
is that *Moving With Math* is designed for mastery of objectives
with long term retention rather than the constant review found
in some of the other programs. For example, two-digit division, which is typically introduced at fourth grade level in
other programs, is introduced at Level C (grades 5-6) where a
child can be expected to master the concept. It is not introduced in Level B since mastery is not intended at that level.

The program should be arranged in the best order for each
child by the teacher, using the diagnostic tests and objective
lists. Help is available in the form of optional Teacher's Guides
for each workbook. The Teacher's Guides make it easier for
parents to learn how to use manipulatives and also include
games. They lay out daily programs, integrating the above
components with *Using Models to Learn Multiplication and
Division Facts. Using Models*, included with the combined
home school set for Level B, will be especially helpful to those
who are unfamiliar with the use of manipulatives.
Manipulative activities need one-on-one presentation as will
many of the worksheet activities, but there are many pages students will be able to do alone. A set of free home school
instructions explains how to integrate the components and suggests the number of days to spend on each objective.

For manipulatives you will need either *Base Ten Blocks* or
Cuisenaire® Rods (cut 10 cm. squares from poster board to use
in place of 100's squares that come with *Base Ten* materials),
fraction circles, and a geoboard (which can be made with a plywood square and nails). Manipulatives are available from MTP.

MTP also offers an introductory calculator kit that includes
a calculator and instruction manual whose lessons will integrate with *Moving with Math.*

Math Teachers Press has an hour-long video, "Moving with
Math: An Overview for Home School," which describes the
philosophy and components of the program, the role of manip-

ulatives in bridging the gap from concrete to abstract, and
practical suggestions from a home-school parent. It also shows
students from various levels working with manipulatives. The
video is free with orders over $125 or it can be purchased for
$19.95. Trained educational consultants are available at Math
Teachers Press' toll free number to answer questions.(S)

Primary Mathematics 3A and 3B
(Family Things)
3A and 3B sets - $18.50 each; teacher's guides - $15
each

See the review of *Primary Mathematics* 1A and 1B. This
level covers further work on addition, subtraction, multiplication, and division, including long division; fractions (equivalent fractions plus adding and subtracting), measurement,
graphs, time, and geometry. It also teaches 2-step word problems and mental calculation. The two coursebooks for this
level are 120-pages each and the four workbooks are 88 pages
each. It will be challenging for most students to begin this program at level 3 if they have been using a different math program. However, the pictorial lessons do help students pick up
concepts they might have not yet been taught. Make sure that
if you are just starting this program, you watch for this problem, and provide the necessary teaching before expecting your
child to do the lessons. Teacher's Guides for this level are not
very helpful. There are no answer keys, so you will have to
solve problems yourself to check answers.(S)

Saxon Math 3
(Saxon Publishers)
home study kit - $94.50; additional
workbooks - $34.50 a set

See the review under "1st Grade
Level." At third grade level, the scope and
sequence is running slightly behind those of the major
Christian publishers with the exception of School of
Tomorrow (which lags quite a distance behind) and BJUP with
which it is almost comparable. It compares almost straight
across with ScottForesman's *Exploring Mathematics* for Grade
3. Children perform all four basic functions, but multiplication
and division are practiced with only single-digit multipliers
and divisors. The slower progression in these areas is compen-
sated for by introduction of other concepts such as social studies and science connections to mathematics, work with positive and negative numbers, learning about lines of symmetry,
and graphing ordered pairs on coordinate graphs.
Manipulatives must be ordered separately, but the same manipulatives are used for all levels. See ordering details in reviews
for younger levels.(S)

Review Help and Extras

See reviews of these recommended resources in the "Helps

for Teaching, Drill, Review, and Fun" section.

ADD-Arithmetic Developed Daily, Grade 3

Addition Facts in 5 Minutes a Day and *Subtraction Facts in 5 Minutes a Day*

Addition, Subtraction, and Multiplication Songs Kits

Arithmetic Practice Books

Calculadder®

Coins Make Change Bingo

Cranium Crackers, Book 1

Creating Line Designs

Designs in Math

Focus on Problem Solving C

Grocery Cart Math

Hive Alive

Holey Cards

Math Fact Fun Packet

Mathematical Reasoning through Verbal Analysis, Book 1

Mental Math, Third Grade

Multiplication Facts in 5 Minutes a Day and *Division Facts in 5 Minutes a Day*

Multiplication Teaching and Learning Made Easy

Musical Math

Musical Math Facts Level 2

The Original Skip Count Kid or *The Skip Count Kid's Bible Heroes*

The Quarter Mile Math Game

Quick Thinks Math, Book A1 or Book B1

Scratch Your Brain Where it Itches

Solving Math Word Problems - Easily, Book 3

Help for Slow Learners

Children who are having trouble mastering basic arithmetic need to slow down and back up. There is no point going on to fractions and decimals without first mastering addition, subtraction, multiplication, and division, since those skills form the foundation for future learning.

Hands-on materials are one of the best ways of reviewing for two reasons. The first reason is that concrete learning methods often work best with children who have difficulty. The second reason is that, because such materials are not age-graded, they do not carry the below-grade-level stigma of younger level texts.

Often, repeated practice is the key, and workbooks can provide a useful format for that practice. However, it is wise to choose workbooks with fewer problems per page since slow students are often overwhelmed by the perceived immensity of the task. Books like the half-size arithmetic practice books from **Essential Learning Products** are much less intimidating than something like an A Beka or MCP worktext.

Some workbooks have been written specifically to help

remedial students. **Computation Basics** (Educators Publishing Service) [$9.30-$10.80 each; answer keys - $1.90 each] is a set of six workbooks designed to help children with the four basic math processes. Each process is "...broken down into small, carefully sequenced steps." There are about twenty problems per page. These books can be used with students of any age, covering concepts up through division with two-digit divisors. Inexpensive answer keys are available for each of the six books.

A similar option is **Building Math Skills Step by Step** (Continental Press) [$6.75 each; teacher's guides -$2.75 each]. This series is a little more comprehensive in that it also covers such topics as geometric shapes, picture graphs, calendar, money, measurement, problem solving, fractions, and decimals. There are six books in the series, broken down into two levels: Primary books cover skills taught in grades K-2, while Intermediate books cover skills for grades 3-5. There are three books at each level. Teacher's Guides with answer keys are available for each workbook.

4th Grade Level

Arithmetic 4, third edition

(A Beka Book)

$11.55; teacher key - $20.95; speed drills/tests - $4.60; key to speed drills - $8.95

The *Arithmetic 4* worktext includes summary presentations of lesson material and exercises. As with the rest of the A Beka Book math program, this book is a little more advanced than some other math programs. However, with the creation of new programs designed to meet the more challenging national math standards, the pace is similar to some others such as the *Horizons Math*. This text does an excellent job of reviewing previously taught concepts, and features periodic review lessons. Supplementary exercises at the back of the book can be used for additional work on particular concepts/skills. Tests and speed drills are contained in a separate book, which some will find helpful. The text includes some work with graphs and charts, but word problems and concept development are still weak in comparison to most other math programs. Supplementing with manipulatives and/or problem-solving books might be helpful to overcome these weaknesses. Explanations within the student text should be adequate for average to above average students to do most of the work independently, which makes this a very efficient option for many families. The teacher key contains answers for the student text. A separate key is needed for the tests and speed drills. The

Curriculum/Lesson Plans book is unnecessary.

Developmental Mathematics

(Mathematics Programs Associates, Inc.)

See description under "1st Grade Level."

Exploring Mathematics Grade 4

(ScottForesman)

hardbound student text - $41.76; teacher's edition - $102.78; manipulatives kit -$273.84

See the review for Grade 3, since the format is very similar. Grade 4 reviews and expands upon place value, addition, subtraction, time, measurement, geometry, statistics, graphing, and probability. Multiplication and division continue on through two-digit multipliers and divisors. Fraction work progresses through addition and subtraction of fractions without common denominators. You need play money (both coins and bills), Base Ten Blocks®, a *Math Sketcher* or other tool for drawing various polygons, and fraction manipulatives to accompany the Grade 4 program. *Fraction Factory* is used in the program. ScottForesman seems to have only classroom-size buckets of *Fraction Factory*, but Creative Publications offers individual sets. As with Grade 3, the *Problem Solving and Critical Thinking Workbook* and supplementary workbooks for practice, enrichment, or review will be useful for some students.(S)

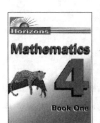

Horizons Mathematics 4

(Alpha Omega)

teacher handbook - $50; students workbooks - $12.50 each ($25 set of 2)

As is true of earlier levels of this program, this course follows an advanced scope and sequence compared to most others. A four-page placement test at the front of the book will help you know whether or not your child is ready for this level. The readiness test asks students to reduce fractions, multiply four-digit numbers by multiples of 10, perform short division, compare values of fractions with unlike denominators, round off numbers, understand ratio, add fractions with common denominators, and solve simple, algebraically-expressed addition equations.

Lessons are designed to be presented by the teacher, but students should be able to do the majority of their work independently. Lesson objectives are clearly spelled out in the teacher handbook. Materials or supplies needed are listed, and you might have to plan ahead to procure some of these. One lesson describes a bingo game for the teacher to construct, but most materials are much more standard—counters, flash cards, rulers, *Base Ten Blocks*, a clock, and play money. While much of the lesson activity takes place within the two student workbooks for this level, there are additional activities such as mental math or manipulative work described in the lesson plans.

About every other lesson uses a worksheet, for which reproducible masters are found in the next to last section of the teacher handbook. (Worksheets are also available in separate packets.) Quarterly tests and a final, plus answer keys for workbooks, worksheets, and tests are all in the teacher handbook. There is also a test after every ten lessons in the student workbooks.

Lessons continue to use the spiral approach, presenting a new concept, then coming back to it a number of times to build toward mastery. Also, concepts are continually reviewed. Because of this, students who might not have previously covered all the concepts taught in *Horizons Mathematics 3* might be able to pick up missing concepts in review lessons. Conversely, some students will have mastered earlier concepts well and might be able to skip some parts of the lessons. Among concepts covered by the end of the course are long division with two-digit divisors, adding and subtracting fractions with unlike denominators, converting fractions to decimals, adding and subtracting decimals, metric measurement, and multiplying or dividing to find equal ratios. Time, money, geometry, and graphs are also covered.

Student workbooks are printed in full color. While there are usually three or four workbook pages per lesson, the amount of work per page is not as bad as it sounds since illustrations, puzzles, and lesson explanations take up some space. I suspect that many parents will be tempted to hand their children the workbooks and ignore the teacher handbooks, but there are some important lessons and presentation ideas in the handbooks you should not skip. You should review the lesson plans and determine how much of each presentation is useful for each student.

Making Math Meaningful 4, second edition

(Cornerstone Curriculum Project)

$40 for Guide and Student Book; extra student books - $18.75 each

The program, designed for home educators, consists of a Parent/Teacher Guide and Student Book. The manipulative kit used for levels K-3 is no longer needed. Math concepts are taught through a variety of discussions and activities presented one-on-one by the teacher. Lessons are scripted for the parent teacher, explaining in detail what to say and do. Students complete workbook pages in conjunction with the lesson presentations. Unique methods of presentation used throughout the program aim for student mastery of concepts and mathematical thinking. Some students might need additional computation practice which can be accomplished with any of a number of supplemental resources. See descriptions under second and third grades. Student books are consumable and may be purchased separately.

Mastering Mathematics

See description under "1st Grade Level."

Math 54

by Stephen Hake and John Saxon
(Saxon Publishers, Inc.)
home study kit - $51.50; extra student book - $ 50.60

This text should be appropriate for most fourth graders and those fifth graders who lag slightly behind grade level. It is similar in format to *Math 65* and *Math 76* rather than the K-3 Saxon program. Lessons and problems are all contained in the student textbook. Like the older level books, hands-on/manipulative work is not included in the program, although the *Saxon Activity Guide for Middle Grades Series* (see review) can be used along with the text to provide some activity. Constant review and introduction of new concepts in small increments make it practical for many students. It is most suitable for children who are able to work abstractly without the need for manipulatives. The Home Study Kit includes the student text, Home Study packet, and Test Forms booklet. The Home Study Packet is the answer key for text problems, speed drills, and tests. The Test Forms booklet contains speed drills, tests and reproducible pages of play money, "hundred number" charts, and a few other forms to be used with the course.(S)

Math for Christian Schools 4

(Bob Jones University Press)
home school kit - $57; worktext - $12; teacher's edition - $22; student materials packet - $5.50; home teacher packet - $8; flip chart - $15; tests and answer key - $10; activity books - $9 each; activity book answer keys - $4.50 each

The fourth grade level has been revised. See the review of the first grade program which is similar in format. The course is designed to be taught from the Teacher's Edition rather than used as an independent-study program. The student worktext serves as an adjunct to the course and cannot be used on its own. The Student Materials Packet includes manipulatives that are used throughout the course. Students study multiplication, division, fractions, decimals, and even positive and negative numbers which are introduced through manipulatives. Mental math activities add yet another dimension. The Flip Chart consists of 42 charts used by the teacher for presenting lessons. Review is presented from the Teacher's Edition. As with other levels, there are three optional activity books from which you might choose for additional practice. This course does require quite a bit of teacher preparation and presentation time. The Math 4 Home School Kit includes the student worktext, home teacher's edition, student materials packet, home teacher packet, and tests with answer key. Activity books and flip chart are optional.

Mathematics Level D

(Modern Curriculum Press)
$9.55; teacher's edition - $20.15

This is a worktext with plenty of thinking skill activity built in. It is a little less advanced than A Beka, but many of the word problems are very challenging. Some hands-on ideas are listed in the Teacher's Edition, to be used or not as you need. The biggest weakness is the lack of review. You must supply your own method of review and application of previously learned concepts. Try skipping occasional problems, then using those for review. Students can generally work independently, although they will often need help on the thought problems. I recommend getting the teacher's edition.(S)

Math-U-See, Intermediate level

See both the general review of the program under "1st Grade Level" and the review of this level under "3rd Grade Level."

Moving with Math Level B

(Math Teachers Press)

See information under third grade since this level is set up to cover both third and fourth grade material. MTP will send you—upon request and at no cost—instructions for dividing the program into separate, one-year courses. This program is the easiest I have seen for picking and choosing objectives to teach.(S)

Primary Mathematics 4A and 4B

(Family Things)
4A and 4B sets - $18.50 each; teacher's guides - $15 each

See the review of *Primary Mathematics* 1A and 1B. By this level, the advanced scope and sequence of the entire program has created a significant gap between what *Primary Mathematics* covers and the content of most other programs. At fourth level students learn all four functions with both fractions and decimals. Geometry coverage is also very advanced as students compute the degrees in angles and complex area and perimeter questions. Students also work with advanced whole number concepts (e.g. factors, multiples, rounding off), money, other geometric concepts, graphs, and averages. In contrast to most other programs, *Primary Mathematics* introduces two-digit multipliers at this level, but doesn't really work on two-digit multipliers and divisors until the fifth level. While students complete quite a few computation problems, the number of word problems seems to gradually increase at this level. One curious typographical style used is certain to raise questions but shouldn't pose any problems: decimals are placed at the mid-height of numbers rather than at the base. The two coursebooks for this level are 120-pages each and the four workbooks are 88 pages each. Students who want to begin work in this program will not be able to go from most third grade programs into this level, but they will need to first work through at least the third level. There is still quite a bit of pictorial lesson presentation, but not as much as in earlier levels. Answer keys for both the coursebook and workbook exercises are found in the Teacher's Guides.(S)

Progressing with Arithmetic 4
(Rod and Staff)
student text - $14.30; teacher's edition (two volumes) - $21; speed drills - $4.70; tests - $1.90

Rod and Staff's math program is black-and-white, straightforward, no-nonsense traditional mathematics with an emphasis on drill and memorization as well as practical application through word problems. Previously taught concepts are continuously reviewed. Conceptual teaching is weaker than in other programs such as BJUP's, Modern Curriculum Press', and ScottForesman's. Sometimes teachers are told to visually illustrate a concept on the board, and there are some illustrations. But manipulative activities are rare. Student books include brief instructions on new concepts. While it is possible to provide adequate math instruction from only the student text, the teacher's editions (two volumes) are extremely useful for more complete lesson presentation, more comprehensive review, oral drill exercises, answers overprinted on reproduced student pages, and coordinating instructions for use of drills. Supplementary drills are at the back of the student book, and speed drills (to be used with every other lesson) are in a separate book. Tests are in a separate booklet, and answers for tests are in the teacher's editions. The extra Speed Drill book emphasizes speed and accuracy, but it should be optional since there is already so much drill within the textbook itself. You should also purchase or make flash cards for addition, subtraction, multiplication, and division to use with this course.

The program is about average in pace. It reviews addition and subtraction, then focuses primarily upon multiplication and division skills and fractions. It takes multiplication up through three-digit multipliers; division through two-digit divisors; fractions through addition, subtraction, and introduction of multiplication; and decimals through addition and subtraction. It covers unit conversions, Roman numerals, time, measurement, money, graphs (picture and bar), perimeter, and area. Time/rate/distance problems are also introduced. A "Handbook of Terms and Rules" can be found at the back of both student and teacher editions.

This program stresses mastery of arithmetic skills as well as mathematical thinking such as estimation, choosing mathematical functions, and mathematical vocabulary. It isn't exciting, but it builds a solid foundation in math. The program's Mennonite background is evident in the illustrations and word problems dealing with farming, canning, building, etc., but none of this limits the program's effectiveness for all children.

Hands-on Math

Use learning materials to assist your child in grasping new concepts and for practice. This is especially important for kinesthetic learners (those who learn by touching and doing). Refer to some of the resources listed under "Review Help and Extras" section or use some of the following ideas:
- household projects such as cooking, building, measuring
- games such as *Budget, Shopping Bag, Allowance,* and *Grocery Cart* (Creative Teaching Associates)
- grocery shopping (let children help determine best buys) small business (e.g., lemonade stand)

Review Help and Extras

See views of these recommended resources in the "Helps for Teaching, Drill, Review, and Fun" section below.
ADD-Arithmetic Developed Daily, Grade 4
Arithmetic Practice Books
Baseball Math
Calculadder®
Cranium Crackers, Book 1
Creating Line Designs
Designs in Math
Equation Golf
Enright® Computation Series
Focus on Problem Solving D
Fraction Mania
Grocery Cart Math
Hive Alive
Holey Cards
Key to Decimals
Key to Fractions
Math Fact Fun Packet
Mathematical Reasoning through Verbal Analysis, Books 1 and 2
Mental Math, Fourth Grade
Multiplication Facts in 5 Minutes a Day and *Division Facts in 5 Minutes a Day*
Multiplication Teaching and Learning Made Easy
One game
Operations
The Original Skip Count Kid or *The Skip Count Kid's Bible Heroes*
The Quarter Mile Math Game
Quick Thinks Math, Book A1 or Book B1
Saxon Activity Guide for Middle Grades Series
SOLUTIONS: Applying Problem-Solving Skills in Math
24 Game: Single Digits or *Double Digits*

CAUTION: Fourth or fifth grade is when the failure to understand concepts which have been taught earlier often shows up. Sometimes children can progress well through math programs by simple rote learning of processes. At upper levels they need to combine a number of processes and understand how and why to do so. If they have not understood what they have been learning, they begin to stumble at this point. If your child is having trouble with fraction functions or word problems at this point, back up and review as much as necessary before continuing. It will probably be necessary to reteach via a different method rather than simply repeating the same instruction the student did not comprehend the first time. Manipulatives are often the key to understanding in such situations.

Of particular interest at this level are *Key To Fractions* (Key Curriculum Press) which is very good for additional help with fraction concepts and the *Focus on Problem Solving* books (Continental Press) [$6.50 each; teacher's guides - $2.25 each] which provide additional practice with word problems.

5th Grade Level

Arithmetic 5, third edition
(A Beka Book)
$11.55; teacher edition - $20.95; speed drills and tests - $4.60; key to speed drills/tests - $8.95

The latest edition of this text is still a challenging math program, strong on computation skill development. Expanded explanations with illustrations are an improvement over earlier editions. There are more story problems, previously one of the weak areas. In keeping with the math standards, there is more work with graphs. One lesson deals with probability, a topic included in the national standards, but not one that really needs to be addressed at this level of math. (A Beka deserves credit for limiting time spent on this topic.)

In addition to the above topics, *Arithmetic 5* continues on through multiplication and division of both fractions and decimals. It reviews and expands coverage of place value, basic operations, Roman numerals (rarely taught in other programs!), measurement, graphs, and introductory geometry. At the end of the book are supplemental sections with more problems arranged by topics (e.g., multiplying fractions, story problems), homework "review" problems for every other lesson, and reference handbook.

It is still not a program that stresses conceptual understanding such as *Math-U-See* or *Exploring Mathematics,* but this is much improved over earlier editions. It should work well for students who are generally good at math and like to work independently. The worktext format is easy to work with—instruction and examples are built into the student book. Also, students appreciate not having to copy problems. You will probably want the Teacher's Edition for an answer key.

Developmental Mathematics
(Mathematics Programs Associates, Inc.)
See description under "1st Grade Level."

Exploring Mathematics Grade 5
(ScottForesman)
hardbound student text - $41.76; teacher's edition - $102.78; manipulatives kit - $273.84

See the review for Grade 3, since the format is very similar. Grade 5 reviews and expands upon place value, addition, subtraction, multiplication, division, measurement, geometry, statistics, graphing, and probability.

Fractions and decimals are emphasized this year. Multiplication continues on through multi-digit multipliers, including multiplication with decimals and fractions. Division includes decimals divided by whole numbers and a pictorial introduction to division of fractions. Although fraction and decimal instruction lags behind programs like BJUP, Saxon, and A Beka, *Exploring Mathematics* jumps ahead with instruction on patterns, coordinate graphing, ratio, proportion, and percent. You need play money (both coins and bills), *Base Ten Blocks®* , a *Math Sketcher* or other tool for drawing various polygons, and fraction manipulatives to accompany the Grade 5 program (essentially the same manipulatives for Grade 4). *Fraction Factory* is used in the program. ScottForesman seems to have only classroom-size buckets of *Fraction Factory*, but Creative Publications offers individual sets. As with Grade 3 and Grade 4, the *Problem Solving and Critical Thinking Workbook* and supplementary workbooks for practice, enrichment, or review will be useful for some students.(S)

Gaining Skill with Arithmetic 5
(Rod and Staff)
student text - $14.25; teacher's edition (two volumes) - $21; speed drills - $4.85; tests - $1.90

Identical in format to *Progressing with Arithmetic 4*, this text continues with multiplication and division, then concentrates on fractions, decimals, ratio, percent, graphing, measurement, unit conversion, and geometry (shapes, perimeter, and area). While it might be possible to work with only the student text, the teacher's editions are valuable for lesson presentation, oral reviews, mental drills, and answer keys. Tests are available in a separate booklet, and test answers are found in the teacher's editions.

Horizons Mathematics 5
(Alpha Omega)
teacher handbook - $50; students workbooks - $12.50 each ($25 set of 2)

See the review of *Horizons Mathematics 4*. The format is identical for level 5. As in level 4, there is a four-page readiness test at the front of the teacher handbook to help determine whether students are ready for this level. Among concepts they are expected to know *before beginning* this course are division of 2-digit divisors into dollar amounts with decimals; acute angles; diameters and radii of circles; similar and congruent figures; simple perimeter, area, and volume; ratios; addition of fractions with unlike denominators, addition and subtraction of mixed numbers, decimal values, and metric measurements. As with earlier levels, there is a great deal of review, so if your child has not yet covered all of these concepts, they might be able to pick them up easily through the review that is built into level 5.

Among concepts taught by the end of this course are multiplying 3-digit by 3-digit numbers, values of exponential numbers, finding averages, division by 2-digit divisors, types of triangles, least common multiples, multiplying and dividing fractions, all four functions applied to decimal numbers, percent, and probability. Calculators are used, primarily for checking answers. This course continues to stress both computation skills and understanding of concepts.

Making Math Meaningful 5, second edition

(Cornerstone Curriculum Project)
$40; additional student books - $20 each

Level 5 is presented in a single, 336-page book. Unlike younger levels, this book is designed for the student to work independently. The answer key is at the back of the book. If you need to, remove it and keep it elsewhere.

Unique methods of presentation stress conceptual understanding. For example, when students learn complex multiplication and division, they are shown why it works rather than just the steps to memorize. Students are occasionally directed to collect materials for hands-on activities: pennies, Lego blocks (or similar math manipulatives), and toothpicks. Such instances are not very frequent, and materials should not be difficult to obtain or find substitutes for. These activities coupled with the illustrations and applications within the lessons help develop conceptual understanding better than do some other popular math programs.

The scope and sequence is also a little different. For example, long division is taught up through single-digit divisors and division by multiples of 10, while most fifth grade programs have moved beyond to multi-digit divisors. However, fraction concepts are presented in algebraic forms advanced beyond most programs at this level.

Students work more on concepts, patterns, logic, and word problems than on computation skills. Supplement if students need more computation practice. The book is consumable, and you will need a separate book for each child taking the course.

Mastering Mathematics

See description under "1st Grade Level."

Math for Christian Schools 5 (second edition)

(Bob Jones University Press)
home school kit - $64; hardbound student text - $23; teacher's edition - $22; home teacher packet - $8; flip chart - $15; student materials packet - $5.50; activity books - $9 each; activity book answer keys - $4.50 each; tests and answer key - $10

This revised edition is designed with a balance of activity, practice, review, and thinking skills, focusing heavily on multiplication and division of fractions and decimals. It also includes an optional pre-algebra chapter. Strong points are excellent word problems and skills application. Centered around an aviation theme, the course is designed to be presented by the teacher from the spiral bound Home Teacher's Edition. Flip Charts are used as optional teaching aids, and students do hands-on work with manipulatives from the Student Materials Packet. We should also select one of the activity books depending upon the abilities of the student. *Spread Your Wings 5* is for the remedial student; *Spring into Action 5* is for the average student; *Stretch Your Mind 5* challenges the advanced student. Or we might use the new Math 5 Review Activity Book which includes cumulative, concept, and fact reviews for extra practice. A separate test packet and answer key is optional. This program will require more parental preparation and presentation time than programs such as Saxon's *Math 65* or A Beka's *Arithmetic 5*.

The *Math 5 Home School Kit* includes the student text, home teacher's edition, student materials packet, home teacher packet, and tests with answer key.

Math 65

by John Saxon and Stephen Hake
(Saxon Publishers, Inc.)
home study kit - $52.50; extra student text - $50.60

This hardback text is appropriate for the average fifth grader. Students who need extra time at this level might spend more time in this text, perhaps skipping the *87* book later on. The Saxon series, as originally written (minus the *87* book) takes one year less to cover grades K-8. The Saxon math series is highly recommended because it teaches new concepts in small segments while continually reviewing previously learned material. It does have a "rules" orientation more like A Beka's rather than a hands-on conceptual orientation like *Math-U-See, Exploring Mathematics*, and others where students use manipulatives to see what actually happens when they tackle problems such as long division. Nevertheless, thinking skills are emphasized more than in most programs. It correlates fairly well (but not completely) with the new math standards, including topics like graphing, probability, and many word problems to develop mathematical thinking skills. However, it does not teach the use of calculators. (See the review of the new *Saxon Activity Guide for Middle Grades Series* which provides additional practice on topics stressed in the new standards. Note that it still does not teach basic calculator usage, although it uses calculators in one division activity.) It continues developing arithmetic skills through multiplication and division of fractions and decimals while also reviewing and expanding concepts of place value, addition and subtraction, geometry, measurement, and probability. Extra math drills for each lesson are at the back of the book.

Saxon sells the Home Study Kit, a package for home schoolers which includes the student text, Home Study Packet, and Test Forms booklet. The Home Study Packet contains all of your answer keys and the Test Forms booklet includes tests, speed drills, and "photocopiable" fraction circles, play money, and place value template. The revised second edition (1996) introduces each lesson with a box that directs the student to do mental math problems, a speed drill, and a word problem.

Parents like Saxon because it allows students to do most of their math lessons independently. A few students have difficulty with this text because it requires them to work in more abstract ways than they might be ready for. These children still need either a manipulative-based program or supplemental work with manipulatives to understand concepts and prevent discouragement.(S)

Mathematics E (grade 5)
(Modern Curriculum Press)
$10.60; teacher's edition - $20.15

Worktext format. You might wish to continue using this series if you began at earlier levels. Exercises include work on thinking skills and application of concepts. Review is a weak point, so make sure you provide supplemental review to aid retention of previously learned concepts. The Teacher's Edition is recommended.(S)

Math-U-See, Intermediate or Advanced level
(Math-U-See)

See the complete review of the program under "1st Grade Level" and the reviews of the *Intermediate* level under third grade or the *Advanced* level under sixth grade. Most fifth grade concepts are covered within the *Intermediate* level, but some fifth graders will be able to move on to the *Advanced* level.

Moving with Math Level C [for 5th-6th grades]
(Math Teachers Press)
Combined Home School Set - reproducible version - $62.95 OR consumable version - $37.95; combined teacher's guides - $28.85; manipulatives sold separately by MTP

Components: *Skill Builders C; Moving with Math* work-books—Part I (Numeration and Problem Solving with Whole Numbers), Part II (Fractions, Decimals, and Percent), Part III (Geometry, Measurement, and Problem Solving); and, *Math Capsules*. See the full description of the components under the early grades above.

Part I stresses problem solving, including a five-step plan for solving word problems and many strategies to help students decide which process is needed to solve problems. At this level, the need for manipulatives is not universal, but for those students who need hands-on work, this program, *Making Math Meaningful*, and *Math-U-See* are the best fully-developed alternatives I have seen.

There is a moderate amount of manipulative work in the *Moving with Math* student workbooks, but it may be enough for many students. Those who need more will benefit from the lessons in *Skill Builders* which often require more manipulative work. (The best way to use these components is to look at the lessons in both components, including lesson presentation ideas in *Skill Builders*, that teach the same concept. Choose as few or as many as your child needs, selecting those lessons that use methods that work best with your child.)

The diagnostic tests (for identifying which areas need attention) and "maintenance tests" (for review) in *Math Capsules* are very important at this level. A free set of home school instructions explains how to integrate the components and suggests the number of days to spend on each objective.

At this level, the need for manipulatives for whole number concepts is often greatly reduced; however, students benefit from the fraction bar activities for developing fraction concepts, *Base Ten Blocks* for developing decimal concepts, and the geoboard activities for increased understanding of geometric concepts. Many students need only occasional use of manipulatives for reviewing concepts but benefit greatly from manipulative use when learning new ones. Manipulatives you will need: either *Base Ten Blocks* (the expensive 1000's cube is unnecessary) or *Cuisenaire® Rods* (cut squares 10 cm. by 10 cm. from poster board to use in place of 100's squares that come with *Base Ten* sets); fraction bars; six- and ten-sided dice; and a geoboard which can easily be made from a square of plywood and nails. Manipulatives are available from MTP or other sources.

The Teacher's Guides (one for each workbook) offer security to parents, save preparation time, lay out daily lesson plans, show us how to teach with manipulatives, and integrate program components. Games and answer keys are also included in the Teacher's Guides.

Math Teachers Press has an hour-long video, "Moving with Math: An Overview for Home School," which describes the philosophy and components of the program, the role of manipulatives in bridging the gap from concrete to abstract, and practical suggestions from a home-school parent. It also shows students from various levels working with manipulatives. The video is free with purchases over $125 or it can be purchased for $19.95. Trained educational consultants are available at Math Teachers Press' toll free phone number to answer questions.(S)

Primary Mathematics 5A and 5B

(Family Things)

5A and 5B sets - $18.50 each; teacher's guides - $15 each

See the review of *Primary Mathematics* 1A and 1B. The scope and sequence continues to be quite advanced beyond other programs typically used by homeschoolers. At the fifth level, students do advanced work with decimals plus multiplication and division with up to four-digit multipliers and divisors. They learn to work with percentages, continue with advanced work on fractions, geometry (e.g., finding the area of a triangle), and graphs. Rate and speed word problems, as well as other types of word problems are given a great deal of attention. At the end of the course, students are doing beginning algebra. Some of the geometry taught at this level is rarely introduced before high school level. For example, a workbook problem asks students to find the ratio of the area of one triangle to another, with only dimensions for the triangles given. The rate and distance problems are not quite as complex as the time/rate/distance problems of high school texts, but they get close.

The two coursebooks for this level are 128-pages each, and there is only one 128-page workbook per coursebook. There are many more time-consuming word problems and fewer drill type problems at this level, which accounts for the reduced number of workbook pages. The coursebooks have answers to practice and review problems at the back of each book, but there are no answers to the lesson presentation problems. Workbook answers are in the Teacher's Guides, which makes them fairly essential at this level.

Students who want to begin work in this program will not be able to go from most fourth grade programs into this level, but they will need to first work through at least the fourth level, and maybe also the third. Pictorial lesson presentation continues to decrease.(S)

Hands-On Help

All of the formal curricula should be supplemented with hands-on presentations and/or applications, both to enhance learning and to make math more enjoyable. Creative Teaching Associates offers board games that are particularly appropriate for this level: I recommend *Budget, Bank Account,* and *Stock Exchange* [$16.95-$21.95] because they cover skills students learn in the middle to upper elementary grades.

Review Help and Extras

See views of these recommended resources in the "Helps for Teaching, Drill, Review, and Fun" section below.

ADD-Arithmetic Developed Daily, Grade 5
Arithmetic Practice Books
Calculadder®
Cranium Crackers, Book 2
Designs in Math
Equation Golf
Enright® Computation Series
Focus on Problem Solving E
Fraction Mania
Grocery Cart Math
Hive Alive
Key to Decimals
Key to Fractions
Key to Geometry
Math Fact Fun Packet
Mathematical Reasoning through Verbal Analysis, Book 2
Mental Math, Fifth Grade
Multiplication Facts in 5 Minutes a Day and *Division Facts in 5 Minutes a Day*
One game
Operations
The Original Skip Count Kid or *The Skip Count Kid's Bible Heroes*
The Quarter Mile Math Game
Quick Thinks Math, Book A1 or Book B1
Saxon Activity Guide for Middle Grades Series
SOLUTIONS: Applying Problem-Solving Skills in Math
24 Game: Fractions Edition

6th Grade Level

Arithmetic 6

(A Beka Book)

$11.55; teacher key - $20.95; speed drills/tests - $4.60; key to speed drills/tests - $8.95

By sixth grade this program has advanced beyond some others. Some concepts such as working with decimals and percent are the same, but the level of difficulty is higher. It stresses computation skills more than applications, although this book does include some consumer math topics such as banking, interest, installment buying, and reading meters. The book is in the easy-to-use worktext format. Also purchase the Teacher's Key which is your answer key.

Developmental Mathematics

(Mathematics Programs Associates, Inc.)

See description under "1st Grade Level."

Exploring Mathematics Grade 6

(ScottForesman)

hardbound student text - $40.97; teacher's edition -

$113.97; manipulatives kit - $198.33

See the review for Grade 3, since the format is very similar for Grades 3 through 6. Grade 6 reviews and expands upon place value, addition, subtraction, multiplication, division, percent, measurement, geometry, statistics, graphing, and probability. Instruction in basic computation is completed with fractions and decimals. *Exploring Mathematics* moves beyond most other programs for sixth grade with entire chapters on statistics (data and graph interpretation), probability, and integers (introduction of negative numbers). It also teaches Cartesian coordinates and a great deal more geometry than others. Grade 6 incorporates calculator exercises throughout the book. (If a student has mastered the math facts and is fairly proficient with them, it is okay for him or her to use a calculator.) Grade 6 requires significantly less manipulative usage than do earlier levels, but students still need *Base Ten Blocks®* (which can also be used in place of rainbow cubes and tiles when those are called for), a protractor, *Math Sketcher* or other tool for drawing various polygons, compass, ruler with both centimeter and inch markings, blank cubes (dice), and fraction manipulatives. (*Fraction Factory* is used in the program. ScottForesman seems to have only classroom-size buckets of *Fraction Factory*, but Creative Publications offers individual sets.) As with Grade 3 through Grade 5, the *Problem Solving and Critical Thinking Workbook* and supplementary workbooks for practice, enrichment, or review will be useful for some students.(S)

Horizons Mathematics 6
(Alpha Omega)
teacher handbook - $50; students workbooks - $12.50 each ($25 set of 2)

See the review of level 4 for a complete description since this level follows the same format. The scope and sequence continues to be advanced beyond most other programs. Students beginning this level are expected to know how to work with fractions, decimals, and percent, although not all types of functions (e.g., division with decimal divisors). Some other concepts covered in *Horizons'* earlier levels might not yet have been taught in other programs: congruency/similarity; diameter, chords, and radius of a circle; and different types of averages. However, the continual review and spiral approach used to teach mean that these concepts are reviewed and/or retaught at this level. Still, the program moves beyond the level of most others. For example, Saxon's *Math 76* introduces the idea of ratio while *Horizons Mathematics 6* teaches cross multiplication to solve for *n*. Geometry coverage is more complex with students learning to construct geometric figures using a compass and straightedge. Students continue to work with fractions, decimals and percent. Consumer math topics such as check writing, banking, budgeting, and figuring interest are covered along with more advanced equations, graphs, meas-

urement, and problem solving.

Making Math Meaningful 6, second edition
(Cornerstone Curriculum Project)
$40; additional student books - $20 each

See description of level 5. The format is the same for level 6, but concepts covered include fractions, decimals, percents, and division to complete basic arithmetic foundations. By the time children complete this level, they are prepared for the study of algebra, although they might not be mature enough to comprehend algebra lessons as presented in most textbooks. Cornerstone has introduced an algebra program that immediately follows Level 6. Students who have completed Level 6 should be ready for Cornerstone's algebra course since it is more concrete in presentation than other algebra courses, and because students already have a foundation of conceptual understanding as a consequence of their studies within the *Making Math Meaningful* curriculum.

Mastering Mathematics

See description under "1st Grade Level." Students completing this program should be ready for most seventh grade programs, Saxon *Math 76*, or *Algebra 1/2* (mature students).

Math for Christian Schools 6
(Bob Jones University Press)
home school kit - $64; hardbound student text - $22; teacher's edition - $22; student materials packet - $5.50; home teacher packet - $8; flip chart - $15; activity books - $9 each; activity book answer keys - $4.50 each; tests and answer key - $10

The revised edition is designed with a balance of activity, practice, review, and thinking skills. Thinking is required in applying math concepts to ensure that children are understanding the concepts, not just memorizing methods. It covers fractions, decimals, percent, ratio, probability, measurement, negative numbers, statistics, and use of both calculators and computers. Centered around the theme "Courage in Crisis," the course is designed to be presented by the teacher from the spiral-bound Home Teacher's Edition rather than used for independent study. Flip Charts are used as optional teaching aids, and students do hands-on work with manipulatives from the Student Materials Packet. You should also select one of the activity books depending upon the abilities of your student. *Spread Your Wings 6* is for the remedial student. *Spring into Action 6* is for the average student. *Stretch Your Mind 6* challenges the advanced student. This program requires more parent preparation and presentation than others. The course content and difficulty level is approximately equivalent to ScottForesman's *Exploring Mathematics 6*. The *Math 6 Home School Kit* includes the student text, home teacher's edition, student materials packet, home teacher packet, and tests with answer key.

Math 76
(Saxon Publishers, Inc.)
home study kit - $53.50; student text only - $50.60 hc

This hardbound math text is advertised as being appropriate for bright sixth graders or average seventh graders, although the average sixth grader should have no trouble with it, especially those coming from fifth grade programs from A Beka Book, BJUP, and Alpha Omega. It reviews all math concepts that have been learned in a spiraling method of constant review. Especially notable are word problems that cause children to think of math concepts in a number of different ways to ensure that they have understanding. Students can work fairly independently in the Saxon series. All these advantages make this the top recommendation for most students at this level. The only criticism is that a few of the word problems talk about ghouls and trolls and such. Skip these if they are offensive to you. Saxon packages the book with an answer key, tests, and speed drills for home educators as the Home Study Kit.(SE)

Mathematics F (grade 6)
(Modern Curriculum Press)
$10.60; teacher's edition - $20.15

This book is in worktext format. You may wish to continue using this series if you began at earlier levels, although you need to supplement for adequate review. It teaches thinking skills and includes application exercises. The Teacher's Edition is recommended.(S)

Math-U-See Advanced level
(Math-U-See)
teacher's manual - $20; student book - $15; instruction video tapes set (2 tapes) - $40; blocks - $30; fraction overlays - $30; extra practice sheets - $17.50; Algebra/Decimal Inserts - $20

See the review under "1st Grade Level" for the basics about this program. For this level, you need to add the Algebra/Decimal Inserts, which are used along with the other manipulatives.

Advanced level covers skills approximating those typical for grades 6-8. This program's methodology is quite different from standard math programs. However, it does include review of concepts taught at previous levels for those just beginning the program with older students.

Concepts covered are decimals; more complicated work with multiplication, division, and fractions; algebra (factoring trinomials, multiplying binomials); positive and negative numbers, surface area (rectangular prisms); circles (area and circumference); Pythagorean Theorem; volume of a cylinder; similar polygons; metric prefixes and conversions; Celsius and Fahrenheit; squares and square roots; mean, median, and mode; ratio and proportion; parallel and perpendicular; linear measure; order of operations; solving for unknowns; rational and irrational numbers; probability; and geometry.

The presentation at this level is more like Saxon than the other two levels. One or two new concepts are taught, then students work on those concepts along with review and practice on previously-learned concepts (usually from four to eight lessons of practice). Unlike Saxon, almost all new concepts are taught with manipulatives as presented on the four hours of lesson-by-lesson video tapes. Lessons must be taught, although parent and student might watch the video presentation together to understand the basic concept. Students cannot work only from their books. An answer key is included in the teacher manual along with tests and word problems..

When students complete the Advanced level they can move on to *Math-U-See's Algebra and Geometry* or to Saxon's *Algebra 1/2*.

Moving with Math Level C [for grades 5-6]
(Math Teachers Press-MTP)

See the description under fifth grade. MTP will send you—upon request and at no charge—an information sheet showing how to divide the program into fifth and sixth grade, one-year programs.(S)

Primary Mathematics 6A and 6B
(Family Things)
6A and 6B sets - $18.50 each; teacher's guides - $15 each

See the review of *Primary Mathematics* 1A and 1B. The scope and sequence is very advanced beyond other programs typically used by homeschoolers. At the sixth level, much of the work is more typical of other high school level texts. Students work with fractions, but a typical problem requires students to perform three different operations on four different fractions within a single problem, much like an advanced Algebra 1 type problem, although without variables. Common geometry problems are set up in proof-style format, although you need not require students to present their solutions in that format. Among other concepts covered at this level are graphs, algebraic expressions, geometry (e.g., volume of solids and radius, diameter and circumference of circles), advanced fractions, ratio, percentage, tessellations, and lots of word problems including those challenging time/rate/distance problems. Instructions for teaching some of the challenging concepts are often quite minimal in the coursebooks. Some assistance is in the Teacher's Guides, but I suspect that even with the Teacher's Guides, some parents might not feel they have enough guidance to teach the advanced topics here without better instructional assistance. Coursebooks have exercise and review answers at the back, but there are no answers to many of the lesson problems that the teacher is to work through with students. Answer keys to workbooks are in the Teacher's Guides. The two coursebooks for this level are 120 and 112-pages each, and the two workbooks are 128 and 104 pages respectively. Students who want to begin work in this program will not be able to go from most fifth grade programs into this level, but they will need to first work through at least the fourth and fifth levels.(S)

○○○○○○○○○

Do not neglect practical application and rely on the textbook to cover everything. Look for life application situations to use math—at the market, figuring wallpaper/carpeting footage, balancing bank accounts, construction projects, and small business ventures. Also, Creative Teaching Associates offers *Big Deal* [$19.95], a board game that concentrates on application of percentage skills—a major concept at sixth grade level.

Review Help and Extras

See views of these recommended resources in the "Helps for Teaching, Drill, Review, and Fun" section below.
ADD-Arithmetic Developed Daily, Grade 6
Arithmetic Practice Books
Calculadder®
Cranium Crackers, Book 2
Designs in Math
Equation Golf
Enright® Computation Series
Focus on Problem Solving F
Fraction Mania
Hive Alive
Key to Percents
Mathematical Reasoning through Verbal Analysis, Book 2
Multiplication Facts in 5 Minutes a Day and *Division Facts in 5 Minutes a Day*
One game
Operations
The Quarter Mile Math Game
Quick Thinks Math, Book A1 or Book B1
Saxon Activity Guide for Middle Grades Series
SOLUTIONS: Applying Problem-Solving Skills in Math
24 Game: Fractions Edition (Item #3497)

Helps for Teaching, Drill, Review, and Fun

ADD-Arithmetic Developed Daily, Grades 1- 8
(GROW Publications)
$23.95 each
This is a math skills maintenance program that can be used

along with any other material or program. A teacher's manual includes reproducible student worksheets. One worksheet is to be used each day, and each worksheet is only one-third of a page and takes just a few minutes to do. Review work includes mental math, word problems, and exercises covering all areas of math appropriate for the grade level. This makes the perfect supplement to Modern Curriculum Press *Mathematics,* which needs more review work.(S)

Addition Facts in 5 Minutes a Day and Subtraction Facts in 5 Minutes a Day
by Susan C. Anthony
(Instructional Resources Co.)
$11.95 each

These are two in a four-book series for reviewing and drilling basic math computation skills. Books contain reproducible worksheets for timed tests along with explanations of procedures and reasons for using them, record keeping forms, and flash cards for practice. The *Subtraction* book also includes a few review sheets for addition. Use these for about five minutes a day along with your basic math curriculum. While these skill improvement strategies should appeal most to students who like competition and racing against time, they should be useable with almost all students who need such practice.

Addition, Subtraction, and Multiplication Songs Kits [audio tapes]
(Audio Memory) cassette - $9.95 each; CD - $12.95 each

Each kit includes a reproducible book and an audio cassette or CD teaching the math facts set to music. *Addition* covers the facts through 9 + 9. *Multiplication* covers the times tables from the 2s through the 12s. *Subtraction* covers facts up through 20 - 12. Time for student response is allowed when each song repeats. Books feature the math facts covered on each tape. At this level, students will most likely be working on addition and/or subtraction facts. Use resources like these with strong auditory learners who have trouble mastering the math tables or those who need a variety of approaches.

Addition Teaching and Learning Made Easy
by Glenda Brown James
(Multiplication Teaching & Learning Made Easy)
$16

Narrowly focused on teaching basic addition facts, this workbook presents strategies for both teaching and practicing. The book includes a set of flash cards along with a variety of reproducible worksheets (puzzles, coloring pages, and games) for working with math facts. Timed tests are included at the end of the book. A book like this works well alongside a program such as *Making Math Meaningful* that needs a little extra work on math facts.(S)

The AIMS Program

The *AIMS Program* is a series of outstanding activity-oriented workbooks combining science with math activities in fun projects. Younger and older levels are offered on many different topics. These are great! See complete description under "Science. "(S)

AL Abacus

(Activities for Learning)

Dr. Joan Cotter has developed a special abacus [$25] and written a book, *Activities for the Abacus* [$18], to show how to teach addition, subtraction, multiplication, division, and other concepts with the abacus. Dr. Cotter is the most widely recognized "abacus specialist" in the country. With the ideas in her book, the inexpensive abacus becomes an excellent, easy-to-use manipulative (and visual tool) that costs far less than some of the other options. Also available are two other books by Dr. Cotter: *Worksheets for the Abacus* [$25] and *Math Card Games* [$18] (which includes instructions for 300 math games), the cards needed for the games [$20], *Drawing Board Geometry Set* [$12], *Place Value Cards* [$5], and *Complete Program K-4* (all of the above items and more) [$120].(S)

Arithmetic Practice Books, Addition or Subtraction

(Essential Learning Products, Co.)
$3.99 each

These half-size books are good for practice and review. Two titles for first and second grade levels are *Addition* and *Subtraction*. *Multiplication, Division, Fractions, Word Problems,* and *Money* are appropriate for third and fourth grade levels. Add *Decimals* and *Metric* books for fifth and sixth grade levels. Each book progresses from easy to more difficult concepts. Print is large with lots of space between problems for those who need to write big. This is much less intimidating than regular workbooks for children who struggle with math. These are not intended to be the primary books for students but serve as supplements.

Essential Learning Products has another series called *Math Practice Books*. One book from that series—*Counting, Measuring, Telling Time,* and *Basic Facts*—works well at kindergarten and first grade levels as a supplement for the topics listed in the title, plus money, fractions, shapes, patterns, and calendars.

Baseball Math

(Good Year Books)
$9.95

Design a better baseball stadium! Calculate how far your favorite team travels. This real-life math and problem solving book for baseball fanatics has a variety of different problems and projects that will help your player sharpen his thinking skills while learning more about his favorite game.(S) [VT]

CalcuLadder®

(The Providence Project)
workbooks - $17.95 each ; MasterPaks - $27.95 each

Available as either consumable workbook or reproducible MasterPaks, these pages of timed drill will help students develop speed and accuracy with math facts. Students repeat a given drill page (12 copies of each provided within each workbook) until they can complete it accurately within a set time. Consumable books come in six levels: 1 covers basic addition and subtraction; 2 covers advanced addition and subtraction plus beginning multiplication; 3 covers intermediate and advanced multiplication and beginning division; 4 covers intermediate and advanced division, beginning fractions, and decimals; 5 covers intermediate and advanced fractions; and 6 covers percents, measurement systems, and geometric concepts, while reviewing fractions. Each book comes with an achievement record, answer keys, and teacher's guide. While we have permission to copy pages as needed, the colored pages sometimes do not reproduce clearly. If we wish to copy pages as needed from black-and-white originals (especially useful for those with more than one child), we should purchase the reproducible MasterPaks. MasterPak 1 covers books 1-3 (plus material from the *ReadyWriter*® penmanship program) and MasterPak 2 covers the last three (plus drill pages from the *AlphaBetter*®). (See reviews of these other two programs under "Language Arts.") MasterPaks consist of copy masters, guides, achievement record, and keys, plus three transparent overlays so we can reuse individual copies.

Centimeter-Gram Cubes

Centimeter-Gram Cubes are seen under a number of names. I think they are manufactured out of the country. Single cubes are one cubic centimeter and also weigh one gram.

Cubes can be snapped together on all sides to build rods, squares, cubes, and other constructions to do the same activities as those done with the rods and blocks. These cubes can be used for science experiments to demonstrate the density of water. (Add salt to make the cubes bob to the surface, add alcohol to make them sink.) Volume can also be demonstrated easily. Cubes can be used as very inexpensive weights to use with a balance. The only disadvantage is that with large constructions it takes too long to snap together all of the cubes. Cubes are listed as *Interlocking Gram Cubes* [$23.95 per thousand] in Nasco's Math catalog and as *Centimeter Cubes* [$32 per thousand] in the Cuisenaire, Dale Seymour Catalog. Guides for using the cubes are sold in both catalogs.(S)

Coins Make Change Bingo

(QNQ, Inc.)
$19.95

Children in first through third grades can practice addition, subtraction, coin identification, and counting with this versatile game. Ten bingo cards feature pictures of coins. Calling cards offer a number of options to challenge learners of varying skill levels. We can simply call the amount and students match it with coins on the bingo card. The reverse side of the calling cards features pictures of the coins, so, with even younger children, we might have them just match the pictures. For a greater challenge, each calling card lists four addition and four subtraction problems with the answer to all problems equivalent to the coins shown on the bingo cards. Additional games (like "war") can be played using only the calling cards. To play beyond simply matching pictures of coins, players need to be able to add together pennies, nickels, dimes, and quarters in amounts up to $0.85. All components are laminated for long life.

Cranium Crackers, Book 1 and Book 2

(Critical Thinking Books & Software)
$19.95 each

Book 1 in this series is suggested for grades 3-4 and Book 2 for grades 5-6, but both can be used by students above and below level because they are not age-graded. Critical thinking is truly the most important goal of these books with mathematics being the vehicle. The purpose is to stretch children beyond rote levels of learning into a wide range of ways of thinking about and applying math skills. There are problems dealing with logic and numbers and even some that deal with organizational and analytical skills that do not include any numbers. "Book 1 requires only the most basic knowledge of fractions and includes no complicated addition or subtraction, no long multiplication or division, and no decimals, percents, or areas." "Book 2 works with integer addition and subtraction, simple long multiplication and division, addition and subtraction of simple mixed numbers, and multiplication and division of simple fractions. Aside from an occasional elementary money problem, no decimals, complicated fractions, three-digit divisors, percents, or areas are included." There is a great deal of variety from lesson to lesson, so much so that few lessons bear resemblance to each other. The student pages are reproducible, and the teacher's manual is part of each book.(S)

Creating Line Designs

(Golden Educational Center)
$6.95

This is a series of four books for working on basic math skills, visual perception, and eye-hand coordination with line designs. The two latter skills improve overall learning ability. Book 2, for grades 1-5, has children connecting letters and numbers to create their designs. Book 3, for grades 3-6, progresses in difficulty and primarily develops perception, coordination, and sequencing skills. Book 4, for grades 4-7, is still more difficult, but works mostly on perception and coordination skills. This is a fun supplement.

Cuisenaire® Rods and/or Base Ten Blocks

(Cuisenaire/Dale Seymour Publications, Creative Publications, Timberdoodle, Builder Books, Shekinah Curriculum Cellar)
starter sets of *Cuisenaire® Rods* are $34.50 for plastic and $37.50 for wood; starter set for *Base Ten Blocks* - $27

Either *Cuisenaire® Rods* or *Base Ten Blocks* can be used for presenting concepts from addition through algebra. Rods are based on a metric scale with one white rod being one cubic centimeter. Rods of different colors are 2 through 10 centimeters long. *Base Ten Blocks* have pieces one centimeter long, 10 centimeters, squares of 100 square centimeters, and cubes of 1000 cubic centimeters, all the same color. Books for working with various materials are available from the sources mentioned in addition to other teacher supply stores. *Mathematics Made Meaningful* by John Kunz [$29.95 for set with plastic rods or $32.95 for set with wooden rods] is a good introductory kit for *Cuisenaire Rods* which includes rods, a basic teacher's manual, and 50 topic cards covering addition, subtraction, multiplication, and division. *The Cuisenaire Alphabet Book* (Cuisenaire, Dale Seymour Publications) [$9.50] is a useful tool for familiarizing children in the early elementary grades with the rods. *Multiplication and Division with Rod Patterns and Graph Paper* [$9.50] is an excellent reproducible workbook for teaching those concepts with rods. The *Super Source* series for *Cuisenaire Rods* [$15.95 each] (Addison-Wesley) is also excellent. There are three books in this series, for K-2, 3-4, and 5-6, although these grade delineations seem very arbitrary. Activities in these books frequently would be appropriate for other grade levels. Unlike most of the other books, these present a range of activities to enhance mathematical thinking and conceptual understanding in general rather than focus upon particular skills such as addition and subtraction. Some activities do focus on such skills, but they do not follow any logical sequence in doing so. Charts at the front of each book show which mathematical concepts/skills are covered within each activity, so you might use this to determine which activities to use when. They can be used in any order you choose. Most activities are interactive, requiring a partner. (Mom will do.) Numerous blackline masters at the back of each book are used to construct game parts, serve as the foundation of activities, or function as worksheets or cut-

and-paste projects to use with activities. Many activities are drawn from the same ideas found in the more specialized, topical Cuisenaire activity books, so you will discover many ways the Rods can be used through these activities which might help you decide which other books you might want to purchase. There are also *Super Source* books for other manipulatives such as *Pattern Blocks, Snap Cubes,* and *Geoboards*, but I suspect that this series and the *Cuisenaire Rods* will be the most useful for homeschoolers.(S)

Graph paper marked in centimeters is difficult to find but is a valuable tool for use with *Cuisenaire Rods*, other manipulatives based on cubic centimeters, or simply to be used for keeping numbers properly aligned in problem solving. If you can't find any, you can create it quite easily on a computer.

Designs in Math
(Golden Educational Center)
$6.95

Geometric designs provide a format for reviewing math facts and equivalencies. Books on addition, subtraction, and multiplication from this series are useful for grade 3, while the books on multiplication, division, and fractions are useful for grades 4-8. Student sheets are reproducible, and an answer key is included.

Early Math Literacy Packet
by Eunice S. Coleman
(Literacy Press, Inc.)
packet - $41.25; board - $33.50

A "One Hundred Board" is the heart of this method for supplementing your program. We can either make the board ourselves with instructions provided or purchase a beautiful, ready-made board from Literacy Press. The packet includes the book, *Early Math Literacy*, 30-blackline ditto masters for seatwork to reinforce learning, 3 math workbooks (from Continental Press) for the primary grades, 100-colored, number tags, and 100 brass cuphooks that go on the One Hundred Board to hold the number tags. The *Packet* can be used to teach addition, subtraction, multiplication, division, fractions, clocks, and money. Lessons are presented by the teacher with children doing hands-on work with the board. The books and ditto masters are used for reinforcement after the teaching.

Enright® Computation Series
(Curriculum Associates, Inc.)
$4.25-$4.45 each; answer keys - $3.50 each

The *Enright® Computation Series* includes eight separate books for review and practice on math concepts. Each book is narrowly targeted. There are four books on the basic functions performed only with whole numbers. The fifth and largest book covers conversion to fractions plus addition and subtraction of fractions. The sixth book covers multiplication and division of fractions. The seventh and eighth books cover addition/subtraction and multiplication/division of decimals. Boxes at the top of some pages review each process very briefly, assuming that this is not the first time a student has encountered the concept. Books primarily consist of drill on each math skill. These are not intended to be comprehensive tools, so they cover each skill, then move on to the next without review. Numerous tests are included throughout each book. Answer Guides feature reduced student pages with answers, and sometimes the solution process overprinted in blue ink. At this level, students might use any of the first four or five books. These might be especially useful for the student who has used or is using a program that is strong on concepts but weak on practice.(S)

Equation Golf
(Creative Teaching Associates)
$11.95

This mental math game uses two card decks—one from which you draw two digits which form a "target" answer, and the other from which cards are drawn one at a time to try to come up with combinations to arrive at the target number. You can use addition, subtraction, multiplication, division, cubes, squares, roots, or other operations as you choose. This is NOT spelled out clearly in the game. You should identify operations that a child has mastered, and allow all players to use *only* those operations. Then include more complex operations as children's abilities expand. The game is set up with four as "par" which means that, typically, you can arrive at the solution by drawing four cards. Using the simpler operations will often make it take longer, so you might change par to six for younger players. The goal remains to use as few cards as possible. This game is actually very flexible, and it should provide great mental math practice. Suggested for grades four and up.

Family Math
(Lawrence Hall of Science)
$19.95

Family Math is a 320-page book that includes creative ways to teach math effectively. It was designed for parents to work with their children at home—to teach, reinforce, and supplement math concepts already covered in a typical math curriculum. It was also designed to turn children (and parents) on to math, which it does very well. It is organized by various mathematical concepts and skills, then broken down into general age levels within each section. The emphasis is on hands-on learning and practical application. Lots of games are used, many of them to be photocopied from the book. Activities use common materials that are easily found around the house or purchased. It would be great for a support group to join together to work through *Family Math*, although it will work very well for individual families.(S)

Flashcards for Kids [website]

(website: www.edu4kids.com/math/)

This website offers free drill type activities on-line, most of which are customizable. Math for elementary grades gets the most attention. There are flashcards, games, math table drills, timed drills, and money drills. We can set the type of problems and number of problems to some extent in most of these. The time it takes for children to complete each activity is shown with their results when they finish each one.

Focus on Problem Solving, books B-G

(Continental Press)

$6.50 each; teacher's guide - $2.25 each

Word problems often pose serious difficulty for children. This series of workbooks helps children learn strategies for attacking such problems, then provides plenty of practice. In addition to traditional word problems, students learn to work with information from graphs, charts, maps, and other sources. These workbooks are suggested for grades 2 through 7, reflecting skills with which children should be familiar at each level. The teacher's guide is your answer key.(S)

Fraction Mania

(Math Concepts, Inc.)

$24.95

Fraction Mania is a very professionally-designed game that offers four game variations to suit different skill levels. Brightly-colored planets are made up of fractional "pie" shapes, with the identifying fraction appearing on only one side. In three of the games, children try to complete their planets by rolling a fraction die and collecting the various pieces they need. *Beginner's Mania* helps children become familiar with fractions. *Fraction Mania*, the second game in difficulty, requires children to "trade up," working on fraction equivalencies. Game cards are also used which add a random element to play. Double Mania becomes even more challenging with another set of game cards and the addition of a whole number die. Children multiply the whole number and fraction dice to determine the total of the fraction pieces they collect. This requires significant work with conversions. The last game, played with the Spacelog tablet and fraction die requires children to do much of the same type fraction converting, but without the fraction pieces. I suspect that creative families will come up with their own additional variations on how to play with *Fraction Mania*.

If you are careful not to lose them, you can also use the fraction pieces as manipulatives as you cover lessons from your math program.

The Good Steward game

(Creative Teaching Associates)

$16.95

Children ages 6 and up can practice math skills while applying Biblical principles of stewardship. They earn money by doing chores and recycling cans, then spend money in the form of tithes, savings, and purchases. Sometimes they win an extra turn for a good deed. Some spaces tell the player to "share a Scripture." The math is fairly simple, appropriate for early elementary grade levels.

Grocery Cart Math

(Common Sense Press)

$8

Many home schooling parents use grocery shopping trips for practical math lessons. This book saves time and energy by mapping out "grocery store lessons" for us with reproducible work sheets. We need to take a few minutes to look over lessons before we go to the store and talk about any new ideas that might need to be covered. However, most lessons simply apply much of what has been introduced already in math texts. For example, one lesson asks students to list fruits and vegetables in the produce section that are sold by the pound. They also record the price per pound. When they get home, they figure out which costs the least per pound and write them in order from least to most expensive. Another lesson has students reading hot dog labels for grams of fat per serving then graphing their answers. Yet another lesson has them record prices for hamburger fixings then compare to restaurant prices. There are 32 lessons altogether with a range of difficulty from approximately third grade level up through fifth or sixth grade. I don't recommend dawdling at the grocery store if you have toddlers or babies in tow, but as long as you only bring along older children, this is a great way to transform grocery shopping trips into practical learning experiences.

Hive Alive

(Aristoplay)

$12

Hive Alive is a math strategy game. It is recommended for ages 7 and up, but I think ages 9 and up might be more appropriate for the level of strategical thinking needed to play this game well. However, if you have seven-year-old chess players, they should be able to play. The game is like a simplified chess game in that two players vie to remove each other's game pieces. Game pieces are plastic stands into which are inserted numbers. As in the card game *War*, the highest number "takes" the lower number—in this case, the game piece. Levels of play are determined by choosing the number cards to be used as inserts for the playing pieces. There are whole numbers, fractions, mixed numbers, decimals, and a few negative numbers. Strategy is important because each player also has a queen bee and a killer bee. If the queen is "captured," a player loses the game. Killer bees are like wild cards, but once you've identified your opponent's killer bee, you can take him out with your own killer bee—a sacrifice move. Placement of playing pieces and movement will probably be more challenging than comparing numerical values. However, for students in fourth and fifth grades, this is a good way to become more familiar with values and conversions of the different types of numbers.

Holey Cards

(available from Greenleaf Press)

$1 each

Holey Cards are very inexpensive, timed-drill tools for working on basic math facts in addition, subtraction, multiplication, and division. The cards (one for each math function) have math facts arranged in rows with holes where answers should be. The cards fold in half. We insert a piece of paper in the middle and students write answers in the holes, completing as many problems as they can within the time limit. Because problems are arranged in random order, and there are 100 problems on each card, students cannot easily memorize the placement of answers.

Key to Decimals

(Key Curriculum Press)

$12.25 for a set

Like the *Fractions* course listed below, this is not a complete math course but a fairly complete course on decimals for children about nine and older. The *Key to...* books generally have lots of white space and less paper and pencil work required per page than other workbooks. They emphasize concepts with pictures and easy-to-understand explanations rather than drill work. The *Decimals* series consists of four student workbooks and a teacher's guide/answer key. An optional *Reproducible Tests* book is also available for $13.50. The folks at Timberdoodle (who sell the *Key to...* books) note that the fourth book requires the use of a <u>scientific</u> calculator (one that shows square roots, pi, etc.) for two pages and also that a calculator will be beneficial in numerous other instances.(S)

Key to Fractions

(Key Curriculum Press)

$12.25 for a set

This is not a complete math course, but it is a fairly complete course on fractions for children about nine and older. The *Fractions* series consists of four student workbooks and a teacher's guide/answer key. (See *Key to*

Decimals description above.) An optional *Reproducible Tests* book is also available for $13.50.(S)

Key to Geometry

(Key Curriculum Press)

books 1-6 - $2.25 each; books 7-8 - $6.95 each; answer keys - $3.25 each

Geometry at fifth or sixth grade? Actually, this is only an introductory geometry course, so it can indeed be used with students below high school level. Some will be ready as early as fifth grade, while sixth to eighth graders are the most likely users. Children learn by using a compass and straight edge to create geometric constructions. They learn the principles (theorems) through discovery rather than by having it explained in words. Children learn concepts rather than computation skills. The format is very user-friendly with lots of white space for drawing and few words. There are eight student workbooks with a total of more than 600 pages; the first six are fairly thin, and the last two are hefty. Four teacher's guides/answer keys cover the eight workbooks. Students can work independently with minimal teacher input when they have problems.(S)

Key to Measurement series

(Key Curriculum Press)

workbooks plus answers and notes for all four books - $12.25

The newest in the *Key to...* series is *Measurement*. It features hands-on activities, games, application situations, word problems—a wonderful variety of learning activities. This four-workbook set should be appropriate for children in second grade and above. Book 1 covers English units of measurement; Book 2 covers measuring length and perimeter; Book 3 covers finding area and volume; and Book 4 covers weight, capacity, temperature, and time. Second graders should be able to do Book 1 with help from a parent. The other books will stretch up into higher grade levels. A single teacher's guide with answers covers all four books.

Key to Percents

(Key Curriculum Press)

$10 for the set

Children should have covered fractions and decimals before tackling percentage. Since the books are ungraded, they can be used with any student who has covered the prerequisite topics. This series of three workbooks uses word problems, illustrations, and easy-to-understand explanations to help children understand this very practical topic. Like the other *Key to....* books, the format is user friendly with plenty of white space and few problems per page. A single teacher's guide/answer key covers all three workbooks. An optional *Reproducible Tests* book is also available for $13.50.(S)

Learning Wrap-Ups
(Learning Wrap-Ups Inc.)
about $8 per individual set;
about $45 for the Math
Intro Kit

Learning Wrap-Ups help to increase speed in fact recognition. Each *Wrap-Up* has twelve items on its left side and twelve on its right that need to be matched properly. For example, the *Wrap-Up* for multiplication by the number 4 has the numbers 1 through 12 in mixed order on the left, with products of 4 times those numbers on the right (in mixed order). Grooves next to each number allow the user to guide the attached string from a groove on the left across to the groove next to the corresponding answer on the right. The string continues around the back and forward through the next groove on the left. When all grooves have been used, the user looks at the back of the *Wrap-Up*. Raised lines show where the string will lie if all grooves have been connected properly. If any lines are showing, there is an error. These are fun to work with, easy to handle (great to take along on trips), and effective learning tools. They are sold in sets of 10 *Wrap-Ups*, with sets available for addition, subtraction, multiplication, division, numbers, shapes and logic, and fractions (identification and equivalencies). There is also a *Math Intro Kit* which includes addition, subtraction, multiplication, division, and fractions, plus a 16-page guide and four accompanying audio-cassette tapes. These can also be purchased individually.

Those working on multiplication might also be interested in a companion book, *10 Days to Multiplication Mastery*[$9.95]. This 128-page book is loaded with ideas for using the multiplication *Wrap-Ups* as well as other simple manipulatives along with worksheets and interactive activities. A few of the activities are classroom-oriented, but most are appropriate for home educators.(S)

Little Spender
(Creative Teaching Associates)
$16.95

Introduce young children to pennies, nickels, dimes, quarters and dollars as they use play money in this board game. They learn to add, subtract, and make change.

Math Drillsters
(Good Apple)
$17.99

Math Drillsters is a reproducible activity book containing 224 pages of math drill activities primarily covering addition, subtraction, multiplication, and division, but also touching on measurement, time, money, temperature, fractions, and mathematical thinking. Most activities are paper-and-pencil tasks presented in a variety of formats, but there are also a number of mental math "chain games." For the chain games, we reproduce the parts to the chain on paper, cut them out as cards, and divide them between the players. One card might read "I have 15. Who has its double?" The player who has the "30" card answers, "I have 30. Who has 1/5 of it?" Chain games, as with all activity pages, are featured for various concepts and levels. *Math Drillsters* makes a good supplement for sharpening math skills for all elementary grades.

Math Generator, version 2.8.3 [computer program]
(Teacher Created Materials)
$19.95

This CD-ROM program will run on either Windows or Macintosh systems. It is a tool for teachers rather than a student program. Teachers can generate math practice sheets or tests for computation skills for grade levels 1 - 6. Select from addition, subtraction, multiplication, division, or "other," then fine tune the selection of problems, requesting the number of digits in divisors and dividends, etc. The "other" category includes number value comparison, improper and mixed fraction conversions, ratios, proportions, equations, and mixed problems. The mixed problems will only mix addition, subtraction, and multiplication. (TCM plans expansions to this program to include even more concepts.) Once you've created a worksheet with the problems you need, print it out. You can also print out the answer key to each page. This is an extremely handy tool for homeschoolers.(S)

Mathematical Reasoning through Verbal Analysis, Book 1 or Book 2
(Critical Thinking Books & Software)
$22.95 each; teacher's manual - $12.95 each; bundle of both books with teacher manuals - $64.95

Book 1 is targeted for students in grades 2-4 and Book 2 for grades 4-8. However, both can be used by older and younger students since they are not age-graded. (Students working below grade level would probably do better in Critical Thinking Books' *Cranium Crackers* series.) The verbal analysis, an essential aspect of the books, occurs through discussion, so it is essential that the parent/teacher plan time to interact with students for these lessons. A group class would be even better. Lessons are challenging, combining visual/spatial skills, logic, math, and verbal skills. An underlying goal is preparation for the thinking skills necessary for abstract high school-level math. There are six categories of lessons in each book: number and numeration, geometry, operations, measurement, relations, and tables and graphs. Although actual mathematical knowledge reflects what is typically taught in grades 2-4 and 4-8 respectively, the lessons are challenging and best address the needs of average to above average students. Both the reproducible student workbook and the teacher's manual are necessary. The teacher's manual is essential for the discussions as well as for an answer key.(S)

Mathematicians are People, Too, volumes one and two

by Luetta Reimer and Wilbert Reimer
(Cuisenaire, Dale Seymour Publications)
$12.95 each

Biographical anecdotes and folklore combine in these stories about mathematicians. Each story uses an incident, discovery, or other such hook to provide the human dimension to some mathematical idea. For example, we read about Pythagoras paying his first student so that he might have the opportunity to teach, then becoming a popular teacher who had some intriguing ideas about numbers and their relationship to the universe. Among mathematicians introduced in volume one are Thales, Archimedes, Galileo, Newton, Euler, and Evariste Galois. Math concepts that show up in this volume are geometry, number systems and number theory, algebra, computation and estimation, probability and statistics, measurement, and mathematical symbols. Volume two introduces Euclid, Descartes, Benjamin Banneker, Albert Einstein, and others touching on geometry, algebra, number systems and theory, probability, calculators and computers, and calculus. Women in mathematics are featured in both books. Some stories will be appropriate for the elementary grades, while others are better saved for junior and senior high when the concepts are more familiar. Each book is 144 pages long, so there are quite a few stories from which to choose. These books help students relate to math, building a bridge from the world of abstractions to the world of real people.(S)

Math-It

(Weimar Institute)
$49.95

Math-It is primarily for mastering addition, subtraction, and multiplication computation skills. It consists of packets of game boards and fact cards plus instructions. This is not a complete math curriculum! Techniques used to master facts are often unusual (compared to traditional math instruction) but very effective. *Math-It* works well for some children but not for others. It is ideal for the child who has difficulty developing speed with math facts. If you can borrow one to try before purchasing, do so. If you use *Math-It*, cover other aspects of a math program in some manner, perhaps using a math text for other concepts. If using *Math-It*, also practice math concepts with games or practical life applications. *Math-It* by itself gets boring quickly. Children are ready for *Math-It* when they can pass this test: Close your eyes tightly, count backwards from 20 down to 0, and tie your shoes at the same time. Most children are seven or eight years old before they can do this. *Math-It* comes with the very useful *Math-It Guide Book*. The *Guide Book* covers all three levels (Pre through Advanced) and features extra teaching helps. It is also available separately for $13.95.

Pre Math-It [$41.95] uses dominoes to teach number facts at early levels. It also includes instructions for many of the identical learning methods used in the regular *Math-It* set. This set is useful with most children.

Advanced Math-It [$24.95] carries on with division, fractions, decimals, percents, and some algebra and geometry using the same techniques used in *Math-It*.

Maximum Math

by Kathryn Stout
(Design-A-Study)
$24

This is one of the most comprehensive tools for determining what to teach and how to teach. It lists objectives and teaching strategies by grade level (K-8). Kathryn particularly recommends the use of hands-on methods for young children, so many such activities are described. Objectives reflect national math standards, including probability, graphing, and the use of calculators in the early grades.

Mental Math series

(Math Concepts)
$19.95 each

In the *Mental Math* series, there is one book per level for each of grades one through five. These books are designed to help students improve mental math skills as well as their grasp of math terminology, especially as used on standardized tests. Five to ten questions per day are presented orally to students who record their answers. There are from 90 to 172 sets of questions in books for the various levels. Reproducible answer sheets and score-graphing page are included. (A few other classroom motivators are included, but these are unlikely to be of use to homeschoolers.) The beginning of each book reviews material from the previous grade level, then moves on to review concepts being learned that year. The exception is first grade level, since almost all concepts are new. It is recommended that *Mental Math* be used only the second semester of the school year for first grade, but throughout the year in succeeding grades. Each *Mental Math* lesson should take less than ten minutes to complete.

Moneywise Kids
(Aristoplay)
$15

Children can apply math their math skills by using play money to handle a typical family budget including such items as food, housing, taxes, and medical care. The game was not designed for Christian audiences, so it doesn't include tithing or charitable giving. Children exchange small bills for larger, make change, and learn to count by multiples of 5, 10, 20, and 50. On the back of one of the playing boards are ideas for parents to discuss budget items with children in more detail. Although the game is suggested for ages 7 and up, I expect that many younger children will also be able to play. Only two can play at a time.(S)

Muggins and other games
(Old Fashioned Products)

Old Fashioned Products offers great games for teaching mathematical thinking as well as improving computation skills. Games are offered in two formats: wooden boards with marbles, dice, and directions [$26.95 each] or enamel wipe-off boards with dice and directions [$9.95 each]. For the wipe-off board versions, the customer supplies either crayons or wipe-off markers to color spaces rather than moving marbles. *Muggins* is the most popular game. Rolling three 6-face dice, players must add, subtract, multiply, and/or divide numbers to produce a total. They have to perform a great deal of mental math while strategizing to score bonus points. *Muggins* is suggested for ages 10 and up, but other games such as *Jelly Beans*, and *Knock-Out* better suit younger children. *Jelly Beans*, geared for ages 4 to 6, works on number recognition, simple addition and subtraction, and thinking skills. *Knock-Out*, for ages 6 to adult, combines addition and subtraction in a challenging strategy game. The wooden boards are also available as two-sided combination game boards [$39.95 each], featuring any combination of the above three games. Old Fashioned Crafts' brochure lists a number of other games that might also be of interest. Their newest game, *Number Neighbors*, covers a number of skills for ages 3 to 9.

Multiplication, Addition, Subtraction, Division [audio tapes and workbooks]
(Twin Sisters Productions)
four audio cassettes and workbooks, sold individually - $9.98 for cassettes and 24-page activity book

Each cassette helps children master their math facts by setting them to rap music. The rapping is light, cheery, and clearly enunciated rather than the driving, pounding style we usually associate with rap. The math facts are presented in order with transition rhymes between each table. Multiplication facts are sung through the twelves, addition through sums of eighteen, and subtraction to eighteen. Division teaches the concept of division on one side, then drills the facts on side 2. The 24-page activity books contain puzzles, brain teasers, and other activities, plus lyrics to all songs.(S)

Multiplication Facts in 5 Minutes a Day and Division Facts in 5 Minutes a Day
by Susan C. Anthony
(Instructional Resources Co.)
Multiplication - $13.95 each; Division - $11.95

These two volumes, along with two others for addition and subtraction comprise a set of books for reviewing and drilling basic math computation skills. Books contain reproducible worksheets for timed tests along with explanations of procedures and reasons for using them, record keeping forms, and flash cards for practice. The *Multiplication* book includes a few review masters for addition and subtraction, a section of extra-challenging tests for advanced students (which also include division facts), and three games. The *Division* volume is a little shorter, but it, too, has review sheets for addition, subtraction, and multiplication. Use these for about five minutes a day along with your basic math curriculum. While these skill improvement strategies should appeal most to students who like competition and racing against time, they should be useable with almost all students who need such practice.

Multiplication Teaching and Learning Made Easy
by Glenda Brown James
(Multiplication Teaching & Learning Made Easy)
$16

Like the *Addition* book from the same author, this one is narrowly focused on teaching and practicing multiplication facts. The book includes a set of flash cards along with a variety of reproducible worksheets (puzzles, coloring pages, and games) for working with basic multiplication facts up through the 11 times table. Timed tests are included at the end of the book. A book like this works well alongside any program when a child needs extra work to master the facts.(S)

Musical Math
(Hear An' Tell Adventures)
$18

Work on multiplication facts and skip counting with this professionally-recorded, musical audio cassette. It uses a story context, different for each times table, to make learning times tables easy and fun. The kit includes blackline masters for students, plus instructions.

Musical Math Facts Level 1 and Level 2

(International Learning Systems of North America, Inc.)
$36 each

An audio cassette features catchy songs covering the 100 addition and 100 subtraction math facts for Level 1 and multiplication and division facts up through the 12's for Level 2. The reason these versions of "musical math facts" are more expensive than others is that the packages also include a substantial teacher's manual, a student book, counting sticks, winks, wipe-off marker and eraser. All of the student book pages are laminated so that students can write on them with the wipe-off pen and reuse them. Multi-sensory learning is promoted through hands-on activities, visual aids (number line, hundreds chart), plus the obvious auditory experience the tape provides. Timed practices help develop computation speed. *Musical Math Facts* is by Sue Dickson, the teacher who developed *Sing, Spell, Read, and Write.*

One game

(Creative Teaching Associates)
$6.50

A simple fraction card deck comes with four game variations that will take children from identifying fraction equivalents through advanced computation with fractions. Thus, this game is recommended for grades 4 - 9. Game instructions are relatively easy to follow, and the games really should be fun for most children.

One Hundred Sheep, Skip Counting Songs from the Gospels

by Roger Nichols
(Common Sense Press)
$10

This skip counting audio tape and accompanying songbook differ from others in that the Biblical content of the songs overshadows the skip counting most of the time. The skip counting usually takes place in the choruses while verses offer solid Bible stories such as the story of the farmer sowing his seed, Jairus' daughter, Mary and Martha, and Zacchaeus. A variety of lively musical styles are used interspersed with a few slower-paced songs. This tape is appealing enough that you might buy it for the Bible songs alone. One possible drawback is that the Bible songs tend to crowd out the skip counting since they sidetrack a child's attention to the stories. Skip counting covers counting by numbers two through ten.

The Original Skip Count Kid or The Skip Count Kid's Bible Heroes

by James McGhee II
(Lifetime Books)
$10 each

Both these tapes come with little books describing hands-on activities for learning skip counting. I, personally, like *The Skip Count Kid's Bible Heroes* best of all the skip count tapes, both musically and mathematically. The music and singing are terrific—I could listen to it over and over. The phrasing of the skip counting is musical enough for children to easily pick up the patterns, and the Bible content actually says something worthwhile.

Primary Fonts I [computer program]

(Teacher Created Materials)
$19.95

Primary Fonts I allows you to add fonts to your computer (Windows or Macintosh system) that will help you create your own math lessons—from groups of objects to count and add, to pie slices and fractions. You will find all the symbols you need to make professional-looking pages as well as several fun fonts for your titles. Also included are dotted line manuscript or cursive letters your child can use for handwriting practice.(S)

The Quarter Mile Math Games [computer programs]

(Barnum Software)
$39 per program; $65 for grades 4-9 or grades K-7 bundles; $95 for K-9 bundle

Math drill in either drag racing or "wild" riderless, running horses format offers a new twist to the challenge of mastering math facts. Programs are available in a number of grade level combination packages. The K-9 cross section package has 16,000 problems drawn from those included in the more topic-specific programs. The grades K-3 program has 22,000 problems covering keyboarding, alphabet, whole numbers, and estimating. The grades 4-7 program has 29,000 problems covering whole numbers, fractions, decimals, percents, and estimation. The grades 5-9 package covers positive and negative number operations and equations with 21,000 problems. A larger grades 4-9 bundle has 50,000 problems, and the even larger K-9 bundle has more than 70,000 problems.

During each race, problems appear one at at time, presented randomly from a pool of problems for each topic. Correct answers increase the player's speed and cause a new problem to appear. Incorrect answers leave the problem on the screen for three tries; then the program gives the correct answer. After each race, the dragster or horse gets an elapsed time. Once the student has raced five times, the top 5 average elapsed times are posted; students then race against their own top five times from then on. More than one player can record scores so they can compete against each other.

Home schoolers can participate in Barnum Software's international *Quarter Mile* tournaments.

Programs come on hybrid CDs or 3.5" disks that will run on either IBM or Macintosh systems.(S)

Quick Thinks Math, Books A1 or B1

by Robert Femiano
(Critical Thinking Books & Software)
$10.95 each

Book A1 in this series is suggested for grades 2-5. Its purpose is to "...introduce and reinforce mathematical concepts in a quick, fun way." Thus, it stresses thinking skills more than computation. Students will need to be able to add and subtract. Multiplication and division are only introduced toward the end of the book as the problems progress in difficulty. Children are encouraged to use objects, draw pictures, and write about their strategies. Reflecting the NCTM standards, emphasis is on the process more than obtaining the correct answer. (It's up to parents whether or not to stress both.) Unlike typical word problems, these often require a number of steps such as deducing one answer before arriving at the final one. For example, "How long will it take a 7 year old to triple his/her age?" This reproducible workbook contains 120 problems, with only 3 or 4 per page to allow plenty of space for children to work. Solutions are at the back of the book. Book B1, suggested for grades 5-8, requires students to have a working knowledge of multiplication and division, focusing on fractions, decimals, and percents. Some of the most difficult problems use a little algebra. The format is the same as A1.(S)

Saxon Activity Guide for Middle Grades Series

(Saxon Publishers)
$25

Students using Saxon's *Math 54, 65,* and possibly even *76,* might benefit from the presentations in this book. The primary Saxon texts give less attention than some other programs to "peripheral" math concepts, focusing on basic computation skills. Since the new math standards emphasize more of the peripheral topics at younger levels, Saxon offers this book to help expand coverage, while also offering more interactive and hands-on learning opportunities. This does not teach basic math concepts with manipulatives, but focusing on topics like calendar reading, thermometers, bar graphs, weather reporting, working with money, maps, compasses, estimation, measurement, symmetry, and computing area. Lessons are written for classroom presentation, and some activities will not work with a single child. Reproducible work sheets and play money are at the back of the book. Those familiar with the K-3 Saxon program will note the similarity in these activities to those used in "The Meeting" time in those courses.

Scratch Your Brain Where It Itches

(Critical Thinking Books & Software)
$9.95

There are five books thus far in this series; Book A-1 is targeted at students in grades 1-3, and Book B-1 for grades 3-6. The books are subtitled "Math Games, Tricks, and Quick Activities," which accurately summarizes the content of these math supplements. Book A-1 covers place value, addition, subtraction, multiplication, and shapes. Unlike the next two books in the series, many of the activities require either a partner or a group, limiting its usefulness for home educating families. Book B-1 covers place value, operations, shapes, measurement, money, time, the calendar, and using calculators. These are primarily "brain teasers" done with paper and pencil, mental math, calculators, and manipulatives. Books are reproducible, and answer keys are at the end of each book.

SOLUTIONS: Applying Problem-Solving Skills in Math

(Curriculum Associates, Inc.)
$6.45 each; teacher guides - $3.95 each

The Solutions series is a great supplement to stretch children's mathematical thinking skills. These are particularly useful if you are using a traditional program that stresses mastery of math facts, but which might be short on thinking and application skills (e.g. A Beka) or a program that is limited in scope such as *Mastering Mathematics.* There are six books in the series (Levels 3-8) which I would judge appropriate for students in grades four through eight or for older students doing remedial work. Levels are not grade designations. (Level 3 includes fraction and decimal concepts that are more appropriate for fourth than third graders.)

All books follow the same lesson sequence, but increasing in difficulty at each level. Each starts with an assessment. In keeping with the emphasis on mathematical thinking, there are sections on interpreting and restating problems, tracking down data from outside sources such as encyclopedias to determine an answer, selecting problem-solving strategies, solving non-routine problems (sometimes you have to work backwards to get to the answer), using calculators, identifying extraneous data, using graphs/charts/maps, and estimating. All of this is packed into a workbook of about 30 pages.

This series better reflects the type of problems students encounter on standardized tests than do some math programs, so they might be especially useful for those preparing their children for testing. The teacher guides also have a reproducible page of open-ended problems that don't appear in the student book; these, too, are commonly seen on new tests. Teachers Guides include answers plus guidance for using each section.(S)

Solving Math Word Problems - Easily, Book 3

(Golden Educational Center)

$7.95

Children who struggle to figure out the proper strategy needed to solve math word problems will appreciate the layout of the problems in this book. Key words (e.g., altogether, both, less, how many more) are in bold type. There are few problems per page, and they are neatly arranged in boxes. An optional enrichment activity is included at the bottom of each page. The book is reproducible and an answer key is included in the back.(S)

Triangle Flash Cards

(Creative Teaching Associates)

$4.95 per set

These are much better than the standard style. Addition/subtraction cards show two addends and the sum on the three "corners" of each flash card. You cover either one of the addends or the sum for drill, effectively doing both addition and subtraction with good visual input for reinforcement. Multiplication and division cards work similarly.

Turbo Math Facts [computer program]

(Nordic Software)

$49.95

This program is a good tool for reinforcing math skills in young children. Although it is recommended for ages 5-12, it is most appropriate for children up to about ages 9 or 10. It covers addition, subtraction, multiplication, and division (covering basic addition and subtraction facts up through 15+9 and 15-9, multiplication and division up through 9 x 9 and its inverse). It includes progress reports so that parents can see exactly how each child is performing. Each progress report contains a record of each problem solved as well as the time it took to solve each time the student encountered the same problem. This will give parents a clear indicator of the student's progress. Students use the program by selecting which of the four problem types to solve. The student must then solve each problem with a timer running. Wrong answers are reviewed by the program before the student can continue. The goal is to answer as many problems correctly as possible to earn "money." With every correct answer, more money is earned. With enough money a student can visit the car lot and purchase a race car. The student then selects one of several race tracks, and they're off in a race that's strictly for fun, not math practice.

This program requires a CD-ROM, Microsoft Windows 95 or higher, 4MB RAM, a sound card, and SVGA display. The program will also run on MAC systems 7.0 or higher with a 13" monitor or larger.(S)

24 Game: Single Digits (Item #33976) or Double Digits (Item #39976)

(Suntex International, Inc.)

$19.95 each

This is one of those deceptively simple ideas that accomplishes much more than one might guess. There are 192, 4" x 4" cards in each set. Each has four single-digit numbers (or a combination of single- and double-digit numbers in *Double Digits*). The challenge is to combine those four numbers using addition, subtraction, multiplication, and division to make a total of 24. Since the cards are divided into three groups, from easy to difficult, children as young as nine (approximately) can play using the easy cards of the *Single Digit* game, while adults will find some of the difficult ones in either game very challenging. The beauty of such a game is the amount of mental math that takes place to find the correct solution. Games can be played in groups or solo. This game has proven so popular that there are *24 Challenge* tournaments across the country. Highly recommended. Those who need easier levels can work with the "Primer" editions: *Add/Subtract Primer* (#31976) and *Multiply/Divide Primer* (#32976). Advanced students should try the *Fractions Edition*.

24 Game: Fractions Fluency Edition (Item #34976)

(Suntex International, Inc.)

$19.95

See the review of the *Single* and *Double Digit* versions. Try both of these editions before moving up to *Fractions Fluency*. *Fractions Fluency Edition* is suggested for students ages 11 and up. "Primer level" cards within this set use easier fraction concepts. The more difficult cards can be extremely challenging, even for older students. As in all editions, there are three levels of difficulty, so start them slowly with the easiest level. The cards have from one to three fractions per card as well as single-digit numbers. Otherwise, play is just like the *Single-Digit* game. For advanced students, also try the *Algebra Readiness* Edition.

Unifix Cubes

(Didax)

Unifix Cubes are large, colorful plastic cubes that snap together. They are useful manipulatives for preschool through second or third grade. Hands-on demonstrations using these snap-together blocks can be extremely helpful in teaching concepts to your children, even if you are using a curriculum. The visual presentation and hands-on practice will help children to better understand what they are doing. Unifix books that you might be interested in are *Developing Number Concepts Using Unifix Cubes* (Didax or Nasco) , *Unifix Teacher's Manual* (Didax), and the *Unifix Teacher's Resource Book* (Didax or

Nasco). Didax also sells the *Unifix Mathematics Home Helper* [$29.95] designed especially for parents working with their own children. The kit includes 110 *Unifix Cubes*, a *Unifix Stair*, number indicators, number/number word cards, crayons, and parent's guide with activity sheets. Unifix materials and books are also available through Creative Publications, Builder Books, Shekinah Curriculum Cellar, and other teacher supply stores.(S)

Wonder Number Learning System

(Interactive Dimensions)
$29.95; workbooks - $12.95 each

Wonder Number Learning System is a board game and more. The board is basically a "100s chart," but it is color and symbol coded for teaching and game playing. The game alone can help children to learn counting, number relationships, odd and even numbers, multiples, place value, definition of prime and square numbers. (Most of this depends on input from a "teacher" to explain what they are dealing with.) Also available are series of reproducible workbooks for various levels. The workbooks use the game to teach an amazing number of mathematical concepts. The 100s chart has been around for years, and many teachers have done some very creative things with it. This game incorporates some of the best ideas into an excellent tool that can be used for kindergarten through eighth grade.

Chip Art [$23.95] is a supplement from the same people which contains 300 "poker chips" in the eleven colors of the *Wonder Number Learning System.* The chips can be used to help identify number patterns and functions on the game board or as a manipulative math tool with or without the board. (S)

Outstanding Math Resource Companies

There are a few companies that specialize in math resources, usually supplemental type materials with some basic curriculum. Those described here have an excellent selection of very helpful products of which you need to be aware. Send for their free catalogs and familiarize yourself with some of the thousands of options that will make teaching and learning easier.

Creative Publications

Although they carry many classroom kits, they still have a huge selection of math teaching aids practical for individual families. They have materials for all levels with most geared for the elementary grades. They carry many books on problem solving and thinking, along with many teaching how to use manipulatives, both for beginners and advanced users. A selection of calculators is offered with fairly lengthy descriptions of each. Most basic manipulatives such as *Unifix, Cuisenaire,* and *Base Ten* are offered along with fraction circles, *LinkerCubes*, pattern blocks, tangrams, counters, dice, and much more.(S)

Creative Teaching Associates

CTA is known for their huge line of math games. They have something for every concept, and they will send you a correlation showing which products help to teach which skills at each level. In addition they sell a few manipulative type items and books. Of particular interest is the outstanding *AIMS Program* math/science series which is reviewed elsewhere in this book.(S)

Delta Education Hands-On Math Catalog

Delta's catalog is very similar to Nasco's (described below) in the assortment and types of materials sold. However, Delta's catalog is smaller than Nasco's, making it a little easier to sort through so many good choices.(S)

Didax

The maker of *Unifix* has a large catalog of math manipulatives and games for preschool through the elementary grades. They have an extra large section of materials for the youngest levels.(S)

Nasco Math Catalog

Nasco is primarily a distributor for other publishers, but they have gathered a huge variety of materials from manipulatives and books to games and software. They carry so much that you have to do a bit of work to figure out things such as which of the six types of a particular item might be best for you.(S)

Cuisenaire/Dale Seymour Publications

The Cuisenaire, Dale Seymour Publications catalog features some of the best math-related books and materials. Their line is large but selective. They emphasize thinking skills, use of manipulative materials, and math applications (generally weak points in most curricula). Materials cover all aspects of math for all levels.(S)

Economics

Economics is often totally ignored at the elementary level, yet it is one of the most important subjects in terms of long-term usefulness. The following resources make it easy and practical to introduce our children to economics.

Whatever Happened to Penny Candy?

by Richard Maybury (Bluestocking Press)
$12.95; guide - $15.95

Children in fifth or sixth grades might be ready for this simple, entertaining introduction to economics. *Penny Candy* introduces the economic facts of life where they touch us most—continuing increases in the cost of things. The book is written as a series of letters from fictional Uncle Eric to his niece or nephew Chris. Uncle Eric explains the economic facts of life, adding interesting historical tidbits along the way. Doses of economic theory in each letter are just enough to prod thinking without overload. The author has also included an excellent annotated bibliography with suggestions for where to go next to learn more about economics. [Note: A new edition of this book is due out in 2000.]

A study guide, *A Bluestocking Guide to Economics*, is available to use along with the book, although it will also be useful along with any other sources for studying economics. It features vocabulary study, essay and discussion questions, activity suggestions, applications, final exam, reprints of a number of articles, and suggestions for further reading. It progresses in level of difficulty in each area, so that we can select activities suitable for children of different ages. This *Guide* really expands the usefulness of *Whatever Happened to Penny Candy?*

Canadians can order a twenty-page supplement to *Penny Candy* that explains the differences between American and Canadian monetary and economic history which will help Canadian students better understand and apply the principles taught.

Check out the other "Uncle Eric" books: *Whatever Happened to Justice?, Ancient Rome: How It Affects You Today,* and *Evaluating Books-What Would Thomas Jefferson Think About This?*, and others.(S)

Chapter 14

Science

Introduction to Science

Science can be an intimidating subject unless we have a proper perspective. Science, in terms of education, means the study of God's creation, its purposes, its functioning, and its beauty. We often tend to limit our definition of science to memorization of plant structure and other laborious details without seeing beyond to God's purposes for each aspect of creation. Obviously, we do not have a total understanding of all of God's purposes, but even with our limited understanding we can develop a sense of awe for God's creative genius.

It is more useful for young children to develop an appreciation for God's creation—our bodies, the earth, plants, animals, the weather, and so on—than it is for them to begin memorizing details. If the interest is first kindled, the details will be easier to learn later. The interest rarely develops when it has been stifled by too much emphasis on meaningless (to them) detail. Field trips, experiments, observations, and nature collections will all stimulate interest in children. They should be a major part of our science curriculum for all ages. Attention to detail becomes more important about the time the child is ready for more academic approaches to school, which is usually around eight to ten years of age.

Our goals in teaching science for elementary levels (kindergarten through sixth grades) should be:
1. to turn children on to science;
2. to expose children to many of the numerous aspects of science; and
3. to teach children the foundations of scientific method—orderly thinking and forming, testing, and evaluating hypotheses.

The best way to meet these goals is <u>not</u> by using science textbooks. We can turn our children on to science by teaching them to observe, experiment, read, and think about the things that surround us. Children are naturally curious about the different areas of science but not usually according to the textbook's scope and sequence. It is far better to respond to an area of interest by an immediate trip to the library or a field trip that gives them information that they are personally seeking.

Also, as children grow, they look beyond the surface and begin to ask, "Why did that happen?" Scientific method begins with that observation and question. We can develop it further by working with our child to form possible answers and ways of testing those possibilities. If we limit science to a textbook, we will be missing much. Although textbooks try to introduce a variety of topics each year at elementary levels, they have no way of predicting what will interest each child.

Even if we are willing to abandon the textbook approach, many of us feel insecure determining at what level our child should be working on a science topic. Does making a model of the body systems equally satisfy learning needs of both a seven-year-old and a twelve-year-old? Probably not. Kathryn Stout's **Science Scope** (Design-A-Study) [$15] helps us identify appropriate activities for different age groups within each science area. This is an extremely useful resource. Divided into four main areas—general science, life science, earth science, and physical science—it takes specific topics under each heading, then suggests methods for use with students at primary, intermediate, junior, and senior high levels. Use of *Science Scope* will make it easier to select appropriate resources for whatever topic is chosen for study.

Summarizing all of this into a recommendation, I suggest choosing three or four science topics per year, taking into account the general topics you feel should be covered as well as your children's interests. Then use information books, experiment/activity books (such as those listed under the general and topical headings in this chapter), and field trips to put together an interesting study for each topic.

Almost all of the home school distributors list a variety of science resources to help you pursue topical studies. The Elijah Company catalog makes selection even easier by grouping science resources under topics.

Those who prefer more direction, should check out the following resources.

Amanda Bennett has written a series of science **Unit Study**  **Adventures** guides for grades K-8 (Holly Hall) [$13.99 each]. The science-oriented guides in this series each develop a single topic. Present science-oriented titles are *Baseball, Electricity, Gardens, Home, Computers, Oceans, Olympics,* and *Dogs.* These guides do a lot of the organization and planning for you, while still leaving in your hands specific decisions about which resources and activities to use. See the complete review in Chapter Five under "Limited Unit Studies."

Kym Wright has already been doing exactly what I've described, and she has put together some of their topical studies in six books thus far which are available through **alwright! Publishing**. (Watch for more titles in the future.) Present titles are *Bird Unit Study, Microscope Adventure!, Goat Unit Study, Sheep Unit Study, Poultry Unit Study,* and *Botany Unit Study.* Most of these stretch easily for use with different age students. As you might guess from some of the titles, they also will work best for those who live in rural areas and can raise farm animals or easily observe different types of birds. These are very detailed studies that include experiments, projects, reading, writing, and numerous other activities. Kym provides lesson plans that you can use as is or adapt to suit your situation. You will need to find some of the resource books she recommends for each topic. Studies also feature related Scripture verses. U.S. dollar prices range from $13.95 to $17.95 per book.

Getting feedback from students is more challenging when you create your own studies. Applying scientific knowledge is the best sort of feedback, but some topics, like nuclear power and lightning don't lend themselves to home applications. Writing about science can be a good alternative. *Science Works* (Pencils Writing Resources) [$12.95] serves as a stimulus to get students writing within six topical areas: oceans, plants, animals, matter and energy, weather, and the solar system. Every one or two pages is a new writing assignment, all of them heavily illustrated for extra appeal. Some assignments simply tell the student what to write about. One such assignment begins, " Imagine you are a shark. Tell how you would feel swimming through the ocean. Describe what type of shark you are, which ocean you live in and how other sea creatures treat you." Other pages are reproducible, formatted pages for students to write on particular topics; an example would be a page decorated with water drops and weather symbols where students are to illustrate and write about the water cycle. At the front of the book is a handy page of tips for helping students master those vocabulary words so important to science lessons. Various assignments will suit students from early elementary grades up through high school. Some ideas can be easily adapted for older or younger students.(S)

If the idea of working without a textbook still makes you feel insecure, here are some guidelines for selection of textbooks.

Selecting Texts

The Christian perspective is vital in studying science. In science we constantly find ourselves wading through "untruth." Evolution is not the only problem. God's plan and purposes are a necessary part of most science studies, and secular materials are incomplete without it. If we are using secular "real" books,

we shouldn't be surprised if we encounter non-Christian philosophy. It is up to us to supply corrections or truth when necessary. This can be a very advantageous way to teach if we have a good Scriptural foundation. It is important to develop discernment to be able to separate truth from untruth.

While it is fairly easy to select and use only those portions of library or supplementary books that are accurate and truthful, it is more difficult to do this with secular textbooks when we intend to use the entire book. The textbooks are generally based entirely on an untruthful premise (which they are trying to influence our children to accept as truth), making the entire book difficult to work with. If we choose to purchase science texts, we should choose Christian books.

Most science textbooks for younger levels simply introduce areas of science with little demand for attention to detail. Often the concepts are presented so broadly there is no new information for the child, and he is bored. While details help make a topic more interesting, trying to present details to young children if they are not interested in the topic to begin with is probably a waste of time. Because of these factors, most science texts for first and second grades are a waste of money. If, in spite of these drawbacks you still wish to use texts, BJUP's and CSI's look more interesting than most.

While detail can make science more interesting, some Christian publishers have put excessive emphasis on *memorization* of detail, so use caution even in choosing texts on older levels.

I generally do not recommend any workbook approach to science where the primary activity is filling in blanks. Workbook activities can be appropriate as reinforcement for learning, but they should not be the main event.

Another problem occurs with workbook courses such as Alpha Omega LifePacs. Even when they include material to be presented by the teacher to expand on the student workbook, many parents skip those parts and use only the workbook. The result is often an inadequate and/or ineffective course.

BJUP, Rod and Staff, Christian Schools International (CSI), and A Beka science texts are good, although I often recommend that A Beka's test and review sheets be omitted. CSI's science program for grades K-2, presented from the teacher's manual without a student text, have a strong hands-on orientation.

Experiments and Investigations

Science experiments and investigations are important in all programs, but there are different methods of presenting them that we find in Christian science texts. One method presents the concept and explanation, then has children perform an experiment to see that what they read is true. Another method has children perform the experiment or investigation to observe what is happening, try to make an educated guess as to the cause, or make other predictions to test. In the second method, children need to be guided to know that there are true, consistent answers. In my opinion, the second method is preferable because children are rarely interested in doing an experiment when they already know what the result will be as they do in the first method. Rod and Staff and A Beka frequently use the first method while BJUP uses the second.

Even better than most textbooks when it comes to activities and experiments are some of the numerous books on science activities available at the library or bookstores. Not all science activity books are good. Some are difficult to follow. Some do not clearly indicate the purpose for the activity either before or after. If children do something interesting but no learning takes place, all you have is entertainment. So why bother?

While the library is an excellent source for activity books on all levels, you might use these guidelines to select those you will use:

- ☛ Look for clearly worded instructions and explanations.
- ☛ Look for a purpose for each activity.
- ☛ Books that allow children to hypothesize (suggest possible solutions) are better than those that present the answer before they begin.
- ☛ For older children, look for activities that will require recording of data for analysis.
- ☛ Look for questions that are thought provoking.
- ☛ Look for books that require simple, easily-available materials.
- ☛ If we want children to experiment on their own, look for an attractive format.

Two examples of what I consider good experiment books are *Science on a Shoestring* (Foresman-Addison Wesley) or any of the *Backyard Scientist* books.

None of these are grade specific, but they are especially good, thought-provoking books which present experiments and activities for children, allowing them to try to predict the answers.

Equipment and Supplies

General science materials and equipment are available by mail from Home Training Tools, Carolina Biological Supply, Delta Education Hands-On Science Catalog, Nasco, Nature's

Workshop, Tobin's Lab, and Wild Goose Company.

Home Training Tools, operated by a Christian, homeschooling family, puts out an exceptional catalog of science resources. The catalog is arranged topically, with very useful "Quick Tips" interspersed with product descriptions and illustrations. To make it even easier, their "Quick Selection Guide" lists topics and all possible resources in index fashion showing catalog page numbers and recom-

mended age group. Another feature of Home Training Tools is special order forms listing materials needed for A Beka, BJUP, Alpha Omega, Apologia, Castle Heights, and Christian Light science texts for each grade level. (Free for courses you are using, but \$.50 for others.) They have even prepackaged Materials Kits for the Alpha Omega LifePacs, Bob Jones texts, Apologia, and Castle Heights, although these don't include the most expensive items like microscopes and balances. These options will make it very easy for you to either pick and choose the resources you need from their lists or purchase the kit and then decide which of the other items you wish to invest in. The catalog includes just about anything you could want including curriculum, chemicals, lab equipment, activity books, science kits, resource and activity books, videos, dissection specimens, microscopes, telescopes, and creation science resources.

Carolina Biological Supply has a free *K-6 Science Catalog* as well as an almost two-inch-thick complete catalog that sells for \$17.95 postage paid. The free catalog should have plenty of resources for those teaching the elementary grades. If you purchase the complete catalog, you receive a coupon worth \$17.95 off your first order of \$25 or more.

Delta sells inexpensive chemistry lab supplies such as plastic graduated cylinders and beakers, as well as equipment and learning aids for nature studies, physics, geology, astronomy, environmental studies, and more.

Tobin's Lab puts out a great catalog especially for home schoolers. Structured to reflect the days of creation, the catalog includes everything for science except traditional textbooks. They do carry lots of topical science books (including some on creation science), videos, microscopes, equipment, kits, chemistry sets, posters, and dissection specimens. I think it would be exciting to use the *Good Science Workshop* video, which presents teaching strategies and experiments correlated with the days of creation, or *Considering God's Creation*, then select resources from this catalog to augment studies for each day since they both follow the same structure and make the job easier for us. Contact Tobin's Lab to get their free catalog.

A source for both usual and unusual science materials is American Science and Surplus. They usually have such things as lab materials and equipment, maps and charts, motors, and magnets plus odds and ends of school supplies at very low prices.

Try dabbling in different areas of science as suggested by the items in these companies' catalogs.

Science Kits

Good textbooks contain science experiments, but we might want to occasionally purchase science kits to help us out. Kits provide us with equipment and instruction, and are often designed to look more like "fun and games" than learning materials. A good kit can save us much time and energy, and the chances of our experiments being successful are much greater than when we do-it-ourselves from scratch. Kits range from miniature laboratory set-ups down to single topic kits. Following are a number of such kits.

Adventures in Science kits

(Educational Insights)
$9.95 each

The *Adventures in Science Kits*, packaged in colorful boxes, offer a real hands-on approach. Twelve kits are available: *Backyard Science, Dinosaurs and Fossils, Electricity, Kitchen Science, Color & Light, Magnetism, How Things Work, Sky Science, Spy Science, Eco Detective, Science Magic Tricks,* and *Human Body.* Each kit features 21 experiments and activities plus an assortment of supplies needed for the projects. Recommended for grade four and up.(SE)

Astronomy, Birds and Magnetism

(Stratton House)
$59.95

Do you want your children to have an activity based science course but you don't have time to look for experiments and gather materials? This hands-on science course in a box is actually a combination of three different "kits" on astronomy, birds, and magnetism. It has a total of 40 lessons along with the materials needed for the activities, such as binoculars, bird seed and magnets. (The Bird kit is pictured here.) Lessons are laid out with clear, illustrated instructions and reproducible worksheets. The Parent Guide has additional ideas and topics for discussion to make the most of your children's curiosity. The kit also includes a bird identification book and star charts.

Enough materials are included for one or two children. Some extra materials can be ordered through the catalog. Each of the subjects in this triple set is also available separately, as well as the titles *The Wonders of Light* and *Microscopic Explorations.* Prices range from $24.95 to $29.95. A second "triple" set, *Microscopic Explorations, Light and Insects,* will be released in the Spring of 2000. The price will also be $59.95. Great family learning for those with children in grades 1-6. Aside from one mention of the Bible in the Parent Guide, the materials seem to present no particular religious perspective.[V.T.]

Delta Education science kits

Delta sells kits, equipment, and books for hands-on science learning. Delta has some interesting but expensive kits for classrooms, but home educators will be more interested in the smaller kits and equipment. Also, teacher's guides for the larger kits are available separately so we can put together our own kits with materials from Delta and do the same experiments.

Examples of the types of kits: *Grow A Frog, Postertube Science: Electric Circuits, Gears at Work,* and *Acid Rain Kit.*

Nasco

Nasco sells mini versions of their large *Sciquest* kits. Each mini kit provides a variety of experiments related to a topic with enough materials in each kit for at least a small group of children. Kits are available on two levels: primary for grades K-4 and intermediate for grades 4-9. The eight primary kits are *Air; Water; Force, Mechanical Energy and Work; Heat; Sound; Light; Magnetism;* and *Earth and Space.* Fourteen kits for intermediate level include *Air, Water, Forces, Mechanical Energy and Work, Motion, Simple Machines, Heat, Sound, Light, Magnetism, Static Electricity, Electromagnetism, Current Electricity,* and *Earth and Space.* A teacher's guide with illustrated instructions and blackline masters for student work sheets come with each kit. Consumable parts of the kits can be replaced so kits can be used over and over again.(S)

Science with Air

by Helen Edom and Moira Butterfield
(Educational Development Corporation)
$15.95

This is part of the Usborne "Kid Kits" series and includes a paperback book of step-by-step experiments nicely packaged with an assortment of materials that can be used for the activities in the book (e.g., straws, "tornado tube," feathers, clothespins). Some experiments require additional readily available items, such as newspaper or empty bottles. Step-by-step, illustrated instructions should make it easy for kids to do experiments on their own. At the back of the book are two pages of notes for parents that will help answer questions that children might ask while carrying out the experiments. This kit is recommended for ages 6-9.

Other *Kid Kits* are available priced at $9.95 to $19.95, with titles such as *Science with Magnets, Things that Fly, The Young Naturalist,* and *Rocks & Fossils.* These might be used as part of topical unit studies or adjuncts to other science lessons, but they should also be great for those days when you need something quick and entertaining to make schooling more fun.(S)[V. Thorpe]

Wild Goose Company science kits

(Wild Goose Company)

Wild Goose has created "science kits with an attitude." Kits with titles such as *Slimey Chemistry, Crash & Burn Chemistry, Kitchen Table Chemistry,* and *Oooh Aaah Chemistry* teach science principles through experiments. You get a hint of their approach from the titles. Cartoon illustrations and irreverent humor abound. Some of it is of questionable taste—e.g., adding raisins to Mountain Dew and telling your friends that sewer maggots are cleaning the dirty water. I reviewed two kits, *Slimey Chemistry* and *Kitchen Table Chemistry*, and we preferred the *Slimey Chemistry* because of the great experiments—making pseudo silly putty and other gelatinous concoctions—and because the humor was more acceptable. Kits come with almost everything you need, but often there is only enough for a single student to do an experiment. The *Kitchen Table* kit tells us to wear goggles, although goggles are not included in the kit. However, Wild Goose sells high-quality, inexpensive goggles that I would recommend to you for any even semi-dangerous experiments. Chemicals in *Kitchen Table Chemistry* were primarily common household items such as baking soda, while *Slimey Chemistry* had more unusual chemicals. These experiments are quick and easy, no measuring required. Kits are $29.99 each. I recommend starting with *Slimey Chemistry*.

If you like the Wild Goose approach, you might be interested in attending or hosting a **Young Scientists and Mathematicians Institute** with those who created the Wild Goose kits. This is a hands-on workshop for kids where they dissect eyeballs; build and launch "rockets;" experiment with rocks, minerals, and fossils; and much more. Contact the Young Scientists' Institute for dates and locations or hosting information.

Covering Science within a Multi-Subject Unit Study Approach

If you are using a unit study approach, you will usually find sufficient material on science included, although the unit studies themselves will generally direct you to other resources for more information about topics being studied. At older levels, make sure students are beginning to learn the basics of scientific method—posing questions, planning and conducting experiments, recording information, analyzing and evaluating results, and reaching conclusions.

Science Fairs

Science fairs can be great fun for home school groups. They can (and should) be totally non-competitive if this is the first time for most participants. Each child can participate at his level. Young children can make and display collections. Experiments or demonstrations can be progressively more challenging as children get older. Every child should get some form of recognition for participation such as a certificate or participation ribbon.

For older or more experienced children, more rigid and challenging guidelines can be set up. The following resources outline typical guidelines for science fairs we can use or adapt as needed. Older children should be encouraged to make an oral presentation to accompany their project. Those who are able can prepare written research reports documenting their presentation.

We should take care that our children are not overwhelmed with difficult and unfamiliar requirements for their first science fair or else they might never again participate.

Beyond the Science Fair
by Ruth M. Young, M.S.Ed.
(Teacher Created Materials)
$11.95

Some educators feel that typical science fair research projects are not as beneficial for younger students as for those in the upper grades. This book gives complete instructions for schools that want to set up alternative events that promote scientific thinking, including ideas that may be of interest to your home school group. Three different events are suggested: Science Discovery Day, which suggests a variety of hands-on activities; Inventor's Convention, which has teams of students working on inventions; and Family Science, which includes a homemade musical instrument recital and science magic show. Fun for grade K-6.(S) [V.Thorpe]

The Complete Science Fair Handbook
by Anthony D. Fredericks and Isaac Asimov
(Good Year Book)
$9.95

Everything we need to put on a science fair is included here. Instructions are given for teachers, parents, and students. There are tips on how to make your science fair a success, timetables for planning, suggestions for projects by grade levels, chapters on conducting research and the scientific method, ideas for presenting and displaying projects, criteria and forms for judging, and more. Even if there is no science fair, students can work on science projects on their own, using guidelines and ideas from this book. Although recommended for grades 4-8, this book is useful at all levels.(S)

Field Trips

Science field trips for most of us mean zoos, nature centers, parks, and other designated wildlife settings. There seem to be plenty of wildlife reserves and nature centers with guided tours and classes where most of us live. While excursions to such places are worthwhile, we do not have to go far to do science field trips. We just need to take time to closely observe the world around us. Have we ever studied the sow bugs under our potted plants? Where do they go when we move the plant? How about trying to identify the different insects or plants that live in a "barren" vacant lot.

Nature study is probably the most important scientific activity we should be doing with young children. Field guides might be our only textbooks for such study. (Nature's Workshop is a good source for field guides, including the very inexpensive "Finders" series for the western states.)

Science field trips need not be limited to the outdoors. Sometimes we are able to tour factories to see how machines work and how products are manufactured. The physics principles involved in manufacturing processes are intriguing. Food processing plants are always popular field trips.

"Behind the scenes" is always interesting. Instead of a trip to the small local post office, visit the regional post office with its huge sorting machines for all types of mail. A field trip to a photo lab offers a look at chemistry in action. In California, the **Institute for Creation Research Museum** (write to ICR for information) has an interesting museum with exhibits and videos on the creationist viewpoint. This is a wonderful field trip for all ages, although older students will benefit more than younger. A video of museum highlights is available for $14.95 for those too far away.

Other ideas are on just about every street corner. Find out where parents in your local home school group work. Usually they mistakenly think others would not be interested in touring their work place, but this often presents a rich source for science-related field trips. Science is much broader than we usually think!

Learning Styles

Different learning styles will usually be obvious when we approach science. Wiggly Willy will probably be too busy to want to take time to learn science from textbooks, but will really "turn on" if we use an activity approach. Perfect Paulas tend to do only that which is set before them, clearly laid out with step-by-step instructions. Competent Carls will study and analyze for hours with no outside prompting. We might have trouble interesting Sociable Sue in science, but we can draw her interest by using integrated learning methods such as found in *KONOS, Alta Vista,* and *The Weaver.*

The *AIMS Program* (AIMS Education Foundation) integrates science with math in hands-on activities that will appeal especially to Wiggly Willy and Sociable Sue, although you might have a little trouble getting some children to follow through with the paper work. The *AIMS Program* offers step-by-step instructions, making it easy for Perfect Paula parents and children to tackle the activities. The stress on application and thinking skills will appeal to Competent Carls.

Backyard Scientist books (Backyard Scientist) and other activity books will appeal to the activity-oriented Wiggly Willys. Posing questions as is done in the *Backyard Scientist* books, intrigues and tantalizes Competent Carls.

Our own learning styles and interests will greatly affect how we teach science to our children. We may have to overcome our own disinterest before we can make science an interesting

subject to our children. We should choose resources that we <u>will</u> work with. It does not matter how good something is for our child if we do not enjoy it enough to pull it off the shelf and use it. If we become enthused about a subject, we will then be in a better position to adapt presentations and activities to meet the learning style needs of our children.

Learning Style Preferences

Wiggly Willy Prefers
- short, hands-on experiments
- outdoor activities
- active field trips
- life science, wildlife studies

Wiggly Willy needs help to work with scientific data and to work on longer term projects.

Perfect Paula Prefers
- science notebooks
- making collections of leaves, rocks, seeds, etc.
- book learning
- biology, botany, physiology—sciences that are less speculative

Perfect Paula needs encouragement to form hypotheses and do experiments.

Competent Carl Prefers
- laws and principles of science
- solving complex problems
- experiments
- devising his own experiments
- chemistry and physics

Competent Carl usually will not need encouragement in science.

Sociable Sue Prefers
- learning about scientists and their discoveries and how these discoveries affected people
- experiments or field trips done with a group

Sociable Sue needs encouragement to pay attention to detail.

Science Resources

About Microscopes

Cheap microscopes (most of those in the under $100 range) are just about useless. In most cases you will be better off with small magnifiers that magnify images ten to thirty times. Hand-held, pocket-size instruments will usually give you clearer views than you can get with cheap microscopes. (Nature's Workshop sells a small 30x illuminating microscope—a pocket instrument that sells for less than ten dollars. This is a good alternative for those who do not want to invest in a microscope.)

Microscopes, even in the $50 to $100 range, usually are difficult or impossible to focus at high magnification. While they can be focused more easily at low magnification, preparing good slides is still a challenge. An exception is the *Blister Microscope* (General Science Service Co.) which sells for $45.95. It comes with a 50x magnification lens (25x and 100x lens are available at extra cost) that can be used to view both slides and thicker, opaque objects that cannot be viewed with a regular microscope. The microscope uses a much more efficient appliance-size light bulb rather than the frustrating mirror set-ups common to lower priced microscopes. It plugs in instead of operating on batteries. Special blister slides make slide preparation much easier than traditional slides, although regular slides might also be used. This microscope is much easier for children to focus and operate successfully. It is made of heavy duty metal, and the cost is much less than for regular microscopes. I have used both a *Blister Microscope* and a seventy dollar microscope (a popular brand carried by many suppliers) in our home school science classes. Opinions are unanimously in favor of the *Blister Microscope*. However, the Blister microscope still does a poor job with high magnification. Unless you are able to invest a few hundred dollars in a high quality microscope, this microscope, together with a hand lens such as the one mentioned above (because it is battery operated), should provide for sufficient indoor and outdoor magnification activities.

If you prefer to purchase a quality, standard microscope, they are available from Nasco, Edmund Scientific, Carolina Biological Supply, and many other sources. The people at Nature's Workshop sound like they have searched for microscopes with home schoolers' needs in mind. They describe their microscopes clearly so you can more easily choose one to meet your needs. (They can also order other microscopes than those described in their catalog.)

○○○○○○○○○○○○○○○

Note: Many of the following resources are from secular publishers and may contain evolution-based material. Watch for the S and SE codes at the end of reviews.

○○○○○○○○○○○○○○○

General and Miscellaneous Science Topics

Note: Be sure to see the more specialized resources under topical headings which follow this section.

AIMS Program
(AIMS Education Foundation)
most books are $16.95

This series of activity-oriented books combines science with math activities in fun projects for experiencing science in action. For example, one activity has to do with the amount of popped corn obtained from various brands of popcorn. As they proceed, students learn about ratio, volume, value-for-cost, etc. Reproducible work sheets are included for recording data from the activities. Books are offered covering various grade levels such as K-3, K-4, and 5-9. There are more than thirty different topics (e.g., food, flight, and the human body) available at the various levels. These are fantastic for all types of learners, although some will not enjoy recording and analyzing the data as much as others. Plan an afternoon once every week or so for each *AIMS* lesson, and I expect it will become one of the highlights of your schooling. The AIMS Education Foundation sends a very detailed booklet about the program upon request. Highly recommended.(S)

Along Came Galileo
by Jeanne Bendick
(Beautiful Feet Books)
9.95

Similar in concept to Bendick's other book reviewed in this chapter, *Archimedes and the Door of Science*, this is a great book to introduce children to a great scientist, some of his scientific forebears, and his significant scientific ideas and discoveries. Told through a series of anecdotes about his life, the book presents just the right amount of information for children in elementary grades to interest them in science. Illustrated with black-and-white drawings, the presentation and lively writing style also make this book visually appealing and fun to read.(S)

Astronomy and the Bible: Questions and Answers, 2nd edition
by Donald B. DeYoung
(Baker Book House)
$9.99

A good reference book for families, *Astronomy and the Bible* gives simple, sensible answers to basic astronomy questions from the viewpoint of a literal Bible interpretation. Many times definite answers cannot be given, so various proposed theories are presented. There are about 170 pages, packed full with information, plus a glossary and a list of other suggested resources for further study. It is divided into six main sections: the earth and moon, the solar system, the stars, galaxies and the universe, general science, and technical terms and ideas. I appreciate the fact DeYoung has included an index so that we can quickly locate specific topics. This is quite a thought provoking book, appropriate for ages ten and up, but especially good for high school level. [Valerie Thorpe/C.D.]

The Backyard Scientist books and kits
books - $8.95; science kits - $10.95

Jane Hoffman, the Backyard Scientist, has written a series of science experiment books. The first three books explore physics and chemistry-related topics. (See description under "Physics and Chemistry.") A fourth book, *The Backyard Scientist Series 3*, features biology experiments. *Backyard Scientist Series 4*, has been designed to involve the entire family in some fascinating experiments, mostly involving physics principles. Jane's exciting dry ice experiments, intriguing viscosity demonstration, and others that thousands have witnessed at her workshops, are now written out in her special, easy-to-do format. Jane's latest book, *Exploring Earthworms with Me*, concentrates exclusively on earthworms. Instructions are clearly written and experiments use convenient materials, most of which we already have in our homes. Exceptions are likely to be the dry ice used in *Series 4*—Jane tells how and where to get it—and earthworms which Jane tells us how to find outdoors. Entertaining illustrations help to clarify instructions. Questions are posed before the experiments are performed, and explanations are given at the end for those of us who are baffled by what we observe. Jane also adds suggestions for further research and study in this book. Experiments in these books, unlike those in some others, really do work. These are good for all learning styles.

The Backyard Scientist also produces three super science kits: *Magical Slime* (non-Newtonian substances), *Magic of Rocks* (geology), and *Magical Super Crystals* (copolymers). Each kit comes with a 24-page activity book that guides students beyond the fun of the experiment into an understanding of scientific principles and methods. More than one child can use each kit, and consumable materials in the kits can be replaced at a grocery or drug store.

Biblical Applications from the Backyard Scientist should be of special interest to Christian home educators. It supplements the other Backyard Scientist books and products with applicable Bible verses, Bible-based explanations, and object lessons.[$8.95].

Bubble Monster and Other Science Fun

(Chicago Review Press)
$17.95

This is not your typical science experiment book, but a compendium of activities that prod young children (ages 3-8) to begin to think scientifically. Children learn to observe, experiment, and analyze as they participate in activities with the assistance of a parent/teacher. The activities are written for a parent and child to work together, although they have been tested and used in day care settings and schools as well as in homes. Easily accessible, inexpensive supplies are required (e.g., graham crackers, marshmallows, colored construction paper, ruler, camera, boxes, food coloring, and a frisbee). Some activities are very simple: build a car out of a cardboard box, then practice stopping and going with red and green lights made from construction paper. A few are more complex: building a water-propelled boat from a paper milk carton, a paper cup, and a straw. There are five general categories of activities:

patterns, matter, communication, the human body, and design and technology. Forty-five basic activities can be stretched to more challenging levels with the extra "Try It" challenges listed in a sidebar for each activity. A "Think About It" section follows each with an explanation of the scientific concept that has been demonstrated. This book should be most useful for the younger end of the suggested age group, although many of these activities, such as building graham cracker and marshmallow castles to learn about architectural strength and design, will make great family fun.(S)

Considering God's Creation

(Eagle's Wings Educational Materials)
$29.95; additional student books - $13.95

This multi-grade science curriculum is for children in grades 3-7. Creation serves as the backdrop for science studies which can be easily adapted for multi-level teaching in the home school setting. The one-year program is contained in a teacher's manual and a student book. It can also be used as a supplement to other curriculum if desired.

The teacher's manual contains the lessons, written in an easy-to-use format. Each lesson first describes preparation needed (generally minimal). Next are vocabulary words listed with definitions and origins. Following is the "introduction"—actually the main idea of the lesson—which can be read to students directly from the book. The words from an original song/poem about the lesson are included. The actual song version is on the accompanying, professionally-recorded audio cassette. Because the authors believe in hands-on activities for effective learning, at least one such activity is described in each lesson. Many of the activities utilize student activity pages from the back of the book. Students also create and maintain a notebook of their own, so a notebook activity is also included. While a Christian view of science is presented throughout each lesson, a special section called Bible Reading directs students to Scripture for verses related to the subject under study. A fun extra, called Evolution Stumpers, provides tidbits of scientific information with which to challenge the theory of evolution. A review section includes questions to pose to our children about each lesson. Since the curriculum is designed for a wide age span, the final section, Digging Deeper, offers suggestions for additional study, activities, investigations, reading, reports, etc., which can be used as is appropriate with each student.

The student workbook is made up of work/activity pages. You are free to make copies for immediate family and classroom use only, although you might prefer to order a separate workbook for each student. These sheets are often the foundation for investigations or experiments, or they are used for cut-and-paste activities, all of which are essential parts of the curriculum. Students compile their own notebooks as they work through these activities and lessons. A few extra items will be needed for activities—crayons, scissors, and glue for most lessons, and items like flashlights, shoe boxes, rocks, and library/resource books on particular topics.

Topical areas include creation, the universe, the earth, rocks and minerals, weather, plant kingdom, ecology, insects, spiders, fish, reptiles, birds, mammals, amphibians, animal structures, food chains, animal reproduction, instinct, man, and scientists. None of these topics is covered thoroughly, since that would be impossible within a one-year curriculum. If you examine the list of topics, you can see that life science receives the most attention with earth science filling the remainder.

We definitely need to make decisions about what to require from each child, since some material will be too challenging for young students and some not challenging enough for older students. However, this curriculum seems to come closer than others to meeting the needs of a home school family that wants a Christian science curriculum that can be used to teach a broad span of grade levels together.

Developing Critical Thinking through Science, Books One and Two

(Critical Thinking Books & Software)
$22.95 and $26.95 respectively

Parents who are reluctant to get into science experiments because they fear they will be unable to explain or understand results will find these books extremely useful. The teacher is not expected to have any science background for these activities. Step-by-step procedures, lists of easy-to-find "equipment" (the only one that might be difficult is an empty ditto fluid can used in one activity), and minimal preparation time all make the books simple for the inexperienced parent/teacher. Even better, questions, explanations and answers are laid out at each step where they are needed, so there is no fumbling around to check the answer key or search for further information. Each book is complete in itself, serving as a teacher's manual. The second book has some data-recording pages that can be copied for student use, but otherwise students simply participate in hands-on activities and discussion.

The critical thinking component of these books is crucial. The underlying philosophy lays out three steps in learning science skills and concepts: "doing through direct, firsthand experiences in an interactive, open atmosphere; constructing by building their knowledge through guided inquiry; [and] connecting by relating their learning to the world around them."

Book One is geared toward grades 1-4, but older students with little science background will find it a good starting place. It is divided into seven units: observing, water, buoyancy and surface tension, air, moving air/air pressure, force, and

space/light/shadows. There are 41 lessons with review lessons at the end of each unit. Because the book was written for the classroom, some lessons describe cooperative activities done in groups. Most are easily adaptable to the home situation.

Book Two has 80 lessons arranged in 17 units. The emphasis is on physics as in the younger volume, but activities are geared toward students in grades 4-6. There appears to be some overlap between both books—some lesson concepts presented in Book One are presented also in Book Two but in a more challenging manner. However, if you use Book One, then follow with Book Two a few years later, any repetition is likely to serve as reinforcement for learning.(S)

Discover the Wonders of Water
by Harold Silviani (Creative Teaching Associates)
$6.95

If you choose water as one of your science topics for the year, this book will fit in perfectly. (You can still use it if you are not following a topical course of study for science.) Here we have 20 experiments/activities, all teaching about the properties of water. The front of the book has a few pages about the properties of water and general information to give us helpful background. See the review of *Kitchen, Garage, and Garbage Can Science* for a description of the layout of that series of books which is similar. The only difference is that this book is aimed at a slightly older age group than *Kitchen....* However, I think younger children will still benefit from the experiments on an introductory level. Necessary materials are mostly found in the kitchen. Suggested for grades 4-12.(S)

DK Publishing, Inc.

DK publishes many beautifully-illustrated "real books" and software programs related to science. Their line includes some Eyewitness books, carefully differentiated from the Knopf Eyewitness books described below. "Carefully" means you will have a difficult time figuring out whose books belong to whom. Some catalogs show both the Knopf *Eyewitness* titles and DK's *Eyewitness* titles! It appears that DK publishes particular series within the line: *Eyewitness Handbooks, Eyewitness Visual Dictionaries, Eyewitness Explorers*, and *Eyewitness Science*. Other DK titles (not from *Eyewitness* lines) seem to come in series with the exception of a few books such as *Young Astronomer* and *My First Batteries and Magnets Book*. Series titles are *See How They Grow* (great for very young children), *Let's Explore Science* (information and experiments for ages 4-7), *Look Closer* (nature series for ages 7-10), and the *ASPCA Pet Care Guides for Kids* (ages 7 and up).

DK Interactive Learning products include a number of intriguing CD-ROM products. See the reviews of the *Eyewitness Encyclopedia of Science* and *The New Way Things*

Work. Among other interactive titles are *Eyewitness Encyclopedia of Space and the Universe, Castle Explorer, Eyewitness World Atlas* (reviewed in Chapter Fifteen), *Ultimate Human Body,* and *Stowaway.* DK is making a big effort to reach home educators, so you should be seeing more of their products in the future. Meanwhile, bookstores and libraries are likely to have at least some of the titles.(SE)

Eyewitness Encyclopedia of Science 2.0 [computer program]

(DK Publishing, Inc.)
$29.95

This interactive reference CD-ROM covers mathematics, physics, chemistry, life sciences, and the earth and the universe. Click on a topic on the impressive 3D interface and you will be connected to a narrated information box with basic information about the subject. Although you could read the box without the narration, your computer must have sound capabilities to profit from any accompanying video clips or animations as the narration for these is not printed out. Evolution is presented as fact. Students of chemistry will appreciate the interactive periodic table and selected 3D molecules. You can find information about important scientists, take a quiz, or try the web link to the Eyewitness Science Online site.

If you need more than basic information you can access more in-depth articles. These pages are not narrated and are not as easy to read on the computer screen as they would be in a book; however you can explore more advanced topics such as higher dimensions, quarks or chaos theory. While suitable for ages 10 and up, this program is probably most interesting for curious 6th or 7th graders. The program will run on either Windows or Apple systems.(SE)[V.Thorpe]

Hands-On Minds-On Science series
(Teacher Created Materials)
$11.95 each

There are a number of titles in this series, and they are divided into three levels: K-2, 2-4, and 4-6. Titles for the first level are *Creepy Crawlies, Animals, Weather, Magnets, The Earth,* and *Our Bodies.* For the second level, titles are *Plants, Animals, Ecology, Endangered Species, Rain Forest, Space, Magnetism and Electricity, Simple Machines, Simple Chemistry,* and *Rocks and Minerals.* Titles for the upper grades are *Plants, Animals, Endangered Species, Environmental Issues, Space, Magnetism and Electricity, Force and Motion, Easy Chemistry, Rain Forest, Matter, Ocean, Flight,* and *Geology.* Since these were created primarily for use in government school classrooms, expect occasional content problems. Although suggested for particular grade levels, most titles should easily stretch to cover students in a slightly broader age span.

This series is intended to attract children's interest to science with fascinating hands-on activities, then lead them into deeper thinking with discussion and follow up research, reading, and writing.

I reviewed only *Magnets* from the first level and the mid-level *Space* and *Animals* books, but the layout is similar for other books.

Magnets and other titles for the first level are designed to teach science to non-writers. Children check off boxes, circle items, and draw pictures as they record their scientific findings. Through hands-on activities children learn basic science concepts, as we present background information, drawing from that provided within the book. These books are not limited to kindergartners and first-graders, since even older children can be involved in the activities and discussions if they have not already covered the concepts. Preparation time is needed, primarily to gather materials, but reproducible activity pages make the books fairly easy to use.

The *Space* book activities assume higher skill levels. In a lesson "3-Stage Rocket," students create their own balloon-propelled "stage" rocket. After launching their rocket, students make observations and comparisons to the real thing. *Space* covers the history of space flight, the solar system, and living and working in space, then adds some cross-curricula activities and some fun "station-to-station" activities. Reproducible worksheets, a glossary, and a bibliography of related resources make all of the activity-oriented learning easier for parents to manage. You will need to plan ahead to gather materials—black poster paint, a tennis ball, empty soda bottles, etc. The most challenging item might be a video showing a rocket launch, but even that should be available through the library. (If unavailable, use pictures.)

The intermediate *Animals* book is particularly good. It really does work on analysis and understanding. For example, in a study about tundras, lakes, and ponds, students begin by freezing a pan partially filled with soil, then adding water over the frozen soil and observing the result. Students keep a journal with photocopied pages from the book. They record their observations and conclusions, then study how this physical/geological action affects animals in tundra regions. Students then follow up with research on tundra regions and/or a specific animal that lives there. Some background information is included within the book, but research in other books is necessary. Activities can be done at home (in or out of doors) for the most part, even though they are written with the classroom in mind. Nothing exotic is required, although some of us might have to go farther than the schoolyard to look for the animal tracks mentioned in one lesson. Although the title is animals, the book encompasses creatures from the single-cell level up through mammals. The book's organizational structure makes it a good tool for beginning study of living things.

It starts with characteristics of living things and classifications. It then divides into sections on the tundra, coniferous forests, deciduous forests, rain forests, deserts, and the sea, studying selected life forms found in the different environments. Reproducible worksheets, a glossary, and a bibliography of suggested resources enhance the book's usefulness.(SE)

The Everyday Science Sourcebook: Ideas for Teaching in the Elementary and Middle School
by Lawrence F. Lowery
(Dale Seymour Publications)
$19.95

This thick book is crammed with more than 1000 activities for grades K-8. The purpose of the book is to supplement basic instruction in many areas of science. Simple materials are used and less time is required than for activities in other books that feature experiments for their own sake rather than as adjuncts to your lessons as these are.(S)

Explorabook: A Kids' Science Museum in a Book
(Exploratorium Mail Order Department)
$18.95

This most unusual book comes complete with a large magnet, Fresnel lens, agar gel, diffraction grating, mirror, and moiré spinner. Activities using these materials can be enjoyed by all ages. Young children will find the effects fascinating, while older children will begin to understand the principles causing the effects. Aside from the bacterial studies using the agar gel, most activities have to do with physics. Instructions are written so that most children from about fourth grade and up can work independently. Explanations are provided along with examples of practical applications of the principles in real life. Intriguing, colorful illustrations along with cartoon characters aid understanding. *Explorabook* is not your typical experiment book but a fun-filled "package."(SE)

The Exploratorium Science Snackbook
(Exploratorium Mail Order Department)
$10.95 each

The San Francisco Exploratorium is one of the world's best hands-on science museums for children. In this series of four books, teachers have adapted Exploratorium exhibits and demonstrations for children to recreate at home. The titles of each of the books are *Perception and Light, Force and Motion, How We See the World,* and *Energy and Matter.* Topics range over the areas of chemistry, physics, and life science, but visual effects seem to be an important part of many activities. Each project has clear directions with illustrations of both the original Exploratorium exhibit and the homemade version. Scientific explanations follow each activity. I appreciate the fact that the explanations are easy to understand, using analogies to familiar phenomena and occasional illustrations. For

those of an investigative bent, there are often follow-up activities under the heading "Etc."

These projects range from simple to very complicated—learning about air with a hair dryer and a ping pong ball as compared to a gravity experiment using clear plastic, rigid-walled tube, rubber stoppers, copper tubing, vacuum tubing, vacuum pump, and clamps. Most materials for projects can be obtained at places such as hardware and toy stores, although you might have to obtain some items from sources listed in the resource guide found in the back of the book. Remember that these projects were designed by teachers for classroom use, so many are more complicated than what a single family might tackle at home. (Consider doing some of the more complicated or expensive projects with home school groups.) Some projects require some serious power tool usage for cutting wood to precise measurements or for routing work. While some projects are simple enough for young children, most are more complicated than those found in books such as the *Backyard Scientist* series or Janice Van Cleave books. However, they offer an excellent challenge for students at about fourth grade level and above. Science concepts will be most easily understood by students at junior high level or older, although younger children can certainly begin to understand some scientific principles. With more than 100 experiments to choose among, this series is likely to provide ideas that can be used over a number of years. Some of these projects might even provide "jumping off" ideas for science fair projects for older students.

Check out the Exploratorium's web site for other unusual science resources and activity ideas.(SE)

Eyewitness Juniors series and Eyewitness Books
(Random House/Knopf)
$10.99-$20.99

Two outstanding series of books from Knopf make excellent science resources. These books are beautifully illustrated, primarily with photographs. Text is well-written and loaded with fascinating information. *Eyewitness Junior* books are written for children ages 6-10, while *Eyewitness* books aim for ages 10 and up. There is less text, and it is printed in larger type in the younger level books. Titles in the Junior series all start with the word "amazing." The *Amazing* titles are *Animal Babies; Armored Animals; Bats; Birds; Birds of Prey; Bikes; Boats; Butterflies and Moths; Cats; Crocodiles and Reptiles; Fish; Flying Machines; Frogs and Toads; Insects; Lizards; Mammals; Monkeys; Poisonous Animals; Snakes; Wolves, Dogs, and Foxes;* and *Spiders.* Older level titles include *Butterfly and Moth, Dinosaur, Fish, Insect, Mammal, Reptile, Car, Crystal and Gem, Early Humans, Flying Machine, Invention, Plant and Flower, Pond and River, Rocks and Minerals, Seashore, Shell, Skeleton, Sports, Tree,* and *Weather.* (SE-some of these titles such as *Mammal* and *Skeleton* have content some parents will find objectionable.)

Facts, Not Fear: A Parent's Guide to Teaching Children About the Environment

by Michael Sanera and Jane Shaw
(Regnery Publishing, Inc.)
$14.95

Christians tend to reject most environmental education resources because they embody animistic or pantheistic worldviews combined with pseudo-science. (Christians shouldn't be the only ones rejecting this nonsense!) Assuming that most young people have been exposed to quite a bit of environmental misinformation, Sanera and Shaw try to set the record straight. While acknowledging the reality of some environmental problems, they balance popularly-held concepts with scientific fact and logical analysis to put things into proper perspective. For example, they tackle global warning by examining the records of temperature change (acknowledging about .5 degree Celcius change over the past 100 years); discussing mathematical computer-generated models; pointing out questionable and unlikely assumptions within those models; addressing common questions; and suggesting activities, field trips, and additional reading. This is a resource book for parents to use with children of all ages. Since *Facts, Not Fear* was not intended for only Christian audiences, it does not address the spiritual worldview issues except for a brief mention that this is an issue to consider. Assuming that most children attend government schools, the authors frequently refer to texts used in those schools. They also provide two lists of "environmental" books—one list of books to avoid, and the other of books to add to your library.(S)

Galileo and the Stargazers [audio CD]

(Greathall Productions, Inc.)
cassette - $9.95; CD - $14.95

Storyteller Jim Weiss mixes folklore, history, and science in these stories of early scientists. For example, the first story of "Archimedes and the Golden Crown" retells Archimedes puzzling through the challenge of determining whether or not the man who constructed the king's crown made it with the seven pounds of gold he was given or a less-precious substitute. In the process, he discovered the principal of atomic mass. Physics, math, and astronomy are critical elements of these stories of Ptolemy, Copernicus, Brahe, Kepler, Galileo, and Newton. Weiss creates different characters with his voice for dramatic effect. Children, even as young as 7 or 8, can understand and learn from these presentations because of the storytelling format. Moreover, the professionalism of the presentations make them appropriate and appealing to teens and adults.(S)

Genesis for Kids: Science Experiments that show God's power in Creation!

by Doug Lambier and Robert Stevenson
(Tommy Nelson/Word Publishing)
$12.99

Using the seven days of creation as the organizing theme, Lambier and Stevenson present more than 100 science experiments and investigations. The book is written directly to children, with the reading level most appropriate for about fourth grade and up. Interest level will extend widely to both younger and older students. Most experiments are similar to those found in other such books, but the presentation is very appealing with cartoon illustrations, interesting presentation, and clear instructions. Scientific explanations are included, although they are fairly brief. This should be a good resource for family science activities.

Hands-On Science!

(Prentice Hall)
$24.95

This science activity book differs from most others with its strong emphasis on practical application. It discusses current science issues without taking the extreme liberal position so prevalent in other non-Christian science books. While there are probably still a few points where Christians will take exception (e.g., lesson on genetic engineering), overall, the book is well-balanced. There are 112 activities designated for various age groupings from fourth through eighth grades. The section headings reflect the content of the book accurately. Some of these headings are Creating an Atmosphere of Science-in-Action in the Classroom, Science for Living, Using the Process Approach in Science, Developing Scientific and Technological Literacy and Competency, Science/Societal Issues, and Personal Aspects of Science. Examples of some activities/experiments are identifying chemical food additives, tracking air pollution, and analyzing muscle fatigue. Some unusual materials are required (houseflies, copper tubing, petri dishes, heavy art paper) but nothing that is extremely difficult or expensive. Even though the book assumes a classroom set up with students working in groups, it sometimes suggests resources not common to the classroom but common to our homes such as "freezing units" and "hot plates." Detailed instructions are easy-to-follow, and activities are followed by analysis and discussion. Some reproducible student recording pages are included. Reluctant science students might be turned on when they experience these science activities that really relate to life. ISBN # 0876289065.(S)

A History of Science: A Literature Based Introduction to Scientific Principles and their Discoverers

by Rebecca Berg
(Beautiful Feet Books)
$12.95

This is a guide to a book and activity-based study of science for children in the primary and intermediate grades. Personally, I think it most appropriate for children in grades 3-6 because of the depth of coverage it offers. You can move through it more slowly with children in first and second grade, selecting age-appropriate activities, while you should go more quickly using almost all of the main lesson activities for older children. Those in fifth and sixth grade should also be challenged with some of the activities from the "Notes for additional research..." at the end of each section of the book. While the book suggests that older students complete three to four lessons per week, I think that parents will need to make their own judgments as to how long to take to complete the lessons. Some lessons can easily be completed in 30 to 60 minutes, while others appear to require much more time. For example, one lesson directs reading from Great Inventors, recording about Da Vinci's discoveries as related in Great Inventors, creation of a new section in their notebook, library research and a short report on Leonardo Da Vinci, and mirror-writing experiments from two resource books. The library research and short report alone might easily take two to three days! The course should take about one school year to complete.

Parents should read some or all of the selections with their children. The entire family can join in the science experiments. Older students will complete reading and research activities on their own. All students create a notebook, to which they add information as they study different topics.

The study uses a combination of biographies and resource books. Essential resource books are *Science Around the House, Explorabook, The Picture History of Great Inventors,* and *The Way Things Work.* Essential biographies are *Archimedes and the Door of Science, Galileo and the Universe, Benjamin Franklin's Adventures with Electricity, The Story of Thomas Alva Edison, Pasteur's Fight Against Microbes, Marie Curie's Search for Radium, Along Came Galileo,* and *Albert Einstein, Young Thinker.* Additional tapes and books are recommended, but they are optional.

Instructions are very clear; this guide directs you to where to find the information or experiment rather than just a vague assignment. While most experiments and activities are detailed in the resource books, a few are found at the back of this guide.

A separate *History of Science Timeline* with preprinted figures relating to this study is available for $8.95.

This is a wonderful way to introduce children to science and scientists since they learn why and how science developed, not just what we know today. This approach stretches across all learning styles because it brings in the human dimension and practical applications (which appeal especially to Sociable Sues and Wiggly Willys) while presenting material through great books and activities that appeal to reluctant science students. It does require parent preparation and presentation time, but parents, too, should find it very enjoyable.

Intermediate Science through Children's Literature

by Carol M. Butzow and John W. Butzow
(Teacher Ideas Press)
$23

Intermediate Science through Children's Literature is written to be either a supplement or a stand-alone approach to science for grades 4 through 7. The authors' intent is to encourage students to go beyond mere comprehension of isolated science facts that are quickly forgotten. Traditional texts, they say, break up science into little bits of knowledge. They contend that by using children's literature, the student must use higher thinking skills, such as inference and comparison, rather than simple memorization. A story involving, for example, a tornado, requires that the characters see the scientific phenomenon as part of their real life, forcing the reader to treat it in the same way.

The activities in the book are addressed to the student, rather than to the teacher. Some of them are for the student to do alone; some should be done in small groups. A few require adult help or supervision, such as those using simple chemicals. They are designed to be done *after* reading the book. The activities center on science, but also make use of math, social studies, writing and field trips, a more integrated approach to the study of science. The book leans heavily towards the life sciences in its topics. Some examples of the books topics included are: *Sarah, Plain and Tall,* the prairie ecosystem; *Night of the Twisters,* tornadoes and weather; and *The Island of the Blue Dolphins,* California coastal islands.

Because of the interesting approach that this book employs, I recommend it especially for children who have trouble learning with a textbook approach. However, I need to include some cautions. Some of the activities reflect a concern with political correctness, and some of the topics (fossils, killer whales, wetlands encroachment) are especially prone to that. I have not read all of the books, but I know that some of the authors, Gary Paulsen, for example, would be objectionable to many parents. However, with 14 books to choose among, there is easily a full year of activities, even leaving out some of the sections.(S)[Kath Courtney]

Kaw Valley Video Sales and Rentals [videos]

(Kaw Valley Video Sales and Rentals)
$10 annual membership fee; $19.95 each for video pur-

chase, $4 for rental with volume discounts

Kaw Valley's catalog features some science related topics that might be used as course supplements or part of topical studies. I particularly recommend to you their videos *Bridges, Irrigation,* and *George Washington Carver. Bridges* is an interesting 22-minute look at the various types of bridges from ancient times through the present. It covers basics of construction principles and building materials on an introductory-physics level that will be interesting to all ages. Especially interesting is footage of an actual, short-lived bridge, nick-named "Galloping Gerty" since it rippled and rolled uncontrollably because wind force was not properly taken into account in its design. Kaw Valley's biographical video on the renowned black scientist George Washington Carver is also excellent. Carter's own words are used, reflecting his Christian beliefs. *Irrigation* is an interesting 32-minute presentation on water, agriculture, conservation, economic issues, drought, and topics related to irrigation. I also reviewed *Paper* and *Wheat* which were not as good, but which you might still find worthwhile.

Most of these are older films, with some out-of-date information, although some, such as *George Washington Carver* are more recent. Other titles in the science section of their catalog are *Mules, Paint, Soap, Wood,* and *Tunnels.* Kaw Valley also offers creation science videos from Films for Christ and Answers in Genesis. Videos published by Kaw Valley come with teacher guides.

A $10 annual fee allows purchase of all Kaw Valley created videos at $19.95 each. A 44-video set is available for $399—about half price. Rentals are for 2 week periods and are $4 each with a volume discount when 5 or more videos are rented at a time.(S)

Kingfisher Books

(Larousse Kingfisher Chambers, Inc.)

Kingfisher publishers a number of titles similar in concept to Usborne but, generally, with more text and less clutter. These are beautiful resource books children love to own, but you will have to watch for content problems. Among their science titles are their two giant volumes *The Kingfisher Science Encyclopedia* (reviewed next) and *The Kingfisher Illustrated Encyclopedia of Animals* [$21.95]. They also have science series: *Young Discovers* (see review of *The Human Body* from this series), *The World Around Us, 1000 Facts About, How Things Work,* and *Visual Factfinders.* You should be able to find many of these books in bookstores and libraries.(SE)

The Kingfisher Science Encyclopedia

(Larousse Kingfisher Chambers, Inc.)
$39.95

This is an exceptionally attractive, single-volume, 768-page encyclopedia for students. It features full color illustrations on every page

and easy-to-read text that presents more information than the typical "picture" reference books. "See for Yourself" boxes show children how to carry out simple experiments that illustrate concepts. The information looks helpful, although there is the typical view of evolution and one diagram of gestation in mammals states that "the longer the gestation period, the longer the offspring has to be taken care of by its parents", which would be true except that a human is pictured along with the mouse, hare, whale and elephant. Aside from this type of inaccuracy, the explanations are for the most part short, clear, and interesting. A Special Features index lists subjects that are treated in more detail in order to be useful for school projects and study. This encyclopedia is appropriate for students in middle and upper elementary grades. (SE)[V.Thorpe]

Kitchen, Garage, and Garbage Can Science series

(Creative Teaching Associates)
$6.95 each

There are six titles in this series: *Experiments With Air; Experiments With Gravity, Magnets & Electricity; Experiments With Water; Human Body: Senses & The Brain; Human Body: Heart, Lungs, Bones & Muscle;* and *Fun With Biology.* These are designed as supplements rather than as foundations for science instruction for students in grade K-8. They may be used with students of all ages by varying the choices of questions and follow-up activities. Younger children will enjoy the activities without much, if any, recording or analysis. In the upper primary and lower intermediate grades, students are challenged to do more comparison and organizing, recording data from the activities and identifying patterns or conclusions. Older students should be analyzing and extending ideas, maybe suggesting additional experiments. So the typical home school family can use the same experiments with all of their children, simply going further with older students.

Each book offers fifteen science experiments/activities. All experiment materials are easily available and typically found in the kitchen, garage, garbage can, or elsewhere around the home. One page of teacher instructions and a one-page student instruction sheet (reproducible) are used for each lesson. Instructions are very easy to follow. Explanations, application examples, and extension activities are given on the teacher's sheet. The student pages use cartoon-like illustrations and large print so they are kid-friendly. Examples of topics: air pressure, chemical changes, balance and the center of gravity, oil and water, exercise and your pulse rate, lung capacity, sensitivity spots on the tongue to different tastes, how sound travels, and reaction times. The experiments themselves are not unusual or unique, but the simple format of this book will be a big help to busy parents who would like to do more hands-on science.

Lyrical Life Science, Volumes 1, 2, and 3
(Lyrical Learning)
each text, tape, and workbook set - $25.50; text and tape only - $19.95; additional workbooks - $5.95

Teacher Doug Eldon struggled to get his sixth graders to remember life science vocabulary and concepts until he hit upon the idea of putting the information to music. The result was the first tape of *Lyrical Life Science*: a recording of eleven life science songs, professionally recorded with a variety of instruments by Bobby Horton, well-known for his historical ballads. Songs on Volume 1 of *Lyrical Life Science* pack an amazing amount of detail into lyrics set to popular tunes like "Dixie," "Clementine," and "Yankee Doodle." For example, "Oh Bacteria" is set to the tune of "Oh Susanna" and begins:

"Oh lacking any nucleus, you do have a cell wall
You live in water, air and soil and anywhere at all...."

The meter and phrasing occasionally leave something to be desired, but you can't beat this approach for liveliness. You can't help laughing when you try to sing along to "Algae and fungi, lichen, moss and liverworts...." Topics Volume 1 addresses include scientific method, living things, invertebrates, coldblooded vertebrates, birds, classification, algae/fungi/nonvascular plants, vascular plants, protozoa, genetics, viruses, and bacteria.

Volume 2 - *Mammals, Ecology, and Biomes*, uses tunes like "Erie Canal," "The Yellow Rose of Texas," and "Irish Washerwoman" to teach about bats, carnivores, insectivores, pinnepeds, ecology, biomes, toothless mammals, manatees, whales, dolphins, and single-family orders. You won't have to wade through evolutionary nonsense.

Volume 3 - *The Human Body,* begins with an introductory song on cells, genes, tissue, organs, and organ systems. Then it focuses on each of the body systems. You will recognize some of the tunes like "Caissons Go Rolling Along" and "Red River Valley," but some others like "Goober Peas," "Old Joe Clark," and "Tarantella" will be less familiar. "The Skeletal System" sung to "Tarantella" is a familiar pirate tune that takes "...the thigh bone is connected to the hip bone...." to a whole other level.

Along with each tape comes a textbook which expands upon the information summarized in the songs. The textbooks, about 100 pages each, are generously illustrated with line drawings and touches of humor. They include song lyrics and simple music. The corresponding workbook lessons offer matching, fill-in-the-blank, essay, and labeling exercises.

Answer keys are at the back. Although originally written for sixth graders, the content reflects some of what we find in typical high school life science texts. Whatever level you choose to use these for, they remain supplements rather than comprehensive courses. While this approach is not for all students, it

does offers a rare alternative for auditory learners when it comes to science. And for those who just want learning to be a little more light-hearted, be aware that it is almost impossible to listen to these tapes without bursting out laughing.

Millbrook Press books
(Millbrook Press)

Millbrook is following the lead of other publishers like DK and Kingfisher with colorful, fun-to-explore, fact-filled books for children. They publish many titles that you will find only in libraries because they are sold only in expensive library-binding editions. However, they do publish some books for the popular market in paperback editions. You might consider their *Simple Experiments for Young Scientists* series, *New Book of ...* series, *How Science Works* series, or their *I Didn't Know That ...* series. Reviews of the books *Planes and Other Aircraft* (from *How Science Works* series) and *New Book of Space* are found elsewhere in this section. A review of *Gravity* from the *Simple Experiments* series is under "Physics and Chemistry."(SE)

Mr. Wizard Supermarket Science
by Don Herbert
(Random House, Inc.)
$10

Check out this and other *Mr. Wizard* books such as *Mr. Wizard's Experiments for Young Scientists* [$10.95]. Experiments in all books are different. *Mr. Wizard's* books are always easy-to-use, requiring simple materials, and they are entertainingly written.(S)

Milliken Transparency Reproducible Books
(Milliken)
$12.95

Milliken publishes a number of titles related to science that can be easily adapted for children over a wide age span. The books have full-color illustrations and transparencies (designed for use on overhead projectors, but just as useful without the projector), information on the topic, and reproducible student work sheets. One series of eight books related to environmental topics is suggested for use with grades 3-5. Another series of ten books on a wide range of topics (human body, nutrition, weather, space, plants, etc.) is suggested for grades 4-9, while still another series of ten books (on birds, electricity and magnetism, machines and work, light and sound, oceanography, etc.) is suggested for grades 5-9. The books do reflect gradually increasing level of difficulties, yet there is still room to stretch beyond these suggested grade level boundaries. Since we copy the worksheets, each book is nonconsumable. Each book also includes a brief teaching guide and answer key. These books are intended to supplement a basic science program rather than be used as the primary resources. (The Weaver suggests their use in conjunction with their unit studies.) The quality of the content and presentation is excellent, although we are likely to encounter philosophical problems with evolution.(SE)

Moody Science Adventures and Moody Science Classics [videos]
(Moody Video)

Moody has produced a number of series of outstanding science videos that rival National Geographic Society in production quality, and, even better, they recognize God as the Divine Architect behind creation. Titles in the Classics series [$9.95 each] are *City of the Bees, Dust or Destiny* (God's amazing creation), *Facts of Faith* (science experiments are used to demonstrate spiritual truths), *God of Creation, Hidden Treasures* (microscopic nature), *Prior Claim* (man's inventions mimic God's creation), *Red River of Life* (circulation), *Signposts Aloft* (flying), *Empty Cities* (examination of the Mayan and Incan cultures), and *Where the Waters Run* (water). The films from the Classics series all have strong spiritual messages that are more the essence of each film than are the science topics.

The Adventures series videos [$14.95 each] are oriented toward science instruction for children. Each video has three, ten-minute segments on different topics. Four videos available are *Treasure Hunt/Animals Move/Eight-Legged Engineer, The Power in Plants/Busy as a Bee/Small World, The Clown-Faced Carpenter/Journey to the Stars/Water,* and *The Wonder of You/A Mystery Story/A Matter of Taste.* The Adventures series are good for all elementary grades, although they are targeted for grades 3-6, and they are very reasonably priced.

Moody has other series which I have not yet reviewed, so you will need to check these out for yourself. The Awesome Forces of God's Creation series includes three videos: *Roaring Waters, Thundering Earth,* and *Whirling Winds.* The Wonders of God's Creation series includes *Planet Earth, Animal Kingdom,* and *Human Life.* Yet another series, The Creation Discovery series, sounds like it was designed with lots of entertainment via songs, games, and experiments. It includes God's Power Plants, God's Rockin' World, and *God's Earth Team.*

The Naturalist's Handbook: Activities for Young Explorers
by Lynn Kuntz
(Gibbs Smith, Publisher)
$14.95

At 64 pages, this book might sound overpriced, but this is not your ordinary book. It has a hard cover with a metal comb binding within the spine so the book can lie flat. The book needs to lie flat because children actually write right in it. Humorous, full-color illustrations are both entertaining and

helpful. Intended to spark young naturalists' interest in exploring nature, it directs children to get outside and get down in the dirt with nature. Children explore plants, photosynthesis, seeds, flowers, medicinal plants, insects, spiders, mammals, birds, water, frogs, fish, ponds, and conservation. Information on each topic is interspersed with activities and questions. Lined sections for children to record information or thoughts about their explorations stimulate children to analyze and react, but I suspect that the space will be too small for older students' reflections and observations. Note that since kids write in the book, each child needs his or her own book unless you have each one maintain a separate notebook—a better idea anyway so that they have enough room to write on each topic. None of the activities require fancy equipment. Aside from nature itself, only a few items are required, items such as plastic soda bottles, plaster for making animal track molds, jars, a banana, and a piece of bread. Some of the activities can be done with access to nothing more than a weedy patch of ground on a vacant lot. Others require ventures closer to habitats where we might locate animal burrows and tracks. Although this book is not written from a Biblical perspective, I didn't spot any evolutionary assumptions, except for the statement that 10,000-year-old lichens have been found, a statement with which young-earthers will take exception.(S)

Nature Club series
(Troll Books)
$4.95 each

This is one of Troll's best series. Inexpensive, colorful, and well-written, these thirty-two page books can be an important part of your science curriculum. Both photographs and art are used for illustration. The content is "meaty," and activity suggestions are included. *Trees and Leaves* is one of the best resources available for the topic for students in elementary grades. Other titles: *Animal Babies, Animal Homes, Animal Journeys, Birds, Fossil Detectives, Insects, Night Creatures, Ponds and Streams,* and *Seashores.*(SE)

Nature Friend magazine
(Nature Friend Magazine)
$22 per year

This magazine is a monthly publication for Christian children. Stories, games, puzzles, and activities—all relating to nature and science topics—are appropriate for ages 4 to 14.

The New Book of Space
by Robin Scagell
(Millbrook Press)
$9.95 pb

Your space buff will enjoy looking through these 32 over-sized pages that beautifully illustrate some of the recent developments in space exploration such as the Hubble Space

Telescope and the proposed International Space Station, as well as the latest information (1997) about planets, moons and comets. Also available, but not reviewed, is *The New Book of Mars*. Recommended for ages 9-11.(S)[V. Thorpe]

Oceans: A Fact Filled Coloring Book [from the Start Exploring series]
(Running Press)
$8.95

Children learn about sea life through the detailed coloring pictures and text in this book. These are appropriate for middle and upper elementary grades because there is a great deal of detail in the pictures.(S)

One Week Off Unit Studies
(Castle Heights Press)
$9.95 each

The Julicher family of Castle Heights Press has combined efforts of both parents and children to produce this series of unit studies, each of which is designed to take about one week. Titles in the series are *Aviation, Cats and Kittens, Dogs and Puppies, Horses,* and *Space Exploration.* While all of these will stretch to cover a fairly wide age span, they do vary in level of difficulty, reflecting the ages of authors involved. The animal titles, particularly those about cats and dogs, seem "younger" than the others. Each study requires extensive research and completion of workbook writing activities. This is coupled with field trips, experiments, drawings, reports, or presentations as is appropriate for each study and age level. These studies do challenge students to go beyond superficial information into serious research. The various activities also require student output that ensures that they are understanding and utilizing what they learn.

Planes and Other Aircraft
by Nigel Hawkes
(Millbrook Press)
$6.95 pb

This 32-page book from Millbrook's *How Science Works* series has a lot of information about aircraft in an attractive and easy-to-read format. Large print and full-color illustrations make this book especially suitable for young learners as well as those with reading difficulties. The scientific principles behind flight are explained and reviewed, and experiments illustrate some of the concepts. Instructions for building a paper glider are integrated into the appropriate chapters. Adult help may be needed for this as the glider parts must be photocopied or transferred from the book and cut out carefully in order to be assembled properly.

Also in the series, but not reviewed, is *Ships and Other Seacraft.* These books are recommended for ages 9- 11.(S)[V. Thorpe]

Project-Oriented Science: A Teacher's Guide
by Kathleen Julicher
(Castle Heights Press)
$16.95

Kathleen Julicher is an advocate of using projects for teaching science, but she recognizes that many children get caught up in the fun aspects of projects and fail to learn the cognitive facts or the critical thinking skills necessary to process and apply them. This book helps us successfully combine project and cognitive learning for children at almost all levels (probably about second grade and up). While this is not a science curriculum in itself, it is a how-to book that can be used along with almost any book about "doing" science. Children will need a source for information and directions for experiments or observations, but this book tells us how to select and organize science studies and how to prepare and present individual lessons. Reproducible planning worksheets are included. The book then tells us how to teach children to record information. There are numerous recording forms for students to use: some for labeled drawings, some for recording specific information, and some general experiment recording sheets appropriate for differing skill levels. Key skill areas covered are drawing, taking and recording measurements, keeping records, and scientific method. Some actual lessons are included to introduce students to each of these skill areas. I envision this book as an ideal introduction to use before getting into books such as the *Unit Adventure Study Guides* which steer you toward subject specific information and ideas. If parents and children first gain experience doing this type of work through *Project-Oriented Science*, they will understand how to create their own recording devices when needed. Some of the reproducible recording pages could even be used to enhance experiments from books such as *The Backyard Scientist.*

Even more help is available from Castle Heights Press in the form of *My First Science Notebook* [$10.95] and *My Science Notebook 2* [$10.95]. The first book is appropriate for children in grades K-3, although young children will probably need help with reading the instructions. It walks them through activities for drawing, measuring, recording, and reporting. A list of "Classic Experiments for Young Scientists" at the back of the book suggests numerous topics that can be pursued, many of them using some of the recording pages in the *Notebook. My Science Notebook 2* is very similar but is written for students second grade and older. It covers drawing, classification, measuring and charting, observing, and scientific method. This is intended to be the student's personal workbook, so, while pages are reproducible (for your family only), each student should have his or her own copy. Both *Notebooks* have some content overlap with *Project-Oriented Science*, which is intended to be the teacher's guide. While the *Notebooks* can stand on their own, they really are best used along with the teacher's guide. (All of the Castle Heights books are written to be used by either home educating families or small schools, although they are not reproducible for school groups.)

Ring of Fire rock and mineral kits
by Myrna Martin
(Ring of Fire)
$24.95 each

Five kits are available thus far: *Igneous Rock, Sedimentary Rock, Metamorphic Rock, Mineral,* and *Rock and Mineral ID*. I received for review the first and last kits. The first seems great for even young children while the last seems targeted at older students. Kits are similar in format with a book and plastic case with rocks and/or minerals, and a pocket microscope. The fifth kit includes a magnet, small vinegar bottle, and a few other identification tools. A review of the *Igneous Rock* kit follows. I would start here, then continue with other kits if this style of learning works well for your children. According to the author, the first three kits "cover the rock cycle"—all the more reason for using them in order. The intensive vocabulary of the book that comes with the *Rock and Mineral ID* kit might be overwhelming for young students. Parents might use it as a reference tool, but I would suggest waiting till the teen years so students can try to make their own identifications using the book.

Igneous Rock kit: Pursue a minor unit study on rocks and minerals with this kit which includes a plastic case with rock samples (including ash from Mt. St. Helens) and 20x magnifier plus a comb-bound book. Activities range from those simple enough for five-year olds to those suitable for students in the upper elementary grades. Most activities have to do with visual identifications and comparisons. Using identification guidelines students can also perform scratch/hardness tests, and they estimate specific gravity of the different rocks through experimentation. Pre- and post-tests are included as well as an answer key. Children do some written work, recording observations and analyses. This is a fun, low-pressure way to introduce children to informally-applied scientific method as well as a hands-on entry-level study of rocks and minerals. (Note: there are no mentions of evolution.)

Science and the Bible, 30 Scientific Demonstrations Illustrating Scriptural Truths, volumes 1 and 2
by Donald B. DeYoung
(Baker Book House)
$8.99 each

Science activities are used to illustrate Bible truths in both of these books, so the primary reason to use it will be to learn Bible knowledge and application. See the review under Bible resources.

Science for Every Kid series
by Janice VanCleave
(John Wiley and Sons, Inc.)
$29.95 hc; $12.95 pb each

Physics for Every Kid was the book from the series I actually reviewed. The subtitle for this book is "101 Easy Experiments in Motion, Heat, Light, Machines, and Sound." Experiments range from extremely easy to slightly involved, but none require fancy equipment. The most complicated activities are things like building a wheel and axle contraption out of pencils, a spool, and string. They are designed for children ages 8 to 12 and have been child-tested. Each experiment lists the purpose, materials needed, step-by-step instructions, results (what should happen if all goes well), and an explanation. Everything is very straightforward and easy to understand, but it lacks the "wonder quotient" we find in books such as *The Backyard Scientist* which prompt kids with "wondering why" questions before they begin. The value of this book is in its organization. We can easily select experiments to go along with whatever topic we are studying because they are divided into categories: electricity, magnets, buoyancy, gravity, balance, flight, simple machines, inertia, motion, light, heat, and sound. Unlike most experiment books for children, it has an index, which also helps identify experiments for particular concepts. Other science titles in the "For Every Kid" series are *Astronomy, Biology, Chemistry, Dinosaurs, Earth Science, The Human Body,* and *Oceans*.(S)

Science Wizardry for Kids
by Margaret Kenda and Phyllis Williams
(Barrons)
$14.95

This book, recommended for children in grades 1-8, features more than 200 experiments in chemistry, physics, astronomy, ecology, biology, weather, and earth science.(S)

Sciencewise, Books 1, 2, and 3
by Dennis Holley
(Critical Thinking Books & Software)
$23.95 each

These activity books make terrific supplements used independently of any text, but the individual activities will be even more useful if you can use them as "hooks" to lead your children into study of particular topics. Each book features 36 "Dynamo Demos" which are demos set up by the teacher. Students are presented with questions or challenges in regard to each "Demo." Reproducible worksheets allow them to write out predictions and conclusions before, during, and after each activity. Each activity has a "For the Teacher" page which lists the objective, materials needed (mostly simple, inexpensive materials), setup instructions, safety concerns (when appropriate), outcomes and explanations, and an application example. For example, in one activity the teacher floats some peanuts on the surface of water. Students are challenged to figure out how to sink a peanut without touching it. An inverted cup can be used to sink the peanut which leads to a discussion on air compression, buoyancy, and early diving chambers that worked by this principle. Book 1 is suggested for grades 4-6 and Book 2 for grades 6-8, although most of the activities will easily stretch to include younger and older students. In addition to the "Dynamo Demos" there are 18 "Creative Challenges" designed for independent student work. Students are given an instruction sheet (reproduced from the book) and one or more items with which to work. For example, a banana and 2 rubber bands are the provided components for a student constructed "bananamobile." They can add whatever elements the teacher allows to create a bananamobile that will travel farther than those of other students. Designed for the classroom, most activities will work fine in home schools, especially if you involve more than one child.

The author stresses science as exploration and experimentation rather than the memorization of facts, saying in the introduction, "What we regard as facts are at best momentary illusions seen through a veil of ignorance." This relativistic, postmodernist viewpoint rejects absolute truth, usually not just in science, but in all areas. So watch that your study of science does not inculcate this same worldview with too much emphasis on individual discovery and not enough on study of factual information.(S)

Simple and Fun Science

(Essential Learning Products)
$5.99 each

There are six 128-page books in this series, designated as books A-F. Each might be used with a span of at least two or three grade levels, so they need not be used strictly for grades 1-6. These are a little larger than other ELP books, but still small enough in size to be unintimidating. They feature a mix of information, activity, and thinking skills covering topics such as biology, chemistry, physics, ecology, health and nutrition, electricity, weather, water, oceans, and geology in each book. None of these books are intended to be a complete science curriculum, but at the younger grade levels, using a few of these along with real books on specific science topics might constitute your science course. You might, for most grade levels, think of them as a combination science and thinking skills supplement. Some activities are paper and pencil, writing or drawing, but others are simple experiments that can easily be done at home without special equipment. Books definitely progress in difficulty from level to level. Evolutionary assumptions (primarily dating issues) appear very infrequently. Hot ecological issues, such as the greenhouse effect and acid rain, are addressed without acknowledging controversy over scien-

tific evidence, a problem we encounter in most science resources these days. Overall, these books are well-balanced and interesting, and they offer a useful variety of activities to supplement your basic curriculum.(SE)

Small Wonders: Hands-on Science Activities for Young Children

by Peggy K. Perdue
(Good Year Books)
$8.95

If you like to organize learning activities for young children, this book will give you some great ideas. There's nothing too complicated here. Each of the twenty-nine experiments or activities is done with easy to find, inexpensive objects. For example, sugar cubes, food coloring, and hot and cold water are used to find out whether hot or cold water will help sugar dissolve more quickly. Learn about topics like floating and sinking, inclined planes, popping corn, and colors and shapes of bubbles. The author includes good observation and thinking questions and comments for teachers to use. Those of you "into" creative movement will appreciate correlations of science activities with creative movement activities (e.g., acting like sugar molecules in cold water, then hot water). Extension activities at the end of each lesson give you more ideas if you want to challenge a curious child.

Usborne Books

(Educational Development Corporation)

I've selected only a few of the science-related titles and series to highlight here. The Usborne books present science topics in beautifully-illustrated formats that just beg to be looked at. The information is also good for the most part with the exception of evolutionary ideas. These books are so appealing that they can be given as gifts. Most children will not realize they are educational.(SE)

The Usborne Science Encyclopedia

$14.95 pb; $22.95 hc

Suggested for ages 8 to 12, this 128-page encyclopedia uses numerous illustrations and limited text to cover selected topics. Topics are arranged according to themes. Not limited to information, articles also include experiments for children to try.

Finding Out About series

$4.50 - $4.95 each; combined books - $12.95 each

Recommended for ages 7 to 9, this series is an introduction to many science topics, appropriate for the early to mid-elementary grades. Among titles in the series are *Deserts; Jungles; Where Food Comes From; How Things Are Built; How Things Are Made; Things That Float; Things That Fly; Our Earth, Sun, Moon, and Planets; Rockets and Spaceflight; Things At Home;* and *Things Outdoors.* Four different combined books—*Everyday Things, Wild Places, Living Long Ago,* and *Wings, Wheels and Water*—each contain three books, although some of the content in combined books is not available in single book form. Illustrations combine with short paragraphs of information, so that children are not overwhelmed. These books include snippets of very specific, intriguing detail to pique children's interest.

Mysteries and Marvels of Nature series
$6.95 each pb; $14.95 hc (not all titles available); $24.95 for combined book

Six titles comprise this nature series: *Ocean Life, Reptile World, Plant Life, Bird Life, Insect Life*, and *Animal World*. The combined book includes all six titles. The individual titles are each 32 pages in length. These books are quite fascinating. They provide some basic information, but they also bring in intriguing and weird aspects of nature that are enthralling to children.

Usborne Famous Lives series
$8.95 pb; $16.95 hc; combined edition - $19.95 pb; $27.95 hc

There are five books in this series, two of which come under science: *Inventors* and *Scientists*. Recommended for ages ten and up, they follow an historical progression. A little biographical information is intermixed with each story of invention or discovery. I particularly like these books because scientific ideas and their progression are much easier to follow when that is the only topic—unlike history books where we usually encounter tidbits on scientific advances thrown in from time to time as if such advances were spontaneously generated. There are plenty of the full-color illustrations for which Usborne is famous. The text in this book flows in regular columns with only occasional, brief picture descriptions and a few sidebars to interrupt the flow. That makes this a better reading book than many other Usborne books that are great for browsing and skipping around.

You will have to deal with evolutionary assumptions. In *Scientists,* the attitude is that scientists were struggling to make sense of things until they finally figured out the process of evolution. Now everything makes sense. You will encounter this at the end of the classification section, then through "The age of the earth" and "Evolution"—five pages. I suggest using this section for your own expanded lesson on critical thinking as well as upon the requirement of replication to prove scientific theories.

If you are also interested in one or more of the other titles in this series—*Explorers, Kings and Queens*, and *Famous Women*—the combined volume titled *Famous Lives*, which includes all five books, is a great buy.(SE)

Usborne Science for Beginners series
$6.95 each pb

Three titles comprise this series recommended for ages 8 and up: *Understanding Your Brain, Understanding Your Muscles and Bones*, and *Understanding Your Senses*. I reviewed only the first title. Children can read through this book on their own, skipping around rather than reading in

order if they please. Mostly cartoon illustrations help children to visualize how the brain functions without "gross" pictures. For example, eleven small cartoons are shown with the larger brain to illustrate the varied brain functions. Comic strip illustrations also help to explain some concepts. A few quizzes, puzzles, and "try this" activities are for fun rather than grading. There are a few subtle problems you might want to address such as the explanation that "...a complicated feeling such as jealousy is a series of electrical and chemical changes." which implies that we are not accountable for or in control of our feelings. I was pleased to see that the book debunks the "science" of phrenology, popular a century ago, which taught that you could determine people's characteristics and talents by measuring and analyzing the shape of their skulls. (Most people have never heard of phrenology, but it was the rationalization for much racism.)

Weather and the Bible, 100 Questions & Answers
by Donald B. DeYoung
(Baker Book House)
$8.99

Similar in concept to DeYoung's excellent book, *Astronomy and the Bible*, this one seems to wander some and is not as compelling as the first book. Also, it repeats some of the same information found in *Astronomy and the Bible*. It is divided into five sections: weather basics; water, wind, and clouds; stormy weather; past weather; and future weather. While some information is presented at a level appropriate for upper elementary and junior high students, much of it is best for high school level.[Valerie Thorpe/C.D.]

Who Says You Can't Teach Science?
(Good Year)
$9.95

This book was written for teachers (and parents) who have to teach science in spite of their lack of background knowledge. This is an activity-based approach to many different science topics for K-6th grades. It is written without scientific jargon in a style designed to encourage the teacher. Ideas are easy, fun, and thought provoking.(S)

Women Scientists and Inventors: A Science Puzzle Book
by Jacquelyn A. Greenblatt
(Good Year Book)
$9.95

The purpose of this book is to encourage young girls with the message that science is not just a "guy thing." It conveys the message through sketches about women scientists, their discoveries, and their work. Women were "...selected on the basis of the creativity and conceptual innovation of their work." A puzzle follows each sketch. Puzzles are a variety of word and letter games such as crosswords and codes. Suggested for grades 4-8.(S)

The Wonder of God's World - Water

by Bonita Searle-Barnes
(Lion Publishing)
$6.99

Hands-on learners should appreciate this approach to the study of water. This hard cover book uses colorful photos and illustrations, including cartoon-like figures, to provide information and experiments about oceans, clouds, rain, snow, water power, frost, ice, surface tension, floating, and sinking. Experiments feature step-by-step instructions accompanied by pictures. Generally, the experiments raise questions which children will be able to answer from their observations, although, occasionally, the illustration reveals the outcome in advance. Since this book comes from a Christian publisher it is no surprise to find paraphrased Scripture scattered here and there, but the overall Christian content is rather general and low key. At only 32-pages, the presentation of each topic is brief and introductory, appropriate for children from about kindergarten to third-grade level.[Valerie Thorpe/C.D.]

Animals, Birds, Insects, and Other Creatures

Backyard Scientist: Exploring Earthworms with Me

(Backyard Scientist)
$8.95

Exploring Earthworms is a kinder, gentler approach to studying these creatures than most of us ever encountered in school. We use live earthworms, which we learn how to locate or purchase if necessary. We carefully handle them and return them to their natural habitats when we are through experimenting. None are killed (except accidentally) or cut up. We learn by observation through experiments with soil, food sources, light, moisture, and other environmental variables. This is a naturalist rather than anatomical approach. Experiments are suggested for ages 4 to 12, and they vary in complexity to suit learners across that age span. Some simple, single-session experiments will suit younger children, while multi-week experiments and data recording are better for older learners. We need to collect various types of soil, screen material, containers, and other equipment as well as the earthworms. None of these items should be very difficult to locate, although we do need to plan ahead.

The Bird Book and The Bird Feeder

(Workman Publishing)
$12.95

This clear plastic bird feeder can hang from a tree, sit on a balcony or platform, or attach to a window, so even children who lack yard space can set up their bird feeder/observation station. The companion book tells how to identify and attract 24 birds that are common in North America. Instructions on types of food and habits help us lure birds likely to be in our area so we can become acquainted with them. This is a simple way to begin studying birds, although children who become interested will need more detailed information such as that found in a Peterson or Audobon field guide.

The Bug Book and The Bug Bottle

(Workman Publishing)
$9.95

It is certainly easier to learn about bugs when we have live models to observe. The bug bottle is an oval plastic case with a perforated plastic lid which can serve as the bug home for our subjects. The companion guide offers notes about 24 common North American bugs with descriptions and illustrations. Guidelines for catching and caring for creatures are included. Since this is basically an introduction to "Bugs," it is best for younger children up through middle elementary grades.(SE)

Character Sketches

(Advanced Training Institute International) $39 each or $105 for the set [three independent volumes]

Character traits are illustrated by animal stories, followed by biological studies, then by Bible studies explaining particular character traits represented by the animals. These are written on an adult level but work well for reading together. For young children, pick and choose from the biological information according to interests and attention spans. A unique feature children especially enjoy is the question posed at the beginning of each chapter and each Bible story. The questions provide clues that readers use to see if they can identify the answers before they are given in the book. We began using these with our children when they were 8, 6, and 3. Our three-year-old was too young, but the others understood and learned more than I thought possible. Coloring books corresponding to these volumes are also available.

Ranger Rick Magazine

(National Wildlife Federation)
$17 for 12 monthly issues

This magazine features lots of animals and is written for children in the elementary grades. The purpose of *Ranger Rick* is to help children better understand the natural world in a creative and entertaining way.(SE)

Young Inventors at Work! Learning Science by Doing Science
by Ed Sobey
(Good Year Books)
$ 13.95

Do you have active, inventive kids who would enjoy designing structures with spaghetti or launching ping pong balls with rubber bands? This program, developed for use as an after-school informal science program for grades 4 through 8, uses simple, easily-obtained materials for activities designed to get kids to experience scientific concepts in an enjoyable way. Each lesson is laid out for you and includes an opening activity to use while kids are arriving, a demonstration, a reading about an inventor, instructions about the activity for the day, suggested reference books, and closing ideas. Contains 24 activities.(S)[V. Thorpe]

Zoobooks
(Wildlife Education, Ltd.)
softcover - $2.95 each; hardcover - $13.95 each. Write for prices and details on sets and teaching guides.

Do your children love the full-color pictures of animals they see in *National Geographic, Ranger Rick*, and other "wildlife" magazines and books? If so, they will love the *Zoobooks*. These are 58 different, twenty-page books that are most economical when purchased in softcover editions. Each one is dedicated to an animal, bird, or reptile, or else to a limited group such as insects, dolphins/porpoises, or birds of prey. Representative titles are *Apes, Baby Animals, Camels, Eagles, Endangered Animals, Hummingbirds, Rattlesnakes, Spiders*, and *Tigers*. Books are heavily illustrated with beautiful photos and drawings. There is not a lot of text, but what there is interestingly written, informative, and appealing to all ages. Each of the books I reviewed features at least two pages on the structure and function of the animal (interesting science lessons here), but like the Usborne books, it breaks the information down into bite-size chunks. Children can read all or part as they prefer. Other topics vary from book to book, but typical are sections on the birth of their young, feeding habits, and where and how they live. Evolutionary assumptions crop up here and there, usually in the form of "70 million years ago....," but there seem to be far fewer of these than we typically find in other such resources. The *Dinosaurs* book is likely to be the most troublesome. *Zoobooks* puts out a separate, ten-book set called *Prehistoric Zoobooks*, which also poses problems. Books are available individually or as grouped sets.

They have also created Teaching Guides/Units on a number of topics such as "Endangered Animals" and "Ocean Ecosystems" which can be used with the related Zoobook to create unit studies. These are described on their web site.

The Human Body and Health Education

These areas of study so often cover the same material in the elementary grades that it makes sense to list them all together, so that is what I've done in this section.

Secular health texts are usually either objectionable or a waste of time for home schoolers. We should be training our children to care for their bodies with good health habits, good nutrition, and proper exercise without a health curriculum directing us. If we do in-depth study of the human body, we will very naturally learn about some good health habits as we learn how the human body functions and the problems we encounter when we mistreat it. While I'm not excited about health textbooks, as you can tell, texts from Christian publishers and other resources can point out topics we might wish to cover and help us focus on particular areas. I've reviewed some health textbooks here, but A Beka's are reviewed under the various sections on textbooks for each grade level since their health texts are intended to be companion texts to their science texts for each grade.

The safety aspects of health education deserves some attention, although there are few resources that I have found worth recommending in that area. Brite Music offers a cassette tape with activity book on personal safety [$10.95 each]; they also have a companion song book [$7.95] and a dialog book with cassette [$10.95]. You should check both Christian and secular bookstores for other books and resources that appeal to you.

A Beka Book Health texts

See the Health Textbooks from A Beka Book listed under textbook recommendations below. They are listed there since they are designed to complete the science curriculum when used in conjunction with the A Beka Book science texts.

Blood and Guts
(Brown Paper School Books) $12.95

This book has great activities for studying the human body. It covers basic information on the body systems with activities integrated throughout each section. Active learners will love this approach. Watch out for evolution—you will need to skip some introductory sections such as those on the brain. It is appropriate for about third grade and above.(SE)

The Bones Book and Skeleton
(Workman Publishing)
$16.95

Children construct a movable skeleton as they read about how bones grow, make blood, protect vital body parts, and help us move. The plastic skeleton has 21 pieces (obviously simplified) and comes with a clear plastic display case.

Suggestions for projects and experiments are included.(SE)

Gray's Anatomy [from the Start Exploring series]
by Fred Stark
(Running Press)
$8.95

The Start Exploring Series books are each a combination of text and blackline coloring book. This *Gray's Anatomy* is not the original "Bible of Anatomy" used in medical circles, but selected drawings and text (128 pages) suitable for upper elementary grades through high school.(S)

Health Quest
(Alpha Omega)
$33.50

Health Quest presents a Christian health program recommended for students in grades 4-7, although I would think most fourth graders too young for this course. This is a LifePac course with five student LifePacs and a Teacher's Guide. Topics covered are physical health, mental health, nutrition, injury and disease, and stewardship of both the environment and our bodies. The material is definitely elementary level, not anywhere near the comprehensive coverage of a high school course. Christian perspective throughout the course lends a moral tone to the entire study. Content is uneven in quality with some sections interestingly written and others less so. Questions present some of the same problems encountered in other LifePacs: students are expected to answer with words used in the text sections, although other answers that a thoughtful student might come up with would also be true. Use discretion on marking incorrect answers. Scripture from the NKJV is used throughout the course. The Teacher's Guide contains alternate pages using the KJV version for those who prefer that version. In addition, the Teacher's Guide contains course management instructions, alternate tests, and keys to all exercises and tests.

The course also comes with a large poster and gold stickers that are to be put on the poster as students complete various sections.

Healthy Living [Levels K-6]
(Christian Schools International)
$17.50; teacher guide - $52.50

Public schools have created a diverse social agenda they now teach under "health." It includes the traditional topics of growth and development, nutrition, personal health, disease prevention, safety, and first aid. In addition we now find drug education, emotional/mental health, AIDS/HIV education, family issues (death and dying), human sexuality (beyond the basics at increasingly younger levels), decision making, social issues, and more. I personally believe that the family is the appropriate arena for discussing many of these topics.

However, many Christians disagree, and the *Healthy Living* series is an example of how Christian publishers adopt the public school system's goals. I have to say their treatment of these topics is definitely from a Christian viewpoint, and, of course, we are free to skip sections we feel are inappropriate.

With that preface, I know that some home educators are looking for a complete Christian health curriculum, and this is one of the most complete available if you want coverage of all of the aforementioned topics.

The curriculum is designed to be taught in the classroom, so lessons are presented by the teacher from the teacher guide and include many classroom activities. The teacher guides are spiral-bound with a hard back cover for ease of handling. They list preparation, needed materials, objectives, step-by-step lesson plans, and related activity ideas. Full-color, illustrated, student books for grades 3-6 serve as texts for student reading. Discussion questions are included at the end of each small section of information. Reproducible blackline masters at the back of the teacher guide are also used for various lessons. Many illustrations (picture and text) as well as directed discussions assume children are in a traditional classroom which is a handicap for home educators. The student books for grades 3-6 can be used on their own, but we will be missing full development of the lessons and some helpful information found in the teacher guide.

The Human Body
(Instructional Fair)
$10.95 (order #IF8754)

The Human Body is a reproducible book of work sheets suggested for grades 5-8 but also useful for a low-level high school course. It serves as a supplement for studying the human body that helps reinforce learning through coloring, labeling, puzzles, and other activities. Most of the work sheets involve identification, but some also deal with function and purpose. Drawings are detailed, yet not cluttered, since they do not include everything we would find in books for older levels. There are 100 different work sheet activities, and an answer key is in the back of the book.(S)

The Human Body
(Larouse Kingfisher Chambers, Inc.)
$6.95 each pb; $13.90 each hb

This book is from the *Young Discoverers* series of 16 books, written for ages 6 though 9. The series is divided into four areas (4 books per area): biology, environment, geography, and physics. These 32-page books feature full-color illustrations, large-print "text," numerous sidebars of information, and experiments and activities.

The Human Body primarily focuses on body systems, presenting information in a very age-appropriate fashion. For example, body systems are drawn in fairly accurate, but not complete, detail. Labels show the correct terminology, but only for major parts of body systems, not all the details. It also covers teeth, diet, inheritance, growth, and fitness. This should serve as a first introduction to these topics for children. Take time to try the suggested activities such as checking reflexes and determining lung capacity since these will provide very personal connections to the subject matter.(S)

Human Body Felt Set

(Betty Lukens and Little Folk Visuals)
economy set - $19.95

Beautiful, life-size, full-color felt pieces for all the body organs and systems come with the pamphlet called *My Body Temple*, which is a teacher's manual with instructions on how to use the set. It also has short readings for children on topics such as air and breathing, diet, cleanliness, and posture. (Note: Betty Lukens includes the "Basic Food Groups" in this package at no additional cost.)

Life Before Birth

by Gary E. Parker
(Master Books)
$12.95

Skipping the sensitive fertilization stage, this book begins with the fertilized egg, then traces the development of the baby through birth. Colorful, appealing illustrations provide visual explanations along with the text which is primarily in a conversation format. Scientific aspects of development are explained extremely well for children at elementary levels—solid science, but not too complicated. The baby is described throughout as God's special creation, and the pro-life message is emphasized at the end of the book in a discussion about children born with defects. Parker goes one step further to include some explanations about aspects of development that are often construed by evolutionists as evidence for evolution. The only negative about this book is that it is a little difficult to read aloud a book that is written as a conversation between three or more people. My suggestion to turn this negative into a positive is to get the whole family, including dad, involved in the reading.

My Body

(Teacher Created Materials)
$7.95

Make a life-size tracing of your child's body outline, then learn about various body parts by coloring, cutting, and pasting them onto the outline. This is a fun way to learn about the body for children in grades 1-4. The catalog number is TCM211 which you might need to differentiate it from a similarly titled TCM book.(S)

Schick Anatomy Atlas

(American Map Corporation)
$29.95

Although written for adults, children will find this a fascinating book to explore. It has 30, full-color anatomy charts with transparent identifying overlays, similar to those we see in college level physiology textbooks. Children can see how the body systems truly fit together. It will be extremely useful for high school biology.(S)

The Science of Health and Nutrition Curriculum

by Helen Schweikert Ph.D., CCN
(Outreach Nutrition Education Services)
$69

This nutrition education program was written for pre-kindergarten through sixth grade, but might be adapted fairly easily for use with older students so that the entire family studies together and applies what they learn. Rather than relying on the concept of "four basic food groups" or the "food pyramid" this program stresses the basic nutrients needed for good health, in which foods they are found, and how they interact in the body. Dr. Schweikert draws on Biblical reasons for maintaining good health and upon the latest research which shows that much of our food is lacking in nutrients or is tainted by chemicals or other harmful processes as it is converted from its natural state. She recommends as natural a diet as possible, the judicious use of vitamins and supplements, and avoidance of junk food. Lessons are divided by units on topics such as "Nutrient Food Groups," "Proteins," and "Essential Fatty Acids." Within each unit are Lesson Guides (detailed lesson plans) and Teacher/Parent Overviews which we should read through for background information on the unit. Following these are projects and worksheets for both upper grades and lower grades which we photocopy for our students as needed. This program is the only comprehensive, Christian nutrition course I have seen that seriously challenges the typical American diet with solid scientific information and offers practical solutions. It even includes recipes, and resource addresses at the end. You can use the course daily over a semester or longer, depending upon how many of the activities you use, or you can use it less frequently over a longer time span.

Total Health: Talking About Life's Changes

by Susan Boe
(RiversEdge Publishing Co.)
$22.95 pb or $28.95 hc, teacher's edition - $36.95, test and quiz book - $15.50, *The Parent Connection* - $12.50

Total Health's high school program was the first health curriculum written specifically for Christian day schools and home schoolers. *Talking About Life's Changes* is the program they have developed for middle school. Both books are definitely written from a Christian perspective. The emphasis on spiritual motivation based on our relationship with God plays a major role. *Talking About Life's Changes* is divided into four large units on physical, mental, social, and spiritual health.

The student book is 336 pages long. Although there is a teacher's edition, you shouldn't need it. (The teacher's edition features chapter outlines, suggested course plans, vocabulary exercises, worksheets, transparency masters, activity suggestions, and discussion questions.)

The Parent Connection correlates with topics covered in the text, supplying background information, discussion topics, problems to watch for (e.g., depression, eating disorders), and suggestions for dealing with "touchy" topics like contraception and masturbation. This book is for parents only!

Talking About Life's Changes covers topics addressed in other texts, although the amount of time devoted to many of them is very different. Positive health and nutrition issues as well as the changes young teens undergo receive far more attention than do the negative issues (drugs, sexually-transmitted diseases, etc.). Also, while other texts address physical, mental, and social health, *Total Health* adds a section on spiritual health.

The layout makes this course very easy to use. Chapter reviews focus on both comprehension and application, providing natural opportunities to expand on topics of special interest.

A student workbook should be available soon, and there is a Test and Quiz Master Book that includes its own answer keys plus keys to chapter reviews.

The Visual Dictionary of the Human Body
(DK Publishing)
$18.95

This stunning, oversized book in the Eyewitness series is filled with exceptionally clear and beautiful illustrations, models and photos that cover the human body and its systems in enough detail to be a useful reference for high school biology students. (Note: the nervous and circulatory systems are shown superimposed on a photo of a nude woman.) This book is great for all ages, but illustrations are realistic and might be overwhelming for some children.(S)[V. T.]

Watch Me Grow: Fun Ways to Learn about Cells, Bones, Muscles, and Joints
by Michelle O'Brien-Palmer
(Chicago Review Press)
$12.95

Suggested for children ages 5 to 9, this is an excellent book for introducing anatomy and physiology. It combines information, data recording, graphing, and hands-on activity in a very balanced fashion. Younger children might do more of the activities and less of the written work than older children, but there's plenty here to involve a wide age span of children. Interestingly, the book starts with children observing and charting plant growth as a lead-in to observations about their own bodies. Many of the best time-tested activities are included: e.g., making cells out of colored dough, chicken bone in vinegar, and making full-size outlines of children's bodies. These and other activities require simple resources, almost all of which can be found around the house. In addition, there are some reproducible, cut-and-paste activity pages plus trivia and bingo match-up type games. This is a particularly good way to introduce children to graphing and other forms of recording and displaying data.(S)

The Weaver's 3-D Body Book
(The Weaver)
$5

This is similar to *My Body* but more complicated and more visually accurate. We make the body out of cardboard covered with pantyhose. Three-dimensional fabric organs (which we make) go inside this "skin." It takes a lot of work (about seven hours according to the publisher), but the great results are worth it. Students also learn sewing skills if Mom will let them do part of the work.

Plants

Backyard Explorer Kit
(Workman Publishing)
$11.95

This kit includes an illustrated, 64-page leaf and tree guide with a 28-page leaf collecting album. Major leaf and needle shapes are described along with common trees. Children learn about the life cycle of trees and how to press and mount leaves they collect from their tree observations. Related activity suggestions are included. Recommended for children ages 5-10 who are just beginning their study of trees.

Botany Unit Study
by Kym Wright
(alWright! Publishing)
$21.95; extra lab sheets - $5; extra flash cards - $5

Students in upper elementary grades through high school can participate in this thoroughly developed unit study. Since it is quite extensive, you will need to plan on one or two semesters to complete it, depending upon the depth of study.

The *Botany Unit Study* is presented in seven sections. The first section covers 13 key topics with suggested readings, research activities, questions to answer, experiments, websites, microscope activities, and further research suggestions. These are quite detailed, providing a "road map" for tackling each topic. If we use every question and activity provided, the result will be a very comprehensive course. The structuring of questions and activities sets this up as primarily a "discovery" approach to learning.

You will need to use additional books for reference, research, and experiments. *Janice Van Cleave's Plants: Mind-Boggling Experiments You Can Turn Into Science Fair Projects* is used for most of the experiments/activities, so you will need to borrow or buy these books to have on hand throughout the course. Additional reference books might be selected from a list in the appendix.

The appendix is next with lengthy vocabulary, supply, source, and book lists. Lesson plan pages make record keeping and planning simple, although a blank lesson plan page allows you to create your own plans. 23 lab sheets correspond with activities either described in the first section or in one of the two required reference books. Practice/review pages and the flashcards help students master essential concepts such as flower parts, leaf shapes, and root types. The lesson plan, lab sheet, and practice/review pages are reproducible, and we can purchase extra sets of the lab sheets and flash cards.

The entire study focuses heavily on learning-by-doing. It will require preparation and presentation time. There is little written work required, although students should complete at least one research report. Students compile a notebook as they work through the study, including their lab sheets, collected specimens, drawings, vocabulary definitions (if required), and other pertinent work. Microscope work is optional.

Since there are no botany texts written for elementary and high school students, until now those of us who wanted to study botany had to create our own courses from the ground up. This unit study solves that problem and does a great job of structuring a botany course that is both enjoyable and educational.

The Garden Book
(Workman Publishing)
$11.95

For those of us who have never sprouted a seed, the idea of nurturing a green thumb in our children is overwhelming. Even though sprouting seeds and growing plants is not very difficult, beginners will appreciate this kit that includes a miniature greenhouse (very small), beginners instruction book, two seed packets, and two peat pellets. Children get to observe and eat some of the fruit of their labor. Recommended for ages 5-10 but only for those with no plant growing experience.

Let's Go Gardening: A Young Person's Guide to the Garden
by Ursula Kruger
(Parkwest Publications)
$16.95

Ideal for children in the middle to upper elementary grades, this book can still be used as the foundation for a "whole-family" unit study on gardening. Plentiful, full-color illustrations are especially appealing to children, and the text is written

directly to children, although parents will probably want to read it aloud with most of them. Solid science combines with practical how-tos for children to actually grow their own plants on windowsills and balconies or in ponds and gardens. This isn't just elementary gardening, but it gets into companion planting, organic solutions for getting rid of bugs, and encouraging helpful garden creatures such as birds and ladybugs. Kruger has done an excellent job of creating this appealing book that teaches both parents and children.

Tree, from the Eyewitness Books series
(Random House/Knopf)
$19

This is one of the best resources for older children (ages 9-10 and older) about trees. Illustrations are beautiful photographs and drawings. The content is detailed, yet not overwhelming. This is a much more comprehensive and useful book than the Usborne books and others that I have seen in the library.(S)

Usborne First Nature: Trees and Usborne First Nature: Flowers
(Educational Development Corporation)
$4.50 each

These titles from the "First Nature" series are written on an introductory level for children age six and older. Drawings are colorful and text is kept relatively short and simple.(S)

The Young Naturalist
(Educational Development Corporation)
$6.95

Introduce children to nature studies with this "user-friendly" Usborne book. This is more of a how-to book than just a nature information book. It directs children in a wide variety of nature study activities. They learn techniques of scientific observation that will help in all science studies.(SE)

Creation Science

Creation Science: A Study Guide to Creation!
by Felice Gerwitz and Jill Whitlock
(Media Angels Science)
$16.95

This is one of a series of unit study guides from Media Angels, a team of two authors, teacher Felice Gerwitz and geologist Jill Whitlock, both of whom are also home schooling moms. The companion volumes are *Creation Anatomy, Creation Astronomy,* and *Creation Geology* [$18.95 each]. Each study should take about six to eight weeks to complete. The guides are set up for multi-grade teaching with activities divided into levels for K-3, 4-8, and 9-12. Activities for each level are further divided under the headings of Reading List,

Vocabulary/Spelling List, Vocabulary/Spelling/Grammar Ideas, Language Arts Ideas, Math Reinforcements, Science Activities and Experiments, Geography/History Ideas, and Art/Music Ideas. Science receives the most attention, with a good deal of background information for the teacher included in a "Teaching Outline" section in each book. (Read through this section in each book before you begin to teach the unit.) Lots of extras are included: bibliography of videos, books, and computer resources; materials list; field trip guide; science experiment copy pages; and reproducible activity pages. Coverage of subjects other than science is spotty, so you will probably want to add other resources to ensure sufficient attention to the other subject areas, or else consider the activities in these studies as supplements to your core curriculum. Activity instructions are fairly well spelled out; they are not just a list or outline of suggestions. The suggested reading list includes titles that are referenced within some of the activities. (Suggested books include titles from both secular and Christian sources.) You will need to plan ahead to determine which activities to do and what resources you will need. All studies are presented from the young-earth perspective and rely on a literal interpretation of the Bible.

A separate *Geology and Creation Science Hands-On Experiment and Activity Pack* [$12.95] features reproducible pages of activities and experiments with step-by-step instructions, questions, games, puzzles, a glossary, and more. It serves as a companion to both the main book and the *Geology* book. Experiments are most appropriate for the elementary grades up through junior high since they do not require any mathematical analysis.

Dinosaurs and The Bible

by Dave Unfred
(Vital Issues Press/Huntington House Publishers)
$14.99; book with teacher's guide - $15.99

This full-color, hardback book presents scientific information about dinosaurs in a very readable format for children ages 8-13. It considers questions about the fate of dinosaurs, including the possibility that some might still exist. The author compares what we think we know about dinosaurs with Scripture, showing that as scientists learn more about them, there is more evidence for Scriptural truth. There's also a teacher's guide for this book.

Discovery: a Monthly Paper of Bible and Science for Kids

(Apologetics Press)
$12 per year

High quality and low price make each of these eight-page resources great science supplements for children. Monthly issues are printed in full-color on quality paper with large, easy-to-read print. Typically, there are arti-

cles on creation science (fossils and dinosaurs), Bible animals, the Bible and history, the human body, nature, and scientists, plus two pages of questions and puzzles. Some earlier editions are available as bound volumes (one-year's worth in each), so if you like *Discovery*, check for those back issues. The reading level and puzzle page are written for about fourth grade level and up, but younger children will enjoy having the paper read to them. (Bulk and/or club subscriptions bring the cost per paper even lower, so see about ordering as a group. 10% discount off all prices for home schoolers.)

History Links, Creation Unit

by Jennifer Alles and Barbara Little
(Wooly Lamb Publishing)
$15

See the review of *History Links* under "Published Unit Studies" in Chapter Five. The *Creation Unit* explores the evolution/creation debate from a Catholic perspective. All the while, carefully explaining that the Church has yet to make a final declaration on the subject, the authors point out the clear theological teaching of the Church in regard to evolution. The authors do not try to hide their bias in favor of creation rather than evolution. They use a selection of resources that are frequently used by Protestant creation proponents such as *Unlocking the Mysteries of Creation*. This unit offers a terrific mix of activities to address all age levels.

The Great Dinosaur Mystery and The Bible

(Chariot Victor Publishing)
$14.99

This is an excellent book about what creation scientists think happened to dinosaurs.

It Couldn't Just Happen

by Lawrence Richards
(Thomas Nelson/Word)
$14.99

The "It" of the title is evolution. Richards tackles the creation/evolution debate, addressing theories about the origin of the universe and life, the fossil record, dinosaurs, missing links, and other hot topics. He mixes stories, illustrations, and science facts to shatter evolutionary teaching. We can jump around in the book, reading about topics most interesting or important to our children at the moment. The last section of the book deals with the Bible as the source of truth, the validity of the Bible, and the Bible's teaching about creation. At the end of each chapter is "Just for Fun"—questions, project ideas, and research assignments.

Full-color illustrations and a lively writing style will hold children's interest far better than science textbooks. This book is ideally suited for homeschooling families with children of all ages.

Master Books

Master Books has a number of titles that are excellent for elementary level. Some recommended titles:

Bombus the Bumblebee is the first of a planned series of books for children ages 3-7. All of these will relate to creationism is some way. In this book, children follow the adventures of Bombus the bumblebee as he explores his world and the special abilities God gave him. [$11.95]

Dinosaurs by Design—the best book for children who want to know about dinosaurs. [$15.95]

Dry Bones and Other Fossils is an excellent introduction to fossils for children of all ages. [$12.95]

God Created Dinosaurs—activity/learning book that includes stickers, coloring, and reading material. [$4.95]

Noah's Ark and the Ararat Adventure— Written in story form, this book relates the biblical story of Noah to recent searches for the ark. Suggested for ages 6 to adult. [$13.95]

What Really Happened to the Dinosaurs answers young children's questions about creation, dinosaurs, and the flood through an adventure story. [$10.95]

Science in the Creation Week

(Noble Books)
$19.95

The creation "outline" from Genesis serves as the foundation for this science curriculum that teaches the physics of light, the chemistry of basic elements, an introduction to astronomy, and the fundamentals of plant and animal biology. This is a multi-level, one-year curriculum suggested for grades 2-5, although I think that it will easily stretch through sixth grade. It is published in a spiral-bound 8 1/2" x 7" format. There are seven units correlating with the biblical days of creation: human senses; light, energy, and matter; water and the atmosphere; land and plants; sun, moon and stars; birds and sealife; and land animals and humans. Within each unit lessons/activities are offered at three levels—explorer, inspector, and researcher—reflecting increasing levels of difficulty in thinking skills. There are from six to seventeen activities within each unit. Students or parents can begin work at whatever level of difficulty they wish. There is more content within this book than we find in typical experiment or activity books or even in some science books for the early grades. (Some topics will be too difficult for younger students and should be saved for later.) However, we still might wish to do further research on some topics using some of the references listed in the back of the book or other sources.

Handy charts in the front of the book designate levels for each activity, skills covered, preparation time, and activity time. Activities use easy-to-find, inexpensive materials, and data recording/activity charts are included within the book.

Unlocking The Mysteries of Creation

by Dennis Petersen
(Creation Resource Foundation)
$22.99; workbook - $19.99

This is an outstanding creation science book for all ages. It incorporates Scripture, science, history, and related information in a nicely-illustrated format. We can pick and choose information to read as we adapt to the ages of our children. This book is great for dads to read aloud in the evening with the family. It is also my personal favorite all-purpose creation science resource. A companion workbook is available. *Unlocking the Mysteries of Creation* is also available as a 12-tape video series [$23/tape or $275 for the series].

The X-Nilo Show: Dinosaurs and the Bible [video]

(American Portrait Films)
$19.95

This high-quality video presentation from the *X-Nilo* series (title comes from the latin "ex nihilo" which means "out of nothing") is intended to promote a biblical world view. It is directed toward children as young as 7, but, ideally, in upper elementary through junior high levels. *Dinosaurs and the Bible* is biblically based, but also addresses scientific issues like fossils, dating, and the flood. It compares and contrasts what the Bible says about dinosaurs with evolutionary viewpoints. It also tackles practical issues such as how all those creatures could have fit on Noah's ark. Designed to entertain as well as to educate, the video features skits, parodies, and running jokes with a variety of "characters" throughout the entire video. Children should really enjoy this 28-minute presentation. The viewpoint is "young earth."

Physics and Chemistry

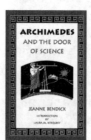

Archimedes and the Door of Science

by Jeanne Bendick
(Bethlehem Books)
$11.95

The story of Archimedes, famous mathematician and scientist, conveys something of the culture of Ancient Greece as well as of this remarkable man and his critical influence. The story is written for children, even when it explains some of Archimedes' scientific and mathematical discoveries. Line drawing illustrations help us visualize many of these concepts. Many anecdotes about Archimedes have come down through history, and the author blends these into her storytelling. The result is a thoroughly enjoyable book that manages to cover a great deal of educational territory.(S)

Bernie Zubrowski books
(HarperCollins)

Bernie Zubrowski has written a series of books designed to teach physics concepts through hands-on learning. Appropriate for third grade and up, the activities in these books stimulate thinking and transmit basic physics principles. These are great fun! Titles in the series: *Balloons, Blinkers and Buzzers, Making Waves, Mirrors, Shadow Play, Soda Science, Tops,* and *Wheels at Work.*

Gravity: Simple Experiments for Young Scientists
(Millbrook Press)
$6.95 pb

What was the experiment that Aristotle never tried? This little book discusses in a simple way some of the views various thinkers have held in the past, and presents a dozen activities that illustrate how gravity works. Not reviewed, but also in the same *Simple Experiments for Young Scientists* series are books on the subjects of water, air and energy. Recommended for grades 2-4.(S)[V. Thorpe]

LEGOS
(LEGO Dacta)
Fischertechnik
(Timberdoodle)

These are both fantastic tools for learning principles of physics. Educational *Technic LEGO* (Sometimes listed as *Simple Machines*) sets come with task cards and guides to learn about pulleys, gear ratios and directions, levers, and much more. Pneumatic and computerized *LEGO* sets are available for older students. New *E-lab* products deal with various forms of energy, using solar panels, capacitors, motors, and other components.

Fischertechnik is more expensive and more ambitious, really getting into robotics and computerization, although they do offer some simpler sets for the less ambitious. Both are excellent investments.(S)

The Junior Boom Academy
(Wild Goose Company)
$11.99

Subtitled, "100 Chemistry Experiments for the Teacher of Anklebiters," this book has a wide variety of chemistry experiments accompanied by cartoon illustrations. About one-third of them can be done using only items you can find around the house. Some of the experiments are the same as those in the Wild Goose kits (described earlier). Wild Goose sells chemicals (in small amounts) and lab supplies so you can select

which experiments you want to do, then purchase the appropriate chemicals. The book is designed for the classroom. Part of the lesson is intended for teacher presentation. Reproducible student pages direct students as they perform experiments and record results. Explanations of results are included. These experiments are, for the most part, more sophisticated than those in other science experiment books reviewed here, so use them with your older students.(S)

The New Way Things Work
by David Macaulay
(Houghton Mifflin Company)
$35

In it's expanded and updated 1998 edition, this book is a guide to the working of machines unlike anything else you have ever seen (unless you are familiar with *Castle, City, Pyramid,* or *Cathedral* also by Macaulay). This book is full of colorful and entertaining drawings, and the text is witty—sometimes silly. Those of us who are intimidated by the technology behind the functioning of a can opener will find that all of that confusing machinery is actually very simple. Macaulay introduces basic mechanical principles, then shows how each principle is applied to different types of machinery. He covers inclined planes, levers, wheels and axles, gears and belts, cams and cranks, pulleys, screws, rotating wheels, springs, friction, floating, flying, pressure, power, exploiting heat, nuclear power, light and images, photography, printing, sound and music, telecommunications, electricity, magnetism, sensors and detectors, computers, and automation. Just think of how many science textbooks you can skip! The book appeals to all ages and removes the intimidation factor from the study of physics. (*The New Way Things Work* is also available on CD-ROM from DK.)(S)

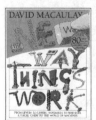

The New Way Things Work [computer program
by David Macaulay
(DK Publishing, Inc.)
$29.95

The CD-ROM *The Way Things Work,* has been made even more fun with this new version with more interactive links and more sound and animation. And of course there is still that silly mammoth demonstrating scientific concepts in his charming prehistoric way. The content has been updated to include digital technology and there is a link to the mammoth.net website. Your child can even print out a mammoth letterhead or a postcard. Recommended for ages 8 and up. This program will run on either Windows or Apple systems.(S)[V. Thorpe]

The Original Backyard Scientist, Backyard Scientist Series 1, and Series 2
(Backyard Scientist)
$8.95 each

These three books contain chemistry and physics experiments we can perform with simple equipment at home. These are highly recommended because questions are presented to stimulate thinking and experiments are simple and really work. Explanations are given at the end of each experiment. See description under General Science materials above.(S)

TOPS Learning System
(TOPS)
$15 each

Individual books (called worksheet modules) titled *Magnetism; Balancing; Electricity; Pendulums; Metric Measuring; More Metrics; Animal Survival; Green Thumbs: Radishes; Green Thumbs: Corn and Beans; The Earth, Moon, and Sun;* and *The Planets and Stars* incorporate math and thinking skills for learning about scientific principles through activities. Activity instructions are simple to understand and easy to do successfully. The *Electricity* book provided the first successful electricity experiments I was able to do with my children after a number of previous attempts with other methods. Equipment needed is minimal and inexpensive. Activity work sheets are reproducible so one book can be used for many children. Lessons can be used with children in grades 3-10.

TOPS also will send their combination catalog/magazine to homeschoolers at no charge. You can read more about the products there, but every issue of the catalog also includes a couple of complete science lessons from the books or their older-level task cards so you can try before buying.

Textbooks and Grade Level Resources

A Beka Book science and health texts
Discovering God's World [Grade 1]
$9.20; teacher edition - $19.45

This full-color text provides some good information, but there is not a lot of material in the student text on its own. The teacher edition provides hands-on activities and other ideas we can use to make a more complete program. It also includes the complete student text, but with answers overprinted in blue. The question and answer aspect of the text at this level is relatively unimportant, and we might choose to purchase only the teacher edition and allow our child to use it as his text. If you choose not to buy the teacher edition, you should supplement the student text with library books or other resources to complete your course. Topics covered are the human body, atmosphere, simple machines, magnets, animals, insects, plants, and seasons.

Enjoying God's World [Grade 2]
$9.20; teacher edition - $19.45

This full-color text is more substantial in content than the first grade book, but the amount of information on any single topic is still sparse. The teacher edition provides hands-on activities and other ideas we can use to make a more complete program. It also includes the complete student text, but with answers overprinted in blue. The question and answer aspect of the text at this level is relatively unimportant, and we might choose to purchase only the teacher edition and allow our child to use it as his text. If you choose not to buy the teacher edition, you should supplement the student text with library books or other resources to complete your course. Topics covered are health, animals, insects, plants, energy, force, friction, atmosphere, weather, the stars and planets, and the earth. While some topics are similar to those in the first grade book, different aspects of those topics are addressed.

Exploring God's World 3
$11.30; teacher's edition - $22.20; answer key - $5.95; cassette tapes - $10.95 each; test and quiz book - $4.45; key to test and quiz book - $8.95; cassettes - $10.20 each

This text teaches about the human body (sense organs), plants and animals, classification, the desert, oceans, ponds, forests, fields, and weather. Two correlated but optional cassette tapes, *Colonel Corn* and *The Fish with a Pole*, are available. The Student Test and Review Sheet Booklet will save test preparation time for those who desire to test their children, but watch for excessive concern for detail at this level. "Something to Try" sidebars suggest experiments and observations that demonstrate concepts in some of the lessons. A Teacher's Edition includes lesson plans, and there is a separate answer key. You probably only need the latter. I suggest supplementing with some "real" books to expand on some of the topics introduced in this course. This course is intended to take one semester. The second semester of science is used by A Beka to cover *Health, Safety, and Manners 3*. I expect that you could cover that material in less than a semester and spend more time on the science topics.

Understanding God's World [Grade 4]
$15.30; teacher edition - $22.20; answer key - $5.95; test/quiz book - $4.45; activity book - $4.45; keys for quiz and activity books - $8.95 each; cassette - $10.20

Understanding God's World includes a wide range of topics: scientific method, insects, plants, birds, matter, energy, geology, oceanography, and astronomy. Comprehension questions for discussion are scattered throughout the book. Written exercises are also included, and students can actually write in the books if we wish. However, there are not that many pages that would be written on, and it seems a shame to ruin a beautiful book by writing in it. Activities are included throughout the book. There is a Teacher's edition with lesson plans plus a separate answer key. The optional cassette tape *Red, Red Robin* corrrelates with the text. A Student Test and Quiz Booklet and a Student Worksheet Booklet, both with teacher's keys, are also available.

Health related information was removed from the older edition and published separately in a new text, *Developing Good Health*. Both books together provide a complete science program.

Developing Good Health [Grade 4]

$9.30; teacher edition - $19.95; answer key - $5.95; test/study book - $4.45; key - $8.95

This book is intended to be used along with *Understanding God's World* for a complete science program. Topics include physical fitness, hygiene, skeletal, muscular and circulatory systems, and interpersonal relationships. It should take about one-fourth of the school year to study this book. There are comprehension questions at the end of each unit. A teacher's edition, separate answer key, Student Test and Study Book, and key to the test and study book are available.

Investigating God's World [Grade 5]

$15.30; teacher's edition - $22.20; answer key - $5.95; test book - $4.45; quiz book - $4.45; keys for test and quiz books - $8.95 each

This fifth grade text teaches students about a combination of life, physical, and earth science topics such as plants, animals, matter, energy, light, minerals, and short biographies of Christian scientists. Review questions are in the book which is in worktext format. Activities and demonstrations are included. The Teacher Edition has includes the student text with overprinted answers. A separate answer key is also available. Supplemental flash cards on insects [$18.95] and *Birds of North America* [$13.95] are available along with quiz and test booklets. This text serves as three-fourths of a complete science course. *Enjoying Good Health* completes the fourth quarter.

Enjoying Good Health [Grade 5]

$9.30; teacher edition - $19.95; answer key - $5.95; student test and study book - $4.45; teacher key - $8.95; cassette - $10.20

Topics in this text include physical fitness, the circulatory system, nutrition, safety, and first aid. It should take one quarter of the school year to cover this material. An optional audio cassette, *The Helicopter Bird,* is available.

Observing God's World [Grade 6]

$14.95; teacher's edition - $20.20; answer key - $5.95; student test and quiz books - $4.20 each; keys for test and quiz books - $8.95 each; flashcards - $18.85

Students study invertebrates, plants, earth, the universe, space, and matter in this newly revised text. The Teacher Edition includes a student text with overprinted answers. A separate answer key is also available. In addition, there are optional *Insect Flashcards*, a Test Booklet, and a Quiz Booklet. Use with *Choosing Good Health* for a complete course.

Choosing Good Health [Grade 6]

$9.20; teacher's edition - $16.95; answer key - $5.95; test and study book - $5.25; key to test/study book - $8.95

Lifestyle is the theme. Endocrine, immune, and nervous systems are studied. Hot topics in the health field such as drug abuse and AIDS are discussed from the standpoint of Biblical values rather than the value-free approach attempted by secular texts.

Bob Jones University Press Science for Christian Schools series
(BJUP)

Grade 1 kit - $51

The text for first grade covers the following topics on an introductory level: senses; heat; sound; wild and tame animals; and the sun, moon, and stars. Students learn through activities and application of "scientific thinking" rather than by memorizing facts. Both the Bible and everyday use of science are incorporated into the course. BJUP sells a Home Teacher's Edition that is much less expensive than the classroom version. The Teacher's Edition is necessary as is the inexpensive *Science 1* Packet which contains reproducible student work pages. A supplementary Listening Cassette is also essential for Chapters One and Eleven. Lessons must be prepared and presented by the teacher. The *Science 1* Kit includes all of these essential components, including the hardbound student text.

Grade 2 kit - $51

Both physical and life sciences are introduced in this text. Topics include bones, plants, shape and movement of the earth, forces, and shorelines. Learning is activity-based and encourages children to develop scientific thinking skills. The teacher's information is in a Home Teacher's Edition; this and the *Science 2* Packet of reproducible student work pages are both essential. The course requires teacher preparation and presentation. All essential components come in the *Science 2* Kit, including the hardbound student text.

Grade 3 kit - $51

This text features more experiments and activities for hands on learning than we find in most classroom-designed texts. The Home Teacher's Edition is very well organized and easy-to-use. Most of the activities are described there. Topics include classification of animals, the solar system, photosynthesis, birds, mass, and weight. The student hardback book; a student Notebook Packet of work sheets for observations; a teacher's packet of visuals, charts, and game pieces; and the Home Teacher's Edition are essential. All of these items are in the *Science 3* Kit. It does require lesson preparation time and one-on-one presentation, but this is interesting and "meaty" material. For those wishing to teach more than one child together, the third grade level could also easily be used for fourth grade, but it would be more difficult to use with second graders.

Grade 4 kit - $63

This revised text helps students further develop scientific skills of observation, classification, and interpretation. The contrast between creation and evolution is introduced with a study of the origin of the moon. Other topics include insects, light, electricity, area and volume, simple machines, digestion, animal defenses, trees, and erosion. Much student learning takes place through activities. Teacher preparation and presentation are essential. In addition to the text, the student Notebook Packet, Teacher's Packet (visuals, charts, and game pieces), and Home Teacher's Edition are necessary. All of these items as well as tests and answer keys are included in the *Science 4* Kit.

Grade 5 kit - $63

This revised text builds on the thinking skills foundation begun in the new fourth grade science text and continues to develop skills of inferring, predicting, and experimenting. However, it is not dependent upon prior study of the fourth grade book. Topics studied include fossils, airplanes, thermal energy, atomic theory, weather, plant and animal reproduction, oceans, forces that cause wind, and tracks. The theme of the limitations of man's understanding and God's omnipotence underlies the study. Lessons need to be prepared and presented by the teacher. In addition to the student text, the Home Teacher's Edition, the student Notebook Packet, and the Home Teacher's Packet (visuals, charts, and game pieces) are essential. All these items as well as tests with answer keys are included in the *Science 5* Kit.

Grade 6 kit - $63

Topics studied in this revised edition include earthquakes, volcanoes, nuclear energy, space exploration, the stars, laws of motion, nuclear energy, animal behavior, respiration, the balance of nature, and a Christian perspective on science. Scientific method is learned through experiments and activities. The student text, Home Teacher's Edition, the Science 6 Notebook Packet, and Home Teacher's Packet are essential. All components as well as tests with answer keys are included in the *Science 6* Kit.

Christian Liberty Press: God's Creation series
Our Father's World

$8.95; teacher's manual - $5.95; test packet - $2.95

This beautiful, full-color first grade text introduces children to science with the theme of "things that God has made." Actual topics are an eclectic collection of general introductions and details of selective examples. For example, insects are introduced, then special attention is given to metamorphosis, anthills, locusts, and a few other topics. While there is quite a bit of overlap in content with the 2nd grade text, this one also covers some health and safety topics and adds a section called "Studying Things"—activities to help children understand concepts of balance, weight, temperature, flotation, and size. A brief teacher's manual and test packet are included.

God's Wonderful Works

$9.25; teacher's manual - $5.95; test packet - $2.95

Suggested as a 2nd grade text, *God's Wonderful Works* might also be used with older students. Subtitled "The Creation in Six Days," the book is organized in six sections reflecting what God brought into existence on each day. Coverage is introductory as is appropriate for this level. Like the first grade book, it is printed in beautiful, full-color with a "glossy" look that is very visually appealing. Simple hands-on activities help convey concepts. Questions, including fill-in-the-blank, at the end of each section require some written work. A brief teacher's manual and test packet are included. Curiously, there is a great deal of repetition of concepts already covered in the first grade book, although coverage is more extensive in this book.

Exploring God's Creation
$8

This third grade text is divided into four units: physics and chemistry, geology and botany, astronomy and weather, and biology and health. Hands-on learning is stressed rather than a reliance on absorbing information strictly from reading the text. Numerous color and black-and-white illustrations, large print, and relatively short text make it practical for young learners. Every lesson includes an experiment/activity, but the thirty-one lessons should require only about two days per week. Some thought-provoking questions are built into the lessons. Unit reviews (quizzes) are provided within the book along with an answer key. A separate test booklet with answers included is available [$1.95]. The situations and needs of homeschoolers were primary considerations in the development of this book, so we find practical experiments that require household items, field trip suggestions that are broader than those that are strictly for classroom groups, and an easy-to-teach, all-in-one book format that saves time and energy.

Christian Schools International science series
student books for grades 3-6 - $31 each; teacher guides - $52.50 each

In CSI's program, science is presented from a Biblical perspective, emphasizing God's creation and our responsibility to be good stewards of His creation. A spiral-bound teacher's manual presents the program without a student textbook. There are some reproducible worksheets in the back, but the program emphasizes learning by doing. The program is designed for schools, so some activities need to be adapted. Each lesson follows a plan: discover, develop, and reinforce/assess. In the "discover" part of the lesson, inductive-learning methods draw students into the lesson by asking questions, creating discussions, and using demonstrations or experiments. The "develop" part helps students understand the concepts, still using discovery methods to guide discussion and activities much of the time. "Reinforce/assess" questions students to determine whether they understand the concepts stated in the lesson objective and sometimes adds a reinforcement activity. We need to plan ahead to gather resources for the various activities, but they are generally easy-to-find items. Background information is provided for the teacher. Some great extension activities can be used to expand each lesson. If you have more than one child in grades K-2, try to use only one level of the program with all children rather than purchasing the book designated for each level.

Topics covered in Grade 1: living and nonliving things; plants; animals; water and air; sun, moon, and earth; weather; matter; machines and magnets; and how we grow.

Topics in Grade 2 are the functions of plant parts; animals; endangered animals; staying healthy; rocks and soil; the solar system; states of matter; the water cycle; and light, heat, and sound.

The third grade program follows the basic design described in the review of the first grade program, but a student text is added for this and all higher levels. The teacher's guide still has quite a few reproducible activity sheets in addition to unit review quizzes. The student text describes and illustrates many of the experiments. Since there is more information at this level, the text provides some of that information directly to the student. Some questions are contained in the student text, but they seem to repeat some questions in the teacher's guide although phrasing is different. Topics covered in Grade 3 are the senses, where animals live, animals, machines and work, electricity, heat and temperature, water, the earth's resources, and the solar system. Although many of these topics were addressed in first and second grade, different aspects are covered at this level.

The fourth grade program is very similar to that for third grade. The student text describes and illustrates many of the experiments. Topics covered in Grade 4 are pond communities, food plants, birds, bones and muscles, energy, sound, packages, the earth's surface, the ocean, and weather.

In the fifth grade program the student text describes and illustrates many of the experiments and presents the bulk of the information to be learned at this level, although lessons still need to be presented from the teacher's guide. Questions are contained in the student text with answers in the teacher's guide. Grade 5 covers cells and heredity, body systems, seed plants, insects, environmental factors, geology, structures, light, and matter.

Grade 6 covers the animal kingdom; simple living things; forest communities; ecology; motion, force, and work; energy; electricity; forecasting weather; and the universe.

Daily Science
(GROW Publications)
$23.95 per level

Daily Science is designed to help students review science knowledge as well as improve their thinking skills. Books for each grade level (grades 1-6) are designed as supplements rather than primary sources for learning. They assume basic science course content has been or is being covered by some other means. Scope and Sequence charts in the front of each book show detailed topic coverage for each level. General headings for the areas covered are earth science, life science, physical science, environmental science, and science reasoning.

Each book is complete in itself with student pages, teaching information, and answers. Students can work directly from the student pages as long as the spiral-bound book is folded back so students are not looking at the facing answer key. Student pages can also be photocopied or copied by the parent onto a chalk or white board. The book for first grade covers 25 weeks with two questions per day, three days per week. Books for grades 2 and 3 have two exercises per day for three days per week for 32 weeks. Books for grades 4-6 also have two exercises per day, three days per week, but for 36 weeks. Exercises sometimes require brief answers but more often require lengthier explanations that encourage deeper thinking. I found no significant evolutionary content in the Grade Five book I reviewed.

These books should be useful for parents who want to reinforce previously studied science knowledge. Questions are general enough to be common to almost all science curriculum. If you have put little emphasis on science in the early grades, choose a book a year or two below grade level.(S)

Five Kids and A Monkey series
(Creative Attic)
7.95 each; $20.25 for the set of
three books; unit studies - $5 each

Suggested for grades 2-6, these are particularly good "health" books for younger children. There are three books in the series. Each title begins "*Five Kids and A Monkey,*" then continues "*Investigate A Vicious Virus,*" "*Solve the Great Cupcake Caper,*" or "*Banish the Stinkies.*" They deal with germs and sickness, nutrition and general health, and hygiene, bacteria, and cleanliness respectively. The same characters are featured in all the books, and each book follows a story line to present information on a topic. Full-color, cartoon illustrations make these very appealing. Silly jokes, questions, and "puzzlers" are added for fun and to stimulate comprehension. These books are especially good at prodding children to consider cause and effects of their own actions in regard to health, although they avoid a "preachy" attitude. The publisher sells nine-page "unit studies" for each book, but these are really a collection of additional activities and reproducible worksheets rather than what most of us would call a unit study. They are only moderately helpful, but the books are super.(S)

Good Science Curriculum, Book I for K-3 and Book II for 4-6
by Dr. Richard Bliss
(Institute for Creation Research)
$59.95 each; extra workbooks - $12.95 each

This curriculum will help us meet all three goals described at the beginning of this chapter while providing a thorough and organized program for us to follow. The attributes of God form a foundation for science studies covering both life and physical science topics. All activities are designed to develop critical thinking skills through pupil hands-on activity and also to lead children into further exploration. Experiments and activities use mostly household items, and a Starter Kit containing the more difficult to find items comes with the curriculum.

Book I of *Good Science* comes in a package which includes a large, softbound book, the Starter Kit, four audio cassette tapes with instructions by the author, and one student workbook.

Science concepts in both physical and life sciences are developed. Physical science topics include the broad headings: objects, systems, variables, relativity, energy, and models. Life science topics include organisms, life cycles, populations, environments, communities, and ecosystems.

This program can be used over a number of years, although you might be able to complete it within one year. You will still need to use other resource books to provide complete explanations of concepts studied in *Good Science*, although the curriculum emphasis is more on process (how to do science) than

on detailed information.

The single volume will suffice as the main text, but unless you are very knowledgeable in science you will probably want to refer to other resources for more information.

The best preparation for using *Good Science* is to first watch the *Good Science Workshop* video featuring Fred Willson [$14.95]. This 75-minute video of a hands-on class for home schooling students and their parents walks us through the days of creation to demonstrate God's attributes through science. Packed with simple experiments, this presentation also demonstrates numerous scientific concepts, many of which you can explore more fully in the *Good Science* curriculum. Parents and children can watch the video together or parents can view the video, then present the same lessons to their own children using easily found materials such as styrofoam trays, toothpicks, pennies, candles, clothespin, feathers, and trail mix. Oat and filaree seeds might be a little more challenging to come by in small quantities so two of each are provided with the video. If you prefer, you can purchase pre-packaged supply kits with all of these items or extra seeds from the Creation Hands-On Science Center in Ohio. Call them at (800) 237-6866. This workshop is suggested for grades K-6, but older students who might have already been exposed to some of the scientific concepts can benefit from the spiritual lessons in the presentation.

Book II of *Good Science* for grades 4-6 is very much like the younger level in format, but the information covered is more advanced. As with the younger level, it comes with the Starter Kit and four audio tapes.

How Does God Do That?
by Paul and Danielle Harris
(Coffeehouse Publishing)
$23.95

This is an intriguing science "text" that is designed for home educators. It covers a mixture of physical and life science with units on the solar system, the earth, and "God's Handiwork" which includes an introductory study of matter, plants, animals, and the human body. It assumes creation as a basic underlying concept of science rather than evolution; it doesn't even discuss evolution as a possibility, leaving that for older grade levels. The book is written directly to the student, expecting that they are completing most work independently. Captain Explorer is a character introduced at the beginning of the book to speak directly to students, but he's mostly "invisible" as the book uses this as a way to justify using a first person "we" to present material. However, the tone is certainly more user-friendly as a result.

Chapter objectives are clearly described at the beginning of each chapter for both student and parent reference. Many activities are included, but materials, equipment, and preparation time are minimal. Cross curriculum activities for writing, math, art, and drama are built in, although writing and drawing are the most common. In addition to such "outside the book" activities, within the book are drawings to label, charts to complete, words to define, and questions to answer. This mix of learning modes helps maintain student interest.

One of the curious design elements of this text is that questions are frequently presented before material has been presented. Children need to be told that they need not expect to fill in all questions when they first encounter them, but they may go back and complete these pages as they discover information. For the chapter reviews, which most of us would try to use as tests, students are encouraged to search back through the chapter for information. They will sometimes have to analyze information presented to come up with answers.

This book is suggested for ages 8 to 12, but it would have benefitted from a narrower target audience in its design. Some vocabulary seems on the 12-year-old level, while some activities such as coloring, are definitely for 8-year-olds. Most younger children will not be able to read this independently; fifth through seventh grades seem the right levels to me.

Black-and-white illustrations satisfy the needs of the course, but the book lacks the visual appeal of other science texts or "real books." The book features a glossary but lacks an index.

Rod and Staff science texts
Patterns of Nature 2
$5.40; teacher's manual - $2.75

This text leads students through a study of nature with an emphasis on observation and identification. God as Creator is a strong theme.

God's Protected World
$9.95; teacher's manual - $10.65; test booklet - $1.90

This text explores materials and their properties; relationship of the sun, moon, and earth; animal classification; and simple machines. God's care of His creation is emphasized as the general theme. "New words" are introduced at the beginning of each lesson, then lessons are divided into two parts: the first is intended for teaching or group work, while children should read the second part on their own. Questions follow the reading assignment. Unit tests are available in a separate booklet. A teacher's manual is available but should not be necessary.

God's Marvelous Works 1
$9.85; teacher's manual - $9.85; test booklet - $1.90

The main topics are insects, birds, flowers, and reptiles, with a strong emphasis on God as Creator. Observation and study are the principle methods of learning.

God's Marvelous Works 2
$11.75; teacher's manual - $10.90; test booklet - $1.90

This text teaches students about algae and fungi, mammals, aquatic creatures, and amphibians. It should follow *God's Marvelous Works 1*. As with other Rod and Staff science texts, learning is primarily through study and observation rather than experimentation and activities.

Science and Living in God's World series
(Our Lady of Victory/Lepanto Press)
grade 1 - $10; grade 2 - $20; grade 3 - $22; grade 4 - $16; grade 5 - $12; grades 6 to 8 - $20 each; teacher manuals for grades 2,3,7,8 - $8 each; grade 1 key - $3; grade 4 key - $4; grade 5 key - $2; grade 5 test and test key - $6; grade 4 workbook with answers - $6

These texts are revised reprints of science texts from the 1950s and 1960s, originally published by Mentzer, Bush and Company and J.B. Lippincott Company. Revisions included some (limited) updating of illustrations and content. Some or all of these were originally used in Catholic schools, and the content should be acceptable to all Christians with the exception of mentions of an old age for the earth. (I reviewed only the third and eighth grade books.) These books still retain the appearance of their ancestors which makes them less visually appealing. Content also seems to lack the sort of serious updating necessary to reflect the enormous growth in technological knowledge in the intervening years. Nevertheless, these texts offer an alternative to those from both secular and Protestant publishers. The first grade book is softcover, and all others are hardbacks. Books for grades 4 and 6 are in the works.

The third grade text is actually more interesting than many others written for this level. Divided into eight sections, each focuses on a particular topic in a sort of story format. Children learn about scientific principles within each context. For example, in one section they learn about electricity by reading about some experiments children are doing, which can easily be imitated at home. Activity suggestions are included for each section.

Topics in the eighth grade text are modern science, animals, respiratory and nervous systems, energy, and machines. It is not particularly exciting, but each chapter does include experiments, thinking- and written-response questions, vocabulary lists, and suggested books for further reading. (The word "evolution" doesn't appear in the sizable glossary at the back of the book!)

Science for Young Catholics series
(Seton Press)
1 - $8; 2- $10; 4 - $17.50

Three books for grades 1, 2, and 4 are available in this series, although more should be developed in the future. Science 1 and 2 are recently-revised courses for first and second grades. Both have a mixture of full-color and black-and white illustrations, which are helpful, but a little distracting since they are a hodgepodge of styles (clip art, line drawings, and photos). Content is interestingly written and clearly Christian. As with almost all science texts, these books try to cover many topics, so each gets minimal space. Level one is a general introduction to science and personal health. The second grade book covers topics such as the solar system, light, magnets, sound, plants, reptiles, and birds.

The fourth grade book is quite different from the younger levels. While there are a few activities suggested in the younger books, this one is loaded with experiments. The worktext format includes fill-in-the-blank questions within each chapter plus chapter reviews (tests) at the end of each chapter. An answer key comes with the book. Illustrations are both full color and black-and-white. Parents will need to spend some time collecting materials, but most required materials are household or easy-to-find items. The major exception is a microscope, but you can get through the course without one if need be. Features such as biographical sketches at the beginning of each chapter make this book more obviously Catholic in content than the younger levels. Topics covered astronomy, space, the sun, the moon, earth, oceans/weather/climate, water, matter, machines, living things, the human body, and health. I suspect that fourth graders will love this mix of information and experiments.

Seton has two *Health for Young Catholics* texts due out in 2000 for grades 5 and 6. Each of these texts has sections about the unborn child that help establish their "personhood." Both books cover nutrition, with lots of practical application and spiritual lessons intermixed with factual information. The fifth grade book also focuses on the senses and sense organs while the sixth grade book focuses on the digestive, circulatory, respiratory, and nervous systems. Books include black-and-white illustrations, activity exercises and tests.

Sex Education

Sex education seems to require a lot of attention in the public schools as a means of counteracting the media and peer influence that generally promotes promiscuity and irresponsibility in sexual conduct. Many young children have been exposed to so much sexual information and misinformation that schools are "forced" into teaching children the "facts of life" at earlier and earlier ages.

At home we certainly should take advantage of the opportunity to shelter our children from too much information too soon, whether by regulating television and other media entry into the home or by maintaining some say over the people with whom our children associate.

Even if we keep things in proper perspective, we will still need to provide our children with explanations of how babies are made and how their own bodies function and change. Fortunately, we have some excellent materials available to help us handle it.

The Wonderful Way Babies are Made by Larry Christenson (Bethany House) [$12.99] is one of the best books I have seen. It discusses babies, the sexual act, and reproduction all in the context of families and God's plan. It also devotes some attention to adoption, using Jesus as the example of an adopted child (adopted by Joseph). An unusual feature is text written on two different levels. On one page the text is written for young children (up to about age nine). On the facing page is text for children about ten and older that provides more detail and information.

Where Do Babies Come From? by Ruth Hummel (Concordia) [$9.99] is written in story form for six- to eight-year-olds. (It should be appropriate for children up to ten years old.) Seven-year-old Suzanne asks questions that come up in a typical family—about grandparents, adopted children, and how babies grow inside their mothers. The author very carefully weaves in information about how babies are conceived. The facts are all here, but scattered through the story and phrased in such a way that children who are not ready to know everything will not be forced to deal with overwhelming information. Concordia is a Christian publishing house (Lutheran affiliation), so all information is presented in a Godly context. This book is part of a series, "Learning About Sex."

How You are Changing by Jane Graver (Concordia) [$9.99] is the next in Concordia's series "Learning About Sex." Intended for eight- to eleven-year-olds, this book is written directly to the reader rather than as a story. It explains sexual differences, adolescence, development, and sexual intercourse in language appropriate for the age group. The cute, cartoon-like illustrations are less intimidating than medically accurate ones. (There is no illustration of the sex act.) Accurate vocabulary words are used, but not overemphasized. As with the younger level book, you might find this appropriate for children a year or two older than the designated age.

Preparing for Adolescence by Dr. James Dobson (Regal Books) [$9.99] is appropriate for many preteens. Dr. Dobson speaks to teens in a friendly, non-threatening tone as he covers physical, emotional, and spiritual angles of physical (primarily sexual) development, boy-girl relationships (accepting popular attitudes rather than a view that dating is not a biblical concept), the sex act, grooming, and more. A *Growth Guide Workbook* [$14.99] for *Preparing for Adolescence* is available from the publisher. The *Family Guide* [$14.99] is a book for families and pre-teens to read through and discuss together. It is set up so that it can be covered in 20, ten-minute sessions. *The Family Tape Pack* [$39.99] covers much of what is covered in the book in six audio tapes for teens and two tapes for parents.

Check your local Christian bookstore for more titles.

C h a p t e r

History/ Geography/ Cultural Studies

Social studies is a comprehensive term which includes history, geography, and cultural studies. Some of us cringe at the term social studies, equating it with all that has gone wrong philosophically with the government school system. The term itself is not the culprit. The problem lies in emphasis and philosophy. The public school system (in general) has overemphasized cultural studies at the expense of history and geography. Social studies has also been perverted into a tool for influencing the minds of our children in favor of secular humanist philosophy.

In reacting to the secular bias in textbooks, Christians have often erred in moving to the other extreme, rejecting cultural studies to concentrate on history and geography. Neither approach is correct.

If we approach social studies as a newspaper reporter, we can see the interrelationships of the three areas: history, geography, and cultural studies. Reporters look for the answers to the questions, Who did what? Where did they do it? When did they do it? and Why did they do it? The first two questions are answered by the names and dates or times (history). The third question of Where? is answered by describing the location (geography). The last question deals with the background of the event and other influences, essentially putting an event in context (cultural studies). Our social studies should be like a good newspaper article, combining all the necessary ingredients.

To carry the above approach a step further from theory to practicality, we need to establish specific goals. What do we wish to accomplish in social studies? I would suggest the following goals for kindergarten through eighth grade [Note: for the sake of continuity, goals continue up through eighth grade rather than sixth, even though that is the highest level covered in this book.]:

1.) To stimulate a life-long interest in social studies;

2.) To provide an overview of state, national, and world history;

3.) To learn geographical definitions and important geographical locations;

4.) To introduce children to other cultures.

Stimulating Interest

If children have no interest in social studies, they might go along with what we force feed them while we have control, but they are not likely to pursue the subject when left to themselves. You may be wondering yourself whether it really matters if your children know history. After all, the three R's are reading, writing, and arithmetic. However, if we wish to have a spiritual impact on society it is essential that we first recognize God's hand on all of history and then understand that we can and should learn from the past.

Throughout the Old Testament God commanded the leaders of Israel to build altars, to set aside special days of remembrance, and to teach the people about what God had done. This was not for God's sake but for the people's—that by knowing the past they would have guidance for the present and the future.

The framers of our Constitution knew both the Bible and history. They had studied how different governmental systems worked. Because of their knowledge of history they recognized the sinfulness of man and the need to provide checks and controls. They applied that historical knowledge to their situation.

Today we seem to be lacking historical wisdom in our government at all levels. If we desire to exert godly influence in government, we need to be good historians. We should strive to instill that vision for godly influence in our children also.

At the same time we must realize that history does not stop when we finish a textbook but is made in each passing moment. Thus, the learning of history is an ongoing, life-long process.

If our goal is life-long learning, then we are working at cross purposes if we are killing our children's interest rather than stimulating it.

Stimulation is not likely to happen with most textbooks that I have seen, especially if the texts are used on their own. It will more likely happen if we substitute biographies, historical novels, geographical activities, construction of time lines, and a variety of field trips and experiential activities that relate to social studies. We can then use texts as supplements or guides if we desire.

I strongly recommend avoiding textbooks below fourth grade. From fourth grade up we might rely more on texts to provide order for studies. However, interest will blossom as we continue to use other methods to help history, geography, and cultural studies come alive.

For instance, as part of our studies of United States History we can read the text for an overview of the American Revolution. Then we can read biographies of Washington, Benjamin Franklin, or other significant figures, along with novels such as *Ben and Me* (by Robert Lawson) and *Johnny Tremain* (by Esther Forbes) that are especially entertaining while also being informative. We could then make figures of British and American soldiers and reenact a battle on a three-dimensional clay or plaster geographical re-creation of the battle scene. To help our children explore beyond superficial information to the important motivating factors, we can include discussion of the beliefs of the Loyalists and the Rebels, the background of the British culture and governmental system, and the spiritual attitudes of the day.

Providing an Overview

With the exception of state history, this second goal is easily accomplished with textbooks as our guides. Textbooks should not be viewed as the best means of providing an overview, but often they are the most efficient. If you choose the textbook route, I strongly recommend use of Christian textbooks for social studies. Secular texts often have glaring problems of which we are aware, but my concern is more for the subtle attitudes and opinions that are not so readily visible. An example is the almost universal portrayal of the expansion of federal government's power and control as a good thing for our country. Christian textbooks often point out the loss of freedom and betrayal of constitutional limitations, subjects ignored by secular texts.

An overview can also be provided by selecting resources (biographies, historical novels, videos, etc.) that relate to each other in chronological order. See "Real Books" for some exciting ways to put together book-based historical studies without textbooks.

Learning Geography

Geography is learned most efficiently when combined with study of particular events. For instance, when studying the Lewis and Clark expedition we use both political and topographical maps of the United States, we discuss land formations in terms of obstacles to be overcome by the explorers, we compare political boundaries of the historical period and changes since that time, and we locate important cities today that are located along the original route.

We should have a globe, maps, atlases, or other geography tools easily accessible whenever we are reading a novel, biography, magazine, textbook, or any other work mentioning geographic locations. Every time a place is mentioned, we should locate it!

We should introduce geography (continents, oceans, land forms) by using the mentioned resources. As children begin to use textbooks, they will find that geography is often included in history texts. Whether it is or not, we still might wish to use other resources for geography and map skills. See suggestions under "Geography" below.

Introduction to Other Worldviews and Cultures

We might object to global education that is slanted toward a homogeneous, God-rejecting government and culture. But we do need to develop a Christian world view that feels with God's heart for the lost and needy. We cannot do that if we know nothing of other cultures. We can teach our children about other cultures in a way that public schools cannot, discussing their history and customs from a godly point of view. We can point out good and evil rather than accept the popular philosophy that each culture is free to set its own standards which we are not to criticize.

Since this is a new way of studying history which many of us have not experienced, I highly recommend to you Diana Waring's two-volume tape series, ***What in the World's Going on Here?*** (Diana Waring-History Alive!) [$20.95 each]. On four, 60-minute audio cassettes per volume, Diana teaches us "how to re-evaluate world history from an eternal perspective: God sovereignly ruling over the affairs of men and nations." Four timespans are covered in each volume. Volume 1 covers creation to the destruction of Assyria, the rise of Babylon to Jesus Christ, destruction of Jerusalem to the fall of Constantinople, and the Renaissance/Reformation to Queen Victoria. Volume 2 overlaps a little with the first tape covering Napoleon through the American Civil War, then continues Queen Victoria to Teddy Roosevelt, Turn of the Century to World War I, and World War II and the Rebirth of Israel. Diana directs her dynamic presentations to parents, although older children might want to listen along as we relearn history. Parents interested in teaching world views (philosophical frameworks that interpret all areas of life) to their children should find this a valuable resource. Three companion study guides use these tapes as background to fairly comprehensive unit studies. See the review of the guides under "Unit Studies."

We can integrate a more narrowly-focused spiritual dimension into our cultural studies in a number of ways. ***Operation World*** by P. J. Johnstone (Zondervan) [$14.99] is a book that gives information on every country in the world, detailing the spiritual status of each along with basic statistics on the population, economy, and political situation. It tells us the government's attitude toward Christianity, the percentages of people of various faiths, and the spiritual/prayer needs for each country. Refer to *Operation World* as you study each country and follow through with prayers for those needs. (Look for the 1993 edition.)

The Voice of the Martyrs publishes the ***Link International*** Homeschool edition, a free newsletter geared for children.

(They also publish *The Voice of the Martyrs*, a 16-page, monthly newsletter for adults.) Their goal is to educate Christians about their persecuted brethren in other countries for spiritual benefit and to build bridges between these Christian communities. Each issue features a country with articles, information, activities, and possible "action items." Newsletters are very colorful and appealing—a marvelous tool for moving from education to action. Although there are no subscription charges, donations are greatly appreciated.

A further step we can take to incorporate the spiritual dimension into history studies is to contact one or more missionary organizations. We can become involved by making donations of any size to these groups which will then put us on their mailing lists. Periodically, we will receive mailings about their missionary efforts that provide specific information about the culture and the spiritual battles being waged. (Keep in mind that these organizations are usually on limited budgets, so make donations to at least offset the cost of the mailings.)

More personal is one-on-one involvement. One of the best ways to do this is to become involved with a particular missions organization or a person or family working oversees in missionary work. Writing to missionaries, supporting them financially and prayerfully, and hosting them on visits home can all be wonderful learning experiences as well as spiritual blessings. First-person reports about other cultures are the most valuable sources we are likely to have. If we are tuned in—looking for those contacts with missionaries—the number of opportunities might even overwhelm us.

Parents who want to incorporate missionary stories into history study should read *From Jerusalem to Irian Jaya* by Ruth A. Tucker (Zondervan) [$21.99]. Missionary stories are arranged geographically and chronologically, and they can be easily incorporated as we study the history of different countries. This is a book for parents to read to children.

There are many, many missionary-related resource books, including stories and biographies written for children. They can be used to supplement history studies as much as we choose. *Kids for the World: A Guidebook to Children's Mission Resources* (U.S. Center for World Mission) [$10.25] has many pages of resource listings so that we can locate materials to fit in with our history study. (See complete review under Bible.) The resource lists in the book are available separately if desired. Contact the Children's Missions Resource Center at the U.S. Center for World Mission for ordering information or check their web site.

Real Books and Biographies

Young children are very much interested in the world and people around them. If we begin reading biographies and enjoyable historical novels to our children before history has a chance to become a boring subject, we are more likely to create a positive lifelong attitude toward history. There are many

"real" books to use for history/geography/social studies. A few publishers seem to have concentrated on publishing high quality information-type books and/or biographies you might want to consider using. I describe a number of them and some of their books below.

Books from the non-Christian publishers will sometimes present evolutionary content and humanistic perceptions and explanations which you will need to discuss. Biographies, even those from Christian publishers, sometimes also need some "editing." In an attempt to show Christian character, some authors idealize their subjects and ignore their human weaknesses. We have to acknowledge that all men and women have the same sinful nature, but some, by the grace of God, have accomplished mighty things. We should lift up the worthy actions of these people while also recognizing that they struggled and had the same failings as other people. If we falsely glorify historical figures, making them sound infallible, we distort history and set an unattainable standard for our children. So, as you read biographies, watch for historical accuracy and realism.

For your auditory learners, you might also want to use biographical audio and video tapes such as **Richard Little Bear Wheeler's (Mantle Ministries)** and some from **Your Story Hour**.

Bethlehem Books has also republished high-quality historical biography and fiction. Their catalog describes a very eclectic booklist. Books seem to have been chosen because they are great books with educational and inspirational value rather than because they fit any particular topic or time frame. Some titles are particularly appealing to Catholic families.

Children often enjoy reading about the childhoods of famous people. A series of books from Macmillan Publishing Co. called **Childhood of Famous Americans** [$4.95 each] tells stories about Clara Barton, Daniel Boone, Thomas Edison, Helen Keller, Robert E. Lee, Teddy Roosevelt and others. Reading level is for grades 2-6; interest level will include children a few years older and younger. These books strongly emphasize positive character by telling stories of famous Americans beginning in their childhood years. Obviously, there will be large proportions of fiction in most cases, but the stories give some idea of how people rose to their great accomplishments.(SE)

DK Publishing offers books and software for broad surveys of history and geography as well as narrower topics. All their publications, including software combine lush graphics with manageable amounts of text. Among their books are *DK Illustrated Book of Great Adventures, Cross Sections: Castle, Cross-Sections: Man-of-War, Aztecs, Castle, Pompeii, Tutankhamun*, and *The Visual Dictionary of Ancient Civilizations*. They also produce "Action Packs" that include

16-page booklets with activity materials. History topics addressed with Action Packs are *Castle, Pyramid, Rome*, and *Tutankhamun and Ancient Egypt*. Among their software titles are *Encyclopedia of History, Chronicle of the 20th Century, Castle Explorer, Eyewitness History of the World*, and *Eyewitness World Atlas*.

The **G.A. Henty** series of historical novels have proven popular with homeschoolers, most especially for young men about ten to fourteen years old. Books fall into the general time periods of Ancient Civilizations, Reformation Times, Exploration, and American History. Henty used the same format for most of these stories: young man fights difficult circumstances as he comes of age, finds himself caught up in major historical event, and proves himself good and courageous in the process. Minor romantic interests are thrown in but don't get much attention. Some of Henty's descriptive passages seem unnecessarily cumbersome to modern readers, but the action and adventure is strong enough to engage young men. Although readers follow the exploits of the young hero, he is always brought into the context of historical figures and events, transforming stories into appealing history lessons. Although there are occasional historic inaccuracies, they are minor given the context. These books have been republished by PrestonSpeed in both beautiful, hardcover heirloom editions [$19.99] and softcover editions [$13.99]. Not all titles are available in both editions. Christian Liberty Press has republished a revised edition of one Henty title: *In Freedom's Cause*.

Even more Henty books are now also available on CD-ROM from Oregon Institute of Science and Medicine [$99]. Ninety-nine Henty books (all of his books), 53, short stories, and 216 other short stories by authors from the same era can be printed out (recommended) or read on the computer screen.

Kingfisher Books are similar in concept to Peter Bedrick and R.J. Unstead books with more information and less clutter than Usborne. They produce a huge, 808-page *Illustrated History of the World, The Kingfisher History Encyclopedia* (see review in this chapter), and the "Visual Factfinder" series which includes the titles *World History* and *Countries of the World*. Among their other titles are The *Kingfisher Reference Atlas* and The *Young People's Atlas of the United States*. (Kingfisher books are ordered from Larousse Kingfisher Chambers, Inc.)

Still at the top of my list for biographies are the old **Landmark** series of books, well over one hundred children's books published around the 1950's and 60's. They went out of print, but some titles have been reprinted. Older books are still available at some libraries and at thrift and used book stores. I have yet to find a "bad" Landmark book. These are typically historical biographies. (I've noted Landmark titles among those listed below when I know they are.)

Mott Media publishes a series of biographies written from the Christian perspective called *The Sower Series* [$7.99 each]. While these vary in quality, they still represent an improvement over many of the fictionalized biographies which have totally omitted important godly aspects of these people's lives. Try first reading a biography from the *Sower Series*, then reading a different biography of the same person and compare. Reading level for the *Sower Series* is grades 4-8; interest level will stretch a few years younger and older. Recommended titles are included in the lists below with an indication that the book is from the series.

Parkwest Publications offers activity books for children ages 7-11. Drawing and coloring projects, puzzles, games, and quizzes combine with easy-to-read text and pictures in books entitled *The Ancient Greeks, The Romans, The Celts*, and *The Anglo-Saxons*. Books for making cut-and-glue models will keep hands-on learners busy. Model building books are *Egyptian Funeral Boat, Viking Ship, Anglo-Saxon Helmet, Sun Dials and Time Dials* (working models), *The Tarquin Globe*, and *The Tarquin Star-Globe* [$4.95 and up].

Peter Bedrick Books are very colorful like the Usborne books (Educational Development Corporation). However, more of them are written for higher grade levels. Their "Inside Story" series is particularly good [$10.95 paperback, $18.95 for hard cover]. Titles include *A Medieval Cathedral, A Medieval Castle, An Egyptian Pyramid, A Frontier Fort, Greek Temple, Roman Fort, Roman Villa, 16th Century Mosque, 16th Century Galleon, Samurai Castle, Shakespeare's Theater*, and *A World War Two Submarine*. Their "History of Everyday Things" series includes *First Civilizations, The Middle Ages, Renaissance*, and *The Roman Empire* [$10.95 for paperback, $17.95 for hard cover]. The Biographical History series [$17.95 each] includes the titles *The Roman Empire, The Crusades, The Rise of Islam*, and *The Black Experience*. I reviewed The first two of these, and both are excellent. However, I was surprised that the reading level of *The Roman Empire* (about fourth grade and up) is significantly easier than *The Crusades* (junior high and up). You might find similar reading level discrepancies within any of these series since books within a series frequently have different authors. Peter Bedrick Books has still other series: "Voyages of Discovery," "First Facts," "What Do We Know About?", and "Timelink."

Spizzirri Publishing, Inc. sells a broad line of educational read-and-color books some with accompanying audio cassettes, with realistic illustrations and museum-curator-approved text. Of most interest are probably the various books on Indians who lived in different sections of the United States, along with *Eskimos, Pioneers, Colonies, Cowboys*, and *California Missions*. Spizzirri publishes 48 such titles. Book/cassette packages are $6.95 each.

 **Usborne** is probably the most well known publisher of such books. (See Educational Development Corporation to order.) Some of their books are reviewed individually under different areas of study. While Usborne has a number of smaller books that cover sections of history, the combination books where they have combined a number of small books into one larger one are usually a much better buy. *Time Traveler* and *The Usborne First Book of History* are examples of these "best buy" combination books. Many other Usborne books are of interest to home educators. Among them are *The Usborne Illustrated Handbook of Invention and Discovery, The Young Scientist Book of Archaeology, The Seas,* and *The Usborne Book of World Geography.* Hands-on learners should also love Usborne's *Cut-Out Models* series. They can create detailed models of a castle, fort, Greek temple, cathedral, and other historical settings by cutting and pasting together the full-color pieces from these books—all printed on sturdy paper.

⟁⟁⟁⟁⟁⟁⟁⟁⟁⟁⟁⟁

I am continually growing in my conviction that these types of books I've mentioned above are more valuable than textbooks in providing the sort of historical knowledge that children will retain. Because of this, I've added lists of such books that you might use for covering history, divided by topic.

"Real" Books by Time Periods/Topics

Listed here are historical biographies and novels as well as a few informational books that read like stories. You can choose an assortment of such books as the core of your curriculum, adding discussion, writing, and activities to accomplish your educational goals.

I've included some titles that are written for adults, but might be read aloud to your older children. I've started using a *very general* coding of (y) to indicate books written for children up through about fourth grade level, and (o) to indicate books written for at least sixth grade level to adult. I've also used (oop) to indicate books that are out of print but worth searching for, as well as some notations for books that are part of recommended series: Landmark = Landmark Books, CFA = Childhood of Famous Americans, and Sower = Sower series. (Coding will be more extensive in the next edition of this *Curriculum Manual.*) Note that titles listed under "Black History" repeat some of those listed under other headings.

Ancient Egypt

The Cat of Bubastes G.A. Henty (o)
Pyramid by David Macaulay
Tales of Ancient Egypt by Roger Lancelyn Green

Golden Goblet and other titles by Eloise Jarvis McGraw
Moses by Leonard Fisher
Motel of the Mysteries by David Macaulay
The Riddle of the Rosetta Stone by James Cross Givlin
Pharaohs of Ancient Egypt by Payne (Landmark)
Into the Mummy's Tomb by Nicholas Reeves

Ancient Greece

The Great Alexander the Great by Joe Lasker (y)
Exploits of Xenophon by Geoffrey Household (oop)
Classic Myths to Read Aloud: The Great Stories of Greek and Roman Mythology by William F. Russell
Tales of the Greek Heroes by Roger Lancelyn Green (o)
The Illiad translated by Lattimore(o)
The Odyssey translated by Lattimore and another translation by Robert Fitzgerald (o)
Adventures of Ulysses translated by Gottlieb
The Wanderings of Odysseus by Rosemary Sutcliff
Black Ships before Troy by Rosemary Sutcliff
The Children's Homer by Padric Colum (o)
Alexander and His Times by Frederic Theule(o)
The Trojan Horse by Little (y)
D'Aulaires Book of Greek Myths (y)
Archimedes and the Door of Science by Jeanne Bendick
The Librarian Who Measured the Earth (Ptolemy) by Lasky

Bible Times and Ancient Rome

Hittite Warrior by Joanne Williamson
Classic Myths to Read Aloud: The Great Stories of Greek and Roman Mythology by William F. Russell
Augustus Caesar's World by Genevieve Foster (o)
The Eagle of the North by Rosemary Sutcliff
The Aeneid of Virgil translated by Robert Fitzgerald
Runaway and other titles by Patricia St. John
Bronze Bow by Elizabeth Speare
For the Temple by G.A. Henty (o)
Festival of Lights by Maida Silverman (y)
Light Another Candle by Miriam Chaikin (oop)
Beric the Briton: A Story of the Roman Invasion by G.A. Henty (o)
Young Carthaginian by G.A. Henty (o)
Cleopatra by Diane Stanley and Peter Vennema
Saint Valentine retold by Robert Sabuda
The Ides of April by Mary Ray
The Lantern Bearers (Britain at the end of the Roman occupation) by Rosemary Sutcliff
Ben Hur by Lew Wallace (read aloud) (o)
The Robe by Lloyd C. Douglas (read aloud) (o)
Quo Vadis by Henryk Sienkiewicz (read aloud) (o)

Explorers and Invaders

Beowulf the Warrior by Ian Serraillier

Dragon Slayer (Beowulf) by Rosemary Sutcliff

Augustine Came to Kent by Barbara Willard

Son of Charlemagne by Barbara Willard

Wulf the Saxon: A Story of the Norman Conquest by G.A. Henty (o)

Leif the Lucky by the D'Aulaires

Beorn the Proud by Madeleine Pollard

Norse Gods and Giants by the D'Aulaires

The Story of Rolf and the Viking Bow by Allen French

Vikings by Janeway (Landmark)

Genghis Khan and the Mongol Hordes by Lamb

The White Stag (Attila the Hun) by Kate Seredy

Under Drake's Flag: A Tale of the Spanish Main by G.A. Henty (o)

By Right of Conquest or With Cortez in Mexico by G.A. Henty (o)

With Pipe, Paddle and Song by Elizabeth Yates

Tristan and Iseult (Ireland and Britain) by Rosemary Sutcliff

Where Do You Think You're Going, Christopher Columbus? by Jean Fritz (y)

Columbus by the D'Aulaires (y)

The World of Columbus and Sons by Genevieve Foster

The World of Captain John Smith by Genevieve Foster

Middle Ages, Reformation, Renaissance, and World History up to Modern History

St. George and the Dragon by Margaret Hodges

Leonardo da Vinci by Diane Stanley

In Freedom's Cause (William Wallace and Robert the Bruce and the battle for Scottish independence) by G.A. Henty (o)

The Red Keep by Allen French

Wulf the Saxon by G.A. Henty (o)

By Pike and Dike by G.A. Henty (o)

Winning His Spurs by G.A. Henty (o)

Magna Charta by James Daugherty (Landmark)

Cathedral by David Macaulay

Joan of Arc by Josephine Poole

A Knight of the White Cross by G.A. Henty (o)

In Freedom's Cause by G.A. Henty (o)

The Dragon and the Raven or the Days of King Alfred by G.A. Henty (o)

St. Bartholomew's Eve: A Tale of the Huguenot Wars by G.A. Henty (o)

Ivanhoe by Sir Walter Scott

The Talisman by Sir Walter Scott

The Trumpeter of Krakow by Eric P. Kelly

The Black Arrow by Robert Louis Stevenson

The Road to Damietta (St. Francis of Assisi) by Scott O'Dell

Adam of the Road by Elizabeth Gray

The Whipping Boy by Sid Fleishman

The Door in the Wall by Marguerite DeAngeli

The Minstrel in the Tower by Gloria Skurzynski

Jackaroo by Cynthia Voight

The Story of King Arthur and His Knights and other Arthurian tales by Howard Pyle

King Arthur by Howard Pyle (y)

Men of Iron by Howard Pyle

The Merry Adventures of Robin Hood by Howard Pyle

Otto of the Silver Hand by Howard Pyle

Sir Gawain and the Green Knight by J.R.R. Tolkien

William Tell retold by Margaret Early

Johannes Kepler by John Hudson Tiner (Sower series)

Isaac Newton by John Hudson Tiner (Sower series)

Ink on His Fingers by Louise Vernon

The Hawk that Dare Not Hunt by Day by Scott O'Dell

Red Hugh: Prince of Donegal by Robert T. Reilly

Martin Luther, The Great Reformer by J.A. Morrison

This Was John Calvin by Thea B. Van Halsema

St. Bartholomew's Eve: A Tale of the Huguenot Wars by G.A. Henty (o)

A Tale of Two Cities by Charles Dickens (read aloud) (o)

The Scarlet Pimpernel by Baroness Orezy (read aloud) (o)

Don Quixote by Miguel Cervantes retold by Michael Harrison

U.S. History

Pocahontas by the D'Aulaires (y)

Diary of an Early American Boy by Eric Sloan

The Last of the Mohicans by James Fenimore Cooper (o)

Witchcraft of Salem Village by Shirley Jackson (Landmark)

Can't You Get Them to Behave, King George? by Jeanne Fritz

And Then What Happened, Paul Revere? by Jeanne Fritz

America's Paul Revere by Esther Forbes

Why Don't You Get a Horse, Sam Adams? By Jeanne Fritz

Sam the Minuteman by Nathaniel Benchley

Ben and Me by Robert Lawson

Mr. Revere and I by Robert Lawson

Ben Franklin of Old Philadelphia by Margaret Cousins (Landmark)

The World of Captain John Smith by Genevieve Foster (o)

George Washington's World by Genevieve Foster (o)

Cabin Faced West by Jeanne Fritz

Fourth of July Story by Dagliesh

The Reb and the Redcoats by Constance Savery.

Benjamin Franklin by the D'Aulaires

Johnny Tremain by Esther Forbes

By the Great Hornspoon by Sid Fleischman

Pioneers Go West by Steward (Landmark)

Patty Reed's Doll by Rachel Laurgaard

The California Gold Rush by May McNeer
Island of the Blue Dolphins by Scott O'Dell
Streams to the River, River to the Sea (Sacagawea) by Scott O'Dell
Paddle to the Sea by Holling C. Holling
Tree in the Trail by Holling C. Holling
Minn of the Mississippi by Holling C. Holling
Caddie Woodlawn by Carol Ryrie Brink
The Courage of Sarah Noble by Alice Dagliesh
The Matchlock Gun by Walter D. Edmonds
Carry on, Mr. Bowditch by Jean Lee Latham
The Sign of the Beaver by Elizabeth Speare
Samuel F.B. Morse by John Hudson Tiner (Sower series)
Sitting Bull: Dakota Boy by Augusta Stevenson (CFA)
Carlota (Mexican War) by Scott O'Dell
Will Clark: Boy Adventurer by Wilkie (CFA)
Meriwether Lewis: Boy Explorer by Charlotta Bebenroth (CFA)
Booker T. Washington by Jan Gleiter
A Pocketful of Goobers: A Story of George Washington Carver by Barbara Mitchell
Alamo by George Sullivan
Make Way for Sam Houston by Jeanne Fritz
Flatboats on the Ohio by Catherine Chambers
Johnny Appleseed by Collins (Sower series)
American Girls series
If You Traveled West in a Covered Wagon by Ellen Levine
Daniel Boone and the Wilderness Road by Catherine Chambers
Iron Dragon Never Sleeps by Stephen Krensky
Dragon's Gate (Chinese immigrants and the railroads) by Laurence Yep
Sing Down the Moon (Navaho Indians) by Scott O'Dell
Clara Barton: Founder of the American Red Cross by Augusta Stevenson (CFA)

Civil War

The Life of Stonewall Jackson by Mary L. Williamson
The Life of J.E.B. Stuart by Mary L. Williamson
Abraham Lincoln by the D'Aulaires (y)
Abe Lincoln: Log Cabin to the Whitehouse by Sterling North (Landmark)
Robert E. Lee, The Christian by William J. Johnson
Robert E. Lee by Lee Roddy (Sower series)
Stonewall by Jeanne Fritz
With Lee in Virginia: A Story of the American Civil War by G.A. Henty (o)
Little Women by Louisa May Alcott (o)
Across Five Aprils by Irene Hunt
Gettysburg by MacKinlay Kantor (o)
The Slave Dancer by Paula Fox (read aloud) (o)
Perilous Road by William O. Steele, Jean Fritz

Uncle Tom's Cabin by Harriet Beecher Stowe (read aloud) (o)
Rifles for Watie by Harold Keith
Pink and Say by Patricia Polacco
Charley Skedaddle by Patricia Beatty
Iron Scouts of the Confederacy by McGriffon
The Red Badge of Courage by Stephen Crane(o)
Amos Fortune: Free Man by Elizabeth Yates
Frederick Douglass Fights for Freedom by Margaret Davidson
The Drinking Gourd by F.N. Monjo

Modern U.S. History

American Girls series
Danger at the Breaker (Industrial Revolution) by Catherine A. Welch
The Story of the Wright Brothers and Their Sister by Lois Mills (y)
Andrew Carnegie: Steel King and Friend to Libraries by Zachary Kent (o)
Henry Ford: Young Man with Ideas by Hazel Aird and Catherine Ruddiman
Dear America: So Far from Home—The Diary of Mary Driscoll, An Irish Mill Girl, Lowell, MA 1847 by Barry Denenberg
Children of the Dust Bowl: The True Story of the School at Weedpatch Camp by Jerry Stanley
The Bracelet (Japanese internment in WWII) by Joanna Yardley and Yoshiko Uchida
Farewell to Manzanar (Japanese internment in WWII) by Houston and Houston (read aloud)
Rosie the Riveter: Women Working on the Home Front in WWII by Penny Colman
Understood Betsy by Dorothy Canfield Fisher
The Yearling by Marjorie Rawlings
Roll of Thunder, Hear My Cry by Mildred D. Taylor (read aloud)
To Kill a Mockingbird by Harper Lee (read aloud) (o)
Amelia Earhart by Beatrice Gormley
Rocket! How a Toy Launched the Space Age by Richard Maurer
Ronald Reagan by Montrew Dunham

Modern World History

Number the Stars (Danish Resistance) by Lois Lowry
The House of Sixty Fathers (China) by Meindert de Jong
The Wheel on the School (Netherlands) by Meindert de Jong
The Winged Watchman (Netherlands) by Hilda Van Stockum
Twenty and Ten (WWII refugee children in France) by Claire Huchet Bishop
The Crystal Snowstorm, Following the Phoenix, Angel and the Dragon, The Rose and Crown (19th century European politics) by Meriol Trevor

The Cay by Theodore Taylor

When Jessie Came across the Sea (Jewish Immigrant) by Amy Hett (y)

Teresa of Calcutta by D. Jeanene Watson (Sower series)

Sweet Dried Apples: A Vietnamese Wartime Childhood by Rosemary Breckler

The Land I Lost: Adventures of a Boy in Vietnam by Huynh Quang Nhuong

Black History

Some families choose to balance their history studies with additional focus on the contributions of blacks, especially if they are using primary texts that entirely omit any mention of them. Lori Harris of Landmark Distributors assisted me by pulling together a recommended reading list for Black History in America according to time periods. All of the following books are available through Landmark, and you can also find some of these titles in Elijah Company's catalog, and, most likely, in some of the other distributors' catalogs. Also see the reviews of *African Americans Thematic Unit, Freedom's Sons: The True Story of the AMISTAD Mutiny,* and *Free Indeed: Heroes of Black Christian History.*

Blacks in the Revolution

• *Amos Fortune: Free Man* by Elizabeth Yates

• *Crispus Attucks: Black Leader of Colonial Patriots* by Gray Morrow (CFA)

• *Phoebe the Spy* by Judith Berry Griffin

• *Poems of Phillis Wheatley* by Phillis Wheatley

• *Hang a Thousand Trees With Ribbons : The Story of Phillis Wheatley* by Ann Rinaldi

• *Story of Phillis Wheatley* by Shirley Graham

Blacks in the War Between the States

• *Booker T. Washington* by Jan Gleiter

• *Freedom Train* by Dorothy Sterling

• *Go Free Or Die: A Story about Harriet Tubman* by Jeri Ferris

• *What Mrs. Fisher Knows about Old Southern Cooking* by Mrs. Fisher (First cookbook by a black)

• *Wanted Dead or Alive: The True Story of Harriet Tubman* by Ann McGovern

Harriet Tubman, The Moses Of Her People by Sarah Bradford

• *Harriet Tubman, the Road To Freedom* by Rae Baines

• *If You Traveled On the Underground Railroad* by Ellen Levine

• *Incidents In The Life Of A Slave Girl* by Harriet A. Jacobs

• *Letters From A Slave Girl* by Mary E. Lyons

• *The Slave Dancer* by Paula Fox

• *Sojourner Truth and The Struggle For by Freedom* by Edward Beecher Claflin

• *Sojourner Truth; Ain't I A Woman* by Pat and Patricia McKissack

• *Pocketful of Goobers: A Story about George Washington Carver* by Barbara Mitchell

• *The Story of George Washington Carver* by Eva Moore

• *Tales From the Underground Railroad* by Kate Connell

• *To Be A Slave* by Julius Lester

• *Uncle Tom's Cabin* by Harriet Beecher Stowe

• *Up From Slavery* by Booker T. Washington

• *Walking The Road To Freedom: Sojourner Truth* by Jeri Ferris

• *Brady* by Jean Fritz

• *Black Soldiers in the The Civil War* - coloring book by Alan Archambault

• *Pink and Say* by Patricia Polacco (oop)

• *Undying Glory: The Story of the Massachusetts Fifty-Fourth Regiment* by Clinton Cox

• *Life and Times of Frederick Douglas* by Frederick Douglass (oop)

Black Pioneers In The American West

• *Black Frontiers : A History of African-American Heroes in the Old West* by Lillian Schlissel

• *The Real McCoy: The Life of an African-American Inventor* by Wendy Towle (y)

• *Mary McLeod Bethune* by Eloise Greenfield (y)

• *John Jasper* by William E. Hatcher (oop)

• *Free Indeed: Heroes Of Black Christian History* by Mark Sidwell

• *George Washington Carver: In His Own Words* by George Washington Carver

• *Samuel Morris* by Lindley Baldwin

• *The Negro Cowboys* by Philip Durham (o)

• *The Life and Adventures of Nat Love* by Nat Love

• *Shadow and Light: Autobiography of M. W. Gibbs*

• *The Life and Adventures of James P. Beckwourth* by T.D. Bonner (oop)

Black Leaders In Modern American History

• *Souls Of Black Folk* by W.E.B. DuBois (This book is important, but DuBois was definitely communist so read with caution.) (o)

• *One More River To Cross: The Stories of Twelve Black Americans* by James Haskins

• *David Robinson* (Today's Heroes series) by Steve Hubbard

• *John Perkins* (Today's Heroes series) by Terry Whalin

More and more home school distributors are offering groups of books (primarily historical novels and biographies) for various historical periods. While most distributors have a number of books that can be used this way, Beautiful Feet Books, Elijah Company, Lifetime Books, *Greenleaf Press*, and *Bluestocking Press* have purposely listed books under time period headings for this reason.

Elijah Company has taken this idea a step further within their catalog than most distributors. In their catalog they describe three approaches to history: the events approach, the people approach, and the ideas approach. Generally, we would use the first two approaches with younger students, reserving the idea approach until upper levels. The catalog then lists materials suitable for each approach, then materials for topical areas of history.

Beautiful Feet Books has produced study guides for a literature-approach to various periods of history. See the reviews under "World History," "American History," and "California History."

There are two resource books I know of that help us select our own books for historical studies. *Turning Back the Pages of Time: A Guide to American History through Literature* is a separate little resource book that helps us put together overview studies of American History with real books. It further divides American History into chronological subtopics. (See the review under "United States History-Primary Resources.")

A much broader resource is *Let the Authors Speak: A Guide to Worthy Books Based on Historical Setting* by Carolyn Hatcher (Old Pinnacle Publishing) [$18.95]. Hatcher uses the first half of the book explaining the rationale for using real books for learning and for literature, and because of this I also discuss *Let the Authors Speak* in the "Reading" chapter. The second half lists books, first by historical setting (time period, location), then by author. A supplemental section lists myths/legends, fantasy, folk tales, fables, and allegories by time period. Few twentieth century titles appear since Hatcher's emphasis is on classical literature and most recent works have not yet had time to establish themselves as classics. Brief comments accompany each entry. Hatcher works from a Judeo-Christian world view and leans toward a western-civilization background which is reflected in the lists. However, all books listed are not necessarily Christian.

One other resource deserves mention here. *History in His Hands, Volume One Ancient History* (Simplified Learning Products) uses a story-telling approach combined with recommended real books, thus it fits partially in this section and partially in the next. You will find the full review under "Textbooks for early levels of social studies."

Learning Styles

In our discussion so far, we have already touched on a wide variety of approaches for teaching social studies. Some of those approaches are strongly recommended for specific learning styles. History becomes interesting to Wiggly Willys and Sociable Sues when we use historical biographies such as those from the Sower Series and historical fiction rather than history textbooks. Biographies will also help Perfect Paulas and Competent Carls go beyond the details of names and dates

and develop an interest in the stories of history that tie things together making it applicable to modern times.

History books from various publishers vary greatly in quality by grade level. Look for those that go beyond names and dates. Some A Beka history texts are excellent, but the overemphasis on trivia in the questions will kill the potential interest of all but the hardiest Perfect Paula. We need to create our own questions for discussion and, with A Beka or any other history text, look for opportunities to use field trips and activities as lessons.

Wiggly Willy Prefers
- heroes (biographies, both written and on tape)
- historically-based adventure stories
- study of wars, possibly through reenactment
- dress-up and acting
- travel/field trips
- three-dimensional map making
- making dioramas or projects if not too complicated

Wiggly Willy needs help to tie together events, people, and places (time lines), and to understand the relevancy of history to us today (tie in with current events).

Perfect Paula Prefers
- names and dates
- studying in chronological order
- tracing maps
- making time lines

Perfect Paula needs encouragement to read biographies, historical fiction, and novels that give life to historical figures.

Competent Carl Prefers
- patterns in history
- studying the relationship of more technical subjects to history
- laws and principles
- What if...? questions

Competent Carl needs help to see God's plan in history and to develop an understanding of people and motivations in history.

Sociable Sue Prefers
- biographies
- historical novels
- studying concepts rather than details
- field trips
- activities/crafts
- acting out historical events

Sociable Sue needs encouragement to learn details of history.

Planning Our Approach

As mentioned above, one of our goals is to provide an overview of state, national, and world history. We sometimes take whatever social studies or history text is offered by our favorite publisher for a grade level without regard to the subject matter or our own scope and sequence (where we are heading and when). We need to lay out a plan of which topics we plan to cover in which year. When we have children of various ages this gets tricky. We may have a fourth grader who needs to cover state history and an eighth grader who has not yet had United States history. It is difficult to cover different areas of history in the same year and still do a decent job. It is better to choose one area on which to concentrate. In the above instance, it might be best to cover United States history with both students, requiring more work and reading from the older student, and postpone state history for a year or two.

I have some prejudices about the sequence of history topics. The history of the United States is very much a reflection of world history. The roots of our country are tightly bound up with European history. However, many publishers offer United States history before world history. (The same thing is true of state history study in most cases.) This is probably because the United States is the more familiar topic. Publishers assume that children can better understand that which is close in time and distance. But in terms of providing a foundation for understanding, it makes little sense, since world history provides the necessary backdrop for United States history.

However, many children are not ready for a full chronological historical study before upper elementary grades. Their grasp of time sequence and relationships of events is too spotty to provide a foundation for future study. In that case, we can introduce United States history whenever we wish, recognizing that we will be covering it more fully later.

Considering these factors, we need not worry about a specific sequence in early elementary grades. However, we should plan for the upper elementary years, or possibly for junior or senior high school, to begin a chronological study of history that begins with world history and follows with United States history.

I would suggest history studies according to a schedule such as the following:

Kindergarten through 3rd grades: families, communities, introduction to history, geography, and other cultures

4th grade: state history with lots of field trips (Note: some states require it to be taught either in the elementary grades or at high school level, so this one is really flexible.)

5th grade: world history through the Middle Ages

6th grade: world history from the Middle Ages through modern times

7th grade: early U.S. history, including study of the Constitution

8th grade: modern U.S. history and current events

Difficulties with Textbook Level

If we follow the above sequence for history, we might run into problems finding a text we like which is written at the appropriate grade level. When we encounter this problem, it is best to choose a text on a higher level, even if that means high school level, since it is easier to use parts of a text or bring it down to a lower level than it is to bring a text up to a usable level.

Completing Your Program

It is important that we not simply assign reading in a text to our child and leave it at that. Especially with younger children, I recommend reading the chosen textbook aloud. Oral discussion, research, and map work are important at all levels. At older levels, include notebooks, written reports, newspaper and magazine reading, and analysis of current events.

History Coverage through a Unit Study

If we use a unit study approach such as *The Classics*, *KONOS*, *The Weaver*, or *Alta Vista's Home School Curriculum*, we will find adequate social studies material included without having to use a separate social studies textbook at younger levels. Wooly Lambs' history-based unit studies focus primarily on history. See the review of their *History Links* in Chapter Five. Thus far they have units on *Creation*, *Mesopotamia*, *Ancient Egypt*, *Ancient Israel*, and *Ancient Greece*, with *Ancient Rome* due soon.

If we wish to use this approach through sixth or eighth grade, we must check the scope and sequence of our program to make sure we will be covering topics (probably not in proper time sequence) that will give a good overview of both United States and world history. A time line used with a unit study will provide the glue that pulls the history studies together. *KONOS* publishes time lines that correspond to each volume of their curriculum along with two special time lines, one on *Artists and Composers* and the other on *The Bible*.

More and more home school distributors and publishers are pulling together a variety of materials to create unit studies for historical periods. See descriptions of the *Greenleaf Guides* and materials from Beautiful Feet Books, Elijah Company, and Bluestocking Press under the various period headings. Also check out the Sonlight Curriculum which coordinates a variety of real books and texts for different topics.

Family History

Studying your family's history and genealogy can be an intriguing way to tackle history studies. This type of research can be as minimal or involved as you wish it to be. It usually requires a bit of work to dig up the information, but it can provide a wonderful avenue for letter writing and conversations with older relatives. If you are focusing on genealogy, the Mormon church is the most widely-recognized source of data. It is easy to create unit studies around historical research, perhaps even including field trips to track down information and visit sites of "family history.".

When we "meet" relatives from the different historical eras, it helps make those time periods come alive in a personal way for our children. This is even more exciting when we identify a well-known ancestor.

There are a number of software programs that help us compile family history, but they are too specialized for me to review for this book. However, *FrontPorch History* includes reviews and recommendations of such programs as well as a number of other resources that you should find helpful.

FrontPorch History: Researching and Telling Your Family's Stories

by Tammy Marshall Cardwell
(Greenleaf Press)
$9.95

Tammy Cardwell describes her personal family history project in this 74-page book. She tells how she sought out historical documents, letters, and memorabilia, then encouraged living family members to write about particular memories. Tammy compiled this collection, to which she added her own writings, to create a beautiful book. She includes details of the actual production of the book and worksheets for collecting and organizing data. Sharing about her experience, Tammy relates many of the pitfalls she encountered and many things she would do differently next time. One of the most important recommendations she makes is that you include your children in the project. Veteran homeschooler, Peggy Flint, then adds a chapter where she describes ways to translate Tammy's ideas into unit studies that involve your children. The appendices with reviews of recommended resources are very helpful to anyone interested in the subject. Although the book sometimes focuses too much on what Tammy thinks she should have done differently, it does serve as a practical guide for tackling such projects.

Time Lines/Memorizing Names and Dates

There is a strong temptation to push our children to memorize names and dates for history rather than focus on the overall picture of events. Along with the temptation comes the danger of instilling in our children a dislike of the subject. A more effective method to help children grasp the relationships of time and people is to have them construct time lines of their own, filling in drawings and written information reflecting what they have learned. This can be a do-it-yourself project, or

we might purchase one of the aids listed below.

Book of the Centuries and History Helps

(Small Ventures) *Book of the Centuries* - $29.95; *History Helps* -$11.95; both books -$39.95

Book of the Centuries is a time line offering the most significantly different option among all of those I have reviewed. It is contained in a large, seven-ring binder so that we can add manila envelopes to hold pictures of projects, research reports or other extras. Children should each have their own book in which they draw, write, color, or paste information, illustrations, etc. from history. Most of the book is set up with one century covering two facing pages. (1600 A.D. to the present is given twice as much space.) Small Ventures solved the problem of beginning dates by providing undated pages for Creation, The Fall, The Flood, and From the Flood to 3500 B.C. From 3500 B.C. on, the time line is marked off in increments of 10 years. These pages are blank, aside from the time line at the top. Inserted between each two pages is a 3/4-size, lined page on which students can write notes. (The time line is visible above the notes.) This layout creates tremendous flexibility. Younger children might begin by entering drawings, then in subsequent years, add notes as they become more proficient writers. Two pages of suggestions for using the book are at the beginning. Durable, laminated covers should help it hold up under constant use.

An optional companion to the *Book of Centuries* is *History Helps: A Parent/Teacher Guide*. *History Helps* explains the "why to" and "how to" for teaching history from a Christian perspective. It is not a curriculum, but it tells us how to select history resources (with descriptions of recommended resources) and combine them with literature, time lines, and activities. A section detailing events for a Biblical time line (following a "literal" interpretation of Scripture for dates) fills the gap we find in most textbooks, even those from Christian publishers. General information about the major civilizations, including religious issues and events, is outlined with dates. At the end of the book is a selection of reproducible maps.

Catholic World History Timeline and Guide

(Marcia Neill)
$89.95

Most timelines represent world history from a Protestant view, breezing over early church fathers and other people and events that receive greater attention in Catholic history texts. This timeline set includes most figures you find in other timelines plus those of especial interest to Catholics. Brightly-colored, heavy-duty paper is cut into strips to mount on the wall. The 700+ figures are engravings, drawings, and photos, mostly from out-of-print resources. Some more recent historical event photos taken by a White House photographer have been included by special permission. Each picture (approx. 2" x 2") is labeled with names or events and dates. These are printed with black ink on cream-colored card stock, and they may be colored in with soft colored pencils, although it isn't necessary. Patterns for additional stick figures are supplied. The 290-page book provides instructions for constructing the timeline and using it as a teaching tool. It includes charts showing the people or events, date for location on timeline, and a brief summary of the "contribution" of the event or person. Many "summaries" are much longer than we find in other timeline books. Extra chapters on American presidents and the Papacy add much more detail on each president and Church history respectively. The book sometimes includes cross references to the Catechism of the Catholic Church, especially in the time periods corresponding to those of the Bible.

Early American History Time Line
by Rea Berg
(Beautiful Feet Books)
$8.95; 2-student pack - $13.95

Covering the period from Leif Erikson through the Civil War, this time line works as a student kit for students to color, cut, and paste (onto the provided strips of heavy paper) as they study events from this time period. It can be used as a supplement with any other methods and ties in particularly well to Rea Berg's *Early American History: A Literature Approach.*

Historical TimeLine Figure Set
(J & K Schooling)
Timeline - $8; basic figure set - $28; all figure sets - $52

This is a make-it-yourself timeline plus a set of more than 400 figures to color, cut, and paste onto the timeline. You are free to photocopy the pages of figures for each of the children in your family. J & K recommends laminating or covering the sheets with contact paper for durability. You might also use temporary tacky glue rather than permanent glue to mount your figures so that you can remove or rearrange them. The timeline itself is only about three inches wide, but it is very long. It has been designed so that it curves back on itself so that it can be put on a single wall (approx. 5' x 7') or even hung on a shower curtain (great idea!). A large proportion of the figures are unique (e.g., the sinking of the Titanic, bombing of Pearl Harbor), but some are generalized pictures with identifications such as the ships for sea-borne explorers and pennants for other types of explorers. The 400 figures are divided into categories: artists, Bible/religious leaders, American history, indians and tribes, miscellaneous, presidents, great thinkers, authors, composers, world history, inventors, poets, states, and wars. Some blank figures are included for our own customization. Additional sets of figures for *More World History; More Bible; Famous Quotes; More American History; The 1900s; Missionaries, Martyrs and More*; and *Conquerers, Rulers and Popes* are available for $4 to $6 per set. All sets (approximate-

ly 700 figures) can be purchased together to save money. If you use Sonlight Curriculum, more than 80% of the figures are represented within J & K's sets.

History of California Time Line
by Rea Berg (Beautiful Feet Books)

See description under resources for California History.

Mark-It Timeline of History
(Geography Matters)
laminated - $9.95; paper - $4.95

The *Mark-It Timeline of History* is a poster-size, two-sided chart on which you create your own time line. On one side are lines already marked off into eras from 4000 BC to 2050 AD. On the reverse are lines only so that you can fill in your own dates to concentrate on a more limited span of history. On the laminated version, you can change information and reuse it over and over again.

Medieval History Time Line
by Rea Berg
(Beautiful Feet Books)
$8.95; 2-student pack - $13.95

The format is the same as the other Beautiful Feet Books time lines. See the review of *A Literature Approach to Medieval History* for an idea on how to use it.

Social Studies for Grades K-3

Many people believe that before we can learn about other places and people we need to learn about ourselves. I am not certain I agree with that conclusion, but it underlies the typical school scope and sequence. The usual approach is to study first those things in closest proximity to the child—each person's uniqueness, his family, home, and community. This is easily accomplished without a textbook. For children ages five to seven, talking about these things throughout the day, taking field trips to the post office, fire station, police station, etc., and reading to them from books that broaden their horizons will accomplish as much or more than textbooks might.

If family history is an uncomfortable subject, we might choose a more popularly recognized area of history to study with a younger child, although it is still not necessary to use a textbook. We might choose to cover some beginning United States history touching on topics such as the Pilgrims, Indians, and our flag. We could also read biographies of famous Americans and books such as *Little House on the Prairie*. If jumping from topic to topic bothers us, we can tie events together with some coherence by choosing materials (biographies, field trips, etc.) that are related to a theme, such as early American history, and by creating a time line.

Typical textbooks for social studies/history for the early

grades are usually a hodgepodge of community helpers, geography, biographies, American history, and other cultures. Most topics are simply being introduced so there is often very minimal content on any one topic. Content is also simplified so that students in the primary grades can read these books on their own. We can usually do as good a job or better by using library books and other resources for the early grades in place of textbooks. Our children can then assimilate much more information from more challenging books if we read the books to them. After third grade is a better time to consider using textbooks as we begin to study topics more in-depth.

I seldom recommend non-Christian social studies textbooks because the secular point of view which tries to ignore God warps the interpretation of events. The few secular books recommended are of such high quality that they are worth editing for non-Christian viewpoints.

Textbooks for Early Levels of Social Studies

If you wish to use textbooks, consider some of the following. Note that suggested grade levels are usually shown after the publisher's name.

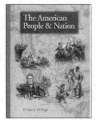

The American People and Nation

(Christian Liberty Press) [first-second grade]

$6; teacher's manual - $4

This book is somewhat similar to the original *Our Christian Heritage* series. It is an 8 1/2" by 11" workbook, printed in black and white, and it teaches a providential view of history. Topics cover a broad range of introductory level material: the Bible as history, great Christians of the past, the Pilgrims, life in early America, the forming of our nation, study of land and oceans, the first and second World Wars, and some of the changes in our country during and since the Civil War. The coverage is very brief. An accompanying Teacher's Manual outlines activities and questions to broaden the study. Very large, clear print is easy for children to read, but the vocabulary is not controlled, so parents must work with their children.

America's Christian History, Christian Self-Government, [Levels A through H for grades 1-8]

by Jean S. Smithies

(Intrepid Books)

$12.95 each

This is a series of study guides based upon the Principle Approach. While they refer to some other Principle Approach books, these study guides will stand alone. These books are about principles and concepts rather than straightforward history, although history certainly is learned in the context of

ideas. The books are designed to be read to younger children. The language has purposely been kept at a higher level. Some of the content for early grades seems much too abstract for most children to absorb, but I know that the author is trying to encourage a higher level of scholarship among our children. In spite of that, I would suggest shifting the series back a few years, beginning in third grade rather than first to ensure that children really learn the concepts. Those who have seen the large, red Principle Approach books or James Rose's book might have felt overwhelmed and shied away from this method of learning, but these books are well-written and concise, making the Principle Approach accessible to everyone.

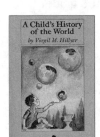

A Child's History of the World

by Virgil M. Hillyer

(Calvert School)

book - $35; CD-ROM - $40

Have you tried to find an out-of-print copy of this classic book and realized how scarce they are? Calvert School has remedied the situation with this newly-printed, updated edition. Hillyer's elementary-level world history is a classic that will continue to grow in popularity with this beautiful new, hardbound edition.

The primary appeal is the writing style. Hillyer speaks to children in ways they understand, yet he doesn't talk down to them in the short, choppy sentences typical of most texts written for this level. The difference is obvious in the page count: 618 pages. Illustrations are minimal: a few maps, line drawings, and, occasionally, words arranged to convey an idea. (Can you imagine any modern publisher offering a textbook this length for fourth graders without color illustrations?) In spite of these contrasts with modern texts, Hillyer's book is far better in my estimation. It offers depth and interest lacking in most textbooks. Children's imaginations will be engaged by the stories of history told in their proper settings with enough detail to make them come alive.

This updated edition covers up through the breakup of the U.S.S.R. It also reaches beyond Europe, the Middle East, and North America with selected coverage of other countries and cultures.

Hillyer clearly asserts Christian belief, although his Biblical references imply a questioning of the truthfulness of Old Testament stories and sometimes slightly misinterpret the text. For instance, he says, "King Saul had a daughter, and she fell in love with this... David the Giant-Killer, and at last they were married." This version overlooks the fact that Saul had promised his daughter in marriage to whoever killed the giant. The beginning of the book also discusses cave men and prehistory in a manner with which some might disagree (e.g., cavemen talked in grunts).

A Child's History of the World really should be read aloud together, so such things as I've mentioned can easily be discussed when you encounter them. I suggest you purchase a copy of this edition just in case it disappears from print again. {Note: this book and associated lessons are included in Calvert's fourth grade curriculum.]

A CD-ROM, multi-media version of this book is also available. It includes illustrations, "...original art, original music, and opportunities for student interaction. Stories are followed by review questions and games that are scored by the computer."(SE)

Great American Heroes (History course)
(Landmark's Freedom Baptist Curriculum) [third grade]
$35

This self-contained course, suggested for third grade, features heroes such as Christopher Columbus, Benjamin Franklin, Patrick Henry, Abraham Lincoln, and Thomas Edison. It also stretches the course title to include discussion of topics such as Indians and their homes, the Pilgrims, and school in pioneer days. Each lesson begins with vocabulary words to define from a dictionary. Students then read the lesson and answer questions, both short answer and essay. In an unusual feature for a course at this grade level, students are asked to write a report (about one per week) on an assigned topic (for which space is provided in the worktext). Students also write and memorize a Bible verse each week, with a "friend's" signature required for accountability on the memorization. Even though this black-and-white worktext includes quite a few illustrations, it isn't particularly appealing visually. However, it is interestingly written and should appeal on that strength to students even a year or two beyond third grade level. Weekly quizzes, quarterly tests, and answer key are included.

Greenleaf Press resources
See the reviews of Greenleaf's books under World History. Many of these are suitable for the early grades, but the *Greenleaf Guide to Old Testament History* and the *Greenleaf Guide to Ancient Egypt* are especially suitable.

Heritage Studies for Christian Schools, Books 1 and 2, 1996 editions
(Bob Jones University Press) [first and second grades]
Kit - $44; tests - $8; answer key - $4.50
These are beautifully-illustrated books, now in their second edition. However, I cannot recommend the first grade book. Even though the vocabulary has not been reduced to three- and four-letter words, sentence length, construction, and content suffered in the effort to write for young children. In comparison, the second grade book significantly

stretches sentence length and coverage of each topic. Still, as is true of most texts written for this level, each topic rates only from two to four paragraphs. Aside from a few digressions into local communities, farming, and brief sketches of a few European monarchs, the text focuses on topics related to early American history. Activity suggestions are included in the text. The Teacher's Edition (now available in a Home Teacher's Edition) offers useful teaching instruction. A Student Notebook (94 pages) provides worksheets for questions, maps, charts, puzzles, games, and other teaching tools. All three components are packaged as a Home School Kit which saves money over buying the items individually. Tests and answer keys are available for both levels, but I would not recommend using them at these levels.

Heritage Studies for Christian Schools 3, second edition
(Bob Jones University Press) [third grade]
Kit - $38; tests - $8; answer key - $4.50
This 1997 edition of BJUP's third grade text is intended to cover U.S. history from the founding of our government up through the Civil War and westward movement. However, it takes a scattershot approach to history, mixing in a few lengthy sections on single topics (e.g., 15 pages on the French Revolution), folk tales (as you would find in a reader), biographical sketches, map/geography lessons, and social studies topics such as transportation, time zones, and cultural approaches to music making. A "Resource Treasury" at the back of the book features pictures and data on presidents, maps, a glossary, and other resource information. *Heritage Studies for Christian Schools 4* continues to follow the historical timeline through modern American history. A companion Timeline is available for this text, but the classroom-size illustrations are probably too large for most home schools. (A smaller *Time Line Snapshots* version, created for home schoolers, is included in the home school kits beginning with fourth grade level.) The Home Teacher's Edition is useful but not essential. Questions, maps, charts, puzzles, and games provide lesson reinforcement in the Student Notebook. All three of these components (text, student notebook, and teacher's edition) plus test and answer key are packaged as a kit which is less expensive than buying the items individually.

History for Little Pilgrims
(Christian Liberty Press) [first and second grades]
text - $9.50; teacher's manual - $5; coloring book - $2
This is a very unusual history book, especially for the early grades. The purpose of this book is to provide a view of history that puts God

at the center. Thus, the first half of this history text is actually more of a Bible and Protestant church history. Then it shifts to highlights of American history for the second half. Aimed at first and second graders, the book features large print and colorful, cartoon illustrations by Vic Lockman. The vocabulary is challenging enough that parents will need to read it to most first graders and some second graders.

Since the purpose is to present "His Story," the authors have selected highlights to illustrate God's working through history rather than trying to cover subject matter comprehensively. For example, the book begins with creation, the flood, and the Tower of Babel. It discusses the beginnings of the church, the spread of the church, and the Reformation (disproportionately large coverage of this topic with entire sections on Luther and Calvin). Then, American History mentions exploration and colonization, the Great Awakening, the Revolution, westward movement, and other selected topics up to the present, with a few pages devoted to each. Brief unit review questions and answers are included in the text.

The teacher's manual expands on topics presented in the text, gives a memory verse to be learned with each unit, defines the words to know (listed in the text without definitions), and offers additional discussion questions and activities. Using the teacher's manual will require some preparation time for parents to read through the material before presenting each lesson. The optional coloring book features black-and-white versions of Lockman's illustrations.

History in His Hands: Volume One Ancient History, A Biblical Perspective *and* Volume Two, New Testament, Early Church, and Middle Ages History
by Joyce Herzog
(Simplified Learning Products)

Vol. 1: read aloud book - $9.95; study guide - $9.95; Vol. 2: read aloud book - $14.95, study guide - $12.95

History is a wonderful vehicle for helping children begin to develop a Biblical Christian worldview, and *History in His Hands* is purposely designed to do just that. Herzog retells ancient history in the *Read Aloud* Volume One, beginning with creation and continuing up to the Roman occupation of Israel just before the arrival of the Messiah. Much of this is a retelling of the Bible for young children (kindergarten through about second grade level), emphasizing the character of God since this is the foundation for our judgments of right and wrong. As children begin to develop a Christian worldview, they can then better understand the story as it branches out to other peoples. We can continue, then, to read about the Greeks, the Chinese, Hindus, and other religious, ethnic, and political groups now that we have a context for understanding.

We can create a timeline to accompany our reading and let

that be the extent of the study. Or, after we finish reading, we can go back and do some real studying by using the Study Guides. Herzog suggests two study options: chronological or interest-directed study. We need our primary resource book which will be *The Children's Bible* (published by Western Publishing Company). She also recommends that we use three other tools: *Halley's Bible Handbook, What the Bible is All About for Young Explorers*, and *30 Days to Understanding the Bible*. She says, "You can complete your study using only the above books appropriate for the age level you are working with and the encyclopedia for the secular history." But there are many wonderful books available to enrich each topic. These are listed in the Resource List in the Study Guide.

A study plan, laid out in chronological order, is designed to highlight people, events and topics, rather than cover the Old Testament in its entirety. Each section has a rough lesson plan which lists Scripture to be read and discussion suggestions. Other elements vary from lesson to lesson but include such things as correlation with other reading, craft and/or activity ideas. Again, the emphasis throughout is on developing worldview understanding, albeit at introductory levels. There are charts (with instructions for how they are to be completed) to accompany some of the lessons. Charts filled in with the appropriate information are included as a sort of answer key. Study of various topics can be expanded with suggested books or others we might choose. The study guides and charts were designed to cover a wide age span with questions to talk about or research, and Biblical principles to apply to life. Some lesson preparation is required once we move beyond the actual "history" reading, but the amount of time required will depend upon how far we want to develop related activities and reading. The basic volume can be used alone, but I recommend you also use the Study Guide and extra resources to get the most out of this valuable study.

Note: *History in His Hands* Volume One should also work well with learning-handicapped children who might be beyond second grade level but who have not grasped the big picture of history.

The second volume tries to cover a huge amount of territory: the New Testament era and the early Church up through the Middle Ages. While it briefly covers a broad range of historical highlights, most emphasis is upon church history from a Protestant perspective. The format is similar to that of the first volume, although it is clearly aimed at an older audience. Many of the ideas brought out in volume two would be very appropriate for high school research and discussion.

History Stories for Children
by Dr. John W. Wayland, Revised and edited by Michael J.

McHugh
(Christian Liberty Press)
$6; answer key - $1

The sixty-four short stories in this book help bring history to life. Stories are designed to be read to children, although they can be read by children independently by third or fourth grade level. With only a few exceptions, stories are from American history rather than world history with a few Bible stories mixed in. Many stories have been adapted to tie in with holidays and anniversaries such as "Saint Valentine," "Easter Lilies," and "Hatchets and Cherries." Because the stories are quite short, this book will not serve as a foundation for study, but it will make an excellent supplement to history studies for most elementary grades. A "Note to the Teacher" follows most stories with brief background information and/or teaching suggestions. Large page and print size make this book very easy to read.

Map Skills A and B

(Continental Press) [second and third grades]
$5.95 each; teacher's guides - $2.50 each

These workbooks cover beginning map skills. Level A introduces maps, symbols, keys, directions, the poles, and the equator. Level B reviews introductory information, then teaches about political, physical, and product maps, continents, oceans, and hemispheres. These simple books might be used with bright students a year younger than suggested.(S)

My America and My World

(A Beka Book) [first grade]
$9.20; teacher edition - $19.45

This very brief overview of the United States and the world is patriotic and upbeat. It offers tidbits about famous people and places (including the fable about George Washington and the cherry tree). "World" study features a few paragraphs about selected countries. The only way I recommend this book to you is if you purchase the teacher edition. The last half of that edition is the student text, so you need not purchase a separate student book. The first half of the teacher edition fleshes out and enlivens lessons with lesson plans that include reading comprehension, vocabulary, geography, and writing activities; additional background information; and other enrichment activities. Of course, this requires teacher presentation, but it should require minimal preparation time.

Our America, third edition

(A Beka Book) [second grade]
$9.20; teacher edition - $19.45

This textbook provides an introduction to our country's history. It teaches about our flag, patriotic holidays and songs (music included), then shifts to brief historical vignettes and/or summaries about the Separatists, Indians, colonists, pioneers,

cowboys, and immigrants. Plenty of full-color pictures and large print make the appearance appealing to children. Although it has a good deal more text than does the first grade book from A Beka, *Our America* still covers topics superficially. Comprehension questions are at the end of each chapter, and vocabulary words are featured in boxes. Enrichment activities sometimes appear at the ends of chapters. You should not need an answer key or the teacher edition for this book. I suggest supplementing with historical stories, biographies, and activities.

Our American Heritage

(A Beka Book) [third grade]
$11.30; teacher edition - $22.20; answer key - $5.95; test/quiz book - $4.20; map study book - $4.20; keys to test/quiz book and map study book - $6.30 each

This colorful book is essentially short biographies of famous Americans. Read excerpts with your child or have him or her read using the text as a reading comprehension tool. Then check out full-length books about people mentioned in the book who interest your child. The teacher edition has lesson plans and answers, but is probably of minimal use. An answer key is available separately. The *Map Study Skills* book should be useful, but the test/quiz book is probably not very important at this level.

Our Christian Heritage, books A and B

[first, second, or third grades]
$7.50 each or complete set for $34.50

These workbooks with fill-in-the-blank exercises are most appropriate for Perfect Paulas but probably also useful for Competent Carls and Sociable Sues. While they can be used as independent workbooks, I recommend using them for reading and discussion rather than as workbooks for children to read and fill in on their own. Book A can be used at first or, more likely, second grade level, depending on the child. The first two books study our globe, the continents, creation, rules and their importance for people living in groups, and beginning information on important events in United States history. Throughout all books runs the providential viewpoint that God's hand is upon all of history. The black-and-white presentation in this series of five books is not particularly appealing, but the content is excellent.

Revised editions, now in print, will eventually replace the first editions reviewed above. The revised editions have about 35% more material in each book, have companion teachers manuals, and are printed in two colors (which I'm not certain is an enhancement from reviewing the sixth grade student book printed in magenta and black). The Principle Approach is also much more evident in these editions. The first grade book covers content fairly similar to the original books A and B. The second grade book discusses self-government, communities, state and national government organization, national holidays, songs, and monuments, the Constitution and Bill of Rights, key figures in American history, directions, climate zones, map legends, and natural resources. Student books are $7.50 each. Teacher manuals that provide lots of background information on both content and teaching strategies as well as worksheets, activity suggestions, quizzes, and tests cost $22.50 each.

Our Christian Heritage C

[third, fourth, or fifth grade]
original edition - $7.50 each or complete set for $34.50

See description above. This book provides an overview of both world and American geography and history. The revised version for third grade discusses God's establishment of government on earth, early forms of government, the Ten Commandments in relation to government, the difference between a democracy and a republic, American expansion, an overview of history from Adam and Eve through the Civil War, church beginnings, physical and political geography, geographical study of the continents and the 50 states, hemispheres, directions, natural resource maps, and key figures such as Luther, Columbus, Squanto, Washington, Lewis and Clark, the Whitmans, and Lincoln. See the description of the revised editions in the review immediately above. [New editions: grade three student book - $8.50; teacher manual - $23.50]

Methods and Materials Recommendations by Topic

In the following section I list textbooks under topic headings rather than grade levels since we may choose to cover the topic areas in a different order than the publishers. The publisher's suggested grade level is listed in brackets.

State History

Somewhere around fourth grade level is the most common time for studying state history, although some states require it at high school level. In some states, only a part of a school year is set aside for state history, in some the entire year is used, while in others there is no state history requirement. We can often determine for ourselves what we wish to do. Actually, we should not be overly concerned about state history. What happens if we move out of state next year? We are certainly not obligated to teach five different states' history if we happen to live in five different states during our home schooling years. On the other hand, state history can be much more fun since we can tie in field trips and activities more easily than with United States and world history. Just keep it in proper perspective.

Many textbook publishers offer regional history coverage, but no specific state history books. Most states require that you cover state history, but coverage as part of a regional study may be adequate although less interesting. Consider putting together your own state history program based on real books, field trips, museums, landmarks, and help from historical societies.

Sometimes textbooks of the larger states' histories are available. If you would like a state history text, contact your local or state Department of Education, if possible, and ask for a textbook recommendation. Do not do this if they are antagonistic toward home educators! Most current state history textbooks appear to be written by formula and are generally very boring.

For those looking for resources related to their states, I have begun to compile information about useful materials as I discover them. Since I live in California, the list is quite obviously lopsided in representing that state. For many states, I have yet to discover what is available, so please send me your suggestions.

Some publishers such as Children's Press have published one book for each state. Check out their "America the Beautiful" series written for grades 5-8, and the "Sea to Shining Sea" series written for grades 3-5. There are 52 volumes in each series, one for each state plus Washington D.C. and Puerto Rico. (Approximately two-thirds of these books are also available in paperback editions.) These can often be found in libraries.

Alpha Omega is developing *Switched On Schoolhouse* programs for each state's history, although these are geared toward high school level.

You might also be interested in having your child create his own *State History Chronicles* notebook using Hewitt Homeschooling Resources book [$17.95]. It comes in a three-ring binder with brief instructions and suggestions. The rest of the book consists of heavyweight, cream-colored pages for students to complete. There are pages for the state tree, song, statistics, and other such data; pages to write about tourism, transportation, and points of interest; pages to record field trip experiences; and much more. This should be a useful tool for students to organize and present their studies based on an assortment of books, activities, and field trips.

Arkansas

Arkansas History In Light of the Cross

(State Histories)
worktext - $12, teacher guide - $7

A providential view of history is presented in this state history worktext. Student worktexts present reading material, activities, and questions, while the teacher guide provides lesson plans, quizzes, teaching helps, and answer keys. The books are presented in comb-bound format, printed in black-and-white, including a few illustrations. They are not fancy, but they present the material from a biblical Christian worldview. The Arkansas study for elementary grades is presented chronologically from the 1500s through the present. State Histories also publishes a high school level text that expands topical coverage into resources, agriculture, railroads, and a few other topics. You might have a younger and older student both working through these texts simultaneously, but completing their workbooks activities designed for the different levels.

California

California Missions

by Randy L. Womack
(Golden Educational Center)
$15.95

This 200+ page book is the most comprehensive book I'm aware of about the California Missions that is written for children. It includes an introductory section of historical background which is extremely helpful. It outlines the political, economic, religious, and geographical issues that are crucial to understanding how the missions came into being and what happened because of them. You might need to expand upon information in the book if your children haven't yet learned about early explorers or some world history events.

The bulk of the book consists of studies of each of the missions. Facts about the mission; about two pages of history; vocabulary and "review questions; a crossword puzzle, wordsearch, or other puzzle in most lessons; and a page about the present-day status of the mission comprise each lesson. Activities within the lessons are varied enough to encourage student interest more than you might expect in such a book. Maps, diagrams, and photos are included.

Craft ideas, a glossary, bibliography, helpful charts, addresses and contact numbers for each, and an answer key are at the back of the book. The overall presentation seems to objectively and accurately portray the motivations and conflicts surrounding the missions. The book is recommended for grades 4-8, but it is so well-written that anyone with an interest in California history should find it useful.

Golden Educational Center also sells a sturdy, full-color poster with a map of California showing mission locations and Indian tribal areas plus photos of each mission [$5.95].

California Weekly Explorer

by Don Oliver
(California Weekly Explorer)
standard set - $33.75

In the *California Weekly Explorer*, thirty-four "newspapers" cover the complete California history and geography curriculum in a much more lively format than we find in textbooks. Although California history is typically taught in fourth grade,

these resources can be used with children from grades 4 through 7. Different topics are featured in each issue along with activity suggestions and a wealth of maps. The *Home School Educator's Standard Set* includes 1 set of 34 issues of CWE plus 1 teacher's manual, all boxed in a permanent container.

Exciting group presentations performed by representatives of the company are also available. These presentations have received rave reviews from all types of school groups for many years. Presentations being offered include "Walk through California," "Walk along the El Camino Real," "Walk through the American Revolution," "Walk through the West," "Walk through the Ancient World," and "Walk through Israel."

Other resources are offered by California Weekly Explorer. The *Student Atlas of California - 1999*, [student edition - $12; teacher edition - $14] has resource information on "...California Indians, missions, people, deserts, forests, farming, wilderness, cities, population, counties, weather, how to use maps, exploration, history time-lines, nature, vocabulary, and more....," all written at fourth grade level.

Lone Woman of Ghalas-Hat [$6 pb] tells the story of an Indian woman who is abandoned on one of the California islands for eighteen years. Unlike the similar fictional story in *Island of the Blue Dolphins,* this story is a non-fiction account for younger readers.

His California Story

by Lesha Myers
(Cameron Academy)
$24.95; teacher's supplement - $22.95

This is a courageously, politically-incorrect, aggressively Christian course in California history. It teaches facts we parents never learned when we attended school, while contradicting secular texts on many points. For example, in discussing the question, "Were the Indians Slaves?" Myers ends with the statement: "Far from treating the Indians as slaves, the Catholic missionaries were training them to be free - free from hunger and want, free from the bondage of their ungodly religion, and free to learn how to honor and serve the Lord" (p. 89).

The 282-page student text contains reading material and comprehension questions. It is heavily illustrated with photos and drawings. The teacher's supplement is essential for the complete course, although the text can stand on its own as a source of information. The teacher's supplement provides activity ideas, projects, oral discussion questions, tests, source documents, field trip ideas, and suggestions for further reading. The source documents are presented with additional discussion regarding some of the challenging topics.

This course can be very simply presented with a student completing the reading independently and by utilizing only a few of the suggestions from the teacher's supplement. Or it can be used as the foundation for extensive unit studies based on each topic. For example, in the Gold Rush Unit, students might do "character sketches" on James Marshall, Lewis Manly, or other significant people; study and memorize key dates, learn a "California History Song," identify geographical locations, add a number of assignments to their notebooks, and answer questions.

History of California: A Literature Approach
by Rea Berg
(Beautiful Feet Books)
Study Guide - $12.95; Basic Pack - $52.95; Jumbo Pack - $146.95

See the full description for Rea Berg's Study Guides under "United States History - Primary Resources." The California guide, *History of California*, follows the same format with 115 lessons. It is unusual in that it lays a foundation for the discovery and settlement of California by tracing back through some of the explorers, including Columbus. This strategy is based on the Principle Approach "idea" that there was a chain of providential settlement and spreading of the Gospel. Thus, books included in the Basic Pack are *Columbus* by the D'Aulaires, *Log of Columbus, Island of the Blue Dolphins, Carlota, Zia, Junipero Serra, Song of the Swallows, Blue Willow*, and *Patty Reed's Doll*. The Jumbo Pack adds *America's Providential History, Our Golden California, The Making of American California: A Providential Approach, History of California Time Line*, three *Story Hour* cassettes, a composition notebook, and the Study Guide. The Guide may be used for grades 4-6.

History of California Time Line
by Rea Berg (Beautiful Feet Books)
$8.95; 2-student pack - $13.95

Covering the period of 1492 through 1860, this time line includes illustrations for students to color (colored pencils recommended), cut, and paste onto the provided time line "strips." Illustrations relate to major people and events in the discovery, exploration, and settlement of California. This time line is useful with any California history study method, but it works especially well with literature-based approaches such the *History of California: A Literature Approach* from Beautiful Feet.

My California 21
(R.C. Law and Company, Inc.)
student packet - $19.90; comprehensive teaching manual - $54; set of both - $65; additional student sets - $14.90 each

This set of more than 30, four- to six-page lesson sheets in "newspaper" format teaches California history in a more appealing format than textbooks. Although *My California* is in a periodical format, the content is actually comparable to most texts. It features interesting presentations on history and geography with photos, and maps, as well as a few paper-and-pencil activities (including puzzles and quizzes), vocabulary words, reading and thinking skill development, and discussion questions. A complete index is included.

My California can be used either as your primary resource for covering California history or as a supplement. If used as your primary resource, you should pull additional activities from the Comprehensive Teacher's Manual or consider supplementing with other books and activities (e.g., field trip to missions or other historical sites, books from Beautiful Feet Books).

The lessons are designed to be interactive with students responding to questions throughout the lessons. The Comprehensive Teaching Manual includes all of the above plus "intensive, lesson-by-lesson review of content, theory, objective, and technique coupled with expanded aids, masters, and resources."(S)

Our Golden California

by Juanita Houston
(ETC Publications)
student book - $16.95; teacher's edition - $20.95; chapter tests - $13.95

Many of us will appreciate this easy-to-use, Christian alternative to California State series books. Juanita Houston's book, *Our Golden California*, was written for Christian students and can be used from about third through sixth grades. The book itself is a large 264-page paperback printed in black-and-white with many illustrations. Large type makes it easy on young eyes. Children can write in the book if we allow them, but having them instead do their writing in a separate notebook will allow us to use the book again with younger children.

Each chapter is followed by review questions to check on fact comprehension and by thought questions to encourage thinking beyond the surface. There are lines for answering questions in the book. Following the questions is an assignment sheet for working on a California notebook. The notebook will consist of written work, drawings, and maps. Those of us who want our children to make such a notebook will appreciate having all of the planning for assignments already done for us.

The writing style of the author is very readable. It is not broken into short, choppy sentences as we so often find in texts for this level. Instead, the author has done a skillful job of writing on a level children can understand even though sentences are longer and more involved than is typical for such books. A glossary is included at the back of the book for words that might be unfamiliar to students.

References to Christianity and God's providence are apparent throughout the book. They seem to present a balanced approach, particularly in regard to the Indians and the missions.

This book has everything we need for a thorough study about California. Historical coverage begins with the explorers and continues up to the present. Geography is used to enhance learning as children study and draw maps relating to the various topics. The only thing we might add would be biographies or historical novels. Student Tests are available in a separate, reproducible book (for class use only). A separate Teacher's Guidebook offers additional teaching and activity suggestions plus the answer keys for questions in both the student text and test book. It is possible to use the student text on its own as long as we do not feel the need for an answer key and teaching suggestions.

Social Studies School Service California

(Social Studies School Service)

This is an extensive catalog of resources primarily focused on teaching California history. Most resources are specialized rather than comprehensive. They include historical novels; biographies; geography studies; books about natural history, Indians, and missions; and broader topical books on the Gold Rush and "The West." If you want to put together your own California history course or if you want to supplement whatever else you are using, this catalog certainly offers a wide selection of resources to choose from.(S)

www.californiamissions.com

This web site features virtual tours of the California missions. Background information, photos, maps, and other illustrations make this a great site for researching the topic.

Colorado

Colorado History In Light of the Cross

(State Histories)

set of four worktexts - $24

A providential view of history is presented in this four-volume state history worktext. Student worktexts present reading material, activities, and questions. The fourth book is actually the teacher guide; it has a final exam, teaching helps, and answer keys. The books are presented in comb-bound format, printed in black-and-white, including a few illustrations. They are not fancy, but they present the material from a biblical Christian worldview. The Colorado study is presented chronologically from the 1500s through the present and also covers agriculture, railroads, natural resources, and education. The chronological coverage is in the first two books, while the other topics are addressed in the third book. If time is short,

you can use only the first two books.

Roadside History of Colorado

(Johnson Books)

$13.95

If the "field trip approach" appeals to you, this is the guide you need. Start traveling one of a number of highways in Colorado. *Roadside History* provides the maps, then stops us at various points along the way, telling the history associated with each place. (If they've built a 7-11 Store on the historical site, you might not bother stopping the car!) At 390 pages, this book covers a significant slice of history. While some of it is narrowly focused within the state, much of it deals with broader historical events such as the transcontinental railroad.(S)

Tales, Trails and Tommyknockers

(Johnson Books)

$8.95

Add still more color to Colorado history with this storybook. The tales are based on history, although some are more folklore- than history-based. Historical photos and illustrations add interest and appeal. Suggestion: read some of these stories while driving one of the suggested routes in *Roadside History*.(S)

District of Columbia

Red Rose Studio

Red Rose Studio publishes a number of books that might serve as supplements in your study. *Flashbacks Volume One:*  *A Cartoon History of the District of Columbia* and *Flashbacks Volume Two: District of Columbia Neighborhoods— A cartoon history* [$14.95 each], both by Patrick M. Reynolds, are collections of cartoons already published in newspapers that depict the actual history of D.C. with brief narratives and detailed drawings. Most are lengthy cartoon panels that actually provide quite a bit of historical fact. In keeping with the cartoon format, humor is injected here and there in the retelling.

Red Rose's photographic books might also be of interest. *Old Washington, D.C. in Early Photographs 1846-1932* [$10.95] features 224 photos by Robert Reed. *Washington, D.C. Then and Now* by Charles S. Kelly [$12.95] focuses on the architectural evolution of the city. *Washington Seen—A Photographic History* by F.M. Miller and H. Gillette, Jr. [$35.95] focuses on the people of Washington-how they lived and worked. Check their catalog for even more such titles.

Florida

Color Historic Florida

(Color Historic America, Inc.)

$3

Highlights of Florida's history, from its discovery by Juan Ponce de Leon to the present, provide coloring activities for children. Brief text on each page explains each picture. This 32-page book will supplement state history studies.

Georgia

Color Historic Atlanta, Color Historic Savannah, and Color Historic Georgia

(Color Historic America, Inc.)

$3 each

These 32-page educational coloring books offer tidbits of history in color book form as supplements to state studies. Brief explanations accompany each picture. Famous events, places, and people featured in *Savannah* are General James Oglethorpe, Tomochichi, the Girl Scouts, Forsyth Park, River Street, and Tybee Island. *Atlanta* features Standing Peachtree, Terminus, Stone Mountain, Zoo Atlanta, Fernbank Science Center, and Martin Luther King, Junior. *Georgia* includes pictures of the state bird, flower, and flag along with General James Oglethorpe, John Wesley, Button Gwinnett, and the first gold rush.

Hawaii

[Bess Press publishes a number of texts and other books on Hawaii and the Pacific Islands as well as resources on languages spoken in those areas such as Hawaiian and Japanese.]

The Hawaiians of Old

by Betty Dunford

(The Bess Press)

hardcover - $34.95, paperback - $29.95; workbook - $8.95; teacher's manual - $9.95

Short sentences and vocabulary appropriate for the elementary grades make this book suitable for students from about third grade through sixth. Illustrations are primarily black-and-white line drawings. The emphasis here is on Hawaiian culture—societal structure, rulers, warriors, fishermen, craftsmen, sports, games, foods, stories, music, religion, and daily life. Science related topics are also introduced, particularly at the beginning when children learn how the islands were formed. This is not a history book as such, although it occasionally mentions specific historical events or people. Treatment of the Hawaiian worship of gods and other practices based on superstitious beliefs is non-judgmental. I recommend that parents read this book along with their students so that they can discuss such issues. The workbook includes a variety of questions

(multiple choice, cause/result, fill-in the blank, true/false), puzzles, and other written activities. It does a commendable job of incorporating reading skill activities that move students beyond the simple recall level. The teacher's manual features discussion suggestions and an answer key for the workbook. There are no questions in the text itself. (SE)

Hawaii: The Pacific State

(The Bess Press)

hardcover - $39.95, paperback - $34.95; workbook - $8.95; answer key - $9.95

This text is suitable for upper elementary grades. It covers the birth of the islands up through present day. I have not reviewed this text (which replaces an earlier edition), but from the catalog description it seems to take a dimmer view of U.S. involvement and influence in Hawaii than do most history books. It deals with the overthrow of the monarchy by the U.S., sugar and pineapple industries as major factors in the state's development, the movement for Hawaiian sovereignty, and the push for return of land to Hawaiian natives.(SE)

Illinois

Illinois: The Prairie State

by Becky Daniel, illustrated by Gary Hoover

(ETC Publications)

$17.95; teacher's guide - $20.95; test booklet - $13.95

This illustrated history of Illinois follows state guidelines but includes "strong ecumenical Christian values." I bring it to your attention, although I have not reviewed it. It is recommended for grades 5-7 and covers both history and geography.

My Illinois

(R.C. Law and Company, Inc.)

student packet - $15.90 (big discounts for more than one packet sent to one address); standard teacher guide - $10; comprehensive teaching manual - $39

See the review of *My California*. Parts relating to U.S. history are identical in both publications, while all state content is different.

Indiana

My Indiana

(R.C. Law and Company, Inc.)

student packet - $15.90 (big discounts for more than one packet sent to one address); comprehensive teaching manual - $39

See the review of *My California*. Parts relating to U.S. history are identical in both publications, while all state content is different. *My Indiana* does not have a Standard Teacher's Guide, but only the Comprehensive Teacher's Manual.

Missouri

Missouri Department of Conservation
(Missouri Department of Conservation)

The Department of Conservation offers free or inexpensive materials to Missouri home schooling parents which can be reproduced for class use. While some items are of general scientific interest, a number are specifically for Missouri. Representative titles include Learning with Otis (practical conservation activities), Biogeography of Missouri, Missouri's Rare and Endangered Species, Prairie Life of Missouri, and Ecology of Missouri Forests. In addition to free items, the Department also has a number of books on outdoor/nature topics for sale. Write for information and an order form for materials. Materials can also be requested through their web site.

New York

Color Historic New York
(Color Historic America, Inc.)
$3

This 32-page educational coloring book offers tidbits of history in color book form as a supplement to state studies. A brief description accompanies each picture. Along with the state bird, flower, and flag, students color pictures of Henry Hudson, Peter Minuit, and the Erie Canal.

Red Rose Studio
Extras for studying about New York state or city are available from Red Rose Studio. Examples of some titles in their catalog are *Big Apple Almanac* (Volumes 1, 2, and 3) [$34.85 for the set] which contains the history of New York in graphic/illustrated format, *All Around the Town, Under the Sidewalks of New York, The Great New York City Trivia and Fact Book,* and *722 Miles—The Building of the Subways of New York.* (Contact Red Rose Studio for a complete catalog.)(SE)

North Carolina

North Carolina in a Nutshell
by Letz Farmer
(Mastery Publications)
$12.95

This is introductory history for children in grades 3 through 7. It features information, maps, puzzles, research activities, writing assignments, an answer key, a list of places of interest

(potential field trips), a bibliography, and more. Home schooling families can reproduce pages, using one book for the entire family. Schools or groups that charge tuition must purchase books for each student.

Oklahoma

Oklahoma History In Light of the Cross
(State Histories)

A providential view of history is presented in this state history course. There are three different format options from which to choose. There is a set of three worktexts with a companion teacher guide for the elementary level [$24]. There is a condensed, single-volume version of the worktexts with a companion teacher guide [$19]. The condensed version skips natural resources, agriculture, education, aviation, and a few other such topics and is designed for a 5-9 week time frame. The third option is to use State Histories' high school level text, the content of which is very similar to the elementary three-volume series, along with the teacher's guide that allows us to teach both high school and elementary grade level students at the same time [$21].

Student worktexts present reading material, activities, and questions, while the teacher guide provides lesson plans, quizzes, teaching helps, and answer keys. The books are presented in comb-bound format, printed in black-and-white, including a few illustrations. They are not fancy, but they present the material from a biblical Christian worldview.

Pennsylvania

Red Rose Studio

Everything you ever wanted to know about Pennsylvania (plus Trivial Pursuit type tidbits) can be found in books from the Red Rose Studio. The *Pennsylvania Profiles* (ten volumes) combine history, legend, and trivia with cartoon illustrations. Each 56-page volume seems to vaguely follow some sort of theme, but they certainly do not read like history books. For instance, Volume Fourteen, subtitled "It Started in Pennsylvania," gives detailed accounts of how the Pennsylvania Turnpike started, the invention of toilet paper and root beer, Pennsylvania's only gold mine, the "Peanut King," the "Dragon Lady," and more. Other informative and

entertaining ways to learn about the commonwealth include *Pennsylvania Firsts—The Famous, Infamous, and Quirky of the Keystone State* by Patrick M. Reynolds [$9.95], *Pennsylvania Tales* by Webb Garrison [$8.95], *Coal and Coke in PA* [$16.95], and *The Delaware Indians* [$19.95]. (Contact Red Rose Studio for a complete catalog.)(SE)

Texas

My Texas
(R.C. Law and Company, Inc.)
student packet - $15.90 (big discounts for more than one packet sent to one address); standard teacher guide - $10; comprehensive teaching manual - $39

My Texas follows the same format as *My California*. See the review under California history.

Red Rose Studio
The *Texas Lore Collection* is similar to the *Pennsylvania Profiles* series described above, both from Red Rose Studio. There are twelve, 56-page volumes covering history, legend, and trivia from Texas' past. Red Rose also offers *The Texas Rangers, The Indians of Texas,* and *Ghost Towns of Texas.* (Contact Red Rose Studio for a complete catalog.)(SE)

Texas History In Light of the Cross
(State Histories)
worktext - $12, teacher guide - $7

A providential view of history is presented in this state history worktext. A student worktext presents reading material, activities, and questions, while the teacher guide provides lesson plans, quizzes, teaching helps, and answer keys. The books are in comb-bound format, printed in black-and-white, including a few illustrations. They are not fancy, but they present the material from a biblical Christian worldview. The Texas study for elementary grades is presented chronologically from the 1500s through the present. State Histories also publishes a high school level text with separate workbook that cover essentially the same material. You might have a younger and older student both working through these texts simultaneously, but completing their workbooks activities designed for the different levels.

Canadian History

I have reviewed only a few resources for Canadian History. Canadian History resources are available from the Canadian distributors listed in this book: Canadian Home Education Resources, Home and Hearth, The Home Works, and Maple Ridge Books. Also see the reviews of *Golden Educational Center Province Studies* and Rod and Staff's *Homelands of North America.*

Canadian Province Notebook
(A Beka Book) [$6.85]

Canadian students will find A Beka's *Canadian Province Notebook* a useful tool for focusing research and organizing the presentation of information for their studies. Instructions at the beginning of the book tell how to do the research. The remaining pages can be used for the actual presentation. Pages have headings, boxes for illustrations, specific spaces such as the one for drawing Canada's flag, and general directions for completing each page. Time line and map pages help children gain historical and geographical perspectives. Research must be done from other sources, but this notebook saves students' time by narrowing research topics and providing a ready-made presentation format. (Suggested for 4th-6th grade levels.)

My First History of Canada
by Donalda Dickie, revised and updated by Rudiger Krause
(Red Leaf Press)
$18.95 (Canadian)

Originally published in 1958, this edition has been updated and slightly revised to bring it up to date. Like many books written during this time period, it has solid content and acknowledges Christian influence in history. The writing style is appropriate for children about grades 3 - 6. The author uses story-telling to make history come alive, and line-drawing illustrations and maps add some visual interest. Questions and activities for each chapter are at the end of the book. The extensive index is also very helpful.

World History—Primary Resources

Beautiful Feet Books selected materials
For a study of medieval history, Beautiful Feet Books offers a selection of books rather than texts. Their list includes titles such as *Adam of the Road, Otto of the Silver Hand, Canterbury Tales, Men of Iron, Ivanhoe, The Door in the Wall, King John and Henry VIII, Tales from Shakespeare, Robin Hood,* and *King Arthur and the Knights of the Round Table.* See *A Literature Approach to Medieval History,* also from Beautiful Feet Books, reviewed below.

Creation to Canaan
(Rod and Staff)
student text - $11.35; workbook - $5.05; teacher's workbook manual - $ 7.70; test booklet - $1.90

Although this book is designated for seventh grade level, the reading level is easy enough for many fifth and sixth graders. Black-and-white photos, maps, and illustrations help children visualize people, places, and events. The Rod and Staff catalog describes the intent of this text well: [to] "center on the place of God's people in history, instead of idealizing military heroes and super-power nations. We want to guide our students to a better understanding of God's unfolding plan for mankind rather than following man's pursuits, achievements, and culture from a humanistic perspective."

The text covers history from Creation through the conquest

and settlement of Canaan. The time period overlaps that of most world history courses, but the emphasis is upon early Biblical history, a time period that is usually breezed over elsewhere. The philosophical approach taken by the authors helps children develop a "God's eye" view of history—to begin to understand that history is the outworking of God's plan rather than a collection of random events. Discussion/study questions follow each chapter.

The accompanying workbook has space for writing answers to discussion/study questions (assuming we want students to write rather than discuss), along with additional exercises. Many activities require Bible research. The *Teacher's Workbook Manual* has the answers for all questions. Tests are available separately. The course requires a significant amount of written work, so we might choose to omit some for younger students.

Cultural Atlas for Young People series
(Facts On File)
$17.95-$19.95 each; $102.75 for the set

This series includes five different titles: *Ancient Egypt* ISBN # 0-8160-1971-1, *Ancient Greece* ISBN #0-8160-1972-X, *Ancient Rome* ISBN # 0-8160-1970-3, *Ancient America* ISBN # 0-8160-2210-0, and *First Civilizations* ISBN # 0-8160-2976-8. Many full-color maps, drawings, and photographs (more than half of each book's content) give these books great eye appeal. The text is very well written and just the right amount of information for upper elementary students. These are much meatier than most other "picture" books and can stand alone for study of the listed topics. I have not reviewed *First Civilizations*, but it might present material in ways that conflict with your beliefs. (SE)

Founders of Freedom
(Neumann Press)
$25

This is the first volume in the Land of Our Lady Catholic history textbook series. These hard-cover editions are reprints of books originally published in the 1950's. The series is obviously Catholic throughout with unit introductions related to Mary the Mother of Jesus, coverage of Catholic missionary efforts, and a consistently Catholic worldview throughout. This is the best series I have seen for those looking for such elements in a history series for the elementary grades.

Intended for fourth graders, this text begins with a biblically-based review of God's creation of Adam and Eve, then continues through ancient civilizations, Egyptians, Greeks, and Romans with special focus on the birth and growth of Christianity. It briefly covers some world history events under units organized around themes having to do with Christianity and its impact upon civilization. Church history receives more

attention than is typical of World History texts for elementary grades, even from Protestant publishers. As is true of most older texts, the content is more extensive than newer texts. Black-and-white illustrations, photos, and maps add visual interest. At the end of each chapter are vocabulary lists, discussion questions, quizzes, and an activity. At the end of each unit is a summary of unit highlights plus a mastery test. No answer key is available.

Genevieve Foster books
(Beautiful Feet Books)
$15.95 each

Beautiful Feet Books is bringing back some of my favorite books for world history for upper elementary grades through high school. Titles in print thus far are *Augustus Caesar's World*, *The World of Columbus and Sons*, *The World of Captain John Smith*, and *George Washington's World*. This is a series of books by Genevieve Foster, which were written around the 1940s. They reflect a Christian culture without being Christian in content. The beauty of these books is the storytelling approach to history. Foster begins with the day the key person was born and traces "goings-on" around the world throughout his lifetime. Foster makes the connections between people and events, even across the globe that are usually lacking in textbooks. Because of this approach, even *George Washington's World* is a world history study. If you read these in chronological sequence you cover world history fairly well. These are great for read aloud time. Contact Beautiful Feet Books to check for other Foster books that might become available.

A Study Guide for these books is due out in the spring of 2000.

Greenleaf Press history resources: Famous Men and Greenleaf Guides
Greenleaf Guide to Old Testament History

by Rob and Cyndy Shearer
(Greenleaf Press)
$10.95

The Old Testament is the perfect place to start teaching history since it truly starts at the beginning. Many of us shy away from such a study because of the difficulties we might encounter, but the Shearer's have made it much easier with this Guide. It covers Genesis, Exodus, Numbers, Deuteronomy, Joshua, and most of Judges. This Guide differs from the others in that it is based upon Bible reading and discussion rather than readings from an assortment of books. (Either *The Children's Bible Atlas* or *The Cultural Atlas of the Bible* is recommended as a visual tool, but nothing else is necessary.) We read through sections of Scripture with our children, then use the Guide's questions to lead a discussion. The Shearers also suggest using Charlotte Mason's "narration" technique where children relate back in their own words what has just been read. The questions generally focus on "who, what, where, when, why, and how" for historical understanding rather than as theology lessons. Background information is included whenever it is useful. The Shearer's also offer practical tips for dealing with the difficult passages like Tamar and Judah. You can tell from the suggestions that they have used all of this with their own family of seven children. This is not like your typical Bible study material that uses stories or incidents to teach spiritual truths or doctrine. But even though this is not the primary focus, children will, indeed, learn foundational spiritual truths. Young children can easily answer most of the questions if they learn to listen carefully, but there are a few questions that will challenge older children to think more deeply. Adults will also enjoy the study, because most will find they have missed many interesting details in their previous readings. It should take a full school year to complete the book.

Famous Men of Greece, Famous Men of Rome, and Famous Men of the Middle Ages

edited and updated by Rob and Cyndy Shearer (Greenleaf Press)
$15.95 each

Instead of reading dry textbooks, children can learn about ancient history through biographical sketches of influential figures in the *Famous Men* books. Stories often build one upon another in chronological order. The effect is like reading a good storybook.

To accompany each book we have *The Greenleaf Guide to Famous Men of Greece, The Greenleaf Guide to Famous Men of Rome*, and *The Greenleaf Guide to Famous Men of the Middle Ages* [$7.95 each]. These *Guides* turn the reading into unit studies with activities, discussion questions, geography (including map building projects), and vocabulary for each chapter of each book. Biblical standards are used as the measuring rod when discussing the lives of the famous men. Chronological summaries of people and events are at the end of each book. Project work is optional, for the most part, with more emphasis on reading and discussion. Frequently, lessons refer to the supplemental resources (available individually or in Greenleaf "packages") for further research and reading on Greece, Rome, or the Middle Ages.

Of particular note in the *Greenleaf Guide to Famous Men of the Middle Ages* are the "worldview" comparison charts. On one chart we compare creation and end of the world stories from Teutonic mythology and the Bible. Greek myths are compared against the other two belief systems as we consider characteristics of God and the gods, what they value, who they honor, what they honor, and man's purpose for living. Another chart compares beliefs of Islam with Christianity. Discussion questions in all of the guides cover names, dates, and events,

but they go much further than textbooks in dealing with character issues and Biblical principles.

Greenleaf also publishes *Famous Men of the Renaissance and Reformation* by Robert Shearer. A companion *Guide* is also available. These two books are best suited to older students at junior and senior high level. I appreciate the unusual selection of biographies in this *Famous Men* book. We meet famous men like Petrarch, Leonardo da Vinci, Erasmus, and some of the standard Reformation leaders, but we also encounter characters such as Lorenzo d' Medici, Cesare Borgia, Niccolo Machiavelli, Albrecht Durer, and representatives of the Anabaptist movement. The result is a richer picture of the period than we typically see.

The *Ancient Greece Study Package* includes *Famous Men, The Greenleaf Guide, The Greeks* (an Usborne book), and *Children's Homer*. The *Ancient Rome Study Package* includes *Famous Men, The Greenleaf Guide, City*, and *The Romans* (an Usborne book). *The Middle Ages Study Package* includes *Famous Men, The Greenleaf Guide, Castle, Cathedral*, and *Cultural Atlas of the Middle Ages*.

The Greenleaf materials more than adequately replace textbook material. The *Famous Men* books can be read to children at very young ages, but the actual studies are more suitable for middle to upper elementary grades. Even though the reading level is a little young, junior and senior high students can read the stories. Guide activities can be stretched to meet the needs of most learning levels, although the Middle Ages guide seems the easiest to use with older students.

The Greenleaf Guide to Ancient Egypt

by Cyndy Shearer (Greenleaf Press) [$7.95]

This *Greenleaf Guide* differs from the Guides on Rome and Greece in that there is no *Famous Men* book to accompany it. Instead it uses six other books and the Bible as resources. The books are *Pharaohs of Ancient Egypt, Time-Traveller Book of Pharaohs and Pyramids, First Travellers: Deserts, Pyramid, Tut's Mummy...Lost and Found*, and *Mummies Made in Egypt*. There are many hands-on activities along with vocabulary and discussion questions. The general tone of this guide seems slightly younger than those for Rome and Greece. Since Egypt figures in chronological order before the others, it makes sense to use this book and the *Greenleaf Guide to Old Testament History* as your starting point, then follow with Greece, then Rome and the Middle Ages. Study can be adapted for children as young as second grade level, although it should be perfect for the middle elementary grades.

Heritage Studies for Christian Schools 5, second edition

(Bob Jones University Press) [fifth grade]

home school kit - $67; student text - $16.50; student notebook - $6.50; teacher's edition - $37; tests - $8; answer key - $4.50

This 1998 text focuses on modern American history, although it inevitably includes world history as it discusses the wars of this century. As with other texts in this series, it includes geography and cultural studies, even though these topics are not well integrated with the history. The first two chapters are on boundaries/geography and transportation. Then history begins abruptly with a discussion of WWI. We then encounter 5 pages on world cultures, 7 on world geography, and a whirlwind tour of U.S. geographical regions before coming back to the Roaring 20s. Following this is an entire chapter devoted to economics which discusses basic, but essential, concepts to which elementary grade levels are rarely exposed. The text then returns to modern history up to the Clinton Administration, interrupting with a chapter on American Homes and Customs. A "Resource Treasury" at the back of the book features flags of the nations, information on presidents and states, maps, and a glossary. The Student Notebook is frequently referred to for activities in the textbook. The Teacher's Edition provides instructional information plus correlation of the Student Notebook with the text.

The home school kit includes the Teacher's Edition, student text, student notebook, tests and key.

Heritage Studies for Christian Schools 6, second edition

(Bob Jones University Press) [sixth grade]

home school kit - $69; student text - $18.50; student notebook - $6.50; teacher's edition - $37

Surprisingly, this text is the first in BJUP's second edition series to address ancient world history. It opens with biblical history, Abraham, and Mesopotamia, then studies ancient times in Egypt, Israel, India, and China. Next, it moves up to the Classical Greek period and the time of the Roman Empire. Following chapters cover ancient African and Mayan history, then the golden age of the orient during part of the dark and middle age periods of Europe. The Byzantine Empire receives special attention, especially in regard to the crusades and relations between the Byantine and Roman Catholic churches (from a Protestant perspective). The book ends with brief discussion of the Middle Ages. Some activity suggestions are in the textbook. They sometimes refer to the Student Notebook which is also used for map work and other exercises. The

Teacher's Edition provides instructional background and presentation information. Tests and answer key are included in the Home School Kit.

History and Geography 400

(Alpha Omega) [fourth grade]

$42.95 for complete set

The fourth grade level LifePac course provides an overview of different types of regions and cultures throughout the world. Check for correct placement level before using Alpha Omega curriculum, in this instance considering both level of difficulty and topic. (Check diagnostic level with Alpha Omega's diagnostic tests described elsewhere in this book.) The complete set includes ten LifePacs and a complete Teacher's Guide with answer keys and teacher helps.

History and Geography 600

(Alpha Omega) [sixth grade]

$42.95 for complete set

This sixth grade level LifePac course provides an overview of world history and an introduction to geography. Check for proper level placement before using Alpha Omega curriculum, checking both level of difficulty and the topics covered. (Use Alpha Omega diagnostic tests for placement help.) The complete set includes ten LifePacs and a complete Teacher's Guide with answer keys and teacher helps.

Into All the World

(Christian Light Publications) [fourth grade]

$15

This text has an even stronger Biblical perspective than do the A Beka and Bob Jones books. The subject matter leans toward culture and geography rather than history. It is meant to be an introductory, survey-type course that lays a foundation for future world history studies. The presentation is "providential"—God is the provider of everything. While there are a variety of questions and activities at the end of each chapter, one of them, entitled "What Does the Bible Say?", directs children to Scripture for their answers. Among the other exercises/activities are fill-in-the-blanks, short answers, thinking/discussion questions, map and globe activities, and research and project suggestions. A glossary and Scripture reference index are unusual features for books at this level. Full-color illustrations and large, clear print make the book appropriate and usable for fourth graders. Christian Light Publications publishes a series of *LightUnit* workbooks with answer keys to accompany this text. However, if a parent works with a child through the questions and activities in the book, there is more than enough material. A teacher's guidebook has answers for textbook questions.

A Literature Approach to Medieval History, 1998 edition

by Rea C. Berg
(Beautiful Feet Books)
Study Guide - $14.95; junior high pack - $149.95; senior high pack - $169.95

Similar to Rea Berg's other *Literature Approach* guides, this one begins with the era of the Magna Carta (about 1215) and continues up through the early seventeenth century in Elizabethan England. "Real" books are used as the basis of the study in conjunction with Rea's *Medieval History* study guide.

This Guide offers a full year program for both junior and senior high level, actually divided into two separate sections. Referred to for either level are Genevieve Foster's *The World of Columbus and Sons* and *The Story of Liberty* by Charles Coffin. While these books serve as the background, other books are incorporated to focus more closely on different aspects and characters of the time period. The Study Guide lessons (some requiring much more than a single day) concentrate on books such as *Castle, Cathedral, Otto of the Silver Hand,* and *The World of Columbus and Sons* for junior high, and *Ivanhoe, Scottish Chiefs, Joan of Arc, Henry VIII,* and *Westward Ho!* for senior high. The Junior High Pack includes the guide and the *Medieval History Time Line,* the aforementioned books plus *Magna Carta, The Story of Liberty, The Door in the Wall, Adam of the Road, The Morning Star of the Reformation, Fine Print, The Hawk That Dare Not Hunt by Day, In Freedom's Cause,* and *The Canterbury Tales.* The Senior High Pack includes the study guide, the aforementioned books plus *Magna Carta, The World of Columbus and Sons, The Story of Liberty, The Canterbury Tales, King John, Martin Luther, Marco Polo and the Medieval Explorers,* and *Men of Iron.*

You could go through the study at junior high level, purchasing the Junior High Pack, then use it again for an older student, purchasing only the individual books you still need.

A *Medieval History Time Line* from Beautiful Feet Books covers the same period as the Study Guide, making a wonderful hands-on/visual supplement.

New World History and Geography

(A Beka Book) [sixth grade]
$15.10; Teacher Edition - $22.60; answer key - $5.95

This is the 1992 revision of A Beka's study of western hemisphere history which emphasizes geography and cultures. (Note that A Beka's *Old* and *New World History* books are not chronologically divided, but geographically.) This book should be used following *Old World History and Geography.*

Some parts of this text are lively, but when it tries to tell all about the geography and history of each country in a very few pages the presentation is very dry. We need to accompany at least some sections of this book with more lively supplements

if we want children to enjoy history. This revised version uses a larger type style, which is easier on the eyes than the previous edition. Text has been rewritten to eliminate wordiness. Sentences are often longer and less choppy. New material on "black history" has been added. Some material has been deleted and some has been condensed, but the overall effect is improvement. The Teacher Edition contains answers to text questions printed in front of the text pages, so you could use the single teacher edition as student text and answer key. A separate answer key is also available.

Consider using A Beka's *Nation Notebook* for in-depth study of one country. The text is generously illustrated in full color.

Maps in the *Student Map/Review Book* are very useful although the question worksheets might be too much for many students. Reading comprehension and map study questions in the book deal mostly with factual information rather than analysis or interpretation. A Student Quiz Booklet and a Student Test Booklet have additional questions, although they tend also to concentrate on factual information.

The Old World and America

by Most Rev. Philip J. Furlong
(TAN Books)
$18.00

This 384-page text, originally published in 1940, gives an overview of history from creation to the founding of the new world from a Catholic viewpoint. With such a wide time span, do not expect an in-depth study of any particular period of history. Instead, the author seeks to give the student a basic foundation for the study of American history. After all, we cannot begin to understand the present if we do not first study the past. Since one cannot truly understand the past without first understanding the impact of Christ and His church on historical events, this text recognizes the Church's contributions throughout history.

Although written for fifth to eighth graders, this text can be used with younger students as a read-aloud or reference book. For example, when my third grader was studying Ancient Rome, I read the chapter entitled "Contribution of Rome to Civilization" to him over the course of several days. This was a nice addition to our year-long immersion into the study of Rome.

Chapters end with objective tests, questions that make you think, activities, questions that test your character, and a vocabulary list. The text also includes illustrations, maps, index, and a pronunciation key.

An answer key, which is a great time saver for the parent/teacher, is available for purchase from TAN for an additional $10. It was written by Maureen McDewitt, a homeschooling mother. (Text has the Imprimatur and the Nihil Obstat.) [Maureen Wittmann]

Old World History and Geography, 1999 edition

(A Beka Book) [fifth grade]

$16.30; teacher edition - $22.20; answer key - $5.95; maps and review sheets - $4.45; key to maps/review sheets - $8.85; test book - $4.45; quiz/activity book - $4.45; keys to tests and quiz/activity book - $8.95 each

This book is an introduction to eastern hemisphere history with an emphasis on geography which dictates the book's organizational structure. Study begins with the Fertile Crescent, moves through the Middle East, central and southern Asia, Egypt, and Africa, then on to Europe and Australia. As students study each geographic area, they are also studying history from ancient times through the present, albeit very briefly. This is really a geography/social studies book more than history. It includes church history, and frequently addresses forms of government, particularly communism. Throughout the book, Christianity and the Bible are used as the standard and measure of comparison for all cultures and ideas. One entire chapter is titled: "Christianity: The Greatest Force in History."

Historical coverage seems more extensive in studies of ancient civilizations than those that are more modern. For example, more than six pages are devoted to Sumer, while France gets about three pages. Treatment of ancient civilizations is also wider ranging, and, consequently, more interesting than treatment of countries such as Italy and France. For example, in reading about Sumer, we learn about archaeology, the invention of the wheel, cuneiform writing, their culture, geography, religion, education, and history. In comparison, the study of France seems very narrowly selective. It begins with its location and geography. Next, two very general paragraphs introduce "People and Events," which includes snippets on famous men and women. Next are two paragraphs on John Calvin and the Huguenots; a single paragraph each on the Enlightenment, the French Revolution, and Napoleon; two paragraphs on modern France; and a few geographical highlights.

There are plenty of maps and full-color illustrations as well as interesting sidebars throughout the text. The first approximately 50 pages comprise a "Geography Handbook" that includes an atlas, continent studies (which students should work through in conjunction with the appropriate chapters), and geography facts.

Comprehension questions follow each subsection within each chapter, and there are "Chapter Checkup" tests at the end of each chapter. The Teacher Edition contains the answer key to text questions as well as a copy of the student text without answers. A separate answer key is also available if you choose not to get the Teacher Edition. It is not difficult to figure out answers without the answer key.

Maps in the *Student Maps and Review Sheets* are very useful, although the question worksheets might be too much for many students. A Student Test Booklet and a Student Quiz and Activity Booklet are available, along with teacher keys for all three supplements.

You should follow this text with *New World History and Geography*. If you begin with *Old World History*, it is difficult to jump to another history book for coverage of the New World because of the organizational structure. For example, Christian School International's *Story of the Old World* covers much of the same territory, but stops at the era of exploration historically, while A Beka's book brings each geographical area up to modern times.

Story of the Old World

(Christian Schools International)

student text - $33; teacher guide - $48.75

The publisher states that this beautiful, hardcover text is written at a sixth-grade reading level, but I would judge it easy enough for children as young as fourth grade. I imagine most eighth graders will find it too young. Some of the subject treatment is superficial in comparison with A Beka's *Old World History and Geography* which makes it more appropriate for younger learners. The book follows the traditional approach to history, concentrating on study of the old world with the exception of a section at the end covering the exploration of North America. (See the comparison of content within the review of A Beka's *Old World History and Geography*. Geography coverage is minimal since that is not the purpose of *Story of the Old World*.) There are a variety of questions that take children beyond the information-recall level. On student text pages are small purple boxes with the headings "discuss," "discover," or "do." ("Do" activities are primarily research and writing, not hands-on.) We can use as many of these as we choose to broaden learning activities. This is a thoroughly Christian history text, continually tying the story of history to the Bible and Biblical principles. Because of this, as well as great thought and application questions throughout the book, *Story of the Old World* is a good resource for developing worldview ideas in the upper elementary grades. The teacher's edition contains the answers to student questions, although it would be possible to use the student text on its own.

Usborne World History: Ancient World and Medieval World

(Educational Development Corporation)

$21.95 each

These beautifully-illustrated, hardcover history books can be used to cover world history up through the Middle Ages for students in grades 4 through 6. History and culture are combined as is appropriate for these grade levels. Although the text is broken up by illustrations, it flows in columns, making it fairly easy to read. Illustrations all have helpful descriptions—children are likely to browse through these books just "reading" illustrations and their descriptions. Time lines running across the bottom of every page are helpful. Coverage is necessarily spotty, but these books should give children a good introduction to world history.

Interestingly, *Ancient World* skips cave men and begins with the first farming communities. It briefly touches on a few examples of ancient towns, then moves on to the Sumerian and Egyptian civilizations. Hittites, Canaanites, Phoenicians, Assyrians, Hebrews, and other ancient civilizations also get brief coverage. Coverage of ancient Greece and Rome is given more space, and China, Japan, Africa, India, and the Americas also get attention.

Medieval World picks up where *Ancient World* leaves off, around 500 A.D. It begins with the Byzantine Empire, skipping over the barbarian invasions to discuss the barbarian kingdoms that arose. Arabs and Islam, Vikings, Anglo-Saxon England, Charlemagne, and the Holy Roman Empire typify the range of topics covered next. Castles, towns, trade, and the Church all receive attention as significant historical factors. Coverage expands beyond western civilization to worldwide, including the rise of the Russians, conquest of North Africa, East Africa, Southern India, Southeast Asia, Pacific Islanders, the Americas, and other civilizations up through about 1400 A.D.

I suggest using these books along with Greenleaf Guides or other books. Christians will probably want more coverage of Christian history than we find here since these books strive for religious neutrality.(SE)

Veritas Press History Studies, Flash Card Sets, and Tapes

(Veritas Press)
$19.95 per set of cards; audio tapes - $6.95 each; sets of cards and a tape - $24.95 each; teacher's manuals - $19.95 each

The folks at Veritas Press developed these resources to provide historical studies that were chronological and included Biblical and church history. The result is five history teacher's manuals, plus history and Bible flash cards and audio tapes, designed primarily for grades 2-6.

The teacher's manuals divide history into five time periods. Volumes are titled *Old Testament and Ancient Egypt; New Testament/Greece & Rome; Middle Ages, Renaissance & Reformation; Explorers to 1815;* and *1815 to the Present.* Each volume includes readings (many from primary sources), worksheets, tests, scripts, maps, projects, crafts, and other activities. Some additional books are required for "literature units."

The emphasis on Biblical/church history is clear even in reading the tables of contents. For example, in the *Middle Ages...* volume, the first three lessons are titled "St. Augustine Converts to Christianity," "Barbarian Invasion and Vikings,"

and "St. Jerome Completes the Vulgate." Lessons often broaden beyond the title, but the goal is to demonstrate links between Biblical/church history and the typical history which most children are taught. The religious perspective is Protestant, but it does include early church fathers, church councils, and other church history often neglected.

These studies deal with much more challenging topics than are typically taught at the designated grade levels (2-6). For example, in the *Middle Ages...* volume, children read and analyze Luther's *95 Theses.* Certainly, parents should adjust any of the activities to the appropriate level for each child. Doing so, you should be able to use any volume with a fairly wide age span. I suspect that these volumes could easily be adapted for students in junior and senior high.

Veritas Press advocates classical education, so these studies also stress student mastery of key people, events, and dates. To assist students, they have created five sets of history cards that correlate with the above volumes and five sets of Bible cards. Each set has thirty-two 5" x 8" cards, printed in full color. A reproduction of a well-known piece of artwork or, occasionally, a photograph depicts the key event or person discussed on each card. On the reverse are the date and a brief summary of the event or topic. At the bottom of the card is a list of resources, including page numbers, where the topic is discussed at length.

Companion audio tapes feature a lilting recitation of the key names, dates, and events set to music; this presentation enhances learning for some students. The tapes are only about 10 to 15 minutes long, with the identical song on the reverse. The phrasing is awkward, although the singing is quite lovely. Tapes are optional.

This entire program has so much more content than other elementary history programs for the same grade levels, some parents might be intimidated. Make adjustments in grade levels if need be, but I suspect you will find that your children are capable of learning at these challenging levels because of the multi-sensory learning experiences. Plan to review some of the deeper ideas as your children mature, since young children don't process ideas as well as do teens and adults.

World History Supplements

Ancient Greece [computer CD program]

(Calvert School)
$40

This CD runs on computers with Windows 95 or higher. It is divided into three main sections: study, explore, and activities. "Study" works through brief historical background, presented in six different sections: Geography, Early Civilizations, City-states, Government, Sparta, and Athens. Students should begin here.

Comprehension questions follow each section. "Explore" focuses on topical areas: society, war, culture, art, and learning, with subsections within each of these areas. Again, comprehension questions are at the end of each section. Background music, voiceovers, and sound effects are present in some sections. Students can choose from three types of "Activities" in the third section: hands-on projects done away from the computer, writing activities (which can be done on the computer or off as you please), and games (on the computer). Games are fairly simple. A Progress Chart checks off areas that each student has completed.

There were a couple occasions where I encountered questions where the information in the questions had not yet been presented within the section being covered. Otherwise, this is a beautifully done program. Graphics are rich and colorful, and there's lots of variety and interaction. The program is suggested for students in grades 4-8, and content is largely accessible to the younger students, although I wouldn't expect them to master all the names and key ideas of the philosophers. Since sports and the Olympics are included, the nudity issue arises. But aside from one fairly discreet picture of athletes, there are no real problems.(S)

At A Glance series

(Peter Bedrick Books)
$14.95 each

There are four books in this series: *Ancient Egyptians, Ancient Greeks, Ancient Romans,* and *The Vikings.* These hardcover books are heavily illustrated in full color, similar in appearance to Usborne and DK books. Although the books are suggested for grades 3 and up, the reading level is a little higher than that. (Read them aloud with younger children.) The text is interestingly written and it flows logically rather than jumping from topic to topic on a single page as we sometimes find in other "picture" books. Timelines, maps, comparisons with simultaneous world events, and charts of military conquests/battles combine with discussion of the history, culture/society, religious practices, political leadership, and forms of government. I was especially impressed with the integration of information about religious beliefs with other areas of life, especially in *Ancient Egyptians.* Although they are only 32 pages each, the books are packed with information. They might be used as primary resource books for studying these time periods for children in the elementary grades.(S)

Canterbury Tales

by Geoffrey Chaucer; selected, translated, and adapted by Barbara Cohen; illustrated by Trina Schart Hyman
(HarperCollins)
$21.95

Most children today are not acquainted with old classics such as *Canterbury Tales* because the archaic language is dif-

ficult to understand and enjoy. This book adapts the *Tales* to offer children a rich retelling of some of Chaucer's stories. It is a large-size picture book with beautifully-lavish illustrations.

Barbara Cohen begins her adaptation with a brief biography of Chaucer and an introduction to the reason for the *Tales*: a group of pilgrims journeying to Canterbury. She includes in the book some of the repartee between the pilgrims (something that makes the original *Canterbury Tales* immensely enjoyable) and four of the tales. The stories she chooses are suitable for children and give a good picture of what life was like in medieval times. By reflecting in her prose Chaucer's love of humanity, the flavor of Chaucer is retained. Cohen succeeds in enticing the reader to delve deeper into the original works of Chaucer.

The illustrations of Trina Schart Hyman do full justice to Cohen's writing. The pictures interspersed throughout the book are beautifully drawn with rich colors and tapestry-like borders. Hyman faithfully pictures each of the pilgrims according to Chaucer's own descriptions.

I used this book with a homeschool co-op elementary class. They loved it and afterward were able to understand some of the "adult" translations of Chaucer. They also enjoyed hearing Chaucer in middle English! This book would be a great supplement for a unit on medieval times. How better to understand life in the fourteenth century than to see it through the eyes of someone who lived it?[Becky Parker]

Castle Explorer [computer program]

(DK Publishing)
$29.95

In this medieval adventure game on CD-ROM, you are a young "spy" who must explore detailed cross-section illustrations of a 14th century castle, looking for information and gold coins. Realistic sound effects evoke the life of the times (although I could have done without the sound effects in the latrine!). In order to visit one of the 3D rooms with live action characters (similar to *Myst*), you will have to answer questions from the suspicious alchemist or the cook. But you'd better research carefully, because if you give the wrong answer you will end up in the dungeon. This program runs on either Windows or Macintosh systems and is recommended for grades 4 and up.(S)[V.Thorpe]

Days of Knights and Damsels: An Activity Guide

by Laurie Carlson
(Chicago Review Press)
$14.95

If you have active learners, this is a perfect addition to whatever curriculum or library books you are using to study the

Middle Ages. Along with some interesting facts about the period, this 11"X 8 ½" paperback has instructions for over 100 inexpensive projects using items you probably already have around the house. Ideas include recipes, simple costumes, heraldry, games and magic tricks, and crafts. Lots of fun for grades K-5.[V. Thorpe]

Eyewitness Books
(Random House/Knopf')
$19-$20.99 each

Ancient Rome, Money, and *Arms and Armor* are history-related titles in this outstanding series. These hardbound books are about 70% illustrations and 30% text. However, even with so much illustration, they are not as busy in appearance as some of the other "picture" history books because text is kept together in larger chunks and related illustrations are grouped. Reading level is about fifth grade and above. However, younger children will learn much by looking at the pictures while an adult or older sibling reads aloud. Although some drawings are used, most illustrations are large, color photographs of actual artifacts. *Ancient Rome*, the volume I reviewed, covered all aspects of Roman civilization—soldiers, emperors, government, family life, engineering, entertainment, religion, music, farming, and transportation. The wealth of detail in both text and illustrations will fascinate readers of all ages. Books in this series make excellent additions to your home library.(SE)

Facts on File Children's Atlas
(Facts On File)
$18.95

Children about age seven and older will enjoy delving into this beautiful book. Full of colorful photos, illustrations, and maps, it is an easy-to-use resource for children who can easily be overwhelmed with adult atlases. The text and extra activities help students learn more than just geography. ISBN # 0-8160-3713-2.(SE)

Golden Educational Center Country Studies and Province Studies
(Golden Educational Center)
$10.95 to $11.95

These reproducible books can be used to supplement studies for children in fourth grade up through junior high. There are at present four country studies books: *Middle East, Far East, South America*, and *North America. Canada* is the only province study book thus far. All books follow the same basic format.

Each country has its own section within each book. The first activity within each section is vocabulary/dictionary work with words relating to the country/province studied plus general geographical terms. The following page is a map. Next is sum-marized detailed information, then brief historical background. The last page for each country has review questions with suggestions for further research reports noted at the bottom of the page. Books vary in size but are around 100 pages each.(S)

Greathall Productions Audio Recordings
by Jim Weiss
(Greathall Productions, Inc.)
$9.95 cassettes; $14.95 CD's

Master storyteller Jim Weiss retells folklore, myths, and tales from past civilizations that help bring history to life. By using his voice to create different characters, Weiss sparks children's imaginations with drama. Among his recordings (available on cassette or CD) that might enhance history and social studies are *Greek Myths, Arabian Nights, The Three Musketeers/Robin Hood, Tales from the Old Testament, King Arthur and His Knights, Tales from Cultures Far and Near, She and He: Adventures in Mythology, Galileo and the Stargazers* (reviewed in Chapter Fourteen), and *Egyptian Treasures: Mummies and Myths.* Even titles such as *Egyptian Treasures,* which some might think likely to be problematic, are presented in an inoffensive fashion. Weiss clearly treats mythology as such, and treatment of mummies is factual and historical—told as a story of tracking down grave robbers.

See additional comments on these recordings in the "Read Aloud" section of Chapter Nine.(SE)

Hands On Activities for Elementary Social Studies
by David Cooper
(Alpha Publishing Company)
$34.95

Those who would like to jazz up their social studies with hands-on activities, but who are reluctant to invest in *KONOS* or *The Weaver*, might find this a practical alternative. Activities are appropriate for grades 3 to 6. They cover the areas of geography (12 lessons), U.S. history (11 lessons), world history (11 lessons), and citizenship and values (6 lessons). Most activities are quite involved and time-consuming; examples are building a cardboard model of the Mayflower, constructing a model of a medieval castle, and making paper.

Evolutionary assumptions pop up occasionally but primarily in the time line assignment which assumes millions of years of earth's history as well as evolutionary development of life. Each lesson has two parts. The first is a "teachers guide" which tells the teacher the goal, student objective, background information, some vocabulary words which will be useful in discussing the topic, and some additional resources which we might want to investigate. The second part is the actual presentation. It begins with an introduction which can be read or otherwise presented to students. Next is a list of materials, then step-by-step procedures, usually with illustrations. Finally, there are some "Suggestions for Further Study" which range from reading and research through more complicated project ideas. The cost is high (around $40), but the ideas provided will be useful through a number of years of social studies.(SE)

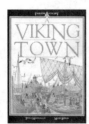

Inside Story Series
(Peter Bedrick Books)
$10.95 each pb; $18.95 each hc

For a learning experience that relies more on illustrations than words, jump into the "Inside Story Series". This series of books includes a number of titles relating to world history: *A Samurai Castle, A Viking Town, A Medieval Cathedral, An Egyptian Pyramid, A Roman Fort, A Greek Temple, A Medieval Castle, Shakespeare's Theater, A 16th Century Mosque,* and *A 16th Century Galleon.*

Each book is packed with information such as customs, traditions, dress, architecture, structural design, and history. Full-color illustrations draw the reader into the text. Young children can look at the pictures, but the text is written for older children (fifth grade and up) and is even interesting enough for adults. These books are available in paperback editions for some titles and sturdy, library hardcover editions for all titles. [Matt Duffy/C.D.]

Jackdaw Portfolios of Historical Documents and Study Guides
(Golden Owl Publishing Company)
Portfolio and Guide sets - $39 each

More than 100 different Portfolios and Study Guides cover historical topics under the broad headings U.S. History; World History; Ancient, Cultural, and Religious History; Government, Law, and Civil Rights; Labor and Industry; and Rebellion and War. Examples of specific titles: *American Revolution, California Gold Rush, Reconstruction, Slavery in the U.S., Columbus and the Age of Explorers, Russian Revolution, Magna Carta, Martin Luther, The New Deal, The Depression, French Revolution,* and *The Holocaust.* Portfolios contain from eight to eighteen historical source documents which are facsimiles of originals. Transcripts are included since some of these are difficult to read. Four to eight "Broadsheets" expand upon selected topics, tying in the source documents. Notes for each portfolio include background on each document, suggested books to read, thought questions, plus assorted extras depending upon the topic (such as a list of places to visit).

The reading level is fairly high, so use these selectively with younger readers. The publisher suggests their use with children fifth grade or above.

The Study Guides help us fully utilize the portfolio material, serving as activity guides. Many activities involve writing, primarily relying upon the source documents and broadsheets for selected information. In addition to writing, there are proj-

ects such as determining the best route to California during the Gold Rush. Activities range from simple questions to involved research/projects. A couple of vocabulary worksheets (reproducible) are included. Both Portfolios and Study Guides are intended for use with a wide range of age groups, but the Guides seem to have more range of activities with some suitable for elementary grade students. Guides are dependent upon the Portfolios, referring to them for information, so they may not be purchased separately.

Although some of the material is better suited to junior and senior high students, some, such as the *California Gold Rush Portfolio and Guide*, are geared for students in upper elementary grades.(SE)

King Arthur through the Ages [computer CD-ROM]
(Calvert School)
$40

This is a well-designed program on not just one Arthurian legend but on many of the written works about him and Camelot. The program actually overlaps history and literature almost equally, and it probably works best as a supplement when you are studying the Middle Ages. From even the opening "wallpaper" of the program, you get the feel that this is a quality piece of work, styled to give it a very artistic and history-laden atmosphere. The program is divided into seven sections: "Tales of Arthur," "Readings from Arthur," "Arthur through History," "Arthur's World," "Picturing Arthur," "The Land of Arthur," and "Quest for the Holy Grail." "Tales" and "Readings" feature a number of Arthurian legends with accompanying illustrations. Click on key words for further descriptions and illustrations. Readings such as *Le Morte D' Arthur, The Lady of Shalott, Idylls of the King,* and *A Connecticut Yankee in King Arthur's Court,* feature beautiful, dramatic readings of excerpts from each of these. "Arthur through History" is actually a timeline running from 50 A.D. up through 1975, with entries that can be selected for further information. "Arthur's World" deals with knights, armor, weapons, castles, the church, customs, etc. Children read about a topic such as castles, and as they hit highlighted words, they can actually watch parts of a castle added to the basic structure.

"Picturing Arthur" presents works of art with background information. "The Land of Arthur" begins with a map of Arthur's Britain. We can then select historical sights for illustrations and information. The "Quest for the Holy Grail" is a game that quizzes children on historical and legendary information contained in the program. The game is probably the least appealing part of the program graphically, but children will still enjoy trying to pass through the different levels. Highlighted words throughout the program have audio clips for pronunciation that can be selected. There is a surprising amount of complexity and depth in this program. You will need a multimedia computer (486 or higher processor) with Windows 3.1 or later and a CD-ROM drive.(S)

Kingfisher History Encyclopedia

(Larousse Kingfisher Chambers, Inc.)
$39.95 hc

"Encyclopedia" is a misnomer for this book since it is arranged in chronological rather than topical order. Beginning with pre-history, it presents a new topic for every two-page spread. Students could conceivably read it through cover-to-cover since it often relates information to previous sections. However, I suspect that it will more likely be used as a reference volume as you try to correlate events and find information about particular people or events.

This book aims for a multicultural presentation, covering Asia, Africa, India, the early Americas, and other civilizations much more than we find in typical textbooks. Timelines running across the top of the pages help students place people and events in perspective. Numerous sidebars and illustrations with their captions are also instructive. Full-color illustrations take up half of each page on average. Consequently, coverage is very selective and cursory because of the limited amount of textual material. For example, the Vietnam War is covered in a single paragraph. Nevertheless, this is a good resource for obtaining a "snapshot" understanding of people, places, and events.

The book is divided into ten sections, each of which opens with a "World at a Glance" overview and ends with general presentations on "The Arts," "Architecture," and "Science and Technology." A "Ready Reference" section at the back lists rulers, dynasties, popes, presidents, and other chronological lists of those in power through history. The pre-history section presents hypothetical information as fact, so you will need to caution children about this. Also, Christianity is treated as just one of many religions. (492 pages) (SE)

Medieval Times Thematic Unit

(Teacher Created Materials)
$9.95

Three novels plus poetry and ballads are the foundation of this thematic approach to medieval history. Novels studied are *Robin Hood of Sherwood Forest, Adam of the Road,* and *The Door in the Wall.*

Lesson plans are provided along with other suggestions to make the book easy-to-use. Medieval Times is the theme, yet studies cross the curriculum, touching on math, science, language arts, art, music, and life skills, as much as they do social studies. Obviously, this is not comprehensive coverage of history, but it uses a method that works well to involve reluctant learners. Reproducible worksheets are included along with complete instructions on all activities. Some activities are

classroom oriented but many will work well in the home school. There might be content problems—I have not seen any in my brief review, but they show up in another book in the same series.(SE)

Milliken Transparency Reproducible Books

(Milliken)
$12.95 each

Milliken publishes a number of world history titles that can be easily adapted for children over a wide age span, even though they suggest using them for grades 7-12. The books have full-color illustrations and transparencies (designed for use on overhead projectors, but just as useful without the projector), information on the subject, maps, and reproducible student worksheets. They have nineteen titles on world history, although those of most interest are likely to be *Sumer and Babylonia; Ancient Egypt; Hebrews, Phoenicians, and Hittites; Greece-The Hellenic Age; Greece-The Hellenistic Age; Rome I; Rome II; The Byzantine and Moslem Empires; Medieval Period I; Medieval Period II; Age of Exploration;* and *French Revolution.* Since we copy the worksheets, each book is non-consumable. These books are intended to supplement our studies rather than be used as the primary resources. (The Weaver suggests their use in conjunction with their unit studies.) The quality of the content and presentation is excellent, although we are likely to encounter philosophical problems.(SE)

Nation Notebook

(A Beka Book)
$6.85

Children can use the *Nation Notebook* to study a single country. Instructions at the beginning teach how to do research, including how to write letters to get information about a country. The book helps students frame their searches for information by designating topics for each page with specific "research questions" in the far left margin. Students paste pictures and postcards directly on the pages, then complete their drawings and written information.

Pages have headings like "Climate," "Capital City," and "Language." The completed pages of this book are the finished product. Parents might want to select which pages to use depending how extensive they want the project to be.

Oxford University Press

prices range from $9.95-$20.95

Numerous titles from Oxford make excellent supplements for world history, particularly for Greek and Roman eras. Among their titles are *Pompeii* by Peter Connolly (recreates this ancient city through essays, fictional "eyewitness" reports, and beautiful illustrations), The Roman Fort by Peter Connolly (life in a Roman Britain fort), and *The Greeks* by Roy Burrell (slices of life and history: "...opening night for a play by Euripedes, the first Olympic Games, Alexander the Great's last battle,..." etc.). Some titles are available in both soft and hard cover editions.(SE)

Picture the Middle Ages

(Golden Owl Publishing)
$26

Children learn to picture the Middle Ages by participating in this extensive, activity-based unit study. Designed to be used for grade levels 4-8, this resource book is loaded with such a variety of activities that it is hard to do it justice. Twelve chapters divide studies into key areas such as "The Town: Craftsmen and Guilds," "The Monastery: Monks and Nuns," and "Making Costumes and Armor."

The entire study is based upon the imaginary medieval world called Higginswold, created at the Higgins Armory Museum in Worcester, Massachusetts.

A huge fold-out picture of Higginswold is included, as well as a timeline; patterns for costumes, shields, helmets, and breastplates; maps, illustrations of coats of arms, banners, and guild signs; and recipes. Students study literature, the arts, and history, including the oft-neglected church history. The vocabulary and writing assignments, together with supplemental reading, are extensive enough to replace other language arts curricula. Of course, we are free to pick and choose from among the wealth of options. The authors suggest allowing five to eight weeks to complete the study. It is designed to culminate in a Medieval Festival complete with tournaments (academic), games, a play, a feast, and a fair. The unit study will work best with a group. It might be worth forming a special group for this purpose even if you don't already have one. There is still plenty to do if a group is not possible.

If you want to extend the study even further, additional resources are listed for each chapter. Among these are some of the *Jackdaw Portfolios of Historical Documents*. (See separate review.)

Sightseers Essential Travel Guides to the Past

(Larousse Kingfisher Chambers, Inc.)
$8.95 each

Spice up your history program with these colorful travel guides to the past that point out where to stay, what to eat, where to shop, sights to see, cultural notes and survival tips. Your children (approximately ages 7 - 11) will learn fun and fascinating facts as they become tourists in a distant time and place. In the back of each book is a quiz and a fold out map.

The titles **Ancient Greece** and **Ancient Egypt** necessarily have information about pagan religions and some discreet nudity is shown where appropriate, but less than some other books on these cultures. Also in the series, but not reviewed, are **California Gold Rush** and **Paris 1789.**(SE)[V. Thorpe]

Thematic Units

(Teacher Created Materials)
$9.95 each

Teacher Created Materials' Thematic Units are available in four levels, Early Childhood, Primary, Intermediate, and Challenging. They are literature-based lesson plans for studying various topics. A diverse field of topics is covered, but those pertaining to world history are *Explorers, Ancient Egypt, Ancient Rome, Ancient China, Ancient India, Ancient Japan, Ancient Middle East, Medieval Times, Industrial Revolution, Archaeology, Ancient Greece, Renaissance, World War I, World War II, Holocaust,* and *Mayans, Aztecs, and Incas.* (*Medieval Times* is reviewed elsewhere in this section.) A parent would want to choose among the titles available, since some such as *Self-Esteem, Peace*, or *Native Americans* might reflect a non-Christian world view.

Time Traveler

(Educational Development Corporation)
$22.95

Usborne's *Time Traveler* is one of their combination books. It brings together the smaller books: *Viking Raiders, Rome and Romans, Knights and Castles,* and *Pharaohs and Pyramids.* Suggested for ages 8 to 11, it consists primarily of full-color illustrations. Two or three paragraphs introduce each topic, then labeled illustrations, maps, diagrams, and sequenced illustrations take over. Two pages at the end of each of the smaller books except *Knights and Castles* provide succinct historical overviews. Otherwise, emphasis is primarily upon what it was like to live in those times and places. *Time Traveler* is interesting, even to adults, but children love this as a means of connecting with the personal side of history.(S)

What Do We Know About...? series

(Peter Bedrick Books)
$8.95-$10.95 each pb; $18.95 each reinforced binding editions

Books in this series are each about 40 to 50 pages long. They feature colorful photographs and drawings interspersed with text written for children about third through eighth grade levels. Factual information is presented in small, "headlined" sections so that it is easy for children to spot what they are looking for as compared to searching through lengthy encyclopedia articles. For example, in the book, *The Middle Ages*, there is a section on food. Within that section are brief presentations under such headings as fish, wine to drink, hunting, the work force, pig-sticking, and table manners.

While most of the information seems accurate, the section on religion misrepresents beliefs and motivations, betraying the author's unfamiliarity with Christian history. We will probably encounter similar problems in other books in the series as well as pro-pagan biases in books about other cultures and religions. Other titles relating to world history: *The Amazonian Indians, The Aztecs, The Celts, The Egyptians, The Greeks, The Inuit, Prehistoric People, The Romans, Judaism, Hinduism*, and *The Vikings*.(SE)

Where in the World is Carmen Sandiego? computer program]

(The Learning Company) [recommended for grades 4 and up]
approx. $40

This popular computer software program (CD-ROM versions for Windows 3.1 or 95 with sound card or Macintosh 7.0.1) requires research through the enclosed *World Almanac* as the player tracks down the villains. The incentive to learn geographical information along with some history is greatly enhanced when the computer rather than the teacher requires a child to look something up. Games can be saved and players advance in rank as they capture gang members until they capture Carmen Sandiego herself. This new edition features animated cartoon characters and video clips with lots of music and sound effects—significant improvements visually over the earlier editions. Animations can be skipped by clicking on a mouse button.

Each time a game begins, the player is told about a crime that has been committed, then left with a few clues to begin tracking the villain around the world. Using references within the program as well as the *Almanac*, players have to determine to which country each clue or group of clues applies. Along the way they ask people they encounter for clues about the villain. When a player accumulates enough clues, he can get a warrant and attempt to arrest the villain. If clues are properly interpreted, catching the villain is almost a certainty, at least at the beginning. Play becomes increasingly difficult as a player gets promoted from Rookie up through the ranks to Super Sleuth.

While there is a time limit for each game, we can take extra time to learn more about each country we visit as we play the game without it being deducted from time available. An on-screen notepad allows us to record clues as we travel from country to country so we don't forget them. Players can take a break from sleuthing and use the Explore Mode to fly around the world and receive "guided tours" of countries. Of course, this is a less efficient way to learn geography than using a book on the subject, but children are likely to consider this play rather than school and use the game often which might result in a great deal of learning in the end. In addition to the *Almanac*, the game comes with the *ACME Agent Handbook*, an excellent guide to the program. Suggested for ages 9 and up.(S)

Where in the World?

(Aristoplay) [for ages 8 to adult]
$32

This board game contains four different game variations. Players of different skill levels can play together by selecting easier or more difficult questions. Play can be concentrated on one geographical region being studied if desired. Along with geography, players learn some economic and cultural information. At the top level, current events are incorporated into game play. Although the game is expensive, I recommend it because of the quality construction, educational value, and great variety of usage.(S)

United States History - Foundational Resources

If you have children in the early elementary grades, as you read through this section, you might also need to check back through the section "Textbooks for Early Levels of Social Studies" for other possibilities.

Note: Many Christian resources on U.S. history were written purposely to balance the distorted presentations that dominate the market. They are often not intended to be the sole resource that we use but should be combined with others for a complete perspective. *America's Christian History, Christian Self-Government* and *America, The First 350 Years* are examples.

America's Christian History, Christian Self-Government, Levels A through H

(Intrepid Books) [grade 1-8]
by Jean S. Smithies
$12.95 each

This is a series of study guides based upon the larger Principle Approach books discussed elsewhere, but these study guides will stand alone. These books are about principles and concepts rather than straightforward history, although history certainly is learned in the context of ideas. The books are designed to be read to younger children. The language has purposely been kept at a higher level. Even at middle elementary grades, some children will find the suggested grade level content difficult to absorb. Feel free to use levels a year or two later than suggested. The author has taken ideas from the Principle Approach and brought them down to an easier level of understanding, although you must judge your own child's ability to understand the abstract ideas.

America, The First 350 Years

(Covenant Publications)
$69.95

Here is a tape series that offers perhaps the most lucid contrast between the false history we have been taught and what actually happened. The author, Pastor Steve Wilkins, pulls the historical facts together and organizes his presentation better than anyone else I know. Pastor Wilkins is speaking to an adult audience on the tapes for sessions of about forty-five minutes each, so they are likely to be too long for the attention span of younger children. However, parents and older children can listen to the entire presentation while younger children listen only to particular sections of the tapes and participate in discussions when appropriate. The set contains sixteen cassette tapes with about ninety minutes of speaking on each. It also comes with a notebook and study guide. The notebook clearly outlines each presentation with the key ideas written out. Documentation of quotations and bibliographies are included. The notebook itself can be used as a refresher course for review. The Study Guide has a page of discussion questions for each tape. This would be a great way for dad to get involved with family learning. The components can be purchased separately or as a complete set.

American History for Young Catholics 1

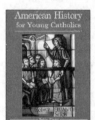

(Seton Press)

$6

This small, 46-page book introduces children to American history and a little Mexican history primarily through biographical sketches. Even in the first section on the first voyages to America, the focus is on two people, Leif Ericson and St. Brendan. Subjects of the sketches are often chosen both for the contributions to history and to the advancement of Catholicism. Some of the black-and-white illustrations make good coloring pages. (There is some overlap in content with Seton's third grade level *The Catholic Faith Comes to America*.)

American Pioneers and Patriots

(Christian Liberty Press)

$8.95; answer key - $1; tests - $1

This history reader features selected stories about different types of pioneers in America's history. Each multi-chaptered story centers around a main character using an engaging, narrative style. For example, the first story is of Pedro and Catalina, two Spanish children, and their trip to St. Augustine (in what is now Florida) in the year 1565. Following this are stories, primarily told through the eyes of children, about pioneers from Holland, pioneers in Virginia, pioneers moving westward, and others. Stories have threads of patriotism and character building although, with the exception of a few statements, the book is not overtly Christian. Each story is followed by comprehension and thinking questions plus activity ideas such as drawing a picture of a scene from a story, identifying

places on maps, and making a quill pen. The book should appeal to children in the middle elementary grades. An answer key and test packet are available.

The Catholic Faith Comes to the Americas

(Seton Press)

$15

Written as a third grade text, this 120-page book uses a biographical approach to present vignettes of exploration, settlement, and development of South, Central, and North America. While a few of the standard characters such as Columbus are featured, most are included because of their advancement of Catholicism. Unique and interesting content plus full-color illustrations make this an interesting resource for this grade level. (There is some overlap in content with the first grade level *American History for Young Catholics*.)

A Child's Story of America, second edition

(Christian Liberty Press)

$8.95; test booklet and answer key - $2 each

This is one of the most delightful history books I have ever come across. It reads like Hillyer's *Child's History of The World* from Calvert Schools which has only recently been reprinted. Both read more like stories than like history texts, giving the reader a sense that the author is conversing directly with him. Unlike Hillyer's book, *A Child's Story of America* includes Christianity in its coverage. The revised second edition markedly expands that coverage with information on the Great Awakening, revivals, and sketches of influential Protestant ministers. This edition now has a strong Protestant flavor that was lacking in the first edition.

It is important to know that both editions of this book have their origins in a much earlier version (written closer to the turn of the last century). The original book reflected attitudes towards Indians that were quite different than today. This second edition reprint has taken pains to update the language and correct inaccurate and incomplete information while still reflecting some of the original attitude. Keep this in mind as you read the book.

Information has been updated through the Clinton administration including the fact of his impeachment.

The new edition features many more illustrations and maps, printed in two colors. Sidebars add extra biographical sketches or vignettes that enhance topic coverage. Chapter review questions are in the book. A separate test booklet and answer key is available.

The Civil War

by Pat Wesolowski

(D.P. & K. Productions)

$20

Ages 9 and up can participate in this unit study on the Civil War. Organized around major battles of the war, the study involves children in activities from history, geography, literature, language arts, speech, journalism, economics, art, home economics, and music. Historical background information is included, although further research will be essential. Right at the beginning, we are challenged to dig into the true history surrounding the war with questions and answers that blow holes in some common beliefs. The author refers us to the book *Facts the Historians Leave Out* as a source about causes of the war. A key part of the study is production of a newsletter (weekly or less frequent depending upon the size of your group). Ideally, the study works best with more than one family, although it can be done with a single family. The more children involved, the more side issues can be developed in individual articles for the newsletter, which expands learning exposure for all. It also means that you have more bodies to participate in reenactments, debates, or other activities you might choose to do. Small group or large, there are plenty of activities to choose from beyond the newsletter. Suggestions and background information are given for geography (blackline map masters included), creating a time line, literature, vocabulary, and economics/statistics. One chapter focuses upon key people and interesting facts. A brief chapter on "Crafts, Cooking, Music & Movies" describes some hands-on activities and supplementary resources. There is an extensive section of reproducible "Puzzles, Games, Codes and More." Suggestions for field trips and activities such as a library scavenger hunt are next, followed by 100 "Quiz Bowl" questions that might be used in a competition, and a book and periodical bibliography. The author used this study with other families, meeting once a week, but you could select from the suggested activities and/or design a different schedule to suit your needs.

Early American History: A Literature Approach

by Rea C. Berg

(Beautiful Feet Books)

Study Guides - $12.95 for primary grades, $14.95 for intermediate grades; costs of books varies

Rea Berg has created two different Study Guides for early American History, one for grades K-3, and one for grades 5-8. The content of the guides and the books selected for inclusion overlap, so we would choose only one of the Study Guides. Rea has successfully pulled together two popular learning approaches—literature-based history and the Principle Approach. The Principle Approach can be intimidating without the sort of help provided here. In fact, Rea describes her method as a simplified Principle Approach. A key book used

at both levels is Principle Approach-based *America's Providential History* by Mark Beliles and Stephen McDowell. At both levels, daily lesson plans are supplied (for 110 days in the K-3 Guide and for 119 days in the 5-8 Guide).

Generally, children are reading (or being read to from) one of the selected books such as *Columbus* by the D'Aulaires. Lessons involve activities such as reading quotes of Columbus from other source books, discussing topics raised in the reading, comparing a person's character with that of someone else the child has read about, drawing or writing in a notebook, working on vocabulary words, drawing maps, completing a time line, or doing research for a report. Activities are appropriate for each level, although we must be careful with kindergarten or first graders to choose activities they can handle. An emphasis on Christian character flows through almost all the lessons. Children maintain a notebook as they do with the Principle Approach.

Study Guides are available by themselves or as part of a package. Beautiful Feet Books has selected literature that is generally available through library loan, but they also sell the books for those who want to own them. There are two packs of books/resources available for each Study Guide. A Literature Pack has the core books, and the Study Guide is purchased separately. The Jumbo Packs include core books, supplemental books, the Study Guide, and Your Story Hour cassettes. The *Early American History Time Line* from Beautiful Feet Books comes with the intermediate grades Jumbo Pack. Selected books are high quality titles that are worth adding to the family library such as titles by the D'Aulaires, *The Fourth of July Story*, *Stories of the Pilgrims*, and *The Courage of Sarah Noble* in the Primary Literature Pack, and *George Washington's World*, *Of Courage Undaunted*, and *Poor Richard* in the Intermediate Literature Pack.

Hats off to Rea Berg for taking a literature-based approach to a deeper level!

Exploring American History

(Christian Liberty Press)

$5.95

This is an expanded and revised version of CLP's *History Book E*. It is much improved. It takes a scattershot approach to U.S. history through short biographies of key figures such as Leif Ericson, Sir Walter Raleigh, Benjamin Franklin, Abraham Lincoln, Eli Whitney, Theodore Roosevelt, and Douglas MacArthur. Even though selective, the biographies paint a fair outline of U.S. history up to the 1990s. The last few chapters are written more broadly, encompassing both the key people and some major events, along with a strong Christian message about the future of our country. Comprehension questions follow each chapter. A separate test booklet and an answer key for both the test booklet and textbook questions are included. (Questions are recall type rather than essay or discussion.) The book itself is in a 6" by 9" format; the print is fairly large, and there are black-and-white illustrations. Reading level is about fifth grade, although interest level will range from about fourth through eighth grade levels.

Heritage Studies for Christian Schools 4, second edition [fourth grade]
(Bob Jones University Press)
home school kit - $67; student text - $15.50; student notebook - $6.50; teacher's edition - $37; tests - $8; answer key - $4.50

This 1997 edition follows United States history from the Constitution through the Industrial Revolution. It is intended to be a continuation of American history studies following Heritage Studies 3. Instead of providing thorough historical coverage, it functions more as a social studies text. Lengthy sections on immigration, Protestant pastors and missionaries, inventions, the Industrial Revolution, and other topics highlight the struggles our country faced as it grew. Each state receives a very brief overview in one chapter. I had trouble figuring out the logic for inclusion of some topics within this book. For example, a chapter titled "Struggles Far Away" covers only two topics: The Boer War, and The Boxer Rebellion. Each of these topics, more typically covered in a world history study, receives about seven pages of attention. I strongly object to the last chapter's explanation of our country as a democracy rather than a Constitutional Republic. The text implies that we make laws under majority rule rather than under the limits of our Constitution. Later comments about the Constitution do not adequately make the limiting connection.

Maps and reference resources are found at the back of the book. A Student Notebook offers worksheets for student activities. Some activities are suggested in the text, and sometimes these make reference to the Student Notebook. Instructional presentation information and instruction on use of Student Notebook pages is in the Teacher Edition. Tests and answer key are are also included in the Home School Kit.

History and Geography 500 series
(Alpha Omega) [fifth grade]
$42.95 for complete set

This LifePac course covers the history of the United States and North America. Check for proper placement by level of difficulty and topic. (Use Alpha Omega diagnostic tests for placement level.) The complete set includes ten LifePacs and a complete Teacher's Guide with answer keys and teacher helps.

The History of Our United States, third edition
(A Beka Book) [fourth grade]
student text - $15.30; teacher edition - $22.20; answer

key for text - $5.95; Geography/Maps - $4.45; activity book teacher key - $8.95; curriculum - $14.95

For a fourth-grade level history book, this has more comprehensive content coverage than average. It covers U.S. history, emphasizing patriotism and the spread of the Gospel. The political view is clearly conservative and the religious perspective non-denominational Protestant. The text includes comprehension questions throughout each chapter, with a lengthier "chapter checkup" at the end. Lush, full-color illustrations, timelines, maps, and photographs give this text unusually strong visual appeal. Although there is a large section of maps at the beginning of the text, you will also want to use the separate *Geography/Maps and Reviews* book. While the majority of the exercises deal with geography, there are also some content exercises. There are separate answer keys for the text and the geography workbook, but there is also a teacher edition of the text which includes answers. Choose one or the other form of answer key. The *History and Geography Curriculum* for this course is primarily lesson plans which correlate the two components and suggest a few additional activities. It is of marginal benefit to homeschoolers. However, since some states require state history in fourth grade, the *Curriculum* does explain how to insert A Beka's *My State Notebook* as a six-week course.

Homelands of North America
(Rod and Staff)
$15.25; teacher's edition - $11; tests - $1.90

Rod and Staff publishes this unique history/geography book for studying the United States and Canada from a Mennonite perspective. It covers geography basics, includes maps for students to copy and fill in, and teaches history with a strong examination of cultures from a Biblical perspective. The Mennonite philosophy is especially evident throughout this book—there are statements about Mennonites (or Anabaptists) starting a church of the only true believers in the early 1500s, that Christians should not tell their government leaders what to do, and promoting nonresistance. This is a far more opinionated book than most from Christian publishers. On the content end, the majority of the book deals with the U.S., but Canada receives significant attention, which those living near the northern border or in Canada will greatly appreciate. It begins with a discussion of Indians, then covers the time period from colonization through modern history.

Land of Our Lady series
(Neumann Press)
$119 for all five volumes

The Land of Our Lady Catholic history textbook series are reprints of books originally published in the 1950s. The series is obviously Catholic throughout with unit introductions related to Mary the Mother of Jesus, coverage of Catholic missionary efforts, and a consistently Catholic worldview throughout. This is the best series I have seen for those looking for such elements in a history series for the elementary grades, although I list below a few cautions about the eighth grade text.

The first book in the series provides the background in world history. (See the review under World History resources.) The rest of the series focuses on United States History with four more texts for grades 5-8. *Bearers of Freedom* [$27], suggested for fifth grade, begins with the growth of world trade, explorations, discovery and settlement of the New World. *Leaders of Freedom* [$25] for sixth grade begins with growing discontent in the American colonies, then continues through the revolution up into the early 1800s. The text of the Declaration of Independence and Constitution are included at the end of this text as well as the next two texts. *The Challenge of Freedom* [$26] picks up with the early 1800s and the populist election of Andrew Jackson, the continues through the expansion of the United States, the Civil War, and Reconstruction. Immigration, science and technology, agriculture, education, and culture are also covered for that time period. *Guardian of Freedom* [$28] covers from the post-Civil War period up into the 1950s. It is important to note that the "political" view in this particular text is supportive of government's expansion into the social arena as well as participation in the United Nations. It also has a very strong anti-Communist flavor as you might well expect in the period just entering into the Cold War. This last text should be used with some caution because of its lack of long-range perspective on issues (e.g., failure of the Great Society, global government goals of the United Nations).

Throughout this series, Church history and "social action" receive more attention than is typical of history texts for elementary grades, even from most Protestant publishers. As is true of most older texts, the content is more extensive than newer texts.

These are all beautiful and durable hard cover books. Black-and-white illustrations, photos, and maps add visual interest. At the end of each chapter are vocabulary lists, discussion questions, quizzes, and ,sometimes, activities. At the end of each unit is a summary of unit highlights plus a mastery test. No answer keys are available.

Notebooks for Families: United States History
by Katherine Mehaffey
(Notebooks for Families)
$75.00; Time Line - $9

If you have decided to use "real" books instead of a textbook to study American History but are concerned about a lack of structure in your program, this may be for you. It will help you construct your own book-based history study, while ensuring that you cover the necessary topics in a meaningful

way. Each of the 194 lessons gives a one page list of notes to be studied, plus a teacher's page giving research topics, lesson starters, discussion questions, and writing and activity ideas relating to the lesson. A comprehensive outline of basic facts is provided, but most of the actual information to flesh out the outline will come from books you get from the library or purchase. A substantial list of suggested books for each topic is included, as well as a separate section of tests with answer keys for those who wish to use tests with the lessons. Part of each lesson and test is marked as suitable for younger children, while older students study the entire lesson, so the program is designed to be used by the entire family studying the topics together. (It is recommended for grades 4-12.) Those with high school students should add essay questions to the tests as suggested in the introduction. The type style used for the teacher's pages and book recommendations is rather hard on the eyes, but the student pages are more readable. The format is loose-leaf for ease of use. A companion, 32-card time line can be used alongside *Notebooks*. The cards can be colored in by children, then arranged in chronological order. Books are not reproducible. At present, you need to buy a separate one for each child. However, separate books of student pages and tests will soon be available.[V. Thorpe/C.D.]

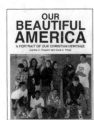

Our Beautiful America
by Juanita C. Houston and Carla B. Perez
(ETC Publications)
student text - $23.95; teacher guide - $21.95; student workbook - $17.95; test booklet - $19.95

The student text for *Our Beautiful America* is hardcover, 280 pages, in a large 8 1/2" x 11" format. There are over 300 illustrations, but all are black-and-white. The book is intended for eighth graders, but really seems more appropriate for 6th-7th grade levels. It is similar in organization to typical textbooks, but it includes significant coverage of Christianity (from a Protestant perspective). It also seems to lean toward a "limited government" view, but not consistently. Abrupt shifts from topic to topic are sometimes disconcerting; for example, within a two page spread we cover three topics: "The Railroad," "Challenges to the Bible," and Chester Arthur's assumption of the presidency following the assassination of James Garfield. The helpful student workbook includes key ideas, people, places, dates, and vocabulary for each chapter plus activity pages with puzzles, maps, charts, and other work pages to reinforce chapter content. Chapter reviews include both recall and analytical questions. Tests are in a separate, reproducible book. Answers for workbook questions/activities and tests are all in the Teacher's Guide. The Teacher's Guide adds a little extra help with lesson presentation plus ideas for field trips, scrapbook entries, further research, and projects.

Our Nation Under God

(Christian Liberty Press)
student book - $7.95; teacher's manual - $4; test booklet - $1.95

Our Nation Under God is written for children about seven to eight years old. It is a brief overview of United States history like most such books for this level. However, I especially liked the opening chapter's discussion of four types of government—self, family, church, and civil—which serves as a foundation for the book in many ways. The rest of the book follows the traditional pattern of teaching from the period of exploration and discovery up through modern times, highlighting key events and people. The teacher's manual is essential since much lesson background is contained therein. Discussion of some topics within the text by itself is inadequate and requires additional input from parents. The teacher's manual also provides lesson plans, discussion questions, activities, answers to exercises when needed, and an answer key for the test booklet.

Our Christian Heritage D

(Our Christian Heritage) [approximately fourth, fifth, or sixth grade]
$7.50 each or complete set for $34.50

These workbooks with fill-in-the-blank exercises are most appropriate for Perfect Paulas, but possibly useful also for Competent Carls and Sociable Sues. While they can be used as independent workbooks, I recommend using them for reading and discussion rather than as workbooks for children to read and fill in on their own. The providential viewpoint is obvious throughout the books. The presentation is in black-and-white and is not particularly appealing, but the content is excellent. Level D focuses on important people in America's history and the beginnings of our nation.

The revised edition for fourth grade [student book - $8.50; teacher manual - $23.50] is printed in two colors and contains about 35% more content. It includes study of various forms of government, self-government, early civilizations, Greece, the Roman Empire, the Dark Ages, the Vikings, the Crusades, colonization, exploration, settlement of the New World, the Great Awakening, reasons for the Civil War, the politics of religious freedom, expanded study of geography, and key figures such as Marco Polo, Leif Ericson, John Smith, Thomas Hooker, George Whitefield, Thomas Paine, and Daniel Boone. The Principle Approach is much more evident in this edition than the first. The teacher's manual provides lots of background information on both content and teaching strategies as well as worksheets, activity suggestions, quizzes, and tests.

Our Christian Heritage E

(Our Christian Heritage) [approximately fifth, sixth, or seventh grade]
$7.50 each or complete set for $34.50
See the description of Level D above. Level E requires more mature levels of thinking than do earlier levels. It studies various influences on our present form of government along with advanced geography.

The revised book for fifth grade [student book -$9.50; teacher manual - $24.50] covers ancient law, the state church of the Middle Ages, a comparison of representative government with dictatorial monarchies, principles of the Declaration of Independence, rights and responsibilities of free men, early civilizations (Sumer, Phoenicia, Egypt, and the ancient Middle East), Greece and Rome as preparation for Christ, introduction to the Reformation, the Revolutionary and Civil Wars, technology and progress, geography of Mesopotamia and the Middle East, physical and political maps (Africa, Asia, Southeast Asia, and Western Europe), latitude and longitude, and key figures such as Tyndale, Jefferson, Franklin, James Madison, Lafayette, Robert E. Lee, Ulysses S. Grant, and Thomas Edison.

Our Christian Heritage, Grade Six

(Our Christian Heritage)
student book - $9.50; teacher manual - $24.50

While the first edition of this series ended with book E, the revised series continues through a sixth book, targeted for sixth grade. Like the other books in this series, United States history and government are primary themes, but world history, government and geography receive substantial coverage. The student book is printed in two-colors, but the magenta/black combination in this book is a bit hard on the eyes.

The organization of this book is quite different from other texts at this level, perhaps owing to the Principle Approach themes that play an important role. Sometimes, the organization seems random as in the first section on early civilizations that inserts geographical overview of the continents. Still, the organizational thread in this book follows chronologically through Greek and Roman civilizations, the Middle Ages, the Reformation, birth of the United States, and modern U.S. history. This is not comprehensive history as we find in most textbooks for this level, but selected "snapshots" with a purpose of demonstrating God's plan unfolding through history. The teacher manual provides lots of background information on both content and teaching strategies as well as worksheets, activity suggestions, quizzes, and tests. Questions require thought and analysis as students answer essay questions (orally or in writing) and fill in charts in addition to filling-in-the-blanks and matching columns.

Our Pioneers and Patriots

by Most Rev. Philip J. Furlong

(TAN Books)

$18

Suggested for grades 5-8, this American history text is written from a Catholic, as well as patriotic, perspective. Bishop Furlong begins with the Norsemen and the exploration of the New World, following through to the English colonies, the birth and growth of our country, civil war, westward expansion, the industrial revolution, and, finally, leaders of the early 20th century. Written in the same format as *The Old World and America* this 508-page text is easy and enjoyable to read.

Chapters begin with a synopsis to pique the student's interest. Chapters end with study summaries and activities to encourage students to look beyond dates and places so they may learn to ask why and how. The study tests are designed to review vocabulary, people, geography, and dates. Well indexed, this text also includes illustrations and maps.

I strongly recommend purchasing the answer key which TAN has available for an additional $10. The answer key can be used by a self-directed student, freeing up time for the parent/teacher.

Originally published in 1940, you will need to supplement this text if you wish to include modern America in your history studies. (Text has the Imprimatur and the Nihil Obstat.)[Maureen Wittmann]

U.S. History Supplements

About Our States

(Bob Jones University Press)

student book - $9; teacher's resource guide - $10

Bob Jones University Press offers this resource for a four-week unit covering each of the fifty states. The Teacher's Resource Guide includes suggested schedule and teaching instructions plus blackline masters for maps and games and a student-constructed booklet on their own state. The colorful, 30-page student book presents a very brief view of each state, highlighting state flags, capitals, flowers, birds, trees, and nicknames.

African Americans Thematic Unit

(Teacher Created Materials)

$9.95

This Thematic Unit on *African Americans* was interesting and fairly evenhanded in its presentation. It is on the Challenging level for grades 5-8. The unit uses three books, *The Talking Eggs; Roll of Thunder, Hear My Cry;* and *One More River to Cross* (short biographies of African Americans throughout America's history). The activities are heavily slanted toward understanding the literary selections, with writing and plot and character analysis, but they also include art, creative writing, maps, science, research, games, drama, and sewing.

I had only two objections to the material in this unit. There was a problem with one of the optional activities centered on Kwanzaa, the African American "holiday." Also, *One More River to Cross* apparently includes a biography on Malcolm X, but the thematic unit does not have any activities that involve this part of the book. Again, like much secular material, it might be necessary to leave out a few objectionable parts. But Teacher Created Materials' prices are generally low enough that it is fine to do that.(SE)

American Adventures, True Stories from America's Past, Part 1 (1770 to 1870) and Part 2 (1870 to the present)

by Morrie Greenberg

(Brooke-Richards Press)

$9.95 each

In each of these two books, fifteen high-interest stories from American history are used for special, self-contained lessons or to supplement a comprehensive history study. Johnny Appleseed, the Orphan Train, and the Camels of the Old West are three of the topics in Part 1, and Theodore Roosevelt, John Ponzi (of the infamous "Ponzi Scheme"), and Rosa Parks are three topics featured in Part 2. Stories are short—about three pages, followed by activities. Activities are grouped into three areas: writing/journal (short writing activities, vocabulary exercises), discussion (good discussion questions and thought-provoking challenges to defend both sides of an issue), and cooperative group (further research and presentation). A timeline and short summary of "What Else Was Happening?" put each story in focus. The books were not written for Christian audiences, so don't expect to hear the "whole story" such as Johnny Appleseed and his gospel preaching. You'll also have to deal with such "perspective" problems as an exercise that asks students to identify "four most important qualities you think a U.S. President should have" from only these eight traits: intelligent, experienced, inspiring, logical, reasonable, caring, healthy, and energetic. Suggested for ages 10 to 15.(SE)

American History Comes Alive Through Narration and Song ⌒

(published by WEM Records, available through Bluestocking Press)

$19.95 per two-cassette volume; $22.95-$26.95 for CDs

Folksongs are a wonderful vehicle for adding the personal dimension to studies of American History. Multi-talented Keith and Rusty McNeil sing and narrate folksongs pertaining to various places and eras in our country's history on these audio cassette sets. I think a quote from their brochure characterizes the purpose of these tapes very well: "Just as the historian provides students with an 'overview' of history by looking from the outside in, the folksong provides an 'innerview' of the attitudes and emotions of the actual participants of historical events, preserving them exactly as they were expressed at the time." Songs are interspersed with narrative details for background and setting to enhance learning and understanding.

There are, at present, eight volumes in this series: *Colonial & Revolution Songs, Moving West Songs, Western Railroad Songs, Civil War Songs, Working and Union Songs, Cowboy Songs*, and two volumes of *California Songs*. There are from 36 to 60 songs contained on two audio cassettes or CDs per volume. Each volume is broken down into theme areas; for example, *Moving West Songs* takes us through "Territorial Expansion and Abolition," "Texas and the Mexican War," "Minstrel Shows and the California Gold Rush," "Western Railroad Songs," and "Immigrants from China, Ireland, and Germany." Each set has supplemental notes that add a few details about the origin of lyrics and tunes as well as history which are not covered in the actual narration. The folksongs are performed with a variety of instruments and, of course, reflect many differing musical styles, so the tapes do not get boring. Those who appreciate folk music already will recognize familiar tunes and musical styles, and those unfamiliar will be getting a musical education. Great for all children up to about eighth grade level.(S)

The American Story series
by Betsy and Giulio Maestro
(HarperCollins)

As series of books is planned to cover the history of the Americas (not just the U.S.). The perspective is non-sectarian throughout the books. While they occasionally acknowledge religious motivations, they do not do so at all important junctures (e.g., Thanksgiving), and sometimes misrepresent religion with broad generalizations. ("Although these explorers were brave men, they were often brutal and cruel to the native people. They tried to force them to accept the Christian religion and to adopt European customs. As a result, the natives did not trust the newcomers and often attacked them" p. 35, *Discovery of the Americas*.) Books are illustrated with full color on every page, and the text is appropriate for early to middle elementary grades. (Reading level is about grades 3-4.)

The first book, titled *The Discovery of the Americas,* covers prehistory through the early explorations. It discusses all of the major, documented explorations as well as some that are hypothetical. A major problem with this book is that it does not distinguish the hypothetical from the factual. For example, it talks about the land bridge connecting Asia and North America, and migrations across that land bridge, as if this were documented fact [$5.95 pb; $16 hc].

The New Americans: Colonial Times 1620-1689 features more text and, consequently, more information than The

Discovery of the Americas. It objectively addresses some of the religious issues, frequently identifying significant roles they played in economics and politics [hardcover only, $16].

Other titles in the series which I have not reviewed are *Exploration and Conquest* and *A More Perfect Union.*

America's Providential History
by Mark A. Beliles and Stephen K. McDowell
(Providence Foundation)
$16.95

Beliles and McDowell have rewritten much of the material from Rosalie Slater, Verna Hall, Arnold Guyot, and others, into a very readable book. The theme, that God in His providence directs both individuals and nations, is prominent. It begins with an overview of geography and ancient history to lay groundwork for presenting the theme in the context of American history, economics, and foreign affairs. It draws on some of Arnold Guyot's ideas in regard to geography and the development of civilizations. (See my comments on Guyot's book, *Physical Geography*.) There is an extensive section on education in America, including the basics of how to apply the Principle Approach. The final chapters describe the "apostasy and decline" of America and a plan for the "reformation" of our country. The authors present a strong call to action and Christian political involvement. This book has a purposeful message with which readers might agree or disagree, but it is nevertheless valuable as a balancing source for the presentation of American history. It is best used as a parent resource book. (The book is 296-pages, softbound, with large print and black-and-white illustrations.)

Bluestocking Press

Bluestocking has selected many titles relating to American history for inclusion in their catalog. Use these for your history curriculum or as supplements. They have items related to the *Little House* books and Laura Ingalls Wilder that will be of special interest to many.

Boys and Girls of Colonial Days
(Christian Liberty Press)
$5; answer key - $1

This revised and edited edition of an original book by Carolyn Sherwin Bailey is an excellent supplement for children from about third grade up through fifth or sixth grade. It contains twelve stories about children in colonial days. In many of the stories the children meet famous people such as Benjamin Franklin, Samuel Adams, George Washington, and Betsy Ross. The writing style sounds like the original was written in the nineteenth century, yet it is very understandable for children. The book also has numerous black-and-white illustrations, most of an older-appearing etched style in keeping with the text. This book is printed in large type in a 6" by

9" format, thus eliminating small-print problems for young readers.

Civil War Thematic Unit
(Teacher Created Materials)
$9.95

This reproducible book uses whole language methods to study all subject areas with the Civil War as the theme. Two novels are the foundation: *Charley Skedaddle* and *Behind Rebel Lines*. Activities cover language arts, math, science, social studies, art, music, and life skills. Lesson plans and teaching suggestions are included as well as a few worksheets and an answer key. This is essentially unit study, packaged on a smaller scale than *KONOS* or *The Weaver*. Many activities are classroom oriented and must either be skipped or adapted for home use. There are also some minor content problems. Appropriate for upper elementary grades.(SE)

Color Historic America
(Color Historic America, Inc.)
$3

This 32-page coloring book features famous people, places, and events from American history. It makes a fun supplement, especially for children who enjoy coloring.

Color Historic America States and Capitals
(Color Historic America, Inc.)
$5

Second through sixth graders can use this 56-page book as a supplement to their studies of the United States. Coloring pictures from each state are accompanied by descriptions and information about the state's bird, flower, and motto. Extra maps are included showing topography, the thirteen original colonies, and locations of capitals.

Free Indeed: Heroes of Black Christian History
by Mark Sidwell
(Bob Jones University Press)
$9

The focus here is upon black Christians in America rather than the typical black heroes. The book opens with a brief history of the black church in America, then presents biographies of thirteen men who demonstrate the work of salvation in their lives. Each story is as much a spiritual journey as an historical one. Parents might read these aloud with students in the upper elementary grades, although the book is geared to reading levels for junior and senior high students. Discussion questions should probably be saved for older students.

Freedom's Sons: The True Story of the AMISTAD Mutiny
by Suzanne Jurmain
(HarperCollins/Lothrop, Lee and Shepard Books imprint)
$15

The mutiny aboard the slave ship Amistad has earned increasing attention since a movie about it was made in 1997. This book presents the story, avoiding sensationalism, but instead using research, documents and drawings for accuracy. The story itself is so gripping without embellishment—the story of slaves who mutinied when they thought they were soon to die, then the legal battle they endured to regain their freedom. A few pages of photos and artwork created at the time highlight the actuality of the event. The story helps children understand a little of the complexity of the slave issue: why Africans sold other Africans into slavery, how slavery was treated differently by different countries, some of the corruption that accompanied the slave trade, and the difficulties faced by captive slaves when they were thrust into unknown situations without the ability to communicate in a common language. Efforts to present the gospel to the Africans are presented in a refreshingly objective manner. The story is appropriate for upper elementary ages through high school. (The large print misleadingly seems to indicate a younger level audience than the vocabulary of the story requires.) I particularly like this book since it is historically accurate and skips the politically-correct interpretations all too common in such stories.(S)

Great Women in American History
by Rebecca Price Janney
(Christian Publications/Horizon Books imprint)
$12.99

Abigail Adams, Anne Bradstreet, Queen Kaahumanu, Catherine Marshall, Rosa Parks, Pocahontas, Harriet Beecher Stowe, and Laura Ingalls Wilder are among 23 women highlighted with brief biographies. They span all periods of U.S. History and a wide range of backgrounds, recognizing the Christian faith of many of these women. The stories are interestingly written, slanted for emotional and inspirational impact. This book will serve as a useful supplement to emphasize the roles many women have played in our country's history. It can be read aloud or assigned as independent reading for ages ten and up.

Hands On Activities for Elementary Social Studies
by David Cooper
(Alpha Publishing Company)

See review under "Supplements" for World History.

History Alive! through Music

(Holly Hall)

$19.99 each

History Alive! through Music offers two book/audio cassette sets entitled *America 1750-1890* and *Westward Ho!*. Books of more than 70 pages each trace these two periods of American history through representative songs. Children can enjoy the stories and illustrations while listening to each professionally-recorded song. There are 16 songs and stories in *America 1750-1890*, and 14 songs and stories in *Westward Ho!*

A new addition is *Favorite Songs from Little House Country*. The tape has 13 songs (folk tunes and hymns), skillfully performed with unusual and interesting instruments and various vocal styles. The book has historic photos, photos of the Ingall's sites, and text written by Bill Anderson, noted "Laura" historian and author.

These high quality products from a home schooling family are designed to add life to history, and they do the job very well.

History Mysteries

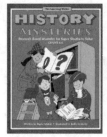

(Learning Works)

$10.95

History Mysteries focuses on U.S. History events, people, presidents, inventions, sports, the arts, Native Americans, monuments, and other topics. Each lesson presents ten mystery questions, each of which is a group of clues leading toward an answer. Some of the lessons are constructed such that the clues build upon answers to preceding questions. To solve the questions, students will need to research through sources like *World Book Encyclopedia*, *Microsoft Encarta*, or history textbooks. This is a fun way to get children to pay attention to historical details as they learn how to research information.(S)

A History of US, second edition

by Joy Hakim

(Oxford University Press)

$13.95 pb/$19.95 hc each volume;
$153.45 pb/$219.45 hc for the set;
teacher's guides - $4.16 each

This eleven-volume U.S. history has garnered lots of attention—good and bad. Some improvements were made in the second edition, such as toning down "anti-Reagan" rhetoric. The books are very well written, presenting history more as story than the recitation of facts. That approach, though, means that the content will necessarily be much more subjective. If parents will read through these books with discernment, discussing alternate points of view on various topics, the series can be a valuable teaching tool. Beautiful Feet Books provides an excellent example as they incorporate some of these books into their *U.S and World History* course, suggesting controversial topics that should be discussed. The eleventh volume, added to the second edition features "94 essential documents with commentary, as well as a glossary and index to the entire series." Teacher's guides are also available from Oxford University Press for the second edition. Although they didn't provide one for review, I suspect that using something like the Beautiful Feet study would be better.(SE)

I Love America, Part 1 and Part 2

(National Center for Constitutional Studies)

Part 1 - $19.95; Part 2 - $24.95; either can be purchased without the three-ring binder for $5 less

I Love America is a two-volume resource that can be used in schools, homes, or other group settings to teach children patriotism. A combination of stories, songs, poems, games, crafts, and projects are presented at two different levels—Part 1 for ages 4-7 and Part 2 for upper elementary grades. Topics covered in Part 1 include the American flag, Christopher Columbus, the first Thanksgiving, Washington, Franklin, Jefferson, Pocahontas, and our American heritage. Part 2 teaches about the Statue of Liberty, the Pilgrims, freedom of religion, the Revolutionary War, Jefferson, the Declaration of Independence, the Constitutional Convention, the Constitution, and the free enterprise system.

Immigration Thematic Unit

(Teacher Created Materials)

$9.95

This whole-language approach to the topic of immigration centers around four books: *Do People Grow on Family Trees?*, *Molly's Pilgrim*, *How Many Days to America? A Thanksgiving Story*, and *Hello, My Name is Scrambled Eggs*. *Immigration* is a teacher's guide with reproducible pages for student activities geared for intermediate level students (middle to upper elementary). Classroom design and politically-correct orientation make some of the material awkward or unusable, but there are plenty of ideas to draw from to help children develop a better understanding of the immigrant experience both in history and at the present time. The first book studied involves children in investigations of their own family history, a very worthwhile activity for building personal connections with topics studied in history, geography, and social studies. (See the reviews of *Medieval* and *Civil War Thematic Units* for more information about the format.)(SE)

Inside Story Series

(Peter Bedrick Books)

$10.95 each pb; $18.95 each hc

See the review under "Supplements" for World History.

Two books in the series —*A Frontier Fort on the Oregon Trail*, and *World War Two Submarine*—can be used while studying U.S. History.

Jackdaw Portfolios of Historical Documents and Study Guides

(Golden Owl Publishing Company)

See review under "Supplements" for World History.

Kaw Valley Video Sales and Rentals [videos]

(Kaw Valley Video Sales and Rentals)

$10 annual membership fee; $19.95 each on purchases, $4 each rental

Among videos in Kaw Valley's catalog are some pertaining to U.S. history. One is entitled *"We Proceeded On..." The Expedition of Lewis and Clark 1804-1806*. This 32-minute video tracks the expedition from the confluence of the Missouri and Mississippi Rivers all the way to the Pacific Coast then back. It capsulizes the hardships of the expedition and their discoveries with enough information to make it interesting without being overwhelming. Members of the expedition and the Indians they met and traveled with are introduced, and we are given biographical insight into the nature of the two strong leaders, Lewis and Clark, who planned and executed this expedition so magnificently. I am told that this is the same video shown at the Fort Clatsop National Park on the Oregon Coast, which was built by the expedition. (If you have seen other such videos at national parks you have an idea of the professional quality.) Likewise *Gettysburg: 1863* is shown at the Gettysburg Visitor's Center. This film describes the events leading up to this fateful battle, then the battle itself. It depicts the battle with a topographical map, arrows, and other markings, then fills in the story about the key generals, the status of the war, and the consequences, both immediate and long term. Another series of videos, *The History of American Railroads* makes a great supplement as you study the period of the westward movement. Four 20-minute videos can be used at the appropriate times in your U.S. History studies. *The 1880s* video is like viewing newspaper headlines about key events of that era—snippets about all kinds of unrelated topics. Interesting but superficial. These are high-quality videos that appeal to all ages.

While I reviewed only these few videos, you should check out others in their catalog such as *Oregon Trail, Pony Express, The Mississippi River*, and *Shiloh*.

A $10 annual membership fee entitles you to a catalog, purchase of videos at the $19.95 price (or a special 44-video package for $399), or two-week rentals for $4 each (volume discounts available).(S)

The Light and the Glory for Children

(Baker Book House)

$9.99

Peter Marshall and David Manuel's popular book *The Light and the Glory* has been rewritten for children by Anna Wilson Fishel. She has added narratives, study questions, and a glossary to make it even more useful. For those unfamiliar with the original, the theme is the providential founding of America and the spiritual significance of our country's history. (Note: this book is actually published by Revell which is a division of Baker Book House.)

Made for Trade: A Game of Early American Life

(Aristoplay)

$25

Learn about the history, culture, trades, and economy of colonial America with this outstanding game that has four different levels of play. For ages eight to adult.

Mantle Ministries/Richard "Little Bear" Wheeler

Little Bear does a wonderful job of teaching both godly principles and American history to all ages. His presentations are on both audio and video cassettes, some with accompanying workbooks. Little Bear is a delight to watch in authentic period costumes with props as he dramatically relives key historical events. Most of his videos are single stories of varying lengths, although *The Pilgrim Adventure* is two sets of three tapes each [$20 per set]. Among other video titles are *Be on Guard, The Fort Story, The Kit Carson Story, The Joseph Walker Story, The John Colter Story, The Showdown of the O.K. Corral, Battle of Monongahela, Battle of Long Island*, and *Battle of Trenton* [priced from $10 to $20 each].

Mantle Ministries also features a collection of reprinted classical literature—fiction and non-fiction. Major publications include nonfiction character-building anthologies such as *Gaining Favor with God and Man* and *Moral Lessons of Yesteryear*; biographical books such as *Illustrious Americans*; and historical accounts such as *Pilgrim Adventure* and the *Price of Liberty*. Most recently, Mantle Ministries has begun reprinting Christ-centered fiction for children and families to enjoy, including the Elsie Dinsmore collection, the Mildred Keith collection (both by Martha Finlay), and the Family Classic collection which includes stories by authors such as Oliver Optic and Horatio Alger Jr.

Milliken Transparency Reproducible Books

(Milliken)

$12.95 each

Milliken publishes a number of United States history titles

that can be easily adapted for children over a wide age span, even though the publisher suggests using them for grades 7-12. The books have full-color illustrations and transparencies (designed for use on overhead projectors, but just as useful without the projector), information on the subject, maps, and reproducible student worksheets. The eleven titles in this series begin with the colonization period just before the American Revolution and continue up through the early twentieth century. These books are intended to supplement our studies rather than be used as the primary resources. (The Weaver suggests their use in conjunction with their unit studies.) Since we copy the worksheets, each book is non-consumable. The quality of the content and presentation is excellent, although we are likely to encounter philosophical problems.(SE)

My American Journey
(Multnomah Publishers)
$19.99 each

This is a series of history "sets," appropriate for children in grades 3-6, on Lewis and Clark, George Washington, Benjamin Franklin, Harriet Tubman, Abraham Lincoln, the Wright brothers, Mark Twain, Thomas Edison, and Teddy Roosevelt.

Each set comes as a well put together package. The two we received for review included a beautifully-illustrated 45-page hardback book, a 22-page activity book with a secret message to decode, 4 picture cards and samples of historical material. Especially worthwhile is a character building workbook with questions about each chapter of the book along with pertinent Biblical examples and suggestions for prayer. The workbook also has hints and suggestions for answers which would be helpful for younger children, but which might make things a little too easy for the older ones.

One title we reviewed, *From Colonies to Country with George Washington,* includes a workbook on *Leadership*, a copy of the Declaration of Independence, a soldiers drill manual and a war-time code. The well-told and exciting story of George Washington is narrated by a fictional character. Interesting and little known facts are included along with some myth (e.g., Betsy Ross).

From East to West with Lewis & Clark includes a workbook on *Endurance,* a map from 1804, and a small sample journal. This story is narrated by "Lewis and Clark", but the introduced, fictional character is not as effective as in the Washington book. The Indian and Black characters are presented in a rather stereotypical way, and you might want to make that a point of discussion. However, the story has lots of adventure, guns and boats, and some children may enjoy reenacting parts of it.(Note: This series may be soon be taken over by another publisher.)[V. Thorpe/C.D.]

Pathways of America series
(Good Apple)
$12.99 each

There are four books in this series for grades 4 through 8: *The Oregon Trail, Lewis and Clark, The California Gold Rush Trail,* and *The Santa Fe Trail.* (Another book, *The California Mission Trail* is due Spring of 2000.) Each is a 96-page book, and although the publisher labels them as activity books, they contain a large amount of text/background material with activity instructions following the various sections. I reviewed *The Oregon Trail* which traces the trail from its origin at Independence, Missouri to its terminus at Oregon City, telling the story of key people and places. Activities range from writing, drawing, and crafts through budgeting and library research.(S)

Revolutionary War Thematic Unit
(Teacher Created Materials)
$9.95

This reproducible book uses whole language methods to study all subject areas with the Revolutionary War as the theme. See the description of *Civil War Thematic Unit* above for the format description. Novels studied are *Johnny Tremain* and *The Fighting Ground.*(SE)

States and Capitals ∩
(Twin Sisters Productions, Inc.)
cassette with activity book set - $9.98

Auditory learners can learn states and their capitals along with other tidbits of state information through songs on the audio cassette tape plus activities in the accompanying 24-page activity book. The activity book features puzzles, writing and poetry, plus lyrics to all the songs. A variety of musical styles, clearly-articulated words, and professional recording earn high marks for the tape. Reinforce learning by using activities in the reproducible 48-page workbook which include creative writing, crosswords, research assignments, drawing, and more. This book also contains the sheet music for all of the songs.(S)

States and Capitals Challenge game
(Creative Teaching Associates)
$18.95

Children about fourth grade level and up can play this fun board game. From two to four players move around the outside rim of the board on flags representing each of the states. As they land on a state, they try to name that state's capital. If correct, they place their marker on that state. Play gets interesting as they land on already "claimed" states. 24 "Challenge" cards, each with three questions, are used. Players spin to identify which question category to use: fact, landmark, or nickname. This game should be fun to play as well as educational. My only concern is the limited number of challenge cards—you might want to make up some of your own to keep things interesting.

States and Capitals Kit [audio cassette]
(Audio Memory)
cassette - $9.95; CD - $12.95

Children can sing along with this audio tape or CD to learn names and locations of the states and their capitals. It comes with a 25" by 36" map which children label and color.

States and Capitals Match Wits game
(Creative Teaching Associates)
$9.95

You'll find my reviews of other *Match Wits* games for other topics scattered through this book. I really like these four-sided, domino-style games. In this one, you try to match not just states and their capitals, but also time zones and regions of the country (e.g., midwestern states). A handy guide to all of these is included. Students score more points if they can manage to match up more than one fact on each tile they place.

Stories of The Pilgrims
(Christian Liberty Press)
$6; answer key - $1

Although this book is listed in the CLP catalog as a reader, it also serves well as a history resource for young children. This updated and revised edition of the original book about the Pilgrims by Margaret B. Pumphrey tells of this brief but important time in America's history in story form. The reading level is appropriate for third or fourth graders, but it makes a good read-aloud book for younger children. The print is large and dark, and the book is in a large, softcover format. There are several black-and-white illustrations scattered throughout the book.

The Story Behind the Scenery series
(KC Publications, Inc.)
$7.95 each

If you have visited some of the national parks or monuments in the U.S., you might have seen in the book store a colorful book full of photographs about the place you are visiting. One publisher of those beautiful books is KC Publications. The "Story Behind the Scenery" series covers such places as *Alcatraz, Bryce Canyon, Cape Cod, Crater Lake, Death Valley*, the *Everglades, Gettysburg, Mammoth Cave, Mesa Verde, Mount Rushmore*, the *Redwoods*, the *Statue of Liberty*, and *Yosemite*. They also have a few more topical books in the series such as the one on *Civil War Parks* and the *Colonial* book on Williamsburg, Yorktown, and

Jamestown. KC offers other series: one titled "in pictures...The Continuing Story" features books on the *Grand Canyon, Mount Rainier*, some of the places included in the first series, and more; and another series of special interest books features topics like *John Wesley Powell, Lewis and Clark*, the *Oregon Trail*, and the *Santa Fe Trail*. I reviewed a number of titles from all but the "in pictures" series. Some books fit together to create topical series; the series titles are "American Early Exploration and Westward Expansion," "American Indian Cultural Series" (particularly concentrating on the tribes of the Southwest), "Civil War Era Series," "Colonial America Series," and "Physical and Cultural Geography Series." All of these books feature beautiful photographs accompanied by well-written text that might explain historical events related to the place, geographical information, explanation of the creation of the park or monument, and/or biographical information about the key people. The authors do make evolutionary assumptions, so be prepared to sift the information. KC is in the process of creating lesson plans for at least some of the titles. Special pricing and discounts are available. These are beautiful books at very reasonable prices.(SE)

Teaching American History Through Art
by Rich and Sharon Jeffus
(Visual Manna)
$14.95

If your Sociable Sue has a hard time studying history, perhaps using art projects tied into the subject would be just the thing to spark her interest. The lessons in this black-and-white paperback are not clear enough for those who need step-by-step instructions, but for teachers who have experience with arts and crafts media and who just need a little inspiration it could serve as a source of ideas. Grades 3-6.[V.Thorpe]

Turning Back the Pages of Time: A Guide to American History through Literature
Compiled by Kathy Keller
(Pilgrim Enterprises)
$4.50

This 35-page booklet is a helpful resource for those who want to study American History by reading "real" books, but who want unbiased recommendations from someone who is not selling the books they recommend. Kathy Keller divides recommendations under time periods and also under age groups (from kindergarten up) to make it easy to spot titles quickly. She also provides a brief annotation for each resource. Titles are a mixture of biographies, historical fiction, classics, and non-fiction. At the end of the book, more general resources are listed as well as some period cookbooks (e.g., *The Little House Cookbook*) and craft books. Books have been pre-screened for content, but those listed are from both Christian and secular publishers. However, under each time period there is an extra section recommending only Christian titles such as those from the Mott Media Sower series and stories of Christian figures such as John Wesley. Also listed at the end of each time period section are additional topics to investigate for other reading material. A symbol-code system lets us know how easy or difficult to locate a book might be.

Unit Study Adventures series
by Amanda Bennett
(Holly Hall)
$13.99 each

Three titles in this series fit under U.S. history studies: *Pioneers, Elections,* and *Thanksgiving.* Suitable for students in grades K-8, these are not comprehensive unit studies such as *KONOS* or *Weaver* but guides that develop single topics. Guides include minimal Christian content with the exception of *Thanksgiving* which is thoroughly Christian in its treatment. See the complete review in Chapter Five under "Limited Unit Studies."

U.S. Geography Map and Card Decks
(Bealls' Learning Games)
map - $5; card deck - $5

A laminated 11" x 17" U.S. Geography map can be used along with the geography card deck or the states and capitals card deck (states on hot pink cards and capitals on bright lime green cards) from Beall's. Geography cards cover topics such as rivers, mountains, mountain ranges, parks, and points of interest.

Bealls' also produce a packet of reproducible masters that can be used with the above items as well as for other subject areas. The packet includes a master for a U.S. States and Capitals map, a master sheet of states and capitals for reference, 10-page reproducible quiz/test that might also be used as a study guide on the states, and game instructions for seven games. Some game ideas require the double-sided game board that comes in the *Phonogram Fun Packet*

Studying the Constitution

The Constitution receives attention within a number of resources reviewed in this chapter. However, there are a few excellent resources dedicated just to that topic.

Our Constitution
by Linda Carlson Johnson
(Millbrook)
$7.46 pb

Millbrook's "I Know America" series features a number of

books that relate to the Constitution and our government. I reviewed only *Our Constitution,* but other related titles in the series are *Our Congress, Our Declaration of Independence, Our Elections, Our Flag, Our Money, Our National Anthem, Our National Capital, Our Presidency,* and *Our Supreme Court.* All of these are 48-page books. You can find many of them in hardcover editions in your library, but more-affordable paperback editions are very reasonably priced. All books feature both full-color and black-and-white illustrations. The catalog suggests using these for children in grades 2 through 4. However, if the detailed information in *Our Constitution* is a fair representation of other books in the series, I would recommend them for grades 3 to 6. *Our Constitution* includes a page on the Magna Carta, a two-page discussion of the Virginia Plan, and an entire chapter on the Bill of Rights. The presentation is balanced. While it refers to the "living Constitution," it does so in regard to the amendment process rather than judicial interpretation. I consider this one of the best topical children's books among others of similar size and price. (S)

Our Living Constitution, Then and Now
(Good Apple)
$14.99

This 168-page book offers a thorough study of the historical and literal facts about the Constitution, and a briefer look at modern applications. The publisher recommends it for students in grades 5 to 8, but it is also appropriate for high school level. It covers the entire text of the Constitution, The Bill of Rights, and the remaining amendments, arranging them in two-column fashion with the original text on the left and a "translation" on the right. Interspersed at various points are explanations, activity pages, and research assignments. With younger students, we might cover selected sections and activities, saving more challenging assignments for older students (e.g., "In the space below cite several examples in today's world where Congress has exercised implied power. Look in newspapers and magazines for additional ideas," or "What is the main essential in a writ of habeas corpus?"). While the perspective is secular, it seems well-balanced. We can use the trivial pursuit type game found towards the end of the book to "quiz" students on their knowledge. The book is reproducible and an answer key is at the back. Plan a semester-long course using this book along with You, Your Child, and the Constitution for the Christian perspective.

The Principle Approach

The Principle Approach requires much study and planning on the part of the teacher/parent, but the results will usually reflect the effort. This methodology can be used with children of all ages. Most people utilizing the Principle Approach have children keep a notebook for recording information that has been researched and studied. The application of concepts is also recorded in the notebook.

History is an important aspect of the Principle Approach with the emphasis upon America's Christian history. In reviewing many Principle Approach history resources, I have found that many authors have attempted to counterbalance the secularization of history by presenting the other extreme. As I mentioned earlier, it is important that we recognize that many times these resources are not intended to present a complete and balanced story, but to compensate for what has been omitted or misrepresented elsewhere. Because of this, you must ensure that you are providing thorough, balanced coverage rather than using only resources that stress America's Christian heritage.

Seven principles are identified, studied, and used as a foundation for further learning. The following phrases summarize the principles:
- God's principle of individuality
- The Christian principle of self-government
- America's heritage of Christian character
- Conscience is the most sacred of all property
- The Christian form of our government
- How the seed of local self-government is planted
- The Christian principle of American political union

The Principle Approach can also be applied to all subject areas as explained in Mr. Rose's book and other resources listed below. The easiest books to work with are *America's Christian History, Christian Self-Government* (Intrepid Books) described above.

Below are listed other books that are based upon the Principle Approach. These are not textbooks for children to use but source books for parents.

Contact Landmark Distributors, F.A.C.E., or the American Christian History Institute for more information. These organizations publish and distribute Principle Approach material. Landmark Distributors has an extensive catalog with the widest range of Principle Approach resources.

Foundational Resources for the Principle Approach

The American Dictionary of the English Language a facsimile 1828 edition
by Noah Webster
(Foundation for American Christian Education)
$60

A dictionary seems an unusual item to list under history, but this one is different. Webster provides Biblical meanings and references within many definitions to clarify the meaning and usage of words. Definitions of many words have changed since 1828, and this dictionary helps us properly interpret source documents from America's beginnings by defining words as their original writers intended. The use of this dictionary is also a vital part of the Principle Approach since one of the first steps to studying a subject is to properly define its terms.

The Christian History of the Constitution of the United States of America, Volumes I and II [Volume II is subtitled Christian Self-Government with Union]
(Foundation for American Christian Education)
$40

These books, compiled by Verna Hall, provide primary sources that help lay the philosophical foundation for the Principle Approach. The primary sources contained in these books document the Christian heritage of America. They should be used as reference tools, particularly in conjunction with other books listed below. These are beautiful hardbound volumes as are the other books from Foundation for American Christian Education.

A Guide to American Christian Education for the Home and School, The Principle Approach, 2nd Edition
by James B. Rose
(American Christian History Institute)
$38

This is THE book about how to teach the various subjects by the Principle Approach. It is a beautifully bound, very large book—550 pages, requiring a significant study effort. However, it attempts to answer all the questions that arise over implementation of the Principle Approach. It defines the Principle Approach and the Seven Principles. It discusses application of the Principle Approach in both the school at home and the Christian school. Probably the most valuable part of the book for most people is that which tells how to 4-R a subject and how to use the Principle Approach to teach literature, typing, geography, history, economics, science, and mathematics.

A Principle Approach for 3 R's and Other Subjects
by Steve C. Dawson
(Landmark Distributors)

Dawson apparently wanted to simplify the Principle Approach and its application so teachers at Providence Christian Academy could use it. This manual is the basic foundation. The principles are summarized. He demonstrates how they apply to reading, writing, grammar, literature, math, and science. He provides teaching notes covering what students need to grasp about why we learn various subjects, along with quizzes (reproducible) and answer keys on this material. This information is offered on two levels, for younger and older students. Since defining terms is a crucial part of the Principle Approach, Dawson provides examples and a reproducible vocabulary worksheet. Those who need or prefer some assistance in tackling the Principle Approach will appreciate this book's simplified handling of the task. However, be forewarned not to expect a polished product. This book was probably compiled in pieces as necessity dictated, so type styles differ, there is no table of contents, and we are left to figure out for ourselves precisely how to use it. Those who have no exposure to the Principle Approach will likely need some more background about the Principle Approach itself to understand how to use it.

Radical Christianity
by Paul Goedecke
(Landmark Distributors)
$20

Goedecke subtitles this book, "A Study into the Theological Basis and Application of the Root Principles of Christ." He uses the same seven basic principles described by Verna Hall, although he simplifies both definitions and explanations. He applies each principle in the realms of home, church and government. This book might well serve as your starting point to understand what the Principle Approach is all about. I believe that it also gives us a clearer picture of how we are to apply the principles than do some of the original works.

Renewing the Mind
by Paul W. Jehle
(Landmark Distributors)
$15

This is a compilation of Jehle's newsletters in which he applies the Principle Approach to various subject areas. He identifies the basic words and definitions from which we begin our studies, relates these to the seven basic principles described above, then offers practical teaching suggestions. Think of this as a greatly simplified version of James Rose's *A Guide to American Christian Education for the Home and School, The Principle Approach.*

Study Guide to the Christian History of the Constitution of the United States of America, Volume II
by Mary-Elaine Swanson
(American Christian History Institute)
$20

The purpose of the *Study Guide* is to focus on materials in *Volume II of Christian History of the Constitution* which show how and where our Founders discovered and developed the

seeds of American unity and union. The principles underlying the choices of our Founding Fathers are emphasized, demonstrating their reliance upon a Biblical view of man and government. The *Guide* may be used by adults or mature high school students. The use of a notebook as outlined in *The Principle Approach* (by Slater) is strongly recommended. The *Study Guide* comes with answers to questions and a ninety-minute cassette tape by the author on how to teach through the 92-page book.

Teaching and Learning America's Christian History: The Principle Approach
by Rosalie Slater
(Foundation for American Christian Education)
$35

This volume outlines the seven basic principles of "America's Christian history and government." Each topic is frequently cross referenced to the above *Christian History Volumes* by Verna Hall. As the seminal volume of the Principle Approach, this book will get you started but will not carry you through into all subject areas as does the book by James Rose.

Topic-Specific Resources for the Principle Approach

Note: some of the following resources are for other subject areas!

The Christian History of The American Revolution
by Verna M. Hall
(Foundation for American Christian Education)
$42

This book provides the Biblical background of the American Revolution by comparing the liberty of the Gospel with American political liberty. It contains early election sermons, and essays on early American education and the use of the Bible in forming a Christian worldview.

Christian Home Learning Guides
by Marshall Foster and Ron Ball
(Mayflower Institute)
$39.95

This is actually a single very large book (almost 500 pages) divided up into numerous sections, many of which correspond to the educational CD-ROMs from the *Zane Home Library*. The book can stand alone as a history-oriented Biblical world view curriculum guide. Foster and Ball explore philosophy and beliefs as they impact all the different subject areas, presenting the rationale for a Biblical Christian view. Elements of the Principle Approach are incorporated; making this a sort of "Principle Approach made simple" course. Marshall Foster's background as a history researcher tilts the entire book more toward history than any other subject. A huge appendix includes important historical documents and writings such as the *Mayflower Compact* and *Declaration of Independence*. An interesting feature is the inclusion of critiques of the Zane CD-ROM programs. Foster and Ball deal with the humanistic, evolutionary assumptions evident in the programs, using them as a way of teaching the alternative Biblical Christian worldview. If you purchase the Zane programs, you really need this book. If you don't have the programs, you can still benefit from the information presented here. Note: the *Zane Home Library* CD-ROMs are being marketed through Amway distributors who will also be selling this book. They did not supply any of their programs for review.

Introduction to Elementary Science: an American Christian Principle Approach
by Steve C. Dawson
(Landmark Distributors)
$20

This ungraded manual can be used with all ages to introduce science topics, although some of the material is better saved for students in the upper elementary levels. We can go through this book a few times, presenting material at increasing depth each time. If used as a one-year course, it will typically require 2 or 3 lessons per week.

The book begins with a review of the Principle Approach upon which the course is based. It then presents the Biblical foundation of science and an historical overview featuring well-known scientists. Brief biographies about the scientists often bring out little-known information about the influence of their Christian beliefs upon their views about science. The remainder of the book is broken down into sections on physical, earth, and life sciences. Typically for each lesson there are notes (for presenting the material), activity pages (paper and pencil), quizzes, and answer keys. Composition assignments are given for older students. Dawson builds most lessons around the "rule of 3" based upon the three-fold nature of God, but I personally tend to view this organizational construction as unnecessarily restrictive rather than illustrative (a minor quibble). Some understanding of the Principle Approach would be extremely helpful before tackling this study because it requires students to use the "4-R" method which the Principle Approach employs. Teacher presentation and preparation time are required. The book is self-contained with reproducible student pages.

The Rudiments of America's Christian History and Government: Student Handbook
by Rosalie J. Slater and Verna M. Hall
(Foundation for American Christian Education)
$13

This book is intended to introduce students to a key Principle Approach idea—the hand of God in the founding of America—and the reasoning and writing of Biblical principles applied in the *Christian History* volumes and *Teaching and Learning America's Christian History.*

Physical Geography
by Arnold Guyot
(American Christian History Institute)
$9.95

This is a reprint of the 1885 edition of this book. It serves as a companion to the section on teaching geography in James Rose's *A Guide to American Christian Education* (American Christian History Institute). It is also quoted and referred to in *Teaching and Learning America's Christian History*, although it is not required for that book. I am not knowledgeable enough to critique the geographic content of the book, and I assume it is accurate, although there are certainly more recent discoveries that would shed more light on some topics (such as earthquakes and plate tectonics.) When he ventures away from geographical facts, the content of the book becomes debatable. I am bothered by Guyot's approach to The Human Family—the white Caucasian is held up as the ideal with every other race as inferior. He also makes a few generalizations about continents and historical movements that I consider to be more philosophical than factual. When reading Guyot, we must keep in mind the time period and culture from which he wrote, since some of his ideas seem out of step with contemporary thought.

This is a heavy-duty geography textbook. It is not very readable alone but would serve better as a source book. According to the publisher, this edition is the only textbook on physical geography written by a dedicated Christian and creation scientist in the twentieth century from the viewpoint that the earth and its geography are God's handiwork. A supplement, *Physical Geography Maps* (American Christian History Institute) [$10], includes 36 maps with instructions and a sample full-color map.

Geography/Map Skills

Map skills and geographical knowledge become increasingly important as students move on to world history. Have a globe, maps, and atlases handy for reference and research. Geography is incorporated into many of the above history textbooks. If not, we can do it ourselves by identifying places where historical events occur, discussing geographical influences upon historical events, and using a supplement such as one of these listed below.

Cultural Atlas for Young People series
(Facts On File)

This series of books begins with geography then incorporates history and cultural studies. Titles in the series are

Ancient Egypt, Ancient Greece, Ancient Rome, Ancient America, and *First Civilizations.* See the description under "World History."(S)

Eyewitness World Atlas [CD-ROM]
(DK Publishing)
$59.95 for school version; $29.95 for CD-ROM only

DK uses multimedia techniques to present geography information with this CD-ROM program. It runs on Windows 95 or higher systems running 75MHz or faster with a sound card. Gorgeous graphics make it very visually appealing.

You can purchase the CD-ROM on its own which is useful, but the school version includes two copies of the CD-ROM plus a binder with lesson plans. The lesson plans are identified for four "levels": grades 4-6, grades 7-9, for ESL students, and for special education students. You might find that younger students can complete some of the lessons from the last category.

This is a fairly complex program, so the first lessons acquaint students with how it operates and where to locate information. There are physical and political views of the globe. Click on a spot and a close-up map of the country appears with additional information: a brief description with a few highlights plus brief data on population, capital, language, currency, and political status. Information on the people, communications, politics, health, climate, education, wealth, tourism, defense and other topics is available by clicking on another sidebar. Religion is not included in this list. Back on the opening page, you have the option of viewing eight "satellite tours" which zoom over a particular geographic area such as the Andes Mountains or the East Coast of the United States providing a brief guided tour. Web connections are included for every country for more research.

Lesson plans have students primarily collect and compare information. For example, one lesson directs students to compare gross national product, rate of inflation, the percent of GNP spent on education and the percent spent on health. It poses two follow-up questions on the relationships between these numbers: "Do you see any patterns with the rate of inflation? What are they?" and "Explain any of the patterns you have noticed." Students also learn how to graph information.

The program is covering much of what is covered in a typical geography course. However, students will selectively cover countries according to the assignments given or their own chosen explorations, so they will not get the thorough coverage of a text. However, I doubt most students retain much from the typical text, so this might not be a problem.(S)

Geography Songs - Sing Around The World [audio cassette]

(Audio Memory)
cassette - $19.95; CD - $22.95

Geography Songs includes a cassette, a workbook, and a giant map. One long-playing cassette tape features 23 "catchy" songs. The workbook has words to each song, maps, a crossword puzzle, a test, and answer key. The giant map shows the world, the 50 states, and the solar system. All of these work together to build familiarity with the locations of planets, continents, countries, and states. Many of the songs are sung in a style that reflects the culture of the geographical area which helps with memory association. Children color and label the world map. This is by no means comprehensive geography but, instead, serves as introduction to further study. Children will probably lose interest if you have them listen through the entire tape at once, so the best way to use *Sing Around The World* is to only use the song, map section and puzzles that relate to whatever country or continent you are studying at the moment. The workbook is reproducible, so one set is all you need for the entire family. The most important thing these songs will do is help students recognize and associate countries, states, etc. in geographical areas.

Hands On Activities for Elementary Social Studies
by David Cooper
(Alpha Publishing Company)
See review under "Supplements" for World History.(S)

Hands-On Geography: Easy & Fun Activities for Exploring God's World, revised edition
by Maggie S. Hogan and Janice Baker
(GeoCreations Limited)
$14.95

Two home school moms have published this helpful activity book which grew out of their hands-on geography workshops they have presented for other home schoolers. The book presents multi-grade (K-4), inexpensive (often free) and practical activities and resources for home schools. It teaches us how to make homemade books, games and notebooks that can be used for studies of any people, country, or other locale. It presents ideas for Biblical geography, genealogy geography, and mission geography. Add instructions, reproducible worksheets and maps, lists of recommended resources, a geography bowl game, and lots of practical tips, and the result is a valuable resource that makes geography more fun to learn and to teach. The revised edition is more professional in appearance, and a few of the activities have been changed to sharpen the focus toward early- to mid-elementary grade levels.

It's Our World, Geography (Books A - F)
(Essential Learning Products)
$3.99 each

These half-size books are appropriate for grades 1-6. They include environmental education and some social studies topics in addition to the geography. Most of the activities are acceptable, but I think there are a number of pages within each book that are a waste of time for home educated children. I suggest choosing appropriate pages for children to do rather than using everything in each book. (These books are so inexpensive that you shouldn't feel guilty skipping some pages.) They are printed in two colors with answers included in the back of each book. I recommend them as inexpensive and unintimidating tools for covering some basic geography skills and knowledge.(SE)

A Literature Approach to Geography, History and Science Using the Holling Clancy Holling Books
by Rea C. Berg
(Beautiful Feet Books)
Guide - $8.95; maps $16.95; books (paperback editions) - $8.95-$11.95 each, hard cover editions - $19.95 each

This is the ideal way to teach geography in my opinion. Rea Berg has selected the wonderful Holling books, *Paddle to the Sea, Minn of the Mississippi, Tree in the Trail*, and *Seabird* to teach geography along with history and science to children in grades 2-6. These books are wonderful classics that home schoolers should add to their library, and this course gives us the perfect excuse to do so. The course consists of the Guide, the four books, and four large maps printed on very heavy paper. Three regions of the U.S. are covered, and students are introduced to World Geography. We adapt the program for different ages by choosing the amount of detail to explore with each one and by having older students compile a notebook. Lesson plans are outlines that direct us to activities such as "Read Chapters 14-15 of Minn of the Mississippi," or "Describe the forces which cause continual change in rivers. How has man altered that to a large degree?", or "Define meander, bayou, spillway, shoal....," or "Do some research on the New Madrid, Missouri earthquake of the early 1800's. Record findings in notebook." Outside research is required. Children color and write on the maps as they "explore." The course should take about one year to complete.

The Map Corner
(Good Year Books)
$12.95

This is a terrific book everyone can use. This 127-page book contains 45 pages of reproducible maps. Lesson plans cover geography, road maps, weather, bird migration, and more. A section on explorers with biographies and map-related activi-

ties is excellent. This book could be used for a number of years as you study different places and time periods, and also as you study some science topics.(S)

Map Mysteries
(Learning Works)
$10.95

Motivate children to become familiar with locations, directions, and geographical features in the U.S. by solving "mysteries." Each lesson presents a series of questions. There are ten questions per lesson, with each question actually a collection of clues to identify a place. A standard atlas or the maps in World Book Encyclopedia can serve as sources for all the answers. Some questions are progressive and must be solved sequentially. Questions are appropriate for grades 4-6.(S)

Map Skills C
(Continental Press) [fourth grade]
$5.95; teacher's guide - $2.50

Level C of this series of reproducible workbooks reviews the basics of map reading, then teaches about weather; scales and distances; hemispheres and climate zones; latitude and longitude; and product, road and population maps.(S)

Map Skills D
(Continental Press) [fifth grade]
$5.95; teacher's guide - $2.50

Level D of this series of reproducible workbooks again reviews the basics, then teaches about special purpose maps; the different bodies of land and water; map keys, scales, and markers; climate and time zones; map projections; and latitude and longitude.(S)

Map Skills E
(Continental Press) [sixth grade]
$5.95; teacher's guide - $2.50

Level E of this series of reproducible workbooks further develops skills taught at younger levels.(S)

Mapping the World by Heart Lite
by David Smith
(Tom Snyder Productions)
$59.95

Would you like your children to be able to draw a map of the entire world, including latitude and longitude markings without copying or referring to another map? David Smith's methods are designed to enable children to do just that. This geography curriculum is recommended for grades 5-12, although it fits most appropriately in upper elementary and junior high levels. I suggest using it either while studying United States and world history studies in upper elementary and junior high levels or else as a concentrated course just before starting U.S. and world history at high school level. I say this because at younger levels students lack knowledge of people, places, and events to which they can relate geographical knowledge, so they are less likely to be interested. Older students need the concrete geographical knowledge to help them understand and link events as they are presented in upper level studies.

The program uses an assortment of activities to develop map skills, but the most important are the actual map-drawing activities. Besides properly locating and identifying places, children learn geographical knowledge that includes map reading skills, i.e., directions, symbols, topographical maps (great activities for learning how to make these!), the various types of map projections, the earth's rotation/seasons, dimensions, and more.

This ungraded program comes in a nicely designed three-ring binder. It can be used as a one-year program or it can be used as a supplement over a number of years, perhaps studying continents in conjunction with history topics. Lessons are well-designed and easy-to-follow. Great illustrations and layout make it especially easy to use.

Lessons need to be presented by the parent/teacher, but after the presentation students do much of the work on their own using reproducible work sheets from the binder. With the binder we get two sets of 9 double-sided 11" x 15" region maps to be used by students for initial work. We also get two sets of projection maps (three different types drawn on grids) and blank, 11" x 17" grids (reproducible) for students to use for their final map which will be done from memory. Additional maps are available in sets, although they are quite expensive. (The classroom edition of the program includes 30 of each map.)

There are lots of extras included in the program that we can use or not as we please—games, activity ideas, mnemonics, addresses for resources, and instructions for putting on a "World's Fair."

This method of learning geography has proven to be more effective and painless than traditional methods since it involves a variety of activities that interest and challenge students.(S)

Maps My Way U.S.A.
(Soteria)
$14

Maps My Way U.S.A. is a set of 46 glossy, black-and-white maps that can be reproduced for use along with history or geography lessons. (Suggestions for other uses are included with the set.) There are essentially 23 different maps since there are two versions of each: a teaching map and a student map. Teaching and student maps feature major rivers, mountain ranges, and bodies of water. There is also a "spotter" map that shows the featured states in context with the entire United States. The teaching map labels major cities, capitals, rivers,

and mountains. The student map is not labeled. All 50 states are included, but most are grouped with two neighboring states (e.g., Delaware, Maryland, and Washington D.C. are grouped together). Maps are three-whole punched for easy storage in a three-ring binder.

Mark-It Maps
(Geography Matters)
large, double-sided maps - $9.95 laminated or $4.95 paper; smaller maps - $6.95 laminated or $2.95 paper

Geography Matters produces an assortment of maps in different formats. Two are available in the larger 23" x 34", double-sided format. One of these has the United States on one side and the world on the reverse. The other, called *3A Map*, has Asia and Australia with the Pacific Ocean and an inset of Antarctica. Single-sided maps 17" x 22" in size are available for *Ancient Civilizations, Israel, Europe, Europe and the Middle East, Africa, North America, South America,* and the *United States*. These are outline maps, printed in black-and-white so children can label and color them. If you get the laminated version, children can erase and reuse them. Maps are also available in two packaged sets. *The Continents Map Set* [$34.95 laminated, $16.95 paper] includes the two large maps plus *Europe, Africa, North America*, and *South America*. The *Ancient Civilizations/Bible Lands Set* [$24.95 laminated, $9.95 paper] includes *Ancient Civilizations, Israel, Europe and the Middle East*, plus the *Timeline of History* from Geography Matters, which is reviewed earlier in this chapter.

Milliken Transparency Reproducible Books
(Milliken)

Milliken publishes *United States Map Skills* and *Canada Map Skills* [$12.95 each], reproducible/transparency books. They cover climate, industry, geography, and population. Each book has 12 full-color transparencies (designed for use on overhead projectors, but just as useful without the projector) plus 28 reproducible activity pages. They are suggested for grades 4-9. The quality of the content and presentation is excellent.

They also publish 22 titles in the "Our Global Village" series for pre-kindergarten through grade 6 [$6.95 each]. They reflect the modern approach to social studies, combining languages, holidays, festivals, costumes, history, legends, foods, creative arts, lifestyles, and children's games. I have not reviewed these personally, so I cannot vouch for the content. (I like the idea of thematic country studies, but sometimes the politically-correct slant turns them into propaganda vehicles. However, I am told by the publisher that they are written by teachers and natives of each particular country.) Since we copy the worksheets, each book is non-consumable. Titles in the series are *Africa, Australia, Brazil, Canada, China, Egypt, England, France, Germany, Greece, India, Ireland, Italy,*

Japan, Korea, Mexico, Poland, Polynesian Hawaii, Russia, Spain, Sweden, and *Turkey*.(SE)

National Geographic 🖥

The Complete National Geographic is a CD-ROM [$99.95] or DVD [$129.95] based program that includes 110 years of National Geographic magazines. Everything that appeared on pages of the magazines is included. Unfortunately, that excludes the supplemental maps. The program runs on either Windows 95 and higher or Macintosh systems. The CD version has 31 disks, while the DVD version has 4. It has extensive searching and printing capability.

If the supplemental maps are what interests you, they are available as a separate program called *National Geographic Maps* [$49.95]. This program runs on Windows 95 or higher systems. The program includes searching capability and zooming. Some thematic "tours" on the program include video clips and audio narration with photos. All maps are included up through May of 1999.

The Nystrom Desk Atlas

(Nystrom)

Atlas $9.95; Student Activities binder - $92

Nystrom's beautiful, full-color desk atlas is a fantastic tool for teaching geography to all ages, but I think it would be especially good for upper elementary and junior high students. It features physical, political, thematic (e.g., land use, population, rainfall), and regional maps of the entire world; graphs; data charts; and some photographs that can be used as research tools or for assigned lessons. The companion *Student Activities* binder is primarily reproducible activity sheets for 46 lessons plus the answer key. Five geographic themes are covered in each lesson: the world in spatial terms (locations); places, regions, and landscapes; human systems; environment and society; and uses of geography. Students are directed to the atlas to search out and analyze information for the lessons. Beyond the obvious geography questions, lessons stretch student thinking with questions like: "Why do you think there is little commercial activity in much of northern Russia?" and "If you were a farmer in South America, in what area would you *not* want to start a farm?". For each activity, students are referred to appropriate sections of the atlas. The binder also has a few pages of teacher instructions, charts showing in which lessons the themes are covered, and a class record page. The cost of the *Student Activities* binder is very high since it was designed for classroom use. However, it is non-consumable and might be used by a number of families to share the cost.(S)

The Travel-the-World Cookbook

by Pamela Marx

(Good Year Books)

$12.95

This book is a neat resource for older elementary or junior high kids who are studying geography or world cultures. It is divided by continent areas, with several recipes for each section. Each recipe is followed by a Food Fact (such as the different forms bread takes around the world), cultural information (mostly crafts or history), and an activity that is an extension of the cultural information. There is not enough of this background information to use this book alone, but it makes a great supplement. *The Travel-the-World Cookbook* is a secular resource, and parents should be aware that some of the cultural information draws on the religious beliefs of other lands.

The recipes are clear and easy to follow, allowing a child to use the book alone. A list of tools needed for each is included. The ingredients are easy to find in a large supermarket. For safety, recipes that traditionally call for frying use baking instead, providing an additional health benefit. The author includes a list of literature readings for each continent at the end of the book and a glossary of cooking terms, but there is no index of recipes. One especially helpful feature is that the book is spiral bound so that it lies flat on counter or table without threatening to close.[Kath Courtney]

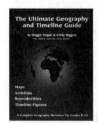

The Ultimate Geography and Timeline Guide

by Maggie Hogan and Cindy Wiggers

(GeoCreations, Ltd.)

$34.95

Maggie Hogan, author of *Hands-On Geography*, and Cindy Wiggers of *Geography Matters,* have combined their wisdom and experience to put together this resource book for teaching geography to children from grades K through 12. It takes a little time to explore the wealth of options found here. The first section, "Planning Your Destination," suggests basic teaching methods, describes notebooks that students might create, and recommends basic supplies. Chapter 2 is sort of a primer course in geography—hopefully a refresher for most of us. It covers basic terminology and concepts, including the five themes of geography identified by the national standards group for geography. Hogan and Wiggers show us how to incorporate the five themes into our studies. Next is a section on maps: different types, how to use them, map games, and more. All this is just the first of six units.

The second unit focuses on fun, games, and food as tools for teaching and enjoying geography. Unit three teaches us how to teach geography through other subject areas. This is especially important since Hogan and Wiggers are unit study fans, and unit studies almost always include more than one subject area. To help us get into unit studies, the authors include two complete unit studies on volcanoes and for the book *Hans Brinker or the Silver Skates*. At the end of this section are tips on teaching geography through the internet, including a list of great sites. Unit four presents what most people think of as the nuts and bolts of geography: lesson directions and data on geographical features, climate, vegetation, etc. Lesson ideas are divided into those for middle school and those for high school. Reproducible maps and activity sheets for games, weather reports, research and other activities described in this book comprise the next two sections. The final unit is all about creating a timeline and includes hundreds of reproducible figures for your own timeline. Another fun feature of this book is a "Who Am I?" game that uses the reproducible pages of game cards. In addition to all this the book includes an answer key, glossary, an index (very useful with a book such as this), and lists of additional resources you might want to use.

In my opinion, this approach to geography will be far more interesting than a standard text on the subject. The fact that one book does it all for every grade level makes it even more appealing.

Uncle Josh's Outline Map Book

by Josh Wiggers
(Geography Matters)
$19.99

This 8.5" x 11" book features more than 100 reproducible, detailed outline maps that can be used by students of all ages. "General Instructions" at the beginning of the book offers suggestions for using the maps, even for literature and science studies. There are maps of the world, countries, ancient civilizations, the United States, and individual states. Maps outlines are extremely detailed, for example, including the little islands off the coast of a country. Rivers and bodies of water are lightly shaded, so they might still be colored. Longitude and latitude lines are shown, and there is scale on each map.

World Geography Mysteries

(Learning Works)
$10.95

Presenting your children with problems to solve rather than names of places to memorize often serves as a better learning motivator. That's the approach used in *World Geography Mysteries*. Suggested for grades 4-6, the activities in this book are the kind the whole family can join in. You will need a world atlas, or even better, a set of *World Book Encyclopedias*. Each of the 27 "lessons" has a geographical theme: e.g., "Mystery Cruise" which works with islands, seaports, reefs, and oceans. The book tries to hit geographic locations all over

the world. Each "lesson" consists of ten, paragraph-style questions that lead students on a route. Each of those questions includes a number of clues for students to identify a particular place. Many of the clues indicate distances and directions from easily identifiable locations. Historical and cultural information is interwoven throughout the questions. Space is provided for students to write the names of places as they identify them. You could set students to work separately (if you have more than one atlas to work with), competing with each other to find all ten places first. You could work as a family to figure them out. Or you could assign them for independent work. This approach should appeal to those who dislike typical geography texts.(S)

Other Sources for Geographical Materials

Both modern day and historical atlases are available from Nystrom Publishers as well as maps and globes. American Map Corporation offers *Student's Atlas of The Bible* [$6.95] along with modern maps and atlases. The George F. Cram Co. also specializes in geographical materials including globes and maps.

Current Events

God's World News for Kids (God's World Publications) makes an excellent supplement for social studies or unit study. Subscriptions to weekly newspapers are offered on four different age levels, summarizing current events and offering Christian commentary. Subscriptions are sent through the school year, but not over the summer. Age-appropriate workpage activities are included in each issue. Extra activities including outlines for unit studies are in the Teacher's Helper. Ordering three or more subscriptions, even of different editions, means significant savings. *God's World* levels are preK-1, grades 2-3, grades 4-6, and grades 7-9. Single subscription prices for a school year are $17.95 for each of the two lower levels and $19.95 for each of the two upper levels. When 3 or more subscriptions are ordered for the same address, price for lower levels drops to $6.95 each and for upper levels to $7.50 each. The cost is extremely reasonable for such a useful resource.

Chapter 16

Art, Music, and Drama

In home schooling, we usually find that we have time to put some real effort into art, music, drama, and other areas that will enrich the lives of our children. It is important that we provide these activities to help our children grow into well-rounded individuals. While these subjects have value in themselves, they also offer a vehicle for stimulating interest in other subject areas. This is particularly true for Wiggly Willys and Sociable Sues who are often more interested in the arts than in academic subjects. By using their own works of art to stimulate writing ideas, music as a tool for teaching parts of speech, drama as a means of studying history, etc., we can use their natural interest to develop the weaker areas.

Learning Styles

Following are typical preferences of each learning style that involve the arts.

Wiggly Willy Prefers
- varied, short projects
- different media
- cardboard and paper construction
- drama or dance
- playing music by ear
- singing

Wiggly Willy usually needs little encouragement in the arts.

Perfect Paula Prefers
- drawing with clear directions to follow
- photography
- craft projects
- note reading music rather than playing by ear

Perfect Paula needs encouragement to draw on her own creativity.

Competent Carl Prefers
- composition and perspective aspects of art
- print making
- architecture
- studying the structure of music
- music composition

Competent Carl needs encouragement to develop appreciation for other artistic qualities such as emotional expression in art.

Sociable Sue Prefers
- figure drawing and painting
- art history
- illustrating stories
- psychological effects of color
- interior design
- choir or band
- social music

Sociable Sue usually needs little encouragement in the arts.

We tend to classify art as a frill subject, partly because the public schools have treated it as such. Throughout history, Christianity has been the motivating force behind much artistic effort. In more recent times, secular forces have dominated the arts to our detriment. If we hope to change this situation, we must not ignore the arts as we work with our children.

By the end of high school they should have at least a minimal foundation in art and music history and appreciation. At the elementary levels, history and appreciation are not as important as actual experience doing art or music. We should encourage the development of artistic talents in our children at young ages before they, like many people, decide they simply have no talent.

Many parents who are very concerned with academic subjects neglect the arts, thinking them unnecessary. But by doing so they actually neglect the development of half our students' resources. Basic academic subjects place more stress on logic, analysis, and sequential thinking. But creativity, intuition, and imagination developed through the arts are equally important for productive and aesthetic living. Having said all this, I will now address art, music, and drama individually.

Art

Art should be one of the basics. It uses all senses for learning, and it heightens our awareness of the world around us. Art uses non-verbal means of expression and can be a very important emotional outlet for the child to balance the academic subjects, especially for those who may be having some stress and difficulty with schoolwork. Besides all of this, art is fun!

Art is a broader subject than some of us realize. Broad headings under art include:

1.) art appreciation—an ability to study and enjoy art

2.) art history—study of art as expressed in different cultures in different times

3.) art creation—learning about and using various techniques and media for art expression

4.) art in the world around us—the usefulness and importance of art in our environment.

Often we concentrate on technique and media without the other elements of true art education. If we approach art as an integral part of our studies, we can see the interrelationships of art, history, language, mathematics, and science in a way that enhances all learning.

Suggestions For Art

Very young children scribble. This is natural and necessary for them to gain control of their arm and hand movements. Let them do as much scribbling as they need. Do not push for recognizable objects before the child is ready. He will naturally move to the next step as he matures. Remember that the process is as important as the product!

Some Do's and Don'ts for Parents

DON'T compare one child's art with another's unless to comment positively about color, design, etc.

DO insist that children respect each other's work and expression of art.

If one child is very good at one type of art, give his brother a different medium to work with so he can be successful and not have to compete. (If sister can paint well, try clay or 3-D paper construction for her brother.)

DO praise the art work only when the child has worked hard and is pleased.

DON'T praise careless work.

Age Appropriate Art Activity		
Grade Level	**Some Subject Ideas for Art Projects**	**Materials**
K - 2 Children can draw and paint from experience and imagination. Sometimes children need help to begin. It is not very motivating just to say, " Draw whatever you want." Help your child think about a recent experience by asking questions such as "What did you see at the zoo?" "What was your favorite animal?" "What kind of fur did it have?"	• my pet • Noah's ark • bug zoo • tree full of birds • fish in the sea • my house • at Grandma's and Grandpa's • a day at the park • wild animals	(those for younger children are listed first, with increasing difficulty further down the list) • crayons • oil pastel on construction paper • cardboard boxes for buildings • poster paint • felt pens
3 - 4 Children can learn to draw from everyday objects, plants, and live animals. Help them to notice details by asking questions such as "Is the stem straight or curved?" or "What kind of edge does the leaf have?"	• flowers in the rain • pet show • airport • trip into space • trains • freeway traffic • design a tree house • city under the sea • friends on bicycles • baseball game	• cut and torn construction paper collage • clay • tempera • tissue paper collage (liquid laundry starch for glue) • styrofoam print (use meat tray or picnic plate)
5 -6 Children can draw landscapes and buildings. Try a sketching field trip to a harbor, airport, zoo, shopping mall, building under construction, or botanical garden. Some children are reluctant to draw people at this age. Sketching from a live model (or mirror) might be helpful. When setting up a still life to draw or paint, do not get stuck in a "vase, fruit bowl" rut. Think about all the interesting objects that kids can relate to. What about a couple of well-worn baseball mitts and a ball? Or a favorite jacket draped over the back of a chair with a pair of old tennis shoes on the seat?	• space stations • musical instruments • knights in armor • our camping trip • Thanksgiving with our family • trees - above and below ground • future cities • sports events • county fair • myself cooking breakfast • plants and animals of the desert, ocean, forest, etc. • cactus garden • portrait of Mom	• cardboard relief print • glue line print • colored pencils • 3-D paper folding • water colors • pen and ink • acrylics

DON'T use coloring books as art activity.

DON'T allow tracing as art work, although tracing can be useful for small muscle coordination, map work, or other subject area activity.

DON'T add to the child's drawing or make models for him to copy—instead, help the child to observe things carefully and think about what it is he is trying to draw.

DO tie your art session to a concrete experience your child has had such as a visit to the zoo or a trip to the snow.

DO remember that one of the purposes of art instruction is to get children to see more, notice more, and become more aware of their environment. Help them to do this by guiding them to express their perceptions rather than by telling them exactly what to do. Working on a project along with them is an encouragement to some children. Give them guidelines and encourage experimentation with alternative methods.

[Suggestions are adapted from *Your Child and His Art* by Viktor Lowenfeld, Macmillan Publishing Co., New York, 1954.]

Crafts

Crafts are not a substitute for art but can, nevertheless, be enjoyable and useful. Crafts come easily to home school families with a whole house full of materials to choose from. Save odds and ends and turn your children loose to create whatever they choose. You will probably be surprised at the amount of creativity you will witness.

Involve your children in crafts you enjoy such as needlework (they can work easily on plastic canvas for needlepoint), woodworking, sewing, and ceramics. There are many lessons available through parks and recreation, private lessons, craft shops, etc. Craft idea books are available by the score from libraries and bookstores.

The *Nasco Arts and Crafts Catalog* is an excellent source for art supplies for those who cannot buy materials they need locally.

Art Resources

Adventures in Art
by Laura H. Chapman
(Davis Publications)
student books, levels 1-6 - $26.95 each; teacher's editions - $46.50 each; kindergarten teacher's resource book - $48

This is the most complete, well-presented art program I have found. It covers all aspects of art—appreciation, history, various media, technique, and activity—except the philosophical ideas behind artistic expression. Each lesson lists preparation and materials needed. It will require some time to gather supplies, so plan ahead. The teacher's manual clearly outlines the lesson presentation (which is based on the student text), then provides directions for the art activity, evaluation time, and extension activities. Safety tips and hints on other ways of doing things are offered.

Lessons are written for the classroom, so they reflect the limitations encountered there. For example, it is not practical for every classroom student to bring the materials for and set up his or her own still life arrangement. You might want to alter some of the lessons to do such things at home.

The program is available for grades K-8. It is not necessary to use the correct grade level text; for example, you might use the 4th grade level if you have 2nd and 5th graders. There is far more within each book (60 lessons) than most of us will accomplish in one year, so you might plan to cover one level every other year. For each level except kindergarten there are a student book (hardback) and a teacher's manual.

The kindergarten program is taught from the teacher's resource book and has no student books. For the other levels, teacher's manuals reproduce student pages (about 1/2 original size) and provide complete instructions. The manuals are essential to the course. You cannot figure out how to do the activities without them. Since the reproduced student pages are too small to observe detail described within the lessons, it is necessary to purchase student books also.

Although this program is not Christian, it avoids problems common to so many other programs—nudity (there are a few nudes in the series, but no frontal views), occult and new age symbols, glorification of pagan cultures, etc. The closest thing to "objectionable" are probably mask making activities. Interestingly, the program of the same name from Cornerstone Curriculum Project provides the philosophical input we miss in any such program written for use in public schools.

This is an excellent program to use for a few families working together or for a group class because of the time needed to prepare for and do the projects. Also, children will enjoy seeing how others tackle the same art projects.(SE)

Adventures in Art
(Cornerstone Curriculum Project)
Gallery 1 - $60; Galleries 2 and 3 - $55 each

Here is the tool to balance any art instruction with the Christian perspective. Those familiar with Francis Schaeffer's book *How Should We Then Live?* will spot his teaching about how philosophy and ideas are reflected in art. Charlotte Mason's ideas (popularized in the book *For the Children's Sake*) also are foundational.

Cornerstone has carefully gathered top quality prints of famous art works that illustrate how art reflects ideas. There are three levels (or galleries) for the series. When we order the first set (or first "gallery") of these prints, we receive the *Comprehensive Study Guide* that is to be used with all three galleries. The *Study Guide* provides detailed instructions for teaching and guiding discussion with our children as we study each print. Material has been written on a level to use with children as young as first grade as well as up through high school. Galleries two and three do not include the *Study Guide*. The *Comprehensive Study Guide* outlines schedules that might be used for younger and older age groups. Younger children are not likely to fully understand the philosophical implications of the study that older children can comprehend, so adjust your lessons accordingly. If you use these with children in the early elementary grades, plan to go back through the lessons again in high school. You might also use some of the individual art works to supplement other studies, particularly for history. (Also consider framing some of these prints when you are through working with them.)

Classical Composers and the Christian World View is a music program, also from Cornerstone Curriculum Project, that serves as a companion to *Adventures in Art*.

Art Adventures at Home: A Curriculum Guide for Home Schools, Level 1, 2 and 3
by Pattye Carlson and M. Jean Soyke
(At Home Publications)
$19.95 each

Level 1 is a foundational art program geared toward the early elementary grades. Level 2 is geared toward upper elementary grades, although students should have spent at least one year in Level 1 before beginning Level 2. Level 3 is for middle-high school.

For those who like lesson plans all spelled out, here is a great program designed specifically for homeschoolers. Starting with goals and wrapping up with evaluation questions, these one-page lesson plans present a step-by-step guide to teaching the basic elements of line, shape/form, color, and texture. Some projects are representational and some are strictly design. A subject index makes it easy to correlate art lessons with unit studies.

There are enough lessons for three years of art instruction in each level if one lesson is used each week of the school year. These fun activities gently build an awareness of the special language of art in the student. You might even find yourself gaining a new appreciation for different art forms.

Although the lessons are structured, there is much room for creativity. The introductory section on teaching art is especially helpful. (Note: one lesson in Level 1 has children using rubber cement. Rubber cement is no longer recommended for use in children's art programs because of the vapors. That particular lesson can easily be omitted or used with caution.)

Level 2 builds upon concepts introduced in Level 1 and includes activities such as printing, drawing, etching, sculpture, mosaics, and dioramas. Level 3 includes chapters on careers in art and Christian artists.[V.T./C.D.]

Art Extension Press
Art Extension Press offers prints of the world's masterpieces

for study in either small (3" x 4") or large (7" x 9") sizes, grouped by levels (primary, intermediate, and upper). The levels seem to be somewhat arbitrary—there is not a great difference in the text or subject matter from primary to upper. I suggest starting with the primary print set with children of all ages. *Learning More About Pictures* by Royal Bailey Farnum [$15] is the teacher's manual for art studies based upon the prints. It provides an outline of art history and commentary on the 100 prints offered. Purchase the book and one or more of the sets of prints. A set of 100 small prints is $22.50; a set of large prints is $130. These are great for those of us who have little art background. Special subject groupings of art prints are also offered.(S)

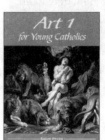

Art for Young Catholics series
(Seton Press)
Art 1 - $10; Art 4 - $12

Seton Press is developing an entire series of art books for Catholic homeschoolers. These combine art appreciation, skill development, and craft-type activities. A number of beautiful, full-color reproductions in each book are used for appreciation lessons as well as design and technique lessons. Basic drawing and color skills are taught. Intermixed are craft activities which are designed to teach or reinforce a concept that has been presented. Books for only two elementary grade levels are available thus far, but others are in the works.

Art Projects A
(A Beka Book)
$11.30

This fourth grade level book is mostly arts and crafts, but it does have some freehand drawing and some instruction in the use of color and perspective. Designs for many of the activities are printed directly in the book on heavy stock. A good percentage of the activities are related to Scripture, and there are certainly no problems such as witch and jack-o'-lantern art for Halloween.

Art Projects B
(A Beka Book)
$11.30

This fifth-grade level book continues with color, drawing and watercolor techniques, using colored pencils, working with one-point perspective, and shading. Some art appreciation is also included. It leans less towards crafts and more towards art than Book A.

Art Projects C
(A Beka Book)
$11.20

This sixth grade level book helps students explore art media such as watercolor, clay, and paper sculpture. In addition, step-by-step instructions help students draw faces, figures, buildings, and vehicles. Some art appreciation is included.

Art Smart
(Prentice Hall)
$79.95

In many ways this program is similar in approach to *Adventures in Art*. Art history and appreciation is taught through illustration and activity, but in one large book rather than smaller grade level books. Children do projects that mimic art works representative of different time periods and types of expression. Painting, architecture, sculpture, and other types of art expression are included. *Art Smart* divides activities chronologically so you can easily integrate art with history. Unit headings are Stone Age, Egyptian, Greek and Roman, Middle Ages, Renaissance, Post-Renaissance, Pre-through Post Impressionism, Modern Art (then breaking away from chronology), Art of the Middle East, Far East, and Africa. Activities vary in difficulty and can be easily tailored to children's ages so the program can be used with all ages. Forty color slides of museum art works come with the book. Content is definitely secular, written from the viewpoint that art is a reflection of differing values which are all equally valid. But the book is a teacher resource manual, not something you hand the children, so screening content is fairly easy. ISBN #0130477540. (SE)

Art With A Purpose
(Share-A-Care Publications)
$5 per Artpac

Artpacs for grades 1-8 each include lesson plans, art sheets, directions, examples, and lists of materials needed. This is basically arts and crafts for the younger grades, although it gets into drawing, painting, and more "true" art at the upper levels.

Bible Arts and Crafts
by Rich and Sharon Jeffus
(Visual Manna)
$7.50

This book is suitable for primary and elementary children (also great for Sunday School classes!), with over fifty craft ideas for various Bible verses. They range from simple coloring to making banners. The authors want children to have a visual picture of ideas contained in the Bible, so the crafts are hands-on, often resulting in products that can be hung on a wall. The book could easily be used in a home with several children or in a Sunday School setting. It is easy to see that the Jeffuses have a real drive to communicate the truth of the Word of God. However, as with other books from Visual Manna, the authors need to be more careful in proofreading their text.

Hopefully, a second edition will take care of such problems. (Note: Some of the ideas used in the Jeffus' book *Real Manna* are adapted here as craft projects.) [Kath Courtney]

Celebrating Art and Appreciating Art
by Debbie and Darrel Trulson
(Christian Liberty Press)
$5 and $5.50 respectively

These two books take a craft-oriented approach to art for young children. They are suggested for kindergarten and first grade, but I think many older children (plus some younger) will enjoy the activities. In fact, many of them would be great for a family evening. Complete instructions with patterns and recipes (when appropriate) are provided for the projects. Examples of projects in *Celebrating Art*: homemade play dough, felt board storytelling, paper doll chains, pop-up cards, personalized wrapping paper, collages, and bird feeders. *Appreciating Art* tells us how to make puffed cereal balls, bakers clay sculptures, yarn bowls, fabric banners, straw paintings, seed wreaths, paper beads, and many more fun projects that might even be used as gifts or decorations. A few basic drawing skills are taught along the way in both volumes. A coding system indicates the level of difficulty (or amount of time and energy required) of the various activities so we can select those best suited for our children.

Child-size Masterpieces sets and How to Use Child-Size Masterpieces for Art Appreciation
by Aline D. Wolf
(Parent Child Press)
$10.95 each except for *Transportation in America* - $12.95

How to Use Child-Size Masterpieces for Art Appreciation is a handbook that can be used by parent/teachers, even if they have no background in art, for introducing children to art masterpieces. You need to also purchase at least one of seven books of postcard-size art reproductions to use with the handbook. Preschoolers begin by matching identical paintings. As they progress, children begin matching similar paintings by the same artist. Then they develop skill in distinguishing works from the various schools of art. A time line helps to illustrate the developments and changes in artistic styles. The postcard art reproductions in the accompanying books increase in level of difficulty. You can begin with any one of the books, but since you will probably eventually wish to have them all, I recommend you start with the starter package [$39.95] that includes the handbook and first three volumes of *Child-Size Masterpieces*. Titles of the books: *Child-Size Masterpieces For Steps 1,2,3-Level 1/Easy*, for ages 3-12; *Child-Size Masterpieces For Steps 1,2,3-Level 2/Intermediate*, for ages 4-12; *Child-Size Masterpieces For Steps 1,2,3-Level*

3/Advanced, for ages 5-12; *Child-Size Masterpieces For Step 4-Artists' Names*, for beginning readers and above; *Child-Size Masterpieces For Step 5-Famous Paintings*, for ages 6-12; *Child-Size Masterpieces-Black Images for Steps 1,2,3, and 4* (paintings of blacks from over a 500 year period); and *Child-Size Masterpieces-Transportation in America* to be used with Step 8. You may also purchase a set that includes the handbook plus all seven volumes of *Child-Size Masterpieces* for $80.(S)

Drawing with Children
by Mona Brookes
(Penguin Putnam, Inc.)
$15.95

Mona Brookes has helped many people discover that art is not only for those who feel they were born with talent, but that anyone can do art with just a few lessons. The first few chapters of the book deal with attitudes and preparation. Brookes gives specific instructions about materials. Expensive art supplies are not necessary—just begin with a pen, then move on to felt pens and colored pencils. If we want to experiment with pastels and watercolors, simple instructions are supplied. Parents can use the book as a guide to work with children as young as three or four, or anyone able to read the book can use it as a self-teaching tool. Lessons begin with the five elements of shape. Next we draw from two-dimensional pictures, then from still life (three-dimensional). Instructions for drawing people are excellent without being overwhelming; she shows the general shapes that can represent body parts, their relationships, and some positions without getting into mathematical proportions. Mona Brookes gives a few specific assignments of things to draw, but for the most part, it is up to us to draw what we wish using the techniques she has taught. ISBN # 0874778271.(S)

Feed My Sheep
by Barry Stebbing
(How Great Thou ART)
$42.95; with paints and brushes - $59.95

This is a combined art text and workbook for teaching drawing, color theory, art appreciation, perspective, portraiture, anatomy, lettering, painting, and more to students in grades 3 through 9. However, students beyond ninth grade (even adults!) without art experience should find this a valuable course. It contains more than 250 lessons plus a packet of 17 paint cards. These are 8 1/2" x 11" in size and are made of a heavy 110 stock. For many of the lessons, students need only drawing pencils, a set of colored pencils, a kneaded eraser, a ruler, an extra-fine marker, sketch book, and poster board. Later lessons on painting use acrylic paints and brushes. A drawing board, triangle, and T-square are also helpful in later lessons, but not essential. Students

learn primarily to draw realistic images but also some cartoon figures. Depending upon the age and ability of the student, it might take a number of years to complete this book. So the painting lessons might be delayed until later. If you want to tackle painting as soon as possible, purchase the book combined with a set of acrylic paints and brushes. Otherwise, start with just the book and purchase paints later so they will be fresh when you want to use them.

Author Barry Stebbing's Christian perspective is evident throughout the course in Bible verses, lesson explanations, art appreciation lessons, and even the choices of examples. The book is written to the student so he or she can work independently. However, younger students will probably need some assistance. Instructions are fairly thorough so even parents with little art background should be able to help students through all of the lessons.

Art appreciation is incorporated into many of the lessons, and more-focused lessons direct students to the library to locate and copy artists' works or examples from particular periods. Students also research answers to questions posed about art history, styles, artists, etc.

Overall, this is a very comprehensive course. For parents who wish to maintain academic accountability, there are occasional quizzes on art theory and appreciation, with an answer key at the back of the book. This single volume offers a tremendous amount of art instruction at very low cost. Since students actually work in the book, it is best to purchase one for each student. However, for parents who would rather copy the lessons for multiple children, this is allowed for in-the-home use only.

I Can Do All Things: A Beginning Book of Drawing and Painting
by Barry Stebbing
(How Great Thou Art)
$42.95; with acrylic paints and brushes set - $63.95

Although it is suggested for ages 6 and up, do not limit this resource to children in the primary grades. Most activities are appropriate for anyone who wants to learn beginning techniques with drawing, colored markers, or acrylic paints. Occasional pictures or assignments do seem directed only at young children, but older students can adapt or skip those. Stebbing provides tips for the teacher. Lessons then address various skills and techniques appropriate for each art medium. Lessons mix text and black-and-white illustrations to provide step-by-step instruction. Each student needs his or her own book since many lessons are done directly on the book's pages. However, copying of the pages for multiple children is allowed within the home.

Some lessons work in a progressive order. For example, students learn to draw circles, then snowmen, faces, cans, jars, and other round things. Other lessons like shading, showing depth, drawing people, and cartoons might be used in random order.

A set of 38, 8 1/2" x 11 marker/painting cards comes with the book. These are printed on heavy card stock for use with the colored markers and acrylic paints. You will need extra sets for additional students.

Toward the end of the book is a small section for students to use for studying "art masters." Students are told to recreate a master's drawing in 3" x 4" box and a portrait of the artist himself in an even smaller box. This really isn't sufficient space unless the students is exceptionally skillful. The task, itself, is more suitable for older students.

The book should easily take more than a year to complete if your child is truly exploring and learning to work with each media. I expect that it will work best for families where parents are confident enough to expand upon lessons and select which lessons to use in what sequence.

Kid Pix® Studio Deluxe [computer program] 🖥

(The Learning Company)
$29.95

This CD-ROM is a powerful graphics program for kids with almost unlimited creative possibilities. The basic *Kid Pix* screen allows the child to draw with a pencil tool or choose the wacky brush and paint with shapes like dots, drips or dog bones. A single brush stroke can form a tree, cloud or mountain. Each type of brush has its own sound effect, which can be a little distracting if you are seriously drawing something as there is the temptation to keep making shapes for the interesting sounds they make, rather than for their contribution to the picture. It is great fun just playing around with the program. The "undo" tool might say "Oops!" or "Yikes!" You can erase your whole picture with a countdown or fadeout, blow it up with a firecracker, or scrub around with one of the eraser tools to reveal a hidden picture.

The youngest children can use the talking alphabet stamps that call out their names as they are selected. A typewriter tool allows children to type sentences (along with old-fashioned typewriter sound effects complete with carriage return). Use the speech menu commands and pick a voice for the computer, and it will read aloud the words you typed. You can even type in your Spanish lesson and have "Carmen" read your words in correct Spanish. Of course all the menu commands will be changed to Spanish also.

After you have typed in your text, you can choose a movie from the "Wacky TV" and glue it onto your project. These movies are of variable quality. Some are actual videos of different sorts of birds, some are animated drawings, and some are 3D animations. You can paste on a scene or have the movie play on your *Kid Pix* screen.

A smaller "Moopies" screen causes everything that is drawn

on it to jiggle. Choose the small stamps of various subjects and they move also. However, I found the effect of a whole screen full of wiggling pictures quite disturbing.

There is also a "Stampimator" screen where you can record a path for the animated stamps and also pick a background and sound effects to go with them. There are hundreds of stamps to choose from. (Some of these are horror types like skulls and monsters.)

The "Digital Puppets" are figures that move as you press different keys on the keyboard. One key will open a mouth or close an eye or cause a smile or frown. You can record the movements and play them back with sound effects or record your own sound.

Older or more organized students can make a multimedia slide show using any of these activities.

Kid Pix® Classic [$14.95] is a "scaled down version of the Deluxe program. It includes silly brushes, multicolor fill patterns, stamps, special effects, Wacky TV video clips, and tools for creating moving slide shows.

In the school version of *Kid Pix Deluxe* [$69.95], along with the usual user's guide is a teacher's guide with tutorials and ideas for projects that various teachers have tried in their classrooms. Browsing through these will help you see how *Kid Pix* can be used to make books and slide shows for various subjects. Even without special assignments, this program gives children good preparation for adult computer graphics programs as many of the tools are similar to those in Adobe *Illustrator*. Fun for grades Pre-K through 6. The program runs on Macintosh or Windows systems with multimedia capability.

The Learning Company and Teacher Created Materials have teamed up to create *Kid Pix Activity Kits* [$19.95 each] (order from Teacher Created Materials]. These kits each combine a group of thematic units from TCM with some of the most popular *Kid Pix* creativity tools on individual program disks. Six "volumes" are available: (1) *Creepy Crawlies, Rocks and Soil, Seasons, and Weather;* (2) *Community Workers, Fairy Tales, My Country, and Native Americans;* (3) *Animals, My Body, Plants, and Sea Animals;* (4) *Electricity, Insects, Oceans, and Space;* (5) *Family, Farm, Our Environment, and Safety;* (6) *Immigration, Inventions, Tall Tales, and Westward Ho!.* (S)[V. Thorpe/C.D.]

KidsArt

KidsArt provides art instruction and activities for all ages and abilities in a series of inexpensive booklets [$4 each]. Each unit features a main topic—for instance, one on "Faces" studies famous portraits (art history and appreciation), gives instruction for drawing portraits, then shows how to enlarge pictures using diagonal or square grids. Face activities include making blockhead portraits and clay sculptures. *KidsArt* also includes tips on art products, materials, and resources.

Activity instructions are complete and easy-to-follow for even the least experienced non-artist. There are enough ideas in these booklets to provide us with all the art we need. Other popular *KidsArt* booklets are *Ancient Egypt, Ancient Greece, Ancient Rome, Rembrandt, Leonardo da Vince,* and *Celtic Ireland.*

KidsArt hosts a site on the internet filled with contests, free art lessons, and a gallery of child-made art for kids to explore. A free catalog of KidsArt art teaching products is available.(S)

Lamb's Book of ART, Books I and II

by Barry Stebbing
(How Great Thou ART)
$14.95 each; teacher's manual - $7.95

Books I and II cover essentially the same territory, offering two sets of lessons that can be used independently, simultaneously (if we want to spend more time on each skill), or consecutively. It does not matter which book comes first. Far more than arts and crafts, *Lamb's Book of ART* is a serious art course for teaching children about drawing, color theory, lettering, perspective, anatomy, cartooning, and graphic design. These books are geared for students in grades 3-8. Students work with colored markers, colored pencils, a drawing pencil, a fine black marker, and a brush to blend colors. You will want to photocopy pages that might "bleed" through since lessons continue on both sides of each page. Most work will be done within the book, and extra blank pages are provided at the back. Barry Stebbing generously illustrates the books with black-line drawings. While children do some copying, they also learn to draw from "still lifes" in Book II—to draw what they actually see. Children also develop creativity through cartooning. Bible verses or quotations are featured on every page, but Christian content is also integrated into some of the lessons. There are 69 lessons in Book I and 73 in Book II. Each book might stretch over one or two years, depending upon a child's rate of progress. A single teacher's manual covering lessons in both books provides further explanation and suggestions for parents. While it is not essential, parents without artistic background will find it useful.

The principle difference between these books and How Great Thou ART's *Feed My Sheep* is in the length of each program and the addition of painting to *Feed My Sheep.*

Those with preschoolers might be interested in *Baby Lambs* [$14.95] for ages 3 to 5. It teaches children numbers, letters, and counting in addition to drawing and basic color theory. There are also a few cut-and-paste activity pages plus ABC's with Scripture.

Mark Kistler's Draw Squad

by Mark Kistler
(Simon and Schuster)
$17

Mark Kistler decided he wanted to help spread the good news that everyone could learn how to draw by learning just a few basic techniques. He teaches basic principles of drawing in lessons that produce immediate results. His techniques are adapted from those of Bruce McIntyre, but Kistler uses a jazzy format with cartoon characters popping up occasionally to make things more interesting. Lessons are well laid out and easy to follow—a fourth or fifth grader can use it on his own. Younger children can draw the lessons with a little help, and the format is such that it appeals equally to adults. ISBN # 0671-656945.(S)

Masterpieces in Art

(Christian Liberty Press)
$7

In many ways this book is similar to *Learning More About Pictures* by Royal Bailey Farnum (Art Extension Press). Black-and-white prints of selected art works are printed in the book (unlike *Learning More About Pictures* which is not illustrated). Fewer art works are covered, but the information is more in-depth. The Christian perspective also offers a contrast to most other art resources which generally approach art from the humanist viewpoint. The book was originally written some time ago and has been revised and updated for the present printing. However, the tone and style are reminiscent of books from the turn of the century. This includes the art selections themselves which are an assortment of primarily religious, family, pastoral, and historical works. I find interesting the comment by the original author that, "The masterpieces which have been selected for study are those which are common to the majority of courses of study outlined for elementary and high schools" (from the Preface). The artworks here stand in strong contrast to those found in most present-day school art texts! Even more anachronistic is the picture of Michelangelo's statue of *David* which sports some minimal "clothing" for modesty that is not present on the original statue. Be reassured that you will find nothing objectionable in this book. Various commentary accompanies each artwork, and we should use as much as is appropriate for learners of different ages. "The Picture" is the primary story about the piece to be read with everyone (elementary through high school levels). Then we can choose from "The Plan for Study" information about "The Artist," "Comments," or "Questions." The book is printed on high quality, glossy paper, but we lose some of the details as well as the color on the reprints of artworks. Think about using this book along with better prints, such as those from sources reviewed here.

Masterpieces
by Mary Martin and Steven Zorn
(Running Press)
$8.95

From the *Start Exploring* series of *Fact-Filled Coloring Books*, this 128-page, full-size book features line drawings of 60 art masterpieces for coloring along with information about the paintings and their artists. Paintings are too detailed for very young children, but by second or third grade they should have no trouble coloring them.(SE)

Multicultural Art Activities Kit
by Dwila Bloom
(Prentice Hall)
$59.95

The word "multicultural" in a title is usually a signal that the content will offend Christians. Dwila Bloom's presentation of art activities was a pleasant surprise. No nude goddesses or grizzly figures. Through 50 lessons, she presents six geographically organized units. Each unit introduces the land and its people, a map, and key art influences. Full-color illustrations of exemplary art are featured. The presentation is nonjudgmental. For example in a sculpture lesson based on masks from the Congo, she tells us "they are extensively employed in religious rituals and other special tribal ceremonies." Information is presented for us to deal with as we wish; she neither glorifies nor criticizes. This leaves the job of critiquing in the hands of parents or teachers using the book. The scope of the book is massive, covering the whole world via a broad array of artistic media. This is a combination art history and application course. The applications require some specialized resources, although they are not terribly expensive (dyes, bamboo brushes, black latex paint, origami paper, silk, etc.). Among the projects are coiled baskets, fabric painting, weaving, batik, rug making, water color, print making, trapunto, calligraphy, sand painting, wood burning, and tin work. (There seem to be quite a few oriented toward fiber arts.) Many of these projects have a folk-art rather than fine-art flavor. It is assumed that the teacher has an art background. Although instructions for selecting and using materials are given, it appears that some knowledge of at least some of the art media is essential for success. At 357 pages, there is so much in this volume you will use it over a number of years. Activities can be adapted for use with all age levels, although some should definitely be saved for high school students. This book would work especially well for a group class. ISBN #0876285876. (SE)

The National Gallery of Art

The National Gallery of Art has an Extension Service Program that has designed audio-visual art programs. The programs are set up as topical studies. Some are historical, such as *700 Years of Art* and *The European Vision of America*. Some are technical, such as *The Artist's Hand: Five Techniques of Painting*. Others are narrow in scope, such as *Picasso and the Circus* and *The Treasures of Tutankhamun*. Programs are available in different media—slide with audio cassette, film, and videocassette; but all programs are not available in all media forms. The only cost for using these materials is that of return postage. Requests must be made many months in advance so planning ahead is essential. Send for the free *Extension Programs Catalog* which describes programs, available formats, and borrowing procedures.

I understand that the National Gallery is also an excellent source for inexpensive prints.(SE)

Telecourses

TV telecourses might be available in your area on beginning sketching or drawing. In some areas these telecourses are also available on video cassette at local libraries and through Video Lending Library.

University Prints

This company lists 7,500 fine art prints in their catalog. These very inexpensive prints, all 5 1/2" by 8", cost only $.08 (black and white) and $.18 (color) each. These would be suitable for study of art history more than technique since the detail is not usually fine enough to make out brush strokes. Prints are not just of paintings but also of sculptures, and some prints are of photographs of famous buildings. Prints can be purchased individually or in topical sets which are very affordable. For instance when you study about ancient Egypt, you might purchase the set of 66 prints entitled *A Visit to Ancient Egypt* for only $5; or for U.S. History, try *Development of America*, 120 prints for $12. The *Topic Study Sets* brochure lists six pages of grade-level prints on hundreds of topics.(SE)

Usborne Story of Painting
(Educational Development Corporation)
$6.95 pb; $14.95 hc

This 32-page book introduces children to the world of art by briefly covering various periods and styles in chronological order for the most part. History, biography, art techniques, and cultural issues combine to create an interesting presentation. Heavy with illustrations—reproductions of famous art work and Usborne's own drawings—this book is appropriate for children in the middle to upper-elementary grades. Unsurprisingly, a few nude figures are included.(SE)

Video Lending Library
membership fee for homeschoolers $25 (yearly) or $45 lifetime (must mention you are a homeschooler for reduced price!)

Buy or rent art videos, choosing from more than 1200 titles. Homeschoolers who choose to rent videos get a special low membership fee. Video rental costs of $6 or $9 are on top of the membership fee. Rental videos can be kept for a full seven days. Most titles are about 60 minutes long. Among the topics are watercolor, Chinese brush painting, drawing, American artists, art history, pastels, acrylics, cartooning, art theory, calligraphy, ceramics, airbrush technique, crafts, and sewing. Request their free brochure so you can determine which topics are of interest, then I suggest calling for advice on appropriate videos before actually ordering.

Visual Manna's Complete Art Curriculum
by Richard and Sharon Jeffus
(Visual Manna)
$68.95; economy edition - $42.95

Visual Manna's Complete Art Curriculum was written for either classroom or home school settings. It is a complete, multi-grade art curriculum that comes in a large binder. While the binder does contain over 300 pages, it looks larger because all pages are placed in vinyl page protectors. (This is to keep intact those pages that have one of the 30 fine art prints attached.) Forty-five lessons teach skills and concepts such as primary colors, symmetry, patterns, positive/negative space, shading, perspective, and proportion through examples and activities.

Children work with many types art media, including pencils, water colors, pastels, crayons, ink, clay, fabric, and yarn. Examples of some of the activities are creating gingerbread houses from various papers, abstract metal sculptures, coiled pots, yarn "paintings," and a mosaic; drawing people (both still and action figures) and bears using shading techniques; painting a seascape; and illustrating a book.

Most lessons offer activity suggestions for younger (grades 1-6) and older (grades 7-12) students. Since there is a vast difference between the abilities of first and sixth graders (or between a seventh grader and a twelfth grader, also!), you will need to select activities that are suitable for the ages and skill levels of your own children. Lessons do not follow a progression of difficulty, so you should also look through all of them before deciding in what order to proceed.

Objectives for each lesson are listed at the front of the book and in each lesson. Lessons also include background and/or instructional information and a supply list. Some lessons include fine art prints, and a few have reproducible activity sheets.

Periodic tests and answer keys are included. At the end of the binder are an art history time line, a list of 55 creative ideas/projects, suggestions for creating a student sketch book, instructions for making an art portfolio, and worksheets for a visit to an art museum and a visit with a professional artist.

This program offers more than most families could accomplish in a year, even if they select only age appropriate activities. Plan on using it for two or more years. The overall thrust of this program is toward creativity in art.

Lessons should be fairly easy to use, although most of them leave much detail for students and parents to figure out on their own. This is at least partially intentional since the authors do not believe in dictating the results of art projects. Grammatical errors and awkward wording are a minor annoyance, especially in the introductory sections of the book.

Visual Manna also publishes *Visual Manna's Project Newsletter*, a quarterly publication with lots more art and craft project ideas plus helpful hints.

Young Masters Home Study Art Program ▭
(Gordon School of Art)
$190; extra student art book - $15; extra supply packs - $7.50

John Gordon believes that anyone can learn to be an artist if he simply puts the time and effort into it. Gordon teaches art as a science composed of numerous techniques that must be mastered in consecutive order. Although younger students have successfully used the program, age 7 or 8 is probably the earliest most students should begin. Gordon tells us success in his program depends upon diligence, perseverance, and concentration rather than innate artistic ability. Students who have sloppy work habits, are careless, or who dislike following instructions exactly are not good candidates for the program, although the program itself might be a tool for developing good work habits. (Tips for working with such students are included in the teacher's manual.) Actually, the same is also true for the parent or teacher who must work very closely with the student, studying the lessons and mastering the techniques in preparation for monitoring the student. (For simplicity's sake, I'll assume the teacher is the parent.) The parent must read through the teacher manual before beginning since the course is built upon principles that must be thoroughly understood. All students must begin with the Foundation Course which is a combination of the first four levels as defined by Gordon. It consists of the teacher manual, a student art book, one set of some of the basic art supplies, and three professional-quality video tapes. The course is restricted for use to no more than 2 students (typically the parent and one child). Additional family members must each purchase their own student art books. We are not permitted to teach non-family members without special permission.

The Introductory video tape describes the program, shows examples of student work, and explains the principles upon which it is based. The other two videos provide lesson instructions. Students develop basic skills in pencil manipulation, line control, line quality, shading, and drawing on grids, while working with pencils, pens, crayons, and colored pencils.

Lesson plans, worksheets, and the worksheet demonstrations video coordinate for each lesson. Skills are broken down into minute steps, which might seem tedious at times, but are designed to develop technical proficiency needed for more challenging projects.

As soon as students demonstrate a minimal level of proficiency, they tackle projects under the direction of the parent while using the project demonstrations video and accompanying worksheets. Projects throughout this level are all small grid drawings of increasing difficulty.

The course functions as a correspondence course. Two free mail evaluations are included with the program, which should be sufficient for a student who seems to be mastering the skills. Additional consultations are available for $25. Students must send in their work and have it approved to graduate from the program. No one who has not mastered the Foundation Course (which includes levels 1-4) will be allowed to purchase higher levels. Thus far, only Level 5 is available beyond this, but the courses should eventually go all the way through Level 12—drawing and painting from life.) The Foundation Course might take from four months to four years to complete depending upon the age and ability of the student.

This is not a Christian course, thus we see samples of student art on the introductory tape that we might not wish our children to draw. However, children are not asked to draw these particular pictures. Those that come with the course are not objectionable. Many of the project drawings are cartoonish but inoffensive. In fact, Gordon tried to include a variety of types of drawing projects to appeal to everyone.

The program is as rigid as it sounds, but purposely so. Gordon believes these are the very techniques learned by the great art masters. He rejects the self-expressive techniques taught in many art courses which lead us to believe that art is an inborn talent owned by few people. On the introductory tape, he shows samples from all of his students (at the time of taping) to buttress his claim that everyone willing to put forth the effort can learn the techniques.

The introductory video is available for one week for a $25 deposit with $20 of that refundable. Since this is an expensive course, check it out for yourself before enrolling.

Music

We can provide our children with musical education no matter what musical knowledge and background we have. If we can play an instrument, children can make drums, tambourines, shakers, or other simple instruments to accompany us. Song flutes and autoharps are easy for children to learn to play successfully. If we have no musical expertise in our family, we might use money saved on tuition to pay for music lessons. We might find another home schooling parent willing to trade music lessons for a skill we have.

If music lessons are out of the question, we can still provide a musical education by studying and enjoying various musical performances, learning about composers and instruments, singing, and finding other personal ways to enjoy music. In fact, the study of music, famous composers, hymns, and styles of music can be a fun family activity.

We should attend concerts of all types to expose our children to a wide range of music, but we need to be sensitive to their attention span and interest level. Often there are concerts for youth offered by major orchestras. Check your area for events. Libraries carry records representative of all musical types. Check out various types of music for sampling.

Make singing a part of everyday life. Songs will lighten the atmosphere of your home, particularly if they are praise songs.

RECOMMENDED RESOURCES

Alfred Complete Catalog
(Alfred Publishing Company)

Alfred Publishing has to be one of the most complete sources for music education resources. Their huge catalog includes lesson and theory books for piano, string, percussion, and wind instruments. They have self-teaching courses for piano, recorder, guitar (*Teach Yourself to Play..* series) and other instruments which each include a book and an "enhanced CD" (computer CD-ROM which can be played in a regular CD player if you don't own a computer with CD-ROM capability) [$19.90 each course]. These courses are great for independent learners about age nine and older. These are a real bargain!

They offer a new, parent-directed beginning keyboard/theory/appreciation course for children ages 4-6, *Music for Little Mozarts,* that uses Mozart Mouse and Beethoven Bear stuffed animals as "co-teachers."

You will also find in their catalog computer-based piano and guitar courses and piano theory games, sheet music for individuals or orchestras, and scripts, scores and accompaniments for musical productions. They offer great music theory courses such as *Practical Theory Complete: A Self Instruction Music Theory Course* (start with the first parts of this book with younger students) and *Essentials of Music Theory. Essentials of Music Theory* is their newest and most comprehensive theory course. It includes books, ear-training CD's, and CD-ROM versions for both student and teacher. (The teacher version allows teachers' to track up to 200 students.) You can try this out on Alfred's web site before purchasing.

Although Alfred doesn't sell instruments, they can direct you to those who do.

Alfred will provide homeschoolers with free catalogs, but they will direct you to local suppliers for actual purchases. They have a home school coordinator who is anxious to assist you in finding the right resources.

Basic Library of the World's Greatest Music 🎧
(World's Greatest Music.)
$199 (specially discounted price for home educators)

This is a broader classical music appreciation resource than

Music and Moments with the Masters, since it includes works from thirty-one different composers representing nearly all the orchestral forms in the world of classical music. However, there are fewer selections per composer than in *MMWM*. Selections are chosen to be representative of various musical forms rather than biographical. Forty-six complete works are presented on sixteen cassettes. They come packaged in a cassette album. An important part of the Library is the Master Volume Listener's Guide. In the *Listener's Guide* are biographies (well-written); background information on the musical pieces; timetable charts of musical periods which also show musical history in relation to other historical events; a dictionary of musical phrases; listening activities; extended activity suggestions in art, writing, dramatization, etc.; questions and answers; and puzzles. The biographies and musical background are the most useful parts of the *Listener's Guide*. Children are unlikely to pick up the Listener's Guide and read on their own, so it will require parent interaction to make full use of this resource.

While the *Listener's Guide* might serve well for many families, those who want more guidance and help might want to use the teachers' edition [$33], student textbook [$25], and student workbook [$4.50] to create a full course. (I haven't had a chance to review these.)(S)

Children Sing the Word Beginning Theory Course
🎧

(Children Sing the Word)
complete set - $49.95: Book 1 - $5; Book 2 - $25; Book 3 - $15; tape - $5; flash cards - $4; teacher's manual - $15

This is a Christian, Biblical approach to teaching music, written especially for home schooling families. The songs are from Scripture, and instruction is built upon Biblical precepts. The course consists of three books and a cassette tape. Optional Flash Cards and Teacher's Manual (containing teacher helps and answer keys) are available. The three books are distinctive in purpose rather than a progression in teaching skills.

Book 1 teaches singing and can be used with very young children through adults. The cassette tape contains recorded versions of the twelve songs. Book 1 also has drawings and brief histories of ancient musical instruments. Book 1, used with the teacher helps found in the Teacher's Manual, is designed for preschool level.

Book 2 contains basic music theory—note reading, key signatures, timing, following step-by-step precepts. Biblical precepts for building good habits for music study are taught first. A practice keyboard, printed on heavy paper and eleven notes long (white piano keys), is provided for children to practice beginning exercises.

Book 3 completes the program (for now) with lessons for guitar and piano. Included in the lessons are staff writing practice, review, and daily practice schedules. The authors do not recommend pushing young children into instrument lessons using Book 3 too soon but encourage waiting until ages nine or ten. However, younger children with strong musical inclination might also be successful.

The entire set is very reasonably priced and appears to be a practical method. As with many small companies, quality is improving with each new printing and revision. They also offer special 30% discounts to missionaries and church schools.

New additions to *Children Sing the Word* materials include: *The Children Sing the Word Primer for the Piano*, for ages 6 and up, complete set - $21.95; *The Children Sing the Word Beginning Recorder Book of Scripture Songs* - $10; an intermediate book entitled *The Dynamics of Music* - $10; and *The Children Sing the Word Scripture Song Book* (with 100+ new songs) - $19.95.

Davidsons Music 🎧

(Davidsons Music)
books for each level - $7.95 each; cassettes - $10.95; Preparatory level and level 1 packages - $27 each; levels 2-5 packages - $17 each

Those who want to learn to play the piano but cannot afford lessons should consider Davidsons guaranteed, self-teaching courses by Madonna Woods. Courses for playing by ear, by note reading, or both are offered.

Much of the music is "church" and "gospel." Courses for organ, guitar, electronic keyboard, and a number of other instruments are offered, but the bulk of the business concentrates on piano instruction and playing for different age and ability levels. Typical piano courses include a book, audio cassette, chord chart, keyboard decals (for learning notes), and sound set-ups for playing the organ. Of special interest to home educators should be the complete *Piano Course for Christians* in six levels. This, like the other courses, can be used as a self-taught course with instruction provided on the cassette tapes. The first two levels (preparatory and level 1) include two audio cassettes and a book, while levels 2 through 5 have one audio cassette and a book. These can be purchased individually or as complete packages for each level. The course can be used by both children and adults. It teaches music theory and note reading from the very beginning. Madonna Woods has taught so many people to play the piano that she knows how to predict trouble spots and make the lessons very understandable. Lesson guides are included with notes to parents explaining how to set up and monitor lessons, encourage practice, select music, watch for danger signals, and assess progress. There might be a few occasions when a student would want to consult with someone who can already play the piano, but for the most part, the tapes and books will do the job. If you have always wanted piano lessons but could not afford them, here is your solution.

While music for songs is already included in the basic course, some people will want or need more practice at each level. Consequently, Davidsons Music also sells supplementary music books of songs that can be played by those working at the various levels of the piano course.

One supplement you might consider is the *Meet the Composers* book and cassette tape designed to accompany the preparatory level. Brief biographical information on composers is interspersed with Madonna Woods playing the composers' songs for which sheet music is provided in the companion book. [$10 for the set.] *Meet the Composers* sets are planned for additional levels of the piano course.

Focus on Composers

(Teacher Created Materials)
$11.95

For a basic course in music appreciation for grade levels 4-8, this has to be one of the most practical resources. Short biographies of composers, overviews of musical periods and styles, information about instruments and music theory, plus plenty of activities combine in one book that should suit many families. The first section tells how to use the lessons plus ideas for extending them. Reproducible composer research forms help students ferret out information for themselves. Brief sections on women in music and music up to the middle ages bring us up to the point where music is presented by periods or styles: middle ages, renaissance, baroque, classical, romantic, modern, and contemporary. The last section of the book pictures musical instruments by families, introduces basic music terms, note values, and rhythm. Activities scattered throughout the book range from simple written answers to complicated projects such as making your own instruments. There are numerous full-page drawings of composers which can be used as coloring pages. Choose activities most appropriate for the ages and interests of your children. Listening activities recommend musical pieces of a composer, a style, or a time period so children get a full range of musical experience.(S)

A Gift of Music-Great Composers and Their Influence

(Crossway)
$15.99

This books teaches us about the influence of Christianity on music and great composers. Here are detailed biographies of composers written on an adult level. Parents need to digest information and whittle it down for a child's attention span unless they have a child with an unusual interest in music and composers.

God Made Music series

(Praise Hymn, Inc.)
student books - $4.98 each; teacher's manuals - $10.98

each; mini-packets range from $21 to $24; music packets range from $28 to $53

This is a Christian music curriculum for kindergarten through high school. Those with younger children (K-3rd grades) might wish to start with the first grade book. Those with 4th through 6th graders might begin with the fourth grade book. Books need not be used in sequence but can be started at any level. K through 6th books require teacher's manuals for presentation. The seventh book presents a course in a single book appropriate for older elementary students through high school.

K through 6th grade books include games, biographies of famous musicians and composers, activities, study of instruments, songs, and sheet music. Folk, patriotic, humorous, and religious songs dominate the song selections and sheet music. The music presents a simple melody line, but separate *We Sing Music Piano Accompaniment* books contain both piano accompaniments and guitar chords. Children are also exposed to classical music throughout the various levels as they listen to selections composed by Beethoven, Handel, Bach, and others. Correlated audio CD's are available at each level.

Student books are illustrated with full color and humorous cartoon drawings, while teacher's manuals are printed in black-and-white and contain reduced pictures of student pages. Lessons are dependent upon presentation from the teacher's manuals and will require some preparation. Teachers should have at least a minimal background in music, but if a parent is starting from the early grades, he or she can learn along with the children. The program is classroom designed, but most activities can be adapted for the home fairly easily. Select only one grade level to work with the entire family if at all possible. Each book has 34 lessons which works out to about once a week for music class. The mix of activities and solid music theory content make this series outstanding.

We can purchase Music Mini-packets for each level which include student workbook, teacher's manual, *We Sing Music* CD, a Flutophone for grade 3, and a Soprano Recorder for grade 4. Complete packets add additional CD's of classical music recordings. We also need one set of *Musicards Music Flash Cards* that will be used for all levels [$14.98 for large-size set or $4.98 for a "mini" set].

Homespun Tapes, Ltd.

Homespun offers hundreds of video and audio tapes for learning to play musical instruments. They offer lessons in country, bluegrass, and folk music rather than traditional. *Gospel Guitar, Flatpick Country Guitar, 5-String Banjo*, and *The Hammer Dulcimer* are typical. Instruments for which they have tapes are guitar (acoustic and electric), fiddle, banjo, mandolin, dobro, jawharp, autoharp, dulcimer, keyboards, flute, bass, synthesizer, harmonica, pennywhistle, and drums. Vocal instruction (including yodeling) is also included. Tapes are for skill levels from beginning through advanced intermediate. Homespun also sells tapes on musicianship as well as books, strings, and small instruments.(S)

Jaffé Strings

(A Beka Book)

$370 per course

A Beka Book offers Jaffé Strings video courses for students ages 10 and up to learn violin, viola, cello, or bass. Courses are offered at two different levels depending upon age and musical background. There are two year courses offered at each level. Students learn to play and also do their practice along with the videos. These courses work best used in a group where a knowledgeable supervisor is present to work with students as needed. Students can work alone, but the supervisor is still essential. Group interaction makes learning easier and more enjoyable. I would recommend these courses to home school groups which have experienced musicians who lack teaching experience.

Keyboard Capers: Music Theory for Children

(Elijah Company) $18.95

The title almost does this book a disservice by designating it only for children. Somehow, with four years of piano and five years of violin plus assorted music classes in school, my music theory knowledge is pitiful. This book really covers the basics and the things I have missed! It is recommended for children because the author presents the material in short lessons with visual aids and games designed for elementary age children. A couple of little poems are used, but the games are not cluttered with too many cutesy gimmicks. Most learning takes place with the visual aids and activities. If you are short on time, purchase the prepared visual aids sold by the publisher. For older students or adults, pick and choose the games that are useful and get right to the heart of the lesson. Lesson plan headings are the musical alphabet, orientation to the piano, musical notation, rhythm, intervals, note identification, music vocabulary, ear training, and major scales. The piano or keyboard is the primary teaching tool used with the book. A xylophone could be substituted, but an inexpensive electronic keyboard would be preferable. The basic knowledge of music learned is applicable to any other musical instrument and to singing.

We need to prepare the manipulatives for *Keyboard Capers* from patterns and instructions within the book. However, if we are short on time, we can purchase the Keyboard Capers book with ready-made manipulatives printed on heavy card stock [$36.95] or with those same manipulatives laminated for durability [$51.95].

Keyboard Theory Learning Wrap-Ups

(Learning Wrap-Ups)

$7.95 individual sets; $35 for intro kit

See the full description of how *Wrap-Ups* are used in the math chapter. There are five music theory sets of ten *Wrap-Ups* each or a larger introductory set that includes all five sets. Skills covered within the five sets are note reading, signs and symbols, rhythm, vocabulary, chords, and intervals. A chart cross references the theory to the major music theory programs (Glover, Bastien, Alfred, Aaron, and Schaum) so we can easily identify which *Wrap-Ups* will correlate with theory lessons. The *Wrap-Ups* will not do all of the teaching, but they are a great reinforcement and practice tool. They are appropriate for any child who is able to read words like "moderately" and "staccato," as well as for older children (and maybe even adults!).

Mr. Bach Comes to Call and other audio recordings ⌒

by the Classical Kids

(Children's Book Store Distribution)

$10.98 cassette; $20.98 CDs;

teacher's guides - $9.98 each;

Classroom Collection - on cassettes: $159.98, on CDs: $279.98

Mr. Bach Comes to Call, Tchaikovsky Discovers America, Hallelujah Handel, Mozart's Magnificent Voyage, Vivaldi's Ring of Mystery, Song of the Unicorn, and *Beethoven Lives Upstairs* are a series of recordings, each an hour long, that intertwine music, biography, history, and humor. In *Mr. Bach,* a little girl practicing her piano lessons is interrupted by a visit from Mr. Bach and his magical orchestra. Fantasy is a major element of these tapes, so "realists" might be uncomfortable with some of the content. Excerpts from more than two dozen of Bach's compositions are woven throughout the "tale." *Tchaikovsky Discovers America, Beethoven Lives Upstairs,* and *Vivaldi's Ring of Mystery* are similar in concept—a story is interwoven with the composer's music. *Mozart's Magnificent Voyage* intertwines biography with a fantasy story involving Mozart's opera, *The Magic Flute. Song of the Unicorn* is a Merlin tale of fantasy that features a collection of traditional English and Celtic songs, Gregorian chant, medieval dance music, and a little Bach and Mozart. Various "actors" supply the voices for the characters, creating truly dramatic presentations. These high-quality tapes are a delightful means of introducing some major composers and their music to children of all ages, but keep in mind the heavy emphasis on fantasy.

Extend the value of these tapes by purchasing companion teacher's guides or the Classroom Collection. The Classroom Collection includes either cassettes or CDs of all six recordings, a 40-minute "music only" CD featuring some of the featured composers' music, Teacher's Guides for each recording, and a lengthier guide to Bach and Beethoven. The Teacher's Guides include additional background information, discussion topics, activities, and ideas for creating "unit study" type lessons that cross over into history geography, language arts, and the fine arts. *Susan Hammond's Classical Kids Teacher's Notes* is a guide for further study of Bach and Beethoven. It features six, 10-day lesson plans which can be used to create short-term unit studies. The Teacher's Guides as well as this guide can also be purchased individually. The Classroom Collection is geared towards grades 4 through 6, although it can be stretched to suit children a few grades younger and older.(SE)

Music and Moments with the Masters, cassette tapes and study guide

(Cornerstone Curriculum Project)
Set 1 - $75; Sets 2, 3 and 4 - $65

CD's and a companion study guide and book comprise a five-year music appreciation and history program. CD's can be purchased separately if you so choose.

Four different sets of excellent quality recordings are available. Each set has eight CD's covering four composers—two CD's per composer. There is a biographical recording that intersperses each composer's music with his story and a CD featuring some of the composer's most popular pieces. Biographical CD's are so well done they appeal to all ages.

Set 1 includes the book *A Gift of Music* for background information, a study guide, and an additional CD of *Peter and the Wolf.* Readings from *A Gift of Music* are incorporated into study guide lessons. The first set features Bach, Handel, Haydn, and Mozart. Set two features Beethoven, Schubert, Berlioz, and Mendelssohn. Schumann, Chopin, Verdi, and Grieg are in set three. Wagner, Brahms, Tchaikovsky, and Dvorak are in set four. This is a wonderful way to introduce your family to classical music if you don't know where to start. While children can listen and learn entirely on their own, using the study guide greatly enhances the value of the CD's.

David and Shirley Quine, with their son Ben, have authored this guide which is best used by the entire family. It begins with an introduction to classical music, music appreciation, and the development of listening skills. Each year focuses on one set of recordings, working through them slowly with repeated listenings so that children become very familiar with the different composers. You will also need some additional recordings beyond the basic sets. They are listed in the front of the study guide, and they should be easy to find. Suggested discussion questions help parents focus children's attention and thinking. Biographical selections from *A Gift of Music* expands beyond biographical sketches on the recordings. The fifth year shifts into the study of the history of music plus world view analysis. As with other materials developed by the Quines, this course draws heavily upon Francis Schaeffer's ideas as presented in his book *How Should We Then Live?* In the fifth year, there is also an optional study using the text, *A History of Western Music* by Donald Grout.

This course is unique in its scope and in its presentation of worldview study. It also serves as a marvelous way for the family to both learn and enjoy music together.

Music Education in the Christian Home

by Dr. Mary Ann Froehlich
(Noble Books)
$14.95

Dr. Froehlich has written this book based on her belief that music education is not an option but a scriptural command for Christians. She uses the first two chapters to buttress her statement by discussing music in Scripture and its practical application.

Once we are convinced that we need to teach music, we then need to know how to go about it. Froehlich discusses the most popular methods of music education (for those of us who have no idea whether Suzuki is the best method or if there are any other possibilities).

The rest of the book is practical information that can be used whether or not we have chosen one of the methods that were discussed. The author assumes that at some point we will be choosing some type of lessons for our child. However, a well-rounded music education will go beyond the scope of what is learned in lessons from a single teacher. It is the parent's responsibility to work on a comprehensive plan for music education. A Music Education Checklist in the book will help us identify goals for music education. The author provides suggestions for meeting those goals. For example, listening is a major part of music education, so the author includes lists of musical examples from medieval times through modern. Since a book this size could not possibly provide us with all of the details that we need to actually teach music, a large proportion of the book consists of listings of music resources including books on education, history, reference, techniques, and theory. Those of us who like the integrated approach might use the timelines in the back of the book to tie musical history to other history-based studies.

The non-musician might find all of this intimidating, but he/she should just choose a starting place such as listening to some of the works by major composers. (Check to see if your library has tapes, records, or CD's for loan.)

It helps to work with a music teacher who includes parents in children's lessons as do Suzuki teachers. In this way we learn along with our children and get guidance on what we can do on our own.

Music for Minors

by Christine J. Dillon
(Hewitt Homeschooling Resources)
$8.95

Parents without musical background should appreciate this practical resource for teaching music. It assumes nothing and begins with ideas for creating a musical environment, followed by simple activities for having fun with sound. These ideas are especially good for young students (preschool-grade 3). Following this, it teaches about pitch and melody, followed by some musical games. The next section helps parents learn some music theory, from which we can select appropriate parts to teach our children. The theory does get fairly involved, so we must decide how far into theory we wish to go. As in earlier sections, game and activity ideas are intermixed. After teaching about rhythm, the book moves on to a brief section of music appreciation, a discussion about music lessons, and ideas for using music to teach other subjects. At the end are a glossary, lists of resources with addresses, lists of songs, a pattern for a game cube, blank music sheets, and simple music for a number of songs.

Music in Motion

This is a mail order source for educational and gift items related to music. Books, audios, and videos are their mainstays, but right brain creativity is strongly in evidence in the catalog selections. While they do not sell band instruments such as violins and clarinets, they do offer children's rhythm band instruments, recorders, bells, and the Omnichord. Other items include music-education visual aids, cassettes, CDs, computer software, and games for songs, dance, and music theory (Orff, Kodaly, and Suzuki methods). The catalog is full of all kinds of fun music-making ideas.(S)

Piano Discovery 🖥

(Jump! Music)
$199.99; levels 2 and 3 software - $59.99 each

This is probably the most painless way to give your children piano lessons. It comes with a MIDI piano, software for Level 1, cables, and a manual on CD. It requires a computer with Windows 3.1, 95, or 98, 8 MB RAM, a 2x CD-ROM drive or better, 100% Sound Blaster 16 compatible sound card, SVGA monitor, and at least 8 MB free disk space. Apparently, you also need a MIDI cable to hook up to a general MIDI keyboard.

Three levels of piano lessons take students from the very beginning to playing fairly simple music with chords. You need to purchase the other two levels of software separately. This is a fantastic course for piano-lesson-averse students as well as for those who want to do it on their own at their own pace.

CD-ROMs offer students their (or a supervisor's) choice of six options: School House, Practice Room, Jam Stage, MIDI Studio, Arcade, and Performance Hall. Total interaction ensures that learning is multisensory as students read, hear, and perform. The School House teaches a lesson. Students should then move to the Practice Room (also referred to as the Practice Bungalo) where they can hear a song played, practice it, play it along with "the teacher," or practice either right or left hand separately. The Arcade sets up three different games that help students practice their music theory knowledge and

playing skills. The Jam Stage and MIDI Studio allow students to perform and record songs accompanied by an "orchestra." In the Performance Hall, students are accompanied by an orchestra as they play through their songs. Their performance is rated; they receive a standing ovation for a correct performance, but a newspaper review will let them know if it is less than perfect. If they pass, the computer displays a certificate which we should be able to print out. However, we could not get ours to print correctly for whatever reason. Musical pieces are an eclectic collection of children's songs, ditties, holiday tunes, classical adaptations, folk songs, patriotic and gospel tunes. Speed, timed by a metronome, can be adjusted to slower or faster speeds as needed. The multimedia quality is excellent, the entire program is easy to figure out and work through, and the layout is entertaining.

Minor problems have to do with the way the program switches from one page of music to the next; in actuality, most pianists read ahead as they play which you can only do if the music is there ahead of time. An irritation for some students might be that if the student makes a mistake in the School House, the program sends the student back to only right or left hand practice after a student has already been playing a piece with both hands.

Two additional CD-ROM's are available for use with the *Piano Discovery* interface: *Piano Discovery Christmas Collection* and *Piano Discovery Gospel Collection* [$24.99 each].

I see no reason that *Piano Discovery* cannot be used with younger children, but Jump Music also sells *Piano Discovery for Kids* for ages 6-12 for $59.99. This might a good starting place because it is a smaller starting investment.

Ready-To-Use Music Reading Activities Kit

(Prentice Hall)
$26.95

Children up through about fourth grade level can learn beginning music reading with the variety of activities presented by Loretta Mitchell, an experienced music teacher and school district music coordinator. Activities begin with a section on beat and rhythm, quarter and eighth notes. Reproducible work and activity sheets, simple games (e.g., rhythm identification), song sheets (with recognizable favorites such as "Twinkle, Twinkle, Little Star" and "This Old Man"), composition worksheets for students to write their own music compositions, award certificates, and bonus activities comprise each section. The paper and pencil work is actually quite minimal, but reading skills are necessary for children to participate in all activities. There are fourteen progressively more challenging sections to the book covering the basic scale, sharps and flats, and dotted half notes. Rhythm sticks are required as well as some sort of pitched musical instrument to hear tones. It might be a keyboard, mallet instrument (xylophone, metallophone), chromatic or resonator bells. Recorders will also work, although illustrations show keyboard and mallet instruments. Activities will work for group or individual learning. I suspect that those working in one-on-one situations will breeze through the various levels very quickly, choosing from among the activities only those that are necessary. The teacher/parent presents the lessons, and it is assumed that person is a music teacher by profession. However, only a minimal amount of musical knowledge should be necessary to present the lessons. ISBN # 0137561644.(S)

Rhythm Band Instruments

Rhythm instruments are the easiest type for young children to use, and Rhythm Band is the place to find them. Here we also find other easy-to-play instruments such as xylophones, handbells, drums, and recorders. More complicated versions of such basic instruments are available along with pianicas, autoharps, guitars, ukuleles and more. To help with teaching, there are books, games, cassettes, and CDs. This is a great catalog for anyone teaching music to children, both for ideas and as a source. Now, they also have an on-line catalog with e-commerce.

Sounds of Praise Christian Music Studies

by Debra Matula
(Sounds of Praise)
Levels O and AO kits - $25; extra student book - $12.50;
Levels 1 and 2 kits -$35; extra student books - $17.50

Debra Matula, a home schooling mom and musician, searched for a comprehensive music course that taught about instruments, composers, hymn writers, and hymn histories, while also providing instruction in music theory. Not finding such a course, she decided to put it together herself. We now have Level O for grades K-2, Level AO (advanced O) to follow level O, Level 1 for third grade and up, and Level 2 for older students or after Level 1.

Each course consists of a student workbook, teacher's edition of the student book with answers, a teacher's guide that provides lesson outlines with background information, two cassette tapes, and a set of flashcards. Level 0 teaches introductory theory—recognition of the staff, notes, and other symbols—and introduces orchestral instruments and their sounds. Forty flashcards can be used to help children with recognition. One cassette tape provides actual instrument sounds, then the second cassette, a performance of *Peter and the Wolf*, is used after children have studied instruments to let them hear how they are used in this musical story. Workbook activities involve coloring and drawing rather than written work. Level AO continues basic theory with study of time and key signatures, placement of instruments into families, and the orchestra. It includes a tape and study guide for the *Nutcracker*. Level 1 reviews and expands upon theory basics. There is more

detailed study of selected instruments (harp, oboe, French horn, timpani, violin, flute, and piano). The composers studied at this level are Handel, Mendlessohn, Tchaikovsky, and Mozart. Hymn writers include Fanny Crosby, Adelaide Pollard, George Stebbins, Ira Sankey, and Harriet Beecher Stowe. The stories behind eight hymns round out the study. Level 1 is the starting place for any student who has not already studied basic music theory and has little familiarity with instruments, no matter their grade level. Level 2 reviews Level 1, then adds advanced theory, additional instruments, composers (Vivaldi, Beethoven, and Bach), hymn writers (Watts, Adams, Bradbury, and Walford), and hymn histories. It includes tapes and flashcards.

This is an ambitious course, particularly Level 1. It touches on many topics that can really use more time and attention. While it makes an ideal supplement for a child who is taking instrument lessons because they can see and apply what they are learning, it can be used with all children. Student materials are reproducible for family use only.

As with so many fledgling home businesses, the product is not polished. Tapes are compilations of professional recordings mixed with Debra's recordings. Hand lettering and uneven print quality are other marks of an amateur publisher. However, as with so many other such businesses, these problems are bound to be rapidly overcome with experience. The quality of the content more than makes up for any flaws in production.

The Spiritual Lives of Great Composers

by Patrick Kavanaugh
(Zondervan)
$10.99

Twelve famous composers are profiled in this book: Handel, Bach, Haydn, Mozart, Beethoven, Schubert, Mendelssohn, Liszt, Wagner, Dvorak, Ives, and Stravinsky. Kavanaugh's approach is not that of a biographer, since there are already numerous such works available. Instead, he chose to concentrate on the spiritual aspects of their lives. Still, there is some biographical information which helps put their spirituality into perspective. Kavanaugh draws on letters and other writings of the composers themselves as well as their friends and families. Such references are footnoted for those wishing to check it out for themselves. Kavanaugh introduces each composer with a brief vignette, then takes a few pages to relate the story of each composer. He ends with a short piece highlighting a key, positive character trait exhibited by each man and "Recommended Listening" suggestions to acquaint us with each composer's music. The writing style is lively and interesting, although I would suggest holding off with younger children and reading it aloud with children ages ten and up. Each section is short enough to be covered in a single sitting.

I found this book to be one of the most readable books about composers I have encountered. I also appreciate the balance it provides in contrast to popular modern images of some of the composers. Mozart is one of the best examples. He was made to look mentally unbalanced and amoral (at least) in the movie *Amadeus*, yet Kavanaugh introduces a deeply spiritual side of Mozart that most of us have never seen. He does not whitewash these men, yet he shows that they are much more than one-dimensional caricatures. Kavanaugh says that although the twelve composers "...come from a wide variety of backgrounds and beliefs....there is a surprising level of agreement on basic Christian beliefs."

Theory Time

by Heather Rathnau and Karen Wallace
(Theory Time)
student books - $7.95 each; teacher's editions - $17.95 each

Music theory books are offered for a primer level and for grades 1-12. Older students need not start at the primer level, but they should begin with one of the lower grade level books if they are just starting their study of theory. Books review basic information up to a certain point, adding additional information of increasing difficulty at each level, so students might also jump from one level to a few levels higher for the next book. This is serious music theory study. For example, the seventh level book covers "rhythm drill, drawing enharmonics, melodic/harmonic intervals, chromatic/diatonic half steps, double sharps & flats, simple/compound meter, conducting patterns, triplets, major keys, I, IV and V triads, relative minors, minor circle of fifths, pure minor scales & key signatures, major & minor thirds & triads." There are three teacher's editions, each covering a span of grade levels. The teacher's edition covering grades 1-6 includes reproductions of selected pages from the first three student books, answers, "ear training guides," and activity pages. The second and third teacher's editions cover grades 7-9 and 10-12 respectively, and both include complete copies of each of the student books with answers. Theory Time does not sell directly, but will direct you to a local or mail order distributor.(S)

Usborne First Book of the Recorder

(Educational Development Corporation)
$10.95

Here is an excellent introduction to music reading and instrument playing. Written for children ages seven to eleven, this book uses cartoon characters and a light-handed approach to music. Children actually learn to play some songs, some recognizable and others new to them.(SE)

The Usborne Story of Music

(Educational Development Corporation)
$6.95

This beautifully illustrated little book from Usborne covers music history, instruments, composers, and musical styles. It is interesting even if you are not a music lover.(S)

Drama

Drama does not have to mean full-scale production of plays, although it is possible to do this through local support groups.

Puppet shows are simple to do with only a few children to manipulate a number of puppets. Or, we can get together with another family or two and present a puppet show or drama for our support group or church.

Role play and reenactment are valuable tools for reinforcing Bible lessons or historical events we have been studying. Children might be encouraged to participate in dramatic productions at church, through community colleges, and in local stage presentations.

Dramatic reading is another form of drama easily overlooked. Choosing a poem or famous writing to memorize and recite is good practice for our children. Encourage the small efforts at first so the big efforts we hope to see in the future do not seem so intimidating.

Studying about drama and dramatists can also be an interesting aspect of our social studies/history lessons. Other than these suggestions, I make no specific recommendations for drama since our individual situations and approaches will vary greatly.

Chapter 17

Physical Education

With all the concern over teaching methods, learning styles, and curriculum, it is easy to overlook an important factor in our child's learning—his ability to perform motor tasks accurately. Too often we take for granted that children will pick up these skills as they grow, and we fail to understand what causes that development to take place.

Physical Education for Proper Development

Recent studies seem to show that a normal child develops his mind by acting on his environment. In fact, even his visual perception seems to be built up by many experiences of moving his body through the spaces around him. If that is so, the young child who is swinging, jumping, and balancing is building up mental and physical abilities he will later use in reading, while the child sitting passively watching *Sesame Street* is not.

Unfortunately, a lot of the movements children need for proper development seem silly and useless to adults. It does not appear that anything important is happening when we watch a child twisting in a swing and then spinning around as the chain unwinds, yet the spinning may be helping develop the muscles of his eyes so that they can work together smoothly. Skipping might look carefree but rather pointless unless we realize how important it is that a child be able to easily use both sides of his body in coordinated movements.

In our modern society, with its play pens, car seats, video games, and television sets, we must be especially careful that our children have enough opportunity for simple, self-directed movement. It might not be as convenient for us to have an adventurous acrobat on our hands as it is to have a sedate and unobtrusive youngster who does not need constant supervision. Yet, the child who is physically exploring and experimenting with his environment will be better prepared developmentally when the time comes for him to use small motor (muscle) skills needed for paper and pencil school activities. We should not expect children to do a lot of fine motor work before they have a foundation of gross motor (large muscle) patterning.

When we think of physical education, we often think of calisthenics such as sit-ups and push-ups, or organized team sports such as baseball and basketball. Yet some children still need to work on very basic movements before moving on to a more complex sport or type of exercise. Some good basic movements for children are:

- jumping with both feet together
- hopping on one foot
- skipping
- hopscotch
- jump rope
- crawling
- swinging
- skating
- forward and backward rolls
- playing catch with beanbags or balls
- walking while throwing a beanbag
- rolling along the floor or down a slope
- balancing
- bouncing balls (also switching hands)
- walking on stepping stones or other patterns
- rope walking (or garden hose walking)—crossing one foot in front of the other
- tracing activities—with lines that move from one side of the page or larger surface to the other

A few things to look for as signals of proper development in a school age child are that he should:

- have a dominant hand
- be able to relax
- be able to walk along a six to eight foot 2" x 4" board—forward, backward, and sideways (right foot leading, then left foot leading)—without losing his balance more than once
- be able to move his eyes smoothly to follow a moving object like a pencil. His eyes should not blink or wobble when crossing a point in front of the middle of his face, and the eyes should work smoothly together.
- be able to keep a rhythm with his hands or feet, alternating right and left sides (right, left, right, left; or right, right, left, right, right, left, etc.)

If your school-age child has difficulty in one or more of these areas, he probably is not able to learn as efficiently as he should. Different parts of the brain need to be working well together, but sometimes conflicting messages from the brain interfere with proper functioning. For example, a common problem, faulty eye movement, is best corrected by getting the rest of the body working together smoothly because the muscles and movements of the body affect those of the eyes.

Many home educators have children with learning disabilities, and they purchase special books and materials to help their children get through challenging academic areas. They often require these children to spend more time doing seat work which ends up taking much longer than normal, when children might be helped more significantly by physical activity. It might be wiser to make sure a child with difficulties has more opportunity for basic, large muscle movements before requiring that he do much school work that requires fine motor skills.

If some of these activities I have suggested sound too babyish for our child, make them into games. If your child skipped that important crawling stage in infancy, design a game where he has to crawl through an obstacle course or race in crawling position. If our child lacks balance, lay out a course with 2" x 4" boards and have him walk along the boards in different ways. For a child who lacks rhythm, have him clap to music, try simple dances, or beat a drum alternating hands. Many movements can be introduced as games, and usually the child enjoys working on things he senses his body really needs.

Physical education is important not only for developmental reasons, but also because good exercise and muscle development are beneficial to academic work. As the parts of the body learn to work well together, eye-brain-hand coordination improves, making school work easier. Physical exercise also increases oxygen flow to the brain, resulting in better brain functioning. Children who spend time exercising are often able to sit still for times in between with better concentration.

While public schools place little emphasis on the arts, they do place strong emphasis on physical education. Most schools have a minimum specified time that is required. Some of us are ignoring physical education because of the difficulties it presents, but we need to explore ways of overcoming those difficulties. As temples of the Holy Spirit, our bodies should be properly cared for. We use this spiritual reasoning in avoidance of drugs, cigarettes, and alcohol, yet overweight and out-of-shape bodies are also being abused.

Some children will very naturally do a wide variety of physical activities. These children need less help than more sedentary children.

Team Sports

We should not attempt to involve our children in organized team sports as a means of compensating for socialization they might be missing in regular school. Group sports are usually fun, and they can be worthwhile for learning to work together with others toward a common goal and for learning good sportsmanship. Group sports are also useful for some of the developmental reasons discussed above, but often our children encounter the same peer pressure and negative socialization in

these settings that many of us are trying to avoid. Consider organizing low-key team sports within home school support groups. If we organize it ourselves, we can keep the amount of time to a reasonable level, shift team members so that pride and animosity are unlikely to be encouraged, and maintain a flexibility that allows for players of varied ages and abilities. Park days can be a prime time for some group game playing with an adult or two to supervise and referee if needed.

Those looking for some guidance in creating a physical fitness/sports program might want to check out *Physical Education for Homeschool Co-ops and Private Schools* (Home School Family Fitness Institute) [$20]. This wide-ranging book covers skills such as body movement activities for younger children, tumbling, gymnastics, rhythm and dance, ball skills, soccer, basketball, football, volleyball, aerobic fitness, and fitness. After discussing management and equipment issues, author Dr. Bruce Whitney presents guidelines for teaching each "skill." Instructions are fairly detailed, including rules of the game when appropriate, checklists, forms, and other helpful tools to help the novice P.E. teacher.

Practical P.E.

Physical education should involve developing an interest in activities that will last beyond school years. This often means independent activity. Sports such as track, jogging, tennis, racquetball, and swimming can be most valuable in the long run as children develop life-long interests that will keep them in shape as adults.

Sono Harris (wife of Gregg Harris) has developed *Fun Physical Fitness for the Home* (Noble Books) [$19.95]. The goals of this program are to develop strength, flexibility, agility, large and small muscle coordination, spatial awareness, and grace of movement. Activities are described for babies, toddlers, and older children (up to about ten years of age). These are simple and fun activities that do not require fancy equipment. Most can be done indoors. Sono even ties in physical education activities with academic subjects. The book includes a CD that will direct the activities. Sono developed this material with four of her children while home schooling, so we know it has been tested and proven in a setting similar to ours.

If we are house bound because of weather or circumstances and do not have Sono's program, consider tuning in to one of the many aerobic exercise programs on television, video tape, record, or cassette.

The President's Challenge Physical Fitness Program might be a help in motivating your children. Young people ages 6-17 can work towards achieving one of three awards: *The Presidential Physical Fitness Award* which recognizes an outstanding level of physical fitness, *The National Physical Fitness Award* for achieving a basic yet challenging level of physical fitness, or *The Participant Physical Fitness Award* just for participating in the program. The first two awards are earned by meeting qualifying standards (according to age and sex) in five areas of fitness: curl-ups, shuttle run, v-sit or sit and reach, one-mile run, and pull-ups or flexed-arm hang. Emblems and/or certificates are the awards. There is a restriction, although I'm not certain if it is enforced: a certified physical education teacher/specialist must oversee instruction and testing to qualify students for the awards. If this is not possible for you, you might want to still use the program for the sake of fitness, possibly creating your own awards. *The President's Challenge Program* is very concerned about assisting home educators, so they have created an entire web page at their site to address homeschoolers' most frequently asked questions, including those on how to administer the program. The web site also allows homeschoolers to order information and awards, view testing protocols, and access other information about the program and physical fitness in general.

Fitness at Home: A Physical Fitness Program for Home Schools offers yet another option suitable for children ages 6 to 17. Similar in many ways to *The President's Challenge*, this program offers a plan for fulfilling physical education requirements with worthwhile and measurable fitness goals. It includes over 20 simple exercises in flexibility, arm and shoulder strength, abdominal muscle strength, and cardiovascular endurance. The exercises are designed to improve a student's overall level of fitness which is measured by a simple physical fitness test outlined in the 10-page Parent Manual. The particular exercises involved differ from *The President's Challenge*. There are two levels of fitness standards so that significant, yet attainable, goals can be set for individual students. A colorful embroidered emblem and four-color award certificate help motivate students. The Student Training Program describes and illustrates the exercises, contains a chart for daily record keeping, and offers a convenient place to record fitness test results. The chart is reproducible, and a master copy is at the back of the Parent Manual. A Christian rationale, Bible verses, and related discussion topics distinguish this program from others. Parent Manuals are $4.75; Student Training Programs (one per child) are $2.95 each (each includes one certificate); emblems are $2.25 each; and additional award certificates are $.50 each.

It is more fun for most children (and adults) to use game playing to achieve physical fitness rather than solitary calisthenics. ***Physical Education for Homeschoolers*** by L.S. McClaine (Nutmeg Publications) [$12.95] offers a combination of group and individual activities for an easy-to-use, low equipment-cost program. A variety of skill-building activities work well with either families or larger groups. Equipment is minimal, and there are ideas for improvising with materials on hand. Variations of each activity are included for children of different skill levels. This is active fun for children in grades K-6. The fact that the book says Volume 1 on the cover, leads me to believe we might see a Volume 2 in the future. [V.

Thorpe]

We Win: A Complete Non-Competitive Physical Education Program for the Entire Family by Alexander D. Marini (Noble Books) [$21.95] is a comprehensive physical education program ideal for Christian home schoolers. In three brief, but crucial, chapters at the beginning of the book, Marini outlines the Biblical basis for physical education, goals, and a "philosophy of games." He tells us that the "focal point must be the maintenance and refreshment of God's temple [our bodies], keeping fun, competition, and sports in their proper place." While acknowledging the usefulness of recreational games and sports, Marini cautions against striving to win at someone else's expense and the dangers of involvement in competitive sport teams. Marini has done the best job I have seen of presenting a Biblical position concerning sports participation. His bottom line is that non-competitive or very mildly competitive games are acceptable as long as everyone participates and enjoys it, the tone remains uplifting, friendly, and fun, and no one receives honor while others are disgraced.

Marini moves from philosophy into specifics for putting together a program that includes fitness, skills, activities, and research projects. Fitness includes flexibility, strength, and aerobic exercises. Skills include running, throwing, catching, etc., as well as developing a sports and fitness vocabulary. Activities are not limited to what we typically think of as P.E. activities but also include work activities such as lawn mowing and chopping wood. Research projects are optional, but we might include studies on the human body or other related topics as part of our program as Marini describes.

For each area, Marini spells out the details with both words and illustrations. We can use the basic flexibility, strength, and aerobic activities, developing a program for each family member in keeping with their personal development. We can choose skill activities according to what is most practical for the season and available equipment and facilities, perhaps spending a few weeks each on a number of different skills throughout the year. *We Win* includes twenty, detailed Skill Units for basic ball skills, basketball, chase games, football, field/gym day, frisbee, volleyball, swimming, and more. The equipment needed is fairly minimal considering the range of activities. Since the emphasis is on skills, we don't even have to have access to basketball courts, baseball diamonds, and volleyball nets to learn the skills. Marini sometimes suggests ways to construct our own equipment, even describing how we can construct a homemade swimming pool with filter for about $250.

Reproducible organizing and planning charts are included along with instructions so that we can create a fitness plan for the entire school year. *We Win* is thorough, easy-to-use, and practical for even the most inexperienced, out-of-shape home schooling parent.

We all know our children need physical education, but

sometimes we don't quite know how to begin. Dr. Bruce Whitney, a professional physical education teacher with experience with all age levels and also a homeschooling father of eight children, has put together an excellent program we can do at home without a lot of expensive equipment called *Home School Family Fitness: A Complete Curriculum Guide* [$18.75] (Home School Family Fitness Institute). This 9" x 11" paperback has a spiral wire binding to lie flat when it is open, and it contains lesson plans, exercise instructions, fitness tests, reproducible lab sheets for specific sport skills, record keeping charts, games, and a special section on anatomy with tests included. The lesson plans, which cover body movement fundamentals, ball skills, rhythm and dance, tumbling and gymnastics, and swimming, are designed for grades K-12. Children playing on competitive sports teams will benefit from the exercises to prevent shoulder and knee injuries. The games include indoor, outdoor, and even snow games suitable for small or large groups. Even though there are so many activities to try, we do not have to be overwhelmed; we are instructed to start with the muscle strengthening program first and then add other activities gradually. A 40-week lesson plan guide makes it easy to figure out what to do when. Best of all, Dr. Whitney shows us how we can strengthen our families as well as our bodies by having some active fun together. [V. Thorpe]

○○○○○○○○○○○

It might be more difficult for us to involve our children in physical education if we are not physically active ourselves. Our children's needs might be just the incentive we need to get into shape. If that is not enough motivation, we should look for an active home schooling family to work with or enroll our children in sports activities.

Chapter 18

Foreign Language

There are two schools of thought on teaching foreign language: one advocates a conversational approach without technical grammar instruction, while the other does the opposite—concentrating on technical grammar and placing conversational ability in a secondary position. We find programs representing both schools of thought and many that combine both.

Neither approach is, in itself, wrong. It depends upon the age of the student and the goal. For young children, we may wish to only introduce them to the language. Early elementary students usually lack knowledge of English grammar, and it is difficult to convey grammatical concepts about a foreign language without the grammatical vocabulary. Thus, we often choose conversation-based programs rather than grammatical ones for children in elementary grades.

While many of us would like to expose our children to a foreign language, this can be difficult if we have no background in the language we wish to teach. For serious grammatical language study, it is best to have a tutor or another person whom we can consult. If we prefer to take a lighter approach, there are numerous materials that can assist us whether or not we have any prior knowledge. My reviews and recommendations reflect my familiarity with Latin and Spanish, so check other sources for more comprehensive reviews of resources for other languages.

Spanish/French/German/Russian/ Etc.

Note: materials that focus exclusively on one of the major languages are listed under those specific language headings (e.g., Latin, Spanish) following this section.

Audio-Forum ◯

Audio-Forum offers *Storybridges to Spanish for Children* [$29.95 each]—popular stories such as *Little Red Riding Hood*, told with a mixture of English and Spanish, to work on beginning Spanish vocabulary. *Storybridges* is now also available in French and German versions. The stories are very professionally performed and taped. Each set has three cassettes with six stories altogether. This is very introductory material.

Audio-Forum also publishes *Phrase-A-Day French* and *Phrase-A-Day Spanish for Young Children*, audio-cassette/coloring book sets for introducing these languages [$24.95 each]. Each set consists of two audio cassettes plus an activity/color-

ing book. Children learn everyday expressions by listening and coloring. The illustrations, vocabulary, and activities are organized by seasons of the year. All voices on the tapes are native speakers, accompanied by original music and sound effects. It provides practice in writing, reading, comprehension, and communication skills.

Phrase-A-Day French for the Macintosh is a computer version of the original *Phrase-A-Day*, appropriate for children ages 5-12. The entire program consists of 28 diskettes and a 24-page booklet. This is also broken down into 4 sections that can be purchased individually. Call for price and system requirements.

Among other Audio-Forum materials for children are *Monopoly* in Spanish and *Scrabble* in Spanish and French [$39.95 each], *Teach Me Japanese, Teach Me Russian,* flash cards with cassettes, videos, foreign language folk songs and much more. Send for their free catalog to see the full range of materials they offer.(S)

Calliope Books

Calliope's catalog features only foreign language materials. Owner Danna Faturos, who is multilingual and loves languages, has carefully selected resources for all the major languages plus many others. (Ever thought about learning Gujarati, Punjabi, or Quecha?) The catalog includes basic and supplemental materials (e.g., grammar guides, games, tapes, videos) but not resources in both categories for all languages. Many imported books in the various languages, from child to adult levels (e.g., *Winnie the Pooh* in German!), offer a fun method of developing language skill.

Hear An' Tell Adventures ◯

prices shown are for complete sets; components are also available individually

Hear An' Tell Adventures offers Biblically-based bilingual story tapes with accompanying readers, flashcards, teaching manuals, and games. They are easy to use and no prior foreign language experience is required. Stories are *Goldilocks, Noah's Ark , Little Lamb , Cinderella* (no magic in this version) [these first four are $19 each], and *Simon, James, and John* [$24]. All are available in English/Spanish, and *Cinderella* is also available in English/French. For Spanish, you might use them in the following order: first, *Goldilocks*; second, *Little Lamb*; third, *Simon, James, and John*; with *Noah* and *ABC's* used as supplements. Older students can skip *Goldilocks* and start with any other story. Teaching manuals tell how to adapt lessons for the various ages. *Simon, James, and John* comes with a full workbook appropriate for third grade and above.

The *ABC's of Spanish* [$25] differs from the other items. It is two hours of Bible-based audio cassette which begins with the phonetic alphabet in Spanish. It continues with lessons presented in both English and Spanish, phrase by phrase. This is followed by Spanish only. All of this is recorded against classical music backgrounds. Simple reading lessons are also presented in the accompanying book in both English and Spanish. The book also has coloring pages for each sound of the Spanish alphabet. While these materials do not form a complete program, they are good introductory materials as well as useful supplements to any Spanish language study for preschool through elementary grades.

The Learnables-French, German, Hebrew, Spanish, Japanese, Russian, Chinese, or English

(The Learnables Foreign Language Courses)

(for most languages) Level 1 - one book with five tapes - $45; Basic Structures 1 - $45 Level 1 and Basic Structures 1 package - $85

The Learnables features an unusual approach that uses picture books (no text with the pictures) and cassettes to build up vocabulary and learn sentence structure from repeated usage. The methodology is to develop understanding and comprehension first, then follow with reading, speaking, and writing skills in that order. The same books are used with each language. For beginners, start with Level 1 which includes a book with five audio cassette tapes. Tapes begin with words and short phrases whose meaning is obvious from the pictures. Translation is not given. If the student is in doubt, repetition of a word in another picture will likely clear things up. Sentences become more complex as do the pictures. This approach is certainly more enjoyable than typical programs of either the textbook variety or the records that have us simply repeat the foreign language phrases after the speaker. The learner must think about what is happening in the pictures to understand the meaning.

The program is set up with four levels for most languages. Each level follows a similar plan, although the other three levels have five to six cassette tapes each.

Spanish students also have available to them a fifth level as well as specialized vocabulary books on eating, transportation, walking, and placement. German students can continue with

Levels 5, 6, 7, and 8, or they might work through any of eight specialized vocabulary study books.

If you use only the basic sets, students do not develop the ability to read or write the language since they are not exposed to the written form. However, the *Basic Structures* programs fill the gap nicely.

Basic Structures programs are designed as companions for each level. Thus far, *Basic Structures* is available in Spanish and German for three levels, French for two levels, and Russian and Hebrew for one level.

Basic Structures, Book 1, has four audio cassette tapes. It provides reading material as well as written exercises. The audio tapes are essential. This provides experience with the written language that is missing from the basic course.

Grammar is not taught directly within the basic program, but students acquire grammatical knowledge from actually using the language. At elementary levels this does not present a problem as it would for high school where formal grammar is often required.

Recognizing this problem, International Linguistics is developing *Grammar Enhancement* programs, with Spanish and German available at this time. Each *Grammar Enhancement* set includes a book and either five audio cassettes or four CDs [$55 and $59 respectively]. These are designed to be used after completion of Level 2. *Grammar Enhancements* give extra practice and examples of the proper use of prepositions, plurals, pronouns and the present continuative and simple past tense of verbs. The book contains the words from the tapes as well as pictures, but no instruction is given in English and no grammar rules are provided. Instead, many examples are given so students learn the sometimes subtle distinctions as they look for patterns and listen to the correct usage. This method may be more effective for some students than the traditional instruction about grammar rules and their many exceptions as it is similar to the way we originally learned our own language.

Pricing for different languages at different levels is complex, but a pricing chart is included in International Linguistics' brochure.(S)[V. Thorpe/C.D.]

Lingua Fun! Language Learning Card Games
(Penton Overseas, Inc.)
$12.95 each

Lingua Fun! "Family Series" is available in Spanish, French, German, Italian, and English (for Spanish speakers). It includes a 45-minute audio tape with native speakers pronouncing words and sentences used in the game. These are presented in alternating Spanish and English with response time allowed. *Lingua Fun!* also comes with a card deck and instruction book. The 54-card deck features numbers on one end, words or phrases on the other (both in the foreign language), with English translations in small print. Instructions for six different card games focus on different skill levels as well as on either the numbers or the words. Some of the games require students to compose complete sentences from the cards. A color-coding system on the cards helps cue students as to how to do this. This is a great tool for building basic conversational vocabulary.(S)

Listen and Learn a Language: Spanish, German, Italian, or French 🎧

(Twin Sisters Productions)
$9.98 each

Introduce your children of all ages to Spanish, French, Italian, or German words and phrases with tape and book combinations. Songs are professionally performed with high-quality recordings that appeal to all, and especially meet the needs of auditory learners. The 24-page books that come with each cassette contain the words to each song, accompanied by illustrations to enhance memory. Songs cover the alphabet (names of the letters in Spanish, Italian, etc.), counting from 1 to 20, days of the week, names of animals, food and eating, families, the ocean, and weather. A few more relationship-oriented songs (e.g., friendship) round out each collection. Side 1 of each tape is recorded for the English speaking person, while side 2 is for the foreign language speaker who wishes to learn English. English speakers should tackle side 2 after mastering side 1 to see how well they can understand and interpret it.(S)

Logos Language Institute 🎧

Introductory Courses - $15 each; Spanish course regular price is $19 per level; homeschoolers get a 10% discount

Logos Language Institute Introductory Courses are in 21 languages. The Logos goal is to help equip people with basic conversational skills needed for evangelism. The Introductory Courses skip the grammar and teach common phrases by using a book and a cassette tape. Tapes are of high quality with male and female speakers alternating in saying phrases for the student to repeat, first slowly, then more quickly. Younger students could begin with the Introductory Courses.

Spanish is also available from Logos in a five level, in-depth course. This is an excellent Spanish course whether or not students are bound for the mission field. A tape and book are provided for each level. Spanish language grammar is taught. (A basic understanding of English grammar would be prerequisite to using the in-depth course. The level one book includes a brief review of English grammar.) Some written exercises are included in the book, but learning takes place primarily through speaking the language rather than by translating. Students should probably be <u>at least</u> fourth or fifth grade to begin the in-depth course.

Lyric Language 🎧▭

(Penton Overseas, Inc.)
audio tapes - $9.95 each; videos - $14.95 each; combination sets - $19.95 each

The *Lyric Language* series features audio and video tapes introducing foreign language vocabulary through songs. Vocabulary centers around topics such as the zoo, the beach, the supermarket, birthdays, rain, the seasons, days of the week, and the alphabet. Ten to eleven lively songs are accompanied by a full-color booklet with lyrics and *Family Circus* cartoon illustrations. French, German, Italian, Japanese, Spanish, and Swedish audio tapes are available, each of which is 35 minutes in length. Videos running 35 to 40 minutes use live action to illustrate the songs. Videos are available in French, German, Italian, Japanese, and Spanish. Advanced level audio and video tapes are offered for French, German, Italian, and Spanish. Combination sets, called *Double Play*, at both beginning and advanced levels are available in the above four languages. These include one audio and one video tape and the booklet. The combination sets are the best buy since they give us three different means of introducing and practicing the vocabulary for real multi-sensory effectiveness.(S)

The Rosetta Stone [CD-ROM computer programs] 🖥

(Fairfield Language Technologies)
$195 per level for each language

Are you looking for a language program that will help your student understand the spoken words as well as the written ones? Do you want your child to learn a language that you do not know? These CD-ROMs are similar to *The Learnables* audio tapes in methodology but are more interactive and give students more options.

First you look at four photos or drawings and listen to words by native speakers that are illustrated by the pictures. Listen to the sequence over and over, or choose a particular photo and hear the words as many times as you wish. You also have the option of having the words appear on the screen if you are one of those who need to see a word in order to hear it correctly. After you go through the ten preview screens of the lesson, pick the style of exercise that is most helpful to you. Hear a word and click on the correct picture, or see a picture and choose the correct word. Especially for languages that look very different, such as Arabic or Chinese, it would be helpful to use the exercises that give you a chance to try matching the sound of the word to its printed form. You can repeat a lesson as often as like, test yourself and keep a record of your progress. If you have a microphone with your computer, you can even evaluate your pronunciation.

The photos are multicultural to be appealing to all types of students, and some even include very short video segments to clarify what is happening (such as showing the difference between tying and untying shoes).

The foreign languages that are available in two levels are: German, Dutch, Spanish, Portuguese, French, Italian, Russian, Japanese and Mandarin Chinese. The first level is also available in Latin, Polish, Welsh, Arabic, Hebrew, Thai ,Vietnamese, Korean, Indonesian and Swahili. There are also English programs in U.S. and U.K. versions.

Those who want a more traditional program with writing practice can order workbooks for the German, Spanish, French and English programs. Currently there are study guides for the first level of those languages, with notes on grammar and usage. (You should plan to use these only with older children.) A quiz book is also available for Spanish.

Programs are recommended for ages 8 and up. The programs run on Windows 3.1 or higher, or Windows NT 4.0 or higher (both require a Pentium system and microphone for speech recognition), or Mac OS 7.0 or higher systems. Rosetta Stone has a free on-line demo, or you can purchase a demo CD for $4.95.(S)

Teach Me Tapes ⌒
$13.95

Available in Spanish, French, Japanese, Russian, Hebrew, Italian, Chinese, German, and English, *Teach Me* tapes are a means of introducing children to foreign languages. An audio cassette has professionally recorded children's songs in whichever language you purchased. A 20-page coloring book provides children with activities related to the songs. English translations are included.

Step up a to a little higher level with *Teach Me More* tapes [$13.95], geared for slightly older children. These are available for Spanish, French, German, Italian, Japanese, Russian, Chinese, or English. Again there is a tape of children's songs and a coloring book, but it moves beyond the introductory level into everyday phrases children can say. The *Teach Me Even More* [$13.95] series for Spanish and French follows the same format, working at a yet higher level. Other options are the *Teach Me French* and *Teach Me Spanish* "Gift Sets" which include an ABC coloring poster for $14.95 each.

All of the above are also available in CD version for $15.95 each.

Optional Teacher's Guides [$6.95] for all series offer additional learning activities and vocabulary. Songbooks for French, Spanish, and English [$7.95] are also available, showing piano accompaniment, chord symbols, and lyrics printed in both the foreign language and English. This is still introductory language study but useful with children as a precursor to more comprehensive instruction in foreign language.

French

Beginning French I and II ⌒
(Calvert School)
cost depends on enrollment option selected. Basic tuition for a single child is $95 for Level I and $95 for Level II.

Like all Calvert courses, these come with everything we need: five audio cassette tapes; teacher's manual with lesson plans and tape script; and student workbook with flashcards, games, worksheets, and tests. Level II includes books for children written in French. There are 96 lessons per course, which should take 32 weeks with three lessons per week. The courses are conversationally rather than grammatically oriented. They are recommended for students fourth grade and higher. Parents can teach the courses without a knowledge of French, but they might wish to pay the extra $70 for the Advisory Teacher Service.(S)

Greek

Since I have not studied Greek, I must rely on the recommendations of those who have. Check out Trivium Pursuit's catalog for classical language materials, including Greek. One Greek program comes highly recommended for use at all levels.

Basic Greek in 30 Minutes a Day
by Jim Found
(Bethany House)
$15.99

Because this book relies heavily on cognates (words that sound very similar to familiar English words), learning is simplified. A parent with no background in Greek should be able to use this book to teach a child (or learn Greek for him or herself.)

Hey, Andrew!! Teach Me Some Greek!
by Karen Mohs
(Greek 'n' Stuff)
Reader - $9.95; book and full answer key for each level: Level One - $12.95 each, Level Two -$15.95 each, Level Three - $18.95 each; Level Four - $18.95 each; Level Five or Six - $20.95 each; abbreviated answer keys - $3 per level; flashcards - Levels One or Two - $4 each; Level Three - $6; Levels Four, Five, or Six - $8; Pronunciation Tapes - $6 each; quiz and exam packets for each level - $4.50 each

Four-year old Andrew, pictured throughout the Reader, introduces children to the Greek alphabet, small letters only. A two-page spread teaches the shape and sound of each letter.

For example, delta is introduced with the rhyme,

An EIGHT that is broken,

you say?

Almost right!

Our friend

the

DELTA

is a funny sight!

The letter is shown with arrows for directionality in forming it, and we are told that "It sounds like 'd' in dog." Once all of the letters have been taught, children are introduced to three Greek words. A letter name and pronunciation key are at the back of this book as well as at the back of each succeeding volume for quick reference.

Level One can be used along with the Reader or, especially with older children, by itself as the starting point. It, too, introduces the letters, sounds, and their formation, but this time adding blank lines for students to actually practice writing. Learning is also expanded with workbook pages for identifying sounds and letter names, plus the use of flashcards (which are either purchased in pre-made sets or fashioned by cutting-and-pasting the flash card pages at the back of the book). A number of Greek words are introduced throughout the book and in a few lessons after individual letters have been taught. The exercises are similar to those found in primary grade (grades 1-3) phonics or language books, so they might seem too young for older students. If so, begin an older student at the next level.

Level Two again reviews all of the letters, this time teaching (or reviewing) two letters per page in keeping with the abilities of older students. By page 37 (out of 162 pages), students are learning words through a variety of exercises. Again, they work with flashcard recognition for both letters and words. (Vocabulary words are repeated and reviewed from book to book except for a few words used for letter or word recognition.)

Level Three condenses presentation of letters and sounds to 10 pages, then concentrates on vocabulary for the remaining 187 pages. While the earlier levels basically use a memorization and drill approach, this level begins to introduce some grammar. Since it is designed for early- to mid- elementary grades it does not assume that students have even learned English grammar. For example, simple verb conjugations are introduced, but without any labels referring to person, number, or tense. By the end of the book, students are translating sentences in their workbooks. At the back of the book are an alphabet chart, glossary, declension charts for second declension masculine and neuter nouns, a conjugation chart for present active indicative verbs, and flash card pages.

Level Four begins with a review of the alphabet (6 pages), vocabulary (10 pages), and Greek grammatical principles (16 pages, now with English grammatical terminology introduced.) The Greek article is taught in all three persons and both numbers. Short and long vowels, diphthongs, breathings, iota subscripts, and syllable names and length are introduced in preparation for the general rules of Greek accent, followed by the special rules for noun and verb accent. Word order and punctuation are discussed. All four feminine declensions are presented. Additional vocabulary is interspersed throughout this 170 page workbook, again with varied activities and sentence translation practice. At the back of the book are Greek-English and English-Greek glossaries, 32 flash card pages, Flash Card Tips, and charts for the alphabet, articles, conjugations, declensions and accent rules.

Levels five and six continue to work on advanced concepts, but most students will not be ready for these before junior high.

Answer keys are separate for each level and are available in two formats: one is a complete student book with answers while the other is answers only. The Reader is not consumable, and one book can be shared by the family, but workbooks for other levels are consumable and we need one for each student.

Quiz and test packets are available for each level. Also, *Flashcards on a Ring* are available for each level. These will save a good deal of preparation time since they are cut and pre-punched. They also come with a heavy-duty metal ring to keep them together. Prices reflect the number of flashcards per set. *Pronunciation Tapes* are now available which present pronunciations of the vocabulary words, covering two levels per tape.

As you might expect, this is a Christian program; the first sentence introduced is, "The Lord is my helper." Because it is designed to be used primarily with younger children, it is slow in introducing any grammar, but integration of grammar increases at the higher levels. Overall, this is an easy-to-use program for parents who have no background in Greek. We should be able to use the books with children spanning a number of grade levels. Children beyond third grade level should still begin at Level One or Two, but they should move through those books much more quickly than younger siblings.

Hebrew

Hebrew World [CD-ROM computer program]
created by Living Israeli Hebrew
(Bridgestone Multimedia Group)
$59.95

Beginning students who want to learn to read and write Hebrew will find this friendly interactive program on CD-ROM to be quite helpful. You begin by learning all the Hebrew letters and then testing yourself. After you become familiar with the vowels, you start practicing reading words of a single syllable and then move up to more advanced words. Tips and simplified rules help make sense of things. When you are ready to try sentences, you can read (and hear) selections from the first 12 chapters of Genesis. Many of the pages can be printed out for study which is handy because you can print off as many writing worksheets as you need. Writing is presented in both block letter form and in cursive. The program also teaches numbers and the calendar as used in Israel. Instruction is in English and the Hebrew pronunciation is that most commonly used in Israel today.

Lists of greetings, commands and other pieces of conversation are given to be listened to, but they are not all presented with pictures that show their context and so are not as easily learned as with immersion programs. It might be ideal to use this program along with an immersion program such as the one from *The Rosetta Stone* by Fairfield Language Technologies if you want to be able to speak modern Hebrew as well as read and write. But if you are mainly interested in studying Hebrew to enhance your study of the Bible, this program can be used on its own as it has a lot of useful information for the beginner. There are lists of names in Hebrew that will teach you how some of those Biblical names were pronounced, but since there is no English equivalent given, some are a little hard to identify. Also they are alphabetized in Hebrew, so you had better know your Hebrew alphabet if you want to look something up. Very interesting for motivated students of all ages. This program runs on Windows 95 or higher with a sound card or Macintosh 7.0 or higher systems.[V.T.]

Latin

Artes Latinae

(Bolchazy-Carducci)
Level I package - $314; Phase I package - $103 (prices include postage)

This is a programmed Latin course for independent learning. It includes texts, readers, reference notebooks, teacher's manuals, test booklets, cassettes, and optional audio-visual materials. Students first become familiar with pronunciation and the sound of the language in sentences. Later they look at sentence elements and develop vocabulary. It does teach Latin grammar but in an unusual way. I have some concern about the methodology. For instance, in Book One, before nominative and accusative cases are named, students are told to identify subjects and objects by endings of *s* or *m*—a fact which will not hold true with plurals and other declensions. Later on, the proper terms and other endings are introduced, but I personally find this confusing. Proper grammar is taught as the program progresses but on a need to know basis. Perhaps this approach is good for younger children who often lack the English grammatical background to fully understand Latin grammar. The program moves slowly (at least through the first half of Book One) with much repetition, although students can zoom ahead through this at whatever rate is comfortable for them. Coordinating the teacher's manual and other materials with the textbook is also quite confusing, but we really do need all the extras except the audio-visual materials which are rec-

ommended but not essential.

My opinion has been influenced by our experience using it with one of our children, which certainly is limited exposure. Many knowledgeable people do not share my misgivings about *Artes Latinae*. I have also solicited reactions from a number of people using the program. The majority of them are pleased with the program, so I feel it is important to balance my misgivings with the fact that I seem to be in the minority.

Components of the program for Level I are two student texts, a Unit Test Booklet, Graded Reader, Reference Notebook, Teacher's Manual (which covers both student texts), teacher edition of the Graded Reader, Teacher Guide for Unit Tests, two filmstrip sets (five filmstrips in each), and 15 audio drill cassettes. We can purchase the entire Level I or only the essentials for the first part of the course which are packaged as Phase I. The Level II package is $303 and Phase 1 of Level II is $112.

Artes Latinae is also available on CD-ROM for IBM compatible computers. [Level I - $276; Level II - $287] The CD-ROM package for each level includes disks, readers, reference notebooks, manuals, and test booklets.(S)

Ecce Romani

(ScottForesman-Addison Wesley)
Note: Ordering numbers follow items and must be used to place orders or obtain information.

This lavishly-illustrated, full-color Latin course is one of the few suitable for intermediate students. It is not as challenging as some other high school courses, yet it is quite comprehensive—equivalent to two and a half years of Latin. It should work with bright fifth or sixth graders, junior high, and high school students. Rather than stories of Caesar's wars, the story of an upper class Roman family is carried through the series. Cultural tidbits also make the text interesting.

You might want to get all the components: student's text or texts, Teacher's Guide, Language Activity Book, and accompanying Activity Book Teacher's Edition for each level. The text assumes the teacher's familiarity with Latin but not to the extent of most other programs. The Teacher's Guide is easy to read and very helpful. It has translations of readings, answers to exercises, teaching instructions, plus explanations of cultural resource materials, unusual constructions, and new concepts. The Teacher's Edition for the Language Activity Book is essentially a student edition with answers. The student text contains both a Latin-English glossary and an English-Latin glossary.

Student texts are available in two different formats: paperback and hardbound. Paperback versions are divided into five student books (all ISBN numbers begin with 0-8013; the last 5 digits of each ISBN are shown for each book): Level IA,#1204-3; IB, #1205-1; IIA, #1206-X; IIB, #1207-8; and III, #1208-6 [$15.30 each]. IA and IB are equivalent to a high school Latin I course, so they should be spread out over two years for most younger students. IIA and IIB are equivalent to Latin II, and III is equivalent to a semester of Latin III. The hardcover editions are contained within only three books reflecting the three years: I, #1201-9; II, #1202-7; and III, #1203-5 [$41.34 for I and II and $32.07 for III]. The same teacher's guides are used with either version, and they are contained in three books for the three years: I, #1217-5 [$40.56]; II, #1218-3 [$40.56]; and III, #1219-1 [$15.48]. There are four Language Activity Books, two each for the first two years, but none for the third. They are IA, #1209-4; IB, #1210-8; IIA, #1211-6; and IIB, #1212-4 [$5.94 each]. Separate teacher's guides for the activity books are required: IA, #1213-2; IB, #1214-0; IIA, #1215-9; and IIB,#1216-7 [$15.18 each]. Test masters for each of the first two levels are $15 each [#1220-5 and 1221-3].

Two other simple Latin readers, *The Romans Speak for Themselves* (2 volumes), can also be used for supplemental readings to accompany the cultural topics in *Ecce Romani*. Send for their catalog for more complete information.(S)

Latin Grammar Book 1

by Douglas Wilson and Karen Craig
(Canon Press)
$20; solutions manual - $8

Wilson has written a traditional Latin program especially for Christian private and home school students in grades six and above. It consists of a worktext designed for independent study and an answer key. The worktext provides instruction and exercises in a straightforward manner. There are no tests and no classroom busywork. It is assumed that the student already has a basic knowledge of English grammar, but brief review is included. Lessons have students translate from Latin into English and the reverse, review pronunciation and grammar, and practice conjugation and declension memorization chants. The teaching method is traditional/grammatically-based rather than conversational. In Book 1, students study through the fourth conjugation verbs (six tenses each), through fifth declension nouns, through third declension adjectives, and through pronouns. A Latin to English glossary is included at the back of the book. I recommend that students get a Latin-English/English-Latin dictionary for easier reference, particularly if they intend to continue study beyond this book. The course requires a significant amount of study and memorization, but the reward is improved knowledge of English grammar, expanded vocabulary, and the world of learning open to those who know Latin. Since the books are paperback and more condensed than classroom-designed material, the cost is much less than for other programs.

Canon Press's Latin Primer series provides an excellent foundation for students before beginning this course. However, the second edition was revised to add more review of the

basics so that older students can comfortably use this for their first Latin course.

Latin Primer I, II, and III

by Martha Wilson
(Canon Press)
Books I and II: student editions - $15 each; teacher's editions - $15 each; Book III - student edition - $18; teacher edition - $18; audio cassette - $3; test and quiz book for Book I - $10

Third graders can begin their study of Latin with the *Latin Primer I*, although some of us might want to wait until fourth or fifth grade to tackle this. In the first year they learn pronunciation (slightly simplified), a vocabulary of about 350 words, how to recognize many Latin derivatives in English, how to use the dictionary for etymology, declensions of the first and second declension nouns, conjugations of the first and second conjugations verbs, simple translation work, and more. Biblical quotes and language are included, reflecting the author's Christian world view. Daily oral chants help children memorize the conjugations and declensions, although they are not expected to understand all of the grammar at this stage. Nevertheless, the program is challenging. For example, on the first test students translate more than 30 Latin words into English, translate English words into Latin, give English derivatives for three Latin words, translate a dozen Latin verbs into English (including person and number), and translate four Latin phrases. The *Latin Pronunciation Aid* audio cassette is an optional tool that provides pronunciations for all vocabulary as well as the chants in *Primer I*. This is a traditional approach to learning with memorization and drill, but it is balanced a little with some suggestions for games. Even though it requires some hard work by students, many of them will be motivated by the growth in their vocabulary and knowledge of the English language as well as by the prestige of tackling Latin at an early age.

The teacher's edition is essential. It has grammatical information, word lists, weekly lesson outlines, tests, and answer key. The first half of the student book is the "textbook," and the second half is weekly worksheets, crossword puzzles, and "Chant Charts." Student books are not reproducible, so we need to purchase one for each student. Lessons should take minimal preparation time but need to be presented and practiced with students. It seems to me that daily lessons should take ten minutes or less most days, with students then taking additional time during the week to complete the weekly worksheet. (Even though students will learn a great deal in the *Latin Primer*, it will not substitute for a year one of a high school Latin course.)

Latin Primer II builds upon the lessons from the first Primer. Students should be working at fourth grade level or above to tackle this level. It covers nouns through the fifth declension, verb tenses and voice, with translations of words and sentences from Latin to English. Book III is suggested for fifth grade. It continues to cover more grammar and vocabulary. Students should be able to move easily from this book into Wilson's *Latin Grammar*.

Logos School has produced a series of three video tapes for the *Latin Primer I* that can replace the teacher's edition. Teacher Julie Garfield presents the lessons, expanding beyond explanations in the teacher's edition. Students watch the videos, reciting chants and stopping to complete written exercises as directed. Logos packages the three videos, a textbook, and a homeschool teachers packet of quizzes, tests, and instructions for $75. Tapes alone are $55 for the set. ▭

The Latin Road to English Grammar, Volumes I-III
by Barbara Beers
(Schola Publications)
Complete Curriculum Set for each level - $129; extra textbook - $24; replacement set of worksheets/tests - $9.95; set of two Verb Tense Posters - $19.95

Forget direct comparisons to other Latin programs; this one is really different. It combines instruction in English grammar with Latin, eliminating the need to use anything else for those subjects except resources covering punctuation and capitalization. The author states that students as young as fourth grade level have successfully worked through Volume I, although it will be more appropriate for most students who are at fifth grade level or beyond. Volumes II and III gradually increase in difficulty. They might be completed by students up through junior and senior high levels.

Some of Barbara Beers' experience comes from teaching *The Writing Road to Reading*, so we find that methodology repeated as children compile their own notebooks of everything they are learning. They create ten sections in their binders for vocabulary, pronunciation, definitions, grammar, cases/declensions, conjugations, text work (answers to text questions/exercises), work sheets, word study, and tests. Even though information is presented in the student text, children record it in their notebooks to enhance learning and provide a ready-reference tool.

My caution against most fourth graders doing this program relates to the speed at which new concepts are introduced. I suspect it comes too fast and furious for young learners. For example, in Chapter 1 children briefly review the eight principal parts of speech (nine if you separate articles from adjectives). In the next day's lesson they are working with syntax, covering subjects, predicates, direct and indirect objects, linking verbs, predicate adjectives, and predicate nominatives. Latin syntax structures are presented immediately following the English syntax. While much of this is introduced superficially—as material for a child to copy into his notebook for

now—it accumulates quickly, and a certain amount of understanding is necessary to make sense of so much data. I think most students will be more successful in this program if they have already studied basic grammar at fourth grade level or higher. There are plans for 140 daily lessons. If we take extra time where needed, it will definitely take a year to get through Volume I.

English grammar is usually taught simultaneously with the Latin as structural similarities are noted. This method is very efficient. It is also a positive motivator for children to see that this grammar knowledge does serve an immediate purpose. Coverage of English grammar in Volume I includes parts of speech, syntax, gender, number, voice, mood, tense, person, principle parts of verbs (stressed more in Latin than in English), types of sentences, prefixes, adjective/noun agreement, and subject/verb agreement. Latin instruction encompasses all of the above plus case, stems, distinctions in ablative case usage, enclitics, and word particles while teaching through the second declension nouns and first conjugation verbs (six tenses). Volume II begins with a review of Volume I, then moves on into more challenging material, tackling second and third conjugation verbs and third declension nouns. Volume III covers much more vocabulary than do the other two volumes and tackles up through fifth declension nouns and fourth conjugation verbs. All three volumes together provide a Latin course equivalent to two years of standard high school courses, so the progression on Latin is slower here (appropriately so if we are teaching pre-high school students). When coupled with the in-depth coverage of English grammar, the program is moving at a pace that should be appropriate for most students, but possibly too quick for some.

The program for each level comes as a Curriculum Set with additional textbooks, worksheets, and tests available separately. The set includes the teacher's binder, an audio cassette tape, flash cards, and a student textbook. The teacher's binder has daily lesson plans and teaching directions, section separators for the teacher to construct her own notebook similar to the students', answer keys, charts to be used with lesson presentation (and posted for reference), and reproducible tests and a map. On the audio cassettes that come with each level, Barbara pronounces the Latin sounds and words pertinent to the various lessons. (The pronunciation method she has chosen differs from that of all the other Latin resources I have examined. She is using what she describes as Church Latin or Italian pronunciation.) The flash cards are printed on heavy card stock, and they are color coded to identify parts of speech as well as gender of nouns. (These cards are great for drilling declension and conjugation endings as well as vocabulary.) Latin/English and English/Latin glossaries are found in each text.

The first half of the student book is the text which has instruction and exercises. (No writing in the book in this section.) Reading practice material in Latin such as The Lord's

Prayer, the Pledge of Allegiance, and the song, "O come All Ye Faithful," is incorporated into the first level student text, while it shifts to incorporate readings/translations from the Bible and historical sources in Volumes II and III. Perforated, tear-out worksheets comprise the last half of the book. We can reuse the text part of a student book, purchasing only replacement worksheets for subsequent students to save money.

The program is designed to be taught rather than used for independent study. Some lesson preparation is necessary, especially the compilation of the teacher's own notebook. According to the author, those without Latin background can teach this course, but I suspect that those without a solid English grammar background might have difficulty. Parents who have an adequate grammar background as well as the time to teach this course properly should find it an excellent tool for building a thorough, solid foundation in both English grammar and Latin.

Latina Christiana, 1998 editions

by Cheryl Lowe
(Memoria Press)
Books I and II - student books - $15 each; teacher's manuals - $20 each; tape - $5; set of student book, teacher's manual and tape - $35

Cheryl Lowe sees Latin as the ideal foundation for education for grades 3 through 8, building on ideas from Dorothy Sayers and others for teaching a classical education. Ideally, Latin study replaces some English language study (particularly grammar and vocabulary) through these years. It also serves as the focus for unit studies for history and geography to a minor extent. Cheryl explains how to integrate your studies in her teacher's manuals, correlating history questions based on *Famous Men of Rome* (from Greenleaf Press) throughout both volumes.

She advocates using *Latina Christiana*, Books I and II, for grades 3 to 5, then using a first year high school Latin text in grades 6 to 8 to complete the foundation. Students are then prepared for reading Latin literature in high school and for further language study, especially in any of the Romance languages and English itself.

Latina Christiana uses the Medieval or "Church" Latin pronunciation rather than the "Classical." Consequently, Catholicism, the primary conduit of Latin through that time period, is reflected in some of the course content such as phrases from the Catholic mass, prayers, and other more subtle influences. Still, Protestants should find nothing theologically offensive here. (The author tells me that those using the course are mostly Protestant.)

Lessons need to be taught following instructions in the teacher's manuals. Lessons are learned through repetition, memorization, and drill, but Cheryl presents a number of ideas for making this interesting: vocabulary flash cards, games (e.g. Latin "Pictionary"), songs, and an audio tape.

The student books are less intimidating than most other foreign language workbooks. Students study vocabulary words and complete exercises in their books (or on blank paper if you wish to reuse the books), then complete additional written work in a separate notebook. Students listen to the audio tape that comes with each level and complete a "Tape Exercise Form" each day.

The courses were developed with small classes of homeschoolers, so Cheryl suggests gathering a small group for class. However, the course should work well for a single student and parent.

Book I covers first and second declension noun and adjective forms, first and second conjugations and three tenses, subject/verb agreement, personal pronouns, gender, and use of the nominative case. Book II covers the third through fifth declensions, third and fourth conjugations, present and imperfect tenses, use of accusative and ablative cases, third person personal pronouns, and principal parts of selected verbs.

Note that the 1998 editions exhibit significant visual improvement over the first editions.

Latin's Not so Tough!, Levels One-Three

(Greek 'n' Stuff)
workbook and full answer key: Level One - $12.95, Level Two - $15.95, Level Three - $18.95; abbreviated answer keys - $3 each level; quiz and exam packets - $4.50 per level; flashcards: Level One - $4, Level Two - $6, Level Three - $7; pronunciation tape - $6

This program introduces Latin in the slowest progression of any of the programs I have reviewed, making it a good choice for young students. Level One is entirely focused upon pronunciation, including some of the peculiar diphthongs we find in Latin but not English. Very large print, instructions on letter formation, and workbook activities match the type activities we find in typical English language workbooks for first and second grades. Sounds are all taught in the context of English vocabulary.

Level Two introduces a beginning Latin vocabulary. It quickly reviews pronunciation, then introduces one Latin word per lesson. Students then circle matching words, fill in the blanks with word meanings, do matching exercises, and answer yes/no questions (think of these as true/false questions). While verbs are taught only in the first person singular forms (e.g., I love), all other words are presented in isolation rather than in sentences. Vocabulary is continually reviewed through subsequent lessons. Vocabulary comes from traditional course approaches teaching Latin for words such as girl, boy, earth, poet, forest, island, horse, sword, gate, love, prepare, carry, and seize. Older students could easily begin with Level Two as long as you make sure that you spend enough time on the pronunciation lessons.

Level Three begins with even briefer pronunciation review, then adds review of the vocabulary words taught in Level Two. On page 27, they start work with sentences. Accusative case words are presented with a note that endings change depending upon the use in sentences, but explanation is withheld. This book avoids grammatical vocabulary, either English (e.g., object of the verb, possessive case) or Latin. For example, when it presents the genitive case, it says, "The new ending is *ae*. It replaces the *a* at the end of words like puella to show that the farmhouse belongs to the girl." Level Three teaches first conjugation verbs and first and second declension nouns in this fashion. Paradigm charts for these are at the back of the book.

Each student book includes flashcard pages that are essential to the program. These are printed on only one side of each page. Instructions tell us to cut out both "sides" of each flashcard, then mount them on 3" x 5" cards. Alternatively, we can purchase pre-printed flashcards that come pre-punched with a hole so that they can be kept together on a ring. The flashcards cover what is taught within each book, so flashcard sets grow in size for each level.

Answer keys are either complete copies of the student book with answers overprinted or the abbreviated answers-only format. If you are drilling through the flashcards with your student and overseeing their lessons, you probably will not need the answer keys, although the significantly greater amount of written work in Level Three might be reason enough to purchase the key for that text.

Matin Latin, Books 1 and 2

by Karen Craig
(Canon Press)
Book 1: student - $25, teacher - $28;
Book 2: student - $30, teacher - $33

Ideal for students from about grades third grade and up, *Matin Latin* combines solid grammatical instruction in Latin with English grammar. In Book 1, children memorize first declension nouns and the first conjugation of verbs (three tenses only). As with a classical approach, children practice with "chants." However, learning is made easier for younger children by the use of drawings to illustrate new vocabulary words rather than word definitions. Children might be offered the choice of illustrating some of their responses or answering orally rather than writing out the words. Parents will need to determine what method is most appropriate for their children, but I suspect that drawing might become too time consuming if done for many responses. For children who are more "word-oriented," you might want to work with them to write the actual English definition under

each picture. Children do work with nouns, verbs, adjectives, and other other parts of speech to construct and read complete but simple sentences.

Book 2 continues through two more noun declensions, through the third conjugation verbs, and through third declension adjectives. The book continues to use illustrations to introduce some of the new vocabulary. It features a section of "Paradigm Summaries" with charts of declensions and conjugations for easy reference.

Both books have vocabulary dictionaries at the back for easy reference. Classical pronunciation is taught. The author uses a variety of exercises throughout both books to maintain student interest.

Some of the reading material is drawn from mythology, but there is also quite a bit of Biblical content. In Book 1, the single mythology reading is clearly presented as myth. The second volume has far more of both types of readings, so the author uses an introductory page to present her rationale for this approach.

This is serious Latin study. Even though it will work for third and fourth graders, I can easily envision both volumes being used with junior and senior high school students as a first year course, particularly those students who begin with a weak foundation in English grammar.

Teacher's Editions are identical to student books except they also have answers printed directly on the related exercise pages. No lesson preparation time is required. Parents will need to work through the lessons with younger children, but older students will be able to do much of the work independently.

Sign Language

Say It by Signing

(Audio-Forum)
$34.95

This is a course on video cassette (VHS format) for learning American sign language that can be used by learners of all ages.

Sign Language for Everyone ▭

by Cathy Rice
(Bill Rice Ranch)
$54.95 for the set; book only - $20; videos only - $39.95

Two 2-hour videos present a course that includes over 600 signs of American Sign Language. This is the only introductory signing course I know of that also teaches signs for witnessing. Many of the signs are taught with logical associations so they are easily remembered. A 170-page, hardback book comes with the videos, making it easier to review and practice what we have watched on the videos. The course is appropriate for all ages.

Spanish

Beginning Spanish I and II
(Calvert School)
Cost depends on enrollment option selected. Basic tuition for a single child is $95 for Level I and $95 for Level II.

Like all Calvert courses, these come with everything we need: five audio cassette tapes; teacher's manual with lesson plans and tape script; and student workbook with flashcards, games, worksheets, and tests. Level II includes books for children written in Spanish. There are 96 lessons per course, which should take 32 weeks with three lessons per week. The courses are conversationally rather than grammatically oriented. They are recommended for students fourth grade and higher. Parents can teach the courses without a knowledge of Spanish, but they might wish to pay the extra $70 for the Advisory Teacher Service.(S)

Learning Wrap-Ups: Spanish Intro Kit
(Learning Wrap-Ups Inc.)
$34.95

See the description under the second grade math recommendations "Review Help." The *Spanish Wrap-Ups* are a great tool to use with students in middle elementary grades and up. Many of them feature picture/word identifications to help build vocabulary. The set includes four different sets of *Wrap-Ups*, two audio tapes, and a teacher's guide. The audio tapes are a great help with pronunciation.

Spanish Made Fun
by Beverly J. North
(Spanish Made Fun)
$55

This interesting, informal introduction to Spanish is most appropriate for the middle elementary grades though usable for younger children. The approach is conversational rather than grammatical, and therefore should not be used to fulfill a high school language requirement. For example, all the verb work is in the present tense. However, after using the course a third-grader would know how to converse in a simple way with someone in Mexico.

The course consists of a teacher's manual in a three-ring binder, 5 audio cassette tapes, one testing cassette tape, directions for flashcards, reproducible pages for games, charts, a few worksheets, and test pages which double as a workbook. Each lesson has a dialogue on tape and a variety of other suggested activities, including vocabulary, directed conversations, and games. There are activities which are adaptable for pre-

readers. The emphasis is Christian, and Mrs. North shares about her experiences in missionary work in Mexico.

The author presents her information in a clear way. She explains the real usage of words, which can sometimes differ radically from the dictionary definition. The lack of grammatical information could be frustrating for someone who has no background in Spanish; however, Mrs. North provides a list of reference books which could easily supply the necessary grammar for the parent. Optional items are *Methods and Techniques for Making Language Learning Fun* (e.g. puppets, games, songs), *Tricky Words and Travel Tips* (very practical for travelers) [$2 each], *Reproducible Activity Calendar* [$5], and a *Spanish/English Storybook* with cassette [$10]. This is considered to be Course 1. Course 2 continues with more songs, drills, and worksheets [$65], and an optional song cassette with words and chords [$10].

You might compare this program with *Speedy Spanish*. There is more conversational practice and greater variety of activities here than in *Speedy Spanish*, although *Speedy Spanish* has more Scripture to memorize and praise songs.[K. Courtney]

Speedy Spanish
books - $12.95 each; tapes for Level I - $32.95, Level II tapes - $40.95; tests - $2 per level; answer key for tests - $2 per level; extra practice sheets - $6; Primer book and cassette - $19

This conversational Spanish course, written by a Christian family, can be used with all ages, although it is best suited for younger learners who need to be taught with a conversational approach.

Components are the Elementary Spanish Book and a set of four, ninety-minute cassette tapes. One book is needed for each student since many activities and exercises are done in the book. One set of tapes will do for all. I was particularly impressed by the creativity and variety of the program.

Each of the thirty-six lessons is set up to take one week of study. New vocabulary words and practice sentences are studied while listening to a cassette tape. Match-up exercises in the book have children identify Spanish and English words and phrases that mean the same thing. Children can check their own answers by listening to the tape. Bible verses and short worship and praise songs are taught in Spanish. (The songs are in the book and on the tape.)

At the end of each lesson, children practice vocabulary with a lotto-type game called Quiz-nish. Vocabulary cards are included at the back of the book, to be cut out and used for study and for Quiz-nish.

The variety of activities is bound to prove interesting to children and encourage learning. The only things lacking in this program are professional polish and grammatical instruction (although declension charts are provided). However, it is intended as an introductory course rather than a complete grammatical course. Even so, many grammatical concepts are picked up through usage. The program's authors believe that children should have fun with the language and learn to speak it correctly, then learn the whys and wherefores later when they get into more formal language study.

Speedy Spanish, Book 2 comes with five, ninety-minute cassettes. It teaches more complicated sentence structure while continuing to build vocabulary. Declension charts are provided in the back of the book, and a pronunciation chart is in the front. Development of a biblical/Christian Spanish vocabulary is stressed throughout, in lessons and songs as before. It is recommended that students obtain and read a Spanish Bible.

Extra Practice Sheets are available for both levels I and II. These provide writing practice as older students translate from English to Spanish and from Spanish to English. This is a reproducible, 30-page book that includes an answer key.

The inclusion of games, songs, and flash cards make the material appropriate for use with young children, although you might eliminate one or more of these elements with an older learner. If you want to teach young children (preschool through first grade level), you should start with the *Speedy Spanish Primer* which teaches over 1,000 words in 16 categories. This 336-page book comes with a cassette.

Chapter 19

Kids and Computers

I believe that home schooling families should have at least one computer. There's no excuse not to when old ones can be had for free. Even those on the most limited budget should be able to acquire a system that will run word processing programs and some educational programs, even if not the latest editions.

However, I am more and more convinced of the importance of computer literacy for preparing for the work world as well as for college. Computer literacy ranks with reading and writing skills in the majority of occupations that pay a living wage. Thorough knowledge of even one or two "production" programs such as *Word, Excel*, or *Access* qualifies an applicant for many jobs.

The starting place for developing computer literacy is keyboard skills. Students should learn to type properly so that they can develop adequate speed and accuracy. I do know some people who hunt and peck accurately at an acceptable rate, but they tend to be rare. So I highly recommend use of some sort of keyboarding program for beginners. *Mavis Beacon* programs, *Typing Tutor*, and *Type to Learn* are some of the more popular typing programs available. I do not recommend starting children on the computer in the first few years of school, because they need to focus on handwriting (printing and cursive) first. If they start to use the computer early on, they often are resistant to mastering handwriting skills which seem more laborious. Once they've gotten over the hump with handwriting and can write with reasonable speed, that's the time to turn them loose on they keyboard.

After basic keyboarding, the most valuable computer usage for elementary grade students is composition work. It is amazing to see how much student writing improves when the computer makes it so easy to rewrite and reorganize, while also letting children add illustrations, fancy fonts, and other formatting that makes a written piece look great. I recommend investing a good word processing program that is easy for children to use. Even the very advanced word processing programs, Word and Word Perfect, can be used by children for the basics with very little instruction. However, if they want to add graphics or get very fancy, these programs might prove too complex. A good word processing program designed for children might be a more useful. Examples of such programs are The Learning Company's *Ultimate Writing & Creativity Center* (for grades 2-5) or *Storybook Weaver Deluxe* (for grades 1-6) or *Student Writing Center* (for grades 5-12)..

Other educational programs come next. Sometimes a student hits a difficult spot with math and needs to focus on fractions, long division, or another concept beyond what the textbook provides. Or maybe a child needs a fun way to master his math facts. Or maybe mom is extremely busy and needs a computer-based phonics program. In such cases, complete or supplemental programs, even if used for only a short time, might be smart investments. *Phonics Tutor*, *Math Blaster* programs, and *Stickybear's Math Splash* are examples of such programs.

The next type programs I would consider are those that are supplemental in other subject areas, helpful for developing thinking or research skills, serve as tools for learning computer and technology skills, or in some way make learning enjoyable, make teaching easier, or otherwise contribute to home schooling. Examples might be *Oregon Trail*, the *Carmen San Diego* series, *King Arthur through the Ages*, and DK Interactive programs.

Games for computers (preferably without the word "educational" anywhere on the label) are probably at the top of most children's lists. And some of these games are so good, that parents will be just as tempted as children to while away hours with the keyboard and joystick, having fun, but accomplishing nothing that seems worthwhile. But games are not necessarily time wasters, no matter how embarrassed you might be trying to justify your own game playing to other adults who have resisted the lure of computer games. Many games require logic and analysis that transfers over to other activities. (*Minesweeper* is one such game that most people seem to have on their computers.) Some of the non-violent "adventure" games also stretch analytic and thinking skills. When it comes to games, just keep children (and yourself) to reasonable time limits.

There was a limit to how many educational programs I could review for this edition of the *Curriculum Manual*. Also, programs are updated from time to time, and this sometimes changes the nature of the program significantly. No book can be republished often enough to stay current with this ever-changing market. So it makes sense to read the magazines that keep current with such developments to get the latest scoop on many of the educational programs. *Practical Homeschooling* magazine seems to do the best job on computer software for home schoolers.

Complete Courses

Many publishers are now producing complete courses for the computer, but the nature of the computer tends to reduce learning to acquisition of facts and skillful regurgitation rather than thoughtful learning. I have been very discouraged by the programs I have reviewed that require exact answers and that cannot respond to children's creative—and, oftentimes, even better—answers.

Although some programs have links to the web (and assuming you have a connection you allow children to use), learning still is constrained by the program's ideas about what a child might be interested in. On the other hand, when a parent directs or is involved in learning, he or she can react to a child's questions or interests by directing him or her to sources that are much more likely to be useful to the child.

Such programs are often little more than glorified and expensive workbooks. However, computer programs still might be valuable in many situations. Children might be able to get more multi-sensory instruction than mom is able to provide. Audio explanations might be easier for an auditory child to grasp than reading from a book. Colorful graphics might hold a child's attention longer than a textbook. The programs that quiz and score a child's responses might help the busy mom who just cannot seem to stay on top of things.

When you are considering such programs, ask yourself why you are getting it—what needs do you expect it to fill—and whether the expense (as compared to a comparable text or workbook) is justifiable.

Do not be misled by salespeople who try to tell you that their computer learning program will do absolutely everything for you, and your child will just love it. Children can become bored with too much computer work just as with too much of anything.

Software Sources

Some of the best sources I have found for computer software are listed here:

Learning Services offers discounted educational software for IBM, Macintosh, and Apple along with computer hardware and accessories. They are selective in their offerings but still have a large selection (over 20,000 items) of quality products.(S)

The Home Computer Market specializes in computers and software for home educators. Their catalog describes hardware plus selected software programs and features a handy chart indicating which programs cover which subjects at which levels. The owners, who are also the software columnists for *Practical Homeschooling* magazine, have reviewed most of the programs on the market. From those programs they have carefully selected those that they feel are best for home educating families. Their catalog features helpful articles about selecting and using computers.

Internet Guides

The Internet for Educators and Homeschoolers
by Steve Jones
(ETC Publications)
$21.95 hc; $14.95 pb

Although titled as a guide to the internet, this book actually answers even more basic questions about computers in general. Still, the bulk of the book has to do with the internet and how home or traditional school educators can utilize it. It explains internet vocabulary, options, etiquette, and dangers, then goes on to explain different forms of learning that can take place. Computer novices should find this very useful, and those who are already on-line are still likely to learn more. Recommended site addresses are included, although listings under "Distance Education and Homeschool Resources" are sparse. I would also have liked to see some step-by-step instructions for accessing some internet tools that are described. Nevertheless, this is a helpful book for figuring out how to make your computer more educationally productive.(S)

Internet Kids & Family Yellow Pages, Third Edition
by Jean Armour Polly
(Osborne/McGraw-Hill)
$34.99

This 744-page guide covers more than 4,000, individually reviewed and selected web sites appropriate for children and families. Research teasers are sprinkled through the book—you'll find the answers on the internet if you check out the web site mentioned next to the question. Find what you're looking for with the table of contents, alphabetical list of sites, or alphabetical index. The book comes with a CD-ROM that makes it super easy to find and access sites. This third edition was published in October 1998.(SE)

Parents' Computer Companion
by Jason D. Baker
(Baker Books)
$9.99

Parents new to computers and/or the internet will appreciate Jason Baker's unassuming approach—he doesn't assume that you have any background, and he provides just enough information to get going without being overwhelmed. He also addresses homeschooling issues directly, while writing from a Christian perspective. He covers questions about purchasing computers, what is available over the internet, how to get access to the internet, "child-proofing" your computer (mechanical protection for your hardware as well as protection against pornography and other evils that inhabit the ether waves), the computer's usefulness for education, and types of programs you might want to use. He includes resource and site lists for on-line educational resources, on-line education (unfortunately, limited to accredited programs), and recommended software programs, with reviews of many of the best software programs of interest to home educators.

The Prentice Hall Directory of Online Education Resources
by Vicki Smith Bigham and George Bigham
(Prentice Hall)
$34.95

This is a much more comprehensive guide to online resources, covering 1,002 educational sites. It should spark all sorts of ideas for unit study type learning as you connect with information, people, and activities related to various topics. Virtual field trips, "visiting" museums to view famous art works, and connecting with specialists in particular fields are only a few of the suggestions. This directory is continuously updated on the web, which helps keep information current—the biggest challenge when you create this sort of book. Although not written from either a Christian or a homeschooling viewpoint, this guide should be very useful to those who want to make the most of their computers.

Useful Web Sites

I have included web sites along with addresses for many of the publishers, distributors, and other companies I mention in this Manual. But there are many web sites of interest to home-schoolers.

Some are useful for making contact with other homeschoolers and for finding and sharing information about homeschooling. Examples of such sites are:

- **www.crosswalk.com**, homeschool channel—Crosswalk is continually building content and links for their home-school site
- **www.home-school.com**—Mary Pride and *Practical Homeschooling's* site. One of the largest and best for all sorts of information
- **www.prestonspeed.com/lobby.html**—sponsored by the folks who publish the Henty books, this site is a great communication point for homeschoolers with scheduled chat sessions, bulletin boards, curriculum "store," and helpful information
- **www.discoveryschool.com**
- **www.familyeducation.com**—this site includes helps for families with children in traditional schools but it also features a significant and useful homeschooling section that is nonsectarian

Reference sources:
- **www.britannica.com** — free complete *Encyclopedia Britannica* available on line—most comprehensive, free encyclopedia available, supported by advertisers
- **www.FunkandWagnalls.com** — free encyclopedia access
- **www.studyweb.com** — links to help with all sorts of educational topics
- **www.encarta.com** — abridged version of Encarta
- **www.Encyclopedia.com** — The Concise Columbia Electronic Encyclopedia
- **www.infoplease.com** — encyclopedia, almanacs, dictionary
- **www.worldbook.com**— subscription access to *World Book* on-line
- **www.eng.usf.edu/~malave/freebies/software.html** — free electronic Bibles, Christian educational software, Christian clip art, and other goodies can be located through the site

Chapter 20
Creative Learning

You might have noticed that I have included many informal learning ideas for different subjects under curriculum recommendations. There are a number of reasons for this.

It is important that we recognize and make use of the advantages we have as home schoolers. In a typical classroom there are a large number of children who are required to learn the same material at certain times, at certain speeds, and under the same conditions. At home we can respond to learning opportunities as they arise. We can respond to a child's interest or readiness when it appears. We can proceed at the best speed for each child. And, best of all, we can change curriculum to suit the child.

We need to change the way most of us think so we can see learning opportunities in our surroundings. We need to change our mindset so we can see other things than textbooks as curriculum material.

Following are some ideas for more creative learning for your children to try.

Carry a camera on field trips, vacations, or anywhere the least bit unusual. Take lots of pictures, then paste them into books. (Rubber cement or spray adhesives work best.) Children can either write or dictate captions for their stories. They learn to put a story into sequence and relate the events, using various language skills.

Newsletter articles can be written by your children about field trips, projects, or ideas they can share with others through local newsletters. They will learn that their communication is valuable.

Pen Pals: Corresponding with a pen pal will give practice in the language arts and, again, will show the value of communication. It might also motivate students to use proper spelling and grammar.

Dictation: Children can tell stories into a tape recorder which they can later transcribe at their own speed. (For younger ones, the parent would transcribe). Many children can express themselves on tape but lose their train of thought too easily trying to write it down at the same time.

Intercession or Spiritual Life Notebook: Intercession notebooks can be done many ways. One suggestion includes social studies. Study different countries in depth, including culture, food, crafts, geography, and spiritual condition. Make maps, flags, crafts, foods, etc. that relate to the country, then begin to intercede in prayer for that country based on a knowledge of the country and its needs. Keep researched information, written reports, drawings, and whatever else will fit in a notebook, along with the intercessory prayer requests. Or children can keep a separate journal of prayer requests and answers. *Operation World* (Zondervan) [$14.99] contains statistical information along with spiritual information on most countries.

Use globe, atlases, and the newspaper for geography and social studies: Read about current events, locating the places on the globe and relating current events to knowledge of other world events. Historical atlases can be especially valuable. This is a good springboard for digging into history.

Science experiments: Let your children experience science. You have few enough children that you can supervise more complicated activities than a classroom teacher can.

Home projects: Have your child help figure the amount of paint, wallpaper, or carpeting needed for your home. Have them plan a garden, keep records of what is planted, when, and how long they take to produce. Sell produce from the garden or figure what it would be worth at market prices.

Plan parties: Children love to plan parties, especially the older child for the younger. They can make a schedule, purchase supplies, and make preparations for food, games, decorations, and prizes. They can also supervise the party with or without parental assistance. (The success of this idea will depend greatly on sibling relationships. Children close in age might resent the other child running things.)

Research projects: Have your child choose something he or she is interested in learning more about such as sewing. This might involve learning sewing techniques, researching patterns and materials at stores, planning and purchasing (lots of math involved here), and possibly socialization skills as your child interacts with others to learn skills.

Grocery shopping: Have your child plan a meal, making a list of all ingredients needed. Allow as much responsibility at the market as he can handle to purchase the ingredients himself. Maybe allot him a certain budget to work within or check over his grocery list beforehand. Try to allow him a few mistakes. You might be surprised how much he has learned from observing you in the market.

Puppet show outreach: Write a script, make puppets (can be very simple), and make a stage for a puppet show with an evangelistic message to be presented for your neighborhood, support group, or church. Get ideas from children's records or scripts found in Bible book stores.

Family business: Organize a family business in which all family members are involved. Successfully tested ideas have been cookie baking and selling; putting on parties, including entertainment; making and selling home school learning materials; operating a mailing service; and child care.

Creative Learning Resources

The A to Z Guide to Field Trips
edited by Gregg Harris
(Noble Books)
$21.95

Do you have trouble coming up with field trip ideas? Do your field trips lack educational value? *The A to Z Guide* offers a broad array of suggestions from advertising agencies to zoos, and shows you how to turn each field trip into a valuable educational experience. 77 different field trip ideas are listed with background information, questions you might want to ask on the field trip, activities that enhance learning from the experience, vocabulary words, and "Tips from Barnabas." The "Tips" offer Scriptural tie-ins for each topic—some great Bible lessons here. There is a convenient, little field trip information box in each section which can be filled in with details to localize the *Guide* for trips you plan.

Video Lending Library 📼
membership fee for homeschoolers - $25 (yearly) or $45 lifetime (must mention you are a homeschooler for reduced price!)

A lengthy description of their art videos for sale or rental is found under "Art." The Video Lending Library has expanded its offerings to include videos on other topics and subject areas. Their brochure lists all their titles.

Bethump'd with words, Discovery Edition
(Mamopalire, Inc.)
$29

Bethump'd with words is a game, similar in concept to *Trivial Pursuit*. It has a game board, cards with questions, and key spots to land on to accumulate letters of the "Game Word." There seem to be many such games on the market, but I like this one better than most

for the quality of the questions. Questions are presented at six levels of difficulty—six questions per card. Questions for all levels are from "language" categories such as idioms, homophones, homographs, homonyms, eponyms, word origins, acronyms, Spoonerisms, euphemisms, calques (direct translations from other languages), "Australianisms," "portmanteau" words (coined by combining words), history of language, slang, and true/false questions about language. The Discovery Edition is recommended for ages 9 and up, and it should provide plenty of challenge for the entire family. However, there is a more challenging Senior Edition for teens and adults. This is a great way to tune students into the intricacies of language without overwhelming them.

Big Book of Books and Activities
by Dinah Zike
(Dinah-Might Activities)
$19.95

Dinah Zike has developed a dazzling array of craft activities through her classroom experience, and home educators can pick and choose from the cornucopia of ideas in this book to jazz up learning at home. Many of the activities are labeled as "books," but Zike stretches the idea of books to lengths most of us never imagined. There are miniature "matchbooks" for drilling math facts, putting together mini-reports on social studies topics, and other creative uses. Layered books, circle-mobile books, top-tab books, and frame books are among the other options that can be used for teaching, reviewing, researching, and reporting across many subject areas as well as for creative art activities. Since books are not the limit here, we also have directions for making giant sidewalk chalk, colored glue, macaroni, and cornmeal (what to do with them also), and much more. Ideas are useful for kindergarten through the elementary grades. Materials required are very basic and inexpensive. Full instructions with illustrations are provided.

BIG Ideas/Small Budget
(D.P. & K. Productions)
$12/year for 6 issues

This monthly newsletter, written by homeschoolers for homeschoolers, is a forum for money saving and money making ideas. Find out how to get paid to shop, how to eat out for free, how to make money at other people's garage sales, where to get free art supplies and discounted books, cottage industry ideas, how to create saleable crafts, and much more. There is something for everyone in every issue. Since back issues of this newsletter are usually just as valuable as current issues, they have been made available as a bound volume for $10. Order a sample issue for $1 plus a SASE.

The Booklet Building Book

by Barbara Edtl Shelton
(Homeschool Seminars and Publications)
$8.50

Christian home schooling parents and kids up to about age twelve should both love this user-friendly resource for making more than 30 "make-my-own" booklets. Reproducible pages with instructions show us how to make booklets such as "A Week in My Life," "Days of Creation," Homeschool Memories," "My Favorite Things," and "Pressed Flowers." Instructions are friendly, humorous, and practical. Shelton also shares ideas for book covers, bindings, and decorative touches. The ideas here are intended to stimulate us to go beyond the samples here to create our own topical booklets.Permission is given for two families to reproduce pages from the same book, so get together with another family to share the fun. [Valerie Thorpe]

Brain Quest

(Workman Publishing)
$10.95 each

Brain Quest is essentially *Trivial Pursuit* without a board. Seven different editions focus on questions appropriate for grade levels 1-7. Each edition comes in a sturdy, plastic box and consists of two sets of cards, each set held together by a plastic hinge. The number of questions in each edition range from 750 in level one to 1,500 at levels 4-7. Questions are from the categories English, history, science and technology, math, geography, and grab bag. Answers are on the reverse of each card. The questions can be used for informal quizzes or game playing, by individuals or by groups. Suggestions for game playing options are included. It is not intended that all students at the designated level should be able to answer all questions, but rather that there be an assortment of easy, moderate, and challenging questions on a broad range of subjects. There are occasional questions relating to the media and popular culture that many of our children will not be able to answer. (It is easy enough to skip inappropriate questions.) I checked out the seventh grade level edition with a car full of junior high students who had a fun time occupying themselves by simply challenging each other with questions as we drove. Since there are two "decks" questioners can very conveniently form teams to challenge each other. I think the big appeal here will be the portability and flexibility. I also think many children will appreciate having questions more narrowly designed for different levels rather than the broad "children's level" of most games. You can find *Brain Quest* in most toy and educational stores.

Brown Paper School Books

(Little Brown and Co.)
$11.95 - $12.95 each for softbound editions

This is a series of books including such titles as *Gee Wiz!*

How to Mix Art and Science (Or the Art of Thinking Scientifically), The Book of Think (Or How to Solve a Problem Twice Your Size), The Night Sky Book (An Everyday Guide to Every Night), The I Hate Mathematics! Book, The Book of Where (Or How to be Naturally Geographic), Good for Me! (All About Food in 32 Bites), and *Blood and Guts.* These books are filled with creative, fun, very original ways of exploring traditional subjects such as math, language, science, astronomy, art, music, and history. They are from a secular publisher and should be screened for objectionable content, but they are well worth the trouble.(SE)

A Christian Homeschooler's Guide to Field Trips and Extra-Curricular Activities

by Barbara Edtl Shelton
(Homeschool Seminars and Publications)
$14.95

This hefty book covers everything we should know about field trips and offers plenty of suggestions for organizing extra-curricular activities. With at least as many pages telling us why and how to do things as there are pages of actual suggestions, the ideas are meant to stimulate us to come up with more of our own. Most of the ideas Barb shares are ones they or people they know have actually done. Ideas are presented for different size groups and for different age levels. Many helpful forms are included among which is a fairly standard "Field Trip Report." However, there are others such as the "Occupational Skills Interview," and "Safety Rule." Extensive details are provided in section six for a "Home School Presentation Night," so if your group is interested in doing such an event, it might well be worth getting the book for this section alone. Unlike many other such books, this one stretches up to the older levels to include ideas for our teens. It also cautions us to seek God's heart about how much involvement in outside activities is right for our family.

Crossword Studio [computer program] 🖥

(Teacher Created Materials)
$19.95

The *Crossword Studio* CD-ROM has attractive, illustrated crossword puzzles on various elementary school type subjects, such as: environmental issues, holidays, famous people, etc. There is also a smaller selection of subjects for junior and senior high students. You can also design puzzles to fit your needs and add your own graphics if you want. These puzzles can either be printed out or solved on the screen, in which case you may pick the option of allowing hints to be displayed. The on-screen puzzles also highlight the square and question the child is working on which is helpful for those who loose their place easily. A tone tells whether the word is correct or incorrect; if you don't care about this you could use the program just as well without sound. The program will run on either Windows or Macintosh systems.(S)[V.Thorpe]

GeoSafari
(Educational Insights)

With *GeoSafari*, children enjoy answering the same type of factual questions they encounter in textbooks (with dislike) because in *GeoSafari* knowledge has been turned into an electronic game. Even though this is not a computer or video game, the flashing lights and sounds encourage play/learning in a very effective manner. A console is the main part, upon which we place two-sided game cards. Answering is simply matching correct words with numbers next to pictures on the display. Flashing lights encourage correct answers, and scores are tallied automatically. The games can be adapted for use by one or more players. *GeoSafari* runs on batteries or with an optional AC adaptor [$9.95]. It comes with a 20-lesson set from the National Geographic Society. Extra games come in packages of twenty games (10, 2-sided cards) to concentrate on geography, animals, history, science, Spanish, French, ecosystems, sports, stamps, learning basic English, the Smithsonian, and thinking skills. Blank cards can also be used to make our own games.

Educational Insights also sells *MathSafari* [$99.95], using the same concept to work on math skills, as well as *GeoSafari Jr.* [$99.95] for pre-kindergarten through second grade.

They also offer the *GeoSafari World*, a 9" diameter electronic globe with game pedestal. There are over 5,000 questions incorporated into this interactive game.(SE)

Good Apple Trivial Pursuit
(Good Apple)
$12.99 each

Good Apple publishes *Trivial Pursuit* type games in book format. Each book contains a fold-out gameboard, over 230 game cards, and card box. We cut out the cards and card box, find a die (or use the cardboard one in the book) and moving pawns, and we are ready to play. Books for math, science, and language arts are offered at two or three different levels within each subject: primary, intermediate, and junior high. Language arts games are heavy on literature (three out of four categories) and light on skills (one category). Science games address the categories of the human body, earth and space, matter and energy, and plants and animals. Math games tackle concepts and applications, computations, geometry, and math for daily living.

Homeschooler's Guide to Free Teaching Aids, 1st edition
(Educators Progress Service, Inc.)
$34.95

If you like to design your own curriculum or enrich lessons

with extras, this guide will help you locate some interesting resources for all grade levels. Most of the free materials are booklets, brochures, fact sheets, lesson plans, or other written material, but they often include pictures or illustrations. Some offerings are kits, stickers, or more substantial items. Materials are listed under headings such as agriculture and animal care, business and computer education, environmental education, fine arts, food and nutrition, home economics, language arts, mathematics, science and social studies. Title, subject, and source indexes make it easy to find items of interest. Listed resources have all been verified as being available to home educators.

A large percentage of the resources are very narrowly targeted upon specific topics and are sponsored by an organization with a promotional interest. Even so, there are thousands of items that will be useful. Following are some examples of interesting items:

The Frog Fact Kit suggested for grades 2-6

"Nine reproducible fact sheets about frogs, a poster, and stickers that allow students to learn all about frogs without dissection."

The Dolls' House

"Describes Faith Bradford's presentation of an artist's dolls' house interpretation of the household life of the early 1900s. Includes illustrations and descriptions of rooms and their inhabitants."

Coal Sample Kit

"Presents samples of peat, lignite, bituminous coal, and anthracite—all packaged in resealable bags. Also included is a brief description of coal formation and the differences in the ranks of coal."

Addresses and other contact numbers are included along with suggested grade levels and the numbers of "copies" you can request.

This book is rewritten every year to keep up with the frequent changes, additions, and deletions in such listings. It might be wisest for a few families or a support group to purchase the book together and share rather than each family buying their own copy.

Also check out Educators Progress Service's *Homeschooler's Guide to Free Videotapes*. Fifteen-day free trial periods allow you time to check out their books before buying.(S)

Homeschooler's Guide to Free Videotapes, 1st edition
(Educators Progress Service, Inc.)
$34.95

See the description of *Homeschooler's Guide to Free Teaching Aids* above. Similar in concept, this guide lists videos under the categories of business and economics, career education, famous people, fine arts, foreign languages, guidance, health, home economics, physical education and recreation, religion and philosophy, safety education, science, and social studies. Almost all video tapes are on loan, and you will have to schedule the viewing time in advance and pay return postage. The Korean Cultural ministry offers a number of tapes, but they ask that you send blank tapes on to which they will copy the presentation—then it's yours.

Among some of the interesting titles:

Wolfgang Amade Mozart from the Austrian Cultural Institute

"Journey to historic places relevant to W.A. Mozart, including excerpts of his work performed by talented students of music."

Partners: Life with a Seeing Eye Dog from Motion Picture Services

"A first-person look at the independence, dignity and confidence that See Eye dogs provide to blind men and women."

The Great Pyramid and the Bible from Chicago Bible Students

"Once an ancient wonder, the Great Pyramid has become a modern mystery."

Otto the Auto (Series H) from Motion Picture Services

"Four vignettes to teach young children about bicycle safety."

Some video titles seem like odd inclusions—e.g., *Training Mature Workers* and a title about "empowering nursing home residents. Many are promotional or propaganda type presentations, but there are many that should be useful. Again, it's probably a great idea to purchase a copy of the book for your support group to share.(S)

How To Set Up Learning Centers In Your Home
by Mary Hood, Ph.D.
(Elijah Company)
$5

Most of us have heard of learning centers in conjunction with schools but it's not a popular concept in home schools. Mary Hood shows us how to adapt nooks and crannies around the home to create learning centers for all ages. She offers specific suggestions for centers for science, writing, reading, math, social studies, art, and music, plus a few other more-specialized possibilities. In keeping with her "relaxed" philosophy of education, she recommends a mix of books and hands-on learning materials with a primary emphasis on creating positive attitudes toward self-education.

The Learning Heart Memory System
(The Learning Heart Workshop)
$18

The Learning Heart Memory System is essentially a folder system that can be used for memory work for any subject. It is a heavy duty vinyl folder with plastic pockets that opens flat. Pockets, labeled daily, weekly, or monthly, hold 1 1/2" x

3 1/2" cards. Instructions are included for a systematic study method whereby we shift cards from pocket to pocket across the rows as we master them. Those that have been properly identified through daily review are reencountered for weekly, then monthly review. Cards can be purchased through The Learning Heart Workshop or directly from Vis-Ed, or we can make our own from scratch. Vis-Ed sells topic-specific sets of cards as well as blank cards at very reasonable prices. Preprinted Vis-Ed cards are primarily for high school and college subjects, so you will probably want to make your own for elementary students for most subjects such as phonics, math facts, and history facts. They do have cards for English grammar, punctuation, and composition. If you are starting foreign language, Vis-Ed has vocabulary cards for just about any language you might choose to study. Each student needs his or her own folder since cards are sorted according to the student's mastery of each. Granted that some students need to use other methods for memorization, this idea will certainly work well to systematize memory work for many home schoolers.

Learning Seeds Activity Library
(Home Team Press)
$44.95

The *Learning Seeds Activity Library* offers entertaining activities that simultaneously help us meet many learning objectives. The *Library* is a brightly-colored, plastic file box, filled with 300 activity cards divided under fifteen subject areas. Labeled dividers separate the color-coded cards. The subject areas are art, biology, character, chemistry, earth science, electricity, fluid mechanics, geography, language, math, music, nature, optics, physics, and thinking skills. Since the *Library* is intended for use by the whole family, there are no age distinctions. Most activities can be adapted for young ones, but children at elementary through junior high levels are likely to get the most out of them. (Parents will enjoy them also!) The activities vary in complexity; time requirements range from 10-20 minutes to 60-90 minutes. A number of activities require some equipment like soda bottles, balloons, hangers, rubber bands, or a hammer, but nothing elaborate or expensive is called for. Each card lists materials needed in the top right hand corner, then the purpose, procedure, what happened, and why (although some of these are skipped when they do not fit the activity). The activities offer significant learning opportunities rather than simple entertainment. For example, some of the art activities borrow from (giving credit where it is due) Bruce McIntyre's principles of drawing. Typical activities from other areas are one from earth science where we make an astrolabe and use it to track the sun; one from fluid mechanics where we make an air rocket with balloon, fishing line, drinking straw, and tape; and one from character where we plan a get-together to learn more about grandparents or other older relatives, or hear about mom and dad's courtship. The set is heaviest on science activities, and they are on a par with those found in the best experiment books available. Helpful extras are the thirty graphing cards provided for use with activities that call for creating a chart. *The Library* was created by a Christian family, and, although it does not contain anything identifying it as a Christian resource, we see Christian values reflected in the "Character" activities. Accompanying the set is a *User Guide and Activity/Topic Index*, which is valuable for locating activities to correlate with subjects we are studying.

Math Games & Activities from Around the World

by Claudia Zaslavsky
(Chicago Review Press)
$14.95

People all over the world enjoy playing games and it is amazing how similar games are found in very different cultures. Along with the interesting cultural tidbits, this 11X8 ½" paperback presents more than 70 games, puzzles and crafts that will help develop logical thinking and problem solving. Game boards can be made from paper or cardboard, with beans, coins, or buttons used as playing pieces. Instructions for each game include "Things to Think About"—questions that suggest strategies or variations that help the player to analyze how the game works. In the games of chance, the child is asked to think about the "probability" involved to decide whether a game is fair to each player.

Many of the games are from Africa and would be a valuable addition to anyone doing a unit study on that continent. There are also Native American games; games from the Philippines, England, Colombia, Sri Lanka, India and Hawaii; magic squares and tangrams from China; tessellations from Islamic culture; and even the U.S. postal code. Some games are used in their countries for fortune telling, and you might want to skip those, but you are sure to find many other interesting activities in this book. Fun for families with children aged 8-12.(SE)[V.Thorpe]

101 Great Homeschool Teaching Tips from the Sycamore Tree

(Sycamore Tree Center for Home Education)
$3.95

Here is a nifty, inexpensive book of creative ideas gathered from monthly newsletters that go out to families enrolled in the Sycamore Tree Center for Home Education program. They are grouped according to subject areas: Bible, language arts, math, writing, social studies, science, and art. When you need some inspiration, pick and choose from 101 well-tested ideas.

School in a Box

by Joyce Herzog
(Simplified Learning Products
booklet - $3.95; box plus booklet - $19.95

This unique "tool" helps parents teach and reinforce basic learning concepts. (There's also a *Toddler School in a Box* booklet [$3.95] for those dealing with preschoolers.) Small and miniature items are used as the basis of informal lessons in concepts (e.g., things that are alike, things that are smooth), math (e.g., how many, size relationships), language (e.g., use of prepositions to show relationships, adjectives to describe), etc. The booklet explains how the box works, how to put your own together, and the type questions you use with the box. You can create your own box or purchase a prepared box. The beauty of this idea is that children learn a great deal through what seems like play. Also, you can carry the box along on trips, to appointments, or visits much more easily than school books.

Scrabble, Boggle, Balderdash, and other language skill games.

Some popular games, especially some of those considered classics, are wonderful learning tools.

St. Joseph Messenger: A Monthly Reader for Catholic Families

(St. Joseph Messenger)
$25/10 issues

Although the *St. Joseph Messenger* is not a home schooling newsletter per se, it makes a great addition to any Catholic home school. A Catholic perspective is presented in each article, allowing the reader to see the beauty of the Church's teaching in art, architecture, music, history, poetry, and science. Each issue also includes a biography, questions (with answer keys), project ideas (essays, research, and creative writing), and a vocabulary list. Articles are intelligently and interestingly written. The $25/year subscription price (for 10 issues per year, sent Sept.-June) is well justified as each 16-page issue contains a wealth of useful information for home schooling families.[M.Wittmann]

The Travel Bug

(The Learning Works)
$9.95

Many home educating families include travel as part of their curriculum, and others just want to make the best use of travel time. *The Travel Bug* serves as a journal for recording information about your travels, a place to glue in pictures and mementos, and as an activity book. Activities range from paper-and-pencil puzzles to design-a-visor and creating an amusement park ride (all on paper). The book assumes you are staying within the boundaries of the United States, so many activities will not be applicable if you travel beyond our borders. The book is suggested for ages 7 to 14, but, as you might guess, some is beyond most seven-year-olds and most is too young for fourteen-year-olds. Kids who have a creative bent will most appreciate the activity pages, and the more workbook oriented child will enjoy filling in the information pages. One caution: most of the activity is "paper and writing instrument" which, when done in a moving vehicle, causes some children to get carsick. In those cases, save it for the campsite or motel room. You might want to photocopy some of the pages to use more than once, particularly ones such as the "State the Facts" where kids record information about a city visited. Limited copying rights are allowed, and an answer key for puzzles is in the book.(S)

Chapter 21

Testing and Special Needs

Why Test?

There are two main types of testing many of us will be considering—the everyday tests that reflect student mastery of material being studied at that time, and standardized tests reflecting the overall level of competence.

Mastery Testing

The first type of test is used widely in schools since teachers have few other means of ensuring that students are learning anything. At home, with one-on-one interaction, testing is not as essential. Home schooling parents generally know how well their children know the subjects they have been studying. (If you need more help with evaluation, read Teresa Moon's book *Evaluating for Excellence*) As children begin to work more independently, testing becomes more helpful. However, written or oral reports can be substituted for testing to give us the feedback we need.

Standardized Testing

We home educators sometimes give our children standardized tests without clearly identifying our reasons for doing so. Many of us feel this is a necessary part of education because the schools do it. In some states the law requires home educated children to be tested periodically. Some of us want to demonstrate to skeptical relatives that we are indeed educating our children. Some of us, whether we admit it or not, want proof that our children are more intelligent than others. Many of us want to find out if we are doing an adequate job as teachers.

Schools test children regularly for a number of reasons, most having little to do with the individual child, but more to do with statistics, politics, and money. We need not be concerned with testing for these purposes. When the state demands standardized testing, there is often little we can do but go along with the requirement.

Skeptical relatives can be a definite problem, and sometimes good test results will relieve the pressure on us. But more often, skeptical relatives are impressed with the results they <u>see</u> in our children after a year or two of home education. All of us want to be proud of our children, but that is not adequate

reason to submit them to standardized testing.

The concern over our adequacy is legitimate. Usually we can tell how well our children are doing just because we are working so closely with them every day. But it can be difficult to step back and objectively examine what we are accomplishing. However, a standardized test will <u>not</u> give us a total picture. It does not measure curiosity, creativity, social wisdom, attitudes, and the other intangibles that can be of utmost importance. A standardized test will tell us to some extent how well our child has mastered basic subject matter.

The most important reason for testing, and one which few of us identify, is to test for gaps in knowledge. If a child misses every problem having to do with fractions but answers correctly every other math problem, there is a definite learning gap. However, using standardized tests for such feedback is becoming increasingly problematic. School restructuring taking place within the government schools significantly influences test content. Outcome-based education and the National Education Goals are dictating content changes in tests to reflect a politically-correct agenda. Thus we find even basic math and language arts questions presented within contexts that make it difficult for children to determine the expected answers. Science and social studies questions are generally worse than those for math and language arts.

We must recognize that the goal of government schools is shaping children for society as they define it, not for God's purposes. Author and educational commentator Jonathan Kozol tells us in his book *The Night is Dark and I Am Far from Home* that "The first goal and primary function of the U.S. public school is not to educate good people, but good citizens. It is the function which we call—in enemy nations— 'state indoctrination.'"

Standardized testing is viewed as a tool for shaping the curriculum to state purposes. Testing drives the curriculum; whatever is tested is what will be taught. While standardized tests covered academic basics, few parents were seriously concerned about testing requirements. But, as tests have changed to support the political agenda, parents began to realize that tests can do far more harm than good.

From a practical standpoint, we need to compare our goals with those of government schools. A test designed to reflect goals we do not share is of little use. Because parents are seldom allowed to review the questions on such tests, we have no way of knowing what questions our children are missing and whether or not they are even valid for our children.

Another consideration regarding standardized testing is that most of them are computer-scored, and the results are retained in centralized data banks along with each child's identification. In this age of enforced political-correctness and governmental invasion of privacy, we should be concerned about how any such data might be used in the future. Sometimes we can request hand-scoring, although generally we will be given much less detailed feedback because hand-scoring prohibits computer analysis of results.

If you have alternatives to standardized tests, I strongly recommend you use them. (If you would like to better understand school restructuring and its impact on home education, read my book, *Government Nannies*, which is published by Noble Books.)

Test Results

Meanwhile, some of us will still be using standardized tests for one reason or another. If so, try to make the experience as productive as possible. It is important that we receive a complete breakdown of standardized test results, demonstrating what particular skill or skills within each subject area show weakness. A general score showing poor language usage is of little value in many cases. More valuable is a breakdown showing that most capitalization problems were answered incorrectly while other skills were satisfactory.

Standardized test results come back to us in various forms, some giving only a minimal amount of information and others showing a thorough breakdown of subject areas. It is important to know what kind of result interpretation we will be given from the testing before we send in our money. If we need a thorough breakdown of results, we must make sure that is what we will receive.

Another important factor to consider with standardized tests is the requirement that the test be administered by a credentialed teacher or someone with a college degree. Many tests have such requirements. Some home educated children are very uncomfortable working under adults other than their parents, so tests under such conditions might be inaccurate.

Standardized tests are of minimal value for children below third grade. Young children often respond according to their mood of the moment which greatly influences test results. Young children also tend to mature by leaps and bounds, especially in dealing with abstractions, so the results of a test taken a month previously are possibly no longer valid.

Standardized tests also can be poor tools to evaluate older children. Some children test well, others do not. This may be because of their learning style, their ability to concentrate, their attitude toward the test, distractions, worry, etc. If we can see that our child is missing questions we are confident he

knows under other circumstances, the validity of the test results is doubtful.

If your state has a testing requirement, check with a home school group to determine which tests are acceptable to the state and if there are administration (who gives the test) requirements. All standardized tests are not accepted in every state.

Testing Services

Bob Jones University Press offers a testing service using either the *Iowa Test of Basic Skills* or the *Stanford Achievement Test* for elementary and junior high. In addition, they offer learning abilities tests for grades 2-12, *Metropolitan Math, Reading*, or *Language* diagnostic tests, and *Personality Profile* testing. For the *Iowa* and *Stanford* tests, results are given in terms of norm-references (percentile, grade equivalents, and stanine) and objectives, accompanied by a narrative report. Tests from BJUP must be administered by either a credentialed teacher or someone with a four-year college degree. Request their Information and Order Form for Testing and Evaluation Service or contact Testing Services Department for more information.

Christian Liberty Academy Independent Achievement Testing Service offers *California Achievement Tests* (CAT) to both enrolled and non-enrolled families. Testing may be administered by parents. Student test form (answer sheet only) and grade equivalent results for individual subjects are returned to us. The cost is very reasonable, and there are no restrictions on who can administer the test, making this a favorable alternative for many families.

For a small additional fee, Christian Liberty Academy will also use the test results to provide you with curriculum recommendations for the coming school year if you so desire. Recommendations are not limited to materials used in CLA courses. While recommendations will be chosen to suit the obvious grade level placement, there is no avenue for evaluating learning styles, family situations, individual interests, or other factors that are important in curriculum selection. This service would probably be most appealing to those just beginning who need to start somewhere and feel unable to evaluate all of these other factors until they have acquired some experience. This service does help to solve the major problem of grade level placement, and it will be likely to pick up learning gaps from earlier years and recommend materials to fill in.

Hewitt Homeschooling Resources offers a specially-designed standardized test, *The Personalized Assessment Summary System (PASS)*, for parents to administer to their children in a home setting. Hewitt does not require that a certified teacher or college graduate administer the test. An initial placement test is with the child to identify the level of test needed. Then the actual *PASS* test is administered. This means the actual test is shorter than other standardized tests.

The interpretation should be more useful for home educators than some of the interpretations provided by other testing services since Hewitt provides parents with a detailed analysis and suggestions for working on areas that were most difficult for the child. Hewitt also tracks testing results for up to three years to give us a larger view of our child's progress and needs. The *PASS* test is accepted by some states who have a testing requirement, but not all. We must check with our local authorities to find out if they will accept the *PASS* as an alternative to other standardized tests. The normal testing schedule is October and/or April. With most of the standardized tests gradually changing to reflect outcome-based education, this test should be a preferable alternative for many families. Tests are $26 each ($50 for both Fall and Spring testing), although discounts are available for purchases of six or more tests.

McGuffey Testing Service (McGuffey Academy) is available to home schoolers in grades K-12 whether or not they are enrolled in McGuffey Academy. The *Stanford Achievement Test* is offered and may be administered by parents without special qualifications unless a certified teacher is required by your state. McGuffey Academy will hand check each test and will send you a copy of the results along with an evaluation and letter that will help you interpret the scores accurately. The results show a detailed breakdown of skills within subject areas.

Covenant Home Curriculum offers an adapted version of the 1964 SAT test. (Older SAT tests were more challenging than present editions.) *Covenant Home Achievement Tests* evaluate English and math skills of students in grades K-12. Tests are hand scored and provide results under general headings such as grammar, reading comprehension, and spelling. Test scorers include some observation comments that might pinpoint specific problems. The English section of the test is tied to the *Warriner English* series although it should adequately evaluate skills of students using other English programs. Tests are available to all home educators, and no credentials or degrees are required for those administering the tests.

Kolbe Academy also offers *Stanford Achievement Tests* for students in grades 1-12 in March each year for $35. Parents may administer the tests as long as they follow proper procedures. Tests are scored by the Psychological Corporation. Students need not be enrolled in Kolbe Academy for testing.

Seton Home Study offers the *California Achievement Test* for grades K-12. The test can be administered by the parent in most states, although some states require a certified teacher. The fee is $40 and test results are usually returned in one to two weeks. Contact Seton at testing@setonhome.org for more information.

Summit Christian Academy offers the *Iowa Test of Basic Skills* in the Spring to students in grades 3-8. Tests are computer graded with results sent to the parents. Cost is $35 for enrolled students and $45 for others.

Sycamore Tree Center for Home Education offers the *Comprehensive Test of Basic Skills* for grades K-12. There are no restrictions on who can administer the test. Tests are professionally scored on May 15 and August 15, providing a very detailed and helpful breakdown. The rest of the year, tests are hand scored and there is an extra $10 charge. Testing is free to families enrolled in Sycamore Tree.

Outside of these testing services (and others not listed), standardized tests such as the *Iowa* test are available only to qualified teachers, schools, and school services.

Diagnostic Testing

If we wish to identify gaps in learning, a shorter diagnostic test might do the job just as well as a standardized test but with a lot less hassle since most diagnostic tests can be administered by parents without strict guidelines. Diagnostic tests are available from Bob Jones University Press, Summit Christian Academy, Alpha Omega [$19.95 a set or $5 per subject area], and School of Tomorrow [$10 a set] for anyone who wishes to order.

Regarding the Alpha Omega and School of Tomorrow tests, use only the Math and English tests, since the others will not be useful for general purposes. These are parent administered and graded. The tests are not perfect. Since they were designed to place students in the publishers' curricula, they do ask some questions that pertain only to each particular curriculum. You should look for and cross out these questions before your child takes the test. The tests also reflect each publisher's scope and sequence, which might differ from yours or that of the publisher whose material you wish to use. Use the results to (1) identify weak areas; (2) compare with your scope and sequence (what you plan to teach when) to identify areas that should already have been mastered or are next to be taught; and (3) plan the child's course of study to either review or teach areas as needed.

Alpha Omega diagnostic tests (in Bible, English, math, science, and history and geography) are offered by **Summit Christian Academy** along with the more widely accepted *Wide Range Achievement Test*. This combination of tests is offered for diagnostic purposes for $35. Tests are teacher graded, and results are sent to parents along with comments after completion of both tests.

If you have the time, money, and experience, you might want to invest in a much more comprehensive do-it-yourself diagnostic tool. One that is available to home educators is the *Brigance Comprehensive Inventory of Basic Skills-Revised* (Curriculum Associates). One huge binder, called the "inventory" [$149], serves as the core of the assessment process. It can be used for students PreK through ninth grade. We are given permission to photocopy pages on which we or students must write. Some responses and all results are recorded in the *Record Book* [$4.25] which we need for each child. The *Student Profile Test Booklet* [$5] is helpful but not essential. The *CIBS* can be used to assess readiness, speech, listening skills, word recognition, oral reading, reading skills, spelling, writing, reference skills, graph and map skills, and math computation and problem solving skills. Assessments ask for oral, written, or physical responses (e.g., pointing to various body parts for identification). Tests are not timed, although time limits are suggested. We select appropriate tests from the inventory; never use all of them for a single student. Select those about one grade level below where you think a student is functioning in those areas that need to be assessed. Assessments are criterion referenced, measuring students against subject matter and skills comparable to those taught in the average public school. To compare results to norm-standardized assessments, you can also purchase the *Standardization and Validation Manual* [$40 or $30 when purchased with the *Inventory*], although I must warn you that if you are not experienced working with these type instruments, you will likely be overwhelmed with that manual. The *CIBS* serves a useful purpose in helping diagnose gaps and weak areas as well as for determining approximate grade level. I would caution you to remember that learning is more than the sum of all these fragmented parts so that you don't fall into the trap of simply teaching children isolated skills.

The Blumenfeld Oral Reading Assessment Test (available from Paradigm) is a diagnostic tool narrowly designed for assessing reading skills. It is designed to analyze a person's ability to decode and pronounce words, progressing from very simple three letter words to difficult multi-syllabic words. Easy administration instructions are on the tape as well as in the printed material which comes with the tests. Words are also pronounced on the tape for the parent/teacher. There are 380 words on the test arranged in increasing order of difficulty. There is also a post-test to use later on to check for improvement. Five copies of each test are included with the kit, and extras are available at reasonable cost from the publisher. While the test can be used with any age from beginning reader through adult, it will be especially useful for the parent who begins home schooling in the mid-elementary grades or later and suspects that her child might have difficulty with decoding or phonics. The test will help to identify whether reading problems are caused by lack of phonetic knowledge or lack of experience with words (vocabulary). It is not designed to identify learning disabilities or comprehension problems, although dyslexic problems might show up during test administration.

There are other diagnostic tests, but these that are mentioned are the most easily accessible to home educators.

Preparing Children for Testing

There are numerous materials to help children do well on standardized tests. There are definite strategies they need to be aware of to do their best. An inexpensive help in this area is Continental Press' *On Target for Tests*, books A (below fourth grade) and B (grades 4-6) [$5.50 each, teacher's guide - $2.75]. These books work on general test-taking skills commonly required for most standardized tests.

Another help for test preparation is the more comprehensive *Scoring High* series (SRA). *Scoring High* books, tailored to the various tests and different levels of each, are available for the *Stanford Achievement Test (SAT)*, the *Comprehensive Test of Basic Skills* (*CTBS*- first or current edition), *California Achievement Tests (CAT), Iowa Test of Basic Skills (ITBS),* and *Metropolitan Achievement Tests (MAT6)*. Each teacher's guide and student book set costs about $14.

In addition, SRA offers preparation books for state competency tests, although these are changing rapidly in response to implementation of outcome-based education.

Curriculum Associates®, Inc. publishes their *Test Ready* series of test preparation books for math, reading and vocabulary, language arts, science, and social studies [$6.95 each; teacher guides - $3 each]. Books range in size from about 30 to 40 pages each. Each book is broken down into a number of "lessons" which might be used over a period of about two weeks. Lessons are essentially practice tests. Most questions are multiple choice with little bubbles to fill in. However, *Test Ready Language Arts, Social Studies*, and *Science* all include some actual writing tasks and test-taking strategies. *Test Ready Language Arts* and *Test Ready Reading & Vocabulary* reflect older style standardized tests which emphasize concrete knowledge and skills. *Test Ready Mathematics* is fairly traditional in approach, focusing a great deal on basic computation skills while also including some problems from geometry, measurement, time, money, and graph interpretation. Science and social studies series all reflect typical government school textbooks in content, so you will encounter some of the same social engineering and philosophical assumptions in both places. However, they do require students to have concrete knowledge in both subject areas. Science and social studies books do not use only questions that rely upon reading skills like those we used to encounter on tests. (Some of these remain, but they are not the bulk of the practice lessons.) These books are primarily for practice with only minimal help as far as test-taking strategies. However, a separate resource book, *Test Ready Tips and Strategies* provides such help for the entire series. *Test Ready* books are available as follows: *Reading* and *Math* - grades 1-8, *Language Arts* - grades 2-8, *Social Studies* - grades 3-8.

Curriculum Associates also offers two more test preparation

ines designed with newer tests in mind: *Plus* and *Omni* series. The *Test Ready Plus Reading* series is more in line with whole language methods. The *Test Ready Plus Mathematics* series reflects the new math standards, so we encounter data interpretation, numeration, geometry, number theory, pre-algebra, and measurement problems presented as word problems rather than mostly numerical problems as in the other math series. It also includes one page of open-ended problems. The plus series for *Reading* and *Math* are available for grades 1-8.

The newest series, *Omni*, also offers *Reading* and *Math* for grades 1-8. *Test Ready Omni Reading* should be used for students preparing for tests that have open-ended writing tasks and significant critical thinking components. Questions require either multiple-choice or extended, written answers. *Omni Math* includes problems that require work with manipulatives (provided with books) as well multiple choice and open-ended, written answers.

It is important to know what kind of test your child will be taking to select the correct preparation series. Teacher Guides are essential for instructions and answer keys.(S)

Developmental Testing, Testing for Special Problems and Learning Disabilities

Some of us will be interested in testing for special purposes. There are many types of testing available that can be selected according to our need.

Developmental tests help us identify maturity levels and learning styles. This knowledge will help guide us in determining timing and methods for teaching each child. If you are thinking of beginning a formal academic program at kindergarten or first grade level, Rod and Staff offers a very inexpensive readiness test (a form of developmental testing) for six-year-olds. This test covers language usage and comprehension, visual perception and discrimination, study skills, attention span, ability to follow directions, and inference and reading skills. No special qualifications are required for parents to use the test with their children. The *Learning Abilities Test* offered by Bob Jones University Press also provides mental development information.

Practitioners such as some of those listed below also offer much more in-depth developmental testing which naturally costs much more.

While developmental testing can help us know how to best teach most children by identifying age and developmentally-appropriate tasks, many home educators are looking for more. They have children who seem to have trouble with learning no matter what they try. They need some help to determine the underlying problem.

For developmental testing or testing for learning disabilities or handicaps, we refer you to the services below. Some of these services will also be helpful in advising methods to overcome problems.

Special Testing Services

Linda Howe, M.A.—Linda Howe has a Masters Degree in Education and is a learning disabilities and perceptual-motor consultant. She has completed advanced study and received special training in perceptual-motor development from Elizabeth Davies. Her methods are often very effective for children with dyslexia, dysgraphia, kinesthetic deficits, and other such problems. Linda Howe has had great success working with many home educated children, even those who have tried other methods that did not work. The cost is reasonable, $150 for the initial perceptual-motor evaluation which includes the remedial program. This is quite different from educational psychologists who often will administer tests but not offer strategies for remediation. The prescribed program is done by parents with their child at home. Occasional re-evaluations and program adjustments are $55 each. Mrs. Howe also works with families that live out of the area through videos. Parents bring the child for the initial assessment if they can, then follow the prescribed program. As they progress, they send videos of the child demonstrating progress for reevaluation. If it is not possible to come to Mrs. Howe, she will work with you to collect information to evaluate the child "long distance."

Lewisville Learning Clinic/Dr. Kenneth A. Lane—offers a developmental testing service and support program. The program for children ages 5-11 consists of school readiness screening with a computerized questionnaire/developmental test administered by the parent and graded by Dr. Lane. Dr. Lane says the program screens for attention deficit disorders and "...potential problems in the following areas: gross motor, ocular motor, visual motor, laterality, directionality, sequential processing, simultaneous processing." Additionally, Dr. Lane creates daily lesson plans of activities for a six-month program taken from *Developing Your Child for Success* and five new workbooks. The workbooks, also available separately, work on specific areas. Titles of the five workbooks are *Visual Memory, Recognition of Reversals, Visual Scanning, Spelling Tracking,* and *Visual Tracking*. We can select parts of the program according to our needs, but the overall cost should be around $200 for everything.

Lindamood-Bell Learning Processes—has offices in California, Florida, Georgia, Illinois, New York, Massachusetts, Ohio, Texas, Washington (state), and Washington D.C. They describe their services: "Lindamood-Bell has pioneered programs to develop the sensory cognitive processes that underlie reading, spelling, language comprehension, math, and visual motor skills. Our research-based programs are for individuals ranging from severely learning disabled to academically gifted—ages 5 years through adult." Comprehensive diagnostic testing is used to identify strengths and weaknesses. A one-hour consultation session explains the results and suggests a "treatment" plan. They offer one-to-one tutoring, small group instruction, parent training, and helpful products. It can be quite expensive, but Lindamood-Bell has developed a solid reputation over time of helping students overcome learning difficulties.

National Academy for Child Development (NACD)/Robert J. Doman, Jr.— based in Utah, but has branches throughout the U.S. They design individualized programs for children on a continuum from brain injured to gifted. In the programs, the parent assumes the role of primary "therapist" with NACD's training. They recognize that parents are the world's greatest experts on their own children. A six-hour audio tape series, "The Miracles of Child Development," [$50] explains the theory and philosophy behind individualized therapeutic programs. NACD has developed a worthy reputation over the years because of their tremendous success. Write or visit their web site for free information. (Non-sectarian organization)

National Institute for Learning Disabilities—Although the NILD is based in Virginia, they can refer you to educational therapists, usually through a local Christian school. NILD's purpose is to help Christian schools or organizations develop programs for students with special learning needs. They train classroom teachers in assessment and therapy to become educational therapists. These educational therapists then work one-on-one with students, including parents in the process. Some therapists will be limited to working with only students enrolled in their school, but others should be willing to work with home educators. NILD uses a variety of methods to help students overcome weaknesses rather than simply providing mechanisms students can use to compensate. Contact the national headquarters for referrals to local therapists. Qualified home educators (bachelor's degree, preferably in education) are invited to take NILD therapist training (with the Executive Director's approval), offered at a number of locations around the country. Request details, cost, and schedule information if you are interested.

Marian S. Soderholm, M.A., MCA Educational Assessment Services—Marian has a masters degree in family counseling and is a credentialed learning disabilities specialist. A former junior and senior high language arts teacher and homeschooling mom of two teenagers, Marian has completed advanced training in the area of special needs assessment testing and curriculum planning. She has been successful in helping families identify and plan educational programs for students with different types of learning and processing difficulties. She also works as a consultant for both ISP leaders and individual families as well as a resource specialist in the edu-

cation community. Her assessment and consulting fees are quite reasonable and include individualized, specific attention paid to the particular needs of the student. She uses a number of cognitive and academic assessment instruments in her evaluations. While she might be able to provide some counsel long distance, most of her services (e.g., testing) require you to travel to her location.

For eye problems, consult a developmental optometrist. Many are listed in the Yellow Pages, but even better is a referral from another patient.

Learning Difficulties/Disabilities

However we choose to label them, there are definitely home educated children who are having difficulty learning. For inexperienced parents, this can create an overwhelmingly frustrating situation. There is a strong temptation to put these children into the public school system so they will get special education. Too often the special education programs provide nothing more than band-aids to pass children ahead in subjects by simply giving them very, very simple work to do as a substitute for normal classroom activities. Rarely do schools take time to address the underlying causes of learning problems, because they do not have the time needed to spend with each individual child to help overcome the problem. It is a lot faster to use band-aids.

To address the specific needs of our learning disabled child, we need to comprehend the individualized time and energy investment it will require on our part. This investment is usually measured in months to years. There is no quick fix or instant-results form of therapy for neurologically training the brain.

However, there are a number of avenues that might lead to cures for learning disabilities. Although most disabilities are still present to some degree no matter what we do, there are things we can do to try to alleviate major problem areas.

Two of the most successful strategies for overcoming learning disabilities seem to be vision therapy and perceptual motor training.

A child's eyes must do more than just see words and numbers—they must send the proper information to the brain. Then the brain must send the proper response to be spoken or written or acted upon. There is much room for errors in transmission. If the eyes do not see well or do not send the proper message to the brain, the result often appears to be a learning disability.

The first thing to check in most situations is visual functioning. This in not what we call 20/20 vision, but rather proper functioning in a variety of situations such as tracking words across a page, following from line to line, and focusing at close range for reading. Over the years, I have seen too many parents spend hundreds of dollars on full range disability testing and therapy, when the problem turned out to be one that could be solved with glasses or fairly simple vision therapy. More and more I am recommending to parents of children exhibiting learning difficulties that their first step should be to visit a developmental or behavioral optometrist for a thorough vision examination. The Optometric Extension Program Foundation, Inc. can give you a referral to a qualified optometrist in the U.S. or any of 35 other countries. Their brochure, *Does Your Child Have a Learning-related Vision Problem?*, includes the following checklist that might alert you to a vision problem.

- Holding a book very close (only 7 or 8 inches away).
- Child holds head at an extreme angle to the book when reading.
- Child covers one eye when reading.
- Child squints when doing near vision work.
- Constant poor posture when working close.
- The child moves his or her head back and forth while reading instead of moving only eyes.
- Poor attention span, drowsiness after prolonged work less than arm's length away.
- Homework requiring reading takes longer than it should.
- Child occasionally or persistently reports seeing blurring or double while reading or writing.
- Child reports blurring or doubling only when work is hard.
- Loses place when moving gaze from desk work to chalkboard, or when copying from text to notebook.
- Child must use a marker to keep their place when reading.
- Writing up or down hill, irregular letter or word spacing.
- Child reverses letter (b for d) or words (saw for was).
- Repeatedly omits "small" words.
- Rereads or skips words or lines unknowingly.
- Fails to recognize the same word in the next sentence.
- Misaligns digits in columns of numbers.
- Headaches after reading or near work.
- Burning or itching eyes after doing near vision work.
- Child blinks excessively when doing near work, but not otherwise.
- Rubs eyes during or after short periods of reading.
- Comprehension declines as reading continues.
- Child fails to visualize (can't describe what they have been reading about).

(Reprinted with permission.)

Sometimes, the solution is glasses, but sometimes it is visual therapy. Visual therapy involves exercises to help improve eye function, which in turn can help the learning process.

Sometimes, "whole-body" therapy is necessary. If the message is properly perceived by the eyes, it may yet be lost in transmission by garbled transmission lines to the brain or hands. If the proper connections are not made by nerve cells, this too interferes with learning. Perceptual motor exercises are designed to help improve the connections within the nervous system so that messages promptly reach their proper destinations.

If some of this sounds like hocus pocus to you, you are not alone. However, I have seen the results of a number of children working through both visual therapy and perceptual motor training. While neither method can guarantee improvement for all children, a large proportion of those who faithfully follow a program of exercises (visual or perceptual motor or both) do achieve some measure of improvement.

Unfortunately, we often have trouble determining whether our child's learning difficulty is caused by a learning disability rather than other factors such as immaturity, laziness, or rebelliousness. This is the question facing many of us when we feel that our child is functioning below level in one area or another. We don't want to shell out hundreds of dollars for a professional evaluation unless we are fairly certain there is a problem. And, even if we are looking for professional evaluation, many of us have no idea where to find an evaluator or what type of evaluator we need.

It is helpful to have some guidelines of symptoms to look for that indicate learning disability problems before rushing off to the professional. A parent might look for problems occurring outside of schoolwork which might indicate learning disabilities. Examples of such problems might be inability to follow directions, difficulty putting ideas into words, or unusual clumsiness. Some of the books described below—*How to Teach Your Child to Read and Spell, How to Identify Your Child's Learning Problems and What to do About Them*, and *20/20 is Not Enough*—provide guidelines for identifying problems. Some of the problems we encounter are minor enough that we can deal with them ourselves with just a little guidance such as is provided in the books described immediately below.

If you suspect your child has a significant problem, you really should see a specialist. They are trained to identify things we might easily miss. Also, with their experience, they can often suggest the best methods to use to try to overcome problems. You can often get recommendations of specialists in your area from other home schoolers.

Resources for Special Needs

Choosing & Using Curriculum For Your Special Child
by Joyce Herzog
(Greenleaf Press)
$9.95

Many parents recognize that their children have learning difficulties; they might even have spent hundreds of dollars having their child "diagnosed." But, too often, they don't know where to go next. How do they find resources to use with their children? How do they know what to do with the resources they have? Joyce Herzog, author of *Learning in Spite of Labels* (and many other books) provides some answers and direction. In this book, she begins with a comparison of four basic types of curricula, comparing their advantages and disadvantages as well as their suitability for children with special needs. She gets into specifics as she addresses the various subject areas such as reading, math, history, and handwriting. She offers teaching tips and curriculum reviews for each area. Much of this is valuable for parents with average children who periodically struggle with subjects, not just those with learning disabilities. She suggests evaluation methods that might be alternatives to norm-referenced testing and includes annotated lists of resources and groups for special education. Joyce does not prescribe one particular program, but offers us a range of choices from which to choose. Even though I review some of the same resources she reviews in her book, her view through "special needs glasses" offers a different and valuable perspective. She also includes quite a few resources that I have not reviewed.

Developing Your Child for Success

by Kenneth A. Lane, O.D. (Learning Potentials Publishers, Inc.)
$24.95; workbooks - $9.95 each or $47 for the set

Dr. Lane has written this book based upon years of work in vision therapy. In the first chapter, he explains the many factors involved in reading (in fairly technical language). Next he explains how we can help children develop perceptual motor skills for reading success. The remainder of the book is divided into eight sections of activities, each focusing on a developmental area. Activities are arranged according to level of difficulty so that parents can begin at easy levels, then work up to more complex levels. The sections are titled as follows:

Section I - "Motor Therapy Procedures: Activities to Develop Balance and Gross Motor Skills"

Section II - "Visual Motor Therapy Procedures: Activities to Improve Eye-Hand Coordination and Writing Skills"

Section III - "Ocular Motor Therapy Procedures: Activities to Improve a Child's Eye Movements and Eliminate Rereading and Losing His Place When He Reads"

Section IV - "Laterality Therapy Procedures: Activities to Develop a Child's Body Imagery and Understanding of His Left and Right"

Section V - "Directionality Therapy Procedures: Activities to Help Children Develop Directionality Skills and Eliminate Reversals"

Section VI - "Sequential Processing Therapy Procedures: Activities to Improve a Child's Ability to Remember Things in Sequence"

Section VII - "Simultaneous Processing Therapy Procedures: Activities to Improve Visual-spatial, Letter Position and Visualization Skills"

Section VIII - "Vision Therapy Procedures: Activities to Improve Focusing, Eye Teaming and Overall Visual Skills"

A list of materials and equipment needed for the exercises is included. (The most expensive item is probably a small trampoline.) Comprehensive explanations and illustrations of activities, and the fact that no special tools are required make this a practical resource.

Dr. Lane does not recommend that this book be used as a substitute for professional evaluation. There are few tools in this book to identify problem areas, and there is no differentiation of therapy programs according to individual needs. Instead, if you relied solely upon this book, all children would do all of the exercises. This would be a very comprehensive program covering a multitude of activities generally recommended for overcoming various learning disabilities, although it would be very time consuming. Parents could work through the activities with their children without professional assistance, although Dr. Lane offers additional assistance through his office. (A book such as *How to Identify Your Child's Learning Problems and What to do About Them* might be useful in helping to pinpoint problem areas if you are unable to afford professional evaluation.)

Dr. Lane has also developed a reasonably-priced diagnostic program. Parents can administer a developmental test to their child that Dr. Lane then grades, or he can screen children through diagnostic software.

In addition, Dr. Lane has developed five workbooks that can be used as part of a total perceptual program to work on specific areas. Workbook titles are *Recognition of Reversals, Spelling Tracking, Visual Tracing, Visual Scanning*, and *Visual Memory*.

Dr. Lane offers even more assistance. He says, "To further help parents, I am also offering a daily lesson plan. Depending on the diagnosis from the computer screen or the developmental test battery, I can write out a daily lesson plan that will give them five activities to do a day for six months. These activities are taken from my workbooks and *Developing Your Child for Success*."

The Gift of Dyslexia: Why Some of the Smartest People Can't Read and How They Can Learn

by Ronald D. Davis with Eldon M. Braun
(Penguin Putnam, Inc.)
$14.95; audiotape set plus book - $29.95

If you work with (or are) someone who has dyslexia, dysgraphia, ADD, ADHD, or autism , here is a different approach to consider. Mr. Davis, himself dyslexic, gives insight into what is going on in the mind of someone with this special visual learning style in a way that explains a lot of otherwise baffling problems. This understanding is worth the price of the book even if you never try out any of the procedures suggested for correcting the learning disabilities associated with dyslexia. These techniques can be done with anyone over the age of eight and include instructions to help the student gain control over the position of his "mind's eye." Modeling clay becomes a learning tool that is used to construct pictures of word meanings and form the alphabet, an idea that can be fun to use with even younger children. This book might even make you thankful for the gift of dyslexia. An audiotape presentation of the book is available on three, 90-minute cassettes; the set is sold with a copy of the book by ordering through Davis Dyslexia Association International, 1601 Old Bayshore Highway, Suite 260C, Burlingame, CA 94010, (888) 999-3324, (415) 692-8995, web site: http://www.dyslexia.com/.[V. Thorpe](S)

Home Schooling Children with Special Needs
by Sharon C. Hensley, M.A.
(Noble Books)
$12.95

Christian parents of children with disabilities or handicaps should read this book, whether they have already begun home-schooling or are at the decision stage. In a little less than 200 pages, Sharon Hensley packs in a tremendous amount of information and encouragement. She offers expert, readable, common-sense comments on available options plus recommendations for further research and reading.

This is a mom who has been there (her own daughter is autistic) and you feel it throughout the book. She even includes her address and phone number at the end of the book and invites readers to write or phone her. Hensley defines various learning difficulty situations such as underachievers, learning disabilities, slow learners, language disorders, mental retardation, and autism. She also tells us what to expect—dealing with our own feelings (grief, anger, and discouragement) and dealing with children's behavior problems—as well as how to set goals, plan our program, write an IEP (Individualized Education Program), and select teaching methods and resources. This is a very practical resource for homeschooling moms, and it offers invaluable advice from a Christian perspective.[Valerie Thorpe/C.D.]

How to Get Your Child off the Refrigerator and on to Learning
by Carol Barnier
(YWAM Publishing)
$8.99

See the review of this book in Chapter One. The first part of the book deals with how to handle a child with hyperactive tendencies. Carol stresses the need to individualize—figure out what works with this child rather than what others think you should do. She addresses issues such as where to do schooling, use of desks, letting children move while working, scheduling, and resources. She writes from her own experience rather than a clinical background, but I believe that there are thousands

and thousands of moms who will relate to and learn from that experience.

How To Identify Your Child's Learning Problems And What To Do About Them
by Duane A. Gagnon
(Pioneer Productions)
$14

Do you suspect your child of having a learning problem but would like to know for sure? Do you have a child who has already been identified as having a learning difficulty but you would like to have activities you can do with him/her at home that will help?.... Or, would you just like some practical activities to do at home with your children to help develop their learning skills? These are the questions the author poses to those who will benefit from this book.

He has written an easy-to-read tool for laymen (parents) who suspect their child can use help with a learning problem. Part one helps us to evaluate strengths and weaknesses in both auditory (hearing) and visual (seeing) skills in nine areas: attention, analysis, synthesis, sequencing, short term memory, long term memory, comprehension, abstract reasoning, and expression.

Part two consists of methods and activities to help in areas that show weakness. These activities are NOT perceptual motor activities such as those found in Lane's book, but are instead more school-like activities typically used by special education teachers. For example, to improve visual comprehension, ...show the child a picture of a person and have him indicate the various parts of the body and what they do. These activities can be useful, but if you identify a serious problem, consider both a professional evaluation and the use of perceptual motor therapy, vision therapy or some other means of addressing the root of the problem. (Watch for a revised editon in 2000.)

How to Teach Your Child to Read and Spell, 1999 revised edition
by Sheldon R. Rappaport, Ph.D.
(Effective Educational Systems, Inc.)
$19.50

Dr. Rappaport has tremendous faith in parents' abilities to diagnose and help their children overcome learning disabilities based on visual or auditory problems. That faith is evident in this do-it-yourself manual. He does advise consulting a professional when necessary, but he also helps us make a preliminary diagnosis so we can figure out whom we need to consult.

He does not just leave us with an identified problem, but he shares strategies to overcome or correct the problem, as well as teaching methods to help a child develop compensating mechanisms. The diagnostic tests are low-pressure, requiring easily found items such as string or a penlight. (The most expensive item mentioned was a $60 light meter, but it is not essential in most situations.) Extensive visual and auditory skills checklists are provided to be used in conjunction with the simple tests.

The book covers visual skills, (including the seven basic visual functions), environmental factors (lighting and posture), auditory functions and processing, readability levels, and reading performance. Since poor spelling is often a side effect of reading problems, there is a special section on spelling strategies and games. Much of the visual and auditory skill development is done through simple games described in the book. The games are excellent for all learners, not just those who have learning difficulties.

Dr. Rappaport directs parents to resources for further assistance. For example, he tells how to determine what type of vision specialist to consult along with an address for obtaining referrals.

This book differs from others reviewed here in that it provides in-depth help for both visual and auditory problems. Dr. Rappaport offers scientific explanations for visual and auditory functioning, although complete understanding is not necessary to apply everything else in the book. *How to Teach Your Child to Read and Spell* is quite comprehensive yet very readable for the average parent.(S)

Learning in Spite of Labels
by Joyce M. Herzog
(Greenleaf Press)
$9.95

Home educators looking for help with their learning disabled children finally have something written just for them. Joyce Herzog, a learning disabilities specialist, shares encouragement and practical strategies based on her many years of experience. On top of that, this book is reader-friendly. Joyce keeps the message short-and-sweet and tells it in plain English instead of educational gobbledygook.

Rather than a step-by-step curriculum guide, this is a collection of ideas: things to think about, things to look for, and things to try. An unusual feature of the book is the chapter on dealing with depression. Teaching children with learning disabilities can be both tiring and discouraging at times, but this book can help you learn to maintain a positive outlook. The creative ideas in Chapter Seven will help you break away from classroom-type thinking, and the teaching tips in Chapter Eight will help you get past some major educational stumbling blocks.

Since children differ in their needs, you will have to decide which of the teaching tips might work for your child. However, the methods of encouragement and the Christian perspective presented here can be used with all children.

(Herzog is also the author of the *Scaredy Cat* reading program, another result of her years of experience helping children with learning difficulties.)[VT]

Special Education: A Biblical Approach
Edited by Joe P. Sutton
(Published by Hidden Treasure Ministries, available through Bob Jones University Press)
$19.95

Hidden Treasure Christian School is a rarity—a Christian school for students with moderate to severe disabilities. Through their experience they have learned a great deal about dealing with children with special needs from a Biblical perspective. That experience has been coupled with the expertise of other learning disabilities specialists to produce this book. Although the presentation assumes that most readers work from within a day school environment rather than a home school, it does acknowledge that part of the audience consists of home educators. The book is intended to primarily assist Christian schools to provide special education, but home educators can glean plenty of practical information. Rather than parrot public school policy for the Christian school environment, the authors integrate a Biblical philosophy of special education throughout each section of the book.

Although there is a section on recognition and identification of problems, this book is not intended to be a diagnostic tool. We understand that better if we realize the authors are addressing far more than learning disabilities. They cover all types of physical, emotional, and learning disabilities, including mental retardation.

The special education world has a vocabulary and structure of its own which the authors translate into everyday language. Individual education plans are described along with a sample form used by Hidden Treasure. Other sample forms for evaluating school work are also provided. Extensive appendices at the back of the book can steer us to resources and organizations for more help.

Smart but Feeling Dumb
by Dr. Harold Levinson
(Warner Books)
$14.95

This intriguing book suggests that many learning disabilities are based upon inner ear problems. Dr. Levinson advocates use of temporary medical treatment to achieve a permanent cure. I know of one well-known learning disability practitioner who incorporates such medical treatment into his program with sometimes successful results. The ISBN number for the revised edition of this book is 0446395455, and the library call number is 616.8553.

20/20 is Not Enough
by Dr. Arthur S. Seiderman and Dr. Steven E. Marcus
(Random House)
$5.99

Experts often find that vision problems are at the root of

learning difficulties or disabilities. Doctors Seiderman and Marcus believe vision therapy can be of tremendous help to many struggling learners and also to those who are near-sighted. Through case histories, they discuss various vision problems, provide the medical explanation, and describe possible treatments. This is not intended to be a do-it-yourself manual, but rather a guide that will help us identify possible problems. (They provide check lists of possible symptoms of vision problems.)

In addition to vision problems that hinder education, the book deals with sports and vision, the work place and video display terminals, aging and vision, and the possibility of curing myopia (near-sightedness).

An appendix summarizes various vision research studies and lists bibliographical information both for the studies cited and for further related reading. Check your library for this book. ISBN# 0449219917.(S)

Also, there are free articles about teaching children with special needs available on the Mastery Publications web site: www.masterypublications.com.

Seriously "Challenged" Homeschoolers

Many children who are being educated at home have difficulties beyond the normal range of learning disabilities. Some are blind, deaf, crippled, have Down's Syndrome and present parents with challenges beyond those facing most of us. A Christian non-profit organization of parents, NATHHAN, works together for mutual support and encouragement. NATHHAN acts as the center of a support network to help unite these families and share information. They publish a quarterly magazine. NATHHAN membership is $25 a year and includes a magazine subscription, lending library privileges, HSLDA membership discount, and a family directory. NATHHAN maintains a current listing of companies and programs that are NATHHAN family favorites. The listing is available by mail, and is also posted on their web page. NATHHAN is a family-operated ministry, founded by Tom and Sherry Bushnell.

Allergies

One further problem some parents have discovered at the root of their child's learning difficulties is allergies. If you have been puzzled by your child's ability to learn well and easily one day, and a seemingly contradictory inability to function the next, maybe allergies or environmental illness are the culprits. In her book, *The Impossible Child*: A Guide for Caring Teachers and Parents/ In School At Home, Dr. Doris J. Rapp (The Practical Allergy Research Foundation) [$7] describes and gives examples of behavioral and appearance clues to help spot allergy-related problems. Next she deals with possible environmental or food sources. Suggestions follow for teach-

ers to deal with problems including behavioral problems (such as unresponsiveness in learning situations) that have been caused secondarily by allergy problems.

A later section provides suggestions for parents to try to help alleviate certain factors under their control. Rapp points out that many children who have been labeled as learning disabled are in reality suffering from allergies. There are a number of methods of dealing with allergies which are discussed. A lengthy section of references will direct parents to sources for more information or assistance. Although written for teachers and parents in typical school settings, almost everything in this book will be equally applicable for home educators.

Is This Your Child? [$12] is a larger, newer book that covers much of the same information, but it is updated and concentrates more upon the types of symptoms some children manifest.

The Practical Allergy Foundation carries a new 635-page book by Dr. Rapp, *Is This Your Child's World?* [$12], and a 90-minute video, *Environmentally Sick Schools* [$15], which also provide helpful information to reduce illness and behavior problems while raising the academic performance in some children. *Is This Your Child's World?* deals with environment, diet, and fast, easy ways for a parent to pinpoint what might be causing problems in their children (and fix them). The emphasis on environmental and chemical pollution differentiates this book from the other books. Too often, children's undiagnosed sensitivities and allergies to environmental and chemical influences cause major learning problems, which might be solved with something as simple as an air purifier.

The Practical Allergy Research Foundation also provides helpful information such as a Multiple Food Elimination Diet that can be used to identify or eliminate possible food allergens.

Chapter 22
Sources for Materials

Now you are ready to order learning materials. How on earth do you go about it? Won't textbook publishers refuse to sell to individuals? It can seem very intimidating to set out to order curriculum on your own. However, there are many different ways to obtain textbooks. The least expensive way is usually to order directly from the publisher or from a distributor. Another way to get textbooks is by enrolling in a program that either provides the textbooks or orders them for you. If you enroll in a correspondence course, independent study program, or school service simply as an easier way to get textbooks, you will be paying more than you need to for books. If the services offered (other providing textbooks) are helpful to you, then enrollment might be the better procedure.

Your choices of methods and materials might be very closely tied to your choice of a correspondence school or independent study program. If you have determined that you have strong preferences in learning materials and methods, you need to make sure your choices are agreeable to any program in which you might be enrolling your children. On the other hand, if you have already determined that you wish to enroll in a particular program, you might find your choices of methods and materials very limited. Basically, you can choose from independent study programs, correspondence courses, or school services, although the distinctions between these different options are increasingly difficult to discern.

Independent Study Programs, Correspondence Schools, and School Services

There are various forms of independent study programs. Some operate under the government school system (e.g., charter schools), while others are private, operating under churches, private schools, organizations, or businesses.

Government school programs make your child part of that system. They offer varying degrees of flexibility in curriculum choices, although legally they are usually forbidden from granting credit for studies done with sectarian (i.e., Christian) materials. Programs through government schools often begin on a very positive basis, but usually public school authorities

will try to increase their control. Watch out for potential problems, or better yet avoid entanglement altogether.

Some Christian schools offer independent study programs where they provide books they are using in the school, and offer testing, field trips, record keeping, and teacher consultation. Sometimes you are limited to a choice of textbooks they recommend, but most seem to be open to a broad range of choices. Check with your local support group for possibilities, or approach Christian schools yourself with the suggestion that they form an independent study program.

Independent study programs are also offered by schools without campuses which have been formed strictly to meet the needs of home educators. These are generally much more open to your individual choice of materials although some promote a particular type of learning (e.g., classical approach or Alpha Omega LifePac curriculum). While many such programs are open only to families who live within a reasonable distance, others enroll students without regard to residency. Typically, local groups offer more field trips, classes, parent training, and other activities than do "distance" programs. Contact your local support group for information on independent study programs in your area if participation in a local group appeals to you.

Correspondence programs are not geographically limited (except, perhaps, to particular countries). They provide texts and learning materials, grade students papers and/or tests, and provide complete record keeping services. Many independent study programs offer these same services along with activities or other services, but independent study programs vary greatly in the amount and type of services offered. The terms "school service" and "umbrella program" are also used by some programs. Any of these is not necessarily better than another. It is important to determine the level of service you need if you are enrolling in a program, then select the one that best suits your purposes.

Following are descriptions of many different types of programs. A listing here does not imply an endorsement of any of them.

A Beka Correspondence School

This program uses A Beka texts, pre-kindergarten through twelfth grade. Students are held to a nine-month school year, although a one-time extension of six months can be obtained for a $25 fee. A Beka prefers that home schoolers enroll in this program rather than buy their books and work independently, but they do not pressure home schoolers to enroll. Teaching methods, like those of Christian Liberty Academy, are traditional with little hands-on activity. This is an academic program, which allows no substitution of other textbooks. Coursework is evaluated every six weeks for grades K-3 and every nine weeks for grades 4-12. A Beka suggests four hours daily to complete daily work for elementary grade students. The cost ranges from $500 to $630.

Enroll early as it takes from four to six weeks to process applications and get the books to you.

A Beka also offers home school **video courses** in addition to their well-known textbook line. We owe A Beka thanks for being the first to make the plunge into video for home educators. They realized that many of us lack time, confidence, or ability to teach, so they brought the classroom teacher to our homes to help us out.

A Beka video courses are of actual school classes with teachers presenting lessons to the children. Our students watch the videos then complete assignments in their A Beka texts. Complete programs are available for kindergarten through high school. Elementary courses come only as complete programs, while we can select individual junior and senior high classes. Jaffé Strings courses for learning to play string instruments are offered as electives for students ages 10 and up. Demo videos of courses are available for $3.95 each. I highly recommend that you review a demo before signing up for courses.

Two basic plans are offered—credit or non credit. For an entire program under the "for credit" option, the cost for kindergarten is $785 and grades 1-7 are $920 per year. For "noncredit courses" the cost for kindergarten is $750, and for grades 1-7 the cost is $879. Payment plans are also available. (All prices includes a $90 refundable retainer fee.) Discounts of 5% are given for additional children in the family enrolling in different grade levels, and significant discounts apply for children in the same family viewing the same courses. At older levels, credits are not issued for individual courses unless A Beka receives a letter from the child's school stating that they will accept the credit. The cost for credit then increases by $55. The refund policy is very forbidding. "Once the course has begun, there are no refunds for the video program.. If all items are returned unused..., your money will be refunded, less a $100 processing charge."

Video tapes are shipped back and forth and remain the property of A Beka. Tapes are sent in groups and must be used on a fairly rigid schedule. All courses must be completed in nine months, but extensions are available at extra cost. In the credit option, student work and tests are sent in, and an evaluation report is issued periodically. Work is evaluated every six weeks for K-3 and every nine weeks for grades 4-12. Permanent school records are maintained for each student.

Courses require a minimal amount of supervision. Kindergarten videos run about 2 1/2 hours a day, with an extra half hour to an hour of seat work and interaction. For elementary grades, videos run 3 hours per day, but combined with seatwork and studying, school time should take a total of 5 to 6 hours a day.

On principal, I do not generally recommend video courses for all subjects for younger students because of the lack of interaction and stimulation. (A Beka has tried to stimulate some reaction from students by having the video teacher call upon children to answer questions aloud.) However, I recognize that there are special situations that make them the most practical alternative, e.g., parent unavailable for interaction and a lack of alternatives, or students taking a course with which parents are unfamiliar. Even for older students, this is a lot of passive viewing. I urge you to break up the sit time with moving around and talking time. I have heard mixed reactions from those who have used the videos. Much depends upon the particular courses used and the child's learning style. Some of the video teachers keep the action moving better than others, encourage student responses, keep the video audience in mind, and otherwise make the course more appealing. We are viewing real classrooms, so we also see some typical classroom interactions, including students uncomfortable being taped, especially when they answer questions incorrectly.

Tape quality is an important issue, especially for children who will be watching three or four hours of these every day. The newer editions of these courses show significant improvement over the first courses. While they still use a single camera placed in the back of each classroom, they have organized the classroom appearance and flow better for video taping. The camera pans from teacher to students to blackboard or illustration fairly smoothly. However, A Beka still does not incorporate external graphics not used in the regular class presentation, failing to take full advantage of the video media.

For parents who want to create the typical, traditional classroom experience at home, this is probably the closest you can come.

Advanced Training Institute International

The Advanced Training Institute was founded in 1982 by Mr. Bill Gothard, founder and president of the Institute in Basic Life Principles (IBLP). The goal of ATI is to equip students with wisdom and understanding starting with Scripture at the core, then relating all academic subjects to it.

The curriculum for home education includes *Wisdom Booklets* and other materials from the Institute, and is designed to be supplemented with your own selected textbooks. These, too, are to be related to the major Scriptural concept currently being studied in the Wisdom Booklet. The focus of ATI is on life training rather than simply academic learning. This program is unique in that it requires familiarity with IBLP and its teachings and principles. In ATI, there is also strong emphasis on parental accountability and involvement. The entire family is enrolled in the program together. Acceptance into the ATI program is completed by attending a two-day Admission Conference. Contact ATI headquarters for dates and locations.

ATI is not a correspondence course; it does, however, offer a comprehensive reporting system designed to assist students in building a transcript that will be recognized at all levels. Write to ATI for more information or request information from ATI Headquarters by phone.

Bridgestone Academy

Formerly known as Alpha Omega Institute, Bridgestone Academy is an accredited, K-12 correspondence school which uses the Alpha Omega LifePacs and the Horizons curriculum. Students take diagnostic tests in math and language arts for proper placement in the curriculum, then they receive one year's LifePacs or the appropriate Horizon course for math, language arts, science, and history/geography. Parents receive training and orientation materials as well as ongoing support. The Academy reviews tests, provides written and oral feedback, records test results, provides report cards and transcripts, and issues diplomas. There is a registration fee of $75. Tuition fees as of winter 1999-2000 are $456 per year ($420 for additional students in the same family). Students may enroll anytime during the school year, but it must be for a minimum of one semester. Students have up to twelve months to complete the curriculum, but if they finish early, they can go ahead and enroll for the next level (paying again as if it were a new school year). Bible LifePacs may be added as an elective with the Academy or may be ordered separately from Alpha Omega.

Bridgestone OnLine Academy

Similar in concept to Bridgestone Academy, the OnLine Academy oversees students who use the *Switched On Schoolhouse Curriculum* which is available for grades 4-12. Tuition as of winter 1999-2000 is $850 per year for the four core subjects. Although students must complete a 180-day school year, the school calendar can be set up however parents wish. Students may also enroll for single subjects rather than full enrollment. Students receive the *Switched On Schoolhouse* curriculum, placement testing, progress reports, report cards, transcripts, and access to certified teachers.

Calvert School

PreK - $270; K - $310; grades 1: - $490; 2 - $505; 3 - $520; 4 - $535; per year; advisory teaching service: K is $200 per year and each grade level goes up $10 per year; there are no shipping charges to the continental U.S. via standard ground service

Calvert offers academic courses for kindergarten through eighth grade with all materials supplied for each course, including such consumable resources as crayons and pencils. Calvert's strength is in their coverage of geography, history, mythology, poetry, and literature, and in their teacher's manuals. Teacher's manuals provide clear, concise instruction for the novice teacher. Even though Calvert makes no such claim, their teachers manuals effectively teach us how to teach. Many of the Calvert courses are very good, although a few of the secular textbooks are mediocre. *A Child's History of the World* and other similar books are much better than typical textbooks. (*History of the World* is now available separately in a beautiful, hardcover edition.) This is not a Christian school and some of the texts contain evolutionary concepts. However, we are welcome to supplement or substitute lessons reflecting our own beliefs and philosophies for the Calvert lessons. Calvert staff seem to have made good judgments about making assignments from some of these books. For example in the K-II science book, there are a couple of pages about space aliens that has little relation to any science topic. The Calvert manual skips these pages, and so should you.

PreK and Kindergarten programs (formerly called Kindergarten I and II), are a little more challenging than some other programs. PreK includes many readiness activities. Reading instruction is introductory and does not use intensive phonics at this level. Kindergarten includes solid phonics instruction through beginning and ending sounds and short vowels. The program includes appropriate work pages and simple readers. Phonics instruction continues in upper grades with new texts and teacher materials for first and second graders that will be introduced in May, 2000.

Since subject studies are integrated to some extent, mixing of grade levels is not allowed with the exception of math. Calvert now offers an option for students to take a placement test and be given a math course at the indicated level. While these courses are a pre-packaged curriculum for each grade level, Calvert will allow students to enroll in the program minus the math curriculum. However, Calvert is introducing their own new math program for grades 1-4 in May of 2000, with grades 4-8 due for completion a year later, that should make this exception unnecessary. A second or third child can now enroll in a course already completed by a sibling at a reduced rate. They get replacements of consumable books, new books when necessary, and a new lesson manual to reflect any changes made. While we are still restricted on the amount of individualizing we can do with Calvert courses, this is a good choice for missionaries or others who have difficulty rounding up all the necessary materials or creating their own lesson plans.

We may enroll our child and work with him or her independently, or we may elect to include the optional Advisory

Teaching Service (ATS) for grades K through eight. With the ATS, tests are sent into Calvert for review and grading by a professional teacher/advisor who also makes comments and suggestions. At kindergarten level, children are given progress sheets rather than tests or grades. Only with the ATS will Calvert issue a certificate of completion for courses.

There is an optional video supplement for the first grade course called *Video Lessons for First Grade* [$50]. It offers expanded teaching help for selected lessons and is directed to students.

Calvert's *Spelling & Vocabulary* CD-ROMs for grades 3-8 are only $10 each when purchased with a complete curriculum.

Calvert also offers enrichment courses: *Beginning French* and *Beginning Spanish* courses for grades 4-8, Levels 1 and 2; *Melody Lane* music course on video for kindergarten through third grade (includes some theory) [$95]; *Discovering Art*, an art appreciation course for grades 4-8 [$125]; and *Classics for Children* literature series (See the review in Chapter Nine.) Enrichment courses are available to those not enrolled in Calvert. Use of enrichment courses for group classes is priced differently. Call for details.

Christian Liberty Academy
(satellite schools are referred to as CLASS)

CLA offers kindergarten through twelfth grades with a program very similar to most Christian schools. They have chosen an assortment of textbooks from various publishers, and they have begun publishing some texts of their own. The textbooks and program reflect a more traditional approach to education, using primarily workbooks and reading. Each course comes with the needed instructions or teacher's manual, and CLA has written their own, simplified teacher's manuals to be used in place of some of the huge volumes offered by many publishers. CLA offers options of either purchasing only books through them with no record keeping or enrollment (The Family Plan) or full enrollment in the correspondence program. If you start with the full enrollment plan, you can change to the Family Plan if you wish. This program is academically sound but does not meet the needs of learners who require hands-on activity. In the past, people have had trouble with the amount of work required, but the program has been changed slightly—requiring less work and offering more flexibility and discretion to parents. CLA has shown a commendable responsiveness to the needs of home educators. They have done an excellent job in their efforts to offer good materials at an affordable price.

Christian Light Education

Christian Light publishes their own LightUnits curriculum. See the description under "Major Publishers" in Chapter Four. While units, courses, and texts can be purchased individually, CLE also offers *Homeschool Plus*. For $100 plus $5 per stu-

dent, you receive parent training and one year of services which includes record-keeping leading to a CLE diploma, access to standardized achievement tests, and academic assistance. Families continuing with *Homeschool Plus* for subsequent years pay $75 plus $5 per student.

Clonlara School Home Based Education Program

Clonlara School is a fully-functioning private day school with a distance learning program to assist home educators. It aims to "create an environment where children and parents are free to guide their own learning. Close team effort with student and parent [is] encouraged and developed." Clonlara truly believes that parents should be directing home education, so they leave day-to-day schooling in parents' hands. Parents are free to choose any method of education with whatever resources they choose. They can use real-life activities, library books, student-designed projects, traditional texts, or other creative alternatives. Clonlara actually encourages us to stay away from textbooks as much as possible, but they will support you if that is your choice. Clonlara is non-sectarian, but they will gladly order Christian textbooks or resources for your use. Standardized testing is recognized as a necessary evil in some states, so Clonlara makes them available to those who need them, but they do not require them from all students. They supply guidelines for what is typically covered in various subjects. They assign a contact teacher who offers guidance and assistance as needed. They keep cumulative files on students, take care of legal and technical details, and issue report cards and transcripts when appropriate. They will also order curriculum and resources for you.

They leave the method of keeping in contact with the school up to the family. They say, "We are not here to badger or coerce...." They describe themselves: "Clonlara School is your shoulder to lean on, your listening ear, your guide, your coach, your file-keeper, your ultimate HELPER." If you want the freedom to do school your way, but you also want the assurance of assistance from an experienced organization, Clonlara fills the bill. Tuition per year is $550 per family with one student; with two to three students, cost is $575; with four or more students, cost is $600. The cost is higher for families living overseas. Clonlara's school year runs from September 1 through August 31. Tuition is prorated for enrollment after January.

Covenant Home Curriculum

Covenant offers kindergarten through twelfth grades for full programs or single courses. They use an assortment of Christian and secular texts with options for tailoring programs to suit the needs of each child—students may work at different grade levels in different subjects. There is more flexibility here than in some other correspondence courses. They will actually encourage you to "double up" so that different aged children work on the same courses when possible. Covenant has their own diagnostic test which can be used to properly place children in math and English.

The basic texts (e.g., S.R.A., Modern Curriculum Press, and Bob Jones) reflect a traditional approach to education, while optional supplementary books offer a more experiential approach. They define their approach as "classical," emphasizing rules, drill, and memorization in the early grades which form a foundation for future learning that stresses concepts and creativity. The phonics program is similar to A Beka's and incorporates *McGuffey Readers* and Covenant Home's updated version of some older phonetically-controlled readers in kindergarten. Like A Beka and *Sing, Spell, Read, and Write*, blending begins with consonant-vowel combinations, then adds following consonants. Bible memorization is required. Covenant teaches a Christian worldview from the Reformed perspective, using books such as the *Westminster Shorter Catechism* and the *God and Government* series.

Covenant integrates classic literature into the curriculum from third grade on. A unique extra with Covenant is *Classic Critiques*—"pamphlet" studies of classic literature for each grade level which also include worldview perspectives.

Covenant has created their "Testset" series of chapter, quarterly, and final tests with answer keys for most of the texts they use. Grading is emphasized. The *Covenant Home Curriculum Preceptor* covers the basics of grading, scheduling, and record keeping. The program, even when tailored, tends to be quite academic.

Course Blueprints show parents an organizational grid for each text and how it is to be used. More detailed help is available in the *Day By Day* daily lesson plan guides which are included with the curriculum for each subject area.

Covenant's program has been used successfully by families who prefer all of their materials provided through one source, yet want more flexibility than they can get from A Beka, Calvert, or Christian Liberty Academy. Covenant now offers the option of selecting course modules rather than complete grade levels, which will appeal to families who already know what they want to do with certain courses but want the help of a correspondence program with others.

The free *Course Inventory Catalog* explains the philosophy and details of Covenant's program. Full curriculum costs range from $365 to $512 for grades K-6. Replacement and "twin" kits are available at significantly reduced costs for families who are reusing a grade level with a second child or teaching two children at the same level simultaneously. Check with Covenant for prices on individual course modules.

Hewitt Homeschooling Resources

This center is a school service originally founded to implement the philosophy of Dr. Raymond Moore, but Dr. Moore is no longer associated with it. They have changed philosophically somewhat over the years. Although they are still advising people against forcing formal academics with young children, they have moved in a more academic direction for the early grades than they used to advocate. *Training Wheels, Here I Grow!, A Bee Sees*, and *Across America* offer activity-based learning for grades K-2.

Curriculum is offered for grades K-12, with other programs available for younger children. They provide testing, evaluation, and textbook recommendations, as well as phone counseling on their toll-free line. Textbook costs are in addition to registration costs. Many options are offered as far as types of programs, and they will tailor a program to suit each child.

If you only want help with curriculum selection, for $40 they will provide you with a questionnaire. After you return it, they create an individualized curriculum guide with book recommendations for your child.

Hewitt will specially tailor programs for children with various disabilities or handicaps. They also sell learning materials and books such as *Training Wheels* and *Winston Grammar* to those who are not enrolled.

Home Study International

Home Study International has been around since 1909, and they offer programs for preschool through college. Two options are available for the elementary grades: the Non-Accredited Plan and the Accredited Plan. The Non-Accredited Plan allows the parent to pick and choose from supplies and parent's guides. Keys for daily work are included in the parent's guides, but keys for exams are not included. The Accredited Plan includes teacher services, transcripts, report cards, etc., under an unaccredited program. An HSI teacher grades all tests, and parents can call or e-mail with any questions.

Home Study International is a Seventh-day Adventist organization, so their Bible courses reflect their doctrine; however, they are optional. Other texts are primarily from secular publishers. According to their catalog, "HSI tries to choose durable books and develop instructional material that appeals to children with varying learning styles." The kindergarten program is a hands-on, activity-oriented readiness program designed to prepare the child for first grade. Curriculum for other grade levels also looks very similar to standard classroom curriculum. They stretch a little further than some correspondence courses by teaching art and music, and by including materials for physical education with courses for grades 3-6. Contact HSI for price information; prices usually change July 1 of each year.

HomeSat

Bob Jones University Press offers home schooling classes through their HomeSat program for grades K5 through high school. Courses for younger grade levels are called BJ HELP.

These courses are delivered via satellite and BJUP has tried to make the courses as accessible as possible by offering a reasonably priced satellite dish, which we can either have installed or install ourselves. We record the broadcast courses on our VCR for use at appropriate times. Aside from the cost of the satellite, we pay $39.95 a month or $359.55 a year for access to all courses plus other programming (e.g., home school seminars, Bible studies, Christian music).

We can record and watch as many courses as we please, but we register for courses by paying $10 per course. Enrolled students receive quizzes, tests, and handouts for each course. (Photocopy the quizzes, tests, and handouts for other students.) No additional fee is required for additional students in your own family. We do need to purchase the BJUP texts, teacher's editions, and other resources for each course. This is not a correspondence course; no student work is sent to BJUP and no records are kept by them. Parents check and grade student work. Parent preparation and participation is extremely minimal, a boon to parents who need their students to accomplish much of their work independently.

The courses for the younger grade levels are presented by experienced teachers. They are filmed on stages with props such as puppets. Video technology is utilized to enhance courses with graphics, film clips, and other elements to add interest. Courses are transmitted via satellite two times each, a real help in case you forget to record it the first time. Tapes are ours to keep. For elementary grades, students should be able to view all grade level courses in three hours per day or less.

Kolbe Academy

Kolbe Academy is a Catholic homeschooling program that views itself as an assistant to parents who are directing the home education of their children. While Kolbe has recommended course material and syllabi, they allow parents to adapt materials and make substitutions as they see fit. This is not a correspondence course; parents make their own evaluations of a child's progress. However, parents may send sample materials or copies of assessments for Kolbe to validate grades given by parents. Quarterly reports containing such items are essential for Kolbe to be able to issue a diploma at high school level. Kolbe's proctor staff is available for consultation concerning any homeschooling questions, and they will comment on quarterly reports upon request.

Kolbe's recommended course of study is orthodox Roman Catholic, "based on the teachings of the Jesuits and the Spiritual Exercises of St. Ignatius Loyola...." This is a classical form of education characterized by the use of Great Books, the study of Greek and Latin, classic literary writings, and an emphasis on the history of western civilization. A solid academic foundation is stressed. Kolbe challenges the typical course of study by including Greek and Latin in the elementary grades and by following a relatively-narrow western civiliza-

tion outline for history studies at the high school level. They also recommend the *Faith and Life* series, *St. Joseph's Baltimore Catechism*, and stories of saints for elementary grade students.

Kolbe offers suggested resources and syllabi/lesson plans, but they also offer alternatives for many subject areas within their catalog and allow parents to use other resources of their own choosing. Many of the selected texts are Catholic (e.g., *Catholic National Readers* series and history texts by Anne Carroll) or "Catholic-friendly" (e.g., Voyages in English series). Kolbe makes Stanford Achievement Tests available to their families.

Kolbe Academy is accredited by the National Association of Private Catholic and Independent Schools.

Kolbe does not recommend enrolling kindergartners unless necessary. The annual fee for kindergarten is $75. The annual fee for students in grades 1-8 is $200 for the first student and $125 for each additional student. Books and resources may be purchased through Kolbe or obtained from other sources.

Landmark's Freedom Baptist Curriculum

Landmark offers a complete curriculum for grades K-12. Students can enroll in the complete program or purchase individual courses. There are three basic plans: Plan A provides all materials, record keeping, testing, report cards, and diplomas for $360 per year for the first child; $325 for the second, third, and fourth children; and $300 for each child thereafter. Plan B is placement and achievement testing which can be "purchased" in conjunction with the other plans as specified ($25 per child with $100 maximum per family). Plan C provides the course basics for any one course for $35. Plans A includes the LFBC Teacherguide which has basic "how-to" information, although it is not absolutely essential. Anyone who purchases four or more courses under Plan C receives the Teacherguide for free, or it can be purchased for $5. Customized samples (samples from two subject sets of the customers choice and a Scope and Sequence) are available for $5.

While LFBC will sell individual courses, they encourage home schooling families to work under an oversight organization for accountability. See further remarks under "Major Publishers" in Chapter Four.

McGuffey Academy International

McGuffey offers assistance to all who home educate their children, not only in America but around the world. Prescribed curricula includes Saxon math, Basic Education, Alpha Omega, Classic Curriculum, A Beka, Bob Jones, and others to meet the needs of students and the goals of parents. Some courses require an extra charge above the basic tuition.

Montgomery Institute

The Montgomery Institute was founded to assist families

who want to implement the Principle Approach. They offer two options: Option 1 - for $10 year you can obtain book service membership and obtain any of their more than 800 books and audio cassettes at discount prices; Option 2 - the Extension Study Program functions as a correspondence course. The required parent training program, taken through correspondence, costs $150. Tuition for the first child is $200, $100 for the second, and $75 for each additional child. As part of the training program you receive essential and valuable resources such as The *1828 American Dictionary of the English Language, The Christian History of the Constitution of the United States of America*, and *Teaching and Learning America's Christian History*, along with a number of audio cassettes and study guides. You also receive book service membership, free admission to the annual Biblical World View conference (held in Idaho) and regional workshop, monthly newsletter, consultation and curriculum selection assistance, teacher notebooks for each grade level you will be teaching (detailed how-to's and lesson plans), achievement tests (plus scoring and recommendations), and annual certificate of completion and or/ final diploma. They will also connect you with any others in your area to form a support group. (Note: At this time the detailed lesson plans are still in development and services are discounted to reflect that. Meanwhile, lesson plan guides, personal consultation, and other helps take their place.) Among the texts used for elementary grades are *Ray's Arithmetic, Our Christian Heritage, Latin Primers, Latin Grammar, Harvey's Grammar, McGuffey Readers, America's Christian History: Christian Self-Government* series, *Natural Science for Homeschooling Families, Spencerian Penmanship* series, as well as a number of Principle Approach oriented resources.

Moore Foundation Curriculum Programs

Dr. and Mrs. Raymond Moore's Moore Foundation now offers membership plus a number of service options.

Moore Foundation Associates (MFA), for families who do not need special services, requires a minimum purchase of materials or donation of $100 and provides an enrollment card which shows that the family is identified with and attached to the Moore Foundation. MFA membership is prerequisite to enrollment in all other programs. MFA members may enroll in any Moore Foundation service programs, as long as there is space.

Moore Academy Full Service Program (MAFSP) is a limited (in enrollment numbers) plan in which those who need more extensive accountability receive more extensive service that includes maintenance of a cumulative record folder, processing of requests for past school records, customized curricula, telephone or letter counseling, an initial evaluation, two progress evaluations, and certificate of completion or transcript. Specialized Full Service Program (SFSP) is for children

who might be "...learning-delayed, learning-different, talented & gifted, handicapped or otherwise in need of special counsel, special materials and perhaps teacher analysis of psychological tests." All programs are available for both elementary and secondary students. Cost varies according to the program.

Mother of Divine Grace

Mother of Divine Grace School offers K-12 classical, Catholic education for homeschooling families. Directed by Laura Berquist, the school reflects many of the ideas she presents in her book *Designing Your Own Classical Curriculum*. Families pay a $265/year enrollment fee plus $195/year consultation fee. Textbooks and learning materials are extra. Every family is required to participate in three consultation sessions. At the first session, a school consultant helps families develop the curriculum for each child. Although the school does try to tailor resources to fit the learning styles of each child, there are many pre-selected resources frequently recommended in keeping with the Catholic and classical learning goals of the school. However, Mother of Divine Grace is open to non-Catholic families who may select curriculum that meets their own needs. The school catalog provides descriptions of resources typically used for each grade level or course. In addition to the consultations, the school provides record keeping services, newsletters and information packets, diplomas, testing, and opportunities for networking with other parents. A "Teacher-Assisted" program is optional; for grades 4-6, the cost is $45 per semester per child for assistance with correcting and grading student work plus help with problem areas. Mother of Divine Grace also has a staff consultant for children with special needs. For a $50 fee, the school provides additional assistance with IEP's and oversight (when required by a state or school district). The school is accredited by NISAC and is seeking WASC accreditation.

Our Lady of Victory School

Established in 1977, this is one of the oldest homeschooling programs in existence. The school is traditional both in education and religion. They enroll students in grades K-12. In kindergarten (called grade 1A) the child will learn Catechism, phonics/reading, arithmetic, and cursive handwriting (if the child is capable). If taking part in the Full Enrollment Program, parents are required to operate regular school hours, assign homework, and maintain logs of time spent on each subject. However, if using the Satellite Program or buying books only, parents are free to create their own schedules.

The school uses a variety of resources including math texts from Steck Vaughan and Saxon, *Little Angel Readers*, the *Baltimore Catechism*, and *Phonics is Fun* from Modern Curriculum Press. They have created their own publishing arm, Lepanto Press, to reprint (sometimes with updates) older texts that used to be used in Catholic schools. Among these reprints are the *Voyages in English* series, *Catholic National Readers*, and the *Science and Living in God's World* series.

The school offers Full Enrollment, Satellite Programs, and book purchasing. Satellite Programs provide lesson plans for $85 for a full load of 6 subjects; no grading or record keeping service is included. Full Enrollment includes record keeping, quarterly progress reports and report cards, diplomas (for grades eight and twelve), and lesson plans. The registration fee is $25 for the first year. Tuition for grades K-6 is $200. The costs of books is additional, with some books available for rental.

Seton Home Study School

Correspondence courses for elementary through high school are offered for full or partial enrollment. Seton offers a traditional, Catholic education at a reasonable cost. They use an assortment of Catholic and other textbooks to provide a quality education. As Seton Press continues to expand the number of books they publish, these are incorporated into Seton's program. At present they publish their own Catholic spelling, English, art, history, religion, handwriting, reading comprehension, and science books, although they do not yet have books for all grade levels. They offer students to enroll in different grade levels for different subjects, and they will sometimes accommodate choices of other resources, but curriculum is mostly predetermined for each subject area.

Because their primary desire is to be of service, Seton offers individual courses (partial enrollment). Some elementary students enroll only in religion courses. This is one of the few programs that allow this. Supplemental software is available for some courses.

They have a large staff of very-experienced teachers and personnel available to assist families enrolled in their program. Seton also serves students with special needs. Contact them for information about the special needs of your child.

Seton also has an office in Southern California to better serve West Coast families. This office offers all of Seton's services. Students who live in California and enroll in Seton need not be covered under another private school affidavit.

Prices vary by grade level and number of children enrolled. Base program fees cover textbooks, workbooks lesson plans, counseling, tuition, tests, grading, and shipping and handling. For grades 1-8, the lesson plans must be returned to Seton at the end of the year. Children may also enroll in single courses at elementary level at a cost of $85 each, except for math courses which are higher.

Seton is accredited by the Southern Association of Colleges and Schools as well as by The Commission on International & Trans-regional Accreditation.

Sonlight Curriculum-International Home Schoolers Curriculum

While Sonlight is not a correspondence course, it is designed like some such courses with a teacher's manual that outlines lessons for each day using specific pages within the materials provided. However, there is no option for sending in work for grading or record keeping.

Sonlight offers a complete, eclectic, literature-based program integrated around historical themes for kindergarten through at least ninth grade (with a tenth level due in 2000). Most levels are designated by years rather than grade levels. World history is taught in grades K-2 and levels 5-6. American history is taught in levels 3, 4, and 7.

Sonlight stresses subject matter over grade level. Because it is a literature (rather than textbook) based program, parents with more than one child are often able to use one year's selection of history, read-aloud, and science books with all their children. In fact, from the fifth year up, Sonlight manuals are specifically designated for use by students in a range of grades. (This is why designations shift from "grade" to "year.") The fifth-year manual, for example is designed for use in any grade from fifth through ninth. The eighth year program is designed for students at any level from eighth through twelfth. You can use the courses at different levels by substituting the appropriate math and language arts materials your student needs, while using the history and science program from just one level.

Sonlight also offers outstanding, mix-and-match loose-leaf teacher's manuals for each subject in every grade. Subjects include Basic (history, readers, read-alouds, and Bible), Language Arts (phonics-oriented reading in early grades, handwriting, dictation, spelling, grammar, vocabulary, creative writing), Science, and Math. All manuals include week-by-week lesson guides with record-keeping calendars, and thorough instructions. Sonlight emphasizes only those activities that have clear educational purposes; make-work projects and crafts are nonexistent. Though parent-child interaction is required at certain times, little time is required for lesson preparation. I am impressed also with the weekly writing assignments built into the curriculum, as this area is lacking in so many other programs.

Sonlight Curriculum features quality literature, a few textbooks and workbooks (e.g., ScottForesman's *Exploring Math*, Saxon *Math*, *A Reason for Writing*, *Italic Handwriting*, *Wordly Wise*), many Usborne and Dorling Kindersley (DK) titles, a huge assortment of literature, historical fiction, topical fiction, and hands-on math and science from the earliest grades. The educational philosophy is generally that of Dr. Ruth Beechick: structured, yet allowing for maximum learning-in-life.

Subjects include language arts (phonics-based reading, writing, spelling, etc.), read-aloud classics and poetry, world history, geography, math, science, Bible (including Christian and missionary biographies), art, and music. Supplemental materials are available for critical thinking, foreign language, art, music, geography, Bible study, typing, creation/evolution, and Canadian history.

Sonlight sells complete curriculum packages for each subject in every grade; it also permits you to purchase any individual items out of the complete packages. The Sonlight science program includes basic science supplies. On its Basic curriculum packages (history, readers, and read-alouds), Sonlight offers an eight-week "use it; if you don't like it, return your program for a complete refund" guarantee. Customers who purchase a complete Basic program have the opportunity to purchase science, math, language arts, and enrichment materials (physical education, art, music, foreign language, etc.) at a 10% discount. Prices for the Basic curricula (ranging from about $300 to $545, depending on the grade) reflect an effective 17% discount when you include the fact that they offer free shipping anywhere in the world. Much of the curriculum is non-consumable, so we can reuse a large percentage of each level with other children. Many of the books used in the curriculum are ones that I would personally be purchasing to build our family library, so, from this perspective, the cost is actually even more reasonable. We save even more if we teach children from the same resources whenever practical even though they might be at different grade levels.

Sonlight is proving to be an excellent option for families that want assistance putting together a "pick and choose" program, but who lack the experience to do it on their own. I strongly recommend reading through Sonlight's catalog before determining which levels or resources to use.

Summit Christian Academy

Programs for first through twelfth grades include testing and placement at appropriate levels in each subject area. They use Alpha Omega for first grade and above, although other materials may be used with their approval. There are three programs to choose from for pre-kindergarten and kindergarten levels. Two of the programs utilize the *Writing Road to Reading* phonics format and the third program is the Alpha Omega *Horizons* program. Summit also offers some alternative and supplementary resources such as *Writing Strands, Reason for Writing, Grammar Songs*, and *Easy Grammar*. They encourage multi-sensory learning and allow some flexibility in designing your program. The toll free telephone number allows parents to consult with the school when necessary.

See both "Testing Services" and "Diagnostic Testing" above for information about Summit's testing services.

A special price of $556 includes enrollment, testing and tuition for four subjects. Or, parents can pay for each item separately. Enrollment is $30 per student; testing is $35 (grades 3-8). Tuition for kindergarten is $111-$285, $325 for grades 1 and 2, and $350 for grades 3-8. Tuition includes all record keeping, report cards, transcripts, and diplomas, as well as

consultation with their toll-free number. Books are extra. Prepayment and family discounts are available on tuition.

Sycamore Tree Center for Home Education

Sycamore Tree Center for Home Education offers full record keeping, educational guidance, supervision, testing, student body cards, 60-80 pages of enrichment learning material every month, and more. They will assist you in developing an individualized program for each child. Guidance is available by phone or mail. A credentialed teacher is on staff during all office hours. Enrollment entitles you to 10 percent discount on curriculum and materials ordered through Sycamore Tree. While this is a good solution for all families, it is especially good for isolated families. (Sycamore Tree has families enrolled from all over the world!) They recommend materials from a wide range of publishers and include both traditional and informal learning materials.

Sycamore Tree has recently added on-line schooling as an option for grades 4 - 12. Under this program, students use Alpha Omega's *Switched On Schoolhouse*, working with credentialed teachers who provide assistance and grading. Classes in Bible, English, Math, Science, and Social Studies are available. English class is $250 and all others are $200 each. All five subjects are $1,000. Also, students might use a combination of these classes and traditional classes if they choose. See Sycamore Tree's web site for more information.

Tree of Life School

Based in New Brunswick, Canada, this school serves home educators in both Canada and the U.S. who are interested in the classical approach to education. They are an affiliate of The Association of Classical and Christian Schools, and they adhere to the Westminster Confession of Faith.

This is a home-based service provided by experienced home educators, Mike and Debbie Flewelling. They offer either monitored and unmonitored enrollment for grades 1-12. For grades 1-6, monitored students submit samples of their work three times a year to Tree of Life for evaluation and comments. With either service, parents receive help in putting together an individualized, classical curriculum for each child. The cost for monitored programs is $165(U.S. dollars) for the first child, $150 for the second and $385 for three or more. For unmonitored programs, cost for the first child is $100, $85 for the second, and $250 for three or more. Materials will cost an additional $150-$400 per child.

Emphasis is on both Christian world view and the classical approach. Students use books such as Saxon *Math, Greenleaf Guides*, Canon Press' *Latin Primer, Vocabulary from Classical Roots*, and *Wordsmith*. Art and music are included in all grade levels. Foreign language is introduced at first grade level and continues through all grade levels. Canadian or U.S. History texts are used at the appropriate grade levels. Read-aloud books are included in each program, and Tree of Life also provides a suggested reading list. The last half of their catalog offers many such books and supplementary curriculum items for sale.

The Westbridge Academy

Westbridge Academy is a college preparatory school service that functions as a correspondence school, but without the rigid limitations common to most. Geared for academically accelerated students, Westbridge helps parents individualize their curriculum and timing to suit each learner. Instead of a prescribed curriculum, goals are set for three levels: Foundations for Learning (approx. grades Pre-K to 3), Basic Studies (approx. grades 4-6), and Advanced Studies (approx. grades 7-12). Those goals include a Judeo-Christian and Classical orientation that stresses the foundations of Western Civilization. While Westbridge is a Christian organization, they will accept non-Christian students. Upon enrollment, students take placement tests and produce writing and grammar samples for evaluation. Individual consultations are scheduled to develop customized academic plans. (It is unlikely that any two students would be using identical books in this program!) Westbridge offers some of their own specially designed courses along with evaluation, counseling, record keeping, transcript, and college application services.

Students may work at different grade levels in various subjects. Credit may be given for alternative learning experiences. The staff of Westbridge Academy includes Kathleen and Mark Julicher of Castle Heights Press and Robert and Kathleen Kustusch of Lightsource Editing Service. Tuition is $800 per year per student with discounts available for more than one student in the family and for early enrollment. Book costs are in addition to tuition costs. Books are ordered by families directly from suppliers, although Rainbow Re-Source acts as their official supplier.

Special Sources

Second-Hand "Stuff"

Schools often discard outdated or unneeded books. Keep your eyes open. Library book sales and thrift stores are often surprising sources for good materials. Used book stores carry all types of books, including some textbooks. Encyclopedia sets, reference books, classic literature, and just about anything else can be found sooner or later at one of these sources.

Ads and Announcements

Magazines, listed and described in Chapter One, include advertisements and product information. They keep you up to date on what is available.

Convention Tapes

O.T. Studios has been taping workshops at home school conventions for many years. They offer tapes from such events for many months afterwards. These tapes address just about

every aspect of home education, although the quality varies from tape to tape because of the convention settings. Write to O.T. for a catalog of their home school tapes. You might also contact your state home school organization to see if they have tapes available.

Free for the Asking, The Resource Guide for Free Educational Materials and Programs

(Hirst)
$17.95

This book tells us where to get all sorts of learning materials for elementary grades through high school including maps, posters, curriculum guides, lesson plans, coloring books, slide presentations, videos, and much more. For example, one listing reads: "Exploring Maps Teachers Packet contains two colorful 22" x 60" posters that feature illustrations of map development from 900 B.C. to present day, as well as map-related texts and a do-it-yourself timeline. The teaching guide includes four activity sheets (themes: location, navigation, information and exploration), notes questions and glossary." Appropriate age levels and the source address follow. An index makes it easy to locate items related to an area of study.

Home School Suppliers

There are a number of businesses set up particularly to serve the home school community with materials. Others offer materials appropriate for home education, although that is not their primary purpose. All of these offer a free catalog or brochure of their materials unless I state otherwise.

Academic Distribution Services, Inc.

This Canadian mail order company carries the complete Alpha Omega line plus Canadian social studies resources and products from publishers like Cadron Creek, School of Tomorrow, Common Sense Press, ISHA Enterprises, Bob Jones University Press, Usborne, Saxon, National Writing Institute, Backyard Scientist, Trend, Mott Media, and Modern Curriculum Press. Their catalog is a combination of the Alpha Omega catalog and their own. They also carry math and science resources not listed in the catalog. Check to see if they have what you need for these areas.

ATCO School Supply, Inc.

ATCO has a walk-in store, open Tuesday through Saturday, and they also fulfill phone and mail orders. They carry thousands of items including Alpha Omega, Saxon and Horizon's math, Modern Curriculum Press, *Learning Language Arts Through Literature*, and *Writing Strands*, plus some not listed in their catalog. Their inventory ranges from traditional texts through creative learning materials, including a large proportion of items reviewed in this book. Credit cards are accepted.

Bluestocking Press

Bluestocking Press carries a different line of materials than any of the other suppliers, concentrating on American history, economics, and law. History resources are carefully selected for historical accuracy. They are listed in the catalog chronologically and under category headings such as fiction, primary source material, historical music, and coloring books. Bluestocking carries the *Little House on the Prairie* books plus many related items such as the *Laura Ingalls Wilder Timetable*. Other products include helps for critical thinking and writing skills, reading guides, basic home schooling books, and their own unique publications: *The Authentic Jane Williams' Home School Market Guide*, *How to Stock a Home Library Inexpensively*, *Whatever Happened to Penny Candy?*, and other "Uncle Eric" titles by Richard Maybury. Send $3 to cover first class shipping of this catalog for immediate delivery. Money back guarantee. MasterCard and Visa accepted.(S)

Builder Books

They sell a full line of carefully-selected educational materials for home education, including many items recommended in this manual such as those from Beautiful Feet Books, Betty Lukens Felts, Saxon math, Progeny Press, Common Sense Press, *Power-glide,* Green Leaf Press, Miquon Math, Modern Curriculum Press, Workman, Aristoplay, and more. This is a good source for those who need educationally-sound, cost-effective alternatives as well as the most effective traditional materials. They ship most orders within 24 hours of receiving them. Credit card orders accepted.

Canadian Home Education Resources

The Baradoys, an experienced home schooling family, have carefully selected resources for their catalog reflecting a consideration for the needs of various learning styles and educational philosophies while being selective as far as content that is not objectionable to Christians. They carry items such as *Pathway Readers, Miquon Math, Horizon Math,* Progeny Press guides, BJUP texts, Greenleaf Press publications, *Easy Grammar, Five in a Row*, Richard Maybury books (*Whatever Happened to Penny Candy?*, etc.), *Considering God's Creation*, Critical Thinking Press books, *K'Nex*™ sets, *The Learnables, World Book Encyclopedia*, and Canadian history and geography resources. All prices in their catalog are shown in Canadian dollars, and they offer a low price guarantee. They accept Visa and MasterCard orders by phone, mail, e-mail, or fax.

Children's Books

This is a source for curriculum and children's reading books that have already been screened for ungodly content. The catalog lists curriculum from publishers such as School of Tomorrow, Easy Grammar, Doorposts, and Christian Liberty along with a few games and flash card sets. Literature/reading books include biographies, classics, beginning reading, preschool, and fiction. They carry books from Troll, Dover, Usborne, and others, including Christian literature from publishers such as Mott, Bethany House, and Moody. Both reading levels and interest levels are listed under literature descriptions. All orders are discounted 15-30%. Visa, Discover, and MasterCard are accepted. Send for free catalog.

Christian Book Distributors (CBD)

CBD is a discount source for Christian books. They carry over 70,000 titles with discounts usually ranging between 20% and 90%. CBD has expanded its focus on home education with a special home education catalog. CBD also publishes special gift, fiction, music, academic, and family catalogs, available upon request. Credit card orders are accepted by mail, phone, and via their secure web site.

Christian Curriculum Cellar

Christian Curriculum Cellar sells used curriculum from A Beka, Bob Jones, and Alpha Omega, along with items from other publishers such as Saxon. They also serve as a reseller

Customized Curriculum Packets

For beginning home educators, curriculum purchases are often a shot-in-the-dark. There is simply too much information to sort out to make the sort of well-informed decisions that they would like to make. Curriculum counseling, aside from that offered through school services, is often hard to find.

Curriculum Cottage's *Homeschool Curriculum Packets* can help solve the problem for many families. They have put together complete curriculum packets that include personalized teaching instructions (including daily lesson plans) for each product in the packet and for all required subjects. You have the option of selecting Bible-based or non Bible-based packets, although the "non" packets will not include materials offensive to Christians. Non-bible based packets include products from publishers such as Modern Curriculum Press, Saxon, and Educators Publishing Service. Bible-based packets include products from publishers such as Association of Christian Schools International, Alpha Omega, and Progeny Press.

They use a personal questionnaire and placement exams (for 2nd grade and up) to determine the child s grade level and the appropriate type of resources. They encourage the use of low-cost materials and multi-grade teaching. Curriculum Cottage will supply you with the resources and included free shipping. Cost for the materials should range between $165-$220 per child for the elementary grades for non Bible-based curriculum and between $185-$245 for Bible based curriculum.

for materials we no longer need by giving us a credit for 30-50% of their selling price. Since the stock is ever-changing, call to see if they have what you want or check their web site. They have an on-line catalog with options for checking availability of items and secure ordering.

Creative Home Teaching

Their 120-page catalog leans towards creative, hands-on resources rather than traditional texts. They list many intriguing items not reviewed in my book, as well as resources such as Backyard Scientist books, Brown Paper School Books, Dale Seymour products, Key Curriculum products, Common Sense Press publications, *Discovery Scope, Memlok*, Critical Thinking Press books, and more. An unusual line they carry is the Reflective Educational Perspectives Learning Style Assessment kits. Request a free catalog. Credit cards are accepted.

Curriculum Cottage

Curriculum Cottage, the Sciscoe family's home business, offers curriculum for preK-12. Their web catalog features descriptions of the broad range of products they offer. Among their products and product lines are Common Sense Press, *Understanding Writing*, Educators Publishing Service, Pathway Readers, *I Love America, Italics Handwriting, The Phonics Game, Cuisenaire Rods*, and *Sing, Spell, Read, and Write*. Credit cards are accepted. Their web site also offers answers to the most commonly asked homeschool questions. (See the box on the previous page for information about their Curriculum Packets.)

Discount Homeschool Supplies

The Tatum's, a homeschooling family, strive to offer materials at about 20% discount. They carry a good selection of resources including *Power-glide* languages, *Easy Grammar,* Bob Jones University Press, Christian Liberty Press publications, Common Sense Press books, *Miquon Math, Saxon Math*, Alpha Omega curriculum, *The Weaver*, and *Five in a Row*. Because of their low prices, returns are accepted only when they ship an item incorrectly. Visa, MasterCard, Discover are accepted.

The Eagle's Nest Educational Supplies

This is a mail order catalog, but they also have a store with limited hours. (Call before coming!) They carry a mix of texts, activity-oriented materials, unit studies, and Bible and history resources promoting a practical approach to creative curriculum for all grade levels. Examples: Saxon *Math, Learning Language Arts Through Literature*, Pathway Readers, *Calculadder, GeoSafari*, Creative Teaching Associates, Ampersand, Aristoplay, Educators Publishing Service, *Cuisenaire Rods, Spelling Power, Easy Grammar*, and

Greenleaf Books. They offer a 15-day money-back guarantee. Credit card orders are accepted. A web site with an on-line catalog is under development.

The Elijah Company

The newest Elijah Company catalog (at 200+ pages) reflects a greatly expanded line of resources for all subject areas. This business, operated by a home schooling family, has selected quality materials that reflect their eclectic philosophy of home education. They describe various educational philosophies extensively at the front of their catalog to provide a better background for making your own selections. At the back of the catalog are grade level recommendations of resources Elijah Company considers to be "best bets." Excellent commentary on what and how to teach is sprinkled throughout the catalog. A large part of the catalog is devoted to history resources, listed by topic/time period. Science resources listed under topic headings is another bonus.

Emmanuel Books

Run by a home schooling family, Emmanuel Books features resources for Catholic home educators. They also specialize in many items of interest to those using a classical approach, particularly following Laura Berquist's recommendations in *Designing Your Own Classical Curriculum*. They seem particularly strong in history, literature, language arts, and religion resources, but they do carry resources for all subject areas. They also carry Laura Berquist's *Syllabi* with lesson plans for classical education. Emmanuel Books accepts phone orders using Visa or MasterCard.

Emmanuel Center

Emmanuel Center sells via mail order, as well as being a walk-in bookstore, Mon-Fri. They have been serving homeschoolers since 1983 and specialize in core curriculum for PreK-12. They also have a used book section in their store, although no in their catalog. Some new items are discounted. All employees have been involved in homeschooling or teaching, and you can talk directly with a curriculum consultant from 9 to 10 a.m. every weekday morning on the inquiry line. Among products and product lines they stock are Common Sense Press products, *Horizons Math*, Modern Curriculum Press, *KONOS*, Educators Publishing Service, Pathway Readers, Saxon Math, and Michigan History resources. They accept phone, fax, mail, and e-mail orders.

Excellence in Education

They describe their catalog as one "specifically designed to bring the joy of learning to your homeschool." Consequently, their catalog is heavy with games, activity-oriented materials, and math manipulatives. They also carry some workbooks, biographies, and curricula such as DK book, Greenleaf Guides,

Educators Publishing Service, Intrepid books, Usborne Books, Beautiful Feet materials, and Modern Curriculum Press *Math*. They accept VISA, MasterCard, Discover, and American Express orders and offer a free catalog. They also have a walk-in store in Monrovia, California with limited hours. Send $1 for catalog. Call to verify current hours and location.

Exodus Provisions

Exodus Provisions operates a walk-in store as well as their mail-order catalog. They carry a large selection of used books in the store, although they are not listed in their catalog. Call to check on items in which you are interested. The catalog offers a broad selection of books, including texts, literature, and theological works reflecting their Reformed/Presbyterian background. Among publishers they carry are Modern Curriculum Press, Canon Press, Christian Liberty Press, ISHA, Saxon, Greenleaf, and Beautiful Feet Books.

Family Learning Center

They are a retail source primarily for Common Sense Press but also for other products. They carry *Creating Books with Children, Learning Language Arts Through Literature, How to Home School, Grocery Cart Math, Record Keeping Sheets, The Great Editing Adventure, Wordsmith* series, and *Math Sense Building Blocks Program*.

Family Resources/Love To Learn

Family Resources, Inc. is operated by veteran homeschoolers. Their *Love to Learn* catalog features a selective line of resources that includes parent helps, books on government and issues, some basic curriculum, but, primarily, homeschooling resources that are fun and multi-sensory: games, puzzles, tapes, math manipulatives, science resources, rhythm instruments, craft kits, sticker books, and their own *Happy Phonics* reading program. Credit card orders are accepted by mail, phone, and through their secure web site.

Farm Country General Store

In spite of its name, this catalog focuses primarily on home education resources, offering many at discounted prices. (The name was chosen because they are farmers located in the midst of beautiful farm country.) In addition to basics such as Saxon math, *Learning Language Arts through Literature*, and *Daily Grams*, they carry a wide variety of books and hands-on resources for all subjects. As a Christian company, they have selected resources carefully without limiting their product line to only Christian publishers. Unlike most other distributors, and in keeping with the name "General Store," they have a section of products for "health, nutrition, and home" that includes cookbooks and a few natural remedies, flour mills, and open-pollinated seeds. MasterCard and VISA are accepted.

Follett Home Education

Follett offers "reconditioned" and out-of-print editions of books from both Christian and non-sectarian publishers such as A Beka, Addison-Wesley, BJUP, Harcourt Brace, Houghton Mifflin, Macmillan, McDougal Littel, Open Court, Riverside, Saxon, and ScottForesman. You can save up to 75% off publisher prices on texts, workbooks, and teacher's editions. They also sell new dictionaries and reference materials at discount prices. Their web site has current information on what's in stock, and you can order on-line 24 hours a day.

Frank Schaffer Publications, Inc.

Frank Schaffer's catalog features posters, Animal PhotoCharts, literature notes to accompany novels, giant puzzles, bulletin board sets, charts for all subjects, stickers, games, and activity books for math, language arts, social studies, and thinking skills. Prices are very reasonable, e.g., 17" by 22" charts at $1.75 each.

God's World Book Club

God's World Book Club offers books, games, and other supplementary educational materials. Their free catalog clearly indicates which are secular and which are Christian resources. Secular books have been screened and objectionable content noted. Titles carried change frequently, especially bargains with limited quantities available. Offerings are primarily for elementary grades, although a few are for older levels. MasterCard, Visa, and Discover accepted. Satisfaction guaranteed.

Greenleaf Press Catalog

Greenleaf's specialty is history. They began with resources for studying Egypt, Greece, and Rome, then grew from there. In addition to their own publications (reviewed in the history section) they list books, tapes, games, and other resources according to historical periods. They also carry home school basics such as *For the Children's Sake; You Can Teach Your Child Successfully; Sing, Spell, Read, and Write;* and *Writing Strands*. Order by phone, mail, e-mail, or on-line at their web site. MasterCard, VISA, and COD orders accepted.

Hearthside Homeschool Helps

Hearthside's homeschooling catalog specializes in KONOS materials and lots of "real books" in addition to ISHA Enterprises products, *Learning Language Arts through Literature*, the *Wordsmith* series, Key Curriculum products, Saxon math series, hands-on math materials, and much more. 33 pages of their catalog list products according to their correlation with each of the *KONOS* volumes. Visa, MasterCard, and Discover are accepted.

Heppner & Heppner Construction

Heppner & Heppner Construction carries a very selective line of carefully-tested (with their 14 children!) resources. They specialize in age- and subject-integrated materials which save us time, energy, and money. The Heppners will help you sort out your home school needs via their 800 telephone number. (They also offer workshops and seminars.) Resources are carefully screened to avoid content problems. Examples of what you will find in their catalog: books by Ruth Beechick and Mary Pride; Betty Lukens felts; Providence Project; Math-It; Greenleaf Press; Common Sense Press; *How Great Thou Art* books; *Backyard Scientist*; biographies; Saxon products; Christian Liberty Press; Alpha Omega; EDC/Usborne; Dover; reprinted classics; and home school journals and organizers. A few items are discounted, and quantity discounts/free shipping are available.

Hewitt Homeschooling Resources

Hewitt is always changing and growing, so if you have not perused their catalog lately, it is time to take another look. They offer their own curricula for grades K-2 and the *PASS* test, plus an assortment of hands-on materials, creative activity books, Saxon Math, *Writing Strands, The Write Source, Winston Grammar*, and *Math-It*. Their catalog is a selective but interesting assortment of traditional and non-traditional resources.

Home and Hearth

Home and Hearth services Canadian home educators through their mail order catalog and retail store. They carry a wide variety of products, including Canadiana and resources from publishers such as Saxon, Alpha Omega, Common Sense Press, Aristoplay, Pathway, Educational Insights, and ISHA. They also specialize in unschooling materials with an extensive selection of hands-on learning tools and educational games. Orders accepted by phone, fax, or e-mail.

The Home Computer Market

The Home Computer Market specializes in software for home educators. Of especial interest is their book *The Homeschooler's Computer Guide: A Resource for Choosing and Using Educational Software and Computers* [$7]. This resource guide also serves as a catalog. This is probably the best single source for the most reviews of software products of interest to home educators. Dan and Tammy Kihlstadius carefully screen programs for home educating families who desire products with educational value but without objectionable content. Most of the worthwhile products are sold by The Home Computer Market. Of course, you should then order those products from Home Computer Market to help support their work in sorting through the new products that come out and saving you money you might have spent on objectionable or worthless software. (Most of their products are discounted 25-35%.) The resource guide also features a number of articles to help you in selection and use of hardware and software, use of the internet, judging software's educational value, programs to avoid (a lengthy list!), and much more. Two super-useful charts will help you in software selection: the Software Planning Grid shows what software to use for different subjects for each grade level, and the Unit Study Guide suggests software programs to be used under a number of different possible unit study headings such as U.S. History, physical science, etc.

The Homeschooler's Computer Guide 2000 will be published sometime in 2000 and will replace this first edition. This next edition will be a "real" book of about 250 pages with lots more reviews. Price should be about $18.

Home School & More

This is primarily a mail order company, based in Canada, although those in the area can make arrangements to visit their warehouse if they call ahead of time. While they carry items found in other catalogs (e.g., Saxon, Common Sense Press, ISHA Enterprises, Teacher Created Materials, Pathway Readers, *American Girls*), they also sell Canadian history, social studies, and handwriting curriculum plus the *Voyages in English* series and a broad selection of "real books," activity books, manipulatives and games. Descriptions in the catalog are very helpful. No credit card orders but they will bill on orders under $250. Checks are accepted in either U.S. or Canadian funds with the exchange rate indicated in the catalog. Most orders are processed within 24 hours within Canada, and within up to two weeks leaving Canada.

The Home School Inc.

Since 1985, The Home School has been providing parents with homeschooling advice from experienced homeschoolers. They also offer a comprehensive selection of over 1500 quality homeschooling resources that can be ordered on a toll-free Advice Line Mon. - Fri., 10am - 10pm (eastern time) or through their secure web site 24 hours a day, 7 days a week. If you are in the Seattle area, they have a store (with regular hours) where you can browse through their huge selection. They accept Visa, Mastercard, Discover, or checks for sales in store or by mail order.

Home School Resource Center

Debra Bell has been presenting home schooling seminars for years, helping thousands of parents educate their own children. The Home School Resource Center grew out of her work as a means of providing many of the resources Debra recommends. With both a retail store and mail order catalog, they carry a wide selection of books, tapes, CD-ROMs, and other resources, including tapes and handouts from some of Debra's seminars. The Resource Center catalog leans toward "real" books but does include some textbooks. They also offer a 15% discount on orders over $200.

Home School Used Book & Curriculum Exchange

Buy and sell used curricula or books on-line through this handy web site. Listings arranged under different headings help you search for books by subject, title, or author, or for curricula under publisher, subject, or grade level. There is no fee for listings, but there is a fee when items are sold: $.50 each for items $5 or less, and 10% of list price for more expensive items. "For Sale" listings are removed when the item sells or after six months, whichever comes first. Check it out at www.homeschoolusedbooks.com.

The Home Works

This Canadian distributor carries a diverse line that includes Saxon math, *Learning Language Arts Through Literature*, Alta Vista curriculum, math manipulatives, games, Usborne books, French materials, and Canadian social studies resources. They accept VISA and Master Card.

Homeschool Potpourri

Colleen and Todd Aukland handle both new and used materials for home education. They will sell your used materials on consignment. (You get 50% of the selling price.) They carry many items reviewed in this book.

John Holt's Book and Music Store (Holt Associates)

They offer a magazine, books, speeches on tape, and more for home educators. While items reflect a wide (primarily non-Christian) philosophical range, they tend to be very creative and unusual. They carry some recommended titles I have found nowhere else. They will accept telephone orders using MasterCard or Visa.(S)

Landmark Distributors

They specialize in Principle Approach resources of all types, including just about everything related to the Principle Approach reviewed in this book. They also carry many other history resources such as the *Greenleaf Guides*, Christian Liberty history books, biographies, historical novels, *Operation World, You Can Change the World*, "Little Bear" Wheeler and David Barton video and audio tapes, as well as selected items for most other subject areas. They accept VISA, MasterCard, and Discover cards. Alan and Lori Harris of Landmark present seminars and book fairs on numerous topics, including many on various aspects of the Principle Approach.

Learning House

The Christian homeschooling House family publishes a catalog of resources targeted primarily at Canadian homeschool-

ers. (Catalog prices are in Canadian dollars.) They have carefully selected items to meet the needs of all types of learners including those with learning disabilities. They offer products such as Bob Jones University Press books, *Play 'N Talk, Mastering Mathematics, Alphabet Island,* Pathway readers, *How Great Thou ART,* literature, Green Leaf Press books, Saxon *Math, Pearable,* and Canadian history, geography, and social studies resources. MasterCard and Visa orders accepted.

Learning Lights

Learning Lights specializes in resources for a non-textbook approach to learning, especially those for hands-on learners. While they carry some books like *Understanding Writing and English from the Roots Up*, they are weighted more toward manipulatives, games, science kits, and fun activity books. They strongly recommend hands-on approaches for preschoolers, and they include extensive, practical suggestions for that age group along with suggested resources. They do not take credit card orders. They offer a 30-day money-back guarantee.

Library and Educational Services

Although they do not carry textbooks, they do offer many other children's books at discounted prices (at least 30% off of list price). Catalogs, published every 8-12 weeks, list books from Bethany House, Focus on the Family, Your Story Hour, and other publishers, and include biographies, classic literature, history, literature (primarily Christian), videos, and many other items for home schooling. They frequently add new items to the catalog, and they include coupon specials and occasional closeout sales. Be sure to identify yourself as a home schooling family because they are a wholesaler, not generally "open to the public."

Lifetime Books and Gifts (Bob and Tina Farewell)

Lifetime's 240-page catalog is titled *The Always Incomplete Resource Guide. Resource Guide* is accurate because product descriptions are more detailed than in most catalogs, and they include many practical tips. Lifetime offers a huge variety of materials for home educators, including good literature, biographies and history (listed under time periods), science and nature (with a section of resources listed under the days of creation), unit study curricula, resources for special needs, and much more. Mrs. Farewell also offers a special book search service for out-of-print books such as old editions of *The Book of Life, Child's History of the World*, and *Child's Geography of the World*. Send $3 for *The Always Incomplete Resource Guide and Catalog*. Credit card orders are accepted.

Maple Ridge Books

Since 1994, the folks at Maple Ridge Books have provided Canadians with a large selection of interesting educational books on topics such as Bible reference, education, geography, history, language arts, foreign languages, literature, math, science, and unit studies. Prices are listed in Canadian dollars.

Mission Resource Catalog
(William Carey Library)

The William Carey Library specializes in missions resources. Their catalog lists books and audio and video tapes for all ages. They sell everything at discounted prices since their goal is to get the resources out rather than making big profits. This is the most complete catalog for such resources I know of. They sell books such as *Operation World, Perspectives on the World Christian Movement, You Can Change the World*, and *Darwin on Trial*.

The Moore Foundation
(Dr. Raymond and Dorothy Moore)

They offer all of Dr. Raymond and Dorothy Moore's books, the *Moore-McGuffey Readers*, a newsletter—*The Moore Report International*, and a variety of materials in accord with their educational philosophy, including *The Weaver, KONOS, Math-It, Winston Grammar*, felt sets, Saxon Math, *Learning Wrap-Ups*, Sower's Series, Usborne books, and more. They plan to increase the number of resources offered, so send for a catalog for a complete list.

More Than Books...

More Than Books publishes two catalogs. One is similar to many others with an assortment of curriculum, literature, parent helps, tapes, and games plus Canadian history, government and social studies resources. Their other catalog focuses on additional resources for Catholic families. Among these are the *Designing Your Own Classical Curriculum Syllabi* for grades K-8, plus selected classes. More Than Books sells many of the resources called for in each of the syllabi, either as individual items are as packaged sets. They sell only to customers in Canada.

Rainbow Resource Center

Rainbow Resource Center is owned and operated by a Christian homeschooling family and offers a wide variety of educational products (books, learning tools, software, and games) in all subject areas and for all grade levels from preK to 12. Over 7,500 items from more than 200 publishers are currently available for a variety of learning and teaching styles. Most prices are discounted, and credit card and check-by-phone orders are accepted. Their free catalog provides detailed descriptions of the products they carry.

Saints & Scholars

Saints & Scholars' catalog features resources for Catholic home educators. In addition to widely used products like *Saxon Math, Learning Language Arts through Literature*, and *Wordly Wise*, they carry a number of different Latin programs plus books from Ignatius Press, TAN Books, Neumann Press, Bethlehem Books, and other Catholic publishers. They include basic curricula, literature, supplements, and fun extras. They will order items for you that are not listed in their catalog. Credit card orders accepted. No returns.

Shekinah Curriculum Cellar

Shekinah features a full line of home education materials, books, and games, including many items recommended in this manual such as A Beka, *Writing Strands, Easy Grammar*, Alpha Omega (English and all high school subjects), Saxon Math, history (reprints of classic editions), science kits, literature, Progeny Press, and Usborne books. They guarantee the lowest prices on all but A Beka. Shekinah also has a store, albeit with limited shopping hours. If you are in their area of Texas, call for a recorded message about store hours. Catalogs are provided free of charge to groups. To request them, send them your group's name, address, and current membership number. Visa, MasterCard, and Discover accepted. Phone orders are welcome and shipped the same day received.

Sonlight Curriculum-International Home Schoolers Curriculum

Sonlight Curriculum is available to all homeschoolers. Even though they offer complete grade-level packages, we can purchase anything from a single book to the complete curriculum. See "Correspondence Schools" for a fuller description of the types of materials offered.

Sycamore Tree Center for Home Education

They offer curriculum from more than 200 publishers plus a huge selection (about 3,500 items) of books, games, and toys carefully selected based upon their years of experience. Sycamore was the first home school supplier on the scene and has a long-standing reputation for dependability. They supply resources primarily through mail order, but their warehouse is open to walk-in customers the first and third Wednesdays of every month.

Catalogs are usually $3, which includes a $3 certificate redeemable on your order, but they are free if you mention *Christian Home Educators' Curriculum Manual*. Visa, MasterCard, American Express, and Discover orders are accepted.

Timberdoodle

Timberdoodle, a business operated for more than fifteen years by a home schooling family, carries an unusual but limited line including such things as Fischertechnik, arts and crafts resources, games, *Cuisenaire Rods, TOPS* science units, the *Learnables, PowerGlide, Switched On Schoolhouse, Piano Discovery*, parent helps, *Lauri Puzzles, Pathway Readers*, computer programs, and more.

Tobin's Lab

I've already described this catalog under "Equipment and Supplies" for science in Chapter Fourteen. However, in addition to being one of the best science resource catalogs, it has now expanded to include history resources including many items for hands-on learning.

Veritas Press

Veritas Press is associated with Veritas Academy, a classical Christian school. Thus, their catalog features resources of particular interest to those wanting to provide that type education. They carry products such as *Saxon Math*, *Shurley Grammar*, Canon Press books, Greenleaf books, *Wheelock's Latin*, and Usborne books, plus a large selection of "real books"—literature, classical works, and reference books. A free Classical Christian Curriculum Guide can be downloaded from the website. They also offer free curriculum counseling by telephone appointments; if you use this service you are under no legal obligation, but you really should purchase materials from Veritas.

Whole Heart Ministries

A ministry of veteran homeschoolers, Sally and Clay Clarkson, Whole Heart presents conferences and seminars as well as offering products through their catalog. The catalog reflects their educational philosophy, with a strong emphasis on family, discipleship, and family-centered learning. They carry many books related to the Charlotte Mason approach including literature and "real" books.

Sources For Special Needs

While in this book we do not address specific learning needs resulting from disabilities, physical handicaps, or (on the other extreme) giftedness, we realize that some children will need materials that are more challenging, move at a slower pace, or are designed to help overcome a particular disability. Following are some sources that we have found useful. All offer free brochures or catalogs. Be sure to check the other sources above, some of whom also carry items for special needs.

Braille Institute

The Braille institute operates only in southern California, but they have a toll free number anyone may call to obtain referrals for assistance in their area. There are many organizations other than the Braille Institute helping those who are blind. Many of them offer classes in life skills, free library loans, and other services. A series of five public service videos dealing with problems encountered by blind people at different ages is available for borrowing at no charge through many video stores.

For referrals call (800) BRA-ILLE. Our local Braille Institute will answer written inquiries. Write to Braille Institute, Orange County Center, 527 North Dale Ave., Anaheim, CA 92801, or call (714) 821-5000.

Educators Publishing Service

EPS offers materials for both average and below average learners. This is one of the best sources of materials for children with "minor" disabilities such as dyslexia and dysgraphia. Books range from general materials useful with all children to those addressing very specific needs, and they are very reasonably priced.(S)

The Learning Home

The Learning Home offers both resources and services for children with special needs. Owners Janine and Paul Seadler specialize in designing and maintaining programs for children with special needs. They will work with you to create an educational program. They can assist with interactions with school districts when necessary.

Modern Signs Press, Inc.

Sign language materials. Send for free catalog.(S)

National Deaf Education Network and Clearinghouse/Info to Go

Info to Go is sponsored by Gallaudet University. Their web site describes their services: "Info to Go, formerly the National Information Center on Deafness, is a centralized source of accurate, up-to-date, objective information on topics dealing with deafness and hearing loss in the age group of 0-21. Info to Go responds to a wide range of questions received from the general public, deaf and hard of hearing people, their families, and professionals who work with them. Info to Go collects, develops, and disseminates information on deafness, hearing loss, and services and programs related to children with hearing loss from birth to age 21."

Phoenix Learning Resources

They offer *Programmed Reading* plus other materials for students with learning disabilities.

Identification

Sometimes we need identification cards for our children. We can create them ourselves by gluing a small photo on a card on which we have typed the child's name and the school name. You might want to add the school year if you don't mind creating a new card each school year. Some home schoolers have found it useful to create identification badges children wear when they are on field trips, even family-size field trips.

The "official" identification makes it easier to deal with questions such as, "Why aren't you in school today?"

Ordering

When ordering from publishers, it is a good idea to use school stationery for a more professional look. Some publishers will sell to us only if orders are written on school letterhead. To create school stationery/letterhead you can have a typesetter create a heading on a plain 8 1/2" by 11" piece of paper as you have seen on other business stationery. It need not be fancy, but it should look professional. It should include school name, address, and phone number. Typesetting and printing can be very expensive. A better option is to use a computer/laser printer service that will create and print stationery for us in the small amount we will need. A source for customized school stationery is **Educational Support Foundation** which offers a stationery package that includes 20 preprinted sheets (plus a master for getting more printed locally), envelopes (unprinted), and second sheets [$25]. They also sell preprinted-custom labels, transcript forms, and report cards. (Send for complete price list.)

A very few publishers have policies stating they will not sell to individuals. Some say they will sell student texts but not teacher's editions to individuals. Their concern is usually to prevent regular school students from getting teacher's editions for purposes of cheating. If we order on school letterhead or send a copy of a school affidavit or other official document showing the school's existence, we will usually have no problem with any of the publishers I have listed. Some publishers charge extra fees for small orders, making it more economical for us to order their materials from one of the sources I show following their listing.

If you have not yet read the first section of this manual, "How to Choose Curriculum," do so before proceeding with ordering.

Generally, you will order on the grade level you feel is appropriate for your child. However, if you have delayed academics until a later age, you might want to go back and review through the earlier grade level material, bringing your child quickly up to the "age appropriate" level. You will find that a child who has been delayed in his approach to traditional academics will learn much more quickly than the younger child in most cases. Do not purchase an entire kindergarten or first grade curriculum for a delayed eight-year-old child, but rather choose materials that are not age specific like *Professor Phonics; Sing, Spell, Read, and Write*; or *Math-U-See* which cover the basics of some subject areas and can be used at whatever speed you desire.

It is a good idea to order books for the fall well in advance, at least by early summer, to avoid back orders and long waits. Many publishers will offer you an examination/return period, although they will ask for payment ahead of time. You could then return books that do not satisfy you. This can be a lot of trouble, and the postage can be expensive, so do try to see textbooks at conventions, other home schoolers' homes, Christian schools, or wherever else you can. However, paying postage affords you the opportunity to review materials in the quiet of your home at your leisure and saves the hassle of vying with many other home schoolers at conventions to see the curriculum and ask questions.

A few last thoughts before ordering

Cost doesn't = quality:

Costs vary greatly among publishers, yet the cost will still be far less than the cost of Christian school. Cost does not always guarantee the best quality. Paying more than is necessary to accomplish our goals is a waste of our resources. On the other hand, choosing the cheapest option may cost more if we have to buy something else to replace it because it did not suit our purposes. Also, paperbacks will generally be less expensive but also less durable than hard cover books. If it is likely that books will be used by more than one child, purchase hard cover books whenever possible.

Don't judge books by their covers:

Do not judge books solely by their appearance. Flashy graphics and color can sometimes be a cover-up for poor content (particularly with the secular publishers). If the appeal of color and pictures is important for our child, that is one thing, but the content needs to be worthwhile.

But appearances do sometimes matter:

Do look for large print in younger children's texts to avoid eyestrain.

Watch the busywork:

Remember, most curricula materials are designed with a certain amount of busy work built in to help occupy children so that the teacher can work individually with students. It is important to be aware of this and not require children to always do all of the problems and exercises.

Don't buy too far ahead:

Don't try to save money or energy by buying curriculum for children too far ahead of schedule. While this strategy might work with other purchases, it rarely works with curriculum since it is impossible to know what will be best for our children a year or two from now.

Appendix

Sources for materials I have referred to in this manual are included here. If you are looking for a publisher with what sounds like a person's name in the title, it will be listed as if the name were a company name (e.g., Wm. B. Eerdmans is under "W"). You can usually contact the publishers directly, but sometimes publishers would rather not sell to individuals. In these cases, they have distributors to sell us their products. In many cases you will pay the same price whether ordering from a distributor or a publisher.

I have referred you to a number of sources that carry lines of products for home educators in the section titled "Sources." It can be very time consuming and expensive to write to every publisher and distributor who might have something of interest. I have tried to make things easier by providing a key to help you identify a source that might carry a number of the items in which you are interested. Then you can place one larger order, saving on shipping costs and hassles.

In the key, I list again some of the sources described more fully under the "Sources" section. These particular sources were chosen because of the number of reviewed products that they carry, their established reputations, and their ability to fill orders from all over the country. (It also reflects their willingness to take time to go through this appendix and identify which items they sell.) Some of the other sources listed in the "Sources" section might fit the same requirements, but I had to make arbitrary selections to keep it manageable.

Obviously it is difficult to keep track of who is selling which items, and that information changes from time to time. Because I do not indicate that an item is carried by a certain distributor, it does not preclude the possibility that they do indeed carry it. The best approach is to obtain catalogs from a number of these sources for reference.

I have included prices unless the publisher did not supply them for some reason. I must caution you that prices change frequently, so you must check the actual price before ordering. In fact, you should expect prices to go up. You will also need to check the cost of shipping and tax on any order. Prices are supplied only so that you will have some idea what a product might cost, an important factor for many of us as we narrow down our choices.

I know that many home educating families operate on very limited budgets and are looking for bargains. However, if you seek information or advice about a product from a distributor who sells at full retail price, then you purchase the item from a discount source, you are taking unfair advantage of that distributor ("...for the worker is worthy of his support." Matt. 10:10).

All of the publishers and sources listed will send a free catalog or brochure unless otherwise specified. SASE means self-addressed stamped envelope. This should be a business-size envelope with a $.33 stamp. Check for more complete details concerning distributors under "Sources for Materials."

Many publishers and sources have toll free telephone numbers. This means that they pay for the cost of our call. These numbers all have (800, 888, or 877) as their area code prefix. If a number is for orders only, please call the other number listed with other types of questions.

I've listed web sites and e-mail addresses for many sources. I've omitted "http://" at the beginning of all web site addresses that start with "www." Technically, the "http://" precedes "www." However, addresses that do not include "www.", since they are unusual, all include "http://".

KEY

ATCO	A
BUILDER BOOKS	B
CHRISTIAN BOOK DISTRIBUTORS	C
ELIJAH COMPANY	D
THE HOME SCHOOL BOOKS AND SUPPLIES	E
HOME SCHOOL RESOURCE CENTER	F
LIFETIME BOOKS AND GIFTS	G
RAINBOW RESOURCE CENTER	H
SHEKINAH CURRICULUM CELLAR	I
SYCAMORE TREE	J

Reading the Codes

The letter following each publisher's name is their code letter. These code letters identify which of the above sources carry which products. Letters [e.g., (C)] immediately following the name of a book or resource indicate that this particular item—but not necessarily any other items from that publisher—is carried by the distributor. The code letters at the end of a publisher's listing (usually following a dash) indicate that the sources represented by their codes carry most or all items I've listed from that publisher.

A

A Beka Book Publications
Box 18000
Pensacola, FL 32532
(877) 223-5226
(800) 874-3590.FAX orders only
web site: www.abeka.org

A Beka Correspondence and Home Video School
Box 18000
Pensacola, FL 32532
(800) 874-3592
(800) 874-3593 FAX

Academic Distribution Services, Inc.
528 Carnarvon St.
New Westminster, BC V3L 1C4
Canada
(604) 524-9758
(800) 276-0078
e-mail: ads@intergate.bc.ca

Action Reading, Inc.
PO Box 4944
Cave Creek, AZ 85327
(800) 378-1046
(602) 465-0274 FAX
e-mail: reading@netzone.com
web site: http://www.actionreading.com
Action Reading Fundamentals

Activities for Learning
21161 York Rd., Dept. CD
Hutchinson, MN 55350-6705
(320) 587-9146
(320) 587-0123 FAX
e-mail: joancott@hutchtel.net
web site: www.alabacus.com
(H)

Addison Wesley Publishing Company
See ScottForesman-Addison Wesley

Advanced Training Institute International
Box 1
Oakbrook, IL 60522-3001
(630) 323-2842

web site: www.ati.iblp.org
Seminars, *Character Sketches* books,
and the Advanced Training Institute of
America

AIMS Education Foundation
PO Box 8120
Fresno, CA 93747
(209) 255-4094
(209) 255-6396 FAX
e-mail: aimsed@fresno.edu
web site: www.aimsedu.org

Alfred Publishing Co. Inc.
PO Box 10003
Van Nuys, CA 91410-0003
(800) 292-6122
(818) 891-5999
(800) 632-1928 FAX
e-mail: jmalone@alfredpub.com
web site: www.alfredpub.com
(C,E)

Alpha Omega
300 North McKemy
Chandler, AZ 85226-2618
(800) 622-3070
(480) 785-8034 FAX
web site: www.home-schooling.com
See "Major Publishers" for a more
detailed description. Publisher of
LifePacs, *Horizons Math* for grades K-6,
Horizons American Language series K,
*Switched On Schoolhouse, Color
Phonics*, and *The Big Books of Home
Learning* (G).—(A,C,E,F,H,J)

Alta Vista Curriculum
Alta Vista College
12324 Road 37
Madera, CA 93638
(800) 544-1397 from U.S. or Canada
(209) 645-4083
e-mail: odysseyone@thegrid.net

alwright! Publishing
PO Box 81124
Conyers, GA 30013
e-mail: KymWright@openarms-
magazine.com
web site: www.openarmsmagazine.com
*Bird Unit Study, Microscope Adventure!,
Goat Unit Study, Sheep Unit Study,
Poultry Unit Study, Botany Unit Study.*
They also have studies on *Photography,
Flower Arranging and Wreaths*, and
Victorian Sewing and Quilting.

Amanda Bennett
5251 C Hwy. 153
#141
Hixson, TN 37343
(423-554-3381
e-mail: amanda@unitstudy.com
web site: www.unitstudy.com
Unit Study Adventures

**Ambleside Educational Press/The Relaxed
Home Schooler**
Mary Hood, Ph.D.
PO Box 2524
Cartersville, GA 30120
(770) 917-9141
e-mail: relaxedhomeschool@juno.com
*Countdown to Consistency: A Workbook
for Home Educators, The Joyful Home
Schooler, The Relaxed Home School*
(B,D,G,H)

American Christian History Institute
James Rose
PO Box 648
Palo Cedro, CA 96073
(916) 547-3535
(916) 547-4045 FAX
web site: www.achipa.com
*A Guide to American Christian
Education for the Home and School* (D)
and other Principle Approach materials.
Also available from Foundation for
American Christian Education.

American Education Corporation
7506 North Broadway
Oklahoma City, OK 73116
(800) 222-2811
(405) 840-6031
(405) 848-3960 FAX
A+ LS Home computer curriculum

American Map Corporation
46-35 54th Road
Maspeth, NY 11378
(800) 432-MAPS orders only
(718) 784-0055
(718) 784-1216 FAX
*Schick Anatomy Atlas, Bible Atlas,
World Atlas*, maps (B,H,I)

American Portrait Films
PO box 19266
Cleveland, OH 44119
(800) 736-4567
(216) 531-8600
(216) 531-8355 FAX

e-mail: amport@amport.com
web site: www.amport.com
*The X-Nilo Show: Dinosaurs and the
Bible* (C)

American Science and Surplus
3605 Howard St.
Skokie, IL 60076
(847) 982-0870
web site: www.sciplus.com

AMG Publishers
PO Box 22000
Chattanooga, TN 37422
(800) 251-7206
Learning English with the Bible series
(C,D,G,H,I)

Apologetics Press
230 Landmark Dr.
Montgomery, AL 36117
(800) 234-8558 for orders
(334) 272-8558
(334) 270-2002 FAX
e-mail: Mail@ApologeticsPress.org
www.DiscoveryMagazine.com
Discovery

Aristoplay Limited
8122 Main St.
Dexter, MI 48130
(800) 634-7738 orders
(734) 424-0123
web site: www.aristoplay.com
Hive Alive, Made for Trade (A,G),
Moneywise Kids, Where in the World?
(A,D,G)—(B,C,E,H,I)

Art Extension Press
PO Box 389
Westport, CT 06881
(203) 256-9920
(203) 259-8160 FAX
web site: www.home-
school.com/mall/artext/

**Association of Christian Schools
International**
PO Box 35097
Colorado Springs, CO 80935-3509
(800) 367-0798
e-mail: order@acsi.org
Spelling (J), *Encyclopedia of Bible
Truths for School Subjects* (C,D)—
(B,E,G,H,I)

At Home Publications
M. Jean Soyke
2826 Roselawn Ave.
Baltimore, MD 21214
(410) 444-1326 voice and FAX
e-mail: Jsoyke@juno.com
web site: www.athomepubs.com
Art Adventures at Home (B,E,F,G,H)

ATCO School Supply, Inc.
425 East Sixth St. #105
Corona, CA 92879
(888) 246-ATCO orders only
(909) 272-2926
(909) 272-3457 FAX
e-mail: atco@atco1.com
web site: http://www.atco1.com
Family Adventure Photo Books

Audio-Forum
96 Broad St.
Guilford, CT 06437
(800) 243-1234
(203) 453-9794
(203) 453-9774 FAX
e-mail: info@audioforum.com
web site: www.audioforum.com
Phrase-A-Day, Storybridges for Children, and other audio cassette programs, plus *Say It by Signing* (E)

Audio Memory Publishing
501 Cliff Dr.
Newport Beach, CA 92663-5810
(800) 365-SING
www.audiomemory.com
Grammar Songs Kit, Geography Songs, Sing Around the World, States and Capitals Kit, Addition Songs, Subtraction Songs, Multiplication Songs Kit (,B,C,E, F,G,H,I,J)

B

Back Home Industries
PO Box 22495
Milwaukie, OR 97260-2495
(503) 654-2300
resource books for history, plus reading and language arts materials: *Teaching Reading at Home & School* (B,G), *The Wise Guide for Spelling, 70 Basic Phonograms and Cassette Tape* (B,G), *TRHS Chart Masters* (B), *The Alpha List, The Primary Learning Log*, Blank Spelling Notebooks, and more— (I)

Backyard Scientist
Jane Hoffman
PO Box 16966
Irvine, CA 92623
(949) 551-2392
(949) 552-5351 FAX
e-mail: backyrdsci@aol.com
web site: www.backyardscientist.com
The Original Backyard Scientist (J), *The Backyard Scientist Series 1-4, Exploring Earthworms*, science kits—(B,C,E,G,H,I)

Baker Book House
PO Box 6287
Grand Rapids, MI 49516-6287
(800) 877-2665
(800) 398-3111 FAX
Astronomy and the Bible, Questions and Answers, How to Raise a Reader, The Light and the Glory for Children (D,F,J), *Parents' Computer Companion, Science and the Bible, Weather and the Bible* (D)—.(B,E,G,H,I,J)

Banner of Truth
PO Box 621
Carlisle, PA 17013
(717) 249-5747
(717) 249-0604 FAX
Sketches from Church History (B,C,G,H)

Barnum Software
3450 Lake Shore Ave., Ste. 200
Oakland, CA 94610
(800) 553-9155
(800) 553-9156 FAX
e-mail: mail@thequartermile.com
The Quarter Mile Math Game (H)

Barron's
250 Wireless Blvd.
Hauppauge, NY 11788
(800) 645-3476 for orders only
(516) 434-3311
web site: www.barronseduc.com
Science Wizardry for Kids

Beacon Hill Press
2923 Troost Ave.
Kansas City, MO 64109-1593
(800) 821-2890
Bible Maps & Charts (H)

Bealls' Learning Games
3375 Edward Beale Rd.

Georgetown, CA 95634
(530) 333-4589
Phonogram Fun Packet (A,I,J)

Beautiful Feet Books
139 Main St.
Sandwich, MA 02563
(800) 889-1978 orders only
(508) 833-8626
(508) 833-2770 FAX
e-mail: russell@bfbooks.com
web site: http://www.bfbooks.com
American History Study Guides; History of California; History of California Time Line; A History of Science; A Literature Approach to Geography, History and Science Using the Holling Clancy Holling Books; A Literature Approach to Ancient History; A Literature Approach to Medieval History, Along Came Galileo, Magna Carta, and *Evaluating for Excellence.* They also publish the series by the D'Aulaires: *George Washington, Leif the Lucky, Pocahontas, Buffalo Bill, Ben Franklin*, and *Columbus* as well as Genevieve Foster titles: *The World of Columbus and Sons, The World of Captain John Smith, George Washington's World* and *Augustus Caesar's World.* (B,D,E,F,G,H,I)

Berean Bible Ministries
26571 Briarwood Ln.
San Juan Capistrano, CA 92675
(949) 364-3138
Train Up a Child

The Bess Press
3565 Harding Ave.
Honolulu, HI 96816
(800) 910-BESS
(808) 734-7159
(808) 732-3627 FAX
e-mail: email@besspress.com
The Hawaiians of Old, Hawaii: The Pacific State

Bethany House Publishers
11400 Hampshire Ave, S
Minneapolis, MN 55438
(612) 829-2500
(800) 328-6109 orders
e-mail: cs@bethanyhouse.com
Basic Greek (D), *Celebrate the Feasts* (G,I),
The Wonderful Way Babies are Made

(G,I,J)—(C)

Bethlehem Books
10194 Garfield St. South
Bathgate, ND 58216
(800) 757-6831
web site: www.bethlehembooks.com
*Archimedes and the Door of Science,
Hittite Warrior, The Story of Rolf and
the Viking Bow*, and other
literature—(B,C,G,H)

Betty Lukens Felts
711 Portal St.
Cotati, CA 94931
(800) 541-9279
(707) 795-2745
(800) 795-8225 FAX
e-mail: info@bettylukens.com
web site: www.bettylukens.com
Sets of felt figures for Bible, the human
body, "Quiet Books," and more. Many
items are identical to those from Little
Folk Visuals. (B,H,I,J)

Bible Memory by Memlok
420 E. Montwood Avenue
La Habra, CA 90631-7411
(800) 373-1947 orders only
(714) 738-0949
(505) 202-2768 FAX
e-mail: memlok@memlok.com
web site: www.memlok.com
Send SASE for free brochure.
(A,B,D,G,I)

Bible Study Guide for All Ages
PO Box 2608
Russellville, AR 72801
(800)530-7995
(501) 967-0577
e-mail: m/wbaker@cei.net
 E,G,H,I)

Bill Rice Ranch
627 Bill Rice Ranch Rd.
Murfreesboro, TN 37128
(615) 893-2767
(615) 898-0656 FAX
e-mail: billriceranch@worldnet.att.net
Sign Language For Everyone. The book
is published by Thomas Nelson
Publishers and can also be obtained
through them. (B,D,G,H,J)

Blackstone Audiobooks
PO Box 969

Ashland, OR 97520
(800) 729-2665

Bluestocking Press
PO Box 2030, Dept. G
Shingle Springs, CA 95682-2030
(800) 959-8586 orders only
(530) 622-8586
(530) 642-9222 FAX
Whatever Happened to Penny Candy?
(D,G,J) and other "Uncle Eric" books
(B,F, H), *American History Comes Alive
Through Narration and Song*, and
more—(I)

Bob Jones University Press
Greenville, SC 29614
(800) 845-5731
web site: www.bjup.com
See "Major Publishers" for a more
detailed description. Publisher of *Best
Books for kindergarten through high
school* and *Special Education: A
Biblical Approach*. Distributor for *Clear
and Lively Writing* (selected items -
A,C,E,H,I,J)

Bolchazy-Carducci Publishers
1000 Brown St., Unit 101
Wauconda, IL 60084
(847) 526-4344
Artes Latinae (D,G)

Books for Results
704 Parkvalley Rd. S.E.
Calgary, AB T2J-4V8
Canada
(403) 271-9085
(403) 278-1160 FAX
Writing with Results

Books on Tape, Inc.
PO Box 7900
Newport Beach, CA 92658
(800) 541-5525
(714) 825-0764 FAX
web site: www.booksontape.com

Bookworm Books of TN
Belinda Couch
200 Deer Ridge Ct.
Kingsport, TN 37663
e-mail: bcouch5@juno.com
My Special School Journal

Bradrick Family Enterprises
1176 West Satsop Rd.

Montesano, WA 98563
(360) 249-2472 (call 9-5 PST)
Understanding Writing (B,E,G,H,I,J)

Braille Institute
Orange County Center
527 North Dale Ave.
Anaheim, CA 92801
(714) 821-5000
(800) Bra-ille for referral information
web site: www.brailleinstitute.org

**Bridgestone Academy and Bridgestone
OnLine Academy**
300 North McKemy Ave.
Chandler, AZ 85226-2618
(800) 682-7396 Academy
(877) 688-2652 OnLine Academy
e-mail: bmgacad@bmgaop.com
website for Academy:
www.home-
schooling.com/Academy.htm
web site for OnLine Academy:
www.switched-onschoolhouse.com

Bridgestone Multimedia Group, Inc.
300 North McKemy Ave.
Chandler, AZ 85226-2618
(800) 523-0988
(480) 940-8924 FAX
web site:
www.bridgestonemultimed.com
*Captain Bible in Dome of Darkness,
Bible Builder, Hebrew World*—(A,C)

Brite Music, Inc.
PO Box 65688
Salt Lake City, UT 84165-0688
(801) 263-9191

Brooke-Richards Press
9420 Reseda Blvd., # 511
Northridge, CA 91324
(818) 893-8126
(818) 349-2558 FAX
American Adventures (B,E,G,J)

Brown Paper School Books
See Little Brown & Co.

Builder Books
PO Box 5789
Lynnwood, WA 98046-5789
(800) 260-5461 orders only
(425) 778-4526
(425) 771-4028 FAX
e-mail: books@televar.com

web site:
www.bbhomeschoolcatalog.com
Writing Step by Step (A,E),
*Diagramming, Humpties, Building
Sentences with the Humpties*, plus mail
order distributor

C

Cactus Game Design
751 Tusquittee Rd.
Hayesville, NC 28904
(800) 365-1711
(757) 366-9907
e-mail: cactusrob@aol.com
www.cactusmarketing.com
The Game of Pilgrim's Progress (B,H)

Cadron Creek Christian Curriculum
4329 Pinos Altos Rd.
Silver City, NM 88061
(505) 534-1496
(505) 534-1499 FAX
e-mail: marigold@gilanet.com
web site: www.cadroncreek.com
The Prairie Primer (B,C,D,E,G,H,I,J)

California Weekly Explorer
285 E. Main, Suite 3
Tustin, CA 92780
(714) 730-5991
(714) 730-3548 FAX
e-mail: eurekacwe.aol.com
web site: californiaweekly.com
*California Weekly Explorer, Lone
Woman of Ghalas-Hat* (A), *Student
Atlas of California -1999* (A)

Calliope Books
Route 3, Box 3395
Saylorsburg, PA 18353
(Calliope expects to move in 2000.
Check web site for new address and
phone.)
(610) 381-2587 phone and fax
web site:
http://calliopebooks.webjump.com

Calvert School
Dept. 2BKS, 105 Tuscany Road
Baltimore, MD 21210-3098
(888) 487-4652
(410) 243-6030
(410) 366-0674 FAX
Correspondence courses, *A Child's
History of the World* (G), *Ancient
Greece, Interactive Spelling &*

*Vocabulary, French, Spanish, Little
House*, and *Beatrix Potter* courses.

Cameron Academy
PO Box 21383
Concord, CA 94521
(925) 798-2097
(925) 689-3769 FAX
His California Story (A,G)

Canadian Home Education Resources
108 1289 Highfield Cr. S.E.
Calgary, AB T2G SM2
(403) 243-4443 order line for Calgary
area
(403) 243-9727 FAX
(800) 345-2952 orders only
e-mail: cher@cadvision.com

Canon Press
PO Box 8729
Moscow, ID 83843
(800) 488-2034
web site: www.canonpress.org
*Latin Primer, Latin Grammar, Matin
Latin* (B,G,H)

Career Publishing, Inc.
905 Allanson Rd.
Mundelein, IL 60060
(800) ICANREAD
(847) 949-0011
*Listen and Learn with Phonics,
Shortcuts to Reading* (B)

Carolina Biological Supply Company
2700 York Rd.
Burlington, NC 27215
(800) 334-5551
e-mail: carolina@carolina.com
web site: www.carolina.com
Bob Knauff at rknauff@carolina.com is
their homeschool contact person.

Castle Heights Press, Inc.
106 Caldwell Drive
Baytown, TX 77520 OR
2578 Alexander Farms Dr.
Marietta, GA 30064
(800) 763-7148 orders only
(770) 218-7998 information
e-mail: julicher@aol.com
web site: www.flash.net/~wx3o/chp
*Project-Oriented Science: A Teacher's
Guide, My First Science Notebook, My
Science Notebook 2, The Homework
Assignment Book, One Week Off Unit*

Studies, Gifted Children at Home
(F)—(G,H)

Castlemoyle Books
PO Box 520
Pomeroy, WA 99347
(509) 843-5009
(509) 843-6098 FAX
(888) SPELLTOO
*Spelling Power, Spelling Power Activity
Task Cards* (B,C,D,E,G,H,I,J)

Catholic Book Publishing Company
77 West End Rd.
Totowa, NJ 07512
(973) 890-2400
(973) 890-2410 FAX
e-mail: cbpcl@bellatlantic.net
www.catholicbkpub.com/
*The New Saint Joseph Baltimore
Catechism*, available through most
Catholic home school catalogs

Catholic Heritage Curricula
PO Box 125
Twain Harte, CA 95383-0125
(800) 490-7713 orders or catalog
requests only
(209) 928-4007 information
(209) 928-1872 FAX
web site: www.chcweb.com
*Little Stories for Little Folks: Catholic
Phonics Readers*

**Center for Applications of Psychological
Type**
2815 N.W. 13th St., Ste. 401
Gainesville, FL 32609
(800) 777-2278
e-mail: capt@capt.org
web site: www.capt.org
People Types and Tiger Stripes

Chariot Victor Publishing
4005 Lee Vance View
Colorado Springs, CO 80918
(800) 437-4337
(800) 664-7167 FAX
web site: www.chariotvictor.com
*The Great Dinosaur Mystery and the
Bible* (A,B,C,E,G,H,I)

Charlotte Mason Communiqué-tions
PMB 500
2522 N. Proctor
Tacoma, WA 98406
(253) 879-0433

A Charlotte Mason Education (B), *More Charlotte Mason Education*—(G,H)

Charlotte Mason Research and Supply Company
PO Box 1142
Rockland, ME 04841
web site: www.charlotte-mason.com
Simply Grammar, Charlotte Mason Companion (F), and teaching resources—(A,B,C,D,E,G,H,I,J)

Chicago Review Press
814 N. Franklin St.
Chicago, IL 60610
web site: www.ipgbook.com
(800) 888-4741
Bubble Monster and Other Science Fun, Days of Knights and Damsels, Math Games & Activities from Around the World, Watch Me Grow

Children Sing the Word
Box 183
Chesterville, OH 43317
(419) 768-3152
e-mail: wordsing@aol.com
web site: http://members.aol.com/wordsing/indexw.htm

Children's Books
PO Box 239
Greer, SC 29652
(864) 968-0391
(864) 968-0393 FAX

Children's Book Store Distribution
67 Wall St., Ste. 2411
New York, NY 10005
(800) 668-0242
Mr. Bach Comes to Call and other audio recordings (B,G,H)

Children's Inductive Bible Studies (CIBS)
David and Janice Southerland
PO Box 720567
Oklahoma City, OK 73172
(405) 728-0290
web site: www.cibsokc.com
Know & Grow Bible studies (C,G,I)

Children's Press
A division of Grolier Publishing Co.
Sherman Turnpike
Danbury, CT 06816
(800) 621-1115
web site: www.publishing.grolier.com

"America the Beautiful" series and "Sea to Shining Sea" series (E). Books available through libraries and secular bookstores.

Christ Centered Publications
PO Box 989
Sapulpa, OK 74067-0989
(800) 884-7858 for information
(800) 778-4318 orders only
web site:
www.christcentercurriculum.com
Christ Centered Curriculum

Christian Book Distributors (CBD)
140 Summit Street
Peabody, MA 01961-6000
(978) 977-5005
e-mail orders:
orders@christianbook.com
e-mail service: customer.service@christianbook.com
web site:
http//www.christianbook.com

Christian Curriculum Cellar
4460 S. Carpenter Rd.
Modesto, CA 95358
(209) 538-3632 1-4 p.m., PST, Tues.-Fri.
(209) 538-3429 FAX
e-mail: kgirouar@ix.netcom.com
web site: http://ccc.simplenet.com

Christian Liberty Academy/Christian Liberty Press
502 W. Euclid Ave.
Arlington Heights, IL 60004
(847) 259-4444
(847) 259-2941 FAX order line
web site: www.homeschools.org
Correspondence school, testing service, publisher of many books. (selected items -C,D,E,F,H,I,J)

Christian Light Publications, Inc.
P. O. Box 1212
Harrisonburg, VA 22801-1212
(540) 434-0768
e-mail: orders@clp.org

Christian Publications/Horizon Books
3825 Hartzdale Drive
Camp Hill, PA 17011
(800) 233-4443
e-mail: orders@cpi-horizon.com
web site: www.cpi-horizon.com

Great Women in American History (A,B,C,E,G,I)

Christian Schools International
3350 East Paris Avenue S.E.
Grand Rapids, MI 49512
(800) 635-8288
Healthy Living, Science

Clonlara School Home Based Education Program
1289 Jewett
Ann Arbor, MI 48104
(734) 769-4515
(734) 769-9629 FAX
e-mail: clonlara@wash.k12.mi.us
web site: www.clonlara.org

Codebusters
9612 Stanford Ave.
Garden Grove, CA 92841
(800) READWAY (B)

Coffeehouse Publishing
32370 SE Judd Rd.
Eagle Creek, OR 97022
(503) 637-3277
(503) 423-7980 FAX
web site: www.coffeehouseink.com
How Does God Do That? (C,E)

Color Historic America, Inc.
3245 Chimney Point Drive
Cumming, GA 30041
(770) 889-0501 (E,G)

Common Sense Press
Wholesale source for Common Sense Press. Retail orders should be placed through the various dealers who carry the materials. Call for dealers in your area.
PO Box 1365
8786 Highway 21
Melrose, FL 32666
(352) 475-5757
(352) 475-6105 FAX
e-mail: info@commonsensepress.com
web site: www.commonsensepress.com
Creating Books with Children, Common Sense Kindergarten Program, Common Sense Reading Program, How to Teach Any Child To Spell, Learning Language Arts Through Literature, How to Home School, Grocery Cart Math (F), *Math Sense Building Blocks Program, Record Keeping Sheets, How to Create Your*

Own Unit Studies, One Hundred Sheep, Unit Study Idea Book, The Great Editing Adventure, Wordsmith, Wordsmith Apprentice, and more. (selected items - B,C,D,E,G,H,I,J)

CompassLearning
9920 Pacific Heights Blvd., #500
San Diego, CA 92121
(800) 247-1380
web site: www.compasslearning.com
Tomorrow's Promise

Concerned Communications
PO Box 1000
Siloam Springs, AR 72761
(501) 549-9000
web site: www.areasonfor.com
A Reason for Writing (G), *A Reason for Spelling*—(B,C,E,H,I,J)

Concordia Publishing House
3558 South Jefferson Ave.
St. Louis, MO 63118
(800) 325-3040
(314) 268-1000
web site: www.cphmall.com
Everyday Life in Bible Times, Learning About Sex series (J). Available through Christian bookstores.—(C)

Continental Press
520 E. Bainbridge St.
Elizabethtown, PA 17022
(800) 233-0759
web site: www.continentalpress.com
Focus on Problem Solving, Reading for Comprehension , Reading and Thinking Skills, Map Skills, Practice Exercises in Basic English (A)*, Building Math Skills Step by Step*—(B,I)

The Core Knowledge Foundation
801 East High St.
Charlotteville, VA 22902
(888) 876-2220
(804) 977-7550
e-mail: coreknow@coreknowledge.org
web site: www.coreknowledge.org
Cultural Literacy, What Your First Grader Needs to Know (series for grades one through 6)*, The Core Knowledge Sequence, Books to Build On* (C,D,E,F,H,I)

Cornerstone Curriculum Project
2006 Flat Creek

Richardson, TX 75080
(972) 235-5149
Let Us Highly Resolve (D.I)*, Music and Moments with the Masters, Making Math Meaningful, Adventures in Art, Science: The Search*—(C,E,G)

Covenant Home Curriculum
N63 W23421 Main St.
Sussex, WI 53089
(800) 578-2421
(262) 246-4760
web site: www.covenanthome.com

Covenant Publications
224 Auburn Ave.
Monroe, LA 71201
(318) 323-3061
e-mail: swilkins@iamerica.net
America, The First 350 Years (B,D,G,H)
Send a SASE for free brochure. They also carry music (cassettes) and books relating to America's history.

Creation Resource Foundation
PO Box 570
El Dorado, CA 95623
(800) 497-1454
e-mail: info@awesomeworks.com
web site: www.awesomeworks.com
Unlocking The Mysteries Of Creation (C,G,H,I)

The Creative Attic, Inc.
PO Box 187
Canterbury, NH 03224
(888) 566-6539
e-mail: the5kids@aol.com
Five Kids and A Monkey series (B)

Creative Home Teaching
PO Box 152581
San Diego, CA 92195
(619) 263-8633 phone and fax
The Basic Skills Book

Creative Learning Systems, Inc.
10966 Via Frontera
San Diego, CA 92127
(800) 458-2880
(858) 592-7055 FAX

Creative Publications
5623 W. 115th St.
Alsip, IL 60803
(800) 624-0822
(800) 624-0821 FAX

web site: www.creativepublications.com

Creative Teaching Associates
PO Box 7766
Fresno, CA 93747
(559) 291-6626
(800) 767-4282
(559) 291-2953 FAX
e-mail: cta@psnw.com
web-site: www.mastercta.com
Educational games; *Equation Golf; Facts in Acts; Triangle Flash Cards* (G,H,I); *One game; Discover the Wonders of Water; The Good Steward; Kitchen, Garage, and Garbage Can Science; Little Spender; Phonics Round-Up; States and Capitals Match Wits; States and Capitals Challenge.* Selected items are available from and teacher supply stores. (selected items-B, C,J)

Critical Thinking Books & Software
PO Box 448
Pacific Grove, CA 93950
(800) 458-4849
(831) 393-3288
(831) 393-3277 FAX
e-mail: ct@criticalthinking.com
web site: www.criticalthinking.com
Thinking skills materials; *Building Thinking Skills* (C); *Cranium Crackers; Developing Critical Thinking through Science; Editor in Chief* series (J); *Mathematical Reasoning through Verbal Analysis* (C); *Quick Thinks Math; Scratch Your Brain Where It Itches; Sciencewise*—(selected items - B,D,E,G,H,I)

Crossway Books
Division of Good News Publishers
1300 Crescent St.
Wheaton, IL 60187
(630) 682-4300
(630) 682-4785 FAX
e-mail: goodnews2@aol.com
For the Children's Sake, Schoolproof (J)*, Books Children Love, The Gift of Music: Composers and Their Influence, Reading Between the Lines.* Available through Christian bookstores and home school suppliers. —(selected items - C,D,E,F,G,H,I)

Cuisenaire, Dale Seymour Publications
Order through Pearson Education
web site: www.cuisenaire-dsp.com

Cuisenaire Rods (A,F,G,H,J), *The Everyday Science Sourcebook* (D,H); *Mathematicians are People, Too* (F,G)—(E)

Curriculum Associates®, Inc.
5 Esquire Rd.
PO Box 2001
N. Billerica, MA 01862-0901
(800) 225-0248
(800) 366-1158 FAX
web site: www.curricassoc.com/cainfo/
Brigance7 Comprehensive Inventory of Basic Skills, Enright7 Computation Series, Solutions: Applying Problem-Solving Skills in Math, Reading Strategies for Literature and Reading Strategies for Nonfiction, Test Ready7 series

Curriculum Cottage
2210 N. Meridian Rd.
Meridian, ID 83642
(800) 808-6606 credit card orders or brochure requests
(208) 887-9292 inquiries
e-mail: ccottage@spro.net
web site: www.curriculumcottage.com

D

D.P. & K. Productions
PO Box 587
Dayton, TN 37321
(423) 570-7172
e-mail: BISB@juno.com
web site: www.dpkproductions.com
Information, Please! (C,G,H,I), *The Civil War* (C,D,G,H), *BIG Ideas/Small Budget* newsletter

Dale Seymour Publications
See Cuisenaire, Dale Seymour Publications
Dandy Lion Publications
3563 Sueldo #L
San Luis Obispo, CA 93401
(800) 776-8032
(805) 544-2823 FAX
web site: www.dandylionbooks.com
Inside Stories, Lollipop Logic, Primarily Logic, Blast Off with Logic series, *Analogies for Beginners, Thinking through Analogies, Advancing through Analogies,* and the *Logic Safari* series.

Dave and Joan Exley
PO Box 0044
W. Melbourne, FL 32912-0044
(877) 321-4646
web site: www.howtohomeschool.com
How to Homeschool the Primary Years

Davidsons Music
6727 Metcalf
Shawnee Mission, KS 66204
(913) 262-4982 for questions
Madonna Woods piano/organ courses (J)

Davis Dyslexia Association International
1601 Old Bayshore Highway, Suite 245
Burlingame, CA 94010
(888) 999-3324
web site: www.dyslexia.com
The Gift of Dyslexia

Davis Publications, Inc.
50 Portland St.
Worcester, MA 01608
(800) 533-2847
(508) 753-3834 FAX
e-mail: acharron@davis-art.com
web site: www.davis-art.com
Adventures in Art series

Delta Education
PO Box 3000
Nashua, NH 03061
(800) 442-5444

Design-A-Study: Resources for Creating a Custom Curriculum
408 Victoria Ave.
Wilmington, DE 19804
(302) 998-3889 phone and FAX
e-mail: kathryn@designastudy.com
www.designastudy.com
Natural Speller (J), *Critical Conditioning, Comprehensive Composition, Maximum Math, Guides to History Plus* (D), *The Maya,* and *Science Scope* (D)—(B,C,F,G,H,I)

Diana Waring-History Alive!
122 W. Grant
Spearfish, SD 57783
(605) 642-7583
e-mail: diana@dianawaring.com
web site: www.dianawaring.com
What in the World's Going on Here?; Ancient Civilizations and the Bible; Romans, Reformers, Revolutionaries; World Empires, World Missions, World

Wars; True Tales from the Times of... (B,C,F,G,H,I,J)

Didax, Inc.
395 Main St.
Rowley, MA 01969
(800) 458-0024
(978) 948-2340
(978) 948-2813 FAX
web site: www.didaxinc.com
Makers of *Unifix Cubes* and other math manipulatives. Large catalog lists many hands-on materials for other subjects. (selected items - H,I,J)

Dinah-Might Activities. Inc.
PO Box 690328
San Antonio, TX 78269-0328
(800) 993-4624
(210) 698-0095 FAX
e-mail: dma@dinah.com
web site: www.dinah.com
Big Book of Books and Activities (H); *Big Book of Books and Activities, Religious Supplements: Old Testament and New Testament*—(A,B,G,I)

Discount Homeschool Supplies
156 Tatum Rd.
Mocksville, NC 27028
(336) 284-4449
(336) 284-2212 FAX
e-mail: books@pipeline.com
web site: www.dhss.com

DK Publishing, Inc.
95 Madison Ave.
New York, NY 10016
(212) 213-4800
(212) 689-1799 FAX
web site: www.dk.com
order through DK Customer Service c/o PRI
1224 Heil Quaker Blvd.
LaVergne, TN 37086
(888) DIAL-DKP (F,J)
Castle Explorer, Eyewitness series (G), *Eyewitness World Atlas, Eyewitness Encyclopedia of Science 2.0* (G,H), *The New Way Things Work (CD)* (C,G,H), *The Visual Dictionary of the Human Body*

Doorposts
5905 SW Lookingglass Dr.
Gaston, OR 97119
(503) 357-4749

(503) 357-4909 FAX
e-mail: doorposts@juno.com
web site: www.doorposts.net
*For Instruction in Righteousness: A
Topical Reference Guide for Biblical
Child-Training, Plants Grown Up,
Polished Cornerstones* (D,E,G,H,J)

Dorbooks
PO Box 2588
Livermore, CA 94551
(925) 449-6983
(800) 852-4890 credit card orders
e-mail: dor@dorbooks.com
web site: www.dorbooks.com
Phonics Pathways, Dorbooks—(H)

E

ETC Publications
700 East Vereda Sur
Palm Springs, CA 92262
(760) 325-5352
(760) 325-8841 FAX
(800) 382-7869
e-mail: etcbooks@earthlink.net
Our Golden California (available
through B,G,I, and Beautiful Feet
Books), *Illinois: The Prairie State, Our
Beautiful America* (A,B,I), *The Internet
for Educators and Homeschoolers*

The Eagle's Nest Educational Supplies
6024 Vivian Rd.
Modesto, CA 95358
(209) 556-9551 orders
(209) 556-9552 FAX
e-mail: enmszabo@aol.com

Eagle's Wings Educational Materials
PO Box 502
Duncan, OK 73534
(580) 252-1555
e-mail: info@EaglesWingsEd.com
web site: www.EaglesWingsEd.com
*Alphabet Island, Kindermath,
Considering God's Creation*
(G)—(B,E,H,I,J)

Edmund Scientific
101 E. Gloucester Pike
Barrington, NJ 08007-1380
(800) 728-6999
web site: www.edmundscientific.com

Education PLUS+
PO Box 1350

Taylors, SC 29687
(864) 609-5411
(864) 609-5678 FAX
e-mail info@edplus.com
web site: www.edplus.com
*Identifying Dangerous "High Places" in
Education, Schooling or Educating:
Which are you doing?, Growing in
Wisdom and Stature* (D,G), *How to
Pattern Learning Upon Scripture*

Educational Development Corporation
PO Box 470663
Tulsa, OK 74147-0663
(800) 475-4522
(800) 747-4509 FAX
e-mail: edc@edcpub.com
web site: www.edcpub.com
U.S. distributors for the Usborne books:
*The Usborne Science Encyclopedia,
Finding Out About* series, *Mysteries and
Marvels of Nature* series, *Usborne Kid
Kits, Science with Air, Time Traveler,
Usborne Famous Lives* series, *Usborne
Science for Beginners* series, Story of
Music, Story of Painting, Living in
Roman Times, Usborne First Book of
the Recorder, Usborne World History
series, and more. Some Usborne titles
are carried by teacher supply stores.
(Selected titles-D,E,G,H,I,J)

Educational Insights
16941 Keegan Ave.
Carson, CA 90746
(800) 933-3277
(310) 886-8850 FAX
web site: www.educationalinsights.com
*GeoSafari, MathSafari, GeoSafari Jr.,
Magnetic AlphaBoard, Adventures in
Science* kits, and other learning materials (selected items -C,D,E,F,H,I,J)

Educational Support Foundation
12954 Westleigh
Houston, TX 77077
(281) 870-9194
(281) 870-9669 FAX
e-mail: hankt@ibm.net
Send SASE for information.

Educators Progress Service, Inc.
214 Center St.
Randolph, WI 53956
(920) 326-3126
(920) 326-3127 FAX
Homeschooler's Guide to Free

*Videotapes, Homeschooler's Guide to
Free Teaching Aids*

Educators Publishing Service
31 Smith Place
Cambridge, MA 02138-1089
(800) 225-5750
(617) 547-6706
(617) 547-0412 FAX
web site: http://www.epsbooks.com
*Learning Grammar through Writing;
The Child's Spelling System: The Rules;
Computation Basics; Explode the Code*
series; *Spellwell* series;*Wordly Wise*
vocabulary series; *Wordly Wise 3000*
series; *Recipe for Reading; Rules of the
Game; A Spelling Dictionary for
Beginning Writers; Type It; Vocabulary
from Classical Roots; Writing Skills for
the Adolescent; A Spelling Workbook for
Early Primary Corrective Work; Writing
Skills; The Alphabet Series; Let's Write
and Spell; Cursive Writing
Skills*—(selected titles -
B,C,D,E,F,G,H,I,J)

Effective Educational Systems, Inc.
164 Ridgecrest Rd.
Heber Springs, AR 72543
(501) 362-0860
(800) 308-8181
e-mail: eesinc@ipa.net
web site: www.eesinc.net
*How to Teach Your Child to Read and
Spell* (D,G)

El Hogar Educador
from outside Mexico
PMB 529
1001 S. 10th St., Ste. G
McAllen, TX 78501
from Mexico
APDO 17
25350 Arteaga, Coahuila
Mexico
phone: 011-528-483-0377
e-mail: vnm@characterlink.net

The Elijah Company
1053 Eldridge Loop
Crossville, TN 38558-0249
(931) 456-6284
(931) 456-6384 FAX
(888) 2-ELIJAH orders only
e-mail: elijahco@elijahco.com
web site: www.elijahco.com
Early Education at Home (B,D,F),

Keyboard Capers (J), *How to Tutor*, *WIN* program , *How To Set Up Learning Centers In Your Home, Relaxed Record Keeping* (J)*, Teaching Children to Use the Library* plus distributor for many more—(selected titles- G,I)

Emmanuel Books
PO Box 321
New Castle, DE 19720
(800) 871-5598 orders only
(302) 325-9515
(302) 325-4336 FAX

Emmanuel Center
4061 Holt Rd.
Holt, MI 48842-1843
(517) 699-2728 inquiries
(800) 256-5044 orders only
(517) 699-2053 FAX
e-mail: emmanuel@tir.com
web site: www.homeschoolcenter.com

Essential Learning Products
PO Box 2590
Columbus, OH 43216-2590
(800) 357-3570
(614) 486-0633
(614) 487-2272 FAX
Supplemental workbooks for math, reading, phonics, grammar, geography, writing, and science, plus other resources listed in their catalog—(C,H)

Eternal Hearts
PO Box 107
Colville, WA 99114
(509) 732-4147
Rummy Roots Card Game (I), *More Roots*; also from Back Home Industries) —(A,B,D,E,G,H)

Evan-Moor
18 Lower Ragsdale Drive
Monterey, CA 93940-5746
(800) 777-4362
(800) 777-4332 FAX
web site: www.evan-moor.com
Making Big Books with Children series and *How to Make Books with Children* series(H)— (C,J)

Excellence in Education
2640 S. Myrtle Ave., Unit A-7
Monrovia, CA 91016
(626) 821-0025
e-mail: mforte@aol.com

www.excellenceineducation.com

Exodus Provisions
19146 S. Molalla Ave., Ste. A
Oregon City, OR 97045
(503) 655-1951 10-5 PST, T.-F.
e-mail: ExodusProvisions@juno.com

Exploratorium Mail Order Department
3601 Lyon Street
San Francisco, CA 94123
(415) 561-0393
web site: www.exploratorium.edu
Exploratorium Science Snackbook, Explorabook (C,F)

F

Facts On File, Inc.
11 Penn Plaza
15th Floor
New York, NY 10001-2006
(800) 322-8755
(212) 967-8800
e-mail: custserv@factsonfile.com
web site: www.factsonfile.com
Ancient Rome, Ancient Egypt (D), Ancient Greece, Ancient America, First Civilizations, Facts on File Children's Atlas—(selected titles - B,G,H

Family Learning Center
221 Long Lake Rd.
Hawthorne, FL 32640
(352) 475-5869

Family Mission/Vision Enterprises
PO Box 1483
Chesapeake, VA 23327-1483
(757) 547-4605
(757) 547-2645 FAX
Teaching With God's Heart for the World (B)

Family Protection Ministries
Roy Hanson
PO Box 730
Lincoln, CA 95648-0730
(916) 786-3523
(916) 434-9470 FAX
Comparing World Views

Family Resources/Love to Learn
741 N. State Road 198
Salem, UT 84653
(888) 771-1034 orders
(801) 423-2009

e-mail: info@lovetolearn.net
web site: www.lovetolearn.net
Happy Phonics

Family Things
PMB # 237
19363 Willamette Dr.
West Linn, OR 97068
(503) 727-5473
(503) 722-5671 FAX
e-mail: FamilyThgs@aol.com
web site: www.Singaporemath.com
Primary Mathematics

Farm Country General Store
412 North Fork Rd.
Metamora, IL 61548
(800) 551-FARM orders only
(309) 367-2844 phone and FAX
e-mail: fcgs@mtco.com
web site: http://homeschoolfcgs.com

FERG N US Services
PO Box 350-D
Richville, NY 13681
(315) 287-9131
(315) 287-9132 FAX
e-mail: fergnus@gisco.net
The Home Schooler's Journal (C,D,F,G,H,I)

First Reader System Inc.
PO Box 495
Alton, IL 62002
(800) 700-5228 (D)
web site: www.eagleforum.org

Fitness at Home
1084 Yale Farm Rd.
Romulus, NY 14541
(315) 585-2248 (D,J)

Five in a Row Publishing
PO Box 707
Grandview, MO 64030-0707
(816) 331-5769
web site: www.fiveinarow.com
Before Five in a Row, Five in a Row, Beyond Five in a Row (C,E,F,G,H,I)

Follett Home Education
1433 Internationale Parkway
Woodbridge, IL 60517
(800) 638-4424 FAX
web site: www.fes.follett.com

Foundation for American Christian Education (F.A.C.E.)
P. O. Box 9588
Chesapeake, VA 23321
(757) 488-6601
(757) 488-5593 FAX
web site: www.face.net
The Noah Plan™, The Christian History of the Constitution Vols. I and II, *Teaching and Learning America's Christian History* (H), *The American Dictionary of the English Language* 1828 facsimile (A,D,G,H), *The Christian History of the American Revolution, The Rudiments of America's Christian History and Government, A Family Program for Reading Aloud* (H), information and materials on the Principle Approach.

Foundation for Biblical Research
2401 W. Southern Ave. #219
Tempe, AZ 85282
(602) 431-8975
No Place Like Home...School

Fountain of Truth Publishing Division
3560 W. Dawson Rd.
Sedalia, CO 80135
(303) 688-6626
web site: www.christiancottage.com
Christian Cottage Unit Studies: *In The Beginning, God!, For God So Loved the World, God Bless America, Blessed To Be A Blessing*—(G,H,I)

4:20 Communications
PO Box 421027
Minneapolis, MN 55442-0027
(888) 420-READ
(612) 397-8569 FAX
e-mail: info@phonicstutor.com
web site: www.phonicstutor.com
PhonicsTutor (H)

Frank Schaffer Publications, Inc.
See Good Apple

Full Gospel Family Publications
419 East Taft Ave.
Appleton, WI 54915
(920) 734-6693
e-mail: pilgrims@juno.com
web site:
www.angelfire.com/wi/characterbuilding
Character Building For Families (B,G,H)

G

Games 2 Learn
150 Paularino Ave., Suite 120
Costa Mesa, CA 92626
(800) 500-GAME
The Phonics Game (H,J), *The Phonics Game Junior*—(A)

Gateway Learning Corporation
2900 S. Harbor Blvd., Ste. 202
Santa Ana, CA 92704
(800) ABC-DEFG
web site: www.hookedonphonics.com
Hooked on Phonics Learn to Read

Gazelle Publications
11560 Red Bud Trail
Berrien Springs, MI 49103
(616) 471-4717 FAX and phone
(800) 650-5076
e-mail: info@hoofprint.com
The Home School Manual (H,J), *Early Years at Home*—(C,E,G)

General Science Service Co.
221 NW 2nd St.
Elbow Lake, MN 56531
(218) 685-4846
Blister Microscope and supplies

GeoCreations LTD, Ltd.
PO Box 31
Magnolia, DE 19962
(877) 492-7879
e-mail: Hogan@inet.net
Retail sales are through Geography Matters (address below) OR Bright Ideas! Educational Resource (same address as GeoCreations) but phone number (877) 492-8081 and e-mail: Hogan@inet.net.
The Ultimate Geography and Timeline Guide (J), *Hands-On Geography, Uncle Josh's Outline Map Book*—(A,,D,F,G,H,I)

Geography Matters
PO Box 92
Nancy, KY 42544
(800) 426-4650
e-mail: geomatters@geomatters.com
web site: www.geomatters.com
Uncle Josh's Outline Map Book (F), *Mark-It Maps, Mark-It Timeline of History*—(C,D,E,G,H,I)

George F. Cram Company, Inc.
PO Box 426
Indianapolis, IN 46206
(800) 227-4199
web site: www.georgefcram.com
Map and geography materials

Gibbs Smith, Publisher
PO Box 667
1877 E. Gentile St.
Layton, UT 84041
(800) 748-5439
(800) 213-3023 FAX
The Naturalist's Handbook: Activities for Young Explorers

Gibson's Curriculum and Counseling Services
Cary Gibson
440 Old Airport Rd.
Auburn, CA 95603
(530) 823-3164
Complete Homeschool Planner plus curriculum counseling for area residents

The Gift of Reading/Homeschool Instructional Services
Trudy Palmer
423 Maplewood Lane
San Antonio, TX 78216
(210) 828-5179
The Gift of Reading, In One Ear and (Hopefully Not) Out the Other!, My Spelling Notebook, Trudy Palmer's Writing Workshop —(G)

God's World Publications, Inc.
85 Tunnel Road
Asheville, NC 28805
(704) 253-8063
(800) 537-0447 Fax order line only
God's World News for Kids customer service (800) 951-5437
e-mail for God's World News: sales@gwnews.com
God's World Book Club customer service (800) 951-2665
God's World Book Club e-mail: GWBooks@aol.com
God's World Book Club web site: www.gwp.org/bookclub/
God's World News for Kids, God's World Books

Golden Educational Center
857 Lake Blvd.
Redding, CA 96003-2233

(800) 800-1791
(530) 244-5939 FAX
e-mail: info@goldened.com
web site: www.goldened.com
Creating Line Designs (H), *Designs in
Math* (H), *Solving Math Word Problems,
California Missions, Country Studies,*
geography and map books

**Golden Owl Publishing/Jackdaw
Publications**
PO Box 503
Amawalk, NY 10501
(800) 789-0022 orders only
(914) 962-6911
(800) 962-9101 FAX
web site: www.jackdaw.com
Picture the Middle Ages (D,H), *Jackdaw
Portfolios and Study Guides*

Good Apple
Division of Frank Schaffer
23740 Hawthorne Blvd.
Torrance, CA 90509
(800) 421-5565 orders
(800) 421-5533 customer service
web site: www.frankschaffer.com
*Math Drillsters, Good Apple Trivial
Pursuit books* (I), *Pathways of America,
Our Living Constitution*
(A,B,H,I)—(C,E,J)

Good Year Books
Order through Pearson Education
web site: www.awl.com
The Poetry Corner, The Map Corner
(H), *Small Wonders, Who Says You
Can't Teach Science?, The Complete
Science Fair Handbook , Baseball Math,
The Travel-the-World Cookbook,Young
Inventors at Work!*—(selected titles -
B,E)

Gordon School of Art
PO Box 28208.
Green Bay, WI 54324-8208
(800) 210-1220
e-mail: gordon@netnet.net
web site: www.newmasters.com
*Young Masters Home Study Art
Program*

The Grammar Key
PO Box 33230
Tulsa, OK 74153
(800) 4800-KEY (G)

Great Expectations Book Co.
PO Box 2067
Eugene, OR 97402
(541) 343-9926
The Write Stuff Adventure (G)

The Great Grammarian
812 Longford Dr.
Stuebenville, OH 43952
(888) 647-5453
(740) 284-1597 FAX

Great Source Education Group
Attn. Order Processing
PO Box 7050
Wilmington, MA 01887
(800) 289-4490
(800) 289-3994 FAX
web site: www.greatsource.com
*Write Source 2000 , Writer's Express
Handbook,* other *Write Source*
resources—(B,E,F,G,H,I)

Greathall Productions
PO Box 5061
Charlottesville, VA 22905-5061
(800) 477-6234
(804) 296-4288
(804) 296-4490 FAX
e-mail: greathall@greathall.com
web site: www.greathall.com
Galileo and the Stargazers (G), *The
Jungle Book, Greek Myths, The Three
Musketeers/Robin Hood, Arabian
Nights, King Arthur and His Knights,
Sherlock Holmes for Children, Egyptian
Treasures: Mummies and Myths*—(H)

Greek 'n' Stuff
PO Box 882
Moline, IL 61266-0882
(309) 796-2707
(309) 796-2706 FAX
e-mail: workbooks@greeknstuff.com
web site: www.greeknstuff.com
*Alone With God Bible Studies, Hey,
Andrew!! Teach me some Greek!* (H,J),
Latin's Not So Tough! (H,J)

Greenleaf Press
3761 Highway 109N, Unit D
Lebanon, TN 37087
(800) 311-1508 for orders only
(615) 449-1617
(615) 449-4018 FAX
e-mail: orders@greenleafpress.com
web site: www.greenleafpress.com

*Choosing & Using Curriculum For Your
Special Child* (G), *English for the
Thoughtful Child, FrontPorch History,
Greenleaf Guides* (C,F), *Learning in
Spite of Labels* (F)
—(D,E,G,H,I)

GROW Publications
222 Wolff St.
Racine, WI 53402-4268
(800) 594-7136
*Arithmetic Developed Daily, Daily
Writing, Daily Science,* plus a calendar
of summer learning activities.

H

Hands to Help Publishing
18550 Timberline Rd.
Lake Elsinore, CA 92532-7325
(909) 245-4082 phone and FAX
e-mail: Caruso@xc.org
web site: www.ioc.net/~abba/B_DC-
txt.htm
Send SASE for brochure.
*Developing Godly Character in
Children.* Available at discounted price
directly from Hands to Help. (C,G)

Harmony Media, Inc.
6601 Brooklake Rd.
Salem, OR 97305
(888) 427-6334
(503) 393-1960
(503) 393-5451 FAX
e-mail: harmonymed@aol.com
web site: www.harmonymediainc.com
Butler's Lives of the Saints

Harold Shaw Publishers
Order through www.amazon.com, local
bookstore, or one of the distributors
from the key.
(800) 742-9782
How to Grow a Young Reader (C,G)

HarperCollins
1000 Keystone Industrial Park
Scranton, PA 18512
(800) 242-7737
web site: www.harpercollins.com
Canterbury Tales (G,H), *Freedom's
Sons, The American Story series,
Balloons, Blinkers and Buzzers* (H),
*Making Waves, Mirrors, Shadow Play,
Soda Science* (H), *Tops, Wheels at Work*

Harvest House Publishers
1075 Arrowsmith
Eugene, OR 97402
(800) 547-8979
(541) 343-0123
(541) 342-6410 FAX
Discover 4 Yourself Bible Studies for Kids

Hear An'Tell Adventures
320 Bunker Hill Rd.
Houston, TX 77024
(713) 784-1273
Foreign language, *Word Maps*, and *Musical Math*. Send SASE for free brochure.

Heart of Wisdom Publishing
13503 Minion St.
Woodbridge, VA 22192
(703) 897-8890 information
(800) 266-5564 orders only
e-mail: Heartofwisdom@home.com
web site: http://heartofwisdom.com
What Your Child Needs to Know When (C,D,H), *A Family Guide to the Biblical Holidays*—(G,I,J)

Hearthside Homeschool Helps
74 Lynn Dr.
Woodbury, NJ 08096
(609) 845-3681 phone and fax
e-mail: hearthside@juno.com

The Helping Hand
PO Box 496316
Garland, TX 75049
(800) 460-7171
(972) 681-5161
e-mail: classics@onramp.net
web site:
http://rampages.onramp.net/~classics
The Classics, Big Little Book of Spelling Fun

Heppner & Heppner Construction
Box 7, 305 Lake St. N.E.
Warroad, MN 56763-0007
(218) 386-1994 phone and FAX
e-mail: family@wiktel.com
web site: www.buildingthefamily.com

Hewitt Homeschooling Resources
PO Box 9
Washougal, WA 98671-0009
(360) 835-8708
FAX (360) 835-8697

e-mail: Hewitt@HomeEducation.org
web site: www.HomeEducation.org
School service, learning materials, books. They publish *A Bee Sees, Across America, Blueprints Organizer, Hewitt Early Readers, Learning Objectives, Music for Minors, State History Chronicles, My First Reports, Training Wheels,* and *Here I Grow!*

Hillside Academy
1804 Melody Lane
Burnsville, MN 55337
(612) 895-0220
e-mail: Tony@LessonsFromHistory.com
web site:
www.LessonsFromHistory.com
Lessons from History (A,B,F,G,H)

Hirst/Pait OR Hirst
PO Box 914
Marshall, VA 20116
(540) 364-3245
Pioneer Boys, Free for the Asking

HIS Publishing Company
1159 County Rd. 16
Plymouth, NY 13832
(607) 334-4628
e-mail: goodkids@netzero.net
The Simplicity of Homeschooling (C,G,H)

Holly Hall Publications
PO Box 254
Elkton, MD 21922
(410) 392-2300
(410) 620-9877 FAX
e-mail: phil@hollyhall.com
Grammar Works (C,J), *Writing to God's Glory* (C,G), *Home Educating with Confidence* (C), *Unit Study Adventures, History Alive! Through Music* (F,G,J and Bluestocking Press)—(I)

Holt Associates/GWS
2380 Massachusetts Ave., Ste. 104
Cambridge, MA 02140-1884
(617) 864-3100
(617) 864-9235 FAX
web site: www.holtgws.com
Growing Without Schooling magazine and John Holt's Book and Music Store (mail order)

Home and Hearth
1914 9 Ave. S.E.

Calgary, AB T2G 0V2
Canada
(403) 281-9644
(403) 281-5229 FAX
e-mail: smshearer

The Home Computer Market
PO Box 385377
Bloomington, MN 55438
(612) 866-4419
(800) 827-7420 order only
web site:
www.homecomputermarket.com

Home Education Magazine
PO Box 1083
Tonasket, WA 98855-1083
(800) 236-3278
(509) 486-2753 FAX
e-mail: HEM-Info@home-ed-maga-zine.com
web site: www.home-ed-magazine.com

H.O.M.E. Inc.
306 Rockhill Rd.
Purvis, MS 39475
(601) 794-8450
e-mail: for-home@netdoor.com
web site:
www.homeschoolingforhome.com
Workshop-in-a-Box: Beginning Homeschooling

Home Life, Inc.
PO Box 1190
Fenton, MO 63026
(800) 346-6322
(636) 343-7203 FAX
e-mail: orders@home-school.com
web site: www.home-school.com
Practical Homeschooling magazine (A), Home Life catalog

Home School & More
Box 458
Maple Creek, Saskatchewan S0N 1N0
Canada
(306) 662-2866

The Home School Inc.
Mail Orders:
PO Box 308
N. Chelmsford, MA 01863-0308
Retail Store:
104 S. West Ave.
Arlington, WA 98223
(800) 788-1221 advice and order line

web site: www.thehomeschool.com

Home School Family Fitness Institute
159 Oakwood Drive
New Brighton, MN 55112
(651) 636-7738
e-mail: whitn003@umn.edu
web site: http://umn.edu/~whitn003
Home School Family Fitness: A Complete Curriculum Guide (H,J), *Physical Education for Homeschool Co-ops and Private Schools*

Home School Legal Defense Association (HSLDA)
Box 3000
Purcellville, VA 20134
(540) 338-5600

Home School Resource Center
1425 E. Chocolate Ave.
Hershey, PA 17033
(800) 937-6311 orders
(717) 533-1669
(717) 533-0413 FAX
e-mail: hsrc@hsrc.com
web site: www.hsrc.com

Home School Used Book & Curriculum Exchange
PO Box 1145
Lansdowne, PA 19050-1145
e-mail: exchange@homeschoolused-books.com
web site:
www.homeschoolusedbooks.com

Home Study International
12501 Old Columbia Pike
Silver Spring, MD 20904-6600
(800) 782-4769
(301) 680-6577 FAX
e-mail: contact@hsi.edu
web site: www.hsi.edu

Home Team Press
2206 20th St.
Cuyahoga Falls, OH 44223
(330) 928-8083
Learning Seeds Activity Library (H)

Home Training Tools
2827 Buffalo Horn Dr.
Laurel, MT 59044-8325
(800) 860-6272
(888) 860-2344 FAX
e-mail: customerservice@hometraining-

tools.com
web site: www.HomeTrainingTools.com

The Home Works
1760 Groves Rd., R.R.#2
Russell, Ontario K4R 1E5
(613) 445-3142
(613) 445-0587 FAX
e-mail: homework@magma.ca
web site: www.magma.ca/~homework

HomeSat
1700 Wade Hampton Blvd.
Greenville, SC 29614
(800) 739-8199
(888) 525-8398 FAX
e-mail: info@homesat.com
web site: www.homesat.com

The Homeschool Planbook
Sarah Crain
164 Strack Farm Lane
Troy, MO 63379
(636) 338-9218
(636) 338-9917 FAX
e-mail: planbooks@hotmail.com
—(C)

Homeschool Potpourri
12815 NE 124th St., Ste. F
Kirkland, WA 98034
(425) 820-4626

Homeschool Seminars and Publications
Barb Shelton
182 No. Columbia Heights Rd.
Longview, WA 98632
(360) 577-1245
e-mail: beshelton@aol.com or beshelton@kalama.com
web site: www.kalama.com/~beshelton/
The Booklet Building Book (D), *A Christian Homeschooler's Guide to Field Trips and Extra-Curricular Activities* (E), *The Homeschool Jumpstart Navigator for Younger Children* (B)

Homeschooling Today® magazine
S Squared Productions, Inc.
PO Box 1608
Ft. Collins, CO 80522
phone calls are handled by Pro Services, Inc.- (954) 962-1930
e-mail: subscriptions@homeschoolto-day.com
web site: www.homeschooltoday.com

—(A)

Homespun Tapes, Ltd.
Box 694, Dept. CHE
Woodstock, NY 12498
(914) 246-2550
(800) 338-2737
(914) 246-5282 FAX
e-mail: hmspn@aol.com
web site: www.homespuntapes.com

Houghton Mifflin
For ordering "school books" see
McDougal Littell/Houghton Mifflin

Houghton Mifflin Publishers
for ordering "non-school" books
222 Berkeley St.
Boston, MA 02116
(800) 225-3362
Curious George and *The New Way Things Work* (E,G,H)—(C)

How Great Thou ART
PO Box 48
McFarlan, NC 28102
(800) 982-3729
(704) 851-3111 FAX
e-mail: howgreat@vnet.net
web site: www.howgreatthouart.com
Lamb's Book of ART, Feed My Sheep (B,G,H)

I

Ignatius Press
PO Box 1339
Fort Collins, CO 80522
(800) 651-1531 credit card orders only
(877) 320-9276 for information
(800) 278-3566 FAX
web site: www.ignatius.com
Faith and Life series (C), *Image of God* series, *A Catholic Homeschool Treasury, Designing Your Own Classical Curriculum* (B,C,G,H), *A Landscape with Dragons, The Harp and Laurel Wreath* (C,G), *Vision Books* series

Incentive Publications/Kids' Stuff
3835 Cleghorn Ave.
Nashville, TN 37215
(800) 421-2830
e-mail: info@incentivepublications.com
web site:
www.incentivepublications.com
Complete Writing Lessons (D), *If You're*

Trying to Teach Kids How to Write...
(J)—(A,B,E,G,H,I)

Individualized Education Systems
PO Box 5136
Fresno, CA 93755
(559) 299-4639
e-mail: Bette1234@aol.com
Beginning Reading at Home, Beginning Math at Home—(H)

Infinite Discovery Inc.
3228 Wilshire Terrace
Oklahoma City, OK 73116
(800) 475-7308
(405) 843-7308
(405) 843-0741 FAX
e-mail: infidisc@theshop.net
web site: www.infinitediscovery.com
Teaching Bible History To Children series

Institute for Creation Research
10946 Woodside Avenue North
Santee, CA 92071
(800) 628-7640 customer service
(619) 448-0900
web site: www.icr.org
Museum and materials. They offer workshops on teaching science and publish *Good Science Curriculum*, the *Good Science Workshop* video, and other creation science items. (E,H,J)

Institute for Excellence in Writing
PO Box 6065
Atascadero, CA 93423
(800) 856-5815
(603) 925-5123 FAX
e-mail: iew@earthlink.net
web site: www.writing-edu.com
Teaching Writing seminar, *Student Writing* seminars, *Student Workshops, Excellence in Spelling*

Instructional Fair
PO Box 1650
Grand Rapids, MI 49501
(800) 253-5469
(800) 543-2690 FAX
web site: www.instructionalfair.com
Series of *Homework Booklets* available through many teacher supply stores, or send for free catalog. (selected items-C,H,J)

Instructional Resources Company
PO Box 111704
Anchorage, AK 99511-1704
(800) 356-9315 orders only
(907) 345-6689
e-mail: santhony@alaska.net
web site: www.susancanthony.com
Facts Plus (D,G,H,J), *Addition Facts in 5 Minutes a Day, Subtraction Facts in 5 Minutes a Day, Multiplication Facts in 5 Minutes a Day, Division Facts in 5 Minutes a Day, Spelling Plus*

Interactive Dimensions
1825 E. Gaviota Court
Simi Valley, CA 93065
(805) 526-7335
Wonder Number Learning System (H)

International Learning Systems
4027 Tampa Rd., Ste. 3800
Oldsmar, FL 34677
(800) 321-8322
web site: www.singspell.com
Sing, Spell, Read, And Write (E,I), *Winning, Grammar Plus Kit, Pre-kindergarten Kit* (I), *Musical Math Facts, Songs That Teach*—(A,B,C,H,J)

Intrepid Books
PO Box 22614
Sacramento, CA 95822-0614
(916) 684-1530 phone and FAX
e-mail: intrepid.books@worldnet.att.net
America's Christian History: Christian Self-Government series (A,B,G)

ISHA Enterprises, Inc.
PO Box 12520
Scottsdale, AZ 85267
(800) 641-6015
(480) 502-9454
(480) 502-9456 FAX
web site: www.easygrammar.com
Easy Grammar, Daily Grams, Easy Writing. Send SASE for free brochure. (A,B,C,D,E,F,G,H,I,J)

J

J & K Schooling
5350 Sunset Lane
Loretto, MN 55357
(612) 479-2286
Historical TimeLine Figure Set (B,H)

John Wiley and Sons, Inc.
1 Wiley Dr.
Somerset, NJ 08875
(800) 225-5945
e-mail: catalog@wiley.com
web site: www.wiley.com
Science For Every Kid series
(A,B,E,F,H)

Johnson Books
1880 South 57th Court
Boulder, CO 80301
(800) 258-5830 orders only
(303) 443-9766
(303) 443-1106 FAX
e-mail: books@jpcolorado.com
Roadside History of Colorado; Tales, Trails and Tommyknockers

Jump! Music
201 San Antonio Circle, Ste. 105
Mountain View, CA 94040
(650) 917-7460
(650) 917-7490 FAX
e-mail: info@jumpmusic.com
web site: www.jumpmusic.com
Piano Discovery

K

KC Publications
PO Box 94558
Las Vegas, NV 89193-4558
(800) 626-9673
(702) 433-3415 in Nevada
(702) 433-3420 FAX
e-mail: kcp@kcpublications.com
web site: www.kcpublications.com
"Story Behind the Scenery" series

Kaw Valley Video Sales and Rentals
15819 W. 127th Terrace
Olathe, KS 66062
(913) 829-4313 after 3 pm central time

Key Curriculum Press
1150 65th St.
Emeryville, CA 94608-1109
(800) 995-MATH
web site: www.keypress.com
Miquon Math, Key To... math series
(A,B,C,E,F,G,H,I,J)

KidsArt
PO Box 274
Mt. Shasta, CA 96067
(530) 926-5076

web site: http://www.kidsart.com
KidsArt booklets

Kolbe Academy Home School
2501 Oak St.
Napa, CA 94559-2226
(707) 255-6499
(707) 255-1581 FAX
web site: http://www.kolbe.org
e-mail: kolbeacad@earthlink.net

KONOS Character Curriculum
PO Box 250
Anna, TX 75409
(972) 924-2712
(972) 924-2733 FAX
e-mail: info@konos.com
web site: www.konos.com
Volumes One, Two, and Three with time
lines, *The Compass*, lesson plans, how-
to audio and video cassettes, *KONOS-
In-A-Box, Dads: The Men in the Gap*
(G)—(J)

Konos Connection
111 Bethea Rd.
Fayetteville, GA 30214
(800) 780-6827
web site: www.konos.org
Learn to Write the Novel Way
(B,C,G,H,J)

K.T. Productions
PO Box 1203
Menomonee Falls, WI 53052
(262) 251-3563
Home School Helper

L

Landmark Distributors
PO Box 849
Fillmore, CA 93016
(805) 524-3263
(805) 524-3263 FAX (call first)
e-mail: landmark@jps.net
www.jps.net\landmark
*A Principle Approach for 3 R's and
Other Subjects, Introduction to
Elementary Science: an American
Christian Principle Approach, Renewing
the Mind, Radical Christianity*

Landmark's Freedom Baptist Curriculum
2222 East Hinson Ave.
Haines City, FL 33844-4902
(800) 700-LFBC

(863) 421-2937

Larousse Kingfisher Chambers, Inc.
95 Madison Ave., Ste. 1205
New York, NY 10016
(800) 497-1657
(212) 686-1082 FAX
Canadian orders and information:
Thomas Allen & Son, Ltd.
390 Steelcase Rd. East
Markham, Ontario L3R 1G2
Canada
(905) 475-9126
www.lkcpub.com
Kingfisher Books, *Sightseers Essential
Travel Guides to the Past, Kingfisher
History Encyclopedia* (B,D,F,G,H), *The
Kingfisher Science Encyclopedia* (B,G),
The Human Body

Lawrence Hall of Science
University of California
Berkeley, CA 94720
(800) 897-5036
(510) 642-1910
web site: www.lhs.berkeley.edu/equals
Family Math (B,G,H)

**The Learnables Foreign Language
Courses**
3505 East Red Bridge
Kansas City, MO 64137
(816) 765-8855
e-mail: learn@qni.com
web site: www.learnables.com
—(B,H)

The Learning Company
1 Athenaeum St.
Cambridge, MA 02142
(617) 761-3000
web site: www.learningco.com
*Ultimate Writing & Creativity Center,
Storybook Weaver Deluxe, Student
Writing Center, Kid Pix Studio Deluxe,
Where in the World is Carmen
Sandiego?*

The Learning Heart Workshop
4 Blue Grouse Circle
Boise, ID 83716-3328
(208) 385-9069
e-mail: lbarry@cyberhighway.net
The Learning Heart Memory System

The Learning Home
5573 Ashbourne Rd.

Baltimore, MD 21227-2813
(410) 242-7826
e-mail: learninghome@aol.com
web site: www.learninghome.com

The Learning House
8 Dunlop Dr., R.R. #4
Goderich, Ontario N7A 3Y1
Canada
(519) 524-5607 (late afternoon and
evenings)
e-mail: tlhouse@hurontel.on.ca
web site: www.learninghouse.on.ca

Learning Lights
PO Box 536
Elmira, OR 97437
(541) 935-6024 M-Th, 2-5:30 p.m. PST
e-mail: VLJensen@aol.com

The Learning Odyssey: ChildU
316 NE Fourth St., Ste. 200
Ft. Lauderdale, FL 33301
(877) 4-CHILDU
(954) 523-1511
(954) 523-1512 FAX
e-mail: info@childu.com
web site: www.childu.com

**Learning Potentials Publishers,
Inc./Lewisville Learning Clinic**
Dr. Kenneth A. Lane
230 West Main St.
Lewisville, TX 75057
(800) 437-7976
(972) 221-2564
Developing Your Child for Success
(B,G)

Learning Services
PO Box 10636
Eugene, OR 97440-2636
(800) 877-9378 (western U.S.) or 877-
3278 (eastern U.S.)
(541) 744-2056 FAX
web site: www.learnserv.com

Learning Works
PO Box 1370
Goleta, CA 93116
(800) 235-5767
(805) 964-1466 FAX
*Analogy Adventure, Book Report
Beagle, Book Report Backpack, History
Mysteries, The How-To-Make-A-Book
Book, Map Mysteries, Poetry Parade,
World Geography Mysteries, The*

Writing Rhino, The Writing Warthog, Spelling Works, The Travel Bug—(selected titles - B,C,J)

Learning Wrap-Ups
2122 East 6550 South
Ogden, UT 84405
(800) 992-4966
FAX (801) 476-0063
Math (H), *Spanish* (C)*, Language, Music,* etc. *Wrap-Ups*; *10 Day to Multiplication Mastery*; *Bring Phonics to Life*—(A,E,I)

LEGO Dacta
PO Box 1707
Pittsburg, KS 66762
(800) 362-4308
Ask for free brochure on the educational Technic sets. You may also request a list of Lego dealers in your area.

The Leonine Press
1331 Red Cedar Circle
Fort Collins, CO 80524
(970) 493-3793
Our Roman Roots

Library and Educational Services
PO Box 146
Berrien Springs, MI 49103
(616) 695-1800

Life in America
2107 N. Sheeran Drive
Milford, MI 48381
(877) 543-3263
web site: www.lifeinamerica.com
Life in the New World, Life in the Colonies, Life Establishing a Nation—(G,H)

Lifetime Books and Gifts
Bob and Tina Farewell
3900 Chalet Suzanne Dr.
Lake Wales, FL 33853-7763
(800) 377-0390 orders only
(863) 676-6311
(863) 676-2732 FAX
e-mail: lifetime@gate.net
web site:
www.LifetimeBooksandGifts.com
Always Incomplete Resource Guide

LifeWay Christian Resources of the Southern Baptist Convention
127 Ninth Avenue North
Nashville, TN 37234
(800) 458-2772
web site: www.lifeway.com
Across the Centuries

Lightsource Editing Service
The Kustusch Family
6064 North Paulina
Chicago, IL 60660
(773) 743-3625
e-mail: Editnow4u@aol.com

Linda Howe, M.A.
4187 Bernardo Court
Chino, CA 91710
(909) 628-9441

Lindamood-Bell Learning Processes
Corporate Headquarters
416 Higuera St.
San Luis Obispo, CA 93401-3865
(800) 300-1818
www.lindamoodbell.org

The Link
PMB 911
587 N. Ventu Park Rd., Ste. F
Newbury Park, CA 91320
(805) 492-1373
(805) 493-9216 FAX
e-mail: hompaper@gte.net
web site:
www.homeschoolnewslink.com

Lion Publishing
Division of Chariot Victor Publishing
4050 Lee Vance View
Colorado Springs, CO 80918
(800) 437-4337
(800) 664-7167 FAX
The Wonder of God's World - Water; How the Bible Came to Us (A,B,H,I)
Send a #10 envelope with 2 stamps to request a catalog.

The Literacy Press
24 Lake Dr.
DeBary, FL 32713
(407) 668-1232
OR contact
Eugene Coleman, Jr.
677 Follett Run
Warren, PA 16365
(804) 726-1788
Phonics program and *Early Math Literacy Packet*

Literacy Unlimited
PO Box 278
Medina, WA 98039-0278
(425) 454-5830
(425) 450-0141 FAX
web site:
http://www.literacyunlimited.com
e-mail: joegilkl@aol.com
English from the Roots Up—(A,B,C,D,E,F,G,H,I)

Little Brown and Co.
attn: Order Dept
3 Center Plaza
Boston, MA 02108
(617) 227-0730
(800) 759-0190
Brown Paper series, *How to Mix Art and Science, The Book of Think* (H), *The Night Sky Book, The I Hate Mathematics! Book* (F,G,H), *The Book of Where*, and Warner Books titles including *Smart but Feeling Dumb.* Available at secular bookstores.—(selected titles-B,I)

Little Folk Visuals
PO Box 14243
Palm Desert, CA 92255-4243
(800) 537-7227
(760) 345-5571
(760) 360-0225 FAX
web site: www.littlefolkvisuals.com
Felts sets - *Fun at the Beach* (H), *Human Body, Pyramid Food Groups, Quiet Book*s (H), *Family Worship*, and more.—(A,B,I,J)

Logos Language Institute
PO Box 55
Belton, TX 76513
(800) 445-6467
(254) 939-6343 FAX
e-mail: LogosLang@aol.com
web site: www.wm.com/Logos/
Brochures are free, but a self-addressed, stamped envelope is appreciated.

Logos School
110 Baker St.
Moscow, ID 83843
(208) 883-3199
web site: www.logosschool.com
Latin Primer I videos (G)

Lowry House Publishers
PO Box 1014

Eugene, OR 97440-1014
(541) 686-2315
(541) 343-3158 FAX
e-mail: gracejanet@aol.com
Freedom Challenge

Loyola Press
3441 North Ashland
Chicago, IL 60657
(800) 621-1008
(773) 281-0555 FAX
Voyages in English (E)

Lynn's Bookshelf
Box 2224
Boise, ID 83701
(208) 331-1987
(208) 331-1987 FAX
e-mail: lynnsbks@cyberhighway.net
web site: www.lynnsbookshelf.faith-
web.com
Proverbs For Parenting (A,B,G,H,I,J)

Lyrical Learning
8008 Cardwell Hill
Corvallis, OR 97330
(541) 754-3579
e-mail: lyricallearning@proaxis.com
web site: www.lyricallearning.com
Lyrical Life Science (B,C,G,H,I,J)

M

Macmillan Publishing Co.
Macmillan is now part of Simon and
Schuster. Order from the Simon and
Schuster address below.

Mamopalire, Inc. of Vermont
PO Box 24
Warren, VT 05674
(802) 496-4095
(802) 4964096
e-mail: bethumpd@wcvt.com
web site: www.bethumpd.com
Bethump'd with words

Managers of Their Homes
2416 S. 15th St.
Leavenworth, KS 66048-4110
(913) 772-0392
(913) 772-6389 FAX
e-mail: managers@we-
communicate.com
web site: www.titus2.com
Managers of Their Homes

Manas Systems
PO Box 5153
Fullerton, CA 92635
(714) 870-4355
*Learning Patterns and Temperament
Styles* (B,G,H,I)

Mantle Ministries
Richard "Little Bear" Wheeler
228 Still Ridge
Bulverde, TX 78163
(210) 438-3777
(210) 438-3370 FAX
e-mail: mantleministries@cs.com
(A,B,D)

Maple Ridge Books
R.R. 6
Markdale, Ontario, N0C 1H0
Canada
(519) 986-2686
e-mail: maplebooks@bmts.com

Marcia Neill
4790 Irvine Blvd., Ste. 105, PMB 286
Irvine, CA 92620
(949) 730-9114 phone and FAX
e-mail: SMAcademy@aol.com
*Catholic World History Timeline and
Guide*

**Marian Soderhom, M.A., MCA
Educational Assessment Services**
3826 Marwick Ave.
Long Beach, CA 90808
(562) 425-7886
e-mail: mercedchristian@yahoo.com

Mary Sturgeon Educational Games
7530 Richards Trail
Duncan, BC V9L 6B3
Canada
(888) 578-4180
(250) 715-1130
web site:
http://www.licketysplit.nisa.com
Lickety Split

Master Books
PO Box 727
Green Forest, AR 72638
(800) 999-3777
web site: www.masterbooks.net
*Life Before Birth, Bombus the
Bumblebee, Dinosaurs by Design, Dry
Bones and Other Fossils, God Created
Dinosaurs, Noah's Ark and the Ararat*

*Adventure, What Really Happened to the
Dinosaurs*—(selected titles -
A,B,C,E,G,H,I,)

**The Master's Press/The Master's
Academy of Fine Arts**
3571 Baywater Trail
Snellville, GA 30039
(770) 978-6324
Rebirth and Reformation (G,H)

Mastery Publications
90 Hillside Lane
Arden, NC 28704
(828) 684-0429
e-mail: masterypub@aol.com
web site: www.masterypublications.com
*F.L.A.G.S, Happy Handwriting,
Mastering Mathematics*—(H)

Math Concepts, Inc.
PMB 372
455 St. Rt. 13 N., # 26
Jacksonville, FL 32259
(800) 574-9936
(904) 287-5051
(904) 287-0363 FAX
web site: www.mathconcepts.com
Fraction Mania, Mental Math series (H)

Math Teachers Press, Inc.
5100 Gamble Dr.
Minneapolis, MN 55416
(800) 852-2435
(612) 546-7502 FAX
web site: www.movingwithmath.com
Moving with Math program. Request a
free sampler; include grade levels with
your request. Tell them you are a home
educator when you write or call so that
you are given the correct ordering information and prices.

Math-U-See
1378 River Road
Drumore, PA 17518
(888) 854-6284
e-mail: mathusee@epix.net
web site: www.mathusee.com

Mathematics Programs Associates, Inc.
PO Box 2118
Halesite, NY 11743
(888) MPA-MATH
(631) 643-9300
(631) 643-9301 FAX
e-mail: mpa@greatpyramid.com

web site: www.greatpyramid.com
Developmental Mathematics (B,G,H)

Mayflower Institute
PO Box 4673
Thousand Oaks, CA 91359
(805) 523-0072
(888) 222-2001 orders only
Christian Home Learning Guides

McGuffey Academy
PO Box 155
Lakemont, GA 30552
(706) 782-7709
e-mail: mcguffey2@juno.com

Media Angels
16450 S. Tamiami Trail, Ste. 3, PMB
#116
Ft. Myers, FL 33908
e-mail: whitlock@sprynet.com OR
MediAngels@aol.com
web site: www.mediaangels.com
*Creation Science, Creation Astronomy,
Creation Geology, Creation
Anatomy*—(C,E,F,G,H,I)

Memoria Press
PO Box 5066
Louisville, KY 40255-0066
(502) 458-5001
e-mail: Magister@memoriapress.com
web site: www.memoriapress.com
Latina Christiana (G,H,I)

Millbrook Press
PO Box 335
2 Old New Milford Road
Brookfield, CT 06804
(800) 462-4703
(203) 740-2223 FAX
web site: www.millbrookpress.com
Our Constitution (C)*, Gravity: Simple
Experiments for Young Scientists, The
New Book of Space, Planes and Other
Aircraft*

Milliken Publishing Company
1100 Research Blvd.
PO Box 21579
St. Louis, MO 63132-0579
(800) 325-4136
web site for SkillWorks: www.skill-
works.com
web site: www.millikenpub.com
Skillworks. Also books available at
teacher supply stores and through The

Weaver. (selected titles - H,I,J)

**Missouri Department of Conservation,
Education Division**
PO Box 180
Jefferson City, MO 65102-0180
web site:
www.conservation.state.mo.us/teacher/

Modern Curriculum Press
4350 Equity Dr.
PO Box 2649
Columbus, OH 43216
(800) 526-9907
(614) 771-7361 FAX
web site: www.mcschool.com
*Plaid Phonics, Phonics Word Study,
Mathematics, Spelling Workout, Phonics
Practice Readers* (selected titles -
A,B,E,H,I,J)

Modern Signs Press, Inc.
PO Box 1181
Los Alamitos, CA 90720
(562) 596-8548 regular phone or (same
number) TDD for hearing impaired.
(562) 795-6614 FAX

Montgomery Institute
PO Box 532
Boise, ID 83701
(208) 362-8060
(208) 362-8061 FAX

Moody Video
820 North LaSalle Blvd.
Chicago, IL 60610
(800) 842-1223
—(C,E,H)

Moody Press
820 North LaSalle Blvd.
Chicago, IL 60610
(312) 329-2102
(312) 2019 FAX
e-mail: pressinfo@moody.edu
web site: www.moodypress.org
*Learning for Life Series Family Activity
Books, Your Child Wonderfully
Made*—(D)

The Moore Foundation
Dr. Raymond and Dorothy Moore
Box 1
Camas, WA 98607
(360) 835-5500
(360) 835-5392 FAX

e-mail: moorefnd@pacifier.com
web site: www.moorefoundation.com
Moore-McGuffey Readers (B), Dr. and
Mrs. Moore's books(C), plus many other
resources and Moore Foundation
Curriculum Programs—(D,H)

More Than Books
146 McClintock Way
Kanata, ON K2L 2A4
Canada
(613) 592-5338
(613) 592-9210 orders
(613) 592-6794 FAX

Mother of Divine Grace School
PO Box 1440
Ojai, CA 93024
(805) 646-5818
(805) 646-0186 FAX
e-mail: modg@mhtc.net

Mott Media
1000 East Huron
Milford, MI 48381
(248) 685-8773
web site: www.mottmedia.com
*A Measuring Scale for Ability in
Spelling; Language and Thinking for
Young Children; Phonics Made Plain;
Original McGuffey Readers; Ray's
Arithmetic; Sower Series* biographies
(distributed by Baker Book House);
*Harvey's Grammar; The Three R'S
(Home Start in Reading, An Easy Start
in Arithmetic, A Strong Start in
Language)*—these three books are sold
individually or as the set; *Dr. Beechick's
Homeschool Answer Book; GENESIS,
Finding Our Roots; You Can Teach Your
Child Successfully* (E)*; Adam and His
Kin*— (selected titles - A,B,C,D,G,H,I,J)

Mountain Meadow Press
PO Box 447
Kooskia, ID 83539
(208) 926-7875
(208) 926-7579 FAX
e-mail: mtmeadow@camasnet.com
*How to Write a Low Cost/No Cost
Curriculum.* Send your name and
address plus a $.33 stamp for brochure.
(B,H,I,J)

**Multiplication Teaching & Learning Made
Easy**
PO Box 1482

Conway, AR 72033
(501) 327-1968
*Addition Teaching and Learning Made
Easy, Multiplication Teaching &
Learning Made Easy*

Multnomah Publishers
PO Box 1720
Sisters, OR 97759
(800) 929-0910
web site: www.multnomahbooks.com
My American Journey (C,H)

Music in Motion
PO Box 869231
Plano, TX 75086-92313
(800) 445-0649
catalog@music-in-motion.com

My Father's World
1706 The Willows Road
San Jacinto, CA 92583
(909) 654-2095
e-mail: teachmfw@aol.com
web site: www.dnc.net/users/triad/mfw
*My Father's World From A to Z, My
Father's World First Grade*—(B,H)

N

Nasco
901 Janesville Ave.
Fort Atkinson, WI 53538 OR
4825 Stoddard Rd.
Modesto, CA 95356-9318
(800) 558-9595 for orders only
web site: www.nascofa.com
Send for free catalogs for math, science,
arts/crafts, learning materials for young
children, and home economics.

NATHHAN
PO Box 39
Porthill, ID 83853
(208) 267-6246
e-mail: NATHANEWS@aol.com
web site: www.NATHHAN.com

**National Academy for Child
Development/N.A.C.D.**
Robert J. Doman, Jr.
PO Box 1639
Ogden, UT 84402
(801) 621-8606
(801) 621-8389 FAX
web site: www.nacd.org

National Center for Constitutional Studies
HC 61 Box 1056
Malta, ID 83342
(800) 388-4512 orders
(208) 645-2625
(208) 645-2667 FAX
e-mail: nccs@xmission.com
web site: www.nccs.net
I Love America (E,G)

National Center for Home Education
PO Box 3000
Purcellville, VA 20134
(540) 338-7600
(540) 338-9333 FAX
web site: www.hslda.org/nationalcenter/

**National Deaf Education Network and
Clearinghouse/Info to Go**
Gallaudet University
800 Florida Avenue N.E.
Washington, DC 20002
(202) 651-5051
(202) 651-5052 TTY
(202) 651-5054 FAX
e-mail: Clearinghouse.Infotogo@gal-
laudet.edu
web site: www.gallaudet.edu/~nicd/

National Gallery of Art
Washington, DC 20565
Send for free Extension Programs
Catalog.

National Geographic Society
Attn. Educational Services
P.O. Box 10041
Des Moines, Iowa 50340-0041
(888) 225-5647
*The Complete National Geographic,
National Geographic Maps*

**National Institute for Learning Disabilities
(NILD)**
107 Seekel St.
Norfolk, VA 23505-4415
(757) 423-8646
(757) 451-0970 FAX
e-mail: NILD@compuserve.net

National Wildlife Federation
310 Tyson Dr.
Winchester, VA 22603
(800) 477-5560
web site: http://catalog.nwf.org
Ranger Rick orders: (800) 588-1650
Ranger Rick magazine

National Writing Institute
810 Damon Court
Houston, TX 77006-1329
(800) 688-5375
(713) 529-9396
(713) 522-1934 FAX
web site: www.writingstrands.com
*Writing Strands,Reading Strands,
Evaluating Writing* (A,B,C,D,E,G,H,I,J)

Nature Friend Magazine
2727 Press Run Rd.
Sugar Creek, OH 44681
(800) 852-4482

Nature's Workshop, Plus!
PO Box 220
Pittsboro, IN 46167-0220
(888) 393-5663

The Neumann Press
Rt. 2, Box 30
Long Prairie, MN 56347
(800) 746-2521
(320) 732-6358
web site: www.nuemannpress.com
*My First Communion Catechism, Land
of Our Lady* history series, *Catholic
National Readers*

Newport Publishers
912 E. Union St.
Pasadena, CA 91106
(800) 579-5532
web site: www.audiobookclassics.com
*Children's Classics Library, Family
Classics Library*

Night Owl Creations, Inc.
10808 Cherith Lane
Clermont, FL 34711
(352) 242-9842

Noble Books
710 N.E. Cleveland St., Ste. 170
Gresham, OR 97030
(503) 667-5084
(800) 225-5259 orders only
e-mail: noblebooks@aol.com
*Classics at Home, The Christian Home
School* (F), *Fun Physical Fitness for the
Home, Government Nannies, Home
Schooling Children with Special Needs,
Home School Organizer, Learning at
Home: Preschool and Kindergarten,
Music Education in the Christian Home,
The Right Choice, Science in the*

Creation Week (D)*, Searching for Treasure, We Win, The A to Z Guide to Field Trips* (D)*, audio tapes, and other books. (selected titles - A,B,C,E,G,H,I,J)

Nordic Software
PO Box 83499
Lincoln, NE 68501-3499
(800) 306-6502
web site: www.nordicsoftware.com
Turbo Math Facts

Notebooks for Families
Katherine Mehaffey
534 Ridgeway Drive
Metairie, LA 70001
(800) 757-9712
web site:
www.notebooksforfamilies.com
Notebooks for Families: United States History

Nutmeg Publications
PO Box 9335
Moscow, ID 83843
e-mail: nutmeg@turbonet.com
Physical Education for Homeschoolers (G,J)

Nystrom, division of Herff Jones, Inc.
3333 Elston Ave.
Chicago, IL 60618
(773) 463-1144 or
(773) 463-0515 FAX
(800) 621-8086
e-mail: orders@nystromnet.com
web site: www.nystromnet.com
The Nystrom Desk Atlas

O

Oh Scrud!
Sylvia Young
41 W. Center
Alton, UT 84710
(801) 648-2164
—(H)

Old Fashioned Products
4860 Burnt Mountain Rd.
Ellijay, GA 30540
(800) 962-8849
e-mail: muggins@ellijay.com
web site: www.mugginsmath.com
Muggins and other games (H)

Old Pinnacle Publishing
1048 Old Pinnacle Rd.
Joelton, TN 37080
(615) 746-3342
e-mail: CAROLYNRH@aol.com
Let the Authors Speak (A,B,E,F,G,H,I)

Optometric Extension Program Foundation, Inc.
1921 E. Carnegie
Santa Ana, CA 92705
(714) 250-8070
(714) 250-8157 FAX
e-mail: oep1@oep.org

Oregon Institute of Science and Medicine and Althouse Press
2251 Dick George Rd.
Cave Junction, OR 97523
(541) 592-4142
Robinson Self-Teaching Home School Curriculum, Robinson Books Henty Collection—(G)

Osborne/McGraw-Hill
2600 Tenth St.
Berkeley, CA 94710
(800) 262-4729
(510) 549-6603 FAX
web site: www.osborne.com
Internet Kids & Family Yellow Pages (F,G)

O. T. Studios
Convention Dept.
11830 E. Washington Blvd.
Whittier, CA 90606
(800) 808-8173
(562) 693-8173
(562) 698-9985 FAX
web site: www.otstudios.com

Our Christian Heritage
7923 W. 62nd Way
Arvada, CO 80004
(303) 421-0444
Send SASE for free brochure. Receive a small discount by purchasing the set of all five books. (C,E,H)

Our Father's House
5530 S. Orcas
Seattle, WA 98118
(206) 725-9026
e-mail: jfogassy@aol.com
The ABC's of Christian Culture

Our Lady of Victory/Lepanto Press
103 E. 10th Ave.
Post Falls, ID 83854
(208) 773-7265
(208) 773-1951 FAX
web site: www.olvs.org
Science and Living in God's World series, *Catholic National Readers, Voyages in English* series

Outreach Nutrition Education Services
11828 E. Washington Blvd.
Whittier, CA 90606
(562) 693-9083
(562) 698-9985 FAX
otstudios@otstudios.com
The Science of Health and Nutrition Curriculum

Oxford University Press
Customer Service Department
2001 Evans Road
Cary, NC 27513
(800) 445-9714
web site: www.oup-usa.org/
A History of Us (A,C,D,F,G,H)*, Any Child Can Write* (C,D,F,G,H,I,J)*, The Legend of Odysseus, Pompeii, The Roman Fort, The Greeks*—(B,E)

P

Paradigm
PO Box 45161
Boise, ID 83711
(208) 322-4440
Samuel Blumenfeld's books: *NEA: Trojan Horse in American Education, Is Public Education Necessary?, The Blumenfeld Oral Reading Assessment Test* (A,H), and *How to Tutor* (A,B,D,G). The last title is distributed by Elijah Company

Parent Child Press
PO Box 675
Hollidaysburg, PA 16648-0675
(814) 696-7512
(814) 696-7510 FAX
web site: www.nb.net\~pcp\
Child-Size Masterpieces program (B,C,G,H,I,J)

Parkwest Publications, Inc.
451 Communipaw Avenue
Jersey City, NJ 07304
(201) 432-3257

(800) PARKWEST FAX
e-mail: parkwest@parkwestpubs.com
web site: www.parkwestpubs.com
Let's Go Gardening, history activity
books.
Check their catalog for other titles for
math, science, and social studies.

Pathway Books
2580 N. 250 W.
Lagrange, IN 46761
In Canada: Pathway Publishers
R.R. 4
Aylmer, Ontario N5H 1R3
Canada (B,H,I,J)

Pearables
PO Box 272000
Fort Collins, CO 80527 (G)

Pearson Education
4350 Equity Dr.
Columbus, OH 43216
(800) 321-3106
(800) 872-1100 orders
source for Cuisenaire-Dale Seymour
Publications and Good Year Books

Pecci Educational Publishing
440 Davis Court #405
San Francisco, CA 94111
(415) 391-8579
e-mail: pecci@sirius.com
web site:
www.OnlineReadingTeacher.com
*At Last! A Reading Method for Every
Child, Super Seatwork, Super Spelling*
(B,G)

Peggy Pickering
12206 Colbarn Pl.
Fishers, IN 46038
(317) 595-9744
(317) 595-0402 FAX
e-mail: peggypickering@hotmail.com
Library Skills for Christian Students

Pencils Writing Resources
PO Box 68235
Raleigh, NC 27613
(800) PENCIL IT
(919) 846-7005
(919) 847-4128 FAX
e-mail: almapwr@aol.com
*Science Works, Writing
Works*

Penguin Putnam, Inc.
PO Box 12289
Newark, NJ 07101
(800) 788-6262
(201) 896-8569 FAX
Drawing With Children (A,D,E,G,H,I),
In Their Own Way (D,G)*, Teaching Your
Child to Write, The Gift of Dyslexia.*
Available from secular bookstores.

Penton Overseas, Inc.
2470 Impala Dr.
Carlsbad, CA 92008-7226
(800) 748-5804
(619) 431-0060
(619) 431-8110 FAX
e-mail: info@pentonoverseas.com
web site: www.pentonoverseas.com
*Lingua Fun! Language Learning Card
Games, Lyric Language*—(H,J)

Personal Touch Planners
Cherry Patterson
PO Box 178
Groveland, CA 95321-0178
(209) 962-4555
e-mail: ptplanners@jps.net

Peter Bedrick Books
156 Fifth Ave.
New York, NY 10010
(212) 206-3738
(212) 206-3741 FAX
"Inside Story" series (G), "What Do We
Know About...?" series, "Biographical
History" series, "At A Glance" series,
and other history books—(selected titles
- H)

**Peter Parker's Magnetic Learning
Systems**
PO Box 1406
Pinehurst, NC 28370
(888) 715-0757
*Magnetic Alphabet, Phonics
Magnets*—(H)

Peterson Directed Handwriting
PO Box 249
Greensburg, PA 15601-0249
(800) 541-6328
(412) 836-4110 FAX
e-mail: mrpencil@peterson-handwrit-
ing.com
web site: www.peterson-
handwriting.com

Phoenix Learning Resources
2349 Chaffee Dr.
St. Louis, MO 63146
(800) 221-1274 orders
(800) 526-6581 information
Special education materials

Phonics Treasure Chest
Marsha King
2126 Turkey Ledge
San Antonio, TX 78232
(210) 494-7860

Pilgrim Enterprises
Kathy Keller
3279 South El Dorado Dr.
New Berlin, WI 53151
(414) 785-8052
Turning Back the Pages of Time (D,H)

Pioneer Productions
PO Box 328
Young, AZ 85554-0328
e-mail: djgagnon@juno.com
*How to Identify Your Child's Learning
Problems and What to Do About Them*
(B,J)

Play 'N Talk
7105 Manzanita St.
Carlsbad, CA 92009
(800) 472-7525 outside CA
(760) 438-4330 in CA
web site: www.playntalk.com

Portico Books
Dept. H
PO Box 9451
St. Louis, MO 63117
(314) 721-7131
(888) 641-5353
e-mail: info@porticobooks.com
web site: http://www.porticobooks.com
Hands-On English

**Portland State University, School of
Extended Studies**
Continuing Education Press
PO Box 1394
Portland, OR 97207
(800) 547-8887, extension 4891
(503) 725-4891
Italic Handwriting series plus *Write
Now* (A,B,C,D,E,G,H,I,J)

Positive Action for Christ
PO Box 1948

Rocky Mount, NC 27802-1948
(800) 688-3008
(252) 977-2181 FAX
web site: www.positiveaction.org
Pro Series Bible Curriculum

The Practical Allergy Research Foundation
PO Box 60
Buffalo, NY 14223-0060
(800) 787-8780
(716) 875-0398
e-mail: parf1421@aol.com
www.drrapp.com
The Impossible Child (G,J), *Is This Your Child?* (G), *Is This Your Child's World?*, *Environmentally Sick Schools*

Praise Hymn, Inc.
PO Box 1325
Taylors, SC 29687
(800) 729-2821
(864) 322-8284 FAX
God Made Music series (C), *Star Light/Star Ways* Bible Curriculum

Precious Memories Educational Resources
18403 N.E. 111th Ave.
Battle Ground, WA 98604
(206) 687-0282
e-mail: lwhittle@ptld.uswest.net
Winston Grammar (D,E,G), *Winston Word Works* (A,B,H,I,J)

Prentice Hall
Order Processing Center
PO Box 11071
Des Moines, IA 50336-1071
(800) 288-4745
(800) 282-0693
web site: www.phdirect.com
Art Smart, Favorite Books Activities Kit, The Prentice Hall Directory of Online Education Resources, Hands-On Science!, Ready-To-Use Music Reading Activities Kit (H), *Multicultural Art Activities Kit*—(selected titles - G)

President's Challenge Physical Fitness Program
Poplars Research Center
400 E. 7th St.
Bloomington, IN 47405
(800) 258-8146
e-mail: preschal@indiana.edu
web site: www.indiana.edu/~preschal

PrestonSpeed Publications
51 Ridge Rd.
Mill Hall, PA 17751
(570) 726-7844
web site: www.prestonspeed.com
G.A. Henty series (B,C,G,H,I)

Prima Publishing
3000 Lava Ridge Ct.
Roseville, CA 95661
(800) 632-8676
(916) 787-7000
(916) 787-7001 FAX
web site: www.primapublishing.com
Homeschooling Almanac 2000-2001 (C), *Discover Your Child's Learning Style* (also available through Reflective Educational Perspectives)—(E)

Professor Phonics-EduCare
4700 Hubble Rd.
Cincinnati, OH 45247
(513) 385-1717
(513) 385-7920 FAX
e-mail: sue@professorphonics.com
web site: www.professorphonics.com
Professor Phonics Gives Sound Advice, Sound Track to Reading (B,I)

Progeny Press
PO Box 223
Eau Claire, WI 54702-0223
(877) 776-4369
(715) 936-0105 FAX
e-mail: progeny@mgprogeny.com
web site: www.mgprogeny.com/progeny (B,D,E,F,H,I)

Prometheus Books
59 John Glenn Dr.
Buffalo, NY 14228-2197
(800) 421-0351
They're Never Too Young for Books

Providence Foundation
PO Box 6759
Charlottesville, VA 22906
(804) 978-4535 phone and FAX
e-mail: provfdn@aol.com
America's Providential History (A,B,C,D,E,F,G,H,I)

The Providence Project
14566 N.W. 110th St.
Whitewater, KS 67154
(888) 776-8776
(316) 799-2112

e-mail: info@providenceproject.com
web site: www.providenceproject.com
Alphabetter®, CalcuLadder® (D,G,J), *ReadyWriter®, SanctiFinder®* (G) —(A,B,E,H,I)

Q

QNQ, Inc.
PO Box 901
New Castle, DE 19720
(302) 323-0723
e-mail: george@qnq.com
Coins Make Change Bingo

R

Rainbow Resource Center
Rt. 1, Box 159A
50 N. 500 E. Rd.
Toulon, IL 61483
(888) 841-3456 orders
(800) 705-8809 FAX
e-mail: rainbowr@cin.net
web site: www.rainbowresource.com

Random House, Inc./Knopf
Customer Service
400 Hahn Rd.
Westminster, MD 21157
(800) 726-0600 customer service
(800) 733-3000 order only
(800) 659-2436 FAX
web site: www.randomhouse.com
Eyewitness series (G), *20/20 is Not Enough* (G), *Mr. Wizard books*—(D)

R. C. Law and Company, Inc.
4861 Chino Ave.
Chino, CA 91710-5132
(800) 777-5292
(909) 627-9475 FAX
My California, My Texas, My Illinois, My Indiana

Red Leaf Press
WT Educational Services
12563 Carrs Landing Road
Winfield, B.C. V4V 1A1
Canada
(250) 766-0568
e-mail: redleaf@cablelan.net
My First History of Canada

Red Rose Studio
358 Flintlock Drive
Willow Street, PA 17584

(717) 464-3873
District of Columbia, Pennsylvania,
New York, and Texas history. Send $1
for catalog.

Reflective Educational Perspectives
M. Pelullo-Willis and V. Kindle-Hodson
1451 E. Main St. #200
Ventura, CA 93001
(805) 648-1739
(805) 643-8633 FAX
e-mail: redp@redp.com
web site: www.redp.com

Regal Books
2300 Knoll Drive
Ventura, CA 93003
(800) 4GOSPEL
*What The Bible Is All About For Young
Explorers* (G,H), *Preparing for
Adolescence* (J)—(A,B,C,D)

Regnery Publishing, Inc.
1 Massachusetts Ave. N.W.
Washington, DC 20001
(202) 216-0600
(202) 216-0612 FAX
web site: www.regnery.com
Facts, Not Fear

Republic Policy Institute Press
POBox 789
Lancaster, CA 93584
(800) 244-7196
(661) 949-6788 FAX
web site:
www.rolnet.com/rpip/cssb.html
The Common Sense Spelling Book

Rhythm Band Instruments
PO Box 126
Fort Worth, TX 76101
(800) 424-4724
(817) 335-2561
(800) 784-9401 FAX
e-mail: rhythmband@aol.com
web site: www.rhythmband.com
—(C,H)

The Riggs Institute
4185 S.W. 102nd Avenue
Beaverton, OR 97005
(503) 646-9459
(503) 644-5191 FAX
Resources and training for *The Writing
Road to Reading (B)*

Ring of Fire
PO Box 489
Scio, OR 97374
(888) 785-5439
(503) 394-3100 FAX
e-mail: myrna@ring-of-fire.com
web site: www.ring-of-fire.com

Ringbound Enterprises
PO Box 102
Dallas, WI 54733
(715) 924-4860
Ringbound Reading

RiversEdge Publishing Co.
PO Box 622
West Linn, OR 97068
(503) 557-1850
(503) 557-8662 FAX
(888) 337-1850
Total Health (E,F,H)

Rod and Staff Publishers
PO Box 3, Highway 172
Crockett, KY 41413
(606) 522-4348
(selected items - H)

Rosetta Stone
165 S. Main St.
Harrisonburg, VA 22801
(800) 788-0822
(540) 432-6166
web site: www.rosettastone.com

Running Press
125 South 22nd St.
Philadelphia, PA 19103
(800) 345-5359
web site: www.runningpress.com
Start Exploring series: *Masterpieces,
Oceans*, and *Gray's Anatomy*
(D,G)—(A,E,H)

S

S & D Publications
18604 Cross Country Lane
Gaithersburg, MD 20879
(301) 330-4658
e-mail: Sdpub@juno.com OR deniseg-
riney@aol.com
web site: www.SDPublication.com
I Love To Read! I Love To Write!

SRA
220 East Danieldale Rd.

DeSoto, TX 75115
(888) 772-4543
(972) 228-1982 FAX
web site: www.sra4kids.com
Scoring High series (F,H,J), *Prescriptive
Spelling*

Saints & Scholars
c/o Palmer House Bookshop
34 N. Main Street
Waynesville, NC 28786
(800) 452-3936
(828) 452-3932 FAX
e-mail: saints@brinet.com
web site: www.saintsandscholars.com

Saxon Publishers
2450 John Saxon Blvd.
Norman, OK 73071
(800) 284-7019
(405) 329-7071
(405) 360-4205 FAX
web site: www.saxonpub.com
Saxon Math (D,F,G), *Saxon Phonics,
Phonics Intervention*—(A,B,C,E,H,I,J)

Schola Publications
1698 Market St. #162
Redding, CA 96001
(530) 275-2064
The Latin Road to English Grammar (J)

Scholastic Inc.
Box 7502
Jefferson City, MO 65102
(800) 325-6149
web site: www.scholastic.com
Bob Books (A,B,C,D,E,G,H,I,J)

School of Tomorrow
PO Box 299000
Lewisville, TX 75029-9000
(800) 925-7777
Publisher of *Readmaster,
Typemaster*—(C,J)

ScottForesman-Addison Wesley
Division of Pearson Edcuation
4350 Equity Dr.
Columbus, OH 43205
(800) 552-2259
web site: www.sf.aw.com
*Ecce Romani, Exploring Mathematics,
D'Nealian* handwriting books
(A,B,E,I,J), *Super Source* series—(C,H)

Scripture Memory Fellowship International
Box 411551
St. Louis, MO 63141
(314) 569-0244

Seton Home Study School/Seton Press
1350 Progress Drive
Front Royal, VA 22630
(540) 636-9990
(540) 636-9996 Seton Press
(540) 636-1602 FAX
e-mail: info@home.org
OR
Seton Home Study California
44751 Date St., Ste. 8
Lancaster, CA 93534
(661) 948-8881
e-mail: setonca@networkone.net
web site: www.setonhome.org
American History for Young Catholics 1, The Art of Writing for Young Catholics, The Catholic Faith Comes to the Americas, English for Young Catholics, Phonics for Young Catholics, Reading for Young Catholics, Religion for Young Catholics, Science for Young Catholics, Spelling for Young Catholics

Share-A-Care Publications
240 Mohns Hill Rd.
Reinholds, PA 17569
e-mail: myronweaver@juno.com
Art with a Purpose (A,H,I)

Shekinah Curriculum Cellar
101 Meador Rd.
Kilgore, TX 75662
(903) 643-2760
(903) 643-2796 FAX
e-mail:
customerservice@shekinahcc.com
web site: www.shekinahcc.com

Shurley Instructional Materials, Inc.
366 SIM Drive
Cabot, AR 72023
(800) 566-2966
(501) 843-3869
(501) 843-0583 FAX
web site: www.shurley.com
The Shurley Method

Simon and Schuster, Inc.
100 Front St.
Riverside, NJ 08075
(800) 223-2336 for orders
web site: www.simonsays.com
Mark Kistler's Draw Squad, Teach Your Child To Read In 100 Easy Lessons (B,G,J), and Macmillan titles, including *Childhood of Famous Americans* series (G,J)—(A,D,E,H,I)

Simplified Learning Products
PO Box 45387
Rio Rancho, NM 87174-5387
(800) 745-8212 phone and FAX
e-mail: NMSLP@aol.com
web site: www.joyceherzog.com
Scaredy Cat Reading System, History in His Hands—(G,I)

Small Ventures
Bonnie Dettmer
11023 Watterson Dr.
Dallas, TX 75228
(972) 681-1728
web site: www.smallventuresbooks.com
Phonics for Reading and Spelling (D), *Phonics Fun, Handbook for The Writing Road to Reading, Spelling Scale for Home Educators, Learning at Home: First Grade and Second Grade, Book of the Centuries* (D), *History Helps*, and more.—(A,B,E,G,H,I,J)

Smartek
7908 Convoy Ct.
San Diego, CA 92111
(800) 858-WORD
(858) 565-8068
web site: www.smartekinc.com
Think Speak and Write Better!, Word Adventure

Social Studies School Service
10200 Jefferson Blvd.
PO Box 802
Culver City, CA 90232-0802
(800) 421-4246
(310) 839-2436
(800) 944-5432 FAX
e-mail: access@socialstudies.com
web site: www.socialstudies.com
Social Studies School Service California catalog

Sonlight Curriculum
8121 S. Grant Way
Littleton, CO 80122-2701
(303) 730-6292
(303) 795-8668 FAX
e-mail: sonlight@crsys.com
web site: www.crsys.com/sonlight

Soteria
order from
AlmaNiche Publishing, LLC
310 Williams St.
Hattiesburg, MS 39401
(601) 584-8932
(800) 299-6974
The Home School Lesson Planner, Maps My Way U.S.A.—(H)

Sounds Of Praise Christian Music Studies
Debra Matula
442 Pennsacola Rd.
Ebensburg, PA 15931-3600
(814) 472-7704

Spalding Education Foundation
2814 W. Bell Road, Suite 1405
Phoenix, AZ 85053
(602) 866-7801
(602) 866-7488 FAX
e-mail: spalding@neta.com
web site: www.spalding.org
The Writing Road to Reading (E,G,H,J)

Spanish Made Fun
PO Box 35832
Tulsa, OK 74153
(918) 665-8245

Speedy Spanish
36107 S.E. Squaw Mountain Road
Estacada, OR 97023
(888) 621-3293
(503) 630-4606 (B,H,J)

Spizzirri Publishing, Inc.
PO Box 9397
Rapid City, SD 57709
(800) 325-9819
(800) 322-9819 FAX
web site: www.spizzirri.com

Spring Street Press
2606 Spring Blvd.
Eugene, OR 97403
(541) 345-6887
(541) 345-7287 FAX
Responding to Literature, Strategies for Reading Nonfiction (B,H)

St. Joseph Messenger
PO Box 11260
Cincinnati, OH 45211-0260
e-mail: stjoseph@erinet.com

web site:
www.aquinas-multimedia.com/stjoseph/

State Histories
14506 E. 380 Rd.
Claremore, OK 74017
(918) 341-7559
e-mail: tllc7559@aol.com
Arkansas, Colorado, Oklahoma, and
Texas History in Light of the Cross

Steck-Vaughn
PO Box 690789
Orlando, FL 32819
(800) 531-5015
web site: www.steck-vaughn.com
*Critical Thinking, Reading, And
Reasoning Skills* (J)

Stone Tablet Press
12 Wallach Drive
Fenton, MO 63026-4964
new address Summer 2000
3348 Whitsetts Fork Rd.
Wildwood, MO 63038
(636) 343-4244
web site:
http://memebers@aol.com/stonetblt
Little Angel Readers

Stratton House
17650 1st Ave. S. #186
Seattle, WA 98148
(800) 694-7225
e-mail: science@jetcity.com
web site: www.homeschoolscience.com
Astronomy, Birds and Magnetism
(B,H,I)

Successful Co-oping
PO Box 3192
Boynton Beach, FL 33424-3192
*The Complete Guide to Successful Co-
oping for Homeschooling Families*
(C,D,G)

Summit Christian Academy
DFW Corporate Park
2100 N. Highway 360, Suite 503
Grand Prairie, TX 75050
(800) 362-9180
(972) 602-8050
(972) 602-8243 FAX
e-mail: sca100@aol.com
web site: www.scahomeschool.com

Summit Ministries
PO Box 207
Manitou Springs, CO 80829
(719) 685-9103
web site: www.summit.org
Understanding the Times book (D,F,G),
published by Harvest House but also
available through Summit

Suntex International, Inc.
118 N. 3rd St.
Easton, PA 18042
(610) 253-5255
(610) 258-2180 FAX
e-mail: math24@aol.com
24 Game (B,F). The publisher does not
accept direct orders. Games may be
ordered from the distributors noted
above.

Susan Mortimer
731 W. Camp Wisdom
Duncanville, TX 75116
(972) 780-1683
Remembering God's Awesome Acts (B)

Swift Learning Resources
88 North West State Rd.
American Fork, UT 84003
(800) 292-2831
web site: www. swiftlearning.com
*McOmber Reading Program; Swift
Placement Screen for Reading*

**Sycamore Tree Center for Home
Education**
2179 Meyer Place
Costa Mesa, CA 92627
School service plus catalog.
(949) 650-4466 for information about
materials or school service
(800) 779-6750 credit card/FAX orders
only
(949) 642-6750 credit card/FAX orders
only
e-mail: sycamoretree@compuserve.com
web site: www.sycamoretree.com
*My Growth in Kindergarten Report
Card, School Forms for Home and
Classroom, Christian Cumulative
Record, Assignment Sheets For Home
And School, My Homeschool Year,
Pretty Pages and Beautiful Border, 101
Great Homeschool Teaching Tips from
the Sycamore Tree*

T

TAN Books and Publishers, Inc.
PO Box 424
Rockford, IL 61105
(800) 437-5876
*Catholic Home Schooling: A Handbook
for Parents, The Old World and
America, Our Pioneers and Patriots*

Teach America to Read and Spell
PO Box 44093
Tacoma, WA 98444
(253) 531-0312
web site: http://verticalphonics.com
The Great Saltmine and Hifwip reading
program

Teach Me tapes
9900 Bren Road East, Ste. B-1, Ste. 100
Minneapolis, MN 55343
(800) 456-4656
(612) 933-8086
(612) 933-0512 FAX
e-mail: teachme@wavetech.net
web site: www.teachmetapes.com
Foreign languages

Teacher Created Materials, Inc.
6421 Industry Way
Westminster, CA 92683
(800) 662-4321
(714) 525-1254 FAX
*African Americans, Beyond the Science
Fair, Brain Teasers, Math Generator,
Hands-On Minds On Science* series, *Kid
Pix Activity Kits, "How To"* Series (I),
Animals, Magnets, Space, My Body
(H,I), *Newspaper Reporters* (I),
Medieval Times, Focus on Composers
(H), *Interdisciplinary Thematic Units,
Thematic Units,* and *Literature
Units*—(selected titles - A,B,C,E,J)

Teacher Ideas Press
PO Box 6633
Englewood, CO 80155-6633
(800) 237-6124
e-mail: lu-books@lu.com
web site: www.lu.com
*Intermediate Science through Children's
Literature, Quizzes for 220 Great
Children's Books, More Quizzes for
Great Children's Books*

Teachers College Press
PO Box 20
Williston, VT 05495-0020
(800) 575-6566
*Gates-Peardon-LaClair Reading
Exercise Books, McCall-Crabbs
Standard Test Lessons in Reading*

Teaching & Learning Company
1204 Buchanan St.
PO Box 10
Carthage, IL 62321-0010
e-mail: tandlcom@adams.net
web site: www.teachinglearning.com
(217) 357-2591
How to Write (C)

The Teaching Home Magazine
PO Box 20219
Portland, OR 97294-9965
(503) 253-9633
e-mail: tth@TeachingHome.com
web site: www.TeachingHome.com (A)

Theory Time
9207 Woodleigh Dr.
Houston, TX 77083
(281) 575-8101
(281) 933-3612 FAX
e-mail: info@theorytime.com
web site: www.theorytime.com

**Thoburn Press/Fairfax Christian
Bookstore**
PO Box 6941
Tyler, TX 75711
(800) 962-5432
(903) 581-0677
McGuffey Readers (J), penmanship program, math—(E)

Tim and Kathy von Duyke
PO Box 7271
Newark, DE 19714-7271
(302) 737-3673
*The Home Education CopyBook and
Planning Guide, The Month by Month
Spelling Guide*

Timberdoodle
1510 E. Spencer Lake Rd.
Shelton, WA 98584
(360) 426-0672
(800) 478-0672 FAX
e-mail: mailbag@timberdoodle.com
web site: www.timberdoodle.com

Tin Man Press
PO Box 219
Stanwood, WA 98292
(800) 676-0459 phone/FAX
web site: www.tinmanpress.com
Play by the Rules

Tobin's Lab
(800) 522-4776
e-mail: mike@tobinlab.com
web site: www.tobinlab.com

Tom Snyder Productions
80 Coolidge Hill Rd.
Watertown, MA 02472-5003
(800) 342-0236
(800) 304-1254 FAX
web site: www.tomsnyder.com
Mapping the World by Heart Lite
(B,D,E,G,H,I,J)

Tools for Godly Living
PO Box 1382
Los Banos, CA 93635
e-mail: AlyceKayGarrett@netscape.net
Language Arts, Book One

Tops Learning Systems
10970 S. Mulino Rd.
Canby, OR 97013
(503) 263-2040 (H)

Total Language Plus, Inc.
PO Box 12622
Olympia, WA 98508
(360) 754-3660
e-mail: tlp@integrityol.com
web site: ww2@intergrityol.com/tlp
(A,B,E,H)

Tree of Life School
443 Weston Rd.
Weston, NB E7K 1B1
Canada
OR
106 Main St., Ste. 518
Houlton, ME 04730-9001
(506) 328-6781
(506) 328-9506 FAX
e-mail: treeoflife@sws.nb.ca
web site: www.sws.nb.ca/treeoflife

Trivium Pursuit
PMB 168
139 Colorado St.
Muscatine, IA 52761
(309) 537-3641

e-mail: trivium@muscanet.com
web site: www.muscanet.com/~trivium
Information on how to apply the classical approach of education to home
schooling. Also, publisher of *Hand that
Rocks the Cradle* (D,G).

Troll Books
Troll Associates
100 Corporate Dr.
Mahwah, NJ 07430
(800) 929-TROLL
(800) 979-TROLL FAX
web site: www.troll.com
Nature Club series, biographies and literature
— (selected titles - B,D,F,H)

The Tutoring Company
PO Box 540111
Waltham, MA 02454-0111
(781) 899-6468
Alpha-Phonics

Twin Sisters Productions
1340 Home Ave., Ste. D
Akron, OH 44310
(800) 248-TWIN
(800) 480-8946 FAX
(330) 633-8900
e-mail: twinsisters@twinsisters.com
web site: www.twinsisters.com
*Multiplication, Addition, Subtraction,
Division, Phonics, States and Capitals,
Listen and Learn a Language* (H)

Tyndale House Publishers
PO Box 80
Wheaton, IL 60189
(800) 323-9400
(630) 668-8300
(630) 668-8905 FAX
The Way They Learn (A,D,J), *Every
Child Can Succeed*—(B,C,F,G,H)

U

United States Center for World Mission
Children's Mission Resource Center
1605 Elizabeth St.
Pasadena, CA 91104
(626) 398-2233 (Mon.-Fri.)
(626) 398-2263 FAX
e-mail: gerry.dueck@wciu.edu
web site: www.uscwm.org/children's-
missionresources/catalog
Kids For The World

University Prints
21 East St.
PO Box 485
Winchester, MA 01890
Send $3 for catalog of art prints or
request a free brochure of Topic Study
Sets.

Usborne Books
See Educational Development
Corporation

V

Veritas Press
1250 Belle Meade Drive
Lancaster, PA 17601
(800) 922-5082 12-5 p.m. EST
(717)519-1974
(717) 519-1978 FAX
e-mail: Veritasprs@aol.com
web site:
http://members.aol.com/Veritasprs
History and Bible Flash Card Sets (G)
and *Teacher's Manuals*

Victory Drill Book
PO Box 2935
Castro Valley, CA 94546-0935
(510) 537-9404 —(E,H)

Video Lending Library
5777 Azalea Dr.
Grants Pass, OR 97526
(541) 479-7140 phone and FAX

Visual Manna
PO Box 553
Salem, MO 65560
(573) 729-2100
*Visual Manna's Complete Art
Curriculum* (G), *Teaching American
History Through Art* (G), *Teaching
English Through Art, Bible Arts and
Crafts*—(H)

Vital Issues Press/Huntington House
PO Box 53788
Lafayette, LA 70505
(800) 749-4009
(318) 237-7060 FAX
web site:
www.huntingtonhousebooks.com
Dinosaurs and the Bible (G,H,I)

Voice of the Martyrs
PO Box 443

Bartlesville, OK 74005
(918) 337-8015
e-mail: vom@linkingup.com
Link International

W

W.W. Norton and Company
500 Fifth Avenue
New York, NY 10110
(800) 233-4830
web site: www.wwnorton.com
The Well-Trained Mind (F,G,H)

Warner Books
Order from Little Brown and Company
See address above.

The Weaver Curriculum Company, Inc.
300 N. McKemy Ave.
Chandler, AZ 85226-2618
(888) 367-9871
(480) 785-8034 FAX
The Weaver "unit study" approach curriculum—*Interlock,* Volumes One, Two,
Three, Four, and Five, *Wisdom Words,
The Literature Program, Teaching Tips
and Techniques, 3-D Body, Skills
Evaluation for The Home School, Day
by Day, Success in Spelling,* and supplementary books, including many Milliken
titles.—(C,H,J)

Weimar Institute
PO Box 486
Weimar, CA 95736
(800) 525-9192
(530) 637-4722 FAX
web site: www.weimar.org
Math-it (A,B,D,E,G,H,I,J)

The Westbridge Academy
1610 West Highland Ave., Box 228
Chicago, IL 60660
(312) 743-3312
e-mail: westbrgA@aol.com

Wheeler Applied Research
38-221 Desert Greens Dr. W.
Palm Desert, CA 92260
(800) 782-4869
(760) 773-9426
(801) 382-4627 FAX
e-mail: cq@writeaddress.com
web site: http://writeaddress.com
EZ Writer

Whole Heart Ministries
PO Box 67
Walnut Springs, TX 76690
(800) 311-2146 orders only
(254) 797-2142 information
(254) 797-2148 FAX
web site: www.wholeheart.org
Educating the Whole Hearted Child
(B,C,D,E,F,G,H,I)

Wild Goose Company
4321 Piedmont Parkway
Greensboro, NC 27410
(888) 621-1040, extension 6
web site: www.wildgoosescience.com
Junior Boom Academy, science kits and
supplies—(D,H,J)

Wildlife Education, Ltd.
12233 Thatcher Court
Poway, CA 92064
(858) 513-7600
(858) 513-7660 FAX
e-mail: animals@zoobooks.com
web site: www.zoobooks.com
Zoobooks

**William B. Eerdmans Publishing
Company**
255 Jefferson Avenue S.E.
Grand Rapids, MI 49503
(800) 253-7521
(616) 459-6540 FAX
e-mail: sales@eerdmans.com
web site: http://www.eerdmans.com
Child's Story Bible (A,D), *Leading Little
Ones to God* (A), *The Christian Eclectic
Readers and Study Guide*—(B,C,G,H,I)

William Carey Library
PO Box 40129
Pasadena, CA 91114
(626) 798-0819
(800) MISSION for orders
Mission Resource Catalog

Wisdom's Gate
PO Box 374
Covert, MI 49043
(800) 343-1943
e-mail: wisgate@characterlink.net
web site: www.homeschooldigest.com
Home School Digest

Wooly Lamb Publishing
PO Box 662
La Center, WA 98629

(360) 263-6568
e-mail:
woolylamb@worldaccessnet.com
web site:
www.wa-net.com/~little/welcome.html
History Links

Thomas Nelson Publishers/Word Publishing
Nelson Place at Elm Hill Pike
PO Box 141000
Nashville, TN 37214-1000
(800) 933-9673, Ext. 2037
Genesis for Kids (), *It Couldn't Just Happen*(A,B,D,E), *The Ultimate Guide To Homeschooling* (D,F)— (C,G,H,I,J)

Wordsmiths
1355 Ferry Rd.
Grants Pass, OR 97526
(541) 476-3080
(541) 474-9756 FAX
e-mail: frodej@chatlink.com
web site: www.jsgrammar.com
A Journey through Grammar Land
(B,E,H,I,J)

Workman Publishing
708 Broadway
New York, NY 10003
(800) 722-7202
(212) 254-5900
The Bug Book and The Bug Bottle, The Bird Book and The Bird Feeder, The Bones Book and Skeleton (H), *Backyard Explorer Kit, The Garden Book, Brain Quest, The Science Book* by Stein—(selected items - B,D,J)

World Book, Inc.
233 N. Michigan Ave.
Chicago, IL 60601
(800) 975-3250
web site: www.worldbook.com
print and CD-ROM Encyclopedia and
Typical Course of Study (A,B).
Local distributors usually have the
Typical Course of Study available.—(J)

World's Greatest Music
PO Box 747
Lobeco. SC 29931
(800) 414-8003
e-mail: amwlee@webtv.net
web site: www.amusicworld.com
Basic Library of the World's Greatest Music (G)

Writing Assessment Services
16 Stanfill Lane
Jackson, TN 38301-4241
(901) 427-8321
e-mail: cmarsch786@aol.com (preferred method of contact)
web site:
http://members.aol.com/cmarsch786 (preferred method of contact)

Y

Young Scientists and Mathematicians Institute
See Young Writers' Institutes for information.

Young Writers' Institutes
1425 E. Chocolate Ave.
Hershey, PA 17033
(717) 520-1303
(717) 533-0413 FAX
e-mail: YWIHershey@aol.com
web site: www.hsrc.com
Also check out their new project, Young Scientists and Mathematicians Institute on their web page.

Your Story Hour Recordings
Box 511
Medina, OH 44258
(330) 725-5767
web site: www.yourstoryhour.com
(B,C,H,J)

YWAM Publishing
PO Box 635
Lynnwood, WA 98046
(800) 922-2143
(425) 775-2383 FAX
web site: www.ywampublishing.com
How to Get Your Child off the Refrigerator and on to Learning

Z

Zephyr Press
PO Box 66006
Tucson, AZ 85728-6006
(520) 322-5090
Unit studies

Zondervan Publishing House
5300 Patterson S.E.
Grand Rapids, MI 49530
(800) 727-1309
web site: www.zondervan.com

Honey For A Child's Heart (A,B,E,F), *From Jerusalem to Irian Jaya* (B), *Operation World* (A,B,), *The Spiritual Lives of Great Composers* (J)—(C,D,G,H,I)

F